Tenney 2-9

Enlightened England

Revised Edition

Books by Wylie Sypher

FOUR STAGES OF RENAISSANCE STYLE
ROCOCO TO CUBISM IN ART AND LITERATURE

Edited by Wylie Sypher

COMEDY
THE RING AND THE BOOK (ROBERT BROWNING)

Enlightened England

Revised Edition

AN ANTHOLOGY OF
*English Literature
from Dryden to Blake*

Edited by Wylie Sypher

SIMMONS COLLEGE

W · W · NORTON *&* COMPANY · INC · *New York*

89

Prefatory Note

THIS NEW EDITION of *Enlightened England* is designed to present the great British writers from Dryden to Blake against the background of their age. The structure is therefore nuclear. Generous and, in most cases, complete selections from the major writers are arranged chronologically, and about these are grouped brief passages—often from "non-literary" books—vital to the understanding of these writers and to the century as a whole. Most of these brief passages are fragments of eighteenth-century works on the fine arts, science, ethics, theology, economics, political theory, history, or aesthetics which have been hitherto generally unavailable. These briefer passages provide background for related works by major authors throughout the whole book. Thus, the excerpt from Newton's *Principia* appears next to Shaftesbury but also bears directly upon selections from Pope, Thomson, Paine, and Blake.

The introductory essay on the eighteenth century as a whole epitomizes the many developments that influenced the contemporaneous literature. If the British eighteenth century was dark enough in many places, it was also the age of the Enlightenment. The foundations of modern political theory, economic society, religion, and aesthetic values were laid in this period. For that reason the collection is called *Enlightened England*.

The novel and the drama are not represented; both are difficult to reduce to the dimensions of an anthology, and both are generally available for supplementary reading. However, while such excerpts as those from Richardson's *Familiar Letters*, Goldsmith's *Life of Richard Nash*, and Hervey's *Meditations among the Tombs* are included chiefly as records of eighteenth-century manners, they can also be read as introductions to the prose fiction and drama of the day.

This collection stresses the personal tone of the age, in Boswell and Johnson particularly. It also stresses the arts which had such a great influence on the British writers of the century—landscape gardening, painting, and architecture.

Selections from the major writers and from the auxiliary material have been made with special regard for the possibilities of contrast and comparison—Johnson's view of his Scottish journey, for example, as contrasted with Boswell's view of the same journey; or the issues that rise between Hume and Reynolds, between Defoe, Mandeville, Shaftesbury, and Steele, between Malthus and Crabbe, between Monboddo and John Brown, between Lord Chesterfield and Wesley. The oppositions and reflections between such writers seem inexhaustible, and should suggest something of the diversity of the century.

The texts are from authoritative editions, in most cases contemporary printings. The prose is in almost every instance modernized. The poetry has been kept as close as seemed wise to eighteenth-century texts on the principle that variations like desert—desart, interest—int'rest, order—Order, pity—Pity do not impede reading and are of possible significance in interpreting meter and even sense.

Special and often extensive help has been given by many, and particularly by Robert M. Gay, Willard Trask, Addison Burnham, J. Jean Hecht, Ruth Emery, Edith Helman, and the librarians of the Landscape Architecture Library, the Architecture Library, and the Fogg Museum Library at Harvard.

In this revised edition John Dryden's work is for the first time generously represented; also, there are new background selections from Thomas Sprat's *History of the Royal Society*, from John Locke's *Essay Concerning Human Understanding* and *Treatises of Government*, and from Isaac Newton's *Opticks*. Since *Gulliver's Travels* is readily available in reprint editions and often read in survey courses, the selection from this work has been replaced by other, seldom-anthologized, selections from Swift's prose and poetry—including the *Journal to Stella*—in order to give a wider representation to this important author. A number of selections from Blake have been added. The bibliographies have been brought up to date throughout. My thanks for suggestions go to Kenneth M. Greene, my colleague, and to the editorial staff of W. W. Norton & Company, Inc., whose efforts have made this revision possible.

W.S.

Boston, Mass.
March 1961

Contents

BACKGROUND SELECTION

WILLIAM SHENSTONE   663

BACKGROUND SELECTIONS

WILLIAM COLLINS   695

DAVID HUME   800

SAMUEL JOHNSON   838

JAMES BOSWELL   896

Illustrations

Illustrations

THE EIGHTEENTH CENTURY offers us perhaps the rarest and most engaging collection of personalities in English literature, and in all the arts. We are always hearing Johnson's own loud voice, slow and deliberate, or the high-pitched arguing of Tom Paine, or the stammer of Goldsmith, or the nursery-rhyme cadences of William Blake. We are always conscious of the writer himself, his very temperament—in the magisterial whimsey of Dr. Johnson saying, for example, "Attack is the reaction; I never think I have hit hard unless it rebounds," or in his complaining that women "give great offense by a contemptuous spirit of noncompliance on petty occasions." In the novels, we are with the gossipy little groups strolling the Pump Room at Bath, where there was a Humane Society for the Recovery of Persons Apparently Drowned. On his second visit to London, Haydn is supposed to have taken rooms in Bury Street to be near Mrs. Schroeter because, as he said, she was "an English widow who loved me. I should in all likelihood have married her if I had been single." In what other century could such a remark have so casually been made? Even the eighteenth-century philosophers were "people." When the matter-of-fact skeptic David Hume contracted a repulsive disease that he knew to be "mortal and incurable," he set about dying with stoicism and poise, writing how he never suffered a moment's abatement in his spirits—"Were I to name a period of my life which I should most choose to pass over again, I might be tempted to point to this later period. It is difficult to be more detached from life than I am at present." There is Pope, the "correct" rhymer, who doubtless released some hidden urge in excavating a little grotto in his garden and making it gaudy with bits of glass, colored stones, and carefully arranged stalactites brought from western England. There are the rakes in the Hell Fire Club who apparently dressed as monks while they performed the Black Mass with all the lewd rituals they could devise. This, too, is the eighteenth century that is supposed to be an age of "reason" and to be "classical" in one way or another. And there was always the full tide of life in old London, the smoky, crowded, noisy city that is felt almost as a personality itself throughout the poems, novels, and dramas of the century.

Although the eighteenth century is ordinarily considered to be an age of formality and the "rules," in fact it was an age of brilliant impromptu talk, with Johnson, Boswell, Swift, the Bluestockings, and all the people who gathered in coffeehouses, clubs, and salons. The air of conversation, of accomplished conversation, is in the witty, shrewd letters of Horace Walpole and Thomas Gray, in the chatty essays by Addison and Goldsmith; it appears, with all the dramatic inflections of London argument, in the great records of Dr. Johnson's life; it is in the closely written diaries like Fanny Burney's, and in the quick accents of Pope's heroic couplet. The century liked to be informal in an easy civilized way. Chesterfield was always advising his illegitimate son to cultivate the graces. The supposedly formal eighteenth century affords us inexhaustibly our most intimate anecdotes of British writers: Swift, fearing that he would go mad, writing out his terrible hatreds and all his thwarted tenderness for that "perfect friend" of his, Stella; Sterne, the sentimental clergyman, bleeding from his poor lungs as he sniggered and leered his way through *Tristram Shandy;* self-centered, defensive Pope, painstakingly contriving to have his own letters "stolen" and printed, and carefully rewriting his impassioned love letters; Boswell with his drunkenness and Rotarian eagerness to know everybody and be liked; cumbrous, earnest Johnson; pursy little Gibbon tapping his snuffbox and writing with an "equal and easy pace" his huge *Decline and Fall of the Roman Empire;* Blake conversing with the ghost of John Milton or with the prophet Ezekiel. The period has a humor and caprice all its own to delight us—as when Boswell argued for an "Asiatic multiplicity" of wives; or when "a lively pretty little woman" was encouraged by the company to sit upon Johnson's knee and to put her hands about his neck and kiss him, to which Johnson responded, "Do it again, and let us see who will tire first"; or when Thomas Gray, the Oxford intellectual, sang and danced through the streets of Rouen at four or five of a spring morning with some of the well-bred ladies of France.

People were also "civilized." The writers of the eighteenth century, in contrast to those of the nineteenth particularly, are ur-

bane. There were certain boors, of course, and some of the poems
and essays moralize a little heavily; but the distinctive eighteenth-
century tone is that of the *Spectator* papers, in which Addison
brought philosophy out of the libraries and scholars' closets to clubs
and tea tables. Johnson, as uncouth a figure as the age presents,
once remarked, "Why, Sir, I am a man of the world. I live in
the world, and I take, in some degree, the color of the world as
it moves along." Milton was not a man of the world in this sense;
nor was Wordsworth or Shelley or even Byron. One might call
the eighteenth the last civilized century.

This urbanity was apparent in the prevailing taste. There
are many discords in the prose and poetry of the seventeenth
century, and the nineteenth century often strained too hard to
gain its effects, and abandoned itself too freely to emotional in-
tensities. Somehow the best writing of the eighteenth century
composes; there are few false notes. The eighteenth-century author was usually very sensitive to "composition" and "fitness." If
he was writing prose, he intended to be "natural" and "correct"
as well as agreeable—to avoid extremes and to be "simple" and
"refined," as Hume put it. If he was writing an essay in verse, he
strove to express attractively the opinions everybody was holding—to be "just" and "regular." Dr. Johnson spoke of taste as an
"intuitive perception of consonance and propriety," and Sir Joshua
Reynolds believed that all the arts depended upon the "sense of
congruity, coherence, and consistency" in the human mind. In
descriptive passages in prose or verse the eighteenth century was
remarkably sensitive to sound and to gradations of light and shade,
or what a painter would call values. The eighteenth-century eye
was much more responsive than ours to subtle pictorial effects;
doubtless, at the opening of Gray's *Elegy*, the reader of 1751 was
far more intimately affected than we by the toll of the curfew and
the herd winding across the glimmering lea. Doubtless he *saw* a
great many of the poetic abstractions like Fear and Pity and Remorse. The eighteenth century had an eye and an ear.

It had, too, a poise that we lack in our century of violences and
perplexity. The eighteenth century had made up its mind upon
certain standards, or at least believed that it had. It was an age of
agreements (or presumed agreements). Its prose and its verse are
apt to lie at the center of normal human experience, or more
nearly at the center than ours, or than the prose and verse of the

seventeenth century. It was able to make assumptions that we find trouble in making—for example, assumptions that man is everywhere the same, that there is a clear order in nature, that Greek and Roman literature set standards by which to measure almost all literature, that Christianity is not a mystery but a collection of plain, evident truths easily understood, that one will prosper if one is industrious, and that society as a whole will benefit if each person energetically seeks his own interest. The poise and soundness of the prose of the eighteenth century—which, at its best, is difficult to parody because it is not in any way freakish or mannered—probably results from this reliance upon accepted standards. The very moralizing of the day often depended upon the large conclusions that everybody seemed able to make: as Boswell said of Johnson, "His maxims carry conviction; for they are founded on the basis of common sense, and a very attentive and minute survey of real life."

This sense of order was one legacy of the seventeenth to the eighteenth century. By 1700 it seemed clear, after the civil wars and tumults and doubts of the early seventeenth century, that the universe is ordered on the invariable simple mathematical principle of gravitation—the physicist Sir Isaac Newton had proved it so. The same kind of order seemed to be in the "state of nature" upon which all political, civil society was held to be founded—the philosopher John Locke had demonstrated this. Similarly, Locke had shown how the human mind itself, gathering in sense impressions and neatly arranging them by association, operated, like the Newtonian universe, by perfectly regular laws. Thus the "rules" in drama, the neat pattern of the formal garden, the tendency to balance in architecture, and the simplified and coherent prose and heroic couplet all manifest this new awareness of order.

The agreements about taste and standards in literature and the arts were not, however, made by reason alone. They were agreements in which traditions and attitudes were influential. Some of the more rationalistic agreements of the eighteenth century were political agreements, concerning the rights of man. The very foundations of democratic political principles were established in the century between the British Revolution of 1688 and the French Revolution of 1789. In 1690, after England had deposed her last absolutist monarch, James II, and had summoned William and Mary to the throne, John Locke had justified this "glorious" revolution by arguing that "men being . . . by nature all free, equal, and independent, no one can be put out of this estate and subjected to the political power of another without his own consent, which is done by agreeing with other men to join and unite into a community for their own comfortable, safe, and peaceable living." Consequently the governors of a state must be directly responsible to the will of the majority. The terms of this compact were restated in various ways in the eighteenth century during the age of Queen Anne (the Augustan age in England), the following long Whig ministry under Robert Walpole, and the reigns of the first three Georges, those unamiable and shambling kings whom the British had called to the throne from the German house of Hanover.

While the British empire was spreading from Hudson's Bay to India, the colonists in America had reaffirmed the political compact in their Declaration of Independence. Then Tom Paine, in *The Rights of Man*, justified the French Revolution on the grounds that "man has no property in man; neither has any generation property in the generations which are to follow." This great agreement in political theory was transmitted to the nineteenth and twentieth centuries as one of the most significant eighteenth-century certainties.

Of course the century was a transitional one, and had *its* own confusions and perplexities and increasing contradictions. For one thing, the eighteenth-century writer was often led by his feelings and sensibility to distrust the very standards that he presumably accepted. Thus the era ended with manifestations of what is commonly called romanticism, which repudiated in general the eighteenth-century "order." The nineteenth-century writers were not only personal but aggressively individual as the eighteenth-century writers were not. The sense of composition and fitness was gone. No doubt the inconsistencies and dilemmas of the nineteenth century developed during the eighteenth, which had its own sort of complexity.

However, the ability of the thinkers and writers of the enlightenment was to arrive at certain large agreements; they formulated standards and made assumptions that were often not "rational" at all, but were accepted nevertheless. One of the most provoking questions is to ask precisely how the eighteenth century *did* make its assumptions and how it *did* hold its agreements. Even if the agreements were general, they were held very personally. It is apparent that we cannot accept some of these standards exactly as the eighteenth century understood them. Yet they are of the greatest value to us because the literature of the last thirty or forty years has been increasingly inspired by the writers of the seventeenth century, which was a period of conflict, doubt, and religious instability. Our recent poetry, our recent literary criticism, and our ideals in religion have been deeply indebted to such seventeenth-century writers as John Donne. There has also been a tendency to depreciate the nineteenth century as "romantic." Because of our admiration of the seventeenth century and our lack of sympathy with the nineteenth, the literature of the eighteenth century, with its personal tone, its agreements, urbanity, taste, and sense of how things "compose," takes on larger meaning in the midst of our own present confusions.

ENLIGHTENED ENGLAND: THE CULTURAL AND INTELLECTUAL MILIEU

I. THE ENLIGHTENMENT AS A TURNING POINT

THOSE who do not wish to look more deeply value the Augustans and Georgians for their graceful living and the anecdotal charm of their writing. For others, the closing years of the seventeenth century and the opening of the eighteenth mark a shift in the very consciousness of Europe. Behind lay the eras of faith, whether that faith was the medieval one of Aquinas, the Elizabethan, Anglican compromise of Richard Hooker, or the aggressive protestantism of John Milton. Ahead opened the scientific, commercial, and democratic nineteenth and twentieth centuries.

The eighteenth century—the period often called the enlightenment—brought not only the minuet, the music of Handel and Mozart, the poetry of Pope, portraiture by Reynolds, and the sedate Georgian architecture, but also the energy and excitement of the industrial revolution, the unshackling of business from state control, or what we now call the change from mercantilism to laissez-faire. Upon thriving iron foundries, textile factories, and potteries was established a British empire extending from the West Indies to India. Between 1710 and 1790 the British consumption of cotton alone rose from 1,000,000 pounds to 22,000,000 pounds. Eighteenth-century England was a nation of amateur devisers and experimenters: Daniel Defoe forever occupied with his projects, Lady Mary Wortley Montagu popularizing inoculation against smallpox, James Watt building steam engines under the patronage of Matthew Boulton, the great Birmingham maker of hardware, Joseph Priestley tinkering with apparatus for analyzing the "phlogiston" in air, Robert Bakewell improving the breed of English sheep, John Wilkinson the ironmaster building iron bridges and iron coffins, Arthur Young composing his *Essay on the Management of Hogs*, and Erasmus Darwin speculating upon the biological evolution that his famous grandson was to formulate into a theory. When James Cook sailed in the "Endeavour" to the South Seas, the Royal Society sent with him their astronomer and botanist Joseph Banks, who on June 3, 1769, carefully observed from Tahiti the transit of Venus. The *Transactions* of the Society were on the shelves of every country house. The same vigor that expressed itself in science and industry appears in the "enlightened" scrutiny of religion, ethics, and politics. The Wesleys and evangelical preachers revivified English piety. Schemes abounded to reform prisons, poorhouses, and asylums. The prevailing revolt against political tyranny and the emphasis upon individual rights were expressed in the American Declaration of Independence, then in the French Declaration of the Rights of Man, which found the support of British republicans. The mechanical ingenuities of a Ben Franklin or a James Watt were accompanied by the revolutionary idealism of a Rousseau, a Tom Paine, or a William Godwin. The sometimes utopian enthusiasms of such visionaries made all too clear the failings of the world as it was. Hence rose a vehement criticism of existing institutions. The enlightenment was nothing if not skeptical.

Accordingly, it is possible to take one of two sharply divergent views of the enlightened eighteenth century, the earliest century in which we recognize clearly the modern situation, its assumptions and temper. To the majority of liberals—those who dislike a religious faith expressed in dogma, an unscientific attitude, or royalism and privilege in the social order—the eighteenth century was a great one, since it fostered a thoroughgoing skepticism, an experimental, empirical mode of thinking, and certain democratic political theories. To a small but influential modern minority—including Anglo-Catholics and those who accept medieval values, as well as critics of literature who admire seventeenth-century "metaphysical" complexities in prose and verse—the eighteenth century was a decline from the seventeenth. These critics find that during the enlightenment man turned from a truth "revealed" by faith to immerse himself in the temporal and rational, and that English poetry made an accelerated descent toward nineteenth-century sentimentalism, superficiality, and prettiness.

Possibly we are still too close to the eighteenth century to place it with entire certainty. Beneath its large agreements were certain inconsistencies. Against almost every current there was a countercurrent, and any attempt to simplify eighteenth-century

English literature as one of "classicism" in which there were "romantic" impulses is misleading. The eighteenth-century literature is of great importance; yet the full significance of its backgrounds in psychology, religion, sentimentalism, and democratic political theory for the twentieth is not only a literary matter. The origins of the twentieth century often lie not in the nineteenth century but in the eighteenth, and the literature of the enlightenment often needs to be interpreted by means of the enlightenment itself.

2. THE POLITICAL BACKGROUND

Many eighteenth-century writers refer to political circumstances that need to be kept in mind.

In 1688 the Stuart monarch James II, last of the absolutist English kings, had been deposed when William and Mary, "limited" monarchs, gained a kingdom bloodlessly and accepted a political settlement upon which the eighteenth century could rest. For more than half that century, during the reign of Queen Anne, and the administrations of Robert Walpole and the elder William Pitt, the influence of Catholicism and popery ceased to appear menacing, and the Crown and Parliament, long at discord, settled into at least a nominal co-operation. In 1689 a Toleration Act had established the right of freedom of worship for those Protestants who did not conform to the Church of England. Like the limitation upon royal power, this act was a kind of answer to the absolute Catholic monarch Louis XIV of France, who to the injury of the French Protestants had shortly before revoked the Edict of Nantes. Although England did not yet have a genuine party system, differing attitudes toward church and state distinguished the Whig from the Tory mentality. The Tories, in general the older landowners, upheld royal prerogative and the Established Church, for both of which the Whigs, in general representing mercantile and dissenting interests, had considerably less enthusiasm.

At the opening of the century the military situation was not satisfactory for England. The Stuart concessions to Louis XIV had nourished the power of France, the traditional enemy of England throughout the eighteenth century. Immediately after the accession of William and Mary (1688) there was war. The Treaty of Ryswick in 1697 merely marked an interval. Within four years England, with the Netherlands and Austria, was again attacking France. The conflict, which spread even to the colonies in the New

World, established British supremacy over France not only at sea but also in Europe, through the Duke of Marlborough's great victories at Blenheim, in 1704, and at Ramillies, in 1706. By these successes Marlborough came to occupy the position that the Duke of Wellington was to occupy a century later, after Napoleon was broken at Waterloo, though Marlborough was perhaps less gratefully used.

The Whigs, who had pushed the war, fell from power in 1710, and the Tory ministry of Bolingbroke and Harley achieved the brilliant Treaty of Utrecht, in 1713, which still further restricted the French. The Tories did not long enjoy their triumph. Since all the children of Queen Anne were dead, the question of the succession split the group asunder, some under Bolingbroke being drawn toward the exiled Stuarts, others supporting George of the German house of Hanover. At the death of Anne in 1714, the Tories—friends of Swift, Pope, Arbuthnot, and Gay, and all the literary brightest "wits"—were dispersed. The long Whig administration under Robert Walpole, minister from 1721 to 1742, followed.

The Walpole era was tranquil. Sir Robert's motto—"Let sleeping dogs lie"—suited the political complacency of the earlier Georgian period, in which vested interests were untroubled by reforming zeal. The Hanoverian George I (1714–27) resigned to his Whig ministers still further prerogatives of the Crown, so that now government was largely in the hands of the Prime Minister, his cabinet, and the House of Commons. Affairs under George II (1727–60) were little different. After a turbulent seventeenth century, England had relaxed into a slothful and even cynical tolerance of the established order—as Pope wrote,

One truth is clear, WHATEVER IS, IS RIGHT.

If the great Whig families controlled matters of state, the countryside got on well enough under beef-eating, fox-hunting squires like Fielding's Squire Western.

The repose was broken by a naval war with Spain in 1739, and by another war with France in 1742, the War of the Austrian Succession, which again spread to the colonies. The followers of the Stuarts had also for the last time taken arms, and in 1745–46 the rash Jacobite invasion of England by Prince Charles Edward and his Highlanders ended disastrously at Culloden. The years between the War of the Austrian Succession and the Seven Years' War (1756–63), again pitting England against France, have been called the most placid of the century. During the latter war the elder Pitt established England's vast colonial empire on a world-wide scope by supporting Clive in India and Wolfe in Canada. Meanwhile, England was aiding Frederick the Great in his struggle against France, Austria, and Russia.

Then came the troublous years of George III (1760–1820). Constitutional issues rose when the King insisted upon ruling through his friends. The witty radical John Wilkes became a popular hero when Parliament attempted to deny him the seat to which he had been duly elected. Above all, the war with the American colonies was a disturbing experience not only because part of the empire was lost but also because basic principles were deeply involved —the coercion of fellow Englishmen, and the personal government of the King. The trial of Warren Hastings for corruption in Indian politics, the vexing Irish-Catholic situation, and the alarming antipapist riots provoked by the fanatical Lord George Gordon unsettled things further.

During the administration of the younger William Pitt, a new sort of Tory who came into power in 1784, democratic ideas were sweeping France and England, and the Foxite Whigs came to be identified with the revolutionary notions of the radicals Tom Paine, Richard Price, and Joseph Priestley.

The onset of the French Revolution began a new era. Although at first England felt no dread of the upheaval in France, and perhaps a certain approval of the French revolutionists, the Terror and the triumphant armies of the Republic soon provoked a violent British conservatism. War was declared against France in 1793, and by 1794 the vise of repression clamped upon democrats like Thomas Hardy, the shoemaker, accused of treason simply because he founded a corresponding society that advocated political reform. Hardy was acquitted, to be sure, but England remained resolutely anti-Jacobin. Affairs were going badly in the West Indies, too, where a British campaign against the French islands was costing scores of thousands of lives. In 1797 the sailors in the home fleet mutinied at Spithead. All the while, in defiance of the conservative *Anti-Jacobin* magazine, writers like John Thelwall were preaching equality and liberty and fraternity. It was a painful hour. The only cheer was the defeat of Napoleon in the Battle of the Nile in

1798. The triumph was inconclusive, however, for England was embarked upon a conflict with France that was to end only in 1815 at Waterloo.

3. SOCIETY: LONDON AND THE COUNTRY

Gradual industrialization—a result of expanding commerce, the increased use of coal, and countless ingenious inventions like the spinning jenny and the steam engine—modified the entire social order of eighteenth-century England. While common lands were being enclosed and the factory system was developing, the great propertyless class, now called "labor," was being swept into the vortex of urban life. The eighteenth century called them "the poor." They wandered about highways everywhere. They swarmed into filthy, windowless lodgings (there was a tax on windows). They perished with cold, hunger, and disease. Yet the population of England increased from six to nine millions within the second half of the century. In 1776 the Bluestocking Mrs. Montagu writes to Mrs. Carter of the workers in her coal mines near Denton, Yorkshire:

The people here are little better than savages, and their countenances bear the marks of hard labor and total ignorance. Our pitmen are literally as black as a coal; they earn much more than laborers, their children get a shilling a day at 9 or 10 years old, but they are so barbarous and uncultivated they know no use of money but to buy much meat and liquor with it. . . . . They are useful persons to the general commonwealth, but considered separately a strange set of barbarians.

London was filled with the unemployed and unemployable who, until the tax on gin in 1751, horribly tried to forget their misery in "Gin Lane." The blind and the maimed flocked to the alleys off Fleet Street, where they could thieve by night and beg by day.

Everyone presumed that expanding industry and commerce meant progress. The poet John Dyer in *The Fleece* exclaims with satisfaction that the textiles of Manchester clothe tribes along the Niger. New industrial and commercial wealth meant the bourgeois revolution that eventually demolished the genteel, aristocratic graces commended by Lord Chesterfield, the tradition of wit and taste; the bourgeoisie meant sentimentality, humanity, and democracy. The nation of shopkeepers expressed itself in Defoe

The Old East India Wharf at London Bridge
Painting by Peter Monamy, 1670–1749

A Perspective View of Whitehall, 1740
After a copperplate by J. Maurer

The Beggars' Opera by William Hogarth

Drury Lane Theatre as It Appeared in 1775

and Samuel Richardson, and, paradoxically, in the radicals Richard Price, Joseph Priestley, and Tom Paine; or in Thrale, the rich brewer at whose suburban villa, with its "improved" garden, Dr. Johnson lolled. In London, pleasure gardens like Vauxhall and Ranelagh profited by the "cit," and resorts like Bath, Epsom, Tunbridge Wells, and Scarborough were filled with businessmen on holiday who strolled the pump rooms and paraded among noble lords and wealthy colonials.

The disruption of the old economic order stimulated thinking upon political economy, and in 1776 Adam Smith's *Wealth of Nations*, with its theories of free enterprise, division of labor, and supply and demand, signified the passing of the old mercantilist policy, whereby the government controlled trade, and the coming heyday of laissez-faire. A glance through the periodicals will show how constant was the interest in foreign trade and colonial enterprise. Speculation in stocks was heavy as early as 1721, when the South Sea Bubble burst. England was becoming a capitalist, imperialist nation of entrepreneurs.

Meanwhile the country squire was left in a dull provincialism that might produce a whimsical Roger de Coverley or a coarse Squire Western. If he owned a London house, he might use it only a few weeks in the year, and then only after an arduous journey over abominable roads, unless he was fortunately near some of the improved highways being built into London. At that, he was in danger of being robbed and beaten by highwaymen; and as he approached London, he might have to hold his nostrils while his coach passed some of the fields of refuse that ringed the city.

Until the later days of the century, when new roads made all travel easier, the country was thus isolated from London. And London meant living. The city itself was for the most part a swarming place of ill-lighted alleys, open kennels or sewers (like Fleet Ditch), chairmen bawling their way through sheep or cattle being driven to slaughter along the streets, coaches pounding day and night over cobblestones, and tradesmen's shops huddled together under their heavy signs. Houses of prostitution were common. Prints (like Hogarth's) or novels (like *Clarissa Harlowe*) show how the guileless country maid might be accosted even as she stepped from the London coach. Then might follow a course of crime ending in the workhouse task of beating hemp. From the pestilential jails the criminal might be transported in some filthy prison ship to bondage in the colonies; or, if condemned, he would be driven, in a tumbril holding his coffin, to Tyburn, where a disorderly mob would witness his execution. Apprentices were given eight holidays a year to enjoy the hangings at Tyburn. After 1783, however, executions took place within Newgate Prison. Before the Paving Act of 1762, one ventured the London streets at night with caution. There were few, if any, lamps; watchmen were indifferent or timid; rakes, "Mohocks," and "scowerers" might be abroad to slit one's face in sport. At the least, one might tumble into gutters or holes.

Until late in the century the coffeehouse or alehouse was the center of social, and often of business, life for men. The Turk's Head, at which Dr. Johnson's Club met Thursday evenings, was only one of innumerable taverns where one ate with friends, read the newspapers, wrote letters, or met clients. There were political clubs, clubs for eating, drinking, gambling, or bullbaiting. For the moneyed there were gambling houses like White's, where fortunes were squandered in an evening; or there were "routs" at large, chill mansions in fashionable Berkeley, Hanover, Grosvenor, or Portman Squares. One could agreeably spend an evening being rowed by a burly waterman along the Thames. All the world was to be seen at Vauxhall gardens or Ranelagh; here even bishops could saunter without injuring their characters. One could linger in the Rotunda at Ranelagh, listening to the organ. Vauxhall, across the Thames, was perhaps more exciting. There one ate thin slices of cold meat, wandered in conveniently darkened alleys, rushed to see fireworks or balloon ascensions, relished the latest song by Arne, or heard with rapture the nightingales sing in the groves. The famous "Gothic" pavilions at Vauxhall were decorated with remarkable paintings—"Two Mahometans Gazing in Astonishment at the Beauties of Vauxhall," "A Shepherd Playing a Pipe and Seducing a Shepherdess into a Wood," "Pamela Revealing Her Wishes to Return Home." There were also the statue of Handel by Roubillac and the vistas down alleys to the painted Ruins of Palmyra. It was all very amusing, particularly the various arrangements in the "Chinese" manner.

The theater of the day was a barnlike place, occasionally filled with those who came to make trouble at some personal or political implication in the play of the evening or at some rise in the price of admission. If the cry of "Ladies out" was raised, it was signal for rioting that might wreck the house. Until the day of Garrick, one might sit upon the stage. Ordinarily there was a full-length play—perhaps Shakespeare recast to conform to the dramatic rules of time and place—and then as afterpiece a brief farce or burletta. One might hear an oratorio by Handel sung at the Haymarket Theater. If one were fortunate, one might be invited to a private concert by Italian singers at Lady Brown's or at Mrs. Fox Lane's. Here one might meet a "nabob" (an Englishman who had amassed a fortune in India) or a West Indian who had come to London to run through his fabulous wealth as showily as he could. London, if callous, was hardly dull.

Neither was London provincial. In the cosmopolitan eighteenth century great French men of letters like Buffon, Montesquieu, Rousseau, or Voltaire might be living there; one might see Gray's Swiss friend Bonstetten on the street. British and French armies might be engaged abroad, but Horace Walpole could inspire the devotion of Mme. du Deffand, leader of a Parisian salon, or the Abbé Raynal, a *philosophe*, might be elected to the Royal Society and talk brilliantly the whole afternoon and evening before a choice group of learned ladies—Bluestockings, as they were called. The eighteenth century had a whole line of them, the most clubbable (in Johnson's phrase) banding into salons somewhat on the French pattern. Mrs. Vesey, Mrs. Boscawen, Mrs. Delany, Fanny Burney—all were intelligent, if not learned. Some seemed learned: Mrs. Montagu achieved an essay on Shakespeare in reply to Voltaire; and she and Elizabeth Carter read Tacitus "so as to always have a subject to correspond upon." Mrs. Carter,[1] who walked or rode from four to five each morning and who is said to have translated Epictetus with a cold towel wrapped about her head, was perhaps more learned than charming. At the age of eighty-eight she coolly remarked, "Nobody knows what *may* happen; I never said I would not marry." Hannah More, who dreaded pedantry, was a sort of moving spirit in every philanthropy. Mrs. Thrale refused to be shouted down by even Dr. Johnson. Mrs. Chapone, author of the official Bluestocking text—*Letters on the Improvement of the Mind*—announced that "*women*, as rational and accountable beings, are free agents as well as *men*." The nineteenth

---

1 The term "Mrs." did not necessarily mean that a woman was married; it was often a term of respect.

century, with its evangelical heritage, was to domesticate the female into a more decent submission.

4. THE APPEAL TO "REASON"—TRENDS IN PHILOSOPHY

The eighteenth century is called the age of reason—and possibly the most difficult problem it offers is to determine what "reason" implied. Like the term "nature," with which it was allied if not often identical, it had scores of meanings. A few among these sundry meanings of reason are easily distinguished: the perfect mathematical-physical order of the universe operating by the gravitational laws discovered by Sir Isaac Newton; the insight or individual conviction about truth called "right reason," a heritage from Milton and the religious thought of the preceding century; an intuitive good sense or "taste," the faculty much admired by French critics and by Horace; the "common" sense of the Scottish thinkers, not unlike American "horse sense"; "judgment," a faculty opposed to cleverness or "wit"; the precedent of the Roman or Greek writers in literary matters, this precedent being solidified in "the rules"; the analytic, destructive, and often cynical criticism of reformers like Voltaire or Tom Paine; the clear abstract ideas and concepts which the French philosopher Descartes supposed to be innate in the human mind; or, exactly the opposite, a reliance upon the experience of the five senses and the impressions they receive, an empiricism inherited from John Locke.

Many of these meanings of reason correspond to the meanings of that other slippery term "nature," which often meant simply human nature. If the eighteenth century admired anything more than reason, it was nature, to which everyone appealed. Both terms implied, generally, that there is an inviolable order in the universe *and* in the minds and feelings of all men of all ages and places. The appeal was to this uniform pattern, which was expressed in the mathematical order of Sir Isaac Newton's universe, in the deistic theological system of Samuel Clarke by which the world is a vast divine order, in John Locke's supposition that before men established governments the original human society existed in an ordered "state of nature," in the literary "rules," in the geometry of the formal garden, and in the neat heroic couplet in verse. Charles Gildon in his *Complete Art of Poetry* (1718) accepted order as a critical standard: "But let *Imagination* be never so strong and fertile of *Ideas*, without the Assistance of Judgment (which can only be informed and directed by the Stated Rules) there can be nothing produced *entirely beautiful*." As the century moved on, its skepticism about a universal order increased because thinkers and writers became keenly aware of whatever is local, singular, or eccentric. The change was manifested, for example, in the theory that differing climates diversify the natures of men everywhere, in the keen interest in outlandish spots like Patagonia and Abyssinia, and in the new enthusiasm for one's own individual experience and "original" genius. Political theory, however, and especially the many programs for democracy, continued to assume that there is an ideal state of nature with its ideal scheme of natural rights.

Biology, also, was changing the direction of scientific thought. After Newton came naturalists like Linnaeus and Buffon. Science also became practical and experimental with many inventions like those by Ben Franklin. A strong empiricism—experiment, and the evidence of the senses—also transformed philosophy into psychology, the interest in *what* we know into the interest in *how* we know. When in 1690 John Locke attempted to show that our abstract ideas are only assimilations and combinations of sense impressions, he began a psychological investigation that was continued by David Hartley and David Hume, and that affected painting, landscape gardening, and poetry. Philosophy was increasingly concerned to prove that the nature of man's mind is determined by the sense experiences with which it has been brought into contact. French and English psychologists developed a completely mechanical fatalism—*l'homme machine*—to prove that we have no free will and that we behave by automatic reflex. This fatalism was employed by "necessitarians" like William Godwin to prove that man is perfectible; for if man *is* a product of the forces operating mechanically upon him, then control of those forces can ameliorate his situation and nature. Thus comes a paradox in the age that devoted itself to proving that man is "free" by "nature." David Hume pressed matters unpleasantly far: to him, abstract knowledge is uncertain and well-nigh impossible, for we "know" only separate and momentary sense impressions. Such "avowed and dogmatical atheism," as James Beattie called it, especially distressed certain hard-headed Scottish thinkers, who replied to Hume by falling back upon the principle that a thing must be true if it seems-to be true to plain common sense; otherwise, we end in mental paralysis. We can see why the age is called skeptical.

In the arts, this appeal to the senses worked a revolution. Addison in saying that the imagination is the remembrance of things seen, Mark Akenside in his poem on *The Pleasures of Imagination*, Edmund Burke in his treatise on the sublime and beautiful, and numberless other critics admitted in one or another way that since man's sensibility is molded by what is heard, touched, or seen, the imagination is a creation of impressions received from nature. There was a religious implication also. Even the orthodox Christian accepted the deistic view that God, the great contriver, is revealed in nature; therefore, one gets in touch with divinity through nature, that can speak memorable things. By 1712 Addison was hymning how

> The Spacious Firmament on high,
> With all the blue Etherial Sky,
> And spangled Heav'ns, a Shining Frame,
> Their great Original proclaim:
> Th' unwearied Sun, from Day to Day,
> Does his Creator's Power display,
> And publishes to every Land
> The Work of an Almighty Hand.

The development of a Wordsworthian "natural piety" was thus possible. Furthermore, since the imagination itself was held to be a kind of recollection of things seen, the imaginative arts became primarily descriptive; and the art of Dryden and Pope was succeeded by the more visual or "retinal" art of Thomson, Dyer, and Cowper. The descriptive poem or painting was reminiscent of what was seen, an exalted language of the sense. Here is another paradox: that the age of reason should evolve an art addressed to the senses.

Samuel Johnson represents a unique value in this age of reason. Like Swift or Burke, he is profoundly distrustful of intellectualism, abstraction, and rationality. Johnson's Rasselas, like Swift's Laputans, cannot live by mind alone. Although Swift represents the Houyhnhnms as living by reason, and although Johnson mistrusts imagination as deeply as he mistrusts reason, yet what Johnson and Swift actually admire is reasonableness—the ability to live satisfactorily rather than to think abstractly. This reasonableness, a practical and ethical talent to determine how to live in the existing circumstances, avoids Tom Paine's or William Godwin's doctrinaire theorizing about man. In fact, throughout the age of reason there was a widespread dislike of intellectualized systems, especially on the part of critics who espoused taste.

5. LIBERTY, EQUALITY, FRATERNITY: THE DEMOCRATIC IDEOLOGY

Toward the end of the century, some shocking opinions about liberty were playing feverishly over the surface, at least, of middle-class society. The Englishman had always cherished his freedom. Although it is hard to say what the cliché "free-born Briton" meant to the writers of the day who used it so often, it certainly implied, among other things, a check upon royal prerogative, a semblance, at least, of equity before the law, an absence of ecclesiastical interference, a degree of representative government, a sense of the integrity of the individual, and the privilege of the moneyed to catch a little of the social glitter. In 1690 John Locke in his *Treatises of Government* had insisted that royal power is not divine and that society is founded upon a contract under which the government is responsible to the governed. Locke's insistence upon men's natural rights was not lost upon the French political thinkers, who with characteristic logic elaborated the social compact into a highly rationalist and even utopian political theory of democracy. Thomas Day, Joseph Priestley, Richard Price, Tom Paine, Thomas Holcroft, John Thelwall, and a number of British "friends of humanity" endorsed this Gallic design for society, and saw first in the American Revolution, then in the French, an omen of the new democracy and man's perfectibility. Many of these levelers belong in the tradition of reason that depends not upon historical and empirical evidence but upon unverifiable abstract ideas: democracy was an ideology. Since England had inherited a tradition of compromise and settlement, the British *philosophe* was less destructive than the French. Nevertheless, to the Jacobin and democrat like Paine it was "rational" enough that "man" was "originally" created "free" and "equal," concepts clear to the enlightenment according to the "system of nature"—whatever that may have been.

6. DEISM: THE DECLINE OF FAITH IN
REVEALED RELIGION

The "rationalistic reason," seeking to represent ideas with almost mathematical clarity, was in part responsible for the widespread disrepute of Christianity and the rise of deism or "natural religion." In 1682 Dryden had presumed that "the things we must believe are few and plain," things comparable, perhaps, to the mathematical principles of gravitation by which Sir Isaac Newton in 1687 simplified and arranged the universe. Dryden spoke prophetically: the seventeenth century had spilled enough blood in contentious religion, and England was weary of Miltonic severity, and zeal in any form. Instead, the easy tolerance recommended by the third Earl of Shaftesbury in the *Characteristics* (1711) sufficed, particularly under the openly corrupt politics of a Robert Walpole. There was, to be sure, the Bangorian uproar (*ca.* 1717) raised by a proposal to disestablish the Church, but before the evangelical and Methodist quickening, the English church was content with sluggish, fox-hunting clergy who forgot the poor at their gates. Meantime the dissenters were becoming a numerous and influential group, chiefly recruited among the shopkeepers.

When about 1729 the Holy Club, a group of Oxford students inspired by Charles and John Wesley, began to receive the sacrament regularly and devoutly, they were called, contemptuously, "Methodists." Whatever may have been his personal failings, John Wesley was not discouraged by contempt, and with prodigious energy he began traveling on horseback thousands of miles each year preaching outdoors to the laboring poor. The evangelicals—low churchmen like Cowper's friend John Newton—also felt the reawakening that swept beyond the shores of England to the colonies. If this impetuous revivalism was heat without light, too often the established Church had neither light nor eat. George Crabbe was able to dismiss Methodism as a "spiritual influenza," and to the Duchess of Buckingham the Methodists were "most repulsive, and strongly tinctured with impertinence and disrespect towards their superiors." "It is monstrous," she went on, "to be told that you have a heart as sinful as the common wretches that crawl the earth." Respectable people were content with subscribing to the thirty-nine articles of belief listed in the Book of Common Prayer; the bare formalities of religion were sometimes not observed either in the slothful universities or in the pluralistic livings beyond their walls. Often the age attempted to comfort itself against religious chill by an emphatic moralizing; it was the age of the moral tale and the apologue.

Tolerating the way of the world also suited the deism inherited from the seventeenth century. In some ways the most influential consequence of enlightened thought, deism was not a system of belief; indeed, it was inconsistent and antidogmatic by its very nature. It was, rather, a certain attitude, full of irreconcilable assumptions. The chief of these assumptions seem to have been the following: the universe is a creation of a highly intelligent mind, and operates upon clearly demonstrable, perhaps mathematical, principles "lest God himself should seem too absolute"; faith is not the evidence of things unseen, but is merely a useful superstition for instilling good behavior among the less enlightened; all the Old Testament and much of the New, particularly the miraculous goings-on, are the language of uninformed superstition; the universe—external nature —can as clearly reveal God as any miracle; in spite of the misadventures of history and natural calamities such as the Lisbon quake of 1755 in which some 60,000 persons perished, the scheme of things is, on the whole, as satisfactory as one could wish; God, emitting his creative energy (a tenet of Neo-Platonism), has penetrated as far as possible, though at times imperfectly, the material substance that is not-God, and in so doing has created the best of possible worlds; good humor and toleration will enable us to get on much better than stiff-necked insistence upon any creed based upon what is not demonstrable to plain reason; one should do good simply because benevolence is man's natural impulse, and not because of any niggling expectation of future heavenly reward from divinity; and, in general, one had better live as naturally as one can, since nature is the norm.

Obviously there are difficulties with these propositions, not the least of which is conceiving a universe that is at the same time a precise machine and a vital organism. Yet deism is of the highest consequence because it made assumptions that are sometimes made today, and because it meant skepticism of revealed religion in favor of a rationalistic quasi-explanation of things. It is a conclusive instance of man's turn from faith to reason and thoroughgoing modern secularism. Its greatest weakness is its extreme plausibility.

Its greatest virtue is toleration, which virtue, however, becomes available in proportion to one's distrust of dogma and one's own uncertainty: toleration may simply be a lack of conviction. Deism replaced belief by easy suppositions. As the century went on, the tenor of deism was often politically and socially radical; the placid optimism of Shaftesbury became the bitter scoffing of Voltaire and Paine, and the devastating sneer of Edward Gibbon, whose *Decline and Fall of the Roman Empire* mocked not only the miracles of the early Church but even the crucifixion of Christ.

Although the English Church began by condemning deists like Toland and Tindal, natural religion so deeply contaminated the orthodox clergy that Joseph Butler's *Analogy of Religion* and William Paley's *Evidences of Christianity* and *Natural Theology* unconsciously accepted the very deistic proposal that God is to be found in nature, or is demonstrated by nature. Edward Young, opposing deism in *Night Thoughts,* urged that we "Renounce St. Evremond, and read St. Paul." In the next breath he appealed to the stars as "nature's system of divinity." The orthodox Cowper, like Wordsworth, discerned a grandeur in the language of the senses—the language of nature. All this admiration for nature was destined to be placed in a new light after the geologist and biologist suggested that nature is really red in tooth and claw. But the eighteenth century was not troubled by this uncomfortable Darwinian observation, even if the Reverend Thomas Malthus insisted in 1798 that population was increasing in a faster ratio than the means of subsistence. Only a few skeptics like Swift or Voltaire mocked the deistic optimism that "whatever is, is right"; and only a Dr. Johnson feared that "Life protracted is protracted woe."

7. PRIMITIVISM: THE STATE OF NATURE

Many supposed that they could behold the state of nature in the South Sea Islands or along the banks of the Ohio, or anywhere else remote enough from Fleet Street. The century had a consuming curiosity about the far places of the earth. Great English navigators like Anson, Byron, and Cook were voyaging the Pacific. Gigantic collections of travels burdened the shelves of polite libraries. Dr. Johnson permitted himself to wonder at the Great Wall of China, and the introspective Cowper, reading of Cook's voyages in his seclusion at Olney, marveled at how South Sea Islanders dance with exquisite grace. While Indian kings and Omiah, the savage prince from Tahiti, visited London, Lord Monboddo was meditating upon Mlle. le Blanc, the wild girl, and upon man's relation to the orangutan. Boswell, too, was serving as press agent for General Paoli and his noble, savage Corsicans oppressed by the French and Genoese. Bluestockings and queens were finding the poetry of nature among lowly Pindars and Sapphos: Stephen Duck, the thresher; Mary Collier, the washerwoman; Ann Yearsley, the milkwoman; James Woodhouse, the shoemaker; Ignatius Sancho and Phillis Wheatley, Negro servants; and Robert Burns, greeted as a "heaven-sent plowman, from his humble and unlettered station."

How seriously did the eighteenth century believe in the noble savage? At times, as seriously as we believe in American life as shown by Hollywood. Each generation has its fantasies, if not its illusions, and the noble savage was a fantasy that provoked, as Rousseau found out, a good many attractive questions. It is said that the explorers stimulated faith in noble savagery; yet the accounts of James Cook or James Bruce will do little to make one admire the Patagonian or the Abyssinian. Rather, the noble savage was a diversion, like the cowboy, or the shepherd of the pastoral. He symbolized the very indiscretions that a polite but bored society could not tolerate. Or else he was a "philosophical" symbol of the state of nature. The state of nature, according to reason, was not nasty and brutish; it was man living uncorrupted by society. Any ideology has its symbols: there was an ideology behind the noble savage. Loud as was the new bourgeois acclaim of civilizing commerce—"social trade," as the poet Thomson called it—a rationalist countertheory insisted that only natural man is admirable. Side by side with Dyer's *Fleece* and odes to commerce were the laments of John Brown, whose *Estimate of the Manners and Principles of the Times* (1757–58) voiced the fear that the arts and commerce had corrupted virtue. The admiration for the primitive everywhere belied the admiration for progress.

8. THE NEW SENSIBILITY: SENTIMENTALISM, HUMANITY, AND MELANCHOLY

Paradoxically enough, the age of reason was likewise the age of feeling. James Thomson gave himself to the "social tear" as readily as to Newtonian science. If reason was common to men in China and Peru, the feelings were also. As Hannah More argued,

> From heads to hearts lies Nature's plain appeal,
> Though few can reason, all mankind can *feel.*

Mary Wollstonecraft, the wife of William Godwin and a very cogitative female indeed, cherished her sensibility—the result, she said, "of acute senses, finely fashioned nerves, which vibrate at the slightest touch." This sensibility took puzzling forms. Those who could enjoy tea in Bedlam watching the antics of the insane, or who relished a hanging day at Tyburn, could dissolve in tears over the dilemmas of *Clarissa Harlowe* or the posturings of *Tristram Shandy.* Even Smollett's robust Roderick Random simpers before his Narcissa.

The ideal eighteenth-century "man of feeling" was, above all, humane. Shaftesbury and the deists suggested that since the uncorrupted instincts of man are benevolent, one is naturally prone to relieve distress, and self-interest is as artificial as it is ungenerous. Francis Hutcheson believed that the "calm, stable, universal good will to all, or the most extensive benevolence," is our most excellent disposition. Presently, this "strong sense of pity" expanded into what Pope called "one close system of benevolence," to embrace, with complacency, the fallen woman, the debtor and beggar, the drunkard, the slave, the imprisoned and orphaned, the insane, the peasant, and even the beasts slaughtered for the table. Thomson pitied men's "thousand nameless ills"; Pope's *Moral Essays* pay tribute to John Kyrle, Man of Ross, whose philanthropy became legendary; Gray gave to misery all he had—a tear; Cowper felt for poor, crazed Kate; Burns pitied wee cowerin' timorous beasties; Blake pled for little black chimney sweeps.

The accepted motive in economic life and the new industry, however, was enlightened selfishness. For example, Bernard Mandeville, harshly insisting on the benefits of competition and division of labor, held that the general weal results from the self-seeking of each member of society. Opposed to this thesis was the stronger benevolent argument that by helping others one helped one's self—that personal happiness is possible only in a society in which happiness is widely diffused. Thus a "feeling" benevolism developed into a full theory of social utilitarianism. As Francis Hutcheson said, "that action is best which procures the greatest happiness for the greatest numbers"; he even calculated social good by convenient mathematical formulas. The principle of "disinterested affection" was accepted and further extended by David Hume and Jeremy Bentham (who complained that when he read Molière he found no facts, but who loved everything with four legs). When in 1776 in the *Wealth of Nations* Adam Smith justified man's eagerness to truck, barter, and exchange, he did not intend to separate man's self-seeking disposition from man's social sympathy for man. In 1759, in his *Theory of Moral Sentiments*, he had urged that acquisitiveness be kept within social bounds by benevolence, for all morality, he had explained, originates in sympathy. Thus the eighteenth century bequeathed to the nineteenth two associated but incompatible views of economic life: that acquisitiveness is the cause of prosperity, and that acquisitiveness is to be tempered by benevolence. Philanthropy was a ready but not conclusive solution to this dilemma, as the nineteenth century found.

When sensibility turned in upon itself unwholesomely, it bred a melancholy that had already been felt in the seventeenth century. Shenstone, Collins, Gray, Johnson, and Cowper often lived under a malady of spirit. When the French wanted to spend what they called an English morning, they shut themselves into the deepest shade of their gardens to enjoy what Wordsworth later called "that sweet mood when pleasant thoughts bring sad thoughts to the mind"; and Voltaire jested about the "dark November days when the English hang themselves." A depression or deficiency of animal vigor, which one suspects may have been in part due to a sodden diet or want of exercise or even to English weather, overtook almost everyone at some time or other. Often it was called the vapors, the spleen, or the hyp. Often it inspired morbid religious doubts—was one saved, really? Cowper and Johnson labored under this blacker mood. It has been conjectured that Dr. Johnson's secret, known only to Mrs. Thrale, was that he thought himself mad. John Wesley, whose followers seemed to have a diseased sensibility, wrote of whole congregations overcome by tears and anguish; "sudden storms" swept over meetinghouses, and benches were broken in the tumult. Sometimes, more grotesquely, this introverted sensibility appeared as "Gothicism," a taste for worms and epitaphs; "graveyard" poets like Young and Blair relished their gloom, and James Hervey chose to meditate among the tombs.

Matthew Gregory Lewis's Gothic novel, *The Monk*, with its murders, rapes, and blasphemies, is as offensive as were some of the hell-fire clubs of the rakes. Byron, Shelley, De Quincey, Poe, and others prolong the malady into the next century. This acute sensibility, "pleasure that is in sorrow," as Shelley was to call it, was responsive to what was picturesque, sublime, or medieval.

9. MEDIEVALISM: THE GOTHIC QUEST

The eighteenth-century enthusiasm for the middle ages expressed itself in complex and freakish ways: in the diseased sensibility of Gothicism, in the antiquarianism of scholars like George Hickes, Thomas Percy, and the Wartons; in the finicking "taste" of Thomas Gray; in the dilettantism of Horace Walpole. The fruits of this medievalism were often strange: odes, like Collin's, on superstitions in the Highlands (composed in a half-Grecian manner), or the extravagance of Gothic romance. Again, Bishop Hurd's *Letters on Chivalry and Romance*, and the "bardic" verse of Ossian—one of the great hoaxes of the time—show how the admiration for the medieval became an admiration for the primitive. There was also an archeological interest: the revival of Gothic architecture by James Wyatt and his forerunners—and the picturesque Gothic style of building that confused Chinese, Hindoo, or Mohammedan architecture with Norman, perpendicular, and even renaissance ornament. In versification, medievalism appears in the allegorical and decorative Spenserian manner—Thomson's *Castle of Indolence* or Shenstone's *Schoolmistress*—or in the ballad as manipulated by Chatterton. In brief, there was a sustained curiosity about the medieval throughout the century. Some of it was affected; there is an air of the precious about Horace Walpole's description of his Gothic estate at Strawberry Hill:

Entering by the great north gate, the first object that presents itself is a small oratory inclosed with iron rails; in front, an altar, on which stands a saint in bronze; open niches, and stone basins for holy water . . .

Here, in 1774, is a foreshadowing of the religiosity of the Victorian Camden Society and the stained-glass attitudes of the Pre-Raphaelites. Nevertheless this sort of thing does not foreshadow the nineteenth century so properly as it belongs within the "rococo Gothic" of the eighteenth.

10. TASTE

Until lately the eighteenth century was spoken of as a time during which romanticism by degrees evolved within classicism or neoclassicism. We are now justly skeptical of such terms. It is, however, true that certain writers are less prone than others to abandon themselves to their subject; that they are more diffident or detached in representing their own personal situation; that they have a quick critical, satiric, or even ironic sense; that they are fonder of certain traditional usages and phrasings than of eccentric or individual statements; that they have an awareness of order and arrangement. Such seem to be some of the "classical" traits to be found in varying degrees among the writers of the century. The talent of Pope or Swift is critical and satiric, or, at moments, ironic. Pope's concern for arrangement is always evident. If these abilities are weak in Thomson, he nevertheless follows a good many traditional Miltonic or Latinized phrasings. Gray shows many of the classical traits, although (or, possibly, because) he is deficient in vitality. Perhaps the romantic attitude can be thought of as a reaction against the classical one, or as an absence of it.

The classicism of the era expresses itself most unmistakably in "taste," a faculty that was infirm in the seventeenth and nineteenth centuries. It seems to be a rococo faculty; at least, it disappeared when the rococo sprightliness and verve—that of the minuet—relaxed into sentimentality and platitude. In the fine arts, rococo implies fragility, balance without precise symmetry, and grace without insipidity. Either pedantry or sentimentality makes what Addison calls "fine taste" impossible. An unmistakable eighteenth-century tone that is in Pope, Addison, Gay, Collins, Gray, and, at moments, Goldsmith, is due to the exercise of this faculty. When Dr. Johnson, writing of Pope, mentioned that poet's "good sense" he defined taste as well as it has been defined: Pope, Johnson said, had "a prompt and intuitive perception of consonance and propriety." This quick, instinctive sense of what is fitting is the characteristic talent of the century at its best. It was the age of *polite* learning and *polite* writing; it was the age of the graces. It was the French moment in English literature, although the British could not so freely give themselves to the bagatelle as the French. Thus rococo leavens the arts of a new middle class. If the seventeenth century represents baroque with its heavy accent, agitation, distortion, and expressiveness—the art of John Donne and Milton—the rococo that followed represents grace, equivalence rather than precise symmetry, a certain cheerfulness, and the tact just to touch a subject without belaboring it. Fragile as the rococo was, it had a certain poise through its care for "justness" and "propriety," its "true wit" that is nature itself—the art of Pope or Addison.

Since the eighteenth century, taste has usually meant what it meant to William Hazlitt or John Ruskin—a relish or gusto, a whim, an impulsive like or dislike, an irresponsible appreciation. To the eighteenth century, taste, although intuitive, was exercised along with judgment; taste was as largely appraisal as gusto. A man of taste did not freely abandon himself to eccentric likes and dislikes, because his preferences were restrained or ordered by certain standards. These standards were not mere rules. The tasteful poem was composed

> . . . by some rule that *guides but not constrains*,
> And finish'd more thro' happiness than pains.

To write by rule was pedantry; and the man of taste would be anything rather than a pedant. The French term for taste, *je ne sais quoi*, indicates how tactfully such standards were held—not rigidly as precepts, but as amenities and as agreements or conclusions about what had been commonly experienced in reading the great writers of the past. The immediate perception of consonance and propriety was a result as largely of being cultivated within a tradition as of relying upon instinct. The eighteenth-century connoisseur, in short, was educated and informed, not ignorant or willful. After being cultivated, taste could be exercised promptly and with some assurance, and without pedantry. Thus Dr. Johnson's definition of good sense involves most of the classical traits—the refusal to abandon one's self to impulse, the awareness of order and arrangement, and particularly the sense of what is fitting, a consequence of understanding a tradition.

There is plenty of lamentable classical verse and prose and criticism by rule in the eighteenth century, but it is lamentable usually because it lacks taste; it is simply conventional and pedantic. As the century wore on, traditional standards were examined and abondoned, and taste softened into mere feeling. A good many "tasteful" dilettanti, like the Della Cruscan group of poets, were only silly. A new kind of imagination, also, began to yearn for the "sublime" and could not be held within polite rococo limits. Unquestionably, however, a Pope, though he may lack warmth, can write tastefully; Swift's taste in prose is as impeccable as Addison's; Gray is as tasteful in his way as Lord Chesterfield with his graces; the charm of Collins is somehow due to his writing in key. The best eighteenth-century prose and verse has an excellent and indispensable note struck only in the enlightenment.

11. ART AND NATURE: LANDSCAPE GARDENING, PAINTING, AND ARCHITECTURE

Throughout the eighteenth century from Pope and Dyer to Thomson, Collins, and Cowper, poets sought a "pleasure of the eye" in the descriptive or topographical poem, the prospect or landscape seen in a contemplative mood. This sort of poem was in the tradition of Milton's *L'Allegro* and *Il Penseroso;* furthermore, Addison's *Spectator* papers claimed that the pleasures of the sight stimulate and replenish the imagination. Addison believed that the imagination is restless; it cannot, he said, be immured within the alleys of formal gardens, where the marks of scissors are upon every shrub. The imagination, he observed, flies on without constraint "and is fed with an infinite variety of images" in the wide fields of nature; "it loves to be filled with an object, or to grasp at anything that is too big for its capacity. We are flung into a pleasing astonishment at such unbounded views." All the while, deists like Shaftesbury were chanting in pantheistic rapture that nature is the manifestation of God, if not God himself. As roads improved in the latter half of the century and travel in the Wye Valley and the Lake Country became less taxing and more fashionable, it began more and more to appear that God made the country as well as the town.

This questing of the eye and the imagination speeded the revolution by which the arts, until the twentieth century, became highly visual and descriptive. The eighteenth century tried to distinguish three qualities that were usually thought to exist in nature or in the work of art itself—beauty, sublimity, and picturesqueness. According to Burke's essay upon *The Sublime and Beautiful* the beautiful depends upon smallness, smoothness, gradual variation, delicacy, and mild color; it evokes a sense of pleasure. The sublime, associated with pain, terror, astonishment, and "imaginative" in the wilder Addisonian sense, depends upon obscurity, power, vastness, infinity, difficulty, gloom, and suddenness. This kind of sublimity has affinities with seventeenth-century baroque. Milton was said to be sublime; so were Mount Snowdon and the Scottish Highlands and *Ossian* and the *Book of Job* and Handel.

But the eighteenth century was filled with judicious persons who found that the excitement of the sublime, without its recklessness, was available in a third quality, the picturesque, which came to be thought of as intermediate between beauty and sublimity—"a savage but respectable terror," as Horace Walpole put it. Instead of being painful or terrible, the picturesque had a sentimental, often a reminiscent, mood; yet at the same moment there might be a shock of mild surprise in the irregularities, roughness, and melodramatic lighting of a picturesque scene. The term was supposed by some to mean a scene that looked like a picture, and in fact at least four picturesque "landscape-with-figure" manners can be distinguished among painters very influential on the seventeenth and eighteenth centuries: the rugged, theatrical scenery of the Italian Salvator Rosa; the "classical" academic pastoral of the French Nicholas and Gaspard Poussin and the Englishman Richard Wilson; the homely countrysides of the Dutch Hobbema and Ruysdael; and the mild glimmering light in the vistas of the French Claude Lorrain (known as Claude). Thus the picturesque at its extremes resembles both the sublime and the beautiful:

> The beauteous shapes of objects near,
> Or distant ones confused in air;
> The golden eve, the blinking dawn,
> Smiling on the lovely lawn!
> And pleasing views of checker'd glades!
> And rivers winding thro' the shades!
> And sunny hills, and pleasant plains!
> And groups of merry nymphs and swains!
> Or some old building, hid with grass,
> Rearing its sad ruin'd face,
> Whose columns, friezes, statues lie
> The grief and wonder of the eye!
> Or swift adown a mountain tall
> A foaming cat'ract's sounding fall . . .
>   (John Dyer, "To a Famous Painter")

English poetry is filled with these picturesque effects inspired by painting. Humphry Repton, the picturesque gardener, speaks of "that disposition of objects which, without exposing all of them equally to view at once, may lead the eye to each by an easy gradation, without flutter, confusion, or perplexity." Uvedale Price, on the other hand, remarks, "I am therefore persuaded, that the two opposite qualities of roughness, and of sudden variation, joined to that of irregularity, are the most efficient causes of the picturesque." All are very fond of "that mellow golden hue so beautiful in itself, and which, when diffused, as in a fine evening, over the whole landscape, creates that rich union and harmony, so enchanting in nature and in Claude." This last cool gleam bathes the upland fallows of Collins's "Ode to Evening." Travelers in the Wye Valley or the Lake Country—Gray, for example—carried a Claude glass, a mirrorlike device, or a tube, to compose any scene agreeably. Surprisingly enough, the special province of many poets of the age of reason is the picturesque "landscape with figures."

At the opening of the century, the "order in variety" of Pope's *Windsor Forest* suggests the carefully arranged scenes of the French painter Watteau. Yet Pope's own taste in gardens was anything but formal. He disliked the grand symmetries of Marlborough's estate at Blenheim, and when he retired to Twickenham, he enjoyed winding his walks and filling his "natural" grotto with bits of glass, stones, shells, and even stalactites fetched from Wookey Hole, Somerset. Neither did the sedate Addison enjoy clipped hedges and parterres; like the landscape architects William Kent and Batty Langley, he began to see all nature as an informal garden. By means of the sunken hedge, called the ha-ha, the English gardeners early in the century avoided formal alleys and opened the various prospects over which the sensitive eye could sweep; sheep were loosed to graze over lawns; streams were encouraged to meander and to gurgle artfully down cascades. Lancelot Brown, one of the leading designers of the "improved" estate, was called "Capability" because of the frightful haste with which he razed avenues of old oaks and beeches to enlarge a "natural" prospect. In poetry, vistas opened more extensively in Dyer's *Grongar Hill*, Thomson's *Seasons*, and Cowper's gently sloping Ouse valley. William Shenstone, who possessed a feeble but correct taste, spent his fortune entangling paths and achieving cataracts on his estate, the Leasowes. The neighboring great Hagley Park of Lord Lyttelton, celebrated by Thomson, offered the tourist more striking prospects of the Wrekin and the Welsh Mountains. "Natural" gardens—Stowe, Envil, Richmond, and Esher—were the great contribution of the English to the arts of the eighteenth century.

The taste for the natural was soon perverted into a taste for the Gothic, and the wild landscapes of the painter Salvator Rosa inspired such absurdity as planting dead trees in Kensington Gardens and hiring Sanderson Miller to construct ruins (as William Gilpin said, "It is not every man who can build a house that can execute a ruin.") The garden grotto also became more bizarre; in 1735 Kent designed for Queen Caroline the famous Merlin's Cave in Richmond: a thatched hut with Gothic windows and wax figures of Merlin and his secretary at a table, the queen of Henry VII, Queen Elizabeth and her nurse, and Minerva. Yew-shaded paths, made entertaining by funerary urns with their polite memorial inscriptions, would suddenly twist toward a ruin, before which the wealthy could afford to hire an ornamental "monk" or a "hermit" to sit when visitors came. Gray's friend William Mason suggested dressing the poor ("children of Penury and Toil in many a tatter'd fold") as shepherds and setting them to wander through a prospect.

The century was nothing if not cosmopolitan, and the Gothic easily assimilated the oriental. Tea, chintz, and porcelain were followed by pagodas, "Chinese" drawing rooms (like Garrick's and Mrs. Montagu's), "oriental" eclogues, "eastern" tales and apologues, and numerous "Chinese," "Persian," or "Hindoo" letters commenting upon the follies of London. Sir William Chambers contrasted the dullness of the natural garden with the surprising variety in Chinese buildings and gardens, and did not hesitate to enliven Kew Gardens by a pagoda near a House of Confucius, set amid a mosque, Roman ruins, and Greek temples. William Beckford, builder of the preposterous medieval Fonthill Abbey and author of that "eastern" novel *Vathek*, typifies the picturesque confusion of Gothic and oriental. Goldfish, an oriental novelty, were valued because they "afford pleasing ideas to every spectator." Lacquer and porcelain inspired many a rococo design. The more classical picturesque—for example, the heaps of Roman ruins in drawings by the Italian Piranesi and paintings by Richard Wilson and the "great quantity of cornices and other fragments spread over the ground" by the architect Chambers—can readily be glimpsed in Dyer's *Ruins of Rome.*

A feeling for the countryside made landscape gardening a singu-

larly English art. The harmony between the painting and the literature of the time is as close, though not so obvious. The cavalier
and somewhat insolent air of the seventeenth-century court of
Charles I had been interpreted by the painter Van Dyck; the
coarser ways of the Restoration court had been caught by Sir Peter
Lely, whose "Windsor beauties" parade their robust charms in the
decent-indecent frankness of the day. By the time of Queen Anne,
Sir Godfrey Kneller and his assistants were mechanically turning
off a great many portraits with a less fleshy look. The sophisticated glitter of Pope's *The Rape of the Lock*, in which women
stain their honor—or their new brocade, is suggested by the toy-
like mannerisms in the French painter Watteau. The really acute
sensitivity of Pope and his almost lyric grace are also caught in
England in the lively "conversation pieces" (dramatic little groups
sitting or walking) by the younger Marcellus Laroon or Joseph
Francis Nollekins. The same rococo touch animates the intimate
little domestic scenes painted by Francis Hayman, Joseph Highmore, Arthur Devis, and Johann Zoffany. Critics mention the
muted harmonies in the fabrics of the period, a tonality also found
in the distinguished portraits of women by Allan Ramsay and the
"breeding" in Gray's *Elegy*.

The whimsicalities, humors, and caricatures of prose fiction,
with its anecdotal variety, correspond to the engravings by Hogarth, who, like Defoe and Smollett, spares us none of the inele-
gancies of low life. Hogarth, in his agitated narrative, and his
theory of the waving line of beauty, is as formless and cluttered
as Smollett's *Roderick Random*. Just as the novelist's moralizing
adhered loosely to his final chapter, so Hogarth's insistent moralizing was somehow external to his consuming appetite for miscellaneous facts. Hogarth protested that he "wished to compose pictures on canvas, similar to representations on the stage." One thinks
of domestic tragedy like George Lillo's *London Merchant* (1731),
the play that evidently inspired Hogarth's *Industrious and Idle Apprentices*. "In these compositions," Hogarth explained, "those subjects that will both entertain and improve the mind bid fair to be
of the greatest public utility, and must therefore be entitled to
rank in the highest class." Fielding claimed that the *Rake's Progress*
and *Harlot's Progress* were as calculated to serve the cause of virtue as a folio of morality; and he might have mentioned *Marriage
à la Mode*, *The Four Stages of Cruelty*, and *Gin Lane*. Hogarth

is as fond of "characters" as Sterne is of My Uncle Toby, and as devoted to odd "humors" as Addison, Steele, or Goldsmith. Joseph Highmore, who illustrated *Pamela* in 1745, has more narrative charm than Samuel Richardson himself.

The English facility in portraiture was great, and the competence and clear-sighted honesty of characterization to be found in the novel or in the newer personal biography dignify the hundreds of family groups and "faces" done in the period. The busts sculptured by Joseph Nollekins show the same integrity. From portraiture alone one might surmise that a Boswell's *Life of Johnson* was inevitable. A scrupulous and even severe interpretation of people distinguishes the portraits by the innumerable groups of painters surrounding Gainsborough and Reynolds. The shrewdness of characterization in novels by Fielding, Fanny Burney, or Jane Austen in varying degrees enlivens the portraits by Romney, Raeburn, Opie, Hoppner, and Lawrence. To see the sentimental heroines of the novel, we may turn to certain portraits of Emma Hart (or Lyon or Lady Hamilton) by Romney. They are not very different from cloying nymphs by the French painter Greuze. Romney, infatuated with the adventuress Emma, lacks that delicate sophistry of the heart to be found in *Clarissa Harlowe;* yet he unpleasantly suggests the languor and false pathos of Richardson's novel. As for the caricatures in prose fiction—Fielding's Thwackum and Square—we may turn not only to scenes by Hogarth, but to those by his talented successors, Thomas Rowlandson or James Gillray.

The heavy opinions of Sir Joshua Reynolds's *Discourses* on painting accord with the massive judgments of Dr. Johnson, who may have had some hand in their composition. Johnson's solid criticism, repeating that great thoughts are always general and that poetry is not to enumerate the streaks of the tulip, was rephrased in Reynolds's insistence that the painter must rise above all singular and local forms and elevate the mind to general truth and general beauty. In his own fashionable work (portrait after portrait of persons who "mattered" in London society) Reynolds usually suppressed his romantic talents—his realism, his humor, his sympathy for the informal and for children—much as Dr. Johnson often suppressed the impulses that once took him journeying with Boswell to the Western Islands of Scotland to ride ponies and suffer a sea change. As Johnson in his verse personified Learning and

Poverty and Time, so when Reynolds painted Mrs. Siddons, he saw her as The Tragic Muse, and Romney chose to paint Lady Hamilton as Medea. Reynolds's portraits with their weak coloring ("flying colors" they were called) are of most interest when they interpret British character as downrightly as Fielding caught Squire Western or as Smollett caught Matt Bramble. Here, Reynolds can compete with the distinguished portraitist Gainsborough. The academic "history" painting, imitating "grand" subjects in the grand manner of Italian painters like Guido Reni, Titian, and Tintoretto collected by travelers to Italy, was never successful in England in spite of the doctrine of Reynolds and the efforts of painters like Benjamin West and James Barry. It was a good deal like tragedy written by the dramatic rules—Dr. Johnson's *Irene*, for instance—much respected but seldom effectively accomplished.

The distinctively English talent for landscape painting made headway against the great difficulty of being unfashionable. Richard Wilson, called the father of English landscape painting, learned his classical rhetoric in Rome by doing landscapes with figures in the academic tradition. In view of that careful "simplicity" of nature contrived in poetry and gardening, it is illuminating that Gainsborough may have achieved his mastery of spatial composition by arranging his landscapes indoors, on a table, with broken stones, dried herbs, and blocks. Thus he emphasizes the classical disregard for photographic details (Wilson contemptuously called Gainsborough's scenes "fried parsley"). The humble country scene, the pastoral, and the picturesque mingle in Gainsborough's landscapes as they do in Goldsmith's *Deserted Village*. With Gainsborough came the vigorous painting of single local subjects that corresponds to the local descriptive poetry of the time. Numerous water-colorists and painters of the English countryside like Paul Sandby, John Crome and the Norwich School, George Morland, Julius Caesar Ibbetson, Thomas Girtin, J. S. Cotman, and John Constable—a distinguished group, many of whom were inspired by the Dutch painters Hobbema and Ruysdael— elevated the picturesque into masterful landscape painting. As truly as Wordsworth, they fixed their eye upon the earth and every common sight. Constable's "dewy freshness" and honesty of detail probably owed something to Cowper, who was the painter's favorite author.

English verse of the period attained its greatest intensity in William Blake. The same intense vision, with a lyrical, sinuous rhythm, is in Blake's engravings for the poems of Milton, Blair, Young, and his own prophetic books. Whatever Blake may owe to Gothicism or to the nightmarish visions of his friend Henry Fuseli or to imitating the muscularity of Michelangelo's style, his intensity is his own, like the intensity of his poetic tiger burning bright in the forests of the night.

The development of taste in architecture is more remote from that of literature. There were four reasonably distinct phases in architecture: a baroque heritage from the preceding century, a reaction toward the classical simplicity of the Renaissance architects Palladio and Inigo Jones, a rococo medievalism already mentioned, and finally a late-century imitation of Greco-Roman designs. Neither the first nor the last phase is clearly echoed in the literature of the century.

The heavy baroque style of the Restoration, never very pronounced in the buildings designed by Sir Christopher Wren, swept over into Sir John Vanbrugh's designs for Castle Howard and Blenheim, with their grandiose "movement." These baroque rhythms were too extravagant for the taste of Pope; he with his friend Richard Boyle, Earl of Burlington and owner of Chiswick, turned back to the plainer renaissance design of Andrea Palladio and Inigo Jones, who in Italy and England followed a classical Roman style. Thence derived Georgian. Colin Campbell, author of the *Vitruvius Britannicus* (1717–25) complained that the baroque is "licentious" and will "debauch Mankind" with chimerical beauties "where the Parts are without Proportion, Solids without their true Bearing, Heaps of Materials without Strength, excessive Ornament without Grace, and the Whole without Symmetry." Like Pope, he wished "correctness." However "natural" Pope and William Kent might be as gardeners, they were academic enough about architecture.

But this revived Palladian style, however correct, proved a little insipid, especially when one's garden was year by year becoming excitingly Gothic. Thus Horace Walpole presently began affixing medieval pinnacles and crockets and ogival curves and mullioned windows to his house at Strawberry Hill, wherever ingenuity could devise. Sanderson Miller began erecting his "medieval ruins" across the countryside, and rococo Gothic culminated in William Beckford's fantastic towering Fonthill Abbey, which James Wyatt could design but could not make stand. The era of "restoring" churches had also come, and Thomas Gray amused himself by taking notes upon Norman cathedrals.

Things were poised between Palladian and Gothic when Pompeii was excavated in 1748, and the Englishmen James Stuart and Nicholas Revett visited Athens in 1751. In the fifties the Italian Piranesi was etching his classical-picturesque ruins of Rome. Johann J. Winckelmann's *History of Art among the Ancients* followed in 1764, and Richard Chandler's *Ionian Antiquities* in 1769. Fashion turned to Herculaneum and Athens. In England the rococo sculptor Roubillac was followed by John Flaxman and Thomas Banks, the Neo-Hellenists. For some years Akenside, Collins, and Gray had been writing Grecian and Horatian odes. In 1769 Josiah Wedgwood called his new pottery factory Etruria and his wares Etruscan; and in London Angelica Kauffmann began to paint in her chocolate-box manner Penelope Weeping over the Bow of Ulysses, and Andromache Weeping over the Ashes of Hector. The taste for rococo, Gothic, and Chinese Chippendale waned, and plainer furniture by Hepplewhite and Sheraton came into vogue. The architect Robert Adam adopted the new low classical reliefs that presently tightened into a dry filigree. Meanwhile in France, Louis David was painting Oaths of the Horatii in stucco-revolutionary fashion. In 1770 Sir William Hamilton brought to England the famous Portland Vase, an urn found in a sarcophagus near Rome. The Elgin Marbles from the Parthenon were to follow in 1803, and Benjamin Robert Haydon spent nights sketching them by candlelight in their chilly shed. Haydon was to inspire Keats to odes on Grecian urns, and a cycle of classicism was complete. But the classicism of Pope and Addison hardly touches the classicism of Keats and Shelley.

12. MUSIC: OPERA AND ORATORIO

After the death of Henry Purcell in 1695, the English turned abroad for their music. John Christopher Pepusch, Handel, Bach, Haydn, and a swarm of Italian singers—Nicolini and Farinelli, Francesca Cuzzoni and Faustina Bordoni, Signora Paganini and Manzuoli—all had their triumphs in London. The critic Johann Mattheson remarked, "The Italians exalt music; the French enliven it; the Germans strive after it; and the English pay well for it."

Young lords on their grand tour stripped Italy of its finest violins. The ballad opera, the songs at Vauxhall and Ranelagh, the unaccompanied glee singing, and the hymns of the Methodists and Evangelicals were the genuinely English music of the century.

Purcell's opera *Dido and Aeneas* was followed by what Dr. Johnson called that "exotic and irrational entertainment," Italian opera, showily baroque, like the opera house designed by Sir John Vanbrugh. Opera demanded the greatest technical skill. Singers were esteemed for their tremolo or "shake"; Farinelli was said to be so accomplished that composers could not write passages difficult enough to display his full virtuosity. There must be six principal singers, three women and three men; the first woman was a high soprano, the first man an artificial soprano; in each act every character must sing an aria; and so on. The authors of the *Spectator* smirked at opera. Dr. Burney gives the reason for their hostility: Steele, who owned shares in a theater and a concert room, had no wish to see opera succeed, and Addison was simply "ignorant of music and impenetrable to its powers."

By 1740, however, as Burney explains, the English appetite for Italian opera waned: "It is vain to ascribe the ruin of operas to faction, opposition, and enmity to Handel; the fact was that the public curiosity being satisfied as to new compositions and singers, the English returned to their homely food, the *Beggar's Opera*, and ballad farces on the same plan, with eagerness and comfort." Yet there was another "splendid period of opera" in the sixties, and Italian singers like Signora Paganini filled the opera house until "caps were lost, and gowns torn to pieces, without number or mercy, in the struggle to get in."

In 1722 the first *ridotto* was given at the opera house: "it was opened with twenty-four select songs, which lasted about two hours; after which the company passed over a bridge, from the pit to the stage, where a duke and duchess led up the ball." These twenty-four songs were chosen from current operas. There were private concerts, too, like that at which Mrs. Thrale first saw Signor Piozzi.

In 1728, Gay's *Beggar's Opera*, with music by Pepusch, founded the English *opéra bouffe* and burletta. Thomas Augustine Arne, whose ballads were sung at Vauxhall, wrote the scores for at least thirty of the many musical pieces like Bickerstaff's *Love in a Village*.

But the English had a tradition of public concert and oratorio rather than of opera. Handel, who had come to England in 1710 to produce the opera *Rinaldo*, was organist for the Duke of Chandos when he composed the oratorio *Esther* for the chapel at Cannons. This oratorio was first sung publicly in April, 1732, in the great room at York Buildings; tickets were five shillings. In May it was sung at the Haymarket. In the same month came *Acis and Galatea*, also at the Haymarket. Burney prints the advertisement:

There will be *no action* on the stage, but the scene will represent, in a picturesque manner, a rural prospect, with rocks, groves, fountains, and grottos, among which will be disposed a chorus of nymphs and shepherds, the habits and every other decoration suited to the subject.

The oratorios, including the great *Messiah*, followed fast upon each other until they became unfashionable about 1750. They were cheap to produce, since fewer major voices were required than for opera.

Even if London continued to welcome the continental masters like Haydn, the English, out of the main current in music, remained amateurs. Burney ventures to say that "keyed instruments are perhaps nowhere on the globe better played" than in England; "not only professors, but dilettanti, who though not public performers, are heard with great pleasure in private." These sprightly groups of singers and players are clustered in the exquisite drawings of the younger Marcellus Laroon. The family of Granville Sharp had a small barge and, each one with a different instrument, they used to play little airs as they floated down the twilight Thames.

13. LITERARY FORMS

Pope was the first modern English author in the sense that he lived by his pen and lived well. Dr. Johnson's squabble with Lord Chesterfield about the *Dictionary* showed that the age of patronage was passing. Not noble lords but the printers and booksellers —Tonson, Lintot, Cave, and Dodsley—were setting the key for the Muses.

The reading public was steadily enlarging. In the *Tatler* and *Spectator* appeared the periodical essay, without which we should be wanting much of Defoe, Addison, Steele, Swift, Johnson, and Goldsmith. Indeed, the periodical "character" like Sir Roger de Coverley, Will Wimble, and Ned Softly prepared the way for the novel, which the eighteenth century saw established on such a scale that no lady or gentleman of quality failed to write at least one novel; and the fiction of hacks like Courtney Melmoth appeared regularly in three, four, five, and six volumes. The line between the novel and the memoir or biography was often blurred, particularly in adventures of persons of rank, or the Life and Opinions of * * * * *. Journals and revelations of the inner life were especially common among the religious. Boswell, with his appetite for confessional and anecdote, is very characteristic. Before Boswell, Dr. Johnson himself was preaching and practicing the informal biography: "A man's intimate friend should mention his faults, if he writes a Life." There is no more gossipy century than the eighteenth, with the tattle of Mary Wortley Montagu, Thomas Gray, Fanny Burney, and Horace Walpole. The letter was a cultivated art. Every gentleman supposed that he was at liberty to touch up his correspondence for publication, and often wrote his friends that he might be assured something to print. It did not strike Richardson as odd that his characters in "high life" should spend their lives at the escritoire; his epistolary novel was simply a projection of the voluminous letter.

It was only natural, also, that the enlightenment should call forth a "philosophic" history, and English and Scottish letters were distinguished by the work of David Hume, William Robertson, and Edward Gibbon. The great collections of voyages and travels often had the same philosophic air.

The drama languished. From September to June one could always see a play at the Covent Garden or Drury Lane; but it was the age of superlative acting rather than superlative drama—the age of Mrs. Clive, Peg Woffington, Mrs. Siddons, Betterton, Cibber, Quin, Macklin, Foote, and, above all, David Garrick. The century seems to have been extraordinarily sensitive to histrionic effects, as the posing in Sterne's novel, *Tristram Shandy*, would go to prove. The license of the Restoration and post-Restoration drama had provoked some spirited tracts, such as Collier's *Short View of the Immorality and Profaneness of the English Stage*, and a good many religious shopkeepers looked gravely askance at the theater. Playwrights like Steele and Cibber made questionable attempts to chasten wit and moralize the stage, but the resulting wishy-washy sentimental drama finally so disgusted Goldsmith and Sheridan that they returned to "laughing comedy." The early social-problem play, like George Lillo's *London Apprentice* (1731), was rare but symptomatic of the new humanitarianism. Many plays were adapted from the French, and melodramas by the German Kotzebue were in great vogue toward the end of the century. After the censorship imposed by the Licensing Act of 1737, especially, the repertory consisted largely of such traditional plays as Southerne's *Oroonoko*, Otway's *Venice Preserved*, and adaptations of Shakespeare. Large playhouses encouraged the broadest effects in acting, until the time of Garrick, who improved the lighting of the stage. Scenery was crude, a number of flats in grooves, used from play to play. Before Garrick introduced historical costuming in mid-century, many heroes wore feathered headdresses and oriental-looking robes or played Othello in a bag wig and cocked hat, and the heroine (as ridiculed in the forty-second *Spectator*) appeared in a gaudy train that was held by a page.

In any literature as topical as that of the eighteenth century, satire is to be expected. Swift's satire is cosmic. Pope, in his more personal furies and spites, is Horatian. The Juvenilian satire appears in Johnson's *London*. In the novel, political and social satire is as vigorous as it is in Charles Churchill's poem *Gotham* or in the verse of the *Anti-Jacobin*.

The eighteenth century is commonly referred to as a century of prose. Yet there was no one way of writing prose. The urbanity of Addison, the negligent ease of Steele and Goldsmith, the clarity and soundness of Swift, the efficiency of Hume, the more rhetorical flow of Shaftesbury or Gibbon, and the density of Johnson all have the tone of the eighteenth century, but each is readily distinguishable.

A good deal of eighteenth-century verse, but not nearly so much as is ordinarily supposed, is heroic couplet, a form that could be adapted to the conversational accent of Pope's *Epistle to Dr. Arbuthnot*, the elegancies of his translations, the labored cadence of Dr. Johnson's line, the starkness of Crabbe, and the pomposities of minor poets like James Grainger or Erasmus Darwin. Pope aimed at correctness, and the heroic couplet, with its dramatic compression, was an apt rhetorical pattern for the neat oppositions of sense in which he specialized. But the concise couplet of Pope could not contain the panoramic vistas in Thomson's *Seasons*, and would have isolated too sharply the microscopic observations of Cowper; these poets turned, like some others, to blank verse.

Especially after Addison's *Spectator* papers praising Milton, the reputation of this poet gained ground everywhere, and among Milton's imitators, also, came a reaction against rhyme. However, most poets strained themselves badly in attempting to be Miltonic organ voices: they could not manipulate Milton's inversions, his complex circumlocutions and appositives, Latinisms, and epithets. A great deal of the meditative verse seems like a travesty of Milton.

The unrhymed descriptive or topographical poem, often in the *Il Penseroso* mood but more lengthy and with many unassimilated themes, was highly characteristic of the period. The poetic technical treatise, or essay in verse, was often modeled after the *Georgics* of Vergil. The more unpromising the subject—raising hops, cultivating sugar cane, making cider, marketing wool—the greater seems to have been the challenge to write poetry upon it. Certain of these treatises were attempted in the Miltonic manner, with every elaboration of language. It is true that most of these efforts are not poetry, but the poetic attitude of mind inspiring them is interesting. Essentially, the metaphysical or seventeenth-century internal complexity of *attitude* was replaced with an external or purely decorative poetic complexity of *phrasing;* Dr. Johnson unfortunately thought of language as a "dress of thought," something external to meaning. It eventually became the task of Coleridge to demonstrate the fallacy of this externalized view of poetry by asserting that language is integral with meaning. In the poetical treatise the poet's special problem was to avoid being "low"—to *seem* not to say that which of necessity had to be said. Thus, a breeze might become a "cool perflation" and a cow a "milky mother of the plain." Every such poem, then, was a feat; it is not surprising that it was done poorly, but it is surprising to us that it was done at all. Yet C. S. Lewis has said that the "treatise poem" of the eighteenth century was not merely a revival of the ancient didactic verse but an original and genuinely new form.

The Spenserian stanza, a form of medievalism like the ballad, was occasionally used, though as Joseph Warton said, the likeness was in a few ancient expressions rather than in catching Spenser's real manner. Even if Thomas Edwards, the younger Thomas Warton, Gray, and others wrote sonnets, the form was of small consequence until the end of the century, when the sonnets of William Lisle Bowles attracted the attention of the young Coleridge. Because of the education of the time, everyone was familiar with the pastoral, of which there were imitations by poets like Ambrose Philips, Pope, and Gay. The ode was frequent, whether it bore the scholarship of Gray or moved with the allusive grace of Collins. The elegy appeared in slighter poets like Shenstone and Gray. The brief lyric of love or nature, although not unknown in the early part of the century, attained a new perfection in Burns; and the lyric of Blake is unique in English verse. Scotland enjoyed a poetic golden age of its own, nurtured upon Scottish themes and Scottish dialect.

In view of such diverse forms and themes, it is hardly proper to generalize about the poetic manner of the century. There was, in one sense, an eighteenth-century poetry. In another sense, Pope was as different from Johnson and Crabbe as Collins was from Thomson and Cowper. Gaudy and inane phraseology, as Wordsworth later called it, was not an invariable habit. It can be found in James Thomson, in William Cowper, and even in William Collins. But there is none in Blake; there is little in Pope's conversational pieces, and that in the *Rape of the Lock* or *Windsor Forest* is put to special uses. Cowper often wrote the language of common men, and Crabbe wavered between the prosaic and the "elegant." Neither was the personification of Collins like the poetic abstraction of Johnson, nor the abstraction of Johnson like the abstraction of Pope. Then too, in spite of their tasteless use in the poetic treatises, the epithet, compound adjectives or adjectives in -y like "flowery" or "feathery," Latinisms like "horrid" or "gelid," inversions, and archaisms like "besprent" or "ycleped" all had a great many connotations to the eighteenth century that for us, without a classical education, cannot be evoked. Poetic diction had not only a descriptive or expository value but a reminiscent one as well, since it recalled the verses of Milton, Vergil, Theocritus, or Homer. If the language of Donne is to be understood only in its setting of seventeenth-century theology and science, the language of eighteenth-century verse demands no less a special competence from the reader. In 1798 Wordsworth expressed his intention to write verse in a language used by men. We can find that, too, in the eighteenth century. But it is not the only language of poetry.

John Dryden

1631–1700

WITHOUT knowing Dryden, we can hardly view the eighteenth century in perspective, for Dryden is the artist who most completely
indicates the ways in which English poetry and prose turned from the
traditions of the seventeenth century to the new mode of eighteenth-
century prose and verse—from the "false magnificence" of much
Restoration art to the "correctness" of the Age of Queen Anne. Few
have written of Dryden better than Samuel Johnson, who said that
Dryden's "compositions are the effects of a vigorous genius operating
upon large materials," and that "whatever subjects employed his pen,
he was still improving our measures and embellishing our language."
In his verse Dryden gradually put aside the "forced conceits" of the
seventeenth century for the more regular harmonies of a "new versification" with "known and settled rule." Dryden's essays on rhyme,
on the language of poetry, and on translation indeed make him, as
Johnson notes, the father of modern criticism—and Dryden's criticism
is always "the criticism of a poet." Thus "it was reserved for Dryden
to fix the limits of poetical liberty, and give us just rules and examples of translation." His "wild and daring sallies of sentiment" are
expressed chiefly in his heroic plays, which, to be sure, often "approach the precipice of absurdity." Particularly in these extravagant
actions Dryden shows his masculine vigor, the abounding energy that
links him with baroque art, a kind of "turbulent delight." Yet his verse
essays also show the operation of a faculty that the eighteenth century
called judgment, even if they do not have the regularity of eighteenth-
century poetry. As Johnson put it, if "Pope hangs upon the ear," then
"Dryden finds the passes of the mind." Dryden's changing religious
course was symptomatic of his age: he moved from Presbyterianism
to Anglicanism and then to Roman Catholicism. However, as Johnson
correctly said, "if he changed, he changed with the nation." Furthermore, Dryden's forthright, if sometimes blustering, art seems to indicate the eagerness in England to reach some settlement in religious
and political problems, a settlement that could be based only upon
"opinions clear." That, perhaps, is why Dryden avoided "disquisitions
vain" and tried to write a "rugged verse, as fittest for discourse and
nearest prose." Doubtless it was nearer prose than was the ornate
verse of earlier poets; but Dryden's verse is anything but prosaic, and
it has its own special poetic strength and virtue.

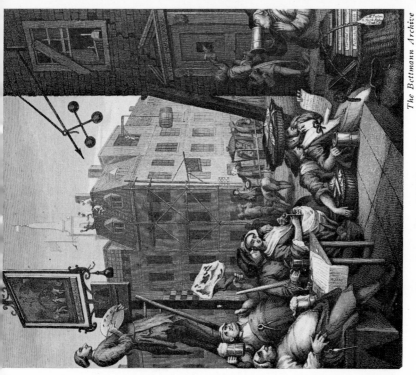

Beer Street by William Hogarth
An engraving from the painting

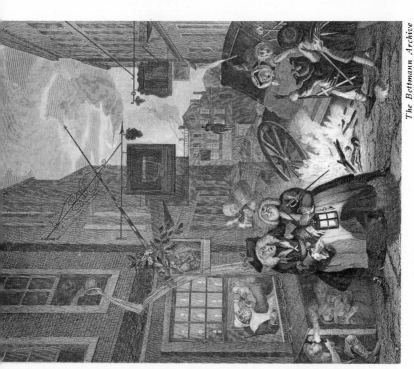

Night by William Hogarth
An engraving from the painting

English Family at Tea

Breakfast Scene from "Marriage à la Mode"
by William Hogarth

BIOGRAPHICAL NOTES

Born at Aldwinckle All Saints as eldest of fourteen children in a
family that seems to have been Presbyterian. Studied under Dr. Busby
at Westminster School, London (*ca.* 1644–50); then at Trinity College,
Cambridge (1650–54). Clerk in Cromwellian government (1657–8)
and wrote "Heroic Stanzas" on the death of Cromwell (1659). Hailed
the Restoration of Charles II by writing "Astraea Redux" (1660) and
was elected to Royal Society (1662). Married Lady Elizabeth Howard,
sister of Sir Robert Howard (1663). After failure of *The Wild Gallant*
wrote heroic plays like *The Indian Queen, The Indian Emperor,
Tyrannic Love, The Conquest of Granada* (1664–70); wrote "Annus
Mirabilis" (1666) on the great fire in London and the English victory
over the Dutch at sea. Appointed Poet Laureate (1668). Wrote tragi-
comedies like *Secret Love* (1667) and *Marriage à la Mode* (1672) and
comedies like *Sir Martin Mar All* (1667) and *The Assignation* (1672).
Satirized as "Mr. Bayes" in Buckingham's play *The Rehearsal* (1671–2),
which ridiculed heroic drama. While recasting Milton's *Paradise Lost*
into an opera, *The State of Innocence* (pub. 1677), wrote *Aureng
Zebe*, another heroic play (1675) and *All For Love* (1677). Dryden
suspected to be the author of "An Essay on Satire" attacking the Earl
of Rochester (the Earl of Mulgrave was actually responsible) and
was beaten by hired ruffians in Rose Alley (1679). Attempted to
defend Charles II against political intrigues by writing *Absalom and
Achitophel* (1681); then "The Medal" (1682) and helped Tate write
the second part of *Absalom and Achitophel* (1682). An unauthorized
version of *Mac Flecknoe* appeared while Dryden was writing *Religio
Laici* (1682) justifying the Church of England. Death of Charles II
(1685), while Dryden finished his opera *Albion and Albanius* and its
sequel *King Arthur*. Dryden received into the Roman communion
after James II acceded; printed *The Hind and the Panther* (1687) to
support his conversion. James II dethroned (1688), and with the
accession of William III Dryden was stripped of his poet laureateship,
now given to Thomas Shadwell, whom he had lampooned in *Mac
Flecknoe*. *Don Sebastian*, a tragedy (1689) and *Amphitryon*, a comedy
(1690); then *Cleomenes*, a tragedy (1692); then *Love Triumphant*
(1693). Meanwhile Dryden was translating Juvenal, Ovid, and Virgil.
The Fables, translations from Ovid, Boccaccio, and Chaucer (1700).
Died May 1, 1700.

BIBLIOGRAPHY: *Works*, edd. E. N. Hooker and H. T. Swedenberg, Jr., 1956– .
Poetical Works, ed. G. R. Noyes, 1950. *Poems*, ed. James Kinsley, 4 vols., 1958.
Dramatic Works, ed. Montagu Summers, 4 vols., 1931–32. *Poetry, Prose, and Plays*,
ed. Douglas Grant, 1952. *Letters*, ed. C. E. Ward, 1942. *Essays*, ed. W. P. Ker, 2
vols., 1900. Beljame, Alexandre, *Men of Letters and the English Public, 1660–1744*,
1948. Bredvold, Louis I., *The Intellectual Milieu of John Dryden*, 1956. Dobrée,
Bonamy, *Dryden*, 1956. Eliot, T. S., *Homage to John Dryden*, 1924; *John Dryden:
The Poet, the Dramatist, the Critic*, 1932. Frost, William, *Dryden and the Art of
Translation*, 1955. Myers, Robert Manson, *Handel, Dryden, and Milton*, 1956. Rus-
sell, Trusten W., *Voltaire, Dryden, and Heroic Tragedy*, 1946. Saintsbury, George,
Dryden, 1881. Smith, David Nichol, *John Dryden*, 1950. Van Doren, Mark, *John
Dryden: A Study of His Poetry*, 1946, 1960. Verrall, A. W., *Lectures on Dryden*,
1914. Young, Kenneth, *John Dryden*, 1954.

From EPISTLE DEDICATORY OF
THE RIVAL LADIES
1664

. . . I here present you, my Lord,[1] with that in print which you
had the goodness not to dislike upon the stage; and account it
happy to have met you here in England; it being, at best, like
small wines, to be drunk out upon the place, and has not body
enough to endure the sea. I know not whether I have been so
careful of the plot and language as I ought; but, for the latter,
I have endeavoured to write English, as near as I could distinguish it from the tongue of pedants, and that of affected travellers. Only I am sorry that (speaking so noble a language as we
do) we have not a more certain measure of it, as they have in
France, where they have an Academy erected for that purpose,
and endowed with large privileges by the present king. I wish
we might at length leave to borrow words from other nations,
which is now a wantonness in us, not a necessity; but so long
as some affect to speak them, there will not want others who will
have the boldness to write them.

But I fear lest, defending the received words, I shall be accused
for following the new way; I mean, of writing scenes in verse.
Though, to speak properly, 'tis not so much a new way amongst
us, as an old way new revived; for many years before Shakespeare's plays was the tragedy of Queen *Gorboduc*,[2] in English
verse written by that famous Lord Buckhurst, afterwards Earl
of Dorset, and progenitor to that excellent person, who (as he
inherits his soul and title) I wish may inherit his good fortune.
But supposing our countrymen had not received this writing till
of late; shall we oppose ourselves to the most polished and civilized
nations of Europe? Shall we, with the same singularity, oppose
the world in this, as most of us do in pronouncing Latin? Or do
we desire that the brand, which Barclay has (I hope unjustly) laid
upon the English, should still continue? *Angli suos ac sua omnia
impensè mirantur; caeteras nationes despectui habent.*[3] All the
Spanish and Italian tragedies I have yet seen are writ in rhyme.

1 The epistle dedicatory is addressed to
Roger Boyle, Earl of Orrery.

2 Gorboduc was king, not queen; and
the play, in blank verse, was by Thomas
Sackville, Lord Buckhurst.

3 Dryden quotes from John Barclay's
satire *Euphormionis Satyricon:* "The English are always keenly admiring themselves and all theirs, looking down upon
other nations."

For the French, I do not name them, because it is the fate of our countrymen to admit little of theirs among us, but the basest of their men, the extravagancies of their fashions, and the frippery of their merchandise. Shakespeare (who, with some errors not to be avoided in that age, had undoubtedly a larger soul of poesy than ever any of our nation) was the first who, to shun the pains of continual rhyming, invented that kind of writing which we call blank verse, but the French, more properly, *prose mesurée;* into which the English tongue so naturally slides, that, in writing prose, it is hardly to be avoided. And therefore I admire some men should perpetually stumble in a way so easy, and inverting the order of their words, constantly close their lines with verbs, which though commended sometimes in writing Latin, yet we were whipt at Westminster if we used it twice together. I know some who, if they were to write in blank verse, *Sir, I ask your pardon,* would think it sounded more heroically to write, *Sir, I your pardon ask.* I should judge him to have little command of English, whom the necessity of a rhyme should force often upon this rock; though sometimes it cannot easily be avoided; and indeed this is the only inconvenience with which rhyme can be charged. This is that which makes them say rhyme is not natural, it being only so when the poet either makes a vicious choice of words, or places them, for rhyme sake, so unnaturally as no man would in ordinary speaking; but when 'tis so judiciously ordered that the first word in the verse seems to beget the second, and that the next, till that becomes the last word in the line, which, in the negligence of prose, would be so; it must then be granted rhyme has all the advantages of prose, besides its own. But the excellence and dignity of it were never fully known till Mr. Waller taught it; he first made writing easily an art; first showed us to conclude the sense most commonly in distichs, which, in the verse of those before him, runs on for so many lines together, that the reader is out of breath to overtake it. This sweetness of Mr. Waller's lyric poesy was afterwards followed in the epic by Sir John Denham, in his *Cooper's Hill,* a poem which your Lordship knows for the majesty of the style is, and ever will be, the exact standard of good writing. But if we owe the invention of it to Mr. Waller, we are acknowledging for the noblest use of it to Sir William D'Avenant, who at once brought it upon the stage, and made it perfect, in *The Siege of Rhodes.*

The advantages which rhyme has over blank verse are so many

that it were lost time to name them. Sir Philip Sidney, in his *Defence of Poesy*, gives us one which, in my opinion, is not the least considerable; I mean the help it brings to memory, which rhyme so knits up by the affinity of sounds that, by remembering the last word in one line, we often call to mind both the verses. Then, in the quickness of repartees (which in discursive scenes fall very often) it has so particular a grace, and is so aptly suited to them, that the sudden smartness of the answer, and the sweetness of the rhyme, set off the beauty of each other. But that benefit which I consider most in it, because I have not seldom found it, is that it bounds and circumscribes the fancy. For imagination in a poet is a faculty so wild and lawless, that like a high-ranging spaniel it must have clogs tied to it, lest it outrun the judgment. The great easiness of blank verse renders the poet too luxuriant; he is tempted to say many things which might better be omitted, or at least shut up in fewer words; but when the difficulty of artful rhyming is interposed, where the poet commonly confines his sense to his couplet, and must contrive that sense into such words that the rhyme shall naturally follow them, not they the rhyme, the fancy then gives leisure to the judgment to come in, which, seeing so heavy a tax imposed, is ready to cut off all unnecessary expenses. This last consideration has already answered an objection which some have made, that rhyme is only an embroidery of sense, to make that which is ordinary in itself pass for excellent with less examination. But certainly that which most regulates the fancy, and gives the judgment its busiest employment, is like to bring forth the richest and clearest thoughts. The poet examines that most which he produceth with the greatest leisure, and which he knows must pass the severest test of the audience, because they are aptest to have it ever in their memory; as the stomach makes the best concoction when it strictly embraces the nourishment, and takes account of every little particle as it passes through. But as the best medicines may lose their virtue by being ill applied, so it is with verse, if a fit subject be not chosen for it. Neither must the argument alone, but the characters and persons be great and noble; otherwise (as Scaliger says of Claudian) the poet will be *ignobiliore materiâ depressus.*[4] The scenes which in my opinion most commend it, are those of argumentation and discourse, on the result of which the doing or not doing some considerable action should depend. . . .

4 "Sunk in a lowly fable."

THE AUTHOR'S APOLOGY FOR HEROIC POETRY AND POETIC LICENCE, PREFIXED TO *THE STATE OF INNOCENCE AND FALL OF MAN*, AN OPERA

1677

To satisfy the curiosity of those who will give themselves the trouble of reading the ensuing poem, I think myself obliged to render them a reason why I publish an opera which was never acted.[1] In the first place, I shall not be ashamed to own that my chiefest motive was the ambition which I acknowledged in the Epistle. I was desirous to lay at the feet of so beautiful and excellent a Princess a work which, I confess, was unworthy her but which, I hope, she will have the goodness to forgive. I was also induced to it in my own defence, many hundred copies of it being dispersed abroad without my knowledge or consent; so that every one gathering new faults, it became at length a libel against me; and I saw, with some disdain, more nonsense than either I, or as bad a poet, could have crammed into it at a month's warning, in which time 'twas wholly written, and not since revised. After this, I cannot, without injury to the deceased author of *Paradise Lost*, but acknowledge that this poem has received its entire foundation, part of the design, and many of the ornaments, from him. What I have borrowed will be so easily discerned from my mean productions that I shall not need to point the reader to the places: and truly I should be sorry, for my own sake, that any one should take the pains to compare them together, the original being undoubtedly one of the greatest, most noble, and most sublime poems which either this age or nation has produced. And though I could not refuse the partiality of my friend [2] who is pleased to commend me in his verses, I hope they will rather be esteemed the effect of his love to me, than of his deliberate and sober judgment. His genius is able to make beautiful what he pleases; yet, as he has been too favourable to me, I doubt not but he will hear of his kindness from many of our

---

1 The opera (written *ca.* 1674) was based on *Paradise Lost* and dedicated to   Mary of Este, Duchess of York.
2 Nat Lee, the dramatist.

contemporaries, for we are fallen into an age of illiterate, censorious, and detracting people who, thus qualified, set up for critics.

In the first place, I must take leave to tell them that they wholly mistake the nature of criticism who think its business is principally to find fault. Criticism, as it was first instituted by Aristotle, was meant a standard of judging well, the chiefest part of which is to observe those excellencies which should delight a reasonable reader. If the design, the conduct, the thoughts, and the expressions of a poem be generally such as proceed from a true genius of poetry, the critic ought to pass his judgment in favour of the author. 'Tis malicious and unmanly to snarl at the little lapses of a pen, from which Virgil himself stands not exempted. Horace acknowledges that Honest Homer nods sometimes: he is not equally awake in every line; but he leaves it also as a standing measure for our judgments,

> . . . Non, ubi plura nitent in carmine, paucis
> Offendi maculis, quas aut incuria fudit,
> Aut humana parum cavit natura . . .[3]

And Longinus, who was undoubtedly, after Aristotle, the greatest critic among the Greeks, in his twenty-seventh chapter *Peri Hupsous*, has judiciously preferred the sublime genius that sometimes errs to the middling or indifferent one which makes few faults, but seldom or never rises to any excellence. He compares the first to a man of large possessions, who has not the leisure to consider of every slight expense, will not debase himself to the management of every trifle: particular sums are not laid out, or spared, to the greatest advantage in his economy, but are sometimes suffered to run to waste, while he is only careful of the main. On the other side, he likens the mediocrity of wit to one of a mean fortune, who manages his store with extreme frugality, or rather parsimony, but who, with fear of running into profuseness, never arrives to the magnificence of living. This kind of genius writes indeed correctly. A wary man he is in grammar,

---

3 *Ars Poetica,* 351:
  "If then a poem charm me in the main,
  Slight faults I'll not too rigidly arraign,

Which frail humanity has here and there
Let fall from oversight or want of care." (Howes)

very nice as to solecism or barbarism, judges to a hair of little decencies, knows better than any man what is not to be written, and never hazards himself as far as to fall, but plods on deliberately, and, as a grave man ought, is sure to put his staff before him; in short, he sets his heart upon it, and with wonderful care makes his business sure; that is, in plain English, neither to be blamed nor praised.—I could, says my author, find out some blemishes in Homer, and am perhaps as naturally inclined to be disgusted at a fault as another man; but after all, to speak impartially, his failings are such as are only marks of human frailty: they are little mistakes, or rather negligences, which have escaped his pen in the fervour of his writing; the sublimity of his spirit carries it with me against his carelessness; and though Apollonius his *Argonauts* and Theocritus his *Eidullia* are more free from errors, there is not any man of so false a judgment, who would choose rather to have been Apollonius or Theocritus than Homer.

'Tis worth our consideration a little to examine how much these hypercritics of English poetry differ from the opinion of the Greek and Latin judges of antiquity; from the Italians and French who have succeeded them; and indeed from the general taste and approbation of all ages. Heroic poetry, which they condemn, has ever been esteemed, and ever will be, the greatest work of human nature: in that rank has Aristotle placed it; and Longinus is so full of the like expressions that he abundantly confirms the other's testimony. Horace as plainly delivers his opinion, and particularly praises Homer in these verses—

> Trojani Belli scriptorem, maxime Lolli,
> Tum tu declamas Romae, Praeneste relegi:
> Qui quid sit pulchrum, quid turpe, quid utile, quid non,
> Plenius ac melius Chrysippo et Crantore dicit.[4]

And in another place, modestly excluding himself from the number of poets, because he only writ odes and satires, he tells you a poet is such an one,

4 *Epistles,* I, 2, 1:
"While you, my Lollius, on some chosen theme,
With youthful eloquence at Rome declaim,
I read the Grecian poets o'er again,
Whose works the beautiful and base contain;

Of vice and virtues more instructive rules
Than all the sober sages of the schools." (Francis)
The following snatch is from *Satires,* I, 4, 43: "great genius, and a grand lofty style."

. . . cui mens divinior, atque os
Magna sonaturum.

Quotations are superfluous in an established truth; otherwise I could reckon up, amongst the moderns, all the Italian commentators on Aristotle's book of poetry; and, amongst the French, the greatest of this age, Boileau and Rapin; the latter of which is alone sufficient, were all other critics lost, to teach anew the rules of writing. Any man who will seriously consider the nature of an epic poem, how it agrees with that of poetry in general, which is to instruct and delight, what actions it describes, and what persons they are chiefly whom it informs, will find it a work which indeed is full of difficulty in the attempt, but admirable when it is well performed. I write not this with the least intention to undervalue the other parts of poetry: for comedy is both excellently instructive and extremely pleasant; satire lashes vice into reformation, and humour represents folly so as to render it ridiculous. Many of our present writers are eminent in both these kinds; and, particularly, the author of the *Plain Dealer*,[5] whom I am proud to call my friend, has obliged all honest and virtuous men by one of the most bold, most general, and most useful satires which has ever been presented on the English theatre. I do not dispute the preference of tragedy; let every man enjoy his taste: but 'tis unjust that they who have not the least notion of heroic writing should therefore condemn the pleasure which others receive from it, because they cannot comprehend it. Let them please their appetites in eating what they like; but let them not force their dish on all the table. They who would combat general authority with particular opinion, must first establish themselves a reputation of understanding better than other men. Are all the flights of heroic poetry to be concluded bombast, unnatural, and mere madness because they are not affected with their excellencies? It is just as reasonable to conclude there is no day because a blind man cannot distinguish of light and colours. Ought they not rather, in modesty, to doubt of their own judgments when they think this or that expression in Homer, Virgil, Tasso, or Milton's *Paradise* to be too far

5 Wycherley.

strained, than positively to conclude that 'tis all fustian, and mere nonsense? 'Tis true there are limits to be set betwixt the boldness and rashness of a poet; but he must understand those limits who pretends to judge as well as he who undertakes to write: and he who has no liking to the whole, ought, in reason, to be excluded from censuring of the parts. He must be a lawyer before he mounts the tribunal; and the judicature of one court, too, does not qualify a man to preside in another. He may be an excellent pleader in the Chancery who is not fit to rule the Common Pleas. But I will presume for once to tell them that the boldest strokes of poetry, when they are managed artfully, are those which most delight the reader.

Virgil and Horace, the severest writers of the severest age, have made frequent use of the hardest metaphors and of the strongest hyperboles; and in this case the best authority is the best argument; for generally to have pleased, and through all ages, must bear the force of universal tradition. And if you would appeal from thence to right reason, you will gain no more by it in effect, than, first, to set up your reason against those authors, and, secondly, against all those who have admired them. You must prove why that ought not to have pleased, which has pleased the most learned and the most judicious; and, to be thought knowing, you must first put the fool upon all mankind. If you can enter more deeply than they have done into the causes and resorts of that which moves pleasure in a reader, the field is open, you may be heard; but those springs of human nature are not so easily discovered by every superficial judge: it requires philosophy as well as poetry to sound the depth of all the passions; what they are in themselves, and how they are to be provoked: and in this science the best poets have excelled. Aristotle raised the fabric of his *Poetry* from observation of those things in which Euripides, Sophocles, and Aeschylus pleased: he considered how they raised the passions, and thence has drawn rules for our imitation. From hence have sprung the tropes and figures for which they wanted a name, who first practised them, and succeeded in them. Thus I grant you that the knowledge of Nature was the original rule; and that all poets ought to study her, as well as Aristotle and Horace, her interpreters. But then this also undeniably follows, that those things which delight all ages, must have been an imitation of Nature; which is all I contend. Therefore is rhetoric made an art; therefore the names of so many tropes and figures were invented; because it was observed they had such and such effect upon the audience. Therefore catachreses and hyperboles have found their place amongst them; not that they were to be avoided, but to be used judiciously, and placed in poetry as heightenings and shadows are in painting, to make the figure bolder, and cause it to stand off to sight.

> Nec retia cervis
> Ulla dolum meditantur [6]

says Virgil in his *Eclogues:* and speaking of Leander in his *Georgics,*

> Nocte natat caeca serus freta, quem super ingens
> Porta tonat coeli, et scopulis illisa reclamant
> Aequora.[7]

In both of these, you see, he fears not to give voice and thought to things inanimate.

Will you arraign your master Horace for his hardness of expression when he describes the death of Cleopatra and says she did *asperos tractare serpentes, ut atrum corpore combiberet venenum,*[8] because the body, in that action, performs what is proper to the mouth?

As for hyperboles, I will neither quote Lucan nor Statius, men of an unbounded imagination, but who often wanted the poise of judgment. The divine Virgil was not liable to that exception; and yet he describes Polyphemus thus—

> . . . . Graditurque per aequor
> Jam medium; necdum fluctus latera ardua tinxit.[9]

In imitation of this place our admirable Cowley thus paints Goliath—

6 *Eclogues,* V, 60: "Nor net against deer plotting any harm."
7 *Georgics,* III, 260:
"Alone by night his wat'ry way he took:
About him, and above, the billows broke;
The sluices of the sky were open spread,
And rolling thunder rattled o'er his head." (Dryden)
8 *Odes,* I, 37, 26: "To handle poisonous asps that she might suck black venom to her heart."
9 *Aeneid,* III, 664:
". . . thro' seas he strides,
And scarce the topmost billows touch'd his sides." (Dryden)

The valley, now, this monster seem'd to fill;
And we, methought, look'd up to him from our hill: [10]

where the two words *seemed* and *methought* have mollified the figure; and yet if they had not been there, the fright of the Israelites might have excused their belief of the giant's stature.

In the eighth of the *Aeneids* Virgil paints the swiftness of Camilla thus:

> Illa vel intactae segetis per summa volaret
> Gramina, nec teneras cursu laesisset aristas;
> Vel mare per medium, fluctu suspensa tumenti,
> Ferret iter, celeres nec tingeret aequore plantas.[11]

You are not obliged, as in history, to a literal belief of what the poet says; but you are pleased with the image without being cozened by the fiction.

Yet even in history Longinus quotes Herodotus on this occasion of hyperboles. The Lacedemonians, says he, at the straits of Thermopylae, defended themselves to the last extremity; and when their arms failed them, fought it out with their nails and teeth; till at length (the Persians shooting continually upon them) they lay buried under the arrows of their enemies. It is not reasonable (continues the critic) to believe that men could defend themselves with their nails and teeth from an armed multitude, nor that they lay buried under a pile of darts and arrows; and yet there wants not probability for the figure, because the hyperbole seems not to have been made for the sake of the description, but rather to have been produced from the occasion.

'Tis true the boldness of the figures is to be hidden sometimes by the address of the poet, that they may work their effect upon the mind without discovering the art which caused it. And therefore they are principally to be used in passion, when we speak more warmly, and with more precipitation than at other times: for then, *si vis me flere, dolendum est primum ipsi tibi* [12]; the poet must put on the passion he endeavours to represent: a man

---

10 *Davideis,* III.
11 *Aeneid,* VII, 808:
  "Outstrip'd the winds in speed upon
    the plain,
  Flew o'er the fields, nor hurt the
    bearded grain:
  She swept the seas, and, as she
  skimm'd along,
  Her flying feet unbath'd on billows
    hung." (Dryden)
12 Horace, *Ars Poetica,* 102:
  "Who claims my tears must first display
    his own." (Howes)

in such an occasion is not cool enough either to reason rightly, or to talk calmly. Aggravations are then in their proper places; interrogations, exclamations, hyperbata, or a disordered connexion of discourse are graceful there, because they are natural. The sum of all depends on what before I hinted, that this boldness of expression is not to be blamed if it be managed by the coolness and discretion which is necessary to a poet.

Yet before I leave this subject, I cannot but take notice how disingenuous our adversaries appear: all that is dull, insipid, languishing, and without sinews in a poem they call an imitation of Nature: they only offend our most equitable judges, who think beyond them; and lively images and elocution are never to be forgiven.

What fustian, as they call it, have I heard these gentlemen find out in Mr. Cowley's *Odes!* I acknowledge myself unworthy to defend so excellent an author, neither have I room to do it here; only in general I will say that nothing can appear more beautiful to me than the strength of those images which they condemn.

Imaging is, in itself, the very height and life of poetry. It is, as Longinus describes it, a discourse which, by a kind of enthusiasm, or extraordinary emotion of the soul, makes it seem to us that we behold those things which the poet paints, so as to be pleased with them, and to admire them.

If poetry be imitation, that part of it must needs be best which describes most lively our actions and passions, our virtues and our vices, our follies and our humours; for neither is comedy without its part of imaging, and they who do it best are certainly the most excellent in their kind. This is too plainly proved to be denied. But how are poetical fictions, how are hippocentaurs and chimeras, or how are angels and immaterial substances to be imaged; which, some of them, are things quite out of nature; others, such whereof we can have no notion? This is the last refuge of our adversaries, and more than any of them have yet had the wit to object against us. The answer is easy to the first part of it: the fiction of some beings which are not in nature (second notions, as the logicians call them) has been founded on the conjunction of two natures which have a real separate being. So hippocentaurs were imaged by joining the natures of a man and horse together; as Lucretius tells us, who has used this word *image* oftener than any of the poets—

Nam certe ex vivo centauri non fit imago,
Nulla fuit quoniam talis natura animai:
Verum ubi equi atque hominis, casu, convenit imago,
Haerescit facile extemplo, &c.[13]

The same reason may also be alleged for chimeras and the rest. And poets may be allowed the like liberty for describing things which really exist not, if they are founded on popular belief. Of this nature are fairies, pigmies, and the extraordinary effects of magic; for 'tis still an imitation, though of other men's fancies: and thus are Shakespeare's *Tempest*, his *Midsummer Night's Dream*, and Ben Jonson's *Masque of Witches* to be defended. For immaterial substances we are authorized by Scripture in their description: and herein the text accommodates itself to vulgar apprehension, in giving angels the likeness of beautiful young men. Thus, after the pagan divinity, has Homer drawn his gods with human faces: and thus we have notions of things above us, by describing them like other beings more within our knowledge.

I wish I could produce any one example of excellent imaging in all this poem. Perhaps I cannot; but that which comes nearest it is in these four lines, which have been sufficiently canvassed by my well-natured censors—

Seraph and cherub, careless of their charge,
And wanton, in full ease now live at large:
Unguarded leave the passes of the sky,
And all dissolved in hallelujahs lie.[14]

I have heard (says one of them) of anchovies dissolved in sauce, but never of an angel in hallelujahs. A mighty witticism! (if you will pardon a new word) but there is some difference between a laugher and a critic. He might have burlesqued Virgil too, from whom I took the image: *Invadunt urbem, somno vino-que sepultam.*[15] A city's being buried is just as proper on occasion as an angel's being dissolved in ease and songs of triumph. Mr. Cowley lies as open too in many places—

Where their vast courts the mother waters keep, &c.

13 Lucretius, *De Rerum Natura*, IV, 737: "For in truth the image of the centaur comes not from a living thing, since there never was the nature of such a living creature, but when by chance the images of man and horse have met, they cling together readily." (Bailey)

14 In Act I, Scene 1 of the opera.

15 *Aeneid*, II, 265: "They enter the city, buried in sleep and wine."

authority supports energy

For if the mass of waters be the mothers, then their daughters, the little streams, are bound, in all good manners, to make courtesy to them, and ask them blessing. How easy 'tis to turn into ridicule the best descriptions, when once a man is in the humour of laughing till he wheezes at his own dull jest! But an image which is strongly and beautifully set before the eyes of the reader will still be poetry when the merry fit is over, and last when the other is forgotten.

I have promised to say somewhat of poetic licence, but have in part anticipated my discourse already. Poetic licence I take to be the liberty which poets have assumed to themselves, in all ages, of speaking things in verse, which are beyond the severity of prose. 'Tis that particular character which distinguishes and sets the bounds betwixt *oratio soluta* and poetry. This, as to what regards the thought or imagination of a poet, consists in fiction: but then those thoughts must be expressed; and here arise two other branches of it: for if this licence be included in a single word, it admits of tropes; if in a sentence or proposition, of figures; both which are of a much larger extent, and more forcibly to be used in verse than prose. This is that birthright which is derived to us from our great forefathers, even from Homer down to Ben; and they who would deny it to us have, in plain terms, the fox's quarrel to the grapes—they cannot reach it.

How far these liberties are to be extended, I will not presume to determine here, since Horace does not. But it is certain that they are to be varied according to the language and age in which an author writes. That which would be allowed to a Grecian poet, Martial tells you, would not be suffered in a Roman. And 'tis evident that the English does more nearly follow the strictness of the latter than the freedoms of the former. Connexion of epithets, or the conjunction of two words in one, are frequent and elegant in the Greek, which yet Sir Philip Sidney, and the translator of Du Bartas, have unluckily attempted in the English; though this, I confess, is not so proper an instance of poetic licence as it is of a variety of idiom in languages.

Horace a little explains himself on this subject of *Licentia Poetica*, in these verses—

.... Pictoribus atque Poetis
Quidlibet audendi semper fuit aequa potestas: ...

Sed non, ut placidis coeant immitia, non ut
Serpentes avibus geminentur, tigribus haedi.[16]

He would have a poem of a piece; not to begin with one thing and
end with another: he restrains it so far that thoughts of an unlike nature ought not to be joined together. That were indeed
to make a chaos. He taxed not Homer, nor the divine Virgil, for
interesting their gods in the wars of Troy and Italy; neither, had
he now lived, would he have taxed Milton, as our false critics
have presumed to do, for his choice of a supernatural argument;
but he would have blamed my author, who was a Christian, had
he introduced into his poem heathen deities, as Tasso is condemned by Rapin on the like occasion; and as Camoens, the author of the *Lusiads*, ought to be censured by all his readers, when
he brings in Bacchus and Christ into the same adventure of his
fable.

From that which has been said it may be collected that the
definition of Wit (which has been so often attempted, and ever
unsuccessfully by many poets) is only this: that it is a propriety
of thoughts and words; or, in other terms, thoughts and words
elegantly adapted to the subject. If our critics will join issue on
this definition, that we may *convenire in aliquo tertio;*[17] if they
will take it as a granted principle, it will be easy to put an end to
this dispute. No man will disagree from another's judgment concerning the dignity of style in heroic poetry; but all reasonable
men will conclude it necessary that sublime subjects ought to be
adorned with the sublimest, and consequently often with the most
figurative, expressions. In the meantime I will not run into their
fault of imposing my opinions on other men, any more than I
would my writings on their taste: I have only laid down, and that
superficially enough, my present thoughts, and shall be glad to be
taught better by those who pretend to reform our poetry.

16 *Ars Poetica,* 9–13:
"Painters (you'll say) and bards, the
world agrees,
Are privileged to dare what flights
they please. . . .

But let them stop where nature stops
at least,
Nor couple tame with savage, bird
with beast." (Howes)
17 To find a third term, a compromise.

ABSALOM AND ACHITOPHEL [1]

1681

In pious times, ere priestcraft did begin,
Before polygamy was made a sin;
When man, on many, multiply'd his kind,
Ere one to one was, cursedly, confin'd;
When nature prompted, and no law deny'd
Promiscuous use of concubine and bride;
Then Israel's monarch after Heaven's own heart,
His vigorous warmth did variously impart
To wives and slaves: and, wide as his command,
Scatter'd his Maker's image thro' the land.
Michal, of royal blood, the crown did wear;
A soyl ungratefull to the tiller's care:
Not so the rest; for several mothers bore
To godlike David several sons before.
But since like slaves his bed they did ascend,
No true succession could their seed attend.
Of all this numerous progeny was none
So beautyfull, so brave as Absolon:
Whether, inspir'd by some diviner lust,
His father got him with a greater gust;
Or that his conscious destiny made way,   20
By manly beauty to imperiall sway.
Early in foreign fields he won renown,
With kings and states ally'd to Israel's crown:
In peace the thoughts of war he could remove,
And seem'd as he were only born for love.
Whate'er he did, was done with so much ease,

---

1 The satire is based upon *II Samuel*, 13-18. Protestant nobles like Shaftesbury and Buckingham were stirring up the Duke of Monmouth, illegitimate son of Charles II, to head a revolution against his father (just as Absalom rebelled against David, Absalom being egged on by Achitophel). Michal is Queen Catherine of Portugal, wife of Charles II. Annabel is Agnes Scott, wife of Monmouth. Amnon is Sir Charles Coventry, beaten by Monmouth's dependents. Saul is Oliver Cromwell, and Ishbosheth is Cromwell's son Richard. Zimri is George Villiers, Duke of Buckingham. Corah is Titus Oates, witness against the Catholics in the Popish Plot. Achitophel is Anthony Ashley Cooper, Earl of Shaftesbury. The Jews are the English; the Jebusites, the Catholics; the Levites, the Presbyterian ministers; the Rabbins, the Anglican clergy. Hebron is Scotland.

In him alone 'twas natural to please:
His motions all accompanied with grace;
And paradise was open'd in his face.
With secret joy indulgent David view'd   30
His youthfull image in his son renew'd:
To all his wishes nothing he deny'd;
And made the charming Annabel his bride.
What faults he had (for who from faults is free?)
His father could not, or he would not see.
Some warm excesses, which the law forbore,
Were constru'd youth that purg'd by boyling o'er,
And Amnon's murther, by a specious name,
Was call'd a just revenge for injur'd fame.   40
Thus prais'd, and lov'd, the noble youth remain'd,
While David, undisturb'd, in Sion raign'd.
But life can never be sincerely blest:
Heaven punishes the bad, and proves the best.
The Jews, a headstrong, moody, murm'ring race,
As ever try'd th' extent and stretch of grace;
God's pamper'd people, whom, debauch'd with ease,
No king could govern, nor no God could please;
(Gods they had tri'd of every shape and size,
That god-smiths could produce, or priests devise:)   50
These Adam-wits, too fortunately free,
Began to dream they wanted libertie;
And when no rule, no precedent was found,
Of men by laws less circumscrib'd and bound,
They led their wild desires to woods and caves,
And thought that all but savages were slaves.
They who, when Saul was dead, without a blow,
Made foolish Ishbosheth the crown forgo;
Who banish't David did from Hebron bring,
And with a generall shout proclaim'd him king: 60
Those very Jews, who, at their very best,
Their humour more than loyalty exprest,
Now wonder'd why so long they had obey'd
An idoll monarch which their hands had made;
Thought they might ruine him they could create,
Or melt him to that golden calf, a State.
But these were randome bolts: no form'd design,
Nor interest made the factious croud to joyn:
The sober part of Israel, free from stain,
Well knew the value of a peacefull raign;   70

And, looking backward with a wise afright,
Saw seames of wounds, dishonest to the sight;
In contemplation of whose ugly scars
They curst the memory of civil wars.
The moderate sort of men, thus qualifi'd,
Inclin'd the ballance to the better side:
And David's mildness manag'd it so well,
The bad found no occasion to rebell.
But when to sin our byast nature leans,
The carefull Devil is still at hand with means;   80
And providently pimps for ill desires:
The Good Old Cause reviv'd, a plot requires.
Plots, true or false, are necessary things,
To raise up commonwealths, and ruin kings.
   Th' inhabitants of old Jerusalem
Were Jebusites: the town so call'd from them;
And theirs the native right——
But when the chosen people grew more strong,
The rightfull cause at length became the wrong:
And every loss the men of Jebus bore,   90
They still were thought God's enemies the more.
Thus worn and weaken'd, well or ill content,
Submit they must to David's government:
Impoverisht and depriv'd of all command,
Their taxes doubled as they lost their land;
And, what was harder yet to flesh and blood,
Their gods disgrac'd, and burnt like common wood.
This set the heathen priesthood in a flame;
For priests of all religions are the same:
Of whatsoe'er descent their godhead be,   100
Stock, stone, or other homely pedigree,
In his defense his servants are as bold
As if he had been born of beaten gold.
The Jewish rabbins, tho' their enemies,
In this conclude them honest men and wise:
For 'twas their duty, all the learned think,
T' espouse his cause, by whom they eat and drink.
From hence began that Plot,[2] the nation's curse,
Bad in itself, but represented worse.
Rais'd in extremes, and in extremes decry'd;   110
With oaths affirm'd, with dying vows deny'd;

2 Titus Oates said there was a plot to murder Charles and put James on the throne.

Not weigh'd or winnow'd by the multitude;   *intricate logic*
But swallow'd in the mass, unchew'd and crude. *every word that*
Some truth there was, but dash'd and brew'd with lies, *Rhymes paral*
To please the fools, and puzzle all the wise. *tels each other*
Succeeding times did equal folly call,
Believing nothing, or believing all.
Th' Egyptian rites [3] the Jebusites imbrac'd;
Where gods were recommended by their tast.
Such savory deities must needs be good,   120
As serv'd at once for worship and for food.
By force they could not introduce these gods;
For ten to one in former days was odds.
So fraud was us'd (the sacrificer's trade),
Fools are more hard to conquer than perswade.
Their busie teachers mingled with the Jews;
And rak'd for converts, even the court and stews:
Which Hebrew priests the more unkindly took,
Because the fleece [4] accompanies the flock.
Some thought they God's anointed meant to slay   *deliberate*
By guns, invented since full many a day: 130 *anachonism*
Our authour swears it not; but who can know
How far the Devil and Jebusites may go?
This Plot, which fail'd for want of common sense,
Had yet a deep and dangerous consequence:
For, as when raging fevers boyl the blood,
The standing lake soon floats into a flood,
And every hostile humor, which before
Slept quiet in its channels, bubbles o'er:
So, several factions from this first ferment   140
Work up to foam, and threat the government.
Some by their friends, more by themselves thought wise,
Oppos'd the pow'r to which they could not rise.
Some had in courts been great, and thrown from thence,
Like fiends were harden'd in impenitence.
Some, by their monarch's fatal mercy grown
From pardon'd rebels kinsmen to the throne,
Were rais'd in power and publick office high:
Strong bands, if bands ungratefull men could tye.
    Of these the false Achitophel was first: *epic label* 150
A name to all succeeding ages curst: *Miltonic*
For close designs, and crooked counsels fit; *vein*
Sagacious, bold, and turbulent of wit: *twisted* *Clinched*
                                         image

3 French Catholic rituals.   4 Tithes.

Restless, unfixt in principles and place;
In power unpleas'd, impatient of disgrace.
A fiery soul, which working out its way,
Fretted the pigmy body to decay,
And o'er-inform'd the tenement of clay.
A daring pilot in extremity;
Pleas'd with the danger, when the waves went high   160
He sought the storms; but, for a calm unfit,
Would steer too nigh the sands, to boast his wit.
Great wits are sure to madness near ally'd;
And thin partitions do their bounds divide:
Else, why should he, with wealth and honour blest,
Refuse his age the needful hours of rest?
Punish a body which he could not please;
Bankrupt of life, yet prodigal of ease?
And all to leave, what with his toyl he won,
To that unfeather'd two-leg'd thing, a son; [5]   170
Got, while his soul did hudled notions try;
And born a shapeless lump, like anarchy.
In friendship false, implacable in hate;
Resolv'd to ruin or to rule the State.
To compass this the triple bond [6] he broke;
The pillars of the publick safety shook;
And fitted Israel for a foreign yoke:
Then, seiz'd with fear, yet still affecting fame,
Usurp'd a patriot's all-attoning name.
So easie still it proves in factious times,   180
With publick zeal to cancel private crimes.
How safe is treason, and how sacred ill,
Where none can sin against the people's will:
Where crouds can wink; and no offense be known,
Since in another's guilt they find their own.
Yet, fame deserv'd, no enemy can grudge;
The statesman we abhor, but praise the judge.
In Israel's courts ne'er sat an Abbethdin [7]
With more discerning eyes, or hands more clean:
Unbrib'd, unsought, the wretched to redress;   190
Swift of dispatch, and easie of access.
Oh, had he been content to serve the crown,
With vertues only proper to the gown;

5 The son of Shaftesbury.   7 Jewish court official: Shaftesbury,
6 Triple Alliance of England, Sweden,   who was Lord Chancellor.
and Holland against France.

Or, had the rankness of the soyl been freed
From cockle, that oppresst the noble seed:
David, for him his tuneful harp had strung,
And Heaven had wanted one immortal song.
But wilde Ambition loves to slide, not stand,
And Fortune's ice prefers to Vertue's land.
Achitophel, grown weary to possess   200
A lawfull fame, and lazy happiness,
Disdain'd the golden fruit to gather free,
And lent the croud his arm to shake the tree.
Now, manifest of crimes contriv'd long since,
He stood at bold defiance with his prince:
Held up the buckler of the people's cause,
Against the crown, and sculk'd behind the laws.
The wish'd occasion of the Plot he takes,
Some circumstances finds, but more he makes.
By buzzing emissaries, fills the ears   210
Of list'ning crowds with jealosies and fears
Of arbitrary counsels brought to light,
And proves the king himself a Jebusite:
Weak arguments! which yet he knew full well
Were strong with people easie to rebell.
For, govern'd by the moon, the giddy Jews
Tread the same track when she the prime renews:
And once in twenty years, their scribes record,
By natural instinct they change their lord.
Achitophel still wants a chief, and none   220
Was found so fit as warlike Absalon:
Not that he wish'd his greatness to create,
(For politicians neither love nor hate,)
But, for he knew, his title not allow'd,
Would keep him still depending on the crowd:
That kingly power, thus ebbing out, might be
Drawn to the dregs of a democracy.
Him he attempts, with studied arts to please,
And sheds his venome in such words as these:
    "Auspicious prince! at whose nativity   230
Some royal planet rul'd the southern sky;
Thy longing country's darling and desire;
Their cloudy pillar and their guardian fire:
Their second Moses, whose extended wand
Divides the seas, and shews the promis'd land;
Whose dawning day, in every distant age,

Has exercis'd the sacred prophets' rage:
The people's prayer, the glad deviners' theam,
The young men's vision, and the old men's dream!
Thee, Saviour, thee, the nation's vows confess,   240
And, never satisfi'd with seeing, bless:
Swift, unbespoken pomps, thy steps proclaim,
And stammerring babes are taught to lisp thy name.
How long wilt thou the general joy detain,
Starve, and defraud the people of thy reign?
Content ingloriously to pass thy days
Like one of Vertue's fools that feeds on praise;
Till thy fresh glories, which now shine so bright,
Grow stale and tarnish with our daily sight.
Believe me, royal youth, thy fruit must be   250
Or gather'd ripe, or rot upon the tree.
Heav'n has to all allotted, soon or late,
Some lucky revolution of their fate;
Whose motions, if we watch and guide with skill,
(For human good depends on humane will,)
Our Fortune rolls, as from a smooth descent,
And, from the first impression, takes the bent:
But, if unseiz'd, she glides away like wind;
And leaves repenting Folly far behind.
Now, now she meets you with a glorious prize,   260
And spreads her locks before her as she flies.
Had thus old David, from whose loyns you spring,
Not dar'd, when Fortune call'd him, to be king,
At Gath [8] an exile he might still remain,
And Heaven's anointing oyle had been in vain.
Let his successfull youth your hopes engage;
But shun th' example of declining age:
Behold him setting in his western skies,
The shadows lengthning as the vapors rise.
He is not now, as when on Jordan's sand   270
The joyfull people throng'd to see him land,
Cov'ring the beach, and blackning all the strand:
But, like the Prince of Angels from his height,
Comes tumbling downward with diminish'd light;
Betray'd by one poor plot to publick scorn,
(Our only blessing since his curst return):
Those heaps of people which one sheaf did bind,
Blown off and scatter'd by a puff of wind.

8 Brussels: Jordan is Dover.

already assuming
Absalom

What strength can he to <u>your designs</u> oppose,
Naked of friends, and round beset with foes?   280
If Pharaoh's [9] doubtfull succor he should use,
A foreign aid would more incense the Jews:
Proud Egypt would dissembled friendship bring;
Foment the war, but not support the king:
Nor would the royal party e'er unite
With Pharaoh's arms t' assist the Jebusite;
Or if they should, their interest soon would break,
And with such odious aid make David weak.
All sorts of men by my successfull arts,
Abhorring kings, estrange their alter'd hearts   290
From David's rule: and 'tis the general cry,
'Religion, commonwealth, and liberty.'
If you as champion of the publique good,
Add to their arms a chief of royal blood,
What may not Israel hope, and what applause
Might such a general gain by such a cause?
Not barren praise alone, that gaudy flower
Fair only to the sight, but solid power:
And nobler is a limited command,
Giv'n by the love of all your native land,   300
Than a successive title, long, and dark,
Drawn from the mouldy rolls of Noah's ark."
    What cannot praise effect in mighty minds,
When flattery sooths, and when ambition blinds!
Desire of power, on earth a vitious weed,
Yet, sprung from high, is of celestial seed:
In God 'tis glory; and when men aspire,
'Tis but a spark too much of heavenly fire.
Th' ambitious youth, too covetous of fame,
Too full of angells' metal in his frame,   310
Unwarily was led from vertue's ways,
Made drunk with honour, and debauch'd with praise.
Half loath, and half consenting to the ill,
(For loyal blood within him strugled still,)
He thus reply'd: "And what pretense have I
To take up arms for publick liberty?
My father governs with unquestion'd right;
The faith's defender, and mankind's delight:
Good, gracious, just, observant of the laws:
And Heav'n by wonders has espous'd his cause.   320

9 Louis XIV.

Whom has he wrong'd in all his peaceful reign?
Who sues for justice to his throne in vain?
What millions has he pardon'd of his foes,
Whom just revenge did to his wrath expose?
Mild, easy, humble, studious of our good;
Enclin'd to mercy, and averse from blood;
If mildness ill with stubborn Israel suit,
His crime is God's beloved attribute.
What could he gain, his people to betray,
Or change his right for arbitrary sway?   330
Let haughty Pharaoh curse with such a reign,
His fruitfull Nile, and yoak a servile train.
If David's rule Jerusalem displease,
The Dog-star heats their brains to this disease.
Why then should I, encouraging the bad,
Turn rebell and run popularly mad?
Were he a tyrant, who, by lawless might
Opprest the Jews, and rais'd the Jebusite,
Well might I mourn; but nature's holy bands
Would curb my spirits and restrain my hands: 340
The people might assert their liberty;
But what was right in them were crime in me.
His favour leaves me nothing to require,
Prevents my wishes, and outruns desire.
What more can I expect while David lives?
All but his kingly diadem he gives:
And that"—But there he paus'd; then sighing, said—
"Is justly destin'd for a worthier head.
For when my father from his toyls shall rest,
And late augment the number of the blest,   350
His lawfull issue shall the throne ascend,
Or the *collateral* line, where that shall end.
His brother, tho' opprest with vulgar spight,
Yet dauntless, and secure of native right,
Of every royal virtue stands possest;
Still dear to all the bravest, and the best.
His courage foes, his friends his truth proclaim;
His loyalty the king, the world his fame.
His mercy even th' offending crowd will find;
For sure he comes of a forgiving kind.
Why should I then repine at Heaven's decree,   360
Which gives me no pretence to royalty?
Yet oh that fate, propitiously enclin'd,

[handwritten margin notes: "fufill wishes before they're requested"; "fate"; "talking in Achitophel's terms"; "watershed in speech, turning point"]

Had rais'd my birth, or had debas'd my mind;
To my large soul not all her treasure lent,
And then betray'd it to a mean descent.
I find, I find my mounting spirits bold,
And David's part disdains my mother's mold.
Why am I scanted by a niggard birth?
My soul disclaims the kindred of her earth: 370
And made for empire, whispers me within,
'Desire of greatness is a godlike sin.' "
    Him staggering so when hell's dire agent found,
While fainting Vertue scarce maintain'd her ground,
He pours fresh forces in, and thus replies:
    "Th' eternal God, supremely good and wise,
Imparts not these prodigious gifts in vain;
What wonders are reserv'd to bless your reign?
Against your will, your arguments have shown,
Such vertue's only given to guide a throne.   380
Not that your father's mildness I contemn;
But manly force becomes the diadem.
'Tis true he grants the people all they crave;
And more perhaps than subjects ought to have:
For lavish grants suppose a monarch tame,
And more his goodness than his wit proclaim.
But when should people strive their bonds to break,
If not when kings are negligent or weak?
Let him give on till he can give no more,
The thrifty Sanhedrin [10] shall keep him poor: 390
And every shekel which he can receive,
Shall cost a limb of his prerogative.
To ply him with new plots shall be my care,
Or plunge him deep in some expensive war;
Which when his treasure can no more supply,
He must, with the remains of kingship, buy.
His faithful friends, our jealousies and fears
Call Jebusites, and Pharaoh's pensioners;
Whom, when our fury from his aid has torn,
He shall be naked left to publick scorn.   400
The next successor, whom I fear and hate,
My arts have made obnoxious to the State;
Turn'd all his vertues to his overthrow,
And gain'd our elders to pronounce a foe.
His right, for sums of necessary gold,

10 The Jewish high court: Parliament.

Shall first be pawn'd, and afterwards be sold:
Till time shall ever-wanting David draw,
To pass your doubtfull title into law:
If not, the people have a right supreme
To make their kings; for kings are made for them.   410
All empire is no more than pow'r in trust,
Which, when resum'd, can be no longer just.
Succession, for the general good design'd,
In its own wrong a nation cannot bind:
If altering that, the people can relieve,
Better one suffer, than a nation grieve.
The Jews well know their power: ere Saul they chose,
God was their king, and God they durst depose.
Urge now your piety, your filial name,
A father's right, and fear of future fame;   420
The publick good, that universal call,
To which even Heav'n submitted, answers all.
Nor let his love enchant your generous mind;
'Tis Nature's trick to propagate her kind.
Our fond begetters, who would never die,
Love but themselves in their posterity.
Or let his kindness by th' effects be try'd,
Or let him lay his vain pretence aside.
God said he lov'd your father; could he bring
A better proof, than to anoint him king?   430
It surely shew'd he lov'd the shepherd well,
Who gave so fair a flock as Israel.
Would David have you thought his darling son?
What means he then, to alienate the crown?
The name of godly he may blush to bear:
'Tis after God's own heart to cheat his heir.
He to his brother gives supreme command;
To you a legacy of barren land:
Perhaps th' old harp, on which he thrums his layes,
Or some dull Hebrew ballad in your praise.   440
Then the next heir, a prince, severe and wise,
Already looks on you with jealous eyes;
Sees thro' the thin disguises of your arts,
And marks your progress in the people's hearts.
Tho' now his mighty soul its grief contains,
He meditates revenge who least complains;
And, like a lyon, slumbring in the way,
Or sleep dissembling, while he waits his prey,

His fearless foes within his distance draws,
Constrains his roaring, and contracts his paws;　450
Till at the last, his time for fury found,
He shoots with sudden vengeance from the ground;
The prostrate vulgar passes o'er, and spares,
But with a lordly rage his hunters teares.
Your case no tame expedients will afford;
Resolve on death, or conquest by the sword,
Which for no less a stake than life, you draw;
And self-defence is nature's eldest law.
Leave the warm people no considering time;
For then rebellion may be thought a crime.　460
Prevail your self of what occasion gives,
But try your title while your father lives:
And that your arms may have a fair pretence,
Proclaim you take them in the king's defence:
Whose sacred life each minute would expose
To plots, from seeming friends, and secret foes.
And who can sound the depth of David's soul?
Perhaps his fear, his kindness may control.
He fears his brother, tho' he loves his son,
For plighted vows too late to be undone.　470
If so, by force he wishes to be gain'd;
Like women's leachery, to seem constrain'd:
Doubt not, but when he most affects the frown,
Commit a pleasing rape upon the crown.
Secure his person to secure your cause;
They who possess the prince, possess the laws."
　He said, and this advice above the rest,
With Absalom's mild nature suited best:
Unblam'd of life, (ambition set aside,)
Not stain'd with cruelty, nor puft with pride;　480
How happy had he been, if destiny
Had higher plac'd his birth, or not so high!
His kingly vertues might have claim'd a throne,
And blest all other countries but his own:
But charming greatness since so few refuse,
'Tis juster to lament him, than accuse.
Strong were his hopes a rival to remove,
With blandishments to gain the publick love;
To head the faction while their zeal was hot,
And popularly prosecute the Plot.　490
To farther this, Achitophel unites

The malcontents of all the Israelites;
Whose differing parties he could wisely joyn,
For several ends, to serve the same design.
The best, (and of the princes some were such,)
Who thought the power of monarchy too much:
Mistaken men, and patriots in their hearts;
Not wicked, but seduc'd by impious arts.
By these the springs of property were bent,
And wound so high, they crack'd the government.   500
The next for interest sought t'embroil the State,
To sell their duty at a dearer rate;
And make their Jewish markets of the throne,
Pretending publick good, to serve their own.
Others thought kings an useless heavy load,
Who cost too much, and did too little good.
These were for laying honest David by,
On principles of pure good husbandry.
With them joyn'd all th' haranguers of the throng,
That thought to get preferment by the tongue.   510
Who follow next, a double danger bring,
Not only hating David, but the king:
The Solymaean rout,[11] well-verst of old
In godly faction, and in treason bold;
Cowring and quaking at a conqueror's sword,
But lofty to a lawfull prince restor'd;
Saw with disdain an Ethnick [12] plot begun,
And scorn'd by Jebusites to be outdone.
Hot Levites [13] headed these; who, pull'd before
From th' ark, which in the Judges' days they bore,   520
Resum'd their cant, and with a zealous cry
Pursued their old belov'd Theocracy:
Where Sanhedrin and priest inslav'd the nation,
And justifi'd their spoils by inspiration;
For who so fit for reign as Aaron's race,
If once dominion they could found in grace.
These led the pack; tho' not of surest scent,
Yet deepest mouth'd against the government.
A numerous host of dreaming saints succeed,
Of the true old enthusiastick breed: 530
'Gainst form and order they their power imploy,

11 The London mob.   13 The priests, who are "Aaron's
12 Popish Plot.   race."

Nothing to build, and all things to destroy.
But far more numerous was the herd of such,
Who think too little, and who talk too much.
These, out of meer instinct, they knew not why,
Ador'd their fathers' God and property;
And, by the same blind benefit of fate,
The Devil and the Jebusite did hate:
Born to be sav'd, even in their own despight,
Because they could not help believing right.   540
Such were the tools; but a whole Hydra more
Remains, of sprouting heads too long to score.
Some of their chiefs were princes of the land:
In the first rank of these did Zimri stand; _Duke of Buckingham_
A man so various, that he seem'd to be
Not one, but all mankind's epitome:
Stiff in opinions, always in the wrong;
Was everything by starts, and nothing long:
But, in the course of one revolving moon,
Was chymist, fiddler, statesman, and buffoon: 550
Then all for women, painting, rhiming, drinking,
Besides ten thousand freaks that dy'd in thinking.
Blest madman, who could every hour employ,
With something new to wish, or to enjoy!
Rayling and praising were his usual theams;
And both (to shew his judgment) in extreams:
So over-violent, or over-civil,
That every man, with him, was God or Devil.
In squandring wealth was his peculiar art:
Nothing went unrewarded but desert.   560
Beggar'd by fools, whom still he found too late:
He had his jest, and they had his estate.
He laught himself from court, then sought relief
By forming parties, but could ne'er be chief:
For, spight of him, the weight of business fell
On Absalom and wise Achitophel:
Thus, wicked but in will, of means bereft,
He left not faction, but of that was left.
    Titles and names 't were tedious to reherse
Of lords, below the dignity of verse.   570
Wits, warriors, Commonwealth's-men, were the best:
Kind husbands, and meer nobles, all the rest.
And, therefore in the name of dulness, be

The well-hung Balaam [14] and cold Caleb, free.
And canting Nadab let oblivion damn,
Who made new porridge for the paschal lamb.
Let friendship's holy band some names assure:
Some their own worth, and some let scorn secure.
Nor shall the rascall rabble here have place,
Whom kings no titles gave, and God no grace: 580
Not bull-fac'd Jonas, who could statutes draw
To mean rebellion, and make treason law.
But he, tho' bad, is follow'd by a worse,
The wretch who Heav'n's anointed dar'd to curse:
Shimei, whose youth did early promise bring
Of zeal to God and hatred to his king,
Did wisely from expensive sins refrain,
And never broke the Sabbath, but for gain:
Nor ever was he known an oath to vent,
Or curse, unless against the government.   590
Thus heaping wealth, by the most ready way
Among the Jews, which was to cheat and pray;
The city, to reward his pious hate
Against his master, chose him magistrate:
His hand a vare of justice did uphold;
His neck was loaded with a chain of gold.
During his office, treason was no crime;
The sons of Belial had a glorious time:
For Shimei, tho' not prodigal of pelf,
Yet lov'd his wicked neighbour as himself.   600
When two or three were gather'd to declaim
Against the monarch of Jerusalem,
Shimei was always in the midst of them.
And if they curst the king when he was by,
Would rather curse, than break good company.
If any durst his factious friends accuse,
He pack'd a jury of dissenting Jews;
Whose fellow-feeling in the godly cause
Would free the suffring saint from humane laws.
For laws are only made to punish those   610
Who serve the king, and to protect his foes.
If any leisure time he had from power,
(Because 'tis sin to misimploy an hour,)

Sheriff of London [handwritten annotation]

14 Theophilus Hastings, Earl of Hunt- is Sir William Jones; and Shimei is
ingdon; Caleb is Lord Grey; Nadab is Slingsby Bethel, sheriff of London.
William, Lord Howard of Escrick; Jonas

His bus'ness was, by writing, to persuade
That kings were useless, and a clog to trade;
And, that his noble stile he might refine,
No Rechabite [15] more shun'd the fumes of wine.
Chast were his cellars, and his shrieval board
The grossness of a city feast abhor'd:
His cooks, with long disuse, their trade forgot;   620
Cool was his kitchen, tho' his brains were hot.
Such frugal vertue malice may accuse,
But sure 'twas necessary to the Jews:
For towns once burnt such magistrates require
As dare not tempt God's providence by fire.
With spiritual food he fed his servants well,
But free from flesh that made the Jews rebel;
And Moses' laws he held in more account,
For forty days of fasting in the mount.
    To speak the rest, who better are forgot,   630
Would tyre a well-breath'd witness of the Plot:
Yet, Corah, thou shalt from oblivion pass;   *panic Titus
Erect thyself, thou monumental brass,   Oates
High as the serpent of thy metall made,
While nations stand secure beneath thy shade.
What tho' his birth were base, yet comets rise
From earthy vapours, ere they shine in skies.
Prodigious actions may as well be done
By weaver's issue, as by prince's son.
This arch-attestor for the publick good   640
By that one deed enobles all his bloud.
Who ever ask'd the witnesses' high race,
Whose oath with martyrdom did Stephen [16] grace?
Ours was a Levite, and as times went then,
His tribe were God Almighty's gentlemen.
Sunk were his eyes, his voyce was harsh and loud,
Sure signs he neither cholerick was, nor proud:
His long chin prov'd his wit; his saintlike grace
A church vermilion, and a Moses' face;
His memory, miraculously great,   650
Could plots, exceeding man's belief, repeat;
Which therefore cannot be accounted lies,
For humane wit could never such devise.

---

[15] A Jew who drank no wine (*Jere-*   [16] St. Stephen, the martyr.
miah, 35).

Some future truths are mingled in his book;
But where the witness fail'd, the prophet spoke:
Some things like visionary flights appear;
The spirit caught him up, the Lord knows where;
And gave him his rabbinical degree
Unknown to foreign university.
His judgment yet his memory did excel;   660
Which piec'd his wondrous evidence so well,
And suited to the temper of the times,
Then groaning under Jebusitick crimes.
Let Israel's foes suspect his heav'nly call,
And rashly judge his writ apocryphal;
Our laws for such affronts have forfeits made:
He takes his life, who takes away his trade.
Were I myself in witness Corah's place,
The wretch who did me such a dire disgrace,
Should whet my memory, tho' once forgot,   670
To make him an appendix of my plot.
His zeal to Heav'n made him his prince despise,
And load his person with indignities;
But zeal peculiar priviledg affords,
Indulging latitude to deeds and words;
And Corah might for Agag's [17] murther call,
In terms as coarse as Samuel us'd to Saul.
What others in his evidence did joyn,
(The best that could be had for love or coyn,)
In Corah's own predicament will fall;   680
For *witness* is a common name to all.
     Surrounded thus with friends of every sort,
Deluded Absalom forsakes the court:
Impatient of high hopes, urg'd with renown,
And fir'd with near possession of a crown.
Th' admiring crowd are dazled with surprize,
And on his goodly person feed their eyes:
His joy conceal'd, he sets himself to show,
On each side bowing popularly low;
His looks, his gestures, and his words he frames,   690
And with familiar ease repeats their names.
Thus form'd by nature, furnish'd out with arts,
He glides unfelt into their secret hearts.
Then, with a kind compassionating look,

17 Sir Edmund Berry Godfrey was found stabbed to death.

And sighs, bespeaking pity ere he spoak,
Few words he said; but easy those and fit,
More slow than Hybla-drops, and far more sweet.
   "I mourn, my countrymen, your lost estate;
Tho' far unable to prevent your fate:
Behold a banisht man, for your dear cause   700
Expos'd a prey to arbitrary laws!
Yet oh! that I alone could be undone,
Cut off from empire, and no more a son!
Now all your liberties a spoil are made;
Egypt and Tyrus intercept your trade,
And Jebusites your sacred rites invade.
My father, whom with reverence yet I name,
Charm'd into ease, is careless of his fame;
And, brib'd with petty summs of forreign gold,
Is grown in Bathsheba's [18] embraces old;   710
Exalts his enemies, his friends destroys;
And all his power against himself employs.
He gives, and let him give, my right away;
But why should he his own, and yours betray?
He only, he can make the nation bleed,
And he alone from my revenge is freed.
Take then my tears, (with that he wip'd his eyes)
'Tis all the aid my present power supplies:
No court-informer can these arms accuse;
These arms may sons against their fathers use: 720
And 'tis my wish, the next successor's reign
May make no other Israelite complain."
   Youth, beauty, graceful action seldom fail;
But common interest always will prevail;
And pity never ceases to be shown
To him who makes the people's wrongs his own.
The croud, (that still believe their kings oppress)
With lifted hands their young Messiah bless:
Who now begins his progress to ordain
With chariots, horsemen, and a numerous train;   730
From east to west his glories he displaies,
And, like the sun, the promis'd land survays.
Fame runs before him as the morning star,
And shouts of joy salute him from afar:
Each house receives him as a guardian god,

18 Louise de Keroualle, Duchess of Portsmouth, mistress of Charless II.

And consecrates the place of his aboad:
But hospitable treats did most commend
Wise Issachar,[19] his wealthy western friend.
This moving court, that caught the people's eyes,
And seem'd but pomp, did other ends disguise: 740
Achitophel had form'd it, with intent
To sound the depths, and fathom where it went,
The people's hearts; distinguish friends from foes,
And try their strength, before they came to blows.
Yet all was colour'd with a smooth pretence
Of specious love, and duty to their prince.
Religion, and redress of grievances,
Two names that always cheat and always please,
Are often urg'd; and good King David's life
Indanger'd by a brother and a wife.[20] *duke of york & Quee*
Thus, in a pageant shew, a plot is made,   *Cathari*
And peace itself is war in masquerade.
O foolish Israel! never warn'd by ill,
Still the same baite, and circumvented still!
Did ever men forsake their present ease,
In midst of health imagine a desease;
Take pains contingent mischiefs to foresee,
Make heirs for monarchs, and for God decree?
What shall we think! Can people give away
Both for themselves and sons, their native sway?   760
Then they are left defencless to the sword
Of each unbounded, arbitrary lord:
And laws are vain, by which we right enjoy,
If kings unquestiond can those laws destroy.
Yet if the crowd be judge of fit and just,
And kings are onely officers in trust,
Then this resuming cov'nant was declar'd
When kings were made, or is for ever barr'd.
If those who gave the scepter could not tye
By their own deed their own posterity,   770
How then could Adam bind his future race?
How could his forfeit on mankind take place?
Or how could heavenly justice damn us all,
Who ne'er consented to our father's fall?

19 Thomas Thynne, who entertained   Catherine were accused of plotting
Monmouth.   against Charles.
20 The Duke of York and Queen

Then kings are slaves to those whom they command,
And tenants to their people's pleasure stand.
Add, that the pow'r for property allowd
Is mischievously seated in the crowd;
For who can be secure of private right,
If sovereign sway may be dissolv'd by might?   780
Nor is the people's judgment always true:
The most may err as grosly as the few;
And faultless kings run down, by common cry,
For vice, oppression, and for tyranny.
What standard is there in a fickle rout,
Which, flowing to the mark, runs faster out?
Nor only crowds, but Sandhedrins may be
Infected with this publick lunacy,
And share the madness of rebellious times,
To murther monarchs for imagin'd crimes.   790
If they may give and take whene'er they please,
Not kings alone, (the Godhead's images,)
But government it self at length must fall
To nature's state, where all have right to all.
Yet, grant our lords the people kings can make,
What prudent men a setled throne would shake?
For whatsoe'er their sufferings were before,
That change they covet makes them suffer more.
All other errors but disturb a state,
But innovation is the blow of fate.   800
If ancient fabricks nod, and threat to fall,
To patch the flaws, and buttress up the wall,
Thus far 'tis duty; but here fix the mark;
For all beyond it is to touch our ark.
To change foundations, cast the frame anew,
Is work for rebels, who base ends pursue,
At once divine and human laws controul,
And mend the parts by ruin of the whole.
The tampering world is subject to this curse,
To physick their disease into a worse.   810
   Now what relief can righteous David bring?
How fatall 'tis to be too good a king!
Friends he has few, so high the madness grows:
Who dare be such, must be the people's foes:
Yet some there were, ev'n in the worst of days;
Some let me name, and naming is to praise.

James Butler, Duke of Ormond

In this short file Barzillai first appears;

Chas. Supporter Barzillai,[21] crown'd with honor and with years:
Long since, the rising rebells he withstood
In regions waste, beyond the Jordan's flood: 820
Unfortunately brave to buoy the State;
But sinking underneath his master's fate:
In exile with his godlike prince he mourn'd;
For him he suffer'd, and with him return'd.
The court he practis'd, not the courtier's art:
Large was his wealth, but larger was his heart:
Which well the noblest objects knew to choose,
The fighting warriour, and recording Muse.
His bed could once a fruitfull issue boast;
Now more than half a father's name is lost.   830
His eldest hope, with every grace adorn'd,
By me (so Heav'n will have it) always mourn'd,
And always honour'd, snatcht in manhood's prime
B' unequal fates, and Providence's crime:
Yet not before the goal of honour won,
All parts fulfill'd of subject and of son;
Swift was the race, but short the time to run.
O narrow circle, but of pow'r divine,
Scanted in space, but perfect in thy line!
By sea, by land, thy matchless worth was known,   840
Arms thy delight, and war was all thy own:
Thy force, infus'd, the fainting Tyrians propp'd;
And haughty Pharaoh found his fortune stopp'd.
Oh ancient honour! Oh unconquer'd hand,
Whom foes unpunish'd never could withstand!
But Israel was unworthy of thy name:
Short is the date of all immoderate fame.
It looks as Heav'n our ruine had design'd,
And durst not trust thy fortune and thy mind.
Now, free from earth, thy disencumberd soul   850
Mounts up, and leaves behind the clouds and starry pole:
From thence thy kindred legions mayst thou bring,
To aid the guardian angel of thy king.
Here stop my Muse, here cease thy painful flight;
No pinions can pursue immortal height:
Tell good Barzillai thou canst sing no more,
And tell thy soul she should have fled before.
Or fled she with his life, and left this verse

21 James Butler, Duke of Ormond, Charles' supporter.

To hang on her departed patron's hearse?
Now take thy steepy flight from heaven, and see   860
If thou canst find on earth another *he:*
Another *he* would be too hard to find;
See then whom thou canst see not far behind.
Zadoc [22] the priest, whom, shunning power and place,
His lowly mind advanc'd to David's grace:
With him the Sagan of Jerusalem,
Of hospitable soul, and noble stem;
Him of the western dome, whose weighty sense
Flows in fit words and heavenly eloquence.
The prophets' sons, by such example led,   870
To learning and to loyalty were bred:
For colleges on bounteous kings depend,
And never rebell was to arts a friend.
To these succeed the pillars of the laws,
Who best could plead, and best can judge a cause.
Next them a train of loyal peers ascend;
Sharp-judging Adriel, the Muses' friend,
Himself a Muse—in Sandhedrin's debate
True to his prince, but not a slave of state:
Whom David's love with honours did adorn,   880
That from his disobedient son were torn.
Jotham of piercing wit, and pregnant thought,
Indued by nature, and by learning taught
To move assemblies, who but onely try'd
The worse a while, then chose the better side;
Nor chose alone, but turn'd the balance too;
So much the weight of one brave man can doe.
Hushai, the friend of David in distress,
In publick storms, of manly steadfastness:
By foreign treaties he inform'd his youth,   890
And join'd experience to his native truth.
His frugal care supply'd the wanting throne,
Frugal for that, but bounteous of his own:
'Tis easy conduct when exchequers flow,
But hard the task to manage well the low;
For sovraign power is too deprest or high,
When kings are forc'd to sell, or crowds to buy.
Indulge one labour more, my weary Muse,

22 William Sancroft, Archbishop of Canterbury; the Sagan is Henry Compton, Bishop of London; Adriel is John Sheffield, Earl of Mulgrave; Jotham, George Savile, Marquis of Halifax; Hushai, Lawrence Hyde, Earl of Rochester; and Amiel is Edward Seymour, Speaker of the Commons.

For Amiel: who can Amiel's praise refuse?
Of ancient race by birth, but nobler yet   900
In his own worth, and without title great:
The Sanhedrin long time as chief he rul'd,
Their reason guided, and their passion cool'd:
So dexterous was he in the crown's defence,
So form'd to speak a loyal nation's sense,
That, as their band was Israel's tribes in small,
So fit was he to represent them all.
Now rasher charioteers the seat ascend,
Whose loose careers his steady skill commend:
They like th' unequal ruler of the day,   910
Misguide the seasons, and mistake the way;
While he withdrawn at their mad labor smiles,
And safe enjoys the sabbath of his toyls.
    These were the chief, a small but faithful band
Of worthies, in the breach who dar'd to stand,
And tempt th' united fury of the land.
With grief they view'd such powerful engines bent,
To batter down the lawful government:
A numerous faction, with pretended frights,
In Sanhedrins to plume the regal rights;   920
The true successor from the court remov'd:
The Plot, by hireling witnesses, improv'd.
These ills they saw, and, as their duty bound,
They shew'd the king the danger of the wound:
That no concessions from the throne would please,
But lenitives fomented the disease;
That Absalom, ambitious of the crown,
Was made the lure to draw the people down;
That false Achitophel's pernitious hate
Had turn'd the Plot to ruin Church and State: 930
The councill violent, the rabble worse;
That Shimei taught Jerusalem to curse.
    With all these loads of injuries opprest,
And long revolving in his carefull breast,
Th' event of things, at last, his patience tir'd,
Thus from his royal throne, by Heav'n inspir'd,
The godlike David spoke: with awfull fear
His train their Maker in their master hear.
    "Thus long have I, by native mercy sway'd,
My wrongs dissembl'd, my revenge delay'd: 940
So willing to forgive th' offending age,

So much the father did the king asswage.
But now so far my clemency they slight,
Th' offenders question my forgiving right.
That one was made for many, they contend;
But 'tis to rule; for that's a monarch's end.
They call my tenderness of blood, my fear;
Tho' manly tempers can the longest bear.
Yet, since they will divert my native course,
'Tis time to shew I am not good by force.   950
Those heap'd affronts that haughty subjects bring,
Are burthens for a camel, not a king:
Kings are the publick pillars of the State,
Born to sustain and prop the nation's weight:
If my young Samson will pretend a call
To shake the column, let him share the fall:
But oh that yet he would repent and live!
How easie 'tis for parents to forgive!
With how few tears a pardon might be won
From nature, pleading for a darling son!   960
Poor pitied youth, by my paternal care
Rais'd up to all the height his frame could bear:
Had God ordain'd his fate for empire born,
He would have given his soul another turn:
Gull'd with a patriot's name, whose modern sense
Is one that would by law supplant his prince:
The people's brave, the politician's tool;
Never was patriot yet, but was a fool.
Whence comes it that religion and the laws
Should more be Absalom's than David's cause?   970
His old instructor, ere he lost his place,
Was never thought indu'd with so much grace.
Good heav'ns, how faction can a patriot paint!
My rebel ever proves my people's saint:
Would *they* impose an heir upon the throne?
Let Sanhedrins be taught to give their own.
A king's at least a part of government,
And mine as requisite as their consent;
Without my leave a future king to choose,
Infers a right the present to depose: 980
True, they petition me t' approve their choice;
But Esau's hands suit ill with Jacob's voice.
My pious subjects for my safety pray,
Which to secure, they take my power away.

From plots and treasons Heaven preserve my years,
But save me most from my petitioners.
Unsatiate as the barren womb or grave;
God cannot grant so much as they can crave.
What then is left but with a jealous eye
To guard the small remains of royalty?   990
The law shall still direct my peacefull sway,
And the same law teach rebels to obey:
Votes shall no more establish'd pow'r control—
Such votes as make a part exceed the whole:
No groundless clamours shall my friends remove,
Nor crowds have power to punish ere they prove:
For gods and godlike kings, their care express,
Still to defend their servants in distress.
O that my power to saving were confin'd:
Why am I forc'd, like Heav'n, against my mind,   1000
To make examples of another kind?
Must I at length the sword of justice draw?
O curst effects of necessary law!
How ill my fear they by my mercy scan!
Beware the fury of a patient man.
Law they require, let Law then shew her face;
They could not be content to look on Grace,
Her hinder parts, but with a daring eye
To tempt the terror of her front and dye.
By their own arts, 'tis righteously decreed,   1010
Those dire artificers of death shall bleed.
Against themselves their witnesses will swear,
Till viper-like their mother Plot they tear:
And suck for nutriment that bloody gore,
Which was their principle of life before.
Their Belial with their Belzebub will fight;
Thus on my foes, my foes shall do me right:
Nor doubt th' event; for factious crowds engage,
In their first onset, all their brutal rage.
Then let 'em take an unresisted course,   1020
Retire and traverse, and delude their force:
But when they stand all breathless, urge the fight,
And rise upon 'em with redoubled might:
For lawful pow'r is still superiour found,
When long driven back, at length it stands the ground."
    He said. Th' Almighty, nodding, gave consent;
And peals of thunder shook the firmament.

the ending disappears almost no action

Henceforth a series of new time began,
The mighty years in long procession ran:
Once more the godlike David was restor'd,   1030
And willing nations knew their lawfull lord.

MAC FLECKNOE

OR, A SATIRE UPON THE TRUE-BLUE-PROTESTANT POET T. S.[1]

1682

All human things are subject to decay,
And, when fate summons, monarchs must obey:
This Flecknoe found, who, like Augustus, young
Was call'd to empire, and had govern'd long:
In prose and verse, was own'd, without dispute,
Thro' all the realms of *Nonsense*, absolute.
This aged prince, now flourishing in peace,
And blest with issue of a large increase,
Worn out with business, did at length debate
To settle the succession of the State: 10
And pond'ring which of all his sons was fit
To reign, and wage immortal war with wit,
Cry'd, " 'Tis resolv'd; for nature pleads, that he
Should onely rule, who most resembles me:
Sh—— alone my perfect image bears,
Mature in dulness from his tender years.
Sh—— alone, of all my sons, is he
Who stands confirm'd in full stupidity.
The rest to some faint meaning make pretence,
But Sh—— never deviates into sense.   20
Some beams of wit on other souls may fall,
Strike thro', and make a lucid intervall;
But Sh——'s genuine night admits no ray,
His rising fogs prevail upon the day:
Besides his goodly fabrick fills the eye,

[Handwritten margin annotations: "Thom Shadwell"; "general propositions"; "stately movement"; "MacFlecknoe, lousy poet, destroys this"; "hold me"; "Closer"; "Tiny Dancer"; "wit, enemy of poet-Shad."]

And seems design'd for thoughtless majesty:
Thoughtless as monarch oakes that shade the plain, *dullness*
And, spread in solemn state, supinely reign.
Heywood and Shirley [2] were but types of thee, *dramatists*
Thou last great prophet of tautology.   30
Even I, a dunce of more renown than they,
Was sent before but to prepare thy way;
And, coarsely clad in Norwich drugget,[3] came *cheap cloth*
To teach the nations in thy greater name.
My warbling lute, the lute I whilom strung,
When to King John of Portugal [4] I sung, *John IV*
Was but the prelude to that glorious day,
When thou on silver Thames didst cut thy way,
With well-tim'd oars before the royal barge,
Swell'd with the pride of thy celestial charge;   40
And big with hymn, commander of a host,
The like was ne'er in Epsom blankets [5] tost. *Shadwell's play*
Methinks I see the new Arion [6] sail, *Greek figure*
The lute still trembling underneath thy nail.
At thy well-sharpend thumb from shore to shore
The treble squeaks for fear, the bases roar;
Echoes from Pissing Alley Sh—— call,
And Sh—— they resound from Aston Hall.
About thy boat the little fishes throng, *sinking couplet*
As at the morning toast, that floats along.   50 *garbage*
Sometimes as prince of thy harmonious band,
Thou wield'st thy papers in thy threshing hand.
St. André's feet [7] ne'er kept more equal time, *dancing master*
Not ev'n the feet of thy own *Psyche's* [8] rhime; *Shadwell's opera*
Tho' they in number as in sense excell:
So just, so like tautology, they fell,
That, pale with envy, Singleton [9] forswore *singer*
The lute and sword, which he in triumph bore,
And vow'd he ne'er would act Villerius more."
Here stopt the good old syre, and wept for joy   60
In silent raptures of the hopefull boy.
All arguments, but most his plays, perswade,
That for anointed dullness he was made.

---

2 Thomas Heywood and James Shirley, earlier dramatists.
3 A cheap cloth.
4 Flecknoe visited John IV of Portugal.
5 Shadwell's play *Epsom Wells*.
6 Arion, a Greek musician (*ca.* 700 B.C.) played his lyre on the prow of a ship, then plunged into the sea.
7 St. André was a dancing master.
8 Shadwell's opera *Psyche*.
9 A singer in operas.

Close to the walls which fair Augusta [10] bind, *London*
(The fair Augusta much to fears inclin'd)
An ancient fabrick rais'd t' inform the sight,
There stood of yore, and Barbican it hight:
A watchtower once; but now, so fate ordains,
Of all the pile an empty name remains.
From its old ruins brothel-houses rise,   70
Scenes of lewd loves, and of polluted joys,
Where their vast courts the mother-strumpets keep,
And, undisturb'd by watch, in silence sleep.
Near these a Nursery erects its head,
Where queens are form'd, and future heroes bred;
Where unfledg'd actors learn to laugh and cry,
Where infant punks their tender voices try,
And little Maximins [11] the gods defy. *hero of Dryden's play*
Great Fletcher never treads in buskins here, *Eliyab.*
Nor greater Jonson dares in socks appear; *Dramatist* 80
But gentle Simkin just reception finds *Charac in farce*
Amidst this monument of vanish'd minds:
Pure clinches the suburbian Muse affords,
And Panton waging harmless war with words. *punster*
Here Flecknoe, as a place to fame well known,
Ambitiously design'd his Sh——'s throne;
For ancient Dekker prophesied long since, *elizabethan dramatist*
That in this pile should reign a mighty prince,
Born for a scourge of wit, and flayle of sense;
To whom true dulness should some *Psyches* owe,   90
But worlds of *Misers* [12] from his pen should flow; *play of Shad.*
Humorists and *Hypocrites* it should produce,
Whole Raymond families, and tribes of Bruce.
   Now Empress Fame had publisht the renown
Of Sh——'s coronation thro' the town.
Rows'd by report of Fame, the nations meet,
From near Bunhill, and distant Watling Street.
No Persian carpets spread th' imperial way,
But scatter'd limbs of mangled poets lay; *sense of Augus.*
From dusty shops neglected authors come,   100
Martyrs of pies, and reliques of the bum. *taste*
Much Heywood, Shirley, Ogleby [13] there lay, *looked down upon*

10 The Romans called London Augusta. Thomas Panton, a punster; and Thomas
11 Maximin was hero of Dryden's own   Dekker, Elizabethan dramatist.
Tyrannic Love; there follow references 12 Shadwell adapted Molière's *Miser.*
to John Fletcher, the Elizabethan drama- 13 John Ogleby, translator.
tist; Simkin, a character in farce;

But loads of Sh—— almost choakt the way.
Bilk't stationers for yeomen stood prepar'd,
And Herringman [14] was captain of the guard.
The hoary prince in majesty appear'd,
High on a throne of his own labours rear'd.
At his right hand our young Ascanius sate, *Son of Aenius*
Rome's other hope, and pillar of the State.
His brows thick fogs, instead of glories, grace,   110
And lambent dulness play'd around his face. *flaming dullness*
As Hannibal did to the altars come,
Sworn by his syre mortal foe to Rome;
So Sh—— swore, nor should his vow be vain,
That he till death true dulness would maintain;
And in his father's right, and realm's defence,
Ne'er to have peace with wit, nor truce with sense.
The king himself the sacred unction made,
As king by office, and as priest by trade:
In his sinister hand, instead of ball,   120
He plac'd a mighty mug of potent ale;
Love's Kingdom [15] to his right he did convey,
At once his scepter, and his rule of sway;
Whose righteous lore the prince had practis'd young,
And from whose loyns recorded *Psyche* sprung.
His temples, last, with poppies were o'erspread,
That nodding seem'd to consecrate his head.
Just at that point of time, if fame not lye,
On his left hand twelve reverend owls did fly.
So Romulus, 'tis sung, by Tiber's brook,   130
Presage of sway from twice six vultures took.
Th'admiring throng loud acclamations make,
And omens of his future empire take.
The syre then shook the honours of his head,
And from his brows damps of oblivion shed
Full on the filial dulness: long he stood,
Repelling from his breast the raging god;
At length burst out in this prophetick mood:
"Heavens bless my son, from Ireland let him reign
To farr Barbadoes on the western main;   140
Of his dominion may no end be known,
And greater than his father's be his throne.
Beyond *Love's Kingdom* let him stretch his pen!"
He paus'd, and all the people cried, "Amen."
Then thus continued he: "My son, advance

---

14 A publisher.   15 Flecknoe's pastoral drama.

Still in new impudence, new ignorance.
Success let others teach, learn thou from me
Pangs without birth, and fruitless industry.
Let *Virtuosos* [16] in five years be writ;
Yet not one thought accuse thy toyl of wit.   150
Let gentle George [17] in triumph tread the stage,
Make Dorimant betray, and Loveit rage;
Let Cully, Cockwood, Fopling, charm the pit,
And in their folly shew the writer's wit.
Yet still thy fools stall stand in thy defence,
And justifie their author's want of sense.
Let 'em be all by thy own model made
Of dulness, and desire no foreign aid:
That they to future ages may be known,
Not copies drawn, but issue of thy own.   160
Nay let thy men of wit too be the same,
All full of thee, and differing but in name.
But let no alien S—dl—y [18] interpose,
To lard with wit thy hungry *Epsom* prose.
And when false flowers of rhetorick thou wouldst cull,
Trust nature, do not labor to be dull;
But write thy best, and top; and, in each line,
Sir Formal's [19] oratory will be thine:
Sir Formal, tho' unsought, attends thy quill,
And does thy northern dedications fill.   170
Nor let false friends seduce thy mind to fame,
By arrogating Jonson's hostile name.
Let father Flecknoe fire thy mind with praise,
And uncle Ogleby thy envy raise.
Thou art my blood, where Jonson has no part;
What share have we in nature, or in art?
Where did his wit on learning fix a brand,
And rail at arts he did not understand?
Where made he love in Prince Nicander's [20] vein,
Or swept the dust in *Psyche's* humble strain?   180
Where sold he bargains, 'whip-stitch, kiss my arse,'
Promis'd a play and dwindled to a farce?
When did his Muse from Fletcher scenes purloin,
As thou whole Eth'rege dost transfuse to thine?
But so transfus'd, as oyl on water's flow,

16 Shadwell's play *The Virtuoso*.
17 George Etherege, whose plays had
the characters Dorimant, Loveit, Cully,
Cockwood, and Sir Fopling Flutter.
18 Charles Sedley wrote a prologue for
Shadwell's *Epsom Wells*.
19 Sir Formal Trifle in *The Virtuoso*.
20 Nicander in *Psyche*.

His always floats above, thine sinks below.
This is thy province, this thy wondrous way,
New humours to invent for each new play:
This is that boasted byas of thy mind,
By which one way, to dulness, 'tis inclin'd;   190
Which makes thy writings lean on one side still,
And in all changes that way bends thy will.
Nor let thy mountain-belly make pretence
Of likeness; thine 's a tympany of sense.
A tun of man in thy large bulk is writ,
But sure thou'rt but a kilderkin [21] of wit.
Like mine, thy gentle numbers feebly creep;
Thy tragick Muse gives smiles, thy comick sleep.
With whate'er gall thou sett'st thyself to write,
Thy inoffensive satyres never bite.   200
In thy fellonious heart tho' venom lies,
It does but touch thy Irish pen, and dyes.
Thy genius calls thee not to purchase fame
In keen iambicks, but mild anagram:
Leave writing plays, and chuse for thy command
Some peacefull province in acrostick land.
There thou may'st wings display and altars raise,
And torture one poor word ten thousand ways.
Or if thou wouldst thy diff'rent talents suit,
Set thy own songs, and sing them to thy lute."   210

     He said: but his last words were scarcely heard,
For Bruce and Longvil had a trap prepar'd,[22]
And down they sent the yet declaiming bard.
Sinking he left his drugget robe behind,
Borne upwards by a subterranean wind.
The mantle fell to the young prophet's part,
With double portion of his father's art.

---

21 Small cask.

22 In *The Virtuoso* Bruce and Longvil
prepare a trap for Sir Formal Trifle.

RELIGIO LAICI

OR, A LAYMAN'S FAITH

1682

Dim, as the borrow'd beams of moon and stars
To lonely, weary, wandring travellers,
Is Reason to the soul: and, as on high
Those rowling fires discover but the sky,
Not light us here, so Reason's glimmering ray
Was lent, not to assure our doubtfull way,
But guide us upward to a better day.
And as those nightly tapers disappear,
When day's bright lord ascends our hemisphere;
So pale grows Reason at Religion's sight;   10
So dyes, and so dissolves in supernatural light.
Some few, whose lamp shone brighter, have been led
From cause to cause, to nature's secret head;
And found that one first principle must be:
But what, or who, that UNIVERSAL HE;
Whether some soul incompassing this ball,
Unmade, unmov'd; yet making, moving All;
Or various atoms' interfering dance
Leapt into form, (the noble work of chance;)
Or this great All was from eternity;   20
Not ev'n the Stagirite [1] himself could see,
And Epicurus guess'd as well as he:
As blindly grop'd they for a future state;
As rashly judg'd of providence and fate:
But least of all could their endeavours find
What most concern'd the good of human kind;
For happiness was never to be found,
But vanish'd from 'em like enchanted ground.
One thought content the good to be enjoy'd:
This, every little accident destroy'd: 30
The wiser madmen did for vertue toyl:
A thorny, or at best a barren soil:
In pleasure some their glutton souls would steep;

[1] Aristotle.

lost hopes

But found their line too short, the well too deep;
And leaky vessels which no bliss could keep.
Thus, anxious thoughts in endless circles roul,
Without a center where to fix the soul:
In this wilde maze their vain endeavours end:
How can the less the greater comprehend?
Or finite reason reach Infinity?   40
For what could fathom God were more than He.
The Deist thinks he stands on firmer ground;
Cries: "Εὕρεχα, the mighty secret 's found:
God is that spring of good; supreme, and best;   *1st princ.*
We, made to serve, and in that service blest."   *2nd princ.*
If so, some rules of worship must be given,
Distributed alike to all by Heaven:

all reasonable

Else God were partial, and to some deny'd
The means his justice should for all provide.
This general worship is to PRAISE and PRAY: *3rd principle*   50
One part to borrow blessings, one to pay:
And when frail nature slides into offence,   *4th prin.*
The sacrifice for crimes is penitence.
Yet, since th' effects of providence, we find,   *5th*
Are variously dispens'd to human kind;
That vice triumphs, and vertue suffers here,
(A brand that sovereign justice cannot bear;)
Our reason prompts us to a future state:
The last appeal from fortune, and from fate:
Where God's all-righteous ways will be declar'd;   60
The bad meet punishment, the good, reward.
   Thus man by his own strength to heaven would soar:
And would not be oblig'd to God for more.
Vain, wretched creature, how art thou misled
To think thy wit these godlike notions bred!
These truths are not the product of thy mind,
But dropt from heaven, and of a nobler kind.
Reveal'd Religion first inform'd thy sight,
And Reason saw not, till Faith sprung the light.
Hence all thy natural worship takes the source: 70
'Tis revelation what thou think'st discourse.
Else, how com'st thou to see these truths so clear,
Which so obscure to heathens did appear?
Not Plato these, nor Aristotle found;
Nor he whose wisedom oracles renown'd.
Hast thou a wit so deep, or so sublime,

Or canst thou lower dive, or higher climb?
Canst thou, by Reason, more of Godhead know
Than Plutarch, Seneca, or Cicero?
Those gyant wits, in happyer ages born,   80
(When arms and arts did Greece and Rome adorn)
Knew no such systeme; no such piles could raise
Of natural worship, built on pray'r and praise,
To One Sole GOD:
Nor did remorse, to expiate sin, prescribe:
But slew their fellow creatures for a bribe:
The guiltless victim groan'd for their offence,
And cruelty, and blood was penitence.
If sheep and oxen could attone for men
Ah! at how cheap a rate the rich might sin!   90
And great oppressours might Heaven's wrath beguile,
By offering his own creatures for a spoil!
    Dar'st thou, poor worm, offend Infinity?
And must the terms of peace be given by thee?
Then thou art Justice in the last appeal;
Thy easy God instructs thee to rebell:
And, like a king remote, and weak, must take
What satisfaction thou are pleas'd to make.
    But if there be a pow'r too just, and strong
To wink at crimes, and bear unpunish'd wrong;   100
Look humbly upward, see his will disclose: *justice*
The forfeit first, and then the fine impose:
A mulct thy poverty could never pay
Had not eternal wisdom found the way:
And with celestial wealth supply'd thy store,
His justice makes the fine, his mercy quits the score.
See God descending in thy human frame;
Th' offended suff'ring in th' offender's name:
All thy misdeeds to him imputed see,
And all his righteousness devolv'd on thee.   110
    For granting we have sin'd, and that th' offence
Of man is made against Omnipotence,   *pride*
Some price, that bears proportion, must be paid,
And infinite with infinite be weigh'd.
See then the Deist lost: remorse for vice,
Not paid; or paid, inadequate in price:
What farther means can Reason now direct,
Or what relief from human wit expect?
That shews us sick; and sadly are we sure

Still to be sick, till Heav'n reveal the cure: 120
If then Heaven's will must needs be understood,
(Which must, if we want cure, and Heaven be good,)
Let all records of will reveal'd be shown;
With Scripture, all in equal ballance thrown,
And our one sacred book will be that one.
   Proof needs not here, for whether we compare
That impious, idle, superstitious ware
Of rites, lustrations, offerings, (which before,
In various ages, various countries bore)
With Christian faith and vertues, we shall find 130
None answ'ring the great ends of human kind,
But this one rule of life: that shews us best
How God may be appeas'd, and mortals blest.
Whether from length of time its worth we draw,
The world is scarce more ancient than the law:
Heav'n's early care prescrib'd for every age;
First, in the soul, and after, in the page.
Or, whether more abstractedly we look,
Or on the writers, or the written book,
Whence, but from heav'n, could men unskill'd in arts, 140
In several ages born, in several parts,
Weave such agreeing truths? or how, or why,
Should all conspire to cheat us with a lye?
Unask'd their pains, ungratefull their advice,
Starving their gain, and martyrdom their price.
   If on the book itself we cast our view,
Concurrent heathens prove the story true;
The doctrine, miracles; which must convince,
For Heav'n in them appeals to human sense:
And tho' they prove not, they confirm the cause, 150
When what is taught agrees with nature's laws.
   Then for the style; majestick and divine,
It speaks no less than God in every line:
Commanding words; whose force is still the same
As the first fiat that produc'd our frame.
All faiths beside, or did by arms ascend,
Or sense indulg'd has made mankind their friend:
This onely doctrine does our lusts oppose,
Unfed by nature's soil, in which it grows;
Cross to our interests, curbing sense, and sin; 160
Oppress'd without, and undermin'd within,
It thrives thro' pain; its own tormentours tires;

And with a stubborn patience still aspires.
To what can Reason such effects assign,
Transcending nature, but to laws divine?
Which in that sacred volume are contain'd;
Sufficient, clear, and for that use ordain'd.
  But stay: the Deist here will urge anew,
No supernatural worship can be true;
Because a general law is that alone   170
Which must to all, and everywhere, be known:
A style so large as not this book can claim,
Nor aught that bears reveal'd Religion's name.
'Tis said the sound of a Messiah's birth
Is gone thro' all the habitable earth;
But still that text must be confin'd alone
To what was then inhabited, and known:
And what provision could from thence accrue
To Indian souls, and worlds discover'd new?
In other parts it helps, that ages past,   180
The Scriptures there were known, and were imbrac'd,
Till Sin spread once again the shades of night:
What 's that to these who never saw the light?
  Of all objections this indeed is chief
To startle Reason, stagger frail Belief:
We grant, 'tis true, that Heav'n from human sense
Has hid the secret paths of Providence:
But boundless wisedom, boundless mercy, may
Find ev'n for those bewilder'd souls a way:
If from his nature foes may pity claim,   190
Much more may strangers who ne'er heard his name.
And tho' no name be for salvation known,
But that of his eternal Son's alone;
Who knows how far transcending goodness can
Extend the merits of that Son to man?
Who knows what reasons may his mercy lead,
Or ignorance invincible may plead?
Not onely charity bids hope the best,
But more the great apostle has exprest:
That if the Gentiles (whom no law inspir'd)   200
By nature did what was by law requir'd;
They, who the written rule had never known,
Were to themselves both rule and law alone:
To nature's plain indictment they shall plead;
And by their conscience be condemn'd or freed.

Most righteous doom! because a rule reveal'd
Is none to those, from whom it was conceal'd.
Then those who follow'd Reason's dictates right,
Liv'd up, and lifted high their natural light;
With Socrates may see their Maker's face,   210
While thousand rubrick-martyrs want a place.
    Nor does it baulk my charity, to find
Th' Egyptian bishop[2] of another mind:
For, tho' his creed eternal truth contains,
'Tis hard for man to doom to endless pains
All who believ'd not all, his zeal requir'd;
Unless he first could prove he was inspir'd.
Then let us either think he meant to say
This faith, where publish'd, was the onely way;
Or else conclude that, Arius to confute,   220
The good old man, too eager in dispute,
Flew high; and, as his Christian fury rose,
Damn'd all for hereticks who durst oppose.
    Thus far my charity this path has try'd;
(A much unskilful, but well-meaning guide:)
Yet what they are, ev'n these crude thoughts were bred
By reading that, which better thou hast read,
Thy matchless author's work; which thou, my friend,
By well translating better dost commend:
Those youthfull hours which of thy equals most   230
In toys have squander'd, or in vice have lost,
Those hours hast thou to nobler use employ'd;
And the severe delights of truth enjoy'd.
Witness this weighty book, in which appears
The crabbed toil of many thoughtfull years,
Spent by thy authour in the sifting care
Of Rabbins' old sophisticated ware
From gold divine; which he who well can sort
May afterwards make algebra a sport.
A treasure, which if country curates buy,   240
They Junius[3] and Tremellius may defy:
Save pains in various readings, and translations,
And without Hebrew make most learn'd quotations.
A work so full with various learning fraught,
So nicely ponder'd, yet so strongly wrought,

_addres.
to Dickinson_

[2] Athansius, Bishop of Alexandria in the third century, who opposed Arius, the heretic who denied the doctrine of the Trinity.

[3] Franciscus Junius and Emmanuel Tremellius, Calvinist clergy of the 16th century.

As nature's height and art's last hand requir'd:
As much as man could compass, uninspir'd.
Where we may see what errours have been made
Both in the copier's and translator's trade;
How Jewish, Popish interests have prevail'd, 250
And where infallibility has fail'd.
　For some, who have his secret meaning guess'd,
Have found our author not too much a priest:
For fashion sake he seems to have recourse
To Pope, and councils, and tradition's force;
But he that old traditions could subdue,
Could not but find the weakness of the new:
If Scripture, tho' deriv'd from heav'nly birth,
Has been but carelessly preserv'd on earth;
If God's own people, who of God before 260
Knew what we know, and had been promis'd more,
In fuller terms, of Heaven's assisting care,
And who did neither time nor study spare
To keep this book untainted, unperplext,
Let in gross errours to corrupt the text,
Omitted paragraphs, embroyl'd the sense,
With vain traditions stopt the gaping fence,
Which every common hand pull'd up with ease:
What safety from such brushwood-helps as these?
If written words from time are not secur'd, 270
How can we think have oral sounds endur'd?
Which thus transmitted, if one mouth has fail'd,
Immortal lyes on ages are intail'd;
And that some such have been, is prov'd too plain;
If we consider interest, Church, and gain.
　"O, but," says one, "tradition set aside,
Where can we hope for an unerring guide?
For since th' original Scripture has been lost,
All copies disagreeing, maim'd the most,
Or Christian faith can have no certain ground, 280
Or truth in Church tradition must be found."
　Such an omniscient Church we wish indeed;
'Twere worth both Testaments; and cast in the Creed:
But if this mother be a guide so sure,
As can all doubts resolve, all truth secure,
Then her infallibility as well
Where copies are corrupt, or lame, can tell;
Restore lost canon with as little pains,

As truly explicate what still remains:
Which yet no council dare pretend to doe,   290
Unless like Esdras [4] they could write it new:
Strange confidence, still to interpret true,
Yet not be sure that all they have explain'd,
Is in the blest original contain'd.
More safe, and much more modest 'tis, to say
God would not leave mankind without a way:
And that the Scriptures, tho' not every where
Free from corruption, or intire, or clear,
Are uncorrupt, sufficient, clear, intire,
In all things which our needful faith require.   300
If others in the same glass better see,
'Tis for themselves they look, but not for me:
For MY salvation must its doom receive,
Not from what OTHERS, but what I believe.
    Must all tradition then be set aside?
This to affirm were ignorance, or pride.
Are there not many points, some needfull sure
To saving faith, that Scripture leaves obscure?
Which every sect will wrest a several way
(For what one sect interprets, all sects may):   310
We hold, and say we prove from Scripture plain,
That Christ is GOD; the bold Socinian [5]
From the same Scripture urges he 's but MAN.
Now what appeal can end th' important suit;
Both parts talk loudly, but the rule is mute?
    Shall I speak plain, and in a nation free
Assume an honest layman's liberty?
I think (according to my little skill,
To my own Mother Church submitting still)
That many have been sav'd, and many may,   320
Who never heard this question brought in play.
Th' unletter'd Christian, who believes in gross,
Plods on to heaven, and ne'er is at a loss;
For the strait gate would be made straiter yet,
Were none admitted there but men of wit.
The few, by nature form'd, with learning fraught,
Born to instruct, as others to be taught,
Must study well the sacred page; and see
Which doctrine, this, or that, does best agree

4 Author of an apocryphal book of   5 The Socinians rejected the doctrine
prophecy.   of the Trinity.

With the whole tenour of the work divine: 330
And plainlyest points to Heaven's reveal'd design:
Which exposition flows from genuine sense,
And which is forc'd by wit and eloquence.
Not that tradition's parts are useless here:
When general, old, disinteress'd and clear:
That ancient Fathers thus expound the page,
Gives truth the reverend majesty of age:
Confirms its force, by biding every test;
For best authority's next rules are best.
And still the nearer to the spring we go, 340
More limpid, more unsoyl'd the waters flow.
Thus, first traditions were a proof alone;
Could we be certain such they were, so known:
But since some flaws in long descent may be,
They make not truth, but probability.
Even Arius and Pelagius [6] durst provoke
To what the centuries preceding spoke.
Such difference is there in an oft-told tale;
But truth by its own sinews will prevail.
Tradition written therefore more commends 350
Authority, than what from voice descends:
And this, as perfect as its kind can be,
Rolls down to us the sacred history,
Which, from the Universal Church receiv'd,
Is try'd, and after, for itself believ'd.
The partial Papists would infer from hence
Their Church, in last resort, should judge the sense.
But first they would assume, with wondrous art,
Themselves to be the whole, who are but part
Of that vast frame, the Church; yet grant they were 360
The handers down, can they from thence infer
A right t' interpret? or would they alone
Who brought the present, claim it for their own?
The book 's a common largess to mankind,
Not more for them, than every man design'd;
The welcome news is in the letter found;
The carrier 's not commission'd to expound.
It speaks it self, and what it does contain,
In all things needfull to be known, is plain.
In times o'ergrown with rust and ignorance, 370
A gainfull trade their clergy did advance:

6 A fifth-century heretic who denied original sin.

When want of learning kept the laymen low,
And none but priests were authoriz'd to know:
When what small knowledge was, in them did dwell,
And he a god who could but read or spell:
Then Mother Church did mightily prevail;
She parcel'd out the Bible by retail:
But still expounded what she sold or gave,
To keep it in her power to damn and save:
Scripture was scarce, and, as the market went,   380
Poor laymen took salvation on content;
As needy men take money, good or bad:
God's word they had not, but the priest's they had.
Yet, whate'er false conveyances they made,
The lawyer still was certain to be paid.
In those dark times they learn'd their knack so well,
That by long use they grew infallible:
At last, a knowing age began t' enquire
If they the book, or that did them inspire;
And, making narrower search they found, tho' late,   390
That what they thought the priest's, was their estate:
Taught by the will produc'd, (the written word)
How long they had been cheated on record.
Then, every man who saw the title fair
Claim'd a child's part, and put in for a share:
Consulted soberly his private good,
And sav'd himself as cheap as e'er he could.
     'Tis true, my friend, (and far be flattery hence)
This good had full as bad a consequence:
The book thus put in every vulgar hand,   400
Which each presum'd he best could understand,
The common rule was made the common prey,
And at the mercy of the rabble lay.
The tender page with horney fists was gall'd,
And he was gifted most that loudest bawl'd:
The spirit gave the doctoral degree;
And every member of a company
Was of his trade and of the Bible free.
Plain truths enough for needfull use they found;
But men would still be itching to expound: 410
Each was ambitious of th' obscurest place,
No measure ta'en from knowledge, all from GRACE.
Study and pains were now no more their care;
Texts were explain'd by fasting, and by prayer:

This was the fruit the private spirit brought;
Occasion'd by great zeal, and little thought.
While crouds unlearn'd, with rude devotion warm,
About the sacred viands buzz and swarm,
The fly-blown text creates a crawling brood,
And turns to maggots what was meant for food.   426
A thousand daily sects rise up and dye;
A thousand more the perish'd race supply:
So all we make of Heaven's discover'd will
Is, not to have it, or to use it ill.
The danger 's much the same; on several shelves
If others wreck us, or we wreck our selves.
      What then remains, but, waving each extreme,
The tides of ignorance, and pride to stem?
Neither so rich a treasure to forgo;
Nor proudly seek beyond our pow'r to know: 430
Faith is not built on disquisitions vain;
The things we must believe, are few, and plain:
But since men will believe more than they need;
And every man will make himself a creed:
In doubtful questions 'tis the safest way
To learn what unsuspected ancients say:
For 'tis not likely we should higher soar
In search of heav'n, than all the Church before:
Nor can we be deceiv'd, unless we see
The Scripture and the Fathers disagree.   440
If, after all, they stand suspected still,
(For no man's faith depends upon his will;)
'Tis some relief, that points not clearly known,
Without much hazard may be let alone:
And, after hearing what our Church can say,
If still our Reason runs another way,
That private Reason 'tis more just to curb,
Than by disputes the publick peace disturb.
For points obscure are of small use to learn:
But common quiet is mankind's concern.   450
      Thus have I made my own opinions clear:
Yet neither praise expect, nor censure fear:
And this unpolish'd, rugged verse, I chose:
As fittest for discourse, and nearest prose:
For while from sacred truth I do not swerve,
Tom Sternhold's,[7] or Tom Sha—ll's rhimes will serve.

7 Translator of the *Psalms*.

Roman Church vs Church of England

THE HIND AND THE PANTHER [1]

—Antiquam exquirite matrem.
*Et vera, incessu, patuit Dea—*Virgil

1687

THE FIRST PART

A milk white Hind, immortal and unchang'd,
Fed on the lawns, and in the forest rang'd;
Without unspotted, innocent within,
She fear'd no danger, for she knew no sin.
Yet had she oft been chas'd with horns and hounds,
And Scythian shafts; and many winged wounds
Aim'd at her heart; was often forc'd to fly,
And doom'd to death, though fated not to dy.
　Not so her young, for their unequal line
Was heroe's make, half humane, half divine.　　　　　10
Their earthly mold obnoxious was to fate,
Th'immortal part assumed immortal state.
Of these a slaughtered army lay in bloud,
Extended o'er the Caledonian wood,
Their native walk; whose vocal bloud arose,
And cry'd for pardon on their perjur'd foes;
Their fate was fruitfull, and the sanguin seed
Endu'd with souls, encreas'd the sacred breed.
So captive Israel multiply'd in chains
A numerous exile, and enjoy'd her pains.　　　　　20
With grief and gladness mixt, their mother view'd
Her martyr'd offspring, and their race renew'd;
Their corps to perish, but their kind to last,
So much the deathless plant the dying fruit surpass'd.

---

1 The epigraph (*Aeneid*, III, 96 and I, 405: "Seek out your ancient mother . . . ; by her bearing is the true goddess known . . .") indicates how this poem justifies the Roman Church (the Hind) against the Church of England (the Panther) and, more sternly, against other protestant sects of "pestilential zeal," especially the Presbyterians (the Wolf, "Isgrim," the "Geneva sect," and "Wickliff's brood," bred of Calvin and Zwingli and at last chased from the "Celtic woods"—that is, England—by the Restoration). The Lion is the British king, James II. The Bear represents the Independents; the Hare, the Quakers; the Ape, the freethinkers; the Boar, the Anabaptists; Reynard the Fox, the Unitarians by "Socinus nurs'd." Faustus Socinus (1539–1604) the Unitarian was born in Siena but later lived on the "Polonian plains."

Panting and pensive now she rang'd alone,
And wander'd in the kingdoms, once her own.
The common hunt, though from their rage restrain'd
By sov'reign pow'r, her company disdain'd:
Grin'd as they pass'd, and with a glaring eye
Gave gloomy signs of secret enmity.   30
'Tis true, she bounded by, and trip'd so light
They had not time to take a steady sight.
For truth has such a face and such a meen
As to be lov'd needs onely to be seen.
    The bloudy Bear an Independent beast, *Independents*
Unlick'd to form, in groans her hate express'd.
Among the timorous kind the quaking Hare *Quackers*
Profess'd neutrality, but would not swear.
Next to her the buffoon Ape, as atheists use, *freethinkers*
Mimick'd all sects, and had his own to chuse: 40
Still when the Lyon look'd his knees he bent, *James II*
And pay'd the church a courtier's complement.
    The bristl'd Baptist Boar, impure as he, *anabaptists*
(But whitn'd with the foam of sanctity)
With fat pollutions fill'd the sacred place,
And mountains levell'd in his furious race,
So first rebellion founded was in grace.
But since the mighty ravage which he made
In German forests, had his guilt betrayd,
With broken tusks, and with a borrow'd name   50
He shunn'd the vengeance, and conceal'd the shame;
So lurk'd in sects unseen. With greater guile
False Reynard fed on consecrated spoil: *Unitarians*
The graceless beast by Athanasius first
Was chas'd from Nice; then by Socinus nurs'd *Faustus, a unitarian*
His impious race their blasphemy renew'd,
And nature's king through nature's opticks view'd.
Revers'd they view'd him lessen'd to their eye,
Nor in an infant could a God descry:
New swarming sects to this obliquely tend,   60
Hence they began, and here they all will end.
    What weight of antient witness can prevail
If private reason hold the publick scale?
But, gratious God, how well dost thou provide
For erring judgments an unerring guide?
Thy throne is darkness in th'abyss of light,
A blaze of glory that forbids the sight;

O teach me to believe Thee thus conceal'd,
And search no farther than thy self reveal'd;
But her alone for my Directour take   70
Whom thou hast promis'd never to forsake!
My thoughtless youth was wing'd with vain desires,
My manhood, long misled by wandring fires,
Follow'd false lights; and when their glimps was gone,
My pride struck out new sparkles of her own.
Such was I, such by nature still I am,
Be thine the glory, and be mine the shame.
Good life be now my task: my doubts are done,
(What could more fright my faith, than Three in One?)
Can I believe eternal God could lye   80
Disguis'd in mortal mold and infancy?
That the great maker of the world could dye?
And after that, trust my imperfect sense
Which calls in question his omnipotence?
Can I my reason to my faith compell,
And shall my sight, and touch, and taste rebell?
Superiour faculties are set aside,
Shall their subservient organs be my guide?
Then let the moon usurp the rule of day,
And winking tapers shew the sun his way;   90
For what my senses can themselves perceive
I need no revelation to believe.
Can they who say the host should be descry'd
By sense, define a body glorify'd?
Impassible, and penetrating parts?
Let them declare by what mysterious arts
He shot that body through th'opposing might
Of bolts and barrs impervious to the light,
And stood before his train confess'd in open sight.
For since thus wondrously he pass'd, 'tis plain   100
One single place two bodies did contain,
And sure the same omnipotence as well
Can make one body in more places dwell.
Let reason then at her own quarry fly,
But how can finite grasp infinity?
'Tis urg'd again that faith did first commence
By miracles, which are appeals to sense,
And thence concluded that our sense must be
The motive still of credibility.
For latter ages must on former wait,   110

And what began belief, must propagate.
But winnow well this thought, and you shall find,
'Tis light as chaff that flies before the wind.
Were all those wonders wrought by pow'r divine
As means or ends of some more deep design?
Most sure as means, whose end was this alone,
To prove the godhead of th'eternal Son.
God thus asserted: man is to believe
Beyond what sense and reason can conceive.
And for mysterious things of faith rely   120
On the proponent, heaven's authority.
If then our faith we for our guide admit,
Vain is the farther search of humane wit,
As when the building gains a surer stay,
We take th'unusefull scaffolding away:
Reason by sense no more can understand,
The game is play'd into another hand.
Why chuse we then like *bilanders* to creep
Along the coast, and land in view to keep,
When safely we may launch into the deep?   130
In the same vessel which our Saviour bore
Himself the pilot, let us leave the shoar,
And with a better guide a better world explore.
Could He his godhead veil with flesh and bloud
And not veil these again to be our food?
His grace in both is equal in extent,
The first affords us life, the second nourishment.
And if he can, why all this frantick pain
To construe what his clearest words contain,
And make a riddle what He made so plain?   140
To take up half on trust, and half to try,
Name it not faith, but bungling biggottry.
Both knave and fool the merchant we may call
To pay great summs, and to compound the small.
For who would break with heav'n, and would not break for all?
Rest then, my soul, from endless anguish freed;
Nor sciences thy guide, nor sense thy creed.
Faith is the best ensurer of thy bliss;
The bank above must fail before the venture miss.
But heaven and heaven-born faith are far from thee   150
Thou first apostate to divinity.
Unkennel'd range in thy Polonian plains;
A fiercer foe th'insatiate Wolf remains.

Presbyterians

Too boastfull Britain please thy self no more,
That beasts of prey are banish'd from thy shoar:
The Bear, the Boar, and every salvage name,
Wild in effect, though in appearance tame,
Lay waste thy woods, destroy thy blissfull bow'r,
And muzl'd though they seem, the mutes devour.
More haughty than the rest the wolfish race,   160
Appear with belly gaunt, and famish'd face:
Never was so deform'd a beast of grace.
His ragged tail betwixt his leggs he wears
Close clap'd for shame, but his rough crest he rears,
And pricks up his predestinating ears.
His wild disorder'd walk, his hagger'd eyes,
Did all the bestial citizens surprize.
Though fear'd and hated, yet he ruled awhile
As captain or companion of the spoil.
Full many a year his hatefull head had been   170
For tribute paid, nor since in Cambria seen:
The last of all the litter scap'd by chance,
And from Geneva first infested France.
Some authours thus his pedigree will trace,
But others write him of an upstart race:
Because of Wickliff's brood no mark he brings
But his innate antipathy to kings.
These last deduce him from th'Helvetian kind
Who near the Leman lake his consort lin'd.
That fi'ry Zuynglius first th'affection bred,   180
And meagre Calvin blest the nuptial bed.
In Israel some believe him whelp'd long since
When the proud Sanhedrim oppress'd the prince.
Or, since he will be Jew, derive him high'r
When Corah with his brethren did conspire,
From Moyses' hand the sov'reign sway to wrest,
And Aaron of his ephod to devest:
Till opening earth made way for all to pass,
And could not bear the burd'n of a class.
The Fox and he came shuffl'd in the dark,   190
If ever they were stow'd in Noah's ark:
Perhaps not made; for all their barking train
The Dog (a common species) will contain.
And some wild currs, who from their masters ran
Abhorring the supremacy of man,
In woods and caves the rebel-race began.

O happy pair, how well have you increas'd,
What ills in church and state have you redress'd!
With teeth untry'd, and rudiments of claws
Your first essay was on your native laws: 200
Those having torn with ease, and trampl'd down
Your fangs you fastn'd on the miter'd crown,
And freed from God and monarchy your town.
What though your native kennel still be small
Bounded betwixt a puddle and a wall,
Yet your victorious colonies are sent
Where the north ocean girds the continent.
Quickn'd with fire below your monsters breed,
In fenny Holland and in fruitfull Tweed.
And like the first the last affects to be 210
Drawn to the dreggs of a democracy.
As where in fields the fairy rounds are seen,
A rank sow'r herbage rises on the green,
So, springing where these midnight elves advance,
Rebellion prints the footsteps of the dance.
Such are their doctrines, such contempt they show
To heav'n above, and to their prince below,
As none but traytours and blasphemers know.
God, like the tyrant of the skyes is plac'd,
And kings like slaves beneath the crowd debas'd. 220
So fulsome is their food, that flocks refuse
To bite, and onely dogs for physick use.
As where the lightning runs along the ground,
No husbandry can heal the blasting wound,
Nor bladed grass, nor bearded corn succeeds,
But scales of scurf, and putrefaction breeds:
Such warrs, such waste, such fiery tracks of dearth
Their zeal has left, and such a teemless earth.
But as the poisons of the deadliest kind
Are to their own unhappy coasts confin'd, 230
As onely Indian shades of sight deprive,
And magick plants will but in Colchos thrive;
So Presbyt'ry and pestilential zeal
Can onely flourish in a commonweal.
   From Celtique woods is chas'd the wolfish crew;
But ah! some pity e'en to brutes is due:
Their native walks, methinks, they might enjoy
Curb'd to their native malice to destroy.
Of all the tyrannies on humane kind

The worst is that which persecutes the mind. 240
Let us but weigh at what offence we strike,
'Tis but because we cannot think alike.
In punishing of this, we overthrow
The laws of nations and of nature too.
Beasts are the subjects of tyrannick sway,
Where still the stronger on the weaker prey.
Man onely of a softer mold is made;
Not for his fellows' ruine, but their aid:
Created kind, beneficent and free,
The noble image of the deity. 250
  One portion of informing fire was giv'n
To brutes, th'inferiour family of heav'n:
The Smith divine, as with a careless beat,
Struck out the mute creation at a heat:
But, when arriv'd at last to humane race,
The godhead took a deep consid'ring space:
And, to distinguish man from all the rest,
Unlock'd the sacred treasures of his breast:
And mercy mix'd with reason did impart;
One to his head, the other to his heart: 260
Reason to rule, but mercy to forgive:
The first is law, the last prerogative.
And like his mind his outward form appear'd;
When issuing naked, to the wondring herd,
He charm'd their eyes, and for they lov'd, they fear'd.
Not arm'd with horns of arbitrary might,
Or claws to seize their furry spoils in fight,
Or with increase of feet t'o'ertake 'em in their flight.
Of easie shape, and pliant ev'ry way;
Confessing still the softness of his clay, 270
And kind as kings upon their coronation day:
With open hands, and with extended space
Of arms, to satisfie a large embrace.
Thus kneaded up with milk, the new made man
His kingdom o'er his kindred world began:
Till knowledge misapply'd, misunderstood,
And pride of empire sour'd his balmy bloud.
Then, first rebelling, his own stamp he coins;
The murth'rer Cain was latent in his loins,
And bloud began its first and loudest cry 280
For diff'ring worship of the deity.

Thus persecution rose, and farther space
Produc'd the mighty hunter of his race.
Not so the blessed Pan his flock encreas'd,
Content to fold 'em from the famish'd beast:
Mild were his laws; the Sheep and harmless Hind
Were never of the persecuting kind.
Such pity now the pious pastor shows,
Such mercy from the British Lyon flows,
That both provide protection for their foes.   290
　Oh happy regions, Italy and Spain,
Which never did those monsters entertain!
The Wolfe, the Bear, the Boar, can there advance
No native claim of just inheritance.
And self-preserving laws, severe in show,
May guard their fences from th'invading foe.
Where birth has plac'd 'em let 'em safely share
The common benefit of vital air.
Themselves unharmfull, let them live unharm'd;
Their jaws disabl'd, and their claws disarm'd: 300
Here, onely in nocturnal howlings bold,
They dare not seize the Hind nor leap the fold.
More pow'rfull, and as vigilant as they,
The Lyon awfully forbids the prey.
Their rage repress'd, though pinch'd with famine sore,
They stand aloof, and tremble at his roar;
Much is their hunger, but their fear is more.
　These are the chief; to number o'er the rest,
And stand, like Adam, naming ev'ry beast,
Were weary work; nor will the muse describe   310
A slimy-born and sun-begotten tribe:
Who, far from steeples and their sacred sound,
In fields their sullen conventicles found:
These gross, half-animated lumps I leave;
Nor can I think what thoughts they can conceive.
But if they think at all, 'tis sure no high'r
Than matter, put in motion, may aspire.
Souls that can scarce ferment their mass of clay;
So drossy, so divisible are they,
As would but serve pure bodies for allay;   320
Such souls as shards produce, such beetle things
As onely buz to heav'n with ev'ning wings;
Strike in the dark, offending but by chance,

Such are the blind-fold blows of ignorance.
They know not beings, and but hate a name,
To them the Hind and Panther are the same.
   The Panther sure the noblest, next the Hind,
And fairest creature of the spotted kind;
Oh, could her in-born stains be wash'd away,
She were too good to be a beast of prey!   330
How can I praise, or blame, and not offend,
Or how divide the frailty from the friend!
Her faults and vertues lye so mix'd, that she
Nor wholly stands condemn'd, nor wholly free.
Then, like her injur'd Lyon, let me speak,
He can not bend her, and he would not break.
Unkind already, and estrang'd in part,
The Wolfe begins to share her wandring heart.
Though unpolluted yet with actual ill,
She half commits, who sins but in her will.   340
If, as our dreaming Platonists report,
There could be spirits of a middle sort,
Too black for heav'n, and yet too white for hell,
Who just dropt half way down, nor lower fell;
So pois'd, so gently she descends from high,
It seems a soft dismission from the sky.
Her house not ancient, whatsoe'er pretence
Her clergy heraulds make in her defence.
A second century not half-way run
Since the new honours of the bloud begun.   350
A Lyon old, obscene, and furious made
By lust, compress'd her mother in a shade.[2]
Then, by a left-hand marr'age weds the dame,
Cov'ring adult'ry with a specious name:
So schism begot; and sacrilege and she,
A well-match'd pair, got graceless heresie.
God's and kings' rebels have the same good cause,
To trample down divine and humane laws:
Both would be call'd reformers, and their hate,
Alike destructive both to church and state: 360
The fruit proclaims the plant; a lawless prince
By luxury reform'd incontinence,
By ruins, charity; by riots, abstinence.
Confessions, fasts and penance set aside;

2 Henry VIII, by wedding Anne Boleyn, brought on the split between Roman and
Anglican churches.

Oh with what ease we follow such a guide!
Where souls are starv'd, and senses gratify'd.
Where marr'age pleasures, midnight pray'r supply,
And mattin bells (a melancholy cry)
Are tun'd to merrier notes, Encrease and multiply.
Religion shows a rosie colour'd face;   370
Not hatter'd out [3] with drudging works of grace;
A down-hill reformation rolls apace.
What flesh and bloud would croud the narrow gate,
Or, till they waste their pamper'd paunches, wait?
All would be happy at the cheapest rate.
    Though our lean faith these rigid laws has giv'n,
The full fed Musulman goes fat to heav'n;
For his Arabian prophet with delights
Of sense, allur'd his eastern proselytes.
The jolly Luther, reading him, began   380
T'interpret scriptures by his Alcoran;
To grub the thorns beneath our tender feet,
And make the paths of Paradise more sweet:
Bethought him of a wife e'er half way gone,
(For 'twas uneasy travailing alone;)
And in this masquerade of mirth and love,
Mistook the bliss of heav'n for Bacchanals above.
Sure he presum'd of praise, who came to stock
Th'etherial pastures with so fair a flock,
Burnish'd, and bat'ning on their food, to show   390
The diligence of carefull herds below.
    Our Panther though like these she chang'd her head,
Yet, as the mistress of a monarch's bed,
Her front erect with majesty she bore,
The crozier wielded, and the miter wore.
Her upper part of decent discipline
Shew'd affectation of an ancient line:
And fathers, councils, church and church's head,
Were on her reverend phylacteries read.
But what disgrac'd and disavow'd the rest,   400
Was Calvin's brand, that stigmatiz'd the beast.
Thus, like a creature of a double kind,
In her own labyrinth she lives confin'd.
To foreign lands no sound of her is come,
Humbly content to be despis'd at home.
Such is her faith, where good cannot be had,

3 Wearied out.

At least she leaves the refuse of the bad.
Nice in her choice of ill, though not of best,
And least deform'd, because reform'd the least.
In doubtfull points betwixt her diff'ring friends,   410
Where one for substance, one for sign contends,
Their contradicting terms she strives to join,
Sign shall be substance, substance shall be sign.
A real presence all her sons allow,
And yet 'tis flat idolatry to bow,
Because the godhead's there they know not how.
Her novices are taught that bread and wine
Are but the visible and outward sign
Receiv'd by those who in communion join.
But th'inward grace, or the thing signify'd,   420
His bloud and body, who to save us dy'd;
The faithfull this thing signify'd receive.
What is't those faithfull then partake or leave?
For what is signify'd and understood,
Is, by her own confession, flesh and blood.
Then, by the same acknowledgment, we know
They take the sign, and take the substance too.
The lit'ral sense is hard to flesh and blood,
But nonsense never can be understood.

Her wild belief on ev'ry wave is tost,   430
But sure no church can better morals boast.
True to her king her principles are found;
Oh that her practice were but half so sound!
Stedfast in various turns of state she stood,
And seal'd her vow'd affection with her bloud;
Nor will I meanly tax her constancy,
That int'rest or obligement made the tye,
(Bound to the fate of murdr'd monarchy:)
(Before the sounding ax so falls the vine,
Whose tender branches round the poplar twine.)   440
She chose her ruin, and resign'd her life,
In death undaunted as an Indian wife:
A rare example: but some souls we see
Grow hard and stiffen in adversity:
Yet these by fortune's favours are undone,
Resolv'd into a baser form they run,
And bore the wind, but cannot bear the sun.
Let this be nature's frailty or her fate,
Or Isgrim's counsel, her new chosen mate;

Still she's the fairest of the fallen crew,⁴⁵⁰
No mother more indulgent but the true.
  Fierce to her foes, yet fears her force to try,
Because she wants innate auctority;
For how can she constrain them to obey
Who has herself cast off the lawfull sway?
Rebellion equals all, and those who toil
In common theft, will share the common spoil.
Let her produce the title and the right
Against her old superiours first to fight;
If she reform by text, ev'n that's as plain ⁴⁶⁰
For her own rebels to reform again.
As long as words a diff'rent sense will bear,
And each may be his own interpreter,
Our ai'ry faith will no foundation find:
The word's a weathercock for ev'ry wind:
The Bear, the Fox, the Wolfe, by turns prevail,
The most in pow'r supplies the present gale.
The wretched Panther crys aloud for aid
To church and councils, whom she first betray'd;
No help from Fathers or tradition's train, ⁴⁷⁰
Those ancient guides she taught us to disdain.
And by that scripture which she once abus'd
To reformation, stands herself accus'd.
What bills for breach of laws can she prefer,
Expounding which she owns herself may err?
And, after all her winding ways are try'd,
If doubts arise she slips herself aside,
And leaves the private conscience for the guide.
If then that conscience set th'offender free,
It barrs her claim to church auctority. ⁴⁸⁰
How can she censure, or what crime pretend,
But scripture may be constru'd to defend?
Ev'n those whom for rebellion she transmits
To civil pow'r, her doctrine first acquits;
Because no disobedience can ensue,
Where no submission to a judge is due.
Each judging for himself, by her consent,
Whom thus absolv'd she sends to punishment.
Suppose the magistrate revenge her cause,
'Tis onely for transgressing humane laws. ⁴⁹⁰
How answ'ring to its end a church is made,
Whose pow'r is but to counsell and persuade?

O solid rock, on which secure she stands!
Eternal house, not built with mortal hands!
Oh sure defence against th'infernal gate,
A patent during pleasure of the state!
　Thus is the Panther neither lov'd nor fear'd,
A mere mock queen of a divided herd;
Whom soon by lawfull pow'r she might controll,
Her self a part submitted to the whole.   500
Then, as the moon who first receives the light
By which she makes our nether regions bright,
So might she shine, reflecting from afar
The rays she borrow'd from a better star:
Big with the beams which from her mother flow
And reigning o'er the rising tides below:
Now, mixing with a salvage croud, she goes
And meanly flatters her invet'rate foes.
Rul'd while she rules, and losing ev'ry hour
Her wretched remnants of precarious pow'r.   510
　One evening while the cooler shade she sought,
Revolving many a melancholy thought,
Alone she walk'd, and look'd around in vain,
With rufull visage for her vanish'd train:
None of her sylvan subjects made their court;
Levées and couchées pass'd without resort.
So hardly can usurpers manage well
Those, whom they first instructed to rebell:
More liberty begets desire for more,
The hunger still encreases with the store.   520
Without respect they brush'd along the wood
Each in his clan, and fill'd with loathsome food
Ask'd no permission to the neighb'ring flood.
The Panther full of inward discontent
Since they would goe, before 'em wisely went:
Supplyng want of pow'r by drinking first,
As if she gave 'em leave to quench their thirst.
Among the rest, the Hind, with fearfull face
Beheld from far the common wat'ring place,
Nor durst approach; till with an awfull roar   530
The sovereign Lyon bad her fear no more.
Encourag'd thus she brought her younglings nigh,
Watching the motions of her patron's eye,
And drank a sober draught; the rest amaz'd
Stood mutely still, and on the stranger gaz'd:

Survey'd her part by part, and sought to find
The ten-horn'd monster in the harmless Hind,
Such as the Wolfe and Panther had design'd.
They thought at first they dream'd, for 'twas offence
With them, to question certitude of sense,   540
Their guide in faith; but nearer when they drew,
And had the faultless object full in view,
Lord, how they all admir'd her heav'nly hiew!
Some, who before her fellowship disdain'd,
Scarce, and but scarce, from inborn rage restrain'd,
Now frisk'd about her, and old kindred feign'd.
Whether for love or int'rest, ev'ry sect
Of all the salvage nation shew'd respect:
The vice-roy Panther could not awe the herd,
The more the company the less they fear'd.   550
The surly Wolfe with secret envy burst,
Yet could not howl, the Hind had seen him first:
But what he durst not speak, the Panther durst.
    For when the herd suffis'd did late repair
To ferny heaths, and to their forest lare,
She made a mannerly excuse to stay,
Proff'ring the Hind to wait her half the way:
That since the sky was clear, an hour of talk,
Might help her to beguile the tedious walk.
With much good-will the motion was embrac'd,   560
To chat awhile on their adventures pass'd:
Nor had the gratefull Hind so soon forgot
Her friend and fellow-suff'rer in the plot.[4]
Yet wondring how of late she grew estrang'd,
Her forehead cloudy, and her count'nance chang'd,
She thought this hour th'occasion would present
To learn her secret cause of discontent,
Which, well she hop'd, might be with ease redress'd,
Consid'ring her a well-bred civil beast,
And more a gentlewoman than the rest.   570
After some common talk what rumours ran,
The lady of the spotted muff began.

4 The various plots against Charles II (see *Absalom and Achitophel*).

A SONG FOR ST. CECILIA'S DAY
1687

I

From harmony, from heav'nly harmony
   This universal frame began:
     When Nature underneath a heap
      Of jarring atomes lay,
     And could not heave her head,
The tuneful voice was heard from high,
   "Arise, ye more than dead."
Then cold, and hot, and moist, and dry,
In order to their stations leap,
     And Musick's pow'r obey.   10
From harmony, from heav'nly harmony
   This universal frame began:
   From harmony to harmony
Thro' all the compass of the notes it ran,
The diapason closing full in Man.

II

What passion cannot Musick raise and quell!
   When Jubal [1] struck the corded shell,
   His list'ning brethren stood around,
   And wond'ring, on their faces fell
   To worship that celestial sound.   20
Less than a god they thought there could not dwell
   Within the hollow of that shell
   That spoke so sweetly and so well.
What passion cannot Music raise and quell!

III

The Trumpet's loud clangor
   Excites us to arms,
With shrill notes of anger,
   And mortal alarms.
The double double double beat
   Of the thundring Drum   30

1 *Genesis* 4:21.

Cryes, "Hark! the foes come;
Charge, charge, 'tis too late to retreat."

IV

    The soft complaining Flute
    In dying notes discovers
    The woes of hopeless lovers,
Whose dirge is whisper'd by the warbling Lute.

V

    Sharp Violins proclaim
Their jealous pangs, and desperation,
Fury, frantick indignation,
Depth of pains, and height of passion,   40
    For the fair, disdainful dame.

VI

    But oh! what art can teach,
    What human voice can reach,
    The sacred Organ's praise?
    Notes inspiring holy love,
Notes that wing their heav'nly ways
    To mend the choires above.

VII

Orpheus could lead the savage race;
And trees unrooted left their place,
    Sequacious of the lyre;   50
But bright Cecilia rais'd the wonder high'r:
When to her Organ vocal breath was giv'n,
An angel heard, and straight appear'd,
    Mistaking earth for heav'n.

GRAND CHORUS

    As from the pow'r of sacred lays
      The spheres began to move,
    And sung the great Creator's praise
      To all the bless'd above;
So, when the last and dreadful hour
This crumbling pageant shall devour,   60
The Trumpet shall be heard on high,
The dead shall live, the living die,
And Musick shall untune the sky.

ALEXANDER'S FEAST

OR, THE POWER OF MUSIC;
AN ODE IN HONOR OF ST. CECILIA'S DAY
1697

I

'Twas at the royal feast, for Persia won,
   By Philip's warlike son:
  Aloft in awful state
  The godlike heroe sate
   On his imperial throne:
His valiant peers were plac'd around;
Their brows with roses and with myrtles bound:
  (So should desert in arms be crown'd.)
The lovely Thais, by his side,
Sate like a blooming Eastern bride   10
In flow'r of youth and beauty's pride.
   Happy, happy, happy pair!
   None but the brave,
   None but the brave,
   None but the brave deserves the fair.

CHORUS

Happy, happy, happy pair!
None but the brave,
None but the brave,
None but the brave deserves the fair.

II

Timotheus, plac'd on high   20
  Amid the tuneful Quire,
   With flying fingers touch'd the lyre:
The trembling notes ascend the sky,
   And heav'nly joys inspire.
The song began from Jove;
Who left his blissful seats above,
(Such is the pow'r of mighty love.)
A dragon's fiery form belied the god:

Sublime on radiant spires he rode,
   When he to fair Olympia press'd;   30
   And while he sought her snowy breast:
Then, round her slender waist he curl'd,
And stamp'd an image of himself, a sov'raign of the world.
The list'ning crowd admire the lofty sound,
"A present deity," they shout around:
"A present deity," the vaulted roofs rebound.
     With ravish'd ears
     The monarch hears,
     Assumes the god,
     Affects to nod,   40
And seems to shake the spheres.

CHORUS

With ravish'd ears
The monarch hears,
Assumes the god,
Affects to nod,
And seems to shake the spheres.

III

The praise of Bacchus then the sweet musician sung,
   Of Bacchus ever fair, and ever young:
     "The jolly god in triumph comes;
     Sound the trumpets; beat the drums;   50
       Flush'd with a purple grace
       He shews his honest face:
Now give the hautboys breath; he comes, he comes.
Bacchus, ever fair and young,
   Drinking joys did first ordain;
Bacchus' blessings are a treasure,
Drinking is the soldier's pleasure:
     Rich the treasure,
     Sweet the pleasure,
   Sweet is pleasure after pain."   60

CHORUS

Bacchus' blessings are a treasure,
Drinking is the soldier's pleasure:
   Rich the treasure,
   Sweet the pleasure,
Sweet is pleasure after pain.

IV

Sooth'd with the sound, the king grew vain;
    Fought all his battles o'er again;
And thrice he routed all his foes; and thrice he slew the slain.
The master saw the madness rise;
    His glowing cheeks, his ardent eyes;   70
And, while he heav'n and earth defy'd,
    Chang'd his hand, and check'd his pride.
      He chose a mournful Muse,
        Soft pity to infuse:
He sung Darius great and good,
      By too severe a fate,
Fallen, fallen, fallen, fallen,
      Fallen from his high estate,
        And welt'ring in his blood;
Deserted, at his utmost need,   80
By those his former bounty fed;
On the bare earth expos'd he lies,
With not a friend to close his eyes.
With downcast looks the joyless victor sate,
    Revolving in his alter'd soul
      The various turns of chance below;
    And, now and then, a sigh he stole,
      And tears began to flow.

CHORUS

Revolving in his alter'd soul
    The various turns of chance below;   90
And, now and then, a sigh he stole,
    And tears began to flow.

V

The mighty master smil'd, to see
That love was in the next degree:
'Twas but a kindred sound to move,
For pity melts the mind to love.
    Softly sweet, in Lydian measures,
    Soon he sooth'd his soul to pleasures.
    "War," he sung, "is toil and trouble;
    Honor, but an empty bubble;   100
      Never ending, still beginning,

Fighting still, and still destroying:
  If the world be worth thy winning,
Think, O think it worth enjoying;
  Lovely Thais sits beside thee,
  Take the good the gods provide thee."
The many rend the skies, with loud applause;
So Love was crown'd, but Music won the cause.
The prince, unable to conceal his pain,
    Gaz'd on the fair   110
  Who caus'd his care.
And sigh'd and look'd, sigh'd and look'd,
  Sigh'd and look'd, and sigh'd again:
At length, with love and wine at once oppress'd,
The vanquish'd victor sunk upon her breast.

CHORUS

The prince, unable to conceal his pain,
  Gaz'd on the fair
  Who caus'd his care,
  And sigh'd and look'd, sigh'd and look'd,
  Sigh'd and look'd, and sigh'd again: 120
At length, with love and wine at once oppress'd,
The vanquish'd victor sunk upon her breast.

VI

Now strike the golden lyre again:
A lowder yet, and yet a lowder strain.
Break his bands of sleep asunder,
And rouze him, like a rattling peal of thunder.
  Hark, hark, the horrid sound
    Has rais'd up his head:
    As awak'd from the dead,
    And amaz'd, he stares around.   130
"Revenge, revenge!" Timotheus cries,
  "See the Furies arise!
  See the snakes that they rear,
  How they hiss in their hair,
And the sparkles that flash from their eyes!
  Behold a ghastly band,
  Each a torch in his hand!
Those are Grecian ghosts, that in battle were slain,
    And unbury'd remain

Inglorious on the plain: 140
  Give the vengeance due
  To the valiant crew.
Behold how they toss their torches on high,
  How they point to the Persian abodes,
And glitt'ring temples of their hostile gods!"
The princes applaud, with a furious joy;
And the king seiz'd a flambeau with zeal to destroy;
   Thais led the way,
   To light him to his prey,
And, like another Helen, fir'd another Troy.   150

CHORUS

And the king seiz'd a flambeau with zeal to destroy;
   Thais led the way,
   To light him to his prey,
And, like another Helen, fir'd another Troy.

VII

  Thus long ago,
  Ere heaving bellows learn'd to blow,
  While organs yet were mute;
  Timotheus, to his breathing flute,
   And sounding lyre,
Could swell the soul to rage, or kindle soft desire. 160
  At last, divine Cecilia came,
  Inventress of the vocal frame;
The sweet enthusiast, from her sacred store,
  Enlarg'd the former narrow bounds,
  And added length to solemn sounds,
With nature's mother wit, and arts unknown before.
  Let old Timotheus yield the prize,
   Or both divide the crown:
  He rais'd a mortal to the skies;
   She drew an angel down.   170

GRAND CHORUS

At last, divine Cecilia came,
  Inventress of the vocal frame;
The sweet enthusiast, from her sacred store,
  Enlarg'd the former narrow bounds,
  And added length to solemn sounds,
With nature's mother wit, and arts unknown before.

Let old Timotheus yield the prize,
Or both divide the crown:
He rais'd a mortal to the skies;
She drew an angel down.   180

A SELECTION

Thomas Sprat

(1635–1713)

THE HISTORY OF THE ROYAL SOCIETY

1667

[As early as 1645 the rising interest in the new "experimental philosophy" led to meetings of "divers worthy persons" in London in
colloquies that became an "Invisible College," soon in communication
with a number of "philosophers" at Wadham College, Oxford. The
growth of these colloquies held at Gresham College, London, led to
the incorporation of The Royal Society in 1662. Like the many
academies of the renaissance, the Society saw no conflict between
science and art, for it was concerned not only to "reason freely upon
the works of Nature" but also to purify and simplify the English
language.]

SECOND PART: Section II: The Meetings at Oxford

Their first purpose was no more than only the satisfaction of
breathing a freer air, and of conversing in quiet one with another,
without being engaged in the passions and madness of that dismal
age. And from the institution of that assembly it had been enough
if no other advantage had come but this, that by this means there
was a race of young men provided, against the next age, whose
minds, receiving from them their first impressions of sober and
generous knowledge, were invincibly armed against all the enchantments of enthusiasm. . . . Nor indeed could it be otherwise; for such spiritual frenzies which did then bear rule can
never stand long before a clear and deep skill in Nature. It is
almost impossible that they who converse much with the subtilty
of *things* should be deluded by such thick deceits. There is but
one better charm in the world than real philosophy to allay the
impulses of the false spirit: and that is the blessed presence and

assistance of the true.

Nor were the good effects of this conversation only confined to Oxford; but they have made themselves known in their printed works, both in our own and in the learned language, which have much conduced to the fame of our nation abroad and to the spreading of profitable light at home. This I trust will be universally acknowledged when I shall have named the men. The principal, and most constant of them, were Doctor Seth Ward, the present Lord Bishop of Exeter, Mr. Boyle, Dr. Wilkins, Sir William Petty, Mr. Matthew Wren, Dr. Wallis, Dr. Goddard, Dr. Willis, Dr. Bathurst, Dr. Christopher Wren, Mr. Rook: besides several others, who joined themselves to them upon occasions. . . .

SECOND PART: Section V: A Model of Their Whole Design

I will here, in the first place, contract into a few words the whole sum of their resolutions, which I shall often have occasion to touch upon in parcels. Their purpose is, in short, to make faithful records of all the works of Nature or Art which can come within their reach: that so the present age and posterity may be able to put a mark on the errors which have been strengthened by long prescription, to restore the truths that have lain neglected, to push on those which are already known to more various uses, and to make the way more passable to what remains unrevealed. This is the compass of their design. And to accomplish this, they have endeavoured to separate the knowledge of Nature from the colours of rhetoric, the devices of fancy, or the delightful deceit of fables. . . .

THIRD PART: Section XII: The Seventh Objection. . . .

From what I have said may be gathered that experimental philosophy will prevent men's spending the strength of their thoughts about disputes, by turning them to works; that it may well be attended by the united labours of many, without wholly devouring the time of those that labour; that it will cure our minds of romantic swelling, by showing all things familiarly to them, just as large as they are; that it will free them from perversity, by not permitting them to be too peremptory in their conclusions; that it accustoms our hands to things which have a near resemblance to the business of life; and that it draws away the shadows which either enlarge or darken human affairs. . . .

A SELECTION

John Locke

(1632–1704)

[In his *Two Treatises of Government* and his *Essay Concerning Human Understanding* John Locke formulated many of the basic notions on which the whole Enlightenment, not only in England but also abroad, developed. Indeed, Locke represents not only the turn from absolutism in English politics of the seventeenth century but also the turn toward theories of the social compact and the rights of man on which the American and French revolutions were fought. Locke's psychology is equally important for the eighteenth century, which adopted and adapted his theories about wit and judgment, the half-empirical, half-rational nature of knowledge, and the association of ideas, imagination, and faith and reason. And Locke's letters *On Toleration* reveal the changing religious temper of the age.]

From TWO TREATISES OF GOVERNMENT

1690

BOOK II

To understand political power aright, and derive it from its original, we must consider what estate all men are naturally in, and that is, a state of perfect freedom to order their actions, and dispose of their possessions and persons as they think fit, within the bounds of the law of Nature, without asking leave or depending upon the will of any other man. . . .

But though this be a state of Liberty, yet it is not a state of license; though man in that state have an uncontrollable liberty to dispose of his person or possessions, yet he has not liberty to destroy himself, or so much as any creature in his possession, but where some nobler use than its bare preservation calls for it. The state of Nature has a law of Nature to govern it, which obliges every one; and reason, which is that law, teaches all mankind who will but consult it, that being all equal and independent, no one ought to harm another in his life, health, liberty, or possessions; for men being all the workmanship of one omnipotent and infinitely wise Maker; all the servants of one sovereign Master, sent into the world by His order and about His business; they are His property, whose workmanship they are, made to last during His, not one another's, pleasure. . . .

. . . For though it would be beside my present purpose to enter here into the particulars of the law of Nature, or its measures of punishment, yet it is certain there is such a law, and that too as intelligible and plain to a rational creature and a studier of that law, as the positive laws of commonwealths, nay, possibly plainer; as much as reason is easier to be understood than the fancies and intricate contrivances of men, following contrary and hidden interests put into words; for truly so are a great part of the municipal laws of countries, which are only so far right, as they are founded on the law of Nature, by which they are to be regulated and interpreted. . . .

[Chapter II]

The natural liberty of man is to be free from any superior power on earth, and not to be under the will or legislative authority of man, but to have only the law of Nature for his rule. The liberty of man in society is to be under no other legislative power but that established by consent in the commonwealth, nor under the dominion of any will, or restraint of any law, but what that legislative shall enact according to the trust put in it. . . .

This freedom from absolute, arbitrary power is so necessary to, and closely joined with, a man's preservation, that he cannot part with it but by what forfeits his preservation and life together. . . .

[Chapter IV]

The freedom then of man, and liberty of acting according to his own will, is grounded on his having reason, which is able to instruct him in that law he is to govern himself by, and make him know how far he is left to the freedom of his own will. To turn him loose to an unrestrained liberty, before he has reason to guide him, is not the allowing him the privilege of his nature to be free, but to thrust him out amongst brutes, and abandon him to a state as wretched and as much beneath that of a man as theirs. . . .

[Chapter VI]

Men being, as has been said, by nature all free, equal, and independent, no one can be put out of this estate and subjected to the political power of another without his own consent, which is done by agreeing with other men, to join and unite into a community for their comfortable, safe, and peaceable living, one amongst another, in a secure enjoyment of their properties, and a greater security against any that are not of it. This any number of men may do, because it injures not the freedom of the rest; they are left, as they were, in the liberty of the state of Nature. When any number of men have so consented to make one community or government, they are thereby presently incorporated, and make one body politic, wherein the majority have a right to act and conclude the rest.

For, when any number of men have, by the consent of every individual, made a community, they have thereby made that community one body, with a power to act as one body, which is only by the will and determination of the majority. For that which acts any community, being only the consent of the individuals of it, and it being one body, must move one way, it is necessary the body should move that way whither the greater force carries it, which is the consent of the majority, or else it is impossible it should act or continue one body, one community, which the consent of every individual that united into it agreed that it should; and so every one is bound by that consent to be concluded by the majority. And therefore we see that in assemblies empowered to act by positive laws where no number is set by that positive law, which empowers them, the act of the majority passes for the act of the whole, and of course determines as having, by the law of Nature and Reason, the power of the whole.

And thus every man, by consenting with others to make one body politic under one government, puts himself under an obligation to every one of that society to submit to the determination of the majority and to be concluded by it. . . .

[Chapter VIII]

From AN ESSAY CONCERNING
HUMAN UNDERSTANDING
1690

Let us then suppose the mind to be, as we say, white paper void of all characters, without any ideas. How comes it to be furnished? Whence comes it by that vast store which the busy and boundless fancy of man has painted on it with an almost endless variety? Whence has it all the materials of reason and knowledge? To this I answer, in one word, from *experience*. In that all our knowledge is founded; and from that it ultimately derives itself. Our observation, employed either about external sensible objects, or about the internal operations of our minds, perceived and reflected on by ourselves, is that which supplies our understandings with all the materials of thinking. These two are the fountains of knowledge, from whence all the ideas we have, or can naturally have, do spring. . . .

[Book II, chapter i]

These simple ideas, the materials of all our knowledge, are suggested and furnished to the mind only by those two ways above mentioned, viz. sensation and reflection. When the understanding is once stored with these simple ideas, it has the power to repeat, compare, and unite them, even to an almost infinite variety, and so can make at pleasure new complex ideas. . . .

[Book II, chapter ii]

Whatsoever the mind perceives in itself or is the immediate object of perception, thought, or understanding, that I call *idea*; and the power to produce any idea in our mind, I call *quality* of the subject wherein that power is. . . .

Qualities thus considered in bodies are:

First, such as are utterly inseparable from the body, in what state soever it be; and such as in all the alterations and changes it suffers, all the force can be used upon it, it constantly keeps; and such as sense constantly finds in every particle of matter which has bulk enough to be perceived; and the mind finds inseparable from every particle of matter, though less than to make itself singly be perceived by our senses: e.g., take a grain of wheat, divide it into two parts; each part has still solidity, extension, figure, and mobility: divide it again, and it retains still the same qualities; and so divide it on, till the parts become insensible; they must retain still each of them all those qualities. For division can never take away either solidity, extension, figure, or mobility from any body, but only makes two or more distinct separate masses of matter, of that which was but one before; all which distinct masses, reckoned as so many distinct bodies, after division, make a certain number. These I call *original* or *primary* qualities of body, which I think we may observe to produce simple ideas in us, viz. solidity, extension, figure, motion or rest, and number.

Secondly, such qualities which in truth are nothing in the objects themselves but powers to produce various sensations in us by their primary qualities, i.e., by the bulk, figure, texture, and motion of their insensible parts, as colours, sounds, tastes, etc. These I call *secondary qualities*. . . .

[Book II, chapter viii]

The next faculty of the mind, whereby it makes a further progress towards knowledge, is that which I call *retention*, or the keeping of those simple ideas which from sensation or reflection it hath received. This is done two ways.

First, by keeping the idea which is brought into it, for some time actually in view, which is called *contemplation*.

The other way of retention is, the power to revive again in our minds those ideas which, after imprinting, have disappeared, or have been as it were laid aside out of sight. And thus we do, when we conceive heat or light, yellow or sweet, the object being removed. This is *memory*, which is as it were the storehouse of our ideas . . . —the mind has a power in many cases to revive perceptions which it has once had, with this additional perception annexed to them, that *it has had them before* . . .

. . . But those which naturally at first make the deepest and most lasting impressions, are those which are accompanied with pleasure or pain . . .

[Book II, chapter x]

. . . For *wit* lying most in the assemblage of ideas, and putting those together with quickness and variety, wherein can be found any resemblance or congruity, thereby to make up pleasant pictures and agreeable visions in the fancy; *judgment*, on the contrary, lies quite on the other side, in separating carefully one from another ideas wherein can be found the least difference, thereby to avoid being misled by similitude, and by affinity to take one thing for another. This is a way of proceeding quite contrary to metaphor and allusion; wherein for the most part lies that entertainment and pleasantry of wit, which strikes so lively on the fancy, and therefore is so acceptable to all people, because its beauty appears at first sight, and there is required no labour of thought to examine what truth or reason there is in it. . . .

[Book II, chapter xi]

. . . The acts of the mind, wherein it exerts its power over its simple ideas, are chiefly these three: Combining several simple ideas into one compound one; and thus all complex ideas are made. The second is bringing two ideas, whether simple or complex, together, and setting them by one another, so as to take a view of them at once, without uniting them into one; by which way it gets all its ideas of relations. The third is separating them from all other ideas that accompany them in their real existence: this is called *abstraction:* and thus all its general ideas are made . . .

[Book II, chapter xii]

. . . And hence it follows that moral knowledge is as capable of real certainty as mathematics. Our moral ideas, as well as mathematical, being archetypes themselves, and so adequate and complete ideas, all the agreement or disagreement which we shall find in them will produce real knowledge, as well as in the mathematical figures . . .

[Book IV, chapter iv]

John Pomfret

1667–1702

The Choice was by repute one of the most-read poems during the eighteenth century, perhaps because it so adequately expressed the circumspect and sedate temper that followed upon the distraught seventeenth century in England. Though Pomfret may seem judicial and tepid, a great many eighteenth-century lives must have been keyed in this even tenor that seeks satisfaction not in overcoming difficulties but in a complacent withdrawal. The same sort of cultivated poise is apparent in such writers as Addison and Gray, a neutrality that gives to the eighteenth century a repose alien to our own day.

BIOGRAPHICAL NOTES

Son of the vicar of Luton, Bedfordshire. Received Bachelor's degree from Queens' College, Cambridge (1684). Married Elizabeth Wingate of Luton (1692). Appointed to the living at Maulden, Bedfordshire (1695). *Poems on Several Occasions* (1699). *The Choice* (1700); four editions within a year. According to report, denied a valuable living by the Bishop of London because *The Choice* recommended "some obliging modest fair" instead of a wife. Died suddenly of smallpox.

BIBLIOGRAPHY: *Poems,* ed. Alexander Chalmers, *Works of the English Poets,* 1810. Johnson, Samuel, *Lives of the English Poets,* 1779–81.

THE CHOICE

1700

If Heav'n the grateful liberty would give,
That I might choose my method how to live;
And all those hours propitious Fate should lend,
In blissful ease and satisfaction spend;
Near some fair town I'd have a private seat,
Built uniform, not little, nor too great:
Better, if on a rising ground it stood;
On this side fields, on that a neighbouring wood.
It should within no other things contain,
But what are useful, necessary, plain: 10

Methinks 'tis nauseous, and I'd ne'er endure,
The needless pomp of gaudy furniture.
A little garden, grateful to the eye;
And a cool rivulet run murm'ring by:
On whose delicious banks a stately row
Of shady limes, or sycamores, should grow.
At th' end of which a silent study plac'd,
Should be with all the noblest authors grac'd:
Horace and Virgil, in whose mighty lines
Immortal wit, and solid learning shines;   20
Sharp Juvenal, and am'rous Ovid too,
Who all the turns of love's soft passion knew:
He that with judgment reads his charming lines,
In which strong art with stronger nature joins,
Must grant his fancy does the best excel;
His thoughts so tender, and express'd so well:
With all those moderns, men of steady sense,
Esteem'd for learning, and for eloquence.
In some of these, as Fancy should advise,
I'd always take my morning exercise: 30
For sure no minutes bring us more content,
Than those in pleasing, useful studies spent.
    I'd have a clear and competent estate,
That I might live genteelly, but not great:
As much as I could moderately spend;
A little more, sometimes t' oblige a friend.
Nor should the sons of Poverty repine
Too much at Fortune, they should taste of mine;
And all that objects of true pity were,
Should be reliev'd with what my wants could spare;   40
For that our Maker has too largely giv'n,
Should be return'd in gratitude to Heav'n.
A frugal plenty should my table spread;
With healthy, not luxurious, dishes fed:
Enough to satisfy, and something more,
To feed the stranger, and the neighb'ring poor.
Strong meat indulges vice, and pamp'ring food
Creates diseases, and inflames the blood.
But what's sufficient to make nature strong,
And the bright lamp of life continue long,   50
I'd freely take; and, as I did possess,
The bounteous Author of my plenty bless.
    I'd have a little vault, but always stor'd

With the best wines each vintage could afford.
Wine whets the wit, improves its native force,
And gives a pleasant flavour to discourse:
By making all our spirits debonair,
Throws off the lees, the sediment of care.
But as the greatest blessing Heaven lends
May be debauch'd, and serve ignoble ends;   60
So, but too oft, the grape's refreshing juice
Does many mischievous effects produce.
My house should no such rude disorders know,
As from high drinking consequently flow;
Nor would I use what was so kindly giv'n,
To the dishonour of indulgent Heav'n.
If any neighbour came, he should be free,
Us'd with respect, and not uneasy be,
In my retreat, or to himself or me.
What freedom, prudence, and right reason give,   70
All men may, with impunity, receive:
But the least swerving from their rule's too much;
For what's forbidden us, 'tis death to touch.
    That life may be more comfortable yet,
And all my joys refin'd, sincere, and great;
I'd choose two friends, whose company would be
A great advance to my felicity:
Well-born, of humours suited to my own,
Discreet, and men as well as books have known;
Brave, gen'rous, witty, and exactly free   80
From loose behaviour, or formality:
Airy and prudent; merry, but not light;
Quick in discerning, and in judging right:
Secret they should be, faithful to their trust;
In reas'ning cool, strong, temperate, and just:
Obliging, open, without huffing, brave;
Brisk in gay talking, and in sober, grave:
Close in dispute, but not tenacious; try'd
By solid reason, and let that decide:
Not prone to lust, revenge, or envious hate;   90
Nor busy meddlers with intrigues of state;
Strangers to slander, and sworn foes to spite;
Not quarrelsome, but stout enough to fight;
Loyal, and pious, friends to Cæsar, true,
As dying martyrs, to their Maker too.
In their society I could not miss

A permanent, sincere, substantial bliss.
   Would bounteous Heav'n once more indulge, I'd choose
(For who would so much satisfaction lose,
As witty nymphs, in conversation, give?)   100
Near some obliging modest fair to live:
For there's that sweetness in a female mind,
Which in a man's we cannot hope to find;
That, by a secret, but a pow'rful art,
Winds up the spring of life, and does impart
Fresh vital heat to the transported heart.
   I'd have her reason all her passions sway:
Easy in company, in private gay:
Coy to a fop, to the deserving free;
Still constant to herself, and just to me.   110
A soul she should have for great actions fit;
Prudence and wisdom to direct her wit:
Courage to look bold danger in the face;
No fear, but only to be proud, or base;
Quick to advise, by an emergence prest,
To give good counsel, or to take the best.
I'd have th' expression of her thoughts be such,
She might not seem reserv'd, nor talk too much:
That shows a want of judgment, and of sense;
More than enough is but impertinence.   120
Her conduct regular, her mirth refin'd;
Civil to strangers, to her neighbours kind:
Averse to vanity, revenge, and pride;
In all the methods of deceit untry'd:
So faithful to her friend, and good to all,
No censure might upon her actions fall:
Then would e'en Envy be compell'd to say,
She goes the least of womankind astray.
   To this fair creature I'd sometimes retire;
Her conversation would new joys inspire;   130
Give life an edge so keen, no surly care
Would venture to assault my soul, or dare,
Near my retreat, to hide one secret snare.
But so divine, so noble a repast
I'd seldom, and with moderation, taste:
For highest cordials all their virtue lose,
By a too frequent and too bold a use;
And what would cheer the spirits in distress,
Ruins our health, when taken to excess.

I'd be concern'd in no litigious jar;   140
Belov'd by all, not vainly popular.
Whate'er assistance I had pow'r to bring,
T' oblige my company, or to serve my king,
Whene'er they call, I'd readily afford,
My tongue, my pen, my counsel, or my sword.
Lawsuits I'd shun, with as much studious care,
As I would dens where hungry lions are;
And rather put up injuries, than be
A plague to him, who'd be a plague to me.
I value quiet at a price too great,   150
To give for my revenge so dear a rate:
For what do we by all our bustle gain,
But counterfeit delight for real [1] pain?
    If Heav'n a date of many years would give,
Thus I'd in pleasure, ease, and plenty live.
And as I near approach'd the verge of life,
Some kind relation (for I'd have no wife)
Should take upon him all my worldly care,
Whilst I did for a better state prepare.
Then I'd not be with any trouble vex'd,   160
Nor have the ev'ning of my days perplex'd;
But by a silent and a peaceful death,
Without a sigh, resign my aged breath.
And when committed to the dust, I'd have
Few tears, but friendly, dropt into my grave.
Then would my exit so propitious be,
All men would wish to live and die like me.

Daniel Defoe

1660?–1731

THIS "middle-sized spare man," with "a hooked nose, a sharp chin,
grey eyes, and a large mole near his mouth," as an advertisement for his
arrest describes him, is perhaps the most successful journalist in the
history of English literature. He seems to have sold his talent upon
both sides of most issues and to have been a slippery person with whom

1 A dissyllable.

to deal. His periodical articles, travel books, political tracts, religious discourses, economic treatises, novels, and topical verse are of a volume and variety that will probably make it impossible ever to determine all that he wrote. The novels, amazingly, were done after he was sixty, when he was no longer needed as a spy and special agent for the government. The characteristic talent of Defoe is his "purely material charm," his ability to make facts seem to matter. No one has keener relish for textures, numbers, and costs. Were spikes and gunpowder and crockery ever made so satisfying to the esthetic sense as they are in *Robinson Crusoe?* Were bills of mortality, in cold tables, ever so suggestive as in *A Journal of the Plague Year?* This indiscriminate appetite for fact of any sort, and the entirely casual tone, make what is really fact look like fiction and what is really fiction look like fact. Herein lies the subtlety of Defoe. Combined with this relish for the most material values of living is a curiosity about the strange, the distant, the horrible. *Crusoe* does precisely what Coleridge proposed to do in *The Ancient Mariner*—it secures a willing suspension of disbelief. Like Stevenson, Defoe specializes in "clean" crime; he has the flavor of the brute incident told with gusto. Everything seems actual enough, but even the most repulsive details are bearable and exhilarating: somehow, man is master of his fate; immersed as he is in things, he is nevertheless able to *act* freely. In this sense Defoe differs from the modern "realist," whose characters succumb to their environment. The exhilarating effects in Defoe arise when a certain kind of difficulty is overcome; dealing with problems of the practical intelligence, he is as full of "projects" as Franklin, Tom Paine, or Erasmus Darwin. Indeed, Defoe so annihilates the inner life of his characters that their states of mind are expressed only in physical action. The bourgeois enterprise, the concern with profit, trade, and one's "calling," are everywhere in Defoe, who in spite of his own lack of conviction is always ready to moralize; he trusts that *Moll Flanders* "will not offend the chastest reader or the modestest hearer; and as the best use is to be made even of the worst story, the moral, 'tis hoped, will keep the reader serious even where the story might incline him to be otherwise."

BIOGRAPHICAL NOTES

Born in St. Giles's, Cripplegate, son of a Presbyterian chandler and butcher; his name actually Daniel Foe. Educated at a dissenting academy at Newington Green (*ca.* 1674); then entered hosiery business. Married Mary Tuffley. Bankrupt, owing £17,000, in 1692. Strong supporter of William III. Established tile business near Tilbury. *Essay on Projects* (1697), proposing miscellaneous reforms. *The True-Born Englishman* (1701), a poem defending William III. *The Shortest Way with the Dissenters* (1702), a satiric pamphlet that led to his imprisonment and standing thrice in the pillory. Rescued from prison by Harley, the Tory leader; hired as government agent and spy, and traveled throughout England and Scotland. Wrote lives of criminals in current journals and pamphlets, and edited *The Review*, a Tory organ, from 1704 to 1713. In 1719 began writing novels—*Robinson Crusoe* (1719), *Memoirs of a Cavalier* (1720), *Captain Singleton* (1720), *Moll Flanders* (1722), *Journal of the Plague Year* (1722), *Colonel Jacque* (1722), *Roxana* (1724). Died in London, in hiding and evidently in debt.

BIBLIOGRAPHY: *Novels and Selected Writings* (Shakespeare Head edition), 14 vols., 1927–28. Fitzgerald, Brian, *Daniel Defoe, A Study in Conflict,* 1954. Moore, John Robert, *Daniel Defoe, Citizen of the Modern World,* 1958. Sen, Chandra, *Daniel Defoe: His Mind and Art,* 1948. Stephen, Leslie, "Defoe's Novels," *Hours in a Library,* Vol. I, 1874, etc. Sutherland, James, *Defoe,* 1950. Trent, W. P., *Daniel Defoe: How to Know Him,* 1916. Watson, Francis, *Daniel Defoe,* 1952. Watt, Ian, *The Rise of the Novel: Studies in Defoe, Richardson, and Fielding,* 1957.

A JOURNAL OF
THE PLAGUE YEAR [1]

1722

It was about the beginning of September 1664, that I, among the rest of my neighbors, heard, in ordinary discourse, that the plague was returned again in Holland; for it had been very violent there, and particularly at Amsterdam and Rotterdam, in the year 1663, whither, they say, it was brought, some said from Italy, others from the Levant, among some goods, which were brought home by their Turkey fleet; others said it was brought from Candia; others from Cyprus. It mattered not from whence it came; but all agreed it was come into Holland again.

We had no such thing as printed newspapers in those days to spread rumors and reports of things, and to improve them by the invention of men, as I have lived to see practiced since. But such things as those were gathered from the letters of merchants and others who corresponded abroad, and from them was handed about by word of mouth only; so that things did not spread instantly over the whole nation, as they do now. But it seems that the Government had a true account of it, and several councils were

---

[1] There had been an outbreak of the plague in Marseilles in 1720. It had caused so much gossip that Defoe produced *Due Preparations for the Plague* (1722). This tract was followed by the *Journal of the Plague Year,* in compiling which Defoe evidently used in altered form several published accounts of the great plague in London. The initials "H.F.," with which he signs the *Journal,* may be taken from his uncle, Henry Foe.

held about ways to prevent its coming over, but all was kept very private. Hence it was that this rumor died off again, and people began to forget it, as a thing we were very little concerned in, and that we hoped was not true; till the latter end of November or the beginning of December, 1664, when two men, said to be Frenchmen, died of the plague in Long Acre, or rather at the upper end of Drury Lane. The family they were in endeavored to conceal it as much as possible, but as it had gotten some vent in the discourse of the neighborhood, the Secretaries of State got knowledge of it. And concerning themselves to inquire about it, in order to be certain of the truth, two physicians and a surgeon were ordered to go to the house and make inspection. This they did; and finding evident tokens of the sickness upon both the bodies that were dead, they gave their opinions publicly that they died of the plague. Whereupon it was given in to the parish clerk, and he also returned them to the Hall; [2] and it was printed in the weekly bill of mortality in the usual manner, thus—

Plague, 2.   Parishes infected, 1.

The people showed a great concern at this, and began to be alarmed all over the town, and the more, because in the last week in December, 1664, another man died in the same house, and of the same distemper. And then we were easy again for about six weeks, when none having died with any marks of infection, it was said the distemper was gone; but after that, I think it was about the 12th of February, another died in another house, but in the same parish and in the same manner.

This turned the people's eyes pretty much towards that end of the town, and the weekly bills showing an increase of burials in St. Giles's parish more than usual, it began to be suspected that the plague was among the people at that end of the town, and that many had died of it, though they had taken care to keep it as much from the knowledge of the public as possible. This possessed the heads of the people very much, and few cared to go through Drury Lane, or the other streets suspected, unless they had extraordinary business that obliged them to it.

This increase of the bills stood thus: the usual number of burials

---

2 Presumably the Guildhall, an administrative center of the Corporation of the City of London.

in a week, in the parishes of St. Giles-in-the-Fields and St. Andrew, Holborn, were from twelve to seventeen or nineteen each, few more or less; but from the time that the plague first began in St. Giles's parish, it was observed that the ordinary burials increased in number considerably. For example:

From December 27 to January	3	.	.	St. Giles's	.	.	16
				St. Andrew's	.	.	17
" January 3 " "	10	.	.	St. Giles's	.	.	12
				St. Andrew's	.	.	25
" January 10 " "	17	.	.	St. Giles's	.	.	18
				St. Andrew's	.	.	18
" January 17 " "	24	.	.	St. Giles's	.	.	23
				St. Andrew's	.	.	16
" January 24 " "	31	.	.	St. Giles's	.	.	24
				St. Andrew's	.	.	15
" January 31 " February	7	.	.	St. Giles's	.	.	21
				St. Andrew's	.	.	23
" February 7 " "	14	.	.	St. Giles's	.	.	24

Whereof one of the plague.

The like increase of the bills was observed in the parishes of St. Bride's, adjoining on one side of Holborn parish, and in the parish of St. James's, Clerkenwell, adjoining on the other side of Holborn; in both which parishes the usual numbers that died weekly were from four to six or eight, whereas at that time they were increased as follows:

From December 20 to December 27	.	.	St. Bride's	.	.	.	0
			St. James's	.	.	.	8
" December 27 to January 3	.	.	St. Bride's	.	.	.	6
			St. James's	.	.	.	9
" January 3 " " 10	.	.	St. Bride's	.	.	.	11
			St. James's	.	.	.	7
" January 10 " " 17	.	.	St. Bride's	.	.	.	12
			St. James's	.	.	.	9
" January 17 " " 24	.	.	St. Bride's	.	.	.	9
			St. James's	.	.	.	15
" January 24 " " 31	.	.	St. Bride's	.	.	.	8
			St. James's	.	.	.	12
" January 31 " February 7	.	.	St. Bride's	.	.	.	13
			St. James's	.	.	.	5
" February 7 " " 14	.	.	St. Bride's	.	.	.	12
			St. James's	.	.	.	6

Besides this, it was observed with great uneasiness by the people that the weekly bills in general increased very much during these weeks, although it was at a time of the year when usually the bills are very moderate.

The usual number of burials within the bills of mortality for a week was from about 240 or thereabouts to 300. The last was esteemed a pretty high bill; but after this we found the bills successively increasing, as follows:

			Buried	Increased
December 20 to the 27th			291	
" 27 "	3rd January		349	58
January 3 "	10th "		394	45
" 10 "	17th "		415	21
" 17 "	24th "		474	59

This last bill was really frightful, being a higher number than had been known to have been buried in one week since the preceding visitation of 1656.

However, all this went off again, and the weather proving cold, and the frost, which began in December, still continuing very severe, even till near the end of February, attended with sharp though moderate winds, the bills decreased again, and the city grew healthy, and everybody began to look upon the danger as good as over; only that still the burials in St. Giles's continued high. From the beginning of April especially they stood at twenty-five each week, till the week from the 18th to the 25th, when there was buried in St. Giles's parish thirty, whereof two of the plague and eight of the spotted fever, which was looked upon as the same thing; likewise the number that died of the spotted fever in the whole increased, being eight the week before, and twelve the week above named.

This alarmed us all again, and terrible apprehensions were among the people, especially the weather being now changed and growing warm, and the summer being at hand. However, the next week there seemed to be some hopes again; the bills were low, the number of the dead in all was but 388; there was none of the plague, and but four of the spotted fever.

But the following week it returned again, and the distemper was spread into two or three other parishes, viz., St. Andrew's, Holborn; St. Clement Danes; and, to the great affliction of the City, one died within the walls, in the parish of St. Mary Woolchurch, that is to say, in Bearbinder Lane, near Stocks Market; in all there were nine of the plague and six of the spotted fever. It was, however, upon inquiry found that this Frenchman who died in Bearbinder Lane was one who, having lived in Long Acre, near the infected houses, had removed for fear of the distemper, not knowing that he was already infected.

This was the beginning of May, yet the weather was temperate, variable, cool enough, and people had still some hopes. That which encouraged them was that the City was healthy, the whole ninety-seven parishes buried but fifty-four, and we began to hope that as it was chiefly among the people at that end of the town, it might go no farther; and the rather because the next week, which was from the 9th of May to the 16th, there died but three, of which not one within the whole City or liberties; and St. Andrew's buried but fifteen, which was very low. 'Tis true St. Giles's buried two-and-thirty, but still, as there was but one of the plague, people began to be easy. The whole bill also was very low, for the week before the bill was but 347, and the week above mentioned but 343. We continued in these hopes for a few days, but it was but for a few, for the people were no more to be deceived thus; they searched the houses, and found that the plague was really spread every way, and that many died of it every day. So that now all our extenuations abated, and it was no more to be concealed; nay, it quickly appeared that the infection had spread itself beyond all hopes of abatement; that in the parish of St. Giles's it was gotten into several streets, and several families lay all sick together; and, accordingly, in the weekly bill for the next week the thing began to show itself. There was indeed but fourteen set down of the plague, but this was all knavery and collusion, for in St. Giles's parish they buried forty in all, whereof it was certain most of them died of the plague, though they were set down of other distempers; and though the number of all the burials were not increased above thirty-two, and the whole bill being but 385, yet there was fourteen of the spotted fever, as well as fourteen of the plague; and we took it for granted upon the whole that there were fifty died that week of the plague.

The next bill was from the 23rd of May to the 30th, when the number of the plague was seventeen. But the burials in St. Giles's were fifty-three—a frightful number!—of whom they set down but nine of the plague; but on an examination more strictly by the justices of the peace, and at the Lord Mayor's request, it was found there were twenty more who were really dead of the plague in that parish, but had been set down of the spotted fever or other distempers, besides others concealed.

But those were trifling things to what followed immediately after; for now the weather set in hot, and from the first week in June the infection spread in a dreadful manner, and the bills rose high; the articles of the fever, spotted fever, and teeth [2] began to swell: for all that could conceal their distempers did it, to prevent their neighbors shunning and refusing to converse with them, and also to prevent authority shutting up their houses, which though it was not yet practiced, yet was threatened, and people were extremely terrified at the thoughts of it.

The second week in June, the parish of St. Giles's, where still the weight of the infection lay, buried 120, whereof, though the bills said but sixty-eight of the plague, everybody said there had been 100 at least, calculating it from the usual number of funerals in that parish, as above.

Till this week the City continued free, there having never any died, except that one Frenchman whom I mentioned before, within the whole ninety-seven parishes. Now there died four within the City, one in Wood Street, one in Fenchurch Street, and two in Crooked Lane. Southwark was entirely free, having not one yet died on that side of the water.

I lived without Aldgate, about midway between Aldgate Church and Whitechapel Bars, on the left hand or north side of the street; and as the distemper had not reached to that side of the City, our neighborhood continued very easy. But at the other end of the town their consternation was very great; and the richer sort of people, especially the nobility and gentry from the west part of the City, thronged out of town with their families and servants in an unusual manner; and this was more particularly seen in Whitechapel; that is to say, the Broad Street, where I lived; indeed, nothing was to be seen but wagons and carts, with goods, women, servants, children, &c.; coaches filled with people of the better sort, and horsemen attending them, and all hurrying away; then empty wagons and carts appeared, and spare horses with servants, who, it was apparent, were returning or sent from the country to fetch more people; besides innumerable numbers of men on horseback, some alone, others with servants, and, generally speaking, all loaded with baggage and fitted out for traveling, as anyone might perceive by their appearance.

This was a very terrible and melancholy thing to see, and as it was a sight which I could not but look on from morning to night,

2 Scurvy.   Through lack of vitamins teeth fell out.

for indeed there was nothing else of moment to be seen, it filled me with very serious thoughts of the misery that was coming upon the City, and the unhappy condition of those that would be left in it.

This hurry of the people was such for some weeks that there was no getting at the Lord Mayor's door without exceeding difficulty; there was such pressing and crowding there to get passes and certificates of health for such as traveled abroad, for without these there was no being admitted to pass through the towns upon the road, or to lodge in any inn. Now as there had none died in the City for all this time, my Lord Mayor gave certificates of health without any difficulty to all those who lived in the ninety-seven parishes, and to those within the liberties too for a while.

This hurry, I say, continued some weeks, that is to say, all the month of May and June, and the more because it was rumored that an order of the Government was to be issued out to place turnpikes and barriers on the road to prevent people traveling, and that the towns on the road would not suffer people from London to pass for fear of bringing the infection along with them, though neither of these rumors had any foundation but in the imagination, especially at first.

I now began to consider seriously with myself concerning my own case, and how I should dispose of myself; that is to say, whether I should resolve to stay in London or shut up my house and flee, as many of my neighbors did. I have set this particular down so fully, because I know not but it may be of moment to those who come after me, if they come to be brought to the same distress, and to the same manner of making their choice; and therefore I desire this account may pass with them rather for a direction to themselves to act by than a history of my actings, seeing it may not be of one farthing value to them to note what became of me.

I had two important things before me: the one was the carrying on my business and shop, which was considerable, and in which was embarked all my effects in the world; and the other was the preservation of my life in so dismal a calamity as I saw apparently was coming upon the whole City, and which, however great it was, my fears perhaps, as well as other people's, represented to be much greater than it could be.

The first consideration was of great moment to me. My trade was a saddler, and as my dealings were chiefly not by a shop or chance trade, but among the merchants trading to the English colonies in America, so my effects lay very much in the hands of such. I was a single man, 'tis true, but I had a family of servants whom I kept at my business; had a house, shop, and warehouses filled with goods; and, in short, to leave them all as things in such a case must be left, that is to say, without any overseer or person fit to be trusted with them, had been to hazard the loss not only of my trade, but of my goods, and indeed of all I had in the world.

I had an elder brother at the same time in London, and not many years before come over from Portugal; and advising with him, his answer was in three words, the same that was given in another case quite different, viz., "Master, save thyself." In a word, he was for my retiring into the country, as he resolved to do himself with his family; telling me what he had, it seems, heard abroad, that the best preparation for the plague was to run away from it. As to my argument of losing my trade, my goods, or debts, he quite confuted me. He told me the same thing which I argued for my staying, viz., that I would trust God with my safety and health, was the strongest repulse to my pretensions of losing my trade and my goods. "For," says he, "is it not as reasonable that you should trust God with the chance or risk of losing your trade, as that you should stay in so eminent a point of danger, and trust Him with your life?"

I could not argue that I was in any strait as to a place where to go, having several friends and relations in Northamptonshire, whence our family first came from; and particularly, I had an only sister in Lincolnshire, very willing to receive and entertain me.

My brother, who had already sent his wife and two children into Bedfordshire, and resolved to follow them, pressed my going very earnestly; and I had once resolved to comply with his desires, but at that time could get no horse; for though it is true all the people did not go out of the City of London, yet I may venture to say that in a manner all the horses did; for there was hardly a horse to be bought or hired in the whole City for some weeks. Once I resolved to travel on foot with one servant, and, as many did, lie at no inn, but carry a soldier's tent with us, and so lie in the fields, the weather being very warm, and no danger from taking cold. I say, as many did, because several did so at last, especially those who had been in the armies in the war which had not been many years past; and I must needs say that, speaking of second causes, had most of the people that traveled done so, the plague had not been carried into so many country towns and houses as it was, to the great damage, and indeed to the ruin, of abundance of people.

But then my servant, whom I had intended to take down with me, deceived me; and being frightened at the increase of the distemper, and not knowing when I should go, he took other measures, and left me, so I was put off for that time; and one way or other, I always found that to appoint to go away was always crossed by some accident or other, so as to disappoint and put it off again. . . .

I went all the first part of the time freely about the streets, though not so freely as to run myself into apparent danger, except when they dug the great pit in the churchyard of our parish of Aldgate. A terrible pit it was, and I could not resist my curiosity to go and see it. As near as I may judge, it was about forty feet in length, and about fifteen or sixteen feet broad, and, at the time I first looked at it, about nine feet deep; but it was said they dug it near twenty feet deep afterwards in one part of it, till they could go no deeper for the water; for they had, it seems, dug several large pits before this. For though the plague was long a-coming to our parish, yet, when it did come, there was no parish in or about London where it raged with such violence as in the two parishes of Aldgate and Whitechapel.

I say they had dug several pits in another ground, when the distemper began to spread in our parish, and especially when the dead-carts began to go about, which was not, in our parish, till the beginning of August. Into these pits they had put perhaps fifty or sixty bodies each; then they made larger holes, wherein they buried all that the cart brought in a week, which, by the middle to the end of August, came to from 200 to 400 a week; and they could not well dig them larger, because of the order of the magistrates confining them to leave no bodies within six feet of the surface; and the water coming on at about seventeen or eighteen feet, they could not well, I say, put more in one pit. But now, at the beginning of September, the plague raging in a dreadful manner, and the number of burials in our parish increasing to more than was ever buried in any parish about London of no larger extent, they ordered this dreadful gulf to be dug, for such it was, rather than a pit.

They had supposed this pit would have supplied them for a month or more when they dug it, and some blamed the churchwardens for suffering such a frightful thing, telling them they were making preparations to bury the whole parish, and the like; but time made it appear the churchwardens knew the condition of the parish better than they did, for the pit being finished the 4th of September, I think, they began to bury in it the 6th, and by the 20th, which was just two weeks, they had thrown into it 1114 bodies, when they were obliged to fill it up, the bodies being then come to lie within six feet of the surface. I doubt not but there may be some ancient persons alive in the parish who can justify the fact of this, and are able to show even in what place of the church-yard the pit lay better than I can. The mark of it also was many years to be seen in the churchyard on the surface, lying in length parallel with the passage which goes by the west wall of the churchyard out of Houndsditch, and turns east again into White-chapel, coming out near the Three Nuns' Inn.

It was about the 10th of September that my curiosity led, or rather drove, me to go and see this pit again, when there had been near 400 people buried in it; and I was not content to see it in the daytime, as I had done before, for then there would have been nothing to have been seen but the loose earth; for all the bodies that were thrown in were immediately covered with earth by those they called the buriers, which at other times were called bearers; but I resolved to go in the night and see some of them thrown in.

There was a strict order to prevent people coming to those pits, and that was only to prevent infection; but after some time that order was more necessary, for people that were infected and near their end, and delirious also, would run to those pits, wrapped in blankets or rugs, and throw themselves in, and, as they said, bury themselves. I cannot say that the officers suffered any willingly to lie there; but I have heard that in a great pit in Finsbury, in the parish of Cripplegate, it lying open then to the fields, for it was not then walled about, they came and threw themselves in, and expired there, before they threw any earth upon them; and that when they came to bury others, and found them there, they were quite dead, though not cold.

This may serve a little to describe the dreadful condition of that day, though it is impossible to say anything that is able to give a true idea of it to those who did not see it, other than this, that it was indeed very, very, very dreadful, and such as no tongue can express.

I got admittance into the churchyard by being acquainted with the sexton who attended, who, though he did not refuse me at all, yet earnestly persuaded me not to go, telling me very seriously, for he was a good, religious, and sensible man, that it was indeed their business and duty to venture, and to run all hazards, and that in it they might hope to be preserved; but that I had no apparent call to it but my own curiosity, which, he said, he believed I would not pretend was sufficient to justify my running that hazard. I told him I had been pressed in my mind to go, and that perhaps it might be an instructing sight, that might not be without its uses. "Nay," says the good man, "if you will venture upon that score, 'Name of God go in; for, depend upon it, 'twill be a sermon to you, it may be, the best that ever you heard in your life. 'Tis a speaking sight," says he, "and has a voice with it, and a loud one, to call us all to repentance"; and with that he opened the door and said, "Go, if you will."

His discourse had shocked my resolution a little, and I stood wavering for a good while, but just at that interval I saw two links [3] come over from the end of the Minories, and heard the bellman, and then appeared a dead-cart, as they called it, coming over the streets; so I could no longer resist my desire of seeing it, and went in. There was nobody, as I could perceive at first, in the churchyard, or going into it, but the buriers and the fellow that drove the cart, or rather led the horse and cart; but when they came up to the pit they saw a man go to and again, [4] muffled up in a brown cloak, and making motions with his hands under his cloak, as if he was in a great agony; and the buriers immediately gathered about him, supposing he was one of those poor delirious or desperate creatures that used to pretend, as I have said, to bury themselves. He said nothing as he walked about, but two or three times groaned very deeply and loud, and sighed as he would break his heart.

When the buriers came up to him they soon found he was neither a person infected and desperate, as I have observed above, or a person distempered in mind, but one oppressed with a dreadful weight of grief indeed, having his wife and several of his children all in the cart that was just come in with him, and he followed in

---

[3] Torches of pitch.   [4] Going to and fro.

an agony and excess of sorrow. He mourned heartily, as it was easy to see, but with a kind of masculine grief that could not give itself vent by tears; and calmly defying the buriers to let him alone, said he would only see the bodies thrown in and go away; so they left importuning him. But no sooner was the cart turned round and the bodies shot into the pit promiscuously, which was a surprise to him, for he at least expected they would have been decently laid in, though indeed he was afterwards convinced that was impracticable; I say, no sooner did he see the sight but he cried out aloud, unable to contain himself. I could not hear what he said, but he went backward two or three steps and fell down in a swoon. The buriers ran to him and took him up, and in a little while he came to himself, and they led him away to the Pie Tavern over against the end of Houndsditch, where, it seems, the man was known, and where they took care of him. He looked into the pit again as he went away, but the buriers had covered the bodies so immediately with throwing in earth, that though there was light enough, for there were lanterns, and candles in them, placed all night round the sides of the pit, upon the heaps of earth, seven or eight, or perhaps more, yet nothing could be seen.

This was a mournful scene indeed, and affected me almost as much as the rest; but the other was awful and full of terror. The cart had in it sixteen or seventeen bodies; some were wrapped up in linen sheets, some in rags, some little other than naked, or so loose that what covering they had fell from them in the shooting out of the cart, and they fell quite naked among the rest; but the matter was not much to them, or the indecency much to anyone else, seeing they were all dead, and were to be huddled together into the common grave of mankind, as we may call it, for here was no difference made, but poor and rich went together; there was no other way of burials, neither was it possible there should, for coffins were not to be had for the prodigious numbers that fell in such a calamity as this.

It was reported, by way of scandal upon the buriers, that if any corpse was delivered to them decently wound up, as we called it then, in a winding sheet tied over the head and feet, which some did, and which was generally of good linen; I say, it was reported that the buriers were so wicked as to strip them in the cart and carry them quite naked to the ground. But as I cannot easily credit anything so vile among Christians, and at a time so filled with terrors as that was, I can only relate it and leave it undetermined. Innumerable stories also went about of the cruel behaviors and practices of nurses who tended the sick, and of their hastening on the fate of those they tended in their sickness. But I shall say more of this in its place.

I was indeed shocked with this sight; it almost overwhelmed me, and I went away with my heart most afflicted, and full of afflicting thoughts, such as I cannot describe. Just at my going out of the church, and turning up the street towards my own house, I saw another cart with links, and a bellman going before, coming out of Harrow Alley in the Butcher Row, on the other side of the way, and being, as I perceived, very full of dead bodies, it went directly over the street also toward the church. I stood awhile, but I had no stomach to go back again to see the same dismal scene over again, so I went directly home, where I could not but consider with thankfulness the risk I had run, believing I had gotten no injury; as indeed I had not.

Here the poor unhappy gentleman's grief came into my head again, and indeed I could not but shed tears in the reflection upon it, perhaps more than he did himself; but his case lay so heavy upon my mind that I could not prevail with myself but that I must go out again into the street, and go to the Pie Tavern, resolving to inquire what became of him.

It was by this time one o'clock in the morning, and yet the poor gentleman was there. The truth was, the people of the house, knowing him, had entertained him, and kept him there all the night, notwithstanding the danger of being infected by him, though it appeared the man was perfectly sound himself.

It is with regret that I take notice of this tavern. The people were civil, mannerly, and an obliging sort of folks enough, and had till this time kept their house open and their trade going on, though not so very publicly as formerly; but there was a dreadful set of fellows that used their house, and who, in the middle of all this horror, met there every night, behaved with all the reveling and roaring extravagances as is usual for such people to do at other times, and indeed to such an offensive degree that the very master and mistress of the house grew first ashamed, and then terrified, at them.

They sat generally in a room next the street; and as they always kept late hours, so when the dead-cart came across the street end to go into Houndsditch, which was in view of the tavern windows, they would frequently open the windows as soon as they heard the bell and look out at them; and as they might often hear sad lamentations of people in the streets or at their windows as the carts went along, they would make their impudent mocks and jeers at them, especially if they heard the poor people call upon God to have mercy upon them, as many would do at those times in their ordinary passing along the streets.

These gentlemen being something disturbed with the clutter of bringing the poor gentleman into the house, as above, were first angry and very high with the master of the house for suffering such a fellow, as they called him, to be brought out of the grave into their house; but being answered that the man was a neighbor, and that he was sound, but overwhelmed with the calamity of his family, and the like, they turned their anger into ridiculing the man and his sorrow for his wife and children, taunted him with want of courage to leap into the great pit and go to heaven, as they jeeringly expressed it, along with them, adding some very profane and even blasphemous expressions. . . .

I acknowledge I was one of those thoughtless ones that had made so little provision that my servants were obliged to go out of doors to buy every trifle by penny and halfpenny, just as before it begun, even till my experience showing me the folly, I began to be wiser so late that I had scarce time to store myself sufficient for our common subsistence for a month.

I had in family only an ancient woman that managed the house, a maidservant, two apprentices, and myself; and the plague beginning to increase about us, I had many sad thoughts about what course I should take, and how I should act. The many dismal objects, which happened everywhere as I went about the streets, had filled my mind with a great deal of horror, for fear of the distemper itself, which was, indeed, very horrible in itself, and in some more than in others. The swellings, which were generally in the neck or groin, when they grew hard and would not break, grew so painful that it was equal to the most exquisite torture; and some, not able to bear the torment, threw themselves out at windows or shot themselves, or otherwise made themselves away, and I saw several dismal objects of that kind. Others, unable to contain themselves, vented their pain by incessant roarings, and such loud and lamentable cries were to be heard as we walked along the streets that would pierce the very heart to think of, especially when it was to be considered that the same dreadful scourge might be expected every moment to seize upon ourselves.

I cannot say but that now I began to faint in my resolutions; my heart failed me very much, and sorely I repented of my rashness. When I had been out, and met with such terrible things as these I have talked of; I say I repented my rashness in venturing to abide in town, and I wished often that I had not taken upon me to stay, but had gone away with my brother and his family.

Terrified by those frightful objects, I would retire home sometimes and resolve to go out no more; and perhaps I would keep those resolutions for three or four days, which time I spent in the most serious thankfulness for my preservation and the preservation of my family, and the constant confession of my sins, giving myself up to God every day, and applying to Him with fasting, humiliation, and meditation. Such intervals as I had I employed in reading books and in writing down my memorandums of what occurred to me every day, and out of which, afterwards, I took most of this work, as it relates to my observations without doors. What I wrote of my private meditations I reserve for private use, and desire it may not be made public on any account whatever.

I also wrote other meditations upon divine subjects, such as occurred to me at that time and were profitable to myself, but not fit for any other view, and therefore I say no more of that.

I had a very good friend, a physician, whose name was Heath, whom I frequently visited during this dismal time, and to whose advice I was very much obliged for many things which he directed me to take, by way of preventing the infection when I went out, as he found I frequently did, and to hold in my mouth when I was in the streets. He also came very often to see me, and as he was a good Christian as well as a good physician, his agreeable conversation was a very great support to me in the worst of this terrible time.

It was now the beginning of August, and the plague grew very violent and terrible in the place where I lived, and Dr. Heath coming to visit me, and finding that I ventured so often out in the streets, earnestly persuaded me to lock myself up, and my family, and not to suffer any of us to go out of doors; to keep all our windows fast, shutters and curtains close, and never to open them;

but first, to make a very strong smoke in the room where the window or door was to be opened, with rosin and pitch, brimstone or gunpowder, and the like; and we did this for some time; but as I had not laid in a store of provision for such a retreat, it was impossible that we could keep within doors entirely. However, I attempted, though it was so very late, to do something towards it; and first, as I had convenience both for brewing and baking, I went and bought two sacks of meal, and for several weeks, having an oven, we baked all our own bread; also I bought malt, and brewed as much beer as all the casks I had would hold, and which seemed enough to serve my house for five or six weeks; also I laid in a quantity of salt butter and Cheshire cheese; but I had no flesh meat, and the plague raged so violently among the butchers and slaughterhouses on the other side of our street, where they are known to dwell in great numbers, that it was not advisable so much as to go over the street among them.

And here I must observe again that this necessity of going out of our houses to buy provisions was in a great measure the ruin of the whole City, for the people catched the distemper on these occasions one of another, and even the provisions themselves were often tainted; at least I have great reason to believe so; and therefore I cannot say with satisfaction what I know is repeated with great assurance, that the market people and such as brought provisions to town were never infected. I am certain the butchers of Whitechapel, where the greatest part of the flesh meat was killed, were dreadfully visited, and that at last to such a degree that few of their shops were kept open, and those that remained of them killed their meat at Mile End and that way, and brought it to market upon horses.

However, the poor people could not lay up provisions, and there was a necessity that they must go to market to buy, and others to send servants or their children; and as this was a necessity which renewed itself daily, it brought abundance of unsound people to the markets, and a great many that went thither sound brought death home with them.

It is true people used all possible precaution; when anyone bought a joint of meat in the market they would not take it off the butcher's hand, but took it off the hooks themselves. On the other hand, the butcher would not touch the money, but have it put into a pot full of vinegar, which he kept for that purpose. The buyer carried always small money to make up any odd sum, that they might take no change. They carried bottles of scents and perfumes in their hands, and all the means that could be used were used; but then the poor could not do even these things, and they went at all hazards.

Innumerable dismal stories we heard every day on this very account. Sometimes a man or woman dropped down dead in the very markets, for many people that had the plague upon them knew nothing of it till the inward gangrene had affected their vitals, and they died in a few moments. This caused that many died frequently in that manner in the streets suddenly, without any warning; others perhaps had time to go to the next bulk or stall, or to any door or porch, and just sit down and die, as I have said before.

These objects were so frequent in the streets that when the plague came to be very raging on one side, there was scarce any passing by the streets but that several dead bodies would be lying here and there upon the ground. On the other hand, it is observable that though at first the people would stop as they went along and call to the neighbors to come out on such an occasion, yet afterward no notice was taken of them; but that, if at any time we found a corpse lying, go across the way and not come near it; or, if in a narrow lane or passage, go back again and seek some other way to go on the business we were upon; and in those cases the corpse was always left till the officers had notice to come and take them away, or till night, when the bearers attending the dead-cart would take them up and carry them away. Nor did those undaunted creatures who performed these offices fail to search their pockets, and sometimes strip off their clothes if they were well dressed, as sometimes they were, and carry off what they could get.

But to return to the markets. The butchers took that care that if any person died in the market they had the officers always at hand to take them up upon handbarrows and carry them to the next churchyard; and this was so frequent that such were not entered in the weekly bill, "Found dead in the streets or fields," as is the case now, but they went into the general articles of the great distemper. . . .

As for my little family, having thus, as I have said, laid in a store of bread, butter, cheese, and beer, I took my friend and physician's advice, and locked myself up, and my family, and resolved to suffer the hardship of living a few months without flesh meat, rather than to purchase it at the hazard of our lives.

But though I confined my family, I could not prevail upon my unsatisfied curiosity to stay within entirely myself; and though I generally came frighted and terrified home, yet I could not restrain; only that indeed I did not do it so frequently as at first.

I had some little obligations, indeed, upon me to go to my brother's house, which was in Coleman Street parish, and which he had left to my care, and I went at first every day, but afterwards only once or twice a week.

In these walks I had many dismal scenes before my eyes, as particularly of persons falling dead in the streets, terrible shrieks and screechings of women, who, in their agonies, would throw open their chamber windows and cry out in a dismal, surprising manner. It is impossible to describe the variety of postures in which the passions of the poor people would express themselves.

Passing through Tokenhouse Yard, in Lothbury, of a sudden a casement violently opened just over my head, and a woman gave three frightful screeches, and then cried, "Oh! death, death, death!" in a most inimitable tone, and which struck me with horror and a chillness in my very blood. There was nobody to be seen in the whole street; neither did any other window open, for people had no curiosity now in any case, nor could anybody help one another, so I went on to pass into Bell Alley.

Just in Bell Alley, on the right hand of the passage, there was a more terrible cry than that, though it was not so directed out at the window; but the whole family was in a terrible fright, and I could hear women and children run screaming about the rooms like distracted, when a garret window opened, and somebody from a window on the other side the alley called and asked, "What is the matter?" upon which, from the first window it was answered, "O Lord, my old master has hanged himself!" The other asked again, "Is he quite dead?" and the first answered, "Ay, ay, quite dead; quite dead and cold!" This person was a merchant and a deputy alderman, and very rich. I care not to mention his name, though I knew his name too; but that would be an hardship to the family, which is now flourishing again.

But this is but one; it is scarce credible what dreadful cases happened in particular families every day. People in the rage of the distemper, or in the torment of their swellings, which was indeed intolerable, running out of their own government, raving and distracted, and oftentimes laying violent hands upon themselves, throwing themselves out at their windows, shooting themselves, &c.; mothers murdering their own children in their lunacy; some dying of mere grief as a passion, some of mere fright and surprise without any infection at all; others frighted into idiotism and foolish distractions, some into despair and lunacy, others into melancholy madness.

The pain of the swelling was in particular very violent, and to some intolerable; the physicians and surgeons may be said to have tortured many poor creatures even to death. The swellings in some grew hard, and they applied violent drawing plasters or poultices to break them; and if these did not do, they cut and scarified them in a terrible manner. In some those swellings were made hard partly by the force of the distemper and partly by their being too violently drawn, and were so hard that no instrument could cut them, and then they burnt them with caustics, so that many died raving mad with the torment, and some in the very operation. In these distresses, some, for want of help to hold them down in their beds, or to look to them, laid hands upon themselves, as above. Some broke out into the streets, perhaps naked, and would run directly down to the river, if they were not stopped by the watchmen or other officers, and plunge themselves into the water wherever they found it.

It often pierced my very soul to hear the groans and cries of those who were thus tormented, but of the two this was counted the most promising particular in the whole infection, for, if these swellings could be brought to a head, and to break and run, or, as the surgeons call it, to digest, the patient generally recovered; whereas those who . . . were struck with death at the beginning, and had the tokens come out upon them, often went about indifferent easy till a little before they died, and some till the moment they dropped down, as in apoplexies and epilepsies is often the case. Such would be taken suddenly very sick, and would run to a bench or bulk, or any convenient place that offered itself, or to their own houses if possible, as I mentioned before, and there sit down, grow faint, and die. This kind of dying was much the same as it was with those who die of common mortifications, who die swooning, and, as it were, go away in a dream. Such as died thus had very little notice of their being infected at all till the gangrene was spread through their whole body; nor could physicians themselves know certainly how it was with them, till they opened their breasts or other parts of their body, and saw the tokens.

But to return to my particular observations during this dreadful part of the visitation. I am now come, as I have said, to the month of September, which was the most dreadful of its kind, I believe, that ever London saw; for, by all the accounts which I have seen of the preceding visitations which have been in London, nothing has been like it, the number in the weekly bill amounting to almost 40,000 from the 22nd of August to the 26th of September, being but five weeks. The particulars of the bills are as follows, viz.:

From August the 22nd to the 29th	7496
To the 5th of September	8252
To the 12th	7690
To the 19th	8297
To the 26th	6460
	38,195

This was a prodigious number of itself, but if I should add the reasons which I have to believe that this account was deficient, and how deficient it was, you would, with me, make no scruple to believe that there died above ten thousand a week for all those weeks, one week with another, and a proportion for several weeks both before and after. The confusion among the people, especially within the City at that time, was inexpressible. The terror was so great at last that the courage of the people appointed to carry away the dead began to fail them; nay, several of them died, although they had the distemper before and were recovered, and some of them dropped down when they have been carrying the bodies even at the pit side, and just ready to throw them in; and this confusion was greater in the City, because they had flattered themselves with hopes of escaping, and thought the bitterness of death was past. One cart, they told us, going up Shoreditch was forsaken of the drivers, or being left to one man to drive, he died in the street, and the horses going on, overthrew the cart, and left the bodies, some thrown here, some there, in a dismal manner. Another cart was, it seems, found in the great pit in Finsbury Fields, the driver being dead, or having been gone and abandoned it, and the horses running too near it, the cart fell in and drew the horses in also. It was suggested that the driver was thrown in with it, and that the cart fell upon him, by reason his whip was seen to be in the pit among the bodies; but that, I suppose, could not be certain.

In our parish of Aldgate the dead-carts were several times, as I have heard, found standing at the churchyard gate full of dead bodies, but neither bellman or driver or anyone else with it; neither in these or many other cases did they know what bodies they had in their cart, for sometimes they were let down with ropes out of balconies and out of windows, and sometimes the bearers brought them to the cart, sometimes other people; nor, as the men themselves said, did they trouble themselves to keep any account of the numbers. . . .

I would be glad if I could close the account of this melancholy year with some particular examples historically; I mean of the thankfulness to God, our preserver, for our being delivered from this dreadful calamity. Certainly the circumstances of the deliverance, as well as the terrible enemy we were delivered from, called upon the whole nation for it. The circumstances of the deliverance were indeed very remarkable, as I have in part mentioned already, and particularly the dreadful condition which we were all in, when we were, to the surprise of the whole town, made joyful with the hope of a stop of the infection.

Nothing but the immediate finger of God, nothing but omnipotent power, could have done it. The contagion despised all medicine; death raged in every corner; and had it gone on as it did then, a few weeks more would have cleared the town of all and everything that had a soul. Men everywhere began to despair; every heart failed them for fear; people were made desperate through the anguish of their souls, and the terrors of death sat in the very faces and countenances of the people.

In that very moment, when we might very well say, "Vain was the help of man"—I say, in that very moment it pleased God, with a most agreeable surprise, to cause the fury of it to abate, even of itself; and the malignity declining, as I have said, though infinite numbers were sick, yet fewer died, and the very first week's bill decreased 1843; a vast number indeed!

It is impossible to express the change that appeared in the very countenances of the people that Thursday morning when the weekly bill came out. It might have been perceived in their countenances that a secret surprise and smile of joy sat on everybody's face. They shook one another by the hands in the streets, who would hardly go on the same side of the way with one another before. Where the streets were not too broad, they would open their windows and call from one house to another, and ask how they did, and if they had heard the good news that the plague was abated. Some would return, when they said good news, and ask, "What good news?" and when they answered that the plague was abated and the bills decreased almost 2000, they would cry out, "God be praised," and would weep aloud for joy, telling them they had heard nothing of it; and such was the joy of the people that it was, as it were, life to them from the grave. I could almost set down as many extravagant things done in the excess of their joy as of their grief; but that would be to lessen the value of it.

I must confess myself to have been very much dejected just before this happened; for the prodigious number that were taken sick the week or two before, besides those that died, was such, and the lamentations were so great everywhere, that a man must have seemed to have acted even against his reason if he had so much as expected to escape; and as there was hardly a house but mine in all my neighborhood but what was infected, so had it gone on it would not have been long that there would have been any more neighbors to be infected. Indeed it is hardly credible what dreadful havoc the last three weeks had made, for if I might believe the person whose calculations I always found very well grounded, there were not less than 30,000 people dead and near 100,000 fallen sick in the three weeks I speak of; for the number that sickened was surprising; indeed it was astonishing, and those whose courage upheld them all the time before, sank under it now.

In the middle of their distress, when the condition of the City of London was so truly calamitous, just then it pleased God, as it were, by His immediate hand to disarm this enemy; the poison was taken out of the sting. It was wonderful; even the physicians themselves were surprised at it. Wherever they visited they found their patients better; either they had sweated kindly, or the tumors were broke, or the carbuncles went down, and the inflammations round them changed color, or the fever was gone, or the violent headache was assuaged, or some good symptom was in the case; so that in a few days everybody was recovering, whole families that were infected and down, that had ministers praying with them, and expected death every hour, were revived and healed, and none died at all out of them.

Nor was this by any new medicine found out, or new method of cure discovered, or by any experience in the operation which the physicians or surgeons attained to; but it was evidently from the secret invisible hand of Him that had at first sent this disease as a judgment upon us; and let the atheistic part of mankind call my saying what they please, it is no enthusiasm. It was acknowledged at that time by all mankind. The disease was enervated and its malignity spent; and let it proceed from whencesoever it will, let the philosophers search for reasons in nature to account for it by, and labor as much as they will to lessen the debt they owe to their Maker, those physicians who had the least share of religion in them were obliged to acknowledge that it was all supernatural, that it was extraordinary, and that no account could be given of it.

If I should say that this is a visible summons to us all to thankfulness, especially we that were under the terror of its increase, perhaps it may be thought by some, after the sense of the thing was over, an officious canting of religious things, preaching a sermon instead of writing a history, making myself a teacher instead of giving my observations of things; and this restrains me very much from going on here, as I might otherwise do. But if ten lepers were healed, and but one returned to give thanks, I desire to be as that one, and to be thankful for myself.

Nor will I deny but there were abundance of people who, to all appearance, were very thankful at that time; for their mouths were stopped, even the mouths of those whose hearts were not extraordinary long affected with it. But the impression was so strong at that time that it could not be resisted, no, not by the worst of the people.

It was a common thing to meet people in the street that were strangers, and that we knew nothing at all of, expressing their surprise. Going one day through Aldgate, and a pretty many people being passing and repassing, there comes a man out of the end of the Minories, and looking a little up the street and down, he throws his hands abroad, "Lord, what an alteration is here! Why, last week I came along here, and hardly anybody was to be seen." Another man, I heard him, adds to his words, " 'Tis all wonderful; 'tis all a dream." "Blessed be God," says a third man, "and let us give thanks to Him, for 'tis all His own doing. Human help and human skill was at an end." These were all strangers to one another. But such salutations as these were frequent in the street every day; and in spite of a loose behavior, the very common people went along the streets giving God thanks for their deliverance.

It was now, as I said before, the people had cast off all apprehensions, and that too fast; indeed we were no more afraid now to pass by a man with a white cap upon his head, or with a cloth wrapped round his neck, or with his leg limping, occasioned by the sores in his groin, all which were frightful to the last degree but the week before. But now the street was full of them, and these poor recovering creatures, give them their due, appeared very sensible of their unexpected deliverance; and I should wrong them very much if I should not acknowledge that I believe many of them were really thankful. But I must own, that for the generality of the people, it might too justly be said of them as was said of the Children of Israel, after their being delivered from the host of Pharaoh, when they passed the Red Sea, and looked back, and saw the Egyptians overwhelmed in the water, viz., that they sang His praise, but they soon forgot His works.

I can go no further here. I should be counted censorious, and perhaps unjust, if I should enter into the unpleasing work of reflecting, whatever cause there was for it, upon the unthankfulness and return of all manner of wickedness among us, which I was so much an eyewitness of myself. I shall conclude the account of this calamitous year therefore with a coarse but sincere stanza of my own, which I placed at the end of my ordinary memorandums the same year they were written:

> A dreadful plague in London was
>   In the year sixty-five,
> Which swept an hundred thousand souls
>   Away; yet I alive!

H.F.

AUGUSTA TRIUMPHANS:
OR, THE WAY TO MAKE LONDON THE MOST FLOURISHING CITY IN THE UNIVERSE

1728

A man who has the public good in view ought not in the least to be alarmed at the tribute of ridicule which scoffers constantly pay to projecting heads. It is the business of a writer who means well to go directly forward, without regard to criticism, but to offer his thoughts as they occur; and if in twenty schemes he hits but on one to the purpose, he ought to be excused failing in the nineteen for the twentieth sake. It is a kind of good action to mean well, and the intention ought to palliate the failure; but the English, of all people in the world, show least mercy to schemists, for they treat them in the vilest manner; whereas other nations give them fair play for their lives, which is the reason why we are esteemed so bad at invention.

I have but a short time to live, nor would I waste my remaining thread of life in vain, but having often lamented sundry public abuses, and many schemes having occurred to my fancy, which to me carried an air of benefit, I was resolved to commit them to paper before my departure, and leave, at least, a testimony of my good will to my fellow creatures.

But of all my reflections, none was more constantly my companion than a deep sorrow for the present decay of learning among us, and the manifest corruption of education; we have been a brave and learned people, and are insensibly dwindling into an effeminate, superficial race. Our young gentlemen are sent to the universities, 'tis true, but not under restraint or correction as formerly; not to study, but to drink; not for furniture for the head, but a feather for the cap, merely to say they have been at Oxford or Cambridge, as if the air of those places inspired knowledge without application. 'Tis true we ought to have those places in reverence for the many learned men they have sent us; but why must we go so far for knowledge? Why should a young gentleman be sent raw from the nursery to live on his own hands, to be liable to a thousand temptations, and run the risk of being snapped up by sharping jilts, with which both universities abound, who make our youth of fortune their prey, and have brought misery into too many good families? Not only the hazard of their healths from debauches of both kinds, but the waste of their precious time renders the sending them so far off very hazardous. Why should such a metropolis as London be without a university? Would it not save considerably the expense we are at in sending our young gentlemen so far from London? Would it not add to the luster of our state and cultivate politeness among us? What benefits may we not in time expect from so glorious a design? Will not London become the scene of science? And what reason have we but to hope we may vie with any neighboring nations? Not that I would have Oxford or Cambridge neglected, for the good they have done. Besides, there are too many fine endowments to be sunk; we may have universities at those places and at London, too, without prejudice. Knowledge will never hurt us, and whoever lives to see an university here, will find it give quite another turn to the genius of our youth in general.

How many gentlemen pass their lives in a shameful indolence, who might employ themselves to the purpose, were such a design set on foot! Learning would flourish, art revive, and not only those who studied would benefit by it, but the blessing would be conveyed to others by conversation. . . .

It may be objected that there is a kind of university at Gresham College,[1] where professors in all sciences are maintained, and obliged to read lectures every day, or at least as often as demanded. The design is most laudable, but it smells too much of the *sine cure;* they only read in term time, and then their lectures are so hurried over, the audience is little the better. They cannot be turned out; 'tis a good settlement for life, and they are very easy in their studies when once fixed. Whereas were the professorship during good behavior, there would be a study to maintain their posts, and their pupils would reap the benefit.

Upon second thought, I think colleges for university education might be formed at Westminster, Eton, the Charter House, St. Paul's, Merchant Taylors', and other public schools, where youth might begin and end their studies; but this may be further considered of.

I had almost forgot the most material point, which is that his Majesty's sanction must first be obtained, and the university proposed have power to confer degrees, etc., and other academical privileges.

As I am quick to conceive, I am eager to have done, unwilling to overwork a subject; I had rather leave part to the conception of the readers than to tire them or myself with protracting a theme, as if, like a chancery man or a hackney author, I wrote by the sheet for hire. So let us have done with this topic, and proceed to another, which is:—

A proposal to prevent murder, dishonor, and other abuses, by erecting an hospital for foundlings.

It is needless to run into a declamation on this head, since not a sessions passes but we see one or more merciless mothers tried for

---

[1] A college founded by the will of Sir Thomas Gresham, who died in 1579. There were seven professors, and lectures upon astronomy, geometry, physics, law, divinity, rhetoric, and music.

the murder of their bastard children; and, to the shame of good government, generally escape the vengeance due to shedders of innocent blood. For it is a common practice now among them to hire a set of old beldams, or pretended midwives, who make it their trade to bring them off for three or four guineas, having got the ready rote of swearing the child was not at its full growth, for which they have a hidden reserve; that is to say, the child was not at man's or woman's growth. Thus do these impious wretches cheat the world and damn their own souls by a double meaning, which too often imposes on a cautious, merciful, and credulous jury, and gives wicked murderers means to escape and commit fresh sins, to which their acquitters, no doubt, are accessory.

I wonder so many men of sense as have been on the jury have been so often imposed upon by the stale pretense of a scrap or two of childbed linen being found in the murderer's box, etc.; when, alas! perhaps it was never put there till after the murder was committed; or if it was, but with a view of saving themselves by that devilish precaution; for so many have been acquitted on that pretense that it is but too common a thing to provide childbed linen beforehand for a poor innocent babe they are determined to murder.

But, alas! what are the exploded murders to those which escape the eye of the magistrate, and die in silence? Add to this procured abortions and other indirect means which wicked wretches make use of to screen themselves from the censure of the world, which they dread more than the displeasure of their Maker.

Those who cannot be so hardhearted to murder their own offspring themselves take a slower, though as sure, a way, and get it done by others, by dropping their children and leaving them to be starved by parish nurses.

Thus is God robbed of a creature, in whom He had breathed the breath of life, and on whom He had stamped His image; the world of an inhabitant, who might have been of use; the King of a subject; and future generations of an issue not to be accounted for, had this infant lived to have been a parent.

It is therefore the height of charity and humanity to provide against this barbarity, to prevent this crying sin, and extract good, even out of evil, by saving these innocent babes from slaughter, and bringing them up in the nurture and fear of the Lord; to be of benefit to themselves and mankind in general.

And what nearer, what better way can we have than to erect and to endow a proper hospital or house to receive them, where we may see them tenderly brought up, as so many living monuments of our charity; every one of them being a convincing proof of a Christian saved and a murder prevented?

Nor will this be attended with so much charge as is imagined, for we find in many parishes that parents have redemanded their children, on increase of circumstances, and paid all costs, with a handsome present in the bargain; and many times when a clandestine marriage is cleared up and openly avowed, they would purchase the first fruits of their loves at any rate. Oftentimes a couple may have no more children, and an infant thus saved may arrive to inherit a good estate, and become a benefactor where it was once an object of charity.

But let us suppose the worst, and imagine the infant begot in sin and without the sanction of wedlock; is it therefore to be murdered, starved, or neglected, because its parents were wicked? Hard fate of innocent children to suffer for their parents' faults! Where God has thought fit to give His image and life, there is nourishment demanded; that calls aloud for our Christian and human assistance, and best shows our nobleness of soul when we generously assist those who cannot help themselves.

If the fault devolved on the children, our church would deny them baptism, burial, and other Christian rites; but our religion carries more charity with it: they are not denied even to partake of our blessed sacraments, and are excluded no one branch or benefit accruing from Christianity; if so, how unjust are those who arraign them for their parents' faults, and how barbarous are those parents who, though able, make no provision for them, because they are not legitimate. My child is my child, let it be begot in sin or wedlock, and all the duties of a parent are incumbent on me so long as it lives; if it survives me, I ought to make a provision for it, according to my ability; and though I do not set it on a footing with my legitimate children, I ought in conscience to provide against want and shame, or I am answerable for every sin or extravagance my child is forced or led into, for want of my giving an allowance to prevent it.

We have an instance very fresh in everyone's memory, of an ingenious, nay, a sober young nobleman, for such I must call him, whose either father was a peer, and his mother a peeress.[2] This unhappy gentleman, tossed from father to father, at last found none, and himself a vagabond forced to every shift; he in a manner starved for many years, yet was guilty of no capital crime, till that unhappy accident occurred, which God has given him grace and sense enough to repent. However, I cannot but think his hard-hearted mother will bear her portion of the guilt, till washed away by a severe repentance.

What a figure might this man have made in life had due care been taken! If his peerage had not been adjusted, he might at least have been a fine gentleman; nay, probably have filled some handsome post in the Government with applause, and called as much for respect as he does now for pity.

Nor is this gentleman the only person begot and neglected by noble, or rather ignoble, parents; we have but too many now living who owe their birth to the best of our peerage, and yet know not where to eat. Hard fate, when the child would be glad of the scraps which the servants throw away! But Heaven generally rewards them accordingly, for many noble families are become extinct, and large estates alienated into other houses, while their own issue want bread.

And now, methinks, I hear some oversqueamish ladies cry: What would this fellow be at? would not he set up a nursery for lewdness, and encourage fornication? who would be afraid of sinning if they can so easily get rid of their bastards? we shall soon be overrun with foundlings when there is such encouragement given to whoredom. To which I answer, that I am as much against bastards being begot as I am for their being murdered; but when a child is once begot, it cannot be unbegotten; and when once born, it must be kept; the fault, as I said before, is in the parents, not the child; and we ought to show our charity towards it as a fellow creature and Christian, without any regard to its legitimacy or otherwise.

The only way to put a stop to this growing evil would be to oblige all housekeepers not to admit a man and woman as lodgers till they were certified of their being lawfully married; for nowa-

---

2 According to his own word (which has not been accepted), Richard Savage, the poet, and friend of Dr. Johnson, was the natural son of the fourth Earl of Rivers and Anne, wife of the second Earl of Macclesfield. He was convicted of murder, but pardoned, in 1728.

days nothing is more common than for a whoremonger and a strumpet to pretend marriage till they have left a child or two on the parish, and then shift to another end of the town.

If there were no receivers, there would be no thieves; if there were no bawdyhouses, there would be no whores; and though persons letting lodgings be not actual procurers, yet, if they connive at the embraces of a couple whose marriage is doubtful, they are no better than bawds, and their houses no more than brothels.

Now should anybody ask how shall this hospital be built? how endowed? to which I answer, follow the steps of the Venetians, the Hamburgers, and other foreign states, etc., who have for ages past prosecuted this glorious design, and found their account therein. As for building a house, I am utterly against it, especially in the infancy of the affair; let a place convenient be hired. Why should such a considerable sum be sunk in building as has in late public structures, which have swallowed up part of the profits and dividend, if not the capital, of unwary stockmongers?

To my great joy I find my project already anticipated, and a noble subscription carrying on for this purpose; to promote which I exhort all persons of compassion and generosity, and I shall think myself happy if what I have said on this head may anyways contribute to further the same.

Having said all I think material on this subject, I beg pardon for leaving my reader so abruptly, and crave leave to proceed to another article, viz.:—

A proposal to prevent the expensive importation of foreign musicians, etc., by forming an academy of our own.

It will no doubt be asked what have I to do with music? to which I answer, I have been a lover of the science from my infancy, and in my younger days was accounted no despicable performer on the viol and lute, then much in vogue. I esteem it the most innocent amusement in life; it generally relaxes, after too great a hurry of spirits, and composes the mind into a sedateness prone to everything that is generous and good; and when the more necessary parts of education are finished, it is a most genteel and commendable accomplishment; it saves a great deal of drinking and debauchery in our sex, and helps the ladies off with many an idle hour, which sometimes might probably be worse employed otherwise.

Our quality, gentry, and better sort of traders must have diversions; and if those that are commendable be denied, they will take to worse; now, what can be more commendable than music, one of the seven liberal sciences, and no mean branch of the mathematics?

Were it for no other reason, I should esteem it because it was the favorite diversion of his late Majesty of glorious memory, who was as wise a prince as ever filled the British throne.[3] Nor is it less esteemed by their present Majesties, whose souls are formed for harmony, and who have not disdained to make it a part in the education of their sacred race.

Our nobility and gentry have shown their love to the science by supporting at such prodigious expense the Italian opera, improperly called an academy; but they have at the same time shown no small partiality in discouraging anything English and overloading the town with such heaps of foreign musicians.

An academy, rightly understood, is a place for the propagation of science, by training up persons thereto from younger to riper years, under the instruction and inspection of proper artists. How then can the Italian opera properly be called an academy when none are admitted but such as are, at least are thought, or ought to be, adepts in music? If that be an academy, so are the theaters of Drury Lane and Lincoln's Inn Fields; nay, Punch's opera may pass for a lower kind of academy. Would it not be a glorious thing to have an opera of our own, in our own most noble tongue, in which the composer, singers, and orchestra should be of our own growth? Not that we ought to disclaim all obligations to Italy, the mother of music, the nurse of Corelli, Handel, Bononcini, Geminiani; but then we ought not to be so stupidly partial to imagine ourselves too brutal a part of mankind to make any progress in the science. By the same reason that we love it, we may excel in it. Love begets application, and application perfection. We have already had a Purcell, and no doubt there are now many latent geniuses who only want proper instruction, application, and encouragement to become great ornaments of the science and make England emulate even Rome itself.

What a number of excellent performers on all instruments have sprung up in England within these few years! That this is owing to the opera I will not deny, and so far the opera is an academy as it refines the taste and inspires emulation.

3 George I (r. 1714–27).

But though we are happy in instrumental performers, we frequently send to Italy for singers, and that at no small expense; to remedy which I humbly propose that the governors of Christ's Hospital will show their public spirit by forming an academy of music on their foundation, after this or the like manner:

That out of their great number of children, thirty boys be selected of good ears and propensity to music.

That these boys be divided into three classes, viz., six for wind instruments, such as the hautboy, bassoon, and German flute.

That sixteen others be selected for string instruments, or at least the most useful, viz., the violin and bass violin.

That the remaining eight be particularly chosen for voice and organ or harpsichord. That all in due time be taught composition. The boys thus chosen, three masters should be elected, each most excellent in his way; that is to say, one for the wind instrument, another for the stringed, and a third for the voice and organ, etc. . . .

Having advanced what I think proper on this head, or at least enough for a hint, I proceed to offer:—

That many youths and servants may be saved from destruction
were the streets cleared of shameless and impudent strumpets,
gaming tables totally suppressed, and a stop put to Sabbath
debauches.

The corruption of our children and servants is of importance sufficient to require our utmost precaution; and moreover, women servants (commonly called maidservants) are such necessary creatures that it is by no means below us to make them beneficial rather than prejudicial to us.

I shall not run into a description of their abuses; we know enough of those already. Our business now is to make them useful, first by ascertaining their wages at a proper standard.

Secondly, by obliging them to continue longer in service, not to stroll about from place to place, and throw themselves on the town on every dislike.

Thirdly, to prevent their being harbored by wicked persons, when out of place; or living too long on their own hands.

As for their wages, they have topped upon us already, and doubled them in spite of our teeth; but as they have had wit enough to get them, so will they, I doubt not, have the same sense to keep them, and much good may it do those indolent oversecure persons who have given them this advantage. However, if they are honest and diligent, I would have them encouraged, and handsome wages allowed them; because, by this means, we provide for the children of the inferior class of people, who otherwise could not maintain themselves; nay, sometimes tradesmen, etc., reduced, are glad when their children cease to hang upon them, by getting into service, and by that means not only maintaining themselves, but being of use in other families. But, then, there ought to be some medium, some limitation to their wages, or they may extort more than can well be afforded.

Nothing calls for more redress than their quitting service for every idle disgust, leaving a master or mistress at a nonplus, and all under plea of a foolish old custom, called warning, nowhere practiced but in London. For in other places they are hired by the year, or by the statute as they call it, which settles them in a place at least for some time; whereas, when they are not limited, it encourages a roving temper and makes them never easy.

If you turn them away without warning, they will make you pay a month's wages, be the provocation or offense never so great; but if they leave you, though never so abruptly, or unprovided, help yourselves how you can, there is no redress; though I think there ought, in all conscience, to be as much law for the master as for the servant.

No servant should quit a place where they are well fed and paid without assigning a good reason before a magistrate. On the other hand, they should receive no abuse which should not be redressed; for we ought to treat them as servants, not slaves; and a medium ought to be observed on both sides. But if they are not restrained from quitting service on every vagary, they will throw themselves on the town, and not only ruin themselves, but others; for example, a girl quits a place and turns whore; if there is not a bastard to be murdered, or left to the parish, there is one or more unwary youths drawn in to support her in lewdness and idleness; in order to which, they rob their parents and masters, nay, sometimes, anybody else, to support their strumpets; so that many thieves owe their ruin and shameful deaths to harlots; not to mention the communication of loathsome distempers and innumerable other evils to which they give birth.

How many youths, of all ranks, are daily ruined! and how justly may be dreaded the loss of as many more if a speedy stop be not put to this growing evil! Generations to come will curse the neglect of the present, and every sin committed for the future may be passed to our account if we do not use our endeavors to the contrary.

And unless we prevent our maidservants from being harbored by wicked persons when out of place, or living too long on their own hands, our streets will swarm with impudent, shameless strumpets; the good will be molested; those prone to evil will be made yet more wicked by having temptations thrown in their way; and, to crown all, we shall have scarce a servant left, but our wives, etc., must do the household work themselves.

If this be not worthy the consideration of a legislature, I would fain know what is. Is it not time to limit their wages, when they are grown so wanton they know not what to ask? Is it not time to fix them, when they stroll from place to place, and we are hardly sure of a servant a month together? Is it not time to prevent the increase of harlots, by making it penal for servants to be harbored in idleness, and tempted to theft, whoredom, murder, etc., by living too long out of place? and I am sure it is high time to begin the work by clearing the public streets of nightwalkers, who are grown to such a pitch of impudence that peace and common decency are manifestly broken in our public streets. I wonder this has so long escaped the eye of the magistrate, especially when there are already in force laws sufficient to restrain this tide of uncleanness, which will one day overflow us.

The lewdest people upon earth, ourselves excepted, are not guilty of such open violations of the laws of decency. Go all the world over, and you'll see no such impudence as in the streets of London, which makes many foreigners give our women in general a bad character, from the vile specimens they meet with from one end of the town to the other. Our sessions' papers are full of the trials of impudent sluts, who first decoy men and then rob them; a meanness the courtesans of Rome and Venice abhor.

How many honest women, those of the inferior sort especially, get loathsome distempers from their husbands' commerce with these creatures, which distempers are often entailed on posterity; nor have we an hospital separated for that purpose which does not contain too many instances of honest poor wretches made miserable by villains of husbands.

And now I have mentioned the villainy of some husbands in the lower state of life, give me leave to propose, or at least to wish, that they were restrained from abusing their wives at that barbarous rate which is now practiced by butchers, carmen, and such inferior sort of fellows, who are public nuisances to civil neighborhoods, and yet nobody cares to interpose, because the riot is between a man and his wife.

I see no reason why every profligate fellow shall have the liberty to disturb a whole neighborhood, and abuse a poor honest creature at a most inhuman rate, and is not to be called to account because it is his wife; this sort of barbarity was never so notorious and so much encouraged as at present, for every vagabond thinks he may cripple his wife at pleasure; and it is enough to pierce a heart of stone to see how barbarously some poor creatures are beaten and abused by merciless dogs of husbands.

It gives an ill example to the growing generation, and this evil will gain ground on us if not prevented; it may be answered, the law has already provided redress, and a woman abused may swear the peace against her husband; but what woman cares to do that? It is revenging herself on herself, and not without considerable charge and trouble.

There ought to be a shorter way, and when a man has beaten his wife (which by the by is a most unmanly action and great sign of cowardice) it behooves every neighbor who has the least humanity or compassion to complain to the next justice of the peace, who should be empowered to set him in the stocks for the first offense; to have him well scourged at the whipping post for the second; and if he persisted in his barbarous abuse of the holy marriage state, to send him to the house of correction till he should learn to use more mercy to his yokefellow.

How hard is it for a poor industrious woman to be up early and late, to sit in a cold shop, stall, or market all weathers, to carry heavy loads from one end of the town to the other, or to work from morning till night, and even then dread going home for fear of being murdered! Some may think this too low a topic for me to expatiate upon, to which I answer that it is a charitable and Christian one, and therefore not in the least beneath the consideration of any man who had a woman for his mother.

The mention of this leads me to exclaim against the vile practice now so much in vogue among the better sort as they are called, but the worst sort in fact; namely, the sending their wives to mad-houses, at every whim or dislike, that they may be more secure and undisturbed in their debaucheries; which wicked custom is got to such a head that the number of private madhouses in and about London are considerably increased within these few years. . . .

I must beg my reader's indulgence, being the most immethodical writer imaginable. It is true I lay down a scheme, but fancy is so fertile I often start fresh hints, and cannot but pursue them; pardon therefore, kind reader, my digressive way of writing, and let the subject, not the style or method, engage thy attention.

Return we, therefore, to complain of destructive gaming houses, the bane of our youth, and ruin of our children and servants.

This is the most unprofitable evil upon earth, for it only tends to alienate the proper current of specie, to maintain a pack of idle sharping rascals, and beggar unwary gentlemen and traders.

I take the itch of gaming to be the most pernicious of vices, it is a kind of avaricious madness, and if people have not sense to com-mand themselves by reason, they ought to be restrained by law; nor suffered to ruin themselves and families, to enrich a crew of sharpers.

There is no playing on the square with these villains; they are sure to cheat you, either by sleight of hand, confederacy, or false dice, etc.; they have so much the odds of their infatuated bubbles that they might safely play a guinea to a shilling, and yet be sure of winning. This is but genteel pocket-picking, or felony with another name, and yet, so fond are we of it that from the footboy to the lord all must have a touch of gaming; and there are sharpers of different stations and denominations, from Southwark Fair to the Groom Porter's.[4] Shame, that gentlemen should suffer every scoundrel to mix with them for gaming sake! And equal shame, that honest laborious tradesmen should be obstructed in crossing the public streets by the gilt chariots of vagabond gamesters, who now infest the land, and brave even our nobility and gentry with their own money.

But the most barbarous part of this hellish trade is what they call setting of young gentlemen, apprentices, and others; this ought to be deemed felony without benefit of clergy; for it is the worst of thievery. Under pretense of taking a bottle, or spending an evening

4 The Groom Porter, whose duty until the days of George III was to provide dice and cards at court and to set the rules for gam-ing, was lodged south of Whitehall Palace, Charing Cross.

gaily, they draw their cull to the tavern, where they sit not long before the devil's bones or books are found accidentally on purpose, by the help of which they strip my gentleman in an instant, and then generously lend him his own money to lose afresh and create a debt which is but too often more justly paid than those more justly due.

If we look into some late bankruptcies, we shall find some noted gamesters the principal creditors; I think in such cases it would be but justice to make void the gamester's debt, and subject his estate to make good the deficiencies of the bankrupt's effects. If traders have no more wit, the public should have pity on them; and make it as penal to lose as to win; and, in truth, if cards, dice, etc., were totally suppressed, industry and arts would increase the more; gaming may make a man crafty, but not polite; one may understand cards and dice perfectly well and be a blockhead in everything else.

I am sorry to see it so prevalent in the City among the trading part of mankind, who have introduced it into their clubs and play so high of late that many bankrupts have been made by this pernicious practice.

It is the bane of all conversation; and those who can't sit an hour without gaming should never go into a club to spoil company. In a word, 'tis mere madness and a most stupid thing to hazard one's fortune and perplex one's mind; nay, to sit up whole nights, poring over toys of pipped ivory and painted pasteboard, making ourselves worse than little children, whose innocent sports we so much ridicule.

To sum up all, I think it would be a noble retribution to subject gamesters' estates to the use and support of the poor widows and orphans of their unfortunate bubbles.

Sunday debauches are abuses that call loud for amendment. 'Tis in this pernicious soil the seeds of ruin are first sown. Instead of a day of rest, we make it a day of labor, by toiling in the devil's vineyard; and but too many surfeit themselves with the fruits of gluttony, drunkenness, and uncleanness.

Not that I am so superciliously strict to have the Sabbath kept as rigidly here as in Scotland, but then there ought to be a medium between the severity of a fast and the riot of Saturnalia. Instead of a decent and cheerful solemnity, our taverns and public houses have more business that day than all the week beside. Our apprentices plume themselves; nay, some scruple not to put on their swords and tie wigs or toupees, and the loose end of the town is their rendezvous, Sunday being market day all round the hundreds of Drury.

While we want servants to do our work, those hundreds, as they call them, are crowded with numbers of idle impudent sluts, who love sporting more than spinning, and inveigle our youth to their ruin; nay, many old lechers (beasts as they are!) steal from their families, and seek these harlots' lurking holes, to practice their unaccountable schemes of new invented lewdnesses; some half hang themselves, others are whipped, some lie under a table and gnaw the bones that are thrown them, while others stand slaving among a parcel of drabs at a washing tub. Strange that the inclination should not die with the power, but that old fools should make themselves the prey and ridicule of a pack of strumpets!

Some heedless youths are wheedled into marriage, which makes them and their unhappy parents miserable all their lives; others are drawn into extravagancies, and but too often run into their masters' cash, and for fear of a discovery make away with themselves, or at least run away and leave their distracted parents in a thousand tears; not to mention the frustration of their fortune and the miseries that attend a vagabond life. Thus honest parents lose their children, and traders their apprentices, and all from a liberty we have of late given our youth of rambling abroad on Sundays; for many nowadays will lie out all night or stay out so late to give no small disturbance in sober families. It therefore behooves every master of a family to have his servants under his eye; and if the going to church, meeting, or whatever place of worship suited their religion were more enforced, it would be so much the better.

In short, the luxury of the age will be the ruin of the nation, if not prevented. We leave trade to game in stocks; we live above ourselves and barter our ready money for trifles; tea and wine are all we seem anxious for, and God has given the blessings of life to an ungrateful people, who despise their own productions. Our very plow fellows drink wine nowadays; our farmers, graziers, and butchers are above malt liquors; and the wholesome breakfast of water gruel and milk pottage is changed for coffee and tea. This is the reason provisions and corn, etc., are so dear; we all work for vintners and raise our prices one upon another to such a degree it will be an impossibility to live, and we shall, of course, become our own devourers.

We strain at a gnat and swallow a camel; and, in this instance, the public houses are kept open to furnish our luxury, while we deny ourselves other necessaries of life, out of a scruple of conscience. For example, in extreme hot weather, when meat will not keep from Saturday to Sunday, we throw, or cause to be thrown, away vast quantities of tainted meat, and have generally stinking dinners, because the butchers dare not sell a joint of meat on a Sunday morning. Now, though I would not have the Sabbath so far violated as to have it a market day, yet, rather than abuse God's mercies by throwing away creatures given for our use, nay, for our own health's and cleanliness' sake, I would have the same indulgence in extreme hot weather as there is for milk and mackerel; that is to say, that meat might be killed in the cool of the morning, viz., one or two of the clock, and sold till nine, and no longer; nor should villainous informers have power to molest them in this innocent and reasonable amendment of a ridiculous vulgar error.

I cannot forbear taking notice of the extravagant use, or rather abuse, of that nauseous liquor called Geneva [5] among our lower sort. Those who deny that an inferior class of people are most necessary in a body politic contradict reason and experience itself, since they are most useful when industrious and as pernicious when lazy. By their industry our manufactures, trade, and commerce are carried on; the merchant in his countinghouse and the captain in his cabin would find but little employment were it not that many hands carried on the different branches of the concern they superintended.

But now, so far are our common people infatuated with Geneva that half the work is not done now as formerly. It debilitates and enervates them, and they are not near so strong and healthy as formerly. This accursed liquor is in itself so diuretic it overstrains the parts of generation, and makes our common people incapable of getting such lusty children as they used to do. Add to this, that the women, by drinking it, spoil their milk, and by giving it to young children, as they foolishly do, spoil the stomach and hinder digestion; so that in less than an age we may expect a fine spindle-shanked generation.

There is not in nature so unhealthy a liquor as Geneva, especially as commonly sold; it curdles the blood, it stupefies the senses, it weakens the nerves, it spoils the eyesight, and entirely ruins the

5 "Holland" gin, very strong.

stomach; nay, some stomachs have been rendered so cold by the use of Geneva that lamp spirits have not been a dram warm enough for them. Surely they will come to drink aquafortis at last!

On the contrary, our own malt liquors, especially common draft beer, is most wholesome and nourishing, and has brought up better generations than the present: it is strengthening, cooling, and balsamic; it helps digestion, and carries nourishment with it; and, in spite of the whims of some physicians, is most pertinent to a human, especially a good wholesome English, constitution. Nay, the honest part of the faculty deny not the use of small beer, well brewed, even in fevers. I myself have found great benefit by it; and if it be good in its kind, it is the finest jalap upon earth.

If this abuse of Geneva be not stopped, we may go whoop for husbandmen, laborers, etc. Trade must consequently stand still and the credit of the nation sink; nor is the abatement of the excise, though very considerable and most worthy of notice, anyways comparable to the corruption of manners, the destruction of health, and all the train of evils we are threatened with from pernicious Geneva.

An effectual method to prevent street robberies.

The principal encouragements and opportunity given to street robbers is that our streets are so poorly watched; the watchmen, for the most part, being decrepit, superannuated wretches, with one foot in the grave and the other ready to follow; so feeble that a puff of breath can blow them down. Poor crazy mortals! much fitter for an almshouse than a watchhouse. A city watched and guarded by such animals is wretchedly watched indeed.

Nay, so little terror do our watchmen carry with them that hardy thieves make a mere jest of them, and sometimes oblige even the very watchman who should apprehend them to light them in their roguery. And what can a poor creature do, in terror of his life, surrounded by a pack of ruffians, and no assistance near?

Add to this, that our rogues are grown more wicked than ever, and vice in all kinds is so much winked at that robbery is accounted a petty crime. We take pains to puff them up in their villainy, and thieves are set out in so amiable a light in *The Beggar's Opera* that it has taught them to value themselves on their profession rather than be ashamed of it. . . .

We ought to begin our endeavors to suppress these villainies, first by heavenly, and then by earthly, means.

By heavenly means, in enforcing and encouraging a reformation of manners, by suppressing of vice and immorality, and punishing profaneness and licentiousness. Our youth are corrupted by filthy, lewd ballads, sung and sold publicly in our streets; nay, unlicensed and unstamped, notwithstanding acts of Parliament to the contrary.

Coachmen, carmen, etc., are indulged in swearing after the most blasphemous, shocking, and unaccountable rate that ever was known. New oaths and blasphemies are daily uttered and invented; and rather than not exercise this hellish talent, they will vent their curses on their very horses; and, oh, stupid! damn the blood of a post rather than want something to curse.

Our common women, too, have learned this vice; and not only strumpets, but laboring women, who keep our markets and vend things about street, swear and curse at a most hideous rate. Their children learn it from their parents, and those of the middle, or even the better sort of people, if they pass through the streets to school or to play, catch the infection and carry home such words as must consequently be very shocking to sober parents.

Our youth, in general, have too much liberty, the Sabbath is not kept with due solemnity; masters and mistresses of families are too remiss in the care of the souls committed to their charge. Family prayer is neglected; and, to the shame of scoffers be it spoken, too much ridiculed. All ages and sexes, if in health, should be obliged to attend public worship, according to their respective opinions. Were it only to keep youth out of harm's way, it would do well. But it is to be hoped, if their parents, masters, or mistresses should oblige their attendance at public devotion, they would edify by what they should hear, and many wicked acts would be stifled in their infancy and checked even in the intention, by good and useful doctrine.

Our common people make it a day of debauch, and get so drunk on a Sunday they cannot work for a day or two following. Nay, since the use of Geneva has become so common, many get so often drunk they cannot work at all, but run from one irregularity to another till at last they become arrant rogues. And this is the foundation of all our present complaints.

We will suppose a man able to maintain himself and family by his trade, and at the same time to be a Geneva-drinker. This fellow first makes himself incapable of working by being continually drunk; this runs him behindhand, and he either pawns or neglects his work, for which reason nobody will employ him. At last, fear of arrests, his own hunger, the cries of his family for bread, his natural desire to support an irregular life, and a propense hatred to labor turn but too many an honest tradesman into an arrant desperate rogue. And these are commonly the means that furnish us with thieves and villains in general.

Thus is a man that might be useful in a body politic rendered obnoxious to the same: and if this trade of wickedness goes on, they will grow and increase upon us insomuch that we shall not dare to stir out of our habitations; nay, it will be well if they arrive not to the impudence of plundering our houses at noonday.

Where is the courage of the English nation, that a gentleman, with six or seven servants, shall be robbed by one single highwayman? Yet we have lately had instances of this; and for this we may thank our effeminacy, our toupee-wigs, and powdered pates, our tea, and other scandalous fopperies; and, above all, the disuse of noble and manly sports, so necessary to a brave people, once in vogue, but now totally lost among us.

Let not the reader think I run from my subject if I search the bottom of the distemper before I propose a cure, which having done, though indeed but slightly, for this is an argument could be carried to a much greater length, I proceed next to propose earthly means in the manner following.

Let the watch be composed of stout, able-bodied men, and of those at least treble the number now subsisting, that is to say, a watchman to every forty houses, twenty on one side of the way and twenty on the other; for it is observable that a man cannot well see distinctly beyond the extent of twenty houses in a row; if 'tis a single row, and no opposite houses, the charge must be greater and their safety less. This man should be elected and paid by the housekeepers themselves, to prevent misapplication and abuse, so much complained of in the distribution of public money. . . .

The watch thus stationed, strengthened, and encouraged, let every watchman be armed with firearms and sword; and let no watchman stand above twenty doors distant from his fellow.

Let each watchman be provided with a bugle-horn, to sound on alarm, or in time of danger; and let it be made penal, if not felony, for any but a watchman to sound a horn in and about the city, from the time of their going on to that of their going off.

An objection will be here made on account of the postboys, to obviate which I had thoughts of a bell, but that would be too ponderous and troublesome for a watchman to carry, besides his arms and lantern. As to a fixed bell, if the watchman is at another part of his walk, how can he give notice? Besides, rogues may play tricks with the bell; whereas a horn is portable, always ready, and most alarming.

Let the postboys therefore use some other signal, since this is most convenient to this more material purpose. They may carry a bell in a holster with ease, and give notice by that, as well as those who collect the letters.

That the watchmen may see from one end of their walks to the other, let a convenient number of lamps be set up, and those not of the convex kind, which blind the eyes and are of no manner of use; they dazzle, but give no distinct light; and further, rather than prevent robberies, many, deceived and blinded by these *ignes fatui*, have been run over by coaches, carts, etc. People stumble more upon one another, even under these very lamps, than in the dark. In short, they are most unprofitable lights, and in my opinion rather abuses than benefits.

Besides, I see no reason why every ten housekeepers cannot find a lamp among themselves, and let their watchman dress it, rather than fatten a crew of directors; but we are so fond of companies it is a wonder we have not our shoes blacked by one, and a set of directors made rich at the expense of our very blackguards. Convenient turnpikes and stoppages may be made to prevent escapes, and it will be proper for a watchman to be placed at one of these, fixed at the end of a lane, court, alley, or other thoroughfare, which may happen in any part of his beat, and so as not to obstruct his view to both ends thereof, or being able to give notice, as aforesaid; for the watch ought to be in view, as well as in the hearing of each other, or they may be overpowered, and much danger may happen.

The streets thus guarded and illuminated, what remains but that the money allotted by the government be instantly paid on conviction of every offender; for delays in this case are of dangerous consequence, and nobody will venture their lives in hopes of a reward if it be not duly and timely paid. If there is reason of complaint on this head, it ought to be looked into by those at the helm; for nothing can be more vile than for underlings to abuse the benevolence of the public, or their superiors, by sinking, abridging, or delaying public or private benefits. And it is by no means below the dignity or care, even of the greatest, to see the disposal of their own bounty and charity; for it loses but too often by the carriage: and where a nobleman or other generous person has ordered five guineas to be given, it is well if the proper object has had even one.

Something allowed by the Chamber of London to every person apprehending a robber would have a good effect, especially if it be not told over a gridiron,[6] but paid without delay or abatement. And what if the fewer custards are eat, so it augment the public safety?

Some of our common soldiery are (and I hope unjustly) suspected. This may be easily confuted if strict orders are enforced that none but commission or warrant officers shall be out of their quarters after ten at night. But if we consider that neither Blewitt, Bunworth, or their gangs were soldiers, and that of those who have been executed for ten years past, not one in ten were soldiers, but, on the contrary, seamen discharged and thrown on the public without present subsistence, which made them desperate: but I hope the act now depending for the encouragement of seamen, &c., will sufficiently remove that obstacle also. This, I hope, will stop the mouths of censorious persons, who unjustly arraign our soldiery for the vices of others. However, to make all easy, I believe the generality of them will gladly submit to the restraint proposed, merely to show their innocence.

Meantime, would his most sacred Majesty let them partake of his bounty, as the officers, etc., have done, and raise their pay, were it but one penny *per diem*, it would be a most royal bounty, would considerably contribute to their support, and put them above any sordid views: and there was never more occasion than now, when provisions of all kinds are so excessive dear.

Having offered my little mite to the public, I beg they will excuse the deficiency of my style and multitude of my errors, for

6 At the sumptuous dinners of the London Corporation charities were sometimes given to those who had earned well of the city.

my intention's sake. I write without prospect of gain; if I am censured, it is what I can but expect; but if among all my schemes one proves of service, my desires and labors are amply answered.

A SELECTION

Isaac Watts

1674–1748

[One of the most distinguished of the hymn-writers for Dissenters, Watts had great influence among the shopkeepers, and earned the respect even of Dr. Johnson. In Watts the "puritan" influence continues strong—a heritage from the preceding century.]

THE DAY OF JUDGMENT

1706

When the fierce northwind with his airy forces
Rears up the Baltick to a foaming fury;
And the red lightning with a storm of hail comes
    Rushing amain down,

How the poor sailors stand amaz'd and tremble!
While the hoarse thunder like a bloody trumpet,
Roars a loud onset to the gaping waters,
    Quick to devour them.

Such shall the noise be and the wild disorder,
(If things eternal may be like these earthly)
Such the dire terror when the great Archangel
    Shakes the creation;

Tears the strong pillars of the vault of Heaven,
Breaks up old marble, the repose of princes;
See the graves open, and the bones arising,
    Flames all around 'em.

10

Hark, the shrill outcries of the guilty wretches!
Lively bright horror and amazing anguish
Stare thro' their eyelids, while the living worm lies
                    Gnawing within them.   20

Thoughts like old vultures prey upon their heartstrings,
And the smart twinges, when the eye beholds the
Lofty Judge frowning, and a flood of vengeance
                    Rolling afore him.

Hopeless immortals! How they scream and shiver,
While devils push them to the pit wide yawning
Hideous and gloomy, to receive them headlong
                    Down to the center.

Stop here, my fancy (all away ye horrid
Doleful ideas); come, arise to Jesus;   30
How he sits God-like! and the saints around him
                    Thron'd, yet adoring!

Oh may I sit there when he comes triumphant
Dooming the nations: then ascend to glory
While our hosannahs all along the passage
                    Shout the Redeemer.

THE SLUGGARD

1720

'Tis the voice of the Sluggard; I hear him complain,
You have wak'd me too soon, I must slumber again.
As the door on its hinges, so he on his bed,
Turns his sides, and his shoulders, and his heavy head.

A little more sleep, and a little more slumber,
Thus he wastes half his days, and his hours without number:
And when he gets up, he sits folding his hands,
Or walks about sauntring, or trifling he stands.

I past by his garden, and saw the wild bryar,
The thorn and the thistle grow broader and higher: 10
The clothes that hang on him are turning to rags;
And his money still wastes, till he starves, or he begs.

I made him a visit, still hoping to find
He had took better care for improving his mind:
He told me his dreams, talk'd of eating and drinking;
But he scarce reads his Bible, and never loves thinking.

Said I then to my heart, *Here's a lesson for me*,
That man's but a picture of what I might be.
But thanks to my friends for their care in my breeding,
Who taught me betimes to love working and reading.   20

A SELECTION

Isaac Newton

1642–1727

THE MATHEMATICAL PRINCIPLES
OF NATURAL PHILOSOPHY
(Revised and enlarged)

1713

[By its "beautiful system" of mechanical laws that ordered the universe, Newton's work profoundly affected religious, philosophical, and moral thought. The personal God of Milton began to look a little quaint and whimsical; and the law of gravitation so neatly arranged the universe that miracles, revelation, and redemption began to look like an unaccountable caprice on the part of any Creator. Newton, of course, considered himself to be an orthodox Christian, and would have been distressed by the conclusions drawn from his mathematics.]

The General Scholium: The six primary planets are revolved about the sun in circles concentric with the sun, and with motions directed towards the same parts, and almost in the same plane. Ten moons are revolved about the earth, Jupiter, and Saturn, in circles concentric with them, with the same direction of motion, and nearly in the planes of the orbits of those planets. But it is not to be conceived that mere mechanical causes could give birth to so many regular motions: since the comets range over all parts of the heavens, in very eccentric orbits. For by that kind of motion they pass easily through the orbs of the planets, and with great rapidity; and in their aphelions, where they move the slowest and are detained the longest, they recede to the greatest distances from each other, and thence suffer the least disturbance from their mutual attractions. This most beautiful system of the sun, planets, and comets, could only proceed from the counsel and dominion of an intelligent and powerful being. And if the fixed stars are the centers of other like systems, these, being formed by the like wise counsel, must be all subject to the dominion of One; especially since the light of the fixed stars is of the same nature with the light of the sun, and from every system light passes into all the other systems. And lest the systems of the fixed stars should by their gravity fall on each other mutually, He hath placed those systems at immense distances from one another.

This Being governs all things, not as the soul of the world, but as Lord over all: and on account of his dominion he is wont to be called Lord God παντοκράτωρ, or *Universal Ruler*. . . . As a blind man has no idea of colors, so have we no idea of the manner by which the all-wise God perceives and understands all things. He is utterly void of all body and bodily figure, and can therefore neither be seen, nor heard, nor touched; nor ought He to be worshiped under the representation of any corporeal thing. . . . We know Him only by his most wise and excellent contrivances of things, and final causes; we admire Him for his perfections; but we reverence and adore Him on account of his dominion. . . .

[Translated by Andrew Motte, 1729]

A SELECTION

Samuel Clarke
1675–1729

A DISCOURSE CONCERNING THE BEING AND ATTRIBUTES OF GOD, THE OBLIGATIONS OF NATURAL RELIGION, AND THE TRUTH AND CERTAINTY OF THE CHRISTIAN REVELATION

1706

[Clarke supposed that he was orthodox enough—at least, he attacked the deists. Yet his own views make possible the bland deism of Shaftesbury whereby the universe becomes one great Newtonian harmony, with moral law operating as demonstrably and regularly as physical law. Gone is the willful and capricious God of Miltonic wrath; in his stead is a benevolent and imperturbable mechanic (a little chilly, possibly, and remote) who guarantees that whatever is, is right.]

THAT there are differences of things, and different relations, respects, or proportions of some things towards others, is as evident and undeniable as that one magnitude or number is greater, equal to, or smaller than another. That from these different relations of different things there necessarily arises an agreement or disagreement of some things with others, or a fitness or unfitness of the application of different things or different relations one to another, is likewise as plain as that there is any such thing as proportion or disproportion in geometry and arithmetic, or uniformity or deformity in comparing together the respective figures of bodies. Further, that there is a fitness or suitableness of certain circumstances to certain persons, and an unsuitableness of others, founded in the nature of things and the qualifications of persons antecedent to all positive appointment whatsoever; also that from the different relations of different persons to one another, there necessarily arises a fitness or unfitness of certain manners of behavior of some persons towards others, is as manifest as that the properties which flow from the essences of different mathematical figures have different congruities or incongruities between themselves, or that, in mechanics, certain weights or powers have very different forces and different effects upon one another according to their different distances or different positions and situations in respect of each other. For instance: that God is infinitely superior to men is as clear as that infinity is larger than a point, or eternity longer than a moment. And 'tis as certainly fit that men should honor and worship, obey and imitate God, rather than on the contrary in all their actions endeavor to dishonor and disobey Him, as 'tis certainly true that they have an entire dependence on Him, and He on the contrary can in no respect receive any advantage from them; and not only so, but also that His will is as certainly and unalterably just and equitable in giving His commands, as His power is irresistible in requiring submission to it. Again: 'tis a thing absolutely and necessarily fitter in itself that the supreme Author and Creator of the universe should govern, order, and direct all things to certain and constant and regular ends, than that everything should be permitted to go on at adventures and produce uncertain effects merely by chance and in the utmost confusion, without any determinate view or design at all. 'Tis a thing manifestly fitter in itself that the all-powerful Governor of the world should always do what is best in the whole, and what tends most to the universal good of the whole creation, than that he should make the whole continually miserable; or that, to satisfy the unreasonable desires of any particular depraved natures, he should at any time suffer the order of the whole to be altered and perverted. Lastly, 'tis a thing evidently and infinitely more fit that any one particular innocent and good being should by the supreme Ruler and Disposer of all things be placed and preserved in an easy and happy estate, than that, without any fault or demerit of its own, it should be made extremely, and remedilessly, and endlessly miserable. In like manner, in men's dealing and conversing one with another, 'tis undeniably more fit, absolutely and in the nature of the thing itself, that all men should endeavor to promote the universal good and welfare of all, than that all men should be continually contriving the ruin and destruction of all. . . .

[VOL. II, proposition i. Ed. of 1725]

Anthony Ashley Cooper, Third Earl of Shaftesbury

1671–1713

SHAFTESBURY believed that to philosophize is "but to carry good breeding a step higher." However well-bred his thought and rhetoric may be, Shaftesbury has far more than simply literary import. He illuminates the philosophy, poetry, religion, ethics, and esthetics of the century, and has had a pervasive influence on English and Continental thought, notably in ethics and esthetics. His suggestion that ridicule is a test of truth is not so much levity as a plea for toleration. His imperturbable good humor, a genteel Stoicism then in fashion, expands into a philosophy of benevolism. Shaftesbury presumes that God is a great humanitarian, that he made the world in a kindly mood, that our natural impulses are trustworthy, and that these impulses are unselfish. "Harmony" is the focus of his thought. The principle of utility follows: the greatest good for the greatest number is not merely benevolence, but the very basis of society—"to have the natural, kindly, or generous affections strong and powerful towards the good of the public is to have the chief means and power of *self*-enjoyment." Furthermore, the good is synonymous with the beautiful; therefore, morality is a matter of good taste. Ethics and religion and esthetics all depend upon cultivating the proper feelings—the natural feelings, for nature is a moral force. In this way Shaftesbury arrives at the very opposite pole from John Milton and the severity of the seventeenth century with its God of justice and its deep conviction of original sin. Sentiment has replaced strenuousness; to be good, holy, or tasteful, one need simply relax, politely, of course. Associated with this admiration for the "natural" is a pantheistic (really a neo-Platonic) sense that nature is divine and alive and organic. The "hymn" of Theocles in the *Characteristics* is a kind of esthetic noble savagery. Enthusiasm for revealed religion now seemed fanaticism; but enthusiasm for nature was a warrant of good breeding. The Miltonic God of judgment looks ill-bred and narrow-minded indeed when compared with this benevolent creative energy pulsing through the universe. Inconsistently enough, Shaftesbury thinks of this cosmic, vital rhythm as behaving not only like a living organism, but also like one of the mechanical or mathematical laws formulated by Isaac Newton. Shaftesbury himself

nature is a moral force [handwritten marginal note]

is quite invulnerable to all polite refutation. He even patronizes God: religion, he remarks, is to be treated with perfect good humor.

BIOGRAPHICAL NOTES

The grandson of the Whig leader of Dryden's *Absalom and Achitophel*. Educated privately under the tutelage of John Locke; conversed easily in Greek and Latin. Entered Winchester School (1683); then made the grand tour of the Continent (1686–89), followed by a period of study at home (1689–94). Entered Parliament (1695), but retired because of ill health (1698). Edited Whichcote's sermons (1698). Succeeded to the family title (1699); health still infirm. *An Inquiry Concerning Virtue* (1699). *A Letter Concerning Enthusiasm* (1708). *The Moralists* and *Sensus Communis, An Essay upon the Freedom of Wit and Humor* (1709). *Soliloquy, or Advice to an Author* (1710). *Characteristics of Men, Manners, Opinions, and Times* (1711), a collection of the above essays and the *Miscellanies*. Traveled in Italy because of ill health.

BIBLIOGRAPHY: Robertson, J. M., ed., *Characteristics*, 2 vols., 1900. Brett, R. L., *The Third Earl of Shaftesbury*, 1951. Rand, Benjamin, *Life, Letters, and Philosophical Regimen of Shaftesbury*, 1900. Schlegel, Dorothy B., *Shaftesbury and the French Deists*, 1956.

CHARACTERISTICS

1711

AN INQUIRY CONCERNING VIRTUE OR MERIT

1699

BOOK I   PART III

SECTION I

The nature of virtue consisting (as has been explained) in a certain just disposition or proportionable affection of a rational creature towards the moral objects of right and wrong, nothing can possibly in such a creature exclude a principle of virtue, or render it ineffectual, except what

1. Either takes away the natural and just sense of right and wrong,

2. Or creates a wrong sense of it,

3. Or causes the right sense to be opposed by contrary affections.

On the other side, nothing can assist or advance the principle of virtue except what either in some manner nourishes and promotes a sense of right and wrong, or preserves it genuine and uncorrupt, or causes it when such to be obeyed, by subduing and subjecting the other affections to it.

We are to consider, therefore, how any of the above-mentioned opinions on the subject of a Deity may influence in these cases, or produce either of these three effects.

1. As to the first case, the taking away the natural sense of right and wrong.

It will not surely be understood that by this is meant the taking away the notion of what is good or ill in the species or society. For of the reality of such a good and ill, no rational creature can possibly be insensible. Every one discerns and owns a public interest, and is conscious of what affects his fellowship or community. When we say, therefore, of a creature that he has wholly lost the sense of right and wrong, we suppose that being able to discern the good and ill of his species, he has at the same time no concern for either, nor any sense of excellency or baseness in any moral action relating to one or the other. So that except merely with respect to a private and narrowly confined self-good, 'tis supposed there is in such a creature no liking or dislike of manners; no admiration or love of anything as morally good, nor hatred of anything as morally ill, be it ever so unnatural or deformed.

There is in reality no rational creature whatsoever who knows not that when he voluntarily offends or does harm to anyone, he cannot fail to create an apprehension and fear of like harm, and consequently a resentment and animosity in every creature who observes him. So that the offender must needs be conscious of being liable to such treatment from everyone as if he had in some degree offended all.

Thus offense and injury are always known as punishable by everyone; and equal behavior (which is therefore called merit) as rewardable and well deserving from everyone. Of this even the wickedest creature living must have a sense. So that if there be any further meaning in this sense of right and wrong, if in reality there be any sense of this kind which an absolute wicked creature has not, it must consist in a real antipathy or aversion to injustice or wrong, and in a real affection or love towards equity and right for its own sake, and on the account of its own natural beauty and worth.

'Tis impossible to suppose a mere sensible creature originally so ill constituted and unnatural as that, from the moment he comes to be tried by sensible objects, he should have no one good passion towards his kind, no foundation either of pity, love, kindness, or social affection. 'Tis full as impossible to conceive that a rational creature coming first to be tried by rational objects, and receiving into his mind the images or representations of justice, generosity, gratitude, or other virtue, should have no liking of these or dislike of their contraries, but be found absolutely indifferent towards whatsoever is presented to him of this sort. A soul, indeed, may as well be without sense as without admiration in the things of which it has any knowledge. Coming therefore to a capacity of seeing and admiring in this new way, it must needs find a beauty and a deformity as well in actions, minds, and tempers, as in figures, sounds, or colors. If there be no real amiableness or deformity in moral acts, there is at least an imaginary one of full force. Though perhaps the thing itself should not be allowed in Nature, the imagination or fancy of it must be allowed to be from Nature alone. Nor can anything besides art and strong endeavor, with long practice and meditation, overcome such a natural prevention or prepossession of the mind in favor of this moral distinction.

Sense of right and wrong therefore being as natural to us as natural affection itself, and being a first principle in our constitution and make, there is no speculative opinion, persuasion, or belief, which is capable immediately or directly to exclude or destroy it. That which is of original and pure nature, nothing beside contrary habit and custom (a second nature) is able to displace. And this affection being an original one of earliest rise in the soul or affectionate part, nothing beside contrary affection, by frequent check and control, can operate upon it, so as either to diminish it in part or destroy it in the whole.

'Tis evident in what relates to the frame and order of our bodies, that no particular odd mien or gesture, which is either natural to us and consequent to our make, or accidental and by habit acquired, can possibly be overcome by our immediate disapproba-tion, or the contrary bent of our will ever so strongly set against it. Such a change cannot be effected without extraordinary means, and the intervention of art and method, a strict attention, and repeated check. And even thus, Nature we find is hardly mastered, but lies sullen, and ready to revolt on the first occasion. Much

A disapproval

more is this the mind's case in respect of that natural affection and anticipating fancy which makes the sense of right and wrong. 'Tis impossible that this can instantly, or without much force and violence, be effaced, or struck out of the natural temper, even by means of the most extravagant belief or opinion in the world.

Neither theism therefore, nor atheism, nor daemonism, nor any religious or irreligious belief of any kind being able to operate immediately or directly in this case, but indirectly, by the intervention of opposite or of favorable affections casually excited by any such belief, we may consider of this effect in our last case, where we come to examine the agreement or disagreement of other affections with this natural and moral one which relates to right and wrong.

SECTION II

2. As to the second case, viz. the wrong sense or false imagination of right and wrong.

This can proceed only from the force of custom and education in opposition to Nature, as may be noted in those countries where, according to custom or politic institution, certain actions naturally foul and odious are repeatedly viewed with applause, and honor ascribed to them. For thus 'tis possible that a man, forcing himself, may eat the flesh of his enemies, not only against his stomach, but against his nature, and think it nevertheless both right and honorable, as supposing it to be of considerable service to his community, and capable of advancing the name and spreading the terror of his nation.

But to speak of the opinions relating to a Deity, and what effect they may have in this place. As to atheism, it does not seem that it can directly have any effect at all towards the setting up a false species of right or wrong. For notwithstanding a man may through custom, or by licentiousness of practice, favored by atheism, come in time to lose much of his natural moral sense, yet it does not seem that atheism should of itself be the cause of any estimation or valuing of anything as fair, noble, and deserving, which was the contrary. It can never, for instance, make it be thought that the being able to eat man's flesh, or commit bestiality, is good and excellent in itself. But this is certain that by means of *corrupt religion* or *superstition*, many things the most horridly unnatural and inhuman come to be received as excellent, good, and laudable in themselves.

like Marx's idea

Nor is this a wonder. For wherever anything, in its nature odious and abominable, is by religion advanced, as the supposed will or pleasure of a supreme Deity, if in the eye of the believer it appears not indeed in any respect the less ill or odious on this account, then must the Deity of necessity bear the blame, and be considered as a being naturally ill and odious, however courted and solicited through mistrust and fear. But this is what religion, in the main, forbids us to imagine. It everywhere prescribes esteem and honor in company with worship and adoration. Whensoever therefore it teaches the love and admiration of a Deity who has any apparent character of ill, it teaches at the same time a love and admiration of that ill, and causes that to be taken for good and amiable which is in itself horrid and detestable.

Religion can be a brain-washer

For instance, if Jupiter be he who is adored and reverenced, and if his history represents him amorously inclined, and permitting his desires of this kind to wander in the loosest manner, 'tis certain that his worshipers, believing this history to be literally and strictly true, must of course be taught a greater love of amorous and wanton acts. If there be a religion which teaches the adoration and love of a God whose character it is to be captious and of high resentment, subject to wrath and anger, furious, revengeful, and revenging himself, when offended, on others than those who gave the offense; and if there be added to the character of this God a fraudulent disposition, encouraging deceit and treachery amongst men, favorable to a few, though for slight causes, and cruel to the rest, 'tis evident that such a religion as this being strongly enforced must of necessity raise even an approbation and respect towards the vices of this kind, and breed a suitable disposition, a capricious, partial, revengeful, and deceitful temper. For even irregularities and enormities of a heinous kind must in many cases appear illustrious to one who considers them in a being admired and contemplated with the highest honor and veneration.

This indeed must be allowed, that if in the cult or worship of such a Deity there be nothing beyond common form, nothing beside what proceeds from mere example, custom, constraint, or fear; if there be, at the bottom, no real heartiness, no esteem or love implied, the worshiper perhaps may not be much misled as to his notion of right and wrong. If in following the precepts of his supposed God, or doing what he esteems necessary towards the satisfying of such his Deity, he is compelled only by fear, and, contrary to his inclination, performs an act which he secretly detests as barbarous and unnatural, then has he an apprehension or sense still of right and wrong, and, according to what has been already observed, is sensible of ill in the character of his God, however cautious he may be of pronouncing anything on this subject, or so thinking of it as to frame any formal or direct opinion in the case. But if by insensible degrees, as he proceeds in his religious faith and devout exercise, he comes to be more and more reconciled to the malignity, arbitrariness, partiality, or revengefulness of his believed Deity, his reconciliation with these qualities themselves will soon grow in proportion, and the most cruel, unjust, and barbarous acts will, by the power of this example, be often considered by him not only as just and lawful, but as divine and worthy of imitation.

For whoever thinks there is a God, and pretends formally to believe that he is just and good, must suppose that there is independently such a thing as justice and injustice, truth and falsehood, right and wrong, according to which he pronounces that God is just, righteous, and true. If the mere will, decree, or law of God be said absolutely to constitute right and wrong, then are these latter words of no significancy at all. For thus, if each part of a contradiction were affirmed for truth by the Supreme Power, they would consequently become true. Thus if one person were decreed to suffer for another's fault, the sentence would be just and equitable. And thus, in the same manner, if arbitrarily and without reason some beings were destined to endure perpetual ill, and others as constantly to enjoy good, this also would pass under the same denomination. But to say of anything that it is just or unjust on such a foundation as this, is to say nothing, or to speak without a meaning.

And thus it appears that where a real devotion and hearty worship is paid to a Supreme Being who in his history or character is represented otherwise than as really and truly just and good, there must ensue a loss of rectitude, a disturbance of thought, and a corruption of temper and manners in the believer. His honesty will of necessity be supplanted by his zeal, whilst he is thus unnaturally influenced, and rendered thus immorally devout.

To this we need only add that as the ill character of a God does injury to the affections of men, and disturbs and impairs the natural sense of right and wrong, so, on the other hand, nothing can more highly contribute to the fixing of right apprehensions, and a sound judgment or sense of right and wrong, than to believe a God who is ever and on all accounts represented such as to be actually a true model and example of the most exact justice and highest goodness and worth. Such a view of divine providence and bounty extended to all, and expressed in a constant good affection towards the whole, must of necessity engage us, within our compass and sphere, to act by a like principle and affection. And having once the good of our species or public in view, as our end or aim, 'tis impossible we should be misguided by any means to a false apprehension or sense of right or wrong.

As to this second case therefore, religion (according as the kind may prove) is capable of doing great good or harm, and atheism nothing positive in either way. For however it may be indirectly an occasion of men's losing a good and sufficient sense of right and wrong, it will not, *as atheism merely*, be the occasion of setting up a false species of it, which only false religion or fantastical opinion, derived commonly from superstition and credulity, is able to effect.

SECTION III

Now as to the last case, the opposition made by other affections to the natural sense of right and wrong.

'Tis evident that a creature having this sort of sense or good affection in any degree must necessarily act according to it, if it happens not to be opposed, either by some settled sedate affection towards a conceived private good, or by some sudden, strong, and forcible passion, as of lust or anger, which may not only subdue the sense of right and wrong, but the very sense of private good itself, and overrule even the most familiar and received opinion of what is conducing to self-interest.

But it is not our business in this place to examine the several means or methods by which this corruption is introduced or increased. We are to consider only how the opinions concerning a Deity can influence one way or another.

That it is possible for a creature capable of using reflection to have a liking or dislike of moral actions, and consequently a sense of right and wrong, before such time as he may have any settled notion of a God, is what will hardly be questioned; it being a thing not expected, or any way possible, that a creature such as man, arising from his childhood slowly and gradually to several degrees of reason and reflection, should at the very first be taken up with those speculations or more refined sort of reflections, about the subject of God's existence.

Let us suppose a creature who, wanting reason and being unable to reflect, has notwithstanding many good qualities and affections, as love to his kind, courage, gratitude, or pity. 'Tis certain that if you give to this creature a reflecting faculty, it will at the same instant approve of gratitude, kindness, and pity; be taken with any show or representation of the social passion, and think nothing more amiable than this, or more odious than the contrary. And this is *to be capable of virtue*, and *to have a sense of right and wrong*.

Before the time, therefore, that a creature can have any plain or positive notion one way or other concerning the subject of a God, he may be supposed to have an apprehension or sense of right and wrong, and be possessed of virtue and vice in different degrees, as we know by experience of those who, having lived in such places and in such a manner as never to have entered into any serious thoughts of religion, are nevertheless very different among themselves, as to their characters of honesty and worth: some being naturally modest, kind, friendly, and consequently lovers of kind and friendly actions; others proud, harsh, cruel, and consequently inclined to admire rather the acts of violence and mere power.

Now as to the belief of a Deity, and how men are influenced by it, we may consider, in the first place, on what account men yield obedience, and act in conformity to such a supreme Being. It must be either in the way of his power, as presupposing some disadvantage or benefit to accrue from him; or in the way of his excellency and worth, as thinking it the perfection of nature to imitate and resemble him.

If (as in the first case) there be a belief or conception of a Deity who is considered only as powerful over his creature, and enforcing obedience to his absolute will by particular rewards and punishments; and if on this account, through hope merely of reward, or fear of punishment, the creature be incited to do the good he hates, or restrained from doing the ill to which he is not otherwise in the least degree averse, there is in this case (as has been already shown) no virtue or goodness whatsoever. The creature, notwithstanding his good conduct, is intrinsically of as little worth as if he acted in his natural way, when under no dread or terror of any sort.

There is no more of rectitude, piety, or sanctity in a creature thus reformed, than there is meekness or gentleness in a tiger strongly chained, or innocence and sobriety in a monkey under the discipline of the whip. For however orderly and well those animals, or man himself upon like terms, may be induced to act, whilst the will is neither gained nor the inclination wrought upon, but awe alone prevails and forces obedience, the obedience is servile, and all which is done through it merely servile. The greater degree of such a submission or obedience is only the greater servility, whatever may be the object. For whether such a creature has a good master or an ill one, he is neither more nor less servile in his own nature. Be the master or superior ever so perfect or excellent, yet the greater submission caused in this case, through this sole principle or motive, is only the lower and more abject servitude, and implies the greater wretchedness and meanness in the creature, who has those passions of self-love so predominant, and is in his temper so vicious and defective as has been explained.

As to the second case. If there be a belief or conception of a Deity who is considered as worthy and good, and admired and reverenced as such, being understood to have, besides mere power and knowledge, the highest excellence of nature, such as renders him justly amiable to all; and if in the manner this Sovereign and mighty Being is represented, or as he is historically described, there appears in him a high and eminent regard to what is good and excellent, a concern for the good of all, and an affection of benevolence and love towards *the whole*, such an example must undoubtedly serve (as above explained) to raise and increase the affection towards virtue, and help to submit and subdue all other affections to that alone.

Nor is this good effected by example merely. For where the theistical belief is entire and perfect, there must be a steady opinion of the superintendency of a supreme Being, a witness and spectator of human life, and conscious of whatsoever is felt or acted in the universe; so that in the perfectest recess or deepest solitude there must be One still presumed remaining with us, whose presence singly must be of more moment than that of the most august assembly on earth. In such a presence, 'tis evident that as the shame of guilty actions must be the greatest of any, so must the honor be of welldoing, even under the unjust censure of a world. And in this case 'tis very apparent how conducing a perfect theism must be to virtue, and how great deficiency there is in atheism.

What the fear of future punishment and hope of future reward, added to this belief, may further contribute towards virtue, we come now to consider more particularly. So much in the meanwhile may be gathered from what has been said above: that neither this fear nor hope can possibly be of the kind called good affections, such as are acknowledged the springs and sources of all actions truly good. Nor can this fear or hope, as above intimated, consist in reality with virtue or goodness, if it either stands as essential to any moral performance, or as a considerable motive to any act, of which some better affection ought alone to have been a sufficient cause.

It may be considered withal that in this religious sort of discipline, the principle of self-love, which is naturally so prevailing in us, being no way moderated or restrained, but rather improved and made stronger every day by the exercise of the passions in a subject of more extended self-interest, there may be reason to apprehend lest the temper of this kind should extend itself in general through all the parts of life. For if the habit be such as to occasion, in every particular, a stricter attention to self-good and private interest, it must insensibly diminish the affections towards public good or the interest of society, and introduce a certain narrowness of spirit, which (as some pretend) is peculiarly observable in the devout persons and zealots of almost every religious persuasion. . . . .

Now as to atheism; though it be plainly deficient and without remedy, in the case of ill judgment on the happiness of virtue, yet it is not, indeed, of necessity the cause of any such ill judgment. For without an absolute assent to any hypothesis of theism, the advantages of virtue may possibly be seen and owned, and a high opinion of it established in the mind. However, it must be confessed that the natural tendency of atheism is very different.

'Tis in a manner impossible to have any great opinion of the happiness of virtue without conceiving high thoughts of the satisfaction resulting from the generous admiration and love of it; and nothing beside the experience of such a love is likely to make this satisfaction credited. The chief ground and support therefore of this opinion of happiness in virtue must arise from the powerful feeling of this generous moral affection, and the knowledge of its power and strength. But this is certain, that it can be no great strengthening to the moral affection, no great support to the pure love of goodness and virtue, to suppose there is neither goodness nor beauty in the *Whole* itself; nor any example or precedent of good affection in any superior Being. Such a belief must tend rather to the weaning the affections from anything amiable or self-worthy, and to the suppressing the very habit and familiar custom of admiring natural beauties, or whatever in the order of things is according to just design, harmony, and proportion. For how little disposed must a person be to love or admire anything as *orderly* in the universe who thinks the universe itself a pattern of *disorder?* How unapt to reverence or respect any particular subordinate beauty of *a part,* when even *the Whole* itself is thought to want perfection, and to be only a vast and infinite deformity?

Nothing indeed can be more melancholy than the thought of living in a distracted universe, from whence many ills may be suspected, and where there is nothing good or lovely which presents itself, nothing which can satisfy in contemplation, or raise any passion besides that of contempt, hatred, or dislike. Such an opinion as this may by degrees embitter the temper, and not only make the love of virtue to be less felt, but help to impair and ruin the very principle of virtue, viz. natural and kind affection.

Upon the whole, whoever has a firm belief of a God whom he does not merely call good, but of whom in reality he believes nothing beside real good, nothing beside what is truly suitable to the exactest character of benignity and goodness; such a person believing rewards or retributions in another life, must believe them annexed to real goodness and merit, real villainy and baseness, and not to any accidental qualities or circumstances, in which respect they cannot properly be styled rewards or punishments, but *capricious distributions of happiness or unhappiness to creatures.* These are the only terms on which the belief of a world to come can happily influence the believer. And on these terms, and by virtue of this belief, man perhaps may retain his virtue and integrity, even under the hardest thoughts of human nature, when either by any ill circumstance or untoward doctrine he is brought to that unfortunate opinion of virtue's being naturally an enemy to happiness in life.

This, however, is an opinion which cannot be supposed consistent with sound theism. For whatever be decided as to a future life, or the rewards and punishments of hereafter, he who, as a sound theist, believes a reigning mind sovereign in Nature, and ruling all things with the highest perfection of goodness, as well as of wisdom and power, must necessarily believe virtue to be naturally good and advantageous. For what could more strongly imply an unjust ordinance, a blot and imperfection in the general constitution of things, than to suppose virtue the natural ill, and vice the natural good of any creature?

And now, last of all, there remains for us to consider a yet further advantage to virtue, in the theistical belief above the atheistical. The proposition may at first sight appear overrefined, and of a sort which is esteemed too nicely philosophical. But after what has been already examined, the subject perhaps may be more easily explained.

There is no creature, according to what has been already proved, who must not of necessity be ill in some degree, by having any affection or aversion in a stronger degree than is suitable to his own private good, or that of the system to which he is joined. For in either case the affection is ill and vicious. Now if a rational creature has that degree of aversion which is requisite to arm him against any particular misfortune, and alarm him against the approach of any calamity, this is regular and well. But if after the misfortune is happened, his aversion continues still, and his passion rather grows upon him, whilst he rages at the accident and exclaims against his private fortune or lot, this will be acknowledged both vicious in present and for the future, as it affects the temper, and disturbs that easy course of the affections on which virtue and goodness so much depend. On the other side, the patient enduring of the calamity, and the bearing up of the mind under it, must be acknowledged immediately virtuous and preservative of virtue. Now, according to the hypothesis of those who exclude a general mind, it must be confessed there can nothing happen in the course of things to deserve either our admiration and love or our anger and abhorrence. However, as there can be no satisfaction at the best in thinking upon what atoms and chance produce, so upon disastrous occasions, and under the circumstances of a calamitous and hard fortune, 'tis scarce possible to prevent a natural kind of abhorrence and spleen, which will be entertained and kept alive by the imagination of so perverse an order of things. But in another hypothesis (that of perfect theism) it is understood *that whatever*

the order of the world produces, is in the main both just and good.
Therefore in the course of things in this world, whatever hardship
of events may seem to force from any rational creature a hard
censure of his private condition or lot, he may by reflection nevertheless come to have patience, and to acquiesce in it. Nor is this
all. He may go further still in this reconciliation, and from the
same principle may make the lot itself an object of his good affection, whilst he strives to maintain this generous fealty, and
stands so well disposed towards the laws and government of his
higher country. . . .

A LETTER CONCERNING ENTHUSIASM
1708

SECTION II

  If the knowing well how to expose any infirmity or vice were
a sufficient security for the virtue which is contrary, how excellent
an age might we be presumed to live in! Never was there in our
nation a time known when folly and extravagance of every kind
were more sharply inspected, or more wittily ridiculed. And one
might hope at least from this good symptom that our age was in
no declining state; since whatever our distempers are, we stand
so well affected to our remedies. To bear the being told of faults
is in private persons the best token of amendment. 'Tis seldom that
a public is thus disposed. For where jealousy of state, or the ill lives
of the great people, or any other cause is powerful enough to restrain the freedom of censure in any part, it in effect destroys the
benefit of it in the whole. There can be no impartial and free censure
of manners where any peculiar custom or national opinion is set
apart, and not only exempted from criticism, but even flattered
with the highest art. 'Tis only in a free nation, such as ours, that
imposture has no privilege; and that neither the credit of a court,
the power of a nobility, nor the awfulness of a church can give
her protection, or hinder her from being arraigned in every shape
and appearance. 'Tis true, this liberty may seem to run too far.
We may perhaps be said to make ill use of it. So everyone will say
when he himself is touched and his opinion freely examined. But

who shall be judge of what may be freely examined and what may not? Where liberty may be used and where it may not? What remedy shall we prescribe to this in general? Can there be a better than from that liberty itself which is complained of? If men are vicious, petulant, or abusive, the magistrate may correct them: but if they reason ill, 'tis reason still must teach them to do better. Justness of thought and style, refinement in manners, good breeding, and politeness of every kind can come only from the trial and experience of what is best. Let but the search go freely on, and the right measure of everything will soon be found. Whatever humor has got the start, if it be unnatural it cannot hold; and the ridicule, if ill placed at first, will certainly fall at last where it deserves.

I have often wondered to see men of sense so mightily alarmed at the approach of anything like ridicule on certain subjects; as if they mistrusted their own judgment. For what ridicule can lie against reason? Or how can anyone of the least justness of thought endure a ridicule wrong placed? Nothing is more ridiculous than this itself. The vulgar, indeed, may swallow any sordid jest, any mere drollery or buffoonery; but it must be a finer and truer wit which takes with the men of sense and breeding. How comes it to pass, then, that we appear such cowards in reasoning, and are so afraid to stand the test of ridicule? Oh! say we, the subjects are too grave.—Perhaps so: but let us see first whether they are really grave or no; for in the manner we may conceive them they may peradventure be very grave and weighty in our imagination, but very ridiculous and impertinent in their own nature. *Gravity* is of the very essence of imposture. It does not only make us mistake other things, but is apt perpetually almost to mistake itself. For even in common behavior, how hard is it for the grave character to keep long out of the limits of the formal one! We can never be too grave if we can be assured we are really what we suppose. And we can never too much honor or revere anything for grave if we are assured the thing is grave, as we apprehend it. The main point is to know always *true* gravity from *the false:* and this can only be by carrying the rule constantly with us, and freely applying it not only to the things about us, but to ourselves. For if unhappily we lose the measure in ourselves, we shall soon lose it in everything besides. Now what rule or measure is there in the world, except in the considering of the real temper of things, to find which are truly serious and which ridiculous? And how can this be done, unless by applying the ridicule, to see whether it will bear? But if we fear to apply this rule in anything, what security can we have against the imposture of formality in all things? We have allowed ourselves to be *formalists* in one point; and the same formality may rule us as it pleases in all other.

'Tis not in every disposition that we are capacitated to judge of things. We must beforehand judge of our own temper, and accordingly of other things which fall under our judgment. But we must never more pretend to judge of things, or of our own temper in judging them, when we have given up our preliminary right of judgment, and under a presumption of gravity have allowed ourselves to be most ridiculous and to admire profoundly the most ridiculous things in nature, at least for aught we know. For having resolved never to try, we can never be sure.

> Ridiculum acri
> Fortius et melius magnas plerumque secat res.[1]

This, my lord,[2] I may safely aver, is so true in itself, and so well known for truth by the cunning formalists of the age, that they can better bear to have their impostures railed at, with all the bitterness and vehemence imaginable, than to have them touched ever so gently in this other way. They know very well that as modes and fashions, so opinions, though ever so ridiculous, are kept up by solemnity; and that those formal notions which grew up probably in an ill mood and have been conceived in sober sadness are never to be removed but in a sober kind of cheerfulness, and by a more easy and pleasant way of thought. There is a *melancholy* which accompanies all enthusiasm. Be it love or religion (for there are enthusiasms in both) nothing can put a stop to the growing mischief of either till the melancholy be removed and the mind at liberty to hear what can be said against the ridiculousness of an extreme in either way.

It was heretofore the wisdom of some wise nations to let people be fools as much as they pleased, and never to punish seriously what deserved only to be laughed at, and was, after all, best cured by that innocent remedy. There are certain humors in mankind which

---

1 Horace *Satires* I. x. 14, 15: "A jest often decides weighty matters better and more forcibly than can asperity." [Robertson]

2 Lord Somers.

of necessity must have vent. The human mind and body are both of them naturally subject to commotions; and as there are strange ferments in the blood, which in many bodies occasion an extraordinary discharge, so in reason, too, there are heterogeneous particles which must be thrown off by fermentation. Should physicians endeavor absolutely to allay those ferments of the body, and strike in the humors which discover themselves in such eruptions, they might, instead of making a cure, bid fair perhaps to raise a plague, and turn a spring ague or an autumn surfeit into an epidemical malignant fever. They are certainly as ill physicians in the body politic who would needs be tampering with these mental eruptions, and, under the specious pretense of healing this itch of superstition and saving souls from the contagion of enthusiasm, should set all nature in an uproar, and turn a few innocent carbuncles into an inflammation and mortal gangrene.

We read in history that Pan, when he accompanied Bacchus in an expedition to the Indies, found means to strike a terror through a host of enemies by the help of a small company whose clamors he managed to good advantage among the echoing rocks and caverns of a woody vale. The hoarse bellowing of the caves, joined to the hideous aspect of such dark and desert places, raised such a horror in the enemy that in this state their imagination helped them to hear voices, and doubtless to see forms too, which were more than human; whilst the uncertainty of what they feared made their fear yet greater, and spread it faster by implicit looks than any narration could convey it. And this was what in aftertimes men called a _panic_. The story indeed gives a good hint of the nature of this passion, which can hardly be without some mixture of enthusiasm and horrors of a superstitious kind.

One may with good reason call every passion panic which is raised in a multitude and conveyed by aspect or, as it were, by contact of sympathy. Thus popular fury may be called panic when the rage of the people, as we have sometimes known, has put them beyond themselves; especially where religion has had to do. And in this state their very looks are infectious. The fury flies from face to face; and the disease is no sooner seen than caught. They who in a better situation of mind have beheld a multitude under the power of this passion, have owned that they saw in the countenances of men something more ghastly and terrible than at other times is expressed on the most passionate occasions. Such force has society in ill as well as in good passions: and so much stronger any affection is for being social and communicative.

Thus, my lord, there are many panics in mankind besides merely that of fear. And thus is religion also panic when enthusiasm of any kind gets up, as oft, on melancholy occasions, it will. For vapors naturally rise; and in bad times especially, when the spirits of men are low, as either in public calamities, or during the unwholesomeness of air or diet, or when convulsions happen in nature, storms, earthquakes, or other amazing prodigies: at this season the panic must needs run high, and the magistrate of necessity give way to it. For to apply a serious remedy, and bring the sword or *fasces* as a cure, must make the case more melancholy and increase the very cause of the distemper. To forbid men's natural fears and to endeavor the overpowering them by other fears must needs be a most unnatural method. The magistrate, if he be any artist, should have a gentler hand; and instead of caustics, incisions, and amputations, should be using the softest balms; and with a kind sympathy entering into the concern of the people, and taking, as it were, their passion upon him should, when he has soothed and satisfied it, endeavor, by cheerful ways, to divert and heal it.

This was ancient policy: and hence (as a notable author [3] of our nation expresses it) 'tis necessary a people should have a *public leading* in religion. For to deny the magistrate a worship, or take away a national church, is as mere enthusiasm as the notion which sets up persecution. For why should there not be public walks as well as private gardens? Why not public libraries as well as private education and home tutors? But to prescribe bounds to fancy and speculation, to regulate men's apprehensions and religious beliefs or fears, to suppress by violence the natural passion of enthusiasm, or to endeavor to ascertain it, or reduce it to one species, or bring it under any one modification, is in truth no better sense, nor deserves a better character, than what the comedian declares of the like project in the affair of love—

Nihilo plus agas
Quam si des operam ut cum ratione insanias.[4]

Not only the visionaries and enthusiasts of all kind were tolerated, your lordship knows, by the ancients; but, on the other side,

[3] James Harrington, author of *The Commonwealth of Oceana* (1656).

[4] Terence *Eunuch* I. i: "You will manage it no better than if you undertook to be rationally insane." [Robertson]

(natural passion of enthusiasm)

philosophy had as free a course, and was permitted as a balance against superstition. And whilst some sects, such as the Pythagorean and latter Platonic, joined in with the superstition and enthusiasm of the times, the Epicurean, the Academic, and others were allowed to use all the force of wit and raillery against it. And thus matters were happily balanced: reason had fair play; learning and science flourished. Wonderful was the harmony and temper which arose from all these contrarieties. Thus superstition and enthusiasm were mildly treated, and, being let alone, they never raged to that degree as to occasion bloodshed, wars, persecutions, and devastation in the world. But a new sort of policy, which extends itself to another world and considers the future lives and happiness of men rather than the present, has made us leap the bounds of natural humanity; and out of a supernatural charity has taught us the way of plaguing one another most devoutly. It has raised an antipathy which no temporal interest could ever do, and entailed upon us a mutual hatred to all eternity. And now *uniformity in opinion* (a hopeful project!) is looked on as the only expedient against this evil. The *saving* of souls is now the heroic passion of exalted spirits, and is become in a manner the chief care of the magistrate, and the very end of government itself.

If magistracy should vouchsafe to interpose thus much in other sciences, I am afraid we should have as bad logic, as bad mathematics, and in every kind as bad philosophy, as we often have divinity in countries where a precise orthodoxy is settled by law. 'Tis a hard matter for a government to settle wit. If it does but keep us sober and honest, 'tis likely we shall have as much ability in our spiritual as in our temporal affairs; and if we can but be trusted, we shall have wit enough to save ourselves when no prejudice lies in the way. But if honesty and wit be insufficient for this *saving* work, 'tis in vain for the magistrate to meddle with it: since if he be ever so virtuous or wise, he may be as soon mistaken as another man. I am sure the only way to save men's sense or preserve wit at all in the world is to give liberty to wit. Now wit can never have its liberty where the *freedom of raillery* is taken away: for against serious extravagances and splenetic humors there is no other remedy than this.

We have indeed full power over all other modifications of spleen. We may treat other enthusiasms as we please. We may ridicule love, or gallantry, or knight-errantry to the utmost; and we find that in these latter days of wit the humor of this kind, which was once so prevalent, is pretty well declined. The crusades, the rescuing of holy lands, and such devout gallantries are in less request than formerly: but if something of this militant religion, something of this soul-rescuing spirit and saint-errantry prevails still, we need not wonder, when we consider in how solemn a manner we treat this distemper, and how preposterously we go about to cure enthusiasm.

I can hardly forbear fancying that if we had a sort of inquisition or formal court of judicature, with grave officers and judges, erected to restrain poetical licence, and in general to suppress that fancy and humor of versification, but in particular that most extravagant passion of love, as it is set out by poets, in its heathenish dress of Venuses and Cupids; if the poets, as ringleaders and teachers of this heresy, were, under grievous penalties, forbid to enchant the people by their vein of rhyming; and if the people, on the other side, were, under proportionable penalties, forbid to hearken to any such charm or lend their attention to any love tale, so much as in a play, a novel, or a ballad—we might perhaps see a new Arcadia arising out of this heavy persecution: old people and young would be seized with a versifying spirit; we should have field coventicles of lovers and poets; forests would be filled with romantic shepherds and shepherdesses, and rocks resound with echoes of hymns and praises offered to the powers of love. We might indeed have a fair chance, by this management, to bring back the whole train of heathen gods and set our cold northern island burning with as many altars to Venus and Apollo as were formerly in Cyprus, Delos, or any of those warmer Grecian climates.

SECTION IV

In short, my lord, the melancholy way of treating religion is that which, according to my apprehension, renders it so tragical, and is the occasion of its acting in reality such dismal tragedies in the world. And my notion is that, provided we treat religion with good manners, we can never use too much *good humor* or examine it with too much *freedom* and *familiarity*. For if it be genuine and sincere, it will not only stand the proof, but thrive and gain advantage from hence; if it be spurious, or mixed with any imposture, it will be detected and exposed.

The melancholy way in which we have been taught religion makes us unapt to think of it in good humor. 'Tis in adversity chiefly, or in ill health, under affliction, or disturbance of mind, or discomposure of temper, that we have recourse to it. Though in reality we are never so unfit to think of it as at such a heavy and dark hour. We can never be fit to contemplate anything above us when we are in no condition to look into ourselves and calmly examine the temper of our own mind and passions. For then it is we see wrath, and fury, and revenge, and terrors in the Deity; when we are full of disturbances and fears within, and have, by sufferance and anxiety, lost so much of the natural calm and easiness of our temper.

We must not only be in ordinary good humor, but in the best of humors, and in the sweetest, kindest disposition of our lives, to understand well what true goodness is, and what those attributes imply which we ascribe with such applause and honor to the Deity. We shall then be able to see best whether those forms of justice, those degrees of punishment, that temper of resentment, and those measures of offense and indignation, which we vulgarly suppose in God, are suitable to those original ideas of goodness, which the same Divine Being, or Nature under him, has implanted in us, and which we must necessarily presuppose, in order to give him praise or honor in any kind. This, my lord, is the best security against all superstition: to remember that there is nothing in God but what is godlike; and that he is either *not at all*, or *truly and perfectly good.* But when we are afraid to use our reason freely, even on that very question whether he really be or not, we then actually presume him bad, and flatly contradict that pretended character of goodness and greatness; whilst we discover this mistrust of his temper, and fear his anger and resentment, in the case of this freedom of inquiry.

We have a notable instance of this freedom in one of our sacred authors. As patient as Job is said to be, it cannot be denied that he makes bold enough with God and takes his providence roundly to task. His friends, indeed, plead hard with him, and use all arguments, right or wrong, to patch up objections, and set the affairs of providence upon an equal foot. They make a merit of saying all the good they can of God, at the very stretch of their reason, and sometimes quite beyond it. But this, in Job's opinion, is flattering God, accepting of God's person, and even mocking him. And no wonder. For what merit can there be in believing God, or his providence, upon frivolous and weak grounds? What virtue in assuming an opinion contrary to the appearance of things, and resolving to hear nothing which may be said against it? Excellent character of the God of truth! that he should be offended at us for having refused to put the lie upon our understandings, as much as in us lay, and be satisfied with us for having believed at a venture, and against our reason, what might have been the greatest falsehood in the world, for anything we could bring as a proof or evidence to the contrary!

It is impossible that any besides an ill-natured man can wish against the being of a God: for this is wishing against the public, and even against one's private good, too, if rightly understood. But if a man has not any such ill will to stifle his belief, he must have surely an unhappy opinion of God, and believe him not so good by far as he knows himself to be, if he imagines that an impartial use of his reason, in any matter of speculation whatsoever, can make him run any risk hereafter; and that a mean denial of his reason and an affectation of belief in any point too hard for his understanding can entitle him to any favor in another world. This is being *sycophants* in religion, mere parasites of devotion. 'Tis using God as the crafty beggars use those they address to when they are ignorant of their quality. The novices amongst them may innocently come out, perhaps, with a "Good sir," or a "Good forsooth"; but with the old stagers, no matter whom they meet in a coach, 'tis always "Good your honor!" or "Good your lordship!" or "Your ladyship!" For if there should be really a lord in the case, we should be undone (say they) for want of giving the title; but if the party should be no lord, there would be no offense; it would not be ill taken.

And thus it is in religion. We are highly concerned how to *beg right*, and think all depends upon hitting the title and making a good guess. 'Tis the most beggarly refuge imaginable, which is so mightily cried up, and stands as a great maxim with many able men, that they should strive to have faith, and believe to the utmost; because if, after all, there be nothing in the matter, there will be no harm in being thus deceived; but if there be anything, it will be fatal for them not to have believed to the full. But they are so far mistaken that, whilst they have this thought, 'tis certain they can never believe either to their satisfaction and happiness in this world, or with any advantage of recommendation to another. For besides that our reason, which knows the cheat, will never rest thoroughly satisfied on such a bottom, but turn us often adrift, and toss us in a sea of doubt and perplexity, we cannot but actually grow worse in our religion, and entertain a worse opinion still of a Supreme Deity whilst our belief is founded on so injurious a thought of him.

To love the public, to study universal good, and to promote the interest of the whole world, as far as lies within our power, is surely the height of goodness, and makes that temper which we call divine. . . .

THE MORALISTS

1709

PART II

SECTION IV

Philocles to Palemon

Theocles then proposed we should walk out, the evening being fine, and the free air suiting better (as he thought) with such discourses than a chamber.

Accordingly we took our evening walk in the fields, from whence the laborious hinds were now retiring. We fell naturally into the praises of a country life, and discoursed a while of husbandry and the nature of the soil. Our friends began to admire some of the plants which grew here to great perfection. And it being my fortune (as having acquired a little insight into the nature of simples) to say something they mightily approved upon this subject, Theocles immediately turning about to me, "O my ingenious friend!" said he, "whose reason in other respects must be allowed so clear and happy, how is it possible that, with such insight and accurate judgment in the particulars of natural beings and operations, you should no better judge of the structure of things in general and of the order and frame of Nature? Who better than yourself can show the structure of each plant and animal body, declare the office of every part and organ, and tell the uses, ends, and advantages to which they serve? How, therefore, should you prove so ill a naturalist in this whole, and understand so little the anatomy of the world and Nature, as not to discern the same relation of parts, the same consistency and uniformity in the universe!

"Some men perhaps there are of so confused a thought, and so irregularly formed within themselves, that 'tis no more than natural for them to find fault and imagine a thousand inconsistencies and defects in this wider constitution. 'Twas not, we may presume, the absolute aim or interest of the universal nature to render every private one infallible and without defect. 'Twas not its intention to leave us without some pattern of imperfection, such as we perceive in minds like these, perplexed with froward thought. *prever* But you, my friend, are master of a nobler mind. You are conscious of better order within, and can see workmanship and exactness in yourself and other innumerable parts of the creation. Can you answer it to yourself, allowing thus much not to allow all? Can you induce yourself ever to believe or think that where there are parts so variously united, and conspiring fitly within themselves, *the Whole* itself should have neither union nor coherence; and where inferior and private natures are often found so perfect, the universal one should want perfection, and be esteemed like whatsoever can be thought of, most monstrous, rude, and imperfect?

"Strange! that there should be in Nature the idea of an order and perfection which Nature herself wants! That beings which arise from Nature should be so perfect as to discover imperfection in her constitution, and be wise enough to correct that wisdom by which they were made!

"Nothing surely is more strongly imprinted on our minds, or more closely interwoven with our souls, than the idea or sense of *order* and *proportion*. Hence all the force of numbers and those powerful arts founded on their management and use. What a difference there is between *harmony* and *discord! cadency* and *convulsion!* What a difference between composed and orderly motion and that which is ungoverned and accidental! between the regular and uniform pile of some noble architect and a heap of sand or stones! between an organized body and a mist or cloud driven by the wind!

"Now, as this difference is immediately perceived by a plain internal sensation, so there is withal in reason this account of it; that whatever things have order, the same have unity of design, and concur in one, are parts constituent of *one whole* or are, in themselves, entire systems. Such is a tree, with all its branches; an animal, with all its members; an edifice, with all its exterior and interior ornaments. What else is even a tune or symphony, or any excellent piece of music, than a certain system of proportioned sounds?

"Now, in this which we call the *Universe*, whatever the perfection may be of any particular systems, or whatever single parts may have proportion, unity, or form within themselves; yet if they are not united all in general, in *one* system, but are, in respect of one another, as the driven sands, or clouds, or breaking waves; then there being no coherence in the whole, there can be inferred no order, no proportion, and consequently no project or design. But if none of these parts are independent, but all apparently united, then is the *Whole a system* complete, according to one *simple*, *consistent*, and *uniform Design*.

"Here then is our main subject insisted on: that neither man nor any other animal, though ever so complete a system of parts as to all within, can be allowed in the same manner complete as to all without, but must be considered as having a further relation abroad to the system of his kind. So even this system of his kind to the animal system, this to the world (our earth), and this again to the bigger world and to the universe.

"All things in this world are united. For as the branch is united with the tree, so is the tree as immediately with the earth, air, and water which feed it. As much as the fertile mold is fitted to the tree, as much as the strong and upright trunk of the oak or elm is fitted to the twining branches of the vine or ivy; so much are the very leaves, the seeds, and fruits of these trees fitted to the various animals; these again to one another and to the elements where they live, and to which they are, as appendices, in a manner fitted and joined, as either by wings for the air, fins for the water, feet for the earth, and by other correspondent inward parts of a more curious frame and texture. Thus in contemplating all on earth, we must of necessity view all in one, as holding to one common stock. Thus too in the system of the bigger world. See there the mutual dependency of things! the relation of one to another; of the sun to this inhabited earth, and of the earth and other

order
union } *Whole*
coherence

planets to the sun! the order, union, and coherence of *the Whole!* and know, my ingenious friend, that by this survey you will be obliged to own the *Universal System* and coherent scheme of things to be established on abundant proof, capable of convincing any fair and just contemplator of the works of Nature. For scarce would anyone, till he had well surveyed this universal scheme, believe a union thus evidently demonstrable, by such numerous and powerful instances of mutual correspondency and relation, from the minutest ranks and orders of beings to the remotest spheres.

"Now, in this mighty UNION if there be such relations of parts one to another as are not easily discovered, if on this account the end and use of things does not everywhere appear, there is no wonder, since 'tis no more indeed than what must happen of necessity; nor could Supreme Wisdom have otherwise ordered it. For in an infinity of things thus relative, a mind which sees not infinitely can see nothing fully. And since each particular has relation to all in general, it can know no perfect or true relation of anything in a world not perfectly and fully known.

"The same may be considered in any dissected animal, plant, or flower; where he who is no anatomist, nor versed in natural history, sees that the many parts have a relation to the whole, for thus much even a slight view affords; but he who like you, my friend, is curious in the works of Nature, and has been let into a knowledge of the animal and vegetable worlds, he alone can readily declare the just relation of all these parts to one another, and the several uses to which they serve.

"But if you would willingly enter further into this thought, and consider how much we ought not only to be satisfied with this our view of things, but even to admire its clearness, imagine only some person entirely a stranger to navigation, and ignorant of the nature of the sea or waters; how great his astonishment would be when finding himself on board some vessel, anchoring at sea, remote from all land prospect, whilst it was yet a calm, he viewed the ponderous machine firm and motionless in the midst of the smooth ocean, and considered its foundations beneath, together with its cordage, masts, and sails above. How easily would he see the whole one regular structure, all things depending on one another; the uses of the rooms below, the lodgments, and conveniences of men and stores? But being ignorant of the intent or design of all above, would he pronounce the masts and cordage to be useless and cumbersome, and for this reason condemn the frame and despise the architect? O my friend! let us not thus betray our ignorance; but consider where we are, and in what a universe. Think of the many parts of the vast machine in which we have so little insight, and of which it is impossible we should know the ends and uses, when, instead of seeing to the highest pendants, we see only some lower deck and are in this dark case of flesh confined even to the hold and meanest station of the vessel.

"Now having recognized this uniform consistent fabric, and owned the Universal System, we must of consequence acknowledge a *Universal Mind*, which no ingenious man can be tempted to disown, except through the imagination of disorder in the universe, its seat. For can it be supposed of anyone in the world that, being in some desert far from men and hearing there a perfect symphony of music, or seeing an exact pile of regular architecture arising gradually from the earth in all its orders and proportions, he should be persuaded that at the bottom there was no design accompanying this, no secret spring of thought, no active mind? Would he, because he saw no hand, deny the handiwork, and suppose that each of these complete and perfect systems were framed, and thus united in just symmetry and conspiring order, either by the accidental blowing of the winds or rolling of the sands?

"What is it, then, should so disturb our views of Nature as to destroy that unity of design and order of a Mind which otherwise would be so apparent? All we can see either of the heavens or earth demonstrates order and perfection; so as to afford the noblest subjects of contemplation to minds, like yours, enriched with sciences and learning. All is delightful, amiable, rejoicing, except with relation to man only, and his circumstances, which seem unequal. Here the calamity and ill arises, and hence the ruin of this goodly frame. All perishes on this account; and the whole order of the universe, elsewhere so firm, entire, and immovable, is here overthrown and lost by this one view, in which we refer all things to ourselves, submitting the interest of the whole to the good and interest of so small a part.

"But how is it you complain of the unequal state of man and of the few advantages allowed him above the beasts? What can a creature claim so little differing from them, or whose merit appears so little above them, except in wisdom and virtue, to which so few conform? Man may be virtuous, and by being so, is happy. His merit is reward. By virtue he deserves, and in virtue only can meet his happiness deserved. But if even virtue itself be unprovided for, and vice, more prosperous, be the better choice; if this (as you suppose) be in the nature of things, then is all order in reality inverted, and supreme wisdom lost; imperfection and irregularity being, after this manner, undoubtedly too apparent in the moral world.

"Have you, then, ere you pronounced this sentence, considered of the state of virtue and vice with respect to this life merely so as to say with assurance when, and how far, in what particulars, and how circumstantiated the one or the other is good or ill? You who are skilled in other fabrics and compositions, both of art and nature, have you considered of the fabric of the mind, the constitution of the soul, the connection and frame of all its passions and affections; to know accordingly the order and symmetry of the part, and how it either improves or suffers; what its force is when naturally preserved in its sound state, and what becomes of it when corrupted and abused? Till this, my friend, be well examined and understood, how shall we judge either of the force of virtue or power of vice? Or in what manner either of these may work to our happiness or undoing?

"Here, therefore, is that inquiry we should first make. But who is there can afford to make it as he ought? If happily we are born of a good nature; if a liberal education has formed in us a generous temper and disposition, well-regulated appetites, and worthy inclinations, 'tis well for us; and so indeed we esteem it. But who is there endeavors to give these to himself or to advance his portion of happiness in this kind? Who thinks of improving, or so much as of preserving, his share in a world where it must of necessity run so great a hazard, and where we know an honest nature is so easily corrupted? All other things relating to us are preserved with care, and have some art or economy belonging to them; this which is nearest related to us and on which our happiness depends, is alone committed to chance, and temper is the only thing ungoverned, whilst it governs all the rest.

"Thus we inquire concerning what is good and suitable to our appetites; but what appetites are good and suitable to us is no part of our examination. We inquire what is according to interest, policy, fashion, vogue; but it seems wholly strange and out of the way to inquire what is according to *Nature*. The balance of Europe, of trade, of power, is strictly sought after; while few have heard of the balance of their passions, or thought of holding these scales even. Few are acquainted with this province or knowing in these affairs. But were we more so, as this inquiry would make us, we should then see beauty and decorum here as well as elsewhere in Nature; and the order of the moral world would equal that of the natural. By this the *beauty of Virtue* would appear, and hence, as has been shown, *the supreme* and *sovereign Beauty*, the original of all which is good or amiable.

"But lest I should appear at last too like an *enthusiast*, I choose to express my sense, and conclude this philosophical sermon in the words of one of those ancient philologists, whom you are used to esteem. For Divinity itself, says he, is surely beauteous, and of all beauties the brightest; though not a beauteous body, but that from whence the beauty of bodies is derived; not a beauteous plain, but that from whence the plain looks beautiful. The river's beauty, the sea's, the heaven's, and heavenly constellations all flow from hence as from a source eternal and incorruptible. As beings partake of this, they are fair and flourishing, and happy; as they are lost to this, they are deformed, perished, and lost. . . ."

PART III

SECTION I

Philocles to Palemon

It was yet deep night (as I imagined) when I waked with the noise of people up in the house. I called to know the matter, and was told that Theocles had a little before parted with his friends, after which he went out to take his morning walk, but would return, they thought, pretty soon: for so he had left word, and that nobody in the mean time should disturb my rest.

This was disturbance sufficient when I heard it. I presently got up, and, finding it light enough to see the hill which was at a little distance from the house, I soon got thither, and at the foot of it overtook Theocles, to whom I complained of his unkindness. For I was not certainly (I told him) so effeminate and weak a friend as to deserve that he should treat me like a woman; nor had I shown such an aversion to his manners or conversation as to be thought fitter for the dull luxury of a soft bed and ease than for business, recreation, or study with an early friend. He had no other way, therefore, of making me amends than by allowing me henceforward to be a party with him in his serious thoughts, as he saw I was resolved to be in his hours and exercises of this sort.

"You have forgot then," said Theocles, "the assignation you had yesterday with the sylvan nymphs at this place and hour?" "No, truly," said I, "for, as you see, I am come punctually to the place appointed. But I never expected you should have come hither without me." "Nay then," said Theocles, "there is hope you may in time become a lover with me, for you already begin to show jealousy. How little did I think these nymphs could raise that passion in you!" "Truly," said I, "for the nymphs you mention, I know little of them as yet. My jealousy and love regard you only. I was afraid you had a mind to escape me; but now that I am again in possession of you, I want no nymph to make me happy here, unless it were perhaps to join forces against you, in the manner your beloved poet makes the nymph Ægle join with his two youths in forcing the god Silenus to sing to them."

"I dare trust your gallantry," replied Theocles, "that if you had such fair company as you speak of, you would otherwise bestow your time than in an adventure of philosophy. But do you expect I should imitate the poet's God you mentioned, and sing 'the rise of things from atoms, the birth of order from confusion, and the origin of union, harmony, and concord from the sole powers of chaos and blind chance'? [1] The song indeed was fitted to the God. For what could better suit his jolly character than such a drunken creation, which he loved often to celebrate by acting it to the life? But even this song was too harmonious for the night's debauch. Well has our poet made it of the morning, when the God was fresh; for hardly should we be brought ever to believe that such harmonious numbers could arise from a mere chaos of the mind. But we must hear our poet speaking in the mouth of some soberer demigod or hero. He then presents us with a different principle of things, and in a more proper order of precedency gives thought the upper hand. He makes mind originally to have governed body, not body mind; for this had been a chaos everlasting, and must

[1] Vergil *Eclogue* IV.

have kept all things in a chaos state to this day, and forever, had it ever been. But

> The active mind, infused through all the space,
> Unites and mingles with the mighty mass;
> Hence men and beasts.[2]

"Here, Philocles, we shall find our sovereign genius, if we can charm the genius of the place (more chaste and sober than your Silenus) to inspire us with a truer song of Nature, teach us some celestial hymn, and make us feel divinity present in these solemn places of retreat."

"Haste then, I conjure you," said I, "good Theocles, and stop not one moment for any ceremony or rite. For well I see, methinks, that without any such preparation some divinity has approached us and already moves in you. We are come to the sacred groves of the Hamadryads, which formerly were said to render oracles. We are on the most beautiful part of the hill; and the sun, now ready to rise, draws off the curtain of night and shows us the open scene of Nature in the plains below. Begin: for now I know you are full of those divine thoughts which meet you ever in this solitude. Give them but voice and accents. You may be still as much alone as you are used, and take no more notice of me than if I were absent."

Just as I had said this, he turned away his eyes from me, musing awhile by himself; and soon afterwards, stretching out his hand, as pointing to the objects round him, he began:

"Ye fields and woods, my refuge from the toilsome world of business, receive me in your quiet sanctuaries, and favor my retreat and thoughtful solitude. Ye verdant plains, how gladly I salute ye! Hail all ye blissful mansions! known seats! delightful prospects! majestic beauties of this earth, and all ye rural powers and graces! Blessed be ye chaste abodes of happiest mortals, who here in peaceful innocence enjoy a life unenvied, though divine; whilst with its blessed tranquillity it affords a happy leisure and retreat for man, who, made for contemplation, and to search his own and other natures, may here best meditate the cause of things, and, placed amidst the various scenes of Nature, may nearer view her works.

"O *glorious Nature!* supremely fair and sovereignly good! all-

2 Vergil *Aeneid* VI. 726 ff.

strains of Romanticism

loving and all-lovely, all-divine! whose looks are so becoming and of such infinite grace; whose study brings such wisdom, and whose contemplation such delight; whose every single work affords an ampler scene, and is a nobler spectacle than all which ever art presented! O mighty *Nature!* wise substitute of Providence! impowered Creatress! Or thou impowering *Deity*, supreme Creator! Thee I invoke and thee alone adore. To thee this solitude, this place, these rural meditations are sacred; whilst thus inspired with harmony of thought, though unconfined by words, and in loose numbers, I sing of Nature's Order in created beings, and celebrate the beauties which resolve in thee, the source and principle of all beauty and perfection.

"Thy Being is boundless, unsearchable, impenetrable. In thy immensity all thought is lost, fancy gives o'er its flight, and wearied imagination spends itself in vain, finding no coast nor limit of this ocean, nor in the widest tract through which it soars one point yet nearer the circumference than the first centre whence it parted. Thus having oft essayed, thus sallied forth into the wide expanse, when I return again within myself, struck with the sense of this so narrow being and of the fulness of that immense one, I dare no more behold the amazing depths nor sound the abyss of *Deity*.

"Yet since by thee, O *sovereign Mind!* I have been formed such as I am, intelligent and rational, since the peculiar dignity of my nature is to know and contemplate Thee, permit that with due freedom I exert those faculties with which thou hast adorned me. Bear with my venturous and bold approach. And since nor vain curiosity, nor fond conceit, nor love of aught save thee alone inspires me with such thoughts as these, be thou my assistant, and guide me in this pursuit, whilst I venture thus to tread the labyrinth of wide Nature and endeavor to trace thee in thy works. . . ."

A SELECTION

Francis Hutcheson

1694–1746

AN INQUIRY INTO THE ORIGINAL OF OUR IDEAS OF BEAUTY AND VIRTUE: TREATISE II, CONCERNING MORAL GOOD AND EVIL

1725

[Hutcheson subscribes to Shaftesbury's opinion that the moral sense is an instinctive one. He adds that if we fully understood our position in society, we should see that benevolent actions are to our own advantage, for in promoting the good of others, we really promote our own good. Thus Hutcheson formulates benevolism into a philosophy of utility—the greatest good for the greatest number. He even furnishes us with somewhat naïve equations by which we can calculate the degrees of benevolence and social good involved in any action.]

It remains, then, that as the author of nature has determined us to receive by our external senses pleasant or disagreeable ideas of objects, according as they are useful or hurtful to our bodies, and to receive from uniform objects the pleasures of beauty and harmony to excite us to the pursuit of knowledge and to reward us for it, or to be an argument to us of his goodness, as the uniformity itself proves his existence, whether we had a sense of beauty in uniformity or not: in the same manner he has given us a *moral sense* to direct our actions, and to give us still nobler pleasures, so that while we are only intending the good of others, we undesignedly promote our own greatest private good.

[Section I, proposition viii]

Now if it can be made to appear that none of these affections which we call virtuous spring from self-love, or desire of private interest (since all virtue is either some such affections or actions consequent upon them), it must necessarily follow that virtue is not pursued from the interest or self-love of the pursuer, or any motives of his own advantage.

[Section II, Proposition ii]

As to the love of benevolence, the very name excludes self-interest. We never call that man benevolent who is in fact useful to others but at the same time only intends his own interest, without any desire of, or delight in, the good of others. If there be any benevolence at all, it must be disinterested; for the most useful action imaginable loses all appearance of benevolence as soon as we discern that it only flowed from self-love or interest. Thus never were any human actions more advantageous than the inventions of fire and iron; but if these were casual, or if the inventor only intended his own interest in them, there is nothing which can be called benevolent in them. Wherever, then, benevolence is supposed, there it is imagined disinterested and designed for the good of others.

But it must here be observed that as all men have self-love as well as benevolence, these two principles may jointly excite a man to the same action: and then they are to be considered as two forces impelling the same body to motion; sometimes they conspire, sometimes are indifferent to each other, and sometimes are in some degree opposite. Thus, if a man have such strong benevolence as would have produced an action without any views of self-interest, that such a man has also in view private advantage, along with public good, as the effect of his action, does no way diminish the benevolence of the action. When he would not have produced so much public good had it not been for prospect of self-interest, then the effect of self-love is to be deducted, and his benevolence is proportioned to the remainder of the good which pure benevolence would have produced. When a man's benevolence is hurtful to himself, then self-love is opposite to benevolence, and the benevolence is proportioned to the sum of the good produced, added to the resistance of self-love surmounted by it. In most cases it is impossible for men to know how far their fellows are influenced by the one or other of these principles; but yet the general truth is sufficiently certain that this is the way in which the benevolence of actions is to be computed. Since, then, no love to rational agents can proceed from self-interest, every action must be disinterested as far as it flows from love to rational agents.

[SECTION II, proposition iii]

In comparing the moral qualities of actions, in order to regulate our election among various actions proposed or to find which of them has the greatest moral excellency, we are led by our moral sense of virtue to judge thus: that in equal degrees of happiness expected to proceed from the action, the virtue is in proportion to the number of persons to whom happiness shall extend (and here the dignity or moral importance of persons may compensate numbers); and in equal numbers, the virtue is as the quantity of the happiness or natural good; or that the virtue is in a compound ratio of the quantity of good, and the number of enjoyers. In the same manner, the moral evil or vice is as the degree of misery, and number of sufferers; so that that action is best which procures the greatest happiness for the greatest numbers; and that worst, which in like manner occasions misery. . . .

To find a universal canon to compute the morality of any actions, with all their circumstances, when we judge of the actions done by ourselves, or by others, we must observe the following propositions or axioms:

1—The moral importance of any agent or the quantity of public good produced by him is in a compound ratio of his benevolence and abilities: or (by substituting the initial letters for the words, as M = moment of good, and m = moment of evil) $M = B \times A$.

2—In like manner, the moment of private good or interest produced by any person to himself, is in a compound ratio of his self-love and abilities: or (substituting the initial letters) $I = S \times A$.

3—When in comparing the virtue of two actions, the abilities of the agents are equal, the moment of public good produced by them in like circumstances is as the benevolence: or $M = B \times I$.

4—When benevolence in two agents is equal and other circumstances alike, the moment of public good is as the abilities: or $M = A \times I$.

5—The virtue, then, of agents, or their benevolence, is always directly as the moment of good produced in like circumstances, and inversely as their abilities: or $B = \dfrac{M}{A}$.

[SECTION III, propositions viii, xi]

Bernard Mandeville

1670–1733

MANDEVILLE, like David Hume, was a gadfly who stung the respectable people of the eighteenth century, especially the clergy and the philanthropists, into a fury. His particular aversion, the third Earl of Shaftesbury, may have been invulnerable to polite refutation—but

Mandeville was not "polite." He admitted that he "took uncommon pains to search into human nature, and left no stone unturned to detect the pride and hypocrisy of it." By a coarse and even brutal glee in laying bare inconsistencies, he unsettled a great many genteel formulas regarding charity, religion, ethics, and economic life. He persisted in the unpleasant opinion, held in the seventeenth century by Thomas Hobbes, that man selfishly "centers everything in himself." His very great value, like Nietzsche's or Machiavelli's, is that his arguments, even for our own day, are so cogent that in order to refute them, we must penetrate deeply beneath the platitudes we usually accept. Mandeville claims, for example, that most charity is a form of exhibitionism for the wealthy, or what the sociologist Thorstein Veblen would call "conspicuous expenditure." He claims that prosperity is really based not upon frugality but upon luxury, that monogamy is unnatural, and that the moral code is a fraud imposed by the strong upon the weak to make them behave. In his offhand and chatty "Remarks" upon *The Fable of the Bees*, he anticipates the later biological, social, and economic theories of the relativity of moral codes, the struggle for survival in nature and society, utilitarianism, and economic laissez-faire. Only one other mind of his day can be compared with Mandeville's— that of Jonathan Swift. If Swift was more agile and perceptive, Mandeville was no less vigorous.

BIOGRAPHICAL NOTES

Born in Rotterdam, the son of a Dutch physician. Studied medicine at the University of Leyden (1685-91), then traveled in Italy and France. Came to London and married Ruth Elizabeth Laurence (1699). Practiced medicine in London, specializing in diseases of the nerves and stomach; was a great frequenter of coffeehouses. *The Grumbling Hive, or Knaves Turned Honest* (1705), a doggerel poem upon the public benefits of private vice. *Treatise of the Hypochondriac and Hysteric Passions* (1711). Reprinted *The Grumbling Hive* as *The Fable of the Bees*, with appended *Remarks* and *An Inquiry into the Origin of Moral Virtue* (1714). Reprinted *Fable of the Bees* with *An Essay on Charity and Charity Schools* and *A Search into the Nature of Society* (1723), which evoked bitter criticism. The Grand Jury of Middlesex presented the book as a menace to society and religion. *A Modest Defense of Public Stews* (1724) published. *The Fable of the Bees*, Part II (1728).

BIBLIOGRAPHY: Kaye, F. B., ed. *The Fable of the Bees*, 2 vols., 1924.   Robertson, John M., *Essays towards a Critical Method*, 1889.

insisted on unpleasant situation like Hobbes — man selfishly centers everything in himself

THE FABLE OF THE BEES: OR, *PRIVATE VICES, PUBLIC BENEFITS*

1714–1723

AN INQUIRY INTO THE ORIGIN OF MORAL VIRTUE

1714

All untaught animals are only solicitous of pleasing themselves, and naturally follow the bent of their own inclinations without considering the good or harm that from their being pleased will accrue to others. This is the reason that in the wild State of Nature those creatures are fittest to live peaceably together in great numbers that discover the least of understanding and have the fewest appetites to gratify; and consequently no species of animals is, without the curb of government, less capable of agreeing long together in multitudes than that of man; yet such are his qualities (whether good or bad I shall not determine) that no creature besides himself can ever be made sociable. But being an extraordinary selfish and headstrong, as well as cunning animal, however he may be subdued by superior strength, it is impossible by force alone to make him tractable and receive the improvements he is capable of.

The chief thing, therefore, which lawgivers and other wise men that have labored for the establishment of society have endeavored has been to make the people they were to govern believe that it was more beneficial for everybody to conquer than indulge his appetites, and much better to mind the public than what seemed his private interest. As this has always been a very difficult task, so no wit or eloquence has been left untried to compass it; and the moralists and philosophers of all ages employed their utmost skill to prove the truth of so useful an assertion. But whether mankind would have ever believed it or not, it is not likely that anybody could have persuaded them to disapprove of their natural inclinations, or prefer the good of others to their own, if at the same time he had not showed them an equivalent to be enjoyed as a reward for the violence which by so doing they of necessity must commit upon themselves. Those that have undertaken to civilize mankind were not ignorant of this; but being unable to give so many real rewards as would satisfy all persons for every individual action, they were forced to contrive an imaginary one that as a general equivalent for the trouble of self-denial should serve on all occasions, and without costing anything either to themselves or others, be yet a most acceptable recompense to the receivers.

They thoroughly examined all the strength and frailties of our nature, and observing that none were either so savage as not to be charmed with praise, or so despicable as patiently to bear contempt, justly concluded that flattery must be the most powerful argument that could be used to human creatures. Making use of this bewitching engine, they extolled the excellency of our nature above other animals, and setting forth with unbounded praises the wonders of our sagacity and vastness of understanding, bestowed a thousand encomiums on the rationality of our souls, by the help of which we were capable of performing the most noble achievements. Having by this artful way of flattery insinuated themselves into the hearts of men, they began to instruct them in the notions of honor and shame, representing the one as the worst of all evils, and the other as the highest good to which mortals could aspire; which being done, they laid before them how unbecoming it was the dignity of such sublime creatures to be solicitous about gratifying those appetites which they had in common with brutes, and at the same time unmindful of those higher qualities that gave them the pre-eminence over all visible beings. They indeed confessed that those impulses of nature were very pressing, that it was troublesome to resist, and very difficult wholly to subdue them. But this they only used as an argument to demonstrate how glorious the conquest of them was on the one hand, and how scandalous on the other not to attempt it.

To introduce, moreover, an emulation amongst men, they divided the whole species in two classes, vastly differing from one another: the one consisted of abject, low-minded people that, always hunting after immediate enjoyment, were wholly incapable of self-denial, and without regard to the good of others, had no higher aim than their private advantage; such as being enslaved by voluptuousness, yielded without resistance to every gross desire, and made no use of their rational faculties but to heighten their sensual pleasure. These vile groveling wretches, they said, were the dross of their kind, and having only the shape of men, differed from brutes in nothing but their outward figure. But the other class was made up of lofty, high-spirited creatures that, free from sordid selfishness, esteemed the improvements of the mind to be their fairest possessions; and setting a true value upon themselves, took no delight but in embellishing that part in which their excellency consisted; such as, despising whatever they had in common with irrational creatures, opposed by the help of reason their most violent inclinations, and making a continual war with themselves to promote the peace of others, aimed at no less than the public welfare and the conquest of their own passion.

He is stronger who conquers himself than

Fortior est qui se quam qui fortissima vincit
Moenia —— —— —— —— —— ——[1]

he who conquers the strongest fortifications

These they called the true representatives of their sublime species, exceeding in worth the first class by more degrees than that itself was superior to the beasts of the field.

As in all animals that are not too imperfect to discover pride we find that the finest and such as are the most beautiful and valuable of their kind have generally the greatest share of it, so in man, the most perfect of animals, it is so inseparable from his very essence (how cunningly soever some may learn to hide or disguise it) that without it the compound he is made of would want one of the chiefest ingredients: which, if we consider, it is hardly to be doubted but lessons and remonstrances so skillfully adapted to the good opinion man has of himself as those I have mentioned, must, if scattered amongst a multitude, not only gain the assent of most of them as to the speculative part, but likewise induce several, especially the fiercest, most resolute, and best among them, to endure a thousand inconveniences and undergo as many hardships that they may have the pleasure of counting themselves men of the second class, and consequently appropriating to themselves all the excellencies they have heard of it.

From what has been said, we ought to expect in the first place that the heroes who took such extraordinary pains to master some of their natural appetites, and preferred the good of others to any visible interest of their own, would not recede an inch from the fine notions they had received concerning the dignity of ra-

pride

[1] "He is stronger who conquers himself than he who conquers the strongest fortifications"; cf. Proverbs 16:32.

(B) high-spirited people — interested in improving their mind, promote peace

tional creatures; and having ever the authority of the government on their side, with all imaginable vigor assert the esteem that was due to those of the second class as well as their superiority over the rest of their kind. In the second, that those who wanted a sufficient stock of either pride or resolution to buoy them up in mortifying of what was dearest to them, followed the sensual dictates of Nature, would yet be ashamed of confessing themselves to be those despicable wretches that belonged to the inferior class, and were generally reckoned to be so little removed from brutes; and that therefore in their own defense they would say as others did, and hiding their own imperfections as well as they could, cry up self-denial and public-spiritedness as much as any: for it is highly probable that some of them, convinced by the real proofs of fortitude and self-conquest they had seen, would admire in others what they found wanting in themselves; others be afraid of the resolution and prowess of those of the second class, and that all of them were kept in awe by the power of their rulers; wherefore it is reasonable to think that none of them (whatever they thought in themselves) would dare openly contradict what by everybody else was thought criminal to doubt of.

This was (or at least might have been) the manner after which savage man was broken; from whence it is evident that the first rudiments of morality, broached by skillful politicians, to render men useful to each other as well as tractable, were chiefly contrived that the ambitious might reap the more benefit from, and govern vast numbers of, them with greater ease and security. This foundation of politics being once laid, it is impossible that man should long remain uncivilized: for even those who only strove to gratify their appetites, being continually crossed by others of the same stamp, could not but observe that whenever they checked their inclinations, or but followed them with more circumspection, they avoided a world of troubles and often escaped many of the calamities that generally attended the too eager pursuit after pleasure.

First, they received, as well as others, the benefit of those actions that were done for the good of the whole society, and consequently could not forbear wishing well to those of the superior class that performed them. Secondly, the more intent they were in seeking their own advantage, without regard to others, the more they were hourly convinced that none stood so much in their way as those that were most like themselves.

preach up public spiritedness

It being the interest, then, of the very worst of them, more than any, to preach up public-spiritedness, that they might reap the fruits of the labor and self-denial of others and at the same time indulge their own appetites with less disturbance, they agreed with the rest to call everything which, without regard to the public, man should commit to gratify any of his appetites, VICE, if in that action there could be observed the least prospect that it might either be injurious to any of the society, or ever render himself less serviceable to others; and to give the name of VIRTUE to every performance by which man, contrary to the impulse of nature, should endeavor the benefit of others, or the conquest of his own passions out of a rational ambition of being good.

It shall be objected that no society was ever anyways civilized before the major part had agreed upon some worship or other of an overruling Power, and consequently that the notions of good and evil, and the distinction between *Virtue* and *Vice*, were never the contrivance of politicians, but the pure effect of religion. Before I answer this objection, I must repeat what I have said already, that in this *Inquiry into the Origin of Moral Virtue* I speak neither of Jews or Christians, but man in his State of Nature and ignorance of the true Deity; and then I affirm that the idolatrous superstitions of all other nations, and the pitiful notions they had of the Supreme Being, were incapable of exciting man to virtue, and good for nothing but to awe and amuse a rude and unthinking multitude. It is evident from history that in all considerable societies, how stupid or ridiculous soever people's received notions have been as to the deities they worshiped, human nature has ever exerted itself in all its branches, and that there is no earthly wisdom or moral virtue but at one time or other men have excelled in it in all monarchies and commonwealths that for riches and power have been anyways remarkable.

distinction between Vice & virtue — effect of Relig.

The Egyptians, not satisfied with having deified all the ugly monsters they could think on, were so silly as to adore the onions of their own sowing; yet at the same time their country was the most famous nursery of arts and sciences in the world, and themselves more eminently skilled in the deepest mysteries of nature than any nation has been since.

No states or kingdoms under Heaven have yielded more or greater patterns in all sorts of moral virtues than the Greek and Roman empires, more especially the latter; and yet how loose, absurd, and ridiculous were their sentiments as to sacred matters! For without reflecting on the extravagant number of their deities, if we only consider the infamous stories they fathered upon them, it is not to be denied but that their religion, far from teaching men the conquest of their passions and the way to virtue, seemed rather contrived to justify their appetites and encourage their vices. But if we would know what made 'em excel in fortitude, courage, and magnanimity, we must cast our eyes on the pomp of their triumphs, the magnificence of their monuments and arches; their trophies, statues, and inscriptions; the variety of their military crowns, their honors decreed to the dead, public encomiums on the living, and other imaginary rewards they bestowed on men of merit; and we shall find that what carried so many of them to the utmost pitch of self-denial was nothing but their policy in making use of the most effectual means that human pride could be flattered with.

It is visible then that it was not any heathen religion or other idolatrous superstition that first put man upon crossing his appetites and subduing his dearest inclinations, but the skillful management of wary politicians; and the nearer we search into human nature, the more we shall be convinced that the moral virtues are the political offspring which Flattery begot upon Pride. . . .

But here I shall be told that besides the noisy toils of war and public bustle of the ambitious, there are noble and generous actions that are performed in silence; that virtue being its own reward, those who are really good have a satisfaction in their consciousness of being so, which is all the recompense they expect from the most worthy performances; that among the heathens there have been men who, when they did good to others, were so far from coveting thanks and applause that they took all imaginable care to be forever concealed from those on whom they bestowed their benefits, and consequently that pride has no hand in spurring man on to the highest pitch of self-denial.

In answer to this I say that it is impossible to judge of a man's performance unless we are thoroughly acquainted with the principle and motive from which he acts. Pity, though it is the most gentle and the least mischievous of all our passions, is yet as much a frailty of our nature as anger, pride, or fear. The weakest minds have generally the greatest share of it, for which reason none are more compassionate than women and children. It must be owned that of all our weaknesses it is the most amiable, and bears the greatest resemblance to virtue; nay, without a considerable mixture of it the society could hardly subsist. But as it is an impulse of Nature that consults neither the public interest nor our own reason, it may produce evil as well as good. It has helped to destroy the honor of virgins and corrupted the integrity of judges; and whoever acts from it as a principle, what good soever he may bring to the society, has nothing to boast of but that he has indulged a passion that has happened to be beneficial to the public. There is no merit in saving an innocent babe ready to drop into the fire. The action is neither good nor bad, and what benefit soever the infant received, we only obliged ourselves; for to have seen it fall, and not strove to hinder it, would have caused a pain which self-preservation compelled us to prevent. Nor has a rich prodigal that happens to be of a commiserating temper, and loves to gratify his passions, greater virtue to boast of when he relieves an object of compassion with what to himself is a trifle.

But such men as, without complying with any weakness of their own, can part from what they value themselves, and from no other motive but their love to goodness, perform a worthy action in silence—such men, I confess, have acquired more refined notions of virtue than those I have hitherto spoke of; yet even in these (with which the world has yet never swarmed) we may discover no small symptoms of pride, and the humblest man alive must confess that the reward of a virtuous action, which is the satisfaction that ensues upon it, consists in a certain pleasure he procures to himself by contemplating on his own worth; which pleasure, together with the occasion of it, are as certain signs of pride as looking pale and trembling at any imminent danger are the symptoms of fear.

If the too scrupulous reader should at first view condemn these notions concerning the origin of moral virtue, and think them perhaps offensive to Christianity, I hope he'll forbear his censures when he shall consider that nothing can render the unsearchable depth of the Divine Wisdom more conspicuous than that man, whom Providence had designed for society, should not only by his own frailties and imperfections be led into the road to temporal happiness, but likewise receive, from a seeming necessity of natural causes, a tincture of that knowledge in which he was afterwards to be made perfect by the True Religion, to his eternal welfare.

AN ESSAY ON CHARITY AND CHARITY SCHOOLS

charity schools — form of conspicuous waste 1723 & *conspicuous leisure*

The rise then and original of all the bustle and clamor that is made throughout the kingdom in behalf of charity schools is chiefly built on frailty and human passion;[1] at least it is more than possible that a nation should have the same fondness and feel the same zeal for them as are shown in ours, and yet not be prompted to it by any principle of virtue or religion. Encouraged by this consideration, I shall with the greater liberty attack this vulgar error, and endeavor to make it evident that far from being beneficial, this forced education is pernicious to the public, the welfare whereof, as it demands of us a regard superior to all other laws and considerations, so it shall be the only apology I intend to make for differing from the present sentiments of the learned and reverend body of our divines, and venturing plainly to deny what I have just now owned to be openly asserted by most of our bishops as well as inferior clergy. As our Church pretends to no infallibility even in spirituals, her proper province, so it cannot be an affront to her to imagine that she may err in temporals, which are not so much under her immediate care.—But to my task.

tends toward patience of social order

The whole earth being cursed and no bread to be had but what we eat in the sweat of our brows, vast toil must be undergone before man can provide himself with necessaries for his sustenance and the bare support of his corrupt and defective nature as he is a single creature; but infinitely more to make life comfortable in a civil society, where men are become taught animals, and great numbers of them have by mutual compact framed themselves into a body politic; and the more man's knowledge increases in this state, the greater will be the variety of labor required to make him easy. It is impossible that a society can long subsist and suffer many of its members to live in idleness, and enjoy all the ease and pleasure they can invent, without having at the same time great multitudes of people that to make good this defect, will con-

---

1 Mandeville has maintained that tradesmen support charity schools because it flatters their pride to manage things and because it helps their business to be known as public benefactors. Charity schools are a form of "conspicuous waste" and "conspicuous leisure."

Bentham — Contentment — no hierarchy of values

descend to be quite the reverse, and by use and patience inure their bodies to work for others and themselves besides.

The plenty and cheapness of provisions depends in a great measure on the price and value that is set upon this labor, and consequently the welfare of all societies, even before they are tainted with foreign luxury, requires that it should be performed by such of their members as in the first place are sturdy and robust and never used to ease or idleness, and in the second, soon contented as to the necessaries of life; such as are glad to take up with the coarsest manufacture in everything they wear, and in their diet have no other aim than to feed their bodies when their stomachs prompt them to eat, and, with little regard to taste or relish, refuse no wholesome nourishment that can be swallowed when men are hungry, or ask anything for their thirst but to quench it.

As the greatest part of the drudgery is to be done by daylight, so it is by this only that they actually measure the time of their labor without any thought of the hours they are employed or the weariness they feel; and the hireling in the country must get up in the morning not because he has rested enough, but because the sun is going to rise. This last article alone would be an intolerable hardship to grown people under thirty who during nonage had been used to lie abed as long as they could sleep; but all three together make up such a condition of life as a man more mildly educated would hardly choose, though it should deliver him from a jail or a shrew.

If such people there must be, as no great nation can be happy without vast numbers of them, would not a wise legislature cultivate the breed of them with all imaginable care, and provide against their scarcity as he would prevent the scarcity of provision itself? No man would be poor and fatigue himself for a livelihood if he could help it. The absolute necessity all stand in for victuals and drink, and in cold climates for clothes and lodging, makes them submit to anything that can be bore with. If nobody did want, nobody would work; but the greatest hardships are looked upon as solid pleasures when they keep a man from starving.

From what has been said, it is manifest that in a free nation, where slaves are not allowed of, the surest wealth consists in a multitude of laborious poor; for besides that they are the never-failing nursery of fleets and armies, without them there could be

extend their capacity to feel pain by educating them

no enjoyment, and no product of any country could be valuable. To make the society happy and people easy under the meanest circumstances, it is requisite that great numbers of them should be ignorant as well as poor. Knowledge both enlarges and multiplies our desires, and the fewer things a man wishes for, the more easily his necessities may be supplied.

The welfare and felicity, therefore, of every state and kingdom require that the knowledge of the working poor should be confined within the verge of their occupations, and never extended (as to things visible) beyond what relates to their calling. The more a shepherd, a plowman, or any other peasant knows of the world and the things that are foreign to his labor or employment, the less fit he'll be to go through the fatigues and hardships of it with cheerfulness and content.

Reading, writing, and arithmetic are very necessary to those whose business requires such qualifications, but where people's livelihood has no dependence on these arts, they are very pernicious to the poor, who are forced to get their daily bread by their daily labor. Few children make any progress at school, but at the same time they are capable of being employed in some business or other, so that every hour those of poor people spend at their book is so much time lost to the society. Going to school in comparison to working is idleness, and the longer boys continue in this easy sort of life, the more unfit they'll be when grown up for downright labor, both as to strength and inclination. Men who are to remain and end their days in a laborious, tiresome, and painful station of life, the sooner they are put upon it at first, the more patiently they'll submit to it forever after. Hard labor and the coarsest diet are a proper punishment to several kinds of malefactors, but to impose either on those that have not been used and brought up to both is the greatest cruelty when there is no crime you can charge them with.

Reading and writing are not attained to without some labor of the brain and assiduity, and before people are tolerably versed in either, they esteem themselves infinitely above those who are wholly ignorant of them, often with so little justice and moderation as if they were of another species. As all mortals have naturally an aversion to trouble and painstaking, so we are all fond of, and apt to overvalue, those qualifications we have purchased at the expense of our ease and quiet for years together. Those who spent a great part of their youth in learning to read, write, and cipher expect, and not unjustly, to be employed where those qualifications may be of use to them; the generality of them will look upon downright labor with the utmost contempt—I mean labor performed in the service of others in the lowest station of life, and for the meanest consideration. A man who has had some education may follow husbandry by choice, and be diligent at the dirtiest and most laborious work; but then the concern must be his own; and avarice, the care of a family, or some other pressing motive must put him upon it; but he won't make a good hireling and serve a farmer for a pitiful reward; at least he is not so fit for it as a day laborer that has always been employed about the plow and dung cart, and remembers not that ever he has lived otherwise.

When obsequiousness and mean services are required, we shall always observe that they are never so cheerfully nor so heartily performed as from inferiors to superiors; I mean inferiors, not only in riches and quality, but likewise in knowledge and understanding. A servant can have no unfeigned respect for his master as soon as he has sense enough to find out that he serves a fool. When we are to learn or to obey, we shall experience in ourselves that the greater opinion we have of the wisdom and capacity of those that are either to teach or command us, the greater deference we pay to their laws and instructions. No creatures submit contentedly to their equals, and should a horse know as much as a man, I should not desire to be his rider. . . .

I would not be thought cruel, and am well assured if I know anything of myself that I abhor inhumanity; but to be compassionate to excess where reason forbids it, and the general interest of the society requires steadiness of thought and resolution, is an unpardonable weakness. I know it will be ever urged against me that it is barbarous the children of the poor should have no opportunity of exerting themselves as long as God has not debarred them from natural parts and genius more than the rich. But I cannot think this is harder than it is that they should not have money as long as they have the same inclinations to spend as others. That great and useful men have sprung from hospitals, I don't deny; but it is likewise very probable that when they were first employed, many as capable as themselves not brought up in hospitals were neglected that with the same good fortune would have done as well as they, if they had been made use of instead of them.

There are many examples of women that have excelled in learning, and even in war, but this is no reason we should bring 'em all up to Latin and Greek or else military discipline, instead of needlework and housewifery. But there is no scarcity of sprightliness or natural parts among us, and no soil or climate has human creatures to boast of better formed either inside or outside than this island generally produces. But it is not wit, genius, or docility we want, but diligence, application, and assiduity.

Abundance of hard and dirty labor is to be done, and coarse living is to be complied with. Where shall we find a better nursery for these necessities than the children of the poor? None certainly are nearer to it or fitter for it. Besides that, the things I called hardships neither seem nor are such to those who have been brought up to 'em and know no better. There is not a more contented people amongst us than those who work the hardest and are the least acquainted with the pomp and delicacies of the world.

These are truths that are undeniable; yet I know few people will be pleased to have them divulged; what makes them odious is an unreasonable vein of petty reverence for the poor that runs through most multitudes, and more particularly in this nation, and arises from a mixture of pity, folly, and superstition. It is from a lively sense of this compound that men cannot endure to hear or see anything said or acted against the poor, without considering how just the one or insolent the other. So a beggar must not be beat though he strikes you first. Journeymen tailors go to law with their masters and are obstinate in a wrong cause; yet they must be pitied; and murmuring weavers must be relieved, and have fifty silly things done to humor them, though in the midst of their poverty they insult their betters, and on all occasions appear to be more prone to make holidays and riots than they are to working or sobriety.

This puts me in mind of our wool, which, considering the posture of our affairs and the behavior of the poor, I sincerely believe ought not upon any account to be carried abroad. But if we look into the reason why suffering it to be fetched away is so pernicious, our heavy complaint and lamentations that it is exported can be no great credit to us. Considering the mighty and manifold hazards that must be run before it can be got off the coast and safely landed beyond sea, it is manifest that the foreigners, before they can work our wool, must pay more for it very considerably than what we can have it for at home. Yet, notwithstanding this great difference in the prime cost, they can afford to sell the manufactures made of it cheaper at foreign markets than ourselves. This is the disaster we groan under, the intolerable mischief, without which the exportation of that commodity could be no greater prejudice to us than that of tin or lead, as long as our hands were fully employed and we had still wool to spare.

There is no people yet come to higher perfection in the woolen manufacture, either as to dispatch or goodness of work, at least in the most considerable branches, than ourselves, and therefore what we complain of can only depend on the difference in the management of the poor between other nations and ours. If the laboring people in one country will work twelve hours in a day, and six days in a week, and in another they are employed but eight hours in a day, and not above four days in a week, the one is obliged to have nine hands for what the other does with four. But if moreover the living, the food and raiment, and what is consumed by the workmen of the industrious costs but half the money of what is expended among an equal number of the other, the consequence must be that the first will have the work of eighteen men for the same price as the other gives for the work of four. I would not insinuate, neither do I think, that the difference either in diligence or necessaries of life between us and any neighboring nation is near so great as what I speak of; yet I would have it considered that half of that difference and much less is sufficient to overbalance the disadvantage they labor under as to the price of wool.

Nothing to me is more evident than that no nation in any manufacture whatever can undersell their neighbors with whom they are at best but equals as to skill and dispatch, and the conveniency for working, more especially when the prime cost of the thing to be manufactured is not in their favor, unless they have provisions and whatever is relating to their sustenance cheaper, or else workmen that are either more assiduous, and will remain longer at their work, or be content with a meaner and coarser way of living than those of their neighbors. This is certain: that where numbers are equal, the more laborious people are, and the fewer hands the same quantity of work is performed by, the greater plenty there is in a country of the necessaries for life, the more considerable and the cheaper that country may render its exports.

It being granted, then, that abundance of work is to be done, the next thing which I think to be likewise undeniable is that the more cheerfully it is done the better, as well for those that perform it as for the rest of the society. To be happy is to be pleased, and the less notion a man has of a better way of living, the more content he'll be with his own; and on the other hand, the greater a man's knowledge and experience is in the world, the more exquisite the delicacy of his taste, and the more consummate judge he is of things in general, certainly the more difficult it will be to please him. I would not advance anything that is barbarous or inhuman. But when a man enjoys himself, laughs and sings, and in his gesture and behavior shows me all the tokens of content and satisfaction, I pronounce him happy, and have nothing to do with his wit or capacity. I never enter into the reasonableness of his mirth; at least I ought not to judge of it by my own standard, and argue from the effect which the thing that makes him merry would have upon me. At that rate a man that hates cheese must call me a fool for loving blue mold. *De gustibus non est disputandum* [2] is as true in a metaphorical as it is in the literal sense, and the greater the distance is between people as to their condition, their circumstances, and manner of living, the less capable they are of judging of one another's troubles or pleasures. . . .

A SEARCH INTO THE NATURE OF SOCIETY

1723

The generality of moralists and philosophers have hitherto agreed that there could be no virtue without self-denial; but a late author, who is now much read by men of sense, is of a contrary opinion, and imagines that men without any trouble or violence upon themselves may be naturally virtuous. He seems to require and expect goodness in his species, as we do a sweet taste in grapes and China oranges, of which, if any of them are sour, we boldly pronounce that they are not come to that perfection their nature is

2 "There is no disputing about tastes."

capable of. This noble writer (for it is the Lord Shaftesbury I mean, in his *Characteristics*) fancies that as man is made for society, so he ought to be born with a kind affection to the whole, of which he is a part, and a propensity to seek the welfare of it. In pursuance of this supposition, he calls every action performed with regard to the public good, virtuous; and all selfishness, wholly excluding such a regard, vice. In respect to our species he looks upon virtue and vice as permanent realities that must ever be the same in all countries and all ages, and imagines that a man of sound understanding, by following the rules of good sense, may not only find out that *Pulchrum & Honestum* both in morality and the works of art and nature, but likewise govern himself by his reason with as much ease and readiness as a good rider manages a well-taught horse by the bridle.

The attentive reader who perused the foregoing part of this book will soon perceive that two systems cannot be more opposite than his Lordship's and mine. His notions, I confess, are generous and refined: they are a high compliment to humankind, and capable by the help of a little enthusiasm of inspiring us with the most noble sentiments concerning the dignity of our exalted nature. What pity it is that they are not true! I would not advance thus much if I had not already demonstrated in almost every page of this treatise that the solidity of them is inconsistent with our daily experience. But to leave not the least shadow of an objection that might be made unanswered, I design to expatiate on some things which hitherto I have but slightly touched upon, in order to convince the reader not only that the good and amiable qualities of man are not those that make him beyond other animals a sociable creature, but moreover that it would be utterly impossible either to raise any multitudes into a populous, rich and flourishing nation, or when so raised, to keep and maintain them in that condition, without the assistance of what we call evil both natural and moral.

The better to perform what I have undertaken, I shall previously examine into the reality of the *Pulchrum & Honestrum*, the τὸ κάλον that the ancients have talked of so much: the meaning of this is to discuss whether there be a real worth and excellency in things, a pre-eminence of one above another, which everybody will always agree to that well understands them; or that there are few things, if any, that have the same esteem paid them, and which the same judgment is passed upon in all countries and all ages. When we first set out in quest of this intrinsic worth, and find one thing better than another, and a third better than that, and so on, we begin to entertain great hopes of success; but when we meet with several things that are all very good or all very bad, we are puzzled and agree not always with ourselves, much less with others. There are different faults as well as beauties that, as modes and fashions alter and men vary in their tastes and humors, will be differently admired or disapproved of.

Judges of painting will never disagree in opinion when a fine picture is compared to the daubing of a novice; but how strangely have they differed as to the works of eminent masters! There are parties among connoisseurs, and few of them agree in their esteem as to ages and countries, and the best pictures bear not always the best prices: a noted original will be ever worth more than any copy that can be made of it by an unknown hand, though it should be better. The value that is set on paintings depends not only on the name of the master and the time of his age he drew them in, but likewise in a great measure on the scarcity of his works, and what is still more unreasonable, the quality of the persons in whose possession they are as well as the length of time they have been in great families; and if the cartoons now at Hampton Court were done by a less famous hand than that of Raphael, and had a private person for their owner who would be forced to sell them, they would never yield the tenth part of the money which with all their gross faults they are now esteemed to be worth. . .

In the works of nature, worth and excellency are as uncertain: and even in human creatures what is beautiful in one country is not so in another. How whimsical is the florist in his choice! Sometimes the tulip, sometimes the auricula, and at other times the carnation shall engross his esteem, and every year a new flower in his judgment beats all the old ones, though it is much inferior to them both in color and shape. Three hundred years ago men were shaved as closely as they are now: since that, they have wore beards, and cut them in vast variety of forms that were all as becoming when fashionable as now they would be ridiculous. How mean and comically a man looks, that is otherwise well dressed, in a narrow-brimmed hat when everybody wears broad ones; and again, how monstrous in a very great hat when the other extreme has been in fashion for a considerable time! Experience has taught us that these modes seldom last above ten or twelve years, and a man of three score must have observed five or six revolutions of 'em at least; yet the beginnings of these changes, though we have seen several, seem always uncouth and are offensive afresh whenever they return. What mortal can decide which is the handsomest (abstract from the mode in being), to wear great buttons or small ones? The many ways of laying out a garden judiciously are almost innumerable, and what is called beautiful in them varies according to the different tastes of nations and ages. In grass plats, knots, and parterres a great diversity of forms is generally agreeable; but a round may be as pleasing to the eye as a square: an oval cannot be more suitable to one place than it is possible for a triangle to be to another; and the pre-eminence an octagon has over an hexagon is no greater in figures, than at hazard eight has above six among the chances. . . .

In morals there is no greater certainty. Plurality of wives is odious among Christians, and all the wit and learning of a great genius in defense of it has been rejected with contempt: but polygamy is not shocking to a Mahometan. What men have learned from their infancy enslaves them, and the force of custom warps nature, and at the same time imitates her in such a manner that it is often difficult to know which of the two we are influenced by. In the East formerly sisters married brothers, and it was meritorious for a man to marry his mother. Such alliances are abominable; but it is certain that, whatever horror we conceive at the thoughts of them, there is nothing in Nature repugnant against them but what is built upon mode and custom. A religious Mahometan that has never tasted any spirituous liquor, and has often seen people drunk, may receive as great an aversion against wine as another with us of the least morality and education may have against lying with his sister, and both imagine that their antipathy proceeds from Nature. Which is the best religion is a question that has caused more mischief than all other questions together. Ask it at Peking, at Constantinople, and at Rome, and you'll receive three distinct answers extremely different from one another, yet all of them equally positive and peremptory. Christians are well assured of the falsity of the pagan and Mahometan superstitions; as to this point there is a perfect union and concord among them; but inquire of the several sects they are divided into, which is the true Church of Christ, and all of them will tell you it is theirs, and to convince you, go together by the ears.

harder sense of morality

a lot in common w. Swift

easy Stoic position

It is manifest then that the hunting after this *Pulchrum & Honestum* is not much better than a wild-goose chase that is but little to be depended upon: but this is not the greatest fault I find with it. The imaginary notions that men may be virtuous without self-denial are a vast inlet to hypocrisy, which being once made habitual, we must not only deceive others, but likewise become altogether unknown to ourselves, and in an instance I am going to give, it will appear how for want of duly examining himself this might happen to a person of quality of parts and erudition, one everyway resembling the author of the *Characteristics* himself.

A man that has been brought up in ease and affluence, if he is of a quiet, indolent nature, learns to shun everything that is troublesome, and chooses to curb his passions, more because of the inconveniencies that arise from the eager pursuit after pleasure, and the yielding to all the demands of our inclinations, than any dislike he has to sensual enjoyments; and it is possible that a person educated under a great philosopher,[1] who was a mild and good-natured as well as able tutor, may in such happy circumstances have a better opinion of his inward state than it really deserves, and believe himself virtuous because his passions lie dormant. He may form fine notions of the social virtues and the contempt of death, write well of them in his closet, and talk eloquently of them in company; but you shall never catch him fighting for his country, or laboring to retrieve any national losses. A man that deals in metaphysics may easily throw himself into an enthusism, and really believe that he does not fear death while it remains out of sight. But should he be asked, why having this intrepidity either from Nature or acquired by philosophy, he did not follow arms when his country was involved in war, or when he saw the nation daily robbed by those at the helm, and the affairs of the Exchequer perplexed, why he did not go to Court, and make use of all his friends and interest to be a Lord Treasurer, that by his integrity and wise management he might restore the public credit, it is probable he would answer that he loved retirement, had no other ambition than to be a good man, and never aspired to have any share in the government, or that he hated all flattery and slavish attendance, the insincerity of courts and bustle of the world. I am willing to believe him: but may not a man of an indolent temper and unactive spirit say, and be sincere in, all this,

[1] The third Earl of Shaftesbury was educated privately under John Locke.

and at the same time indulge his appetites without being able to subdue them, though his duty summons him to it? Virtue consists in action, and whoever is possessed of this social love and kind affection to his species, and by his birth or quality can claim any post in the public management, ought not to sit still when he can be serviceable, but exert himself to the utmost for the good of his fellow subjects. Had this noble person been of a warlike genius or a boisterous temper, he would have chose another part in the drama of life, and preached a quite contrary doctrine: for we are ever pushing our reason which way soever we feel passion to draw it, and self-love pleads to all human creatures for their different views, still furnishing every individual with arguments to justify their inclinations.

That boasted middle way, and the calm virtues recommended in the *Characteristics,* are good for nothing but to breed drones, and might qualify a man for the stupid enjoyments of a monastic life, or at best a country justice of peace; but they would never fit him for labor and assiduity, or stir him up to great achievements and perilous undertakings. Man's natural love of ease and idleness, and proneness to indulge his sensual pleasures, are not to be cured by precept: his strong habits and inclinations can only be subdued by passions of greater violence. Preach and demonstrate to a coward the unreasonableness of his fears and you'll not make him valiant, more than you can make him taller by bidding him to be ten foot high; whereas the secret to raise courage, as I have made it public in *Remark R,* is almost infallible.[2]

The fear of death is the strongest when we are in our greatest vigor, and our appetite is keen; when we are sharp-sighted, quick of hearing, and every part performs its office. The reason is plain, because then life is most delicious and ourselves most capable of enjoying it. How comes it then that a man of honor should so easily accept of a challenge, though at thirty and in perfect health? It is his pride that conquers his fear: for when his pride is not concerned, this fear will appear most glaringly. If he is not used to the sea, let him but be in a storm, or if he never was ill before, have but a sore throat or a slight fever, and he'll show a thousand anxieties, and in them the inestimable value he sets on life. Had man been naturally humble and proof against flattery, the politician could never have had his ends, or known what to have made of him.

2 That is, by arousing anger.

Without vices the excellency of the species would have ever remained undiscovered, and every worthy that has made himself famous in the world is a strong evidence against this amiable system. . . .

What I have endeavored hitherto, has been to prove that the *Pulchrum & Honestum*, excellency and real worth of things, are most commonly precarious and alterable as modes and customs vary; that consequently the inferences drawn from their certainty are insignificant, and that the generous notions concerning the natural goodness of man are hurtful as they tend to mislead, and are merely chimerical. The truth of this latter I have illustrated by the most obvious examples in history. I have spoke of our love of company and aversion to solitude, examined thoroughly the various motives of them, and made it appear that they all center in self-love. I intend now to investigate into the nature of society, and diving into the very rise of it, make it evident that not the good and amiable, but the bad and hateful qualities of man, his imperfections and the want of excellencies which other creatures are endued with, are the first causes that made man sociable beyond other animals the moment after he lost Paradise; and that if he had remained in his primitive innocence, and continued to enjoy the blessings that attended it, there is no shadow of probability that he ever would have become that sociable creature he is now.

How necessary our appetites and passions are for the welfare of all trades and handicrafts has been sufficiently proved throughout the book, and that they are our bad qualities, or at least produce them, nobody denies. It remains then that I should set forth the variety of obstacles that hinder and perplex man in the labor he is constantly employed in, the procuring of what he wants; and which in other words is called the business of self-preservation: while at the same time I demonstrate that the sociableness of man arises only from these two things, viz. the multiplicity of his desires, and the continual opposition he meets with in his endeavors to gratify them.

The obstacles I speak of relate either to our own frame, or the globe we inhabit; I mean the condition of it, since it has been cursed. I have often endeavored to contemplate separately on the two things I named last, but could never keep them asunder; they always interfere and mix with one another, and at last make up together a frightful chaos of evil. All the elements are our enemies;

water drowns and fire consumes those who unskillfully approach them. The earth in a thousand places produces plants and other vegetables that are hurtful to man, while she feeds and cherishes a variety of creatures that are noxious to him; and suffers a legion of poisons to dwell within her: but the most unkind of all the elements is that which we cannot live one moment without. It is impossible to repeat all the injuries we receive from the wind and weather; and though the greatest part of mankind have ever been employed in defending their species from the inclemency of the air, yet no art or labor have hitherto been able to find a security against the wild rage of some meteors.

Hurricanes, it is true, happen but seldom, and few men are swallowed up by earthquakes or devoured by lions; but while we escape those gigantic mischiefs, we are persecuted by trifles. What a vast variety of insects are tormenting to us; what multitudes of them insult and make game of us with impunity! The most despicable scruple not to trample and graze upon us as cattle do upon a field: which yet is often bore with, if moderately they use their fortune; but here again our clemency becomes a vice, and so encroaching are their cruelty and contempt of us on our pity, that they make laystalls of our heads, and devour our younger ones if we are not daily vigilant in pursuing and destroying them.

There is nothing good in all the universe to the best-designing man if either through mistake or ignorance he commits the least failing in the use of it; there is no innocence or integrity that can protect a man from a thousand mischiefs that surround him: on the contrary, everything is evil which art and experience have not taught us to turn into a blessing. Therefore how diligent in harvest time is the husbandman in getting in his crop and sheltering it from rain, without which he could never have enjoyed it! As seasons differ with the climates, experience has taught us differently to make use of them, and in one part of the globe we may see the farmer sow while he is reaping in the other; from all which we may learn how vastly this earth must have been altered since the fall of our first parents. For should we trace man from his beautiful, his divine original, not proud of wisdom acquired by haughty precept or tedious experience, but endued with consummate knowledge the moment he was formed; I mean the state of innocence, in which no animal nor vegetable upon earth, nor mineral under ground was noxious to him, and himself secure from the injuries of the air as well as all other harms, was contented with the necessaries of life, which the globe he inhabited furnished him with, without his assistance. When yet not conscious of guilt, he found himself in every place to be the well-obeyed unrivaled lord of all, and unaffected with his greatness, was wholly rapt up in sublime meditations on the infinity of his Creator, who daily did vouchsafe intelligibly to speak to him, and visit without mischief.

In such a Golden Age no reason or probability can be alleged why mankind ever should have raised themselves into such large societies as there have been in the world as long as we can give any tolerable account of it. Where a man has everything he desires, and nothing to vex or disturb him, there is nothing can be added to his happiness; and it is impossible to name a trade, art, science, dignity or employment that would not be superfluous in such a blessed state. If we pursue this thought, we shall easily perceive that no societies could have sprung from the amiable virtues and loving qualities of man, but on the contrary that all of them must have had their origin from his wants, his imperfections, and the variety of his appetites: we shall find likewise that the more their pride and vanity are displayed and all their desires enlarged, the more capable they must be of being raised into large and vastly numerous societies.

Was the air always as inoffensive to our naked bodies, and as pleasant as to our thinking it is to the generality of birds in fair weather, and man had not been affected with pride, luxury, and hypocrisy, as well as lust, I cannot see what could have put us upon the invention of clothes and houses. I shall say nothing of jewels, of plate, painting, sculpture, fine furniture, and all that rigid moralists have called unnecessary and superfluous: but if we were not soon tired with walking afoot, and were as nimble as some other animals; if men were naturally laborious, and none unreasonable in seeking and indulging their ease, and likewise free from other vices, and the ground was everywhere even, solid, and clean, who would have thought of coaches or ventured on a horse's back? What occasion has the dolphin for a ship, or what carriage would an eagle ask to travel in?

I hope the reader knows that by society I understand a body politic, in which man either subdued by superior force, or by persuasion drawn from his savage state, is become a disciplined creature that can find his own ends in laboring for others, and where under one head or other form of government each member is rendered subservient to the whole, and all of them by cunning management are made to act as one. For if by society we only mean a number of people that without rule or government should keep together out of a natural affection to their species or love of company, as a herd of cows or a flock of sheep, then there is not in the world a more unfit creature for society than man; an hundred of them that should be all equals, under no subjection or fear of any superior upon earth, could never live together awake two hours without quarreling, and the more knowledge, strength, wit, courage, and resolution there was among them, the worse it would be.

It is probable that in the wild State of Nature parents would keep a superiority over their children, at least while they were in strength, and that even afterwards the remembrance of what the others had experienced might produce in them something between love and fear, which we call reverence: it is probable likewise that the second generation following the example of the first, a man with a little cunning would always be able, as long as he lived and had his senses, to maintain a superior sway over all his own offspring and descendants, how numerous soever they might grow. But the old stock once dead, the sons would quarrel, and there could be no peace long, before there had been war. Eldership in brothers is of no great force, and the pre-eminence that is given to it only invented as a shift to live in peace. Man, as he is a fearful animal, naturally not rapacious, loves peace and quiet, and he would never fight, if nobody offended him and he could have what he fights for without it. To this fearful disposition and the aversion he has to his being disturbed, are owing all the various projects and forms of government. Monarchy without doubt was the first. Aristocracy and democracy were two different methods of mending the inconveniences of the first, and a mixture of these three an improvement on all the rest.

But be we savages or politicians, it is impossible that man, mere fallen man, should act with any other view but to please himself while he has the use of his organs, and the greatest extravagancy either of love or despair can have no other center. There is no difference between will and pleasure in one sense, and every motion made in spite of them must be unnatural and convulsive. Since, then, action is so confined, and we are always forced to do what we please, and at the same time our thoughts are free and uncontrolled, it is impossible we could be sociable creatures without hypocrisy. The proof of this is plain, since we cannot prevent the ideas that are continually arising within us; all civil commerce would be lost if by art and prudent dissimulation we had not learned to hide and stifle them; and if all we think was to be laid open to others in the same manner as it is to ourselves, it is impossible that endued with speech we could be sufferable to one another. I am persuaded that every reader feels the truth of what I say; and I tell my antagonist that his conscience flies in his face, while his tongue is preparing to refute me. In all civil societies men are taught insensibly to be hypocrites from their cradle; nobody dares to own that he gets by public calamities, or even by the loss of private persons. The sexton would be stoned should he wish openly for the death of the parishioners, though everybody knew that he had nothing else to live upon. . . .

The greater the variety of trades and manufactures, the more operose they are, and the more they are divided in many branches, the greater numbers may be contained in a society without being in one another's way, and the more easily they may be rendered a rich, potent, and flourishing people. Few virtues employ any hands, and therefore they may render a small nation good, but they can never make a great one. To be strong and laborious, patient in difficulties, and assiduous in all business, are commendable qualities; but as they do their own work, so they are their own reward, and neither art nor industry have ever paid their compliments to them; whereas the excellency of human thought and contrivance has been and is yet nowhere more conspicuous than in the variety of tools and instruments of workmen and artificers, and the multiplicity of engines that were all invented either to assist the weakness of man, to correct his many imperfections, to gratify his laziness, or obviate his impatience.

It is in morality as it is in Nature, there is nothing so perfectly good in creatures that it cannot be hurtful to anyone of the society, nor anything so entirely evil, but it may prove beneficial to some part or other of the creation: so that things are only good and evil in reference to something else, and according to the light and position they are placed in. What pleases us is good in that regard, and by this rule every man wishes well for himself to the best of his capacity, with little respect to his neighbor. There never was any rain yet, though in a very dry season when public prayers had been made for it, but somebody or other who wanted to go abroad wished it might be fair weather only for that day. When the corn stands thick in the spring, and the generality of the country rejoice at the pleasing object, the rich farmer who kept his last year's crop for a better market, pines at the sight, and inwardly grieves at the prospect of a plentiful harvest. Nay, we shall often hear your idle people openly wish for the possessions of others, and not to be injurious forsooth add this wise proviso, that it should be without detriment to the owners: but I'm afraid they often do it without any such restriction in their hearts.

It is a happiness that the prayers as well as wishes of most people are insignificant and good for nothing; or else the only thing that could keep mankind fit for society, and the world from falling into confusion, would be the impossibility that all the petitions made to Heaven should be granted. A dutiful pretty young gentleman newly come from his travels lies at the Briel waiting with impatience for an easterly wind to waft him over to England, where a dying father, who wants to embrace and give him his blessing before he yields his breath, lies honing after him, melted with grief and tenderness: in the meanwhile a British minister who is to take care of the Protestant interest in Germany is riding post to Harwich, and in violent haste to be at Ratisbon before the Diet breaks up. At the same time a rich fleet lies ready for the Mediterranean, and a fine squadron is bound for the Baltic. All these things may probably happen at once; at least there is no difficulty in supposing they should. If these people are not atheists or very great reprobates, they will all have some good thoughts before they go to sleep, and consequently about bedtime they must all differently pray for a fair wind and a prosperous voyage. I don't say but it is their duty, and it is possible they may be all heard, but I am sure they can't be all served at the same time.

After this I flatter myself to have demonstrated that, neither the friendly qualities and kind affections that are natural to man, nor the real virtues he is capable of acquiring by reason and self-denial, are the foundation of society; but that what we call evil in this world, moral as well as natural, is the grand principle that makes us sociable creatures, the solid basis, the life and support of all trades and employments without exception: that there we must look for the true origin of all arts and sciences, and that the moment evil ceases, the society must be spoiled, if not totally dissolved.

I could add a thousand things to enforce and further illustrate this truth with abundance of pleasure; but for fear of being troublesome I shall make an end, though I confess that I have not been half so solicitous to gain the approbation of others as I have studied to please myself in this amusement; yet if ever I hear that by following this diversion I have given any to the intelligent reader, it will always add to the satisfaction I have received in the performance. In the hope my vanity forms of this I leave him with regret, and conclude with repeating the seeming paradox, the substance of which is advanced in the title page: that private vices by the dextrous management of a skillful politician may be turned into public benefits.

Joseph Addison

1672–1719

Richard Steele

1672–1729

IT has been suspected that Joseph Addison is the first of the Victorians because he is so respectable. His is not the respectability of the Victorians, however, although one of the few matters that could kindle him to rapture was that "grand scene of happiness," the Royal Exchange. Dr. Johnson remarked that Addison thinks justly but faintly. The Augustan regard for propriety or "justness" is everywhere in Addison; this, with his ability to touch a subject gracefully and without pedantry, marks him as belonging to the eighteenth, not the nineteenth, century. He is, above all others of his day, a "polite" writer. His "justness," his wit, his feeling, and his cheerfulness are held in nice balance. His satire has the exquisite poise of the rococo. His moralizing is of a genteel sort, of low density. Anything more emphatic would savor of zeal, and Addison dreads zeal quite as much as does Chesterfield. Contrast the insinuating platitudes of Addison with the vehemence of Milton: nothing could better show the revolution that occurred between the seventeenth and eighteenth centuries. Addison is cautious. There is something inscrutable in his temperament. Although he was a "party" man, he was never very aggressive. Pope's famous sketch of Atticus is evidently just:

> Willing to wound, and yet afraid to strike,
> Just hint a fault, and hesitate dislike;
> Alike reserv'd to blame, or to commend,
> A tim'rous foe, and a suspicious friend.

His letters show almost nothing of the man—circumspect, colorless, placid. In spite of this negative disposition, Addison has a cultivated mind and a surprising curiosity. He is a literary critic of major proportions; his papers on Milton, the imagination, wit and taste, and gardening are of the first importance. His criticism, like his moralizing, is governed by taste; he holds his principles as a kind of social grace, and would evaluate not by rule but by "beauties." He has also the distinctively British relish for the odd or "humorous." The De Coverley papers, the "characters" of Tom Folio, Ned Softly, and Will Wimble belong in the continuous tradition of "humors" running from Chaucer and Shakespeare to Fielding, Goldsmith, and Dickens. These characters move in the social milieu so agreeably drawn in the *Spectator* papers—Lucinda's library, the coffeehouse, the parish church, the country house, the exchange, Westminster Abbey. The material for prose fiction is here; the whole thing is done easily and genially with a gusto one hardly expects.

It is reported that Addison pressed his friend Steele for a debt until a breach between them resulted. Steele, who composed many of the happiest *Spectators* and who carried the burden of the *Tatler*, was a man of perfect "good humor." All he wished was to please and to be pleased, his friends said. He has the Augustan grace, but he is a more full-blooded person than Addison, less judicial and more impulsive. The Augustan propriety begins to melt a little under the sentimentalism of Steele, who like Thomson cultivates "the social passions." Whenever we find a *Spectator* paper pleading for the fallen woman or for charity to the poor, it is almost certain to be Steele's. The tear shed for its own sake begins to glitter in his eye; he shuts himself in his room determined to be sorrowful by thinking upon his dead friends. He is less tactfully moral than Addison; his exhortations are more warmly thrown out. He conducts a campaign against dueling; he writes *The Conscious Lovers* "to chasten wit and moralize the stage." Though his taste is not so certain as Addison's, we cannot help liking Dick Steele as we cannot help liking Oliver Goldsmith. He is not of the same order of Augustans as his chilly friend Addison, who thawed out only in the fellowship of the coffeehouse.

Addison

Son of the Rector of Milston, Wiltshire (later Dean of Lichfield). Attended Charterhouse (1686–87), where he knew Steele; then entered
Queen's College, Oxford (1687). *An Account of the Greatest English
Poets* (1694). Translated classical authors for Tonson. Elected fellow
of Magdalen College (1698). Traveled in France and Italy upon a fellowship gained through Lord Halifax (1699–1703). Again in London,
became one of the Whig Kit-Kat Club. Printed *The Campaign* (1705)
for the Whigs to celebrate Marlborough's victory at Blenheim. Appointed Under-Secretary of State. Comic opera *Rosamund* (1707) was
acted, but failed. Elected M.P. for Lostwithiel. Appointed Secretary
to the Lord Lieutenant of Ireland (1709); in Ireland, met Swift, who
was a good friend until Swift went over to the Tories. Back in London,
Addison began to contribute to Steele's *Tatler* (1709). Presided over
his "little senate" in Button's Coffeehouse. *The Spectator* begun
(1710/11), for which Addison wrote 274 numbers and Steele 236. Addison's *Cato* produced (1713), with a run of at least twenty nights.
Contributed to *The Guardian* (1713). Rupture with Pope, chiefly due
to Addison's promoting Tickell's translation of the *Iliad*. Wrote *The
Drummer*, a comedy (1715). Conducted *Freeholder* to support Whigs
(1715). Married the Countess Dowager of Warwick (1716), by report
unhappily. Gradual estrangement from Steele over political and personal issues. Appointed Commissioner for Trade and the Colonies
(1716) and Secretary of State (1717–18). Gradual decline from dropsy
and asthma.

Steele

Son of a Dublin attorney. Entered Charterhouse (1684), where he knew
Addison. Entered Christ Church College, Oxford (1689). Left college
to enlist in the army (1694). Knew Congreve and Vanbrugh; fought
duel with Captain Kelly (1700). Printed *The Christian Hero* (1701)
"to fix upon his own mind a strong impression of virtue." *The Funeral*,
a comedy, acted at Drury Lane (1701). *The Lying Lover*, a comedy,
acted at Drury Lane (1703). *The Tender Husband* produced at Drury
Lane, with a prologue by Addison (1705). Married Mrs. Stretch, a
widow with estates in Barbados (1705); she died the next year. Appointed gazetteer by Harley (1707). Married Mary Scurlock (1707).
Financial difficulties. Issued *The Tatler* (1709–11), composing 188 of
the 271 numbers. Appointed Commissioner of Stamps (1710). Began
aiding Addison with *The Spectator* (1711). Political disputes with
Swift and the Tories. Edited *The Guardian* and *The Englishman*
(1713–14). Obtained patent at Drury Lane theater (1715). Knighted
(1715). His wife died (1718). Estranged from Addison (*ca.* 1719). *The
Conscious Lovers* acted at the Drury Lane (1722). Last days clouded
by debts.

BIBLIOGRAPHY

The Tatler, ed. G. A. Aitken, 4 vols., 1898–99. *The Spectator,* ed. G. A. Aitken, 8 vols., 1898. *The Spectator,* ed. G. G. Smith, 8 vols., 1897–98.

ADDISON: *Letters,* ed. Walter Graham, 1941. Aikin, Lucy, *Life of Joseph Addison,* 2 vols., 1843. Courthope, W. J., *Addison,* 1911. Dobrée, Bonamy, *Essays in Biography,* 1925. Lannering, Jan, *Studies in the Prose Style of Joseph Addison,* 1951. Lewis, C. S., *Essays on the Eighteenth Century Presented to D. Nichol Smith,* 1945. Smithers, Peter, *Life of Joseph Addison,* 1954.

STEELE: *Correspondence,* ed. Rae Blanchard, 1941. Connely, Willard, *Sir Richard Steele,* 1934.

THE TATLER

1709–1711

No. 1.

[Steele]   Tuesday, April 12, 1709.

Quicquid agunt homines . . . nostri farrago libelli
—Juvenal.[1]

Though the other papers which are published for the use of the good people of England have certainly very wholesome effects and are laudable in their particular kinds, they do not seem to come up to the main design of such narrations, which, I humbly presume, should be principally intended for the use of politic persons who are so public-spirited as to neglect their own affairs to look into transactions of state. Now these gentlemen, for the most part, being men of strong zeal and weak intellects, it is both a charitable and necessary work to offer something whereby such worthy and well-affected members of the commonwealth may be instructed, after their reading, *what to think;* which shall be the end and purpose of this my paper: wherein I shall from time to time report and consider all matters of what kind soever that shall occur to me, and publish such my advices and reflections every Tuesday, Thursday, and Saturday in the week for the convenience of the post. I resolve also to have something which may be of entertainment to the fair sex, in honor of whom I have taken the title of this paper. I therefore earnestly desire all persons, without distinction, to take it in for the present gratis and hereafter at the price of one penny, forbidding all hawkers to take more for it at their peril. And I desire all persons to consider that I am at a very great charge for proper materials for this work, as well as that before I resolved upon it, I had settled a correspondence in all parts of the

1 *Satires* I. 85, 86: "Whatever mankind does shall be the motley substance of my book."

known and knowing world. And forasmuch as this globe is not trodden upon by mere drudges of business only, but that men of spirit and genius are justly to be esteemed as considerable agents in it, we shall not, upon a dearth of news, present you with musty foreign edicts or dull proclamations, but shall divide our relation of the passages which occur in action or discourse throughout this town, as well as elsewhere, under such dates of places as may prepare you for the matter you are to expect, in the following manner:

All accounts of gallantry, pleasure, and entertainment shall be under the article of White's Chocolatehouse; poetry, under that of Will's Coffeehouse; learning, under the title of Grecian; foreign and domestic news, you will have from St. James's Coffeehouse; and what else I shall on any other subject offer shall be dated from my own apartment.

I once more desire my readers to consider that as I cannot keep an ingenious man to go daily to Will's under twopence each day merely for his charges, to White's under sixpence, nor to the Grecian without allowing him some plain Spanish, to be as able as others at the learned table; and that a good observer cannot speak with even Kidney [2] at St. James's without clean linen; I say, these considerations will, I hope, make all persons willing to comply with my humble request (when my gratis stock is exhausted) of a penny apiece; especially since they are sure of some proper amusement, and that it is impossible for me to want means to entertain them, having, besides the force of my own parts, the power of divination, and that I can, by casting a figure, tell you all that will happen before it comes to pass.

But this last faculty I shall use very sparingly, and speak of but few things until they are passed, for fear of divulging matters which may offend our superiors.

No. 181.

[Steele] Tuesday, June 6, 1710.

―――Dies, ni fallor, adest, quem sempeɪ acerbum,
Semper honoratum (sic di voluistis), habebo.

—Vergil.[1]

―――――――

2 One of the waiters.
1 *Aeneid* V. 49: "If I err not, that day is at hand which shall to me be ever bitter yet ever honored (So, O gods, have ye willed)."

From my own Apartment, June 5.

There are those among mankind who can enjoy no relish of their being except the world is made acquainted with all that relates to them, and think everything lost that passes unobserved; but others find a solid delight in stealing by the crowd and modeling their life after such a manner as is as much above the approbation as the practice of the vulgar. Life being too short to give instances great enough of true friendship or goodwill, some sages have thought it pious to preserve a certain reverence for the manes of their deceased friends, and have withdrawn themselves from the rest of the world at certain seasons to commemorate in their own thoughts such of their acquaintance who have gone before them out of this life; and indeed, when we are advanced in years, there is not a more pleasing entertainment than to recollect in a gloomy moment the many we have parted with that have been dear and agreeable to us, and to cast a melancholy thought or two after those with whom, perhaps, we have indulged ourselves in whole nights of mirth and jollity. With such inclinations in my heart, I went to my closet yesterday in the evening, and resolved to be sorrowful; upon which occasion, I could not but look with disdain upon myself, that, though all the reasons which I had to lament the loss of many of my friends are now as forcible as at the moment of their departure, yet did not my heart swell with the same sorrow which I felt at that time; but I could, without tears, reflect upon many pleasing adventures I have had with some who have long been blended with common earth. Though it is by the benefit of nature that length of time thus blots out the violence of afflictions, yet with tempers too much given to pleasure it is almost necessary to revive the old places of grief in our memory, and ponder step by step on past life, to lead the mind into that sobriety of thought which poises the heart and makes it beat with due time, without being quickened with desire, or retarded with despair, from its proper and equal motion. When we wind up a clock that is out of order to make it go well for the future, we do not immediately set the hand to the present instant, but we make it strike the round of all its hours before it can recover the regularity of its time. "Such," thought I, "shall be my method this evening; and since it is that day of the year which I dedicate to the memory of such in another life as I much delighted in when living, an hour or two shall be sacred to sorrow and their memory, while I run over all the melancholy circumstances of this kind which have occurred to me in my whole life."

The first sense of sorrow I ever knew was upon the death of my father, at which time I was not quite five years of age, but was rather amazed at what all the house meant than possessed with a real understanding why nobody was willing to play with me. I remember I went into the room where his body lay, and my mother sat weeping alone by it. I had my battledore in my hand, and fell a-beating the coffin, and calling "Papa"; for I know not how I had some slight idea that he was locked up there. My mother catched me in her arms, and, transported beyond all patience of the silent grief she was before in, she almost smothered me in her embrace, and told me, in a flood of tears, papa could not hear me, and would play with me no more, for they were going to put him underground, whence he could never come to us again. She was a very beautiful woman, of a noble spirit, and there was a dignity in her grief amidst all the wildness of her transport, which, methought, struck me with an instinct of sorrow which, before I was sensible of what it was to grieve, seized my very soul, and has made pity the weakness of my heart ever since. The mind in infancy is, methinks, like the body in embryo, and receives impressions so forcible that they are as hard to be removed by reason as any mark with which a child is born is to be taken away by any future application. Hence it is that good nature in me is no merit; but, having been so frequently overwhelmed with her tears before I knew the cause of any affliction, or could draw defenses from my own judgment, I imbibed commiseration, remorse, and an unmanly gentleness of mind which has since ensnared me into ten thousand calamities, and from whence I can reap no advantage, except it be that in such a humor as I am now in I can the better indulge myself in the softnesses of humanity, and enjoy that sweet anxiety which arises from the memory of past afflictions.

We that are very old are better able to remember things which befell us in our distant youth than the passages of later days. For this reason it is that the companions of my strong and vigorous years present themselves more immediately to me in this office of sorrow. Untimely or unhappy deaths are what we are most apt to lament, so little are we able to make it indifferent when a thing happens, though we know it must happen. Thus we groan under life, and bewail those who are relieved from it. Every object that returns to our imagination raises different passions according to the circumstance of their departure. Who can have lived in an army, and in a serious hour reflect upon the many gay and agreeable men that might long have flourished in the arts of peace, and not join with the imprecations of the fatherless and widow on the tyrant to whose ambition they fell sacrifices? But gallant men who are cut off by the sword move rather our veneration than our pity, and we gather relief enough from their own contempt of death, to make it no evil, which was approached with so much cheerfulness and attended with so much honor. But when we turn our thoughts from the great parts of life on such occasions, and, instead of lamenting those who stood ready to give death to those from whom they had the fortune to receive it—I say, when we let our thoughts wander from such noble objects, and consider the havoc which is made among the tender and the innocent, pity enters with an unmixed softness, and possesses all our souls at once.

Here (were there words to express such sentiments with proper tenderness) I should record the beauty, innocence, and untimely death of the first object my eyes ever beheld with love. The beauteous virgin! How ignorantly did she charm, how carelessly excel! O Death! thou hast right to the bold, to the ambitious, to the high, and to the haughty; but why this cruelty to the humble, to the meek, to the undiscerning, to the thoughtless? Nor age, nor business, nor distress can erase the dear image from my imagination. In the same week, I saw her dressed for a ball and in a shroud. How ill did the habit of Death become the pretty trifler! I still behold the smiling earth— A large train of disasters were coming on to my memory, when my servant knocked at my closet door and interrupted me with a letter, attended with a hamper of wine, of the same sort with that which is to be put to sale on Thursday next at Garraway's Coffeehouse. Upon the receipt of it, I sent for three of my friends. We are so intimate that we can be company in whatever state of mind we meet, and can entertain each other without expecting always to rejoice. The wine we found to be generous and warming, but with such a heat as moved us rather to be cheerful than frolicsome. It revived the spirits without firing the blood. We commended it till two of the clock this morning, and, having today met a little before dinner, we found that, though we drank two bottles a man, we had much more reason to recollect than forget what had passed the night before.

THE SPECTATOR

No. 18.
[Addison]   Wednesday, March 21, 1710/11.

——Equitis quoque jam migravit ab aure voluptas
Omnis ad incertos oculos et gaudia vana.

—Horace.[1]

It is my design in this paper to deliver down to posterity a faithful account of the Italian opera, and of the gradual progress which it has made upon the English stage: for there is no question but our great-grandchildren will be very curious to know the reason why their forefathers used to sit together like an audience of foreigners in their own country, and to hear whole plays acted before them in a tongue which they did not understand.

Arsinoe [2] was the first opera that gave us a taste of Italian music. The great success this opera met with produced some attempts of forming pieces upon Italian plans, which should give a more natural and reasonable entertainment than what can be met with in the elaborate trifles of that nation. This alarmed the poetasters and fiddlers of the town, who were used to deal in a more ordinary kind of ware; and therefore laid down an established rule, which is received as such to this day, *that nothing is capable of being well set to music, that is not nonsense.*

This maxim was no sooner received but we immediately fell to translating the Italian operas; and as there was no great danger of hurting the sense of those extraordinary pieces, our authors would often make words of their own which were entirely foreign to the meaning of the passages they pretended to translate; their chief care being to make the numbers of the English verse answer

---

1 *Epistles* II. i. 187:
"But sound no longer pleases ev'n the knight;
He loves the vain capricious joys of sight."
[Boscawen]

2 Adapted from the Italian with a score by Thomas Clayton, and produced at Drury Lane on Jan. 16, 1705.

to those of the Italian, that both of them might go to the same
tune. Thus the famous song in *Camilla*,[3]

Barbara si t' intendo, &c.
Barbarous woman, yes, I know your meaning,

which expresses the resentments of an angry lover, was translated
into that English lamentation,

Frail are a lover's hopes, &c.

And it was pleasant enough to see the most refined persons of the
British nation dying away and languishing to notes that were
filled with a spirit of rage and indignation. It happened also very
frequently, where the sense was rightly translated, the necessary
transposition of words, which were drawn out of the phrase of
one tongue into that of another, made the music appear very absurd
in one tongue that was very natural in the other. I remember an
Italian verse that ran thus word for word,

And turn'd my rage into pity:

which the English for rhyme sake translated,

And into pity turn'd my rage.

By this means the soft notes that were adapted to *pity* in the Italian
fell upon the word *rage* in the English, and the angry sounds that
were turned to *rage* in the original were made to express *pity* in
the translation. It oftentimes happened likewise that the finest notes
in the air fell upon the most insignificant words in the sentence.
I have known the word *and* pursued through the whole gamut,
have been entertained with many a melodious *the*, and have heard
the most beautiful graces, quavers, and divisions bestowed upon
then, *for*, and *from;* to the eternal honor of our English particles.

The next step to our refinement was the introducing of Italian
actors into our opera; who sung their parts in their own language,
at the same time that our countrymen performed theirs in our
native tongue. The king or hero of the play generally spoke in
Italian, and his slaves answered him in English: the lover frequently made his court, and gained the heart of his princess, in a
language which she did not understand. One would have thought
it very difficult to have carried on dialogues after this manner with-

---

3 By Bononcini, produced at Drury Lane in 1706. The hero sang in Italian, the heroine
in English.

out an interpreter between the persons that conversed together; but this was the state of the English stage for about three years.

At length the audience grew tired of understanding half the opera and therefore, to ease themselves entirely of the fatigue of thinking, have so ordered it at present that the whole opera is performed in an unknown tongue. We no longer understand the language of our own stage; insomuch that I have often been afraid, when I have seen our Italian performers chattering in the vehemence of action, that they have been calling us names, and abusing us among themselves; but I hope, since we do put such an entire confidence in them, they will not talk against us before our faces, though they may do it with the same safety as if it were behind our backs. In the meantime, I cannot forbear thinking how naturally an historian who writes two or three hundred years hence, and does not know the taste of his wise forefathers, will make the following reflection: *In the beginning of the eighteenth century the Italian tongue was so well understood in* England *that operas were acted on the public stage in that language.*

One scarce knows how to be serious in the confutation of an absurdity that shows itself at the first sight. It does not want any great measure of sense to see the ridicule of this monstrous practice; but what makes it the more astonishing, it is not the taste of the rabble, but of persons of the greatest politeness, which has established it.

If the Italians have a genius for music above the English, the English have a genius for other performances of a much higher nature, and capable of giving the mind a much nobler entertainment. Would one think it was possible (at a time when an author lived that was able to write the *Phaedra and Hippolytus* [4]) for a people to be so stupidly fond of the Italian opera as scarce to give a third day's hearing to that admirable tragedy? Music is certainly a very agreeable entertainment, but if it would take the entire possession of our ears, if it would make us incapable of hearing sense, if it would exclude arts that have a much greater tendency to the refinement of human nature, I must confess I would allow it no better quarter than Plato has done, who banishes it out of his commonwealth.

At present, our notions of music are so very uncertain that we do not know what it is we like; only, in general, we are transported

4 By Edmund Smith (1707); Addison wrote the Prologue.

with anything that is not English. So if it be of a foreign growth, let it be Italian, French, or High Dutch, it is the same thing. In short, our English music is quite rooted out and nothing yet planted in its stead.

When a royal palace is burnt to the ground, every man is at liberty to present his plan for a new one; and though it be but indifferently put together, it may furnish several hints that may be of use to a good architect. I shall take the same liberty in a following paper, of giving my opinion upon the subject of music; which I shall lay down only in a problematical manner, to be considered by those who are masters in the art.   C.

No. 37.
[Addison]
                                        Thursday, April 12, 1711.

——Non illa colo calathisve Minervae
Foemineas assueta manus.

                                        —Vergil.[1]

Some months ago my friend Sir Roger, being in the country, enclosed a letter to me, directed to a certain lady whom I shall here call by the name of Leonora, and, as it contained matters of consequence, desired me to deliver it to her with my own hand. Accordingly I waited upon her ladyship pretty early in the morning, and was desired by her woman to walk into her lady's library till such time as she was in a readiness to receive me. The very sound of a lady's library gave me a great curiosity to see it; and, as it was some time before the lady came to me, I had an opportunity of turning over a great many of her books, which were ranged together in a very beautiful order. At the end of the folios (which were finely bound and gilt) were great jars of china placed one above another in a very noble piece of architecture. The quartos were separated from the octavos by a pile of smaller vessels, which rose in a delightful pyramid. The octavos were bounded by tea-dishes of all shapes, colors, and sizes, which were so disposed on a wooden frame that they looked like one continued pillar indented with the finest strokes of sculpture, and stained with the greatest variety of dyes. That part of the library which was designed for the reception of plays and pamphlets and other loose papers was enclosed in a kind of square, consisting of one of the prettiest

1 *Aeneid* VII. 805: "Unbred to spinning, in the loom unskill'd." [Dryden]

grotesque works that ever I saw, and made up of scaramouches, lions, monkeys, mandarins, trees, shells, and a thousand other odd figures in chinaware. In the midst of the room was a little japan table, with a quire of gilt paper upon it, and on the paper a silver snuffbox made in the shape of a little book. I found there were several other counterfeit books upon the upper shelves, which were carved in wood, and served only to fill up the number, like fagots in the muster of a regiment. I was wonderfully pleased with such a mixed kind of furniture as seemed very suitable both to the lady and the scholar, and did not know at first whether I should fancy myself in a grotto or in a library.

Upon my looking into the books, I found there were some few which the lady had bought for her own use, but that most of them had been got together either because she had heard them praised or because she had seen the authors of them. Among several that I examined, I very well remember these that follow: [2]

Ogleby's Vergil.
Dryden's Juvenal.
Cassandra.
Cleopatra.
Astraea.
Sir Isaac Newton's Works.
The Grand Cyrus: with a pin stuck in one of the middle leaves.
Pembroke's Arcadia.
Lock of Human Understanding: with a paper of patches in it.
A Spelling Book.
A Dictionary for the explanation of hard words.
Sherlock upon Death.
The fifteen Comforts of Matrimony.
Sir William Temple's Essays.
Father Malbranche's Search after Truth, translated into English.
A Book of Novels.

2 Of the books mentioned, *Cassandra* and *Cleopatra* (La Calprenède), *Astraea* (D'Urfé), *The Grand Cyrus* and *Clelia* (Mlle. de Scudéry) were seventeenth-century French romances from three to ten volumes long. *The New Atalantis* (1709) was a "secret memoir" from the unsavory pen of Mrs. Mary Manley. *The Fifteen Comforts of Matrimony* was translated from the French book of the same name in 1682. *The Ladies' Calling* (ca. 1700) was by the author of *The Whole Duty of Man. The Academy of*

Compliments appeared in 1705. The remaining books include William Sherlock's *Discourse concerning Death* (1689), Sir Richard Baker's *Chronicle of the Kings of England* (1643), George Savile, Marquess of Halifax's *Advice to a Daughter* (1688), the *Speech* of Henry Sacheverell, the Tory clergyman impeached in 1710 for attacking prominent Whigs under disguised names, and an account of the trial of Robert Feilding (1706), accused of "having two wives."

The Academy of Compliments.

Culpepper's Midwifery.

The Ladies' Calling.

Tales in Verse by Mr. Durfey: bound in red leather, gilt on the back, and doubled down in several places.

All the Classic Authors in Wood.

A set of Elzevirs by the same Hand.

Clelia: which opened of itself in the place that describes two lovers in a bower.

Baker's Chronicle.

Advice to a Daughter.

The New Atalantis, with a Key to it.

Mr. Steele's Christian Hero.

A Prayer-book: with a bottle of Hungary water [3] by the side of it.

Dr. Sacheverell's Speech.

Fielding's Trial.

Seneca's Morals.

Taylor's Holy Living and Dying.

La Ferte's Instructions for Country Dances.

I was taking a catalogue in my pocket-book of these, and several other authors, when Leonora entered, and upon my presenting her with a letter from the knight, told me, with an unspeakable grace, that she hoped Sir Roger was in good health. I answered, "Yes," for I hate long speeches, and after a bow or two retired.

Leonora was formerly a celebrated beauty, and is still a very lovely woman. She has been a widow for two or three years, and, being unfortunate in her first marriage, has taken a resolution never to venture upon a second. She has no children to take care of, and leaves the management of her estate to my good friend Sir Roger. But as the mind naturally sinks into a kind of lethargy, and falls asleep, that is not agitated by some favorite pleasures and pursuits, Leonora has turned all the passions of her sex into a love of books and retirement. She converses chiefly with men (as she has often said herself), but it is only in their writings; and admits of very few male visitants, except my friend Sir Roger, whom she hears with great pleasure, and without scandal. As her reading has lain very much among romances, it has given her a very particular

3 Hungary water was used as a cordial and a lotion as well as a perfume.

turn of thinking, and discovers itself even in her house, her gardens, and her furniture. Sir Roger has entertained me an hour together with a description of her countryseat, which is situated in a kind of wilderness, about an hundred miles distant from London, and looks like a little enchanted palace. The rocks about her are shaped into artificial grottoes, covered with woodbines and jessamines. The woods are cut into shady walks, twisted into bowers, and filled with cages of turtles. The springs are made to run among pebbles, and by that means taught to murmur very agreeably. They are likewise collected into a beautiful lake that is inhabited by a couple of swans, and empties itself by a little rivulet which runs through a green meadow, and is known in the family by the name of the Purling Stream. The knight likewise tells me that this lady preserves her game better than any of the gentlemen in the country; not (says Sir Roger) that she sets so great a value upon her partridges and pheasants as upon her larks and nightingales. For she says that every bird which is killed in her ground will spoil a consort, and that she shall certainly miss him the next year.

When I think how oddly this lady is improved by learning, I look upon her with a mixture of admiration and pity. Amidst these innocent entertainments which she has formed to herself, how much more valuable does she appear than those of her sex who employ themselves in diversions that are less reasonable, though more in fashion! What improvements would a woman have made, who is so susceptible of impressions from what she reads, had she been guided to such books as have a tendency to enlighten the understanding and rectify the passions, as well as to those which are of little more use than to divert the imagination!

But the manner of a lady's employing herself usefully in reading shall be the subject of another paper, in which I design to recommend such particular books as may be proper for the improvement of the sex. And as this is a subject of a very nice nature, I shall desire my correspondents to give me their thoughts upon it.   C.

No. 42.
[Addison]   Wednesday, April 18, 1711.

> Garganum mugire putes nemus aut mare Tuscum,
> Tanto cum strepitu ludi spectantur, et artes,
> Divitiaeque peregrinae; quibus oblitus actor

Cum stetit in scena, concurrit dextera laevae.
Dixit adhuc aliquid? Nil sane. Quid placet ergo?
Lana Tarentino violas imitata veneno.

—Horace.[1]

Aristotle has observed that ordinary writers in tragedy endeavor
to raise terror and pity in their audience not by proper sentiments
and expressions, but by the dresses and decorations of the stage.
There is something of this kind very ridiculous in the English
theater. When the author has a mind to terrify us, it thunders;
when he would make us melancholy, the stage is darkened. But
among all our tragic artifices I am the most offended at those which
are made use of to inspire us with magnificent ideas of the persons
that speak. The ordinary method of making an hero is to clap a
huge plume of feathers upon his head, which rises so very high that
there is often a greater length from his chin to the top of his head
than to the sole of his foot. One would believe that we thought a
great man and a tall man the same thing. This very much em-
barrasses the actor, who is forced to hold his neck extremely stiff
and steady all the while he speaks; and notwithstanding any
anxieties which he pretends for his mistress, his country, or his
friends, one may see by his action that his greatest care and concern is to keep the plume of feathers from falling off his head.
For my own part, when I see a man uttering his complaints
under such a mountain of feathers, I am apt to look upon him
rather as an unfortunate lunatic than a distressed hero. As these
superfluous ornaments upon the head make a great man, a princess
generally receives her grandeur from those additional encum-
brances that fall into her tail: I mean the broad sweeping train
that follows her in all her motions, and finds constant employment for a boy who stands behind her to open and spread it to advantage. I do not know how others are affected at this sight, but
I must confess my eyes are wholly taken up with the page's part;
and as for the queen, I am not so attentive to anything she speaks
as to the right adjusting of her train, lest it should chance to trip

1 *Epistles* II. i. 202:
"Loud as the Gargan grove when tempests roar,
Or waves rebellowing on the Tuscan shore,
Such at the shows the thundering din we hear
When dresses wrought with foreign wealth appear.

O'erspread with these whene'er the actor stands
In sight conspicuous, what a peal of hands!
But has he spoken?—Not a single word.
What charms you then?—The violet robe, that dy'd
At soft Tarentum, shines in mimic pride."
[Boscawen]

up her heels or incommode her as she walks to and fro upon the stage. It is, in my opinion, a very odd spectacle to see a queen venting her passion in a disordered motion and a little boy taking care all the while that they do not ruffle the tail of her gown. The parts that the two persons act on the stage at the same time are very different: the princess is afraid lest she should incur the displeasure of the king, her father, or lose the hero, her lover, whilst her attendant is only concerned lest she should entangle her feet in her petticoat.

We are told that an ancient tragic poet, to move the pity of his audience for his exiled kings and distressed heroes, used to make the actors represent them in dresses and clothes that were threadbare and decayed. This artifice for moving pity seems as ill contrived as that we have been speaking of to inspire us with a great idea of the persons introduced upon the stage. In short, I would have our conceptions raised by the dignity of thought and sublimity of expression rather than by a train of robes or a plume of feathers.

Another mechanical method of making great men and adding dignity to kings and queens is to accompany them with halberts and battle-axes. Two or three shifters of scenes, with the two candle-snuffers, make up a complete body of guards upon the English stage; and by the addition of a few porters dressed in red coats can represent above a dozen legions. I have sometimes seen a couple of armies drawn up together upon the stage when the poet has been disposed to do honor to his generals. It is impossible for the reader's imagination to multiply twenty men into such prodigious multitudes, or to fancy that two or three hundred thousand soldiers are fighting in a room of forty or fifty yards in compass. Incidents of such nature should be told, not represented.

> ——Non tamen intus
> Digna geri promes in scenam: multaque tolles
> Ex oculis, quae mox narret facundia praesens.
> —Horace.[2]
>
> Yet there are things improper for a scene,
> Which men of judgment only will relate.
> —Ld. Roscommon.

I should therefore in this particular recommend to my countrymen the example of the French stage, where the kings and queens

2 *Ars Poetica* 182–84.

always appear unattended and leave their guards behind the scenes. I should likewise be glad if we imitated the French in banishing from our stage the noise of drums, trumpets, and huzzas; which is sometimes so very great that when there is a battle in the Haymarket Theater, one may hear it as far as Charing Cross.

I have here only touched upon those particulars which are made use of to raise and aggrandize the persons of a tragedy; and shall show in another paper the several expedients which are practiced by authors of a vulgar genius to move terror, pity, or admiration in their hearers.

The tailor and the painter often contribute to the success of a tragedy more than the poet. Scenes affect ordinary minds as much as speeches; and our actors are very sensible that a well-dressed play has sometimes brought them as full audiences as a well-written one. The Italians have a very good phrase to express this art of imposing upon the spectators by appearances: they call it the *fourberia della scena*, the knavery or trickish part of the drama. But however the show and outside of the tragedy may work upon the vulgar, the more understanding part of the audience immediately see through it and despise it.

A good poet will give the reader a more lively idea of an army or a battle in a description than if he actually saw them drawn up in squadrons and battalions or engaged in the confusion of a fight. Our minds should be opened to great conceptions and inflamed with glorious sentiments by what the actor speaks, more than by what he appears. Can all the trappings or equipage of a king or hero give Brutus half that pomp and majesty which he receives from a few lines in Shakespeare?

C.

No. 62.
[Addison]   Friday, May 11, 1711.

popular. of advanced thought of day

Scribendi recte sapere est et principium et fons.
—Horace.[1]

Mr. Locke has an admirable reflection upon the difference of wit and judgment, whereby he endeavors to show the reason why they are not always the talents of the same person. His words are as follow: "And hence, perhaps, may be given some reason of that common observation, that men who have a great deal of wit and

1 *Ars Poetica* 309: "Sound judgment is the ground of writing well." [Roscommon]

prompt memories have not always the clearest judgment or deepest reason. For wit lying most in the assemblage of ideas, and putting those together with quickness and variety wherein can be found any resemblance or congruity, thereby to make up pleasant pictures and agreeable visions in the fancy; judgment, on the contrary, lies quite on the other side, in separating carefully one from another ideas wherein can be found the least difference, thereby to avoid being misled by similitude, and by affinity to take one thing for another. This is a way of proceeding quite contrary to metaphor and allusion; wherein, for the most part, lies that entertainment and pleasantry of wit which strikes so lively on the fancy, and is therefore so acceptable to all people." [2]

That is, I think, the best and most philosophical account that I have ever met with of wit, which generally, though not always, consists in such a resemblance and congruity of ideas as this author mentions. I shall only add to it, by way of explanation, that every resemblance of ideas is not that which we call wit unless it be such a one that gives delight and surprise to the reader. These two properties seem essential to wit, more particularly the last of them. In order, therefore, that the resemblance in the ideas be wit, it is necessary that the ideas should not lie too near one another in the nature of things; for where the likeness is obvious, it gives no surprise. To compare one man's singing to that of another, or to represent the whiteness of any object by that of milk and snow, or the variety of its colors by those of the rainbow, cannot be called wit, unless, besides this obvious resemblance, there be some further congruity discovered in the two ideas that is capable of giving the reader some surprise. Thus when a poet tells us the bosom of his mistress is as white as snow, there is no wit in the comparison; but when he adds, with a sigh, that it is as cold too, it then grows into wit. Every reader's memory may supply him with innumerable instances of the same nature. For this reason the similitudes in heroic poets, who endeavor rather to fill the mind with great conceptions than to divert it with such as are new and surprising, have seldom anything in them that can be called wit. Mr. Locke's account of wit, with this short explanation, comprehends most of the species of wit, as metaphors, similitudes, allegories, enigmas, mottoes, parables, fables, dreams, visions, dramatic writings, burlesque, and all the methods of allusion: as there

2 *Essay Concerning Human Understanding* chap. XI.

are many other pieces of wit (how remote soever they may appear at first sight from the foregoing description) which upon examination will be found to agree with it.

As *true wit* generally consists in this resemblance and congruity of ideas, *false wit* chiefly consists in the resemblance and congruity sometimes of single letters, as in anagrams, chronograms, lipograms, and acrostics; sometimes of syllables, as in echoes and doggerel rhymes; sometimes of words, as in puns and quibbles; and sometimes of whole sentences or poems, cast into the figures of eggs, axes, or altars. Nay, some carry the notion of wit so far as to ascribe it even to external mimicry, and to look upon a man as an ingenious person, that can resemble the tone, posture, or face of another.

As true wit consists in the resemblance of ideas, and false wit in the resemblance of words, according to the foregoing instances, there is another kind of wit which consists partly in the resemblance of ideas and partly in the resemblance of words; which for distinction sake I shall call mixed wit. This kind of wit is that which abounds in Cowley more than in any other author that ever wrote. Mr. Waller has likewise a great deal of it. Mr. Dryden is very sparing in it. Milton had a genius much above it. Spenser is in the same class with Milton. The Italians, even in their epic poetry, are full of it. Monsieur Boileau, who formed himself upon the ancient poets, has everywhere rejected it with scorn. If we look after mixed wit among the Greek writers, we shall find it nowhere but in the epigrammatists. There are indeed some strokes of it in the little poem ascribed to Musaeus, which by that, as well as many other marks, betrays itself to be a modern composition. If we look into the Latin writers, we find none of this mixed wit in Vergil, Lucretius, or Catullus; very little in Horace, but a great deal of it in Ovid, and scarce anything else in Martial.

Out of the innumerable branches of mixed wit, I shall choose one instance which may be met with in all the writers of this class. The passion of love in its nature has been thought to resemble fire; for which reason the words *fire* and *flame* are made use of to signify love. The witty poets therefore have taken an advantage from the double meaning of the word fire to make an infinite number of witticisms. Cowley, observing the cold regard of his mistress's eyes, and at the same time their power of producing love in him, considers them as burning glasses made of ice; and, finding himself able to live in the greatest extremities of love, concludes the torrid zone to be habitable. When his mistress has read his letter written in juice of lemon by holding it to the fire, he desires her to read it over a second time by love's flames. When she weeps, he wishes it were inward heat that distilled those drops from the limbec. When she is absent, he is beyond eighty, that is, thirty degrees nearer the pole than when she is with him. His ambitious love is a fire that naturally mounts upwards; his happy love is the beams of Heaven, and his unhappy love flames of Hell. When it does not let him sleep, it is a flame that sends up no smoke; when it is opposed by counsel and advice, it is a fire that rages the more by the wind's blowing upon it. Upon the dying of a tree in which he had cut his loves, he observes that his written flames had burnt up and withered the tree. When he resolves to give over his passion, he tells us that one burnt like him forever dreads the fire. His heart is an Aetna, that instead of Vulcan's shop encloses Cupid's forge in it. His endeavoring to drown his love in wine is throwing oil upon the fire. He would insinuate to his mistress that the fire of love, like that of the sun (which produces so many living creatures), should not only warm but beget. Love in another place cooks pleasure at his fire. Sometimes the poet's heart is frozen in every breast, and sometimes scorched in every eye. Sometimes he is drowned in tears and burnt in love, like a ship set on fire in the middle of the sea.

The reader may observe in every one of these instances that the poet mixes the qualities of fire with those of love; and in the same sentence speaking of it both as a passion and as real fire, surprises the reader with those seeming resemblances or contradictions that make up all the wit in this kind of writing. Mixed wit therefore is a composition of pun and true wit, and is more or less perfect as the resemblance lies in the ideas or in the words. Its foundations are laid partly in falsehood and partly in truth: reason puts in her claim for one half of it, and extravagance for the other. The only province therefore for this kind of wit is epigram, or those little occasional poems that in their own nature are nothing else but a tissue of epigrams. I cannot conclude this head of mixed wit without owning that the admirable poet out of whom I have taken the examples of it had as much true wit as any author that ever writ and indeed all other talents of an extraordinary genius.

It may be expected, since I am upon this subject, that I should take notice of Mr. Dryden's definition of wit; which, with all the deference that is due to the judgment of so great a man, is not so properly a definition of wit as of good writing in general. Wit, as he defines it, is "a propriety of words and thoughts adapted to the subject." [3] If this be a true definition of wit, I am apt to think that Euclid was the greatest wit that ever set pen to paper. It is certain that never was a greater propriety of words and thoughts adapted to the subject than what that author has made use of in his *Elements*. I shall only appeal to my reader if this definition agrees with any notion he has of wit. If it be a true one, I am sure Mr. Dryden was not only a better poet, but a greater wit, than Mr. Cowley, and Vergil a much more facetious man than either Ovid or Martial. *elegant + Refined*

Bouhours,[4] whom I look upon to be the most penetrating of all the French critics, has taken pains to show that it is impossible for any thought to be beautiful which is not just, and has not its foundation in the nature of things; that the basis of all wit is truth; and *basis of all wit is truth from French criticism* that no thought can be valuable of which good sense is not the groundwork. Boileau has endeavored to inculcate the same notion in several parts of his writings, both in prose and verse. This is that natural way of writing, that beautiful simplicity, which we so much admire in the compositions of the ancients, and which nobody deviates from but those who want strength of genius to make a thought shine in its own natural beauties. Poets who want this strength of genius to give that majestic simplicity to nature which we so much admire in the works of the ancients are forced to hunt after foreign ornaments, and not to let any piece of wit of what kind soever escape them. I look upon these writers as Goths in poetry, who, like those in architecture, not being able to come up to the beautiful simplicity of the old Greeks and Romans, have endeavored to supply its place with all the extravagances of an irregular fancy. Mr. Dryden makes a very handsome observation on Ovid's writing a letter from Dido to Aeneas, in the following words: "Ovid," says he,[5] speaking of Vergil's fiction of Dido and Aeneas, "takes it up after him, even in the same age, and makes an ancient heroine of Vergil's new-created Dido; dictates a letter for her just before her death to the ungrateful fugitive; and, very unluckily for himself, is for measuring a sword with a man so much superior in force to

3 *Apology for Heroic Poetry,* prefacing *The State of Innocence* (1677).

4 Dominique Bouhours, *La Manière de bien penser* (1687).

5 *Dedication of the Aeneis* (1697).

him, on the same subject. I think I may be judge of this, because I have translated both. The famous author of *The Art of Love* has nothing of his own; he borrows all from a greater master in his own profession, and, which is worse, improves nothing which he finds. Nature fails him, and being forced to his old shift, he has recourse to witticism. This passes indeed with his soft admirers, and gives him the preference to Vergil in their esteem."

Were not I supported by so great an authority as that of Mr. Dryden, I should not venture to observe that the taste of most of our English poets, as well as readers, is extremely Gothic. He quotes Monsieur Segrais[6] for a threefold distinction of the readers of poetry, in the first of which he comprehends the rabble of readers, whom he does not treat as such with regard to their quality, but to their numbers and the coarseness of their taste. His words are as follows: "Segrais has distinguished the readers of poetry, according to their capacity of judging, into three classes. [He might have said the same of writers, too, if he had pleased.] In the lowest form he places those whom he calls *Les Petits Esprits,* such things as are our upper-gallery audience in a playhouse; who like nothing but the husk and rind of wit, prefer a quibble, a conceit, an epigram, before solid sense and elegant expression: these are mob-readers. If Vergil and Martial stood for Parliament men, we know already who would carry it. But though they make the greatest appearance in the field and cry the loudest, the best on't is they are but a sort of French Huguenots, or Dutch boors, brought over in herds but not naturalized; who have not lands of two pounds per annum in Parnassus, and therefore are not privileged to poll. Their authors are of the same level, fit to represent them on a mountebank's stage, or to be masters of the ceremonies in a bear garden: yet these are they who have the most admirers. But it often happens, to their mortification, that as their readers improve their stock of sense (as they may be reading better books and by conversation with men of judgment) they soon forsake them."

I must not dismiss this subject without observing that as Mr. Locke in the passage above mentioned has discovered the most fruitful source of wit, so there is another of a quite contrary nature to it, which does likewise branch itself out into several kinds. For not only the *resemblance,* but the *opposition* of ideas, does very often produce wit; as I could show in several little points, turns,

6 Translator of Vergil into French verse.

and antitheses, that I may possibly enlarge upon in some future speculation. C.

No. 69.
[Addison] Saturday, May 19, 1711.

Hic segetes, illic veniunt felicius uvae:
Arborei foetus alibi atque injussa virescunt
Gramina. Nonne vides, croceos ut Tmolus odores,
India mittit ebur, molles sua thura Sabaei?
At Chalybes nudi ferrum, virosaque Pontus
Castorea, Eliadum palmas Epirus equarum?
Continuo has leges aeternaque foedera certis
Imposuit Natura locis.

—Vergil.[1]

There is no place in the town which I so much love to frequent as the Royal Exchange. It gives me a secret satisfaction, and in some measure gratifies my vanity, as I am an Englishman, to see so rich an assembly of countrymen and foreigners consulting together upon the private business of mankind, and making this metropolis a kind of emporium for the whole earth. I must confess I look upon High Change to be a great council in which all considerable nations have their representatives. Factors in the trading world are what ambassadors are in the politic world: they negotiate affairs, conclude treaties, and maintain a good correspondence between those wealthy societies of men that are divided from one another by seas and oceans or live on the different extremities of a continent. I have often been pleased to hear disputes adjusted between an inhabitant of Japan and an alderman of London, or to see a subject of the Great Mogul entering into a league with one of the Czar of Muscovy. I am infinitely delighted in mixing with these several ministers of commerce as they are distinguished by their different walks and their different languages. Sometimes I am jostled among a body of Armenians; sometimes I am lost in a crowd of Jews; and sometimes make one in a group of Dutchmen. I am a Dane, Swede,

1 *Georgics* I. 54:
"This ground with Bacchus, that with Ceres, suits.
That other loads the trees with happy fruits:
A fourth with grass unbidden decks the ground.
Thus Tmolus is with yellow saffron crowned:
India black ebon and white ivory bears;

And soft Idume weeps her od'rous tears.
Thus Pontus sends her beaver-stones from far;
And naked Spaniards temper steel for war:
Epirus, for the Elian chariot, breeds
(In hopes of palms) a race of running steeds.
This is the original contract; these the laws
Imposed by Nature, and by Nature's cause." [Dryden]

or Frenchman at different times, or rather fancy myself like the old philosopher who upon being asked what countryman he was, replied, that he was a citizen of the world.[2]

Though I very frequently visit this busy multitude of people, I am known to nobody there but my friend Sir Andrew, who often smiles upon me as he sees me bustling in the crowd, but at the same time connives at my presence without taking any further notice of me. There is, indeed, a merchant of Egypt who just knows me by sight, having formerly remitted me some money to Grand Cairo; but as I am not versed in the modern Coptic, our conferences go no further than a bow and a grimace.

This grand scene of business gives me an infinite variety of solid and substantial entertainments. As I am a great lover of mankind, my heart naturally overflows with pleasure at the sight of a prosperous and happy multitude, insomuch that at many public solemnities I cannot forbear expressing my joy with tears that have stolen down my cheeks. For this reason I am wonderfully delighted to see such a body of men thriving in their own private fortunes and at the same time promoting the public stock; or in other words, raising estates for their own families by bringing into their country whatever is wanting, and carrying out of it whatever is superfluous.

Nature seems to have taken a particular care to disseminate her blessings among the different regions of the world with an eye to this mutual intercourse and traffic among mankind, that the natives of the several parts of the globe might have a kind of dependence upon one another, and be united together by their common interest. Almost every degree produces something peculiar to it. The food often grows in one country, and the sauce in another. The fruits of Portugal are corrected by the products of Barbados; the infusion of a China plant sweetened with the pith of an Indian cane. The Philippic Islands give a flavor to our European bowls. The single dress of a woman of quality is often the product of an hundred climates. The muff and the fan come together from the different ends of the earth. The scarf is sent from the torrid zone, and the tippet from beneath the pole. The brocade petticoat rises out of the mines of Peru, and the diamond necklace out of the bowels of Indostan.

If we consider our country in its natural prospect, without any

2 Diogenes, the Cynic.

of the benefits and advantages of commerce, what a barren uncomfortable spot of earth falls to our share! National historians
tell us that no fruit grows originally among us besides hips and
haws, acorns and pignuts, with other delicacies of the like nature;
that our climate of itself and without the assistance of art can
make no further advances towards a plum than to a sloe, and carries
an apple to no greater a perfection than a crab; that our melons,
our peaches, our figs, our apricots and cherries are strangers among
us, imported in different ages and naturalized in our English
gardens; and that they would all degenerate and fall away into
the trash of our own country if they were wholly neglected by
the planter and left to the mercy of our sun and soil. Nor has
traffic more enriched our vegetable world than it has improved
the whole face of nature among us. Our ships are laden with the
harvest of every climate; our tables are stored with spices and oils
and wines; our rooms are filled with pyramids of china, and
adorned with the workmanship of Japan; our morning's draught
comes to us from the remotest corners of the earth; we repair our
bodies by the drugs of America, and repose ourselves under Indian
canopies. My friend Sir Andrew calls the vineyards of France our
gardens; the Spice Islands our hotbeds; the Persians our silk-
weavers; and the Chinese our potters. Nature indeed furnishes
us with the bare necessaries of life, but traffic gives us a great
variety of what is useful, and at the same time supplies us with
everything that is convenient and ornamental. Nor is it the least
part of this our happiness that whilst we enjoy the remotest
products of the north and south, we are free from those extremities of weather which give them birth; that our eyes are refreshed with the green fields of Britain at the same time that our
palates are feasted with fruits that rise between the tropics.

For these reasons there are not more useful members in a
commonwealth than merchants. They knit mankind together in a
mutual intercourse of good offices, distribute the gifts of nature,
find work for the poor, add wealth to the rich, and magnificence to
the great. Our English merchant converts the tin of his own country into gold, and exchanges his wool for rubies. The Mahometans
are clothed in our British manufacture, and the inhabitants of the
frozen zone warmed with the fleeces of our sheep.

When I have been upon the Change, I have often fancied one
of our old kings standing in person where he is represented in

effigy, and looking down upon the wealthy concourse of people with which that place is every day filled. In this case, how would he be surprised to hear all the languages of Europe spoken in this little spot of his former dominions, and to see so many private men who in his time would have been the vassals of some powerful baron, negotiating like princes for greater sums of money than were formerly to be met with in the royal treasury! Trade, without enlarging the British territories, has given us a kind of additional empire: it has multiplied the number of the rich, made our landed estates infinitely more valuable than they were formerly, and added to them an accession of other estates as valuable as the lands themselves. C.

No. 113.
[Steele]   Tuesday, July 10, 1711.

——Haerent infixi pectore vultus.
                                                    —Vergil.[1]

In my first description of the company in which I pass most of my time, it may be remembered that I mentioned a great affliction which my friend Sir Roger had met with in his youth, which was no less than a disappointment in love. It happened this evening that we fell into a very pleasing walk at a distance from his house. As soon as we came into it, "It is," quoth the good old man, looking round him with a smile, "very hard that any part of my land should be settled upon one who has used me so ill as the perverse widow did; and yet I am sure I could not see a sprig of any bough of this whole walk of trees but I should reflect upon her and her severity. She has certainly the finest hand of any woman in the world. You are to know this was the place wherein I used to muse upon her; and by that custom I can never come into it but the same tender sentiments revive in my mind as if I had actually walked with that beautiful creature under these shades. I have been fool enough to carve her name on the bark of several of these trees; so unhappy is the condition of men in love, to attempt the removing of their passion by the methods which serve only to imprint it deeper. She has certainly the finest hand of any woman in the world."

1 *Aeneid* IV. 4: "His looks imprinted in her heart."

Here followed a profound silence; and I was not displeased to observe my friend falling so naturally into a discourse which I had ever before taken notice he industriously avoided. After a very long pause, he entered upon an account of this great circumstance in his life, with an air which I thought raised my idea of him above what I had ever had before, and gave me the picture of that cheerful mind of his before it received that stroke which has ever since affected his words and actions. But he went on as follows:

"I came to my estate in my twenty-second year, and resolved to follow the steps of the most worthy of my ancestors who have inhabited this spot of earth before me, in all the methods of hospitality and good neighborhood, for the sake of my fame, and in country sports and recreations, for the sake of my health. In my twenty-third year I was obliged to serve as sheriff of the county; and in my servants, officers, and whole equipage, indulged the pleasure of a young man (who did not think ill of his own person) in taking that public occasion of showing my figure and behavior to advantage. You may easily imagine to yourself what appearance I made, who am pretty tall, rid well, and was very well dressed, at the head of a whole county, with music before me, a feather in my hat, and my horse well bitted. I can assure you I was not a little pleased with the kind looks and glances I had from all the balconies and windows as I rode to the hall where the assizes were held. But when I came there, a beautiful creature in a widow's habit sat in court to hear the event of a cause concerning her dower. This commanding creature (who was born for the destruction of all who behold her) put on such a resignation in her countenance, and bore the whispers of all around the court with such a pretty uneasiness, I warrant you, and then recovered herself from one eye to another, until she was perfectly confused by meeting something so wistful in all she encountered, that at last, with a murrain to her, she casts her bewitching eye upon me. I no sooner met it but I bowed like a great surprised booby; and knowing her cause to be the first which came on, I cried, like a captivated calf as I was, 'Make way for the defendant's witnesses.' This sudden partiality made all the county immediately see the sheriff also was become a slave to the fine widow. During the time her cause was upon trial, she behaved herself, I warrant you, with such a deep attention to her business, took opportunities to have little billets handed to her counsel, then would be in such a pretty confusion, occasioned, you must know, by acting before so much company, that not only I but the whole court was prejudiced in her favor; and all that the next heir to her husband had to urge was thought so groundless and frivolous that when it came to her counsel to reply, there was not half so much said as everyone besides in the court thought he could have urged to her advantage. You must understand, sir, this perverse woman is one of those unaccountable creatures that secretly rejoice in the admiration of men, but indulge themselves in no further consequences. Hence it is that she has ever had a train of admirers, and she removes from her slaves in town to those in the country, according to the seasons of the year. She is a reading lady, and far gone in the pleasures of friendship. She is always accompanied by a confidante, who is witness to her daily protestations against our sex, and consequently a bar to her first steps towards love, upon the strength of her own maxims and declarations.

"However, I must need say this accomplished mistress of mine has distinguished me above the rest, and has been known to declare Sir Roger de Coverley was the tamest and most human of all the brutes in the country. I was told she said so by one who thought he rallied me; but upon the strength of this slender encouragement of being thought least detestable, I made new liveries, new-paired my coach horses, sent them all to town to be bitted, and taught to throw their legs well and move all together, before I pretended to cross the country and wait upon her. As soon as I thought my retinue suitable to the character of my fortune and youth, I set out from hence to make my addresses. The particular skill of this lady has ever been to inflame your wishes, and yet command respect. To make her mistress of this art, she has a greater share of knowledge, wit, and good sense than is usual even among men of merit. Then she is beautiful beyond the race of women. If you won't let her go on with a certain artifice with her eyes and the skill of beauty, she will arm herself with her real charms, and strike you with admiration instead of desire. It is certain that if you were to behold the whole woman, there is that dignity in her aspect, that composure in her motion, that complacency in her manner, that if her form makes you hope, her merit makes you fear. But then again, she is such a desperate scholar that no country gentleman can approach her without being a jest. As I was going to

tell you, when I came to her house I was admitted to her presence
with great civility; at the same time she placed herself to be first
seen by me in such an attitude as I think you call the posture of a
picture, that she discovered new charms, and I at last came towards
her with such an awe as made me speechless. This she no sooner
observed but she made her advantage of it, and began a discourse to
me concerning love and honor, as they both are followed by pretenders and the real votaries to them. When she discussed these
points in a discourse which, I verily believe, was as learned as the
best philosopher in Europe could possibly make, she asked me
whether she was so happy as to fall in with my sentiments on these
important particulars. Her confidante sat by her, and upon my being in the last confusion and silence, this malicious aide of hers,
turning to her, says, 'I am very glad to observe Sir Roger pauses
upon this subject, and seems resolved to deliver all his sentiments
upon the matter when he pleases to speak.' They both kept their
countenances, and after I had sat half an hour meditating how to
behave before such profound casuists, I rose up and took my leave.
Chance has since that time thrown me very often in her way, and
she as often has directed a discourse to me which I do not understand. This barbarity has kept me ever at a distance from the most
beautiful object my eyes ever beheld. It is thus also she deals with
all mankind, and you must make love to her as you would conquer
the sphinx, by posing her. But were she like other women, and
that there were any talking to her, how constant must the pleasure
of that man be who could converse with a creature— But, after all,
you may be sure her heart is fixed on some one or other; and yet I
have been credibly informed—but who can believe half that is
said! After she had done speaking to me, she put her hand to her
bosom and adjusted her tucker. Then she cast her eyes a little
down, upon my beholding her too earnestly. They say she sings
excellently: her voice in her ordinary speech has something in it
inexpressibly sweet. You must know I dined with her at a public
table the day after I first saw her, and she helped me to some tansy
in the eye of all the gentlemen in the country. She has certainly
the finest hand of any woman in the world. I can assure you, sir,
were you to behold her, you would be in the same condition; for as
her speech is music, her form is angelic. But I find I grow irregular
while I am talking of her; but indeed it would be stupidity to
be unconcerned at such perfection. Oh the excellent creature,

she is as inimitable to all women as she is inaccessible to all men!"

I found my friend begin to rave, and insensibly led him towards the house, that we might be joined by some other company; and am convinced that the widow is the secret cause of all that inconsistency which appears in some parts of my friend's discourse; though he has so much command of himself as not directly to mention her, yet according to that of Martial which one knows not how to render into English, *dum tacet hanc loquitur*. I shall end this paper with that whole epigram, which represents with much humor my honest friend's condition.

> Quicquid agit Rufus, nihil est nisi Naevia Rufo:
>   Si gaudet, si flet, si tacet, hanc loquitur:
> Caenat, propinat, poscit, negat, annuit, una est
>   Naevia; si non sit Naevia, mutus erit.
> Scriberet hesterna patri cum luce salutem,
>   Naevia lux, inquit, Naevia numen, ave.[2]

> Let Rufus weep, rejoice, stand, sit, or walk,
> Still he can nothing but of Naevia talk;
> Let him eat, drink, ask questions, or dispute,
> Still he must speak of Naevia, or be mute.
> He writ to his father, ending with this line,
> I am, my lovely Naevia, ever thine.

R.

No. 266.
[Steele]   Friday, January 4, 1711/12.

> Id vero est, quod ego mihi puto palmarium,
> Me reperisse, quomodo adolescentulus
> Meretricum ingenia et mores posset noscere:
> Mature ut cum cognorit perpetuo oderit.
>   —Terence.[1]

No vice or wickedness which people fall into from indulgence to desires which are natural to all ought to place them below the compassion of the virtuous part of the world; which indeed often makes me a little apt to suspect the sincerity of their virtue who are too warmly provoked at other people's personal sins. The unlawful commerce of the sexes is of all other the hardest to avoid; and yet there is no one which you shall hear the rigider part of

---

2 Martial *Epigrams* I. lxviii.
1 *Eunuch* V. iv: "This I conceive to be my masterpiece: that I have discovered how unexperienced youth may detect the artifices and the ways of bad women, and by knowing them early, detest them forever."

womankind speak of with so little mercy. It is very certain that a modest woman cannot abhor the breach of chastity too much; but pray let her hate it for herself, and only pity it in others. Will Honeycomb calls these overoffended ladies the "outrageously virtuous."

I do not design to fall upon failures in general with relation to the gift of chastity, but at present only enter upon that large field, and begin with the consideration of poor and public whores. The other evening passing along near Covent Garden, I was jogged on the elbow as I turned into the piazza, on the right hand coming out of James Street, by a slim young girl of about seventeen, who with a pert air asked me if I was for a pint of wine. I do not know but I should have indulged my curiosity in having some chat with her, but that I am informed the man of the Bumper [2] knows me; and it would have made a story for him not very agreeable to some part of my writings, though I have in others so frequently said that I am wholly unconcerned in any scene I am in, but merely as a spectator. This impediment being in my way, we stood under one of the arches by twilight; and there I could observe as exact features as I had ever seen, the most agreeable shape, the finest neck and bosom, in a word the whole person of a woman exquisitely beautiful. She affected to allure me with a forced wantonness in her look and air; but I saw it checked with hunger and cold. Her eyes were wan and eager, her dress thin and tawdry, her mien genteel and childish. This strange figure gave me much anguish of heart, and to avoid being seen with her I went away, but could not forbear giving her a crown. The poor thing sighed, curtsied, and with a blessing, expressed with the utmost vehemence, turned from me. This creature is what they call "newly come upon the town," but who, I suppose, falling into cruel hands, was left in the first month from her dishonor, and exposed to pass through the hands and discipline of one of those hags of hell whom we call bawds. But lest I should grow too suddenly grave on this subject, and be myself outrageously good, I shall turn to a scene in one of Fletcher's plays, where this character is drawn, and the economy of whoredom most admirably described. The passage I would point to is in the third scene of the second act of *The Humorous Lieutenant*. Leucippe, who is agent for the king's lust, and bawds at the same time for the whole court, is very pleasantly introduced,

2 The Bumper was a tavern.

reading her minutes as a person of business, with two maids, her
undersecretaries, taking instructions at a table before her. Her
women, both those under her present tutelage and those which she
is laying wait for, are alphabetically set down in her book; and she
is looking over the letter C, in a muttering voice, as if between
soliloquy and speaking out, she says,

> Her maidenhead will yield me; let me see now;
> She is not fifteen, they say: For her complexion—
> Cloe, Cloe, Cloe, here I have her,
> Cloe, the daughter of a country gentleman;
> Her age upon fifteen. Now her complexion,
> A lovely brown: here 'tis: Eyes black and rolling,
> The body neatly built: she strikes a lute well,
> Sings most enticingly: these helps consider'd,
> Her maidenhead will amount to some three hundred,
> Or three hundred and fifty crowns, 'twill bear it handsomely,
> Her father's poor, some little share deducted,
> To buy him a hunting nag—

These creatures are very well instructed in the circumstances
and manners of all who are in any way related to the fair one whom
they have a design upon. As Cloe is to be purchased with 350
crowns, and the father taken off with a pad, the merchant's wife
next to her, who abounds in plenty, is not to have downright
money, but the mercenary part of her mind is engaged with a
present of plate and a little ambition: she is made to understand
that it is a man of quality who dies for her. The examination of a
young girl for business, and the crying down her value for being a slight thing, together with every other circumstance in the
scene, are inimitably excellent, and have the true spirit of comedy;
though it were to be wished the author had added a circumstance
which should make Leucippe's baseness more odious.

It must not be thought a digression from my intended speculation
to talk of bawds in a discourse upon wenches; for a woman of the
town is not thoroughly and properly such without having gone
through the education of one of these houses; but the compassionate case of very many is that they are taken into such hands without any the least suspicion, previous temptation, or admonition to
what place they are going. The last week I went to an inn in the
City to inquire for some provisions which were sent by a wagon
out of the country; and as I waited in one of the boxes till the
chamberlain had looked over his parcels, I heard an old and a young

voice repeating the questions and responses of the Church catechism. I thought it no breach of good manners to peep at a crevice
and look in at people so well employed; but who should I see there
but the most artful procuress in the town examining a most beautiful country girl, who had come up in the same wagon with my
things, "Whether she was well educated, could forbear playing
the wanton with servants and idle fellows, of which this town,"
says she, "is too full"; at the same time, "Whether she knew enough
of breeding as that if a squire or a gentleman, or one that was her
betters, should give her a civil salute, she could curtsy and be
humble nevertheless." Her innocent forsooth's, yes's, an 't please
you's, and she would do her endeavor, moved the good old lady to
take her out of the hands of a country bumpkin her brother, and
hire her for her own maid. I stayed till I saw them all marched out
to take coach, the brother loaded with a great cheese he prevailed
upon her to take for her civilities to sister. This poor creature's
fate is not far off that of hers whom I spoke of above; and it is
not to be doubted but after she has been long enough a prey to
lust she will be delivered over to famine; the ironical commendation
of the industry and charity of these antiquated ladies, these directors of sin, after they can no longer commit it, makes up the beauty
of the inimitable dedication to *The Plain Dealer*, and is a masterpiece of raillery on this vice. But to understand all the purlieus
of this game the better, and to illustrate this subject in future discourses, I must venture myself, with my friend Will, into the
haunts of beauty and gallantry; from pampered vice in the habitations of the wealthy, to distressed indigent wickedness expelled
the harbors of the brothel.   T.

No. 267.

[Addison]   Saturday, January 5, 1711/12

Cedite Romani scriptores, cedite Graii.
—Propertius.[1]

There is nothing in nature so irksome as general discourses,
especially when they turn chiefly upon words. For this reason I
shall waive the discussion of that point which was started some
years since, whether Milton's *Paradise Lost* may be called an heroic
poem. Those who will not give it that title may call it (if they

1 *Elegies* III. xxxiv. 65: "Make way, ye writers of Greece and Rome."

please) a divine poem. It will be sufficient to its perfection if it
has in it all the beauties of the highest kind of poetry; and as for
those who allege it is not an heroic poem, they advance no more
to the diminution of it than if they should say Adam is not Aeneas,
nor Eve Helen.

I shall therefore examine it by the rules of epic poetry, and
see whether it falls short of the *Iliad* or *Aeneid* in the beauties which
are essential to that kind of writing. The first thing to be considered in an epic poem is the fable, which is perfect or imperfect
according as the action which it relates is more or less so. This
action should have three qualifications in it. First, it should be but
one action; secondly, it should be an entire action; and thirdly, it
should be a great action. To consider the action of the *Iliad*, *Aeneid*,
and *Paradise Lost* in these three several lights. Homer, to preserve
the unity of his action, hastens into the midst of things, as Horace
has observed. Had he gone up to Leda's egg, or begun much later,
even at the rape of Helen, or the investing of Troy, it is manifest
that the story of the poem would have been a series of several actions. He therefore opens his poem with the discord of his princes,
and with great art interweaves in the several succeeding parts of
it an account of everything material which relates to them, and
had passed before that fatal dissension. After the same manner
Aeneas makes his first appearance in the Tyrrhene seas, and within
sight of Italy, because the action proposed to be celebrated was
that of his settling himself in Latium. But because it was necessary
for the reader to know what had happened to him in the taking of
Troy, and in the preceding parts of his voyage, Vergil makes his
hero relate it by way of episode in the second and third books of
the *Aeneid*. The contents of both which books come before those
of the first book in the thread of the story, though for preserving
of this unity of action, they follow them in the disposition of the
poem. Milton, in imitation of these two great poets, opens his
Paradise Lost with an infernal council plotting the fall of man,
which is the action he proposed to celebrate; and as for those
great actions which preceded in point of time, the battle of the
angels and the creation of the world (which would have entirely
destroyed the unity of his principal action had he related them in
the same order that they happened), he cast them into the fifth,
sixth, and seventh books, by way of episode to this noble poem.

Aristotle himself allows that Homer has nothing to boast of as to the unity of his fable, though at the same time that great critic and philosopher endeavors to palliate this imperfection in the Greek poet by imputing it in some measure to the very nature of an epic poem. Some have been of opinion that the *Aeneid* labors also in this particular, and has episodes which may be looked upon as excrescences rather than as parts of the action. On the contrary, the poem which we have now under our consideration hath no other episodes than such as naturally arise from the subject, and yet is filled with such a multitude of astonishing incidents that it gives us at the same time a pleasure of the greatest variety, and of the greatest simplicity.

I must observe also that as Vergil, in the poem which was designed to celebrate the original of the Roman empire, has described the birth of its great rival, the Carthaginian commonwealth, Milton with the like art in his poem on the fall of man has related the fall of those angels who are his professed enemies. Besides the many other beauties in such an episode, its running parallel with the great action of the poem hinders it from breaking the unity so much as another episode would have done, that had not so great an affinity with the principal subject. In short, this is the same kind of beauty which the critics admire in *The Spanish Friar; or The Double Discovery*,[2] where the two different plots look like counterparts and copies of one another.

The second qualification required in the action of an epic poem is that it should be an entire action. An action is entire when it is complete in all its parts; or, as Aristotle describes it, when it consists of a beginning, a middle, and an end. Nothing should go before it, be intermixed with it, or follow after it, that is not related to it. As, on the contrary, no single step should be omitted in that just and regular process which it must be supposed to take from its original to its consummation. Thus we see the anger of Achilles in its birth, its continuance, and effects; and Aeneas's settlement in Italy, carried on through all the oppositions in his way to it both by sea and land. The action in Milton excels (I think) both the former in this particular; we see it contrived in Hell, executed upon earth, and punished by Heaven. The parts of it are told in the most distinct manner, and grow out of one another in the most natural method.

The third qualification of an epic poem is its greatness. The anger

2 By Dryden (1681).

of Achilles was of such consequence that it embroiled the kings of
Greece, destroyed the heroes of Troy, and engaged all the gods
in factions. Aeneas's settlement in Italy produced the Caesars,
and gave birth to the Roman empire. Milton's subject was still
greater than either of the former; it does not determine the fate
of single persons or nations, but of a whole species. The united
powers of Hell are joined together for the destruction of mankind, which they effected in part, and would have completed had
not Omnipotence itself interposed. The principal actors are man
in his greatest perfection and woman in her highest beauty. Their
enemies are the fallen angels; the Messiah their friend, and the
Almighty their protector. In short, everything that is great in
the whole circle of being, whether within the verge of nature or
out of it, has a proper part assigned it in this noble poem.

In poetry, as in architecture, not only the whole, but the principal members, and every part of them, should be great. I will not
presume to say that the book of games in the *Aeneid*, or that in the
Iliad, are not of this nature, nor to reprehend Vergil's simile of a
top,[3] and many others of the same nature in the *Iliad*, as liable
to any censure in this particular; but I think we may say, without
derogating from those wonderful performances, that there is an
unquestionable magnificence in every part of *Paradise Lost*, and
indeed a much greater than could have been formed upon any
pagan system.

But Aristotle, by the greatness of the action, does not only mean
that it should be great in its nature, but also in its duration, or, in
other words, that it should have a due length in it, as well as what
we properly call greatness. The just measure of the kind of magnitude he explains by the following similitude. An animal no bigger
than a mite cannot appear perfect to the eye because the sight
takes it in at once, and has only a confused idea of the whole, and
not a distinct idea of all its parts; if on the contrary you should
suppose an animal of ten thousand furlongs in length, the eye would
be so filled with a single part of it that it could not give the mind
an idea of the whole. What these animals are to the eye a very short
or a very long action would be to the memory. The first would be,
as it were, lost and swallowed up by it, and the other difficult to
be contained in it. Homer and Vergil have shown their principal
art in this particular; the action of the *Iliad*, and that of the *Aeneid*,

3 *Aeneid* VII. 378–84.

were in themselves exceeding short, but are so beautifully extended and diversified by the invention of episodes and the machinery of gods, with the like poetical ornaments, that they make up an agreeable story sufficient to employ the memory without overcharging it. Milton's action is enriched with such a variety of circumstances that I have taken as much pleasure in reading the contents of his books as in the best-invented story I ever met with. It is possible that the traditions on which the *Iliad* and *Aeneid* were built had more circumstances in them than the history of the fall of man, as it is related in Scripture. Besides, it was easier for Homer and Vergil to dash the truth with fiction, as they were in no danger of offending the religion of their country by it. But as for Milton, he had not only a very few circumstances upon which to raise his poem, but was also obliged to proceed with the greatest caution in everything that he added out of his own invention. And indeed, notwithstanding all the restraints he was under, he has filled his story with so many surprising incidents, which bear so close an analogy with what is delivered in Holy Writ, that it is capable of pleasing the most delicate reader, without giving offense to the most scrupulous.

The modern critics have collected from several hints in the *Iliad* and *Aeneid* the space of time which is taken up by the action of each of those poems; but as a great part in Milton's story was transacted in regions that lie out of the reach of the sun and the sphere of day, it is impossible to gratify the reader with such a calculation, which indeed would be more curious than instructive; none of the critics, either ancient or modern, having laid down rules to circumscribe the action of an epic poem with any determined number of years, days, or hours.

This piece of criticism on Milton's *Paradise Lost* shall be carried on in the following Saturdays' papers.　　　　　　　　　　L.

No. 294.
[Steele]　　　　　　　　　　　　　Wednesday, February 6, 1711/12.

Difficile est plurimum virtutem revereri qui semper secunda fortuna sit usus.—Cicero, *Ad Herennium*.[1]

Insolence is the crime of all others which every man is most apt to rail at; and yet is there one respect in which almost all men

1 "The man who is always fortunate cannot easily have much reverence for virtue."

living are guilty of it, and that is in the case of laying a greater
value upon the gifts of fortune than we ought. It is here in England
come into our very language, as a propriety of distinction, to say,
when we would speak of persons to their advantage, they are
people of condition. There is no doubt but the proper use of riches
implies that a man should exert all the good qualities imaginable;
and if we mean by a man of condition or quality one who, according to the wealth he is master of, shows himself just, beneficent,
and charitable, that term ought very deservedly to be had in the
highest veneration; but when wealth is used only as it is the support
of pomp and luxury, to be rich is very far from being a recommendation to honor and respect. It is indeed the greatest insolence
imaginable, in a creature who would feel the extremes of thirst
and hunger if he did not prevent his appetites before they call
upon him, to be so forgetful of the common necessity of human
nature as never to cast an eye upon the poor and needy. The
fellow who escaped from a ship which struck upon a rock in the
west, and joined with the country people to destroy his brother-
sailors and make her a wreck, was thought a most execrable
creature; but does not every man who enjoys the possession of
what he naturally wants, and is unmindful of the unsupplied
distress of other men, betray the same temper of mind? When a
man looks about him and with regard to riches and poverty beholds some drawn in pomp and equipage, and they and their very
servants with an air of scorn and triumph overlooking the multitude that pass by them; and in the same street a creature of the
same make crying out in the name of all that is good and sacred
to behold his misery, and give him some supply against hunger
and nakedness: who would believe these two beings were of the
same species? But so it is that the consideration of fortune has
taken up all our minds, and, as I have often complained, poverty and
riches stand in our imaginations in the places of guilt and innocence.
But in all seasons there will be some instances of persons who have
souls too large to be taken with popular prejudices, and while the
rest of mankind are contending for superiority in power and wealth,
have their thoughts bent upon the necessities of those below them.
The charity schools which have been erected of late years are the
greatest instances of public spirit the age has produced; but indeed
when we consider how long this sort of beneficence has been on
foot, it is rather from the good management of those institutions

than from the number or value of the benefactions to them, that they make so great a figure. One would think it impossible that in the space of fourteen years there should not have been five thousand pounds bestowed in gifts this way, nor sixteen hundred children, including males and females, put out into methods of industry. It is not allowed me to speak of luxury and folly with the severe spirit they deserve; I shall only therefore say, I shall very readily compound with any lady in a hoop-petticoat if she gives the price of one-half yard of the silk towards clothing, feeding, and instructing an innocent helpless creature of her own sex in one of these schools. The consciousness of such an action will give her features a nobler life on this illustrious day than all the jewels that can hang in her hair, or can be clustered in her bosom. It would be uncourtly to speak in harsher words to the fair, but to men one may take a little more freedom. It is monstrous how a man can live with so little reflection as to fancy he is not in a condition very unjust and disproportioned to the rest of mankind while he enjoys wealth and exerts no benevolence or bounty to others. As for this particular occasion of these schools, there cannot any offer more worthy a generous mind. Would you do an handsome thing without return? Do it for an infant that is not sensible of the obligation. Would you do it for public good? Do it for one who would be an honest artificer. Would you do it for the sake of Heaven? Give it to one who shall be instructed in the worship of Him for whose sake you gave it. It is, methinks, a most laudable institution, this, if it were of no other expectation than that of producing a race of good and useful servants, who will have more than a liberal, a religious education. What would not a man do, in common prudence, to lay out in purchase of one about him who would add to all his orders he gave the weight of the Commandments to enforce an obedience to them? for one who would consider his master as his father, his friend, and benefactor upon the easy terms, and in expectation of no other return but moderate wages and gentle usage? It is the common vice of children to run too much among the servants; from such as are educated in these places they would see nothing but lowliness in the servant, which would not be disingenuous in the child. All the ill offices and defamatory whispers which take their birth from domestics would be prevented if this charity could be made universal; and a good man might have a knowledge of the whole life of the persons he designs to take into his house for his own service, or that of his family or children, long before they were admitted. This would create endearing dependencies; and the obligation would have a paternal air in the master, who would be relieved from much care and anxiety from the gratitude and diligence of an humble friend attending him as his servant. I fall into this discourse from a letter sent to me, to give me notice that fifty boys would be clothed and take their seats (at the charge of some generous benefactors) in St. Bride's Church on Sunday next. I wish I could promise to myself anything which my correspondent seems to expect from a publication of it in this paper; for there can be nothing added to what so many excellent and learned men have said on this occasion. But that there may be something here which would move a generous mind, like that of him who writ to me, I shall transcribe an handsome paragraph of Dr. Snape's sermon on these charities, which my correspondent enclosed with this letter.

"The wise Providence has amply compensated the disadvantages of the poor and indigent in wanting many of the conveniencies of this life, by a more abundant provision for their happiness in the next. Had they been higher born or more richly endowed, they would have wanted this manner of education, of which those only enjoy the benefit who are low enough to submit to it; where they have such advantages without money, and without price, as the rich cannot purchase with it. The learning which is given is generally more edifying to them than that which is sold to others. Thus do they become more exalted in goodness by being depressed in fortune, and their poverty is, in reality, their preferment."   T.

No. 324.
[Steele]   Wednesday, March 12, 1711/12.

O curvae in terris animae et coelestium inanes.
                                                          —Persius.[1]

MR. SPECTATOR:

The materials you have collected together towards a general history of clubs make so bright a part of your speculations that I think it is but a justice we all owe the learned world to furnish

1 *Satires* II. 61:
"O souls in whom no heavenly fire is found,
Flat minds, and ever groveling on the
   ground."   [Dryden]

you with such assistances as may promote that useful work. For this reason I could not forbear communicating to you some imperfect informations of a set of men (if you will allow them a place in that species of being) who have lately erected themselves into a nocturnal fraternity under the title of the Mohock Club, a name borrowed, it seems, from a sort of cannibals in India, who subsist by plundering and devouring all the nations about them. The president is styled Emperor of the Mohocks; and his arms are a Turkish crescent, which his imperial majesty bears at present in a very extraordinary manner engraven upon his forehead. Agreeable to their name, the avowed design of their institution is mischief; and upon this foundation all their rules and orders are framed. An outrageous ambition of doing all possible hurt to their fellow creatures is the great cement of their assembly, and the only qualification required in the members. In order to exert this principle to its full strength and perfection, they take care to drink themselves to a pitch, that is, beyond the possibility of attending to any motions of reason or humanity; then make a general sally, and attack all that are so unfortunate as to walk the streets through which they patrol. Some are knocked down, others stabbed, others cut and carbonadoed. To put the watch to a total rout, and mortify some of those inoffensive militia, is reckoned a *coup d'éclat*. The particular talents by which these misanthropes are distinguished from one another consist in the various kinds of barbarities which they execute upon their prisoners. Some are celebrated for a happy dexterity in tipping the lion upon them; which is performed by squeezing the nose flat to the face and boring out the eyes with their fingers. Others are called the dancing masters, and teach their scholars to cut capers by running swords through their legs; a new invention, whether originally French I cannot tell. A third sort are the tumblers, whose office it is to set women upon their heads, and commit certain indecencies, or rather barbarities, on the limbs which they expose. But these I forbear to mention because they can't but be very shocking to the reader as well as the spectator. In this manner they carry on a war against mankind; and by the standing maxims of their policy, are to enter into no alliances but one, and that is offensive and defensive with all bawdyhouses in general, of which they have declared themselves protectors and guarantees.

I must own, sir, these are only broken incoherent memoirs of this wonderful society, but they are the best I have been yet able to procure; for, being but of late establishment, it is not ripe for a just history, and, to be serious, the chief design of this trouble is to hinder it from ever being so. You have been pleased, out of a concern for the good of your countrymen, to act under the character of Spectator, not only the part of a looker-on, but an overseer of their actions; and whenever such enormities as this infest the town, we immediately fly to you for redress. I have reason to believe that some thoughtless youngsters, out of a false notion of bravery and an immoderate fondness to be distinguished for fellows of fire, are insensibly hurried into this senseless, scandalous project. Such will probably stand corrected by your reproofs, especially if you inform them that it is not courage for half a score fellows, mad with wine and lust, to set upon two or three soberer than themselves; and that the manners of Indian savages are no becoming accomplishments to an English fine gentleman. Such of them as have been bullies and scourers of a long standing, and are grown veterans in this kind of service, are, I fear, too hardened to receive any impressions from your admonitions. But I beg you would recommend to their perusal your ninth speculation. They may there be taught to take warning from the club of Duellists, and be put in mind that the common fate of those men of honor was to be hanged.

> I am,
> Sir,
> Your most humble servant,
> PHILANTHROPOS.

March 10, 1711/12.   T.

No. 409.
[Addison]   Thursday, June 19, 1712.

——Musaeo contingere cuncta lepore.
—Lucretius.[1]

Gracian[2] very often recommends *the fine Taste* as the utmost perfection of an accomplished man. As this word arises very often in conversation, I shall endeavor to give some account of it, and

1 *De Rerum Natura* I. 934: "To touch all with the grace of the Muses."

2 Baltasar Gracián (1601–58), a Spanish Jesuit writer upon rhetoric who was very influential in promoting "taste."

to lay down rules how we may know whether we are possessed of it, and how we may acquire that fine taste of writing which is so much talked of among the polite world.

Most languages make use of this metaphor to express that faculty of the mind which distinguishes all the most concealed faults and nicest perfections in writing. We may be sure this metaphor would not have been so general in all tongues had there not been a very great conformity between that mental taste which is the subject of this paper and that sensitive taste which gives us a relish of every different flavor that affects the palate. Accordingly we find there are as many degrees of refinement in the intellectual faculty as in the sense which is marked out by this common denomination.

I knew a person who possessed the one in so great a perfection that after having tasted ten different kinds of tea, he would distinguish, without seeing the color of it, the particular sort which was offered him; and not only so, but any two sorts of them that were mixed together in an equal proportion; nay, he has carried the experiment so far as, upon tasting the composition of three different sorts, to name the parcels from whence the three several ingredients were taken. A man of a fine taste in writing will discern after the same manner, not only the general beauties and imperfections of an author, but discover the several ways of thinking and expressing himself which diversify him from all other authors, with the several foreign infusions of thought and language, and the particular authors from whom they were borrowed.

After having thus far explained what is generally meant by a fine taste in writing, and shown the propriety of the metaphor which is used on this occasion, I think I may define it to be *that faculty of the soul which discerns the beauties of an author with pleasure, and the imperfections with dislike*. If a man would know whether he is possessed of this faculty, I would have him read over the celebrated works of antiquity, which have stood the test of so many different ages and countries; or those works among the moderns which have the sanction of the politer part of our contemporaries. If upon the perusal of such writings he does not find himself delighted in an extraordinary manner, or if, upon reading the admired passages in such authors, he finds a coldness and indifference in his thoughts, he ought to conclude, not (as is too usual among tasteless readers) that the author wants those perfections which have been admired in him, but that he himself wants the faculty of discovering them.

He should, in the second place, be very careful to observe whether he tastes the distinguishing perfections, or, if I may be allowed to call them so, the specific qualities of the author whom he peruses; whether he is particularly pleased with Livy for his manner of telling a story, with Sallust for his entering into those internal principles of action which arise from the characters and manners of the persons he describes, or with Tacitus for his displaying those outward motives of safety and interest which give birth to the whole series of transactions which he relates.

He may likewise consider how differently he is affected by the same thought which presents itself in a great writer from what he is when he finds it delivered by a person of an ordinary genius. For there is as much difference in apprehending a thought clothed in Cicero's language and that of a common author as in seeing an object by the light of a taper or by the light of the sun.

It is very difficult to lay down rules for the acquirement of such a taste as that I am here speaking of. The faculty must in some degree be born with us, and it very often happens that those who have other qualities in perfection are wholly void of this. One of the most eminent mathematicians of the age has assured me that the greatest pleasure he took in reading Vergil was in examining Aeneas his voyage by the map; as I question not but many a modern compiler of history would be delighted with little more in that divine author than the bare matters of fact.

But notwithstanding this faculty must in some measure be born with us, there are several methods for cultivating and improving it, and without which it will be very uncertain, and of little use to the person that possesses it. The most natural method for this purpose is to be conversant among the writings of the most polite authors. A man who has any relish for fine writing either discovers new beauties or receives stronger impressions from the masterly strokes of a great author every time he peruses him: besides that, he naturally wears himself into the same manner of speaking and thinking.

Conversation with men of a polite genius is another method for improving our natural taste. It is impossible for a man of the greatest parts to consider anything in its whole extent, and in all its variety of lights. Every man, besides those general observations which are to be made upon an author, forms several reflections that are peculiar to his own manner of thinking; so that conversation will naturally furnish us with hints which we did not attend to, and make us enjoy other men's parts and reflections as well as our own. This is the best reason I can give for the observation which several have made, that men of great genius in the same way of writing seldom rise up singly, but at certain periods of time appear together and in a body; as they did at Rome in the reign of Augustus, and in Greece about the age of Socrates. I cannot think that Corneille, Racine, Molière, Boileau, La Fontaine, Bruyère, Bossu, or the Daciers would have written so well as they have done, had they not been friends and contemporaries.

It is likewise necessary for a man who would form to himself a finished taste of good writing to be well versed in the works of the best critics both ancient and modern. I must confess that I could wish there were authors of this kind, who, beside the mechanical rules which a man of very little taste may discourse upon, would enter into the very spirit and soul of fine writing, and show us the several sources of that pleasure which rises in the mind upon the perusal of a noble work. Thus although in poetry it be absolutely necessary that the unities of time, place, and action, with other points of the same nature, should be thoroughly explained and understood, there is still something more essential to the art, something that elevates and astonishes the fancy and gives a greatness of mind to the reader, which few of the critics besides Longinus have considered.

Our general taste in England is for epigram, turns of wit, and forced conceits, which have no manner of influence, either for the bettering or enlarging the mind of him who reads them, and have been carefully avoided by the greatest writers, both among the ancients and moderns. I have endeavored in several of my speculations to banish this Gothic taste which has taken possession among us. I entertained the town for a week together with an essay upon wit, in which I endeavored to detect several of those false kinds which have been admired in the different ages of the world; and at the same time to show wherein the nature of true wit consists. I afterwards gave an instance of the great force which lies in a natural simplicity of thought to affect the mind of the reader, from such vulgar pieces as have little else besides this single qualification to recommend them. I have likewise examined the works of the greatest poet which our nation or perhaps any other has produced, and particularized most of those rational and manly beauties which give a value to that divine work. I shall next Saturday enter upon an essay on *the Pleasures of the Imagination*, which, though it shall consider that subject at large, will perhaps suggest to the reader what it is that gives a beauty to many passages of the finest writers both in prose and verse. As an undertaking of this nature is entirely new, I question not but it will be received with candor.   O.

No. 411.
[Addison]   Saturday, June 21, 1712.

—Avia Pieridum peragro loca, nullius ante
Trita solo; juvat integros accedere fonteis,
Atque haurire.
                                                            —Lucretius.[1]

Our sight is the most perfect and most delightful of all our senses. It fills the mind with the largest variety of ideas, converses with its objects at the greatest distance, and continues the longest in action without being tired or satiated with its proper enjoyments. The sense of feeling can indeed give us a notion of extension, shape, and all other ideas that enter at the eye, except colors; but at the same time it is very much straitened and confined in its operations to the number, bulk, and distance of its particular objects. Our sight seems designed to supply all these defects, and may be considered as a more delicate and diffusive kind of touch, that spreads itself over an infinite multitude of bodies, comprehends the largest figures, and brings into our reach some of the most remote parts of the universe.

It is this sense which furnishes the imagination with its ideas; so that by the pleasures of the imagination or fancy (which I shall use promiscuously) I here mean such as arise from visible objects, either when we have them actually in our view, or when we call up their ideas into our minds by paintings, statues, descriptions, or any the like occasion. We cannot indeed have a single image in the fancy that did not make its first entrance through the sight; but we have the power of retaining, altering, and compounding

---

1 *De Rerum Natura* I. 925–27: "I traverse the untrod wastes of the Pierides; I love to reach the virgin springs to drink."

those images, which we have once received, into all the varieties of picture and vision that are most agreeable to the imagination; for by this faculty a man in a dungeon is capable of entertaining himself with scenes and landskips more beautiful than any that can be found in the whole compass of nature.

There are few words in the English Language which are employed in a more loose and uncircumscribed sense than those of the fancy and the imagination. I therefore thought it necessary to fix and determine the notion of these two words, as I intend to make use of them in the thread of my following speculations, that the reader may conceive rightly what is the subject which I proceed upon. I must therefore desire him to remember that by the pleasures of the imagination I mean only such pleasures as arise originally from sight, and that I divide these pleasures into two kinds: my design being first of all to discourse of those primary pleasures of the imagination, which entirely proceed from such objects as are before our eyes; and in the next place to speak of those secondary pleasures of the imagination which flow from the ideas of visible objects when the objects are not actually before the eye, but are called up into our memories, or formed into agreeable visions of things that are either absent or fictitious.

The pleasures of the imagination, taken in the full extent, are not so gross as those of sense, nor so refined as those of the understanding. The last are, indeed, more preferable, because they are founded on some new knowledge or improvement in the mind of man; yet it must be confessed that those of the imagination are as great and as transporting as the other. A beautiful prospect delights the soul as much as a demonstration; and a description in Homer has charmed more readers than a chapter in Aristotle. Besides, the pleasures of the imagination have this advantage above those of the understanding: that they are more obvious, and more easy to be acquired. It is but opening the eye, and the scene enters. The colors paint themselves on the fancy, with very little attention of thought or application of mind in the beholder. We are struck, we know not how, with the symmetry of anything we see, and immediately assent to the beauty of an object without inquiring into the particular causes and occasions of it.

A man of a polite imagination is let into a great many pleasures that the vulgar are not capable of receiving. He can converse with a picture and find an agreeable companion in a statue. He meets with a secret refreshment in a description, and often feels a greater satisfaction in the prospect of fields and meadows than another does in the possession. It gives him, indeed, a kind of property in everything he sees, and makes the most rude uncultivated parts of nature administer to his pleasures; so that he looks upon the world, as it were, in another light, and discovers in it a multitude of charms that conceal themselves from the generality of mankind.

There are, indeed, but very few who know how to be idle and innocent, or have a relish of any pleasures that are not criminal; every diversion they take is at the expense of some one virtue or another, and their very first step out of business is into vice or folly. A man should endeavor, therefore, to make the sphere of his innocent pleasures as wide as possible that he may retire into them with safety, and find in them such a satisfaction as a wise man would not blush to take. Of this nature are those of the imagination, which do not require such a bent of thought as is necessary to our more serious employments, nor, at the same time, suffer the mind to sink into that negligence and remissness which are apt to accompany our more sensual delights, but, like a gentle exercise to the faculties, awaken them from sloth and idleness, without putting them upon any labor or difficulty.

We might here add that the pleasures of the fancy are more conducive to health than those of the understanding, which are worked out by dint of thinking, and attended with too violent a labor of the brain. Delightful scenes, whether in nature, painting, or poetry, have a kindly influence on the body, as well as the mind, and not only serve to clear and brighten the imagination, but are able to disperse grief and melancholy, and to set the animal spirits in pleasing and agreeable motions. For this reason Sir Francis Bacon, in his essay upon health, has not thought it improper to prescribe to his reader a poem or a prospect where he particularly dissuades him from knotty and subtile disquisitions, and advises him to pursue studies that fill the mind with splendid and illustrious objects, as histories, fables, and contemplations of nature.

I have in this paper, by way of introduction, settled the notion of those pleasures of the imagination which are the subject of my present undertaking, and endeavored, by several considerations, to recommend to my reader the pursuit of those pleasures. I shall, in my next paper, examine the several sources from whence these pleasures are derived.   O.

C.S. Lewis —
Collec. of Essays on
Addison —
one finds a
turning point

No. 412.
[Addison]

Monday, June 23, 1712.

——Divisum sic breve fiet opus.

——Martial[1]

I shall first consider those pleasures of the imagination which arise from the actual view and survey of outward objects. And these, I think, all proceed from the sight of what is great, uncommon, or beautiful. There may, indeed, be something so terrible or offensive, that the horror or loathsomeness of an object may overbear the pleasure which results from its greatness, novelty, or beauty; but still there will be such a mixture of delight in the very disgust it gives us, as any of these three qualifications are most conspicuous and prevailing.

By greatness, I do not only mean the bulk of any single object, but the largeness of a whole view, considered as one entire piece. Such are the prospects of an open champaign country, a vast uncultivated desert, of huge heaps of mountains, high rocks and precipices, or a wide expanse of waters, where we are not struck with the novelty or beauty of the sight, but with that rude kind of magnificence which appears in many of these stupendous works of nature. Our imagination loves to be filled with an object, or to grasp at anything that is too big for its capacity. We are flung into a pleasing astonishment at such unbounded views, and feel a delightful stillness and amazement in the soul at the apprehension of them. The mind of man naturally hates everything that looks like a restraint upon it, and is apt to fancy itself under a sort of confinement, when the sight is pent up in a narrow compass, and shortened on every side by the neighborhood of walls or mountains. On the contrary, a spacious horizon is an image of liberty, where the eye has room to range abroad, to expatiate at large on the immensity of its views, and to lose itself amidst the variety of objects that offer themselves to its observation. Such wide and undetermined prospects are as pleasing to the fancy as the speculations of eternity or infinitude are to the understanding. But if there be a beauty or uncommonness joined with this grandeur, as in a troubled ocean, a heaven adorned with stars and meteors, or a spacious landskip cut out into rivers, woods, rocks, and meadows,

Striking
Roman.
ideas of
imaginat,

Retreat
to pleasure

1 *Epigrams* IV. lxxxii. 8: "Divided, the work will be brief."

Sense of Secur.

Augustan pleasing astonish-
ment in basic ideas
standing firm on accepted variances

the pleasure still grows upon us, as it arises from more than a single principle.

Everything that is *new* or *uncommon* raises a pleasure in the imagination, because it fills the soul with an agreeable surprise, gratifies its curiosity, and gives it an idea of which it was not before possessed. We are indeed so often conversant with one set of objects, and tired out with so many repeated shows of the same things, that whatever is *new* or *uncommon* contributes a little to vary human life, and to divert our minds, for a while, with the strangeness of its appearance. It serves us for a kind of refreshment, and takes off from that satiety we are apt to complain of in our usual and ordinary entertainments. It is this that bestows charms on a monster, and makes even the imperfections of nature please us. It is this that recommends variety, where the mind is every instant called off to something new, and the attention not suffered to dwell too long, and waste itself on any particular object. It is this, likewise, that improves what is great or beautiful, and makes it afford the mind a double entertainment. Groves, fields, and meadows are at any season of the year pleasant to look upon, but never so much as in the opening of the spring, when they are all new and fresh, with their first gloss upon them, and not yet too much accustomed and familiar to the eye. For this reason there is nothing that more enlivens a prospect than rivers, *jets d'eau*, or falls of water, where the scene is perpetually shifting, and entertaining the sight every moment with something that is new. We are quickly tired with looking upon hills and valleys, where everything continues fixed and settled in the same place and posture, but find our thoughts a little agitated and relieved at the sight of such objects as are ever in motion, and sliding away from beneath the eye of the beholder. . . .　　　　　　　O.

No. 419.
[Addison]　　　　　　　　　　　　　　　Tuesday, July 1, 1712.

————Mentis gratissimus error.
　　　　　　　　　　　　　　　　　　　　—Horace.[1]

There is a kind of writing wherein the poet quite loses sight of nature, and entertains his reader's imagination with the characters and actions of such persons as have, many of them, no existence

1 *Epistles* II. ii. 140: "A sweet delusion of the mind."

but what he bestows on them. Such are fairies, witches, magicians, demons, and departed spirits. This Mr. Dryden [2] calls "the fairy way of writing," which is indeed more difficult than any other that depends on the poet's fancy, because he has no pattern to follow in it, and must work altogether out of his own invention.

There is a very odd turn of thought required for this sort of writing, and it is impossible for a poet to succeed in it who has not a particular cast of fancy, and an imagination naturally fruitful and superstitious. Besides this, he ought to be very well versed in legends and fables, antiquated romances, and the traditions of nurses and old women, that he may fall in with our natural prejudices, and humor those notions which we have imbibed in our infancy. For, otherwise, he will be apt to make his fairies talk like people of his own species, and not like other sets of beings, who converse with different objects and think in a different manner from that of mankind.

> Sylvis deducti caveant, me judice, fauni
> Ne velut innati triviis, ac pene forenses,
> Aut nimium teneris juvenentur versibus.
>
> —Horace.[3]

> Let not the wood-born satyr fondly sport
> With am'rous verses, as if bred at court.
>
> —Francis.

I do not say, with Mr. Bayes in *The Rehearsal*,[4] that spirits must not be confined to speak sense, but it is certain their sense ought to be a little discolored that it may seem particular, and proper to the person and condition of the speaker.

These descriptions raise a pleasing kind of horror in the mind of the reader, and amuse his imagination with the strangeness and novelty of the persons who are represented in them. They bring up into our memory the stories we have heard in our childhood and favor those secret terrors and apprehensions to which the mind of man is naturally subject. We are pleased with surveying the different habits and behaviors of foreign countries; how much more must we be delighted and surprised when we are led, as it were, into a new creation and see the persons and manners of another species! Men of cold fancies and philosophical dispositions

2 *Apology for Heroic Poetry.*

3 *Ars Poetica*, 244–246.

4 Dryden (as Bayes) was satirized in *The Rehearsal* (1671–72), a play by George Villiers, Duke of Buckingham, and others.

object to this kind of poetry that it has not probability enough to affect the imagination. But to this it may be answered that we are sure, in general, there are many intellectual beings in the world besides ourselves, and several species of spirits who are subject to different laws and economies from those of mankind. When we see, therefore, any of these represented naturally, we cannot look upon the representation as altogether impossible; nay, many are prepossessed with such false opinions as dispose them to believe these particular delusions; at least we have all heard so many pleasing relations in favor of them that we do not care for seeing through the falsehood, and willingly give ourselves up to so agreeable an imposture.

The ancients have not much of this poetry among them; for, indeed, almost the whole substance of it owes its original to the darkness and superstition of later ages, when pious frauds were made use of to amuse mankind and frighten them into a sense of their duty. Our forefathers looked upon nature with more reverence and horror before the world was enlightened by learning and philosophy, and loved to astonish themselves with the apprehensions of witchcraft, prodigies, charms, and enchantments. There was not a village in England that had not a ghost in it, the churchyards were all haunted, every large common had a circle of fairies belonging to it, and there was scarce a shepherd to be met with who had not seen a spirit.

Among all the poets of this kind our English are much the best, by what I have yet seen; whether it be that we abound with more stories of this nature, or that the genius of our country is fitter for this sort of poetry. For the English are naturally fanciful, and very often disposed, by that gloominess and melancholy of temper which is so frequent in our nation, to many wild notions and visions to which others are not so liable.

Among the English, Shakespeare has incomparably excelled all others. That noble extravagance of fancy which he had in so great perfection thoroughly qualified him to touch this weak superstitious part of his reader's imagination, and made him capable of succeeding where he had nothing to support him besides the strength of his own genius. There is something so wild and yet so solemn in the speeches of his ghosts, fairies, witches, and the like imaginary persons that we cannot forbear thinking them natural, though we have no rule by which to judge of them, and must confess, if there are such beings in the world, it looks highly probable they should talk and act as he has represented them.

There is another sort of imaginary beings that we sometimes meet with among the poets when the author represents any passion, appetite, virtue, or vice under a visible shape, and makes it a person or an actor in his poem. Of this nature are the descriptions of Hunger and Envy in Ovid, of Fame in Vergil, and of Sin and Death in Milton. We find a whole creation of the like shadowy persons in Spenser, who had an admirable talent in representations of this kind. I have discoursed of these emblematical persons in former papers, and shall therefore only mention them in this place. Thus we see how many ways poetry addresses itself to the imagination, as it has not only the whole circle of nature for its province, but makes new worlds of its own, shows us persons who are not to be found in being, and represents even the faculties of the soul, with her several virtues and vices, in a sensible shape and character. . . .   O.

John Gay

1685–1732

No ONE of his time except Matthew Prior and Pope himself has so lively an artistry of the bagatelle as John Gay. This graceful, attractive spoiled child of the Augustans was a literary opportunist, always profiting from the success of others. His poem *Wine* echoed John Philips' *Cyder; Rural Sports* was patterned after Pope's *Windsor Forest; The Shepherd's Week* was instigated by Pope as a burlesque of Ambrose Philips' *Pastorals; Trivia* owed something to Swift's "Description of the Morning" and "Description of a City Shower"; *The Beggar's Opera* was provoked by the absurdities of the Italian opera and, again, suggested by Swift's remark that Gay should write a "Newgate pastoral"; the *Fables* were preceded by those of La Fontaine. Howbeit, Gay is (in the phrase of Dr. Johnson) sprightly, various, and pleasant. As with Goldsmith, what Gay touched, he adorned. Besides, as Dr. Johnson also observed, "we owe to Gay the ballad opera." The three parts of *Trivia* so authentically and vividly portray the London scene that as we read we may for the moment live amid the streets that the Spectator knew.

BIOGRAPHICAL NOTES

Born of poor parents at Barnstaple. Orphaned in 1695. Apprenticed to a silk merchant in London. Revolted; turned author with the help of Aaron Richmond. *Wine* (1708), imitating John Philips' *Cyder*. *The Present State of Wit* (1711), a pamphlet on periodicals. Met Pope. Secretary to the Duchess of Monmouth (1712). *Rural Sports* (1713), imitating *Windsor Forest*. Patronized by Pope; friendships with the Tories of the Scriblerus Club. *The Fan* (1714), a mock-heroic. *The Shepherd's Week* (1714), a burlesque of Ambrose Philips' *Pastorals*. Appointed secretary to Lord Clarendon (1714); accompanied him to Hanover. Death of Queen Anne, and end of Tory power. Published *Trivia* (1716), which was very profitable. With Pope and Arbuthnot wrote the farce *Three Hours after Marriage* (1717). Visited the Continent with Pulteney. *Poems* published by Tonson and Lintot (1720). Lost everything in South Sea Bubble (1720). Appointed (by Walpole) to a sinecure, lottery commissioner (1722). Lived in lodgings in Whitehall, granted by the Earl of Lincoln. The *Fables* (1727), written for the Duke of Cumberland, whom he tutored. *The Beggar's Opera* ran sixty-odd nights at Lincoln's Inn Fields (1728). *Polly* suppressed for political reasons but printed in 1729. During his last years enjoyed the patronage of the Duke of Queensberry and his wife and lived with them. Died of the "colic" and was buried in Westminster under the epitaph written by himself:

> "Life is a jest, and all things show it;
> I thought so once, and now I know it."

BIBLIOGRAPHY: *Poetical Works*, ed. G. C. Faber, 1926. *Trivia*, ed. W. H. Williams, 1922. Armens, Sven M., *John Gay, Social Critic*, 1954. Gaye, Phoebe Fenwick, *John Gay, His Place in the 18th Century*, 1938. Irving, William H., *John Gay, Favorite of the Wits*, 1940. Johnson, Samuel, *Lives of the Poets*, 1779–81. Melville, Lewis, *Life and Letters of John Gay*, 1921.

TRIVIA;[1] OR, THE ART OF WALKING THE STREETS OF LONDON

1716

BOOK II

Of Walking the Streets by Day

Thus far the Muse has trac'd in useful lays,
The proper implements for wintry ways;

[1] Plural of the Latin *trivium*, or "meeting of three streets"; likewise the name applied to Diana when she was worshiped at the intersection of three streets.

Has taught the walker, with judicious eyes,
To read the various warnings of the skies.
Now venture, Muse, from home to range the town,
And for the publick safety risque thy own.
　For ease and for dispatch, the morning's best:
No tides of passengers the street molest.
You'll see a draggl'd damsel, here and there,
From Billingsgate her fishy traffick bear;
On doors the sallow milk-maid chalks her gains;   10
Ah! how unlike the milk-maid of the plains!
Before proud gates attending asses bray,[2]
Or arrogate with solemn pace the way;
These grave physicians with their milky chear,
The love-sick maid and dwindling beau repair;
Here rows of drummers stand in martial file,
And with their vellom-thunder shake the pile,
To greet the new-made bride. Are sounds like these
The proper prelude to a state of peace?   20
Now industry awakes her busy sons,
Full charg'd with news the breathless hawker runs:
Shops open, coaches roll, carts shake the ground,
And all the streets with passing cries resound.
　If cloath'd in black, you tread the busy town,
Or if distinguish'd by the rev'rend gown,
Three trades avoid; oft in the mingling press,
The barber's apron soils the sable dress;
Shun the perfumer's touch with cautious eye,
Nor let the baker's step advance too nigh: 30
Ye walkers too that youthful colours wear,
Three sullying trades avoid with equal care;
The little chimney-sweeper skulks along,
And marks with sooty stains the heedless throng;
When "Small-coal" murmurs in the hoarser throat,
From smutty dangers guard thy threaten'd coat:
The dust-man's cart offends thy cloaths and eyes,
When through the street a cloud of ashes flies;
But whether black or lighter dyes are worn,
The chandler's basket, on his shoulder born,   40
With tallow spots thy coat; resign the way,
To shun the surly butcher's greasy tray,
Butchers, whose hands are dy'd with blood's foul stain,
And always foremost in the hangman's train.

---

[2] Asses' milk was sold from door to door.

Let due civilities be strictly paid.
The wall surrender to the hooded maid;
Nor let thy sturdy elbow's hasty rage
Jostle the feeble steps of trembling age:
And when the porter bends beneath his load,
And pants for breath; clear thou the crouded road.   50
But, above all, the groping blind direct,
And from the pressing throng the lame protect.
You'll sometimes meet a fop, of nicest tread,
Whose mantling peruke veils his empty head,
At ev'ry step he dreads the wall to lose,
And risques, to save a coach, his red-heel'd shoes;
Him, like the miller, pass with caution by,
Lest from his shoulder clouds of powder fly.
But when the bully, with assuming pace,
Cocks his broad hat, edg'd round with tarnish'd lace,   60
Yield not the way; defie his strutting pride,
And thrust him to the muddy kennel's side;
He never turns again, nor dares oppose,
But mutters coward curses as he goes.
    If drawn by bus'ness to a street unknown,
Let the sworn porter point thee through the town;
Be sure observe the signs, for signs remain,
Like faithful land-marks to the walking train.
Seek not from prentices to learn the way,
Those fabling boys will turn thy steps astray;   70
Ask the grave tradesman to direct thee right,
He ne'er deceives, but when he profits by 't.
    Where fam'd St. Giles's ancient limits [3] spread,
An inrail'd column rears its lofty head,
Here to sev'n streets sev'n dials count the day,
And from each other catch the circling ray.
Here oft the peasant, with enquiring face,
Bewilder'd, trudges on from place to place;
He dwells on ev'ry sign, with stupid gaze,
Enters the narrow alley's doubtful maze,   80
Tries ev'ry winding court and street in vain,
And doubles o'er his weary steps again.
Thus hardy Theseus with intrepid feet,
Travers'd the dang'rous labyrinth of Crete;
But still the wandring passes forc'd his stay,

---

3 In the parish of St. Giles in the Fields there was an intersection of seven streets with a sundial facing each street.

Till Ariadne's clue unwinds the way.
But do not thou, like that bold chief, confide
Thy ventrous footsteps to a female guide;
She'll lead thee with delusive smiles along,
Dive in thy fob,[4] and drop thee in the throng.   90

When waggish boys the stunted besom ply
To rid the slabby pavement; pass not by
E'er thou hast held their hands; some heedless flirt
Will over-spread thy calves with spatt'ring dirt.
Where porters hogsheads roll from carts aslope,
Or brewers down steep cellars stretch the rope,
Where counted billets are by carmen tost
Stay thy rash step, and walk without the post.[5]

Where elevated o'er the gaping croud,
Clasp'd in the board [6] the perjur'd head is bow'd,   100
Betimes retreat; here, thick as hailstones pour,
Turnips, and half-hatch'd eggs, (a mingled show'r)
Among the rabble rain: some random throw
May with the trickling yolk thy cheek o'erflow.

Though expedition bids, yet never stray
Where no rang'd posts defend the rugged way.
Here laden carts with thundring waggons meet,
Wheels clash with wheels, and bar the narrow street;
The lashing whip resounds, the horses strain,
And blood in anguish bursts the swelling vein.   110
O barb'rous men, your cruel breasts asswage,
Why vent ye on the gen'rous steed your rage?
Does not his service earn your daily bread?
Your wives, your children, by his labours fed!
If, as the Samian [7] taught, the soul revives,
And, shifting seats, in other bodies lives;
Severe shall be the brutal coachman's change,
Doom'd in a hackney horse the town to range:
Carmen, transform'd, the groaning load shall draw,
Whom other tyrants with the lash shall awe.   120

Who would of Watling-street the dangers share,
When the broad pavement of Cheap-side is near?
Or who that rugged street would traverse o'er,
That stretches, O Fleet-ditch,[8] from thy black shore
To the Tow'r's moated walls? Here steams ascend

---

4 A small pocket in breeches.
5 Posts marked the edge of the pavement.
6 The pillory.

7 Pythagoras, who believed in the transmigration of souls.
8 This ditch carried off sewage, offal, and all sorts of refuse.

That, in mix'd fumes, the wrinkled nose offend.
Where chandlers' cauldrons boil; where fishy prey
Hide the wet stall, long absent from the sea;
And where the cleaver chops the heifer's spoil,
And where huge hogsheads sweat with trainy oil,[9]   130
Thy breathing nostril hold; but how shall I
Pass, where in piles Cornavian cheeses [10] lye;
Cheese, that the table's closing rites denies,
And bids me with th' unwilling chaplain rise.

O bear me to the paths of fair Pell-mell,
Safe are thy pavements, grateful is thy smell!
At distance rolls along the gilded coach,
Nor sturdy carmen on thy walks encroach;
No lets would bar thy ways were chairs deny'd,
The soft supports of laziness and pride;   140
Shops breathe perfumes, thro' sashes ribbons glow,
The mutual arms of ladies, and the beau.
Yet still ev'n here, when rains the passage hide,
Oft' the loose stone spirts up a muddy tide
Beneath thy careless foot; and from on high,
Where masons mount the ladder, fragments fly;
Mortar, and crumbled lime in show'rs descend,
And o'er thy head destructive tiles impend.

But sometimes let me leave the noisie roads,
And silent wander in the close abodes   150
Where wheels ne'er shake the ground; there pensive stray,
In studious thought, the long uncrouded way.
Here I remark each walker's diff'rent face,
And in their look their various bus'ness trace.
The broker here his spacious beaver wears,
Upon his brow sit jealousies and cares;
Bent on some mortgage (to avoid reproach)
He seeks bye streets, and saves th' expensive coach.
Soft, at low doors, old letchers tap their cane,
For fair recluse, that travels Drury-lane; [11]   160
Here roams uncomb'd the lavish rake, to shun
His Fleet-street draper's everlasting dun.

Careful observers, studious of the town,
Shun the misfortunes that disgrace the clown;
Untempted, they contemn the jugler's feats,

---

9 Oil obtained from fish; whale oil.
10 Cheshire cheeses. The chaplain in a great family often withdrew after the first course of a meal and returned only to say grace. See *Tatlers* 255 and 258.
11 Drury Lane was the haunt of prostitutes.

Pass by the Meuse, nor try the thimble's cheats.[12]
When drays bound high, they never cross behind,
Where bubbling yest is blown by gusts of wind:
And when up Ludgate-hill huge carts move slow,
Far from the straining steeds securely go,   170
Whose dashing hoofs behind them fling the mire,
And mark with muddy blots the gazing 'squire.
The Parthian thus his jav'lin backward throws,
And as he flies infests pursuing foes.

  The thoughtless wits shall frequent forfeits pay,
Who 'gainst the centry's box discharge their tea.
Do thou some court, or secret corner seek,
Nor flush with shame the passing virgin's cheek.

  Yet let me not descend to trivial song,
Nor vulgar circumstance my verse prolong;   180
Why should I teach the maid when torrents pour,
Her head to shelter from the sudden show'r?
Nature will best her ready hand inform,
With her spread petticoat to fence the storm.
Does not each walker know the warning sign,
When wisps of straw depend upon the twine
Cross the close street; that then the paver's art
Renews the ways, deny'd to coach and cart?
Who knows not that the coachman lashing by,
Oft with his flourish cuts the heedless eye;   190
And when he takes his stand, to wait a fare,
His horses' foreheads shun the winter's air?
Nor will I roam, when summer's sultry rays
Parch the dry ground, and spread with dust the ways;
With whirling gusts the rapid atoms rise,
Smoak o'er the pavement, and involve the skies.

  Winter my theme confines; whose nitry wind
Shall crust the slabby mire, and kennels bind;
She bids the snow descend in flaky sheets,
And in her hoary mantle cloath the streets.   200
Let not the virgin tread these slipp'ry roads,
The gath'ring fleece the hollow patten loads;
But if thy footsteps slide with clotted frost,
Strike off the breaking balls against the post.
On silent wheel the passing coaches roll;
Oft' look behind, and ward the threatning pole.[13]

---

[12] A game played with three thimbles and a ball. The Meuse (or Mews), where falcons were formerly kept, was in Trafalgar Square.

[13] The shafts of the coach.

In harden'd orbs the school-boy moulds the snow,
To mark the coachman with a dextrous throw.
Why do ye, boys, the kennel's surface spread,
To tempt with faithless pass the matron's tread?   210
How can ye laugh to see the damsel spurn,
Sink in your frauds, and her green stocking mourn?
At White's the harness'd chairman idly stands,
And swings around his waste his tingling hands:
The sempstress speeds to 'Change [14] with red-tipt nose;
The Belgian stove beneath her footstool glows;
In half-whipt muslin needles useless lie,
And shuttle-cocks across the counter fly.
These sports warm harmless; why then will ye prove,
Deluded maids, the dang'rous flame of love?   220

Where Covent-garden's famous temple [15] stands,
That boasts the work of Jones' immortal hands;
Columns with plain magnificence appear,
And graceful porches lead along the square:
Here oft' my course I bend, when lo! from far,
I spy the furies of the foot-ball war:
The 'prentice quits his shop, to join the crew,
Encreasing crouds the flying game pursue.
Thus, as you roll the ball o'er snowy ground,
The gath'ring globe augments with ev'ry round.   230
But whither shall I run? the throng draws nigh,
The ball now skims the street, now soars on high;
The dextr'ous glazier strong returns the bound,
And gingling sashes on the pent-house sound.

O roving Muse, recal that wond'rous year, [16]
When winter reign'd in bleak Britannia's air;
When hoary Thames, with frosted oziers crown'd,
Was three long moons in icy fetters bound.
The waterman, forlorn along the shore,
Pensive reclines upon his useless oar,   240
Sees harness'd steeds desert the stony town;
And wander roads unstable, not their own:
Wheels o'er the harden'd waters smoothly glide,
And rase with whiten'd tracks the slipp'ry tide.
Here the fat cook piles high the blazing fire,
And scarce the spit can turn the steer entire.
Booths sudden hide the Thames, long streets appear,

14 The New Exchange, a place of business
for seamstresses.
15 St. Paul's, designed by Inigo Jones.

16 In 1709–10, when booths were set up
on the frozen Thames, as they had been in
the severe winter of 1683–84.

And num'rous games proclaim the crouded fair.
So when a gen'ral bids the martial train
Spread their encampment o'er the spacious plain;   250
Thick-rising tents a canvas city build,
And the loud dice resound thro' all the field.
　　'Twas here the matron found a doleful fate:
Let elegiac lay the woe relate,
Soft as the breath of distant flutes, at hours
When silent ev'ning closes up the flow'rs;
Lulling as falling water's hollow noise;
Indulging grief, like Philomela's voice.
　　Doll ev'ry day had walk'd these treach'rous roads;
Her neck grew warpt beneath autumnal loads   260
Of various fruit; she now a basket bore,
That head, alas! shall basket bear no more.
Each booth she frequent past, in quest of gain,
And boys with pleasure heard her shrilling strain.
Ah Doll! all mortals must resign their breath,
And industry itself submit to death!
The cracking crystal yields, she sinks, she dyes,
Her head, chopt off, from her lost shoulders flies:
Pippins she cry'd, but death her voice confounds,
And pip-pip-pip along the ice resounds.   270
So when the Thracian furies Orpheus tore,
And left his bleeding trunk deform'd with gore,
His sever'd head floats down the silver tide,
His yet warm tongue for his lost consort cry'd;
"Eurydice," with quiv'ring voice he mourn'd,
And Heber's banks "Eurydice" return'd.
　　But now the western gale the flood unbinds,
And black'ning clouds move on with warmer winds,
The wooden town its frail foundation leaves,
And Thames' full urn rolls down his plenteous waves;   280
From ev'ry penthouse streams the fleeting snow,
And with dissolving frost the pavements flow.
　　Experienc'd men, inur'd to city ways,
Need not the calendar to count their days.
When through the town with slow and solemn air,
Led by the nostril, walks the muzled bear; [17]
Behind him moves majestically dull,
The pride of Hockley-hole, the surly bull;
Learn hence the periods of the week to name,

[17] Bear and bull baitings were held at Hockley Hole.

Mondays and Thursdays are the days of game.   290
  When fishy stalls with double store are laid;
The golden-belly'd carp, the broad-finn'd maid,
Red-speckled trouts, the salmon's silver joul,
The jointed lobster, and unscaly soale,
And luscious 'scallops, to allure the tastes
Of rigid zealots to delicious fasts;
Wednesdays and Fridays you'll observe from hence,
Days, when our sires were doom'd to abstinence.
  When dirty waters from balconies drop,
And dext'rous damsels twirle the sprinkling mop,   300
And cleanse the spatter'd sash, and scrub the stairs;
Know Saturday's conclusive morn appears.
  Successive crys the season's change declare,
And mark the monthly progress of the year.
Hark, how the streets with treble voices ring,
To sell the bounteous product of the spring!
Sweet-smelling flow'rs, and elder's early bud,
With nettle's tender shoots, to cleanse the blood:
And when June's thunder cools the sultry skies,
Ev'n Sundays are prophan'd by mackrell cries.   310
  Wallnuts the fruit'rer's hand, in autumn, stain,
Blue plumbs and juicy pears augment his gain;
Next oranges the longing boys entice,
To trust their copper fortunes to the dice.
  When rosemary, and bays, the poet's crown,
Are bawl'd, in frequent cries, through all the town,
Then judge the festival of Christmas near,
Christmas, the joyous period of the year.
Now with bright holly all your temples strow,
With laurel green, and sacred misletoe.   320
Now, heav'n-born Charity, thy blessings shed;
Bid meagre Want uprear her sickly head:
Bid shiv'ring limbs be warm; let plenty's bowle
In humble roofs make glad the needy soul.
See, see, the heav'n-born maid her blessings shed;
Lo! meagre Want uprears her sickly head;
Cloath'd are the naked, and the needy glad,
While selfish Avarice alone is sad.
  Proud coaches pass, regardless of the moan
Of infant orphans, and the widow's groan;   330
While Charity still moves the walker's mind,
His lib'ral purse relieves the lame and blind.

Judiciously thy half-pence are bestow'd,
Where the laborious beggar sweeps the road.
Whate'er you give, give ever at demand,
Nor let old-age long stretch his palsy'd hand.
Those who give late, are importun'd each day,
And still are teaz'd, because they still delay.
If e'er the miser durst his farthings spare,
He thinly spreads them through the publick square,   340
Where, all beside the rail, rang'd beggars lie,
And from each other catch the doleful cry;
With heav'n, for two-pence, cheaply wipes his score,
Lifts up his eyes, and hasts to beggar more.

    Where the brass knocker, wrapt in flannel band,
Forbids the thunder of the footman's hand;
Th' upholder,[18] rueful harbinger of death,
Waits with impatience for the dying breath;
As vultures, o'er a camp, with hov'ring flight,
Snuff up the future carnage of the fight.   350
Here canst thou pass, unmindful of a pray'r,
That heav'n in mercy may thy brother spare?

    Come, F * * * [19] sincere, experienc'd friend,
Thy briefs, thy deeds, and ev'n thy fees suspend;
Come let us leave the Temple's silent walls,
Me bus'ness to my distant lodging calls:
Through the long Strand together let us stray:
With thee conversing I forget the way.
Behold that narrow street which steep descends,
Whose building to the slimy shore extends;   360
Here Arundel's fam'd structure [20] rear'd its frame,
The street alone retains an empty name:
Where Titian's glowing paint the canvas warm'd,
And Raphael's fair design, with judgment, charm'd,
Now hangs the bell-man's song, and pasted here
The colour'd prints of Overton [21] appear.
Where statues breath'd, the work of Phidias' hands,
A wooden pump, or lonely watch-house stands.
There Essex' stately pile adorn'd the shore,
There Cecil's, Bedford's, Villers', now no more.   370
Yet Burlington's fair palace still remains:
Beauty within, without proportion reigns.

---

18 Undertaker.
19 William Fortescue, a famous barrister, and schoolboy friend of Gay.
20 Arundel House, with a famous collection of paintings.
21 John Overton, seller of mezzotints.

Beneath his eye declining art revives,[22]
The wall with animated picture lives;
There Hendel strikes the strings, the melting strain
Transports the soul, and thrills through ev'ry vein;
There oft I enter (but with cleaner shoes)
For Burlington's belov'd by ev'ry Muse.

O ye associate walkers, O my friends,
Upon your state what happiness attends!   380
What, though no coach to frequent visit rolls,
Nor for your shilling chairmen sling their poles;
Yet still your nerves rheumatic pains defye,
Nor lazy jaundice dulls your saffron eye;
No wasting cough discharges sounds of death,
Nor wheezing asthma heaves in vain for breath;
Nor from your restless couch is heard the groan
Of burning gout, or sedentary stone.
Let others in the jolting coach confide,
Or in the leaky boat the Thames divide;   390
Or, box'd within the chair, contemn the street,
And trust their safety to another's feet,
Still let me walk; for oft the sudden gale
Ruffles the tide, and shifts the dang'rous sail.
Then shall the passenger, too late, deplore
The whelming billow, and the faithless oar;
The drunken chairman in the kennel spurns,
The glasses shatters, and his charge o'erturns.
Who can recount the coach's various harms,
The legs disjointed, and the broken arms?   400

I've seen a beau, in some ill-fated hour,
When o'er the stones choak'd kennels swell the show'r
In gilded chariot loll; he with disdain
Views spatter'd passengers all drench'd in rain;
With mud fill'd high, the rumbling cart draws near,
Now rule thy prancing steeds, lac'd charioteer!
The dust-man lashes on with spiteful rage,
His pond'rous spokes thy painted wheel engage,
Crush'd is thy pride, down falls the shrieking beau,
The slabby pavement crystal fragments strow,   410
Black floods of mire th' embroider'd coat disgrace,
And mud enwraps the honours of his face.
So when dread Jove the son of Phœbus hurl'd,
Scarr'd with dark thunder, to the nether world;[23]

22 The front of Burlington House was de-   23 Phaethon.
signed after Palladio.

The headstrong coursers tore the silver reins,
And the sun's beamy ruin gilds the plains.
    If the pale walker pant with weak'ning ills,
His sickly hand is stor'd with friendly bills:
From hence he learns the seventh-born doctor's fame,
From hence he learns the cheapest tailor's name.   420
    Shall the large mutton smoak upon your boards?
Such, Newgate's copious market best affords.
Would'st thou with mighty beef augment thy meal?
Seek Leaden-hall; St. James's sends thee veal.
Thames-street gives cheeses; Covent-garden fruits;
Moor-fields old books; and Monmouth-street old suits.
Hence may'st thou well supply the wants of life,
Support thy family, and cloath thy wife.
    Volumes, on shelter'd stalls, expanded lye,
And various science lures the learned eye;   430
The bending shelves with pond'rous scholiasts groan,
And deep divines to modern shops unknown:
Here, like the bee, that on industrious wing
Collects the various odours of the spring,
Walkers, at leisure, learning's flow'rs may spoil,
Nor watch the wasting of the midnight oil,
May morals snatch from Plutarch's tatter'd page,
A mildew'd Bacon, or Stagyra's [24] sage.
Here saunt'ring prentices o'er Otway weep,
O'er Congreve smile, or over D * * [25] sleep;   440
Pleas'd sempstresses the Lock's fam'd Rape unfold,
And Squirts [26] read Garth, 'till apozems grow cold.
    O Lintot,[27] let my labours obvious lie,
Rang'd on thy stall, for ev'ry curious eye;
So shall the poor these precepts gratis know,
And to my verse their future safeties owe.
    What walker shall his mean ambition fix
On the false lustre of a coach and six?
Let the vain virgin, lur'd by glaring show,
Sigh for the liv'ries of th' embroider'd beau.   450
    See yon bright chariot on its harness swing,
With Flanders mares, and on an arched spring;
That wretch to gain an equipage and place,
Betray'd his sister to a lewd embrace.

---

24 Aristotle.
25 John Dennis, who had quarreled with
Pope.
26 Squirt was the name of the apothecary's boy in Garth's *Dispensary*.
27 Bernard Lintot, who published poems
by Pope and Gay.

This coach that with the blazon'd 'scutcheon glows,
Vain of his unknown race, the coxcomb shows.
Here the brib'd lawyer, sunk in velvet, sleeps;
The starving orphan, as he passes, weeps;
There flames a fool, begirt with tinsell'd slaves,
Who wastes the wealth of a whole race of knaves.   460
That other, with a clustring train behind,
Owes his new honours to a sordid mind.
This next in court-fidelity excells,
The publick rifles, and his country sells.
May the proud chariot never be my fate,
If purchas'd at so mean, so dear a rate;
O rather give me sweet content on foot,
Wrapt in my virtue, and a good surtout!

A SELECTION

Paul Aler

1656–1727

GRADUS AD PARNASSUM

1686, 1702, etc.

[During the eighteenth century the English schoolboy composed Latin verses as exercises in composition. These verses were often done with the aid of a *Gradus ad Parnassum*—a thesaurus of Latin words that were listed with appropriate poetic epithets, synonyms, and poetic phrases. The "poetic diction" of the time was undoubtedly influenced by this sort of "theme-writing." Two typical entries from the standard Paul Aler's *Gradus ad Parnassum, sive Novus Synonymorum, Epithetorum, Versuum, ac Phrasum Poeticarum Thesaurus* follow.]

arbor, -oris—et mala radices altius arbor agit. Ovid. SYN.—arbos, arbustum, virgultum, ramus, frondes. EPITH.—sylvestris, umbrosa, opaca, patula, fructifera, frondens, florens, virens, fertilis, ferax, foliata, alta, procera, ramosa, alticoma, ardua, viridis, rigida, foeta, curvata, nobilis, odorifera, virescens, culta, inculta, ambitiosa, celsa, rediviva, fructuosa, amoena, luxuriosa, annosa, caduca. PHRAS.—pandens, extendens late sua brachia ramis diffusa. Sublimi vertice nutans. infixis alte radicibus haerens. patulis luxuriosa comis. ingentem quae sustinet umbram. Largis fructibus onerata, onusta. Frondibus arbos Luxuriat foecunda novis. avibus frondosa praebens hospitia. Fructibus decora. excelsos tendens ad sydera ramos. Tollens se vertice ad auras. Novis collucens, *vel* decorata floribus arbos.

Fama—Magnas it Fama per urbes. Virg. Aen. 4. 173. *Poetae fabulantur Titanis & Terrae filium, quae pennis instructa. tubam unum, aut duas gerit. Hanc Virgilius exhibet ut monstrum alatum, quod oculos, aures, ora, linguasque innumerabiles habet.* SYN.—Rumor, murmur, sermo. EPITH.—pennata, volitans, mendax, vaga, incerta, garrula, turbida, superstes, memor, velox, perannis, maligna, procax, praenuncia, vivax, celer, verbosa, potens, praepes, pernix, subita, repentina. PHR.—Rerum praenuncia Fama. Tam ficti pavique tenax, quam nuncia veri. innumeras solvens falsa in praeconia linguas. Volitans per regna per urbes. Vacuans implens sermonibus aures. Magnarum nuncia rerum. incertae murmura Famae. VERS.—Fama malum, quo non aliud velocius ullum Mobilitate viget, viresque acquirit eundo. Nuncia fama ruit populisque allabitur aures. Fama loquax pervenit ad aures. Fama loquax, quae veris addere falsa Gaudet, et e minimo sua per mendacia crescit. ad nos vix tenuis famae perlabitur aura. interea pavidam volitans pennata per urbem Nuncia fama ruit. et jam Fama volans tanti praenuncia luctus Evandrum Evandrique domos, et moenia complet. V. RUMOR.

A SELECTION

John Dennis
1657–1734

THE GROUNDS OF CRITICISM IN POETRY
1704

[The following passage is a vigorous statement of the early eighteenth-century impulse toward "order" and "regularity" in poetry.]

. . . SINCE therefore 'tis for want of knowing by what rules [poets] ought to proceed that poetry is fallen so low, it follows then that it is the laying down of those rules alone that can re-establish it. In short, poetry is either an art, or whimsey and fanaticism. If it is an art, it follows that it must propose an end to itself, and afterwards lay down proper means for the attaining that end: for this is undeniable, that there are proper means for the attaining of every end, and those proper means in poetry we call the rules. Again, if the end of poetry be to instruct and reform the world, that is, to bring mankind from irregularity, extravagance, and confusion, to rule and order, how this should be done by a thing that is in itself irregular and extravagant is difficult to be conceived. Besides, the work of every reasonable creature must derive its beauty from regularity; for reason is rule and order, and nothing can be irregular either in our conceptions or our actions any further than it swerves from rule, that is, from reason. As man is the more perfect, the more he resembles his Creator; the works of man must needs be more perfect, the more they resemble his Maker's. Now the works of God, though infinitely various, are extremely regular.

The universe is regular in all its parts, and it is to that exact regularity that it owes its admirable beauty. The microcosm owes the beauty and health both of its body and soul to order, and the deformity and distempers of both to nothing but the want of order. Man was created, like the rest of the creatures, regular, and as long as he remained so, he continued happy; but as soon as he fell from his primitive state by transgressing order, weakness and misery was the immediate consequence of that disorder that immediately followed in his conceptions, in his passions and actions.

The great design of art is to restore the decays that happened to human nature by the fall, by restoring order: The design of logic is to bring back order and rule and method to our conceptions, the want of which causes most of our ignorance, and all our errors. The design of moral philosophy is to cure the disorder that is found in our passions, from which proceeds all our unhappiness, and all our vice; as from the due order that is seen in them comes all our virtue and all our pleasure. But how should these arts re-establish order unless they themselves were regular? Those arts that make the senses instrumental to the pleasure of the mind, as painting and music, do it by a great deal of rule and order: since, therefore, poetry comprehends the force of all these arts of logic, of ethics, of eloquence, of painting, of music, can anything be more ridiculous than to imagine that poetry itself should be without rule and order?

[CHAP. II]

A SELECTION

Samuel Johnson

1709–1784

LIVES OF THE ENGLISH POETS

1779–1781

Abraham Cowley

[The following passage is a classic statement of the eighteenth-century objection against the "metaphysical" or baroque "wit" of the seventeenth century. Addison, in his distinction between "true" and "false" wit, and Pope, in his *Essay on Criticism*, reveal the same regard for "propriety" rather than eccentric "novelty."]

WIT, like all other things subject by their nature to the choice of man, has its changes and fashions, and at different times takes different forms. About the beginning of the seventeenth century appeared a race of writers that may be termed the metaphysical poets: of whom, in a criticism on the works of Cowley, it is not improper to give some account. . . .

If wit be well described by Pope, as being "that which has been often thought, but was never before so well expressed," [1] they certainly never attained, nor ever sought it; for they endeavored to be singular in their thoughts, and were careless of their diction. But Pope's account of wit is undoubtedly erroneous: he depresses it below its natural dignity, and reduces it from strength of thought to happiness of language.

If by a more noble and more adequate conception that be considered as wit which is at once natural and new, that which, though not obvious, is, upon its first production, acknowledged to be just; if it be that which he that never found it, wonders how he missed; to wit of this kind the metaphysical poets have seldom risen. Their thoughts are often new, but seldom natural; they are not obvious, but neither are they just; and the reader, far from wondering that he missed them, wonders more frequently by what perverseness of industry they were ever found.

But wit, abstracted from its effects upon the hearer, may be more rigorously and philosophically considered as a kind of *discordia*

---

[1] *Essay on Criticism* 297–98 (paraphrased).

concors; a combination of dissimilar images, or discovery of occult resemblances in things apparently unlike. Of wit thus defined, they have more than enough. The most heterogeneous ideas are yoked by violence together; nature and art are ransacked for illustrations, comparisons, and allusions; their learning instructs, and their subtlety surprises; but the reader commonly thinks his improvement dearly bought, and, though he sometimes admires, is seldom pleased.

From this account of their compositions it will be readily inferred that they were not successful in representing or moving the affections. As they were wholly employed on something unexpected and surprising, they had no regard to that uniformity of sentiment which enables us to conceive and to excite the pains and the pleasure of other minds: they never inquired what, on any occasion, they should have said or done; but wrote rather as beholders than partakers of human nature; as beings looking upon good and evil, impassive and at leisure; as Epicurean deities, making remarks on the actions of men, and the vicissitudes of life, without interest and without emotion. Their courtship was void of fondness, and their lamentation of sorrow. Their wish was only to say what they hoped had been never said before.

Nor was the sublime more within their reach than the pathetic; for they never attempted that comprehension and expanse of thought which at once fills the whole mind, and of which the first effect is sudden astonishment, and the second rational admiration. Sublimity is produced by aggregation, and littleness by dispersion. Great thoughts are always general, and consist in positions not limited by exceptions, and in descriptions not descending to minuteness. It is with great propriety that subtlety, which in its original import means exility of particles, is taken in its metaphorical meaning for nicety of distinction. Those writers who lay on the watch for novelty could have little hope of greatness; for great things cannot have escaped former observation. Their attempts were always analytic; they broke every image into fragments; and could no more represent, by their slender conceits and labored particularities, the prospects of nature or the scenes of life, than he who dissects a sunbeam with a prism can exhibit the wide effulgence of a summer noon. . . .

Alexander Pope

1688-1744

AFTER a century or more of believing that poetry is the spontaneous overflow of powerful feeling, critics are again asking, with Dr. Johnson, "If Pope be not a poet, where is poetry to be found?" Pope embodies the Augustan wit that was so "just," yet so quick. His sophistication, his cultivated taste, would never permit him to abandon himself to "unnatural flights." But his sensibilities were very lively. Pope once said to Spence that he was always moved by the scene in Homer in which Priam's grief breaks out against his servants and sons, and that he could never read it without weeping; whereupon Pope read the passage and was interrupted by his tears. He also cherished an intention of writing a Persian fable, in which he would "have given a full loose to description and imagination. It would have been a very wild thing." In its way, the *Eloisa to Abelard* is a very wild thing. The sensibility of Pope is more characteristically expressed in the exquisite observations of *Windsor Forest*, the shot bird, for instance—

> Oft, as the mounting larks their notes prepare
> They fall, and leave their little lives in air—

or in the filigree realism of the *Rape of the Lock*—

> This casket India's glowing gems unlocks,
> And all Arabia breathes from yonder box.
> The Tortoise here and Elephant unite,
> Transformed to combs, the speckled, and the white.
> Here files of pins extend their shining rows,
> Puffs, Powders, Patches, Bibles, Billet-doux. *love letters*

Some of the "toughness" of metaphysical poetry is transmitted to Pope, but there is no metaphysical distortion. Instead, there is a "propriety," true wit, moving

> From grave to gay, from lively to severe,
> Correct with spirit, eloquent with ease.

The toughness is nowhere more apparent than in the satires. With a sternness not altogether un-Miltonic, Pope rejoices to behold

> Men not afraid of God afraid of me.

The dramatic address of the metaphysicals also descends to the Augustans in the conversational accents of Pope's couplet. Portions of the *Rape of the Lock* are a puppetlike drama. Pope, however, has the art that the metaphysicals lacked—a "correctness," a grace of movement that is clearest in his easy transitions. Pope's is by no means a "simple" poetry; its texture is as complex as the intricate balance of rococo designs. The couplet permits him to adjust antitheses in parallels. Geoffrey Tillotson calls his meanings "stratified." His couplets usually counterpoint meaning against meaning, sound against sound, cadence against cadence. There is likewise the connotative value of many traditions—phrasings from the classics, and forms from the epic, mock-epic, pastoral, satire, and georgic. Above all, the complexity is not a mechanical one, neat though it be, because Pope had the literary taste that Johnson called an instinctive sense of consonance. Pope's very conviction that

> Expression is the dress of thought, and still
> Appears more decent, as more suitable,

prevented his using "poetic diction" except for special effects. All this is not to deny that Pope has limitations—the venom of personal spite, the occasional nastiness of his fun, the shallowness of his deistic platitudes, and the want of magnanimity. But within these limitations his excellence is unequalled.

BIOGRAPHICAL NOTES

Born in London, son of a Roman Catholic linen merchant. Privately educated at the small estate in Binfield, near Windsor Forest. Read "English, French, Italian, Latin, and Greek poets," injuring his health. The *Pastorals* said to have been composed when he was sixteen. Of unattractive appearance: stunted, weak, thin, and crooked: said to have worn stays and padding in his clothes. Early acquaintance with William Walsh, who encouraged him to be a "correct" poet. Tonson published the *Pastorals* (1709), which led to a quarrel with Ambrose Philips, author of other *Pastorals*. Knew Wycherley, and became hanger-on at London coffeehouses, meeting Steele, Addison, and the painter Jervas. Published the *Essay on Criticism* (1711), with a sneer at John Dennis, who replied bitterly, calling Pope a hunchbacked toad. First version of the *Rape of the Lock* (1712). Published *Windsor Forest* (1713) and became one of the Tory wits and Scriblerus Club, with Swift, Gay, Arbuthnot, and Atterbury. Second version of the *Rape of the Lock* (1714). Began to publish the translation of the *Iliad* (1715), a translation by Addison's friend Tickell appearing the following day: Pope suspected Addison of treachery, and wrote the "Atticus" portrait later included in the *Epistle to Dr. Arbuthnot*. Pope's poems collected (1717). Moved to his Twickenham estate (1719); friendships with Teresa and Martha Blount and Lady Mary Wortley Montagu, with whom he later quarreled bitterly, possibly because she spurned his suit.

Translated the *Odyssey* with William Broome and Elijah Fenton (1725–26). Edited Shakespeare (1725); the edition ridiculed by Lewis Theobald, who became the hero of the first *Dunciad* (1728). Under the influence of Bolingbroke's friendship, Pope composed *An Essay on Man* (1733–34); the *Moral Essays* (1731–35) and *Satires* (*Imitations of Horace*) (1733–38) also composed. Managed to have Curll pirate his correspondence, giving an excuse for an authorized edition (1735–37). Tricked Swift into seeming to approve of publishing the correspondence between them (1741). *The Dunciad* revised (1742–43) with Colley Cibber, poet laureate, as the new hero. William Warburton became his literary executor. Died of dropsy and asthma.

BIBLIOGRAPHY: *Works,* edd. W. Elwin and W. J. Courthope, 10 vols., 1871–79. *Poems,* ed. J. Butt (Twickenham edition), 6 vols., 1939– . *Correspondence,* ed. G. Sherburn, 5 vols., 1956. Ault, N., *New Light on Pope,* 1949. Beljame, A., *Men of Letters and the English Public, 1660–1744,* 1948. Brower, R., *Alexander Pope, The Poetry of Allusion,* 1959. Dobrée, B., *Alexander Pope,* 1951. Goldstein, M., *Pope and the Augustan Stage,* 1958. Knight, D., *Pope and the Heroic Tradition,* 1951. Knight, G. W., *Laureate of Peace,* 1955. MacDonald, W. L., *Pope and His Critics,* 1951. Parkin, R. P., *Poetic Workmanship of Alexander Pope,* 1955. Rogers, R. W., *The Major Satires of Alexander Pope,* 1955. Root, R. K., *The Poetical Career of Alexander Pope,* 1938. Sherburn, G., *The Early Career of Alexander Pope,* 1930. Sitwell, E., *Alexander Pope,* 1930. Tillotson, G., *The Moral Poetry of Pope,* 1946; *On the Poetry of Pope,* 1938; *Pope and Human Nature,* 1958. Thornton, F. B., *Alexander Pope, Catholic Poet,* 1952. Warren, A., *Alexander Pope as Critic and Humanist,* 1929.

AN ESSAY ON CRITICISM

1711

PART I

'Tis hard to say, if greater want of skill
Appear in writing or in judging ill;
But, of the two, less dang'rous is th' offence
To tire our patience, than mislead our sense.
Some few in that, but numbers err in this,
Ten censure wrong for one who writes amiss;
A fool might once himself alone expose,
Now one in verse makes many more in prose.
'Tis with our judgments as our watches, none
Go just alike, yet each believes his own.   10
In poets as true genius is but rare,
True taste as seldom is the critic's share;
Both must alike from Heav'n derive their light,
These born to judge, as well as those to write.
Let such teach others who themselves excel,
And censure freely who have written well.
Authors are partial to their wit, 'tis true,
But are not critics to their judgment too?

Yet if we look more closely, we shall find
Most have the seeds of judgment in their mind: 20
Nature affords at least a glimm'ring light;
The lines, tho' touch'd but faintly, are drawn right.
But as the slightest sketch, if justly trac'd,
Is by ill-colouring but the more disgrac'd,
So by false learning is good sense defac'd:
Some are bewilder'd in the maze of schools,
And some made coxcombs Nature meant but fools.
In search of wit these lose their common sense,
And then turn critics in their own defence:
Each burns alike, who can, or cannot write, 30
Or with a rival's or an eunuch's spite.
All fools have still an itching to deride,
And fain would be upon the laughing side.
If Mævius scribble in Apollo's spight,
There are, who judge still worse than he can write.

Some have at first for wits, then poets past,
Turn'd critics next, and prov'd plain fools at last.
Some neither can for wits nor critics pass,
As heavy mules are neither horse nor ass.
Those half-learn'd witlings, num'rous in our isle, 40
As half-form'd insects on the banks of Nile;
Unfinish'd things, one knows not what to call,
Their generation's so equivocal:
To tell 'em, would a hundred tongues require,
Or one vain wit's, that might a hundred tire.

But you who seek to give and merit fame,
And justly bear a critic's noble name,
Be sure yourself and your own reach to know,
How far your genius, taste, and learning go;
Launch not beyond your depth, but be discreet, 50
And mark that point where sense and dullness meet.

Nature to all things fix'd the limits fit,
And wisely curb'd proud man's pretending wit.
As on the land while here the ocean gains,
In other parts it leaves wide sandy plains;
Thus in the soul while memory prevails,
The solid pow'r of understanding fails;
Where beams of warm imagination play,
The memory's soft figures melt away.
One science only will one genius fit; 60
So vast is art, so narrow human wit:

Not only bounded to peculiar arts,
But oft in those confin'd to single parts.
Like kings, we lose the conquests gain'd before,
By vain ambition still to make them more;
Each might his sev'ral province well command,
Would all but stoop to what they understand.
  First follow Nature, and your judgment frame
By her just standard, which is still the same:
Unerring Nature, still divinely bright,   70
One clear, unchang'd, and universal light,
Life, force, and beauty, must to all impart,
At once the source, and end, and test of Art.
Art from that fund each just supply provides,
Works without show, and without pomp presides:
In some fair body thus th' informing soul
With spirits feeds, with vigour fills the whole,
Each motion guides, and ev'ry nerve sustains;
Itself unseen, but in th' effects, remains.
Some, to whom Heav'n in wit has been profuse,   80
Want as much more, to turn it to its use;
For wit and judgment often are at strife,
Tho' meant each other's aid, like man and wife.
'Tis more to guide, than spur the Muse's steed;
Restrain his fury, than provoke his speed;
The winged courser, like a gen'rous horse,
Shows most true mettle when you check his course.
  Those rules of old discover'd, not devis'd,
Are Nature still, but Nature methodiz'd;
Nature, like liberty, is but restrain'd   90
By the same laws which first herself ordain'd.
  Hear how learn'd Greece her useful rules indites,
When to repress, and when indulge our flights:
High on Parnassus' top her sons she show'd,
And pointed out those arduous paths they trod;
Held from afar, aloft, th' immortal prize,
And urg'd the rest by equal steps to rise.
Just precepts thus from great examples giv'n,
She drew from them what they deriv'd from Heav'n.
The gen'rous critic fann'd the poet's fire,   100
And taught the world with reason to admire.
Then Criticism the Muse's handmaid prov'd,
To dress her charms, and make her more belov'd:
But following wits from that intention stray'd,

Who could not win the mistress, woo'd the maid;
Against the poets their own arms they turn'd,
Sure to hate most the men from whom they learn'd.
So modern 'pothecaries, taught the art
By doctor's bills to play the doctor's part,
Bold in the practice of mistaken rules,   110
Prescribe, apply, and call their masters fools.
Some on the leaves of ancient authors prey,
Nor time nor moths e'er spoil'd so much as they.
Some drily plain, without invention's aid,
Write dull receipts how poems may be made.
These leave the sense, their learning to display,
And those explain the meaning quite away.

    You then whose judgment the right course would steer,
Know well each ancient's proper character;
His fable, subject, scope in ev'ry page;   120
Religion, country, genius of his age:
Without all these at once before your eyes,
Cavil you may, but never criticize.
Be Homer's works your study and delight,
Read them by day, and meditate by night;
Thence form your judgment, thence your maxims bring,
And trace the Muses upward to their spring.
Still with itself compar'd, his text peruse;
And let your comment be the Mantuan Muse.[1]

    When first young Maro in his boundless mind   130
A work t' outlast immortal Rome design'd,
Perhaps he seem'd above the critic's law,
And but from Nature's fountains scorn'd to draw:
But when t' examine ev'ry part he came,
Nature and Homer were, he found, the same.
Convinc'd, amaz'd, he checks the bold design;
And rules as strict his labour'd work confine,
As if the Stagirite[2] o'erlook'd each line.
Learn hence for ancient rules a just esteem;
To copy nature is to copy them.   140

    Some beauties yet no precepts can declare,
For there's a happiness as well as care.
Music resembles poetry; in each
Are nameless graces which no methods teach,
And which a master-hand alone can reach.
If, where the rules not far enough extend

---

[1] Vergil, born near Mantua.   [2] Aristotle, born at Stagira, Macedonia.

(Since rules were made but to promote their end),
Some lucky licence answer to the full
Th' intent propos'd, that licence is a rule.
Thus Pegasus, a nearer way to take,   150
May boldly deviate from the common track;
From vulgar bounds with brave disorder part,
And snatch a grace beyond the reach of art,
Which, without passing thro' the judgment, gains
The heart, and all its end at once attains.
In prospects thus, some objects please our eyes,
Which out of nature's common order rise,
The shapeless rock, or hanging precipice.
Great wits sometimes may gloriously offend,
And rise to faults true critics dare not mend.   160
But tho' the ancients thus their rules invade
(As kings dispense with laws themselves have made),
Moderns, beware! or if you must offend
Against the precept, ne'er transgress its end;
Let it be seldom, and compell'd by need;
And have, at least, their precedent to plead.
The critic else proceeds without remorse,
Seizes your fame, and puts his laws in force.
I know there are, to whose presumptuous thoughts
Those freer beauties, ev'n in them, seem faults.   170
Some figures monstrous and mis-shap'd appear,
Consider'd singly, or beheld too near,
Which, but proportion'd to their light, or place,
Due distance reconciles to form and grace.
A prudent chief not always must display
His pow'rs in equal ranks, and fair array,
But with th' occasion and the place comply,
Conceal his force, nay seem sometimes to fly.
Those oft are stratagems which errors seem,
Nor is it Homer nods, but we that dream.   180
Still green with bays each ancient altar stands,
Above the reach of sacrilegious hands;
Secure from flames, from Envy's fiercer rage,
Destructive War, and all-involving Age.
See from each clime the learn'd their incense bring!
Hear, in all tongues consenting pæans ring!
In praise so just let ev'ry voice be join'd,
And fill the gen'ral chorus of mankind.
Hail, bards triumphant! born in happier days;

Immortal heirs of universal praise!   190
Whose honours with increase of ages grow,
As streams roll down, enlarging as they flow;
Nations unborn your mighty names shall sound,
And worlds applaud that must not yet be found!
Oh may some spark of your celestial fire,
The last, the meanest of your sons inspire
(That on weak wings, from far, pursues your flights;
Glows while he reads, but trembles as he writes)
To teach vain wits a science little known,
T' admire superior sense, and doubt their own!   200

PART II

Of all the causes which conspire to blind
Man's erring judgment, and misguide the mind,
What the weak head with strongest bias rules
Is pride, the never-failing vice of fools.
Whatever Nature has in worth deny'd,
She gives in large recruits of needful pride;
For as in bodies, thus in souls, we find
What wants in blood and spirits, swell'd with wind:
Pride, where wit fails, steps in to our defence,
And fills up all the mighty void of sense.   210
If once right reason drives that cloud away,
Truth breaks upon us with resistless day.
Trust not yourself; but your defects to know,
Make use of ev'ry friend—and ev'ry foe.
A little learning is a dang'rous thing;
Drink deep, or taste not the Pierian spring: [3]
There shallow draughts intoxicate the brain,
And drinking largely sobers us again.
Fir'd at first sight with what the Muse imparts,
In fearless youth we tempt the heights of arts,   220
While from the bounded level of our mind,
Short views we take, nor see the lengths behind;
But more advanc'd, behold with strange surprize
New distant scenes of endless science rise!
So pleas'd at first the tow'ring Alps we try,
Mount o'er the vales, and seem to tread the sky;
Th' eternal snows appear already past,
And the first clouds and mountains seem the last;

---

3 Pieria, in Macedonia, was, traditionally, the place at which the Muses were worshiped in early times.

But, those attain'd, we tremble to survey
The growing labours of the lengthen'd way,   230
Th' increasing prospect tires our wand'ring eyes,
Hills peep o'er hills, and Alps on Alps arise!
   A perfect judge will read each work of wit
With the same spirit that its author writ:
Survey the whole, nor seek slight faults to find
Where nature moves, and rapture warms the mind;
Nor lose, for that malignant dull delight,
The gen'rous pleasure to be charm'd with wit.
But in such lays as neither ebb, nor flow,
Correctly cold, and regularly low,   240
That shunning faults, one quiet tenour keep,
We cannot blame indeed—but we may sleep.
In Wit, as Nature, what affects our hearts
Is not th' exactness of peculiar parts;
'Tis not a lip, or eye, we beauty call,
But the joint force and full result of all.
Thus when we view some well-proportion'd dome,
(The world's just wonder, and ev'n thine, O Rome! [4])
No single parts unequally surprize,
All comes united to th' admiring eyes;   250
No monstrous height, or breadth, or length appear;
The whole at once is bold, and regular.
   Whoever thinks a faultless piece to see,
Thinks what ne'er was, nor is, nor e'er shall be.
In ev'ry work regard the writer's end,
Since none can compass more than they intend;
And if the means be just, the conduct true,
Applause, in spight of trivial faults, is due;
As men of breeding, sometimes men of wit,
T' avoid great errors, must the less commit: 260
Neglect the rules each verbal critic lays,
For not to know some trifles, is a praise.
Most critics, fond of some subservient art,
Still make the whole depend upon a part:
They talk of principles, but notions prize,
And all to one lov'd folly sacrifice.
   Once on a time, La Mancha's knight, they say,
A certain bard encount'ring on the way,
Discours'd in terms as just, with looks as sage,

4 Pope evidently refers to the dome of St. Peter's, although the dome of the Pantheon
would not be impossible.

As e'er could Dennis,[5] of the Grecian stage;   270
Concluding all were desp'rate sots and fools,
Who durst depart from Aristotle's rules.
Our author, happy in a judge so nice,
Produc'd his play, and begg'd the knight's advice;
Made him observe the subject, and the plot,
The manners, passions, unities; what not?
All which, exact to rule, were brought about,
Were but a combat in the lists left out.
"What! leave the combat out?" exclaims the knight;
"Yes, or we must renounce the Stagirite."   280
"Not so, by Heav'n," he answers in a rage,
"Knights, squires, and steeds, must enter on the stage."
"So vast a throng the stage can ne'er contain."
"Then build a new, or act it in a plain."

   Thus critics, of less judgment than caprice,
Curious, not knowing, not exact but nice,
Form short ideas; and offend in arts
(As most in manners) by a love to parts.

   Some to conceit alone their taste confine,
And glitt'ring thoughts struck out at ev'ry line;   290
Pleas'd with a work where nothing's just or fit;
One glaring chaos and wild heap of wit.
Poets, like painters, thus, unskill'd to trace
The naked nature and the living grace,
With gold and jewels cover ev'ry part,
And hide with ornaments their want of art.
True Wit is Nature to advantage dress'd,
What oft was thought, but ne'er so well express'd;
Something, whose truth convinc'd at sight we find,
That gives us back the image of our mind.   300
As shades more sweetly recommend the light,
So modest plainness sets off sprightly wit.
For works may have more wit than does 'em good,
As bodies perish thro' excess of blood.

   Others for language all their care express,
And value books, as women men, for dress:
Their praise is still,—the style is excellent;
The sense, they humbly take upon content.
Words are like leaves; and where they most abound,

5 John Dennis, writer of bombastic trag- *cal* (1711); Pope retorted with a *Narrative*
edy and "judicious" critic. Pope attacked *Concerning the Frenzy of Mr. John Denn—*
his *Appius and Virginia* in line 585; Dennis (1713).
replied with *Reflections, Critical and Satiri-*

Much fruit of sense beneath is rarely found.   310
False eloquence, like the prismatic glass,
Its gaudy colours spreads on ev'ry place;
The face of Nature we no more survey,
All glares alike, without distinction gay:
But true expression, like th' unchanging sun,
Clears, and improves whate'er it shines upon;
It gilds all objects, but it alters none.
Expression is the dress of thought, and still
Appears more decent, as more suitable;
A vile conceit in pompous words express'd,   320
Is like a clown in regal purple dress'd:
For diff'rent styles with diff'rent subjects sort,
As several garbs with country, town, and court.
Some by old words to fame have made pretence,
Ancients in phrase, meer moderns in their sense;
Such labour'd nothings, in so strange a style,
Amaze th' unlearn'd, and make the learned smile.
Unlucky, as Fungoso [6] in the play,
These sparks with aukward vanity display
What the fine gentleman wore yesterday;   330
And but so mimic ancient wits at best,
As apes our grandsires, in their doublets drest.
In words, as fashions, the same rule will hold;
Alike fantastic, if too new, or old:
Be not the first by whom the new are try'd,
Nor yet the last to lay the old aside.
    But most by numbers judge a poet's song;
And smooth or rough, with them, is right or wrong:
In the bright Muse tho' thousand charms conspire,
Her voice is all these tuneful fools admire;   340
Who haunt Parnassus but to please their ear,
Not mend their minds; as some to church repair,
Not for the doctrine, but the music there.
These equal syllables alone require,
Tho' oft the ear the open vowels tire;
While expletives their feeble aid do join;
And ten low words oft creep in one dull line:
While they ring round the same unvary'd chimes,
With sure returns of still expected rhymes;
Where'er you find "the cooling western breeze,"   350
In the next line, it "whispers thro' the trees":

6 A fop in Jonson's *Every Man Out of His Humor.*

trochee — unstressed followed by stressed

iamb

If crystal streams "with pleasing murmurs creep,"
The reader's threaten'd (not in vain) with "sleep":
Then, at the last and only couplet fraught
With some unmeaning thing they call a thought,
A needless Alexandrine ends the song,
That, like a wounded snake, drags its slow length along.

makes one stagger along

Leave such to tune their own dull rhymes, and know
What's roundly smooth, or languishingly slow;
And praise the easy vigour of a line,
Where Denham's strength, and Waller's sweetness join.   360
True ease in writing comes from art, not chance,
As those move easiest who have learn'd to dance.
'Tis not enough no harshness gives offence,
The sound must seem an echo to the sense:
Soft is the strain when Zephyr gently blows,
And the smooth stream in smoother numbers flows;
But when loud surges lash the sounding shoar,
The hoarse, rough verse should like the torrent roar:

builds up sound effect

When Ajax strives some rock's vast weight to throw,   370
The line too labours, and the words move slow;
Not so, when swift Camilla [7] scours the plain,   *Alexandrine*
Flies o'er th' unbending corn, and skims along the main.
Hear how Timotheus' [8] varied lays surprize,
And bid alternate passions fall and rise!
While, at each change, the son of Libyan Jove
Now burns with glory, and then melts with love;
Now his fierce eyes with sparkling fury glow,
Now sighs steal out, and tears begin to flow:
Persians and Greeks like turns of nature found,   380
And the world's victor stood subdu'd by sound!
The pow'r of music all our hearts allow,
And what Timotheus was, is Dryden now.

    Avoid extremes; and shun the fault of such,
Who still are pleas'd too little or too much.
At ev'ry trifle scorn to take offence;
That always shows great pride, or little sense;
Those heads, as stomachs, are not sure the best,
Which nauseate all, and nothing can digest.
Yet let not each gay turn thy rapture move;   390
For fools admire, but men of sense approve:
As things seem large which we thro' mists descry,

7 *Aeneid* VII. 803 ff.
8 See Dryden's *Alexander's Feast, or The Power of Music.*

Dullness is ever apt to magnify.
    Some foreign writers, some our own despise;
The ancients only, or the moderns prize.
Thus wit, like faith, by each man is apply'd
To one small sect, and all are damn'd beside.
Meanly they seek the blessing to confine,
And force that sun but on a part to shine,
Which not alone the southern wit sublimes,   400
But ripens spirits in cold northern climes;
Which from the first has shone on ages past,
Enlights the present, and shall warm the last;
Tho' each may feel increases and decays,
And see now clearer and now darker days.
Regard not then if wit be old or new,
But blame the false, and value still the true.
    Some ne'er advance a judgment of their own,
But catch the spreading notion of the town;
They reason and conclude by precedent,   410
And own stale nonsense which they ne'er invent.
Some judge of authors' names, not works, and then
Nor praise nor blame the writings, but the men.
Of all this servile herd, the worst is he
That in proud dullness joins with quality.
A constant critic at the great man's board,
To fetch and carry nonsense for my lord.
What woful stuff this madrigal would be,
In some starv'd hackney sonneteer, or me!
But let a lord once own the happy lines,   420
How the wit brightens! how the style refines!
Before his sacred name flies ev'ry fault,
And each exalted stanza teems with thought!
    The vulgar thus through imitation err;
As oft the learn'd by being singular;
So much they scorn the croud, that if the throng
By chance go right, they purposely go wrong:
So schismatics the plain believers quit,
And are but damn'd for having too much wit.
Some praise at morning what they blame at night;   430
But always think the last opinion right.
A Muse by these is like a mistress us'd,
This hour she's idoliz'd, the next abus'd;
While their weak heads, like towns unfortify'd,
'Twixt sense and nonsense daily change their side.

Ask them the cause; they're wiser still, they say:
And still to-morrow's wiser than to-day.
We think our fathers fools, so wise we grow;
Our wiser sons, no doubt, will think us so.
Once school-divines this zealous isle o'erspread;   440
Who knew most sentences,[9] was deepest read;
Faith, gospel, all, seem'd made to be disputed,
And none had sense enough to be confuted:
Scotists and Thomists, now, in peace remain,
Amidst their kindred cobwebs in Duck Lane.[10]
If faith itself has diff'rent dresses worn,
What wonder modes in wit should take their turn?
Oft, leaving what is natural and fit,
The current folly proves the ready wit;
And authors think their reputation safe,   450
Which lives as long as fools are pleas'd to laugh.

Some, valuing those of their own side or mind,
Still make themselves the measure of mankind:
Fondly we think we honour merit then,
When we but praise ourselves in other men.
Parties in wit attend on those of state,
And public faction doubles private hate.
Pride, Malice, Folly, against Dryden rose,
In various shapes of parsons, critics, beaus;
But sense surviv'd, when merry jests were past;   460
For rising merit will buoy up at last.
Might he return, and bless once more our eyes,
New Blackmores and new Milbourns [11] must arise:
Nay, should great Homer lift his awful head,
Zoilus [12] again would start up from the dead.
Envy will merit, as its shade, pursue;
But like a shadow, proves the substance true;
For envy'd wit, like Sol eclips'd, makes known
Th' opposing body's grossness, not its own.
When first that sun too pow'rful beams displays,   470
It draws up vapours which obscure its rays;
But ev'n those clouds at last adorn its way,

---

9 Peter Lombard, *Magister Sententiarum* or "Master of the Sentences," composed his scholastic *Sententiae* between 1145 and 1150; the work was a compendium of theological opinions.

10 A place where old and second-hand books were sold formerly, near Smithfield. [Pope]

11 Sir Richard Blackmore in his *Satyr against Wit* (1700) and Luke Milbourne in his *Notes on Dryden's Vergil* (1698) both attacked Dryden.

12 Zoilus, who attacked Homer and Plato in the fourth century B.C., is the classic instance of the tasteless critic.

Reflect new glories, and augment the day.
Be thou the first true merit to befriend;
His praise is lost, who stays till all commend.
Short is the date, alas, of modern rhymes,
And 'tis but just to let them live betimes.
No longer now that golden age appears,
When Patriarch-wits surviv'd a thousand years:
Now length of fame (our second life) is lost,   480
And bare threescore is all ev'n that can boast;
Our sons their fathers' failing language see,
And such as Chaucer is, shall Dryden be.
So when the faithful pencil has design'd
Some bright idea of the master's mind,
Where a new world leaps out at his command,
And ready Nature waits upon his hand;
When the ripe colours soften and unite,
And sweetly melt into just shade and light;
When mellowing years their full perfection give,   490
And each bold figure just begins to live,
The treach'rous colours the fair art betray,
And all the bright creation fades away!
Unhappy Wit, like most mistaken things,
Atones not for that envy which it brings.
In youth alone its empty praise we boast,
But soon the short-liv'd vanity is lost:
Like some fair flow'r the early spring supplies,
That gayly blooms, but ev'n in blooming dies.
What is this Wit, which must our cares employ?   500
The owner's wife, that other men enjoy;
Then most our trouble still when most admir'd,
And still the more we give, the more requir'd;
Whose fame with pains we guard, but lose with ease,
Sure some to vex, but never all to please;
'Tis what the vicious fear, the virtuous shun,
By fools 'tis hated, and by knaves undone!
If Wit so much from ign'rance undergo,
Ah let not Learning too commence its foe!
Of old, those met rewards who could excell,   510
And such were prais'd who but endeavour'd well:
Tho' triumphs were to gen'rals only due,
Crowns were reserv'd to grace the soldiers too.
Now they who reach Parnassus' lofty crown
Employ their pains to spurn some others down;

And while self-love each jealous writer rules,
Contending wits become the sport of fools:
But still the worst with most regret commend,
For each ill author is as bad a friend.
To what base ends, and by what abject ways,   520
Are mortals urg'd thro' sacred lust of praise!
Ah, ne'er so dire a thirst of glory boast,
Nor in the critic let the man be lost.
Good-nature and good-sense must ever join;
To err is human, to forgive, divine.
    But if in noble minds some dregs remain
Not yet purg'd off, of spleen and sour disdain;
Discharge that rage on more provoking crimes,
Nor fear a dearth in these flagitious times.
No pardon vile obscenity should find,   530
Tho' wit and art conspire to move your mind;
But dullness with obscenity must prove
As shameful sure as impotence in love.
In the fat age of pleasure, wealth, and ease,
Sprung the rank weed, and thriv'd with large increase:
When love was all an easy monarch's care;[13]
Seldom at council, never in a war.
Jilts rul'd the state, and statesmen farces writ;
Nay, wits had pensions, and young lords had wit:
The fair sat panting at a courtier's play,   540
And not a mask went unimprov'd away:
The modest fan was lifted up no more,
And virgins smil'd at what they blush'd before.
The following license of a foreign reign [14]
Did all the dregs of bold Socinus drain;
Then unbelieving priests reform'd the nation,
And taught more pleasant methods of salvation;
Where Heav'n's free subjects might their rights dispute,
Lest God himself should seem too absolute:
Pulpits their sacred satire learn'd to spare,   550
And Vice admir'd to find a flatt'rer there!
Encourag'd thus, Wit's Titans brav'd the skies,
And the press groan'd with licens'd blasphemies.
These monsters, critics! with your darts engage,
Here point your thunder, and exhaust your rage!
Yet shun their fault, who, scandalously nice

---

13 During the reign of Charles II.
14 The reign of William III, at which time the doctrines of Lelio and Fausto Sozzini were popular; these doctrines denied the divinity of Christ and the mystery of the sacraments.

Will needs mistake an author into vice;
All seems infected that th' infected spy,
As all looks yellow to the jaundic'd eye.

PART III

  Learn then what morals critics ought to show,   560
For 'tis but half a judge's task, to know.
'Tis not enough, taste, judgment, learning, join;
In all you speak, let truth and candour shine:
That not alone what to your sense is due
All may allow; but seek your friendship too.
  Be silent always, when you doubt your sense;
And speak, tho' sure, with seeming diffidence:
Some positive, persisting fops we know,
Who, if once wrong, will needs be always so;
But you, with pleasure own your errors past,   570
And make each day a critic on the last.
  'Tis not enough your counsel still be true;
Blunt truths more mischief than nice falsehoods do;
Men must be taught as if you taught them not,
And things unknown propos'd as things forgot.
Without good-breeding, truth is disapprov'd;
That only makes superior sense belov'd.
  Be niggards of advice on no pretence;
For the worst avarice is that of sense.
With mean complacence ne're betray your trust,   580
Nor be so civil as to prove unjust.
Fear not the anger of the wise to raise;
Those best can bear reproof, who merit praise.
  'Twere well might critics still this freedom take,
But Appius [15] reddens at each word you speak,
And stares, tremendous, with a threat'ning eye,
Like some fierce tyrant in old tapestry.
Fear most to tax an honourable fool,
Whose right it is, uncensur'd, to be dull;
Such, without wit, are poets when they please,   590
As without learning they can take degrees.
Leave dang'rous truths to unsuccessful satires,
And flattery to fulsome dedicators,
Whom, when they praise, the world believes no more,
Than when they promise to give scribbling o'er.

15 John Dennis, attacked in line 270, above: Dennis was the author of *Appius and Virginia* (1709).

'Tis best sometimes your censure to restrain,
And charitably let the dull be vain:
Your silence there is better than your spite,
For who can rail so long as they can write?
Still humming on, their drouzy course they keep,   600
And lash'd so long, like tops, are lash'd asleep.
False steps but help them to renew the race,
As, after stumbling, jades will mend their pace.
What crouds of these, impenitently bold,
In sounds and jingling syllables grown old,
Still run on poets, in a raging vein,
Ev'n to the dregs and squeezings of the brain,
Strain out the last dull droppings of their sense,
And rhyme with all the rage of impotence.

    Such shameless bards we have; and yet 'tis true,   610
There are as mad, abandon'd critics too.
The bookful blockhead, ignorantly read,
With loads of learned lumber in his head,
With his own tongue still edifies his ears,
And always list'ning to himself appears.
All books he reads, and all he reads assails,
From Dryden's *Fables* down to Durfey's *Tales*.
With him, most authors steal their works, or buy;
Garth did not write his own *Dispensary*.
Name a new play, and he's the poet's friend;   620
Nay, show'd his faults—but when would poets mend?
No place so sacred from such fops is barr'd,
Nor is Paul's church more safe than Paul's churchyard: [16]
Nay, fly to altars; there they'll talk you dead:
For fools rush in where angels fear to tread.
Distrustful sense with modest caution speaks,
It still looks home, and short excursions makes;
But rattling nonsense in full vollies breaks,
And never shock'd, and never turn'd aside,
Bursts out, resistless, with a thund'ring tide.   630

    But where's the man, who counsel can bestow,
Still pleas'd to teach, and yet not proud to know?
Unbias'd, or by favour, or by spite;
Not dully prepossess'd, nor blindly right;
Tho' learn'd, well-bred; and tho' well-bred, sincere;
Modestly bold, and humanly severe:
Who to a friend his faults can freely show,

[16] A center for booksellers.

And gladly praise the merit of a foe?
Blest with a taste exact, yet unconfin'd;
A knowledge both of books and humankind;   640
Gen'rous converse; a soul exempt from pride;
And love to praise, with reason on his side?
    Such once were critics; such the happy few,
Athens and Rome in better ages knew.
The mighty Stagirite first left the shore,
Spread all his sails, and durst the deeps explore;
He steer'd securely, and discover'd far,
Led by the light of the Mæonian star.[17] *Homer*
Poets, a race long unconfin'd, and free,
Still fond and proud of savage liberty,   650
Receiv'd his laws; and stood convinc'd 'twas fit,
Who conquer'd Nature, should preside o'er Wit.[18] *Aristotle*
    Horace still charms with graceful negligence,
And without method talks us into sense,
Will, like a friend, familiarly convey
The truest notions in the easiest way.
He who supreme in judgment, as in wit,
Might boldly censure, as he boldly writ,
Yet judg'd with coolness, tho' he sung with fire;
His precepts teach but what his works inspire.   660
Our critics take a contrary extreme,
They judge with fury, but they write with phlegm:
Nor suffers Horace more in wrong translations
By wits, than critics in as wrong quotations.
See Dionysius [19] Homer's thoughts refine,
And call new beauties forth from ev'ry line!
Fancy and art in gay Petronius [20] please,
The scholar's learning, with the courtier's ease.
    In grave Quintilian's copious work,[21] we find
The justest rules, and clearest method join'd: 670
Thus useful arms in magazines we place,
All rang'd in order, and dispos'd with grace,
But less to please the eye, than arm the hand,
Still fit for use, and ready at command.
    Thee, bold Longinus! [22] all the Nine inspire,

17 Homer, supposed to have been a native of Mæonia, or Lydia.

18 Aristotle, who wrote on both science and poetry.

19 Dionysius of Halicarnassus (first century B.C.), a rhetorician.

20 Petronius Arbiter (died A.D. 66), author of the *Satyricon*.

21 *De Institutione Oratoria* by Quintilian (A.D. 40-ca. 100).

22 Greek critic of the third century who was said to have written the treatise *On the Sublime*.

And bless their critic with a poet's fire.
An ardent judge, who, zealous in his trust,
With warmth gives sentence, yet is always just;
Whose own example strengthens all his laws;
And is himself that great Sublime he draws.   680

Thus long succeeding critics justly reign'd,
License repress'd, and useful laws ordain'd.
Learning and Rome alike in empire grew;
And arts still follow'd where her eagles flew;
From the same foes, at last, both felt their doom,
And the same age saw Learning fall, and Rome.
With Tyranny, then Superstition join'd,
As that the body, this enslav'd the mind;
Much was believ'd, but little understood,
And to be dull was constru'd to be good;   690
A second deluge Learning thus o'errun,
And the monks finish'd what the Goths begun.

At length Erasmus, that great injur'd name,
(The glory of the priesthood, and the shame!)
Stemm'd the wild torrent of a barb'rous age,
And drove those holy Vandals off the stage.

But see! each Muse, in Leo's golden days,[23]
Starts from her trance, and trims her wither'd bays,
Rome's ancient Genius, o'er its ruins spread,
Shakes off the dust, and rears his rev'rend head.   700
Then Sculpture and her sister-arts revive;
Stones leap'd to form, and rocks began to live;
With sweeter notes each rising temple rung;
A Raphael painted, and a Vida [24] sung.
Immortal Vida! on whose honour'd brow
The poet's bays and critic's ivy grow:
Cremona now shall ever boast thy name,
As next in place to Mantua, next in fame!

But soon by impious arms from Latium chas'd,
Their ancient bounds the banish'd Muses pass'd;   710
Thence arts o'er all the northern world advance,
But critic-learning flourish'd most in France:
The rules a nation, born to serve, obeys;
And Boileau still in right of Horace sways.
But we, brave Britons, foreign laws despis'd,
And kept unconquer'd, and unciviliz'd;

---

23 Pope Leo X (1475–1521), patron of
arts and letters.

24 The ecclesiastic who wrote an *Art of
Poetry* (ca. 1527).

Fierce for the liberties of wit, and bold,
We still defy'd the Romans, as of old.
Yet some there were, among the sounder few
Of those who less presum'd, and better knew,   720
Who durst assert the juster ancient cause,
And here restor'd Wit's fundamental laws.
Such was the Muse, whose rules and practice tell,
"Nature's chief masterpiece is writing well." [25]
Such was Roscommon,[26] not more learn'd than good.
With manners gen'rous as his noble blood;
To him the wit of Greece and Rome was known,
And ev'ry author's merit, but his own.
Such late was Walsh [27]—the Muse's judge and friend,
Who justly knew to blame or to commend;   730
To failings mild, but zealous for desert;
The clearest head, and the sincerest heart.
This humble praise, lamented shade! receive,
This praise at least a grateful Muse may give:
The Muse whose early voice you taught to sing,
Prescrib'd her heights, and prun'd her tender wing,
(Her guide now lost) no more attempts to rise,
But in low numbers short excursions tries:
Content, if hence th' unlearn'd their wants may view,
The learn'd reflect on what before they knew: 740
Careless of censure, nor too fond of fame;
Still pleas'd to praise, yet not afraid to blame;
Averse alike to flatter, or offend;
Not free from faults, nor yet too vain to mend.

[25] From *An Essay on Poetry* (1682) by John Sheffield, Duke of Buckingham and Normanby.

[26] Wentworth Dillon, Earl of Roscommon, who composed a verse *Essay on Translated Verse* (1684) and who praised Milton's *Paradise Lost*.

[27] William Walsh (1663–1708), who advised Pope upon poetry.

THE RAPE OF THE LOCK
AN HEROIC-COMICAL POEM

Nolueram, Belinda, tuos violare capillos;
Sed juvat, hoc precibus me tribuisse tuis.

             MART., *Epigr.* XII, 84.[1]

epic machinery   *mock-heroic*

1712–1714

CANTO I

What dire offence from am'rous causes springs,
What mighty contests rise from trivial things,
I sing—This verse to Caryll, Muse! is due:
This, ev'n Belinda may vouchsafe to view:
Slight is the subject, but not so the praise,
If she inspire, and he approve my lays.
   Say what strange motive, Goddess! could compel
A well-bred lord t' assault a gentle belle?
Oh say what stranger cause, yet unexplor'd,
Could make a gentle belle reject a lord?   10
In tasks so bold, can little men engage,
And in soft bosoms dwells such mighty rage?
   Sol thro' white curtains shot a tim'rous ray,   *eyes of lovely ladies*
And op'd those eyes that must eclipse the day;
Now lapdogs give themselves the rousing shake,
And sleepless lovers, just at twelve, awake:
Thrice rung the bell, the slipper knock'd the ground,
And the press'd watch return'd a silver sound.
Belinda still her downy pillow prest,
Her guardian Sylph prolong'd the balmy rest: 20
'Twas he had summon'd to her silent bed
The morning-dream that hover'd o'er her head,
A youth more glitt'ring than a birth-night beau
(That ev'n in slumber caus'd her cheek to glow)
Seem'd to her ear his winning lips to lay,
And thus in whispers said, or seem'd to say:

1 "I was loath, Belinda, to violate your locks; yet I rejoice to have yielded this much to your entreaties." Lord Petre had actually clipped a lock from the hair of Lady Arabella Fermor (Belinda). John Caryll, a relative of Lord Petre, suggested that Pope compose the resulting ill feeling by writing this poem, originally (1711) in only two cantos. In 1713 Pope recast it into five cantos, introducing the "machinery" of sylphs and gnomes.

"Fairest of mortals, thou distinguish'd care
Of thousand bright inhabitants of air!
If e'er one vision touch'd thy infant thought,
Of all the nurse and all the priest have taught;   30
Of airy elves by moonlight shadows seen,
The silver token,[2] and the circled green,
Or virgins visited by angel-pow'rs,
With golden crowns and wreaths of heav'nly flow'rs;
Hear and believe! thy own importance know,
Nor bound thy narrow views to things below.
Some secret truths, from learned pride conceal'd,
To maids alone and children are reveal'd:
What tho' no credit doubting wits may give?
The fair and innocent shall still believe.   40
Know then, unnumber'd spirits round thee fly,
The light militia of the lower sky:
These, tho' unseen, are ever on the wing,
Hang o'er the box, and hover round the Ring.[3]
Think what an equipage thou hast in air,
And view with scorn two pages and a chair.
As now your own, our beings were of old,
And once inclos'd in woman's beauteous mold;
Thence, by a soft transition, we repair
From earthly vehicles to these of air.   50
Think not, when woman's transient breath is fled,
That all her vanities at once are dead;
Succeeding vanities she still regards,
And tho' she plays no more, o'erlooks the cards.
Her joy in gilded chariots, when alive,
And love of ombre, after death survive.
For when the fair in all their pride expire,
To their first elements their souls retire:
The sprites of fiery termagants in flame
Mount up, and take a salamander's name.   60
Soft yielding minds to water glide away,
And sip, with nymphs, their elemental tea.
The graver prude sinks downward to a gnome,
In search of mischief still on earth to roam.
The light coquettes in sylphs aloft repair,
And sport and flutter in the fields of air.
"Know farther yet; whoever fair and chaste

[handwritten margin note: Woman's vanity becomes a sylph]

---

2 Possibly the silver coins said to be
dropped by fairies into the shoes of maids
who kept things tidy. [Croker-Moore]

3 The box at the theater, and the short
circular driveway (the Ring) in Hyde Park.

Rejects mankind, is by some sylph embrac'd:
For spirits, freed from mortal laws, with ease
Assume what sexes and what shapes they please.
What guards the purity of melting maids,
In courtly balls, and midnight masquerades,
Safe from the treach'rous friend, the daring spark,
The glance by day, the whisper in the dark,
When kind occasion prompts their warm desires,
When music softens, and when dancing fires?
'Tis but their sylph, the wise celestials know,
Tho' honour is the word with men below.

    "Some nymphs there are, too conscious of their face,
For life predestin'd to the gnomes' embrace.
These swell their prospects and exalt their pride,
When offers are disdain'd, and love deny'd:
Then gay ideas crowd the vacant brain,
While peers, and dukes, and all their sweeping train,
And garters, stars, and coronets appear,
And in soft sounds, 'Your Grace' salutes their ear.
'Tis these that early taint the female soul,
Instruct the eyes of young coquettes to roll,
Teach infant-cheeks a bidden blush to know,
And little hearts to flutter at a beau.
    "Oft, when the world imagine women stray,
The sylphs thro' mystic mazes guide their way,
Thro' all the giddy circle they pursue,
And old impertinence expel by new.
What tender maid but must a victim fall
To one man's treat, but for another's ball?
When Florio speaks, what virgin could withstand,
If gentle Damon did not squeeze her hand?
With varying vanities, from ev'ry part,
They shift the moving toyshop of their heart;
Where wigs with wigs, with sword-knots sword-knots strive,
Beaux banish beaux, and coaches coaches drive.
This erring mortals levity may call;
Oh blind to truth! the sylphs contrive it all.
    "Of these am I, who thy protection claim,
A watchful sprite, and Ariel is my name.
Late, as I rang'd the crystal wilds of air,
In the clear mirror of thy ruling star
I saw, alas! some dread event impend,
Ere to the main this morning sun descend;

But Heav'n reveals not what, or how, or where:
Warn'd by the sylph, oh pious maid, beware!
This to disclose is all thy guardian can:
Beware of all, but most beware of man!"

He said; when Shock, who thought she slept too long, *Belinda*
Leap'd up, and wak'd his mistress with his tongue.
'Twas then, Belinda, if report say true,
Thy eyes first open'd on a billet-doux; *love letter*
Wounds, charms, and ardours were no sooner read, *what letter*
But all the vision vanish'd from thy head. *is full of—wounds* 120
etc.
And now, unveil'd, the toilet stands display'd,
Each silver vase in mystic order laid.
First, rob'd in white, the nymph intent adores, *make-up*
With head uncover'd, the cosmetic pow'rs. *physical*
A heav'nly image in the glass appears,
To that she bends, to that her eyes she rears;
Th' inferior priestess, at her altar's side,
Trembling begins the sacred rites of Pride.
Unnumber'd treasures ope at once, and here
The various off'rings of the world appear; 130
From each she nicely culls with curious toil,
And decks the goddess with the glitt'ring spoil.
This casket India's glowing gems unlocks,
And all Arabia breathes from yonder box.
The tortoise here and elephant unite,
Transform'd to combs, the speckled, and the white.
Here files of pins extend their shining rows,
Puffs, powders, patches, bibles, billet-doux.
Now awful beauty puts on all its arms;
The fair each moment rises in her charms, 140
Repairs her smiles, awakens ev'ry grace,
And calls forth all the wonders of her face;
Sees by degrees a purer blush arise,
And keener lightnings quicken in her eyes.
The busy sylphs surround their darling care,
These set the head, and those divide the hair,
Some fold the sleeve, whilst others plait the gown;
And Betty's prais'd for labours not her own.

CANTO II

Not with more glories, in th' ethereal plain,
The sun first rises o'er the purpled main,
Than, issuing forth, the rival of his beams

Launch'd on the bosom of the silver Thames.
Fair nymphs, and well-drest youths around her shone,
But ev'ry eye was fix'd on her alone.
On her white breast a sparkling cross she wore,
Which Jews might kiss, and infidels adore.
Her lively looks a sprightly mind disclose,
Quick as her eyes, and as unfix'd as those: 10
Favours to none, to all she smiles extends;
Oft she rejects, but never once offends.
Bright as the sun, her eyes the gazers strike,
And, like the sun, they shine on all alike.
Yet graceful ease, and sweetness void of pride,
Might hide her faults, if belles had faults to hide:
If to her share some female errors fall,
Look on her face, and you'll forget 'em all.
     This nymph, to the destruction of mankind,
Nourish'd two locks, which graceful hung behind   20
In equal curls, and well conspir'd to deck
With shining ringlets the smooth iv'ry neck.
Love in these labyrinths his slaves detains,
And mighty hearts are held in slender chains.
With hairy springes we the birds betray,
Slight lines of hair surprize the finny prey,
Fair tresses man's imperial race insnare,
And Beauty draws us with a single hair.
     Th' advent'rous baron the bright locks admir'd;
He saw, he wish'd, and to the prize aspir'd: 30
Resolv'd to win, he meditates the way,
By force to ravish, or by fraud betray;
For when success a lover's toil attends,
Few ask, if fraud or force attain'd his ends.
     For this, ere Phœbus rose, he had implor'd
Propitious Heav'n, and ev'ry pow'r ador'd,
But chiefly Love—to Love an altar built,
Of twelve vast French romances, neatly gilt.
There lay three garters, half a pair of gloves;
And all the trophies of his former loves.   40
With tender billet-doux he lights the pyre,
And breathes three am'rous sighs to raise the fire.
Then prostrate falls, and begs with ardent eyes
Soon to obtain, and long possess the prize:
The pow'rs gave ear, and granted half his pray'r,
The rest, the winds dispers'd in empty air.

But now secure the painted vessel glides,
The sunbeams trembling on the floating tides:
While melting music steals upon the sky,
And soften'd sounds along the waters die;
Smooth flow the waves, the zephyrs gently play, 50
Belinda smil'd, and all the world was gay.
All but the sylph—with careful thoughts opprest,
Th' impending woe sat heavy on his breast.
He summons straight his denizens of air;
The lucid squadrons round the sails repair:
Soft o'er the shrouds aërial whispers breathe,
That seem'd but zephyrs to the train beneath.
Some to the sun their insect-wings unfold,
Waft on the breeze, or sink in clouds of gold;
Transparent forms, too fine for mortal sight, 60
Their fluid bodies half dissolv'd in light.
Loose to the wind their airy garments flew,
Thin glitt'ring textures of the filmy dew,
Dipt in the richest tincture of the skies,
Where light disports in ever-mingling dyes,
While ev'ry beam new transient colours flings,
Colours that change whene'er they wave their wings.
Amid the circle, on the gilded mast,
Superior by the head, was Ariel plac'd; 70
His purple pinions op'ning to the sun,
He rais'd his azure wand, and thus begun:
    "Ye sylphs and sylphids, to your chief give ear,
Fays, fairies, genii, elves, and dæmons, hear!
Ye know the spheres, and various tasks assign'd
By laws eternal to th' aërial kind.
Some in the fields of purest æther play,
And bask and whiten in the blaze of day.
Some guide the course of wand'ring orbs on high,
Or roll the planets thro' the boundless sky. 80
Some less refin'd, beneath the moon's pale light
Pursue the stars that shoot athwart the night,
Or suck the mists in grosser air below,
Or dip their pinions in the painted bow,
Or brew fierce tempests on the wintry main,
Or o'er the glebe distil the kindly rain.
Others on earth o'er human race preside,
Watch all their ways, and all their actions guide:
Of these the chief the care of nations own,

And guard with arms divine the British throne.　90
　　"Our humbler province is to tend the fair,
Not a less pleasing, though less glorious care;
To save the powder from too rude a gale,
Nor let th' imprison'd essences exhale;
To draw fresh colours from the vernal flow'rs;
To steal from rainbows ere they drop in show'rs
A brighter wash; to curl their waving hairs,
Assist their blushes, and inspire their airs;
Nay oft, in dreams, invention we bestow,
To change a flounce, or add a furbelow.　100
　　"This day, black omens threat the brightest fair,
That e'er deserv'd a watchful spirit's care;
Some dire disaster, or by force, or slight;
But what, or where, the Fates have wrapt in night.
Whether the nymph shall break Diana's law,
Or some frail china jar receive a flaw;
Or stain her honour, or her new brocade;
Forget her pray'rs, or miss a masquerade;
Or lose her heart, or necklace, at a ball;
Or whether Heav'n has doom'd that Shock must fall.　110
Haste then, ye spirits! to your charge repair:
The flutt'ring fan be Zephyretta's care;
The drops to thee, Brillante, we consign;
And, Momentilla, let the watch be thine;
Do thou, Crispissa, tend her fav'rite lock;
Ariel himself shall be the guard of Shock.
　　"To fifty chosen sylphs, of special note,
We trust th' important charge, the petticoat:
Oft have we known that seven-fold fence to fail,
Tho' stiff with hoops, and arm'd with ribs of whale;　120
Form a strong line about the silver bound,
And guard the wide circumference around.
　　"Whatever spirit, careless of his charge,
His post neglects, or leaves the fair at large,
Shall feel sharp vengeance soon o'ertake his sins,
Be stopp'd in vials, or transfix'd with pins;
Or plung'd in lakes of bitter washes lie,
Or wedg'd whole ages in a bodkin's eye:
Gums and pomatums shall his flight restrain,
While clogg'd he beats his silken wings in vain;　130
Or alum styptics with contracting pow'r
Shrink his thin essence like a rivell'd flow'r:

Or, as Ixion fix'd, the wretch shall feel
The giddy motion of the whirling mill,
In fumes of burning chocolate shall glow,
And tremble at the sea that froths below!"
   He spoke; the spirits from the sails descend;
Some, orb in orb, around the nymph extend;
Some thrid the mazy ringlets of her hair;
Some hang upon the pendants of her ear;   140
With beating hearts the dire event they wait,
Anxious, and trembling for the birth of Fate.

CANTO III

Close by those meads, forever crown'd with flow'rs,
Where Thames with pride surveys his rising tow'rs,
There stands a structure of majestic frame,
Which from the neighb'ring Hampton takes its name.
Here Britain's statesmen oft the fall foredoom
Of foreign tyrants and of nymphs at home;
Here thou, great Anna! whom three realms obey,
Dost sometimes counsel take—and sometimes tea.   *Effect of bathos find a lofty line be trivial*
  Hither the heroes and the nymphs resort,
To taste a while the pleasures of a court;   10
In various talk th' instructive hours they past,
Who gave the ball, or paid the visit last;
One speaks the glory of the British Queen,   *Sinking from one realm of*
And one describes a charming Indian screen;   *value to another*
A third interprets motions, looks, and eyes;
At ev'ry word a reputation dies.   *Gossip*
Snuff, or the fan, supply each pause of chat,
With singing, laughing, ogling, *and all that*.
  Meanwhile, declining from the noon of day,
The sun obliquely shoots his burning ray;   20
The hungry judges soon the sentence sign,
And wretches hang that jurymen may dine;
The merchant from th' Exchange returns in peace,
And the long labours of the toilette cease.   *juxta of merchant,*
Belinda now, whom thirst of fame invites,   *lady - collab of*
Burns to encounter two advent'rous knights,   *outer world +*
At ombre [4] singly to decide their doom;   *illusion of*
And swells her breast with conquests yet to come.   *inner world*

[4] In the fashionable game of ombre, the "Matadores" were the three highest cards: in this case, the ace of spades (Spadillio), the two of clubs (Manillio), and the ace of clubs (Basto). The jack of clubs was called "Pam"; in the game of loo it was the highest card. "Codille" was failing to take the necessary number of tricks.

Straight the three bands prepare in arms to join,
Each band the number of the sacred Nine. 30
Soon as she spreads her hand, th' aërial guard
Descend, and sit on each important card:
First Ariel perch'd upon a Matadore,
Then each, according to the rank they bore;
For sylphs, yet mindful of their ancient race,
Are, as when women, wondrous fond of place.

Behold, four kings in majesty rever'd,
With hoary whiskers and a forky beard;
And four fair queens, whose hands sustain a flow'r,
Th' expressive emblem of their softer pow'r; 40
Four knaves in garbs succinct, a trusty band,
Caps on their heads, and halberts in their hand;
And parti-colour'd troops, a shining train,
Draw forth to combat on the velvet plain.

The skillful nymph reviews her force with care:
"Let spades be trumps!" she said, and trumps they were.

Now move to war her sable Matadores,
In show like leaders of the swarthy Moors.
Spadillio first, unconquerable lord!
Led off two captive trumps, and swept the board. 50
As many more Manillio forc'd to yield,
And march'd a victor from the verdant field.
Him Basto follow'd, but his fate more hard
Gain'd but one trump and one plebeian card.
With his broad sabre next, a chief in years,
The hoary Majesty of Spades appears,
Puts forth one manly leg, to sight reveal'd,
The rest, his many-colour'd robe conceal'd.
The rebel Knave, who dares his prince engage,
Proves the just victim of his royal rage. 60
Even mighty Pam, that kings and queens o'erthrew
And mow'd down armies in the fights of Loo,
Sad chance of war! now destitute of aid,
Falls undistinguish'd by the victor spade!

Thus far both armies to Belinda yield;
Now to the baron fate inclines the field.
His warlike Amazon her host invades,
Th' imperial consort of the crown of spades.
The club's black tyrant first her victim dy'd,
Spite of his haughty mien, and barb'rous pride: 70
What boots the regal circle on his head,

His giant limbs, in state unwieldy spread;
That long behind he trails his pompous robe,
And, of all monarchs, only grasps the globe?
 The baron now his diamonds pours apace;
Th' embroider'd King who shows but half his face,
And his refulgent Queen, with pow'rs combin'd
Of broken troops an easy conquest find.
Clubs, diamonds, hearts, in wild disorder seen,
With throngs promiscuous strow the level green. 80
Thus when dispers'd a routed army runs,
Of Asia's troops, and Afric's sable sons,
With like confusion different nations fly,
Of various habit, and of various dye,
The pierc'd battalions disunited fall,
In heaps on heaps; one fate o'erwhelms them all.
 The Knave of Diamonds tries his wily arts,
And wins (oh shameful chance!) the Queen of Hearts.
At this, the blood the virgin's cheek forsook,
A livid paleness spreads o'er all her look; 90
She sees, and trembles at th' approaching ill,
Just in the jaws of ruin, and codille.
And now (as oft in some distemper'd state)
On one nice trick depends the gen'ral fate.
An Ace of Hearts steps forth: the King unseen
Lurk'd in her hand, and mourn'd his captive Queen:
He springs to vengeance with an eager pace,
And falls like thunder on the prostrate Ace.
The nymph exulting fills with shouts the sky;
The walls, the woods, and long canals reply. 100
 Oh thoughtless mortals! ever blind to fate,
Too soon dejected, and too soon elate.
Sudden, these honours shall be snatch'd away,
And curs'd forever this victorious day.
 For lo! the board with cups and spoons is crown'd,
The berries crackle, and the mill turns round; [5]
On shining altars of japan they raise
The silver lamp; the fiery spirits blaze:
From silver spouts the grateful liquors glide,
While China's earth receives the smoking tide: 110
At once they gratify their scent and taste,
And frequent cups prolong the rich repast.
Strait hover round the fair her airy band;

---

[5] Coffee was ground and roasted at the table.

Some, as she sipp'd, the fuming liquor fann'd,
Some o'er her lap their careful plumes display'd,
Trembling, and conscious of the rich brocade.
Coffee (which makes the politician wise,
And see thro' all things with his half-shut eyes)
Sent up in vapours to the baron's brain
New stratagems, the radiant lock to gain.   120
Ah cease, rash youth! desist ere 'tis too late,
Fear the just gods, and think of Scylla's fate! [6]
Chang'd to a bird, and sent to flit in air,
She dearly pays for Nisus' injur'd hair!

But when to mischief mortals bend their will,
How soon they find fit instruments of ill!
Just then, Clarissa drew with tempting grace
A two-edg'd weapon from her shining case:
So ladies in romance assist their knight,
Present the spear, and arm him for the fight.   130
He takes the gift with rev'rence, and extends
The little engine on his fingers' ends;
This just behind Belinda's neck he spread,
As o'er the fragrant steams she bends her head.
Swift to the lock a thousand sprites repair,
A thousand wings, by turns, blow back the hair;
And thrice they twitch'd the diamond in her ear;
Thrice she look'd back, and thrice the foe drew near.
Just in that instant, anxious Ariel sought
The close recesses of the virgin's thought;   140
As on the nosegay in her breast reclin'd,
He watch'd th' ideas rising in her mind,
Sudden he view'd, in spite of all her art,
An earthly lover lurking at her heart.
Amaz'd, confus'd, he found his pow'r expir'd,
Resign'd to fate, and with a sigh retir'd.
    The peer now spreads the glitt'ring forfex wide,
T' enclose the lock; now joins it, to divide.
Ev'n then, before the fatal engine clos'd,
A wretched sylph too fondly interpos'd;   150
Fate urg'd the shears, and cut the sylph in twain,
(But airy substance soon unites again)
The meeting points the sacred hair dissever

---

6 Scylla, daughter of King Nisus of Megara, fell in love with Minos, who was be-
sieging Megara. She gave to Minos the lock
of her father's hair upon which his safety
depended. As punishment, she was changed
into a bird.

From the fair head, for ever, and for ever!
   Then flash'd the living lightning from her eyes,
And screams of horror rend th' affrighted skies.
Not louder shrieks to pitying Heav'n are cast,
When husbands, or when lapdogs breathe their last;
Or when rich china vessels fall'n from high,
In glitt'ring dust and painted fragments lie!   160
   "Let wreaths of triumph now my temples twine,"
The victor cry'd, "the glorious prize is mine!
While fish in streams, or birds delight in air,
Or in a coach and six the British fair,
As long as *Atalantis* [7] shall be read,
Or the small pillow grace a lady's bed,
While visits shall be paid on solemn days,
When num'rous wax-lights in bright order blaze,
While nymphs take treats, or assignations give,
So long my honour, name, and praise shall live!   170
What time would spare, from steel receives its date,
And monuments, like men, submit to fate!
Steel could the labour of the gods destroy,
And strike to dust th' imperial tow'rs of Troy;
Steel could the works of mortal pride confound,
And hew triumphal arches to the ground.
What wonder then, fair nymph! thy hairs should feel
The conqu'ring force of unresisted steel?"

CANTO IV

But anxious cares the pensive nymph opprest,
And secret passions labour'd in her breast.
Not youthful kings in battle seiz'd alive,
Not scornful virgins who their charms survive,
Not ardent lovers robb'd of all their bliss,
Not ancient ladies when refus'd a kiss,
Not tyrants fierce that unrepenting die,
Not Cynthia when her manteau's pinn'd awry,
E'er felt such rage, resentment, and despair,
As thou, sad virgin! for thy ravish'd hair.   10
   For, that sad moment, when the sylphs withdrew,
And Ariel weeping from Belinda flew,
Umbriel, a dusky, melancholy sprite,
As ever sully'd the fair face of light,

---

[7] *The New Atalantis* (1709), a novel by the notorious Mrs. Mary Manley. The slan- derous attacks in it upon persons of note led to prosecution of the author.

Down to the central earth, his proper scene,
Repair'd to search the gloomy cave of Spleen.
    Swift on his sooty pinions flits the gnome,
And in a vapour reach'd the dismal dome.
No chearful breeze this sullen region knows,
The dreaded east is all the wind that blows.   20
Here in a grotto, shelter'd close from air,
And screen'd in shades from day's detested glare,
She sighs for ever on her pensive bed,
Pain at her side, and Megrim at her head.
Two handmaids wait the throne: alike in place,
But diff'ring far in figure and in face.
Here stood Ill-nature like an ancient maid,
Her wrinkled form in black and white array'd;
With store of pray'rs, for mornings, nights, and noons,
Her hand is fill'd; her bosom with lampoons.   30
    There Affectation, with a sickly mien,
Shows in her cheek the roses of eighteen,
Practis'd to lisp, and hang the head aside,
Faints into airs, and languishes with pride,
On the rich quilt sinks with becoming woe,
Wrapt in a gown, for sickness, and for show.
The fair ones feel such maladies as these,
When each new night-dress gives a new disease.
    A constant vapour o'er the palace flies;
Strange phantoms rising as the mists arise;   40
Dreadful as hermits' dreams in haunted shades,
Or bright, as visions of expiring maids.
Now glaring fiends, and snakes on rolling spires,
Pale spectres, gaping tombs, and purple fires:
Now lakes of liquid gold, Elysian scenes,
And crystal domes, and angels in machines.
    Unnumber'd throngs on ev'ry side are seen,
Of bodies chang'd to various forms by Spleen.
Here living teapots stand, one arm held out,
One bent; the handle this, and that the spout: 50
A pipkin there, like Homer's tripod walks;
Here sighs a jar, and there a goose-pye talks;
Men prove with child, as pow'rful fancy works,
And maids turn'd bottles, call aloud for corks.
    Safe past the gnome through this fantastic band,
A branch of healing spleenwort [8] in his hand.

8 A remedy for the spleen.

Then thus address'd the pow'r—"Hail, wayward Queen!
Who rule the sex to fifty from fifteen:
Parent of vapours and of female wit,
Who give th' hysteric, or poetic fit,   60
On various tempers act by various ways,
Make some take physic, others scribble plays;
Who cause the proud their visits to delay,
And send the godly in a pet, to pray.
A nymph there is, that all thy pow'r disdains,
And thousands more in equal mirth maintains.
But oh! if e'er thy gnome could spoil a grace,
Or raise a pimple on a beauteous face,
Like citron-waters matrons' cheeks inflame,
Or change complexions at a losing game;   70
If e'er with airy horns I planted heads,
Or rumpled petticoats, or tumbled beds,
Or caus'd suspicion when no soul was rude,
Or discompos'd the head-dress of a prude,
Or e'er to costive lapdog gave disease,
Which not the tears of brightest eyes could ease:
Hear me, and touch Belinda with chagrin,
That single act gives half the world the spleen."
    The goddess with a discontented air
Seems to reject him, tho' she grants his pray'r.   80
A wondrous bag with both her hands she binds,
Like that where once Ulysses held the winds;
There she collects the force of female lungs,
Sighs, sobs, and passions, and the war of tongues.
A vial next she fills with fainting fears,
Soft sorrows, melting griefs, and flowing tears.
The gnome rejoicing bears her gifts away,
Spreads his black wings, and slowly mounts to day.
    Sunk in Thalestris' [9] arms the nymph he found,
Her eyes dejected, and her hair unbound.   90
Full o'er their heads the swelling bag he rent,
And all the Furies issu'd at the vent.
Belinda burns with more than mortal ire,
And fierce Thalestris fans the rising fire.
"Oh wretched maid!" she spread her hands, and cry'd,
(While Hampton's echoes, "Wretched maid!" reply'd)
"Was it for this you took such constant care
The bodkin, comb, and essence to prepare;

9 Said to be Mrs. Morley, the sister of Sir Plume (Sir George Brown).

small hair pin, long & slender

For this your locks in paper durance bound,
For this with tort'ring irons wreath'd around?   100
For this with fillets strain'd your tender head,
And bravely bore the double loads of lead?
Gods! shall the ravisher display your hair,
While the fops envy, and the ladies stare!
Honour forbid! at whose unrival'd shrine
Ease, pleasure, virtue, all, our sex resign.
Methinks already I your tears survey,
Already hear the horrid things they say,
Already see you a degraded toast,
And all your honour in a whisper lost!   110
How shall I, then, your helpless fame defend?
'Twill then be infamy to seem your friend!
And shall this prize, th' inestimable prize,
Expos'd thro' crystal to the gazing eyes,
And heighten'd by the diamond's circling rays,
On that rapacious hand forever blaze?
Sooner shall grass in Hyde Park Circus grow,
And wits take lodgings in the sound of Bow; [10]
Sooner let earth, air, sea, to chaos fall,
Men, monkeys, lapdogs, parrots, perish all!"   120
    She said; then raging to Sir Plume repairs,
And bids her beau demand the precious hairs
(Sir Plume of amber snuff-box justly vain,
And the nice conduct of a clouded cane):
With earnest eyes, and round unthinking face,
He first the snuff-box open'd, then the case,
And thus broke out—"My Lord, why, what the devil?
Z—ds! damn the lock! 'fore Gad, you must be civil!
Plague on't! 'tis past a jest—nay prithee, pox!
Give her the hair"—he spoke, and rapp'd his box.   130
    "It grieves me much," replied the peer again,
"Who speaks so well should ever speak in vain.
But by this lock, this sacred lock, I swear
(Which never more shall join its parted hair;
Which never more its honours shall renew,
Clip'd from the lovely head where late it grew),
That while my nostrils draw the vital air,
This hand, which won it, shall forever wear."
He spoke, and speaking, in proud triumph spread
The long-contended honours of her head.   140

10 Near St. Mary-le-Bow (not far from St. Paul's), an unfashionable district.

But Umbriel, hateful gnome! forbears not so;
He breaks the vial whence the sorrows flow.
Then see! the nymph in beauteous grief appears,
Her eyes half-languishing, half-drown'd in tears;
On her heav'd bosom hung her drooping head,
Which, with a sigh, she rais'd; and thus she said:
  "Forever curs'd be this detested day,
Which snatch'd my best, my fav'rite curl away!
Happy! ah ten times happy, had I been,
If Hampton Court these eyes had never seen!   150
Yet am not I the first mistaken maid,
By love of courts to num'rous ills betray'd.
Oh had I rather unadmir'd remain'd
In some lone isle, or distant northern land;
Where the gilt chariot never marks the way,
Where none learn ombre, none e'er taste bohea! [11]
There kept my charms conceal'd from mortal eye,
Like roses, that in deserts bloom and die.
What mov'd my mind with youthful lords to roam?
Oh had I stay'd, and said my pray'rs at home!   160
'Twas this, the morning omens seem'd to tell,
Thrice from my trembling hand the patch-box fell;
The tott'ring china shook without a wind,
Nay, Poll sat mute, and Shock was most unkind!
A sylph too warn'd me of the threats of fate,
In mystic visions, now believ'd too late!
See the poor remnants of these slighted hairs!
My hands shall rend what ev'n thy rapine spares:
These, in two sable ringlets taught to break,
Once gave new beauties to the snowy neck;   170
The sister-lock now sits uncouth, alone,
And in its fellow's fate foresees its own;
Uncurl'd it hangs, the fatal shears demands,
And tempts, once more, thy sacrilegious hands.
Oh hadst thou, cruel! been content to seize
Hairs less in sight, or any hairs but these!"

CANTO V

She said: the pitying audience melt in tears;
But Fate and Jove had stopp'd the baron's ears.
In vain Thalestris with reproach assails,
For who can move when fair Belinda fails?

11 Black tea.

Not half so fix'd the Trojan could remain,
While Anna begg'd and Dido rag'd in vain.
Then grave Clarissa graceful wav'd her fan;
Silence ensu'd, and thus the nymph began:
   "Say, why are beauties prais'd and honour'd most,
The wise man's passion, and the vain man's toast?   10
Why deck'd with all that land and sea afford,
Why angels call'd, and angel-like ador'd?
Why round our coaches crowd the white-glov'd beaux,
Why bows the side-box from its inmost rows?
How vain are all these glories, all our pains,
Unless good-sense preserve what beauty gains:
That men may say, when we the front-box grace,
'Behold the first in virtue as in face!'
Oh! if to dance all night, and dress all day,
Charm'd the smallpox, or chas'd old age away;   20
Who would not scorn what housewife's cares produce,
Or who would learn one earthly thing of use?
To patch, nay ogle, might become a saint,
Nor could it sure be such a sin to paint.
But since, alas! frail beauty must decay,
Curl'd or uncurl'd, since locks will turn to grey;
Since painted, or not painted, all shall fade,
And she who scorns a man, must die a maid;
What then remains, but well our pow'r to use,
And keep good-humour still whate'er we lose?   30
And trust me, dear! good-humour can prevail,
When airs, and flights, and screams, and scolding fail.
Beauties in vain their pretty eyes may roll;
Charms strike the sight, but merit wins the soul."
   So spoke the dame, but no applause ensu'd;
Belinda frown'd, Thalestris call'd her prude.
"To arms, to arms!" the fierce virago cries,
And swift as lightning to the combat flies.
All side in parties, and begin th' attack;
Fans clap, silks russle, and tough whalebones crack;   40
Heroes' and heroines' shouts confus'dly rise,
And base and treble voices strike the skies.
No common weapons in their hands are found,
Like gods they fight, nor dread a mortal wound.
   So when bold Homer makes the gods engage,
And heav'nly breasts with human passions rage;
'Gainst Pallas, Mars; Latona, Hermes arms;

And all Olympus rings with loud alarms:
Jove's thunder roars, Heav'n trembles all around,
Blue Neptune storms, the bell'wing deeps resound: 50
Earth shakes her nodding tow'rs, the ground gives way,
And the pale ghosts start at the flash of day!

    Triumphant Umbriel on a sconce's height,
Clap'd his glad wings, and sate to view the fight:
Prop'd on their bodkin spears, the sprites survey
The growing combat, or assist the fray.

    While thro' the press enrag'd Thalestris flies,
And scatters death around from both her eyes,
A beau and witling perish'd in the throng,
One dy'd in metaphor, and one in song.   60
"O cruel nymph! a living death I bear,"
Cry'd Dapperwit, and sunk beside his chair.
A mournful glance Sir Fopling upwards cast,
"Those eyes are made so killing"—was his last.
Thus on Mæander's flow'ry margin lies
Th' expiring swan, and as he sings he dies.

    When bold Sir Plume had drawn Clarissa down,
Chloe stepp'd in, and kill'd him with a frown;
She smil'd to see the doughty hero slain,
But, at her smile, the beau reviv'd again.   70

    Now Jove suspends his golden scales in air,
Weighs the men's wits against the lady's hair;
The doubtful beam long nods from side to side;
At length the wits mount up, the hairs subside.

    See fierce Belinda on the baron flies,
With more than usual lightning in her eyes:
Nor fear'd the chief th' unequal fight to try,
Who sought no more than on his foe to die.
But this bold lord with manly strength endu'd,
She with one finger and a thumb subdu'd: 80
Just where the breath of life his nostrils drew,
A charge of snuff the wily virgin threw;
The gnomes direct, to ev'ry atom just,
The pungent grains of titillating dust.
Sudden, with starting tears each eye o'erflows,
And the high dome re-echoes to his nose.

    "Now meet thy fate," incens'd Belinda cry'd,
And drew a deadly bodkin from her side.
(The same, his ancient personage to deck,
Her grand-great-grandsire wore about his neck,   90

In three seal-rings; which after, melted down,
Form'd a vast buckle for his widow's gown:
Her infant grandame's whistle next it grew,
The bells she jingled, and the whistle blew;
Then in a bodkin grac'd her mother's hairs,
Which long she wore, and now Belinda wears.[12])

　　"Boast not my fall," he cry'd, "insulting foe!
Thou by some other shalt be laid as low,
Nor think, to die dejects my lofty mind:
All that I dread, is leaving you behind!　　　　　100
Rather than so, ah let me still survive,
And burn in Cupid's flames—but burn alive."

　　"Restore the lock!" she cries; and all around
"Restore the lock!" the vaulted roofs rebound.
Not fierce Othello in so loud a strain
Roar'd for the handkerchief that caus'd his pain.
But see how oft ambitious aims are cross'd,
And chiefs contend 'till all the prize is lost!
The lock, obtain'd with guilt, and kept with pain,
In ev'ry place is sought, but sought in vain:　　　110
With such a prize no mortal must be blest,
So Heav'n decrees! with Heav'n who can contest?
Some thought it mounted to the lunar sphere,
Since all things lost on earth, are treasur'd there.
There heroes' wits are kept in pond'rous vases,
And beaus' in snuff-boxes and tweezer-cases.
There broken vows, and deathbed alms are found,
And lovers' hearts with ends of ribband bound,
The courtier's promises, and sick man's pray'rs,
The smiles of harlots, and the tears of heirs,　　120
Cages for gnats, and chains to yoke a flea,
Dried butterflies, and tomes of casuistry.

　　But trust the Muse—she saw it upward rise,
Tho' mark'd by none but quick, poetic eyes:
(So Rome's great founder to the heav'ns withdrew,
To Proculus alone confess'd in view).[13]
A sudden star, it shot thro' liquid air,
And drew behind a radiant trail of hair.
Not Berenice's locks first rose so bright,
The heav'ns bespangling with dishevel'd light.　130
The sylphs behold it kindling as it flies,

12 In imitation of the progress of Agamemnon's sceptre in Homer, II. ii. [Pope]
13 Julius Proculus, the Roman Senator,
said to have had a vision of the deified Romulus.

And pleas'd pursue its progress thro' the skies.
  This the beau monde shall from the Mall survey,
And hail with music its propitious ray.
This the blest lover shall for Venus take,
And send up vows from Rosamonda's lake.[14]
This Partridge [15] soon shall view in cloudless skies,
When next he looks thro' Galileo's eyes;
And hence th' egregious wizard shall foredoom
The fate of Louis, and the fall of Rome.   140
  Then cease, bright nymph! to mourn thy ravish'd hair,
Which adds new glory to the shining sphere!
Not all the tresses that fair head can boast,
Shall draw such envy as the lock you lost.
For, after all the murders of your eye,
When, after millions slain, yourself shall die;
When those fair suns shall set, as set they must,
And all those tresses shall be laid in dust,
This lock, the Muse shall consecrate to fame,
And 'midst the stars inscribe Belinda's name.   150

WINDSOR FOREST

TO THE RIGHT HONOURABLE GEORGE LORD LANSDOWN.

Non injussa cano:—te nostræ, Vare, myricæ,
Te Nemus omne canet: nec Phœbo gratior ulla est,
Quam sibi quæ Vari præscripsit pagina nomen.
                    VIRG., *Ecl.* VI. 10–12.[1]

1713

Thy forests, Windsor! and thy green retreats,
At once the Monarch's and the Muse's seats,
Invite my lays. Be present, sylvan maids!
Unlock your springs, and open all your shades.
Granville commands: your aid, O Muses, bring!
What muse for Granville can refuse to sing?
  The groves of Eden, vanish'd now so long,

---

14 A pond in St. James's Park, a resort of despondent lovers.

15 John Partridge, astrologer and almanac-maker, ridiculed by Swift in the "Bickerstaff" papers.

1 "I do not sing unbidden; our tamarisks, Varus, and the whole grove sing of thee: and no page is more pleasing to Apollo than that which bears the name of Varus."

Live in description, and look green in song:
These, were my breast inspir'd with equal flame,
Like them in beauty, should be like in fame.   10
Here hills and vales, the woodland and the plain,
Here earth and water seem to strive again;
Not chaos-like together crush'd and bruis'd,
But, as the world, harmoniously confus'd:
Where order in variety we see,
And where, though all things differ, all agree.
Here waving groves a chequer'd scene display,
And part admit, and part exclude the day;
As some coy nymph her lover's warm address
Nor quite indulges, nor can quite repress.   20
There, interspers'd in lawns and op'ning glades,
Thin trees arise that shun each other's shades.
Here in full light the russet plains extend:
There wrapt in clouds the blueish hills ascend.
Ev'n the wild heath displays her purple dyes,
And 'midst the desart fruitful fields arise,
That crown'd with tufted trees and springing corn,
Like verdant isles the sable waste adorn.
Let India boast her plants, nor envy we
The weeping amber or the balmy tree,   30
While by our oaks the precious loads are born,
And realms commanded which those trees adorn.
Not proud Olympus yields a nobler sight,
Tho' gods assembled grace his tow'ring height,
Than what more humble mountains offer here,
Where, in their blessings, all those gods appear.
See Pan with flocks, with fruits Pomona crown'd,
Here blushing Flora paints th' enamel'd ground,
Here Ceres' gifts in waving prospect stand,
And nodding tempt the joyful reaper's hand;   40
Rich Industry sits smiling on the plains,
And peace and plenty tell, a Stuart reigns.
    Not thus the land appear'd in ages past,
A dreary desert, and a gloomy waste,
To savage beasts and savage laws a prey,
And kings more furious and severe than they;
Who claim'd the skies, dispeopled air and floods,
The lonely lords of empty wilds and woods:
Cities laid waste, they storm'd the dens and caves
(For wiser brutes were backward to be slaves).   50

What could be free, when lawless beasts obey'd,
And ev'n the elements a tyrant sway'd?
In vain kind seasons swell'd the teeming grain,
Soft show'rs distill'd, and suns grew warm in vain;
The swain with tears his frustrate labour yields,
And famish'd dies amidst his ripen'd fields.
What wonder then, a beast or subject slain
Were equal crimes in a despotic reign?
Both doom'd alike, for sportive tyrants bled,
But while the subject starv'd, the beast was fed.   60
Proud Nimrod first the bloody chace began,
A mighty hunter, and his prey was man:
Our haughty Norman [2] boasts that barb'rous name,
And makes his trembling slaves the royal game.
The fields are ravish'd from th' industrious swains,
From men their cities, and from gods their fanes:
The levell'd towns with weeds lie cover'd o'er;
The hollow winds thro' naked temples roar;
Round broken columns clasping ivy twin'd;
O'er heaps of ruin stalk'd the stately hind;   70
The fox obscene to gaping tombs retires,
And savage howlings fill the sacred choirs.
Aw'd by his nobles, by his commons curst,
Th' oppressor rul'd tyrannic where he durst,
Stretch'd o'er the poor and Church his iron rod,
And serv'd alike his vassals and his God.
Whom ev'n the Saxon spar'd and bloody Dane,
The wanton victims of his sport remain.
But see, the man who spacious regions gave
A waste for beasts, himself denied a grave!   80
Stretch'd on the lawn his second hope [3] survey,
At once the chaser, and at once the prey:
Lo Rufus, tugging at the deadly dart,
Bleeds in the Forest like a wounded hart.
Succeeding monarchs heard the subjects' cries,
Nor saw displeas'd the peaceful cottage rise.
Then gath'ring flocks on unknown mountains fed,
O'er sandy wilds were yellow harvests spread,
The forest wonder'd at th' unusual grain,
And secret transport touch'd the conscious swain.   90
Fair Liberty, Britannia's Goddess, rears

[2] William the Conqueror.
[3] Richard, the second son of William the Conqueror, was killed by a stag in New Forest; in the same forest William's son Rufus was killed by an arrow.

Her chearful head, and leads the golden years.
   Ye vig'rous swains! while youth ferments your blood,
And purer spirits swell the sprightly flood,
Now range the hills, the gameful woods beset,
Wind the shrill horn, or spread the waving net.
When milder autumn summer's heat succeeds,
And in the new-shorn field the partridge feeds,
Before his lord the ready spaniel bounds,
Panting with hope, he tries the furrow'd grounds;   100
But when the tainted gales the game betray,
Couch'd close he lies, and meditates the prey:
Secure they trust th' unfaithful field beset,
'Till hov'ring o'er 'em sweeps the swelling net.
Thus (if small things we may with great compare)
When Albion sends her eager sons to war,
Some thoughtless town, with ease and plenty blest,
Near, and more near, the closing lines invest;
Sudden they seize th' amaz'd, defenceless prize,
And high in air Britannia's standard flies.   110
   See! from the brake the whirring pheasant springs,
And mounts exulting on triumphant wings:
Short is his joy; he feels the fiery wound,
Flutters in blood, and panting beats the ground.
Ah! what avail his glossy, varying dyes,
His purple crest, and scarlet-circled eyes,
The vivid green his shining plumes unfold,
His painted wings, and breast that flames with gold?
   Not yet, when moist Arcturus clouds the sky,
The woods and fields their pleasing toils deny.   120
To plains with well-breath'd beagles we repair,
And trace the mazes of the circling hare:
(Beasts, urg'd by us, their fellow-beasts pursue,
And learn of man each other to undo).
With slaught'ring guns th' unwearied fowler roves,
When frosts have whiten'd all the naked groves;
Where doves in flocks the leafless trees o'ershade,
And lonely woodcocks haunt the wat'ry glade.
He lifts the tube, and levels with his eye;
Strait a short thunder breaks the frozen sky: 130
Oft, as in airy rings they skim the heath,
The clam'rous lapwings feel the leaden death:
Oft, as the mounting larks their notes prepare,
They fall, and leave their little lives in air.

In genial spring, beneath the quiv'ring shade,
Where cooling vapours breathe along the mead,
The patient fisher takes his silent stand,
Intent, his angle trembling in his hand:
With looks unmov'd, he hopes the scaly breed,
And eyes the dancing cork, and bending reed.   140
Our plenteous streams a various race supply,
The bright-ey'd perch with fins of Tyrian dye
The silver eel, in shining volumes roll'd,
The yellow carp, in scales bedropp'd with gold,
Swift trouts, diversify'd with crimson stains,
And pikes, the tyrants of the wat'ry plains.

Now Cancer glows with Phœbus' fiery car:
The youth rush eager to the sylvan war,
Swarm o'er the lawns, the forest walks surround,
Rouze the fleet hart, and chear the opening hound.   150
Th' impatient courser pants in ev'ry vein,
And pawing, seems to beat the distant plain:
Hills, vales, and floods appear already cross'd,
And e'er he starts, a thousand steps are lost.
See the bold youth strain up the threat'ning steep,
Rush thro' the thickets, down the valleys sweep,
Hang o'er their coursers' heads with eager speed,
And earth rolls back beneath the flying steed.
Let old Arcadia boast her ample plain,
Th' immortal huntress, and her virgin-train;   160
Nor envy, Windsor! since thy shades have seen
As bright a Goddess, and as chaste a Queen;
Whose care, like hers, protects the sylvan reign,
The earth's fair light, and Empress of the Main.

In that blest moment from his oozy bed
Old father Thames advanc'd his rev'rend head.
His tresses drop'd with dews, and o'er the stream
His shining horns diffus'd a golden gleam:
Grav'd on his urn appear'd the moon, that guides
His swelling waters, and alternate tides;   170
The figur'd streams in waves of silver roll'd,
And on their banks Augusta rose in gold.
Around his throne the sea-born brothers stood,
Who swell with tributary urns his flood;
First the fam'd authors of his ancient name,

The winding Isis and the fruitful Thame:
The Kennet swift, for silver eels renown'd;
The Lodden slow, with verdant alders crown'd;
Cole, whose dark streams his flow'ry islands lave;
And chalky Wey, that rolls a milky wave:　　　180
The blue, transparent Vandalis appears;
The gulphy Lee his sedgy tresses rears;
And sullen Mole, that hides his diving flood;
And silent Darent, stain'd with Danish blood.

High in the midst, upon his urn reclin'd
(His sea-green mantle waving with the wind),
The god appear'd: he turn'd his azure eyes
Where Windsor-domes and pompous turrets rise;
Then bow'd and spoke; the winds forget to roar,
And the hush'd waves glide softly to the shore.　　　190

"Hail, sacred Peace! hail long-expected days,
That Thames's glory to the stars shall raise!
Tho' Tiber's streams immortal Rome behold,
Tho' foaming Hermus [4] swells with tides of gold,
From heav'n itself tho' sev'n-fold Nilus flows,
And harvests on a hundred realms bestows;
These now no more shall be the Muse's themes,
Lost in my fame, as in the sea their streams.
Let Volga's banks with iron squadrons shine,
And groves of lances glitter on the Rhine,　　　200
Let barb'rous Ganges arm a servile train;
Be mine the blessings of a peaceful reign.
No more my sons shall dye with British blood
Red Iber's sands, or Ister's foaming flood: [5]
Safe on my shore each unmolested swain
Shall tend the flocks, or reap the bearded grain;
The shady empire shall retain no trace
Of war or blood, but in the sylvan chase;
The trumpet sleep, while chearful horns are blown,
And arms employ'd on birds and beasts alone.　　　210
Behold! th' ascending villas on my side,
Project long shadows o'er the crystal tide,
Behold! Augusta's glitt'ring spires increase,
And temples rise, the beauteous works of peace.
I see, I see, where two fair cities bend
Their ample bow, a new Whitehall ascend!

4 The Sarabat, a river in Aeolis.　　　5 The Iber is the Ebro in Spain; the Ister
is the Danube.

There mighty nations shall inquire their doom,
The world's great oracle in times to come;
There kings shall sue, and suppliant states be seen
Once more to bend before a British Queen.   220

"Thy trees, fair Windsor! now shall leave their woods,
And half thy forests rush into thy floods,
Bear Britain's thunder, and her cross display,
To the bright regions of the rising day;
Tempt icy seas, where scarce the waters roll,
Where clearer flames glow round the frozen pole:
Or under southern skies exalt their sails,
Led by new stars, and borne by spicy gales!
For me the balm shall bleed, and amber flow,
The coral redden, and the ruby glow,   230
The pearly shell its lucid globe infold,
And Phœbus warm the rip'ning ore to gold.
The time shall come, when free as seas or wind,
Unbounded Thames shall flow for all mankind,
Whole nations enter with each swelling tide,
And seas but join the regions they divide;
Earth's distant ends our glory shall behold,
And the new world launch forth to seek the old.
Then ships of uncouth form shall stem the tyde,
And feather'd people croud my wealthy side,   240
And naked youths and painted chiefs admire
Our speech, our colour, and our strange attire!
O stretch thy reign, fair Peace! from shore to shore,
Till conquest cease, and slav'ry be no more;
Till the freed Indians in their native groves
Reap their own fruits, and woo their sable loves,
Peru once more a race of kings behold,
And other Mexicos be roof'd with gold.
Exil'd by thee from earth to deepest hell,
In brazen bonds shall barb'rous Discord dwell;   250
Gigantic Pride, pale Terror, gloomy Care,
And mad Ambition shall attend her there:
There purple Vengeance bath'd in gore retires,
Her weapons blunted, and extinct her fires:
There hated Envy her own snakes shall feel,
And Persecution mourn her broken wheel:
There Faction roar, Rebellion bite her chain,
And gasping Furies thirst for blood in vain."

Here cease thy flight, nor with unhallow'd lays

Touch the fair fame of Albion's golden days: 260
The thoughts of gods let Granville's verse recite,
And bring the scenes of op'ning fate to light.
My humble Muse, in unambitious strains,
Paints the green forests and the flow'ry plains,
Where Peace descending bids her olives spring,
And scatters blessings from her dove-like wing.
Ev'n I more sweetly pass my careless days,
Pleas'd in the silent shade with empty praise;
Enough for me, that to the list'ning swains
First in these fields I sung the sylvan strains.   270

ELOISA TO ABELARD

1717

ARGUMENT

ABELARD and Eloisa flourished in the twelfth century;
they were two of the most distinguished persons of their
age in learning and beauty; but for nothing more famous
than for their unfortunate passion. After a long course of
calamities, they retired each to a several Convent, and consecrated the remainder of their days to religion. It was many
years after this separation, that a letter of Abelard's to a
friend, which contained the history of his misfortune, fell
into the hands of Eloisa. This awakening all her tenderness,
occasioned those celebrated letters (out of which the following is partly extracted) which give so lively a picture of
the struggles of grace and nature, virtue and passion.

IN THESE deep solitudes and awful cells,
Where heav'nly-pensive contemplation dwells,
And ever-musing melancholy reigns;
What means this tumult in a Vestal's veins?
Why rove my thoughts beyond this last retreat?
Why feels my heart its long-forgotten heat?
Yet, yet I love!—From Abelard it came,
And Eloïsa yet must kiss the name.
Dear fatal name! rest ever unreveal'd,
Nor pass these lips in holy silence seal'd: 10

Hide it, my heart, within that close disguise,
Where mix'd with God's, his lov'd idea lies:
O write it not my hand—the name appears
Already written—wash it out, my tears!
In vain lost Eloïsa weeps and prays,
Her heart still dictates, and her hand obeys.
    Relentless walls! whose darksome round contains
Repentant sighs, and voluntary pains:
Ye rugged rocks! which holy knees have worn;
Ye grots and caverns shagg'd with horrid thorn!
Shrines! where their vigils pale-ey'd virgins keep,
And pitying saints, whose statues learn to weep!
Tho' cold like you, unmov'd and silent grown,
I have not yet forgot myself to stone.
All is not Heav'n's while Abelard has part,
Still rebel nature holds out half my heart;
Nor pray'rs nor fasts its stubborn pulse restrain,
Nor tears for ages taught to flow in vain.
    Soon as thy letters trembling I unclose,
That well-known name awakens all my woes.
Oh name for ever sad! for ever dear!
Still breath'd in sighs, still usher'd with a tear.
I tremble too, where'er my own I find,
Some dire misfortune follows close behind.
Line after line my gushing eyes o'erflow,
Led thro' a sad variety of woe:
Now warm in love, now with'ring in my bloom,
Lost in a convent's solitary gloom!
There stern Religion quench'd th' unwilling flame,
There dy'd the best of passions, Love and Fame.
    Yet write, oh write me all, that I may join
Griefs to thy griefs, and echo sighs to thine.
Nor foes nor fortune take this pow'r away;
And is my Abelard less kind than they?
Tears still are mine, and those I need not spare,
Love but demands what else were shed in pray'r;
No happier task these faded eyes pursue;
To read and weep is all they now can do.
    Then share thy pain, allow that sad relief;
Ah, more than share it, give me all thy grief.
Heav'n first taught letters for some wretch's aid,
Some banish'd lover, or some captive maid;
They live, they speak, they breathe what love inspires,

Warm from the soul, and faithful to its fires,
The virgin's wish without her fears impart,
Excuse the blush, and pour out all the heart,
Speed the soft intercourse from soul to soul,   *class*
And waft a sigh from Indus to the Pole.

Strong element of eroticism

Thou know'st how guiltless first I met thy flame,
When Love approach'd me under Friendship's name;   60
My fancy form'd thee of angelic kind,
Some emanation of th' all-beauteous Mind.
Those smiling eyes, attemp'ring ev'ry ray,
Shone sweetly lambent with celestial day.
Guiltless I gaz'd; heav'n listen'd while you sung;

Spirit down to sensual

And truths divine came mended from that tongue.
From lips like those what precept fail'd to move?
Too soon they taught me 'twas no sin to love:

gothic type of landscape—disordered passion rendered to disordered landscape

Back thro' the paths of pleasing sense I ran,
Nor wish'd an angel whom I lov'd a man.   70
Dim and remote the joys of saints I see;
Nor envy them that heav'n I lose for thee.
How oft, when press'd to marriage, have I said,
Curse on all laws but those which Love has made?
Love, free as air, at sight of human ties,
Spreads his light wings, and in a moment flies.
Let wealth, let honour, wait the wedded dame,
August her deed, and sacred be her fame;
Before true passion all those views remove,
Fame, wealth, and honour! what are you to Love?   80
The jealous God, when we profane his fires,
Those restless passions in revenge inspires,
And bids them make mistaken mortals groan,
Who seek in love for aught but love alone.
Should at my feet the world's great master fall,
Himself, his throne, his world, I'd scorn 'em all:
Not Cæsar's empress would I deign to prove;
No, make me mistress to the man I love;
If there be yet another name more free,
More fond than mistress, make me that to thee!   90
Oh! happy state! when souls each other draw,
When love is liberty, and nature, law:
All then is full, possessing, and possest,
No craving void left aking in the breast:
Ev'n thought meets thought, ere from the lips it part,
And each warm wish springs mutual from the heart.

This sure is bliss (if bliss on earth there be)
And once the lot of Abelard and me.
　　Alas how chang'd! what sudden horrors rise!
A naked lover bound and bleeding lies!   100
Where, where was Eloïse? her voice, her hand,
Her ponyard had oppos'd the dire command.
Barbarian, stay! that bloody stroke restrain;
The crime was common, common be the pain.
I can no more, by shame, by rage suppress'd,
Let tears, and burning blushes speak the rest.
　　Canst thou forget that sad, that solemn day,
When victims at yon altar's foot we lay?
Canst thou forget what tears that moment fell,
When, warm in youth, I bade the world farewell?   110
As with cold lips I kiss'd the sacred veil,
The shrines all trembled, and the lamps grew pale:
Heav'n scarce believ'd the conquest it survey'd,
And saints with wonder heard the vows I made.
Yet then, to those dread altars as I drew,
Not on the Cross my eyes were fix'd, but you:
Not grace, or zeal, love only was my call,
And if I lose thy love, I lose my all.
Come! with thy looks, thy words, relieve my woe;
Those still at least are left thee to bestow.   120
Still on that breast enamour'd let me lie,
Still drink delicious poison from thy eye,
Pant on thy lip, and to thy heart be press'd;
Give all thou canst—and let me dream the rest.
Ah no! instruct me other joys to prize,
With other beauties charm my partial eyes,
Full in my view set all the bright abode,
And make my soul quit Abelard for God.
　　Ah think at least thy flock deserves thy care,
Plants of thy hand, and children of thy pray'r.   130
From the false world in early youth they fled,
By thee to mountains, wilds, and deserts led.
You rais'd these hallow'd walls; the desert smil'd,
And Paradise was open'd in the Wild.
No weeping orphan saw his father's stores
Our shrines irradiate, or emblaze the floors;
No silver saints, by dying misers giv'n,
Here brib'd the rage of ill-requited heav'n:
But such plain roofs as Piety could raise,

And only vocal with the Maker's praise.   140
In these lone walls (their days eternal bound)
These moss-grown domes with spiry turrets crown'd,
Where awful arches make a noon-day night,
And the dim windows shed a solemn light;
Thy eyes diffus'd a reconciling ray,
And gleams of glory brighten'd all the day.
But now no face divine contentment wears,
'Tis all blank sadness, or continual tears.
See how the force of others pray'rs I try,
(O pious fraud of am'rous charity!)   150
But why should I on others' pray'rs depend?
Come thou, my father, brother, husband, friend!
Ah let thy handmaid, sister, daughter move,
And all those tender names in one, thy love!
The darksome pines that o'er yon rocks reclin'd
Wave high, and murmur to the hollow wind,
The wand'ring streams that shine between the hills,
The grots that echo to the tinkling rills,
The dying gales that pant upon the trees,
The lakes that quiver to the curling breeze;   160
No more these scenes my meditation aid,
Or lull to rest the visionary maid.
But o'er the twilight groves and dusky caves,
Long-sounding isles, and intermingled graves,
Black Melancholy sits, and round her throws
A death-like silence, and a dread repose:
Her gloomy presence saddens all the scene,
Shades ev'ry flow'r, and darkens ev'ry green,
Deepens the murmur of the falling floods,
And breathes a browner horror on the woods.   170

    Yet here for ever, ever must I stay;
Sad proof how well a lover can obey!
Death, only death, can break the lasting chain;
And here, ev'n then, shall my cold dust remain,
Here all its frailties, all its flames resign,
And wait till 'tis no sin to mix with thine.
    Ah wretch! believ'd the spouse of God in vain,
Confess'd within the slave of love and man.
Assist me, heav'n! but whence arose that pray'r?
Sprung it from piety, or from despair?   180
Ev'n here, where frozen chastity retires,
Love finds an altar for forbidden fires.

I ought to grieve, but cannot what I ought;
I mourn the lover, not lament the fault;
I view my crime, but kindle at the view,
Repent old pleasures, and sollicit new;
Now turn'd to heav'n, I weep my past offence,
Now think of thee, and curse my innocence.
Of all affliction taught a lover yet,
'Tis sure the hardest science to forget!
How shall I lose the sin, yet keep the sense,
And love th' offender, yet detest th' offence?
How dear the object from the crime remove,
Or how distinguish penitence from love?
Unequal task! a passion to resign,
For hearts so touch'd, so pierc'd, so lost as mine.
Ere such a soul regains its peaceful state,
How often must it love, how often hate!
How often hope, despair, resent, regret,
Conceal, disdain,—do all things but forget.
But let heav'n seize it, all at once 'tis fir'd;
Not touch'd, but rapt; not waken'd, but inspir'd!
Oh come! oh teach me nature to subdue,
Renounce my love, my life, myself—and you.
Fill my fond heart with God alone, for he
Alone can rival, can succeed to thee.
  How happy is the blameless Vestal's lot?
The world forgetting, by the world forgot:
Eternal sun-shine of the spotless mind!
Each pray'r accepted, and each wish resign'd;
Labour and rest, that equal periods keep;
"Obedient slumbers that can wake and weep;"
Desires compos'd, affections ever ev'n;
Tears that delight, and sighs that waft to heav'n.
Grace shines around her with serenest beams,
And whisp'ring angels prompt her golden dreams.
For her th' unfading rose of Eden blooms,
And wings of seraphs shed divine perfumes,
For her the Spouse prepares the bridal ring,
For her white virgins hymenæals sing,
To sounds of heav'nly harps she dies away,
And melts in visions of eternal day.
  Far other dreams my erring soul employ,
Far other raptures, of unholy joy:
When at the close of each sad, sorrowing day,

190

200

210

220

Fancy restores what vengeance snatch'd away,
Then conscience sleeps, and leaving nature free,
All my loose soul unbounded springs to thee.
O curst, dear horrors of all-conscious night!
How glowing guilt exalts the keen delight!   230
Provoking dæmons all restraint remove,
And stir within me ev'ry source of love.
I hear thee, view thee, gaze o'er all thy charms,
And round thy phantom glue my clasping arms.
I wake:—no more I hear, no more I view,
The phantom flies me, as unkind as you.
I call aloud; it hears not what I say:
I stretch my empty arms; it glides away.
To dream once more I close my willing eyes;
Ye soft illusions, dear deceits, arise!   240
Alas, no more! methinks we wand'ring go
Thro' dreary wastes, and weep each other's woe,
Where round some mould'ring tow'r pale ivy creeps,
And low-brow'd rocks hang nodding o'er the deeps.
Sudden you mount, you beckon from the skies;
Clouds interpose, waves roar, and winds arise.
I shriek, start up, the same sad prospect find,
And wake to all the griefs I left behind.
     For thee the fates, severely kind, ordain
A cool suspense from pleasure and from pain;   250
Thy life a long dead calm of fix'd repose;
No pulse that riots, and no blood that glows.
Still as the sea, ere winds were taught to blow,
Or moving spirit bade the waters flow;
Soft as the slumbers of a saint forgiv'n,
And mild as op'ning gleams of promis'd heav'n.
     Come, Abelard! for what hast thou to dread?
The torch of Venus burns not for the dead.
Nature stands check'd; Religion disapproves;
Ev'n thou art cold—yet Eloïsa loves.   260
Ah hopeless, lasting flames! like those that burn
To light the dead, and warm th' unfruitful urn.
     What scenes appear where'er I turn my view?
The dear ideas, where I fly, pursue,
Rise in the grove, before the altar rise,
Stain all my soul, and wanton in my eyes.
I waste the matin lamp in sighs for thee,
Thy image steals between my God and me,

Thy voice I seem in ev'ry hymn to hear,
With ev'ry bead I drop too soft a tear. *tears of devotion* 270
When from the censer clouds of fragrance roll,
And swelling organs lift the rising soul,
One thought of thee puts all the pomp to flight,
Priests, tapers, temples, swim before my sight:
In seas of flame my plunging soul is drown'd,
While altars blaze, and angels tremble round. *very powerful*
  While prostrate here in humble grief I lie,
Kind, virtuous drops just gath'ring in my eye,
While praying, trembling, in the dust I roll,
And dawning grace is op'ning on my soul: 280
Come, if thou dar'st, all charming as thou art!
Oppose thyself to heav'n; dispute my heart;
Come, with one glance of those deluding eyes
Blot out each bright idea of the skies;
Take back that grace, those sorrows, and those tears;
Take back my fruitless penitence and pray'rs;
Snatch me, just mounting, from the blest abode;
Assist the fiends, and tear me from my God!
  No, fly me, fly me, far as pole from pole;
Rise Alps between us! and whole oceans roll!   290
Ah, come not, write not, think not once of me,
Nor share one pang of all I felt for thee.
Thy oaths I quit, thy memory resign;
Forget, renounce me, hate whate'er was mine.
Fair eyes, and tempting looks (which yet I view!)
Long lov'd, ador'd ideas, all adieu!
O Grace serene! oh virtue heav'nly fair!
Divine oblivion of low-thoughted care!
Fresh blooming Hope, gay daughter of the sky!
And Faith, our early immortality!   300
Enter, each mild, each amicable guest;
Receive, and wrap me in eternal rest!
  See in her cell sad Eloïsa spread,
Propt on some tomb, a neighbour of the dead.
In each low wind methinks a Spirit calls,
And more than Echoes talk along the walls.
Here, as I watch'd the dying lamps around,
From yonder shrine I heard a hollow sound.
"Come, sister, come! (it said, or seem'd to say)
Thy place is here, sad sister, come away!   310
Once like thyself, I trembled, wept, and pray'd,

Love's victim then, tho' now a sainted maid:
But all is calm in this eternal sleep;
Here grief forgets to groan, and love to weep,
Ev'n superstition loses ev'ry fear:
For God, not man, absolves our frailties here."
    I come, I come! prepare your roseate bow'rs,
Celestial palms, and ever-blooming flow'rs.
Thither, where sinners may have rest, I go,
Where flames refin'd in breasts seraphic glow: 320
Thou, Abelard! the last sad office pay,
And smooth my passage to the realms of day;
See my lips tremble, and my eye-balls roll,
Suck my last breath, and catch my flying soul!
Ah no—in sacred vestments may'st thou stand,
The hallow'd taper trembling in thy hand,
Present the Cross before my lifted eye,
Teach me at once, and learn of me to die.
Ah then, thy once-lov'd Eloïsa see!
It will be then no crime to gaze on me.   330
See from my cheek the transient roses fly!
See the last sparkle languish in my eye!
'Till ev'ry motion, pulse, and breath be o'er;
And ev'n my Abelard be lov'd no more.
O Death, all-eloquent! you only prove
What dust we doat on, when 'tis man we love.
    Then too, when fate shall thy fair frame destroy,
(That cause of all my guilt, and all my joy)
In trance extatic may thy pangs be drown'd,
Bright clouds descend, and angels watch thee round,   340
From op'ning skies may streaming glories shine,
And saints embrace thee with a love like mine.
    May one kind grave unite each hapless name,
And graft my love immortal on thy fame!
Then, ages hence, when all my woes are o'er,
When this rebellious heart shall beat no more;
If ever chance two wand'ring lovers brings
To Paraclete's white walls and silver springs,
O'er the pale marble shall they join their heads,
And drink the falling tears each other sheds;   350
Then sadly say, with mutual pity mov'd,
"Oh may we never love as these have lov'd!"
From the full choir when loud hosannas rise,
And swell the pomp of dreadful sacrifice,

Amid that scene if some relenting eye
Glance on the stone where our cold relicks lie,
Devotion's self shall steal a thought from heav'n,
One human tear shall drop, and be forgiv'n.
And sure if fate some future bard shall join
In sad similitude of griefs to mine,   360
Condemn'd whole years in absence to deplore,
And image charms he must behold no more;
Sure if there be, who loves so long, so well;
Let him our sad, our tender story tell;
The well-sung woes will sooth my pensive ghost;
He best can paint 'em who shall feel 'em most.

[handwritten: mock heroic]

THE DUNCIAD [1]

1728-1729

[handwritten: attributed to the dunces of the world]

BOOK THE FIRST

Books and the man I sing, the first who brings
The Smithfield Muses to the ear of kings.
Say great patricians! (since your selves inspire
These wond'rous works; so Jove and Fate require)
Say from what cause, in vain decry'd and curst,
Still Dunce the second reigns like Dunce the first.
    In eldest time, e'er mortals writ or read,
E'er Pallas issued from the Thund'rers head,
Dulness o'er all possess'd her antient right,
Daughter of Chaos and eternal Night: 10
Fate in their dotage this fair idiot gave,
Gross as her sire, and as her mother grave,
Laborious, heavy, busy, bold, and blind,
She rul'd, in native anarchy, the mind.

[handwritten: style sets high epic level]
[handwritten: — latinate words]
[handwritten: see epic movement of words as Rape of the Lock is too]

1 Lewis Theobald (Tibbald) in 1726 had published *Shakespeare Restored, or A Specimen of the Many Errors as Well Committed as Unamended by Mr. Pope,* exposing the shortcomings of Pope's edition of Shakespeare. Apparently at the suggestion of Swift, Pope decided to make Theobald the hero of a Scriblerian poem against dullness that was already partially composed. The consequence was the first edition of *The Dunciad* in 1728; this was followed in 1729 by another edition, with notes added. Pope continued to tinker with the poem, and as late as 1742 appeared *The New Dunciad,* which was incorporated in another *Dunciad* printed in 1743. In this revised version, Colley Cibber replaced Theobald as the hero-dullard; against Cibber, Pope had nourished a variety of grudges since 1717. The version of 1728-29 embodies the hate of the "wits"—the Scriblerus Club of Pope, Swift, Gay, and Arbuthnot—for dullness whether in poetry or learning.

[handwritten: Martinus Scriblerus footnotes accred. to]

Still her old empire to confirm, she tries,
For born a goddess, Dulness never dies.
　　O thou! whatever title please thine ear,
Dean, Drapier, Bickerstaff, or Gulliver!　*address to Swift*
Whether thou chuse Cervantes' serious air,
Or laugh and shake in Rab'lais' easy chair,　　　　　20
Or praise the court, or magnify mankind,
Or thy griev'd country's copper chains unbind;
From thy Bæotia tho' her pow'r retires,
Grieve not at ought our sister realms acquire:
Here pleas'd behold her mighty wings out-spread,
To hatch a new Saturnian age of lead.
　　Where wave the tatter'd ensigns of Rag-Fair,[2]
A yawning ruin hangs and nods in air;
Keen, hollow winds howl thro' the bleak recess,
Emblem of music caus'd by emptiness:　　　　　30
Here in one bed two shiv'ring sisters lye,
The cave of Poverty and Poetry.
This, the Great Mother dearer held than all
The clubs of quidnunc's, or her own guild-hall.
Here stood her opium, here she nurs'd her owls,
And destin'd here th' imperial seat of fools.
Hence springs each weekly muse, the living boast
Of Curl's chaste press, and Lintot's rubric's post,[3]
Hence hymning Tyburn's elegiac lay,
Hence the soft sing-song on Cecilia's day,　　　　　40
Sepulchral lyes our holy walls to grace,
And new-year's odes, and all the Grubstreet race.
　　'Twas here in clouded majesty she shone;
Four guardian Virtues, round, support her Throne;
Fierce champion Fortitude, that knows no fears
Of hisses, blows, or want, or loss of ears:
Calm Temperance, whose blessings those partake
Who hunger, and who thirst, for scribling sake:
Prudence, whose glass presents th' approaching jayl:
Poetic Justice, with her lifted scale;　　　　　50
Where in nice balance, truth with gold she weighs,
And solid pudding against empty praise.
　　Here she beholds the Chaos dark and deep,
Where nameless somethings in their causes sleep,

---

2 Rag-Fair is a place near the Tower of London where old clothes and frippery are sold. [Pope]

3 Edmund Curll, publisher of obscenities; Bernard Lintot adorned his bookseller's shop with red letters.

'Till genial Jacob, or a warm third-day [4]
Call forth each mass, a poem or a play.
How hints, like spawn, scarce quick in embryo lie,
How new-born Nonsense first is taught to cry,
Maggots half-form'd, in rhyme exactly meet,
And learn to crawl upon poetic feet.
Here one poor word a hundred clenches makes,
And ductile dulness new meanders takes;
There motley Images her fancy strike,
Figures ill-pair'd, and Similes unlike.
She sees a mob of Metaphors advance,
Pleas'd with the madness of the mazy dance:
How Tragedy and Comedy embrace;
How Farce and Epic get a jumbled race;
How Time himself stands still at her command,
Realms shift their place, and ocean turns to land.   70
Here gay Description Ægypt glads with showers;
Or gives to Zembla fruits, to Barca [5] flowers;
Glitt'ring with ice here hoary hills are seen,
There painted vallies of eternal green,
On cold December fragrant chaplets blow,
And heavy harvests nod beneath the snow.

All these and more, the cloud-compelling Queen
Beholds thro' fogs that magnify the scene:
She, tinsel'd o'er in robes of varying hues,
With self-applause her wild creation views.   80
Sees momentary monsters rise and fall,
And with her own fool's colours gilds them all.
'Twas on the day, when Thorold,[6] rich and grave,
Like Cimon triumph'd, both on land and wave:
(Pomps without guilt, of bloodless swords and maces,
Glad chains, warm furs, broad banners, and broad faces)
Now night descending, the proud scene was o'er,
But liv'd, in Settle's numbers, one day more.
Now may'rs and shrieves all hush'd and satiate lay,
Yet eat in dreams the custard of the day;   90
While pensive poets painful vigils keep,
Sleepless themselves to give their readers sleep.

4 Jacob Tonson, bookseller and publisher;
on the "third day" of a play, the proceeds of
the performance were for the author's benefit.
5 Novaya Zemlya is two barren islands in
the Arctic Ocean; Barca is a city on the
sands of Cyrenaica, northern Africa.

6 The procession of Sir George Thorold,
Lord Mayor of London in 1720. Elkanah
Settle (1648-1724) was appointed City Poet
in 1691.

Much to the mindful Queen the feast recalls,
What city-swans, once sung within the walls;
Much she revolves their arts, their ancient praise,
And sure succession down from Heywood's [7] days.
She saw with joy the line immortal run,
Each sire imprest and glaring in his son;
So watchful bruin forms with plastic care
Each growing lump, and brings it to a bear.   100
She saw old Pryn in restless Daniel shine,[8]
And Eusden eke out Blackmore's endless line; [9]
She saw slow Philips creep like Tate's poor page,[10]
And all the mighty mad in Dennis [11] rage.

In each she marks her image full exprest,
But chief, in Tibbald's monster-breeding breast; *hero introduced*
Sees God with Dæmons in strange league ingage,
And earth, and heav'n, and hell her battles wage.
She ey'd the bard, where supperless he sate,
And pin'd, unconscious of his rising fate;   110
Studious he sate, with all his books around,
Sinking from thought to thought, a vast profound!
Plung'd for his sense, but found no bottom there;
Then writ, and flounder'd on, in mere despair.
He roll'd his eyes that witness'd huge dismay,
Where yet unpawn'd, much learned lumber lay,
Volumes, whose size the space exactly fill'd;
Or which fond authors were so good to gild;
Or where, by sculpture made for ever known,
The page admires new beauties, not its own.   120
Here swells the shelf with Ogilby [12] the great:
There, stamp'd with arms, Newcastle shines compleat,
Here all his suff'ring brotherhood retire,
And 'scape the martyrdom of jakes and fire;
A Gothic Vatican! of Greece and Rome
Well-purg'd, and worthy Withers, Quarles, and Blome.[13]
But high above, more solid learning shone,

[handwritten marginal note: Tibbald's thought process dulness taking over all]

7 John Heywood (1497?–1580?), writer of interludes.
8 William Prynne, the Puritan pamphleteer and author of *Histrio-mastix* (1632), who was condemned, like "restless Daniel" [Defoe] to have his ears cropped in the pillory.
9 Lawrence Eusden was poet laureate (1718–30); Sir Richard Blackmore was the author of dull epics.
10 Ambrose Philips, author of the *Pastorals* (1709) at which Pope sneered; Nahum Tate was poet laureate from 1692 to 1715.
11 John Dennis, already attacked in the *Essay on Criticism*, as well as in the *Narrative concerning the Frenzy of Mr. J. Denn––*.
12 John Ogilby, like Margaret Cavendish, Duchess of Newcastle, was a voluminous writer.
13 George Wither and Francis Quarles, poets of the seventeenth century. Richard Blome (d. 1705) was a compiler of learned volumes.

The classicks of an age that heard of none;
There Caxton slept, with Wynkin at his side,[14]
One clasp'd in wood, and one in strong cow-hide.   130
There sav'd by spice, like mummies, many a year,
Old bodies of philosophy appear.
De Lyra [15] here a dreadful front extends,
And there, the groaning shelves Philemon bends.
   Of these twelve volumes, twelve of amplest size,
Redeem'd from tapers and defrauded pyes,
Inspir'd he seizes: These an altar raise:
An hecatomb of pure, unsully'd lays
That altar crowns: A folio common-place
Founds the whole pyle, of all his works the base;   140
Quarto's, octavo's, shape the less'ning pyre,
And last, a little Ajax [16] tips the spire.
   Then he: "Great Tamer of all human art!
First in my care, and nearest at my heart:
Dulness! whose good old cause I yet defend,
With whom my muse began, with whom shall end!
O thou, of business the directing soul,
To human heads like byass to the bowl,
Which as more pond'rous makes their aim more true,
Obliquely wadling to the mark in view.   *very low kind of word* [1500]
O ever gracious to perplex'd mankind!
Who spread a healing mist before the mind,
And, lest we err by wit's wild, dancing light,
Secure us kindly in our native night.
Ah! still o'er Britain stretch that peaceful wand,
Which lulls th' Helvetian and Batavian land.
Where rebel to thy throne if Science rise,
She does but shew her coward face and dies:
There, thy good scholiasts with unweary'd pains
Make Horace flat, and humble Maro's strains;   160
Here studious I unlucky moderns save,
Nor sleeps one error in its father's grave,
Old puns restore, lost blunders nicely seek,
And crucify poor Shakespear once a week.[17]
For thee I dim these eyes, and stuff this head,

---

14 William Caxton and Wynkyn de
Worde, the first printers in England.
15 Nicholas de Lyra (ca. 1475) was a
voluminous commentator. Philemon Holland
was a voluminous translator of the seventeenth century.

16 A translation of the *Ajax* of Sophocles
by Theobald.
17 Theobald used to print every week or
fortnight in *Mist's Journal* a single remark
or note upon the text of Shakespeare. *Mist's
Weekly Journal* (1716–28) was a Tory periodical.

With all such reading as was never read;
For thee supplying, in the worst of days,
Notes to dull books, and prologues to dull plays;
For thee explain a thing till all men doubt it,
And write about it, Goddess, and about it;   170
So spins the silkworm small its slender store,
And labours, 'till it clouds itself all o'er.
Not that my quill to critiques was confin'd,
My verse gave ampler lessons to mankind;
So gravest precepts may successless prove,
But sad examples never fail to move.
As forc'd from wind-guns, lead itself can fly,
And pond'rous slugs cut swiftly thro' the sky;
As clocks to weight their nimble motion owe,
The wheels above urg'd by the load below;   180
Me, Emptiness and Dulness could inspire,
And were my elasticity and fire.
Had heav'n decreed such works a longer date,
Heav'n had decreed to spare the Grubstreet-state.
But see great Settle to the dust descend,
And all thy cause and empire at an end!
Cou'd Troy be sav'd by any single hand,
His gray-goose-weapon must have made her stand.
But what can I? my Flaccus cast aside,
Take up th' *Attorney's* (once my better) *Guide?* [18]   190
Or rob the Roman geese of all their glories,
And save the state by cackling to the Tories?
Yes, to my Country I my pen consign,
Yes, from this moment, mighty Mist! am thine,
And rival, Curtius! of thy fame and zeal,
O'er head and ears plunge for the publick weal.
Adieu my children! better thus expire
Un-stall'd, unsold; thus glorious mount in fire
Fair without spot; than greas'd by grocer's hands,
Or shipp'd with Ward [19] to ape and monkey lands,   200
Or wafting ginger, round the streets to go,
And visit alehouse where ye first did grow."
      With that, he lifted thrice the sparkling brand,
And thrice he dropt it from his quiv'ring hand:
Then lights the structure, with averted eyes;

18 In allusion to his first profession of an
attorney. [Pope]
19 Edward Ward, a very voluminous poet
in Hudibrastic verse. Great numbers of his
works are yearly sold into the plantations.
[Pope]

The rowling smokes involve the sacrifice.
The opening clouds disclose each work by turns,
Now flames old Memnon, now Rodrigo burns,[20]
In one quick flash see Proserpine expire,
And last, his own cold Æschylus took fire.   210
Then gush'd the tears, as from the Trojan's eyes
When the last blaze sent Ilion to the skies.

    Rowz'd by the light, old Dulness heav'd the head,
Then snatch'd a sheet of *Thulè* [21] from her bed;
Sudden she flies, and whelms it o'er the pyre:
Down sink the flames, and with a hiss expire.

    Her ample presence fills up all the place;
A veil of fogs dilates her awful face;
Great in her charms! as when on shrieves and may'rs
She looks, and breathes her self into their airs.   220
She bids him wait her to the sacred dome; [22]
Well-pleas'd he enter'd, and confess'd his home:
So spirits ending their terrestrial race,
Ascend, and recognize their native place:
Raptur'd, he gazes round the dear retreat,
And in sweet numbers celebrates the seat.

    Here to her chosen all her works she shows;
Prose swell'd to verse, verse loit'ring into prose;
How random thoughts now meaning chance to find,
Now leave all memory of sense behind: 230
How prologues into prefaces decay,
And these to notes are fritter'd quite away.
How index-learning turns no student pale,
Yet holds the eel of science by the tail.
How, with less reading than makes felons 'scape,[23]
Less human genius than God gives an ape,
Small thanks to France and none to Rome or Greece,
A past, vamp'd, future, old, reviv'd, new piece,
'Twixt Plautus, Fletcher, Congreve, and Corneille,

---

20 Memnon, a hero in *The Persian Princess*, very apt to take fire, as appears by these lines with which he begins the play:

By heav'n it fires my frozen blood with rage,
And makes it *scald* my aged trunk—.

Roderigo, the chief personage of *The Perfidious Brother*, a play written between T. and a watchmaker. *The Rape of Proserpine*, one of the farces of this author, in which Ceres sets fire to a corn-field, which endangered the burning of the play-house. He had been about [translating] Aeschylus for ten years. [Pope]

21 An unfinished poem of that name, of which one sheet was printed fifteen years ago, by A[mbrose] Ph[ilips], a northern author. It is an usual method of putting out a fire to cast wet sheets upon it. Some critics have been of the opinion that this sheet was of the nature of the asbestos, which cannot be consumed by fire; but I rather think it only an allegorical allusion to the coldness and heaviness of the writing. [Pope]

22 The Cave of Poverty; Theobald wrote a poem of this name in 1715 (?).

23 A reference to benefit of clergy.

Can make a Cibber, Johnson, or Ozell.[24]   240
   The Goddess then, o'er his anointed head,
With mystic words, the sacred opium shed;
And lo! her Bird (a monster of a fowl!
Something betwixt a H * * *[25] and Owl)
Perch'd on his crown. "All hail! and hail again,
My son! the promis'd land expects thy reign.
Know, Settle, cloy'd with custard and with praise,
Is gather'd to the dull of antient days,
Safe, where no criticks damn, no duns molest,
Where Gildon, Banks, and high-born Howard rest.[26]   250
I see a king! who leads my chosen sons
To lands, that flow with clenches and with puns:
'Till each fam'd theatre my empire own,
'Till Albion, as Hibernia, bless my throne!
I see! I see!"—Then rapt, she spoke no more.
"God save King Tibbald!" Grubstreet alleys roar.
   So when Jove's block descended from on high,
(As sings thy great fore-father, Ogilby,)
Loud thunder to its bottom shook the bog,
And the hoarse nation croak'd, "God save King Log!"   260

AN ESSAY ON MAN, IN FOUR EPISTLES

To Henry St. John, Lord Bolingbroke

1733–1734

EPISTLE I

OF THE NATURE AND STATE OF MAN, WITH RESPECT TO THE UNIVERSE

Awake, my St. John! leave all meaner things
To low ambition, and the pride of kings.
Let us (since life can little more supply
Than just to look about us and to die)

[handwritten annotations: "large concession Pope makes – what is man", "life offers", "little", "aesthetic unity for our mind"]

24 Charles Johnson, famous for writing a play every season, and for being at Button's every day. Mr. John Ozell . . . has obliged the world with many translations of French plays. [Pope]

25 John James Heidegger, a Swiss who managed the Haymarket Opera House; he had the name of being the ugliest man in London. Pope calls him "a strange bird from Switzerland."

26 Charles Gildon, a critic who "abused Mr. P. very scandalously in an anonymous pamphlet of the life of Mr. Wycherly printed by Curll, in another called *The New Rehearsal*, printed in 1714, in a third entitled *The Complete Art of English Poetry*." John Banks was a lawyer-dramatist. Sir Robert Howard had collaborated with Dryden in writing *The Indian Queen* (1664-65).

[handwritten annotations at bottom: "aesthetic more general", "looks for harmony, of parts to whole"]

Expatiate free o'er all this scene of man;
A mighty maze! but not without a plan;   *eludes, brings*
A wild, where weeds and flow'rs promiscuous shoot;   *in garden—*
Or garden, tempting with forbidden fruit.
Together let us beat this ample field,   *alternate visions*
Try what the open, what the covert yield;   *of same reality*
The latent tracts, the giddy heights, explore   10
Of all who blindly creep, or sightless soar;
Eye Nature's walks, shoot folly as it flies,
And catch the manners living as they rise;   *Characters of man*
Laugh where we must, be candid where we can;
But vindicate the ways of God to man.   *that of looking, very*

   I. Say first, of God above, or man below,   *aesthetic way*
What can we reason, but from what we know?   *of looking*
Of man, what see we but his station here,
From which to reason, or to which refer?   20
Thro' worlds unnumber'd tho' the God be known,
'Tis ours to trace him only in our own.
He, who thro' vast immensity can pierce,
See worlds on worlds compose one universe,
Observe how system into system runs,
What other planets circle other suns,
What vary'd Being peoples ev'ry star,
May tell why Heav'n has made us as we are.
But of this frame the bearings, and the ties,
The strong connections, nice dependencies,   30
Gradations just, has thy pervading soul
Look'd thro'? or can a part contain the whole?
   Is the great chain, that draws all to agree,
And drawn supports, upheld by God, or thee?
   II. Presumptuous man! the reason wouldst thou find,
Why form'd so weak, so little, and so blind?
First, if thou canst, the harder reason guess,
Why form'd no weaker, blinder, and no less?
Ask of thy mother earth, why oaks are made
Taller or stronger than the weeds they shade?   40
Or ask of yonder argent fields above,
Why Jove's satellites are less than Jove? [1]
   Of systems possible, if 'tis confest
That Wisdom infinite must form the best,
Where all must full or not coherent be,
And all that rises, rise in due degree;

[1] A "headless" line, lacking the initial light stress.

ethical are they Right or wrong — punishment or reward

Then, in the scale of reas'ning life, 'tis plain,
There must be, somewhere, such a rank as man:
And all the question (wrangle e'er so long)
Is only this, if God has plac'd him wrong?   50
   Respecting man, whatever wrong we call,
May, must be right, as relative to all.
In human works, tho' labour'd on with pain,
A thousand movements scarce one purpose gain;
In God's, one single can its end produce;
Yet serves to second too some other use.
So man, who here seems principal alone,
Perhaps acts second to some sphere unknown,
Touches some wheel, or verges to some goal;
'Tis but a part we see, and not a whole.   60
   When the proud steed shall know why man restrains
His fiery course, or drives him o'er the plains;
When the dull ox, why now he breaks the clod,
Is now a victim, and now Ægypt's god:
Then shall man's pride and dulness comprehend
His actions', passions', being's use and end;
Why doing, suff'ring, check'd, impell'd; and why
This hour a slave, the next a deity.
   Then say not man's imperfect, Heav'n in fault;
Say rather, man's as perfect as he ought: 70
His knowledge measur'd to his state and place;
His time a moment, and a point his space.
If to be perfect in a certain sphere,
What matter, soon or late, or here or there?
The blest to-day is as completely so,
As who began a thousand years ago.
   III. Heav'n from all creatures hides the book of Fate,
All but the page prescrib'd, their present state:
From brutes what men, from men what spirits know:
Or who could suffer being here below?   80
The lamb thy riot dooms to bleed to-day,
Had he thy reason, would he skip and play?
Pleas'd to the last, he crops the flow'ry food,
And licks the hand just rais'd to shed his blood.
Oh blindness to the future! kindly giv'n,
That each may fill the circle mark'd by Heav'n:
Who sees with equal eye, as God of all,
A hero perish, or a sparrow fall,
Atoms or systems into ruin hurl'd,

[handwritten annotations: "compared w Rope of Lock", "juxtaposition of big + little", "Ironic world — oddly divided", "God's eye view"]

And now a bubble burst, and now a world.　　　　　　90

Hope humbly then; with trembling pinions soar;
Wait the great teacher Death: and God adore.
What future bliss, he gives not thee to know,
But gives that hope to be thy blessing now.
Hope springs eternal in the human breast:
Man never is, but always to be blest:
The soul, uneasy and confin'd from home,
Rests and expatiates in a life to come.

Lo, the poor Indian! whose untutor'd mind
Sees God in clouds, or hears him in the wind;　　　100
His soul, proud Science never taught to stray
Far as the solar walk, or milky way;
Yet simple Nature to his hope has giv'n,
Behind the cloud-topt hill, an humbler heav'n;
Some safer world in depth of woods embrac'd,
Some happier island in the wat'ry waste,
Where slaves once more their native land behold,
No fiends torment, no Christians thirst for gold.
To be, contents his natural desire,
He asks no angel's wing, no seraph's fire;　　　110
But thinks, admitted to that equal sky,
His faithful dog shall bear him company.

IV. Go, wiser thou! and, in thy scale of sense,
Weigh thy opinion against Providence;
Call imperfection what thou fancy'st such,
Say, here he gives too little, there too much:
Destroy all creatures for thy sport or gust,
Yet cry, If man's unhappy, God's unjust;
If man alone ingross not Heav'n's high care,
Alone made perfect here, immortal there:　　　120
Snatch from his hand the balance and the rod,
Re-judge his justice, be the God of God.
In pride, in reas'ning pride, our error lies;
All quit their sphere, and rush into the skies.
Pride still is aiming at the blest abodes,
Men would be angels, angels would be gods.
Aspiring to be gods, if angels fell,
Aspiring to be angels, men rebel:
And who but wishes to invert the laws
Of Order, sins against th' Eternal Cause.　　　130

V. Ask for what end the heav'nly bodies shine,
Earth for whose use? Pride answers, " 'Tis for mine:

For me kind Nature wakes her genial pow'r,
Suckles each herb, and spreads out ev'ry flow'r;
Annual for me, the grape, the rose, renew
The juice nectareous, and the balmy dew;
For me, the mine a thousand treasures brings;
For me, health gushes from a thousand springs;
Seas roll to waft me, suns to light me rise;
My footstool earth, my canopy the skies."   140
    But errs not Nature from this gracious end,
From burning suns when livid deaths descend,
When earthquakes swallow, or when tempests sweep
Towns to one grave, whole nations to the deep?
"No," 'tis reply'd, "the first Almighty Cause
Acts not by partial, but by gen'ral laws;
Th' exceptions few; some change since all began:
And what created perfect?"—Why then man?
If the great end be human happiness,
Then Nature deviates; and can man do less?   150
As much that end a constant course requires
Of show'rs and sunshine, as of man's desires;
As much eternal springs and cloudless skies,
As men for ever temp'rate, calm, and wise.
If plagues or earthquakes break not Heav'n's design,
Why then a Borgia, or a Catiline?
Who knows but he whose hand the lightning forms,
Who heaves old ocean, and who wings the storms;
Pours fierce ambition in a Cæsar's mind,
Or turns young Ammon loose to scourge mankind?   160
From pride, from pride, our very reas'ning springs;
Account for moral, as for nat'ral things:
Why charge we Heav'n in those, in these acquit?
In both, to reason right is to submit.
    Better for us, perhaps, it might appear,
Were there all harmony, all virtue here;
That never air or ocean felt the wind;
That never passion discompos'd the mind.
But ALL subsists by elemental strife;
And passions are the elements of life.   170
The gen'ral ORDER, since the whole began,
Is kept in Nature, and is kept in man.
    VI. What would this man? Now upward will he soar,
And little less than angel, would be more;
Now looking downwards, just as griev'd appears

To want the strength of bulls, the fur of bears.
Made for his use all creatures if he call,
Say what their use, had he the pow'rs of all?
Nature to these, without profusion, kind,
The proper organs, proper pow'rs assign'd;   180
Each seeming want compensated of course,
Here with degrees of swiftness, there of force;
All in exact proportion to the state;
Nothing to add, and nothing to abate.
Each beast, each insect, happy in its own:
Is Heav'n unkind to man, and man alone?
Shall he alone, whom rational we call,
Be pleas'd with nothing, if not bless'd with all?
    The bliss of man (could pride that blessing find)
Is not to act or think beyond mankind;   190
No pow'rs of body or of soul to share,
But what his nature and his state can bear.
Why has not man a microscopic eye?
For this plain reason, man is not a fly.
Say what the use, were finer optics giv'n,
T'' inspect a mite, not comprehend the heav'n?
Or touch, if tremblingly alive all o'er,
To smart and agonize at ev'ry pore?
Or quick effluvia darting thro' the brain,
Die of a rose in aromatic pain?   200
If nature thunder'd in his op'ning ears,
And stunn'd him with the music of the spheres,
How would he wish that Heav'n had left him still
The whisp'ring zephyr, and the purling rill?
Who finds not Providence all good and wise,
Alike in what it gives, and what denies?
    VII. Far as creation's ample range extends,
The scale of sensual, mental pow'rs ascends:
Mark how it mounts, to man's imperial race,
From the green myriads in the peopled grass: 210
What modes of sight betwixt each wide extreme,
The mole's dim curtain, and the lynx's beam:
Of smell, the headlong lioness between,
And hound sagacious on the tainted green:
Of hearing, from the life that fills the flood,
To that which warbles thro' the vernal wood:
The spider's touch, how exquisitely fine!
Feels at each thread, and lives along the line:

In the nice bee, what sense so subtly true
From pois'nous herbs extracts the healing dew?   220
How instinct varies in the grov'ling swine,
Compar'd, half-reas'ning elephant, with thine!
'Twixt that, and reason, what a nice barrier;
For ever sep'rate, yet for ever near!
Remembrance and reflection how ally'd;
What thin partitions sense from thought divide:
And middle natures, how they long to join,
Yet never pass th' insuperable line!
Without this just gradation, could they be
Subjected, these to those, or all to thee?   230
The pow'rs of all subdu'd by thee alone,
Is not thy reason all these pow'rs in one?

*Reason
Separates
his*

VIII. See, thro' this air, this ocean, and this earth,
All matter quick, and bursting into birth.
Above, how high, progressive life may go!
Around, how wide! how deep extend below!
Vast chain of Being! which from God began,
Natures æthereal, human, angel, man,
Beast, bird, fish, insect, what no eye can see,
No glass can reach; from Infinite to thee,   240
From thee to Nothing.—On superior pow'rs
Were we to press, inferior might on ours:
Or in the full creation leave a void,
Where, one step broken, the great scale's destroy'd:
From Nature's chain whatever link you strike,
Tenth or ten thousandth, breaks the chain alike.
And, if each system in gradation roll
Alike essential to th' amazing Whole,
The least confusion but in one, not all
That system only, but the Whole must fall.   250
Let earth unbalanc'd from her orbit fly,
Planets and suns run lawless thro' the sky;
Let ruling angels from their spheres be hurl'd,
Being on being wreck'd, and world on world;
Heav'n's whole foundations to their center nod,
And Nature trembles to the throne of God.
All this dread ORDER break—for whom? for thee?
Vile worm!—oh madness! pride! impiety!
IX. What if the foot, ordain'd the dust to tread,
Or hand, to toil, aspir'd to be the head?   260
What if the head, the eye, or ear repin'd

*Everything
is Connected*

To serve mere engines to the ruling Mind?
Just as absurd for any part to claim
To be another, in this gen'ral frame:
Just as absurd, to mourn the tasks or pains,
The great directing MIND of ALL ordains.
    All are but parts of one stupendous whole,
Whose body Nature is, and God the soul;
That, chang'd thro' all, and yet in all the same;
Great in the earth, as in th' æthereal frame;   270
Warms in the sun, refreshes in the breeze,
Glows in the stars, and blossoms in the trees,
Lives thro' all life, extends thro' all extent,
Spreads undivided, operates unspent;
Breathes in our soul, informs our mortal part,
As full, as perfect, in a hair as heart;
As full, as perfect, in vile man that mourns,
As the rapt seraph that adores and burns:
To him no high, no low, no great, no small;
He fills, he bounds, connects, and equals all.   280
    X. Cease then, nor ORDER imperfection name:
Our proper bliss depends on what we blame.
Know thy own point; this kind, this due degree
Of blindness, weakness, Heav'n bestows on thee.
Submit.—In this, or any other sphere,
Secure to be as blest as thou canst bear:
Safe in the hand of one disposing Pow'r,
Or in the natal, or the mortal hour.
All Nature is but Art, unknown to thee;
All Chance, Direction, which thou canst not see;   290
All Discord, Harmony not understood;
All partial Evil, universal Good:
And, spite of pride, in erring reason's spite,
One truth is clear, WHATEVER IS, IS RIGHT.

EPISTLE II

OF THE NATURE AND STATE OF MAN WITH RESPECT TO HIMSELF,
AS AN INDIVIDUAL

    I. Know then thyself, presume not God to scan;
The proper study of mankind is Man.
Plac'd on this isthmus of a middle state,
A being darkly wise, and rudely great:
With too much knowledge for the sceptic side,
With too much weakness for the Stoic's pride,

He hangs between; in doubt to act, or rest;
In doubt to deem himself a god, or beast;
In doubt his mind or body to prefer;
Born but to die, and reas'ning but to err;   10
Alike in ignorance, his reason such,
Whether he thinks too little, or too much:
Chaos of thought and passion, all confus'd;
Still by himself abus'd, or disabus'd;
Created half to rise, and half to fall;
Great lord of all things, yet a prey to all;
Sole judge of truth, in endless error hurl'd:
The glory, jest, and riddle of the world!

    Go, wondrous creature! mount where science guides,
Go, measure earth, weigh air, and state the tides;   20
Instruct the planets in what orbs to run,
Correct old time, and regulate the sun;
Go, soar with Plato to th' empyreal sphere,
To the first good, first perfect, and first fair;
Or tread the mazy round his follow'rs trod,
And quitting sense call imitating God;
As Eastern priests in giddy circles run,
And turn their heads to imitate the sun.
Go, teach Eternal Wisdom how to rule—
Then drop into thyself, and be a fool!   30
    Superior beings, when of late they saw
A mortal man unfold all Nature's law,
Admir'd such wisdom in an earthly shape,
And shew'd a Newton as we shew an ape.

    Could he, whose rules the rapid comet bind,
Describe or fix one movement of his mind?
Who saw its fires here rise, and there descend,
Explain his own beginning, or his end?
Alas what wonder! Man's superior part
Uncheck'd may rise, and climb from art to art;   40
But when his own great work is but begun,
What reason weaves, by passion is undone.
    Trace science then, with modesty thy guide;
First strip off all her equipage of pride;
Deduct what is but vanity, or dress,
Or learning's luxury, or idleness;
Or tricks to shew the stretch of human brain,
Mere curious pleasure, or ingenious pain;
Expunge the whole, or lop th' excrescent parts

Of all our vices have created arts; 50
Then see how little the remaining sum,
Which serv'd the past, and must the times to come!
    II. Two principles in human nature reign;
Self-love, to urge, and reason, to restrain;
Nor this a good, nor that a bad we call,
Each works its end, to move or govern all:
And to their proper operation still,
Ascribe all good; to their improper, ill.
    Self-love, the spring of motion, acts the soul;
Reason's comparing balance rules the whole. 60
Man, but for that, no action could attend,
And, but for this, were active to no end:
Fix'd like a plant on his peculiar spot,
To draw nutrition, propagate, and rot;
Or, meteor-like, flame lawless thro' the void,
Destroying others, by himself destroy'd.
    Most strength the moving principle requires;
Active its task, it prompts, impels, inspires.
Sedate and quiet the comparing lies,
Form'd but to check, delib'rate, and advise. 70
Self-love still stronger, as its objects nigh;
Reason's at distance, and in prospect lie:
That sees immediate good by present sense;
Reason, the future and the consequence.
Thicker than arguments, temptations throng,
At best more watchful this, but that more strong.
The action of the stronger to suspend
Reason still use, to reason still attend.
Attention, habit and experience gains;
Each strengthens reason, and self-love restrains. 80
    Let subtle schoolmen teach these friends to fight,
More studious to divide than to unite;
And grace and virtue, sense and reason split,
With all the rash dexterity of wit.
Wits, just like fools, at war about a name,
Have full as oft no meaning, or the same.
Self-love and reason to one end aspire,
Pain their aversion, pleasure their desire;
But greedy *that*, its object would devour,
This taste the honey, and not wound the flow'r: 90
Pleasure, or wrong or rightly understood,
Our greatest evil, or our greatest good.

III. Modes of self-love the passions we may call:
'Tis real good, or seeming, moves them all:
But since not ev'ry good we can divide,
And reason bids us for our own provide;
Passions, tho' selfish, if their means be fair,
List under reason, and deserve her care;
Those, that imparted, court a nobler aim,
Exalt their kind, and take some virtue's name.   100

In lazy apathy let Stoics boast
Their virtue fix'd; 'tis fix'd as in a frost;
Contracted all, retiring to the breast;
But strength of mind is exercise, not rest:
The rising tempest puts in act the soul,
Parts it may ravage, but preserves the whole.
On life's vast ocean diversely we sail,
Reason the card, but passion is the gale;
Nor God alone in the still calm we find,
He mounts the storm, and walks upon the wind.   110

Passions, like elements, tho' born to fight,
Yet, mix'd and soften'd, in his work unite:
These 'tis enough to temper and employ;
But what composes man, can man destroy?
Suffice that reason keep to Nature's road,
Subject, compound them, follow her and God.
Love, hope, and joy, fair pleasure's smiling train,
Hate, fear, and grief, the family of pain,
These mix'd with art, and to due bounds confin'd,
Make and maintain the balance of the mind: 120
The lights and shades, whose well accorded strife
Gives all the strength and colour of our life.

Pleasures are ever in our hands or eyes;
And when, in act, they cease, in prospect, rise:
Present to grasp, and future still to find,
The whole employ of body and of mind.
All spread their charms, but charm not all alike;
On diff'rent senses diff'rent objects strike;
Hence diff'rent passions more or less inflame,
As strong or weak, the organs of the frame;   130
And hence one Master Passion in the breast,
Like Aaron's serpent, swallows up the rest.

As man, perhaps, the moment of his breath,
Receives the lurking principle of death;
The young disease, that must subdue at length,

Grows with his growth, and strengthens with his strength:
So, cast and mingled with his very frame,
The mind's disease, its Ruling Passion came;
Each vital humour which should feed the whole,
Soon flows to this, in body and in soul: 140
Whatever warms the heart, or fills the head,
As the mind opens, and its functions spread,
Imagination plies her dang'rous art,
And pours it all upon the peccant part.
   Nature its mother, Habit is its nurse;
Wit, Spirit, Faculties, but make it worse;
Reason itself but gives it edge and pow'r,
As Heav'n's blest beam turns vinegar more sowr.
   We, wretched subjects tho' to lawful sway,
In this weak queen, some fav'rite still obey: 150
Ah! if she lend not arms, as well as rules,
What can she more than tell us we are fools?
Teach us to mourn our nature, not to mend,
A sharp accuser, but a helpless friend!
Or from a judge turn pleader, to persuade
The choice we make, or justify it made;
Proud of an easy conquest all along,
She but removes weak passions for the strong:
So, when small humours gather to a gout,
The doctor fancies he has driv'n them out. 160
   Yes, Nature's road must ever be preferr'd;
Reason is here no guide, but still a guard:
'Tis hers to rectify, not overthrow,
And treat this passion more as friend than foe:
A mightier pow'r the strong direction sends,
And sev'ral men impels to sev'ral ends:
Like varying winds, by other passions tost,
This drives them constant to a certain coast.
Let pow'r or knowledge, gold or glory, please,
Or (oft more strong than all) the love of ease; 170
Thro' life 'tis follow'd ev'n at life's expence;
The merchant's toil, the sage's indolence,
The monk's humility, the hero's pride,
All, all alike, find reason on their side.
   Th' eternal art, educing good from ill,
Grafts on this passion our best principle:
'Tis thus the mercury of man is fix'd,
Strong grows the virtue with his nature mix'd;

The dross cements what else were too refin'd,
And in one interest body acts with mind.   180
   As fruits, ungrateful to the planter's care,
On savage stocks inserted, learn to bear;
The surest virtues thus from passions shoot,
Wild nature's vigour working at the root.
What crops of wit and honesty appear
From spleen, from obstinacy, hate, or fear!
See anger, zeal and fortitude supply;
Ev'n av'rice, prudence; sloth, philosophy;
Lust, thro' some certain strainers well refin'd
Is gentle love, and charms all womankind;   190
Envy, to which th' ignoble mind's a slave,
Is emulation in the learn'd or brave;
Nor virtue, male or female, can we name,
But what will grow on pride, or grow on shame.
   Thus Nature gives us (let it check our pride)
The virtue nearest to our vice ally'd:
Reason the bias turns to good from ill,
And Nero reigns a Titus, if he will.
The fiery soul abhor'd in Catiline,
In Decius charms, in Curtius is divine: 200
The same ambition can destroy or save,
And makes a patriot as it makes a knave.
   IV. This light and darkness in our chaos join'd,
What shall divide? The God within the mind.
   Extremes in nature equal ends produce,
In man they join to some mysterious use;
Tho' each by turns the other's bound invade,
As, in some well-wrought picture, light and shade,
And oft so mix, the diff'rence is too nice
Where ends the virtue, or begins the vice.   210
   Fools! who from hence into the notion fall,
That vice or virtue there is none at all.
If white and black blend, soften, and unite
A thousand ways, is there no black or white?
Ask your own heart, and nothing is so plain;
'Tis to mistake them, costs the time and pain.
   V. Vice is a monster of so frightful mien,
As, to be hated, needs but to be seen;
Yet seen too oft, familiar with her face,
We first endure, then pity, then embrace.   220
But where th' extreme of vice, was ne'er agreed:

Ask where's the north? at York, 'tis on the Tweed;
In Scotland, at the Orcades; and there,
At Greenland, Zembla, or the Lord knows where.
No creature owns it in the first degree,
But thinks his neighbour farther gone than he;
Ev'n those who dwell beneath its very zone,
Or never feel the rage, or never own;
What happier natures shrink at with affright,
The hard inhabitant contends is right.   230
   VI. Virtuous and vicious ev'ry man must be,
Few in th' extreme, but all in the degree;
The rogue and fool, by fits, is fair and wise;
And ev'n the best, by fits, what they despise.
'Tis but by parts we follow good or ill;
For, vice or virtue, self directs it still;
Each individual seeks a sev'ral goal;
But Heav'n's great view is One, and that the Whole.
That counter-works each folly and caprice;
That disappoints th' effect of ev'ry vice;   240
That, happy frailties to all ranks apply'd;
Shame to the virgin, to the matron pride,
Fear to the statesman, rashness to the chief,
To kings presumption, and to crowds belief:
That, virtue's ends from vanity can raise,
Which seeks no int'rest, no reward but praise;
And build on wants, and on defects of mind,
The joy, the peace, the glory of mankind.
   Heav'n forming each on other to depend,
A master, or a servant, or a friend,   250
Bids each on other for assistance call,
Till one man's weakness grows the strength of all.
Wants, frailties, passions, closer still ally
The common int'rest, or endear the tie.
To these we owe true friendship, love sincere,
Each home-felt joy that life inherits here;
Yet from the same we learn, in its decline,
Those joys, those loves, those int'rests to resign;
Taught half by reason, half by mere decay,
To welcome death, and calmly pass away.   260
   Whate'er the passion, knowledge, fame, or pelf,
Not one will change his neighbour with himself.
The learn'd is happy nature to explore,
The fool is happy that he knows no more;

The rich is happy in the plenty giv'n,
The poor contents him with the care of Heav'n.
See the blind beggar dance, the cripple sing,
The sot a hero, lunatic a king;
The starving chemist in his golden views
Supremely blest, the poet in his muse.   270

   See some strange comfort ev'ry state attend,
And pride bestow'd on all, a common friend;
See some fit passion ev'ry age supply,
Hope travels thro', nor quits us when we die.

   Behold the child, by Nature's kindly law,
Pleas'd with a rattle, tickled with a straw:
Some livelier plaything gives his youth delight,
A little louder, but as empty quite:
Scarfs, garters, gold, amuse his riper stage;
And beads and pray'r-books are the toys of age: 280
Pleas'd with this bauble still, as that before;
Till tir'd he sleeps, and life's poor play is o'er.

   Meanwhile opinion gilds with varying rays
Those painted clouds that beautify our days;
Each want of happiness by hope supply'd,
And each vacuity of sense by pride:
These build as fast as knowledge can destroy;
In Folly's cup still laughs the bubble, joy;
One prospect lost, another still we gain;
And not a vanity is giv'n in vain;   290
Ev'n mean self-love becomes, by force divine,
The scale to measure others' wants by thine.
See! and confess, one comfort still must rise,
'Tis this, Tho' man's a fool, yet GOD IS WISE.

EPISTLE TO DR. ARBUTHNOT [1] *wit & phys.*

1735 *to Queen Anne*

ADVERTISEMENT TO THE FIRST PUBLICATION OF THIS EPISTLE

This paper is a sort of bill of complaint, begun many years since, and drawn up by snatches, as the several occasions offered. I had no thoughts of publishing it, till it pleased some persons of rank and fortune (the authors of "Verses to the Imitator of Horace," and of an "Epistle to a Doctor of Divinity from a Nobleman at Hampton Court") to attack, in a very extraordinary manner, not only my writings (of which, being public, the public is judge) but my *person*, *morals*, and *family*, whereof, to those who know me not, a truer information may be requisite. Being divided between the necessity to say something of *myself*, and my own laziness to undertake so awkward a task, I thought it the shortest way to put the last hand to this Epistle. If it have anything pleasing, it will be that by which I am most desirous to please, the *truth* and the *sentiment;* and if anything offensive, it will be only to those I am least sorry to offend, *the vicious* or *the ungenerous*.

Many will know their own pictures in it, there being not a circumstance but what is true; but I have, for the most part, spared their *names*, and they may escape being laughed at, if they please.

I would have some of them know, it was owing to the request of the learned and candid friend to whom it is inscribed, that I make not as free use of theirs as they have done of mine. However, I shall have this advantage, and honour, on my side, that whereas, by their proceeding, any abuse may be directed at any man, no injury can possibly be done by mine, since a nameless character can never be found out, but by its *truth* and *likeness*.

P. Shut, shut the door, good John! [2] fatigu'd, I said,
Tie up the knocker! say I'm sick, I'm dead.
The dog-star rages! nay, 'tis past a doubt,
All Bedlam, or Parnassus, is let out:
Fire in each eye, and papers in each hand,
They rave, recite, and madden round the land.
What walls can guard me, or what shades can hide?

[handwritten margin notes: one extreme / Colloq. - Rhythm low, middle to low diction]

1 Dr. John Arbuthnot (1667–1735), wit and physician to Queen Anne, was the moving spirit of the Scriblerus Club, which included Swift, Gay, and Pope. He was the creator of "John Bull" in *The History of John Bull* (1712), "an honest plain-dealing fellow, choleric, bold, and of a very inconstant temper." *The Memoirs of Martinus Scriblerus* (printed in Pope's works in 1741), satirizing dullness and false taste in learning and literature, was largely the work of Arbuthnot. Knowing that he was mortally ill, Arbuthnot asked Pope to continue to write satire "more to reform than chastise," and the *Epistle* was Pope's response. Pope had been attacked by the squibs he mentions in the Advertisement; squibs for which Lord John Hervey and Lady Mary Wortley Montagu were evidently responsible. Pope had quarreled bitterly with Lady Mary about 1727. Pope believed that Lady Mary and Hervey were the authors of the *Pop upon Pope* (1728), telling how Pope had been beaten while he was out walking.

2 John Searle, his old servant.

[handwritten notes at bottom: Bedlam — mad house / Parnassus — mountain of art]

They pierce my thickets, thro' my grot they glide.
By land, by water, they renew the charge,
They stop the chariot, and they board the barge.
No place is sacred, not the church is free,
Ev'n Sunday shines no Sabbath-day to me:
Then from the Mint [3] walks forth the man of rhyme,
Happy! to catch me just at dinner-time.
    Is there a parson much be-mus'd in beer,
A maudlin poetess, a rhyming peer,
A clerk, foredoom'd his father's soul to cross,
Who pens a stanza when he should engross?
Is there, who, lock'd from ink and paper, scrawls
With desp'rate charcoal round his darken'd walls?   20
All fly to Twit'nam, and in humble strain
Apply to me, to keep them mad or vain.
Arthur,[4] whose giddy son neglects the laws,
Imputes to me and my damn'd works the cause:
Poor Cornus [5] sees his frantic wife elope,
And curses wit, and poetry, and Pope.
    Friend to my life! (which did not you prolong,
The world had wanted many an idle song)
What drop or nostrum can this plague remove?
Or which must end me, a fool's wrath or love?   30
A dire dilemma! either way I'm sped,
If foes, they write, if friends, they read me dead.
Seiz'd and ty'd down to judge, how wretched I!
Who can't be silent and who will not lye:
To laugh, were want of goodness and of grace,
And to be grave exceeds all pow'r of face.
I sit with sad civility, I read
With honest anguish and an aching head;
And drop at last, but in unwilling ears,
This saving counsel, "Keep your piece nine years."   40
    "Nine years!" cries he who, high in Drury Lane,
Lull'd by soft zephyrs thro' the broken pane,
Rhymes ere he wakes, and prints before Term [6] ends,
Oblig'd by hunger, and request of friends:
    "The piece, you think, is incorrect? why take it:
I'm all submission, what you'd have it, make it."

---

3 Debtors were exempt from arrest in the district of the Mint; debtors in all London were exempt from arrest on Sunday.

4 Arthur Moore, a politician; father of the poetaster James Moore.

5 Sir Robert Walpole's wife left him in 1734; the Latin for "horn" is *cornus*.

6 A session of the law courts.

Three things another's modest wishes bound,
My friendship, and a prologue, and ten pound.
Pitholeon [7] sends to me: "You know his Grace:
I want a patron; ask him for a place."   50
Pitholeon libell'd me—"But here's a letter
Informs you, Sir, 'twas when he knew no better.
Dare you refuse him? Curll [8] invites to dine;
He'll write a *Journal*, or he'll turn divine."
    Bless me! a packet.—" 'T is a stranger sues,
A virgin tragedy, an orphan Muse."
If I dislike it, "Furies, death, and rage!"
If I approve, "Commend it to the stage."
There (thank my stars) my whole commission ends,
The play'rs and I are, luckily, no friends.   60
Fir'd that the house reject him, " 'Sdeath I'll print it,
And shame the fools—your int'rest, Sir, with Lintot." [9]
"Lintot, dull rogue! will think your price too much."
"Not, Sir, if you revise it, and retouch."
All my demurs but double his attacks;
At last he whispers, "Do; and we go snacks."
Glad of a quarrel, strait I clap the door,
"Sir, let me see your works and you no more."
    'Tis sung, when Midas' ears began to spring
(Midas, a sacred person and a king),   70
His very minister who spy'd them first
(Some say his queen) was forc'd to speak, or burst.
And is not mine, my friend, a sorer case,
When ev'ry coxcomb perks them in my face?
A. Good friend, forbear! you deal in dang'rous things;
I'd never name queens, ministers, or kings.
Keep close to ears, and those let asses prick;
'Tis nothing—*P.* Nothing? if they bite and kick?
Out with it, *Dunciad!* let the secret pass,
That secret to each fool, that he's an ass.   80
The truth once told (and wherefore should we lie?),
The queen of Midas slept, and so may I.
    You think this cruel? Take it for a rule,
No creature smarts so little as a fool.
Let peals of laughter, Codrus! [10] round thee break,
Thou unconcern'd canst hear the mighty crack:

7 A poetaster of Rhodes; evidently a reference to Leonard Welsted, a minor poet and translator.
8 Edmund Curll, the piratical publisher.
9 Bernard Lintot, the publisher of many of Pope's works.
10 A poet satirized by Juvenal.

Pit, box, and gall'ry in convulsions hurl'd,
Thou stand'st unshook amidst a bursting world.
Who shames a scribler? break one cobweb thro',
He spins the slight, self-pleasing thread anew: 90
Destroy his fib or sophistry, in vain,
The creature's at his dirty work again,
Thron'd in the center of his thin designs,
Proud of a vast extent of flimzy lines!
Whom have I hurt? has poet yet, or peer
Lost the arch'd eyebrow, or Parnassian sneer?
And has not Colley [11] still his lord, and whore?
His butchers Henley, his free-masons Moore?
Does not one table Bavius still admit?
Still to one bishop Philips seem a wit?   100
Still Sappho—A. Hold! for God's sake—you'll offend,
No names—be calm—learn prudence of a friend.
I too could write, and I am twice as tall;
But foes like these—P. One flatt'rer's worse than all.
Of all mad creatures, if the learn'd are right,
It is the slaver kills, and not the bite.
A fool quite angry is quite innocent:
Alas! 'tis ten times worse when they repent.
    One dedicates in high heroic prose,
And ridicules beyond a hundred foes: 110
One from all Grub Street will my fame defend,
And, more abusive, calls himself my friend.
This prints my letters, that expects a bribe,
And others roar aloud, "Subscribe, subscribe."
    There are, who to my person pay their court:
I cough like Horace, and, tho' lean, am short,
Ammon's great son [12] one shoulder had too high,
Such Ovid's nose, and, "Sir! you have an eye"—
Go on, obliging creatures, make me see
All that disgrac'd my betters, met in me: 120
Say for my comfort, languishing in bed,
"Just so immortal Maro held his head":
And when I die, be sure you let me know
Great Homer dy'd three thousand years ago.

11 Colley Cibber, actor, dramatist, and poet laureate; the hero of the second *Dunciad.* "Orator" John Henley preached to the "butchers" and other tradesmen in market places in London. James Moore was the son of the Arthur Moore of l. 23. Bavius was a poetaster of the first century A.D. Ambrose Philips, author of the *Pastorals,* was patronized by Bishop Hugh Boulter. Sappho is Pope's term for Lady Mary Wortley Montagu.

12 Alexander the Great, traditionally descended from Jupiter Ammon.

Why did I write? what sin to me unknown
Dipt me in ink, my parents', or my own?
As yet a child, nor yet a fool to fame,
I lisp'd in numbers, for the numbers came.
I left no calling for this idle trade,
No duty broke, no father disobey'd.
The Muse but serv'd to ease some friend, not wife,
To help me thro' this long disease, my life,
To second, Arbuthnot! thy art and care,   130
And teach the being you preserv'd, to bear.
    But why then publish? Granville [13] the polite,
And knowing Walsh, would tell me I could write;
Well-natur'd Garth inflam'd with early praise;
And Congreve lov'd, and Swift endur'd my lays;
The courtly Talbot, Somers, Sheffield read,[14]
Ev'n mitred Rochester [15] would nod the head,   140
And St. John's self (great Dryden's friends before)
With open arms receiv'd one poet more.
Happy my studies, when by these approv'd!
Happier their author, when by these belov'd!
From these the world will judge of men and books,
Not from the Burnets, Oldmixons, and Cookes.[16]
    Soft were my numbers; who could take offense,
While pure description held the place of sense?
Like gentle Fanny's [17] was my flow'ry theme,
A painted mistress, or a purling stream.   150
Yet then did Gildon [18] draw his venal quill;
I wish'd the man a dinner, and sate still.
Yet then did Dennis rave in furious fret;
I never answer'd—I was not in debt.
If want provok'd, or madness made them print,
I wag'd no war with Bedlam or the Mint.
    Did some more sober critic come abroad?
If wrong, I smil'd; if right, I kiss'd the rod.
Pains, reading, study are their just pretence,
And all they want is spirit, taste, and sense.   160
Commas and points they set exactly right,

13 George Granville, Lord Lansdowne, the politician to whom Pope dedicated *Windsor Forest*.
14 Charles Talbot, Duke of Shrewsbury; John, Baron Somers, Lord Chancellor; and John Sheffield, Duke of Buckingham.
15 Francis Atterbury, Bishop of Rochester.
16 Burnets, etc.—Authors of secret and scandalous history. [Pope]
17 Fanny and Sporus were Pope's names for Lord Hervey, friend of Lady Mary Wortley Montagu.
18 Charles Gildon was believed by Pope to have written at least part of the *True Character of Mr. Pope* (1716), perhaps at the suggestion of Addison.

And 'twere a sin to rob them of their mite.
Yet ne'er one sprig of laurel grac'd these ribalds,
From slashing Bentley down to piddling Tibbalds.[19]
Each wight who reads not, and but scans and spells,
Each word-catcher, that lives on syllables,
Ev'n such small critics some regard may claim,
Preserv'd in Milton's or in Shakespear's name.
Pretty! in amber to observe the forms
Of hairs, or straws, or dirt, or grubs, or worms![17]
The things, we know, are neither rich nor rare,
But wonder how the devil they got there.

Were others angry: I excus'd them too:
Well might they rage, I gave them but their due.
A man's true merit 'tis not hard to find,
But each man's secret standard in his mind,
That casting-weight pride adds to emptiness,
This, who can gratify? for who can guess?
The bard whom pilfer'd pastorals renown,
Who turns a Persian tale for half a crown,[20]   180
Just writes to make his barrenness appear,
And strains from hard-bound brains eight lines a year;
He, who still wanting, tho' he lives on theft,
Steals much, spends little, yet has nothing left;
And he, who now to sense, now nonsense leaning,
Means not, but blunders round about a meaning;
And he, whose fustian's so sublimely bad,
It is not poetry, but prose run mad:
All these, my modest satire bade translate,
And own'd that nine such poets made a Tate.[21]   190
How did they fume, and stamp, and roar, and chafe!
And swear, not Addison himself was safe.

    Peace to all such! But were there one [22] whose fires
True genius kindles and fair fame inspires;
Blest with each talent and each art to please,
And born to write, converse, and live with ease:

[margin notes, handwritten:] pretense, want / sense though— / two things / linked closely / preserve in / amber of Shakes.— / tendency's down

[left margin, handwritten:] Addison / portrait

19 Richard Bentley, the Cambridge scholar who had "slashed" Sir William Temple, Swift's patron, in the Phalaris controversy. Bentley is supposed to have remarked that Pope's translation of the *Iliad* was "a pretty poem, but not Homer." Lewis Theobald was hero of the first *Dunciad*.

20 Ambrose Philips had printed a volume of *Persian Tales*.

21 Nahum Tate, laureate from 1692 to 1715.

22 The celebrated portrait of Atticus, or Addison. Pope suspected that Addison, with his "little senate" at Button's Coffeehouse, had instigated attacks on him. He suspected that Addison had encouraged Tickell to translate the *Iliad* exactly while Pope was doing so, and that Addison had inspired Charles Gildon's attack on Pope in a *Life of Wycherley*.

Should such a man, too fond to rule alone,
Bear, like the Turk, no brother near the throne,
View him with scornful, yet with jealous eyes,
And hate for arts that caus'd himself to rise;   200
Damn with faint praise, assent with civil leer,
And without sneering, teach the rest to sneer;
Willing to wound, and yet afraid to strike,
Just hint a fault, and hesitate dislike;
Alike reserv'd to blame, or to commend,
A tim'rous foe, and a suspicious friend;
Dreading ev'n fools, by flatterers besieg'd,
And so obliging, that he ne'er oblig'd;
Like Cato, give his little senate laws,
And sit attentive to his own applause;   210
While wits and Templars ev'ry sentence raise,
And wonder with a foolish face of praise—
Who but must laugh, if such a man there be?
Who would not weep, if ATTICUS were he!
    What tho' my name stood rubric on the walls,
Or plaister'd posts, with claps,[23] in capitals?
Or smoking forth, a hundred hawkers' load,
On wings of winds came flying all abroad?
I sought no homage from the race that write;
I kept, like Asian monarchs, from their sight: 220
Poems I heeded (now be-rym'd so long)
No more than thou, great George![24] a birthday song.
I ne'er with wits or witlings pass'd my days,
To spread about the itch of verse and praise;
Nor like a puppy, daggled thro' the town,
To fetch and carry sing-song up and down;
Nor at rehearsals sweat, and mouth'd, and cry'd,
With handkerchief and orange at my side;
But sick of fops, and poetry, and prate,
To Bufo[25] left the whole Castalian state.   230
    Proud as Apollo on his forked hill,
Sat full-blown Bufo, puff'd by ev'ry quill;
Fed with soft dedication all day long,
Horace and he went hand in hand in song.
His library (where busts of poets dead
And a true Pindar stood without a head)

---

23 Posters.
24 George II.

25 Charles Montagu, Lord Halifax, patron of Tickell; the latter's translation of
the *Iliad* rivaled Pope's.

Receiv'd of wits an undistinguish'd race,
Who first his judgment ask'd, and then a place:
Much they extoll'd his pictures, much his seat,
And flatter'd ev'ry day, and some days eat: 240
Till grown more frugal in his riper days,
He paid some bards with port, and some with praise,
To some a dry rehearsal was assign'd,
And others (harder still) he paid in kind.
Dryden alone (what wonder?) came not nigh,
Dryden alone escap'd this judging eye:
But still the great have kindness in reserve,
He help'd to bury whom he help'd to starve.
    May some choice patron bless each grey-goose quill!
May ev'ry Bavius have his Bufo still!   250
So when a statesman wants a day's defence,
Or envy holds a whole week's war with sense,
Or simple pride for flatt'ry makes demands,
May dunce by dunce be whistled off my hands!
Blest be the great! for those they take away,
And those they left me—for they left me Gay;
Left me to see neglected genius bloom,
Neglected die, and tell it on his tomb:
Of all thy blameless life the sole return
My verse and Queensb'ry [26] weeping o'er thy urn!   260
    Oh, let me live my own, and die so too!
(To live and die is all I have to do:)
Maintain a poet's dignity and ease,
And see what friends, and read what books I please:
Above a patron, tho' I condescend
Sometimes to call a minister my friend.
I was not born for courts or great affairs;
I pay my debts, believe, and say my pray'rs;
Can sleep without a poem in my head,
Nor know, if Dennis be alive or dead.   270
    Why am I ask'd what next shall see the light?
Heav'ns! was I born for nothing but to write?
Has life no joys for me? or (to be grave)
Have I no friend to serve, no soul to save?
"I found him close with Swift"—"Indeed? no doubt,"
Cries prating Balbus,[27] "something will come out."
'Tis all in vain, deny it as I will:

26 The Duke of Queensbury, and his wife,   27 George Hay, Earl of Kinnoul, with
patrons of John Gay.   whom Pope had quarreled (?).

"No, such a genius never can lye still";
And then for mine obligingly mistakes
The first lampoon Sir Will or Bubo [28] makes.   280
Poor guiltless I! and can I chuse but smile,
When ev'ry coxcomb knows me by my style?

   Curs'd be the verse, how well soe'er it flow,
That tends to make one worthy man my foe,
Give virtue scandal, innocence a fear,
Or from the soft-ey'd virgin steal a tear!
But he who hurts a harmless neighbour's peace,
Insults fall'n worth, or beauty in distress,
Who loves a lie, lame slander helps about,
Who writes a libel, or who copies out: 290
That fop, whose pride affects a patron's name,
Yet absent, wounds an author's honest fame;
Who can your merit selfishly approve,
And show the sense of it without the love;
Who has the vanity to call you friend,
Yet wants the honour, injur'd, to defend;
Who tells whate'er you think, whate'er you say,
And, if he lye not, must at least betray:
Who to the *Dean* and *silver bell* can swear,[29]
And sees at Canons what was never there: 300
Who reads, but with a lust to misapply,
Make satire a lampoon, and fiction lye.
A lash like mine no honest man shall dread,
But all such babbling blockheads in his stead.

   Let Sporus [30] tremble—*A.* What? that thing of silk,
Sporus, that mere white curd of ass's milk?
Satire or sense, alas! can Sporus feel?
Who breaks a butterfly upon a wheel?

   P. Yet let me flap this bug with gilded wings,
This painted child of dirt, that stinks and stings;   310
Whose buzz the witty and the fair annoys,
Yet wit ne'er tastes, and beauty ne'er enjoys:
So well-bred spaniels civilly delight
In mumbling of the game they dare not bite.
Eternal smiles his emptiness betray,
As shallow streams run dimpling all the way.

28 Sir William Yonge, Whig politician; and Bubb Dodington, time-serving politician and tasteless patron of letters.

29 Meaning the man who would have persuaded the Duke of Chandos that Mr. P.

meant him in those circumstances ridiculed in the Epistle on Taste. [Pope]

30 The famous and embittered attack on Lord Hervey.

Whether in florid impotence he speaks,
And, as the prompter breathes, the puppet squeaks;
Or at the ear of Eve, familiar toad,
Half froth, half venom, spits himself abroad,　　320
In puns, or politics, or tales, or lies,
Or spite, or smut, or rhymes, or blasphemies;
His wit all sea-saw, between *that* and *this*,
Now high, now low, now master up, now miss,
And he himself one vile antithesis.
Amphibious thing! that acting either part,
The trifling head or the corrupted heart,
Fop at the toilet, flatt'rer at the board,
Now trips a lady, and now struts a lord.
Eve's tempter thus the Rabbins have exprest,　　330
A cherub's face, a reptile all the rest,
Beauty that shocks you, parts that none will trust,
Wit that can creep, and pride that licks the dust.

　　Not Fortune's worshipper, nor Fashion's fool,
Not Lucre's madman, nor Ambition's tool,
Not proud, nor servile, be one poet's praise,
That, if he pleas'd, he pleas'd by manly ways;
That flatt'ry, ev'n to kings, he held a shame,
And thought a lye in verse or prose the same,
That not in fancy's maze he wander'd long,　　340
But stoop'd to truth and moraliz'd his song:
That not for fame, but virtue's better end,
He stood the furious foe, the timid friend,
The damning critic, half-approving wit,
The coxcomb hit, or fearing to be hit;
Laugh'd at the loss of friends he never had,
The dull, the proud, the wicked, and the mad;
The distant threats of vengeance on his head,
The blow unfelt, the tear he never shed; [31]
The tale reviv'd, the lye so oft o'erthrown,　　350
Th' imputed trash, and dulness not his own;
The morals blacken'd when the writings 'scape,
The libel'd person, and the pictur'd shape; [32]
Abuse, on all he lov'd, or lov'd him, spread,
A friend in exile, or a father, dead;

---

[31] Evidently a denial of the story in the *Pop upon Pope* (supposed to have been written by Lady Mary Wortley Montagu and Lord Hervey) that when Pope was beaten he shed tears.

[32] Pope was represented in caricature (that by Hogarth, for example) as being hunchbacked.

The whisper that to greatness still too near,
Perhaps, yet vibrates on his sov'reigns ear—
Welcome for thee, fair Virtue! all the past:
For thee, fair Virtue! welcome ev'n the last!
    A. But why insult the poor, affront the great?   360
    P. A knave's a knave, to me, in ev'ry state:
Alike my scorn, if he succeed or fail,
Sporus at court, or Japhet [33] in a jail,
A hireling scribler, or a hireling peer,
Knight of the post corrupt,[34] or of the shire;
If on a pillory, or near a throne,
He gain his prince's ear, or lose his own.
    Yet soft by nature, more a dupe than wit,
Sappho can tell you how this man was bit;
This dreaded sat'rist Dennis will confess   370
Foe to his pride, but friend to his distress;
So humble he has knock'd at Tibbald's door,
Has drunk with Cibber, nay has rhym'd for Moore.
Full ten years slander'd, did he once reply?
Three thousand suns went down on Welsted's lye.[35]
To please a mistress one aspers'd his life;
He lash'd him not, but let her be his wife;[36]
Let Budgell charge low Grub Street on his quill,
And write whate'er he pleas'd, except his will.[37]
Let the two Curlls [38] of town and court, abuse   380
His father, mother, body, soul, and Muse.
Yet why? that father held it for a rule,
It was a sin to call our neighbour fool;
That harmless mother thought no wife a whore:
Hear this, and spare his family, James Moore! [39]
Unspotted names, and memorable long!
If there be force in virtue, or in song.
    Of gentle blood (part shed in honour's cause,
While yet in Britain honour had applause)
Each parent sprung.—*A*. What fortune, pray?

---

33 Japhet Crook had lost his nose and ears as punishment for forging.

34 "Knights of the post" waited near sheriff's posts outside courts to sell their testimony to whoever would pay for it.

35 Leonard Welsted in *Of Dullness and Scandal* had implied that "Mr. P. had occasioned a lady's death" (cp. Pope's "Verses to the Memory of an Unfortunate Lady"); he had also "published that he libeled the Duke of Chandos."

36 Teresa Blount (?).

37 Eustace Budgell, one of the followers of Addison who had attacked Pope in the *Bee* and was suspected to have forged a will.

38 Edmund Curll and Lord Hervey, both "publishers" of scandal.

39 James Moore, who had abused Pope, was reputedly illegitimate.

—P. Their own,　　　　　　　　　　　　　　　390
And better got, than Bestia's [40] from the throne.
Born to no pride, inheriting no strife,
Nor marrying discord in a noble wife, [41]
Stranger to civil and religious rage,
The good man walk'd innoxious thro' his age.
No courts he saw, no suits would ever try,
Nor dar'd an oath, nor hazarded a lye.
Unlearn'd, he knew no schoolman's subtle art,
No language, but the language of the heart.
By nature honest, by experience wise,　　　400
Healthy by temp'rance, and by exercise;
His life, tho' long, to sickness past unknown,
His death was instant, and without a groan.
Oh grant me thus to live, and thus to die!
Who sprung from kings shall know less joy than I.

O Friend! may each domestic bliss be thine!
Be no unpleasing melancholy mine:
Me, let the tender office long engage,
To rock the cradle of reposing age,
With lenient arts extend a mother's breath,　　410
Make languor smile, and smooth the bed of death;
Explore the thought, explain the asking eye,
And keep a while one parent from the sky! [42]
On cares like these if length of days attend,
May Heav'n, to bless those days, preserve my friend,
Preserve him social, chearful, and serene,
And just as rich as when he serv'd a queen!

A. Whether that blessing be deny'd or giv'n,
Thus far was right, the rest belongs to Heav'n.

EPIGRAM ENGRAVED ON THE COLLAR OF A DOG

1738

I am His Highness' dog at Kew:
Pray tell me, Sir, whose dog are you?

[40] L. Capurnius Bestia was a Roman pro-
consul who accepted bribes; Pope probably
refers to the emoluments received by the
Duke of Marlborough.

[41] Addison had married the Countess of
Warwick, and apparently was not happy in
his domestic life.
[42] Pope's mother had died in 1733; this
poem was published in January, 1735.

THE UNIVERSAL PRAYER

1738

Father of All! in ev'ry age,
   In ev'ry clime ador'd,
By saint, by savage, and by sage,
   Jehovah, Jove, or Lord!

Thou Great First Cause, least understood:
   Who all my sense confin'd
To know but this, that thou art good,
   And that myself am blind;

Yet gave me, in this dark estate,
   To see the good from ill;
And binding Nature fast in Fate,
   Left free the human will.

What conscience dictates to be done,
   Or warns me not to do,
This, teach me more than Hell to shun,
   That, more than Heav'n pursue.

What blessings thy free bounty gives,
   Let me not cast away;
For God is paid when man receives,
   T' enjoy is to obey.

Yet not to earth's contracted span,
   Thy goodness let me bound,
Or think thee Lord alone of man,
   When thousand worlds are round:

Let not this weak, unknowing hand
   Presume thy bolts to throw,
And deal damnation round the land,
   On each I judge thy foe.

If I am right, thy grace impart,
　　Still in the right to stay;   30
If I am wrong, oh teach my heart
　　To find that better way.

Save me alike from foolish pride,
　　Or impious discontent,
At aught thy wisdom has deny'd,
　　Or aught thy goodness lent.

Teach me to feel another's woe,
　　To hide the fault I see;
That mercy I to others show,
　　That mercy show to me.   40

Mean tho' I am, not wholly so
　　Since quicken'd by thy breath;
Oh lead me wheresoe'er I go,
　　Thro' this day's life or death.

This day, be bread and peace my lot:
　　All else beneath the sun,
Thou know'st if best bestow'd or not,
　　And let thy will be done.

To thee, whose temple is all space,
　　Whose altar, earth, sea, skies!
One chorus let all being raise!   50
　　All Nature's incense rise!

A SELECTION

William Law
1686–1761

A SERIOUS CALL TO A DEVOUT AND HOLY LIFE
1728

[Although William Law is among the most distinguished of English
mystics (he was a follower, like Blake, of Jacob Boehme) everyone

chooses to consider his more "practical" and evangelical piety, and to regard him as the particular inspiration of John and Charles Wesley and the entire Methodist revival.]

CHAPTER I

DEVOTION is neither private nor public prayer; but prayers, whether private or public, are particular parts or instances of devotion. Devotion signifies a life given, or devoted, to God.

He, therefore, is the devout man who lives no longer to his own will, or the way and spirit of the world, but to the sole will of God; who considers God in everything, who serves God in everything, who makes all the parts of his common life parts of piety by doing everything in the name of God and under such rules as are conformable to his glory.

We readily acknowledge that God alone is to be the rule and measure of our prayers; that in them we are to look wholly unto him, and act wholly for him; that we are only to pray in such a manner, for such things and such ends, as are suitable to his glory.

Now let any one but find out the reason why he is to be thus strictly pious in his prayers, and he will find the same as strong a reason to be as strictly pious in all the other parts of his life. For there is not the least shadow of a reason why we should make God the rule and measure of our prayers, why we should then look wholly unto him, and pray according to his will, but what equally proves it necessary for us to look wholly unto God, and make him the rule and measure of all the other actions of our life. For any ways of life, any employment of our talents, whether of our parts, our time, or money, that is not strictly according to the will of God, that is not for such ends as are suitable to his glory, are as great absurdities and failings as prayers that are not according to the will of God. For there is no other reason why our prayers should be according to the will of God, why they should have nothing in them but what is wise and holy and heavenly; there is no other reason for this but that our lives may be of the same nature, full of the same wisdom, holiness, and heavenly tempers, that we may live unto God in the same spirit that we pray unto him. Were it not our strict duty to live by reason, to devote all the actions of our lives to God, were it not absolutely necessary to walk before him in wisdom and holiness and all heavenly conversation, doing everything in his name and for his glory, there would be no excellency or wisdom in the most heavenly prayers. Nay, such prayers would be absurdities; they would be like prayers for wings when it was no part of our duty to fly.

As sure, therefore, as there is any wisdom in praying for the Spirit of God, so sure is it that we are to make that Spirit the rule of all our actions; as sure as it is our duty to look wholly unto God in our prayers, so sure is it that it is our duty to live wholly unto God in our lives. But we can no more be said to live unto God unless we live unto him in all the ordinary actions of our life, unless he be the rule and measure of all our ways, than we can be said to pray unto God, unless our prayers look wholly unto him. So that unreasonable and absurd ways of life, whether in labor or diversion, whether they consume our time or our money, are like unreasonable and absurd prayers, and are as truly an offense unto God.

It is for want of knowing, or at least considering this, that we see such a mixture of ridicule in the lives of many people. You see them strict as to some times and places of devotion, but when the service of the church is over, they are but like those that seldom or never come there. In their way of life, their manner of spending their time and money, in their cares and fears, in their pleasures and indulgences, in their labor and diversions, they are like the rest of the world. This makes the loose part of the world generally make a jest of those that are devout, because they see their devotion goes no farther than their prayers, and that when they are over, they live no more unto God, till the time of prayer returns again; but live by the same humor and fancy, and in as full an enjoyment of all the follies of life as other people. This is the reason why they are the jest and scorn of careless and worldly people; not because they are really devoted to God, but because they appear to have no other devotion but that of occasional prayers. . . .

CHAPTER IV

A tradesman may justly think that it is agreeable to the will of God for him to sell such things as are innocent and useful in life, such as help both himself, and others, to a reasonable support, and enable them to assist those that want to be assisted. But if, instead of this, he trades only with regard to himself, without any other rule than that of his own temper; if it be his chief end in it to grow rich that he may live in figure and indulgence, and to be able to retire from business to idleness and luxury, his trade, as to him, loses all its innocency, and is so far from being an acceptable service to God that it is only a more plausible course of covetousness, self-love, and ambition. For such a one turns the necessities of employment into pride and covetousness, just as the sot and epicure turn the necessities of eating and drinking into gluttony and drunkenness. Now he that is up early and late, that sweats and labors for these ends, that he may be some time or other rich, and live in pleasure and indulgence, lives no more to the glory of God than he that plays and games for the same ends. For though there is a great difference between trading and gaming, yet most of that difference is lost when men once trade with the same desires and tempers, and for the same ends that others game. Charity and fine dressing are things very different; but if men give alms for the same reasons that others dress fine, only to be seen and admired, charity is then but like the vanity of fine clothes. In like manner, if the same motives make some people painful and industrious in their trades, which make others constant at gaming, such pains are but like the pains of gaming.

Calidus has traded above thirty years in the greatest city of the kingdom: he has been so many years constantly increasing his trade and his fortune. Every hour of the day is with him an hour of business; and though he eats and drinks very heartily, yet every meal seems to be in a hurry, and he would say grace if he had time. Calidus ends every day at the tavern, but has not leisure to be there till near nine o'clock. He is always forced to drink a good hearty glass to drive thoughts of business out of his head, and make his spirits drowsy enough for sleep. He does business all the time that he is rising, and has settled several matters before he can get to his counting room. His prayers are a short ejaculation or two, which he never misses in stormy, tempestuous weather, because he has always something or other at sea. Calidus will tell you, with great pleasure, that he has been in this hurry for so many years, and that it must have killed him long ago but that it has been a rule with him to get out of town every Saturday, and make Sunday a day of quiet, and good refreshment in the country.

He is now so rich that he would leave off his business, and amuse his old age with building and furnishing a fine house in the country, but that he is afraid he should grow melancholy if he was to quit his business. He will tell you with great gravity, that it is a dangerous thing for a man that has been used to get money, ever to leave it off. If thoughts of religion happen at any time to steal into his head, Calidus contents himself with thinking that he never was a friend to heretics, and infidels, that he has always been civil to the minister of his parish, and very often given something to the charity schools.

Now this way of life is at such a distance from all the doctrines and discipline of Christianity that no one can live in it through ignorance or frailty. Calidus can no more imagine that he is "born again of the Spirit"; that he is "in Christ a new creature"; that he lives "here as a stranger and a pilgrim, setting his affections on things above, and laying up treasures in heaven"—he can no more imagine this than he can think that he has been all his life an Apostle working miracles, and preaching the Gospel.

It must also be owned that the generality of trading people, especially in great towns, are too much like Calidus. You see them all the week buried in business, unable to think of anything else; and then spending the Sunday in idleness and refreshment, in wandering into the country, in such visits and jovial meetings as make it often the worst day of the week.

Now they do not live thus because they cannot support themselves with less care and application to business; but they live thus because they want to grow rich in their trades, and to maintain their families in some such figure and degree of finery as a reasonable Christian life has no occasion for. Take away but this temper, and then people of all trades will find themselves at leisure to live every day like Christians, to be careful of every duty of the Gospel, to live in a visible course of religion, and be every day strict observers both of private and public prayer.

Now the only way to do this is for people to consider their trade as something that they are obliged to devote to the glory of God, something that they are to do only in such a manner as that they may make it a duty to Him. Nothing can be right in business that is not under these rules. . . .

CHAPTER XV

You have seen . . . how early you are to begin your prayers, and what is to be the subject of your first devotions in the morning.

There is one thing still remaining that you must be required to observe, not only as fit and proper to be done, but as such as cannot be neglected without great prejudice to your devotions: and that is to begin all your prayers with a psalm.

This is so right, is so beneficial to devotion, has so much effect upon our hearts, that it may be insisted upon as a common rule for all persons.

I do not mean that you should read over a psalm, but that you should chant or sing one of those psalms, which we commonly call the reading psalms. For singing is as much the proper use of a psalm as devout supplication is the proper use of a form of prayer; and a psalm only read is very much like a prayer that is only looked over.

Now the method of chanting a psalm, such as is used in the colleges in the universities, and in some churches, is such as all persons are capable of. The change of the voice in thus chanting of a psalm is so small and natural that everybody is able to do it, and yet sufficient to raise and keep up the gladness of our hearts.

You are therefore to consider this chanting of a psalm as a necessary beginning of your devotions, as something that is to awaken all that is good and holy within you, that is to call your spirits to their proper duty, to set you in your best posture towards heaven, and tune all the powers of your soul to worship and adoration.

For there is nothing that so clears a way for your prayers, nothing that so disperses dullness of heart, nothing that so purifies the soul from poor and little passions, nothing that so opens heaven, or carries your heart so near it, as these songs of praise.

They create a sense and delight in God, they awaken holy desires, they teach you how to ask, and they prevail with God to give. They kindle a holy flame, they turn your heart into an altar, your prayers into incense, and carry them as a sweet-smelling savor to the throne of grace.

A SELECTION

Joseph Butler

1692–1752

THE ANALOGY OF RELIGION, NATURAL AND REVEALED

1736

[Straddling between revelation and deism, Butler in this profoundly influential work argues that the whole course of nature proves the existence of a God who will reward and punish. Life is a period of "probation." Therefore, if we have not faith, it is at least *prudential* to believe that "our future interest depends upon our present behavior."]

Now the divine government of the world, implied in the notion of religion in general and of Christianity, contains in it: That mankind is appointed to live in a future state; that there everyone shall be rewarded or punished; rewarded or punished respectively for all that behavior here which we comprehended under the words virtuous or vicious, morally good or evil; that our present life is a probation, a state of trial and of discipline, for that future one; notwithstanding the objections, which men may fancy they have, from notions of Necessity, against there being any such moral plan as this at all; and whatever objections may appear to lie against the wisdom and goodness of it, as it stands so imperfectly made known to us at present; that this world being in a state of apostasy and wickedness, and consequently of ruin, and the sense both of their condition and duty being greatly corrupted amongst men, this gave occasion for an additional dispensation of Providence of the utmost importance, proved by miracles, but containing in it many things appearing to us strange, and not to have been expected; a dispensation of Providence, which is a scheme or system of things, carried on by the mediation of a divine person, the Messiah, in order to the recovery of the world; yet not revealed to all men, nor proved with the strongest possible evidence to all those to whom it is revealed; but only to such a part of mankind, and with such particular evidence, as the wisdom of God thought fit. The design, then, of the following treatise will be to show that the several parts principally objected against in this moral and Christian dispensation, including its scheme, its publication, and the proof which God has afforded us of its truths that the particular parts principally objected against in this whole dispensation, are analogous to what is experienced in the constitution of and course of Nature, or Providence; that the chief objections themselves which are alleged against the former are no other than what may be alleged with like justness against the latter where they are found in fact to be inconclusive; and that this argument from analogy is in general unanswerable, and undoubtedly of weight on the side of religion.

[INTRODUCTION]

Nor ought it to be entirely passed over that tranquillity, satisfaction, and external advantages, being the natural consequences of prudent management of ourselves and our affairs; and rashness, profligate negligence, and willful folly, bringing after them many inconveniences and sufferings; these afford instances of a right constitution of nature: as the correction of children, for their own sakes, and by way of example, when they run into danger or hurt themselves, is a part of right education. And thus, that God governs the world by general fixed laws, that he has endued us with capacities of reflecting upon this constitution of things, and foreseeing the good and bad consequences of our behavior, plainly implies some sort of moral government; since from such a constitution of things it cannot but follow that prudence and imprudence, which are of the nature of virtue and vice, must be, as they are, respectively rewarded and punished.

[PART I, chap. iii]

Jonathan Swift

1667–1745

SWIFT'S genius is the most perplexing among the Augustans. Even his personal life raises questions that may never be answered. Did he marry his "perfect friend" Stella? How ought we explain the *Journal to Stella* and the poems to her? How ought we explain his living intimately with her yet never seeing her without the company of a third person? What were his relations with Hester Vanhomrigh, "Vanessa"? Was he always a little mad? Only his genius is certain, and that genius will always strongly attract or strongly repel. In spite of his witty "easy comedy," he admitted the desire to vex the world rather than to divert it. Swift is Augustan in that he speaks the soundest English prose; he is Augustan, too, in that his satire is brilliant and topical. But the satire of Swift is often more than Augustan: it is of cosmic proportions. Behind his scorn of the Anglican Church, the Dissenters, the Roman Catholics, the Irish, women, most Whigs, and many Tories there is an awful arraignment of human nature. Swift cannot justify the ways of man to God, or to his own sense of what is decent and reasonable. An almost maniacal fury at folly and corruption rouses Swift to a severity that is more destructive than Milton's, an anguished sensibility to human failing. In one way, Swift is the most fastidious of men—"A nice man," he wrote, "is a man of nasty ideas." He is so repelled by animalism that he reacts in a hysteria of nastiness. He is so revolted by unrighteousness that he despairs of man with the medieval sin of *desperatio*. The Yahoo is an appalling parody upon the Christian doctrine of man. Only occasionally is Swift driven beside himself, as when at the close of *Gulliver* he accepts a pickpocket, a fool, a lord, a gamester, a politician, a whoremonger, a physician, a suborner, an attorney, or a traitor as "the due course of things: but when I behold a lump of deformity, and diseases both in body and mind, smitten with *pride*, it immediately breaks all measures of my patience." Usually he has a deadly control of understatement, as in the *Modest Proposal* or the diabolical defense of madness in *A Tale of a Tub*. Even his most lenient critics cannot, however, deny a superfluity of foulness, a Rabelaisianism that is not wholesome. Herein is a further paradox. Swift, who himself betrays unsoundness of mind, is above all concerned that man live sanely and reasonably. He is consistently anti-intellectualist, perceiving that man cannot live by his brain alone. Man's reason simply rationalizes, as *A Tale of a Tub* proves; or else it is a sterile incompetence to deal with life, as it is among the Laputians. The Houyhnhnms live by "reason"; but their reason is not rationalism or logic. It is a kind of Socratic ability to deal with situations reasonably and not theoretically, an ability to live well rather than to think systematically. Yet Swift values intelligence as much as he despises affectation. It is hard to say whether he was a religious man; it is hard to say what his creed might have been. His mind is styptic. Few literary experiences can be more humbling than reading his digression on madness or the final chapters of *Gulliver*.

BIOGRAPHICAL NOTES

Born November 30, 1667; said to be the posthumous son of an English father who was steward of the King's Inns, Dublin. Uncles enabled him to attend Trinity College, Dublin (1682–86); took degree "by special grace": *bene* for Greek and Latin, *male* for philosophy, and *negligenter* for theology. Entered the household of Sir William Temple at Moor Park, Surrey, as secretary (1689). Suffered attacks of "giddiness." Tutored Esther Johnson ("Stella"), then seven, daughter of one of Temple's dependents. Told by his cousin John Dryden that he would never be a poet. Took M.A. at Oxford (1692); ordained priest (1694/5); appointed prebend at Kilroot, Ireland. Affair with Jane Waring ("Varina"). Resigned from Kilroot (1698) after returning to Moor Park until the death of Temple. Appointed vicar of Laracor and prebend of St. Patrick's Cathedral, Dublin (1700). Stella and her companion, Rebecca Dingley, followed Swift to Ireland. Published *A Tale of a Tub* and *The Battle of the Books* (1703/4). Frequent trips to England seeking preferment and negotiating Church business. Met Addison and his "little senate" (1707–9). Met Esther Vanhomrigh ("Vanessa") while in England. Abandoned Whigs, edited the Tory *Examiner*, and wrote *Conduct of the Allies* (1710/11). Became one of the Tory wits—Pope, Gay, Arbuthnot, and Prior—and a member of the Brothers' Club. Composed the *Journal to Stella*. Failed of preferment; appointed merely Dean of St. Patrick's, Dublin (1713). Death of Queen Anne (1714); Swift returned to Ireland in bitterness to agitate against the mistreatment of the Irish. (Married Stella?—1716?) Vanessa followed him to Ireland; when she died (1723) she disregarded him in her will.

Swift composed *Drapier's Letters* (1724); went to England to publish *Gulliver* (1726) and to visit old friends. Printed *Miscellanies* with Pope (1727-32). Stella died (1728). Swift began to "die at the top" (*ca.* 1738) and was declared of unsound mind (1741/42). Complete mental eclipse until death (1745). Buried in St. Patrick's near Stella.

BIBLIOGRAPHY: *Prose Works*, ed. H. Davis, 1939- . *Prose Works*, ed. T. Scott, 12 vols., 1907-25. *Poems*, ed. H. Williams, 3 vols., 1958. Bullitt, J. M., *Jonathan Swift and the Anatomy of Satire*, 1953. Davis, H., *The Satire of Jonathan Swift*, 1947; *Stella, a Gentlewoman*, 1942. Ehrenpreis, I., *The Personality of Jonathan Swift*, 1958. Ewald, W. B., *The Masks of Jonathan Swift*, 1954. Gold, M. B., *Swift's Marriage to Stella*, 1937. Greenacre, P., *Swift and Carroll*, 1955. Hardy, E., *The Conjured Spirit, Swift*, 1949. Johnson, M. O., *The Sin of Wit*, 1950. Johnston, D., *In Search of Swift*, 1959. Landa, L., *Swift and the Church of Ireland*, 1954. Murry, J. M., *Jonathan Swift*, 1954. Price, M., *Swift's Rhetorical Art*, 1953. Quintana, R., *The Mind and Art of Jonathan Swift*, 1953; *Swift*, 1955. Van Doren, C., *Swift*, 1930. Watkins, W. B. C., *Perilous Balance: The Tragic Genius of Swift, Johnson, and Sterne*, 1939. Williams, K., *Jonathan Swift and the Age of Compromise*, 1958.

A TALE OF A TUB
1704

SECTION IX

A digression concerning the original, the use, and improvement of madness in a commonwealth

Nor shall it anyways detract from the just reputation of this famous sect[1] that its rise and institution are owing to such an author as I have described Jack to be; a person whose intellectuals were overturned, and his brain shaken out of its natural position; which we commonly suppose to be a distemper, and call by the name of madness or frenzy. For if we take a survey of the greatest actions that have been performed in the world under the influence of single men, which are the establishment of new empires by conquest, the advance and progress of new schemes in philosophy, and the contriving, as well as the propagating, of new religions, we shall find the authors of them all to have been persons whose natural reason had admitted great revolutions, from their diet, their education, the prevalency of some certain temper, together with the particular influence of air and climate. Besides, there is something individual in human minds that easily kindles at the accidental approach and collision of certain circumstances, which, though of paltry and mean appearance, do often flame out into the greatest

---

1 The Aeolists, who "maintain the original cause of all things to be wind." Jack represents the more extreme sects of protestantism.

emergencies of life. For great turns are not always given by strong hands, but by lucky adaption and at proper seasons; and it is of no import where the fire was kindled if the vapor has once got up into the brain. For the upper region of man is furnished like the middle region of the air; the materials are formed from causes of the widest difference, yet produce at last the same substance and effect. Mists arise from the earth, steams from dunghills, exhalations from the sea, and smoke from fire; yet all clouds are the same in composition as well as consequences, and the fumes issuing from a jakes will furnish as comely and useful a vapor as incense from an altar. Thus far, I suppose, will easily be granted me; and then it will follow that, as the face of nature never produces rain but when it is overcast and disturbed, so human understanding, seated in the brain, must be troubled and overspread by vapors ascending from the lower faculties to water the invention and render it fruitful. Now, although these vapors (as it hath been already said) are of as various original as those of the skies, yet the crop they produce differs both in kind and degree, merely according to the soil. I will produce two instances to prove and explain what I am now advancing.

A certain great prince [2] raised a mighty army, filled his coffers with infinite treasures, provided an invincible fleet, and all this without giving the least part of his design to his greatest ministers or his nearest favorites. Immediately the whole world was alarmed; the neighboring crowns in trembling expectation towards what point the storm would burst; the small politicians everywhere forming profound conjectures. Some believed he had laid a scheme for universal monarchy; others, after much insight, determined the matter to be a project for pulling down the Pope, and setting up the reformed religion, which had once been his own. Some, again, of a deeper sagacity, sent him into Asia to subdue the Turk and recover Palestine. In the midst of all these projects and preparations, a certain state-surgeon [3] gathering the nature of the disease by these symptoms, attempted the cure; at one blow performed the operation, broke the bag, and out flew the vapor; nor did anything want to render it a complete remedy, only that the prince unfortunately happened to die in the performance. Now is the reader exceeding curious to learn whence this vapor took its rise,

leveling tendency

2 Henry IV of France.   3 Ravillac, who stabbed Henry the Great in his coach. [Swift]

which had so long set the nations at a gaze? What secret wheel, what hidden spring, could put into motion so wonderful an engine? It was afterwards discovered that the movement of this whole machine had been directed by an absent female, whose eyes had raised a protuberancy, and, before emission, she was removed into an enemy's country. What should an unhappy prince do in such ticklish circumstances as these? He tried in vain the poet's never-failing receipt of *corpora quaeque;* for,

> Idque petit corpus mens unde est saucia amore:
> Unde feritur, eo tendit, gestitque coire.
>
> —LUCR.[4]

Having to no purpose used all peaceable endeavors, the collected part of the semen, raised and inflamed, became adust, converted to choler, turned head upon the spinal duct, and ascended to the brain: the very same principle that influences a bully to break the windows of a whore who has jilted him naturally stirs up a great prince to raise mighty armies and dream of nothing but sieges, battles, and victories.

> ——Teterrima belli
> Causa——[5]

The other instance is what I have read somewhere in a very ancient author, of a mighty king,[6] who, for the space of above thirty years, amused himself to take and lose towns, beat armies, and be beaten, drive princes out of their dominions; fright children from their bread and butter; burn, lay waste, plunder, dragoon, massacre subject and stranger, friend and foe, male and female. It is recorded that the philosophers of each country were in grave dispute upon causes, natural, moral, and political, to find out where they should assign an original solution of this phenomenon. At last, the vapor or spirit which animated the hero's brain, being in perpetual circulation, seized upon that region of the human body so renowned for furnishing the *zibeta occidentalis,*[7] and, gathering there into a tumor, left the rest of the world for that time in

[margin, handwritten: instance of moral blindness of speaker from materialism]

---

4 Lucretius *De Rerum Natura* IV. 1048 ff.: "And the body seeks that object by which the mind is wounded by love. He is drawn towards what wounds him, and is eager to unite with it."

5 Horace *Satires* I. iii. 107: "A most foul cause of war."

6 Louis XIV of France.

7 Paracelsus, who was so famous for chemistry, tried an experiment upon human excrement, to make a perfume of it; which when he had brought to perfection he called *zibeta occidentalis,* or western civet, the back parts of man (according to the division mentioned by the author) being the west. [Swift]

peace. Of such mighty consequence it is where those exhalations fix, and of so little from whence they proceed. The same spirits which, in their superior progress, would conquer a kingdom, descending upon the anus, conclude in a fistula.[8]

Let us next examine the great introducers of new schemes in philosophy, and search till we can find from what faculty of the soul the disposition arises in mortal man of taking it into his head to advance new systems, with such an eager zeal, in things agreed on all hands impossible to be known; from what seeds this disposition springs, and to what quality of human nature these grand innovators have been indebted for their number of disciples. Because it is plain that several of the chief among them, both ancient and modern, were usually mistaken by their adversaries, and indeed by all except their own followers, to have been persons crazed, or out of their wits; having generally proceeded, in the common course of their words and actions, by a method very different from the vulgar dictates of unrefined reason; agreeing for the most part in their several models with their present undoubted successors in the academy of modern Bedlam (whose merits and principles I shall farther examine in due place). Of this kind were Epicurus, Diogenes, Apollonius, Lucretius, Paracelsus, Descartes, and others, who, if they were now in the world, tied fast, and separate from their followers, would, in this our undistinguishing age, incur manifest danger of phlebotomy, and whips, and chains, and dark chambers, and straw. For what man, in the natural state or course of thinking, did ever conceive it in his power to reduce the notions of all mankind exactly to the same length, and breadth, and height of his own? Yet this is the first humble and civil design of all innovators in the empire of reason. Epicurus modestly hoped that, one time or other, a certain fortuitous concourse of all men's opinions, after perpetual justlings, the sharp with the smooth, the light and the heavy, the round and the square, would, by certain *clinamina*,[9] unite in the notions of atoms and void, as these did in the originals of all things. Cartesius reckoned to see, before he died, the sentiments of all philosophers, like so many lesser stars in his romantic system, rapt and drawn within his own vortex. Now I would gladly be informed how it is possible to account for such imaginations as these in particular men without recourse to my

8 A complaint suffered by Louis XIV.
9 The "declinations" of atoms from straight lines into clusters (the theory of Lucretius).

silly + mechanistic — v. Epicurus

phenomenon of vapors ascending from the lower faculties to over-
shadow the brain, and thence distilling into conceptions for which
the narrowness of our mother tongue has not yet assigned any
other name beside that of madness or frenzy. Let us therefore now
conjecture how it comes to pass that none of these great prescribers
do ever fail providing themselves and their notions with a number
of implicit disciples. And I think the reason is easy to be assigned;
for there is a peculiar string in the harmony of human understanding which, in several individuals, is exactly of the same tuning.
This, if you can dextrously screw up to its right key, and then
strike gently upon it, whenever you have the good fortune to light
among those of the same pitch, they will, by a secret necessary
sympathy, strike exactly at the same time. And in this one circumstance lies all the skill or luck of the matter; for, if you chance
to ajar the string among those who are either above or below your
own height, instead of subscribing to your doctrine, they will tie
you fast, call you mad, and feed you with bread and water. It is
therefore a point of the nicest conduct to distinguish and adapt
this noble talent with respect to the differences of persons and of
times. Cicero understood this very well, when writing to a friend
in England, with a caution, among other matters, to beware of
being cheated by our hackney coachmen (who, it seems, in those
days were as arrant rascals as they are now), has these remarkable
words: *Est quod gaudeas te in ista loca venisse, ubi aliquid sapere
viderere.*[10] For to speak a bold truth, it is a fatal miscarriage so ill
to order affairs as to pass for a fool in one company, when in another you might be treated as a philosopher. Which I desire
some certain gentlemen of my acquaintance to lay up in their
hearts as a very seasonable *innuendo*.

This, indeed, was the fatal mistake of that worthy gentleman, my
most ingenious friend, Mr. Wotton;[11] a person in appearance ordained for great designs, as well as performances, whether you
will consider his notions or his looks. Surely no man ever advanced
into the public with fitter qualifications of body and mind for the
propagation of a new religion. Oh, had those happy talents, misapplied to vain philosophy, been turned into their proper channels
of dreams and visions, where distortion of mind and countenance

---

10 *Familiar Letters* VII. x. 1: "You may
rejoice to have come to a place where you
may seem to know something."

11 William Wotton in 1694 attacked Sir
William Temple in defense of modern learn-
ing; Swift, in turn, satirized Wotton in *The
Battle of the Books.*

are of such sovereign use, the base detracting world would not then have dared to report that something is amiss, that his brain has undergone an unlucky shake; which even his brother Modernists themselves, like ungrates, do whisper so loud that it reaches up to the very garret I am now writing in.

Lastly, whosoever pleases to look into the fountains of enthusiasm, from whence, in all ages, have eternally proceeded such fattening streams, will find the springhead to have been as troubled and muddy as the current; of such great emolument is a tincture of this vapor, which the world calls madness, that without its help the world would not only be deprived of those two great blessings, conquests and systems, but even all mankind would unhappily be reduced to the same belief in things invisible. Now the former *postulatum* being held, that it is of no import from what originals this vapor proceeds, but either in what angles it strikes and spreads over the understanding, or upon what species of brain it ascends, it will be a very delicate point to cut the feather and divide the several reasons to a nice and curious reader, how this numerical difference in the brain can produce effects of so vast a difference from the same vapor as to be the sole point of individuation between Alexander the Great, Jack of Leyden, and Monsieur Descartes. The present argument is the most abstracted that ever I engaged in; it strains my faculties to their highest stretch; and I desire the reader to attend with the utmost propensity, for I now proceed to unravel this knotty point.

There is in mankind a certain

* * * * *
* * * * * * *
Hic multa   * * * * *
desiderantur.[12]   * * * *
                            * * * And this I take to be a
clear solution of the matter.

Having therefore so narrowly passed through this intricate difficulty, the reader will, I am sure, agree with me in the conclusion that if the Moderns mean by madness only a disturbance or transposition of the brain, by force of certain vapors issuing up from the lower faculties, then has this madness been the parent

---

12 Here is another defect in the manuscript, but I think the author did wisely, and that the matter which thus strained his faculties was not worth a solution; and it were well if all metaphysical cobweb problems were no otherwise answered. [Swift]

of all those mighty revolutions that have happened in empire, philosophy, and in religion. For the brain in its natural position and state of serenity disposeth its owner to pass his life in the common forms, without any thoughts of subduing multitudes to his own power, his reasons, or his visions; and the more he shapes his understanding by the pattern of human learning, the less he is inclined to form parties after his particular notions, because that instructs him in his private infirmities, as well as in the stubborn ignorance of the people. But when a man's fancy gets astride on his reason; when imagination is at cuffs with the senses, and common understanding, as well as common sense, is kicked out of doors; the first proselyte he makes is himself; and when that is once compassed, the difficulty is not so great in bringing over others; a strong delusion always operating from without as vigorously as from within. For cant and vision are to the ear and the eye the same that tickling is to the touch. Those entertainments and pleasures we most value in life are such as dupe and play the wag with the senses. For if we take an examination of what is generally understood by happiness, as it has respect either to the understanding or the senses, we shall find all its properties and adjuncts will herd under this short definition: that it is a perpetual possession of being well deceived. And, first, with relation to the mind or understanding, it is manifest what mighty advantages fiction has over truth; and the reason is just at our elbow, because imagination can build nobler scenes, and produce more wonderful revolutions, than fortune or nature will be at expense to furnish. Nor is mankind so much to blame in his choice thus determining him, if we consider that the debate merely lies between things past and things conceived; and so the question is only this: whether things that have place in the imagination may not as properly be said to exist as those that are seated in the memory, which may be justly held in the affirmative, and very much to the advantage of the former, since this is acknowledged to be the womb of things, and the other allowed to be no more than the grave. Again, if we take this definition of happiness, and examine it with reference to the senses, it will be acknowledged wonderfully adapt. How fading and insipid do all objects accost us that are not conveyed in the vehicle of delusion! How shrunk is everything as it appears in the glass of nature! So that if it were not for the assistance of artificial mediums, false lights, refracted angles, varnish and tinsel, there would be a mighty level in the felicity and enjoyments of mortal men. If this were seriously considered by the world, as I have a certain reason to suspect it hardly will, men would no longer reckon among their high points of wisdom the art of exposing weak sides and publishing infirmities; an employment, in my opinion, neither better nor worse than that of unmasking, which, I think, has never been allowed fair usage either in the world or the playhouse.

In the proportion that credulity is a more peaceful possession of the mind than curiosity, so far preferable is that wisdom which converses about the surface to that pretended philosophy which enters into the depth of things, and then comes gravely back with informations and discoveries that in the inside they are good for nothing. The two senses to which all objects first address themselves are the sight and the touch; these never examine farther than the color, the shape, the size, and whatever other qualities dwell or are drawn by art upon the outward of bodies; and then comes reason officiously with tools for cutting, and opening, and mangling, and piercing, offering to demonstrate that they are not of the same consistence quite through. Now I take all this to be the last degree of perverting nature; one of whose eternal laws it is to put her best furniture forward. And therefore, in order to save the charges of all such expensive anatomy for the time to come, I do here think fit to inform the reader that in such conclusions as these, reason is certainly in the right, and that in most corporeal beings which have fallen under my cognizance, the *outside* has been infinitely preferable to the *in;* whereof I have been farther convinced from some late experiments. Last week I saw a woman flayed, and you will hardly believe how much it altered her person for the worse. Yesterday I ordered the carcass of a beau to be stripped in my presence, when we were all amazed to find so many unsuspected faults under one suit of clothes. Then I laid open his brain, his heart, and his spleen; but I plainly perceived at every operation that the farther we proceeded we found the defects increase upon us in number and bulk: from all which, I justly formed this conclusion to myself, that whatever philosopher or projector can find out an art to solder and patch up the flaws and imperfections of nature will deserve much better of mankind, and teach us a more useful science than that so much in present esteem, of widening and exposing them, like him who held anatomy to be the ultimate end of physic. And he whose fortunes and dispositions have placed him in a convenient station to enjoy the fruits of this noble art; he that can, with Epicurus, content his ideas with the films and images that fly off upon his senses from the superficies of things; such a man, truly wise, creams off nature, leaving the sour and the dregs for philosophy and reason to lap up. This is the sublime and refined point of felicity, called *the possession of being well deceived;* the serene peaceful state of being a fool among knaves.

But to return to madness. It is certain that, according to the system I have above deduced, every species thereof proceeds from a redundancy of vapors; therefore, as some kinds of frenzy give double strength to the sinews, so there are of other species which add vigor, and life, and spirit to the brain. Now it usually happens that these active spirits, getting possession of the brain, resemble those that haunt other waste and empty dwellings, which, for want of business, either vanish and carry away a piece of the house, or else stay at home and fling it all out of the windows. By which are mystically displayed the two principal branches of madness, and which some philosophers, not considering so well as I, have mistaken to be different in their causes, overhastily assigning the first to deficiency and the other to redundance.

I think it therefore manifest, from what I have here advanced, that the main point of skill and address is to furnish employment for this redundancy of vapor, and prudently to adjust the season of it; by which means it may certainly become of cardinal and catholic emolument in a commonwealth. Thus one man, choosing a proper juncture, leaps into a gulf, from thence proceeds a hero, and is called the saver of his country; another achieves the same enterprise, but, unluckily timing it, has left the brand of madness fixed as a reproach upon his memory; upon so nice a distinction are we taught to repeat the name of Curtius with reverence and love, that of Empedocles with hatred and contempt. Thus also it is usually conceived that the elder Brutus only personated the fool and madman for the good of the public; but this was nothing else than a redundancy of the same vapor long misapplied, called by the Latins *ingenium par negotiis;* or (to translate it as nearly as I can) a sort of frenzy, never in its right element till you take it up in the business of the state.

Upon all which, and many other reasons of equal weight, though not equally curious, I do here gladly embrace an opportunity I have long sought for, of recommending it as a very noble undertaking to Sir Edward Seymour, Sir Christopher Musgrave, Sir John Bowls, John How, Esq., and other patriots concerned, that they would move for leave to bring in a bill for appointing commissioners to inspect into Bedlam, and the parts adjacent; who shall be empowered to send for persons, papers, and records, to examine into the merits and qualifications of every student and professor, to observe with utmost exactness their several dispositions and behavior, by which means, duly distinguishing and adapting their talents, they might produce admirable instruments for the several offices in a state, * * * * civil and military; proceeding in such methods as I shall here humbly propose. And I hope the gentle reader will give some allowance to my great solicitudes in this important affair, upon account of the high esteem I have borne that honorable society, whereof I had some time the happiness to be an unworthy member.

Is any student tearing his straw in piecemeal, swearing and blaspheming, biting his grate, foaming at the mouth, and emptying his pisspot in the spectators' faces? Let the right worshipful the commissioners of inspection give him a regiment of dragoons, and send him into Flanders among the rest. Is another eternally talking, sputtering, gaping, bawling in a sound without period or article? What wonderful talents are here mislaid! Let him be furnished immediately with a green bag and papers, and threepence in his pocket, and away with him to Westminster Hall. You will find a third gravely taking the dimensions of his kennel, a person of foresight and insight, though kept quite in the dark; for why, like Moses, *ecce cornuta erat ejus facies*.[13] He walks duly in one pace, entreats your penny with due gravity and ceremony, talks much of hard times, and taxes, and the whore of Babylon, bars up the wooden window of his cell constantly at eight o'clock, dreams of fire, and shoplifters, and court customers, and privileged places. Now what a figure would all these acquirements amount to if the owner were sent into the City among his brethren! Behold a fourth in much and deep conversation with himself, biting his thumbs at proper junctures, his countenance checkered with business and design; sometimes walking very fast, with his eyes nailed to a paper that he holds in his hands; a great saver of time, somewhat

13 "Behold his face was shining." (*Cornutus* means either "horned" or "shining.")

thick of hearing, very short of sight, but more of memory; a man ever in haste, a great hatcher and breeder of business, and excellent at the famous art of whispering nothing; a huge idolator of monosyllables and procrastination, so ready to give his word to everybody that he never keeps it; one that has forgot the common meaning of words, but an admirable retainer of the sound; extremely subject to the looseness, for his occasions are perpetually calling him away. If you approach his grate in his familiar intervals, "Sir," says he, "give me a penny, and I'll sing you a song; but give me the penny first." (Hence comes the common saying, and commoner practice, of parting with money for a song.) What a complete system of court skill is here described in every branch of it, and all utterly lost with wrong application! Accost the hole of another kennel, first stopping your nose, you will behold a surly, gloomy, nasty, slovenly mortal, raking in his own dung, and dabbling in his urine. The best part of his diet is the reversion of his own ordure, which, expiring into steams, whirls perpetually about, and at last reinfunds. His complexion is of a dirty yellow, with a thin scattered beard, exactly agreeable to that of his diet upon its first declination, like other insects who, having their birth and education in an excrement, from thence borrow their color and their smell. The student of this apartment is very sparing of his words, but somewhat overliberal of his breath; he holds his hand out ready to receive your penny, and immediately upon receipt withdraws to his former occupations. Now is it not amazing to think the society of Warwick Lane [14] should have no more concern for the recovery of so useful a member, who, if one may judge from these appearances, would become the greatest ornament to that illustrious body? Another student struts up fiercely to your teeth, puffing with his lips, half squeezing out his eyes, and very graciously holds you out his hand to kiss. The keeper desires you not to be afraid of this professor, for he will do you no hurt: to him alone is allowed the liberty of the antechamber, and the orator of the place gives you to understand that this solemn person is a tailor run mad with pride. This considerable student is adorned with many other qualities, upon which at present I shall not farther enlarge. * * * Hark in your ear * * * I am strangely mistaken if all his address, his motions, and his airs would not then be very natural, and in their proper element.

14 The Royal College of Physicians.

I shall not descend so minutely as to insist upon the vast number of beaux, fiddlers, poets, and politicians that the world might recover by such a reformation; but what is more material, besides the clear gain redounding to the commonwealth, by so large an acquisition of persons to employ, whose talents and acquirements, if I may be so bold as to affirm it, are now buried, or at least misapplied; it would be a mighty advantage accruing to the public from this inquiry that all these would very much excel and arrive at great perfection in their several kinds; which, I think, is manifest from what I have already shown, and shall enforce by this one plain instance, that even I myself, the author of these momentous truths, am a person whose imaginations are hard-mouthed and exceedingly disposed to run away with his reason, which I have observed, from long experience, to be a very light rider, and easily shaken off; upon which account, my friends will never trust me alone, without a solemn promise to vent my speculations in this or the like manner, for the universal benefit of humankind; which perhaps the gentle, courteous, and candid reader, brimful of that modern charity and tenderness usually annexed to his office, will be very hardly persuaded to believe.

[handwritten: to reveal shocking implications of]

AN ARGUMENT to prove that the *[handwritten: casual lip service]*

[handwritten: written actually in support of Christian religion was]

ABOLISHING OF CHRISTIANITY IN ENGLAND *[handwritten: to Church of England]*

[handwritten: really an element of stability - advantage to the nation]

may, as things now stand, be attended with some inconveniences, and perhaps not produce those many good effects proposed thereby.

WRITTEN IN THE YEAR 1708.

I am very sensible what a weakness and presumption it is, to reason against the general humour and disposition of the world. I remember it was with great justice, and a due regard to the freedom both of the public and the press, forbidden upon several

[handwritten: victim of satire here is the nominal Christian-lip service church member]

penalties to write, or discourse, or lay wagers against the Union,[1] even before it was confirmed by Parliament, because that was looked upon as a design to oppose the current of the people, which, besides the folly of it, is a manifest breach of the fundamental law that makes this majority of opinion the voice of God. In like manner, and for the very same reasons, it may perhaps be neither safe nor prudent to argue against the abolishing of Christianity at a juncture when all parties appear so unanimously determined upon the point, as we cannot but allow from their actions, their discourses, and their writings. However, I know not how, whether from the affectation of singularity, or the perverseness of human nature, but so it unhappily falls out that I cannot be entirely of this opinion. Nay, though I were sure an order were issued for my immediate prosecution by the attorney-general, I should still confess that in the present posture of our affairs at home or abroad, I do not yet see the absolute necessity of extirpating the Christian religion from among us.

This perhaps may appear too great a paradox even for our wise and paradoxical age to endure: therefore I shall handle it with all tenderness, and with the utmost deference to that great and profound majority which is of another sentiment.

And yet the curious may please to observe how much the genius of a nation is liable to alter in half an age: I have heard it affirmed for certain by some very old people that the contrary opinion was even in their memories as much in vogue as the other is now; and that a project for the abolishing of Christianity would then have appeared as singular, and been thought as absurd, as it would be at this time to write or discourse in its defence.

Therefore I freely own that all appearances are against me. The system of the Gospel, after the fate of other systems, is generally antiquated and exploded; and the mass or body of the common people, among whom it seems to have had its latest credit, are now grown as much ashamed of it as their betters; opinions, like fashions, always descending from those of quality to the middle sort, and thence to the vulgar, where at length they are dropped and vanish.

But here I would not be mistaken, and must therefore be so bold as to borrow a distinction from the writers on the other side, when they make a difference between nominal and real

[1] England and Scotland were united in 1707.

the persona begins his argument by accepting the equation of liberty of conscience w liberty to blaspheme;

Trinitarians. I hope no reader imagines me so weak to stand up in the defence of real Christianity, such as used in primitive times (if we may believe the authors of those ages) to have an influence upon men's belief and actions: to offer at the restoring of that would indeed be a wild project; it would be to dig up foundations; to destroy at one blow all the wit, and half the learning of the kingdom; to break the entire frame and constitution of things; to ruin trade, extinguish arts and sciences with the professors of them; in short, to turn our courts, exchanges, and shops into deserts; and would be full as absurd as the proposal of Horace,[2] where he advises the Romans all in a body to leave their city and seek a new seat in some remote part of the world, by way of cure for the corruption of their manners.

Therefore I think this caution was in itself altogether unnecessary, (which I have inserted only to prevent all possibility of cavilling) since every candid reader will easily understand my discourse to be intended only in defence of nominal Christianity, the other having been for some time wholly laid aside by general consent as utterly inconsistent with all our present schemes of wealth and power.

But why we should therefore cast off the name and title of Christians, although the general opinion and resolution be so violent for it, I confess I cannot (with submission) apprehend the consequence necessary. However, since the undertakers propose such wonderful advantages to the nation by this project, and advance many plausible objections against the system of Christianity, I shall briefly consider the strength of both, fairly allow them their greatest weight, and offer such answers as I think most reasonable. After which I will beg leave to show what inconveniences may possibly happen by such an innovation, in the present posture of our affairs.

First, one great advantage proposed by the abolishing of Christianity is that it would very much enlarge and establish liberty of conscience, that great bulwark of our nation, and of the protestant religion, which is still too much limited by priestcraft, notwithstanding all the good intentions of the legislature, as we have lately found by a severe instance. For it is confidently reported that two young gentlemen of real hopes, bright wit, and profound

2 *Epode* XVI, 15 *ff.*

judgment, who upon a thorough examination of causes and effects, and by the mere force of natural abilities, without the least tincture of learning, having made a discovery that there was no God, and generously communicating their thoughts for the good of the public, were some time ago, by an unparalleled severity, and upon I know not what obsolete law, broke only for blasphemy. And as it hath been wisely observed, if persecution once begins, no man alive knows how far it may reach, or where it will end.

In answer to all which, with deference to wiser judgments, I think this rather shows the necessity of a nominal religion among us. Great wits love to be free with the highest objects; and if they cannot be allowed a God to revile or renounce, they will speak evil of dignities, abuse the government, and reflect upon the ministry; which I am sure few will deny to be of much more pernicious consequence, according to the saying of Tiberius, *Deorum offensa diis curæ*.[3] As to the particular fact related, I think it is not fair to argue from one instance; perhaps another cannot be produced; yet (to the comfort of all those who may be apprehensive of persecution) blasphemy we know is freely spoken a million of times in every coffeehouse and tavern, or wherever else good company meet. It must be allowed indeed, that to break an English freeborn officer only for blasphemy, was, to speak the gentlest of such an action, a very high strain of absolute power. Little can be said in excuse for the general; perhaps he was afraid it might give offence to the allies[4] among whom, for aught we know, it may be the custom of the country to believe a God. But if he argued, as some have done, upon a mistaken principle, that an officer who is guilty of speaking blasphemy may some time or other proceed so far as to raise a mutiny, the consequence is by no means to be admitted: for, surely the commander of an English army is likely to be but ill obeyed whose soldiers fear and reverence him as little as they do a Deity.

It is further objected against the gospel system that it obliges men to the belief of things too difficult for free-thinkers, and such who have shaken off the prejudices that usually cling to a confined education. To which I answer that men should be cautious how they raise objections which reflect upon the wisdom

3 "Offenses against the gods are the concern of the gods" (Tacitus, *Annals,* I, lxxiii).

4 During the War of the Spanish Succession England was allied with Austria and the Netherlands against France.

of the nation. Is not everybody freely allowed to believe whatever he pleases, and to publish his belief to the world whenever he thinks fit, especially if it serves to strengthen the party which is in the right? Would any indifferent foreigner who should read the trumpery lately written by Asgil, Tindal, Toland, Coward,[5] and forty more, imagine the Gospel to be our rule of faith, and confirmed by parliaments? Does any man either believe, or say he believes, or desire to have it thought that he says he believes one syllable of the matter? And is any man worse received upon that score, or does he find his want of nominal faith a disadvantage to him in the pursuit of any civil or military employment? What if there be an old dormant statute or two against him? Are they not now obsolete to a degree that Empson and Dudley[6] themselves, if they were now alive, would find it impossible to put them in execution?

It is likewise urged that there are by computation in this kingdom above ten thousand parsons whose revenues, added to those of my lords the bishops, would suffice to maintain at least two hundred young gentlemen of wit and pleasure, and free-thinking enemies to priestcraft, narrow principles, pedantry, and prejudices; who might be an ornament to the court and town. And then again, so great a number of able [-bodied] divines might be a recruit to our fleet and armies. This indeed appears to be a consideration of some weight: but then, on the other side, several things deserve to be considered likewise: as, first, whether it may not be thought necessary that in certain tracts of country, like what we call parishes, there shall be one man at least of abilities to read and write. Then it seems a wrong computation that the revenues of the Church throughout this island would be large enough to maintain two hundred young gentlemen, or even half that number, after the present refined way of living; that is, to allow each of them such a rent as, in the modern form of speech, would make them easy. But still there is in this project a greater mischief behind; and we ought to beware of the woman's folly who killed the hen that every morning laid her a golden egg. For, pray, what would become of the race of men in the next age if we had nothing to trust to beside the scrofulous, consumptive productions, furnished by our men of wit and pleasure, when,

5 Deistic writers of the day.
6 Two ministers of Henry VII known for their corruption in levying taxes; they were executed by Henry VIII.

having squandered away their vigour, health, and estates, they are forced by some disagreeable marriage to piece up their broken fortunes, and entail rottenness and politeness on their posterity? Now here are ten thousand persons reduced by the wise regulations of Henry the Eighth to the necessity of a low diet and moderate exercise, who are the only great restorers of our breed, without which the nation would in an age or two become one great hospital.

Another advantage proposed by the abolishing of Christianity is the clear gain of one day in seven, which is now entirely lost, and consequently the kingdom one-seventh less considerable in trade, business, and pleasure; besides the loss to the public of so many stately structures now in the hands of the clergy, which might be converted into playhouses, exchanges, market-houses, common dormitories, and other public edifices.

I hope I shall be forgiven a hard word, if I call this a perfect cavil. I readily own there hath been an old custom, time out of mind, for people to assemble in the churches every Sunday, and that shops are still frequently shut, in order, as it is conceived, to preserve the memory of that ancient practice; but how this can prove a hindrance to business or pleasure is hard to imagine. What if the men of pleasure are forced, one day in the week, to game at home instead of the chocolate-house? Are not the taverns and coffee-houses open? Can there be a more convenient season for taking a dose of physic? Are fewer claps got upon Sundays than other days? Is not that the chief day for traders to sum up the accounts of the week, and for lawyers to prepare their briefs? But I would fain know how it can be pretended that the churches are misapplied? Where are more appointments and rendezvouzes of gallantry? Where more care to appear in the foremost box with greater advantage of dress? Where more meetings for business? Where more bargains driven of all sorts? And where so many conveniences or incitements to sleep?

There is one advantage greater than any of the foregoing proposed by the abolishing of Christianity: that it will utterly extinguish parties among us by removing those factious distinctions of High and Low Church, of Whig and Tory, Presbyterian and Church of England, which are now so many mutual clogs upon public proceedings, and dispose men to prefer the gratifying themselves, or depressing their adversaries, before the most important interest of the state.

I confess, if it were certain that so great an advantage would redound to the nation by this expedient, I would submit and be silent: but will any man say that if the words *whoring, drinking, cheating, lying, stealing,* were by act of Parliament ejected out of the English tongue and dictionaries, we should all awake next morning chaste and temperate, honest and just, and lovers of truth? Is this a fair consequence? Or, if the physicians would forbid us to pronounce the words *pox, gout, rheumatism* and *stone,* would that expedient serve like so many talismans to destroy the diseases themselves? Are party and faction rooted in men's hearts no deeper than phrases borrowed from religion, or founded upon no firmer principles? And is our language so poor that we cannot find other terms to express them? Are *envy, pride, avarice* and *ambition* such ill nomenclators that they cannot furnish appellations for their owners? Will not *heydukes* and *mamalukes, mandarins* and *patshaws,* or any other words formed at pleasure, serve to distinguish those who are in the ministry from others who would be in it if they could? What, for instance, is easier than to vary the form of speech, and instead of the *church,* make it a question in politics whether the Monument[7] be in danger? Because religion was nearest at hand to furnish a few convenient phrases, is our invention so barren we can find no others? Suppose, for argument sake, that the Tories favoured Margarita, the Whigs Mrs. Tofts, and the Trimmers Valentini,[8] would not *Margaritians, Toftians* and *Valentinians* be very tolerable marks of distinction? The *Prasini* and *Veniti,*[9] two most virulent factions in Italy, began (if I remember right) by a distinction of colours in ribbons, which we might do with as good a grace about the dignity of the blue and the green, and would serve as properly to divide the court, the Parliament, and the kingdom between them, as any terms of art whatsoever borrowed from religion. Therefore I think there is little force in this objection against Christianity, or prospect of so great an advantage as is proposed in the abolishing of it.

'Tis again objected as a very absurd, ridiculous custom that a

---

7 The Monument, near London Bridge, commemorating the Great Fire of 1666.

8 Margarita, Mrs. Katharine Tofts, and Valentini were singers in the Italian opera. Valentini, the male soprano, is to be supported by the "trimmers"—those committed to no certain party.

9 Possibly a reference to the factions at chariot races in Rome.

set of men should be suffered, much less employed and hired, to bawl one day in seven against the lawfulness of those methods most in use toward the pursuit of greatness, riches and pleasure, which are the constant practice of all men alive on the other six. But this objection is, I think, a little unworthy so refined an age as ours. Let us argue this matter calmly: I appeal to the breast of any polite freethinker whether in the pursuit of gratifying a predominant passion he hath not always felt a wonderful incitement, by reflecting it was a thing forbidden: and therefore we see, in order to cultivate this taste, the wisdom of the nation hath taken special care that the ladies should be furnished with prohibited silks, and the men with prohibited wine. And indeed, it were to be wished that some other prohibitions were promoted in order to improve the pleasures of the town; which, for want of such expedients begin already, as I am told, to flag and grow languid, giving way daily to cruel inroads from the spleen.

'Tis likewise proposed as a great advantage to the public that if we once discard the system of the Gospel, all religion will of course be banished for ever; and consequently, along with it, those grievous prejudices of education, which under the names of *virtue, conscience, honour, justice,* and the like, are so apt to disturb the peace of human minds, and the notions whereof are so hard to be eradicated by right reason or free-thinking, sometimes during the whole course of our lives.

Here first I observe how difficult it is to get rid of a phrase which the world is once grown fond of, though the occasion that first produced it be entirely taken away. For several years past, if a man had but an ill-favoured nose, the deep-thinkers of the age would some way or other contrive to impute the cause to the prejudice of his education. From this fountain were said to be derived all our foolish notions of justice, piety, love of our country, all our opinions of God, or a future state, heaven, hell, and the like: and there might formerly perhaps have been some pretence for this charge. But so effectual care hath been since taken to remove those prejudices by an entire change in the methods of education that (with honour I mention it to our polite innovators) the young gentlemen who are now on the scene, seem to have not the least tincture of those infusions, or string of those weeds; and, by consequence, the reason for abolishing nominal Christianity upon that pretext is wholly ceased.

For the rest, it may perhaps admit a controversy whether the banishing of all notions of religion whatsoever would be convenient for the vulgar. Not that I am in the least of opinion with those who hold religion to have been the invention of politicians to keep the lower part of the world in awe by the fear of invisible powers; unless mankind were then very different from what it is now: for I look upon the mass or body of our people here in England to be as freethinkers, that is to say, as staunch unbelievers, as any of the highest rank. But I conceive some scattered notions about a superior power to be of singular use for the common people, as furnishing excellent materials to keep children quiet when they grow peevish, and providing topics of amusement in a tedious winter night.

Lastly, it is proposed as a singular advantage that the abolishing of Christianity will very much contribute to the uniting of Protestants, by enlarging the terms of communion so as to take in all sorts of Dissenters, who are now shut out of the pale upon account of a few ceremonies which all sides confess to be things indifferent; that this alone will effectually answer the great ends of a scheme for comprehension, by opening a large noble gate, at which all bodies may enter: whereas the chaffering with Dissenters, and dodging about this or t'other ceremony, is but like opening a few wickets, and leaving them at jar, by which no more than one can get in at a time, and that, not without stooping, and sideling, and squeezing his body.

To all this I answer that there is one darling inclination of mankind, which usually affects to be a retainer to religion, though she be neither its parent, its godmother, or its friend; I mean the spirit of opposition, that lived long before Christianity, and can easily subsist without it. Let us, for instance, examine wherein the opposition of sectaries among us consists; we shall find Christianity to have no share in it at all. Does the Gospel any where prescribe a starched, squeezed countenance, a stiff, formal gait, a singularity of manners and habit, or any affected modes of speech different from the reasonable part of mankind? Yet, if Christianity did not lend its name to stand in the gap, and to employ or divert these humours, they must of necessity be spent in contraventions to the laws of the land, and disturbance of the public peace. There is a portion of enthusiasm assigned to every nation, which, if it hath not proper objects to work on. will burst out. and set all in a flame.

If the quiet of a state can be bought by only flinging men a few ceremonies to devour, it is a purchase no wise man would refuse. Let the mastiffs amuse themselves about a sheep-skin stuffed with hay, provided it will keep them from worrying the flock. The institution of convents abroad seems in one point a strain of great wisdom, there being few irregularities in human passions that may not have recourse to vent themselves in some of those orders, which are so many retreats for the speculative, the melancholy, the proud, the silent, the politic and the morose, to spend themselves, and evaporate the noxious particles; for each of whom we in this island are forced to provide a several sect of religion, to keep them quiet. And whenever Christianity shall be abolished, the legislature must find some other expedient to employ and entertain them. For what imports it how large a gate you open if there will be always left a number who place a pride and a merit in refusing to enter?

Having thus considered the most important objections against Christianity and the chief advantages proposed by the abolishing thereof, I shall now with equal deference and submission to wiser judgments as before, proceed to mention a few inconveniences that may happen if the Gospel should be repealed; which perhaps the projectors may not have sufficiently considered.

And first, I am very sensible how much the gentlemen of wit and pleasure are apt to murmur, and be choked at the sight of so many daggled-tail parsons who happen to fall in their way, and offend their eyes. But at the same time, these wise reformers do not consider what an advantage and felicity it is for great wits to be always provided with objects of scorn and contempt, in order to exercise and improve their talents, and divert their spleen from falling on each other or on themselves; especially when all this may be done without the least imaginable danger to their persons.

And to urge another argument of a parallel nature: if Christianity were once abolished, how could the free-thinkers, the strong reasoners, and the men of profound learning, be able to find another subject so calculated in all points whereon to display their abilities? What wonderful productions of wit should we be deprived of from those whose genius by continual practice hath been wholly turned upon raillery and invectives against religion, and would therefore never be able to shine or distinguish themselves upon any other subject! We are daily complaining of the great decline of wit among us, and would we take away the greatest, perhaps the only, topic we have left? Who would ever have suspected Asgil for a wit, or Toland for a philosopher, if the inexhaustible stock of Christianity had not been at hand to provide them with materials? What other subject, through all art or nature, could have produced Tindal for a profound author, or furnished him with readers? It is the wise choice of the subject that alone adorns and distinguishes the writer. For had a hundred such pens as these been employed on the side of religion, they would have immediately sunk into silence and oblivion.

Nor do I think it wholly groundless, or my fears altogether imaginary, that the abolishing of Christianity may perhaps bring the Church in danger, or at least put the senate to the trouble of another securing vote. I desire I may not be mistaken; I am far from presuming to affirm or think that the Church is in danger at present, or as things now stand; but we know not how soon it may be so when the Christian religion is repealed. As plausible as this project seems, there may a dangerous design lurk under it. Nothing can be more notorious than that the atheists, deists, Socinians, Anti-trinitarians, and other subdivisions of free-thinkers are persons of little zeal for the present ecclesiastical establishment: their declared opinion is for repealing the Sacramental Test; [10] they are very indifferent with regard to ceremonies; nor do they hold the *jus divinum* of Episcopacy. Therefore this may be intended as one politic step toward altering the constitution of the Church established, and setting up Presbytery in the stead, which I leave to be further considered by those at the helm.

In the last place, I think nothing can be more plain than that by this expedient, we shall run into the evil we chiefly pretend to avoid; and that the abolishment of the Christian religion will be the readiest course we can take to introduce popery. And I am the more inclined to this opinion because we know it has been the constant practice of the Jesuits to send over emissaries with instructions to personate themselves members of the several prevailing sects among us. So it is recorded that they have at sundry times appeared in the guise of Presbyterians, Anabaptists, Independents, and Quakers, according as any of these were most in credit; so, since the fashion hath been taken up of exploding reli-

---

10 The Test Act of 1673 by which tak-ing communion in the Established Church was made requisite for political office-holding.

gion, the popish missionaries have not been wanting to mix with the freethinkers; among whom, Toland, the great oracle of the Antichristians, is an Irish priest, the son of an Irish priest; and the most learned and ingenious author of a book called *The Rights of the Christian Church*,[11] was in a proper juncture reconciled to the Romish faith, whose true son, as appears by an hundred passages in his treatise, he still continues. Perhaps I could add some others to the number; but the fact is beyond dispute, and the reasoning they proceed by is right: for, supposing Christianity to be extinguished, the people will never be at ease till they find out some other method of worship; which will as infallibly produce superstition as this will end in popery.

And therefore, if notwithstanding all I have said, it still be thought necessary to have a bill brought in for repealing Christianity, I would humbly offer an amendment; that instead of the word *Christianity* may be put *religion* in general; which I conceive will much better answer all the good ends proposed by the projectors of it. For, as long as we leave in being a God and his providence, with all the necessary consequences which curious and inquisitive men will be apt to draw from such premises, we do not strike at the root of the evil, though we should ever so effectually annihilate the present scheme of the Gospel. For of what use is freedom of thought, if it will not produce freedom of action, which is the sole end, how remote soever in appearance, of all objections against Christianity? And, therefore, the freethinkers consider it as a sort of edifice wherein all the parts have such a mutual dependence on each other that if you happen to pull out one single nail, the whole fabric must fall to the ground. This was happily expressed by him who had heard of a text brought for proof of the Trinity, which in an ancient manuscript was differently read; he thereupon immediately took the hint, and by a sudden deduction of a long *sorites*,[12] most logically concluded, "Why, if it be as you say, I may safely whore and drink on, and defy the parson." From which, and many the like instances easy to be produced, I think nothing can be more manifest than that the quarrel is not against any particular points of hard digestion in the Christian system, but against religion in general; which, by laying restraints on human nature, is supposed the great enemy to

11 Matthew Tindal.
12 A sequence of syllogisms in which the conclusion of one furnishes the premise of the following.

in final Refutation, Swift entirely resigned to inevit. of religious dissent, believing that religion provides the safest stuffed dog for the opposition

442 ENLIGHTENED ENGLAND

the freedom of thought and action.

Upon the whole, if it shall still be thought for the benefit of Church and State that Christianity be abolished, I conceive, however, it may be more convenient to defer the execution to a time of peace, and not venture in this conjuncture to disoblige our allies, who, as it falls out, are all Christians; and many of them, by the prejudices of their education, so bigoted as to place a sort of pride in the appellation. If upon being rejected by them, we are to trust to an alliance with the Turk, we shall find ourselves much deceived: for, as he is too remote, and generally engaged in war with the Persian emperor, so his people would be more scandalized at our infidelity than our Christian neighbours. Because the Turks are not only strict observers of religious worship, but what is worse, believe a God; which is more than required of us even while we preserve the name of Christians.

To conclude: Whatever some may think of the great advantages to trade by this favourite scheme, I do very much apprehend that in six months time after the act is passed for the extirpation of the Gospel, the Bank and East-India Stock may fall at least one *per cent*. And since that is fifty times more than ever the wisdom of our age thought fit to venture for the preservation of Christianity, there is no reason we should be at so great a loss merely for the sake of destroying it.

laws of land & public peace are institutions which are separat from church & he values their security more highly than Christianity

A DESCRIPTION OF THE MORNING

1709

Now hardly here and there an hackney-coach
Appearing, show'd the ruddy morn's approach.
Now Betty from her master's bed had flown,
And softly stole to discompose her own.
The slipshod 'prentice from his master's door
Had par'd the dirt, and sprinkled round the floor.
Now Moll had whirl'd her mop with dext'rous airs,
Prepar'd to scrub the entry and the stairs.
The youth with broomy stumps began to trace
The kennel-edge, where wheels had worn the place. 10

The smallcoal-man was heard with cadence deep,
Till drown'd in shriller notes of chimney-sweep:
Duns at his lordship's gate began to meet,
And brickdust Moll had scream'd through half the street.
The turnkey now his flock returning sees,
Duly let out a-nights to steal for fees:
The watchful bailiffs take their silent stands,
And schoolboys lag with satchels in their hands.

A DESCRIPTION OF A CITY SHOWER

1710

Careful observers may foretel the hour
(By sure prognosticks) when to dread a show'r:
While rain depends, the pensive cat gives o'er
Her frolicks, and pursues her tail no more.
Returning home at night, you'll find the sink
Strike your offended sense with double stink.
If you be wise, then go not far to dine,
You'll spend in coach-hire more than save in wine.
A coming show'r your shooting corns presage,
Old aches throb, your hollow tooth will rage: 10
Sauntering in coffee-house is Dulman seen;
He damns the climate and complains of spleen.
    Meanwhile the South, rising with dabbled wings,
A sable cloud athwart the welkin flings,
That swill'd more liquor than it could contain,
And like a drunkard gives it up again.
Brisk Susan whips her linen from the rope,
While the first drizzling show'r is borne aslope,
Such is that sprinkling which some careless quean
Flirts on you from her mop, but not so clean.   20
You fly, invoke the gods; then turning, stop
To rail; she singing, still whirls on her mop,
Not yet, the dust had shunn'd th' unequal strife,
But aided by the wind, fought still for life;
And wafted with its foe by violent gust,
'Twas doubtful which was rain, and which was dust.
Ah! where must needy poet seek for aid,

When dust and rain at once his coat invade?
His only coat, where dust confus'd with rain,
Roughen the nap, and leave a mingled stain.   30
   Now in contiguous drops the flood comes down,
Threat'ning with deluge this devoted town.
To shops in crouds the dagged females fly,
Pretend to cheapen goods, but nothing buy.
The Templar spruce, while ev'ry spout's abroach,
Stays till 'tis fair, yet seems to call a coach.
The tuck'd-up sempstress walks with hasty strides,
While streams run down her oil'd umbrella's sides.
Here various kinds, by various fortunes led,
Commence acquaintance underneath a shed.   40
Triumphant Tories and desponding Whigs,
Forget their fewds, and join to save their wigs.
Box'd in a chair the beau impatient sits,
While spouts run clatt'ring o'er the roof by fits,
And ever and anon with frightful din
The leather sounds, he trembles from within.
So when Troy chairmen bore the wooden steed,
Pregnant with Greeks impatient to be freed
(Those bully Greeks, who, as the moderns do,
Instead of paying chairmen, run them thro'),   50
Laocoön struck the outside with his spear,
And each imprison'd hero quak'd for fear.
   Now from all parts the swelling kennels flow,
And bear their trophies with them as they go:
Filth of all hues and odours seem to tell
What street they sail'd from, by their sight and smell.
They, as each torrent drives, with rapid force,
From Smithfield, or St. Pulchre's shape their course,
And in huge confluent join at Snow Hill Ridge,
Fall from the conduit prone to Holborn Bridge.   60
Sweepings from butchers' stalls, dung, guts, and blood,
Drowned puppies, stinking sprats, all drench'd in mud,
Dead cats, and turnip-tops, come tumbling down the flood.

JOURNAL TO STELLA

1710–1713

LETTER I

Chester, *Septr.* 2, 1710.

Jo will give you an Account of me till I got into te [1] Boat, after which the Rogues made a new bargain & forced me to give them 2 Crowns, and talkt as if we should not be able to overtake any Ship; but in half an Hour we got to te Yatcht; for the Ships lay by wait for My Ld Lt's Steward. We made our Voyage in 15 hours just; last night I came to this Town, and shall leave it I believe on Monday. The first man I mett in Chestr was Dr Raymd, He & Mrs Raymond were come here about levying a Fine in order to have Power to sell their Estate. They have found every Thing answer very well. They both desire to present their humble services to you: They do not think of Ireld till next Year. I got a Fall off my Horse riding here from Parkgate; but no Hurt, the Horse understanding Falls very well, and lying quitely till I got up. My Duty to te Bp of Cl.[2] I saw him returning from Dunlary, but he saw not me. I take it ill He was not at Convocation, & that I have not His Name to My Powers. I beg y will hold yr Resolution of going to Trim, and riding there as much as y can. Let te Bp of Cloghr remind te Bp of Killala to send me a Letter with one inclosd to te Bp of Lichfield. Let all who write to me inclose to Richd Steele Esqr at his Office at te Cockpitt, near Whitehall. But not MD. I will pay for their Lettrs at St James's Coffee house,

---

[1] "The." This letter introduces Swift's "little language," which he used when writing to Stella and Rebecca Dingley ("When I am writing in our language, I make up my mouth just as if I was speaking it"). This "little language" is a kind of code: thus *l* replaces *r* (as "vely" for "very," "deelest" for "dearest," "sollahs" for "sirrahs," etc.); other recurrent words or abbreviations are MD ("my dear," "my dears"), Ppt ("poor pretty thing" or "poppet"), DD ("dear Dingley," or Stella), ME

("Madam Elderly," Dingley), Pdfr ("poor dear foolish rogue" or "poor dear fellow"—i.e., Swift), FW ("farewell" or "foolish wenches"), richar ("little"), sinkerton ("simpleton"), lele ("there, there, there" or, perhaps, "little"). "Presto" is Swift (in Italian). Patrick is Swift's servant; Bernage is a friend of Swift's who is in the army. Full identifications are in editions of the *Journal* by J. K. Moorhead (Everyman) and Harold Williams (Oxford).

[2] Clogher.

that I may have them the sooner—My Ld Mountjoy is now in te humr that we should begin our Journey this afternoon, so that I have stole here again to finish this Lettr, wch must be short or long accordingly. I write this Post to Mrs Wesly, and will tell her that I have taken care she may have her Bill of 115ll whenever she pleases to send for it, and in that Case I desire you will send it her inclosed & sealed; and have it ready so in Case she should send for it otherwise keep it. I will say no more till I hear whether I go to day or no, if I do, the Lettr is almost at an end. My Cozn Abigail is grown prodigiously old—God almight bless poodee-richar MD & for God sake be merry, gett oo health—I am perfectly resolved to return as soon as I hav done my Commission [3] whethr it succeeds or no I neer went to Engd with so little desire in my Life. If Mrs Curry makes any difficulty about te Lodgings; I will quitt them, and pay her from July. 9. last, and Mrs Brent must write to Parvisol with orders accordingly. The Post is come from London ad just going out; so I have only time to pray Gd to bress poor richr MD FW FW MD MD Me Me M.

LETTER V

London, *Sept.* 30, 1710.

Han't I brought myself into a fine *premunire* [1] to begin writing letters in whole sheets, and now I dare not leave it off. I can't tell whether you like these journal letters: I believe they would be dull to me to read them over; but, perhaps, little MD is pleased to know how Presto passes his time in her absence. I always begin my last the same day I ended my former. I told you where I dined to-day at a tavern with Stratford: Lewis, who is a great favourite of Harley's, was to have been with us; but he was hurried to Hampton-court, and sent his excuse; and that next Wednesday he would introduce me to Harley. 'Tis good to see what a lamentable confession the Whigs all make me of my ill usage: but I mind them not. I am already represented to Harley

---

3 To have the Queen remit the first-fruits and twentieth parts paid to the Crown by the Irish clergy.

1 A penalty.

as a discontented person, that was used ill for not being Whig enough; and I hope for good usage from him. The Tories dryly tell me, I may make my fortune, if I please; but I do not understand them, or rather, I do understand them.

Oct. 1. To-day I dined at Molesworth's, the Florence envoy: and sat this evening with my friend Darteneuf, whom you have heard me talk of; the greatest punner of this town next myself. Have you smoakt [2] the *Tatler* that I writ? It is much liked here, and I think it is a pure one. To-morrow I go with Delaval the Portugal envoy, to dine with Lord Halifax near Hampton-court. Your Manley's brother, a parliament-man here, has gotten an employment; and I am informed uses much interest to preserve his brother and, to-day, I spoke to the elder Frankland to engage his father, (post-master here) and I hope he will be safe, although he is cruelly hated by all the Tories of Ireland. I have almost finished my lampoon, and will print it for revenge on a certain great person. [3] It has cost me but three shillings in meat and drink since I came here, as thin as the town is. I laugh to see myself so disengaged in these revolutions. Well, I must leave off and go write to sir John Stanley, to desire him to engage lady Hyde, as my mistress to engage lord Hyde, in favour of Mr. Pratt.

2. Lord Halifax was at Hampton-court at his lodgings, and I dined with him there with Methuen, and Delaval, and the late attorney-general. I went to the drawing-room before dinner, (for the queen was at Hampton-court) and expected to see *nobody;* but I met acquaintance enough. I walked in the gardens, saw the cartons of Raphael, and other things, and with great difficulty got from lord Halifax, who would have kept me to-morrow to show me his house and park, and improvements. We left Hampton-court at sun-set, and got here in a chariot and two horses time enough by star-light. That's something charms me mightily about London; that you go dine a dozen miles off in October, stay all day, and return so quickly: you cannot do any thing like this in Dublin. I writ a second penny-post letter to your mother, and hear nothing of her. Did I tell you that earl Berkeley died last Sunday was se'n-night, at Berkeley-castle, of a dropsy? Lord

---

2 Suspected, guessed.　　　　　3 *Virtues of Sid Hamet,* a satire on Godolphin.

Halifax began a health to me to-day: it was the Resurrection of
the Whigs, which I refused unless he would add their Reformation too: and I told him he was the only Whig in England I
loved, or had any good opinion of.

3. This morning Stella's sister [4] came to me with a letter from
her mother, who is at Sheene; but will soon be in town, and will
call to see me: she gave me a bottle of palsy water,[5] a small one,
and desired I would send it you by the first convenience, as I
will; and she promises a quart bottle of the same: your sister lookt
very well, and seems a good modest sort of girl. I went then to
Mr. Lewis, first secretary to lord Dartmouth, and favourite to
Mr. Harley, who is to introduce me to-morrow morning. Lewis
had with him one Mr. Dyet, a justice of peace, worth twenty
thousand pounds, a commissioner of the stamp-office, and married
to a sister of sir Philip Meadows, envoy to the emperor. I tell you
this, because it is odds but this Mr. Dyet will be hanged; for he
is discovered to have counterfeited stampt paper, in which he was
a commissioner; and, with his accomplices, has cheated the queen
of a hundred thousand pounds. You will hear of it before this
come to you, but may be not so particularly; and it is a very
odd accident in such a man. Smoak Presto writing news to MD.
I dined to-day with Lord Mountjoy at Kensington, and walked
from thence this evening to town like an emperor. Remember
that yesterday, October 2, was a cruel hard frost, with ice;
and six days ago I was dying with heat. As thin as the town is,
I have more dinners than ever, and am asked this month by some
people, without being able to come for pre-engagements. Well,
but I should write plainer, when I consider Stella can't read, and
Dingley is not so skilful at my ugly hand. I had, to-night, a
letter from Mr. Pratt, who tells me, Joe will have his money when
there are trustees appointed by the lord lieutenant for receiving
and disposing the linen fund; and whenever those trustees are
appointed, I will solicit whoever is lord lieutenant, and am in no
fear of succeeding. So pray tell or write him word, and bid him
not be cast down; for Ned Southwell and Mr. Addison both think
Pratt in the right. Do not lose your money at Manley's to-night,

4 Ann Johnson.
5 An infusion of cowslips (palsyworts).

sirrahs.

4. After I had put out my candle last night, my landlady came into my room, with a servant of lord Halifax, to desire I would go dine with him at his house near Hampton-court; but I sent him word I had business of great importance that hindered me, &c. And, to-day, I was brought privately to Mr. Harley, who received me with the greatest respect and kindness imaginable: he has appointed me an hour on Saturday at four, afternoon, when I will open my business to him; which expression I would not use if I were a woman. I know you smoakt it; but I did not till I writ it. I dined to-day at Mr. Delaval's, the envoy for Portugal, with Nic. Rowe the poet, and other friends; and I gave my lampoon to be printed. I have more mischief in my heart; and I think it shall go round with them all, as this hits, and I can find hints. I am certain I answered your 2d letter, and yet I do not find it here. I suppose it was in my 4th; and why N. 2d, 3d; is it not enough to say, as I do, 1, 2, 3? &c. I am going to work at another *Tatler:* I'll be far enough but I say the same thing over two or three times, just as I do when I am talking to little MD; but what care I? they can read it as easily as I can write it: I think I have brought these lines pretty straight again. I fear it will be long before I finish two sides at this rate. Pray, dear MD, when I occasionally give you any little commission mixt with my letters, don't forget it, as that to Morgan and Joe, &c. for I write just as I can remember, otherwise I would put them all together. I was to visit Mr. Sterne to-day, and gave him your commission about handkerchiefs: that of chocolate I will do myself, and send it him when he goes, and you'll pay me when *the givers bread*, &c. To-night I will read a pamphlet, to amuse myself. God preserve your dear healths.

5. This morning Delaval came to see me, and we went together to Kneller's,[6] who was not in town. In the way we met the electors for parliament-men: and the rabble came about our coach, crying A Colt, a Stanhope, &c. we were afraid of a dead cat, or our glasses broken, and so were always of their side. I dined again at Delaval's; and in the evening at the Coffee-house, heard sir Andrew Fountain was come to town. This has been but

6 Sir Godfrey Kneller, the painter.

an insipid sort of day, and I have nothing to remark upon it worth three-pence: I hope MD had a better, with the dean, the bishop, or Mrs. Walls. Why, the reason you lost four and eight-pence last night but one at Manley's, was because you played bad games: I took notice of six that you had ten to one against you: Would any but a mad lady go out twice upon Manilio, Basto,[7] and two small diamonds? Then in that game of spades, you blundered when you had ten-ace; I never saw the like of you: and now you are in a huff because I tell you this. Well, here's two and eight-pence half-penny towards your loss.

6. Sir Andrew Fountain came this morning, and caught me writing in bed. I went into the city with him; and we dined at the Chop-house with Will Pate, the learned woollen-draper: then we sauntered at china-shops and booksellers; went to the tavern, drank two pints of white wine, and never parted till ten: and now I am come home, and must copy out some papers I intend for Mr. Harley, whom I am to see, as I told you, to-morrow afternoon; so that this night I shall say little to MD, but that I heartily wish myself with them, and will come as soon as I either fail, or compass my business. We now hear daily of elections; and, in a list I saw yesterday of about twenty, there are seven or eight more Tories than in the last Parliament; so that I believe they need not fear a majority, with the help of those who will vote as the Court pleases. But I have been told, that Mr. Harley himself would not let the Tories be too numerous, for fear they should be insolent, and kick against him; and for that reason they have kept several Whigs in employments, who expected to be turned out every day; as sir John Holland the comptroller, and many others. And so get you gone to your cards, and your claret and orange, at the dean's, and I'll go write.

7. I wonder when this letter will be finished: it must go by Tuesday, that's certain; and if I have one from MD before, I will not answer it, that's as certain too! 'Tis now morning, and I did not finish my papers for Mr. Harley last night; for you must understand Presto was sleepy, and made blunders and blots. Very pretty that I must be writing to young women in a morning fresh and fasting, faith. Well, good morrow to you; and so I go

7 Trumps in the game of ombre.

to business, and lay aside this paper till night, sirrahs.—At night. Jack How told Harley, that if there were a lower place in Hell than another, it was reserved for his porter, who tells lies so gravely, and with so civil a manner. This porter I have had to deal with, going this evening at four to visit Mr. Harley, by his own appointment. But the fellow told me no lie, though I suspected every word he said. He told me, his master was just gone to dinner, with much company, and desired I would come an hour hence, which I did, expecting to hear Mr. Harley was gone out; but they had just done dinner. Mr. Harley came out to me, brought me in, and presented me to his son-in-law, lord Doblane (or some such name) and his own son, and, among others, Will Penn the quaker: we sat two hours drinking as good wine as you do; and two hours more he and I alone; where he heard me tell my business; entered into it with all kindness; askt for my powers, and read them; and read likewise a memorial I had drawn up, and put it in his pocket to show the queen; told me the measures he would take; and, in short, said every thing I could wish: told me he must bring Mr. St. John (secretary of state) and me acquainted; and spoke so many things of personal kindness and esteem for me, that I am inclined half to believe what some friends have told me, That he would do every thing to bring me over. He has desired to dine with me (what a comical mistake was that) I mean he has desired me to dine with him on Tuesday; and after four hours being with him, set me down at St. James's Coffee-house, in a hackney-coach. All this is odd and comical, if you consider him and me. He knew my Christian name very well. I could not forbear saying thus much upon this matter, although you will think it tedious. But I'll tell you; you must know, 'tis fatal [8] to me to be a scoundrel and a prince the same day: for being to see him at four, I could not engage myself to dine at any friend's; so I went to Tooke, to give him a ballad and dine with him; but he was not at home: so I was forced to go to a blind chophouse,[9] and dine for ten-pence upon gill-ale, bad broth, and three chops of mutton; and then go reeking from thence to the first minister of state. And now I am going in charity

---

[8] Fated.

[9] An obscure, out-of-the-way chophouse serving ale by the gill.

to send Steele a *Tatler*, who is very low of late. I think I am civiller than I used to be; and have not used the expression of (*you in* Ireland) and (*we in* England), as I did when I was here before, to your great indignation. —— They may talk of the *you know what;* [10] but, gad, if it had not been for that, I should never have been able to get the access I have had; and if that helps me to succeed, then that *same thing* will be serviceable to the church. But how far we must depend upon new friends, I have learnt by long practice, though I think among great ministers, they are just as good as old ones. And so I think this important day has made a great hole in this side of the paper; and the fiddle faddles of to-morrow and Monday will make up the rest; and, besides, I shall see Harley on Tuesday before this letter goes.

8. I must tell you a great piece of refinement of Harley. He charged me to come to him often: I told him I was loth to trouble him in so much business as he had, and desired I might have leave to come at his levee; which he immediately refused, and said, That was not a place for friends to come to. Tis now but morning, and I have got a foolish trick, I must say something to MD when I wake, and wish them a good morrow; for this is not a shaving-day, Sunday, so I have time enough: but get you gone, you rogues, I must go write: yes, 'twill vex me to the blood if any of these long letters should miscarry: if they do, I will shrink to half sheets again; but then what will you do to make up the journal? there will be ten days of Presto's life lost; and that will be a sad thing, faith and troth.—At night. I was at a loss to-day for a dinner, unless I would have gone a great way, so I dined with some friends that board hereabout, as a spunger; and this evening sir Andrew Fountain would needs have me go to the tavern, where, for two bottles of wine, Portugal and Florence, among three of us, we had sixteen shillings to pay; but if ever he catches me so again, I'll spend as many pounds: and therefore I have put it among my extraordinaries: but we had a neck of mutton dressed *à la Maintenon,* that the dog could not eat: and it is now twelve o'clock, and I must go sleep. I hope this letter will go before I have MD's third. Do you believe me? and yet, faith, I long

10 *Tale of a Tub.*

for MD's third too: and yet I would have it to say, that I write five for two. I am not fond at all of St. James's Coffee-house, as I used to be. I hope it will mend in winter; but now they are all out of town at elections, or not come from their country houses. Yesterday I was going with Dr. Garth to dine with Charles Main, near the Tower, who has an employment there: he is of Ireland; the bishop of Clogher knows him well: an honest goodnatured fellow, a thorough hearty laugher, mightily beloved by the men of wit: his mistress is never above a cook maid. And so, good night, &c.

9. I dined to-day at sir John Stanley's; my lady Stanley is one of my favourites; I have as many here as the bishop of Killala has in Ireland. I am thinking what scurvy company I shall be to MD when I come back: they know every thing of me already: I will tell you no more, or I shall have nothing to say, no story to tell, nor any kind of thing. I was very uneasy last night with ugly, nasty, filthy wine, that turned sour on my stomach. I must go to the tavern: oh, but I told you that before. To-morrow I dine at Harley's, and will finish this letter at my return; but I can write no more now, because of the archbishop: faith 'tis true; for I am going now to write to him an account of what I have done in the business with Harley: and faith, young women, I'll tell you what you must count upon, that I never will write one word on the third side in these long letters.

10. Poor MD's letter was lying so huddled up among papers I could not find it: I mean poor Presto's letter. Well, I dined with Mr. Harley to-day, and hope some things will be done; but I must say no more: and this letter must be sent to the post-house, and not by the bell-man. I am to dine again there on Sunday next; I hope to some good issue. And so now, soon as ever I can in bed, I must begin my 6th to MD as gravely as if I had not written a word this month: fine doings, faith. Methinks I don't write as I should, because I am not in bed: see the ugly wide lines. God Almighty ever bless you, &c.

Faith, this is a whole treatise; I'll go reckon the lines on t'other sides. I've reckoned them.

LETTER VI

London, *Oct.* 10, 1710.

So as I told you just now in the letter I sent half an hour ago, I dined with Mr. Harley to-day, who presented me to the attorney-general sir Simon Harcourt, with much compliment on all sides, &c. Harley told me he had shown my memorial to the queen, and seconded it very heartily; and he desires me to dine with him again on Sunday, when he promises to settle it with her majesty, before she names a governor; and I protest I am in hopes it will be done, all but the forms, by that time; for he loves the church: this is a popular thing, and he would not have a governor share in it; and, besides, I am told by all hands, he has a mind to gain me over. But in the letter I writ last post (yesterday) to the archbishop, I did not tell him a syllable of what Mr. Harley said to me last night, because he charged me to keep it secret; so I would not tell it to you, but that before this goes, I hope the secret will be over. I am now writing my poetical *Description of a Shower in London,* and will send it to the *Tatler.* This is the last sheet of a whole quire I have written since I came to town. Pray, now it comes into my head, will you, when you go to Mrs. Walls, contrive to know whether Mrs. Wesley be in town, and still at her brother's, and how she is in health, and whether she stays in town. I writ to her from Chester, to know what I should do with her note; and I believe the poor woman is afraid to write to me: so I must go to my business, &c.

11. To-day at last I dined with lord Montrath, and carried lord Mountjoy and sir Andrew Fountain with me; and was looking over them at ombre till eleven this evening like a fool: they played running ombre half crowns; and sir Andrew Fountain won eight guineas of Mr. Coote: so I am come home late, and will say but little to MD this night. I have gotten half a bushel of coals, and Patrick, the extravagant whelp, had a fire ready for me; but I pickt off the coals before I went to-bed. It is a sign London is now an empty place, when it will not furnish me with matter for above five or six lines in a day. Did you smoak in my last how I told you the very day and the place you were playing

at ombre? But I interlined and altered a little, after I had received a letter from Mr. Manley, that said you were at it in his house, while he was writing to me; but without his help I guess'd within one day. Your town is certainly much more sociable than ours. I have not seen your mother yet, &c.

12. I dined to-day with Dr. Garth and Mr. Addison, at the Devil tavern, by Temple-bar, and Garth treated; and 'tis well I dine every day, else I should be longer making out my letters: for we are yet in a very dull state, only enquiring every day after new elections, where the Tories carry it among the new members six to one. Mr. Addison's election has passed easy and undisputed; and I believe, if he had a mind to be chosen king, he would hardly be refused. An odd accident has happened at Colchester: one captain Lavallin coming from Flanders or Spain, found his wife with child by a clerk of Doctors Commons, whose trade, you know, it is to prevent fornications: and this clerk was the very same fellow that made the discovery of Dyet's counterfeiting the stamp paper. Lavallin has been this fortnight hunting after the clerk to kill him; but the fellow was constantly employed at the Treasury about the discovery he made: the wife had made a shift to patch up the business, alledging that the clerk had told her her husband was dead, and other excuses; but t'other day somebody told Lavallin his wife had intrigues before he married her: upon which he goes down in a rage, shoots his wife through the head, then falls on his sword; and, to make the matter sure, at the same time discharges a pistol through his own head, and died on the spot, his wife surviving him about two hours; but in what circumstances of mind and body is terrible to imagine. I have finished my poem on the *Shower,* all but the beginning, and am going on with my *Tatler.* They have fixt about fifty things on me since I came: I have printed but three. One advantage I get by writing to you daily, or rather you get, is, that I shall remember not to write the same things twice; and yet I fear I have done it often already: but I'll mind and confine myself to the accidents of the day; and so get you gone to ombre, and be good girls, and save your money, and be rich against Presto comes, and write to me now and then: I am thinking it would be a pretty thing to hear sometimes from sawcy MD but don't hurt your eyes, Stella, I charge you.

13. O Lord, here's but a trifle of my letter written yet; what shall Presto do for prittle prattle to entertain MD? The talk now grows fresher of the duke of Ormond for Ireland, though Mr. Addison says he hears it will be in commission, and lord Gallaway one. These letters of mine are a sort of journal, where matters open by degrees; and, as I tell true or false, you will find by the event whether my intelligence be good; but I don't care twopence whether it be or no.—At night. To-day I was all about St. Paul's, and up at the top like a fool, with sir Andrew Fountain and two more; and spent seven shillings for my dinner like a puppy: this is the second time he has served me so; but I'll never do it again, though all mankind should persuade me, unconsidering puppies! There's a young fellow here in town we are all fond of, and about a year or two come from the university, one Harrison, a little pretty fellow, with a great deal of wit, good sense, and good nature; has written some mighty pretty things; that in your 6th *Miscellanea*, about the Sprig of an Orange, is his: he has nothing to live on but being governor to one of the duke of Queensbury's sons for forty pounds a year. The fine fellows are always inviting him to the tavern, and make him pay his club. Henley is a great crony of his: they are often at the tavern at six or seven shillings reckoning, and always makes the poor lad pay his full share. A colonel and a lord were at him and me the same way to-night: I absolutely refused, and made Harrison lag behind, and persuaded him not to go to them. I tell you this, because I find all rich fellows have that humour of using all people without any consideration of their fortunes; but I'll see them rot before they shall serve me so. Lord Halifax is always teazing me to go down to his country house, which will cost me a guinea to his servants, and twelve shillings coach hire; and he shall be hanged first. Is not this a plaguy silly story? But I am vext at the heart; for I love the young fellow, and am resolved to stir up people to do something for him: he is a Whig, and I'll put him upon some of my cast Whigs; for I have done with them, and they have, I hope, done with this kingdom for our time. They were sure of the four members for London above all places, and they have lost three in the four. Sir Richard Onslow, we hear, has lost for Surry; and they are overthrown in most places. Lookee, gentle-

women, if I write long letters, I must write you news and stuff, unless I send you my verses; and some I dare not; and those on the Shower in London I have sent to the *Tatler*, and you may see them in Ireland. I fancy you'll smoak me in the *Tatler* I am going to write; for I believe I have told you the hint. I had a letter sent me to-night from sir Matthew Dudley, and found it on my table when I came in. Because it is extraordinary I will transcribe it from beginning to end. It is as follows (Is the Devil in you? Oct. 13, 1710.) I would have answered every particular passage in it, only I wanted time. Here's enough for to-night, such as it is, &c.

14. Is that tobacco at the top of the paper, or what? I don't remember I slobbered. Lord, I dreamt of Stella, &c. so confusedly last night, and that we saw dean Bolton and Sterne go into a shop; and she bid me call them to her, and they proved to be two parsons I know not; and I walked without till she was shifting, and such stuff, mixt with much melancholy and uneasiness, and things not as they should be, and I know not how: and it is now an ugly gloomy morning.—At night. Mr. Addison and I dined with Ned Southwell, and walkt in the Park; and at the Coffee-house I found a letter from the bishop of Clogher, and a pacquet from MD. I opened the bishop's letter; but put up MD's, and visited a lady just come to town, and am now got into bed, and going to open your little letter: and God send I may find MD well, and happy, and merry, and that they love Presto as they do fires. Oh, I won't open it yet! yes I will! no I won't; I am going; I can't stay till I turn over. What shall I do? My fingers itch; and I now have it in my left hand; and now I'll open it this very moment.—I have just got it, and am cracking the seal, and can't imagine what's in it; I fear only some letter from a bishop, and it comes too late: I shall employ nobody's credit but my own. Well, I see though—Pshaw, 'tis from sir Andrew Fountain: What, another! I fancy that is from Mrs. Barton; she told me she would write to me; but she writes a better hand than this: I wish you would inquire; it must be at Dawson's office at the Castle. I fear this is from Patty Rolt, by the scrawl. Well, I'll read MD's letter. Ah, no; it is from poor lady Berkeley, to invite me to Berkeley-castle this winter; and now it grieves my heart: she says she hopes my Lord is in a fair way of recovery; poor lady. Well, now I go to MD's letter: faith, 'tis all right; I hoped it

was wrong. Your letter, N. 3, that I have now received, is dated Sept. 26, and Manley's letter, that I had five days ago, was dated Oct. 3, that's a fortnight difference: I doubt it has lain in Steele's office, and he forgot. Well, there's an end of that: he is turned out of his place; and you must desire those who send me pacquets, to inclose them in a paper directed to Mr. Addison, at St. James's Coffee-house: not common letters, but pacquets: the bishop of Clogher may mention it to the archbishop when he sees him. As for your letter, it makes me mad: slidikins, I have been the best boy in Christendom, and you come with your two eggs a penny.[1] —Well; but stay, I'll look over my book; adad, I think there was a *chasm* between my N. 2 and N. 3. Faith, I won't promise to write to you every week; but I'll write every night, and when it is full I will send it; that will be once in ten days, and that will be often enough: and if you begin to take up the way of writing to Presto, only because it is Tuesday, a Monday bedad, it will grow a task; but write when you have a mind.—No, no, no, no, no, no, no, no—Agad, agad, agad, agad, agad, agad; no, poor Stellakins. Slids, I would the horse were in your—chamber. Have not I ordered Parvisol to obey your directions about him? And han't I said in my former letters, that you may pickle him, and boil him, if you will? What do you trouble me about your horses for? Have I any thing to do with them?—Revolutions a hindrance to me in my business; Revolutions—to me in my business? If it were not for the revolutions, I could do nothing at all; and now I have all hopes possible, though one is certain of nothing; but to-morrow I am to have an answer, and am promised an effectual one. I suppose I have said enough in this and a former letter how I stand with new people; ten times better than ever I did with the old; forty times more caressed. I am to dine to-morrow at Mr. Harley's; and if he continues as he has begun, no man has been ever better treated by another. What you say about Stella's mother, I have spoken enough to it already. I believe she is not in town; for I have not yet seen her. My lampoon is cried up to the skies; but nobody suspects me for it, except sir Andrew Fountain: at least they say nothing of it to me. Did not I tell you of a great man who received me very coldly? That's he; but say nothing;

1 A silly story.

'twas only a little revenge: I'll remember to bring it over. The bishop of Clogher has smoaked my *Tatler* about shortening of words, &c. But God so! &c.

15. I will write plainer if I can remember it; for Stella must not spoil her eyes, and Dingley can't read my hand very well; and I am afraid my letters are too long: then you must suppose one to be two, and read them at twice. I dined to-day with Mr. Harley: Mr. Prior dined with us. He has left my memorial with the queen, who has consented to give the First-Fruits and Twentieth Parts, and will, we hope, declare it to-morrow in the cabinet. But I beg you to tell it to no person alive; for so I am ordered, till in publick: and I hope to get something of greater value. After dinner came in lord Peterborow: we renewed our acquaintance, and he grew mightily fond of me. They began to talk of a paper of verses called *Sid Hamet*. Mr. Harley repeated part, and then pulled them out, and gave them to a gentleman at the table to read, though they had all read them often: lord Peterborow would let nobody read them but himself: so he did; and Mr. Harley bobbed me at every line to take notice of the beauties. Prior rallied lord Peterborow for author of them; and lord Peterborow said, he knew them to be his; and Prior then turned it upon me, and I on him. I am not guessed at all in town to be the author; yet so it is: but that is a secret only to you. Ten to one whether you see them in Ireland; yet here they run prodigiously. Harley presented me to lord president of Scotland, and Mr. Benson, lord of the treasury. Prior and I came away at nine, and sat at the Smyrna till eleven, receiving acquaintance.

16. This morning early I went in a chair, and Patrick before it, to Mr. Harley, to give him another copy of my memorial, as he desired; but he was full of business, going to the queen, and I could not see him; but he desired I would send up the paper, and excused himself upon his hurry. I was a little baulkt; but they tell me it is nothing. I shall judge by next visit. I tipped his porter with half a crown; and so I am well there for a time at least. I dined at Stratford's in the city, and had Burgundy and Tockay: came back afoot like a scoundrel; then went to Mr. Addison and supt with lord Mountjoy, which made me sick all night. I forgot that I bought six pound of chocolate for Stella, and a little

wooden box: and I have a great piece of Brazil tobacco for Dingley, and a bottle of palsy water for Stella: all which, with the two handkerchiefs that Mr. Sterne has bought, and you must pay him for, will be put in the box directed to Mrs. Curry's, and set [?sent] by Dr. Hawkshaw, whom I have not seen; but Sterne has undertaken it. The chocolate is a present, madam, for Stella. Don't read this, you little rogue, with your little eyes; but give it to Dingley, pray now; and I'll write as plain as the skies: and let Dingley write Stella's part, and Stella dictate to her, when she apprehends her eyes, &c.

17. This letter should have gone this post, if I had not been taken up with business, and two nights being late out; so it must stay till Thursday. I dined to-day with your Mr. Sterne, by invitation, and drank Irish wine; but, before we parted, there came in the prince of puppies, colonel Edgworth; so I went away. This day came out the *Tatler* made up wholly of my *Shower*, and a preface to it. They say 'tis the best thing I ever writ, and I think so too. I suppose the bishop of Clogher will shew it you. Pray tell me how you like it. Tooke is going on with my *Miscellany*. I'd give a penny the letter to the bishop of Kilaloe was in it: 'twould do him honour. Could not you contrive to say you hear they are printing my *Things* together; and that you wish the bookseller had that letter among the rest: but don't say any thing of it as from me. I forgot whether it was good or no; but only having heard it much commended, perhaps it may deserve it. Well, I have to-morrow to finish this letter in, and then I'll send it next day. I am so vext that you should write your third to me, when you had but my second, and I had written five, which now I hope you have all: and so I tell you, you are sawcy, little, pretty, dear rogues, &c.

18. To-day I dined, by invitation, with Stratford and others, at a young merchant's in the city, with Hermitage and Tockay, and staid till nine, and am now come home. And that dog Patrick is abroad, and drinking, and I can't get my nightgown. I have a mind to turn that puppy away: he has been drunk ten times in three weeks. But I han't time to say more; so good night, &c.

19. I am come home from dining in the city with Mr. Addison, at a merchant's; and just now, at the Coffee-house, we have notice that the duke of Ormond was this day declared lord lieutenant, at Hampton-court, in council. I have not seen Mr. Harley since;

but hope the affair is done about First-Fruits. I will see him, if possible, to-morrow morning; but this goes to-night. I have sent a box to Mr. Sterne, to send to you by some friend: I have directed it for Mr. Curry, at his house; so you have warning when it comes, as I hope it will soon. The handkerchiefs will be put in some friend's pocket, not to pay custom. And so here ends my sixth, sent when I had but three of MD's: now I am beforehand, and will keep so; and God Almighty bless dearest MD, &c.

LETTER XIV

London, *Jan.* 16, 1710–11.

O faith, young women, I have sent my letter N. 13, without one crumb of an answer to any of MD's, there is for you now; and yet Presto ben't angry faith, not a bit, only he will begin to be in pain next Irish post, except he sees MD's little hand-writing in the glass-frame at the bar of St. James's Coffee-house, where Presto would never go but for that purpose. Presto's at home, God help him, every night from six till bed-time, and has as little enjoyment or pleasure in life at present as any body in the world, although in full favour with all the ministry. As hope saved, nothing gives Presto any sort of dream of happiness but a letter now and then from his own dearest MD. I love the expectation of it, and when it does not come, I comfort myself, that I have it yet to be happy with. Yes faith, and when I write to MD, I am happy too; it is just as if methinks you were here and I prating to you, and telling you where I have been: Well, says you, Presto, come, where have you been to-day? come, let's hear now. And so then I answer; Ford and I were visiting Mr. Lewis, and Mr. Prior, and Prior has given me a fine Plautus, and then Ford would have had me dine at his lodgings, and so I would not; and so I dined with him at an eating-house; which I have not done five times since I came here; and so I came home, after visiting sir Andrew Fountain's mother and sister, and sir Andrew Fountain is mending, though slowly.

17. I was making, this morning, some general visits, and at twelve I called at the Coffee-house for a letter from MD; so the man said, he had given it to Patrick; then I went to the court of requests and treasury, to find Mr. Harley, and after some time spent in mutual reproaches, I promised to dine with him; I staid

there till seven, then called at Sterne's and Leigh's to talk about your box, and to have it sent by Smyth; Sterne says he has been making enquiries, and will set things right as soon as possible. I suppose it lies at Chester, at least I hope so, and only wants a lift over to you. Here has little Harrison been to complain, that the printer I recommended to him for his *Tatler*, is a coxcomb; and yet to see how things will happen; for this very printer is my cousin, his name is Dryden Leach; did you never hear of Dryden Leach, he that prints the *Postman?* he acted Oronoko, he's in love with miss Crosse.—Well, so I came home to read my letter from Stella, but the dog Patrick was abroad; at last he came. and I got my letter; I found another hand had superscribed it; when I opened it, I found it written all in French, and subscribed Bernage: faith I was ready to fling it at Patrick's head. Bernage tells me, he had been to desire your recommendation to me to make him a captain, and your cautious answer, "That he had as much power with me as you," was a notable one; if you were here I would present you to the ministry as a person of ability. Bernage should let me know where to write to him; this is the second letter I have had without any direction; however, I beg I may not have a third, but that you will ask him, and send me how I shall direct to him. In the mean time, tell him, that if regiments are to be raised here, as he says, I will speak to George Granville, secretary at war, to make him a captain; and use what other interest I conveniently can. I think that is enough, and so tell him, and don't trouble me with his letters, when I expect them from MD; do you hear, young women, write to Presto.

18. I was this morning with Mr. secretary St. John, and we were to dine at Mr. Harley's alone, about some business of importance; but there were two or three gentlemen there. Mr. secretary and I went together from his office to Mr. Harley's, and thought to have been very wise; but the deuce a bit, the company staid, and more came, and Harley went away at seven, and the secretary and I staid with the rest of the company till eleven; I would then have had him come away, but he was in for't; and though he swore he would come away at that flask, there I left him. I wonder at the civility of these people; when he saw I would drink no more, he would always pass the bottle by me, and yet I could not keep

the toad from drinking himself, nor he would not let me go neither, nor Masham, who was with us. When I got home, I found a parcel directed to me, and opening it, I found a pamphlet written entirely against myself, not by name, but against something I writ: it is pretty civil, and affects to be so, and I think I will take no notice of it; 'tis against something written very lately; and indeed I know not what to say, nor do I care: and so you are a sawcy rogue for losing your money to-day at Stoite's; to let that bungler beat you, fye, Stella, an't you ashamed? Well, I forgive you this once, never do so again; no, noooo. Kiss and be friends, sirrah.—Come, let me go sleep, I go earlier to bed than formerly; and have not been out so late these two months; but the secretary was in a drinking humour. So good night, myown-littledearsaucyinsolentrogues.

19. Then you read that long word in the last line, no, faith han't you. Well, when will this letter come from our MD? to-morrow or next day without fail; yes faith, and so it is coming. This was an insipid snowy day, no walking day, and I dined gravely with Mrs. Vanhomrigh, and came home, and am now got to bed a little after ten; I remember old Culpepper's maxim. Would you have a settled head, You must early go to bed; I tell you and I tell't again, You must be in bed at ten.

20. And so I went to-day with my new wig, o hoao, to visit lady Worsley, whom I had not seen before, although she was near a month in town; then I walkt in the Park to find Mr. Ford, whom I had promised to meet, and coming down the Mall, who should come towards me but Patrick, and gives me five letters out of his pocket. I read the superscription of the first, Pshoh, said I; of the second, Pshoh again; of the third, Pshah, Pshah, Pshah; of the fourth, A Gad, A Gad, A Gad, I'm in a rage; of the fifth and last, O hoooa; aye marry this is something, this is our MD, so truly we opened it, I think immediately, and it began the most impudently in the world, thus; Dear Presto, We are even thus far. Now we are even, quoth Stephen, when he gave his wife six blows for one. I received your ninth four days after I had sent my thirteenth. But I'll reckon with you anon about that, young women. Why did not you recant at the end of your letter when you got my eleventh, tell me that huzzies base, were we even then,

were we, sirrah? But I won't answer your letter now, I'll keep it
for another time. We had a great deal of snow to-day, and 'tis
terrible cold. I dined with Ford, because it was his Opera-day
and snowed, so I did not care to stir further. I will send to-morrow
to Smyth.

21. Morning. It has snowed terribly all night, and is vengeance
cold. I am not yet up, but cannot write long; my hands will freeze.
Is there a good fire, Patrick? Yes, Sir; then I'll rise, come take
away the candle. You must know I write on the dark side of my
bed-chamber, and am forced to have a candle till I rise, for the
bed stands between me and the window, and I keep the curtains
shut this cold weather. So pray let me rise, and, Patrick, here
take away the candle.—At night. We are now here in high frost
and snow, the largest fire can hardly keep us warm. It is very
ugly walking, a baker's boy broke his thigh yesterday. I walk
slow, make short steps, and never tread on my heel. 'Tis a good
proverb the Devonshire people have; Walk fast in snow, In frost
walk slow, And still as you go, Tread on your toe: When frost
and snow are both together, Sit by the fire and spare shoe-leather.
I dined to-day with Dr. Cockburn, but will not do so again in
haste, he has generally such a parcel of Scots with him.

22. Morning. Starving, starving, Uth, uth, uth, uth, uth.—
Don't you remember I used to come into your chamber, and turn
Stella out of her chair, and rake up the fire in a cold morning, and
cry Uth, uth, uth? &c. O faith I must rise, my hand is so cold I
can write no more. So good morrow, sirrahs.—At night. I went
this morning to lady Giffard's house, and saw your mother, and
made her give me a pint bottle of palsey water, which I brought
home in my pocket; and sealed and tyed up in a paper, and sent
it to Mr. Smyth, who goes to-morrow for Ireland, and sent a
letter to him to desire his care of it, and that he would enquire
at Chester about the box. He was not within, so the bottle and letter were left for him at his lodgings, with strict orders to give them
to him; and I will send Patrick in a day or two, to know whether
it was given, &c. Dr. Stratford and I dined to-day with Mr. Stratford in the city, by appointment; but I chose to walk there for
exercise in the frost. But the weather had *given* a little, as you
women call it, so it was something slobbery. I did not get home

till nine, And now I'm in bed To break your head.

23. Morning. They tell me it freezes again, but 'tis not so cold as yesterday: so now I will answer a bit of your letter.—At night. O faith, I was just going to answer some of our MD's letter this morning, when a printer came in about some business, and staid an hour; so I rose, and then came in Ben Tooke, and then I shaved and scribbled, and it was such a terrible day I could not stir out till one, and then I called at Mrs. Barton's, and we went to lady Worsley's, where we were to dine by appointment. The earl of Berkeley is going to be married to lady Louisa Lenox, the duke of Richmond's daughter. I writ this night to dean Sterne, and bid him to tell you all about the bottle of palsey water by Smyth, and to-morrow morning I will say something to your letter.

24. Morning. Come now to your letter. As for your being even with me, I have spoken to that already. So now, my dearly beloved, let us proceed to the next. You are always grumbling that you han't letters fast enough, surely we shall have your tenth; and yet before you end your letter, you own you have my eleventh.—And why did not MD go into the country with the bishop of Clogher? faith such a journey would have done you good; Stella should have rode, and Dingley gone in the coach. The bishop of Kilmore I know nothing of; he is old and may dye; he lives in some obscure corner, for I never heard of him. As for my old friends, if you mean the Whigs, I never see them, as you may find by my journals, except lord Hallifax, and him very seldom; lord Somers never since the first visit, for he has been a false deceitful rascal. My new friends are very kind, and I have promises enough, but I do not count upon them, and besides my pretences are very young to them. However, we will see what may be done, and if nothing at all, I shall not be disappointed; although perhaps poor MD may, and then I shall be sorryer for their sakes than my own.—Talk of a merry Christmas (why did you write it so then young women? sawce for the goose is sawce for the gander) I have wisht you all that two or three letters ago. Good lack; and your news, that Mr. St. John is going to Holland; he has no such thoughts to quit the great station he is in, nor if he had, could I be spared to go with him. So faith, politick Madam Stella, you come with your two eggs a penny, &c. Well, Madam Dingley,

and so Mrs. Stoite invites you, and so you stay at Donnybrook, and so you could not write. You are plaguy exact in your journals from Dec. 25, to Jan. 4th. Well, Smyth and the palsey water I have handled already, and he does not lodge (or rather did not, for poor man, now he is gone) at Mr. Jesse's and all that stuff; but we found his lodging, and I went to Stella's mother on my own head, for I never remembered it was in the letter to desire another bottle; but I was so fretted, so tosticated, and so impatient, that Stella should have her water (I mean decently, don't be rogues) and so vext with Sterne's carelessness.—Pray God Stella's illnesses may not return. If they come seldom, they begin to be weary; I judge by myself; for when I seldom visit, I grow weary of my acquaintance.—Leave a good deal of my tenth unanswered! —Impudent slut, when did you ever answer my tenth, or ninth, or any other number? or who desires you to answer, provided you write? I defy the D— to answer my letters; sometimes there may be one or two things I should be glad you would answer, but I forget them, and you never think of them. I shall never love answering letters again, if you talk of answering. Answering, quotha; pretty answerers truly.—As for the pamphlet you speak of, and call it scandalous, and that one Mr. Presto is said to write it, hear my answer. Fye, child, you must not mind what every idle body tells you.—I believe you lie, and that the dogs were not crying it when you said so; come, tell truth. I am sorry you go to St. Mary's so soon, you'll be as poor as rats; that place will drain you with a vengeance: besides, I would have you think of being in the country in Summer. Indeed, Stella, pippins produced plentifully; Parvisol could not send from Laracor: there were about half a score, I would be glad to know whether they were good for any thing.—Mrs. Walls at Donnybrook with you; why is not she brought to bed? Well, well, well, Dingley, pray be satisfied; you talk as if you were angry about the bishop's not offering you conveniencies for the journey; and so he should.—- What sort of Christmas? Why I have had no Christmas at all; and has it really been Christmas of late? I never once thought of it. My service to Mrs. Stoite, and Catherine, and let Catherine get the coffee ready against I come, and not have so much care on her countenance; for all will go well—Mr. Bernage, Mr. Bernage

Mr. Fiddlenage, I have had three letters from him now succes- sively; he sends no directions, and how the D— shall I write to him? I would have burnt his last, if I had not seen Stella's hand at the bottom: his request is all nonsense. How can I assist him in buying? and if he be ordered to go to Spain, go he must, or else sell, and I believe one can hardly sell in such a juncture. If he had staid, and new regiments raised, I would have used my en- deavour to have had him removed; although I have no credit that way, or very little: but if the regiment goes, he ought to go too; he has had great indulgence, and opportunities of saving; and I have urged him to it a hundred times. What can I do? whenever it lies in my power to do him a good office, I will do it. Pray draw up this into a handsome speech, and represent it to him from me, and that I would write, if I knew where to direct to him; and so I have told you, and desired you would tell him, fifty times. Yes, Madam Stella, I think I can read your long concluding word, but you can't read mine after bidding you good night. And yet, methinks, I mend extremely in my writing; but when Stella's eyes are well, I hope to write as bad as ever.—So now I have an- swered your letter, and mine is an answer; for I lay yours before me, and I look and write, and write and look, and look and write again.—So good morrow, Madams both, and I'll go rise, for I must rise; for I take pills at night, and so I must rise early, I don't know why.——

25. Morning. I did not tell you how I past my time yesterday, nor bid you good night, and there was good reason. I went in the morning to secretary St. John about some business; he had got a great Whig with him; a creature of the duke of Marlborough, who is a Go-between to make peace between the duke and the ministry; so he came out of his closet; and after a few words, de- sired I would dine with him at three, but Mr. Lewis staid till six before he came; and there we sat talking, and the time slipt so, that at last, when I was positive to go, it was past two of clock; so I came home and went straight to bed. He would never let me look at his watch, and I could not imagine it above twelve when we went away. So I bid you good night for last night, and now I bid you good morrow, and I am still in bed, though it be near ten, but I must rise.

26, 27, 28, 29, 30. I have been so lazy and negligent these last four days that I could not write to MD. My head is not in order, and yet it is not absolutely ill, but giddyish, and makes me listless; I walk every day, and take drops of Dr. Cockburn, and I have just done a box of pills, and to-day lady Kerry sent me some of her bitter drink which I design to take twice a day, and hope I shall grow better. I wish I were with MD, I long for Spring and good weather, and then I will come over. My riding in Ireland keeps me well. I am very temperate, and eat of the easiest meats as I am directed, and hope the malignity will go off; but one fit shakes me a long time. I dined to-day with lord Mountjoy, yesterday at Mr. Stone's in the city, on Sunday at Vanhomrigh's, Saturday with Ford, and Friday I think at Vanhomrigh's, and that's all the journal I can send MD, for I was so lazy while I was well, that I could not write. I thought to have sent this to-night, but 'tis ten, and I'll go to bed, and write on t'other side to Parvisol to-morrow, and send it on Thursday; and so good night my dears, and love Presto, and be healthy, and Presto will be so too, &c.

Cut off these notes handsomely, d'ye hear, sirrahs, and give Mrs. Brent hers, and keep yours till you see Parvisol, and then make up the letter to him, and send it him by the first opportunity, and so God Almighty bless you both, here and ever, and poor Presto.

What, I warrant you thought at first that these last lines were another letter.

Dingley, Pray pay Stella six fishes, and place them to the account of your humble servant, Presto.

Stella, Pray pay Dingley six fishes, and place them to the account of your humble servant, Presto.

There's Bills of Exchange for you.

LETTER XV

London, *Jan.* 31, 1710–11.

I am to send you my fourteenth to-morrow, but my head having some little disorders, confounds all my journals. I was early this morning with Mr. secretary St. John about some business, so I could not scribble my morning lines to MD. They are here intending to tax all little printed penny papers a half penny every half-sheet, which will utterly ruin Grub-street, and I am endeavouring to prevent it. Besides, I was forwarding an impeachment against a certain great person; that was two of my businesses with the secretary, were they not worthy ones? It was Ford's Birth-day, and I refused the secretary and dined with Ford. We are here in as smart a frost for the time as I have seen; delicate walking weather, and the Canal and Rosamond's Pond [1] full of the rabble sliding and with skates, if you know what those are. Patrick's bird's water freezes in the gally-pot, and my hands in bed.

Feb. 1. I was this morning with poor lady Kerry, who is much worse in her head than I. She sends me bottles of her bitter, and we are so fond of one another, because our ailments are the same; don't you know that, Madam Stella? Han't I seen you conning ailments with Joe's wife, and some others, sirrah? I walkt into the city to dine, because of the walk, for we must take care of Presto's health you know, because of poor little MD. But I walkt plaguy carefully, for fear of sliding against my will; but I am very busy.

2. This morning Mr. Ford came to me to walk into the city, where he had business, and then to buy books at Bateman's; and I laid out one pound five shillings for a Strabo and Aristophanes, and I have now got books enough to make me another shelf, and I will have more, or it shall cost me a fall; and so as we came back, we drank a flask of right French wine at Ben Tooke's chamber; and when I got home, Mrs. Vanhomrigh sent me word her eldest daughter was taken suddenly very ill, and desired I would come and see her; I went, and found it was a silly trick of Mrs. Armstrong, lady Lucy's sister, who, with Moll Stanhope, was visiting there: however, I rattled off the daughter.

3. To-day I went and dined at lady Lucy's, where you know I have not been this long time; they are plaguy Whigs, especially the sister Armstrong, the most insupportable of all women, pretending to wit, without any taste. She was running down the last *Examiner*, the prettiest I had read, with a character of the present ministry.—I left them at five, and came home. But I for-

1 In St James's Park.

got to tell you, that this morning my cousin Dryden Leach the printer, came to me with a heavy complaint, that Harrison the new *Tatler* had turned him off, and taken the last *Tatler*'s printers again. He vowed revenge; I answered gravely, and so he left me, and I have ordered Patrick to deny me to him from henceforth: and at night comes a letter from Harrison, telling me the same thing, and excused his doing it without my notice, because he would bear all the blame; and in his *Tatler* of this day he tells you the story, how he has taken his old officers, and there is a most humble letter from Morphew and Lilly to beg his pardon, &c. And lastly, this morning Ford sent me two letters from the Coffee-house (where I hardly ever go) one from the archbishop of Dublin, and t'other from ———. Who do you think t'other was from?——I'll tell you, because you are friends; why then it was, faith it was from my own dear little MD, N. 10. Oh, but won't answer it now, no noooooh, I'll keep it between the two sheets; here it is, just under; oh, I lifted up the sheet and saw it there: lie still, you shan't be answered yet, little letter; for I must go to bed, and take care of my head.

4. I avoid going to church yet, for fear of my head, though it has been much better these last five or six days, since I have taken lady Kerry's bitter. Our frost holds like a dragon. I went to Mr. Addison's, and dined with him at his lodgings; I had not seen him these three weeks, we are grown common acquaintance; yet what have not I done for his friend Steele? Mr. Harley reproached me the last time I saw him, that to please me he would be reconciled to Steele, and had promised and appointed to see him, and that Steele never came. Harrison, whom Mr. Addison recommended to me, I have introduced to the secretary of state, who has promised me to take care of him; and I have represented Addison himself so to the ministry, that they think and talk in his favour, though they hated him before.——Well; he is now in my debt, and there's an end; and I never had the least obligation to him, and there's another end. This evening I had a message from Mr. Harley, desiring to know whether I was alive, and that I would dine with him to-morrow. They dine so late, that since my head has been wrong I have avoided being with them.—— Patrick has been out of favour these ten days; I talk dry and cross

to him, and have called him Friend three or four times. But, sirrahs, get you gone.

5. Morning. I am going this morning to see Prior, who dines with me at Mr. Harley's; so I cannot stay fiddling and talking with dear little brats in a morning, and 'tis still terribly cold.— I wish my cold hand was in the warmest place about you, young women, I'd give ten guineas upon that account with all my heart, faith; oh, it starves my thigh; so I'll rise, and bid you good morrow, my ladies both, good morrow. Come stand away, let me rise: Patrick, take away the candle. Is there a good fire?—So—up a-dazy.—At night. Mr. Harley did not sit down till six, and I staid till eleven; henceforth I will chuse to visit him in the evenings, and dine with him no more if I can help it. It breaks all my measures, and hurts my health; my head is disorderly, but not ill, and I hope it will mend.

6. Here has been such a hurry with the Queen's Birth-day, so much fine cloaths, and the Court so crowded that I did not go there. All the frost is gone. It thawed on Sunday, and so continues, yet ice is still on the Canal (I did not mean that of Laracor, but St. James's Park) and boys sliding on it. Mr. Ford pressed me to dine with him in his chamber.—Did not I tell you Patrick has got a bird, a linnet, to carry over to Dingley? It was very tame at first, and 'tis now the wildest I ever saw. He keeps it in a closet, where it makes a terrible litter; but I say nothing: I am as tame as a clout. When must we answer our MD's letter? One of these odd-come-shortlies. This is a week old, you see, and no further yet. Mr. Harley desired I would dine with him again to-day; but I refused him, for I fell out with him yesterday, and will not see him again till he makes me amends: and so I go to bed.

7. I was this morning early with Mr. Lewis of the secretary's office, and saw a letter Mr. Harley had sent to him, desiring to be reconciled; but I was deaf to all intreaties, and have desired Lewis to go to him, and let him know I expect further satisfaction. If we let these great ministers pretend too much, there will be no governing them. He promises to make me easy, if I will but come and see him; but I won't, and he shall do it by message, or I will cast him off. I'll tell you the cause of our quarrel when I see you, and refer it to yourselves. In that he did something,[2] which he

2 Harley sent Swift £50, which Swift sent back, offended.

intended for a favour; and I have taken it quite otherwise, dis-
liking both the thing and the manner, and it has heartily vexed
me, and all I have said is truth, though it looks like jest; and I
absolutely refused to submit to his intended favour, and expect
further satisfaction. Mr. Ford and I dined with Mr. Lewis. We
have a monstrous deal of snow, and it has cost me two shillings
to-day in chair and coach, and walk'd till I was dirty besides. I
know not what it is now to read or write after I am in bed. The
last thing I do up is to write something to our MD, and then get
into bed, and put out my candle, and so go sleep as fast as ever
I can. But in the mornings I do write sometimes in bed, as you
know.

8. Morning. *I have desired* Apronia *to be always careful, especially about the legs.* Pray, do you see any such great wit in
that sentence? I must freely own that I do not. But party carries
every thing now-a-days, and what a splutter have I heard about
the wit of that saying, repeated with admiration above a hundred
times in half an hour. Pray read it over again this moment, and
consider it. I think the word is *advised*, and not *desired*. I should
not have remembered it if I had not heard it so often. Why—aye
—You must know I dreamt it just now, and waked with it in my
mouth. Are you bit, or are you not, sirrahs? I met Mr. Harley in
the court of requests, and he askt me how long I had learnt the
trick of writing to myself? He had seen your letter through the
glass-case at the Coffee-house, and would swear it was my hand;
and Mr. Ford, who took and sent it me, was of the same mind.
I remember others have formerly said so too. I think I was little
MD's writing-master.—But come, what's here to do, writing to
young women in a morning? I have other fish to fry; so good
morrow, my ladies all, good morrow. Perhaps I'll answer your
letter to-night, perhaps I won't; that's as saucy little Presto takes
the humour.—At night. I walk'd in the park to-day in spight of
the weather, as I do always when it does not actually rain. Do
you know what? It has gone and done; we had a thaw for three
days, then a monstrous dirt and snow, and now it freezes, like
a pot-lid, upon our snow. I dined with lady Betty Germain, the
first time since I came for England; and there did I sit, like a
booby, till eight, looking over her and another lady at picquet,

when I had other business enough to do. It was the coldest day
I felt this year.

9. Morning. After I had been a-bed an hour last night, I was
forced to rise and call to the landlady and maid to have the fire
removed in a chimney below stairs, which made my bed-chamber
smoke, though I had no fire in it. I have been twice served so. I
never lay so miserable an hour in my life. Is it not plaguy vexatious?—It has snowed all night, and rains this morning.—Come,
where's MD's letter? Come, Mrs. Letter, make your appearance.
Here am I, says she, answer me to my face.—Oh, faith, I am
sorry you had my twelfth so soon; I doubt you will stay longer
for the rest. I'm so 'fraid you have got my fourteenth while I am
writing this; and I would always have one letter from Presto reading, one travelling, and one writing. As for the box, I now believe
it lost. It is directed for Mr. Curry at his house in Capel street, &c.
I had a letter yesterday from Dr. Raymond in Chester, who says,
he sent his man every where, and cannot find it; and God knows
whether Mr. Smyth will have better success. Sterne spoke to
him, and I writ to him with the bottle of palsy-water; that bottle
I hope, will not miscarry: I long to hear you have it. Oh, faith,
you have too good an opinion of Presto's care. I am negligent
enough of every thing but MD, and I should not have trusted
Sterne.—But it shall not go so: I will have one more tug for it.—
As to what you say of goodman Peasly and Isaac, I answer as I
did before. Fye, child, you must not give yourself the way to
believe any such thing: and afterwards, only for curiosity, you
may tell me how those things are approved, and how you like
them; and whether they instruct you in the present course of
affairs, and whether they are printed in your town, or only sent
from hence.—Sir Andrew Fountain is recovered; so take your
sorrow again, but don't keep it, fling it to the dogs. And does
little MD walk, indeed?—I'm glad of it at heart.—Yes, we have
done with the plague here: it was very saucy in you to pretend
to have it before your betters. Your intelligence that the story
is false about the officers forced to sell, is admirable. You may
see them all three every day, no more in the Army than you.
Twelve shillings for mending the strong box; that is, for putting
a farthing's worth of iron on a hinge, and gilding it; give him six

shillings, and I'll pay it, and never employ him or his again.—No
—indeed, I put of preaching as much as I can. I am upon another
foot: no-body doubts here whether I can preach, and you are
fools.—The account you give of that weekly paper [3] agrees with
us here. Mr. Prior was like to be insulted in the street for being
supposed the author of it; but one of the last papers cleared him.
No-body knows who it is, but those few in the secret, I suppose,
the ministry and the printer.—Poor Stella's eyes, God bless them,
and send them better. Pray spare them, and write not above two
lines a day in broad day-light. How does Stella look, madam
Dingley? Pretty well; a handsome young woman still. Will she
pass in a crowd? Will she make a figure in a country church?—
Stay a little, fair ladies. I this minute sent Patrick to Sterne: he
brings back word that your box is very safe with one Mr. Earl's
sister in Chester, and that Colonel Edgworth's widow goes for
Ireland on Monday next, and will receive the box at Chester, and
deliver it you safe: so there is some hopes now.—Well, let us go
on to your letter.—The warrant is passed for the First-Fruits.
The queen does not send a letter; but a patent will be drawn here,
and that will take up time. Mr. Harley of late has said nothing
of presenting me to the queen:—I was overseen [4] when I mentioned it to you. He has such a weight of affairs on him, that he
cannot mind all; but he talk'd of it three or four times to me, long
before I dropt it to you. What, is not Mrs. Walls' business over
yet? I had hopes she was up and well, and the child dead before
this time.—You did right, at last, to send me your accounts; but
I did not stay for them, I thank you. I hope you have your bill
sent in my last, and there will be eight pounds interest soon due
from Hawkshaw; pray look at his bond. I hope you are good
managers, and that when I say so, Stella won't think I intend she
should grudge herself wine. But going to those expensive lodgings
requires some fund. I wish you had staid till I came over, for some
reasons. That Frenchwoman [5] will be grumbling again in a little
time, and if you are invited any where to the country, it will vex
you to pay in absence; and the country may be necessary for poor
Stella's health: but do as you like, and don't blame Presto.—Oh,

3 *The Examiner.*   5 Stella's landlady.
4 Mistaken.

but you are telling your reasons.—Well, I have read them; do as you please.—Yes, Raymond says, he must stay longer than he thought, because he cannot settle his affairs. M——is in the country at some friend's, comes to town in Spring, and then goes to settle in Herefordshire. Her husband is a surly ill-natured brute, and cares not she should see any body. O Lord, see how I blundered, and left two lines short; it was that ugly score in the paper that made me mistake.——I believe you lie about the story of the fire, only to make it more odd. Bernage must go to Spain, and I will see to recommend him to the duke of Argyle, his general, when I see the duke next: but the officers tell me it would be dishonourable in the last degree for him to sell now, and he would never be preferred in the army; so that unless he designs to leave it for good and all, he must go. Tell him so, and that I would write if I knew where to direct to him; which I have said four-score times already. I had rather any thing almost than that you should strain yourselves to send a letter when it is inconvenient; we have settled that matter already. I'll write when I can, and so shall MD; and upon occasions extraordinary I will write, though it be a line; and when we have not letters soon, we agree that all things are well; and so that's settled for ever, and so hold your tongue.—Well, you shall have your pins; but for candles ends, I cannot promise, because I burn them to the stumps; besides, I remember what Stella told Dingley about them many years ago, and she may think the same thing of me.—And Dingley shall have her hinged spectacles.—Poor dear Stella, how durst you write those two lines by candle-light; bang your bones. Faith, this letter shall go to-morrow, I think, and that will be in ten days from the last, young women; that's too soon of all conscience: but answering yours has filled it up so quick, and I don't design to use you to three pages in folio, no nooooh. All this is one morning's work in bed;—and so good morrow, little sirrahs; that's for the rhyme. You want politicks: faith, I can't think of any; but may be at night I may tell you a passage. Come, sit off the bed, and let me rise will you?—At night. I dined to day with my neighbour Vanhomrigh; it was such dismal weather I could not stir further. I have had some threatenings with my head, but no fits. I still drink Dr. Radcliffe's bitter, and will continue it.

10. I was this morning to see the secretary of state, and have engaged him to give a memorial from me to the duke of Argyle in behalf of Bernage. The duke is a man that distinguishes people of merit, and I will speak to him myself; but the secretary backing it will be very effectual, and I will take care to have it done to purpose. Pray tell Bernage so, and that I think nothing can be luckier for him, and that I would have him go by all means. I will order it that the duke shall send for him when they are in Spain; or, if he fails, that he shall receive him kindly when he goes to wait on him. Can I do more? Is not this a great deal?—I now send away this letter, that you may not stay.—I dined with Ford upon his Opera-day, and am now come home, and am going to study; don't you presume to guess, sirrahs, impudent saucy dear boxes. Toward the end of a letter I could not say saucy boxes without putting *dear* between. En't that right now? Farewel. *This* should *be* longer, *but* that *I* send *it* to-*night,*

O silly, silly loggerhead!

I send a letter this post to one Mr. Staunton, and I direct it to Mr. Acton's in St. Michael's-Lane. He formerly lodged there, but he has not told me where to direct. Pray send to that Acton, whether the letter is come there, and whether he has sent it to Staunton.

If Bernage designs to sell his commission and stay at home, pray let him tell me so, that my recommendation to the duke of Argyle may not be in vain.

LETTER XVI

London, *Feb.* 10, 1710–11.

I have just dispatched my fifteenth to the post; I tell you how things will be, after I have got a letter from MD. I am in furious haste to finish mine, for fear of having two of MD's to answer in one of Presto's, which would be such a disgrace, never saw the like; but before you write to me I write at my leisure, like a gentleman, a little every day, just to let you know how matters go, and so and so; and I hope before this comes to you, you'll have got your box and chocolate, and Presto will take more care another time.

11. Morning. I must rise and go see my lord keeper, which will cost me two shillings in coach-hire. Don't call them two thirteens? [1]—At night. It has rained all day, and there was no walking. I read prayers to sir Andrew Fountain in the forenoon, and dined with three Irishmen at one Mr. Cope's lodgings; the other two were one Morris an archdeacon, and Mr. Ford. When I came home this evening, I expected that little jackanapes Harrison would have come to get help about his *Tatler* for Tuesday: I have fixed two evenings in the week which I allow him to come. The toad never came, and I expecting him fell a reading, and left off other business.—Come, what are you doing? How do you pass your time this ugly weather? Gaming and drinking, I suppose: fine diversions for young ladies, truly. I wish you had some of our Seville oranges, and we some of your wine. We have the finest oranges for two-pence apiece, and the basest wine for six shillings a bottle. They tell me wine grows cheap with you. I am resolved to have half a hogshead when I get to Ireland, if it be good and cheap, as it used to be; and I'll treat MD at my table in an evening, oh hoa, and laugh at great ministers of state.

12. The days are grown fine and long, —— be thanked. O faith, you forget all our little sayings, and I am angry. I dined to-day with Mr. secretary St. John: I went to the court of requests at noon, and sent Mr. Harley into the house to call the secretary, to let him know I would not dine with him if he dined late. By good luck the duke of Argyle was at the lobby of the house too, and I kept him in talk till the secretary came out, then told them I was glad to meet them together, and that I had a request to the duke which the secretary must second, and his grace must grant. The duke said he was sure it was something insignificant, and wished it was ten times greater. At the secretary's house I writ a memorial, and gave it to the secretary to give the duke, and shall see that he does it. It is, that his Grace will please to take Mr. Bernage into his protection; and if he finds Bernage answers my character, to give him all encouragement. Colonel Masham and Colonel Hill (Mrs. Masham's brother) tell me my request is reasonable, and they will second it heartily to the duke too: so I

1 In Ireland a shilling was worth thirteen pence.

reckon Bernage is on a very good foot when he goes to Spain. Pray tell him this, though perhaps I will write to him before he goes; yet where shall I direct? for I suppose he has left Conolly's.

13. I have left off lady Kerry's bitter, and got another box of pills. I have no fits of giddiness, but only some little disorders towards it; and I walk as much as I can. Lady Kerry is just as I am, only a great deal worse: I dined to-day at lord Shelburn's, where she is, and we conn ailments, which makes us very fond of each other. I have taken Mr. Harley into favour again, and called to see him, but he was not within; I will use to visit him after dinner, for he dines too late for my head: then I went to visit poor Congreve, who is just getting out of a severe fit of the gout, and I sat with him till near nine o'clock. He gave me a *Tatler* he had written out, as blind as he is, for little Harrison. 'Tis about a scoundrel that was grown rich, and went and bought a Coat of Arms at the Herald's, and a set of ancestors at Fleet-ditch; 'tis well enough, and shall be printed in two or three days, and if you read those kind of things, this will divert you. 'Tis now between ten and eleven, and I am going to bed.

14. This was Mrs. Vanhomrigh's daughter's Birth-day, and Mr. Ford and I were invited to dinner to keep it, and we spent the evening there drinking punch. That was our way of beginning Lent; and in the morning lord Shelburn, lady Kerry, Mrs. Pratt and I went to Hyde-park, instead of going to church; for till my head is a little settled, I think it better not to go; it would be so silly and troublesome to go out sick. Dr. Duke died suddenly two or three nights ago; he was one of the wits when we were children, but turned parson, and left it, and never writ further than a prologue or recommendatory copy of verses. He had a fine living given him by the bishop of Winchester about three months ago; he got his living suddenly, and he got his dying so too.

15. I walked purely to-day about the Park, the rain being just over, of which we have had a great deal, mixt with little short frosts, I went to the court of requests, thinking if Mr. Harley dined early, to go with him. But meeting Leigh and Sterne, they invited me to dine with them, and away we went. When we got into his room, one H——, a worthless Irish fellow, was there

ready to dine with us, so I stept out and whispered them, that I would not dine with that fellow; they made excuses, and begged me to stay, but away to Mr. Harley's, and he did not dine at home, and at last I dined at Sir John Germain's, and found lady Betty but just recovered of a miscarriage. I am writing an inscription for lord Berkeley's tomb: you know the young rake his son, the new earl, is married to the duke of Richmond's daughter, at the duke's country house, and are now coming to town. She'll be fluxed in two months, and they'll be parted in a year. You ladies are brave, bold venturesome folks; and the chit is but seventeen, and is ill-natured, covetous, vicious, and proud in extreams. And so get you gone to Stoite to-morrow.

16. Faith this letter goes on but slow, 'tis a week old, and the first side not written. I went to-day into the city for a walk, but the person I designed to dine with was not at home; so I came back and called at Congreve's, and dined with him and Eastcourt, and laughed till six, then went to Mr. Harley's, who was not gone to dinner; there I staid till nine, and we made up our quarrel, and he has invited me to dinner to-morrow, which is the day of the week (Saturday) that lord keeper and secretary St. John dine with him privately, and at last they have consented to let me among them on that day. Atterbury and Prior went to bury poor Dr. Duke. Congreve's nasty white wine has given me the heart-burn.

17. I took some good walks in the Park to-day, and then went to Mr. Harley. Lord Rivers was got there before me, and I chid him for presuming to come on a day when only lord keeper and the secretary and I were to be there; but he regarded me not; so we all dined together, and sat down at four; and the secretary has invited me to dine with him to-morrow. I told them I had no hopes they could ever keep in, but that I saw they loved one another so well, as indeed they seem to do. They call me nothing but Jonathan; and I said, I believed they would leave me Jonathan as they found me; and that I never knew a ministry do any thing for those whom they make companions of their pleasures; and I believe you will find it so; but I care not. I am upon a project of getting five hundred pounds, without being obliged to any body; but that is a secret, till I see my dearest MD; and so

hold your tongue, and don't talk, sirrahs, for I am now about it. 18. My head has no fits, but a little disordered before dinner; yet I walk stoutly, and take pills, and hope to mend. Secretary St. John would needs have me dine with him to-day, and there I found three persons I never saw, two I had no acquaintance with, and one I did not care for: so I left them early and came home, it being no day to walk, but scurvy rain and wind. The secretary tells me he has put a cheat on me; for lord Peterborow sent him twelve dozen flasks of Burgundy, on condition that I should have my share; but he never was quiet till they were all gone, so I reckon he owes me thirty-six pound. Lord Peterborow is now got to Vienna, and I must write to him to-morrow. I begin now to be towards looking for a letter from some certain ladies of Presto's acquaintance, that live at St. Mary's, and are called in a certain language our little MD. No, stay, I don't expect one these six days, that will be just three weeks; an't I a reasonable creature? We are plagued here with an October Club; that is, a set of above a hundred parliament-men of the country, who drink October beer at home, and meet every evening at a tavern near the parliament, to consult affairs, and drive things on to extreams against the Whigs, to call the old ministry to account, and get off five or six heads. The ministry seem not to regard them, yet one of them in confidence told me, that there must be something thought on to settle things better. I'll tell you one great state-secret; The queen, sensible how much she was governed by the late ministry, runs a little into t'other extream, and is jealous in that point, even of those who got her out of the others hands. The ministry is for gentler measures, and the other Tories for more violent. Lord Rivers, talking to me the other day, cursed the paper called The *Examiner*, for speaking civilly of the duke of Marlborough; this I happened to talk of to the secretary, who blamed the warmth of that lord and some others, and swore, that if their advice were followed, they would be blown up in twenty-four hours. And I have reason to think that they will endeavour to prevail on the queen to put her affairs more into the hands of a ministry than she does at present; and there are, I believe, two men thought on, one of them you have often met the name of in my letters. But so much for politicks.

19. This proved a terrible rainy day, which prevented my walk into the city, and I was only able to run and dine with my neighbour Vanhomrigh, where Sir Andrew Fountain dined too, who has just began to sally out, and has shipt his mother and sister, who were his nurses, back to the country. This evening was fair, and I walkt a little in the Park, till Prior made me go with him to the Smyrna Coffee-house, where I sat a while, and saw four or five Irish persons, who are very handsome genteel fellows, but I know not their names. I came away at seven, and got home. Two days ago I writ to Bernage, and told him what I had done, and directed the letter to Mr. Curry's to be left with Dingley. Brigadiers Hill and Masham, brother and husband to Mrs. Masham, the queen's favourite, colonel Disney and I have recommended Bernage to the duke of Argyle; and secretary St. John has given the duke my memorial; and besides, Hill tells me, that Bernage's colonel, Fielding, designs to make him his captain lieutenant: but I believe I said this to you before, and in this letter, but I will not look.

20. Morning. It snows terribly again, and 'tis mistaken, for I now want a little good weather; I bid you good morrow, and if it clear up, get you gone to poor Mrs. Walls, who has had a hard time of it, but it is now pretty well again; I am sorry it is a girl; the poor archdeacon too, see how simply he lookt when they told him: what did it cost Stella to be gossip? I'll rise, so d'ye hear, let me see you at night, and don't stay late out, and catch cold, sirrahs.—At night. It grew good weather, and I got a good walk, and dined with Ford upon his Opera-day: but now all his wine is gone, I shall dine with him no more. I hope to send this letter before I hear from MD, methinks there's—something great in doing so, only I can't express where it lies; and faith this shall go by Saturday, as sure as you're a rogue. Mrs. Edgworth was to set out but last Monday, so you won't have your box so soon perhaps as this letter; but Sterne told me since, that it is safe at Chester, and that she will take care of it. I'd give a guinea you had it.

21. Morning. Faith, I hope it will be fair for me to walk into the city, for I take all occasions of walking.—I should be plaguy busy at Laracor if I were there now, cutting down willows, plant-

ing others, scouring my canal, and every kind of thing. If Raymond goes over this summer, you must submit, and make them a visit, that we may have another eel and trout fishing; and that Stella may ride by and see Presto in his morning-gown in the garden, and so go up with Joe to the Hill of Bree, and round by Scurlock's Town; O Lord, how I remember names; faith it gives me short sighs: therefore no more of that if you love me. Good morrow, I'll go rise like a gentleman, my pills say I must.—At night. Lady Kerry sent to desire me to engage some lords about an affair she has in their house here: I called to see her, but found she had already engaged every lord I knew, and that there was no great difficulty in the matter, and it rained like a dog; so I took coach, for want of better exercise, and dined privately with a hang-dog in the city, and walkt back in the evening. The days are now long enough to walk in the Park after dinner; and so I do whenever it is fair. This walking is a strange remedy; Mr. Prior walks to make himself fat, and I to bring myself down; he has generally a cough, which he only calls a cold: we often [walk] round the Park together. So I'll go sleep.

22. It snowed all this morning prodigiously, and was some inches thick in three or four hours. I dined with Mr. Lewis of the secretary's office at his lodgings: the chairmen that carried me squeezed a great fellow against a wall, who wisely turned his back, and broke one of the side glasses in a thousand pieces. I fell a scolding, pretended I was like to be cut to pieces, and made them set down the chair in the Park, while they pickt out the bits of glasses: and when I paid them, I quarrelled still, so they dared not grumble, and I came off for my fare: but I was plaguily afraid they would have said, God bless your honour, won't you give us something for our glass? Lewis and I were forming a project how I might get three or four hundred pounds, which I suppose may come to nothing. I hope Smyth has brought you your palsy drops; how does Stella do? I begin more and more to desire to know. The three weeks since I had your last is over within two days, and I'll allow three for accidents.

23. The snow is gone every bit, except the remainder of some great balls made by the boys. Mr. Sterne was with me this morning about an affair he has before the treasury. That drab Mrs. Edgworth is not yet set out, but will infallibly next Monday, and this is the third infallible Monday, and pox take her! So you

will have this letter first; and this shall go to-morrow; and if I have one from MD in that time, I will not answer it till my next; only I will say, Madam, I received your letter, and so, and so. I dined to-day with my Mrs. Butler, who grows very disagreeable.

24. Morning. This letter certainly goes this evening, sure as you're alive, young women, and then you'll be so shamed that I have had none from you; and if I was to reckon like you, I would say, I were six letters before you, for this is N. 16, and I have had your N. 10. But I reckon you have received but fourteen and have sent eleven. I think to go to-day a minister-of-state-hunting in the court of requests; for I have something to say to Mr. Harley. And 'tis fine cold sunshiny weather; I wish dear MD would walk this morning in your Stephen's-Green: 'tis as good as our Park, but not so large. Faith this summer we'll take a coach for six-pence to the Green Well, the two walks, and thence all the way to Stoite's. My hearty service to goody Stoite and Catherine, and I hope Mrs. Walls had a good time. How inconstant I am? I can't imagine I was ever in love with her. Well, I'm going; what have you to say? *I don't care how I write now.* I don't design to write on this side, these few lines are but so much more than your due, so I'll write *large* or small as I please. Oh, faith, my hands are starving in bed; I believe it is a hard frost. I must rise, and bid you good bye, for I'll seal this letter immediately, and carry it in my pocket, and put it into the post-office with my own fair hands. Farewel.

This letter is just a fortnight's journal to-day. Yes, and so it is, I'm sure, says you, with your two eggs a penny.

There, there, there.

O Lord, I am saying There, There, to myself in all our little keys: and now you talk of keys, that dog Patrick broke the key general of the chest of drawers with six locks, and I have been so plagued to get a new one, beside my good two shillings.

LETTER XLIV

London. *Mar.* 22d. 1711–12.

Ugly nasty Weather. I was in te City to day with Mrs Wesly & Mr Percivll to get money from a Banker for Mrs Wesly, who goes to te Bath on Thursday. . I left them there, & dined with a friend, & went to see Ld Treasr; but he had People with him I did not know, so I went to Ldy Mashams, and lost a Crown with her at Picquet, and then sate with Ld Masham, & Ld Treasr &c there till past one, but I had my Man with me to come hom; I gave in my 43d and one for te Bp of Cl. to te Post office as I came from te City, and so oo know tis late now, and I have nothing to say for this day, Our Mohocks are all vanisht; however I shall take care of my Person. Nite my own two deelest nuntyes MD.

23. I was this morning before Church with te Secrty about Ld Abercorn's Business, & some others. My Solliciting Season is come, and will last as long as te Sessions. I went late to Court, and te Company was almost gone. Th Court serves me for a Coffeehouse, once a week I meet acquaintance there that I should not otherwise see in a quarter. There is a flying Report that te French have offerd a Cessation of Arms, and to give us Dunkerk, & te Dutch Namur for security till te Peace is made. Th D. of Ormd thy say goes in a week. Abundance of his Equipage is already gone. Is [His] Friends are afraid te Expence of this Employmt will ruin him, since he must lose te Governmt of Ireld. I dined privately with a Friend, and refused all Dinners offerd me at Court, wch however were but two, and I did not like eithr Did I tell y of a Scoundrel about te Court, that sells Employnts to ignorant People, and cheats them of their Money. he lately made a Bargain for te Vicechamberlns Place for 7000ll, and had received some Guinneas Earnest, but te whole Thing was discoverd tothr day, and Examination taken of it by Ld Dartmouth, & I hope he will be swingd. Th Vicechambrln told me sevll Particulars of it last night at Ld Mashams. Can Dd play at Ombre yet? enough hod [? to hold] te Cards while ppt steps into next Room —Nite deelest sollahs.

24. This morning I recommended Newcomb agn to te D. of Ormd, and left Dick Stewart to [do] it furthr; then I went to visit te Dutchess of Hamilton who was not awake; so I went to te Dutchess of Shrewsbury and sate an hour at her Toilet. I [talkt] to her about the Dukes being Ld Lt; she sayd she knew nothing of it, but I rallyd her out of that, and she resolves not to stay behind te Duke. I intend to recommd te Bp of Cl— to her

for an Acquaintance. He will like her very well. She is indeed a most agreeable woman, & a great Favorite of mine. I know not whethr te Ladyes in Ireld will like her. I was at te Court of Requests to get some Lds to be at a Commtee to morrow about a Friends Bill; & then [? there] te Duke of Beaufort gave me a Poem finely bound in Folio, printed at Stamford, & writt by a Country Squire. Ld Exetr desired te Duke to give it te Qu— because te Authr is his Friend: but te Duke desird I would let him know whethr it was good for any thing; I brought it home & will return it to morrow, as te dullest thing I ever read; & advise te Duke not to present it. I dined with Domvile at his Lodgings by Invitation, for he goes in a few days for Ireld. Nite dee MD.

25. There is a mighty Feast at a Tory Sheriffs to day in te City, 12 hundred dishes of meat, about 5 Lds, and sevll hundrd Gentlemen will be there, and give 4 or 5 Guinneas a Piece, according to Custom. Dr Coghill & I dined by Invitation at Mrs Van's. It has raind or mizzled all day as my Pockets feel. There are two new Answers come out to te Conduct of te Allyes Th last years Examiners printd togethr in a small Volume, go off but slowly. Th Printer overprintd himself by at least a thousand, so soon out of Fashion are Party papers however so well writt. Th Medlys are coming out in te same Volume, & perhaps may sell better. Our news about a Cessation of Arms begins to flag; and I have not these two days since [? seen] any body in Business, to ask them about it. We had a terrible Fire last night in Drury lane, or thereabouts, and 3 or 4 People destroyd. One of te Maids of Honor has te Small-pox, but the best is, she can lose no Beauty, & we have one new handsom Md of Honr. Nite MD.

26. I forgot to tell y that on Sunday last about 7 at night, it lightend above 50 times as I walkt te Mall, wch I think is extdy at this time of te Year. & te Weathr was very hot. Had y any thing of this in Dublin? I intended to dine with Ld Treasr to day: but Ld Mansel & Mr Lewis made me dine with them at Kit Musgrave's. Now y don't know who Kit Musgrave is. I sate te Evening with Mrs Wesley who goes to morrow morning to te Bath. She is much better than she was. Th News of te French desiring a Cessation of Arms &c was but Town talk.. We shall know in a few days as I am told, whethr there will be a Peace or

no. Th D. of Ormd will go in a Week for Flanders, they say: Our Mohawks go on still, & cut Peoples faces every night; fais they shan't cut mine, I like it better as it is, the Dogs will cost me at least a Crown a Week in Chairs. I believe te souls of yr Houghers [1] of Cattle have gott into them, and now they don't distinguish between a Cow and a Christian. I forgot to wish y yesterday a happy new Year, y know te 25 of March is te first day of te Year,[2] And now y must leave of Cards, and put out yr fire: I'll put out mine th 1st of April, cold or not cold. I believe I shall lose Credit with y by not coming over at te Beginning of April: but I hoped te Session would be ended, and I must stay till then, & yet I would fain be at te Beginning of my Willows growing. Percivall tells me that te Quicksetts upon te flatt in te Garden, do not grow so well as those famous ones on te Ditch. They want digging about them; The Cherry trees by te River side my Heart is sett upon. Nite MD.

27. Society day. Y know that I suppose. Dr Arthburnett was Presidt. His dinner was dresst in te Qu—s Kitchin, and was mighty fine; & we eat it at Ozinda's Chocolate house just by St James's. We were never merryer nor bettr company, and did not part till after 11 I did not summon Ld Lansdown: He and I are fallen out. There was something in an Examiner a fortnight ago that he thought reflected on te Abuses in his Office, (he is Secrtry at War) & he writt to te Secty that he had heard I had inserted that Paragraph. This I resented highly, that he should comlain of me before he spoke to me; and I sent him a peppering Letter, and would not summon him by a Note as I do the rest; nor ever will have anything to say to him till he begs my Pardon. I mett Ld Treasr to day at Ldy Masham's he would have fain carryed me home to dinner, but I beggd his Pardon; what? upon a Society day? No no. Tis rate Sollahs; I ant dlunk. Nite MD.

28. I was with my Friend Lewis to day getting Materials for a little Mischief; and I dined with Ld Treasr, and 3 or 4 fellows I never saw before; I left them at 7, and came home, and have been writing to te A.Bp Dubln, and Cozn Dean in answer to one of his of 4 months old, that I spied by chance routing among my Papers.

---

1 Slaughterers.   2 Not until 1752 was the Gregorian calendar accepted.

I have a Pain these 2 days exactly upon te Top of my left Shouldr, I fear it is something Rheumatick, it winches now and then. Shall I putt Flannell to it? Domvile is going to Ireld; he came here this morning to take leave of me; but I shall dine with him to-morrow. Does te Bp of Cl talk of coming for Engd this Summer? I think Ld Molesworth told me so about 2 Months ago. Th weathr is bad again, rainy and very cold this Evening. Do y know what te Longitude is? a Projector has been applying himself to me to recommend him to te Ministry, because he pretends to have found out te Longitude I believe he has no more found it out, than he has found out mine *** However I will gravely hear what he says, and discover him a Knave or Fool. Nite MD.

29. I am plagued with these Pain in my Shouldr; I believe it is Rheumatick; I will do something for to Night. Mr Lewis & I dined with Mr. Domvile to take our Leave of him; I drunk 3 or 4 Glasses of Champigne by perfect teazing thō it is bad for my Pain; but if it continues I will not drink any wine without Water till I am well. The Weathr is abominably cold and wet.— I am got into bed and have put some old Flannel for want of new to my Shouldr, and rubbd it with Hungary water.[3]—Tis plaguy hard; I never would drink any Wine if it were not for my Head, and drinking has given me this Pain. I will try Abstemiousness for a while. How does MD do now? how does Dd & ppt? You must know I hate Pain, as te old woman sd—But I'll try to go seep; My Flesh sucks up Hungary water rarely. My Man's an awkward Rascal, and makes me peevish. Do yo know that tother day he was forced to beg my Pardon that he could not shave my Head, his Hand shook so. He is drunk every day & I design to turn him off soon as ever I get to Ireld. I ll write no more now, but go to Sleep, and see whether Sleep & Flannell will cure my Shouldr. Nite deelest MD.

30. I was not able to go to Church or Court to day, for my Shouldr; th Pain has left my Shouldr and crept to my neck and Collar bone. It makes me think of poop't's bladebone. Urge, urge, urge, dogs gnawing.. I went in a Chair at 2 and dined with Mrs Van, where I could be easy; & came back at 7, My Hungary water is gone, & to night I use Spirits of wine, wch my Landlady

3 Rosemary flowers distilled with spirit of wine.

tells me is very good. It has raind terribly all day long; & is extreamly cold: I am very uneasy, and such cruell Twinges every moment. Nite deelest MD.

31. Ap. 1, 2, 3, 4, 5, 6, 7,—8. All these days I have been extreamly ill, tho I twice crawld out a week ago; but am now recovering, thō very weak. The violence of my Pain abated the night before last; I will just tell y how I was & then send away this Lettr wch ought to have gone Saterday last. Th Pain encreasd with mighty Violence in my left Shouldr & Collar bone & that side of my Neck. On Thursday morning appeared great Red Spots in all those Places where my Pain was, & te violence of te Pain was confined to my Neck behind a little on te left side; which was so violent that I [had] not a minutes ease nor hardly a minutes sleep in 3 days & nights. te Spots encreasd every day & had little Pimples which are now grown white & full of corruption [thō] small. te Red still continues too, and most prodigious hott & inflamed. The Disease is te Shingles th I eat nothing but Water gruell; I am very weak but out of all violent Pain. Th Doctrs say it would have ended in some violent Disease if it had not come out thus. I shall now recover fast. I have been in no danger of Life, but miserable Torture. I must not write too much —so adieu deelest MD MD MD FW FW Me Me Me Lele I can say lele yet oo see—Fais I dont conceal a bitt. as hope savd

I must purge & clystr after this; and my next Letter will not be in te old order of Journall till I have done with Physick. An't oo surprisd to see te Lettr want half a side

LETTER XLV

London. *Apr.* 24. 1712

I had yr 28th 2 or 3 days ago. I can hardly answer it now— Since my last I have been extremely ill. Tis this day just a Month since I felt a small pain on te tip of my left Shoulder, which grew worse & spread for 6 days; then broke all out by my collar, & left side of my neck in monstrous red Spotts, inflamed, & these grew to small Pimples. for 4 days I had no rest nor nights for a Pain in my neck; then I grew a little bettr; afterwards, where my Pains were a cruell Itching seised me beyond what ever I could imagine, & kept me awake severall Nights. I rubbd it vehemently but did not scratch it. Then it grew into three or for great Sores like Blisters and run; at last I advised te Dr to use it like a Blister; so I did, with Melilot Plaisters, which still run, and I am now in pain enough; but am daily mendeng: I kept my Chambr a fortnight; then went out a day or 2; but then confined my self again. 2 days ago, I a went to a Neighbr to dine, but yesterday again kept at home: to day I will venture abroad a little; and hope to be well in a week or ten days. I never suffered so much in my life; I have taken my Breeches in above 2 Inches, so I am leaner, wch answers one Question in yr Letter. Th Weathr is mighty fine, I write in te morning, because I am better then. I will go and try to walk a little; I will give Dd's Certificate to Took to morrow farewell MD MD MD Me Me FW FW Me M—.

LETTER XLVI

London. *May.* 10. 1712.

I have not yet ease or Humor enough to go on in my Journall Method, thō I have left my Chambr these 10 days. My Pain continues still in my Shouldr and Collar I keep Flannel on it, and rub it with Brandy; and take a nasty dyet Drink I still Itch terribly, & have some few Pimples; I am weak & sweat, & then te Flannell makes me mad with Itching; but I think my Pain lessens. A Journall while I was sick would have been a noble thing, made up of Pain; and Physick, & Visits & Messages. The 2 last were almost as troublesome as te 2 first. One good Circumstance is that I am grown much leaner, I believe I told you, that I have taken in my Breeches 2 Inches. I had yr N. 29 last night. In answer to yr good opinion of my disease, te Drs sd they never saw any thing so odd of the Kind; they were not properly Shingles, but Herpes miliaris, and 20 other hard names.. I can never be sick like othr People, but always something out of te common way; and as for yr notion of it coming without Pain, it neither came, nor stayd, nor went without Pain, & th most pain I ever bore in my Life—Madameris is retired in te Country with te Beast her Husband long ago—I thank te Bp of Cl for his Proxy; I will write to him soon. Here is Dilly's Wife in Town, but I have not seen her yet—No, Sinkerton tis not a Sign of Health, but a Sign that if it had not come out some terrible Fitt of Sickness would have followd. I was at our Society last Thursday, to receive a new Membr, te Chancellor of th

Exchequr; but I drink nothing above wine & water—We shall have a Peace I hope soon, or at least entirely broke, but I believe te first. My Lettr to Ld Treasr about te Engl. Tongue is now printing; and I suffer my name to be put at te End of it, wch I nevr did before in my Life. The Appendix to th 3d Part of John Bull was published yesterday; tis equall to te rest. I hope y read John Bull. It was a Scotch Gentleman a friend of mine that writ it; but they put it upon me. The Parlmt will hardly be up till June. We were like to be undone some days ago with a Tack,[1] but we carryed it bravely, and the Whigs came in to help us. Poor Ldy Masham I am afraid will lose her onely son, about a twelve Month old, with te King's Evil. I never would let Mrs Fenton see me in my Illness, tho she often came, but she has been once here since I recovered.. Bernage has been twice to see me of late. His Regimt will be broke, and he onely upon half pay; so perhaps he thinks he will want me again. I am told here that te Bp of Cloghr & Family are coming over, but he says nothing of it himself.—I have been returning th Visits of those that sent Howdees in my Sickness, particularly te Dutchess of Hamilton, who came & satt with me 2 hours; I make Bargains with all People that I dine with, to let me scrub my Back agst a Chair, & te Dutchess of Ormd was forced to bear it tother day: Many of my Friends are gone to Kensington where te Qu— has been removed for some time—This is a long Lettr for a kick body; I will begin te next in te Journall way, thō my Journals will be sorry ones.—My left Hand is very weak & trembles; but my right side has not been toucht This is a pitifull Letter for want of a better, but plagud with a Tetter, my Fancy does fetter—Ah my poor willows & Quicksets,—Well, but y must read John Bull. Do y understand it all? Did I tell y that young Parson Geree is going to be marryed, and asked my Advice when it was too late to break off. He tells me Elwick has purchasd 40ll a year in Land adjoyning to his Living. Ppt does not say one word of her own little Health. I'm angry almost; but I won't tause see im a dood dallar in odle sings, iss and so im Dd too. Gd bless MD & FW & Me, ay & pdfr too. farewell MD MD MD FW FW FW Me Me. Lele I can say lele it ung oomens iss I tan, well as oo.

1 A rider tacked to a bill.

LETTER LXV

Chester. *Jun.* 6. 1713.

I am come here after 6 days; I sett out on Monday last, and gott here to day about 11 in the morning. A Noble Rider fais; and all the Ships and People went off yesterday with a rare wind. This was told me to my Comfort upon my Arrivall. Having not used riding these 3 years, made me terrible weary; yet I resolve on Monday to sett out for Holyhead, as weary as I am Tis good for my Health mun. When I came here I found MD's Letter of te 26th of May sent down to me,—had y writt a Post sooner, I might have brought some Pins; but yo were lazy, & would not write yr orders immediatly as I desired you— I will come when God Pleases, perhaps I may be with you in a week; I will be 3 days going to Holyhead; I cannot ride faster; say hat oo will. I am upon Stay-behind's mare. I have te whole Inn to my self, I would fain scape this Holy-head Journy, but I have no Prospect of Ships, and it will be almost necessary I shoud be in Dublin before te 25th instant, to take the [oaths]; otherwise I must wait to a quarter Sessions. I will lodge as I can; therefore take no lodgings for me, to pay in my absence, the poor Dean can't afford it. I spoke again to D. Ormd about Moimed for Raymd, & hope he may yet have it. for I laid it strongly to te Duke, & gave him te Bp of Meath's Memoriall: I am sorry for Raymd's Fistula, tell him so. I will speak to Ld Tr— about Mrs South to morrow—Odso, I forgot; I thought I had been in London. Mrs Tisdal is very big, ready to ly down. Her Husband is a puppy. Do his feet stink still:—The Letters to Ireld go at so uncertain an Hour, that I am forced to conclude—farewell

MD MD MD FW FW FW Me Me Me

lele lele

lele Logues ad

Ladies bose fais

and ******

I mightily approve ppt's Project of *hanging te blind* Parson—when I read that Passage upon Chester walls, as I was coming into Town, & just receivd te Lettr: I sd aloud — Agreable B—tch—

STELLA'S BIRTHDAY, 1720/21

1727

All travellers at first incline
Where'er they see the fairest sign:
And if they find the chambers neat,
And like the liquor and the meat,
Will call again, and recommend
The Angel-inn to every friend.
What though the painting grows decay'd,
The house will never lose its trade:
Nay, though the treach'rous tapster Thomas
Hangs a new angel two doors from us,   10
As fine as daubers' hands can make it
In hopes that strangers may mistake it,
We think it both a shame and sin
To quit the true old Angel-inn.
  Now this is Stella's case in fact,
An angel's face, a little crack'd,
Could poets, or could painters fix
How angels look at thirty-six:
This drew us in at first to find
In such a form an angel's mind;   20
And ev'ry virtue now supplies
The fainting rays of Stella's eyes:
See at her levee crowding swains,
Whom Stella freely entertains
With breeding, humour, wit, and sense,
And puts them but to small expence,
Their mind so plentifully fills,
And makes such reasonable bills,
So little gets for what she gives
We really wonder how she lives!   30
And had her stock been less, no doubt
She must have long ago run out.
  Then who can think we'll quit the place
When Doll hangs out a newer face?
Or stop and light at Cloe's head,

With scraps and leavings to be fed?
   Then, Cloe, still go on to prate
Of thirty-six, and thirty-eight;
Pursue your trade of scandal-picking,
Your hints, that Stella is no chicken;   40
Your innuendos, when you tell us
That Stella loves to talk with fellows:
And let me warn you to believe
A truth for which your soul should grieve,
That, should you live to see the day
When Stella's locks must all be grey,
When age must print a furrow'd trace
On every feature of her face;
Though you, and all your senseless tribe,
Could art or time or nature bribe   50
To make you look like beauty's queen,
And hold for ever at fifteen,
No bloom of youth can ever blind
The cracks and wrinkles of your mind:
All men of sense will pass your door,
And crowd to Stella's at fourscore.

THE FURNITURE OF A WOMAN'S MIND

1727

A set of phrases learn't by rote;
A passion for a scarlet-coat;
When at a play to laugh, or cry,
You cannot tell the reason why:
Never to hold her tongue a minute;
While all she prates has nothing in it.
Whole hours can with a coxcomb sit,
And take his nonsense all for wit:
Her learning mounts to read a song,
But, half the words pronouncing wrong;   10
Has ev'ry repartee in store,
She spoke ten thousand times before.
Can ready compliments supply
On all occasions, cut and dry.
Such hatred to a parson's gown,

The sight will put her in a swown.
For conversation well endu'd;
She calls it witty to be rude;
And, placing raillery in railing,
Will tell aloud your greatest failing;   20
Nor makes a scruple to expose
Your bandy leg, or crooked nose.
Can, at her morning tea, run o'er
The scandal of the day before.
Improving hourly in her skill,
To cheat and wrangle at quadrille.

In chusing lace a critick nice,
Knows to a groat the lowest price;
Can in her female clubs dispute
What lining best the silk will suit;   30
What colours each complexion match:
And where with art to place a patch.

If chance a mouse creeps in her sight,
Can finely counterfeit a fright;
So, sweetly screams if it comes near her,
She ravishes all hearts to hear her.
Can dext'rously her husband teize,
By taking fits whene'er she please:
By frequent practice learns the trick
At proper seasons to be sick;   40
Thinks nothing gives one airs so pretty;
At once creating love and pity.
If Molly happens to be careless,
And but neglects to warm her hair-lace,
She gets a cold as sure as death;
And vows she scarce can fetch her breath.
Admires how modest women can
Be so *robustious* like a man.

In party, furious to her power;
A bitter Whig, or Tory sow'r;   50
Her arguments directly tend
Against the side she would defend:
Will prove herself a Tory plain,

From principles the Whigs maintain;
And, to defend the Whiggish cause,
Her topicks from the Tories draws.

O yes! If any man can find
More virtues in a woman's mind,
Let them be sent to Mrs. Harding; [1]
She'll pay the charges to a farthing: 60
Take notice, she has my commission
To add them in the next edition;
They may out-sell a better thing;
So, holla, boys; God save the king.

[1] "The widow of John Harding, printer of the Drapier's Letters." (Harold Williams)

[handwritten: an address to + assault upon Ireland — they themselves are plainly taxed w bringing about their own deplorable condition]

A MODEST PROPOSAL

[handwritten: Reveal Ireland's economic situation]

FOR PREVENTING THE CHILDREN OF POOR PEOPLE IN IRELAND FROM BEING A BURTHEN TO THEIR PARENTS OR COUNTRY, AND FOR MAKING THEM BENEFICIAL TO THE PUBLIC

1729 *[handwritten: object of attack — English legislators, landlords]*

It is a melancholy object to those who walk through this great town, or travel in the country, when they see the streets, the roads, and cabin doors crowded with beggars of the female sex, followed by three, four, or six children, *all in rags*, and importuning every passenger for an alms. These mothers instead of being able to work for their honest livelihood, are forced to employ all their time in strolling, to beg sustenance for their helpless infants, who, as they grow up, either turn thieves for want of work, or leave their dear Native Country to fight for the Pretender in Spain, or sell themselves to the Barbados.

I think it is agreed by all parties that this prodigious number of

[handwritten: the proposal is no more shocking than the state of affairs which exists]

children —
grievance of
state

pride

children, in the arms, or on the backs, or at the heels of their mothers, and frequently of their fathers, is in the present deplorable state of the kingdom a very great additional grievance; and therefore whoever could find out a fair, cheap, and easy method of making these children sound, useful members of the commonwealth would deserve so well of the public as to have his statue set up for a preserver of the nation.

But my intention is very far from being confined to provide only for the children of professed beggars; it is of a much greater extent, and shall take in the whole number of infants at a certain age who are born of parents in effect as little able to support them as those who demand our charity in the streets.

As to my own part, having turned my thoughts, for many years, upon this important subject, and maturely weighed the several schemes of other projectors, I have always found them grossly mistaken in their computation. It is true a child, just dropped from its dam, may be supported by her milk for a solar year with little other nourishment, at most not above the value of two shillings, which the mother may certainly get, or the value in scraps, by her lawful occupation of begging; and it is exactly at one year old that I propose to provide for them, in such a manner, as, instead of being a charge upon their parents, or the parish, or wanting food and raiment for the rest of their lives, they shall, on the contrary, contribute to the feeding and partly to the clothing of many thousands.

There is likewise another great advantage in my scheme: that it will prevent those voluntary abortions, and that horrid practice of women murdering their bastard children, alas, too frequent among us, sacrificing the poor innocent babes, I doubt, more to avoid the expense than the shame, which would move tears and pity in the most savage and inhuman breast.

The number of souls in this kingdom being usually reckoned one million and a half, of these I calculate there may be about two hundred thousand couple whose wives are breeders, from which number I substract thirty thousand couple who are able to maintain their own children, although I apprehend there cannot be so many under the present distresses of the kingdom; but this being granted, there will remain an hundred and seventy thousand breeders. I again subtract fifty thousand for those women who miscarry, or whose children die by accident or disease within the year. There only remain an hundred and twenty thousand children

Swift outraged morally

of poor parents annually born: the question therefore is, how this number shall be reared and provided for, which, as I have already said, under the present situation of affairs, is utterly impossible by all the methods hitherto proposed, for we can neither employ them in handicraft or agriculture; we neither build houses (I mean in the country) nor cultivate land: they can very seldom pick up a livelihood *by stealing* till they arrive at six years old, except where they are of towardly parts, although I confess they learn the rudiments much earlier, during which time they can however be properly looked upon only as *probationers*, as I have been informed by a principal gentleman in the County of Cavan, who protested to me that he never knew above one or two instances under the age of six, even in a part of the kingdom so renowned for the quickest proficiency in that art.

I am assured by our merchants that a boy or a girl, before twelve years old, is no saleable commodity, and even when they come to this age, they will not yield above three pounds, or three pounds and half-a-crown at most on the Exchange, which cannot turn to account either to the parents or kingdom, the charge of nutriment and rags having been at least four times that value.

I shall now therefore humbly propose my own thoughts, which I hope will not be liable to the least objection.

I have been assured by a very knowing American of my acquaintance in London that a young healthy child well nursed is at a year old a most delicious, nourishing, and wholesome food, whether stewed, roasted, baked, or boiled, and I make no doubt that it will equally serve in a fricassee, or a ragout.

I do therefore humbly offer it to public consideration that of the hundred and twenty thousand children already computed, twenty thousand may be reserved for breed, whereof only one fourth part to be males, which is more than we allow to sheep, black-cattle, or swine, and my reason is that these children are seldom the fruits of marriage, a circumstance not much regarded by our savages; therefore one male will be sufficient to serve four females. That the remaining hundred thousand may at a year old be offered in sale to the persons of quality and fortune, through the kingdom, always advising the mother to let them suck plentifully in the last month, so as to render them plump and fat for a good table. A child will make two dishes at an entertainment for friends, and when the family dines alone, the fore or hind quarter

direct expression of Swift's Rage

will make a reasonable dish, and seasoned with a little pepper or salt will be very good boiled on the fourth day, especially in winter.

I have reckoned upon a medium, that a child just born will weigh twelve pounds, and in a solar year if tolerably nursed increaseth to twenty-eight pounds.

I grant this food will be somewhat dear, and therefore very proper for landlords, who, as they have already devoured most of the parents, seem to have the best title to the children.

Infants' flesh will be in season throughout the year, but more plentiful in March, and a little before and after, for we are told by a grave author, an eminent French physician, that fish being a prolific diet, there are more children born in Roman Catholic countries about nine months after Lent than at any other season; therefore reckoning a year after Lent, the markets will be more glutted than usual, because the number of Popish infants is at least three to one in this kingdom, and therefore it will have one other collateral advantage by lessening the number of Papists among us.

I have already computed the charge of nursing a beggar's child (in which list I reckon all cottagers, laborers, and four-fifths of the farmers) to be about two shillings *per annum*, rags included, and I believe no gentleman would repine to give ten shillings for the carcass of a good fat child, which, as I have said, will make four dishes of excellent nutritive meat, when he hath only some particular friend or his own family to dine with him. Thus the squire will learn to be a good landlord, and grow popular among his tenants, the mother will have eight shillings net profit, and be fit for work till she produces another child.

Those who are more thrifty (as I must confess the times require) may flay the carcass; the skin of which, artificially dressed, will make admirable gloves for ladies, and summer boots for fine gentlemen.

As to our City of Dublin, shambles may be appointed for this purpose in the most convenient parts of it, and butchers we may be assured will not be wanting, although I rather recommend buying the children alive, and dressing them hot from the knife, as we do roasting pigs.

A very worthy person, a true lover of his country, and whose virtues I highly esteem, was lately pleased, in discoursing on this matter, to offer a refinement upon my scheme. He said that many gentlemen of this kingdom having of late destroyed their deer, he conceived that the want of venison might be well supplied by the bodies of young lads and maidens, not exceeding fourteen years of age, nor under twelve, so great a number of both sexes in every country being now ready to starve for want of work and service: and these to be disposed of by their parents if alive, or otherwise by their nearest relations. But with due deference to so excellent a friend, and so deserving a patriot, I cannot be altogether in his sentiments; for as to the males, my American acquaintance assured me, from frequent experience, that their flesh was generally tough and lean, like that of our schoolboys, by continual exercise, and their taste disagreeable, and to fatten them would not answer the charge. Then as to the females, it would, I think with humble submission, be a loss to the public, because they soon would become breeders themselves: and besides, it is not improbable that some scrupulous people might be apt to censure such a practice (although indeed very unjustly) as a little bordering upon cruelty; which, I confess, hath always been with me the strongest objection against any project, however so well intended.

But in order to justify my friend, he confessed that this expedient was put into his head by the famous Psalmanazar, a native of the island Formosa, who came from thence to London above twenty years ago, and in conversation told my friend that in his country when any young person happened to be put to death, the executioner sold the carcass to persons of quality, as a prime dainty, and that, in his time, the body of a plump girl of fifteen, who was crucified for an attempt to poison the emperor, was sold to his Imperial Majesty's Prime Minister of State, and other great Mandarins of the Court, in joints from the gibbet, at four hundred crowns. Neither indeed can I deny that if the same use were made of several plump young girls in this town, who, without one single groat to their fortunes, cannot stir abroad without a chair, and appear at the playhouse and assemblies in foreign fineries, which they never will pay for, the kingdom would not be the worse.

Some persons of a desponding spirit are in great concern about that vast number of poor people who are aged, diseased, or maimed, and I have been desired to employ my thoughts what course may be taken to ease the nation of so grievous an encumbrance. But I am not in the least pain upon that matter, because it is very well known that they are every day dying and rotting, by cold, and famine, and filth, and vermin, as fast as can be reasonably expected.

And as to the younger laborers, they are now in almost as hopeful a condition. They cannot get work, and consequently pine away for want of nourishment to a degree that if at any time they are accidentally hired to common labor, they have not strength to perform it; and thus the country and themselves are in a fair way of being soon delivered from the evils to come.

I have too long digressed, and therefore shall return to my subject. I think the advantages by the proposal which I have made are obvious and many, as well as of the highest importance.

For *first*, as I have already observed, it would greatly lessen the number of Papists, with whom we are yearly overrun, being the principal breeders of the nation, as well as our most dangerous enemies, and who stay at home on purpose with a design to deliver the kingdom to the Pretender, hoping to take their advantage by the absence of so many good Protestants, who have chosen rather to leave their country [1] than stay at home and pay tithes, against their conscience, to an Episcopal curate.

Secondly, The poorer tenants will have something valuable of their own, which by law may be made liable to distress, and help to pay their landlords rent, their corn and cattle being already seized, and *money a thing unknown.*

Thirdly, Whereas the maintenance of an hundred thousand children, from two years old and upwards cannot be computed at less than ten shillings apiece *per annum,* the nation's stock will be thereby increased fifty thousand pounds *per annum,* besides the profit of a new dish, introduced to the tables of all gentlemen of fortune in the kingdom, who have any refinement in taste, and the money will circulate among ourselves, the goods being entirely of our own growth and manufacture.

Fourthly, The constant breeders, besides the gain of eight shillings sterling *per annum,* by the sale of their children, will be rid of the charge of maintaining them after the first year.

Fifthly, This food would likewise bring great custom to taverns, where the vintners will certainly be so prudent as to procure the best receipts for dressing it to perfection, and consequently have their houses frequented by all the fine gentlemen who justly value themselves upon their knowledge in good eating; and a skillful

[1] One of the grievous burdens Ireland bore was the absentee landlord, who spent in England what he wrenched from Ireland.

cook, who understands how to oblige his guests, will contrive to make it as expensive as they please.

Sixthly, This would be a great inducement to marriage, which all wise nations have either encouraged by rewards, or enforced by laws and penalties. It would increase the care and tenderness of mothers toward their children when they were sure of a settlement for life to the poor babes, provided in some sort by the public to their annual profit instead of expense. We should see an honest emulation among the married women, which of them could bring the fattest child to the market; men would become as fond of their wives during the time of their pregnancy as they are now of their mares in foal, their cows in calf, or sows when they are ready to farrow, nor offer to beat or kick them (as it is too frequent a practice) for fear of a miscarriage.

Many other advantages might be enumerated: for instance, the addition of some thousand carcasses in our exportation of barreled beef; the propagation of swine's flesh, and improvement in the art of making good bacon, so much wanted among us by the great destruction of pigs, too frequent at our tables, which are noway comparable in taste or magnificence to a well-grown, fat yearling child, which roasted whole will make a considerable figure at a Lord Mayor's feast, or any other public entertainment. But this, and many others, I omit, being studious of brevity.

Supposing that one thousand families in this city would be constant customers for infants' flesh, besides others who might have it at merry meetings, particularly weddings and christenings, I compute that Dublin would take off annually about twenty thousand carcasses, and the rest of the kingdom (where probably they will be sold somewhat cheaper) the remaining eighty thousand.

I can think of no one objection that will possibly be raised against this proposal, unless it should be urged that the number of people will be thereby much lessened in the kingdom. This I freely own, and was indeed one principal design in offering it to the world. I desire the reader will observe that I calculate my remedy *for this one individual Kingdom of Ireland, and for no other that ever was, is, or, I think, ever can be upon earth.* Therefore let no man talk to me of other expedients: *Of taxing our absentees at five shillings a pound: Of using neither clothes, nor household furniture, except what is of our own growth and manufacture: Of utterly rejecting the materials and instruments that promote foreign luxury: Of curing the expensiveness of pride, vanity, idleness, and gaming in our women: Of introducing a vein of parsimony, prudence, and temperance: Of learning to love our Country, wherein we differ even from* LAPLANDERS, *and the inhabitants of* TOPINAMBOO: *Of quitting our animosities and factions, nor act any longer like the Jews, who were murdering one another at the very moment their city was taken: Of being a little cautious not to sell our country and consciences for nothing: Of teaching landlords to have at least one degree of mercy toward their tenants. Lastly, of putting a spirit of honesty, industry, and skill into our shopkeepers, who, if a resolution could now be taken to buy only our native goods, would immediately unite to cheat and exact upon us in the price, the measure, and the goodness, nor could ever yet be brought to make one fair proposal of just dealing, though often and earnestly invited to it.*

Therefore, I repeat, let no man talk to me of these and the like expedients till he hath at least some glimpse of hope that there will ever be some hearty and sincere attempt to put them in practice.

But as to myself, having been wearied out for many years with offering vain, idle, visionary thoughts, and at length utterly despairing of success, I fortunately fell upon this proposal, which as it is wholly new, so it hath something solid and real, of no expense and little trouble, full in our own power, and whereby we can incur no danger in *disobliging* ENGLAND. For this kind of commodity will not bear exportation, the flesh being of too tender a consistence to admit a long continuance in salt, *although perhaps I could name a country, which would be glad to eat up our whole nation without it.*

After all, I am not so violently bent upon my own opinion as to reject any offer, proposed by wise men, which shall be found equally innocent, cheap, easy, and effectual. But before something of that kind shall be advanced in contradiction to my scheme, and offering a better, I desire the author or authors will be pleased maturely to consider two points. *First*, as things now stand, how they will be able to find food and raiment for an hundred thousand useless mouths and backs. And *secondly*, there being a round million of creatures in human figure, throughout this kingdom, whose whole subsistence put into a common stock would leave them in debt two millions of pounds sterling; adding those who are beggars by profession to the bulk of farmers, cottagers, and laborers with their wives and children, who are beggars in effect; I desire those politicians who dislike my overture, and may perhaps be so bold to attempt an answer, that they will first ask the parents of these mortals whether they would not at this day think it a great happiness to have been sold for food at a year old, in the manner I prescribe, and thereby have avoided such a perpetual scene of misfortunes as they have since gone through by the oppression of landlords, the impossibility of paying rent without money or trade, the want of common sustenance, with neither house nor clothes to cover them from the inclemencies of the weather, and the most inevitable prospect of entailing the like, or greater, miseries upon their breed forever.

I profess in the sincerity of my heart that I have not the least personal interest in endeavoring to promote this necessary work, having no other motive than the *public good of my country by advancing our trade, providing for infants, relieving the poor, and giving some pleasure to the rich.* I have no children by which I can propose to get a single penny; the youngest being nine years old, and my wife past childbearing.

VERSES ON THE DEATH OF DR. SWIFT, OCCASIONED BY READING THE FOLLOWING MAXIM IN ROCHEFOUCAULD

Written in Nov. 1731

Dans l'adversité de nos meilleurs amis nous trouvons toujours quelque chose, qui ne nous déplaît pas.
In the adversity of our best friends we always find something that doth not displease us.

1739

As Rochefoucault his maxims drew
From nature, I believe 'em true:
They argue no corrupted mind
In him; the fault is in mankind.

This maxim more than all the rest
Is thought too base for human breast:
"In all distresses of our friends
We first consult our private ends,
While nature, kindly bent to ease us,
Points out some circumstance to please us."   10
    If this perhaps your patience move,
Let reason and experience prove.
    We all behold with envious eyes
Our equal rais'd above our size.
Who would not at a crowded show
Stand high himself, keep others low?
I love my friend as well as you:
But would not have him stop my view;
Then let him have the higher post;
I ask but for an inch at most.   20
    If in battle you should find
One, whom you love of all mankind,
Had some heroick action done,
A champion kill'd, or trophy won;
Rather than thus be over-topt,
Would you not wish his lawrels cropt?
    Dear honest Ned is in the gout,
Lies rackt with pain, and you without:
How patiently you hear him groan!
How glad the case is not your own!   30
    What poet would not grieve to see
His brethren write as well as he?
But rather than they should excel,
He'd wish his rivals all in hell.
    Her end when emulation misses,
She turns to envy, stings, and hisses:
The strongest friendship yields to pride,
Unless the odds be on our side.
    Vain human kind! fantastick race!
Thy various follies, who can trace?   40
Self-love, ambition, envy, pride,
Their empire in our hearts divide:
Give others riches, power, and station;
'Tis all on me an usurpation;
I have no title to aspire;
Yet, when you sink, I seem the higher.
In Pope, I cannot read a line,

But with a sigh I wish it mine:
When he can in one couplet fix
More sense than I can do in six;   50
It gives me such a jealous fit,
I cry, "Pox take him and his wit!"

   Why must I be outdone by Gay
In my own hum'rous biting way.

   Arbuthnot is no more my friend,
Who dares to irony pretend;
Which I was born to introduce,
Refin'd it first, and show'd its use.

   St. John,[1] as well as Pulteney knows
That I had some repute for prose;   60
And, till they drove me out of date,
Could maul a minister of state:
If they have mortify'd my pride,
And made me throw my pen aside;
If with such talents Heav'n hath blest 'em,
Have I not reason to detest 'em?

   To all my foes, dear Fortune, send
Thy gifts, but never to my friend:
I tamely can endure the first;
But this with envy makes me burst.   70

   Thus much may serve by way of proem,
Proceed we therefore to our poem.

   The time is not remote, when I
Must by the course of nature dye:
When I foresee my special friends
Will try to find their private ends:
Tho' it is hardly understood
Which way my death can do them good;
Yet thus, methinks, I hear 'em speak;
"See, how the Dean begins to break: 80
Poor gentleman! he droops apace!
You plainly find it in his face.
That old vertigo in his head
Will never leave him, till he's dead.
Besides, his memory decays,

1 Henry St. John, Viscount Boling-broke, Secretary of State in 1710 and founder of the Tory Brothers' Club; at the accession of George I, he was attainted and fled to France, where he became secretary to James the Pretender. He returned to London, pardoned, in 1723. William Pulteney deserted Robert Walpole for Bolingbroke in 1726. Bolingbroke and Pulteney became the center of a group (including Pope, Thomson, Akenside, and Swift) that opposed Walpole.

He recollects not what he says;
He cannot call his friends to mind;
Forgets the place where last he din'd:
Plyes you with stories o'er and o'er,
He told them fifty times before.   90
How does he fancy we can sit
To hear his out-of-fashion'd wit?
But he takes up with younger folks,
Who for his wine will bear his jokes:
Faith, he must make his stories shorter,
Or change his comrades once a quarter:
In half the time he talks them round;
There must another sett be found.

    "For poetry, he's past his prime,
He takes an hour to find a rhime: 100
His fire is out, his wit decay'd,
His fancy sunk, his Muse a jade.
I'd have him throw away his pen;—
But there's no talking to some men."

And, then their tenderness appears
By adding largely to my years:
"He's older than he would be reckon'd,
And well remembers Charles the Second.

    "He hardly drinks a pint of wine;
And that, I doubt, is no good sign.   110
His stomach, too, begins to fail:
Last year we thought him strong and hale;
But now he's quite another thing:
I wish he may hold out till spring."

    Then hug themselves, and reason thus;
"It is not yet so bad with us."

    In such a case they talk in tropes,
And, by their fears express their hopes.
Some great misfortune to portend
No enemy can match a friend;   120
With all the kindness they profess,
The merit of a lucky guess
(When daily how-d'ye's come of course,
And servants answer, "Worse and worse")
Would please 'em better, than to tell,
That, "God be prais'd! the Dean is well."
Then he, who prophecy'd the best,
Approves his foresight to the rest:

"You know I always fear'd the worst,
And often told you so at first." 130
He'd rather chuse that I should dye,
Than his prediction prove a lye.
Not one foretels I shall recover;
But, all agree, to give me over.

Yet should some neighbour feel a pain,
Just in the parts where I complain;
How many a message would he send?
What hearty prayers that I should mend?
Enquire what regimen I kept;
What gave me ease, and how I slept? 140
And more lament, when I was dead,
Than all the sniv'llers round my bed.

My good companions, never fear;
For though you may mistake a year,
Though your prognosticks run too fast,
They must be verify'd at last.

Behold the fatal day arrive!
"How is the Dean?" "He's just alive.
Now the departing prayer is read;
He hardly breathes"—"The Dean is dead." 150
Before the passing-bell begun,
The news thro' half the town has run.
"O, may we all for death prepare!
What has he left? and who's his heir?"
"I know no more than what the news is,
'Tis all bequeath'd to publick uses."
"To publick use! a perfect whim!
What had the publick done for him!
Meer envy, avarice, and pride!
He gave it all—but first he dy'd. 160
And had the Dean, in all the nation,
No worthy friend, no poor relation?
So ready to do strangers good,
Forgetting his own flesh and blood!"

Now Grub Street wits are all employ'd;
With elegies, the town is cloy'd:
Some paragraph in ev'ry paper
To curse the Dean, or bless the Drapier.

The doctors, tender of their fame,
Wisely on me lay all the blame. 170
"We must confess his case was nice;

But he would never take advice:
Had he been rul'd, for aught appears,
He might have liv'd these twenty years:
For, when we open'd him, we found,
That all his vital parts were sound."

From Dublin soon to London spread,
'Tis told at court, "The Dean is dead."
Kind Lady Suffolk, in the spleen,
Runs laughing up to tell the Queen.   180
The Queen, so gracious, mild, and good,
Cries, "Is he gone! 'tis time he should.
He's dead, you say; why, let him rot;
I'm glad the medals were forgot.
I promis'd them, I own; but when?
I only was a princess then;
But now, as consort of the king,
You know 'tis quite a diff'rent thing."

Now Chartres,[2] at Sir Robert's levee,
Tells, with a sneer, the tidings heavy: 190
"Why, is he dead without his shoes?"
(Cries Bob) [3] "I'm sorry for the news;
Oh, were the wretch but living still,
And in his place my good friend Will; [4]
Or had a mitre on his head,
Provided Bolingbroke were dead!"

Now Curll [5] his shop from rubbish drains;
Three genuine tomes of Swift's remains.
And then, to make them pass the glibber,
Revis'd by Tibbalds, Moore, and Cibber.[6]   200
He'll treat me as he does my betters,
Publish my will, my life, my letters;
Revive the libels born to dye;
Which Pope must bear, as well as I.

Here shift the scene, to represent
How those I love my death lament.
Poor Pope will grieve a month; and Gay

2 Francis Charteris, notorious lecher and rake; he was dismissed from the army for cheating.
3 Sir Robert Walpole, Prime Minister.
4 William Pulteney.
5 Edmund Curll, the bookseller notorious for pirating, indecent publications, and frauds. He was involved in the plots and counter-plots attending the publication of Pope's correspondence.

6 Lewis Theobald, author of *Shakespeare Restored* (1726), exposed the weaknesses of Pope's edition of Shakespeare; in revenge, Pope made him the first hero of the *Dunciad*, James Moore was likewise satirized in the *Dunciad*. Colley Cibber, actor, dramatist, and poet laureate, replaced Theobald as hero of the second edition of the *Dunciad*.

A week; and Arbuthnot a day.
   St. John himself will scarce forbear
To bite his pen, and drop a tear.   210
The rest will give a shrug and cry,
"I'm sorry; but we all must die!"
Indifference clad in wisdom's guise
All fortitude of mind supplies:
For how can stony bowels melt
In those who never pity felt?
When *we* are lash'd, *they* kiss the rod,
Resigning to the will of God.
   The fools, my juniors by a year,
Are tortur'd with suspense and fear;   220
Who wisely thought my age a screen,
When death approach'd, to stand between:
The screen remov'd, their hearts are trembling,
They mourn for me without dissembling.
   My female friends, whose tender hearts
Have better learn'd to act their parts,
Receive the news in doleful dumps:
"The Dean is dead (and what is trumps?)
Then, Lord, have mercy on his soul!
(Ladies, I'll venture for the vole.)   230
Six deans, they say, must bear the pall.
(I wish I knew what king to call.)
Madam, your husband will attend
The funeral of so good a friend?"
"No, madam, 'tis a shocking sight;
And he's engag'd to-morrow night!
My Lady Club would take it ill,
If he should fail her at quadrill.
He lov'd the Dean—(I lead a heart)
But dearest friends, they say, must part.   240
His time was come, he ran his race;
We hope he's in a better place."
   Why do we grieve that friends should dye?
No loss more easy to supply.
One year is past; a different scene;
No further mention of the Dean;
Who now, alas, no more is mist,
Than if he never did exist.
Where's now this fav'rite of Apollo?
Departed:—and his works must follow: 250

Must undergo the common fate;
His kind of wit is out of date.
Some country 'squire to Lintot [7] goes,
Inquires for Swift in verse and prose.
Says Lintot, "I have heard the name;
He dy'd a year ago." "The same."
He searcheth all the shop in vain;
"Sir, you may find them in Duck Lane:
I sent them, with a load of books,
Last Monday to the pastry-cook's.   260
To fancy they could live a year!
I find, you're but a stranger here.
The Dean was famous in his time;
And had a kind of knack at rhyme:
His way of writing now is past;
The town has got a better taste:
I keep no antiquated stuff;
But, spick and span I have enough.
Pray, do but give me leave to shew 'em:
Here's Colley Cibber's birthday poem.   270
This ode you never yet have seen
By Stephen Duck,[8] upon the Queen.
Then here's a letter finely penn'd
Against the *Craftsman* [9] and his friend;
It clearly shows that all reflection
On ministers, is disaffection.
Next, here's Sir Robert's vindication,
And Mr. Henley's last oration: [10]
The hawkers have not got 'em yet,
Your honour please to buy a set?   280
    "Here's Wolston's tracts,[11] the twelfth edition;
'Tis read by ev'ry politician:
The country members, when in town,
To all their boroughs send them down:
You never met a thing so smart;
The courtiers have them all by heart:
Those maids of honour (who can read)

7 Bernard Lintot, publisher for Pope, Gay, and Steele.
8 Stephen Duck, the "thresher-poet," made librarian at Richmond and keeper of the "Hermitage" there.
9 Founded by Bolingbroke and Pulteney to oppose Walpole.

10 The Rev. John Henley, supporter of Walpole, he preached from a tub in the market-places.
11 Thomas Woolston, the deist, prosecuted for blasphemy and imprisoned; in 1727-9 he had published *Discourses on the Miracles of our Saviour.*

Are taught to use them for their creed.
The rev'rend author's good intention,
Has been rewarded with a pension: 290
He does an honour to his gown,
By bravely running priestcraft down:
He shews, as sure as God's in Gloucester,
That Jesus was a grand impostor;
That all his miracles were cheats,
Perform'd as jugglers do their feats:
The Church had never such a writer:
A shame he hath not got a mitre!"

Suppose me dead; and then suppose
A club assembled at the Rose; 300
Where, from discourse of this and that,
I grow the subject of their chat:
And, while they toss my name about,
With favour some, and some without,
One, quite indiff'rent in the cause,
My character impartial draws:
"The Dean, if we believe report,
Was never ill receiv'd at court.
As for his works in verse and prose,
I own myself no judge of those: 310
Nor can I tell what criticks thought 'em;
But, this I know, all people bought 'em;
As with a moral view design'd
To cure the vices of mankind:
His vein, ironically grave,
Expos'd the fool, and lash'd the knave:
To steal a hint was never known,
But what he writ was all his own.
"He never thought an honour done him,
Because a duke was proud to own him: 320
Would rather slip aside and chuse
To talk with wits in dirty shoes:
Despis'd the fools with stars and garters,
So often seen caressing Chartres.
He never courted men in station,
Nor persons had in admiration;
Of no man's greatness was afraid,
Because he sought for no man's aid.
Though trusted long in great affairs,

He gave himself no haughty airs: 330
Without regarding private ends,
Spent all his credit for his friends:
And only chose the wise and good;
No flatt'rers; no allies in blood:
But succour'd virtue in distress,
And seldom fail'd of good success;
As numbers in their hearts must own,
Who, but for him, had been unknown.
    "With princes kept a due decorum,
But never stood in awe before 'em.   340
He follow'd David's lesson just,
In princes never put thy trust.
And, would you make him truly sour;
Provoke him with a slave in pow'r:
The Irish senate if you nam'd,
With what impatience he declaim'd!
Fair Liberty was all his cry;
For her he stood prepar'd to die;
For her he boldly stood alone;
For her he oft expos'd his own.   350
Two kingdoms, just as faction led,
Had set a price upon his head;
But not a traytor could be found,
To sell him for six hundred pound.
    "Had he but spar'd his tongue and pen,
He might have rose like other men:
But power was never in his thought;
And, wealth he valu'd not a groat:
Ingratitude he often found,
And pity'd those who meant the wound: 360
But kept the tenor of his mind,
To merit well of human kind:
Nor made a sacrifice of those
Who still were true, to please his foes.
He labour'd many a fruitless hour,
To reconcile his friends in power;
Saw mischief by a faction brewing,
While they pursued each other's ruin.
But, finding vain was all his care,
He left the court in meer despair.   370
    "And, oh! how short are human schemes!

Here ended all our golden dreams.
What St. John's skill in state affairs,
What Ormond's valour, Oxford's cares,
To save their sinking country lent,
Was all destroy'd by one event.[12]
Too soon that precious life was ended,
On which alone, our weal depended.
When up a dang'rous faction starts,
With wrath and vengeance in their hearts: 380
By solemn League and Cov'nant bound,
To ruin, slaughter, and confound;
To turn religion to a fable,
And make the government a Babel:
Pervert the law, disgrace the gown,
Corrupt the senate, rob the crown;
To sacrifice old England's glory,
And make her infamous in story:
When such a tempest shook the land,
How could unguarded Virtue stand!   390
    "With horror, grief, despair, the Dean
Beheld the dire destructive scene:
His friends in exile, or the Tower,
Himself within the frown of power;
Pursued by base envenom'd pens,
Far to the land of slaves and fens;
A servile race in folly nurs'd,
Who truckle most, when treated worst.
    "By innocence and resolution,
He bore continual persecution;   400
While numbers to preferment rose;
Whose merits were, to be his foes.
When *ev'n his own familiar friends*
Intent upon their private ends,
Like renegadoes now he feels,
Against him lifting up their heels.
    "The Dean did by his pen defeat
An infamous destructive cheat.[13]
Taught fools their int'rest how to know,

12 The death of Queen Anne in 1714. "Ormond" was James Butler, Duke of Ormonde, Commander in Chief after the Tories dismissed Marlborough. "Oxford" was Robert Harley, Earl of Oxford, Tory leader, with Bolingbroke.

13 William Wood, attacked in the *Drapier's Letters* for manipulating the Irish coinage.

And gave them arms to ward the blow.   410
Envy has own'd it was his doing,
To save that hapless land from ruin,
While they who at the steerage stood,
And reapt the profit, sought his blood.
     "To save them from their evil fate
In him was held a crime of state.
A wicked monster on the bench,[14]
Whose fury blood could never quench;
As vile and profligate a villain,
As modern Scroggs, or old Tressilian;   420
Who long all justice had discarded,
Nor fear'd he God, nor man regarded;
Vow'd on the Dean his rage to vent,
And make him of his zeal repent:
But Heav'n his innocence defends,
The grateful people stand his friends;
Not strains of law, nor judge's frown,
Nor topicks brought to please the crown,
Nor witness hir'd, nor jury pick'd,
Prevail to bring him in convict.   430
     "In exile with a steady heart,
He spent his life's declining part;
Where folly, pride, and faction sway,
Remote from St. John, Pope, and Gay.
     "His friendship there to few confin'd,
Were always of the midling kind:
No fools of rank, a mungril breed,
Who fain would pass for lords indeed:
Where titles give no right or power,
And peerage is a wither'd flower,   440
He would have held it a disgrace,
If such a wretch had known his face.
On rural squires, that kingdom's bane,
He vented oft his wrath in vain;
Biennial squires to market brought;
Who sell their souls and votes for naught;
The nation stript go joyful back,
To rob the church, their tenants rack,
Go snacks with thieves and rapparees,[15]

---

14 Swift's enemy William Whitshed, Lord Chief Justice of Ireland. Swift compares him to the notorious Chief Justices William Scroggs (1678) and Robert Tresilian (1381).
15 Highwaymen of Ireland.

And keep the peace to pick up fees: 450
In every job to have a share,
A jayl or barrack to repair;
And turn the tax for publick roads,
Commodious to their own abodes.
    "Perhaps I may allow, the Dean,
Had too much satyr in his vein;
And seem'd determin'd not to starve it,
Because no age could more deserve it.
Yet malice never was his aim;
He lash'd the vice, but spar'd the name.   460
No individual could resent,
Where thousands equally were meant.
His satyr points at no defect,
But what all mortals may correct;
For he abhorr'd that senseless tribe,
Who call it humour when they jibe:
He spar'd a hump, or crooked nose,
Whose owners set not up for beaux.
True genuine dullness moved his pity,
Unless it offer'd to be witty.   470
Those, who their ignorance confess'd,
He ne'er offended with a jest;
But laugh'd to hear an idiot quote
A verse from Horace, learn'd by rote.
    "He knew an hundred pleasant stories,
With all the turns of Whigs and Tories:
Was chearful to his dying day;
And friends would let him have his way.
    "He gave the little wealth he had
To build a house for fools and mad: 480
And shew'd by one satyric touch,
No nation wanted it so much:
That kingdom he hath left his debtor,
I wish it soon may have a better."

A SELECTION

Jonathan Richardson, Jr. [and Sr.]

1694–1771

AN ACCOUNT OF THE STATUES, BAS-RELIEFS, DRAWINGS AND PICTURES IN ITALY, FRANCE, &c., WITH REMARKS

1722

[This passage suggests the importance of "landscape" in painting—and poetry.]

LANDSKIPS are in imitation of rural nature, of which therefore there may be as many kinds as there are appearances of this sort of nature; and the scene may be laid in any country or age, with figures or without; but if there are any, as 'tis necessary there should be, generally speaking, they must be suitable, and only subservient to the landskip, to enrich or animate it; otherwise the picture loses its denomination: it becomes history, a battle piece, &c., or at least 'tis of an equivocal kind. This sort of painting is like pastoral in poetry; and of all the landskip painters *Claude Lorrain* has the most beautiful and pleasing ideas; the most rural, and of our own times. *Titian* has a style more noble. So has *Nicholas Poussin*, and the landskips of the latter are usually antique, as is seen by the buildings and figures. *Gaspar's* [1] figures are such; otherwise he has a mixture of *Nicholas* and *Claude*. *Salvator Rosa* has generally chosen to represent a sort of wild and savage nature; his style is great and noble; *Rubens* is pleasant, and loves to enrich his landskips with certain accidents of nature, as winds, a rainbow, lightning, &c. All these masters are excellent in their several kinds. . . .

1 Gaspar Poussin.

John Dyer

1699–1758

DYER once studied painting under Jonathan Richardson, Sr., and *Grongar Hill* is one of the purest examples of the Miltonic-picturesque, the natural-literary prospect elaborated in the half observant, half contemplative mood of *Il Penseroso* or *L'Allegro*. The *Ruins of Rome*, more academic, is in the classical-picturesque manner, like those fashionable "Views of Rome" sketched by the Italian Piranesi. The coloring of Dyer is often the mellow glow diffused over the landscapes by Claude Lorrain, although William Gilpin complained that *Grongar Hill* lacks "that beautiful obscurity which melts a variety of objects into one rich whole." What Dyer mistakenly supposed his major work, *The Fleece*, is a pitiless instance of the eighteenth-century treatise in verse, in this case a georgic. Like others, Dyer assumed that this sort of poem can be accomplished by Vergilian devices and Miltonic circumlocution and epithet. *The Fleece* is more than a museum of poetic diction, however, because it so confidently asserts the prevailing faith in the "progress" that commercial expansion is to effect.

BIOGRAPHICAL NOTES

Son of a solicitor of Aberglasney, Wales. Became a pupil of Dr. Freind at Westminster School, then returned to Wales to study law. At the death of his father in 1720, studied painting under Richardson, Sr. Travel in Italy (1724). Return to London to join the group including Thomson, Richard Savage, and Aaron Hill. *Grongar Hill* and *The Country Walk* (1726). Became itinerant painter in Wales. Farmed at Mapleton, Herefordshire (1734). Married a Miss Ensor (*ca.* 1738) and entered Church (1741), with the living at Catthorpe, Leicestershire (1742). Died of a consumption.

BIBLIOGRAPHY: *Minor Poets of the Eighteenth Century*, ed. H. I'A. Fausset (1929). *Grongar Hill*, ed. Richard C. Boys (1941). Williams, Ralph M., *Poet, Painter, and Parson*, 1956.

*like Milton —
personification
of Penseroso & L'Allegro*

GRONGAR HILL

1726

Silent Nymph, with curious eye!
Who, the purple ev'ning, lie
On the mountain's lonely van,
Beyond the noise of busy man,
Painting fair the form of things,
While the yellow linet sings;
Or the tuneful nightingale
Charms the forest with her tale;
Come with all thy various hues,
Come, and aid thy sister Muse;   10
Now while Phœbus riding high
Gives lustre to the land and sky!
Grongar Hill [1] invites my song,
Draw the landskip bright and strong;
Grongar, in whose mossy cells
Sweetly-musing Quiet dwells;
Grongar, in whose silent shade,
For the modest Muses made,
So oft I have, the evening still,
At the fountain of a rill,   20
Sate upon a flow'ry bed,
With my hand beneath my head;
While stray'd my eyes o'er Towy's flood,
Over mead, and over wood,
From house to house, from hill to hill,
'Till Contemplation had her fill.
    About his chequer'd sides I wind,
And leave his brooks and meads behind,
And groves, and grottoes where I lay,
And vistoes shooting beams of day: 30
Wide and wider spreads the vale;
As circles on a smooth canal:
The mountains round, unhappy fate!
Sooner or later, of all height,
Withdraw their summits from the skies,
And lessen as the others rise:
Still the prospect wider spreads,

1 On the river Towy, Carmarthenshire

Adds a thousand woods and meads,
Still it widens, widens still,
And sinks the newly-risen hill.   40
　　Now, I gain the mountain's brow,
What a landskip lies below!
No clouds, no vapours intervene,
But the gay, the open scene
Does the face of nature show,
In all the hues of heaven's bow!
And, swelling to embrace the light,
Spreads around beneath the sight.
　　Old castles on the cliffs arise,
Proudly tow'ring in the skies!   50
Rushing from the woods, the spires
Seem from hence ascending fires!
Half his beams Apollo sheds
On the yellow mountain-heads!
Gilds the fleeces of the flocks:
And glitters on the broken rocks!
　　Below me trees unnumber'd rise,
Beautiful in various dyes:
The gloomy pine, the poplar blue,
The yellow beech, the sable yew,   60
The slender fir, that taper grows,
The sturdy oak with broad-spread boughs.
And beyond the purple grove,
Haunt of Phillis, queen of love!
Gaudy as the op'ning dawn,
Lies a long and level lawn
On which a dark hill, steep and high,
Holds and charms the wand'ring eye!
Deep are his feet in Towy's flood,
His sides are cloath'd with waving wood,   70
And ancient towers crown his brow,
That cast an awful look below;
Whose ragged walls the ivy creeps,
And with her arms from falling keeps;
So both a safety from the wind
On mutual dependence find.
　　'Tis now the raven's bleak abode;
'Tis now th' apartment of the toad;
And there the fox securely feeds;
And there the pois'nous adder breeds   80

Conceal'd in ruins, moss and weeds;
While, ever and anon, there falls
Huge heaps of hoary moulder'd walls.
Yet time has seen, that lifts the low,
And level lays the lofty brow,
Has seen this broken pile compleat,
Big with the vanity of state;
But transient is the smile of fate!
A little rule, a little sway,
A sun beam in a winter's day,   90
Is all the proud and mighty have
Between the cradle and the grave.

    And see the rivers how they run,
Thro' woods and meads, in shade and sun,
Sometimes swift, sometimes slow,
Wave succeeding wave, they go
A various journey to the deep,
Like human life to endless sleep!
Thus is nature's vesture wrought,
To instruct our wand'ring thought;   100
Thus she dresses green and gay,
To disperse our cares away.

    Ever charming, ever new,
When will the landskip tire the view!
The fountain's fall, the river's flow,
The woody vallies, warm and low;
The windy summit, wild and high,
Roughly rushing on the sky!
The pleasant seat, the ruin'd tow'r,
The naked rock, the shady bow'r;   110
The town and village, dome and farm,
Each give each a double charm,
As pearls upon an Æthiop's arm.

    See on the mountain's southern side,
Where the prospect opens wide,
Where the evening gilds the tide;
How close and small the hedges lie!
What streaks of meadows cross the eye!
A step methinks may pass the stream,
So little distant dangers seem;   120
So we mistake the future's face,
Ey'd thro' hope's deluding glass;
As yon summits soft and fair

Clad in colours of the air,
Which to those who journey near,
Barren, brown, and rough appear;
Still we tread the same coarse way,
The present's still a cloudy day.

  O may I with myself agree,
And never covet what I see: 130
Content me with an humble shade,
My passions tam'd, my wishes laid;
For while our wishes wildly roll,
We banish quiet from the soul:
'Tis thus the busy beat the air;
And misers gather wealth and care.

  Now, ev'n now, my joys run high,
As on the mountain-turf I lie;
While the wanton Zephyr sings,
And in the vale perfumes his wings;   140
While the waters murmur deep;
While the shepherd charms his sheep;
While the birds unbounded fly,
And with musick fill the sky,
Now, ev'n now, my joys run high.

  Be full, ye courts, be great who will;
Search for Peace with all your skill:
Open wide the lofty door,
Seek her on the marble floor,
In vain you search, she is not there;   150
In vain ye search the domes of care!
Grass and flowers Quiet treads,
On the meads, and mountain-heads,
Along with Pleasure, close ally'd,
Ever by each other's side:
And often, by the murm'ring rill,
Hears the thrush, while all is still,
Within the groves of Grongar Hill.

THE RUINS OF ROME
1740

Enough of Grongar, and the shady dales
Of winding Towy, Merlin's fabled haunt,
I sung inglorious. Now the love of arts,
And what in metal or in stone remains
Of proud antiquity, through various realms
And various languages and ages fam'd,
Bears me remote, o'er Gallia's woody bounds,
O'er the cloud-piercing Alps remote; beyond
The vale of Arno purpled with the vine,
Beyond the Umbrian and Etruscan hills,   10
To Latium's wide champaign, forlorn and waste,
Where yellow Tiber his neglected wave
Mournfully rolls. Yet once again, my Muse,
Yet once again, and soar a loftier flight;
Lo the resistless theme, imperial Rome!

Fall'n, fall'n, a silent heap; her heroes all
Sunk in their urns; behold the pride of pomp,
The throne of nations fall'n; obscur'd in dust;
Ev'n yet majestical: the solemn scene
Elates the soul, while now the rising sun   20
Flames on the ruins, in the purer air
Tow'ring aloft, upon the glitt'ring plain,
Like broken rocks, a vast circumference;
Rent palaces, crush'd columns, rifted moles,
Fanes roll'd on fanes, and tombs on buried tombs.

Deep lies in dust the Theban obelisc,
Immense along the waste; minuter art,
Glyconian [1] forms, or Phidian, subtly fair,
O'erwhelming; as th' immense Leviathan
The finny brood, when near Ierne's shore   30
Out-stretch'd, unwieldy, his island length appears,
Above the foamy flood. Globose and huge,
Grey-mould'ring temples swell, and wide o'ercast
The solitary landskape, hills and woods,
And boundless wilds; while the vine-mantled brows
The pendant goats unveil, regardless they

1 Glycon (1st century B.C.) and Phidias (ca. 490–432 B.C.) were Athenian sculptors.

Of hourly peril. though the clefted domes
Tremble to ev'ry wind. The pilgrim oft
At dead of night, 'mid his oraison hears
Aghast the voice of Time, disparting tow'rs, 40
Tumbling all precipitate down dash'd,
Rattling around, loud thund'ring to the moon:
While murmurs sooth each awful interval
Of ever-falling waters; shrouded Nile,[2]
Eridanus, and Tiber with his twins,
And palmy Euphrates; they with dropping locks,
Hang o'er their urns, and mournfully among
The plaintive-ecchoing ruins pour their streams.
  Yet here advent'rous in the sacred search
Of antient arts, the delicate of mind, 50
Curious and modest, from all climes resort,
Grateful society! with these I raise,
The toilsome step up the proud Palatine,
Through spiry cypress groves, and tow'ring pine,
Waving aloft o'er the big ruin's brows,
On num'rous arches rear'd; and frequent stopp'd,
The sunk ground startles me with dreadful chasm,
Breathing forth darkness from the vast profound
Of aisles and halls, within the mountain's womb.
Nor these the nether works; all these beneath, 60
And all beneath the vales and hills around,
Extend the cavern'd sewers, massy, firm,
As the Sibylline grot beside the dead
Lake of Avernus; such the sewers huge,
Whither the great Tarquinian genius dooms
Each wave impure; and proud with added rains,
Hark how the mighty billows lash their vaults,
And thunder; how they heave their rocks in vain;
Though now incessant time has roll'd around
A thousand winters o'er the changeful world, 70
And yet a thousand, since th' indignant floods
Roar loud in their firm bounds, and dash, and swell,
In vain; convey'd to Tiber's lowest wave.
  Hence over airy plains, by crystal founts,
That weave their glitt'ring waves with tuneful lapse,
Among the sleeky pebbles, agate clear,
Cerulian ophite, and the flow'ry vein
Of orient jasper, pleas'd I move along,

---

[2] Nile, Eridanus, Tiber. and Euphrates were statues on fountains in Rome.

And vases boss'd, and huge inscriptive stones,
And intermingling vines; and figur'd nymphs,   80
Floras and Chloes of delicious mould,
Chearing the darkness; and deep empty tombs,
And dells, and mould'ring shrines, with old decay
Rustic and green, and wide-embow'ring shades,
Shot from the crooked clefts of nodding tow'rs;
A solemn wilderness! With error sweet,
I wind the ling'ring step, where'er the path
Mazy conducts me, which the vulgar foot
O'er sculptures maimed has made; Anubis, Sphinx,
Idols of antique guise, and horned Pan,   90
Terrific, monstrous shapes! prepost'rous gods,
Of Fear and Ignorance, by sculptor's hand
Hewn into form, and worship'd; as ev'n now
Blindly they worship at their breathless mouths
In varied appellations: men to these
(From depth to depth in darkening error fall'n)
At length ascrib'd th' inapplicable name.

A SELECTION

Isaac Newton

1642–1727

From OPTICKS: OR, A TREATISE OF THE REFLECTIONS,
REFRACTIONS, INFLECTIONS AND COLOURS OF LIGHT

1704 etc.

[Newton's study of light and his experiments analyzing the spectrum
had their effect on the descriptive poetry of the century. Indeed, the
Optics shows that the eighteenth-century interest in color was common to poetry, painting, and science, and Newton astonishingly lays
the groundwork for the impressionist art of the nineteenth century.
The following passages are from the fourth edition, corrected, 1730.]

Book I. Proposition ii: *The Light of the Sun consists of Rays
differently Refrangible:*

The Proof by Experiments

Exper. 3. In a very dark Chamber, at a round Hole, about one
third Part of an Inch broad, made in the Shut of a Window, I
placed a Glass Prism, whereby the Beam of the Sun's Light, which
came in at that Hole might be refracted upwards toward the
opposite Wall of the Chamber, and there form a colour'd Image
of the Sun. The Axis of the Prism (that is, the Line passing
through the middle of the Prism from one end of it to the other
end parallel to the edge of Refracting Angle) was in this and
the following Experiments perpendicular to the incident Rays.
About this Axis I turned the Prism slowly, and saw the refracted
Light on the Wall, or coloured Image of the Sun, first to descend,
and then to ascend. Between the Descent and Ascent, when the
Image seemed Stationary, I stopp'd the Prism, and fix'd it in
that Posture, that it should be moved no more. For in that Posture
the Refractions of the Light at the two Sides of the refracting
Angle, that is, at the Entrance of the Rays into the Prism, and
at their going out of it, were equal to one another. . . . The
Prism therefore being placed in this Posture, I let the refracted
Light fall perpendicularly upon a Sheet of white Paper at the
opposite Wall of the Chamber, and observed the Figure and

Dimensions of the Solar Image formed on the Paper by that Light. This Image was Oblong and not Oval, but terminated with two Rectilinear and Parallel Sides, and two Semicircular Ends. On its Sides it was bounded pretty distinctly, but on its Ends very confusedly and indistinctly, the Light there decaying and vanishing by degrees. . . .

Now seeing that in all this variety of Experiments, whether the Trial be made in Light reflected, and that either from natural Bodies, as in the first and second Experiment, or specular, as in the ninth; or in Light refracted, and that either before the unequally refracted Rays are by diverging separated from one another, and losing their whiteness which they have altogether, appear severally of several Colours, as in the fifth Experiment; or after they are separated from one another, and appear colour'd as in the sixth, seventh, and eighth Experiments; or in Light trajected through parallel Superficies, destroying each others Effects, as in the tenth Experiment; there are always found Rays, which at equal Incidences on the same Medium suffer unequal Refractions, and that without any splitting or dilating of single Rays, or contingence in the inequality of the Refractions, as is proved in the fifth and sixth Experiments. And seeing the Rays which differ in Refrangibility may be parted and sorted from one another, and that either by Refraction, as in the third Experiment, or by Reflexion, as in the tenth, and then the several sorts apart at equal Incidences suffer unequal Refractions, and those sorts are more refracted than others after separation, which were more refracted before it, as in the sixth and following Experiments, and if the Sun's Light be trajected through three or more cross Prisms successively, those Rays which in the first Prism are refracted more than others, are in all the following Prisms refracted more than others in the same Rate and Proportion, as appears by the fifth Experiment; it's manifest that the Sun's Light is an heterogeneous Mixture of Rays, some of which are constantly more refrangible than others, as was proposed.

Book I. Proposition v. *Whiteness and all grey Colours between white and black, may be compounded Colours, and the whiteness of the Sun's Light is compounded of all the primary Colours mix'd in a due Proportion.* . . .

Book I. Proposition ix. *By the discovered Properties of Light to explain the Colours of the Rain-bow.*

This Bow never appears, but where it rains in the Sun-shine, and may be made artifically by spouting up Water which may break aloft, and scatter into Drops, and fall down like Rain. For the Sun, shining upon these Drops certainly causes the Bow to appear to a Spectator standing in a due Position to the Rain and Sun. And hence it is now agreed upon, that this Bow is made by Refraction of the Sun's Light in Drops of falling Rain. This was understood by some of the Antients. . . .

Book I. Proposition x. *By the discovered Properties of Light to explain the permanent Colours of Natural Bodies.*

These Colours arise from hence, that some natural Bodies reflect some sorts of Rays, others other sorts more copiously than the rest. Minium reflects the least refrangible or red-making Rays most copiously, and thence appears red. Violets reflect the most refrangible most copiously, and thence have their Colour, and so of other Bodies. Every Body reflects the Rays of its own Colour more copiously than the rest, and from their excess and predominance the reflected Light has its Colour. . . .

A SELECTION

Henry Baker

1698–1774

THE MICROSCOPE MADE EASY

1743

[The following passage, from the chapter called "Some Reasonable Reflections on Discoveries made by the Microscope," shows how to the eighteenth century science appeared to support the "great chain of being" and the "universal order." Much of the passage is a loose paraphrase of Addison's *Spectator* No. 519.]

As the microscope discovers almost every drop of water, every blade of grass, every leaf, flower, and grain swarming with inhabitants, all of which enjoy not only life but happiness, a thinking mind can scarce forbear considering that part of the Scale of

Beings which descends from himself to the lowest of all sensitive creatures, and may consequently be brought under his examination. Amongst these, some are raised so little above dead matter that it is difficult to determine whether they live or no. Others, but one step higher, have no other sense besides feeling and taste. Some, again, have the additional one of hearing; others of smell, and others of sight.

It is wonderful to observe by what a gradual progression the world of life advances through a prodigious variety of species before a creature is formed that is complete in all its senses: and, even amongst these, there is such a different degree of perfection in the senses which one animal enjoys beyond what appears in another, that though the sense in different animals be distinguished by the same common denomination, it seems almost of a different nature. If, after this, we look into the several inward perfections of cunning and sagacity, or what we generally call instinct, we find them rising in the same manner, imperceptibly, one above another, and receiving additional improvements according to the species in which they are implanted.

This progress in nature is so very gradual that the whole chasm from a plant to a man is filled up with divers kinds of creatures, rising one over another by such gentle and easy ascent that the little transitions and deviations from one species to another are almost insensible. And the intermediate space is so well husbanded and managed that there is scarce a degree of perception which does not appear in some one part of the world of life. Since then the Scale of Being advances by such regular steps so high as man, we may by parity of reason suppose that it still proceeds gradually upwards through numberless orders of beings of a superior nature to him: as there is an infinitely greater space and room for different degrees of perfection between the Supreme Being and man, than between man and the most despicable insect.

[CHAPTER LII]

James Thomson

1700–1748

THOMSON is the most painter-like of eighteenth-century poets. The prospects that follow one another throughout *The Seasons* are almost operatic. Their elaborateness and melodramatic coloring, particularly the masses of light and shadow, suggest that this kind of picturesque owes something to the baroque; and there are affinities between *The Seasons* and the landscapes of Rubens, whose full-blooded performance, like Thomson's, is that of a colorist. Frequently this sensuousness is diluted into sentimentality, like that in the canvases of Romney or Greuze; the poet's attitude toward what he calls "the British fair" is usually saccharine. Besides the fleshiness of Rubens and the sentimentality of Greuze, Thomson recalls the shagginess and louring atmosphere of Salvator or Fragonard in the blacker and more ominous mood of *Autumn* and *Winter*, which are "sublime" in the sense that Burke understood the term. Again, passages in *The Seasons* and the first canto of *The Castle of Indolence* (one of the eighteenth-century imitations of Spenser) are suffused with the mellow, lyrical hues of Claude. On the whole, the talent of Thomson is a visual one, and his effects are diffuse. He has difficulty in articulating his freely handled passages, a difficulty heightened by the many digressions upon humanity, patriotism, commerce, and religion. The benevolism of Shaftesbury appears in his "social tear" and "social sigh," his devotion to "all the social offspring of the heart." The sensuousness of his temperament sometimes expresses itself in a virile, almost Whitmanesque, abandon to the biological urges; *Spring* is a hymn to fecundity, a deistic *O altitudo* like Theocles' hymn to nature in Shaftesbury's *Characteristics*. A mathematical, rationalistic deism of different origin inspires the lines in memory of Sir Isaac Newton, in which God is a mechanical engineer instead of a vitalistic urge. This poem, like the others, has also a Hebraic, psalmlike tone. The primitivism of Thomson's religion of "nature" is inconsistently yoked with an enthusiasm for commerce and "progress." The famous *Rule Britannia* expresses his jingoism. Thomson's verse is of great external complexity. His rhythms are too broad to be contained within the precision of the couplet; consequently he reverts to Miltonic blank verse. He is addicted to the cumbrous Miltonic splendor by which bees become "happy people in their waxen cells." The first canto, particularly, of *The Castle of Indolence* is a notable instance of the decorative Spenserian manner which even Dr. Johnson admits "fills the imagination." Personally, Thomson is said to have been fat and clumsy, and so lazy that he ate peaches off the wall.

BIOGRAPHICAL NOTES

Son of a Presbyterian minister at Ednam, Roxburghshire. Entered the University of Edinburgh (1715) and studied divinity but left without degree. Went to London (1725), tutored Lord Binning's son, and published a brief version of *Winter* (1726). Patronized by the Countess of

Hertford. *Summer* (1727) and *To the Memory of Newton* (1727). *Spring* (1728). *The Seasons*, including the *Hymn* and *Autumn* (1730). The tragedy *Sophonisba* (1730) produced at Drury Lane. Became tutor to Charles Talbot and traveled with him in France and Italy (1731). Appointed Secretary of Briefs in the Court of Chancery, a sinecure (1733). *Liberty* (1735-36), a jingoistic poem. Moved to Kew Foot Lane, Richmond, near Pope (1736) and cultivated friendship of a group including Collins, Dyer, Armstrong, Mallet, Lord Lyttelton, and Shenstone. Awarded a pension of £100 a year from the Prince of Wales (1737). *The Masque of Alfred*, including "Rule, Britannia" (1740). Visit with Lord Lyttelton at Hagley Park (1743). Philandered with Elizabeth Young ("Amanda"), (1736-44). New edition of *The Seasons* (1744) prepared at Hagley. *Tancred and Sigismunda* produced at the Drury Lane (1745). Frequent visits to Hagley. Visit with Shenstone at The Leasowes (1747). *The Castle of Indolence* published (1748). Died at Richmond after a short illness.

BIBLIOGRAPHY: *Poetical Works*, ed. J. Logie Robertson, 1908. Grant, Douglas, *James Thomson*, 1951. Macaulay, G. C., *James Thomson*, 1908. McKillop, A. D., *The Background of Thomson's Seasons*, 1942. Morel, Léon, *James Thomson, Sa Vie et ses Œuvres*, 1895. Spacks, Patricia Mayer, *The Varied God*, 1959.

THE SEASONS
1726–1744

SPRING

Come, gentle Spring,—ethereal mildness, come,
And from the bosom of yon dropping cloud,
While music wakes around, veil'd in a shower
Of shadowing roses, on our plains descend.
O Hartford,[1] fitted or to shine in courts
With unaffected grace, or walk the plain
With innocence and meditation join'd
In soft assemblage, listen to my song,
Which thy own season paints—when nature all
Is blooming and benevolent, like thee.   10
    And see where surly Winter passes off,
Far to the north, and calls his ruffian blasts:
His blasts obey, and quit the howling hill,
The shatter'd forest, and the ravag'd vale;
While softer gales succeed, at whose kind touch,

1 The Countess of Hertford, to whom *Spring* was dedicated. The poem was in part composed, apparently, at Marlborough Cas-tle, Wiltshire, seat of the Earl of Hertford, to which Thomson was invited in the summer of 1727.

Dissolving snows in livid torrents lost,
The mountains lift their green heads to the sky.
    As yet the trembling year is unconfirm'd,
And Winter oft at eve resumes the breeze,
Chills the pale morn, and bids his driving sleets   20
Deform the day delightless; so that scarce
The bittern knows his time, with bill ingulf'd,
To shake the sounding marsh; or, from the shore,
The plovers when to scatter o'er the heath,
And sing their wild notes to the listening waste.
    At last from Aries rolls the bounteous sun,
And the bright Bull receives him.[2] Then no more
Th' expansive atmosphere is cramp'd with cold;
But, full of life and vivifying soul,
Lifts the light clouds sublime, and spreads them thin,   30
Fleecy, and white, o'er all-surrounding heaven.
    Forth fly the tepid Airs; and unconfin'd,   *Strong use of negatives*
Unbinding earth, the moving softness strays.
Joyous, th' impatient husbandman perceives   *to relate positive*
Relenting nature, and his lusty steers
Drives from their stalls to where the well-us'd plow
Lies in the furrow, loosen'd from the frost.
There, unrefusing, to the harness'd yoke   *awkward usage*
They lend their shoulder, and begin their toil,
Chear'd by the simple song and soaring lark.   40
Meanwhile, incumbent o'er the shining share
The master leans, removes th' obstructing clay,
Winds the whole work, and sidelong lays the glebe.
    White, thro' the neighbouring fields the sower stalks
With measur'd step; and, liberal, throws the grain
Into the faithful bosom of the ground:
The harrow follows harsh, and shuts the scene.
    Be gracious, Heaven! for now laborious man   *push syntactical*
Has done his part. Ye fostering breezes, blow!   *unit to end*
Ye softening dews, ye tender showers, descend!   *of line —Miltonic*   50
And temper all, thou world-reviving sun,
Into the perfect year! Nor ye who live
In luxury and ease, in pomp and pride,
Think these lost themes unworthy of your ear:
Such themes as these the rural Maro [3] sung
To wide-imperial Rome, in the full height
Of elegance and taste, by Greece refin'd.

2 In latter April.   3 Vergil.

In ancient times the sacred plow employ'd
The kings and awful fathers of mankind;
And some, with whom compar'd, your insect-tribes   60
Are but the beings of a summer's day,
Have held the scale of empire, rul'd the storm
Of mighty war; then, with victorious hand,
Disdaining little delicacies, seiz'd
The plow, and, greatly independant, scorn'd
All the vile stores corruption can bestow.

Ye generous Britons, venerate the plow;
And o'er your hills and long withdrawing vales
Let Autumn spread his treasures to the sun,
Luxuriant and unbounded! As the sea,   70
Far thro' his azure turbulent domain,
Your empire owns, and from a thousand shores
Wafts all the pomp of life into your ports;
So with superior boon may your rich soil,
Exuberant, Nature's better blessings pour
O'er every land, the naked nations cloath,
And be th' exhaustless granary of a world!

Nor only through the lenient air this change,
Delicious, breathes: the penetrative sun,
His force deep-darting to the dark retreat   80
Of vegetation, sets the steaming power
At large, to wander o'er the vernant earth
In various hues; but chiefly thee, gay green!
Thou smiling Nature's universal robe!
United light and shade! where the sight dwells
With growing strength and ever-new delight.

From the moist meadow to the wither'd hill,
Led by the breeze, the vivid verdure runs,
And swells, and deepens, to the cherish'd eye.
The hawthorn whitens; and the juicy groves   90
Put forth their buds, unfolding by degrees,
Till the whole leafy forest stands display'd,
In full luxuriance, to the sighing gales;
Where the deer rustle thro' the twining brake,
And the birds sing conceal'd. At once, array'd
In all the colours of the flushing year
By Nature's swift and secret-working hand,
The garden glows, and fills the liberal air
With lavish fragrance; while the promis'd fruit
Lies yet a little embryo, unperceiv'd,   100

Within its crimson folds, Now from the town,
Buried in smoke, and sleep, and noisom damps,
Oft let me wander o'er the dewy fields,
Where freshness breathes, and dash the trembling drops
From the bent bush, as thro' the verdant maze
Of sweet-briar hedges I pursue my walk;
Or taste the smell of dairy: or ascend
Some eminence, Augusta,[4] in thy plains,
And see the country, far diffus'd around,
One boundless blush, one white-empurpled shower   110
Of mingled blossoms; where the raptur'd eye
Hurries from joy to joy, and, hid beneath
The fair profusion, yellow Autumn spies.

    If, brush'd from Russian wilds, a cutting gale
Rise not, and scatter from his humid wings
The clammy mildew; or, dry-blowing, breathe
Untimely frost—before whose baleful blast
The full-blown Spring thro' all her foliage shrinks,
Joyless and dead, a wide-dejected waste.
For oft, engender'd by the hazy north,   120
Myriads on myriads, insect armies waft
Keen in the poison'd breeze, and wasteful eat,
Through buds and bark, into the blacken'd core,
Their eager way. A feeble race! yet oft
The sacred sons of vengeance! on whose course
Corrosive famine waits, and kills the year.
To check this plague, the skillful farmer chaff
And blazing straw before his orchard burns;
Till, all involv'd in smoke, the latent foe
From every cranny suffocated falls: 130
Or scatters o'er the blooms the pungent dust
Of pepper, fatal to the frosty tribe;
Or, when th' envenom'd leaf begins to curl,
With sprinkled water drowns them in their nest:
Nor, while they pick them up with busy bill,
The little trooping birds unwisely scares.

    Be patient, swains; these cruel-seeming winds
Blow not in vain. Far hence they keep, repress'd,
Those deepening clouds on clouds, surcharg'd with rain,
That, o'er the vast Atlantic hither borne,   140
In endless train, would quench the summer blaze,
And, chearless, drown the crude unripen'd year.

4 London.

The north-east spends his rage; and now, shut up
Within his iron caves, th' effusive south
Warms the wide air, and o'er the void of heaven
Breathes the big clouds with vernal showers distent.
At first a dusky wreath they seem to rise,
Scarce staining ether; but by fast degrees,
In heaps on heaps, the doubling vapour sails
Along the loaded sky, and, mingling deep,   150
Sits on th' horizon round a settled gloom:
Not such as wintry storms on mortals shed,
Oppressing life; but lovely, gentle, kind,
And full of every hope and every joy;
The wish of Nature. Gradual sinks the breeze
Into a perfect calm; that not a breath
Is heard to quiver through the closing woods,
Or rustling turn the many-twinkling leaves
Of aspin tall. Th' uncurling floods, diffus'd
In glassy breadth, seem thro' delusive lapse   160
Forgetful of their course. 'Tis silence all,
And pleasing expectation. Herds and flocks
Drop the dry sprig, and, mute-imploring, eye
The falling verdure. Hush'd in short suspense,
The plumy people streak their wings with oil
To throw the lucid moisture, trickling, off;
And wait th' approaching sign to strike, at once,
Into the general choir. Even mountains, vales,
And forests seem, impatient, to demand
The promis'd sweetness. Man superior walks   170
Amid the glad creation, musing praise,
And looking lively gratitude. At last,
The clouds consign their treasures to the fields,
And, softly shaking on the dimpled pool
Prelusive drops, let all their moisture flow,
In large effusion o'er the freshen'd world.
The stealing shower is scarce to patter heard,
By such as wander thro' the forest-walks,
Beneath th' umbrageous multitude of leaves.
But who can hold the shade while Heaven descends   180
In universal bounty, shedding herbs,
And fruits, and flowers, on Nature's ample lap?
Swift fancy fir'd anticipates their growth;
And, while the milky nutriment distills,
Beholds the kindling country colour round.

Thus all day long the full-distended clouds
Indulge their genial stores, and well-shower'd earth *means fertilizing*
Is deep enrich'd with vegetable life;
Till, in the western sky, the downward sun
Looks out, effulgent, from amid the flush   190
Of broken clouds, gay-shifting to his beam.
The rapid radiance instantaneous strikes
Th' illumin'd mountain, thro' the forest streams,
Shakes on the floods, and in a yellow mist,
Far smoking o'er th' interminable plain,
In twinkling myriads lights the dewy gems.
Moist, bright, and green, the landskip laughs around.
Full swell the woods; their every musick wakes,
Mix'd in wild concert, with the warbling brooks
Increas'd, the distant bleatings of the hills,   200
The hollow lows responsive from the vales,
Whence, blending all, the sweeten'd zephyr springs.
Meantime, refracted from yon eastern cloud,
Bestriding earth, the grand ethereal bow
Shoots up immense; and every hue unfolds
In fair proportion running from the red
To where the violet fades into the sky.
Here, awful Newton, the dissolving clouds
Form, fronting on the sun, thy showery prism;
And to the sage-instructed eye unfold   210
The various twine of light, by thee disclos'd
From the white mingling maze. Not so the swain:
He, wondering, views the bright enchantment bend,
Delightful, o'er the radiant fields, and runs
To catch the falling glory; but, amaz'd,
Beholds th' amusive arch before him fly;
Then vanish quite away. Still night succeeds,
A soften'd shade, and saturated earth
Awaits the morning beam, to give to light,
Rais'd thro' ten thousand different plastic tubes,   220
The balmy treasures of the former day.
     Then spring the lively herbs, profusely wild,
O'er all the deep-green earth, beyond the power
Of botanist to number up their tribes:
Whether he steals along the lonely dale,
In silent search; or thro' the forest, rank
With what the dull incurious weeds account,
Bursts his blind way; or climbs the mountain-rock,

Fir'd by the nodding verdure of its brow.
With such a liberal hand has Nature flung   230
Their seeds abroad, blown them about in winds,
Innumerous mix'd them with the nursing mold,
The moistening current, and prolifick rain.
    But who their virtues can declare? Who pierce
With vision pure, into these secret stores
Of health, and life, and joy? The food of man,
While yet he liv'd in innocence, and told
A length of golden years, unflesh'd in blood,
A stranger to the savage arts of life,
Death, rapine, carnage, surfeit, and disease—   240
The lord, and not the tyrant, of the world.
    The first fresh dawn then wak'd the gladden'd race
Of uncorrupted man, nor blush'd to see
The sluggard sleep beneath its sacred beam;
For their light slumbers gently fum'd away,
And up they rose as vigorous as the sun,
Or to the culture of the willing glebe,
Or to the chearful tendance of the flock. _Latina_
Meantime the song went round; and dance and sport,
Wisdom and friendly talk, successive stole   250
Their hours away. While in the rosy vale
Love breath'd his infant sighs, from anguish free,
And full replete with bliss; save the sweet pain,
That, inly thrilling, but exalts it more.
Nor yet injurious act, nor surly deed,
Was known among these happy sons of heaven;
For reason and benevolence were law.
Harmonious Nature too look'd smiling on.
Clear shone the skies, cool'd with eternal gales,
And balmy spirit all. The youthful sun   260
Shot his best rays, and still the gracious clouds
Drop'd fatness down; as o'er the swelling mead,
The herds and flocks, commixing, play'd secure.
This when, emergent from the gloomy wood,
The glaring lion saw, his horrid heart
Was meeken'd, and he join'd his sullen joy.
For music held the whole in perfect peace:
Soft sigh'd the flute; the tender voice was heard,
Warbling the vary'd heart; the woodlands round
Apply'd their choir; and winds and waters flow'd   270
In consonance. Such were those prime of days.

But now those white unblemish'd minutes, whence
The fabling poets took their golden age,
Are found no more amid these iron times,
These dregs of life! Now the distemper'd mind
Has lost that concord of harmonious powers,
Which forms the soul of happiness; and all
Is off the poise within: the passions all
Have burst their bounds; and reason half extinct,
Or impotent, or else approving, sees   280
The foul disorder. Senseless, and deform'd,
Convulsive anger storms at large; or, pale
And silent, settles into fell revenge.
Base envy withers at another's joy,
And hates that excellence it cannot reach.
Desponding fear, of feeble fancies full,
Weak and unmanly, loosens every power.
Even love itself is bitterness of soul—
A pensive anguish pining at the heart;
Or, sunk to sordid interest, feels no more   290
That noble wish, that never-cloy'd desire,
Which, selfish joy disdaining, seeks alone
To bless the dearer object of its flame.
Hope sickens with extravagance; and grief,
Of life impatient, into madness swells;
Or in dead silence wastes the weeping hours.
These, and a thousand mix'd emotions more,
From ever-changing views of good and ill,
Form'd infinitely various, vex the mind
With endless storm; whence, deeply rankling, grows   300
The partial thought, a listless unconcern,
Cold, and averting from our neighbour's good;
Then dark disgust and hatred, winding wiles,
Coward deceit, and ruffian violence.
At last, extinct each social feeling, fell
And joyless inhumanity pervades
And petrifies the heart. Nature disturb'd
Is deem'd, vindictive, to have chang'd her course.
　　Hence, in old dusky time, a deluge came:
When the deep-cleft disparting orb, that arch'd   310
The central waters round, impetuous rush'd,
With universal burst, into the gulf,
And o'er the high-pil'd hills of fractur'd earth
Wide-dash'd the waves, in undulation vast;

Till, from the center to the streaming clouds,
A shoreless ocean tumbled round the globe.
  The Seasons since have, with severer sway,
Oppress'd a broken world: the Winter keen
Shook forth his waste of snows; and Summer shot
His pestilential heats. Great Spring, before,   320
Green'd all the year; and fruits and blossoms blush'd,
In social sweetness, on the self-same bough.
Pure was the temperate air; an even calm
Perpetual reign'd; save what the zephyrs bland
Breath'd o'er the blue expanse: for then nor storms
Were taught to blow, nor hurricanes to rage;
Sound slept the waters; no sulphureous glooms
Swell'd in the sky, and sent the lightning forth;
While sickly damps, and cold autumnal fogs,
Hung not, relaxing, on the springs of life.   330
But now, of turbid elements the sport,
From clear to cloudy tost, from hot to cold,
And dry to moist, with inward-eating change,
Our drooping days are dwindled down to naught;
Their period finish'd ere 'tis well begun.
  And yet the wholesome herb, neglected, dies;
Though with the pure exhilarating soul
Of nutriment, and health, and vital powers,
Beyond the search of art, 'tis copious blest.
For, with hot ravine fir'd, ensanguin'd man   340
Is now become the lion of the plain,
And worse. The wolf, who from the nightly fold
Fierce drags the bleating prey, ne'er drunk her milk,
Nor wore her warming fleece; nor has the steer,
At whose strong chest the deadly tiger hangs,
E'er plow'd for him. They too are temper'd high,
With hunger stung, and wild necessity;
Nor lodges pity in their shaggy breast.
But man, whom Nature form'd of milder clay,
With every kind emotion in his heart,   350
And taught alone to weep—while from her lap
She pours ten thousand delicacies, herbs,
And fruits, as numerous as the drops of rain,
Or beams that gave them birth—shall he, fair form!
Who wears sweet smiles, and looks erect on heaven,
E'er stoop to mingle with the prowling herd,
And dip his tongue in gore? The beast of prey,

Blood-stain'd, deserves to bleed: but you, ye flocks,
What have ye done; ye peaceful people, what,
To merit death? You, who have given us milk   360
In luscious streams, and lent us your own coat
Against the Winter's cold? And the plain ox,
That harmless, honest, guileless animal,
In what has he offended? He, whose toil,
Patient and ever ready, clothes the land
With all the pomp of harvest—shall he bleed,
And struggling groan beneath the cruel hands
Even of the clowns he feeds? And that, perhaps,
To swell the riot of th' autumnal feast,
Won by his labour? This the feeling heart   370
Would tenderly suggest: but 'tis enough,
In this late age, adventurous, to have touch'd
Light on the numbers of the Samian Sage.[5]
High Heaven forbids the bold presumptuous strain,
Whose wisest will has fix'd us in a state
That must not yet to pure perfection rise.
Besides, who knows, how, rais'd to higher life,
From stage to stage, the vital scale ascends?
    Now, when the first foul torrent of the brooks,
Swell'd with the vernal rains, is ebb'd away;   380
And, whitening, down their mossy-tinctur'd stream
Descends the billowy foam; now is the time,
While yet the dark-brown water aids the guile,
To tempt the trout. The well-dissembled fly,
The rod fine-tapering with elastic spring,
Snatch'd from the hoary steed the floating line,
And all thy slender wat'ry stores prepare.
But let not on thy hook the tortur'd worm,
Convulsive, twist in agonizing folds;
Which, by rapacious hunger swallow'd deep,   390
Gives, as you tear it from the bleeding breast
Of the weak, helpless, uncomplaining wretch,
Harsh pain and horror to the tender hand.
    When, with his lively ray, the potent sun
Has pierc'd the streams, and rous'd the finny race,
Then, issuing chearful, to thy sport repair;
Chief should the western breezes curling play,
And light o'er ether bear the shadowy clouds.
High to their fount, this day, amid the hills,

5 Pythagoras, who believed in the transmigration of souls.

And woodlands warbling round, trace up the brooks; 400
The next, pursue their rocky-channel'd maze
Down to the river, in whose ample wave
Their little naiads love to sport at large.
Just in the dubious point, where with the pool
Is mix'd the trembling stream, or where it boils
Around the stone, or from the hollow'd bank,
Reverted, plays in undulating flow,
There throw, nice-judging, the delusive fly;
And, as you lead it round in artful curve,
With eye attentive mark the springing game. 410
Straight as above the surface of the flood
They wanton rise, or urg'd by hunger leap,
Then fix, with gentle twitch, the barbed hook;
Some lightly tossing to the grassy bank,
And to the shelving shore slow-dragging some,
With various hand proportion'd to their force.
If yet too young, and easily deceiv'd,
A worthless prey scarce bends your pliant rod,
Him, piteous of his youth, and the short space
He has enjoy'd the vital light of heaven, 420
Soft disengage, and back into the stream
The speckled infant throw. But should you lure
From his dark haunt, beneath the tangled roots
Of pendent trees, the monarch of the brook,
Behoves you then to ply your finest art.
Long time he, following cautious, scans the fly,
And oft attempts to seize it, but as oft
The dimpled water speaks his jealous fear.
At last, while haply o'er the shaded sun
Passes a cloud, he, desperate, takes the death, 430
With sullen plunge. At once he darts along,
Deep-struck, and runs out all the lengthen'd line;
Then seeks the farthest ooze, the sheltering weed,
The cavern'd bank, his old secure abode;
And flies aloft, and flounces round the pool,
Indignant of the guile. With yielding hand,
That feels him still, yet to his furious course
Gives way, you, now retiring, following now
Across the stream, exhaust his idle rage;
Till floating broad upon his breathless side, 440
And to his fate abandon'd, to the shore
You gaily drag your unresisting prize.

Thus pass the temperate hours: but when the sun
Shakes from his noon-day throne the scattering clouds,
Even shooting listless languor through the deeps,
Then seek the bank where flowering elders croud,
Where scatter'd wild the lily of the vale
Its balmy essence breathes, where cowslips hang
The dewy head, where purple violets lurk,
With all the lowly children of the shade;   450
Or lie reclin'd beneath yon spreading ash,
Hung o'er the steep; whence, borne on liquid wing,
The sounding culver shoots; or where the hawk,
High in the beetling cliff, his eyry builds.
There let the classic page thy fancy lead
Thro' rural scenes; such as the Mantuan swain
Paints in the matchless harmony of song;
Or catch thyself the landscape, gliding swift
Athwart imagination's vivid eye;
Or, by the vocal woods and waters lull'd,   460
And lost in lonely musing, in a dream,
Confus'd, of careless solitude, where mix
Ten thousand wandering images of things,
Soothe every gust of passion into peace—
All but the swellings of the soften'd heart,
That waken, not disturb, the tranquil mind.

Behold, yon breathing prospect bids the Muse
Throw all her beauty forth. But who can paint
Like Nature? Can imagination boast,
Amid its gay creation, hues like hers?   470
Or can it mix them with that matchless skill,
And lose them in each other, as appears
In every bud that blows? If fancy, then,
Unequal, fails beneath the pleasing task;
Ah, what shall language do? Ah, where find words
Ting'd with so many colours; and whose power,
To life approaching, may perfume my lays
With that fine oil, those aromatic gales,
That inexhaustive flow continuous round?

Yet, tho' successless, will the toil delight.   480
Come then, ye virgins and ye youths, whose hearts
Have felt the raptures of refining love;
And thou, Amanda,[6] come, pride of my song!

6 Elizabeth Young, wooed by Thomson in vain—evidently because her mother objected
to the poet.

Form'd by the Graces, loveliness itself!
Come with those downcast eyes, sedate and sweet,
Those looks demure, that deeply pierce the soul—
Where, with the light of thoughtful reason mix'd,
Shines lively fancy, and the feeling heart:
Oh come! and while the rosy-footed May
Steals blushing on, together let us tread   490
The morning-dews, and gather in their prime
Fresh-blooming flowers, to grace thy braided hair,
And thy lov'd bosom that improves their sweets.
   See, where the winding vale its lavish stores,
Irriguous, spreads. See, how the lily drinks
The latent rill, scarce oozing through the grass,
Of growth luxuriant; or the humid bank,
In fair profusion, decks. Long let us walk,
Where the breeze blows from yon extended field
Of blossom'd beans. Arabia cannot boast   500
A fuller gale of joy than, liberal, thence
Breathes thro' the sense, and takes the ravish'd soul.
Nor is the mead unworthy of thy foot;
Full of fresh verdure, and unnumber'd flowers,
The negligence of Nature, wide and wild;
Where, undisguis'd by mimic art, she spreads
Unbounded beauty to the roving eye.
Here their delicious task the fervent bees,
In swarming millions, tend. Around, athwart,
Thro' the soft air, the busy nations fly,   510
Cling to the bud, and, with inserted tube,
Suck its pure essence, its ethereal soul.
And oft, with bolder wing, they, soaring, dare
The purple heath, or where the wild-thyme grows,
And yellow load them with the luscious spoil.
   At length the finish'd garden to the view
Its vistas opens, and its alleys green.
Snatch'd thro' the verdant maze, the hurried eye
Distracted wanders; now the bowery walk
Of covert close, where scarce a speck of day   520
Falls on the lengthen'd gloom, protracted sweeps;
Now meets the bending sky, the river now
Dimpling along, the breezy-ruffled lake,
The forest darkening round, the glittering spire,
Th' ethereal mountain, and the distant main.
But why so far excursive? when at hand,

Along these blushing borders, bright with dew,
And in yon mingled wilderness of flowers,
Fair-handed Spring unbosoms every grace:
Throws out the snow-drop and the crocus first;   530
The daisy, primrose, violet darkly blue,
And polyanthus of unnumber'd dyes;
The yellow wall-flower, stain'd with iron brown;
And lavish stock that scents the garden round.
From the soft wing of vernal breezes shed,
Anemones; auriculas, enrich'd
With shining meal o'er all their velvet leaves;
And full ranunculus, of glowing red.
Then comes the tulip-race, where beauty plays
Her idle freaks: from family diffus'd   540
To family, as flies the father-dust,
The varied colours run; and, while they break
On the charm'd eye, th' exulting florist marks,
With secret pride, the wonders of his hand.
No gradual bloom is wanting; from the bud,
First-born of Spring, to Summer's musky tribes:
Nor hyacinths, of purest virgin-white,
Low-bent, and blushing inward; nor jonquils,
Of potent fragrance; nor narcissus fair,
As o'er the fabled fountain hanging still;   550
Nor broad carnations; nor gay-spotted pinks;
Nor, shower'd from every bush, the damask-rose.
Infinite numbers, delicacies, smells,
With hues on hues expression cannot paint,
The breath of Nature, and her endless bloom.
    Hail, Source of Beings! Universal Soul
Of heaven and earth! Essential Presence, hail!
To thee I bend the knee; to thee my thoughts,
Continual, climb; who, with a master-hand,
Hast the great whole into perfection touch'd.   560
By thee the various vegetative tribes,
Wrapt in a filmy net, and clad with leaves,
Draw the live ether, and imbibe the dew.
By thee dispos'd into congenial soils,
Stands each attractive plant, and sucks, and swells
The juicy tide, a twining mass of tubes.
At thy command the vernal sun awakes
The torpid sap, detruded to the root
By wintry winds, that now in fluent dance,

And lively fermentation, mounting, spreads   570
All this innumerous-colour'd scene of things.
    As rising from the vegetable world
My theme ascends, with equal wing ascend,
My panting Muse; and hark, how loud the woods
Invite you forth in all your gayest trim.
Lend me your song, ye nightingales! oh pour
The mazy-running soul of melody
Into my varied verse! while I deduce,
From the first note the hollow cuckoo sings,
The symphony of Spring, and touch a theme   580
Unknown to fame, the passion of the groves.
    When first the soul of love is sent abroad,
Warm thro' the vital air, and on the heart
Harmonious seizes, the gay troops begin,
In gallant thought, to plume the painted wing;
And try again the long-forgotten strain,
At first faint-warbled. But no sooner grows
The soft infusion prevalent and wide,
Than, all alive, at once their joy o'erflows
In musick unconfin'd. Up-springs the lark,   590
Shrill-voic'd and loud, the messenger of morn:
Ere yet the shadows fly, he mounted sings
Amid the dawning clouds, and from their haunts
Calls up the tuneful nations. Every copse
Deep-tangled, tree irregular, and bush
Bending with dewy moisture, o'er the heads
Of the coy choristers that lodge within,
Are prodigal of harmony. The thrush
And woodlark, o'er the kind-contending throng
Superior heard, run thro' the sweetest length   600
Of notes; when listening Philomela deigns
To let them joy, and purposes, in thought
Elate, to make her night excel their day.
The blackbird whistles from the thorny brake;
The mellow bullfinch answers from the grove:
Nor are the linnets, o'er the flowering furze
Pour'd out profusely, silent. Join'd to these
Innumerous songsters, in the freshening shade
Of new-sprung leaves, their modulations mix
Mellifluous. The jay, the rook, the daw,   610
And each harsh pipe, discordant heard alone,
Aid the full concert: while the stock-dove breathes

A melancholy murmur through the whole.
'Tis love creates their melody, and all
This waste of music is the voice of love;
That even to birds, and beasts, the tender arts
Of pleasing teaches. Hence the glossy kind
Try every winning way inventive love
Can dictate, and in courtship to their mates
Pour forth their little souls. First, wide around,   620
With distant awe, in airy rings they rove,
Endeavouring by a thousand tricks to catch
The cunning, conscious, half-averted glance
Of their regardless charmer. Should she seem
Softening, the least approvance to bestow,
Their colours burnish, and, by hope inspir'd,
They brisk advance; then, on a sudden struck,
Retire disorder'd; then again approach;
In fond rotation spread the spotted wing,
And shiver every feather with desire.   630
    Connubial leagues agreed, to the deep woods
They haste away, all as their fancy leads,
Pleasure, or food, or secret safety prompts;
That Nature's great command may be obey'd;
Nor all the sweet sensations they perceive
Indulg'd in vain. Some to the holly-hedge
Nestling repair, and to the thicket some;
Some to the rude protection of the thorn
Commit their feeble offspring. The cleft tree
Offers its kind concealment to a few,   640
Their food its insects, and its moss their nests.
Others, apart, far in the grassy dale,
Or roughening waste, their humble texture weave.
But most in woodland solitudes delight,
In unfrequented glooms, or shaggy banks,
Steep, and divided by a babbling brook,
Whose murmurs soothe them all the livelong day,
When by kind duty fix'd. Among the roots
Of hazel, pendent o'er the plaintive stream,
They frame the first foundation of their domes;   650
Dry sprigs of trees, in artful fabrick laid,
And bound with clay together. Now 'tis naught
But restless hurry thro' the busy air,
Beat by unnumber'd wings. The swallow sweeps
The slimy pool, to build his hanging house

Intent. And often, from the careless back
Of herds and flocks, a thousand tugging bills
Pluck hair and wool; and oft, when unobserv'd,
Steal from the barn a straw: till soft and warm,
Clean and compleat, their habitation grows.　　　660
　　As thus the patient dam assiduous sits,
Not to be tempted from her tender task,
Or by sharp hunger, or by smooth delight,
Though the whole loosen'd Spring around her blows,
Her sympathizing lover takes his stand
High on th' opponent bank, and ceaseless sings
The tedious time away; or else supplies
Her place a moment, while she sudden flits
To pick the scanty meal. Th' appointed time
With pious toil fulfill'd, the callow young,　　　670
Warm'd and expanded into perfect life,
Their brittle bondage break, and come to light;
A helpless family, demanding food
With constant clamour. Oh, what passions then,
What melting sentiments of kindly care,
On the new parents seize! Away they fly,
Affectionate, and, undesiring, bear
The most delicious morsel to their young,
Which equally distributed, again
The search begins. Even so a gentle pair,　　　680
By fortune sunk, but form'd of generous mold,
And charm'd with cares beyond the vulgar breast,
In some lone cott amid the distant woods,
Sustain'd alone by providential Heaven,
Oft, as they, weeping, eye their infant train,
Check their own appetites, and give them all.
　　Nor toil alone they scorn: exalting love,
By the great Father of the Spring inspir'd,
Gives instant courage to the fearful race,
And to the simple, art. With stealthy wing,　　　690
Should some rude foot their woody haunts molest,
Amid a neighbouring bush they silent drop,
And whirring thence, as if alarm'd, deceive
Th' unfeeling schoolboy. Hence, around the head
Of wandering swain, the white-wing'd plover wheels
Her sounding flight, and then directly on
In long excursion skims the level lawn,
To tempt him from her nest. The wild duck, hence,

O'er the rough moss, and o'er the trackless waste
The heath-hen flutters (pious fraud!) to lead 700
The hot pursuing spaniel far astray.
  Be not the Muse asham'd, here to bemoan
Her brothers of the grove, by tyrant man
Inhuman caught, and in the narrow cage
From liberty confin'd, and boundless air.
Dull are the pretty slaves, their plumage dull,
Ragged, and all its brightening lustre lost;
Nor is that sprightly wildness in their notes,
Which, clear and vigorous, warbles from the beech.
O then, ye friends of love and love-taught song, 710
Spare the soft tribes, this barbarous art forbear!
If on your bosom innocence can win,
Music engage, or piety persuade.
  But let not chief the nightingale lament
Her ruin'd care, too delicately fram'd
To brook the harsh confinement of the cage.
Oft when, returning with her loaded bill,
Th' astonish'd mother finds a vacant nest,
By the hard hand of unrelenting clowns
Robb'd, to the ground the vain provision falls; 720
Her pinions ruffle, and, low-drooping, scarce
Can bear the mourner to the poplar shade;
Where, all abandon'd to despair, she sings
Her sorrows through the night; and, on the bough
Sole-sitting, still at every dying fall
Takes up again her lamentable strain
Of winding woe, till, wide around, the woods
Sigh to her song, and with her wail resound.
  But now the feather'd youth their former bounds,
Ardent, disdain; and, weighing oft their wings, 730
Demand the free possession of the sky.
This one glad office more, and then dissolves
Parental love at once, now needless grown:
Unlavish wisdom never works in vain.
'Tis on some evening, sunny, grateful, mild,
When nought but balm is breathing thro' the woods,
With yellow lustre bright, that the new tribes
Visit the spacious heavens, and look abroad
On Nature's common, far as they can see,
Or wing, their range and pasture. O'er the boughs 740
Dancing about, still at the giddy verge

Their resolution fails—their pinions still,
In loose libration stretch'd, to trust the void
Trembling refuse—till down before them fly
The parent-guides, and chide, exhort, command,
Or push them off. The surging air receives
The plumy burden; and their self-taught wings
Winnow the waving element. On ground
Alighted, bolder up again they lead,
Farther and farther on, the lengthening flight;   750
Till, vanish'd every fear, and every power
Rouz'd into life and action, light in air
Th' acquitted parents see their soaring race,
And, once rejoicing, never know them more.

   High from the summit of a craggy cliff,
Hung o'er the deep, such as amazing frowns
On utmost Kilda's [7] shore, whose lonely race
Resign the setting sun to Indian worlds,
The royal eagle draws his vigorous young,
Strong-pounc'd, and ardent with paternal fire.   760
Now fit to raise a kingdom of their own,
He drives them from his fort, the towering seat,
For ages, of his empire; which, in peace,
Unstain'd he holds, while many a league to sea
He wings his course, and preys in distant isles.

   Should I my steps turn to the rural seat,
Whose lofty elms and venerable oaks
Invite the rook, who, high amid the boughs,
In early Spring, his airy city builds,
And ceaseless caws amusive; there, well-pleas'd,   770
I might the various polity survey
Of the mixt household-kind. The careful hen
Calls all her chirping family around,
Fed and defended by the fearless cock,
Whose breast with ardour flames, as on he walks,
Graceful, and crows defiance. In the pond,
The finely-checker'd duck, before her train,
Rows garrulous. The stately-sailing swan
Gives out his snowy plumage to the gale;
And, arching proud his neck, with oary feet   780
Bears forward fierce, and guards his osier-isle,
Protective of his young. The turkey nigh,
Loud-threatening, reddens; while the peacock spreads

[7] The farthest of the Western Islands of Scotland. [Thomson]

His every-colour'd glory to the sun,
And swims in radiant majesty along.
O'er the whole homely scene, the cooing dove
Flies thick in amorous chase, and wanton rolls
The glancing eye, and turns the changeful neck.
   While thus the gentle tenants of the shade
Indulge their purer loves, the rougher world   790
Of brutes, below, rush furious into flame
And fierce desire. Thro' all his lusty veins
The bull, deep-scorch'd, the raging passion feels.
Of pasture sick, and negligent of food,
Scarce seen, he wades among the yellow broom,
While o'er his ample sides the rambling sprays
Luxuriant shoot; or thro' the mazy wood
Dejected wanders, nor th' enticing bud
Crops, tho' it presses on his careless sense.
And oft, in jealous maddening fancy wrapt,   800
He seeks the fight, and, idly-butting, feigns
His rival gor'd in every knotty trunk.
Him should he meet, the bellowing war begins:
Their eyes flash fury; to the hollow'd earth,
Whence the sand flies, they mutter bloody deeds,
And groaning deep th' impetuous battle mix:
While the fair heifer, balmy-breathing, near,
Stands kindling up their rage. The trembling steed,
With this hot impulse seiz'd in every nerve,
Nor hears the rein, nor heeds the sounding thong;   810
Blows are not felt; but, tossing high his head,
And by the well-known joy to distant plains
Attracted strong, all wild he bursts away;
O'er rocks, and woods, and craggy mountains flies;
And, neighing, on the aërial summit takes
Th' exciting gale; then, steep-descending, cleaves
The headlong torrents foaming down the hills,
Even where the madness of the straiten'd stream
Turns in black eddies round: such is the force
With which his frantic heart and sinews swell.   820
   Nor undelighted by the boundless Spring
Are the broad monsters of the foaming deep:
From the deep ooze and gelid cavern rous'd,
They flounce and tumble in unwieldy joy.
Dire were the strain, and dissonant, to sing
The cruel raptures of the savage kind:

[handwritten marginalia: clars — why not just say delighted — non functional to verse — Milton]

[handwritten marginalia: nonulli - not none (Latin) double negative]

How by this flame their native wrath sublim'd,
They roam, amid the fury of their heart,
The far-resounding waste in fiercer bands,
And growl their horrid loves. But this the theme   830
I sing, enraptur'd, to the British fair,
Forbids, and leads me to the mountain-brow,
Where sits the shepherd on the grassy turf,
Inhaling, healthful, the descending sun.
Around him feeds his many-bleating flock,
Of various cadence; and his sportive lambs,
This way and that convolv'd, in friskful glee,
Their frolics play. And now the sprightly race
Invites them forth; when swift, the signal given,
They start away, and sweep the massy mound   840
That runs around the hill; the rampart once
Of iron war, in ancient barbarous times,
When disunited Britain ever bled,
Lost in eternal broil: ere yet she grew
To this deep-laid indissoluble state,
Where Wealth and Commerce lift the golden head;
And, o'er our labours, Liberty and Law,
Impartial, watch—the wonder of a world!
    What is this mighty breath, ye curious say,
That, in a powerful language, felt not heard,   850
Instructs the fowls of heaven; and thro' their breast
These arts of love diffuses? What, but God?
Inspiring God! who, boundless spirit all,
And unremitting energy, pervades,
Adjusts, sustains, and agitates the whole.
He, ceaseless, works alone, and yet alone
Seems not to work; with such perfection fram'd
Is this complex stupendous scheme of things.
But, tho' conceal'd, to every purer eye
Th' informing Author in his works appears: 860
Chief, lovely Spring, in thee, and thy soft scenes,
The smiling God is seen; while water, earth,
And air attest his bounty; which exalts
The brute creation to this finer thought,
And, annual, melts their undesigning hearts
Profusely thus in tenderness and joy.
    Still let my song a nobler note assume,
And sing th' infusive force of Spring on man;
When heaven and earth, as if contending, vie

To raise his being, and serene his soul,   870
Can he forbear to join the general smile
Of Nature? Can fierce passions vex his breast,
While every gale is peace, and every grove
Is melody? hence! from the bounteous walks
Of flowing Spring, ye sordid sons of earth,
Hard, and unfeeling of another's woe,
Or only lavish to yourselves: away!
But come, ye generous minds, in whose wide thought, *class*
Of all his works, creative bounty burns
With warmest beam; and on your open front *brow*   880
And liberal eye sits, from his dark retreat,   *personifications*
Inviting modest Want. Nor, till invok'd,   *inviting poor to come*
Can restless Goodness wait: your active search
Leaves no cold wintry corner unexplor'd;
Like silent-working heaven, surprizing oft
The lonely heart with unexpected good.
For you the roving spirit of the wind
Blows Spring abroad; for you the teeming clouds   *Searching out*
Descend in gladsome plenty o'er the world;
And the sun sheds his kindest rays for you,   *all wintry corners*
Ye flower of human race!—In these green days,   890
Reviving sickness lifts her languid head;
Life flows afresh; and young-ey'd Health exalts
The whole creation round. Contentment walks   *man walks*
The sunny glade, and feels an inward bliss
Spring o'er his mind, beyond the power of kings   *Shaftesbury*
To purchase. Pure serenity apace
Induces thought, and contemplation still.   *and Thomson —*
By swift degrees the love of nature works,   *have rising*
And warms the bosom; till at last sublim'd   900
To rapture and enthusiastic heat,   *(invoking for man*
We feel the present Deity, and taste   *rational*
The joy of God to see a happy world!   *enthusiasm from Shaftes.*
   These are the sacred feelings of thy heart,
Thy heart inform'd by reason's purer ray,
O Lyttelton,[8] the friend! thy passions thus
And meditations vary, as at large,
Courting the Muse, thro' Hagley Park you stray;
Thy British Tempé! there along the dale,
With woods o'erhung, and shagg'd with mossy rocks,   910

8 George, Lord Lyttelton, of Hagley Park, Worcestershire. In 1743 Thomson visited
Hagley while he was revising *The Seasons*.

[handwritten left margin: extent]
[handwritten top right: presents to mind the generosity of man]

Whence on each hand the gushing waters play, *[handwritten: milton]*
And down the rough cascade white-dashing fall, *[handwritten: Reflects Il Penseroso]*
Or gleam in lengthen'd vista thro' the trees,
You silent steal; or sit beneath the shade *[handwritten: melancholy man]*

[handwritten left margin: emphasis on space - ethically significant —]

Of solemn oaks, that tuft the swelling mounts
Thrown graceful round by Nature's careless hand,
And pensive listen to the various voice

[handwritten left margin: Romanticism]

Of rural peace: the herds, the flocks, the birds,

[handwritten left margin: mind's ex-pansive power]

The hollow-whispering breeze, the plaint of rills,
That, purling down amid the twisted roots   920
Which creep around, their dewy murmurs shake

[handwritten left margin: spatial quality important]

On the sooth'd ear. From these abstracted oft,
You wander thro' the philosophic world;
Where in bright train continual wonders rise,
Or to the curious or the pious eye.
And oft, conducted by historic truth,
You tread the long extent of backward time:
Planning, with warm benevolence of mind *[handwritten: Shaftesburian]*
And honest zeal unwarp'd by party rage,
Britannia's weal; how from the venal gulf   930
To raise her virtue, and her arts revive.

[handwritten left margin: between taste and morality]

Or, turning thence thy view, these graver thoughts
The Muses charm; while, with sure taste refin'd,
You draw th' inspiring breath of antient song,
Till nobly rises, emulous, thy own.
Perhaps thy lov'd Lucinda [9] shares thy walk,
With soul to thine attun'd. Then Nature all
Wears to the lover's eye a look of love;
And all the tumult of a guilty world,
Tost by ungenerous passions, sinks away.   940
The tender heart is animated peace; *[handwritten: Augustan line—form]*
And as it pours its copious treasures forth, *[handwritten: like nature throwing itself upon]*
In vary'd converse, softening every theme,
You, frequent-pausing, turn, and from her eyes,
Where meeken'd sense, and amiable grace
And lively sweetness dwell, enraptur'd drink
That nameless spirit of ethereal joy,
Inimitable happiness! which love
Alone bestows, and on a favour'd few.

[handwritten left margin: Class]

Meantime you gain the height, from whose fair brow   950
The bursting prospect spreads immense around;
And snatch'd o'er hill and dale, and wood and lawn,

[handwritten left margin: activity]

9 Lucy (Fortescue), wife of Lord Lyttelton.

[handwritten bottom: eye makes landscape burst]

Renders act of discovery, of coming upon scene

whole scene rushed in

And verdant field, and darkening heath between,
And villages embosom'd soft in trees,
And spiry towns by surging columns mark'd
Of houshold smoak, your eye excursive roams: *eye was snatched*
Wide-stretching from the hall, in whose kind haunt
The hospitable genius lingers still,
To where the broken landskip, by degrees *eye created & beheld*
Ascending, roughens into rigid hills;
O'er which the Cambrian mountains, like far clouds
That skirt the blue horizon, dusky, rise.

Flush'd by the spirit of the genial year,
Now from the virgin's cheek a fresher bloom
Shoots, less and less, the live-carnation round;
Her lips blush deeper sweets; she breathes of youth;
The shining moisture swells into her eyes
In brighter flow; her wishing bosom heaves
With palpitations wild; kind tumults seize
Her veins, and all her yielding soul is love.
From the keen gaze her lover turns away,
Full of the dear exstatic power, and sick
With sighing languishment. Ah then, ye fair!
Be greatly cautious of your sliding hearts:
Dare not th' infectious sigh; the pleading look,
Downcast and low, in meek submission drest,
But full of guile. Let not the fervent tongue,
Prompt to deceive, with adulation smooth,
Gain on your purpos'd will. Nor in the bower
Where woodbines flaunt and roses shed a couch,
While evening draws her crimson curtains round,
Trust your soft minutes with betraying man.

And let th' aspiring youth beware of love,
Of the smooth glance beware; for 'tis too late,
When on his heart the torrent-softness pours.
Then wisdom prostrate lies, and fading fame
Dissolves in air away; while the fond soul,
Wrapt in gay visions of unreal bliss,
Still paints th' illusive form, the kindling grace,
Th' enticing smile, the modest-seeming eye,
Beneath whose beauteous beams, belying Heaven,
Lurk searchless cunning, cruelty, and death:
And still, false-warbling in his cheated ear,
Her syren voice, enchanting, draws him on
To guileful shores and meads of fatal joy.

960

970

980

990

Even present, in the very lap of love
Inglorious laid; while musick flows around,
Perfumes, and oils, and wine, and wanton hours;
Amid the roses, fierce repentance rears
Her snaky crest: a quick-returning pang   1000
Shoots thro' the conscious heart; where honour still,
And great design, against th' oppressive load
Of luxury, by fits, impatient heave.
But absent, what fantastic woes, arrous'd,
Rage in each thought, by restless musing fed,
Chill the warm cheek, and blast the bloom of life!
Neglected fortune flies; and sliding swift,
Prone into ruin fall his scorn'd affairs.
'Tis nought but gloom around. The darken'd sun
Loses his light. The rosy-bosom'd Spring   1010
To weeping fancy pines; and yon bright arch,
Contracted, bends into a dusky vault.
All nature fades extinct; and she alone
Heard, felt, and seen, possesses every thought,
Fills every sense, and pants in every vein.
Books are but formal dullness, tedious friends;
And sad amid the social band he sits,
Lonely, and unattentive. From the tongue
Th' unfinish'd period falls: while borne away,
On swelling thought, his wafted spirit flies   1020
To the vain bosom of his distant fair;
And leaves the semblance of a lover, fix'd
In melancholy site, with head declin'd,
And love-dejected eyes. Sudden he starts,
Shook from his tender trance, and restless runs
To glimmering shades and sympathetic glooms;
Where the dun umbrage o'er the falling stream,
Romantic, hangs; there thro' the pensive dusk
Strays, in heart-thrilling meditation lost,
Indulging all to love: or on the bank   1030
Thrown, amid drooping lilies, swells the breeze
With sighs unceasing, and the brook with tears.
Thus in soft anguish he consumes the day,
Nor quits his deep retirement, till the moon
Peeps thro' the chambers of the fleecy east,
Enlighten'd by degrees, and in her train
Leads on the gentle hours; then forth he walks,
Beneath the trembling languish of her beam,

With soften'd soul, and wooes the bird of eve
To mingle woes with his: or, while the world   1040
And all the sons of care lie hush'd in sleep,
Associates with the midnight shadows drear;
And, sighing to the lonely taper, pours
His idly-tortur'd heart into the page
Meant for the moving messenger of love;
Where rapture burns on rapture, every line
With rising frenzy fir'd. But if on bed
Delirious flung, sleep from his pillow flies.
All night he tosses, nor the balmy power
In any posture finds; till the grey morn   1050
Lifts her pale lustre on the paler wretch,
Exanimate by love: and then perhaps
Exhausted nature sinks a while to rest,
Still interrupted by distracted dreams,
That o'er the sick imagination rise,
And in black colours paint the mimick scene.
Oft with th' enchantress of his soul he talks;
Sometimes in crouds distress'd; or, if retir'd
To secret-winding flower-enwoven bowers,
Far from the dull impertinence of man,   1060
Just as he, credulous, his endless cares
Begins to lose in blind oblivious love,
Snatch'd from her yielded hand, he knows not how,
Thro' forests huge, and long untravel'd heaths
With desolation brown, he wanders waste,
In night and tempest wrapt; or shrinks aghast,
Back from the bending precipice; or wades
The turbid stream below, and strives to reach
The farther shore, where, succourless and sad,
She with extended arms his aid implores,   1070
But strives in vain: borne by th' outragious flood
To distance down, he rides the ridgy wave,
Or whelm'd beneath the boiling eddy sinks.
These are the charming agonies of love,
Whose misery delights. But thro' the heart
Should jealousy its venom once diffuse,
'Tis then delightful misery no more,
But agony unmix'd, incessant gall,
Corroding every thought, and blasting all
Love's paradise. Ye fairy prospects, then,   1080
Ye beds of roses, and ye bowers of joy,

Farewel! ye gleamings of departed peace,
Shine out your last! the yellow-tinging plague
Internal vision taints, and in a night
Of livid gloom imagination wraps.
Ah! then, instead of love-enliven'd cheeks,
Of sunny features, and of ardent eyes
With flowing rapture bright, dark looks succeed,
Suffus'd and glaring with untender fire—
A clouded aspect, and a burning cheek,   1090
Where the whole poison'd soul, malignant, sits,
And frightens love away. Ten thousand fears
Invented wild, ten thousand frantic views
Of horrid rivals, hanging on the charms
For which he melts in fondness, eat him up
With fervent anguish and consuming rage.
In vain reproaches lend their idle aid,
Deceitful pride, and resolution frail,
Giving false peace a moment. Fancy pours,
Afresh, her beauties on his busy thought;   1100
Her first endearments, twining round the soul
With all the witchcraft of ensnaring love.
Straight the fierce storm involves his mind anew,
Flames thro' the nerves, and boils along the veins;
While anxious doubt distracts the tortur'd heart:
For even the sad assurance of his fears
Were peace to what he feels. Thus the warm youth,
Whom love deludes into his thorny wilds,
Thro' flowery-tempting paths, or leads a life
Of fever'd rapture, or of cruel care;   1110
His brightest aims extinguish'd all, and all
His lively moments running down to waste.

But happy they! the happiest of their kind!
Whom gentler stars unite, and in one fate
Their hearts, their fortunes, and their beings blend.
'Tis not the coarser tie of human laws,
Unnatural oft, and foreign to the mind,
That binds their peace, but harmony itself,
Attuning all their passions into love;
Where friendship full-exerts her softest power,   1120
Perfect esteem enliven'd by desire
Ineffable, and sympathy of soul;
Thought meeting thought, and will preventing will,
With boundless confidence: for naught but love

Can answer love, and render bliss secure.
Let him, ungenerous, who, alone intent
To bless himself, from sordid parents buys
The loathing virgin, in eternal care,
Well-merited, consume his nights and days:
Let barbarous nations, whose inhuman love   1130
Is wild desire, fierce as the suns they feel;
Let eastern tyrants from the light of heaven
Seclude their bosom-slaves, meanly possess'd
Of a meer lifeless, violated form:
While those whom love cements in holy faith
And equal transport, free as Nature live,
Disdaining fear. What is the world to them,
Its pomp, its pleasure, and its nonsense all!
Who in each other clasp whatever fair
High fancy forms, and lavish hearts can wish;   1140
Something than beauty dearer, should they look
Or on the mind, or mind-illumin'd face—
Truth, goodness, honour, harmony, and love,
The richest bounty of indulgent Heaven.
Meantime a smiling offspring rises round,
And mingles both their graces. By degrees,
The human blossom blows; and every day,
Soft as it rolls along, shews some new charm—
The father's lustre, and the mother's bloom.
Then infant reason grows apace, and calls   1150
For the kind hand of an assiduous care.
Delightful task! to rear the tender thought,
To teach the young idea how to shoot,
To pour the fresh instruction o'er the mind,
To breathe th' enlivening spirit, and to fix
The generous purpose in the glowing breast.
O, speak the joy! ye, whom the sudden tear
Surprizes often, while you look around,
And nothing strikes your eye but sights of bliss;
All various Nature pressing on the heart: 1160
An elegant sufficiency, content,
Retirement, rural quiet, friendship, books,
Ease and alternate labour, useful life,
Progressive virtue, and approving Heaven.
These are the matchless joys of virtuous love;
And thus their moments fly. The Seasons thus,
As ceaseless round a jarring world they roll,

Still find them happy; and consenting Spring
Sheds her own rosy garland on their heads:
Till Evening comes at last, serene and mild; 1170
When after the long vernal day of life,
Enamour'd more, as more remembrance swells
With many a proof of recollected love,
Together down they sink, in social sleep;
Together freed, their gentle spirits fly
To scenes where love and bliss immortal reign.

A HYMN

These, as they change, Almighty Father, these
Are but the varied God. The rolling year
Is full of thee. Forth in the pleasing Spring
Thy beauty walks, thy tenderness and love.
Wide-flush the fields; the softening air is balm;
Echo the mountains round; the forest smiles;
And every sense, and every heart, is joy.
Then comes thy glory in the summer months,
With light and heat refulgent. Then thy sun
Shoots full perfection through the swelling year: 10
And oft thy voice in dreadful thunder speaks;
And oft at dawn, deep noon, or falling eve,
By brooks and groves, in hollow-whispering gales.
Thy bounty shines in Autumn unconfin'd,
And spreads a common feast for all that lives.
In Winter, awful thou! with clouds and storms
Around thee thrown, tempest o'er tempest roll'd,
Majestic darkness! on the whirlwind's wing,
Riding sublime, thou bid'st the world adore,
And humblest nature with thy northern blast. 20
　　Mysterious round! what skill, what force divine,
Deep-felt, in these appear! a simple train,
Yet so delightful mix'd, with such kind art,
Such beauty and beneficence combin'd;
Shade, unperceiv'd, so softening into shade;
And all so forming an harmonious whole;
That, as they still succeed, they ravish still.
But wandering oft, with brute unconscious gaze,
Man marks not thee, marks not the mighty hand,
That, ever busy, wheels the silent spheres; 30
Works in the secret deep; shoots, steaming, thence
The fair profusion that o'erspreads the Spring:

Flings from the sun direct the flaming day;
Feeds every creature; hurls the tempest forth;
And, as on earth this grateful change revolves,
With transport touches all the springs of life.
    Nature, attend! join every living soul,
Beneath the spacious temple of the sky,
In adoration join; and, ardent, raise
One general song! To Him, ye vocal gales,   40
Breathe soft, whose spirit in your freshness breathes:
Oh! talk of Him in solitary glooms,
Where, o'er the rock, the scarcely-waving pine
Fills the brown shade with a religious awe.
And ye, whose bolder note is heard afar,
Who shake th' astonish'd world, lift high to Heaven
Th' impetuous song, and say from whom you rage.
His praise ye brooks attune, ye trembling rills;
And let me catch it as I muse along.
Ye headlong torrents, rapid and profound;   50
Ye softer floods, that lead the humid maze
Along the vale; and thou, majestic main,
A secret world of wonders in thyself,
Sound His stupendous praise; whose greater voice
Or bids you roar, or bids your roarings fall.
Soft-roll your incense, herbs, and fruits, and flowers,
In mingled clouds to Him, whose sun exalts,
Whose breath perfumes you, and whose pencil paints.
Ye forests bend, ye harvests wave, to Him;
Breathe your still song into the reaper's heart,   60
As home he goes beneath the joyous moon.
Ye that keep watch in Heaven, as earth asleep
Unconscious lies, effuse your mildest beams,
Ye constellations, while your angels strike,
Amid the spangled sky, the silver lyre.
Great source of day! best image here below
Of thy Creator, ever pouring wide,
From world to world, the vital ocean round,
On nature write with every beam His praise.
The thunder rolls: be hush'd the prostrate world;   70
While cloud to cloud returns the solemn hymn.
Bleat out afresh, ye hills; ye mossy rocks,
Retain the sound; the broad responsive low,
Ye valleys, raise; for the Great Shepherd reigns;
And His unsuffering kingdom yet will come.

Ye woodlands all, awake: a boundless song
Burst from the groves; and when the restless day,
Expiring, lays the warbling world asleep,
Sweetest of birds! sweet Philomela, charm
The listening shades, and teach the night His praise.   80
Ye chief, for whom the whole creation smiles,
At once the head, the heart, and tongue of all,
Crown the great hymn! in swarming cities vast,
Assembled men, to the deep organ join
The long-resounding voice, oft breaking clear,
At solemn pauses, thro' the swelling bass;
And, as each mingling flame increases each,
In one united ardour rise to Heaven.
Or if you rather choose the rural shade,
And find a fane in every sacred grove;   90
There let the shepherd's flute, the virgin's lay,
The prompting seraph, and the poet's lyre,
Still sing the God of Seasons, as they roll.
For me, when I forget the darling theme,
Whether the blossom blows, the summer ray
Russets the plain, inspiring Autumn gleams,
Or Winter rises in the blackening east,
Be my tongue mute, may fancy paint no more,
And, dead to joy, forget my heart to beat!
     Should fate command me to the farthest verge   100
Of the green earth, to distant barbarous climes,
Rivers unknown to song––where first the sun
Gilds Indian mountains, or his setting beam
Flames on th' Atlantic isles––'tis nought to me;
Since God is ever present, ever felt,
In the void waste as in the city full;
And where He vital spreads there must be joy.
When even at last the solemn hour shall come,
And wing my mystic flight to future worlds,
I chearful will obey; there, with new powers,   110
Will rising wonders sing: I cannot go
Where Universal Love not smiles around,
Sustaining all yon orbs, and all their sons;
From seeming evil still educing good,
And better thence again, and better still,
In infinite progression.––––But I lose
Myself in Him, in Light ineffable!
Come then, expressive silence, muse His praise.

A POEM SACRED TO THE MEMORY OF
SIR ISAAC NEWTON

1727

nov 20th

Confident assertion of truth

Shall the great soul of Newton quit this earth,
To mingle with his stars; and every Muse,
Astonish'd into silence, shun the weight
Of honours due to his illustrious name?
But what can man?—Even now the sons of light,
In strains high-warbled to seraphic lyre,
Hail his arrival on the coast of bliss.
Yet am not I deterr'd, tho' high the theme,
And sung to harps of angels, for with you,
Ethereal flames! ambitious, I aspire   10
In Nature's general symphony to join.

   And what new wonders can ye show your guest!
Who, while on this dim spot, where mortals toil
Clouded in dust, from motion's simple laws,
Could trace the secret hand of Providence,
Wide-working thro' this universal frame.

   Have ye not listen'd while he bound the suns
And planets to their spheres! th' unequal task
Of humankind till then. Oft had they roll'd
O'er erring man the year, and oft disgrac'd   20
The pride of schools, before their course was known
Full in its causes and effects to him,
All-piercing sage! who sat not down and dream'd
Romantic schemes, defended by the din
Of specious words, and tyranny of names;
But, bidding his amazing mind attend,
And with heroic patience years on years
Deep-searching, saw at last the system dawn,
And shine, of all his race, on him alone.

   What were his raptures then! how pure! how strong!   30
And what the triumphs of old Greece and Rome,
By his diminish'd, but the pride of boys
In some small fray victorious! when instead
Of shatter'd parcels of this earth usurp'd
By violence unmanly, and sore deeds
Of cruelty and blood, Nature herself

nature conquered by newton

Stood all subdu'd by him, and open laid
Her every latent glory to his view.
   All intellectual eye, our solar round
First gazing thro', he by the blended power   40
Of gravitation and projection, saw
The whole in silent harmony revolve.
From unassisted vision hid, the moons
To chear remoter planets numerous form'd,
By him in all their mingled tracts were seen.
He also fix'd the wandering Queen of Night,
Whether she wanes into a scanty orb,
Or, waxing broad, with her pale shadowy light,
In a soft deluge overflows the sky.
Her every motion clear-discerning, he   50
Adjusted to the mutual main, and taught
Why now the mighty mass of water swells
Resistless, heaving on the broken rocks,
And the full river turning; till again
The tide revertive, unattracted, leaves
A yellow waste of idle sands behind.
   Then breaking hence, he took his ardent flight
Thro' the blue infinite; and every star,
Which the clear concave of a winter's night
Pours on the eye, or astronomic tube,   60
Far-stretching, snatches from the dark abyss,
Or such as farther in successive skies
To fancy shine alone, at his approach
Blaz'd into suns, the living center each
Of an harmonious system: all combin'd,
And rul'd unerring by that single power,
Which draws the stone projected to the ground.
   O unprofuse magnificence divine!
O wisdom truly perfect! thus to call
From a few causes such a scheme of things,   70
Effects so various, beautiful, and great,
An universe compleat! and O belov'd
Of heaven! whose well-purg'd penetrative eye,
The mystic veil transpiercing, inly scan'd
The rising, moving, wide-establish'd frame.
   He, first of men, with awful wing pursu'd
The comet thro' the long eliptic curve,
As round innumerous worlds he wound his way;
Till, to the forehead of our evening sky

Scientific spirit of newton [handwritten marginal note]

Return'd, the blazing wonder glares anew,   80
And o'er the trembling nations shakes dismay.
  The heavens are all his own; from the wide rule
Of whirling vortices, and circling spheres,
To their first great simplicity restor'd.
The schools astonish'd stood; but found it vain
To keep at odds with demonstration strong,
And, unawaken'd, dream beneath the blaze
Of truth. At once their pleasing visions fled,
With the gay shadows of the morning mix'd,
When Newton rose, our philosophic sun.   90
  Th' aërial flow of sound was known to him,
From whence it first in wavy circles breaks,
Till the touch'd organ takes the meaning in.
Nor could the darting beam, of speed immense,
Escape his swift pursuit, and measuring eye.
Even light itself, which everything displays,
Shone undiscover'd, till his brighter mind
Untwisted all the shining robe of day;
And, from the whitening undistinguish'd blaze,
Collecting every ray into his kind,   100
To the charm'd eye educ'd the gorgeous train
Of parent-colours. First the flaming red
Sprung vivid forth; the tawny orange next;
And next delicious yellow; by whose side
Fell the kind beams of all-refreshing green.
Then the pure blue, that swells autumnal skies,
Ethereal play'd; and then, of sadder hue,
Emerg'd the deepen'd indigo, as when
The heavy-skirted evening droops with frost.
While the last gleamings of refracted light   110
Dy'd in the fainting violet away.
These, when the clouds distil the rosy shower,
Shine out distinct adown the wat'ry bow;
While o'er our heads the dewy vision bends
Delightful, melting on the fields beneath.
Myriads of mingling dyes from these result,
And myriads still remain—Infinite source
Of beauty, ever-flushing, ever-new!
  Did ever poet image aught so fair,
Dreaming in whispering groves, by the hoarse brook!   120
Or prophet, to whose rapture heaven descends!
Even now the setting sun and shifting clouds,

Seen, Greenwich, from thy lovely heights, declare
How just, how beauteous the refractive law.
  The noiseless tide of time, all bearing down
To vast Eternity's unbounded sea
Where the green islands of the happy shine,
He stemm'd alone; and to the source (involv'd
Deep in primæval gloom) ascending, rais'd
His lights at equal distances, to guide   130
Historian, wilder'd on his darksome way.
  But who can number up his labours? who
His high discoveries sing? when but a few
Of the deep-studying race can stretch their minds
To what he knew: in fancy's lighter thought,
How shall the Muse then grasp the mighty theme?
  What wonder thence that his devotion swell'd
Responsive to his knowledge! for could he,
Whose piercing mental eye diffusive saw
The finish'd University of things,   140
In all its order, magnitude, and parts,
Forbear incessant to adore that Power
Who fills, sustains, and actuates the whole?
  Say, ye who best can tell, ye happy few,
Who saw him in the softest lights of life,
All unwithheld, indulging to his friends
The vast unborrow'd treasures of his mind,
Oh speak the wondrous man! how mild, how calm,
How greatly humble, how divinely good;
How firm establish'd on eternal truth;   150
Fervent in doing well, with every nerve
Still pressing on, forgetful of the past,
And panting for perfection: far above
Those little cares, and visionary joys,
That so perplex the fond impassion'd heart
Of ever-cheated, ever-trusting man.
  This, Conduit,[1] from thy rural hours we hope;
As thro' the pleasing shade, where Nature pours
Her every sweet, in studious ease you walk;
The social passions smiling at thy heart,   160
That glows with all the recollected sage.
  And you, ye hopeless gloomy-minded tribe,
You who, unconscious of those nobler flights

---

[1] John Conduit married Newton's niece; he planned a biography of Newton which
was never published.

That reach impatient at immortal life,
Against the prime endearing privilege
Of being dare contend, say, can a soul
Of such extensive, deep, tremendous powers,
Enlarging still, be but a finer breath
Of spirits dancing thro' their tubes a while,
And then forever lost in vacant air?   170
   But hark! methinks I hear a warning voice,
Solemn as when some awful change is come,
Sound thro' the world—" 'Tis done!—The measure's full;
And I resign my charge."—Ye mouldering stones,
That build the towering pyramid, the proud
Triumphal arch, the monument effac'd
By ruthless ruin, and whate'er supports
The worship'd name of hoar antiquity,
Down to the dust! what grandeur can ye boast
While Newton lifts his column to the skies,   180
Beyond the waste of time?—Let no weak drop
Be shed for him. The virgin in her bloom
Cut off, the joyous youth, and darling child,
These are the tombs that claim the tender tear,
And elegiac song. But Newton calls
For other notes of gratulation high,
That now he wanders thro' those endless worlds
He here so well descried, and wondering talks,
And hymns their Author with his glad compeers.
   O Britain's boast! whether with angels thou   190
Sittest in dread discourse, or fellow-blest,
Who joy to see the honour of their kind;
Or whether, mounted on cherubic wing,
Thy swift career is with the whirling orbs,
Comparing things with things, in rapture lost,
And grateful adoration, for that light
So plenteous ray'd into thy mind below,
From Light Himself; oh look with pity down
On humankind, a frail erroneous race!
Exalt the spirit of a downward world!   200
O'er thy dejected country chief preside,
And be her Genius call'd! her studies raise,
Correct her manners, and inspire her youth.
For, tho' deprav'd and sunk, she brought thee forth,
And glories in thy name; she points thee out
To all her sons, and bids them eye thy star·

While in expectance of the second life,
When Time shall be no more, thy sacred dust
Sleeps with her kings, and dignifies the scene.

THE CASTLE OF INDOLENCE

1748

CANTO I

The castle hight of indolence,
And its false luxury;
Where for a little time, alas!
We liv'd right jollily.

I

O mortal man, who livest here by toil,
Do not complain of this thy hard estate;
That like an emmet thou must ever moil,
Is a sad sentence of an antient date:
And, certes, there is for it reason great;
For, though sometimes it makes thee weep and wail,
And curse thy star, and early drudge and late,
Withouten that would come an heavier bale,
Loose life, unruly passions, and diseases pale.

II

In lowly dale, fast by a river's side,   10
With woody hill o'er hill encompass'd round,
A most enchanting wizard did abide,
Than whom a fiend more fell is nowhere found.
It was, I ween, a lovely spot of ground;
And there a season atween June and May,
Half prankt with spring, with summer half imbrown'd,
A listless climate made, where, sooth to say,
No living wight could work, ne cared even for play.

III

Was nought around but images of rest:
Sleep-soothing groves, and quiet lawns between;   20
And flowery beds that slumbrous influence kest,
From poppies breath'd; and beds of pleasant green,

Where never yet was creeping creature seen.
Meantime unnumber'd glittering streamlets play'd,
And hurled everywhere their waters sheen;
That, as they bicker'd through the sunny glade,
Though restless still themselves, a lulling murmur made.

IV

Join'd to the prattle of the purling rills,
Were heard the lowing herds along the vale,
And flocks loud-bleating from the distant hills,   30
And vacant shepherds piping in the dale:
And now and then sweet Philomel would wail,
Or stock-doves plain amid the forest deep,
That drowsy rustled to the sighing gale;
And still a coil the grasshopper did keep:
Yet all these sounds yblent inclined all to sleep.

V

Full in the passage of the vale, above,
A sable, silent, solemn forest stood;
Where nought but shadowy forms were seen to move,
As Idless fancied in her dreaming mood.   40
And up the hills, on either side, a wood
Of blackening pines, ay waving to and fro,
Sent forth a sleepy horror through the blood;
And where this valley winded out, below,
The murmuring main was heard, and scarcely heard, to flow.

VI

A pleasing land of drowsy-hed it was:
Of dreams that wave before the half-shut eye;
And of gay castles in the clouds that pass,
For ever flushing round a summer-sky:
There eke the soft delights, that witchingly   50
Instil a wanton sweetness through the breast,
And the calm pleasures always hover'd nigh;
But whate'er smack'd of noyance, or unrest,
Was far, far off expell'd from this delicious nest.

VII

The landskip such, inspiring perfect ease,
Where Indolence (for so the wizard hight)
Close-hid his castle mid embowering trees,

That half shut out the beams of Phœbus bright,
And made a kind of checker'd day and night.
Meanwhile, unceasing at the massy gate,   60
Beneath a spacious palm, the wicked wight
Was plac'd; and to his lute, of cruel fate,
And labour harsh, complain'd, lamenting man's estate.

. . . .

XXXI

Ye gods of quiet, and of sleep profound!
Whose soft dominion o'er this castle sways,
And all the widely-silent places round,
Forgive me, if my trembling pen displays
What never yet was sung in mortal lays.
But how shall I attempt such arduous string?
I who have spent my nights and nightly days,   70
In this soul-deadening place, loose-loitering?
Ah! how shall I for this uprear my moulted wing?

XXXII

Come on, my Muse, nor stoop to low despair,
Thou imp of Jove, touch'd by celestial fire!
Thou yet shalt sing of war, and actions fair,
Which the bold sons of Britain will inspire;
Of antient bards thou yet shalt sweep the lyre;
Thou yet shalt tread in tragic pall the stage,
Paint love's enchanting woes, the heroe's ire,
The sage's calm, the patriot's noble rage,   80
Dashing corruption down through every worthless age.

XXXIII

The doors, that knew no shrill alarming bell,
Ne cursed knocker ply'd by villain's hand,
Self-open'd into halls, where, who can tell
What elegance and grandeur wide expand
The pride of Turkey and of Persia land?
Soft quilts on quilts, on carpets carpets spread,
And couches stretch around in seemly band;
And endless pillows rise to prop the head;
So that each spacious room was one full-swelling bed.   90

XXXIV

And everywhere huge cover'd tables stood,
With wines high-flavour'd and rich viands crown'd;
Whatever sprightly juice or tasteful food
On the green bosom of this earth are found,
And all old ocean genders in his round:
Some hand unseen these silently display'd,
Even undemanded, by a sign or sound;
You need but wish, and, instantly obey'd,
Fair-rang'd the dishes rose, and thick the glasses play'd.

XXXV

Here freedom reign'd, without the least alloy;   100
Nor gossip's tale, nor antient maiden's gall,
Nor saintly spleen durst murmur at our joy,
And with envenom'd tongue our pleasures pall.
For why? there was but one great rule for all;
To wit, that each should work his own desire,
And eat, drink, study, sleep, as it may fall,
Or melt the time in love or wake the lyre,
And carol what, unbid, the Muses might inspire.

XXXVI

The rooms with costly tapestry were hung,
Where was inwoven many a gentle tale;   110
Such as of old the rural poets sung,
Or of Arcadian or Sicilian vale:
Reclining lovers, in the lonely dale,
Pour'd forth at large the sweetly-tortur'd heart;
Or, looking tender passion, swell'd the gale,
And taught charm'd echo to resound their smart,
While flocks, woods, streams, around repose and peace impart.

XXXVII

Those pleas'd the most, where, by a cunning hand,
Depainted was the patriarchal age;
What time Dan Abraham left the Chaldee land,   120
And pastur'd on from verdant stage to stage,
Where fields and fountains fresh could best engage.
Toil was not then. Of nothing took they heed,
But with wild beasts the silvan war to wage,
And o'er vast plains their herds and flocks to feed:
Blest sons of nature they! true golden age indeed!

XXXVIII

Sometimes the pencil,[1] in cool airy halls,
Bade the gay bloom of vernal landskips rise,
Or autumn's varied shades imbrown the walls:
Now the black tempest strikes th' astonish'd eyes;   130
Now down the steep the flashing torrent flies;
The trembling sun now plays o'er ocean blue,
And now rude mountains frown amid the skies;
Whate'er Lorrain light-touch'd with softening hue,
Or savage Rosa dash'd, or learned Poussin drew.

XXXIX

Each sound too here to languishment inclin'd,
Lull'd the weak bosom, and induced ease.
Aërial music in the warbling wind,
At distance rising oft, by small degrees,
Nearer and nearer came, till o'er the trees   140
It hung, and breath'd such soul-dissolving airs,
As did, alas! with soft perdition please:
Entangled deep in its enchanting snares,
The listening heart forgot all duties and all cares.

XL

A certain music, never known before,
Here lull'd the pensive, melancholy mind;
Full easily obtain'd. Behoves no more,
But sidelong, to the gently-waving wind,
To lay the well-tun'd instrument reclin'd;
From which, with airy flying fingers light,   150
Beyond each mortal touch the most refin'd,
The god of winds drew sounds of deep delight:
Whence, with just cause, the harp of Æolus it hight.

XLI

Ah me! what hand can touch the strings so fine?
Who up the lofty diapason roll
Such sweet, such sad, such solemn airs divine,
Then let them down again into the soul?
Now rising love they fann'd; now pleasing dole
They breath'd, in tender musings, through the heart;
And now a graver sacred strain they stole,   160

1 From the Latin *penicillum* (brush); the word "pencil" was used throughout the century in the sense of "painter's brush."

As when seraphic hands an hymn impart:
Wild warbling nature all, above the reach of art!

XLII

Such the gay splendour, the luxurious state,
Of Caliphs old, who on the Tygris' shore,
In mighty Bagdat, populous and great,
Held their bright court, where was of ladies store;
And verse, love, music still the garland wore:
When sleep was coy, the bard, in waiting there,
Chear'd the lone midnight with the Muse's lore;
Composing music bade his dreams be fair,   170
And music lent new gladness to the morning air.

XLIII

Near the pavilions where we slept, still ran
Soft-tinkling streams, and dashing waters fell,
And sobbing breezes sigh'd, and oft began
(So work'd the wizard) wintry storms to swell,
As heaven and earth they would together mell:
At doors and windows, threatening, seem'd to call
The demons of the tempest, growling fell,
Yet the least entrance found they none at all;
Whence sweeter grew our sleep, secure in massy hall.   180

XLIV

And hither Morpheus sent his kindest dreams,
Raising a world of gayer tinct and grace;
O'er which were shadowy cast Elysian gleams,
That play'd, in waving lights, from place to place,
And shed a roseate smile on nature's face.
Not Titian's pencil e'er could so array,
So fleece with clouds the pure ethereal space;
Ne could it e'er such melting forms display,
As loose on flowery beds all languishingly lay.

. . . .

LXVIII

A bard [2] here dwelt, more fat than bard beseems;   190
Who, void of envy, guile, and lust of gain,
On virtue still, and nature's pleasing themes,

2 This bard is Thomson himself. (The following lines of this stanza were writ by a friend
of the author. [Thomson])

Pour'd forth his unpremeditated strain,
The world forsaking with a calm disdain:
Here laugh'd he careless in his easy seat;
Here quaff'd encircled with the joyous train,
Oft moralizing sage: his ditty sweet
He loathed much to write, ne cared to repeat.

LXIX

Full oft by holy feet our ground was trod,
Of clerks good plenty here you mote espy.   200
A little, round, fat, oily man of God [3]
Was one I chiefly mark'd among the fry:
He had a roguish twinkle in his eye,
And shone all glittering with ungodly dew,
If a tight damsel chaunc'd to trippen by;
Which when observ'd, he shrunk into his mew,
And strait would recollect his piety anew.

LXX

Nor be forgot a tribe, who minded nought
(Old inmates of the place) but state affairs:
They look'd, perdie, as if they deeply thought;   210
And on their brow sat every nation's cares.
The world by them is parcel'd out in shares,
When in the Hall of Smoak they congress hold,
And the sage berry sun-burnt Mocha bears
Has clear'd their inward eye: then, smoak-enroll'd,
Their oracles break forth mysterious as of old.

LXXI

Here languid Beauty kept her pale-fac'd court:
Bevies of dainty dames, of high degree,
From every quarter hither made resort;
Where, from gross mortal care and business free,   220
They lay, pour'd out in ease and luxury.
Or should they a vain shew of work assume,
Alas! and well-a-day! what can it be?
To knot, to twist, to range the vernal bloom;
But far is cast the distaff, spinning-wheel, and loom.

[3] The Rev. Patrick Murdoch, who completed the preceding stanza and wrote a biography of Thomson (1762).

LXXII

Their only labour was to kill the time;
And labour dire it is, and weary woe.
They sit, they loll, turn o'er some idle rhyme;
Then rising sudden, to the glass they go,
Or saunter forth, with tottering step and slow;   230
This soon too rude an exercise they find;
Strait on the couch their limbs again they throw,
Where hours on hours they sighing lie reclin'd,
And court the vapoury god soft-breathing in the wind.

LXXIII

Now must I mark the villainy we found,
But ah! too late, as shall eftsoons be shewn,
A place here was, deep, dreary, under ground;
Where still our inmates, when unpleasing grown,
Diseas'd, and loathsome, privily were thrown.
Far from the light of heaven, they languish'd there,   240
Unpitied uttering many a bitter groan;
For of these wretches taken was no care:
Fierce fiends, and hags of hell, their only nurses were.

LXXIV [4]

Alas! the change! from scenes of joy and rest,
To this dark den, where sickness tost alway.
Here Lethargy, with deadly sleep opprest,
Stretch'd on his back, a mighty lubbard lay,
Heaving his sides, and snored night and day;
To stir him from his traunce it was not eath,
And his half-open'd eyne he shut straightway: 250
He led, I wot, the softest way to death,
And taught withouten pain and strife to yield the breath.

LXXV

Of limbs enormous, but withal unsound,
Soft-swoln and pale, here lay the Hydropsy:
Unwieldy man! with belly monstrous round,
For ever fed with watery supply;
For still he drank, and yet he still was dry.
And moping here did Hypochondria sit,
Mother of spleen, in robes of various dye,

[4] The four concluding stanzas are by Dr. John Armstrong.

Who vexed was full oft with ugly fit;   260
And some her frantic deem'd, and some her deem'd a wit.

LXXVI

A lady proud she was, of antient blood,
Yet oft her fear her pride made crouchen low:
She felt, or fancied in her fluttering mood,
All the diseases which the 'spitals know,
And sought all physick which the shops bestow,
And still new leaches and new drugs would try,
Her humour ever wavering to and fro;
For sometimes she would laugh, and sometimes cry,
Then sudden waxed wroth, and all she knew not why.   270

LXXVII

Fast by her side a listless maiden pin'd,
With aching head, and squeamish heart-burnings;
Pale, bloated, cold, she seem'd to hate mankind,
Yet lov'd in secret all forbidden things.
And here the Tertian shakes his chilling wings;
The sleepless Gout here counts the crowing cocks,
A wolf now gnaws him, now a serpent stings;
Whilst Apoplexy cramm'd Intemperance knocks
Down to the ground at once, as butcher felleth ox,

A SELECTION

Samuel Richardson

1689–1761

LETTERS WRITTEN TO AND FOR PARTICULAR FRIENDS, ON THE MOST IMPORTANT OCCASIONS, DIRECTING NOT ONLY THE REQUISITE STYLE AND FORMS TO BE OBSERVED IN WRITING FAMILIAR LETTERS; BUT HOW TO THINK AND ACT JUSTLY AND PRUDENTLY, IN THE COMMON CONCERNS OF HUMAN LIFE. CONTAINING ONE HUNDRED AND SEVENTY-THREE LETTERS, NONE OF WHICH WERE EVER BEFORE PUBLISHED.

1741

[In the eighteenth century the letter was a cultivated "form" of writing from which sprang the epistolary novel. *Pamela* was written as "a series of familiar letters from a beautiful young damsel to her parents," as the original title has it. The *Familiar Letters*, done by Richardson at the request of two other friendly printers, is of great interest because it so adequately represents certain middle-class attitudes of the day. Richardson published this "letter-writer" anonymously.]

LETTER XIII

A Young Man in business, to a Father, desiring leave to address his Daughter

SIR,

I hope the justness of my intentions will excuse the freedom of these few lines, whereby I am to acquaint you of the great affection and esteem I have for your daughter. I would not, sir, offer at any indirect address that should have the least appearance of inconsistency with her duty to you, and my honorable views to her; choosing, by your influence, if I may approve myself to you worthy of that honor, to commend myself to her approbation. You are not insensible, sir, by the credit I have hitherto preserved in the world, of my ability, by God's blessing, to make her happy:

and this the rather emboldens me to request the favor of an evening's conversation with you, at your first convenience, when I
will more fully explain myself, as I earnestly hope, to your satisfaction, and take my encouragement or discouragement from your
own mouth. I am, sir, meantime, with great respect,

Your most obedient humble servant.

LETTER XIV

*To the Daughter (on the Father's allowance) apprising her of his
intended visit*

MADAM,

I have ventured to make known to your honored father the
great desire I have to be thought worthy of a relation to him by
your means. And, as he has not discouraged me in the hopes I have
entertained that I may possibly be not unacceptable to him, and
to all your worthy family, I propose to do myself the honor of a
visit to you next Monday. Though he has been so good as to promise to introduce me, and I make no doubt has acquainted you with
it, I give you, nevertheless, the trouble of these lines that I might
not appear wanting in any outward demonstration of that inviolable respect with which I am, dear Madam,

Your most devoted humble servant.

LETTER XV

*From a Young Lady to her Father, acquainting him with a pro-
posal of marriage made to her*

Nottingham, Apr. 4.

HONORED SIR,

I think it is my duty to acquaint you that a gentleman of this
town, by name Derham, and by business a linen-draper, has made
some overtures to my cousin Morgan, in the way of courtship to
me. My cousin has brought him once or twice into my company,
which he could not well decline doing because he has dealings with
him, and has an high opinion of him and his circumstances. He has
been set up three years, and has very good business, and lives in
credit and fashion. He is about twenty-seven years old, and a likely
man enough: he seems not to want sense or manners, and is come
of a good family. He has broken his mind to me, and boasts how
well he can maintain me. But, I assure you, sir, I have given him
no encouragement, and told him that I had no thoughts of chang-

ing my condition yet a while; and should never think of it but in obedience to my parents; and I desired him to talk no more on that subject to me. Yet he resolves to persevere, and pretends extraordinary affection and esteem. I would not, sir, by any means omit to acquaint you with the *beginnings* of an affair that would be want of duty in me to conceal from you, and show a guilt and disobedience unworthy of the kind indulgence and affection you have always shown to, sir,

Your most dutiful daughter.

My humble duty to my honored mother; love to my brother and sister; and respects to all friends. Cousin Morgan and his wife and sister desire their kind respects. I cannot speak enough of their civility to me.

LETTER XVI

The Father's Answer, on a supposition that he approves not of the Young Man's addresses

Northampton, Apr. 10.

DEAR POLLY,

I have received your letter dated the 4th instant, wherein you acquaint me of the proposals made to you, through your cousin Morgan's recommendation, by one Mr. Derham. I hope, as you assure me, that you have given no encouragement to him, for I by no means approve of him for your husband. I have inquired of one of his townsmen, who knows him and his circumstances very well; and I am neither pleased with them, nor with his character, and wonder my cousin would so inconsiderately recommend him to you. Indeed, I doubt not Mr. Morgan's good intentions, but I insist upon it that you think nothing of the matter, if you would oblige

Your indulgent father.

Your mother gives her blessing to you, and joins with me in the above advice. Your brother and sister, and all friends, send their love and respects to you.

LETTER XVII

The Father's Answer, on a supposition that he does not disapprove of the Young Man's addresses

Northampt., Apr. 10.

MY DEAR DAUGHTER,

In answer to yours of the 4th instant, relating to the addresses of Mr. Derham, I would have you neither wholly encourage nor discourage his suit; for if, on inquiry into his character and circumstances, I shall find that they are answerable to your cousin's good opinion of them, and his own assurances, I know not but his suit may be worthy of attention. But, my dear, consider that men are deceitful, and always put the best side outwards; and it may possibly, on the strict inquiry, which the nature and importance of the case demands, come out far otherwise than it at present appears. Let me advise you, therefore, to act in this matter with great prudence, and that you make not yourself too cheap; for men are apt to slight what is too easily obtained. Your cousin will give him hope enough, while you don't absolutely deny him; and, in the mean time, he may be told that you are not at your own disposal, but entirely resolved to abide by my determination and direction in an affair of this great importance. And this will put him upon applying to me, who, you need not doubt, will in this case, as in all others, study your good; as becomes

Your indulgent father.

Your mother gives her blessing to you, and joins with me in the above advice. Your brother and sister, and all friends, send their love and respects to you.

LETTER XVIII

The young Gentleman's Letter to the Father, apprising him of his affection for his Daughter

Nottingham, Apr. 12.

SIR,

I take the liberty, though personally unknown to you, to declare the great value and affection I have for your worthy daughter, whom I have had the honor to see at my good friend Mr. Morgan's. I should think myself entirely unworthy of *her* favor, and of *your* approbation, if I could have a thought of influencing her resolution but in obedience to your pleasure; as I should, on such a supposition, offer an injury likewise to that prudence in *herself*, which, I flatter myself, is not the least of her amiable perfections. If I might have the honor of your countenance, sir, on this occasion, I would open myself and circumstances to you, in that frank and honest manner which should convince you of the sincerity of my affection for your daughter, and at the same time of the honorableness of my intentions. In the mean time I will in general say that I have been set up in business in the linen-drapery way upwards of three years; that I have a very good trade for the time; that I had £1000 to begin with, which I have improved to £1500, as I am ready to make appear to your satisfaction; that I am descended of a creditable family; have done nothing to stain my character; and that my trade is still farther improvable, as I shall, I hope, enlarge my bottom. This, sir, I thought but honest and fair to acquaint you with that you might know something of a person who sues to you for your countenance, and that of your good lady, in an affair that I hope may prove one day the greatest happiness of my life; as it *must* be if I can be blessed with that, and your daughter's approbation. In hope of which, and the favor of a line, I take the liberty to subscribe myself, good sir,

Your most obedient humble servant.

LETTER XIX

From the Cousin to the Father and Mother, in commendation of the Young Gentleman

Nottingham, April 12.

DEAR COUSINS,

I give you both thanks for so long continuing with us the pleasure of Cousin Polly's company. She has entirely captivated a worthy friend of mine, Mr. Derham, a linen-draper of this town. And I would have acquainted you with it myself, but that I knew and advised Cousin Polly to write to you about it; for I would not for the world anything of this sort should be carried on unknown to you, at my house especially. Mr. Derham has shown me his letter to you, and I believe every tittle of it to be true; and really, if you and my cousin approve it, as also Cousin Polly, I don't know where she can do better. I am sure I should think so if I had a daughter he could love.

Thus much I thought myself obliged to say; and with my kind love to your other self, and all my cousins, as also my wife's and sister's, I remain

Your affectionate cousin.

LETTER XX

From the Father, in answer to the Young Gentleman

Northampton, April 16.

SIR,

I have received yours of the 12th, and am obliged to you for the good opinion you express for my daughter: but I think she is yet full young to alter her condition, and embark in the cares of a family. I cannot but say, that the account you give of yourself, and your application to *me*, rather than first to try to engage the affections of my daughter, carry a very honorable appearance, and such as must be to the advantage of your character. As to your beginning, sir, that is not to be so much looked upon as the *improvement;* and I doubt not that you can make good proof of what you assert on this occasion. But still I must needs say that I think, and so does her mother, that it is too early to encumber her with the cares of the world; and as I am sure she will do nothing in so important an affair without our advice, so I would not for the world, in a case so nearly concerning her, and her future welfare, constrain her in the least. I intend shortly to send for her home, for she has been longer absent from us than we intended; and then I shall consult her inclinations; and you will excuse me to say (for she is my daughter, and a very good child, though I say it) that I shall then determine myself by that, and by what shall appear to offer most for her good. In the mean time, sir, I thank you for the civility and commendable openness of yours; and am

Your humble servant.

[The father in this letter referring pretty much to the daughter's choice, the young gentleman cannot but construe it as an encouragement to him to prosecute his addresses to *her;* in which he doubles his diligence (on the hint that she will soon return to Northampton) in order to gain a footing in her good will; and she, finding her father and mother not averse to the affair, ventures to give him some room to think his addresses not indifferent to her; but still altogether on condition of her parents' consent and approbation. By the time, then, that she is recalled home (nothing disagreeable having appeared in the young gentleman's behavior, and his general character being consistent with his pretensions) there may be supposed some degree of familiarity and confidence to have passed between them; and she gives him hope that she will receive a letter from him, though she shall not promise an answer, entirely referring to her duty to her parents and their good pleasure. He attends her on her journey a good part of the way, as far as she will permit; and when her cousin, his friend, informs him of her safe arrival at Northampton, he sends the following letter.]

LETTER XXI

From a Young Gentleman to his Mistress, on her arrival at her Father's

May 25.

DEAR MADAM,

I have understood, with great pleasure, your safe arrival at your father's house, of which I take the liberty to congratulate your good parents as well as your dear self. I will not, Madam, fill this letter with the regret I had to part with you, because I have no reason nor merit, at present, to expect that you should be concerned for me on this score. Yet, Madam, I am not without hope from the sincerity of my affection for you, and the honesty of my intentions, to deserve, in time, those regards which I cannot at present flatter myself with. As your good father, in his kind letter to me, assured me that he should consult your inclinations and determine by them, and by what should offer most for your good, how happy should I be *if* I could find my humble suit not quite indifferent to your dear self, and not rejected by him! If what I have already opened to him, as to my circumstances, be not unacceptable, I should humbly hope for leave to pay you and him a visit at Northampton; or if this be too great a favor, till he has made further inquiry, that he would be pleased to give himself that trouble and put it in my power as soon as possible to convince him of the truth of my allegations, upon which I desire to stand or fall in my hopes of your favor and his. For I think, far different from many in the world, that a deception in an affair of this weighty nature should be less forgiven than in any other. Since, then, dearest Madam, I build my hopes more on the truth of affection for you, and the honor of my intentions, than any other merit or pretensions, I hope you will condescend, if not to become an advocate for me, which would be too great a presumption to expect, yet to let your good parents know that you have no aversion to the person or address of, dearest Madam,

Your for ever obliged, and affectionate humble servant.

My best respects attend your good father and mother, and whole family.

[As this puts the matter into such a train as may render more writing unnecessary, the next steps to be taken being the inquiry into the truth of the young man's assertions and a confirmation of his character, and then the proposals on the father's part of what he will give with his daughter, all which may be done best by word of mouth or interposition of friends, so shall we have no occasion to pursue this instance of courtship farther.]

LETTER XXVIII

From a Maidservant in town, acquainting her Father and Mother in the country with a proposal of marriage, and asking their consents

HONORED FATHER AND MOTHER,

I think it my duty to acquaint you that I am addressed to for change of condition by one Mr. John Tanner, who is a glazier, and lives in the neighborhood by us. He is a young man of a sober character, and has been set up about two years, has good business for his time, and is well beloved and spoken of by everyone. My friends here think well of it, particularly my master and mistress; and he says he doubts not by God's blessing on his industry, to maintain a family very prettily. And I have fairly told him how little he has to expect with me. But I would not conclude on anything, however, till I had acquainted you with his proposals, and asked your blessings and consents. For I am, and ever will be,

Your dutiful daughter.

LETTER XXIX

From the Parents, in answer to the preceding

DEAR NANNY,

We have received your dutiful letter. We can only pray to God to direct and bless you in all your engagements. Our distance from you must make us leave everything to your own discretion; and as you are so well satisfied in Mr. Tanner's character, as well as all friends, and your master and mistress, we give our blessings and consents with all our hearts. We are only sorry we can do no more for you. But let us know when it is done, and we will do some little matters, as far as we are able, towards housekeeping. Our respects to Mr. Tanner. Everybody joins with us in wishes for your happiness; and may God bless you, is all that can be said by

Your truly loving Father and Mother.

LETTER XXXVI

*A Father to a Son, to dissuade him from the vice of drinking to
excess*

My dear Son,

It is with a grief proportioned to my love, which is extreme, that
I understand you have of late neglected your studies, and given
yourself up to the odious vice of drinking. What shall I say, what
shall I do, to engage you to quit this pernicious practice before it
becomes such an habit that it will be impossible, or at least very
difficult, for you to cast it off? Let me require, let me entreat you,
to give a suitable attention to what I have to say on this head, which
I shall offer rather as a warm friend than an angry father; and as I
address myself to your reason, I will leave it to yourself to judge of
the truth of the observations I have to make to you.

In the first place, with respect to *health*, the greatest jewel of this
life, it is the most destructive of all vices: *asthmas, vertigoes, palsies,
apoplexies, gouts, colics, fevers, dropsies, consumptions, stone*, and
hypochondriac diseases are naturally introduced by excessive
drinking.

All the rest of the vices together are not so often punished with
sudden death as this one. What fatal accidents, what quarrels, what
breaches between friend and friend are owing to it!

Then, in the second place, how does it deface reason, destroy all
the tender impulses of nature, make a wise man a fool, and subject
persons of the brightest parts to the contempt of the weakest, and
even, in time, extinguish those shining qualities which constitute
the difference between a man of sense and a blockhead! For, as a
certain very eminent author well observes, fools having generally
stronger nerves, and less volatile spirits, than men of fine understandings, that which will rouse the one will make the other either
stupid or frantic; and though it sometimes, while the fit continues,
strengthens the imagination, yet it always depresses the judgment;
and after the fit is over, both those faculties languish together till in
time it quenches the imagination, impairs the memory, and drowns
the judgment.

Most other vices are compatible, as the same author observes,
with several virtues; but drunkenness runs counter to all the duties
of life. A great drinker can hardly be either a good husband, a good
father, a good son, a good brother, or a good friend. It lays him
open to the worst company, and this company frequently subjects
him to lewd women, gaming, quarrels, riots, and often murders.

All other vices, even the greatest of vices, as ambition, unchastity, bigotry, avarice, hypocrisy, detest this unnatural and worse than beastly vice; for the beasts themselves, even the uncleanest of them, know nothing of it, much less practice it.

Other vices, indeed, make men worse, says this judicious author; but this alters men from themselves to that degree that they differ not more from their present companions than from their former selves. An habitude of it will make the prudent inconsiderate, the ambitious indolent, the active idle, and the industrious slothful; so that their affairs are ruined for want of application or by being entrusted in the hands of those who turn them wholly to their own advantage, and in the end to the ruin of those who employ them.

I have written a long letter already: yet have I still more to say; which, that I may not tire you, I will leave to another letter, which the next post shall bring you. And I am, meantime, in hopes *this* will not lose its proper effect,

Your most indulgent father.

LETTER LIV

From a Mother to a Daughter, jealous of her Husband

DEAR BET,

I am sorry to find you are grown jealous of your husband. 'Tis a most uneasy passion, and will be fatal not only to your present quiet, but to your future happiness, and probably to that of your family, if you indulge it.

You either *have*, or have *not*, cause for it. If you have cause, look into yourself and your own conduct, to see if you have not, by any change of temper or disagreeableness of behavior, alienated your husband's affections; and if so, set about amending both in order to recover them. For once he loved you, and you were satisfied he did, above all your sex, or you would not have had him. If it be owing to his inconstant temper, that is indeed unhappy; but then, so long as you are clear from blame, you have nothing to reproach *yourself* with: and as the creatures wicked men follow omit nothing to oblige them, you must try to avoid such uneasy and disturbing resentments as will make you more and more distasteful to him. Show him that no guilty wretch's *pretended* love can be equal to your *real* one; show him that such creatures shall not outdo you in an obliging behavior and sweetness of temper; and that let him fly off from *his* duty if he will, you will persevere in *yours*. This conduct will, if not immediately, in time, flash conviction in his face: he will see what a goodness he injures, and will be softened

by your softness. But if you make his home uneasy to him, he will
fly both that and you. And to whom will he fly but, most probably,
to one who will allow his pleas, and aggravate everything against
you; who will side with him, inflame his passions, and thereby secure him to herself? And would *you* contribute to such a wretch's
power over him, and furnish opportunities for *her* to triumph over
you? For while you exasperate his passions and harden his mind
against you, she will, by wicked blandishments, show him how
obliging *she* can be, and so a course of life that he would follow
privately and by stealth, as it were, he will more openly pursue; he
will grow shameless in it; and so common is the vice (more's the
pity!) will find those who will extenuate it for *their own* sakes and
throw the blame on the violence of your temper, and say you drive
him into these excesses. Thus much I write supposing you have
reason to be jealous. I will write yet another letter on this important
subject. I hope they will have the weight intended them by

Your ever indulgent mother.

LETTER CXXXVIII

A Father to a Daughter in service, on hearing of her master's
attempting her virtue

MY DEAR DAUGHTER,

I understand, with great grief of heart, that your master has made
some attempts on your virtue, and yet that you stay with him. God
grant that you have not already yielded to his base desires! For
when once a person has so far forgotten what belongs to himself,
or his character, as to make such an attempt, the very continuance
with him, and in his power, and under the same roof, is an encouragement to him to prosecute his designs. And if he carries it better
and more civil, at present, it is only the more certainly to undo you
when he attacks you next. Consider, my dear child, your reputation
is all you have to trust to. And if you have not already (which God
forbid!) yielded to him, leave it not to the hazard of another temptation; but come away directly (as you ought to have done on your
own motion) at the command of

Your grieved and indulgent father.

LETTER CXXXIX

The Daughter's Answer

HONORED SIR,

I received your letter yesterday, and am sorry I stayed a moment in my master's house after his vile attempt. But he was so full of his promises of never offering the like again, that I hoped I might believe him; nor have I yet seen anything to the contrary: but am so much convinced that I ought to have done as you say, that I have this day left the house; and hope to be with you soon after you will have received the letter. I am

Your dutiful daughter.

A SELECTION

Henry Fielding

1707–1754

PREFACE TO *JOSEPH ANDREWS*

1742

[This Preface not only defines Fielding's attitude toward the novel— "the comic epic poem in prose"—but is among the greatest statements in English upon the nature of comedy.]

. . . The Ridiculous only, as I have before said, falls within my province in the present work. Nor will some explanation of this word be thought impertinent by the reader if he considers how wonderfully it hath been mistaken, even by writers who have professed it: for to what but such a mistake can we attribute the many attempts to ridicule the blackest villainies; and what is yet worse, the most dreadful calamities? What could exceed the absurdity of an author who should write the comedy of Nero with the merry incident of ripping up his mother's belly; or what would give a greater shock to humanity than an attempt to expose the miseries of poverty and distress to ridicule? And yet the reader will not want much learning to suggest such instances to himself.

Besides, it may seem remarkable that Aristotle, who is so fond and free of definitions, hath not thought proper to define the Ridiculous. Indeed, where he tells us it is proper to comedy, he hath remarked that villainy is not its object: but he hath not, as I remember, positively asserted what is. Nor doth the Abbé Bellegarde, who hath written a treatise [1] on this subject, though he shows us many species of it, once trace it to its fountain.

The only source of the true Ridiculous (as it appears to me) is affectation. But though it arises from one spring only, when we consider the infinite streams into which this one branches, we shall presently cease to admire at the copious field it affords to an observer. Now affectation proceeds from one of these two causes: vanity, or hypocrisy; for as vanity puts us on affecting false characters in order to purchase applause, so hypocrisy sets us on an endeavor to avoid censure by concealing our vices under an appearance of their opposite virtues. And though these two causes are often confounded (for there is some difficulty in distinguishing them), yet as they proceed from very different motives, so they are as clearly distinct in their operations: for indeed, the affectation which arises from vanity is nearer to truth than the other; as it hath not that violent repugnancy of nature to struggle with which that of the hypocrite hath. It may be likewise noted that affectation doth not imply an absolute negation of those qualities which are affected: and therefore, though, when it proceeds from hypocrisy, it be nearly allied to deceit, yet when it comes from vanity only, it partakes of the nature of ostentation: for instance, the affectation of liberality in a vain man differs visibly from the same affectation in the avaricious; for though the vain man is not what he would appear, or hath not the virtue he affects, to the degree he would be thought to have it; yet it sits less awkwardly on him than on the avaricious man, who is the very reverse of what he would seem to be.

From the discovery of this affectation arises the Ridiculous, which always strikes the reader with surprise and pleasure; and that in a higher and stronger degree when the affectation arises from hypocrisy, than when from vanity: for to discover anyone to be the exact reverse of what he affects, is more surprising, and consequently more ridiculous, than to find him a little deficient in the quality he desires the reputation of. I might observe that our Ben Jonson, who of all men understood the Ridiculous the best, hath chiefly used the hypocritical affectation.

Now from affectation only, the misfortunes and calamities of life, or the imperfections of nature, may become the objects of ridicule. Surely he hath a very ill-framed mind who can look on ugliness, infirmity, or poverty, as ridiculous in themselves: nor do I believe any man living who meets a dirty fellow riding through

---

1 *Réflexions sur le ridicule*, by Jean-Baptiste Morvan de Bellegarde.

the streets in a cart is struck with an idea of the Ridiculous from it; but if he should see the same figure descend from his coach and six, or bolt from his chair with his hat under his arm, he would then begin to laugh, and with justice. In the same manner, were we to enter a poor house and behold a wretched family shivering with cold and languishing with hunger, it would not incline us to laughter (at least we must have very diabolical natures if it would): but should we discover there a grate, instead of coals, adorned with flowers, empty plate or china dishes on the sideboard, or any other affectation of riches and finery either on their persons or in their furniture, we might then indeed be excused for ridiculing so fantastical an appearance. Much less are natural imperfections the object of derision: but when ugliness aims at the applause of beauty, or lameness endeavors to display agility; it is then that these unfortunate circumstances, which at first moved our compassion, tend only to raise our mirth.

The poet carries this very far:

> None are for being what they are in fault,
> But for not being what they would be thought.

Where if the meter would suffer the word Ridiculous to close the first line, the thought would be rather more proper. Great vices are the proper objects of our detestation; smaller faults of our pity: but affectation appears to me the only true source of the Ridiculous. . . .

Edward Young

1683–1765

Young's accomplishment is so various that he can hardly be "placed." Over his *Poem on the Last Day*, written in the mood of Isaac Watts' *Day of Judgment*, fall the shadows of the seventeenth-century religious dread; although Young attempts Miltonic severity, he achieves only the theatric. The tragedies *Busiris* and *The Revenge* are violent enough to recall the Elizabethan tragedy of blood. The *Epistles to Mr. Pope*, concerned with "some needful precepts how to write and live," restate many of the platitudes that Pope himself had crystallized in his own *Essay on Criticism*, although the couplets are not so decisively managed. The group of satires called *The Love of Fame*, however, often glitter with the brilliance of Pope's own hard antitheses; Young moves easily in the very medium that Pope was presently to exploit. Even if he had not lost his wife, his daughter, and his son-in-law, Young probably would have written *Night Thoughts*, one of the "graveyard" poems. He was not disinclined to melancholy and seems to have had tender nerves: "a door clapt, or a dog running before me, on a sudden, gave me a shock. A great laziness and lowness hangs on me," he complains. Then too, there is the story that when he preached before George II and his Majesty was inattentive, Young "raised his voice very much, and when this had no effect, burst into tears." All this is in the temper of his query in *Night Thoughts*

> Lorenzo, hast thou ever weighed a sigh,
> Or studied the philosophy of tears?

In these nine books the poet's concern is only superficially with the gloom of death; the poem is actually an extended argument against deism and atheism—"Truths which at church you might have heard in prose." Rejecting the placid optimism of Shaftesbury, Young asserts that a religion of reward and punishment is necessary: "A God of mercy is a God unjust." Nevertheless, he somehow finds place for the deistic proof of divinity: "The course of Nature is the art of God." Though written in blank verse, the *Night Thoughts* have the pithiness of the heroic couplet, and are filled with quotable lines. In 1759 Young arrived at the opposite pole from the *Epistles to Mr. Pope* with his *Conjectures on Original Composition*, which is one of the critical documents marking the downfall of the "classical" principles of imitation and restraint. This essay, in the form of a letter to Samuel Richardson, had repercussions on the Continent. Here the "romantic" heresy that within a century was to be formulated into a creed by Carlyle and Emerson is first whispered: "Thyself so reverence as to prefer the native growth of thy own mind to the richest import from abroad."

BIOGRAPHICAL NOTES

Son of the rector at Upham, near Winchester. Attended Winchester School (1695) and New College and Christ's College, Oxford (1702). Nominated to law fellowship at All Souls College (1708). Friendship with Thomas Tickell and Addison. *The Last Day* (1714). Began an almost lifelong quest for patronage. Tutor to the Marquis of Wharton (1715). *Busiris* (1719) and *The Revenge* (1721) produced. Friendship with Bubb Dodington; met Voltaire at Eastbury, Dodington's estate (1722). *The Love of Fame* (1725–28), satires. Gained a pension through Robert Walpole (1726). Took orders and was appointed chaplain to George II (1728). Rector of Welwyn (1730); sought vainly for promotion. Married Lady Elizabeth Lee, daughter of the Earl of Lichfield (1731). Deaths of his stepdaughter ("Narcissa"), her husband, and his own wife (1736–41). Retired to Welwyn. Friendship with Colley Cib-

ber and Samuel Richardson. *The Complaint, or Night Thoughts*
(1742–47). Increasing melancholy. *Conjectures on Original Composition* (1759). Last days embittered by a quarrel with his son.

BIBLIOGRAPHY: *Poetical Works*, ed. J. Mitford, 2 vols., 1844, etc. Mackail, J. W.,
Studies of the English Poets, 1926. Shelley, Henry C., *Life and Letters of Edward
Young*, 1914. Wicker, C. V., *Edward Young and the Fear of Death*, 1952.

THE COMPLAINT, OR NIGHT THOUGHTS ON LIFE, DEATH, AND IMMORTALITY

1742

NIGHT THE FIRST

Tir'd Nature's sweet restorer, balmy Sleep!
He, like the world, his ready visit pays
Where Fortune smiles; the wretched he forsakes;
Swift on his downy pinion flies from woe,
And lights on lids unsullied with a tear.
    From short (as usual) and disturbed repose,
I wake: how happy they who wake no more!
Yet that were vain, if dreams infest the grave.
I wake, emerging from a sea of dreams
Tumultuous; where my wreck'd desponding thought   10
From wave to wave of fancied misery,
At random drove, her helm of reason lost.
Tho' now restor'd, 'tis only change of pain,
(A bitter change!) severer for severe.
The day too short for my distress; and Night,
Even in the zenith of her dark domain,
Is sunshine to the colour of my fate.
    Night, sable goddess! from her ebon throne,
In rayless majesty now stretches forth
Her leaden scepter o'er a slumb'ring world.   20
Silence, how dead! and darkness, how profound!
Nor eye, nor list'ning ear, an object finds;
Creation sleeps. 'Tis as the gen'ral pulse
Of life stood still, and Nature made a pause;
An awful pause! prophetic of her end.
And let her prophecy be soon fulfill'd;
Fate! drop the curtain; I can lose no more.
    Silence and Darkness! solemn sisters! twins
From ancient Night, who nurse the tender thought

To reason, and on reason build resolve, 30
(That column of true majesty in man),
Assist me: I will thank you in the grave;
The grave, your kingdom: there this frame shall fall
A victim sacred to your dreary shrine.
But what are ye?—Thou who didst put to flight
Primeval silence, when the morning stars,
Exulting, shouted o'er the rising ball;
O Thou, whose word from solid darkness struck
That spark, the sun; strike wisdom from my soul;
My soul, which flies to Thee, her trust, her treasure, 40
As misers to their gold, while others rest.

   Through this opaque of nature, and of soul,
This double night, transmit one pitying ray,
To lighten and to cheer. O lead my mind,
(A mind that fain would wander from its woe),
Lead it thro' various scenes of life and death;
And from each scene, the noblest truths inspire.
Nor less inspire my conduct than my song;
Teach my best reason, reason; my best will
Teach rectitude; and fix my firm resolve 50
Wisdom to wed, and pay her long arrear:
Nor let the phial of thy vengeance, pour'd
On this devoted head, be pour'd in vain.

   The bell strikes one. We take no note of time
But from its loss. To give it then a tongue
Is wise in man. As if an angel spoke,
I feel the solemn sound. If heard aright,
It is the knell of my departed hours:
Where are they? With the years beyond the flood.
It is the signal that demands dispatch: 60
How much is to be done? My hopes and fears
Start up alarm'd, and o'er life's narrow verge
Look down—On what? a fathomless abyss;
A dread eternity! how surely mine!
And can eternity belong to me,
Poor pensioner on the bounties of an hour?

   How poor, how rich, how abject, how august,
How complicate, how wonderful, is man!
How passing wonder He, who made him such!
Who centered in our make such strange extremes! 70
From diff'rent natures marvellously mixt,
Connection exquisite of distant worlds!

Distinguish'd link in being's endless chain!
Midway from nothing to the Deity!
A beam ethereal, sullied and absorpt!
Tho' sullied, and dishonour'd, still divine!
Dim miniature of greatness absolute!
An heir of glory! a frail child of dust!
Helpless immortal! insect infinite!
A worm! a god!—I tremble at myself,   80
And in myself am lost! At home a stranger,
Thought wanders up and down, surpris'd, aghast,
And wond'ring at her own: how reason reels!
O what a miracle to man is man,
Triumphantly distress'd! what joy, what dread!
Alternately transported and alarm'd!
What can preserve my life? or what destroy?
An angel's arm can't snatch me from the grave;
Legions of angels can't confine me there.
    'Tis past conjecture; all things rise in proof: 90
While o'er my limbs sleep's soft dominion spread,
What tho' my soul fantastic measures trod
O'er fairy fields; or mourned along the gloom
Of pathless woods; or down the craggy steep
Hurl'd headlong, swam with pain the mantled pool;
Or scal'd the cliff, or danced on hollow winds,
With antic shapes, wild natives of the brain?
Her ceaseless flight, tho' devious, speaks her nature
Of subtler essence than the trodden clod;
Active, aërial, tow'ring, unconfin'd,   100
Unfetter'd with her gross companion's fall.
Ev'n silent night proclaims my soul immortal:
Ev'n silent night proclaims eternal day.
For human weal, Heaven husbands all events;
Dull sleep instructs, nor sport vain dreams in vain.
    Why then their loss deplore, that are not lost?
Why wanders wretched thought their tombs around,
In infidel distress? Are angels there?
Slumbers, rak'd up in dust, ethereal fire?
    They live! they greatly live a life on earth   110
Unkindled, unconceiv'd; and from an eye
Of tenderness let heavenly pity fall
On me, more justly number'd with the dead.
This is the desert, this the solitude:
How populous, how vital, is the grave!

This is creation's melancholy vault,
The vale funereal, the sad cypress gloom;
The land of apparitions, empty shades!
All, all on earth is shadow, all beyond
Is substance; the reverse is Folly's creed: 120
How solid all, where change shall be no more!
     This is the bud of being, the dim dawn,
The twilight of our day, the vestibule.
Life's theatre as yet is shut, and Death,
Strong Death, alone can heave the massy bar,
This gross impediment of clay remove,
And makes us embryos of existence free.
From real life, but little more remote
Is he, not yet a candidate for light,
The future embryo, slumb'ring in his sire.   130
Embryos we must be, till we burst the shell,
Yon ambient azure shell, and spring to life,
The life of gods, O transport! and of man.
     Yet man, fool man! here buries all his thoughts;
Inters celestial hopes without one sigh.
Prisoner of earth, and pent beneath the moon,
Here pinions all his wishes; wing'd by Heaven
To fly at infinite; and reach it there,
Where seraphs gather immortality,
On life's fair tree, fast by the throne of God.   140
What golden joys ambrosial clust'ring glow
In His full beam, and ripen for the just,
Where momentary ages are no more!
Where Time, and Pain, and Chance, and Death expire!
And is it in the flight of threescore years,
To push eternity from human thought,
And smother souls immortal in the dust?
A soul immortal, spending all her fires,
Wasting her strength in strenuous idleness,
Thrown into tumult, raptur'd or alarm'd   150
At aught this scene can threaten or indulge,
Resembles ocean into tempest wrought,
To waft a feather, or to drown a fly.
     Where falls this censure? It o'erwhelms myself;
How was my heart incrusted by the world!
Oh, how self-fetter'd was my grov'ling soul!
How, like a worm, was I wrapped round and round
In silken thought, which reptile Fancy spun,

Till darkened Reason lay quite clouded o'er
With soft conceit of endless comfort here,   160
Nor yet put forth her wings to reach the skies!
   Night-visions may befriend (as sung above):
Our waking dreams are fatal. How I dreamt
Of things impossible! (Could sleep do more?)
Of joys perpetual in perpetual change!
Of stable pleasures on the tossing wave!
Eternal sunshine in the storms of life!
How richly were my noon-tide trances hung
With gorgeous tapestries of pictur'd joys!
Joy behind joy, in endless perspective!   170
Till at Death's toll, whose restless iron tongue
Calls daily for his millions at a meal,
Starting I woke, and found myself undone.
Where now my frenzy's pompous furniture?
The cobweb'd cottage, with its ragged wall
Of mould'ring mud, is royalty to me!
The spider's most attenuated thread
Is cord, is cable, to man's tender tie
On earthly bliss; it breaks at every breeze.
   Oh, ye blest scenes of permanent delight!   180
Full above measure! lasting beyond bound!
A perpetuity of bliss is bliss.
Could you, so rich in rapture, fear an end,
That ghastly thought would drink up all your joy,
And quite unparadise the realms of light.
Safe are you lodg'd above these rolling spheres,
The baleful influence of whose giddy dance
Sheds sad vicissitude on all beneath.
Here teems with revolutions every hour;
And rarely for the better; or the best,   190
More mortal than the common births of Fate.
Each Moment has its sickle, emulous
Of Time's enormous scythe, whose ample sweep
Strikes empires from the root; each Moment plays
His little weapon in the narrower sphere
Of sweet domestic comfort, and cuts down
The fairest bloom of sublunary bliss.
   Bliss! sublunary bliss!—proud words, and vain!
Implicit treason to divine decree!
A bold invasion of the rights of Heaven!   200
I clasp'd the phantoms, and I found them air.

O had I weigh'd it ere my fond embrace!
What darts of agony had miss'd my heart!
Death! great proprietor of all! 'tis thine
To tread out empire and to quench the stars.
The sun himself by thy permission shines,
And, one day, thou shalt pluck him from his sphere.
Amid such mighty plunder, why exhaust
Thy partial quiver on a mark so mean?
Why thy peculiar rancour wreak'd on me?   210
Insatiate archer! could not one suffice?
Thy shaft flew thrice; and thrice my peace was slain;
And thrice, ere thrice yon moon had filled her horn.
O Cynthia! why so pale? dost thou lament
Thy wretched neighbour? Grieve to see thy wheel
Of ceaseless change outwhirl'd in human life?
How wanes my borrow'd bliss! from Fortune's smile
Precarious courtesy! not virtue's sure,
Self-given, solar ray of sound delight.
   In ev'ry varied posture, place, and hour,   220
How widow'd ev'ry thought of ev'ry joy!
Thought, busy thought! too busy for my peace!
Thro' the dark postern of time long elaps'd
Led softly, by the stillness of the night,
Led like a murderer (and such it proves!)
Strays (wretched rover!) o'er the pleasing past;
In quest of wretchedness perversely strays;
And finds all desart now; and meets the ghosts
Of my departed joys; a num'rous train!
I rue the riches of my former fate;   230
Sweet comfort's blasted clusters I lament;
I tremble at the blessings once so dear;
And ev'ry pleasure pains me to the heart.
   Yet why complain? or why complain for one?
Hangs out the sun his lustre but for me,
The single man? Are angels all beside?
I mourn for millions: 'Tis the common lot;
In this shape, or in that, has fate entail'd
The mother's throes on all of woman born,
Not more the children, than sure heirs, of pain.   240
   War, famine, pest, volcano, storm, and fire,
Intestine broils, Oppression, with her heart
Wrapt up in triple brass, besiege mankind.
God's image disinherited of day,

Here, plung'd in mines, forgets a sun was made.
There, beings deathless as their haughty lord,
Are hammer'd to the galling oar for life;
And plough the winter's wave, and reap despair.
Some, for hard masters, broken under arms,
In battle lopt away, with half their limbs,   250
Beg bitter bread thro' realms their valour sav'd,
If so the tyrant, or his minion, doom:
Want, and incurable disease (fell pair!)
On hopeless multitudes remorseless seize
At once; and make a refuge of the grave.
How groaning hospitals eject their dead!
What numbers groan for sad admission there!
What numbers, once in Fortune's lap high-fed,
Solicit the cold hand of Charity!
To shock us more, solicit it in vain!   260
Ye silken sons of Pleasure! since in pains
You rue more modish visits, visit here,
And breathe from your debauch: give, and reduce
Surfeit's dominion o'er you; but, so great
Your impudence, you blush at what is right.
    Happy! did sorrow seize on such alone.
Not prudence can defend, or virtue save;
Disease invades the chastest temperance;
And punishment the guiltless; and alarm
Thro' thickest shades pursues the fond of peace.   270
Man's caution often into danger turns,
And, his guard falling, crushes him to death.
Not Happiness itself makes good her name!
Our very wishes give us not our wish.
How distant oft the thing we doat on most,
From that for which we doat, felicity!
The smoothest course of nature has its pains;
And truest friends, thro' error, wound our rest.
Without misfortune, what calamities!
And what hostilities, without a foe!   280
Nor are foes wanting to the best on earth.
But endless is the list of human ills,
And sighs might sooner fail, than cause to sigh.
    A part how small of the terraqueous globe
Is tenanted by man! the rest a waste,
Rocks, desarts, frozen seas, and burning sands:
Wild haunts of monsters, poisons, stings, and death.

Such is earth's melancholy map! But, far
More sad! this earth is a true map of man.
So bounded are its haughty lord's delights 290
To woe's wide empire; where deep troubles toss,
Loud sorrows howl, envenom'd passions bite,
Rav'nous calamities our vitals seize,
And threat'ning Fate wide opens to devour.
What then am I, who sorrow for myself?
In age, in infancy, from others' aid
Is all our hope; to teach us to be kind.
That, Nature's first, last lesson to mankind;
The selfish heart deserves the pain it feels;
More gen'rous sorrow, while it sinks, exalts; 300
And conscious virtue mitigates the pang.
Nor virtue, more than prudence, bids me give
Swoln thought a second channel; who divide,
They weaken too, the torrent of their grief.
Take then, O world! thy much-indebted tear:
How sad a sight is human happiness,
To those whose thought can pierce beyond an hour!
O thou! whate'er thou art, whose heart exults!
Wouldst thou I should congratulate thy fate?
I know thou wouldst; thy pride demands it from me. 310
Let thy pride pardon what thy nature needs,
The salutary censure of a friend.
Thou happy wretch! by blindness art thou blest;
By dotage dandled to perpetual smiles.
Know, smiler! at thy peril art thou pleas'd;
Thy pleasure is the promise of thy pain.
Misfortune, like a creditor severe,
But rises in demand for her delay;
She makes a scourge of past prosperity,
To sting thee more, and double thy distress. 320
Lorenzo,[1] Fortune makes her court to thee,
Thy fond heart dances, while the siren sings.
Dear is thy welfare; think me not unkind;
I would not damp, but to secure thy joys.
Think not that fear is sacred to the storm:
Stand on thy guard against the smiles of Fate.
Is Heaven tremendous in its frowns? Most sure;
And in its favours formidable too:
Its favours here are trials, not rewards;

1 Young addresses the poem to "Lorenzo" (possibly his patron, the Duke of Wharton)

A call to duty, not discharge from care;   330
And should alarm us, full as much as woes;
Awake us to their cause and consequence;
And make us tremble, weigh'd with our desert;
Awe Nature's tumult and chastise her joys,
Lest while we clasp, we kill them; nay, invert
To worse than simple misery, their charms.
Revolted joys, like foes in civil war,
Like bosom friendships to resentments sour'd,
With rage envenom'd rise against our peace.
Beware what earth calls happiness; beware   340
All joys, but joys that never can expire.
Who builds on less than an immortal base,
Fond as he seems, condemns his joys to death.

    Mine died with thee, Philander! [2] thy last sigh
Dissolv'd the charm; the disenchanted earth
Lost all her lustre. Where her glitt'ring towers?
Her golden mountains, where? all darken'd down
To naked waste; a dreary vale of tears:
The great magician's dead! Thou poor, pale piece
Of out-cast earth, in darkness! what a change   350
From yesterday! Thy darling hope so near,
(Long-laboured prize!) O, how ambition flush'd
Thy glowing cheek! Ambition truly great,
Of virtuous praise. Death's subtle seed within,
(Sly, treacherous miner!) working in the dark,
Smil'd at thy well-concerted scheme, and beckon'd
The worm to riot on that rose so red,
Unfaded ere it fell; one moment's prey!

    Man's foresight is conditionally wise;
Lorenzo, wisdom into folly turns   360
Oft, the first instant, its idea fair
To labouring thought is born. How dim our eye!
The present moment terminates our sight;
Clouds, thick as those on doomsday, drown the next;
We penetrate, we prophesy in vain.
Time is dealt out by particles; and each,
Ere mingled with the streaming sands of life,
By fate's inviolable oath is sworn
Deep silence, "Where eternity begins."

    By Nature's law, what may be, may be now;   370
There's no prerogative in human hours.

2 Supposed to be Young's son-in-law, who died in 1740.

In human hearts what bolder thought can rise
Than man's presumption on to-morrow's dawn?
Where is to-morrow? In another world.
For numbers this is certain; the reverse
Is sure to none; and yet on this perhaps,
This peradventure, infamous for lies,
As on a rock of adamant, we build
Our mountain hopes; spin out eternal schemes,
As we the fatal sisters could out-spin,   380
And, big with life's futurities, expire.
   Not even Philander had bespoke his shroud.
Nor had he cause; a warning was denied:
How many fall as sudden, not as safe!
As sudden, though for years admonish'd home.
Of human ills the last extreme beware,
Beware, Lorenzo! a slow-sudden death.
How dreadful that deliberate surprise!
Be wise to-day; 'tis madness to defer;
Next day the fatal precedent will plead;   390
Thus on, till wisdom is push'd out of life.
Procrastination is the thief of time;
Year after year it steals, till all are fled,
And to the mercies of a moment leaves
The vast concerns of an eternal scene.
If not so frequent, would not this be strange?
That 'tis so frequent, this is stranger still.
   Of man's miraculous mistakes, this bears
The palm, "That all men are about to live,"
Forever on the brink of being born.   400
All pay themselves the compliment to think
They one day shall not drivel: and their pride
On this reversion takes up ready praise;
At least, their own; their future selves applauds;
How excellent that life they ne'er will lead!
Time lodg'd in their own hands is Folly's vails; [3]
That lodg'd in Fate's, to wisdom they consign;
The thing they can't but purpose, they postpone;
'Tis not in folly, not to scorn a fool;
And scarce in human wisdom to do more.   410
All promise is poor dilatory man,
And that thro' every stage: when young, indeed,
In full content we, sometimes, nobly rest,

[3] Gratuities.

Unanxious for ourselves; and only wish,
As duteous sons, our fathers were more wise.
At thirty man suspects himself a fool;
Knows it at forty, and reforms his plan;
At fifty chides his infamous delay,
Pushes his prudent purpose to resolve;
In all the magnanimity of thought   420
Resolves; and re-resolves; then dies the same.

And why? Because he thinks himself immortal.
All men think all men mortal, but themselves;
Themselves, when some alarming shock of Fate
Strikes thro' their wounded hearts the sudden dread;
But their hearts wounded, like the wounded air,
Soon close; where past the shaft, no trace is found.
As from the wing no scar the sky retains,
The parted wave no furrow from the keel;
So dies in human hearts the thought of death.   430
Ev'n with the tender tear which Nature sheds
O'er those we love, we drop it in their grave.
Can I forget Philander? That were strange!
O my full heart—But should I give it vent,
The longest night, though longer far, would fail,
And the lark listen to my midnight song.

    The spritely lark's shrill matin wakes the morn;
Grief's sharpest thorn hard-pressing on my breast,
I strive, with wakeful melody, to cheer
The sullen gloom, sweet Philomel! like thee,   440
And call the stars to listen: every star
Is deaf to mine, enamour'd of thy lay.
Yet be not vain; there are, who thine excel,
And charm thro' distant ages: wrapt in shade,
Pris'ner of darkness! to the silent hours,
How often I repeat their rage divine,
To lull my griefs, and steal my heart from woe!
I roll their raptures, but not catch their fire.
Dark, though not blind, like thee, Maeonides! [4]
Or, Milton! thee; ah, could I reach your strain!   450
Or his, who made Maeonides our own,[5]
Man too he sung: immortal man I sing;
Oft bursts my song beyond the bounds of life;
What, now, but immortality can please?
Oh, had he press'd his theme, pursu'd the track,

---

[4] Homer (son of Maeon).   [5] Pope, who translated Homer.

Which opens out of darkness into day!
O had he, mounted on his wing of fire,
Soar'd where I sink, and sung immortal man!
How had it blest mankind, and rescu'd me!

CONJECTURES ON ORIGINAL COMPOSITION

In a Letter to the Author of *Sir Charles Grandison*

1759

It is with thoughts as it is with words; and with both as with men; they may grow old and die. Words tarnished by passing through the mouths of the vulgar are laid aside as inelegant and obsolete. So thoughts when become too common should lose their currency; and we should send new metal to the mint, that is, new meaning to the press. The division of tongues at Babel did not more effectually debar men from making themselves a name (as the Scripture speaks), than the too great concurrence, or union of tongues will do forever. We may as well grow good by another's virtue, or fat by another's food, as famous by another's thought. The world will pay its debt of praise but once; and, instead of applauding, explode a second demand as a cheat.

If it is said that most of the Latin classics, and all the Greek, except, perhaps, Homer, Pindar, and Anacreon, are in the number of imitators, yet receive our highest applause, our answer is that they, though not real, are accidental originals; the works they imitated, few excepted, are lost; they, on their father's decease, enter as lawful heirs on their estates in fame: the fathers of our copyists are still in possession; and secured in it, in spite of Goths and flames, by the perpetuating power of the press. Very late must a modern imitator's fame arrive if it waits for their decease.

An original enters early on reputation: Fame, fond of new glories, sounds her trumpet in triumph at its birth; and yet how few are awakened by it into the noble ambition of like attempts? Ambition is sometimes no vice in life; it is always a virtue in composition. High in the towering Alps is the fountain of the Po; high in fame and in antiquity is the fountain of an imitator's undertaking; but the river and the imitation humbly creep along the vale. So few are our originals that if all other books were to be burnt, the lettered world would resemble some metropolis in flames, where a few incombustible buildings, a fortress, temple, or tower, lift their heads, in melancholy grandeur, amid the mighty ruin. Compared with this conflagration, old Omar [1] lighted up but a small bonfire, when he heated the baths of the barbarians for eight months together with the famed Alexandrian library's inestimable spoils, that no profane book might obstruct the triumphant progress of his holy Alcoran round the globe.

But why are originals so few? not because the writer's harvest is over, the great reapers of antiquity having left nothing to be gleaned after them; nor because the human mind's teeming time is past, or because it is incapable of putting forth unprecedented births; but because illustrious examples engross, prejudice, and intimidate. They engross our attention, and so prevent a due inspection of ourselves; they prejudice our judgment in favor of their abilities, and so lessen the sense of our own; and they intimidate us with the splendor of their renown, and thus under diffidence bury our strength. Nature's impossibilities, and those of diffidence lie wide asunder.

Let it not be suspected that I would weakly insinuate anything in favor of the moderns as compared with ancient authors; no, I am lamenting their great inferiority. But I think it is no necessary inferiority; that it is not from divine destination, but from some cause far beneath the moon: I think that human souls, through all periods, are equal; that due care and exertion would set us nearer our immortal predecessors than we are at present; and he who questions and confutes this will show abilities not a little tending toward a proof of that equality which he denies.

After all, the first ancients had no merit in being originals; they could not be imitators. Modern writers have a choice to make, and therefore have a merit in their power. They may soar in the regions of liberty, or move in the soft fetters of easy imitation; and imitation has as many plausible reasons to urge as pleasure had to offer to Hercules. Hercules made the choice of an hero, and so became immortal.

1 The Caliph under whom Alexandria was captured in 641.

Yet let not assertors of classic excellence imagine that I deny the tribute it so well deserves. He that admires not ancient authors betrays a secret he would conceal, and tells the world that he does not understand them. Let us be as far from neglecting as from copying their admirable compositions; sacred be their rights, and inviolable their fame. Let our understanding feed on theirs; they afford the noblest nourishment; but let them nourish, not annihilate, our own. When we read, let our imagination kindle at their charms; when we write, let our judgment shut them out of our thoughts; treat even Homer himself as his royal admirer was treated by the cynic; [2] bid him stand aside, nor shade our composition from the beams of our own genius; for nothing original can rise, nothing immortal can ripen, in any other sun.

Must we then, you say, not imitate ancient authors? Imitate them by all means; but imitate aright. He that imitates the divine *Iliad* does not imitate Homer; but he who takes the same method which Homer took for arriving at a capacity of accomplishing a work so great. Tread in his steps to the sole fountain of immortality; drink where he drank, at the true Helicon, that is, at the breast of nature: imitate; but imitate not the composition but the man. For may not this paradox pass into a maxim? viz. "The less we copy the renowned ancients, we shall resemble them the more."

But possibly you may reply that you must either imitate Homer or depart from nature. Not so: for suppose you was to change place, in time, with Homer; then, if you write naturally, you might as well charge Homer with an imitation of you. Can you be said to imitate Homer for writing so as you would have written if Homer had never been? As far as a regard to nature and sound sense will permit a departure from your great predecessors, so far, ambitiously, depart from them; the farther from them in similitude, the nearer are you to them in excellence; you rise by it into an original, become a noble collateral, not an humble descendant from them. Let us build our compositions with the spirit and in the taste of the ancients, but not with their materials: thus will they resemble the structures of Pericles at Athens, which Plutarch commends for having had an air of antiquity as soon as they were built. All eminence and distinction lies out of the beaten road; excursion and deviation are necessary to find it; and the more remote your path from the highway, the more reputable, if, like poor

2 Diogenes.

Gulliver (of whom anon), you fall not into a ditch in your way to glory. . . .

But farther still: a spirit of imitation hath many ill effects; I shall confine myself to three. First, it deprives the liberal and politer arts of an advantage which the mechanic enjoy: in these, men are ever endeavoring to go beyond their predecessors; in the former, to follow them. And since copies surpass not their originals, as streams rise not higher than their spring, rarely so high; hence, while arts mechanic are in perpetual progress and increase, the liberal are in retrogradation and decay. These resemble pyramids, are broad at bottom, but lessen exceedingly as they rise; those resemble rivers which, from a small fountainhead, are spreading ever wider and wider as they run. Hence it is evident that different portions of understanding are not (as some imagine) allotted to different periods of time; for we see, in the same period, understanding rising in one set of artists and declining in another. Therefore nature stands absolved and our inferiority in composition must be charged on ourselves.

Nay, so far are we from complying with a necessity which nature lays us under, that, secondly, by a spirit of imitation we counteract nature, and thwart her design. She brings us into the world all originals: no two faces, no two minds, are just alike; but all bear nature's evident mark of separation on them. Born originals, how comes it to pass that we die copies? That meddling ape, Imitation, as soon as we come to years of indiscretion (so let me speak), snatches the pen and blots out nature's mark of separation, cancels her kind intention, destroys all mental individuality; the lettered world no longer consists of singulars: it is a medley, a mass; and a hundred books, at bottom, are but one. Why are monkeys such masters of mimicry? Why receive they such a talent at imitation? Is it not as the Spartan slave received a licence for ebriety, that their betters might be ashamed of it?

The third fault to be found with a spirit of imitation is that with great incongruity it makes us poor and proud: makes us think little, and write much; gives us huge folios, which are little better than more reputable cushions to promote our repose. . . .

Since it is plain that men may be strangers to their own abilities, and by thinking meanly of them without just cause may possibly lose a name, perhaps a name immortal, I would find some means to prevent these evils. Whatever promotes virtue, promotes something more, and carries its good influence beyond the moral man; to prevent these evils, I borrow two golden rules from ethics, which are no less golden in composition than in life. 1. *Know thyself;* 2dly, *Reverence thyself:* I design to repay ethics in a future letter, by two rules from rhetoric for its service.

1st. *Know thyself.* Of ourselves it may be said, as Martial says of a bad neighbor,

Nil tam prope, proculque nobis.[3]

Therefore dive deep into thy bosom; learn the depth, extent, bias, and full fort of thy mind; contract full intimacy with the stranger within thee; excite and cherish every spark of intellectual light and heat, however smothered under former negligence or scattered through the dull, dark mass of common thoughts; and collecting them into a body, let thy genius rise (if a genius thou hast) as the sun from chaos; and if I should then say, like an Indian, "Worship it" (though too bold), yet should I say little more than my second rule enjoins, (viz.) "Reverence thyself."

That is, let not great examples or authorities browbeat thy reason into too great a diffidence of thyself: thyself so reverence as to prefer the native growth of thy own mind to the richest import from abroad; such borrowed riches make us poor. The man who thus reverences himself will soon find the world's reverence to follow his own. His works will stand distinguished; his the sole property of them; which property alone can confer the noble title of an author; that is, of one who (to speak accurately) thinks and composes; while other invaders of the press, how voluminous and learned soever, (with due respect be it spoken) only read and write.

This is the difference between those two luminaries in literature, the well-accomplished scholar, and the divinely-inspired enthusiast; the first is as the bright morning star; the second, as the rising sun. The writer who neglects those two rules above will never stand alone; he makes one of a group, and thinks in wretched unanimity with the throng: incumbered with the notions of others, and impoverished by their abundance, he conceives not the least embryo of new thought, opens not the least vista through the gloom of ordinary writers into the bright walks of rare imagination and singular design; while the true genius is crossing all

[3] "No one so near to, and so far from, us" (*Epigrams* I. lxxxvi. 1e).

public roads into fresh untrodden ground, he, up to the knees in antiquity, is treading the sacred footsteps of great examples, with the blind veneration of a bigot saluting the papal toe; comfortably hoping full absolution for the sins of his own understanding from the powerful charm of touching his idol's infallibility. . . .

Shakespeare mingled no water with his wine, lowered his genius by no vapid imitation. Shakespeare gave us a Shakespeare, nor could the first in ancient fame have given us more! Shakespeare is not their son, but brother; their equal; and that, in spite of all his faults. Think you this too bold? Consider, in those ancients what is it the world admires? Not the fewness of their faults but the number and brightness of their beauties; and if Shakespeare is their equal (as he doubtless is) in that which in them is admired, then is Shakespeare as great as they; and not impotence, but some other cause, must be charged with his defects. When we are setting these great men in competition, what but the comparative size of their genius is the subject of our inquiry? And a giant loses nothing of his size though he should chance to trip in his race. But it is a compliment to those heroes of antiquity to suppose Shakespeare their equal only in dramatic powers; therefore, though his faults had been greater, the scale would still turn in his favor. There is at least as much genius on the British as on the Grecian stage, though the former is not swept so clean—so clean from violations not only of the dramatic, but moral rule; for an honest heathen on reading some of our celebrated scenes might be seriously concerned to see that our obligations to the religion of nature were canceled by Christianity.

Jonson, in the serious drama, is as much an imitator as Shakespeare is an original. He was very learned, as Samson was very strong, to his own hurt: blind to the nature of tragedy, he pulled down all antiquity on his head, and buried himself under it; we see nothing of Jonson, nor indeed of his admired (but also murdered) ancients; for what shone in the historian is a cloud on the poet; and *Catiline* might have been a good play if Sallust had never writ.

Who knows whether Shakespeare might not have thought less if he had read more? Who knows if he might not have labored under the load of Jonson's learning, as Enceladus under Etna? His mighty genius, indeed, through the most mountainous oppression would have breathed out some of his inextinguishable fire; yet, possibly, he might not have risen up into that giant, that much more than common man, at which we now gaze with amazement and delight. Perhaps he was as learned as his dramatic province required; for whatever other learning he wanted, he was master of two books, unknown to many of the profoundly read, though books which the last conflagration alone can destroy: the book of nature, and that of man. These he had by heart, and has transcribed many admirable pages of them into his immortal works. These are the fountainhead whence the Castalian streams of original composition flow; and these are often mudded by other waters, though waters in their distinct channel most wholesome and pure: as two chemical liquors, separately clear as crystal, grow foul by mixture, and offend the sight. So that he had not only as much learning as his dramatic province required, but, perhaps, as it could safely bear. If Milton had spared some of his learning, his Muse would have gained more glory than he would have lost by it.

Dryden, destitute of Shakespeare's genius, had almost as much learning as Jonson, and, for the buskin, quite as little taste. He was a stranger to the pathos, and, by numbers, expression, sentiment, and every other dramatic cheat strove to make amends for it; as if a saint could make amends for the want of conscience; a soldier, for the want of valor; or a vestal, of modesty. The noble nature of tragedy disclaims an equivalent; like virtue, it demands the heart; and Dryden had none to give. Let epic poets think; the tragedian's point is rather to feel; such distant things are a tragedian and a poet that the latter indulged, destroys the former. Look on Barnwell, and Essex,[4] and see how as to these distant characters Dryden excels, and is excelled. But the strongest demonstration of his no-taste for the buskin are his tragedies fringed with rhyme; which, in epic poetry, is a sore disease, in the tragic, absolute death. To Dryden's enormity, Pope's was a light offense. As lacemen are foes to mourning, these two authors, rich in rhyme, were no great friends to those solemn ornaments which the noble nature of their works required.

Must rhyme then, say you, be banished? I wish the nature of our language could bear its entire expulsion; but our lesser poetry stands in need of a toleration for it; it raises that, but sinks the great; as spangles adorn children, but expose men. Prince Henry bespangled all over in his oylet-hole suit, with glittering pins, and an Achilles,

---

4 Young refers to *The London Merchant: or, The History of George Barnwell* (1731) by George Lillo, and *The Unhappy Favorite: or, The Earl of Essex* (1681) by John Banks; both were popular "pathetic" tragedies.

or an Almanzor, in his Gothic array, are very much on a level as
to the majesty of the poet, and the prince. Dryden had a great, but
a general capacity; and as for a general genius, there is no such
thing in nature: a genius implies the rays of the mind concentered,
and determined to some particular point; when they are scattered
widely, they act feebly, and strike not with sufficient force, to
fire, or dissolve, the heart. As what comes from the writer's heart
reaches ours; so what comes from his head sets our brains at work,
and our hearts at ease. It makes a circle of thoughtful critics, not of
distressed patients; and a passive audience is what tragedy requires.
Applause is not to be given, but extorted; and the silent lapse of a
single tear does the writer more honor than the rattling thunder of
a thousand hands. Applauding hands and dry eyes (which during
Dryden's theatrical reign often met) are a satire on the writer's
talent and the spectator's taste. When by such judges the laurel
is blindly given, and by such a poet proudly received, they resemble an intoxicated host, and his tasteless guests, over some
sparkling adulteration, commending their champagne.

   But Dryden has his glory, though not on the stage. What an
inimitable original is his ode! A small one, indeed, but of the first
luster, and without a flaw; and, amid the brightest boasts of antiquity, it may find a foil. . . .

Robert Blair

1699-1746

ONE of the recognized "graveyard" poems, Blair's chief work is not
so macabre as its name implies. There are the customary paraphernalia—
skulls and coffins, epitaphs and worms, as well as a "supernumerary
horror" of slime—but there is a good deal of platitude as well; and as
the poem moves on, it settles into the rigorous didacticism so satisfying to eighteenth-century orthodoxy. There is less raw sensationalism
than in Hervey's *Meditation among the Tombs.* Its popularity was
very great, and even today it is valued because in certain passages the
blank verse moves with a grand cadence that suggests the Elizabethans.
In 1808 appeared an edition with designs by Blake.

BIOGRAPHICAL NOTES
Son of a Scottish minister of the Old Church, Edinburgh. Studied at
the University of Edinburgh and in the Netherlands. Settled in Edinburgh as unemployed probationer (1718–30). Appointed to the living
at Athelstaneford, East Lothian (1731). Studied botany and early English poetry. Married Isabella Law, daughter of William Law (1738).
After at least two rejections, published *The Grave* (1743). Died of a
fever.

BIBLIOGRAPHY: *Poetical Works*, ed. C. C. Clarke, 1854. Draper, John W., *The Funeral
Elegy and the Rise of English Romanticism*, 1929.

THE GRAVE

1743

While some affect the sun, and some the shade,
Some flee the city, some the hermitage;
Their aims as various as the roads they take
In journeying through life;—the task be mine
To paint the gloomy horrors of the tomb;
The appointed place of rendezvous, where all
These travellers meet.—Thy succours I implore,
Eternal king! whose potent arm sustains
The keys of Hell and Death.—The Grave, dread thing!
Men shiver when thou'rt named: Nature appall'd   10
Shakes off her wonted firmness.—Ah! how dark
Thy long-extended realms and rueful wastes!
Where naught but silence reigns, and night, dark night,
Dark as was chaos, ere the infant Sun
Was roll'd together, or had tried his beams
Athwart the gloom profound.—The sickly taper,
By glimmering through thy low-brow'd misty vaults
(Furr'd round with mouldy damps, and ropy slime)
Lets fall a supernumerary horror,
And only serves to make thy night more irksome.   20
Well do I know thee by thy trusty yew,
Cheerless, unsocial plant! that loves to dwell
'Midst skulls and coffins, epitaphs and worms:
Where light-heel'd ghosts, and visionary shades,
Beneath the wan cold moon (as fame reports)
Embodied, thick, perform their mystic rounds:
No other merriment, dull tree! is thine.

See yonder hallow'd fane—the pious work
Of names once famed, now dubious or forgot,
And buried 'midst the wreck of things which were;   30
There lie interr'd the more illustrious dead.
The wind is up: hark! how it howls! Methinks
Till now I never heard a sound so dreary:
Doors creak, and windows clap, and night's foul bird,
Rook'd [1] in the spire, screams loud: the gloomy aisles,
Black-plaster'd, and hung round with shreds of 'scutcheons
And tatter'd coats of arms, send back the sound,
Laden with heavier airs, from the low vaults,
The mansions of the dead.—Roused from their slumbers,
In grim array the grisly spectres rise,   40
Grin horrible, and, obstinately sullen
Pass and repass, hush'd as the foot of night.
Again the screech-owl shrieks: ungracious sound!
I'll hear no more; it makes one's blood run chill.

Quite round the pile, a row of reverend elms,
Coeval near with that, all ragged show,
Long lash'd by the rude winds: some rift half down
Their branchless trunks; others so thin at top
That scarce two crows could lodge in the same tree.
Strange things, the neighbours say, have happen'd here: 50
Wild shrieks have issued from the hollow tombs;
Dead men have come again, and walk'd about;
And the great bell has toll'd, unrung, untouch'd!
(Such tales their cheer at wake or gossiping,
When it draws near to witching time of night.)
Oft in the lone church yard at night I've seen,
By glimpse of moonshine chequering through the trees,
The schoolboy with his satchel in his hand,
Whistling aloud to bear his courage up,
And lightly tripping o'er the long flat stones   60
(With nettles skirted and with moss o'ergrown)
That tell in homely phrase who lie below.
Sudden he starts! and hears, or thinks he hears,
The sound of something purring at his heels;
Full fast he flies, and dares not look behind him,
Till out of breath he overtakes his fellows;
Who gather round, and wonder at the tale
Of horrid apparition, tall and ghastly,
That walks at dead of night, or takes his stand

1 Cowering.

O'er some new-open'd grave, and, strange to tell!   70
Evanishes at crowing of the cock.
The new-made widow too, I've sometimes spied,
Sad sight! slow moving o'er the prostrate dead:
Listless, she crawls along in doleful black,
Whilst bursts of sorrow gush from either eye,
Fast falling down her now untasted cheek.
Prone on the lowly grave of the dear man
She drops; whilst busy meddling memory
In barbarous succession, musters up
The past endearments of their softer hours,   80
Tenacious of its theme. Still, still she thinks
She sees him, and, indulging the fond thought,
Clings yet more closely to the senseless turf,
Nor heeds the passenger who looks that way.
   Invidious grave!—how dost thou rend in sunder
Whom love has knit, and sympathy made one!
A tie more stubborn far than nature's band.
Friendship! mysterious cement of the soul;
Sweetener of life, and solder of society!
I owe thee much: Thou hast deserved from me,   90
Far, far beyond what I can ever pay.
Oft have I proved the labours of thy love,
And the warm efforts of the gentle heart,
Anxious to please.—Oh! when my friend and I
In some thick wood have wander'd heedless on,
Hid from the vulgar eye, and sat us down
Upon the sloping cowslip-cover'd bank,
Where the pure limpid stream has slid along
In grateful errors through the underwood,
Sweet murmuring—methought the shrill-tongued thrush   100
Mended his song of love; the sooty blackbird
Mellow'd his pipe and soften'd every note;
The eglantine smelled sweeter, and the rose
Assumed a dye more deep; whilst every flower
Vied with its fellow-plant in luxury
Of dress.—Oh! then the longest summer's day
Seem'd too, too much in haste: still the full heart
Had not imparted half! 'twas happiness
Too exquisite to last. Of joys departed,
Not to return, how painful the remembrance!   110
   Dull Grave!—thou spoil'st the dance of youthful blood,
Strik'st out the dimple from the cheek of mirth,

And every smirking feature from the face;
Branding our laughter with the name of madness.
Where are the jesters now? the men of health
Complexionally pleasant? Where the droll,
Whose very look and gesture was a joke
To clapping theatres and shouting crowds,
And made even thick-lipp'd musing Melancholy
To gather up her face into a smile   120
Before she was aware? Ah! sullen now,
And dumb as the green turf that covers them.
　　Where are the mighty thunderbolts of war?
The Roman Cæsars, and the Grecian chiefs,
The boast of story? Where the hot-brain'd youth,
Who the tiara at his pleasure tore
From kings of all the then discover'd globe,
And cried, forsooth, because his arm was hamper'd,
And had not room enough to do its work?—
Alas! how slim, dishonourably slim,   130
And cramm'd into a space we blush to name!
Proud Royalty! How alter'd in thy looks!
How blank thy features, and how wan thy hue!
Son of the morning, whither art thou gone?
Where hast thou hid thy many-spangled head,
And the majestic menace of thine eyes,
Felt from afar? Pliant and powerless now;
Like new-born infant wound up in his swathes,
Or victim tumbled flat upon its back,
That throbs beneath the sacrificer's knife.   140
Mute must thou bear the strife of little tongues,
And coward insults of the base-born crowd,
That grudge a privilege thou never hadst,
But only hoped for in the peaceful grave,
Of being unmolested and alone!
Arabia's gums and odoriferous drugs,
And honours by the heralds duly paid
In mode and form even to a very scruple:
Oh cruel irony! these come too late;
And only mock whom they were meant to honour.   150
Surely there's not a dungeon slave that's buried
In the highway, unshrouded and uncoffin'd,
But lies as soft and sleeps as sound as he.
Sorry preëminence of high descent,
Above the vulgar born, to rot in state!

But see! the well plumed hearse comes nodding on,
Stately and slow; and properly attended
By the whole sable tribe, that painful watch
The sick man's door, and live upon the dead,
By letting out their persons by the hour,   160
To mimic sorrow when the heart's not sad.
How rich the trappings, now they're all unfurl'd
And glittering in the sun! Triumphant entries
Of conquerors, and coronation pomps,
In glory scarce exceed. Great gluts of people
Retard the unwieldly show; whilst from the casements
And houses' tops, ranks behind ranks close wedged
Hang bellying o'er. But tell us, why this waste?
Why this ado in earthing up a carcase
That's fallen into disgrace, and in the nostril   170
Smells horrible?—Ye undertakers, tell us,
'Midst all the gorgeous figures you exhibit,
Why is the principal conceal'd, for which
You make this mighty stir?—'Tis wisely done;
What would offend the eye in a good picture,
The painter casts discreetly into shades.

Proud lineage! now how little thou appear'st!
Below the envy of the private man!
Honour, that meddlesome officious ill,
Pursues thee even to death, nor there stops short;   180
Strange persecution! when the grave itself
Is no protection from rude sufferance.

Absurd to think to overreach the grave,
And from the wreck of names to rescue ours!
The best-concerted schemes men lay for fame
Die fast away: only themselves die faster.
The far-famed sculptor and the laurell'd bard,
Those bold insurancers of deathless fame,
Supply their little feeble aids in vain.
The tapering pyramid, the Egyptian's pride,   190
And wonder of the world; whose spiky top
Has wounded the thick cloud, and long outlived
The angry shaking of the winter's storm;
Yet spent at last by the injuries of heaven,
Shatter'd with age and furrow'd o'er with years,
The mystic cone, with hieroglyphics crusted,
At once gives way. Oh, lamentable sight!
The labour of whole ages lumbers down,

A hideous and misshapen length of ruins.
Sepulchral columns wrestle but in vain   200
With all-subduing Time: her cankering hand
With calm deliberate malice wasteth them:
Worn on the edge of days, the brass consumes,
The busto moulders, and the deep-cut marble,
Unsteady to the steel, gives up its charge.
Ambition, half convicted of her folly,
Hangs down the head, and reddens at the tale.
      Here all the mighty troublers of the earth,
Who swam to sovereign rule through seas of blood;
The oppressive, sturdy, man-destroying villains   210
Who ravaged kingdoms, and laid empires waste,
And in a cruel wantonness of power
Thinn'd states of half their people, and gave up
To want the rest; now, like a storm that's spent,
Lie hush'd, and meanly sneak behind the covert.
Vain thought! to hide them from the general scorn
That haunts and dogs them like an injured ghost
Implacable! Here too the petty tyrant
Whose scant domains geographer ne'er noticed,
And, well for neighbouring grounds, of arm as short;   220
Who fix'd his iron talons on the poor,
And gripp'd them like some lordly beast of prey;
Deaf to the forceful cries of gnawing hunger,
And piteous, plaintive voice of misery
(As if a slave was not a shred of nature,
Of the same common nature with his lord);
Now tame and humble, like a child that's whipp'd,
Shakes hands with dust, and calls the worm his kinsman;
Nor pleads his rank and birthright: Under ground
Precedency's a jest; vassal and lord,   230
Grossly familiar, side by side consume.
      When self-esteem, or others' adulation,
Would cunningly persuade us we were something
Above the common level of our kind,
The Grave gainsays the smooth-complexion'd flattery,
And with blunt truth acquaints us what we are.

      .   .   .   .   .   .

A SELECTION

James Hervey
1714–1758

MEDITATIONS AMONG THE TOMBS, IN
A LETTER TO A LADY
1745/6–1747

[The "Gothic" and graveyard-schoolish aspects of the eighteenth century were not due to mere sensibility, but also to a somewhat morbid religious concern with death that was inherited from the seventeenth century. Hervey's *Meditations among the Tombs*, running through many editions before the end of the century, has obvious affiliations with the graveyard poetry and with Gothicism; it also indicates the hold that his type of religion had over the common mind. Its merciless insistence upon every terror of death is perhaps not so important as its melodramatic vignettes, in woeful taste, that recall the death of Richardson's heroine Clarissa Harlowe, or the theatrical preaching of the French painter Greuze.]

MADAM:

Traveling lately into Cornwall, I happened to alight at a considerable village in that county, where finding myself under an unexpected necessity of staying a little, I took a walk to the church.[1] The doors, like the heaven to which they lead, were wide open, and readily admitted an unworthy stranger. Pleased with the opportunity, I resolved to spend a few minutes under the sacred roof.

In a situation so retired and awful I could not avoid falling into a train of meditations, serious and mournfully pleasing; which I trust were in some degree profitable to me, while they possessed and warmed my thoughts; and if they may administer any satisfaction to you, Madam, now they are recollected, and committed to writing, I shall receive a fresh pleasure from them.

It was an ancient pile, reared by hands that ages ago were mouldered into dust.—Situate in the center of a large burial-ground, remote from the noise and hurry of tumultuous life.—The body

1 The church was that at Kilkhampton, Cornwall.

spacious; the structure lofty; the whole magnificently plain. A row of regular pillars extended themselves through the midst, supporting the roof with simplicity and with dignity.—The light that passed through the windows seemed to shed a kind of luminous obscurity, which gave every object a grave and venerable air.—The deep silence added to the gloomy aspect, and both heightened by the loneliness of the place, greatly increased the solemnity of the scene.—A sort of religious dread stole insensibly on my mind, while I advanced, all pensive and thoughtful, along the inmost aisle: such a dread as hushed every ruder passion and dissipated all the gay images of an alluring world. . . .

Legions, legions of disasters, such as no prudence can foresee and no care prevent, lie in wait to accomplish our doom. A starting horse may throw his rider, may at once dash his body against the stones and fling his soul into the invisible world. A stack of chimneys may tumble into the street and crush the unwary passenger under the ruins. Even a single tile dropping from the roof may be as fatal as the fall of the whole structure.—So frail, so very attenuated is the thread of life that it not only bursts before the storm but breaks even at a breeze. The most common occurrences, those from which we suspect not the least harm, may prove the weapons of our destruction. A grape stone, a despicable fly, may be more mortal than Goliath, with all his formidable armor.—Nay, if God give command, our very comforts become killing. The air we breathe is our bane; the food we eat, the vehicle of death. . . .

Here a small plain stone is placed upon the ground; purchased, one would imagine, from the little fund and formed by the hand of frugality itself. Nothing costly; not one decoration added: only a very short inscription; and that so effaced as to be scarcely intelligible.—Was the depositary unfaithful to its trust? Or were the letters worn by the frequent resort of the surviving family to mourn over the grave of a most valuable and beloved relative?—For I perceive, upon a closer inspection that it covers the remains of a father; a religious father; snatched from his growing offspring before they were settled in the world, or so much as their principles fixed by a thorough education.

This, sure, is the most complicated distress that has hitherto come under our consideration. The solemnities of such a dying chamber are some of the most melting and melancholy scenes imaginable. —There lies the affectionate husband, the indulgent parent, the faithful friend, and the generous master. He lies in the last extremities and on the very point of dissolution. Art has done its all. The raging disease mocks the power of medicine. It hastens with resistless impetuosity to execute its dreadful errand; to rend asunder the silver cord of life, and the more delicate tie of social attachment, and conjugal affection.

A servant or two, from a revering distance, cast many a wishful look, and condole their honored master in the language of sighs. The condescending mildness of his commands was wont to produce an alacrity of obedience and render their service a pleasure. The remembrance of both embitters their grief, and makes it trickle plentifully down their honest cheeks.—His friends, who have so often shared his joys and gladdened his mind with their enlivening converse, now are miserable comforters. A sympathizing and mournful pity is all the relief they are able to contribute; unless it be augmented by their silent prayers for the divine succor, and a word of consolation suggested from the scriptures.—Those poor innocents, the children, crowd around the bed; drowned in tears, and almost frantic with grief, they sob out their little souls and passionately cry, "Will he leave us? Leave us in a helpless condition! Leave us to an injurious world!"

These separate streams are all united in the distressed spouse, and overwhelm her breast with an impetuous tide of sorrows. In her the lover weeps, the wife mourns, and all the mother yearns. To her, the loss is beyond measure aggravated by months and years of delightful society and exalted friendship.—Where, alas! can she meet with such unsuspected fidelity or repose such unreserved confidence? Where find so discreet a counselor, so improving an example, and a guardian so sedulously attentive to the interests of herself and her children?—See! how she hangs over the languishing bed; most tenderly solicitous to prolong a life important and desirable far beyond her own; or, if that be impracticable, no less tenderly officious to soothe the last agonies of her dearer self.—Her hands, trembling under direful apprehensions, wipe the cold dews from the livid cheeks; and sometimes stay the sinking head on her gentle arms, sometimes rest it on her compassionate bosom.—See! how she gazes with a speechless ardor on the pale countenance and meager features. Speechless her tongue; but she looks unutterable things. While all her soft passions throb with unavailing fondness, and her very soul bleeds with exquisite anguish.

The sufferer, all patient and adoring, submits to the divine will; and, by submission, becomes superior to his affliction. He is sensibly touched with the disconsolate state of his attendants, and pierced with an anxious concern for his wife and children; his wife, who will soon be a destitute widow; his children, who will soon be helpless orphans. "Yet though cast down, not in despair." He is greatly refreshed by his trust in the everlasting covenant, and his hope of approaching glory. Religion gives a dignity to distress. At each interval of ease, he comforts his very comforters, and suffers with all the majesty of woe.

The soul, just going to abandon the tottering clay, collects all her force and exerts her last efforts. The good man raises himself on his pillow; extends a kind hand to his servants, which is bathed in tears; takes an affecting farewell of his friends; clasps his wife in a feeble embrace; kisses the dear pledges of their mutual love; and then pours all that remains of life and of strength in the following words:—"I die, my dear children: but God, the everlasting God, will be with you.—Though you lose an earthly parent, you have a Father in heaven, who lives for evermore.—Nothing, nothing but an unbelieving heart, an irreligious life, can ever separate you from the regards of his providence—from the endearments of his love."

He could proceed no farther. His heart was full; but utterance failed. After a short pause, with difficulty, great difficulty, he added—"You, the dear partner of my soul, you are now the only protector of our orphans.—I leave you under a weight of cares.—But God, who defendeth the cause of the widow—God, whose promise is faithfulness and truth—God hath said *I will never leave thee nor forsake thee.*—This revives my drooping spirits—Let this support the wife of my bosom—And now, O Father of compassion, into thy hands I commend my spirit.—Encouraged by thy promised goodness, I leave my fatherless"—

Here he fainted; fell back upon the bed, and lay for some minutes bereft of his senses. As a taper upon the very point of extinction is sometimes suddenly rekindled and leaps into a quivering flame, so life, before it totally expired, gave a parting struggle, and once more looked abroad from opening eyelids.—He would fain have spoke, fain have uttered the sentence he began. More than once he essayed: but the organs of speech were become like a broken vessel, and nothing but the obstructing phlegm rattled in his throat. His aspect, however, spoke affection inexpressible. With all the father, all the husband, still living in his looks, he takes one more view of those dear children whom he had often beheld with a parental triumph. He turns his dying eyes on that beloved woman whom he never beheld but with a glow of delight. Fixed in this posture, amidst smiles of love, and under a gleam of heaven, they shine out their last.

Upon this, the silent sorrow bursts into loud laments. . . .

Yonder entrance leads, I suppose, to the vault. Let me turn aside and take one view of the habitation and its tenants.—The sullen door grates upon its hinges: not used to receive many visitants, it admits me with reluctance and murmurs.—What meaneth this sudden trepidation while I descend the steps and am visiting the pale nations of the dead?—Be composed, my spirits; there is nothing to fear in these quiet chambers. "Here even the wicked cease from troubling."

Good heavens! what a solemn scene!—How dismal the gloom! Here is perpetual darkness and night even at noonday.—How doleful the solitude! Not one trace of cheerful society; but sorrow and terror seem to have made this their dreaded abode.—Hark! how the hollow dome resounds at every tread. The echoes, that long have slept, are awakened, and lament, and sigh along the walls.

A beam or two finds its way through the grates, and reflects a feeble glimmer from the nails of the coffins. So many of those sad spectacles, half concealed in shades, half seen dimly by the baleful twilight, add a deeper horror to these gloomy mansions.—I pore upon the inscriptions, and am just able to pick out that these are the remains of the rich and renowned. . . .

Having cast a superficial view upon these receptacles of the dead, curiosity prompts my inquiry to a more intimate survey. Could we draw back the covering of the tomb; could we discern what those are now who once were mortals—O! how would it surprise and grieve us! Surprise us, to behold the prodigious transformation which has taken place on every individual; grieve us, to observe the dishonor done to our nature in general within these subterranean lodgments.

Here the sweet and winning aspect, that wore perpetually an attractive smile, grins horribly a naked, ghastly skull.—The eye that outshone the diamond's brilliancy and glanced its lovely lightning into the most guarded heart: alas! where is it? Where shall we find the rolling sparkler! How are all its sprightly beams eclipsed! totally eclipsed! . . .

Could the lover have a sight of his once-enchanting fair one, what a startling astonishment would seize him!—"Is this the object I not long ago so passionately admired! I said she was divinely fair, and thought her somewhat more than mortal. Her form was symmetry itself; every elegance breathed in her air; all the graces waited on her motions.—'Twas music when she spoke: but, when she spoke encouragement, 'twas little less than rapture. How my heart danced to those charming accents!—And can that which some weeks ago was to admiration lovely be now so insufferably loathsome?—Where are those blushing cheeks? Where the coral lips? Where that ivory neck on which the curling jet, in such glossy ringlets, flowed? With a thousand other beauties of person and ten thousand delicacies of action?—Amazing alteration! delusory bliss!—Fondly I gazed upon the glittering meteor. It shone brightly, and I mistook it for a star, for a permanent and substantial good. But how is it fallen! fallen from an orb not its own! And all that I can trace on earth is but a putrid mass."

A SELECTION

David Hartley
1705–1757

OBSERVATIONS ON MAN, HIS FRAME, HIS DUTY, AND HIS EXPECTATIONS
1749

[Hartley's theories, derived from Locke and related to Addison's notions on imagination, clearly exhibit the tendency to explain the operation of the mind by some such mechanical principles as Newton saw operating in the external world. The mechanical principle of association by which complex ideas were evolved from simple sense impressions has a twofold bearing: first, it encouraged the necessitarian dogmas of thinkers like William Godwin (and, later, Shelley); secondly, it developed into a Wordsworthian "organic sensibility" and the "inward eye" that re-creates experience in tranquillity. Akenside proclaimed in his poem on the imagination that the pleasures of sight could lead to the most exalted ideas, and finally to God; thus the "language of the sense" opens the way to divinity. Hartley's book was popular; Coleridge named his first son Hartley.]

MAN consists of two parts, body and mind.

The first is subjected to our senses and inquiries, in the same manner as the other parts of the external material world.

The last is that substance, agent, principle, &c. to which we refer the sensations, ideas, pleasures, pains, and voluntary motions.

Sensations are those internal feelings of the mind which arise from the impressions made by external objects upon the several parts of our bodies.

All our other internal feelings may be called *ideas*. Some of these appear to spring up in the mind of themselves; some are suggested by words; others arise in other ways. Many writers comprehend *sensations* under *ideas;* but I everywhere use these words in the senses here ascribed to them.

The ideas which resemble sensations are called *ideas of sensation:* all the rest may therefore be called *intellectual ideas.*

It will appear in the course of these observations that the *ideas of sensation* are the elements of which all the rest are compounded. Hence *ideas of sensation* may be termed *simple; intellectual* ones, *complex.*   [PART I, Introduction]

And upon the whole, it may appear to the reader that the simple ideas of sensation must run into clusters and combinations by association; and that each of these will, at last, coalesce into one complex idea by the approach and commixture of the several compounding parts.

It appears also from observation that many of our intellectual ideas, such as those that belong to the heads of beauty, honor, moral qualities, &c. are, in fact, thus composed of parts which, by degrees, coalesce into one complex idea.

                    [PART I, chap. i, sec. ii, prop. 12]

Here we may observe,

First, That our passions or affections can be no more than aggregates of simple ideas united by association. For they are excited by objects, and by the incidents of life. But these, if we except the impressed sensations, can have no power of affecting us but what they derive from association. . . .

Secondly, Since therefore the passions are states of considerable pleasure or pain, they must be aggregates of the ideas, or traces of the sensible pleasures and pains, which ideas make up, by their number and mutual influence upon one another, for the faintness and transitory nature of each singly taken. . . .

Thirdly, As sensation is the common foundation of all these, so each in its turn, when sufficiently generated, contributes to generate and model all the rest. We may conceive this to be done in the following manner. Let sensation generate imagination; then will sensation and imagination together generate ambition; sensation, imagination, and ambition, self-interest; sensation, imagination, ambition, and self-interest, sympathy; sensation, imagination, ambition, self-interest, and sympathy, theopathy; sensation, imagination, ambition, self-interest, sympathy, and theopathy, the moral sense, and, in an inverted order, imagination will new-model sensation;

ambition, sensation and imagination; self-interest, sensation, imagination, and ambition; sympathy, sensation, imagination, ambition, and self-interest; theopathy, sensation, imagination, ambition, self-interest, and sympathy; and the moral sense, sensation, imagination, ambition, self-interest, sympathy, and theopathy: till at last, by the numerous reciprocal influences of all these upon each other, the passions arrive at that degree of complexness which is observed in fact, and which makes them so difficult to be analyzed.

[PART I, chap. 3, sec. iii, prop. 89]

Mark Akenside

1721–1770

WE are told that this physician-poet, son of a Presbyterian butcher, had a somewhat brutal nature and "evinced a particular disgust to females" among his patients. He is often included among those devoted to the "genius of ancient Greece" who hoped to write the ode with Attic art: at least the charge cannot be brought against his odes and hymns which Dr. Johnson brought against *The Pleasures of Imagination*—that "the words are multiplied till the sense is hardly perceived." Pope advised Dodsley that this latter poem was the performance of "no everyday writer" and should bring no niggardly sum. The poem is significant to us because it explains how the attitude toward imagination was changing. Addison, parroting John Locke, had said that the imagination is only a recollection of what is seen. At the same time the deists had asserted that nature is either itself divine or the evidence of divinity. Akenside drew the inescapable conclusion:

> Thus the men
> Whom Nature's works can charm with God himself
> Hold converse.

Wordsworth, later, merely concluded matters: the imagination, by which one enters into harmony with God, was to him a divine faculty. Instead of being looked upon as it was in the seventeenth century, as a "hot-mouthed jade," or as a faculty that deludes, or instead of being a passive faculty, as with Addison, the imagination to Akenside was coming to be a godlike power in man, a pulse of the great I AM, an "esemplastic," shaping force, as Coleridge was to put it.

BIOGRAPHICAL NOTES

Son of a butcher of Newcastle upon Tyne. Lamed for life by a cleaver in his father's shop. Attended a dissenting academy in Newcastle. Published five poems in the *Gentleman's Magazine* (1737–39). Entered the University of Edinburgh; studied medicine (1739). Practiced as surgeon in Newcastle (1741–42). Went to London (1743) and sold *Pleasures of Imagination* (1744), to Dodsley for £120. Studied medicine at Leyden (1744) and returned to practice at Northampton. *Odes on Several Subjects* (1745). Became editor of Dodsley's *Museum*. Gained a fashionable medical practice; became physician to Queen Charlotte (1761). Said by a fellow medical man, Dr. Lettsom, to have been brutal to the poor at Christ's and St. Thomas's Hospitals. Turned Tory. Died suddenly of a fever at height of fashionable success.

BIBLIOGRAPHY: *Poetical Works*, ed. Alexander Dyce, 1864. Houpt, Charles T., *Mark Akenside*, Philadelphia, 1944.

THE PLEASURES OF IMAGINATION [1]

1744–1757

BOOK THE THIRD

. . . .

Such are the various aspects of the mind—
Some heavenly genius, whose unclouded thoughts
Attain that secret harmony which blends
The aetherial spirit with its mould of clay;
O! teach me to reveal the grateful charm
That searchless Nature o'er the sense of man
Diffuses, to behold, in lifeless things,
The inexpressive semblance of himself,
Of thought and passion. Mark the sable woods
That shade sublime yon mountain's nodding brow;   10
With what religious awe the solemn scene
Commands your steps! as if the reverend form
Of Minos or of Numa should forsake
The Elysian seats, and down the embowering glade
Move to your pausing eye. Behold the expanse
Of yon gay landscape, where the silver clouds
Flit o'er the heavens, before the sprightly breeze:
Now their gray cincture skirts the doubtful sun;

1 Akenside's poem needs to be read with the theory of "association" in mind; see the selection from David Hartley.

Now streams of splendour, through their opening veil
Effulgent, sweep from off the gilded lawn   20
The aerial shadows, on the curling brook,
And on the shady margin's quivering leaves,
With quickest lustre glancing: while you view
The prospect, say, within your cheerful breast,
Plays not the lively sense of winning mirth,
With clouds and sunshine chequer'd; while the round
Of social converse, to the inspiring tongue
Of some gay nymph amid her subject train,
Moves all obsequious? Whence is this effect,
This kindred power of such discordant things?   30
Or flows their semblance from that mystic tone
To which the new-born mind's harmonious powers
At first were strung? Or rather from the links
Which artful custom twines around her frame?
    For when the different images of things
By chance combin'd have struck the attentive soul
With deeper impulse, or, connected long,
Have drawn her frequent eye; howe'er distinct
The external scenes, yet oft the ideas gain
From that conjunction an eternal tie   40
And sympathy unbroken. Let the mind
Recall one partner of the various league,
Immediate, lo! the firm confederates rise,
And each his former station strait resumes;
One movement governs the consenting throng,
And all at once with rosy pleasure shine,
Or all are sadden'd with the glooms of care.
'Twas thus, if ancient fame the truth unfold,
Two faithful needles from the informing touch
Of the same parent-stone together drew   50
Its mystic virtue, and at first conspir'd
With fatal impulse quivering to the pole;
Then, though disjoin'd by kingdoms, though the main
Roll'd its broad surge betwixt, and different stars
Beheld their wakeful motions, yet preserv'd
The former friendship, and remember'd still
Th' alliance of their birth: whate'er the line
Which one possess'd, nor pause nor quiet knew
The sure associate, ere with trembling speed
He found its path, and fix'd unerring there.   60
Such is the secret union when we feel

A song, a flower, a name, at once restore
Those long-connected scenes where first they mov'd
The attention, backward through her mazy walks
Guiding the wanton fancy to her scope,
To temples, courts, or fields, with all the band
Of painted forms, of passions and designs
Attendant: whence, if pleasing in itself,
The prospect from that sweet accession gains
Redoubled influence o'er the listening mind.   70

.   .   .   .

By what fine ties hath God connected things
When present in the mind, which in themselves
Have no connection? Sure the rising sun
O'er the caerulean convex of the sea,
With equal brightness and with equal warmth
Might roll his fiery orb; nor yet the soul
Thus feel her frame expanded, and her powers
Exulting in the splendor she beholds;
Like a young conqueror moving through the pomp
Of some triumphal day. When, joined at eve,   80
Soft murmuring streams and gales of gentlest breath,
Melodious Philomela's wakeful strain
Attemper, could not man's discerning ear
Through all its tones the symphony pursue;
Nor yet this breath divine of nameless joy
Steal through his veins, and fan the awakened heart;
Mild as the breeze, yet rapturous as the song?
     But were not nature still endow'd at large
With all which life requires, though unadorn'd
With such inchantment; wherefore then her form   90
So exquisitely fair? her breath perfum'd
With such aethereal sweetness? whence her voice
Inform'd at will to raise or to depress
The impassion'd soul? and whence the robes of light
Which thus invest her with more lovely pomp
Than fancy can describe? Whence, but from thee,
O Source Divine of everflowing love!
And thy unmeasur'd goodness? Not content
With every food of life to nourish man,
By kind illusions of the wondering sense   100
Thou mak'st all nature beauty to his eye,
Or music to his ear: well pleas'd he scans

The goodly prospect, and with inward smiles
Treads the gay verdure of the painted plain,
Beholds the azure canopy of heaven,
And living lamps that over-arch his head
With more than regal splendour; bends his ears
To the full choir of water, air, and earth;
Nor heeds the pleasing error of his thought,
Nor doubts the painted green or azure arch,   110
Nor questions more the music's mingling sounds,
Than space or motion, or eternal time;
So sweet he feels their influence to attract
The fixed soul, to brighten the dull glooms
Of care, and make the destin'd road of life
Delightful to his feet. So fables tell
The adventurous hero, bound on hard exploits,
Beholds with glad surprise, by secret spells
Of some kind sage, the patron of his toils,
A visionary paradise disclos'd   120
Amid the dubious wild; with streams, and shades,
And airy songs, the enchanted landscape smiles,
Cheers his long labours, and renews his frame.
    What then is taste, but these internal powers
Active, and strong, and feelingly alive
To each fine impulse? a discerning sense
Of decent and sublime, with quick disgust
From things deform'd, or disarrang'd, or gross
In species? This nor gems, nor stores of gold,
Nor purple state, nor culture, can bestow,   130
But God alone, when first his active hand
Imprints the secret bias of the soul.
He, mighty parent! wise and just in all,
Free as the vital breeze or light of heaven,
Reveals the charms of nature. Ask the swain
Who journeys homeward from a summer day's
Long labour, why, forgetful of his toils
And due repose, he loiters to behold
The sunshine gleaming as through amber clouds
O'er all the western sky? Full soon, I ween,   140
His rude expression and untutor'd airs
Beyond the power of language will unfold
The form of beauty smiling at his heart,
How lovely! how commanding! But though heaven
In every breast hath sown these early seeds

Of love and admiration, yet in vain,
Without fair culture's kind parental aid,
Without inlivening suns and genial showers,
And shelter from the blast, in vain we hope
The tender plant should rear its blooming head,   150
Or yield the harvest promis'd in its spring.
Nor yet will every soil with equal stores
Repay the tiller's labour, or attend
His will, obsequious, whether to produce
The olive or the laurel. Different minds
Incline to different objects: one pursues
The vast alone, the wonderful, the wild;
Another sighs for harmony, and grace,
And gentlest beauty. Hence when lightning fires
The arch of heaven, and thunders rock the ground,   160
When furious whirlwinds rend the howling air,
And ocean, groaning from his lowest bed,
Heaves his tempestuous billows to the sky;
Amid the mighty uproar, while below
The nations tremble, Shakespeare looks abroad
From some high cliff superior, and enjoys
The elemental war. But Waller longs
All on the margin of some flowery stream
To spread his careless limbs amid the cool
Of plantane shades, and to the listening deer   170
The tale of slighted vows and love's disdain
Resound soft-warbling all the livelong day:
Consenting Zephyr sighs, the weeping rill
Joins in his plaint melodious, mute the groves,
And hill and dale with all their echoes mourn.
Such and so various are the tastes of men!
    Oh blest of heaven! whom not the languid songs
Of luxury, the Siren, not the bribes
Of sordid wealth, nor all the gaudy spoils
Of pageant honour, can seduce to leave   180
Those ever-blooming sweets which from the store
Of nature fair imagination culls
To charm the inliven'd soul! What though not all
Of mortal offspring can attain the heights
Of envied life, though only few possess
Patrician treasures or imperial state;
Yet nature's care, to all her children just,
With richer treasures, and an ampler state,

Indows at large whatever happy man
Will deign to use them. His the city's pomp,   190
The rural honours his. Whate'er adorns
The princely dome, the column and the arch,
The breathing marbles and the sculptur'd gold,
Beyond the proud possessor's narrow claim,
His tuneful breast enjoys. For him the spring
Distills her dews, and from the silken gem
Its lucid leaves unfolds; for him the hand
Of autumn tinges every fertile branch
With blooming gold and blushes like the morn.
Each passing hour sheds tribute from her wings,   200
And still new beauties meet his lonely walk,
And loves unfelt attract him. Not a breeze
Flies o'er the meadow, not a cloud imbibes
The setting sun's effulgence, not a strain
From all the tenants of the warbling shade
Ascends, but whence his bosom can partake
Fresh pleasure unreprov'd. Nor thence partakes
Fresh pleasure only: for the attentive mind
By this harmonious action on her powers
Becomes herself harmonious: wont so oft   210
In outward things to meditate the charm
Of sacred order, soon she seeks at home
To find a kindred order, to exert
Within herself this elegance of love,
This fair inspir'd delight: her temper'd powers
Refine at length, and every passion wears
A chaster, milder, more attractive mien.
But if to ampler prospects, if to gaze
On nature's form, where, negligent of all
These lesser graces, she assumes the port   220
Of that eternal majesty that weigh'd
The world's foundations; if to these the mind
Exalts her daring eye, then mightier far
Will be the change, and nobler. Would the forms
Of servile custom cramp her generous powers?
Would sordid policies, the barbarous growth
Of ignorance and rapine, bow her down
To tame pursuits, to indolence and fear?
Lo! she appeals to nature, to the winds
And rolling waves, the sun's unwearied course,   230
The elements and seasons: all declare

For what the eternal maker has ordain'd
The powers of man: we feel within ourselves
His energy divine: he tells the heart
He meant, he made, us to behold and love
What he beholds and loves, the general orb
Of life and being; to be great like him,
Beneficent and active. Thus the men
Whom nature's works can charm with God himself
Hold converse, grow familiar day by day   240
With his conceptions, act upon his plan,
And form to his, the relish of their souls.

INSCRIPTION FOR A GROTTO

1758

To me, whom in their lays the shepherds call
Actæa, daughter of the neighbouring stream,
This cave belongs. The fig-tree and the vine,
Which o'er the rocky entrance downward shoot,
Were plac'd by Glycon. He with cowslips pale,
Primrose, and purple lychnis, deck'd the green
Before my threshold, and my shelving walls
With honeysuckle cover'd. Here at noon,
Lull'd by the murmur of my rising fount,
I slumber: here my clustering fruits I tend;   10
Or from the humid flowers, at break of day,
Fresh garlands weave, and chace from all my bounds
Each thing impure or noxious. Enter-in,
O stranger, undismay'd. Nor bat nor toad
Here lurks: and if thy breast of blameless thoughts
Approve thee, not unwelcome shalt thou tread
My quiet mansion: chiefly, if thy name
Wise Pallas and the immortal Muses own.

ODE TO THE EVENING STAR

1772

To-night retir'd the queen of heaven
  With young Endymion stays:
And now to Hesper is it given
Awhile to rule the vacant sky,
Till she shall to her lamp supply
  A stream of brighter rays.

O Hesper, while the starry throng
  With awe thy path surrounds,
Oh listen to my suppliant song,
If haply now the vocal sphere   10
Can suffer thy delighted ear
  To stoop to mortal sounds.

So may the bridegroom's genial strain
  Thee still invoke to shine:
So may the bride's unmarried train
To Hymen chaunt their flattering vow,
Still that his lucky torch may glow
  With lustre pure as thine.

Far other vows must I prefer
  To thy indulgent power.   20
Alas, but now I paid my tear
On fair Olympia's virgin tomb:
And lo, from thence, in quest I roam
  Of Philomela's bower.

Propitious send thy golden ray,
  Thou purest light above:
Let no false flame seduce to stray
Where gulph or steep lie hid for harm:
But lead where music's healing charm
  May sooth afflicted love.   30

To them, by many a grateful song
    In happier seasons vow'd,
These lawns, Olympia's haunt, belong:
Oft by yon silver stream we walk'd,
Or fix'd, while Philomela talk'd,
    Beneath yon copses stood.

Nor seldom, where the beachen boughs
    That roofless tower invade,
We came while her inchanting Muse
The radiant moon above us held:
Till by a clamorous owl compell'd
    She fled the solemn shade.

But hark; I hear her liquid tone.
    Now, Hesper, guide my feet
Down the red marle with moss o'ergrown,
Through yon wild thicket next the plain,
Whose hawthorns choke the winding lane
    Which leads to her retreat.

See the green space: on either hand
    Inlarg'd it spreads around:
See, in the midst she takes her stand,
Where one old oak his awful shade
Extends o'er half the level mead
    Inclos'd in woods profound.

Hark, how through many a melting note
    She now prolongs her lays:
How sweetly down the void they float!
The breeze their magic path attends:
The stars shine out: the forest bends:
    The wakeful heifers gaze.

Whoe'er thou art whom chance may bring
    To this sequester'd spot,
If then the plaintive Syren sing,
Oh softly tread beneath her bower,
And think of heaven's disposing power,
    Of man's uncertain lot.

Oh think, o'er all this mortal stage,
  What mournful scenes arise:
What ruin waits on kingly rage:
How often virtue dwells with woe: 70
How many griefs from knowledge flow:
  How swiftly pleasure flies.

O sacred bird, let me at eve,
  Thus wandering all alone,
Thy tender counsel oft receive,
Bear witness to thy pensive airs,
And pity nature's common cares
  Till I forget my own.

A SELECTION

John Winstanley

1678–1750

THE HAPPY SAVAGE

1732

Oh, happy he who never saw the face
Of man, nor heard the sound of human voice!
But soon as born was carry'd and expos'd
In some vast desart, suckled by the wolf,
Or shaggy bear more kind than our fell race;
Who with his fellow-brutes can range around
The ecchoing forest: his rude artless mind
Uncultivated as the soil—he joins
The dreadful harmony of howling wolves,
And the fierce lyon's roar; while far away   10
Th' affrighted traveller retires and trembles.
Happy the lonely savage! nor deceiv'd,
Nor vex'd, nor griev'd—in ev'ry darksome cave,
Under each verdant shade, he takes repose.
Sweet are his slumbers—of all human arts
Happily ignorant, nor taught by wisdom,
Numberless woes; nor polish'd into torment.

A SELECTION

John Brown
1715–1766

AN ESTIMATE OF THE MANNERS AND PRINCIPLES
OF THE TIMES

1757

[This book, famous in its day, was devoted to the thesis that "our situation seems most dangerous: We are rolling to the brink of a precipice that must destroy us." This calamity, Brown thought, was due to the manners of the times, which "appear to be that of a *vain, luxurious*, and *selfish* EFFEMINACY."]

THE effects of commerce on manners has by most writers, I think, been considered as uniform. Even the sage and amiable Montesquieu says only, in general terms, "that commerce polishes manners, but corrupts [morals]." Whereas, from a candid view of its nature and effects, we shall probably find that in its first and middle stages it is beneficent; in its last, dangerous and fatal.

If we view commerce in its first stages, we shall see that it supplies mutual necessities, prevents mutual wants, extends mutual knowledge, eradicates mutual prejudice, and spreads mutual humanity.

If we view it in its middle and more advanced period, we shall see it provides conveniencies, increaseth numbers, coins money, gives birth to arts and science, creates equal laws, diffuses general plenty and general happiness.

If we view it in its third and highest stage, we shall see it change its nature and effects. It brings in superfluity and vast wealth, begets avarice, gross luxury, or effeminate refinement among the higher ranks, together with general loss of principle.

[PART III, sec. ii]

Thus our present exorbitant degree of trade and wealth, in a mixed state like that of England, naturally tends to produce luxurious and effeminate manners in the higher ranks, together with a general defect of principle. And as the internal strength of a nation will always depend chiefly on the manners and principles of its leading members, so these effeminate manners and this defect of principle operate powerfully, and fatally, on the national conduct and affairs. They have produced a general incapacity, have weakened the national spirit of defense, have heightened the national disunion: and this national disunion, besides its proper and immediate effects, being founded in avarice for the ends of dissipation, hath again weakened the small remainder of public capacity and defense; and thus seems to have fitted us for a prey to the insults and invasions of our most powerful enemy [France].

[PART III, sec. vii]

We have seen that the ruling evils of our age and nation have arisen from the unheeded consequences of our trade and wealth; that these have produced effeminate manners, and occasioned loss of principle; that these have brought on a national debility. But would the lessening this exorbitant trade and wealth bring back manners and principles, and restore the nation's strength?—I very much question the event.

But whatever the consequences might be at home, those abroad would certainly be fatal. The French are every day gaining upon us in commerce; and if ours should lessen, theirs would increase to our destruction.

Thus are we fallen into a kind of dilemma: If our commerce be maintained or increased, its effects bid fair to destroy us; if commerce be discouraged and lessened, the growing power of our enemy threatens the same consequence.

There seems, then, no other expedient than this: that commerce and wealth be not discouraged in their growth, but checked and controlled in their effects.

And even in attempting this, care must be had lest in controlling the effects of commerce, we should destroy commerce itself.

[PART III, sec. x]

Joseph Warton

1722–1800

Thomas Warton, Junior

1728–1790

THE Wartons can be considered as members of a select and influential group of scholar-poets that included Gray. Their verse is largely derivative in the sense that it was bookishly inspired; the echoes of Milton, Spenser, and Chaucer are clearly audible. Although their scholarship is assertive enough and they are not without wit, there is something wistful in their poetry: they quaver a little, as though afraid to speak out. Their taste, a little precious, is for the most part impeccable. Even if their abilities are not of a major order, their antiquarian interests, and their devotion to what Addison had called "the fairy way of writing" and the sublimity of the "Gothic," make them important in literary history. They stand in opposition to what might be called the official usage of Pope. In them comes a shift in "tone" that marks a break with the eighteenth-century poetry of statement.

BIOGRAPHICAL NOTES

JOSEPH WARTON: Son of Thomas Warton, Senior, Professor of Poetry at Oxford. Entered Winchester in 1735, where he became the friend of Collins. Attended Oriel College, Oxford (1740–44). "The Enthusiast" (1744). *Odes on Various Subjects* (1746). Became his father's curate at Basingstoke (1744), then (1748) rector at Winslade. Contributed to *The Adventurer* (1753–54). Appointed second master at Winchester (1755). *Essay on the Genius and Writings of Pope* (Vol. I, 1756; Vol. II, 1782). Friendships with Johnson, Burke, Garrick, Reynolds, and Bishop Percy. Became headmaster at Winchester (1766), with very ill success. Elected to the Literary Club (1773). Retired to the rectory at Wickham (1793). Edited Pope (1797).

THOMAS WARTON, JUNIOR: Son of Thomas Warton; educated by his father at Basingstoke, then at Trinity College, Oxford (1744–50). Elected fellow in 1751. Had great interest in Gothic architecture and antiquities. *The Pleasures of Melancholy* (1747); *Observa-*

tions on the Faerie Queen (1754). Obtains M.A. for Johnson in 1755. Appointed Professor of Poetry at Oxford (1757–67). *The Suicide* (1770), once supposed to be a poem suggested by the death of Chatterton. Elected a fellow of the London Society of Antiquaries (1771). *History of English Poetry from the Twelfth to the Close of the Sixteenth Century* (1774, 1778, 1781). Elected to the Literary Club (1782). Edited Milton's minor poems (1785). Appointed Camden Professor of History at Oxford, and Poet Laureate (1785). Died suddenly at Trinity of a stroke.

BIBLIOGRAPHY: Warton, Joseph, *Poems,* ed. Alexander Chalmers, *Works of the English Poets,* 1810. Warton, Thomas, Junior, *Poems,* ed. Alexander Chalmers, *Works of the English Poets,* 1810. *The Three Wartons; A Choice of Their Verse,* ed. Eric Partridge, 1927. Rinaker, Clarissa, *Thomas Warton [Junior], A Biographical and Critical Study,* 1916.

Joseph Warton

THE ENTHUSIAST

OR THE LOVER OF NATURE

[1744], 1748

Ye green-rob'd Dryads, oft at dusky eve
By wondering shepherds seen, to forests brown,
To unfrequented meads, and pathless wilds,
Lead me from gardens deck'd with art's vain pomps.
Can gilt alcoves, can marble-mimic gods,
Parterres embroider'd, obelisks, and urns,
Of high relief; can the long, spreading lake
Or vista lessening to the sight; can Stow,
With all her Attic fanes, such raptures raise,
As the thrush-haunted copse, where lightly leaps   10
The fearful fawn the rustling leaves along,
And the brisk squirrel sports from bough to bough,
While from an hollow oak, whose naked roots
O'erhang a pensive rill, the busy bees
Hum drowsy lullabies? The bards of old,
Fair Nature's friends, sought such retreats, to charm
Sweet Echo with their songs; oft too they met
In summer evenings, near sequester'd bowers,
Or mountain-nymph, or muse, and eager learnt

The moral strains she taught to mend mankind.   20
As to a secret grot Ægeria stole
With patriot Numa,[1] and in silent night
Whisper'd him sacred laws, he list'ning sat,
Rapt with her virtuous voice, old Tiber lean'd
Attentive on his urn, and hush'd his waves.
   Rich in her weeping country's spoils, Versailles
May boast a thousand fountains, that can cast
The tortur'd waters to the distant heavens;
Yet let me choose some pine-topt precipice
Abrupt and shaggy, whence a foamy stream,   30
Like Anio,[2] tumbling roars; or some bleak heath,
Where straggling stands the mournful juniper,
Or yew-tree scath'd; while in clear prospect round,
From the grove's bosom spires emerge, and smoke
In bluish wreaths ascends, ripe harvests wave,
Low, lonely cottages, and ruin'd tops
Of Gothic battlements appear, and streams
Beneath the sunbeams twinkle.—The shrill lark,
That wakes the wood-man to his early task,
Or love-sick Philomel, whose luscious lays   40
Soothe lone night-wanderers, the moaning dove
Pitied by listening milk-maid, far excel
The deep-mouth'd viol, the soul-lulling lute,
And battle-breathing trumpet. Artful sounds!
That please not like the choristers of air,
When first they hail th' approach of laughing May.
   Can Kent[3] design like Nature? Mark where Thames
Plenty and pleasure pours through Lincoln's meads;
Can the great artist, though with taste supreme
Endu'd, one beauty to this Eden add?   50
Though he, by rules unfetter'd, boldly scorns
Formality and method, round and square
Disdaining, plans irregularly great.
   Creative Titian, can thy vivid strokes,
Or thine, O graceful Raphael, dare to vie
With the rich tints that paint the breathing mead?
The thousand-colour'd tulip, violet's bell
Snow-clad and meek, the vermeil-tinctur'd rose,
And golden crocus?—Yet with these the maid,
Phillis or Phœbe at a feast or wake,   60

1 Numa Pompilius, king of Rome and
lawgiver, who is said to have met the nymph
Egeria.
2 The river that cascades down the falls
at Tivoli.
3 William Kent, the landscape gardener.

Her jetty locks enamels; fairer she,
In innocence and homespun vestments dress'd,
Than if cerulean sapphires at her ears
Shone pendent, or a precious diamond-cross
Heav'd gently on her panting bosom white.
  Yon shepherd idly stretch'd on the rude rock,
Listening to dashing waves, and sea-mew's clang
High-hovering o'er his head, who views beneath
The dolphin dancing o'er the level brine,
Feels more true bliss than the proud admiral,   70
Amid his vessels bright with burnish'd gold
And silken streamers, though his lordly nod
Ten thousand war-worn mariners revere.
And great Æneas gaz'd with more delight
On the rough mountain shagg'd with horrid shades
(Where cloud-compelling Jove, as fancy dream'd,
Descending, shook his direful ægis black)
Than if he enter'd the high Capitol
On golden columns rear'd, a conquer'd world
Exhausted, to enrich its stately head.   80
More pleas'd he slept in poor Evander's cot
On shaggy skins, lull'd by sweet nightingales,
Than if a Nero, in an age refin'd,
Beneath a gorgeous canopy had plac'd
His royal guest, and bade his minstrels sound
Soft slumb'rous Lydian airs, to soothe his rest.
  Happy the first of men, ere yet confin'd
To smoky cities; who in sheltering groves,
Warm caves, and deep-sunk vallies liv'd and lov'd,
By cares unwounded; what the sun and showers,   90
And genial earth untillag'd, could produce,
They gather'd grateful, or the acorn brown,
Or blushing berry; by the liquid lapse
Of murmuring waters call'd to slake their thirst,
Or with fair nymphs their sun-brown limbs to bathe;
With nymphs who fondly clasp'd their favourite youths,
Unaw'd by shame, beneath the beechen shade,
Nor wiles, nor artificial coyness knew.
Then doors and walls were not; the melting maid
Nor frown of parents fear'd, nor husband's threats;   100
Nor had curs'd gold their tender hearts allur'd:
Then beauty was not venal. Injur'd Love,
O! whither, god of raptures, art thou fled?

While Avarice waves his golden wand around,
Abhorr'd magician, and his costly cup
Prepares with baneful drugs, t' enchant the souls
Of each low-thoughted fair to wed for gain.
  In Earth's first infancy (as sung the bard [4]
Who strongly painted what he boldly thought),
Though the fierce north oft smote with iron whip   110
Their shiv'ring limbs, though oft the bristly boar
Or hungry lion woke them with their howls,
And scar'd them from their moss-grown caves, to rove
Houseless and cold in dark tempestuous nights;
Yet were not myriads in embattl'd fields
Swept off at once, nor had the raging seas
O'erwhelm'd the foundering bark and shrieking crew;
In vain the glassy ocean smil'd to tempt
The jolly sailor, unsuspecting harm,
For Commerce ne'er had spread her swelling sails,   120
Nor had the wondering Nereids ever heard
The dashing oar: then famine, want, and pine
Sunk to the grave their fainting limbs; but us,
Diseaseful dainties, riot, and excess,
And feverish luxury destroy. In brakes,
Or marshes wild unknowingly they crop'd
Herbs of malignant juice; to realms remote
While we for powerful poisons madly roam,
From every noxious herb collecting death.
What though unknown to those primeval sires   130
The well-arch'd dome, peopled with breathing forms
By fair Italia's skillful hand, unknown
The shapely column, and the crumbling busts
Of awful ancestors in long descent?
Yet why should man mistaken, deem it nobler
To dwell in palaces, and high-roof'd halls,
Than in God's forests, architect supreme!
Say, is the Persian carpet, than the field's
Or meadow's mantle gay, more richly wov'n;
Or softer to the votaries of ease   140
Than bladed grass, perfum'd with dew-dropt flow'rs?
Oh taste corrupt! that luxury and pomp,
In specious names of polish'd manners veil'd,
Should proudly banish Nature's simple charms!
All-beauteous Nature! by thy boundless charms

4 Lucretius (*De Rerum Natura* V).

Oppress'd, O where shall I begin thy praise,
Where turn th' ecstatic eye, how ease my breast
That pants with wild astonishment and love!
Dark forests, and the op'ning lawn, refresh'd
With ever-gushing brooks, hill, meadow, dale,   150
The balmy bean-field, the gay-clover'd close,
So sweetly interchang'd, the lowing ox,
The playful lamb, the distant water-fall
Now faintly heard, now swelling with the breeze,
The sound of pastoral reed from hazel-bower,
The choral birds, the neighing steed, that snuffs
His dappled mate, stung with intense desire,
The ripen'd orchard when the ruddy orbs
Betwixt the green leaves blush, the azure skies,
The cheerful sun that through earth's vitals pours   160
Delight and health and heat; all, all conspire
To raise, to soothe, to harmonize the mind,
To lift on wings of praise, to the great Sire
Of being and of beauty, at whose nod
Creation started from the gloomy vault
Of dreary Chaos, while the grisly king
Murmur'd to feel his boisterous power confin'd.
        What are the lays of artful Addison,
Coldly correct, to Shakespear's warblings wild?
Whom on the winding Avon's willow'd banks   170
Fair Fancy found, and bore the smiling babe
To a close cavern: (still the shepherds show
The sacred place, whence with religious awe
They hear, returning from the field at eve,
Strange whisp'rings of sweet music through the air)
Here, as with honey gather'd from the rock,
She fed the little prattler, and with songs
Oft sooth'd his wond'ring ears; with deep delight
On her soft lap he sat, and caught the sounds.
        Oft near some crowded city would I walk,   180
Listening the far-off noises, rattling cars,
Loud shouts of joy, sad shrieks of sorrow, knells
Full slowly tolling, instruments of trade,
Striking mine ears with one deep-swelling hum.
Or wand'ring near the sea, attend the sounds
Of hollow winds, and ever-beating waves.
Ev'n when wild tempests swallow up the plains,
And Boreas' blasts, big hail, and rains combine

To shake the groves and mountains, would I sit,
Pensively musing on the outrageous crimes   190
That wake Heav'n's vengeance: at such solemn hours,
Dæmons and goblins through the dark air shriek,
While Hecat, with her black-brow'd sisters nine,
Rides o'er the earth, and scatters woes and death.
Then too, they say, in drear Ægyptian wilds
The lion and the tiger prowl for prey
With roarings loud! the list'ning traveller
Starts fear-struck, while the hollow echoing vaults
Of pyramids increase the deathful sounds.
But let me never fail in cloudless nights,   200
When silent Cynthia in her silver car
Through the blue concave slides, when shine the hills,
Twinkle the streams, and woods look tipt with gold,
To seek some level mead, and there invoke
Old Midnight's sister, Contemplation sage
(Queen of the rugged brow, and stern-fixt eye)
To lift my soul above this little earth,
This folly-fetter'd world: to purge my ears,
That I may hear the rolling planets' song,
And tuneful turning spheres: if this be barr'd,   210
The little Fays that dance in neighbouring dales,
Sipping the night-dew, while they laugh and love,
Shall charm me with aërial notes.—As thus
I wander musing, lo, what awful forms
Yonder appear! sharp-ey'd Philosophy
Clad in dun robes, an eagle on his wrist,
First meets my eye; next, virgin Solitude
Serene, who blushes at each gazer's sight;
Then Wisdom's hoary head, with crutch in hand,
Trembling, and bent with age; last, Virtue's self,   220
Smiling, in white array'd, who with her leads
Sweet Innocence, that prattles by her side,
A naked boy!—Harass'd with fear, I stop,
I gaze, when Virtue thus—"Whoe'er thou art,
Mortal, by whom I deign to be beheld
In these my midnight-walks; depart, and say
That henceforth I and my immortal train
Forsake Britannia's isle; who fondly stoops
To Vice, her favourite paramour."—She spoke,
And as she turn'd, her round and rosy neck,   230
Her flowing train, and long ambrosial hair,

Breathing rich odours, I enamour'd view.
O who will bear me then to western climes
(Since Virtue leaves our wretched land), to fields
Yet unpolluted with Iberian swords:
The isles of Innocence, from mortal view
Deeply retir'd, beneath a plantane's shade,
Where Happiness and Quiet sit enthron'd,
With simple Indian swains, that I may hunt
The boar and tiger through savannahs wild,   240
Through fragrant deserts, and through citron groves?
There, fed on dates and herbs, would I despise
The far-fetch'd cates of luxury, and hoards
Of narrow-hearted avarice; nor heed
The distant din of the tumultuous world.
So when rude whirlwinds rouse the roaring main,
Beneath fair Thetis sits, in coral caves,
Serenely gay, nor sinking sailors' cries
Disturb her sportive nymphs, who round her form
The light fantastic dance, or for her hair   250
Weave rosy crowns, or with according lutes
Grace the soft warbles of her honied voice.

ODE TO SOLITUDE

1746

Thou, that at deep dead of night
Walk'st forth beneath the pale moon's light,
In robe of flowing black array'd,
While cypress-leaves thy brows o'ershade;
List'ning to the crowing cock,
And the distant sounding clock;
Or, sitting in the cavern low,
Dost hear the bleak winds loudly blow,
Or the hoarse death-boding owl,
Or village mastiff's wakeful howl,   10
While through thy melancholy room
A dim lamp casts an awful gloom;
Thou, that on the meadow green
Or daisy'd upland art not seen,
But wand'ring by the dusky nooks,

And the pensive falling brooks,
Or near some rugged, herbless rock,
Where no shepherd keeps his flock!
Musing maid, to thee I come,
Hating the tradeful city's hum;   20
O let me calmly dwell with thee,
From noisy mirth and bus'ness free,
With meditation seek the skies,
This folly-fetter'd world despise!

ODE TO EVENING

1749

Hail, meek-ey'd maiden, clad in sober grey,
Whose soft approach the weary woodman loves,
As, homeward bent to kiss his prattling babes,
He jocund whistles thro' the twilight groves.

When Phœbus sinks beneath the gilded hills,
You lightly o'er the misty meadows walk,
The drooping daisies bathe in dulcet dews,
And nurse the nodding violet's slender stalk.

The panting Dryads, that in day's fierce heat
To inmost bowers and cooling caverns ran,   10
Return to trip in wanton evening dance,
Old Sylvan too returns, and laughing Pan.

To the deep woods the clamorous rooks repair,
Light skims the swallow o'er the wat'ry scene,
And from the sheep-cotes, and fresh-furrow'd field,
Stout ploughmen meet to wrestle on the green.

The swain that artless sings on yonder rock,
His nibbling sheep and length'ning shadow spies,
Pleas'd with the cool, the calm, refreshful hour,
And with hoarse hummings of unnumber'd flies.   20

Now every passion sleeps; desponding Love,
And pining Envy, ever-restless Pride;
An holy calm creeps o'er my peaceful soul,
Anger and mad Ambition's storms subside.

O modest Evening, oft let me appear
A wandering votary in thy pensive train,
List'ning to every wildly-warbling throat
That fills with farewell notes the dark'ning plain.

THE DYING INDIAN

1782

The dart of Izdabel prevails! 'twas dipt
In double poison—I shall soon arrive
At the blest island, where no tigers spring
On heedless hunters; where ananas bloom
Thrice in each moon; where rivers smoothly glide,
Nor thund'ring torrents whirl the light canoe
Down to the sea; where my forefathers feast
Daily on hearts of Spaniards! O my son,
I feel the venom busy in my breast;
Approach, and bring my crown, deck'd with the teeth　10
Of that bold Christian who first dar'd deflow'r
The virgins of the Sun; and, dire to tell!
Robb'd Pachacamac's altar of its gems!
I mark'd the spot where they interr'd this traitor,
And once at midnight stole I to his tomb,
And tore his carcass from the earth, and left it
A prey to poisonous flies. Preserve this crown
With sacred secrecy: if e'er returns
Thy much-lov'd mother from the desert woods,
Where, as I hunted late, I hapless lost her,　20
Cherish her age. Tell her, I ne'er have worshipp'd
With those that eat their God. And when disease
Preys on her languid limbs, then kindly stab her
With thine own hands, nor suffer her to linger,
Like Christian cowards, in a life of pain.
I go! great Copac beckons me! Farewell!

A SELECTION

AN ESSAY ON THE GENIUS AND
WRITINGS OF POPE
1782

[A modern critic, F. R. Leavis, has stated that the assumptions we usually make about poetry were first formulated in the prefatory letter to Warton's essay; these assumptions have been attacked by the most recent critics.]

To THE REVEREND DR. YOUNG, RECTOR OF WELWYN IN HERTFORD-SHIRE

DEAR SIR,

Permit me to break into your retirement, the residence of virtue and literature, and to trouble you with a few reflections on the merits and real character of an admired author, and on other collateral subjects of criticism that will naturally arise in the course of such an inquiry. No love of singularity, no affectation of paradoxical opinions, gave rise to the following work. I revere the memory of Pope, I respect and honor his abilities; but I do not think him at the head of his profession. In other words, in that species of poetry wherein Pope excelled, he is superior to all mankind: and I only say that this species of poetry is not the most excellent one of the art.

We do not, it should seem, sufficiently attend to the difference there is betwixt a *man of wit*, a *man of sense*, and a *true poet*. Donne and Swift were undoubtedly men of wit and men of sense: but what traces have they left of *pure poetry*? It is remarkable that Dryden says of Donne, "He was the greatest wit, though not the greatest poet of this nation." Fontenelle and La Motte are entitled to the former character; but what can they urge to gain the latter? Which of these characters is the most valuable and useful is entirely out of the question: all I plead for is to have their several provinces kept distinct from each other, and to impress on the reader that a clear head and acute understanding are not sufficient, alone, to make a *poet;* that the most solid observations on human life, expressed with the utmost elegance and brevity, are *morality* and not *poetry;* that the *Epistles* of Boileau in rhyme are no more poetical than the *Characters* of La Bruyère in prose; and that it is a creative and glowing *imagination*, "acer spiritus ac vis," and that alone, that can stamp a writer with this exalted and very uncommon character, which so few possess, and which so few can properly judge. . . .

The sublime and the pathetic are the two chief nerves of all genuine poesy. What is there transcendently sublime or pathetic in Pope? In his works there is, indeed, "nihil inane, nihil arcessitum; —puro tamen fonti quam magno flumini proprior," [1] as the excellent Quintilian remarks of Lysias. And because I am perhaps unwilling to speak out in plain English, I will adopt the following passage of Voltaire, which, in my opinion, as exactly characterizes Pope as it does his model Boileau, for whom it was originally designed: "Incapable peut-être du sublime qui élève l'âme, et du sentiment qui l'attendrit, mais fait pour éclairer ceux à qui la nature accorda l'un et l'autre, laborieux, sévère, précis, pur, harmonieux, il devint, enfin, le poète de la raison." [2]

Our English poets may, I think, be disposed in four different classes and degrees. In the first class I would place our only three sublime and pathetic poets: Spenser, Shakespeare, Milton. In the second class should be ranked such as possessed the true poetical genius in a more moderate degree, but who had noble talents for moral, ethical, and panegyrical poesy. At the head of these are Dryden, Prior, Addison, Cowley, Waller, Garth, Fenton, Gay, Denham, Parnell. In the third class may be placed men of wit, of elegant taste, and lively fancy in describing familiar life, though not the higher scenes of poetry. Here may be numbered Butler, Swift, Rochester, Donne, Dorset, Oldham. In the fourth class the mere versifiers, however smooth and mellifluous some of them may be thought, should be disposed. Such as Pitt, Sandys, Fairfax, Broome, Buckingham, Lansdown. This enumeration is not intended as a complete catalogue of writers, and in their proper order, but only to mark out briefly the different species of our celebrated authors. In which of these classes Pope deserves to be placed, the following work is intended to determine.

I am, Dear Sir,

Your affectionate

And faithful servant.

. . . .

1 "Nothing empty, nothing far-fetched—rather like a pure spring than a great river." Quintilian, *Institutes* X. i.

2 "Perhaps incapable of sublimity, which elevates the soul, or of tenderness, which softens it, but made to enlighten those to whom nature has granted both—industrious, exacting, precise, clear, harmonious, he became, in fine, the poet of reason."

Correctness is a vague term, frequently used without meaning and precision. It is perpetually the nauseous cant of the French critics, and of their advocates and pupils, that the English writers are generally *incorrect*. If *correctness* implies an absence of petty faults, this perhaps may be granted. If it means, that, because their tragedians have avoided the irregularities of Shakespeare, and have observed a juster economy in their fables, therefore the *Athalia*,[3] for instance, is preferable to *Lear*, the notion is groundless and absurd. The *Henriade* is free from any very gross faults; but who will dare to rank it with the *Paradise Lost?* The declamations with which some of their most perfect tragedies abound may be reckoned as contrary to the nature of that species of poetry, and as destructive of its end, as the fools or grave-diggers of Shakespeare. That the French may boast some excellent critics, particularly Bossu, Boileau, Fénelon, and Brumoy, cannot be denied; but that these are sufficient to form a taste upon, without having recourse to the genuine fountains of all polite literature, I mean the Grecian writers, no one but a superficial sciolist can allow.

I conclude these reflections with a remarkable fact. In no polished nation, after criticism has been much studied and the rules of writing established, has any very extraordinary work ever appeared. This has visibly been the case in Greece, in Rome, and in France; after Aristotle, Horace, and Boileau, had written their *Arts of Poetry*. In our own country, the rules of the drama, for instance, were never more completely understood than at present: yet what *uninteresting*, though *faultless*, tragedies, have we lately seen? So much better is our judgment than our execution. How to account for the fact here mentioned, adequately and justly, would be attended with all those difficulties that await discussions relative to the productions of the human mind; and to the delicate and secret causes that influence them. Whether or no the natural powers be not confined and debilitated by that timidity and caution which is occasioned by a rigid regard to the dictates of art; or whether that philosophical, that geometrical, and systematical spirit so much in vogue, which has spread itself from the sciences even into polite literature, by consulting only *reason*, has not diminished and destroyed *sentiment;* and made our poets write from and to the *head* rather than the *heart:* or whether, lastly, when just models, from which the rules have necessarily been drawn, have once appeared, succeeding writers, by vainly and ambitiously striving to surpass those just models, and to shine and surprise, do not

---

3 By Racine. The *Henriade* was an epic by Voltaire (1723).

become stiff, and forced, and affected in their thoughts and diction. . . .

Thus I have endeavored to give a critical account, with freedom, but it is hoped with impartiality, of each of Pope's works; by which review it will appear that the largest portion of them is of the didactic, moral, and satiric kind; and consequently, not of the most poetic species of poetry; whence it is manifest that good sense and judgment were his characteristical excellencies, rather than fancy and invention: not that the author of *The Rape of the Lock* and *Eloisa* can be thought to want imagination; but because his imagination was not his predominant talent, because he indulged it not, and because he gave not so many proofs of this talent as of the other. This turn of mind led him to admire French models; he studied Boileau attentively, formed himself upon him, as Milton formed himself upon the Grecian and Italian sons of Fancy. He stuck to describing modern manners; but those manners, because they are familiar, uniform, and polished, are, in their very nature, unfit for any lofty effort of the Muse. He gradually became one of the most correct, even, and exact poets that ever wrote; polishing his pieces with a care and assiduity that no business or avocation ever interrupted; so that if he does not frequently ravish and transport his reader, yet he does not disgust him with unexpected inequalities, and absurd improprieties. Whatever poetical enthusiasm he actually possessed, he withheld and stifled. The perusal of him affects not our minds with such strong emotions as we feel from Homer and Milton; so that no man of a true poetical spirit, is master of himself while he reads them. Hence, he is a writer fit for universal perusal; adapted to all ages and stations; for the old and for the young; the man of business and the scholar. He who would think *The Faerie Queen, Palamon and Arcite, The Tempest,* or *Comus* childish and romantic might relish Pope. Surely, it is no narrow and niggardly encomium, to say he is the great Poet of Reason, the first of ethical authors in verse. And this species of writing is, after all, the surest road to an extensive reputation. It lies more level to the general capacities of men, than the higher flights of more genuine poetry. We all remember when even a Churchill was more in vogue than a Gray. He that treats of fashionable follies and the topics of the day, that describes present persons and recent events, finds many readers whose understandings and whose passions he gratifies. The name of Chesterfield on one hand, and of Walpole on the other, failed not to make a poem bought up and talked of. And it cannot be doubted that the odes of Horace which celebrated, and the satires which ridiculed, well-known and real characters at Rome, were more frequently cited, than the *Aeneid* and the *Georgic* of Vergil.

Where, then, according to the question proposed at the beginning of this essay, shall we with justice be authorized to place our admired Pope? Not, assuredly, in the same rank with Spenser, Shakespeare, and Milton; however justly we may applaud the *Eloisa* and *Rape of the Lock;* but, considering the correctness, elegance, and utility of his works, the weight of sentiment, and the knowledge of man they contain, we may venture to assign him a place next to Milton, and just above Dryden. Yet, to bring our minds steadily to make this decision, we must forget, for a moment, the divine *Music Ode* of Dryden; and may perhaps then be compelled to confess that though Dryden be the greater genius, yet Pope is the better artist.

The preference here given to Pope above other modern English poets, it must be remembered, is founded on the excellencies of his works in general, and taken all together; for there are parts and passages in other modern authors, in Young and in Thomson, for instance, equal to any of Pope; and he has written nothing in a strain so truly sublime, as *The Bard* of Gray.

Thomas Warton, Junior

1728-1790

THE PLEASURES OF MELANCHOLY

*Praecipe lugubres
Cantus, Melpomene!* [1]

[1747], 1757

Mother of musings, Contemplation sage,
Whose grotto stands upon the topmost rock
Of Teneriffe; 'mid the tempestuous night,
On which, in calmest meditation held,
Thou hear'st with howling winds the beating rain
And drifting hail descend; or if the skies

---

[1] "Begin your mournful songs, Melpomene!"

Unclouded shine, and thro' the blue serene
Pale Cynthia rolls her silver-axled car,
Whence gazing steadfast on the spangled vault
Raptur'd thou sitt'st, while murmurs indistinct   10
Of distant billows soothe thy pensive ear
With hoarse and hollow sounds; secure, self-blest,
There oft thou listen'st to the wild uproar
Of fleets encount'ring, that in whispers low
Ascends the rocky summit, where thou dwell'st
Remote from man, conversing with the spheres!
O lead me, Queen sublime, to solemn glooms
Congenial with my soul; to cheerless shades,
To ruin'd seats, to twilight cells and bowers,
Where thoughtful Melancholy loves to muse,   20
Her fav'rite midnight haunts. The laughing scenes
Of purple Spring, where all the wanton train
Of Smiles and Graces seem to lead the dance
In sportive round, while from their hands they shower
Ambrosial blooms and flow'rs, no longer charm;
Tempe,[2] no more I court thy balmy breeze,
Adieu, green vales! ye broider'd meads, adieu!
  Beneath yon ruin'd abbey's moss-grown piles
Oft let me sit, at twilight hour of eve,
Where thro' some western window the pale moon   30
Pours her long-levell'd rule of streaming light;
While sullen sacred silence reigns around,
Save the lone screech-owl's note, who builds his bower
Amid the mould'ring caverns dark and damp,
Or the calm breeze, that rustles in the leaves
Of flaunting ivy, that with mantle green
Invests some wasted tow'r. Or let me tread
Its neighb'ring walk of pines, where mus'd of old
The cloister'd brothers: through the gloomy void
That far extends beneath their ample arch   40
As on I pace, religious horror wraps
My soul in dread repose. But when the world
Is clad in Midnight's raven-colour'd robe,
'Mid hollow charnel let me watch the flame
Of taper dim, shedding a livid glare
O'er the wan heaps; while airy voices talk
Along the glimm'ring walls, or ghostly shape
At distance seen, invites with beck'ning hand

2 The vale in Thessaly through which flows the Peneus.

My lonesome steps, thro' the far-winding vaults.
Nor undelightful is the solemn noon 50
Of night, when haply wakeful from my couch
I start: lo, all is motionless around!
Roars not the rushing wind; the sons of men
And every beast in mute oblivion lie;
All nature's hush'd in silence and in sleep.
Oh then how fearful is it to reflect,
That thro' the still globe's awful solitude,
No being wakes but me! till stealing sleep
My drooping temples bathes in opiate dews.
Nor then let dreams, of wanton folly born, 60
My senses lead thro' flow'ry paths of joy;
But let the sacred Genius of the night
Such mystic visions send as Spenser saw,
When through bewild'ring Fancy's magic maze,
To the fell house of Busyrane, he led
Th' unshaken Britomart; or Milton knew,
When in abstracted thought he first conceiv'd
All heav'n in tumult, and the seraphim
Come tow'ring, arm'd in adamant and gold.
Let others love soft Summer's ev'ning smiles, 70
As listening to the distant water-fall,
They mark the blushes of the streaky west;
I choose the pale December's foggy glooms.
Then, when the sullen shades of ev'ning close,
Where thro' the room a blindly-glimm'ring gleam
The dying embers scatter, far remote
From Mirth's mad shouts, that thro' th' illumin'd roof
Resound with festive echo, let me sit,
Blest with the lowly cricket's drowsy dirge.
Then let my thought contemplative explore 80
This fleeting state of things, the vain delights,
The fruitless toils, that still our search elude,
As thro' the wilderness of life we rove.
This sober hour of silence will unmask
False Folly's smile, that like the dazzling spells
Of wily Comus cheat th' unweeting eye
With blear illusion, and persuade to drink
That charmed cup, which Reason's mintage fair
Unmolds, and stamps the monster on the man.
Eager we taste, but in the luscious draught 90
Forget the poisonous dregs that lurk beneath.

Few know that elegance of soul refin'd,
Whose soft sensation feels a quicker joy
From Melancholy's scenes, than the dull pride
Of tasteless splendour and magnificence
Can e'er afford. Thus Eloïse, whose mind
Had languish'd to the pangs of melting love,
More genuine transport found, as on some tomb
Reclin'd, she watch'd the tapers of the dead;
Or through the pillar'd aisles, amid pale shrines   100
Of imag'd saints, and intermingled graves,
Mus'd a veil'd votaress; than Flavia feels,
As thro' the mazes of the festive ball,
Proud of her conquering charms, and beauty's blaze,
She floats amid the silken sons of dress,
And shines the fairest of th' assembled fair.

When azure noontide cheers the dædal globe,
And the blest regent of the golden day
Rejoices in his bright meridian tower,
How oft my wishes ask the night's return   110
That best befriends the melancholy mind!
Hail, sacred Night! thou too shalt share my song!
Sister of ebon-sceptred Hecate, hail!
Whether in congregated clouds thou wrap'st
Thy viewless chariot, or with silver crown
Thy beaming head encirclest, ever hail!
What tho' beneath thy gloom the sorceress-train,
Far in obscured haunt of Lapland moors,
With rhymes uncouth the bloody cauldron bless;
Tho' Murder wan beneath thy shrouding shade   120
Summons her slow-ey'd votaries to devise
Of secret slaughter, while by one blue lamp
In hideous conf'rence sits the list'ning band,
And starts at each low wind, or wakeful sound:
What tho' thy stay the pilgrim curseth oft,
As all benighted in Arabian wastes
He hears the wilderness around him howl
With roaming monsters, while on his hoar head
The black-descending tempest ceaseless beats;
Yet more delightful to my pensive mind   130
Is thy return, than blooming morn's approach,
Ev'n then, in youthful pride of opening May,
When from the portals of the saffron east
She sheds fresh roses, and ambrosial dews.

The Honorable Frances Duncombe by Thomas Gainsborough

English Tavern and Coffee House
From a copper engraving

Gaming Room by Rowlandson
From a wash drawing

Yet not ungrateful is the morn's approach,
When dropping wet she comes, and clad in clouds,
While thro' the damp air scowls the louring south,
Blackening the landscape's face, that grove and hill
In formless vapours undistinguish'd swim:
Th' afflicted songsters of the sadden'd groves   140
Hail not the sullen gloom; the waving elms
That, hoar thro' time, and rang'd in thick array,
Enclose with stately row some rural hall,
Are mute, nor echo with the clamours hoarse
Of rooks rejoicing on their airy boughs;
While to the shed the dripping poultry crowd,
A mournful train; secure the village hind
Hangs o'er the crackling blaze, nor tempts the storm;
Fix'd in th' unfinish'd furrow rests the plough:
Rings not the high wood with enliven'd shouts   150
Of early hunter: all is silence drear;
And deepest sadness wraps the face of things.
    Thro' Pope's soft song tho' all the Graces breathe,
And happiest art adorn his Attic page;
Yet does my mind with sweeter transport glow,
As at the root of mossy trunk reclined,
In magic Spenser's wildly-warbled song
I see deserted Una wander wide
Thro' wasteful solitudes, and lurid heaths,
Weary, forlorn; than when the fated fair   160
Upon the bosom bright of silver Thames
Launches in all the lustre of brocade,
Amid the splendours of the laughing sun.
The gay description palls upon the sense,
And coldly strikes the mind with feeble bliss.
    Ye youths of Albion's beauty-blooming isle,
Whose brows have worn the wreath of luckless love,
Is there a pleasure like the pensive mood,
Whose magic wont to soothe your soften'd souls?
Oh tell how rapturous the joy, to melt   170
To Melody's assuasive voice; to bend
Th' uncertain step along the midnight mead,
And pour your sorrows to the pitying moon,
By many a slow trill from the bird of woe
Oft interrupted; in embow'ring woods
By darksome brook to muse, and there forget
The solemn dullness of the tedious world,

While Fancy grasps the visionary fair;
And now no more th' abstracted ear attends
The water's murm'ring lapse, th' entranced eye   180
Pierces no longer through th' extended rows
Of thick-ranged trees; till haply from the depth
The woodman's stroke, or distant tinkling team,
Or heifers rustling through the brake, alarms
Th' illuded sense, and mars the golden dream.
These are delights that absence drear has made
Familiar to my soul, e'er since the form
Of young Sapphira, beauteous as the spring,
When from her violet-woven couch awaked
By frolic Zephyr's hand, her tender cheek   190
Graceful she lifts, and blushing from her bower
Issues to clothe in gladsome-glistering green
The genial globe, first met my dazzled sight:
These are delights unknown to minds profane,
And which alone the pensive soul can taste.
   The taper'd choir, at the late hour of prayer,
Oft let me tread, while to th' according voice
The many-sounding organ peals on high
The clear slow-dittied chaunt, or varied hymn,
Till all my soul is bath'd in ecstasies,   200
And lapp'd in Paradise. Or let me sit
Far in sequester'd aisles of the deep dome,
There lonesome listen to the sacred sounds,
Which, as they lengthen thro' the Gothic vaults,
In hollow murmurs reach my ravish'd ear.
Nor when the lamps expiring yield to night,
And solitude returns, would I forsake
The solemn mansion, but attentive mark
The due clock swinging slow with sweepy sway,
Measuring Time's flight with momentary sound.   210
   Nor let me fail to cultivate my mind
With the soft thrillings of the tragic Muse,
Divine Melpomene, sweet Pity's nurse,
Queen of the stately step, and flowing pall.
Now let Monimia [3] mourn with streaming eyes
Her joys incestuous, and polluted love:
Now let soft Juliet in the gaping tomb
Print the last kiss on her true Romeo's lips,
His lips yet reeking from the deadly draught:

___
[3] In Otway's *The Orphan* (1680).

Or Jaffier [4] kneel for one forgiving look.   220
Nor seldom let the Moor on Desdemone
Pour the misguided threats of jealous rage.
By soft degrees the manly torrent steals
From my swoln eyes; and at a brother's woe
My big heart melts in sympathizing tears.
What are the splendours of the gaudy court,
Its tinsel trappings, and its pageant pomps?
To me far happier seems the banish'd lord,
Amid Siberia's unrejoicing wilds
Who pines all lonesome, in the chambers hoar   230
Of some high castle shut, whose windows dim
In distant ken discover trackless plains,
Where Winter ever whirls his icy car;
While still repeated objects of his view,
The gloomy battlements, and ivied spires,
That crown the solitary dome, arise;
While from the topmost turret the slow clock,
Far heard along th' inhospitable wastes,
With sad-returning chime awakes new grief;
Ev'n he far happier seems than is the proud,   240
The potent satrap, whom he left behind
'Mid Moscow's golden palaces, to drown
In ease and luxury the laughing hours.
Illustrious objects strike the gazer's mind
With feeble bliss, and but allure the sight,
Nor rouse with impulse quick th' unfeeling heart.
Thus seen by shepherd from Hymettus' [5] brow,
What dædal landscapes smile! here palmy groves
Resounding once with Plato's voice, arise,
Amid whose umbrage green her silver head   250
Th' unfading olive lifts; here vine-clad hills
Lay forth their purple store, and sunny vales
In prospect vast their level laps expand,
Amid whose beauties glistering Athens towers.
Tho' thro' the blissful scenes Ilissus roll
His sage-inspiring flood, whose winding marge
The thick-wove laurel shades; tho' roseate Morn
Pour all her splendours on th' empurpled scene;
Yet feels the hoary hermit truer joys,
As from the cliff, that o'er his cavern hangs,   260
He views the piles of fall'n Persepolis

4 In Otway's *Venice Preserved* (1682).   5 A mountain near Athens.

In deep arrangement hide the darksome plain.
Unbounded waste! the mould'ring obelisk
Here, like a blasted oak, ascends the clouds;
Here Parian domes their vaulted halls disclose
Horrid with thorn, where lurks th' unpitying thief,
Whence flits the twilight-loving bat at eve,
And the deaf adder wreathes her spotted train,
The dwellings once of elegance and art.
Here temples rise, amid whose hallow'd bounds   270
Spires the black pine, while thro' the naked street,
Once haunt of tradeful merchants, springs the grass:
Here columns heap'd on prostrate columns, torn
From their firm base, increase the mould'ring mass.
Far as the sight can pierce, appear the spoils
Of sunk magnificence! a blended scene
Of moles, fanes, arches, domes, and palaces,
Where, with his brother Horror, Ruin sits.
    O, come then, Melancholy, queen of thought!
O, come, with saintly look, and steadfast step,   280
From forth thy cave embower'd with mournful yew,
Where ever to the curfew's solemn sound
List'ning thou sitt'st, and with thy cypress bind
Thy votary's hair, and seal him for thy son.
But never let Euphrosyne [6] beguile
With toys of wanton mirth my fixed mind,
Nor in my path her primrose garland cast.
Tho' 'mid her train the dimpled Hebe bare
Her rosy bosom to th' enamour'd view;
Though Venus, mother of the Smiles and Loves,   290
And Bacchus, ivy-crown'd in citron bower,
With her on nectar-streaming fruitage feast.
What tho' 'tis hers to calm the lowring skies,
And at her presence mild th' embattled clouds
Disperse in air, and o'er the face of heaven
New day diffusive gleam at her approach;
Yet are these joys that Melancholy gives,
Than all her witless revels happier far;
These deep-felt joys, by Contemplation taught.
    Then ever, beauteous Contemplation, hail!   300
From thee began, auspicious maid, my song,
With thee shall end; for thou art fairer far

6 The Grace presiding over social pleasures.

Than are the nymphs of Cirrha's [7] mossy grot;
To loftier rapture thou canst wake the thought
Than all the fabling poet's boasted powers.
Hail, queen divine! whom, as tradition tells,
Once in his evening walk a Druid found,
Far in a hollow glade of Mona's [8] woods;
And piteous bore with hospitable hand
To the close shelter of his oaken bower.   310
There soon the sage admiring mark'd the dawn
Of solemn musing in your pensive thought;
For, when a smiling babe, you lov'd to lie
Oft deeply list'ning to the rapid roar
Of wood-hung Meinai, stream of Druids old.

SONNET III

WRITTEN IN A BLANK LEAF OF DUGDALE'S MONASTICON [1]

1777

Deem not, devoid of elegance, the sage,
By Fancy's genuine feelings unbeguil'd,
Of painful Pedantry the poring child;
Who turns, of these proud domes, th' historic page,
Now sunk by Time, and Henry's fiercer rage.
Think'st thou the warbling Muses never smil'd
On his lone hours? Ingenuous views engage
His thoughts, on themes, unclassic falsely styl'd,
Intent. While cloister'd Piety displays
Her mouldering roll, the piercing eye explores   10
New manners, and the pomp of elder days,
Whence culls the pensive bard his pictur'd stores.
Nor rough, nor barren, are the winding ways
Of hoar Antiquity, but strown with flowers.

7 Cirra, one of the two peaks of Parnassus.
8 Mona (Anglesey) was inhabited by Druids.

1 William Dugdale's *Monasticon Anglicanum* (1655–73), a history of English monasteries.

When a building or other object has been once viewed from its proper point, the foot should never travel to it by the same path which the eye has traveled over before. Lose the object, and draw nigh obliquely.

The side trees and vistas should be so circumstanced as to afford a probability that they grew by nature.

Ruinated structures appear to derive their power of pleasing from the irregularity of surface which is variety, and the latitude they afford the imagination to conceive an enlargement of their dimensions or to recollect any events or circumstances appertaining to their pristine grandeur, so far as concerns grandeur and solemnity. The breaks in them should be as bold and abrupt as possible.—If mere beauty be aimed at (which, however, is not their chief excellence) the waving line with more easy transitions will become of greater importance.—Events relating to them may be simulated by numberless little artifices; but it is ever to be remembered that high hills and sudden descents are most suitable to castles, and fertile vales near wood and water most imitative of the usual situation for abbeys and religious houses; large oaks in particular are essential to these latter,

> Whose branching arms, and reverend height,
> Admit a dim religious light.

A cottage is a pleasing object partly on account of the variety it may introduce; on account of the tranquillity that seems to reign there; and perhaps (I am somewhat afraid) on account of the pride of human nature:

> Longi alterius spectare laborem.[3]

In a scene presented to the eye objects should never lie so much to the right or left as to give it any uneasiness in the examination. Sometimes, however, it may be better to admit valuable objects even with this disadvantage. They should else never be seen beyond a certain angle. The eye must be easy before it can be pleased.

No mere slope from one side to the other can be agreeable ground. The eye requires a balance—i.e., a degree of uniformity;

---

3 "To see another's labor from afar." [Lucretius, *De Rerum Natura*, II 2]

but this may be otherwise effected, and the rule should be understood with some limitation.

—Each alley has its brother,
And half the platform just reflects the other.[4]

Let us examine what may be said in favor of that regularity which Mr. Pope exposes. Might he not seemingly as well object to the disposition of an human face because it has an eye or cheek that is the very picture of its companion? Or does not Providence, who has observed this regularity in the external structure of our bodies and disregarded it within, seem to consider it as a beauty? The arms, the limbs, and the several parts of them correspond, but it is not the same case with the thorax and the abdomen. I believe one is generally solicitous for a kind of balance in a landskip; and if I am not mistaken the painters generally furnish one: a building, for instance, on one side contrasted by a group of trees, a large oak, or a rising hill on the other. Whence then does this taste proceed but from the love we bear to regularity in perfection? After all, in regard to gardens, the shape of ground, the disposition of trees, and the figure of water must be sacred to nature, and no forms must be allowed that make a discovery of art.

Urns are more solemn if large and plain; more beautiful if less and ornamented. Solemnity is perhaps their point, and the situation of them should still co-operate with it.

Concerning scenes, the more uncommon they appear, the better, provided they form a picture and include nothing that pretends to be of nature's production and is not. The shape of ground, the site of trees, and the fall of water are nature's province. Whatever thwarts her is treason.

On the other hand, buildings and the works of art need have no other reference to nature than that they afford the *eusemnon* [5] with which the human mind is delighted.

Art should never be allowed to set a foot in the province of nature otherwise than clandestinely and by night. Whenever she is allowed to appear here, and men begin to compromise the differ-

---

4 Pope *Moral Essays* IV. 117–18.　　　　5 Embellishment.

ence—night, Gothicism, confusion, and absolute chaos are come again.

Hedges, appearing as such, are universally bad. They discover art in nature's province.

Trees in hedges partake of their artificiality, and become a part of them. There is no more sudden and obvious improvement than a hedge removed and the trees remaining; yet not in such a manner as to mark out the former hedge.

Water should ever appear as an irregular lake or winding stream.

Grandeur and beauty are so very opposite that you often diminish the one as you increase the other. Variety is most akin to the latter, simplicity to the former.

A SELECTION

Horace Walpole

1717–1797

ESSAY ON MODERN GARDENING

1771

[Although a number of Walpole's statements—his attribution of the ha-ha to Bridgman, for example—are inaccurate, his essay remains a valuable commentary upon the "natural" garden and the taste for "nature."]

IT is more extraordinary that having so long ago stumbled on the principle of modern gardening, we should have persisted in retaining its reverse, symmetrical and unnatural gardens. . .

One man, one great man we had, on whom nor education nor custom could impose their prejudices; who, *on evil days though fallen, and with darkness and solitude compassed round,* judged that the mistaken and fantastic ornaments he had seen in gardens were unworthy of the almighty hand that planted the delights of

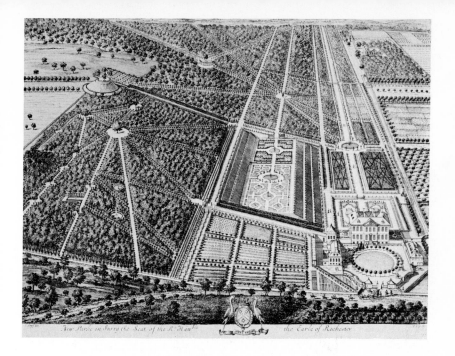

Garden, New Park, Surrey

The Mall in St. James's Park
by Thomas Gainsborough

View of the Chapel in the
Garden at Strawberry Hill

North Front of Strawberry Hill

Paradise. He seems with the prophetic eye of taste (as I have heard taste well defined) to have conceived, to have foreseen, modern gardening, as Lord Bacon announced the discoveries since made by experimental philosophy. The description of Eden is a warmer and more just picture of the present style than Claude Lorrain could have painted from Hagley or Stourhead. The first lines I shall quote exhibit Stourhead on a more magnificent scale:

> Thro' Eden went a river large,
> Nor chang'd his course, but thro' the shaggy hill
> Pass'd underneath ingulph'd, for God had thrown
> That mountain as his garden-mound, high rais'd
> Upon the rapid current—

Hagley seems pictured in what follows:

> which thro' veins
> Of porous earth with kindly thirst updrawn,
> Rose a fresh fountain, and with many a rill
> Water'd the garden—

What coloring, what freedom of pencil, what landscape in these lines:

> ——from that sapphire fount the crisped brooks,
> Rolling on orient pearl and sands of gold,
> With mazy error under pendant shades
> Ran nectar, visiting each plant, and fed
> Flow'rs worthy of Paradise, which not *nice art*
> In beds and curious knots, but *nature* boon
> Pour'd forth profuse on hill and dale and plain,
> Both where the morning sun first warmly smote
> The *open field*, and where the unpierc'd shade
> Imbrown'd the noon-tide bow'rs.—*Thus was this place*
> *A happy rural seat of various view.*

Read this transporting description, paint to your mind the scenes that follow, contrast them with the savage but respectable terror with which the poet guards the bounds of his Paradise, fenced

> ——with the champaign head
> Of a steep wilderness, whose hairy sides
> With thicket overgrown, grotesque and wild
> Access denied; and over head upgrew
> Insuperable height of loftiest shade,
> Cedar and pine, and fir, and branching palm,
> A sylvan scene, and as the ranks ascend,
> Shade above shade, a woody theatre
> Of stateliest view—

and then recollect that the author of this sublime vision had never seen a glimpse of anything like what he has imagined, that his favorite ancients had dropped not a hint of such divine scenery, and that the conceits in Italian gardens and Theobalds and None-such [1] were the brightest originals that his memory could furnish. His intellectual eye saw a nobler plan, so little did he suffer by the loss of sight. It sufficed him to have seen the materials with which he could work. The vigor of a boundless imagination told him how a plan might be disposed that would embellish nature and restore art to its proper office, the just improvement or imitation of it.

It is necessary that the concurrent testimony of the age should swear to posterity that the description above quoted was written about half a century before the introduction of modern garden-ing, or our incredulous descendants will defraud the poet of half his glory by being persuaded that he copied some garden or gardens he had seen—so minutely do his ideas correspond with the present standard. But what shall we say for that intervening half century who could read that plan and never attempt to put it in execution?

Now let us turn to an admired writer posterior to Milton and see how cold, how insipid, how tasteless is his account of what he pro-nounced a perfect garden. I speak not of his style, which it was not necessary for him to animate with the coloring and glow of poetry. It was his want of ideas, of imagination, of taste that I censure, when he dictated on a subject that is capable of all the graces that a knowledge of beautiful nature can bestow. Sir William Temple [2] was an excellent man; Milton a genius of the first order. . . .

We have seen what Moor Park was when pronounced a stand-ard. But as no succeeding generation in an opulent and luxurious country contents itself with the perfection established by its an-cestors, more perfect perfection was still sought; and improve-ments had gone on till London and Wise had stocked our gardens with giants, animals, monsters, coats of arms and mottoes in yew, box, and holly. Absurdity could go no farther, and the tide turned. Bridgman, the next fashionable designer of gardens, was far more chaste; and whether from good sense, or that the nation had been struck and reformed by the admirable paper in the *Guardian*, No. 173,[3] he banished verdant sculpture, and did not even revert to the square precision of the foregoing age. He enlarged his plans, dis-

---

1 Theobalds was the famous garden of Lord Burleigh, in Hertfordshire; Nonesuch was the famous estate of Henry VIII.

2 The reference is to the essay *Upon the Gardens of Epicurus: or Of Gardening in*

1685 (1690) by Sir William Temple, of Moor Park, early patron of Swift.

3 Written by Pope to ridicule "Adam and Eve in yew" and "Ben Jonson in laurel."

dained to make every division tally to its opposite, and though he still adhered much to straight walks with high clipped hedges, they were only his great lines; the rest he diversified by wilderness, and with loose groves of oak, though still within surrounding hedges. I have observed in the garden at Gubbins [4] in Hertfordshire many detached thoughts that strongly indicate the dawn of modern taste. As his reformation gained footing, he ventured farther, and in the royal garden at Richmond dared to introduce cultivated fields, and even morsels of a forest appearance, by the sides of those endless and tiresome walks that stretched out of one into another without intermission. But this was not till other innovators had broke loose too from rigid symmetry.

But the capital stroke, the leading step to all that has followed, was (I believe the first thought was Bridgman's) the destruction of walls for boundaries, and the invention of fosses—an attempt then deemed so astonishing that the common people called them *Ha!Ha's!* to express their surprise at finding a sudden and unperceived check to their walk.

One of the first gardens planted in this simple though still formal style was my father's at Houghton. It was laid out by Mr. Eyre, an imitator of Bridgman. It contains three-and-twenty acres, then reckoned a considerable portion.

I call a sunk fence the leading step for these reasons: No sooner was this simple enchantment made, than leveling, mowing, and rolling followed. The contiguous ground of the park without the sunk fence was to be harmonized with the lawn within; and the garden in its turn was to be set free from its prim regularity that it might assort with the wilder country without. The sunk fence ascertained the specific garden, but that it might not draw too obvious a line of distinction between the neat and the rude, the contiguous outlying parts came to be included in a kind of general design; and when nature was taken into the plan, under improvements, every step that was made pointed out new beauties and inspired new ideas. At that moment appeared Kent, painter enough to taste the charms of landscape, bold and opinionative enough to dare and to dictate, and born with a genius to strike out a great system from the twilight of imperfect essays. He leaped the fence, and saw that all nature was a garden. He felt the delicious contrast of hill and valley, changing imperceptibly into each other, tasted the beauty of the gentle swell or concave scoop, and remarked how loose groves crowned an easy eminence with happy ornament, and

---

[4] More Hall, in the parish of North Mimms, Hertfordshire; also known as More. Gobions, or Gubbins. The gardens by Bridgman were famous.

while they called in the distant view between their graceful stems, removed and extended the perspective by delusive comparison.

Thus the pencil of his imagination bestowed all the arts of landscape on the scenes he handled. The great principles on which he worked were perspective, and light and shade. Groups of trees broke too uniform or too extensive a lawn; evergreens and woods were opposed to the glare of the champaign, and where the view was less fortunate, or so much exposed as to be beheld at once, he blotted out some parts by thick shades, to divide it into variety, or to make the richest scene more enchanting by reserving it to a farther advance of the spectator's steps. Thus, selecting favorite objects, and veiling deformities by screens of plantation, sometimes allowing the rudest waste to add its foil to the richest theater, he realized the compositions of the greatest masters in painting. Where objects were wanting to animate his horizon, his taste as an architect could bestow immediate termination. His buildings, his seats, his temples were more the works of his pencil than of his compasses. We owe the restoration of Greece and the diffusion of architecture to his skill in landscape.

But of all the beauties he added to the face of this beautiful country, none surpassed his management of water. Adieu to canals, circular basins, and cascades tumbling down marble steps, that last absurd magnificence of Italian and French villas. The forced elevation of cataracts was no more. The gentle stream was taught to serpentize seemingly at its pleasure, and where discontinued by different levels, its course appeared to be concealed by thickets properly interspersed, and glittered again at a distance where it might be supposed naturally to arrive. Its borders were smoothed, but preserved their waving irregularity. A few trees scattered here and there on its edges sprinkled the tame bank that accompanied its meanders; and when it disappeared among the hills, shades descending from the heights leaned towards its progress, and framed the distant point of light under which it was lost, as it turned aside to either hand of the blue horizon.

Thus dealing in none but the colors of nature, and catching its most favorable features, men saw a new creation opening before their eyes. The living landscape was chastened or polished, not transformed. Freedom was given to the forms of trees; they extended their branches unrestricted, and where any eminent oak or master beech had escaped maiming and survived the forest, bush and bramble was removed, and all its honors were restored to distinguish and shade the plain. Where the united plumage of an ancient wood extended wide its undulating canopy and stood venerable in its darkness, Kent thinned the foremost ranks, and left but so many detached and scattered trees as softened the approach of gloom and blended a checkered light with the thus-lengthened shadows of the remaining columns. . . .

A SELECTION

Joseph Heely

fl. 1777

LETTERS ON THE BEAUTIES OF HAGLEY, ENVIL, AND THE LEASOWES

1777

[Heely, delighting in "a sympathizing irregularity," writes one of the most intimate accounts of these three celebrated "natural" gardens; he shows how carefully arranged were the effects of eighteenth-century "simplicity."]

The Leasowes [1]

THE day was yet young; I therefore in passing the small town of Halesowen took a slight but necessary repast, and after traveling about half a mile along the road leading to the large and opulent town of Birmingham, a shady, pleasant lane on my right led me into a steep, gloomy glen, covered with trees, to a rude wall, where a small gate, overarched with stones, proclaimed

THE PRIORY WALK

The moment I entered this quiet and sequestered valley, the superlative genius of Shenstone stood confessed on every object, and struck me with silent admiration.—I turned to a bench under the wall, and sat so absorbed with the charms of a cascade, so powerfully conducted in the very image of nature herself, plunging down a bed of shelving rock and huge, massy stones, that for a long while my attention was lost to everything else. . . .

On emerging from the serene melancholy gloom of the Priory Walk, a semicircular piece of water, winding into another valley that rises from the opposite side of the farm, is generally much admired; as is the landscape, gradually opening as you approach the

1 Which in 1777 was owned by Edward Horne; Shenstone had died in 1763.

pool; of few parts indeed, but makes a pretty lively picture, Hales steeple, wood, pasture, some houses, and an agreeable range of country ending with the lofty hills of Clent. . . .

That much attention has been paid by the designer to the genius of this part of the Leasowes is visible wherever we tread; and by that distinction it is rendered one of the most agreeably finished recesses these grounds have the power of affording.—The hanging declivities that surround the whole valley naturally mark it for obscurity; and these, being mantled with tall forest trees and thicket, happily co-operate in giving it a still more opacious cast, particularly in the narrower part, and yet not wanting a becoming cheerfulness.

The space left by so well-varied an outline is a rambling glade, widening into a circular area, running up and ending in a bold sweep of wood, in which the eye is led to a statue of Faunus, fancifully glancing within a break of the trees.—Hence we learn that part of the dell to be dedicated to the rural deities—pleasingly reminding us of those excursive flights of poetical invention, giving revelry and dance to the ideal god and his jolly crew; while on the other hand, the soft murmurs of a rill, and a lone urn in a solitary nook, have equal power to call the mind from festivity to solemn meditation, and to fill it with those tender feelings of which we are susceptible when any circumstance recurs to revive the memory of a lost friend.

> Ingenio, et amicitae
> Gulielmi Somerville
> G. S. posuit
> Debita spargens lacrima favillam
> Vatis amici

> To the genius and friendship
> Of William Somerville,[2]
> William Shenstone erected this urn,
> Sprinkling with tears the ashes
> Of his poetical friend.

Novelty, the most unexpected, accompanied me wherever I stepped: I no sooner left this scene of entertainment, but another at

THE WOODHOUSE

among a thick plantation of chestnuts, larches, and willows fixed me delighted, as well as in astonishment, at the genius of the de-

2 Author of *The Chase* (1735).

signer, who could so easily call in, from the insignificant place it once was, so much beauty and invention.

A bold, artless cascade, in the very life of nature, precipitately rushes down a rugged heap of rock, huge stones, and cinders, at least one hundred and fifty paces, in a constant succession of abrupt falls, till more calm, it finds its way in a subterraneous passage under the seat into the valley below.

I really find it the greatest difficulty in the world even to attempt a relation that shall convey to you the least idea of its charms. —However, the intermediate ground rises steeply, studded with tall distant oaks, and an urn extremely in character—on each side the plunging torrent, from the bottom to the top, is seen closely connected a variety of different shrubby bushes, alders, yews, ashes, spindling among others of a more capacious bulk, the exposed roots of which, grown over with moss, running over, sideways, or into the stream, have a very singular appearance; nor will you less admire the wild disorder of the numerous trees that clothe the whole glen; you will see some well grown, strong, and upright; others aslant; the trunks of many apparently growing out of the torrent; others touching it with their very branches—thus promiscuously irregular, they not only appear confusion itself, but greatly add to the strange, grotesque appearance of everything about it.

The interweaving of the branches of the trees, and the disposition of them, form a kind of long Gothic arch, with pendant foliage, as you have seen ivy from the breaks of an old ruin—and the water rushing from the farthermost part of it, within the deepest gloom, is truly romantic. . . .

In walking from the priory scene, the ascent soon becomes exceedingly bold: and though I observed to you little appears at this place very interesting, yet the inequality of the ground will have some influence; and when wearied with many a tiresome step, you possess that pleasing relief, offered at

SHEPHERD'S BUSH,

where the acceptable face of variety, shown in a rich, extensive country, so engagingly fills the eye that you forget the toil of climbing it, and the deadness of the preceding walk.

It is here [the] prospect first opens in all its dignity; and with it you will find every accompaniment taste can give in different changes to vary the scene through all the upper range of the Leasowes.

From hence, though the eye only takes in part of the variety which appears from above, the variegated line before you has charms sufficiently attractive to fasten it in delight.—Brierly Hill chapel, over green fields and rambling woods filling the adjacent valley, at a distance of about six or eight miles, is too visible among the gay objects not to merit your attention, so strikingly is it surrounded by a picturesque diversity of hanging woodlands, sloping hills and valleys, intermixed with pasture grounds in the luxury of cultivation. . . .

An easy rise now brought me into a rough sort of quarry ground, on the loftiest eminence of the farm, where, in the midst of a small grove of alders and beeches, stands an antique building called

THE GOTHIC ALCOVE

On the back of which you will read these lines [3] in old black print:

> O you that bathe in courtlye blisse,
>   Or toyle in fortune's giddye spheare;
> Do not too rashlye deeme amysse,
>   Of him that 'bides contented here.
>
> Nor yet disdeigne the russet stoale,
>   Which o'er each carelesse lymbe he flyngs:
> Nor yet deryde the beechen bowle
>   In which he quaffs the lympid springs.
>
> Forgive him, if at eve or dawne,
>   Devoide of worldly cark he stray:
> Or all besyde some flowerye lawne
>   He waste his inofensive daye.
>
> So may he pardonne fraud and stryf,
>   If such in courtlye haunt he see:
> For faults there beene in busye lyfe,
>   From whyche these peaceful glennes are free.

There would have appeared too visible a sameness in the features of the distant horizon here, had not the happy taste of the designer, who well knew how acceptable variety is, stepped in and showed it by secluding some particular objects so lately familiar to the eye.—The Clent Hills, Witchberry Wood, and obelisk, on one side, by a straggling group of trees, which one would imagine was dropped there by the hand of Nature herself, are entirely shut out; as are likewise on the other, by the same device, the hanging wood and part of the grounds. By this he brings novelty; and the

3 By Shenstone himself.

prospect is equally as flattering, although the more distant objects dress in the same direction as at the preceding seat.

But one is rather led here to admire the domain itself—so pastoral —so rich in its appearance—so luxuriant its fields—and in cattle, for whom water, shade, and every domestic accommodation is seen for their repose and use.—Animals not only enrich the landscape, but are indisputably as necessary to finish it as grove, hill, and lawn are to complete it.

From this delightful summit, the path gently descends under a hedge of branching oaks to another bench, where no stroke of art has been used to hinder the eye from ranging over an unlimited and beautiful country. . . .

[Shenstone's] taste, however, notwithstanding he was debarred from showing it in the manner in which his inclination might prompt him, nowhere is seen more striking than in what he has done—he knew that to surprise was to please; that in starting from one extreme to another would have all the effect he wished for; and that his favored recess below, by the rudest approach, even to neglect, down the hedge side and through a glenny wilderness of hazel, alder, and poplar, would by such a circumstance be rendered more agreeably interesting.—I apprehend it is impossible for any man of taste not to notice the niceness of his judgment, after he has passed the dreary way, and finds himself within the shady bowers of

THE LOVER'S WALK

The moment you step into this perfect scene of nature, you will stand in pleasure and delight—and conclude that no sudden transition from the melancholy ever had a finer effect—it is here the Naiades again welcome your approach, and here that variety, in all its enticing smiles, frolics in every corner—not that you enter into the splendid, but into the shady, far-winding recess, formed for contemplation—a recess where one would wish to linger and live.

The principal object your eye is led to, from the first bench, is a piece of water that will ever speak its superior charms from the great difficulty of knowing where to fix upon its bounds; so artfully has the designer concealed them. On one side rises a noble cluster of beeches, rearing from the lawn their bulky trunks, entwining their arms in the luxury of foliage, and impending over the surface of the stream: while more opposite, a bed of spindling alders and willows ranges to some scattered old oaks, through which a perspective of Hales steeple, in the valley, bounded by woods, will not escape your notice.—A ray like this, darting into obscurity, is always pleasing—here in particular, and what I think is considered with much judgment.

You will hardly know how to pass from this amusing spot, though you be assured that every step you take from it is accompanied with something new and entertaining; particularly in the intricate form of the water, which though not large, puzzles, and raises conceptions of a real magnitude; and so various are its changes that in a few paces you will be ready to determine it another.—Sometimes, as the path continues, you will at one place have another glimpse of the spire;—again, through some natural breaks, a windmill, or a cottage, till you arrive at

THE ASSIGNATION SEAT

The late bard of the Leasowes, if some say true, though naturally extremely reserved, even to bashfulness when in company with the ladies, had, notwithstanding, a heart too susceptible to withstand the irresistible glances of acquiescing beauty;—and, I am inclined to believe, he had been known frequently to spend a few of his leisure hours here with a favorite nymph in amorous dalliance—or so—But you know fame is not always to be depended upon.—Why we may not as well suppose he meant only to show by the delicacy of his taste the local propriety of such amusements, and that this place seemed the only one suitably adapted for the cooing of those fond turtles who might occasionally meet here—to improve—

For my own part, I confess I felt its influence, and could not sit without indulging a thousand agreeable ideas—everything around me seemed calculated to infuse the tenderest, warmest wishes—concealment—delicious shade—spreading trees—a calm, transparent stream—to the ear, the soft melody of the adjoining grove, and the distant tinkling of a falling rill.

The subsequent scenery of this arcadian recess runs similarly beautiful with the other. The parts are relative, though they often vary: you will find the lake now changed into a rambling rill, dropping artlessly from above, down rocky breaks: sometimes dividing in its course, running round a bush, large stones, or tree: chirping its intricate meanders into the pool below: while the negligent path on its margin, under the umbrage of the copse, creeps between the thinly scattered trees, some young and flourishing, others crooked and old, slanting over the bubbling current and quivering in the breeze.—Cheerfulness, in the Lover's Walk, hovers about you wherever you tread; and though solitary, it knows no gloom: yet will the urn, as you pass it, in a shrubby angle, when you are sensible of the occasion, demand the tribute of a sigh.

This urn originally was richly gilt and placed here in remembrance of a young lady, a relation of Mr. Shenstone, whom he much loved, and whose death he most sincerely lamented.

Peramabili suae consobrinae
M.D.

To his most amiable cousin
MARIA DOLMAN

On the other side:

AH MARIA!
Puellarum elegantissima
Ah flore venustatis abrepta
Vale!
Heu quanto minus est
Cum reliquis versari,
Quam tui
Meminisse!

AH MARIA!
The most elegant of maidens;
Alas! snatch'd away in
The bloom of beauty;
Farewell!
How much less pleasure there is in surviving
Than in remembering thee!

The path in easy serpentine from hence still continues within the covert of the copse in gradual ascent, retired and close; till an opening (though it is now partly grown up) leads the eye over variegated ground to a glimpse of the house among the trees, and scenes of cultivation beyond, rising up the woody sides of Clent— a cheerful view, succeeded soon after by one as melancholy, at the foot of a precipice, with this line

"Divine oblivion of low-thoughted care."

William Collins (695-78)
Nov 13

1721–1759

WHAT Dr. Johnson called the "enchantment" of Collins is perhaps the most inexplicable of the century. Certain passages are in the same minor key that we detect in Gray and the Wartons. However, a fitfulness, even a wildness, of fancy confuses almost all that Collins wrote, and his classical "forms" like the ode suggest, but do not define. In the "Ode on the Poetical Character" he speaks of "the shad'wy tribes of Mind," and, indeed, he is an oddly "mental" poet, moving in a

> world unknown,
> With all its shadowy shapes.

Collins used to sketch, and his disordered personifications have, individually, a sculpturesque quality not unlike his drawing for a medallion with two antique heads, "over the lower part of the necks of which there shall be a veil thrown, from under which a little *Art* shall appear writing on a Roman scroll, & a Satyr either in contrast holding up another, or writing on part of the same, or suppose the veil to be upheld by Friendship, who may at the same time point to the relievo of the medallion." Here is the academic personification of those odes intended to "revive the just designs of Greece." With an almost painful discontinuity, Collins apostrophizes some quality—Simplicity or Fear —and then enumerates a "train" of attendant qualities. The dislocation of imagery is sometimes as fascinating and disturbing as that in surrealist painting:

> High on some cliff, to Heav'n up-pil'd,
> Of rude access, of prospect wild,
> Where, tangled round the jealous steep,
> Strange shades o'erbrow the valleys deep,
> And holy Genii guard the rock,
> Its glooms embrown, its springs unlock . . .

Some believe that Collins was simply too lazy to correct his verses. It is certain that he suffered from infirmity of mind, which Dr. Johnson attributed to a deficiency of vital rather than intellectual powers. So filled are the poems with ambiguities that it is often difficult to say precisely what the subject is; yet the confusion, the false notes, the discontinuous progress take on a rarely poetical character.

BIOGRAPHICAL NOTES

Son of a Chichester hatter. Attended Winchester School (1733), knew Joseph Warton, and composed the *Persian Eclogues*. Entered Queen's College, Oxford (1740), to prepare for the Church. Transferred to Magdalen (1741). The *Persian Eclogues* printed (1742). Received B.A. (1743) but failed to gain a fellowship. Went to London (1744) and frequented theaters and coffeehouses; met Garrick and Johnson. Formed friendships with Thomson, Armstrong, and Mallet. Was said to be "too indolent even for the army." Dodsley refused to print his poems, which appeared as *Odes on Several Descriptive and Allegorical*

Subjects (1746)—a complete failure. Returned to Chichester to live on a small legacy. Composed *Ode on the Popular Superstitions of the Highlands*, a milestone in "romanticism," and sent it to John Home; the verses were not printed until 1788. Signs of insanity appeared (*ca.* 1751). Cared for during last years by Mrs. Sempell, his sister, who destroyed all his papers at his death.

BIBLIOGRAPHY: *Poems,* ed. Edmund Blunden, 1929. *Drafts and Fragments of Verse from the Manuscripts,* ed. J. S. Cunningham, 1956. Ainsworth, Edward G., *Poor Collins,* 1937. Garrod, H. W., *The Poetry of Collins,* 1928.

PERSIAN ECLOGUES

1742

THE PREFACE

It is with the writings of mankind, in some measure, as with their complexions or their dress; each nation hath a peculiarity in all these to distinguish it from the rest of the world.

The gravity of the Spaniard and the levity of the Frenchman are as evident in all their productions as in their persons themselves; and the style of my countrymen is as naturally strong and nervous as that of an Arabian or Persian is rich and figurative.

There is an elegancy and wildness of thought which recommends all their compositions; and our geniuses are as much too cold for the entertainment of such sentiments as our climate is for their fruits and spices. If any of these beauties are to be found in the following *Eclogues,* I hope my reader will consider them as an argument of their being original. I received them at the hands of a merchant, who had made it his business to enrich himself with the learning, as well as the silks and carpets, of the Persians. The little information I could gather concerning their author was that his name was Abdallah, and that he was a native of Tauris.

It was in that city that he died of a distemper fatal in those parts whilst he was engaged in celebrating the victories of his favorite monarch, the great Abbas. As to the *Eclogues* themselves, they give a very just view of the miseries and inconveniences as well as the felicities that attend one of the finest countries in the East.

The time of the writing them was probably in the beginning of Sha Sultan Hosseyn's reign, the successor of Sefi or Solyman the Second.

Whatever defects, as, I doubt not, there will be many, fall under the reader's observation, I hope his candor will incline him to make the following reflection:

That the works of Orientals contain many peculiarities, and that through defect of language few European translators can do them justice.

ECLOGUE THE THIRD

ABRA; OR, THE GEORGIAN SULTANA

Scene, A forest. Time, The evening.

In Georgia's land, where Tefflis' tow'rs are seen,
In distant view along the level green,
While ev'ning dews enrich the glitt'ring glade,
And the tall forests cast a longer shade,
What time 'tis sweet o'er fields of rice to stray,
Or scent the breathing maize at setting day;
Amidst the maids of Zagen's peaceful grove,
Emyra sung the pleasing cares of love.
    Of Abra first began the tender strain,
Who led her youth with flocks upon the plain: 10
At morn she came those willing flocks to lead,
Where lillies rear them in the wat'ry mead;
From early dawn the live-long hours she told,
Till late at silent eve she penn'd the fold.
Deep in the grove, beneath the secret shade,
A various wreath of od'rous flow'rs she made:
Gay-motley'd pinks and sweet jonquils she chose,
The violet blue that on the moss-bank grows;
All sweet to sense, the flaunting rose was there:
The finish'd chaplet well adorn'd her hair. 20
    Great Abbas chanc'd that fated morn to stray
By Love conducted from the chace away;
Among the vocal vales he heard her song,
And sought the vales and echoing groves among:
At length he found and woo'd the rural maid;
She knew the monarch, and with fear obey'd.
    Be ev'ry youth like royal Abbas mov'd,
And ev'ry Georgian maid like Abra lov'd!

    The royal lover bore her from the plain;
Yet still her crook and bleating flock remain: 30
Oft, as she went, she backward turn'd her view,
And bade that crook and bleating flock adieu.
Fair happy maid! to other scenes remove,
To richer scenes of golden pow'r and love!
Go leave the simple pipe, and shepherd's strain;

With love delight thee, and with Abbas reign.
   Be ev'ry youth like royal Abbas mov'd,
   And ev'ry Georgian maid like Abra lov'd!

Yet, midst the blaze of courts, she fix'd her love
On the cool fountain, or the shady grove;   40
Still with the shepherd's innocence, her mind
To the sweet vale and flow'ry mead inclin'd;
And oft as Spring renew'd the plains with flow'rs,
Breath'd his soft gales, and led the fragrant Hours,
With sure return she sought the sylvan scene,
The breezy mountains, and the forests green.
Her maids around her mov'd, a duteous band!
Each bore a crook, all rural, in her hand:
Some simple lay of flocks and herds they sung;
With joy the mountain and the forest rung.   50
   Be ev'ry youth like royal Abbas mov'd,
   And ev'ry Georgian maid like Abra lov'd!

And oft the royal lover left the care
And thorns of state, attendant on the fair;
Oft to the shades and low-roof'd cots retir'd,
Or sought the vale where first his heart was fir'd:
A russet mantle, like a swain, he wore,
And thought of crowns and busy courts no more.
   Be ev'ry youth like royal Abbas mov'd,
   And ev'ry Georgian maid like Abra lov'd!   60

Blest was the life that royal Abbas led:
Sweet was his love, and innocent his bed.
What if in wealth the noble maid excel;
The simple shepherd girl can love as well.
Let those who rule on Persia's jewell'd throne,
Be fam'd for love, and gentlest love alone;
Or wreathe, like Abbas, full of fair renown,
The lover's myrtle with the warrior's crown.
Oh happy days! the maids around her say;
Oh haste, profuse of blessings, haste away!   70
   Be ev'ry youth like royal Abbas mov'd,
   And ev'ry Georgian maid like Abra lov'd!

ODE TO PITY

1747

O thou, the friend of man assign'd,
With balmy hands his wounds to bind,
    And charm his frantic woe:
When first Distress with dagger keen
Broke forth to waste his destin'd scene,
    His wild unsated foe!

By Pella's bard,[1] a magic name,
By all the griefs his thought could frame,
    Receive my humble rite:
Long, Pity, let the nations view   10
Thy sky-worn robes of tend'rest blue,
    And eyes of dewy light!

But wherefore need I wander wide
To old Ilissus'[2] distant side,
    Deserted stream, and mute?
Wild Arun[3] too has heard thy strains,
And Echo, 'midst my native plains,
    Been sooth'd by Pity's lute.

There first the wren thy myrtles shed
On gentlest Otway's infant head,   20
    To him thy cell was shown;
And while he sung the female heart,
With youth's soft notes unspoil'd by art,
    Thy turtles mix'd their own.

Come, Pity, come, by Fancy's aid,
Ev'n now my thoughts, relenting maid,
    Thy temple's pride design:
Its southern site, its truth compleat
Shall raise a wild enthusiast heat,
    In all who view the shrine.   30

1 Euripides, who died in Pella.
2 The Ilissus flowed through Athens.

3 The River Arun runs by the village in
Sussex where Otway had his birth. [Collins]

There Picture's toils shall well relate,
How Chance, or hard involving Fate,
 O'er mortal bliss prevail:
The buskin'd Muse shall near her stand,
And sighing prompt her tender hand,
 With each disastrous tale.

There let me oft, retir'd by day,
In dreams of passion melt away,
 Allow'd with thee to dwell:
There waste the mournful lamp of night,   40
Till, Virgin, thou again delight
 To hear a British shell!

ODE TO FEAR [1]

1747

STROPHE

Thou, to whom the world unknown
With all its shadowy shapes is shown;
Who see'st appall'd th' unreal scene,
While Fancy lifts the veil between:
 Ah Fear! Ah frantic Fear!
 I see, I see thee near.
I know thy hurried step, thy haggard eye!
Like thee I start, like thee disorder'd fly,
For lo what monsters in thy train appear!
Danger, whose limbs of giant mold   10
What mortal eye can fix'd behold?
Who stalks his round, an hideous form,
Howling amidst the midnight storm,
Or throws him on the ridgy steep
Of some loose hanging rock to sleep:
And with him thousand phantoms join'd,
Who prompt to deeds accurs'd the mind:
And those, the fiends, who near allied,
O'er Nature's wounds and wrecks preside;
Whilst Vengeance, in the lurid air,   20

1 Evidently the "fear" mentioned by Aristotle in discussing tragedy. The preceding ode refers to tragic "pity."

Lifts her red arm, expos'd and bare:
On whom that rav'ning brood of Fate,
Who lap the blood of Sorrow, wait;
Who, Fear, this ghastly train can see,
And look not madly wild, like thee?

EPODE

In earliest Greece to thee with partial choice,
    The grief-full Muse addresst her infant tongue;
The maids and matrons, on her awful voice,
    Silent and pale in wild amazement hung.

Yet he, the bard who first invok'd thy name,[2]   30
    Disdain'd in Marathon its pow'r to feel:
For not alone he nurs'd the poet's flame,
    But reach'd from virtue's hand the patriot's steel.

But who is he whom later garlands grace,
    Who left a while o'er Hybla's dews to rove,[3]
With trembling eyes thy dreary steps to trace,
    Where thou and Furies shar'd the baleful grove?

Wrapt in thy cloudy veil, th' incestuous queen [4]
    Sigh'd the sad call her son and husband heard,
When once alone it broke the silent scene,   40
    And he, the wretch of Thebes, no more appear'd.

O Fear, I know thee by my throbbing heart,
    Thy with'ring pow'r inspir'd each mournful line;
Tho' gentle Pity claim her mingled part,
    Yet all the thunders of the scene are thine!

ANTISTROPHE

Thou who such weary lengths hast past,
Where wilt thou rest, mad nymph, at last?
Say, wilt thou shroud in haunted cell,
Where gloomy Rape and Murder dwell?
Or, in some hollow'd seat,   50
'Gainst which the big waves beat,
Hear drowning seamen's cries in tempests brought!

---

2 Aeschylus, who fought at Marathon.
3 The reference is to Sophocles, whose *Oedipus in Colonus* is set in a "grove."

Hybla was a Sicilan city famed for honey.
4 Jocasta, who unwittingly weds her son Oedipus.

Dark pow'r, with shudd'ring meek submitted thought
Be mine, to read the visions old,
Which thy awak'ning bards have told:
And lest thou meet my blasted view,
Hold each strange tale devoutly true,
Ne'er be I found, by thee o'eraw'd,
In that thrice-hallow'd eve abroad,
When ghosts, as cottage-maids believe,   60
Their pebbled beds permitted leave,
And goblins haunt from fire, or fen,
Or mine, or flood, the walks of men!
   O thou whose spirit most possest
The sacred seat of Shakespear's breast!
By all that from thy prophet broke,
In thy divine emotions spoke:
Hither again thy fury deal,
Teach me but once like him to feel:
His cypress wreath my meed decree,   70
And I, O Fear, will dwell with thee!

ODE TO SIMPLICITY

1747

   O thou by Nature taught,
   To breathe her genuine thought,
In numbers warmly pure, and sweetly strong:
   Who first on mountains wild,
   In Fancy, loveliest child,
Thy babe, or Pleasure's, nurs'd the pow'rs of song!

   Thou, who with hermit heart
   Disdain'st the wealth of art,
And gauds, and pageant weeds, and trailing pall:
   But com'st a decent maid   10
   In Attic robe array'd,
O chaste unboastful nymph, to thee I call!

   By all the honey'd store
   On Hybla's [1] thymy shore,

1 Hybla was a Sicilian city famed for its honey.

By all her blooms, and mingled murmurs dear,
　By her,[2] whose love-lorn woe
　In ev'ning musings slow
Sooth'd sweetly sad Electra's poet's ear: [3]

　By old Cephisus [4] deep,
　Who spread his wavy sweep   20
In warbled wand'rings round thy green retreat,
　On whose enamel'd side
　When holy Freedom died
No equal haunt allur'd thy future feet.

　O sister meek of Truth,
　To my admiring youth,
Thy sober aid and native charms infuse!
　The flow'rs that sweetest breathe,
　Tho' beauty cull'd the wreath,
Still ask thy hand to range their order'd hues.   30

　While Rome could none esteem
　But Virtue's patriot theme,
You lov'd her hills, and led her laureate band:
　But stay'd to sing alone
　To one distinguish'd throne,[5]
And turn'd thy face, and fled her alter'd land.

　No more, in hall or bow'r
　The passions own thy pow'r;
Love, only love, her [6] forceless numbers mean:
　For thou hast left her shrine;   40
　Nor olive more, nor vine,
Shall gain thy feet to bless the servile scene.

　Tho' taste, tho' genius bless,
　To some divine excess,
Faints the cold work till thou inspire the whole;
　What each, what all supply,
　May court, may charm our eye,
Thou, only thou canst raise the meeting soul!

---

2 The nightingale.
3 Sophocles, author of *Electra*.
4 The Cephisus flowed by Athens.

5 That of Augustus.
6 The reference evidently is to Rome after the time of Augustus.

Of these let others ask,
To aid some mighty task,
I only seek to find thy temp'rate vale:
Where oft my reed might sound
To maids and shepherds round,
And all thy sons, O Nature, learn my tale.

50

ODE ON THE POETICAL CHARACTER

1747

I

As once, if not with light regard,
I read aright that gifted bard
(Him whose school above the rest
His loveliest Elfin Queen has blest),
One, only one, unrival'd fair,
Might hope the magic girdle[1] wear,
At solemn turney hung on high,
The wish of each love-darting eye;
Lo! to each other nymph in turn applied,
As if, in air unseen, some hov'ring hand,   10
Some chaste and angel-friend to virgin-fame,
With whisper'd spell had burst the starting band,
It left unblest her loath'd dishonour'd side;
Happier, hopeless fair, if never
Her baffled hand with vain endeavour
Had touch'd that fatal zone to her denied!
Young Fancy thus, to me divinest name,
To whom, prepar'd and bath'd in Heav'n
The cest of amplest pow'r is giv'n:
To few the godlike gift assigns,   20
To gird their blest, prophetic loins,
And gaze her visions wild, and feel unmix'd her flame!

II

The band, as fairy legends say,
Was wove on that creating day,
When He, who call'd with thought to birth
Yon tented sky, this laughing earth,

1 The girdle of Florimel in the *Faerie Queene* IV. v.

[handwritten left margin: giving dignity to fancy]

And drest with springs, and forests tall,
And pour'd the main engirting all,
Long by the lov'd Enthusiast [2] woo'd,
Himself in some diviner mood,   30
Retiring, sate with her alone,
And plac'd her on his sapphire throne;
The whiles, the vaulted shrine around, *[handwritten: all thru heavens]*
Seraphic wires were heard to sound,
Now sublimest triumph swelling,
Now on love and mercy dwelling;
And she, from out the veiling cloud,
Breath'd her magic notes aloud:

[handwritten left margin: Appollo →]

And thou, thou rich-hair'd Youth of Morn,[3]
And all thy subject life was born!   40
The dang'rous Passions kept aloof,
Far from the sainted growing woof:
But near it sate ecstatic Wonder,
List'ning the deep applauding thunder: *[handwritten: Miltonic]*
And Truth, in sunny vest array'd,
By whose the tarsel's eyes were made; *[handwritten: eagle's eye]*
All the shad'wy tribes of Mind, *[handwritten: subjects of]*
In braided dance their murmurs join'd, *[handwritten: imagin, poetry]*
And all the bright uncounted Pow'rs *[handwritten: personific: pity]* 50
Who feed on Heav'n's ambrosial flow'rs. *[handwritten: fear]*
Where is the bard, whose soul can now *[handwritten: Simplicity]*
Its high presuming hopes avow?
Where he who thinks, with rapture blind,
This hallow'd work [4] for him design'd?

[handwritten left margin: wonder & fancy & Truth present when creation of world occurs]

III

High on some cliff, to Heav'n up-pil'd,
Of rude access, of prospect wild,
Where, tangled round the jealous steep,
Strange shades o'erbrow the valleys deep,
And holy Genii guard the rock,
Its gloomes embrown, its springs unlock,   60
While on its rich ambitious head,
An Eden, like his own, lies spread:
I view that oak, the fancied glades among,
By which as Milton lay, his ev'ning ear,
From many a cloud that dropp'd ethereal dew,

2 Young Fancy, mentioned in line 17.   4 The cestus or girdle.
3 Apollo. god of the sun and poetry.

Nigh spher'd in Heav'n its native strains could hear:
On which that ancient trump he reach'd was hung;
   Thither oft, his glory greeting,
   From Waller's [5] myrtle shades retreating,
With many a vow from Hope's aspiring tongue,   70
My trembling feet his guiding steps pursue;
   In vain—such bliss to one alone,[6]
   Of all the sons of soul was known,   *laments poets*
   And Heav'n, and Fancy, kindred pow'rs,
   Have now o'erturn'd th' inspiring bow'rs,
Or curtain'd close such scene from ev'ry future view.

ODE

WRITTEN IN THE BEGINNING OF THE YEAR 1746 [1]

1747

How sleep the brave, who sink to rest,
By all their country's wishes blest!
When Spring, with dewy fingers cold,
Returns to deck their hallow'd mold,
She there shall dress a sweeter sod,
Than Fancy's feet have ever trod.

By fairy hands their knell is rung,
By forms unseen their dirge is sung;
There Honour comes, a pilgrim grey,
To bless the turf that wraps their clay,   10
And Freedom shall a while repair,
To dwell a weeping hermit there!

5 Edmund Waller (1606–87).
6 Milton.
1 Possibly referring to the English lost in the Battle of Fontenoy (1745) in the War of the Austrian Succession; or in the battles against the Young Pretender during the Jacobite Rebellion.

ODE TO EVENING

1747

If ought of oaten stop, or pastoral song,
May hope, chaste Eve, to sooth thy modest ear,
   Like thy own solemn springs,
   Thy springs and dying gales,
O nymph reserv'd, while now the bright-hair'd sun
Sits in yon western tent, whose cloudy skirts,
   With brede ethereal wove,
   O'erhang his wavy bed:
Now air is hush'd, save where the weak-ey'd bat,
With short shrill shriek, flits by on leathern wing,   10
   Or where the beetle winds,
   His small but sullen horn,
As oft he rises 'midst the twilight path,
Against the pilgrim borne in heedless hum:
   Now teach me, maid compos'd,
   To breathe some soften'd strain,
Whose numbers, stealing thro' thy dark'ning vale,
May not unseemly with its stillness suit,
   As, musing slow, I hail
   Thy genial lov'd return!   20
For when thy folding-star arising shews
His paly circlet, at his warning lamp
   The fragrant Hours, and elves
   Who slept in flow'rs the day,
And many a nymph who wreaths her brows with sedge,
And sheds the fresh'ning dew, and lovelier still,
   The pensive Pleasures sweet,
   Prepare thy shadowy car.
Then lead, calm vot'ress, where some sheety lake
Cheers the lone heath, or some time-hallow'd pile   30
   Or upland fallows grey
   Reflect its last cool gleam.
But when chill blust'ring winds, or driving rain,
Forbid my willing feet, be mine the hut
   That from the mountain's side,
   Views wilds, and swelling floods,
And hamlets brown, and dim-discover'd spires,

And hears their simple bell, and marks o'er all
   Thy dewy fingers draw
   The gradual dusky veil.   40
While Spring shall pour his show'rs, as oft he wont,
And bathe thy breathing tresses, meekest Eve!
   While Summer loves to sport
   Beneath thy ling'ring light;
While sallow Autumn fills thy lap with leaves;
Or Winter yelling thro' the troublous air,
   Affrights thy shrinking train,
   And rudely rends thy robes;
So long, sure-found beneath the sylvan shed,
Shall Fancy, Friendship, Science, rose-lipp'd Health,   50
   Thy gentlest influence own,
   And hymn thy fav'rite name!

THE PASSIONS, AN ODE FOR MUSIC

1747

When Music, heav'nly maid, was young,
While yet in early Greece she sung,
The Passions oft, to hear her shell,
Throng'd around her magic cell,
Exulting, trembling, raging, fainting,
Possess'd beyond the Muse's painting;
By turns they felt the glowing mind
Disturb'd, delighted, rais'd, refin'd.
Till once, 'tis said, when all were fir'd,
Fill'd with fury, rapt, inspir'd,
From the supporting myrtles round,   10
They snatch'd her instruments of sound,
And, as they oft had heard apart
Sweet lessons of her forceful art,
Each, for madness rul'd the hour,
Would prove his own expressive pow'r.

First Fear his hand, its skill to try,
   Amid the chords bewilder'd laid,
And back recoil'd he knew not why,
   Ev'n at the sound himself had made.   20

Next Anger rush'd, his eyes on fire,
  In lightnings own'd his secret stings;
In one rude clash he struck the lyre,
  And swept with hurried hand the strings.

With woeful measures wan Despair
  Low, sullen sounds his grief beguil'd;
A solemn, strange, and mingled air;
  'Twas sad by fits, by starts 'twas wild.

But thou, O Hope, with eyes so fair,
  What was thy delightful measure?   30
Still it whisper'd promis'd pleasure,
  And bad the lovely scenes at distance hail!

Still would her touch the strain prolong,
  And from the rocks, the woods, the vale,
She call'd on Echo still thro' all the song;
  And where her sweetest theme she chose,
  A soft responsive voice was heard at ev'ry close,
And Hope enchanted smil'd, and wav'd her golden hair.

And longer had she sung,—but with a frown,
  Revenge impatient rose,   40
He threw his blood-stain'd sword in thunder down,
  And with a with'ring look,
  The war-denouncing trumpet took,
And blew a blast so loud and dread,
Were ne'er prophetic sounds so full of woe.
  And ever and anon he beat
  The doubling drum with furious heat;
And tho' sometimes, each dreary pause between,
  Dejected Pity at his side,
  Her soul-subduing voice applied,   50
Yet still he kept his wild unalter'd mien,
While each strain'd ball of sight seem'd bursting from his head.

Thy numbers, Jealousy, to naught were fix'd,
  Sad proof of thy distressful state;
Of diff'ring themes the veering song was mix'd,
  And now it courted Love, now raving call'd on Hate.

With eyes up-rais'd, as one inspir'd,
Pale Melancholy sate retir'd,
And from her wild sequester'd seat,
In notes by distance made more sweet, 60
Pour'd through the mellow horn her pensive soul:
    And, dashing soft from rocks around,
    Bubbling runnels join'd the sound;
Through glades and glooms the mingled measure stole,
Or o'er some haunted stream with fond delay,
    Round an holy calm diffusing,
    Love of peace, and lonely musing,
In hollow murmurs died away.
But oh how alter'd was its sprightlier tone!
When Chearfulness, a nymph of healthiest hue, 70
    Her bow across her shoulder flung,
    Her buskins gemm'd with morning dew,
Blew an inspiring air, that dale and thicket rung,
    The hunter's call to Faun and Dryad known!
    The oak-crown'd Sisters, and their chaste-ey'd Queen,
    Satyrs and sylvan boys were seen,
    Peeping from forth their alleys green;
Brown Exercise rejoic'd to hear,
    And Sport leapt up, and seiz'd his beechen spear.

Last came Joy's ecstatic trial, 80
He, with viny crown advancing,
    First to the lively pipe his hand addrest,
But soon he saw the brisk awak'ning viol,
    Whose sweet entrancing voice he lov'd the best.
    They would have thought who heard the strain,
    They saw in Tempe's vale her native maids,
    Amidst the festal sounding shades,
To some unwearied minstrel dancing,
    While, as his flying fingers kiss'd the strings,
    Love fram'd with Mirth a gay fantastic round; 90
    Loose were her tresses seen, her zone unbound,
    And he, amidst his frolic play,
    As if he would the charming air repay,
    Shook thousand odours from his dewy wings.

O Music, sphere-descended maid,
Friend of Pleasure, Wisdom's aid,
Why, Goddess, why to us denied,

Lay'st thou thy ancient lyre aside?
As in that lov'd Athenian bow'r,
You learn'd an all-commanding pow'r,   100
Thy mimic soul, O Nymph endear'd,
Can well recall what then it heard.
Where is thy native simple heart,
Devote to virtue, fancy, art?
Arise as in that elder time,
Warm, energic, chaste, sublime!
Thy wonders in that godlike age
Fill thy recording Sister's page—
'Tis said, and I believe the tale,
Thy humblest reed could more prevail,   110
Had more of strength, diviner rage,
Than all which charms this laggard age,
Ev'n all at once together found,
Cecilia's mingled world of sound—
Oh bid our vain endeavors cease,
Revive the just designs of Greece,
Return in all thy simple state!
Confirm the tales her sons relate!

A SONG FROM SHAKESPEAR'S CYMBELINE SUNG BY GUIDERUS AND ARVIRAGUS OVER FIDELE, SUPPOSED TO BE DEAD

1749

To fair Fidele's grassy tomb
    Soft maids and village hinds shall bring
Each op'ning sweet, of earliest bloom,
    And rifle all the breathing Spring.

No wailing ghost shall dare appear
    To vex with shrieks this quiet grove:
But shepherd lads assemble here,
    And melting virgins own their love.

No wither'd witch shall here be seen,
    No goblins lead their nightly crew: 10
The female fays shall haunt the green,
    And dress thy grave with pearly dew!

The red-breast oft at ev'ning hours
  Shall kindly lend his little aid:
With hoary moss, and gather'd flow'rs,
  To deck the ground where thou art laid.

When howling winds, and beating rain,
  In tempests shake the sylvan cell;
Or 'midst the chace on ev'ry plain,
  The tender thought on thee shall dwell.   20

Each lonely scene shall thee restore,
  For thee the tear be duly shed:
Belov'd till life can charm no more,
  And mourn'd, till Pity's self be dead.

AN ODE ON THE POPULAR SUPERSTITIONS
OF THE HIGHLANDS OF SCOTLAND

CONSIDERED AS THE SUBJECT OF POETRY

1788

I

H——,[1] thou return'st from Thames, whose Naiads long
  Have seen thee ling'ring, with a fond delay,
Mid those soft friends, whose hearts, some future day,
  Shall melt, perhaps, to hear thy tragic song.
Go, not unmindful of that cordial youth,[2]
  Whom, long endear'd, thou leav'st by Lavant's side;
Together let us wish him lasting truth,
  And joy untainted, with his destin'd bride.
Go! nor regardless, while these numbers boast
  My short-liv'd bliss, forget my social name;   10
But think far off how, on the southern coast,
  I met thy friendship with an equal flame!
Fresh to that soil thou turn'st, whose ev'ry vale
  Shall prompt the poet, and his song demand:
To thee thy copious subjects ne'er shall fail;
  Thou need'st but take the pencil to thy hand,
And paint what all believe who own thy genial land.

1 John Home, author of the tragedy
Douglas (1756); he had been in London to
offer. in vain. his tragedy *Agis* to Garrick.

2 John Barrow, friend of Home and Collins.

II

There must thou wake perforce thy Doric quill,
  'Tis Fancy's land to which thou sett'st thy feet;
Where still, 'tis said, the fairy people meet,   20
  Beneath each birken shade on mead or hill.
There each trim lass that skims the milky store
  To the swart tribes [3] their creamy bowl allots;
By night they sip it round the cottage-door,
  While airy minstrels warble jocund notes.
There every herd, by sad experience, knows
  How, wing'd with fate, their elf-shot arrows fly;
When the sick ewe her summer food foregoes,
  Or, stretch'd on earth, the heart-smit heifers lie.
Such airy beings awe th' untutor'd swain: 30
  Nor thou, though learn'd, his homelier thoughts neglect;
Let thy sweet Muse the rural faith sustain;
  These are the themes of simple, sure effect,
That add new conquests to her boundless reign,
  And fill, with double force, her heart-commanding strain.

III

Ev'n yet preserv'd, how often mayst thou hear,
  Where to the pole the Boreal mountains run,
Taught by the father to his list'ning son,
  Strange lays, whose power had charm'd a Spenser's ear.
At ev'ry pause, before thy mind possest,   40
  Old Runic bards shall seem to rise around,
With uncouth lyres, in many-colour'd vest,
  Their matted hair with boughs fantastic crown'd:
Whether thou bid'st the well-taught hind repeat
  The choral dirge, that mourns some chieftain brave,
When ev'ry shrieking maid her bosom beat,
  And strew'd with choicest herbs his scented grave;
Or whether, sitting in the shepherd's shiel,[4]
  Thou hear'st some sounding tale of war's alarms;
When, at the bugle's call, with fire and steel,   50
  The sturdy clans pour'd forth their bony swarms,
And hostile brothers met to prove each other's arms.

IV

'Tis thine to sing, how, framing hideous spells,
  In Sky's lone isle the gifted wizard seer,

---

3 Brownies   4 A hut used in summer.

Lodg'd in the wintry cave with [   ]
    Or in the depth of Uist's [5] dark forests dwells:
How they, whose sight such dreary dreams engross,
    With their own visions oft astonish'd droop,
When o'er the wat'ry strath [6] or quaggy moss,
    They see the gliding ghosts unbodied troop.   60
Or, if in sports, or on the festive green,
    Their [ ] glance some fated youth descry,
Who, now perhaps in lusty vigour seen
    And rosy health, shall soon lamented die.
For them the viewless forms of air obey,
    Their bidding heed, and at their beck repair.
They know what spirit brews the stormful day,
    And heartless, oft like moody madness stare
To see the phantom train their secret work prepare.

[Twenty-five lines lost.]

VI

What though far off, from some dark dell espied
    His glimm'ring mazes cheer th' excursive sight,
Yet turn, ye wand'rers, turn your steps aside,
    Nor trust the guidance of that faithless light;
For watchful, lurking 'mid th' unrustling reed,
    At those mirk hours the wily monster lies,   100
And listens oft to hear the passing steed,
    And frequent round him rolls his sullen eyes,
If chance his savage wrath may some weak wretch surprise.

VII

Ah, luckless swain, o'er all unblest indeed!
    Whom late bewilder'd in the dank, dark fen,
Far from his flocks and smoking hamlet then!
    To that sad spot [   ]
On him, enrag'd, the fiend, in angry mood,
    Shall never look with pity's kind concern,
But instant, furious, raise the whelming flood   110
    O'er its drown'd bank, forbidding all return.
Or, if he meditate his wish'd escape
    To some dim hill that seems uprising near,
To his faint eye the grim and grisly shape,
    In all its terrors clad, shall wild appear.
Meantime, the wat'ry surge shall around him rise,

<hr>

[5] An island near Skye.   [6] Valley.

Pour'd sudden forth from ev'ry swelling source.
What now remains but tears and hopeless sighs?
His fear-shook limbs have lost their youthly force,
And down the waves he floats, a pale and breathless corse.   120

VIII

For him, in vain, his anxious wife shall wait,
Or wander forth to meet him on his way;
For him, in vain, at to-fall of the day,
His babes shall linger at th' unclosing gate.
Ah, ne'er shall he return! Alone, if night
Her travell'd limbs in broken slumbers steep,
With dropping willows drest, his mournful sprite
Shall visit sad, perchance, her silent sleep:
Then he, perhaps, with moist and wat'ry hand,
Shall fondly seem to press her shudd'ring cheek,   130
And with his blue swoln face before her stand,
And, shiv'ring cold, these piteous accents speak:
"Pursue, dear wife, thy daily toils pursue,
At dawn or dusk, industrious as before;
Nor e'er of me one hapless thought renew,
While I lie welt'ring on the ozier'd shore,
Drown'd by the Kælpie's [7] wrath, nor e'er shall aid thee more!"

IX

Unbounded is thy range; with varied stile
Thy Muse may, like those feath'ry tribes which spring
From their rude rocks, extend her skirting wing   140
Round the moist marge of each cold Hebrid isle,
To that hoar pile which still its ruin shows: [8]
In whose small vaults a pigmy-folk is found,
Whose bones the delver with his spade upthrows,
And culls them, wond'ring, from the hallow'd ground!
Or thither where beneath the show'ry west
The mighty kings of three fair realms are laid: [9]
Once foes, perhaps, together now they rest.
No slaves revere them, and no wars invade:
Yet frequent now, at midnight's solemn hour,   150
The rifted mounds their yawning cells unfold,
And forth the monarchs stalk with sov'reign pow'r

7 Water fiend's.
8 On the island of Benbecula miniature bones were said to have been found among the ruins of a chapel.

9 Kings of Scotland, Ireland, and Norway, buried on Iona.

In pageant robes, and wreath'd with sheeny gold,
And on their twilight tombs aërial council hold.

X

But O! o'er all, forget not Kilda's race,
  On whose bleak rocks, which brave the wasting tides, *pure & upright*
Fair Nature's daughter, Virtue, yet abides.
  Go, just, as they, their blameless manners trace!
Then to my ear transmit some gentle song
  Of those whose lives are yet sincere and plain, 160
Their bounded walks the rugged cliffs along,
  And all their prospect but the wintry main.
With sparing temp'rance, at the needful time,
  They drain the sainted spring, or, hunger-prest,
Along th' Atlantic rock undreading climb,
  And of its eggs despoil the solan's nest.
Thus blest in primal innocence they live,
  Suffic'd and happy with that frugal fare
Which tasteful toil and hourly danger give.
  Hard is their shallow soil, and bleak and bare; 170
Nor ever vernal bee was heard to murmur there!

XI

Nor need'st thou blush, that such false themes engage *Equivocal*
  Thy gentle mind, of fairer stores possest; *regard*
For not alone they touch the village breast,
  But fill'd in elder time th' historic page.
There Shakespeare's self, with ev'ry garland crown'd, *based on*
  In musing hour, his wayward Sisters found, *falsehoods &*
And with their terrors drest the magic scene.
From them he sung, when mid his bold design,
  Before the Scot afflicted and aghast, 180 *yet some truth*
The shadowy kings of Banquo's fated line *in it*
  Through the dark cave in gleamy pageant past.
Proceed, nor quit the tales which, simply told,
  Could once so well my answ'ring bosom pierce;
Proceed, in forceful sounds and colours bold
  The native legends of thy land rehearse; *nostalgia*
To such adapt thy lyre and suit thy pow'rful verse.

XII

In scenes like these, which, daring to depart *break through*
  From sober truth, are still to nature true,

And call forth fresh delight to fancy's view,   190
  Th' heroic muse employ'd her Tasso's art!
How have I trembled, when at Tancred's stroke, *distortion —*
  Its gushing blood the gaping cypress pour'd;
When each live plant with mortal accents spoke, *wants animated*
  And the wild blast up-heav'd the vanish'd sword! *nature*
How have I sat, when pip'd the pensive wind,
  To hear his harp, by British Fairfax [10] strung.
Prevailing poet, whose undoubting mind
  Believ'd the magic wonders which he sung!
Hence at each sound imagination glows;   200
Hence his warm lay with softest sweetness flows;
  Melting it flows, pure, num'rous, strong and clear,
And fills th' impassion'd heart, and wins th' harmonious ear.

XIII

All hail, ye scenes that o'er my soul prevail,
  Ye [ ] friths and lakes which, far away,
  Are by smooth Annan fill'd, or past'ral Tay,
  Or Don's romantic springs, at distance, hail!
The time shall come when I, perhaps, may tread
  Your lowly glens, o'erhung with spreading broom,
Or o'er your stretching heaths by fancy led: 210
  Then will I dress once more the faded bow'r,
  Where Jonson sat in Drummond's [ ] shade; [11]
Or crop from Tiviotdale each [   ],
  And mourn on Yarrow's banks [   ].
Meantime, ye pow'rs, that on the plains which bore
  The cordial youth, on Lothian's plains attend,
Where'er he dwell, on hill, or lowly muir,
  To him I lose, your kind protection lend,
And, touch'd with love like mine, preserve my absent friend.

10 Edward Fairfax, translator of Tasso's   11 Ben Jonson visited William Drummond
Jerusalem Delivered in 1600.   at Hawthornden, near Edinburgh, in 1619.

relationship between fancy & truth

A SELECTION

James Stuart *and* Nicholas Revett
1713–1788   1720–1804

THE ANTIQUITIES OF ATHENS
1762

[While the odes of Akenside, Collins, and Gray were assuming a tone more and more Grecian, the excavations at Herculaneum and Pompeii, the activities of the Dilettanti Society, and volumes upon the ruins of Palmyra and Ionia were emancipating the arts from the age-old tyranny of Rome. Winckelmann's researches and the *Laocoön* by Lessing (1766) suggest the full impact of Greece upon the latter half of the century. Not the least important volumes in the history of neo-Hellenism are those by two Englishmen, Stuart and Revett, patronized by the Dilettanti Society. They regarded Athens, not Rome, as "the mother of elegance and politeness."]

THE ruined edifices of Rome have for many years engaged the attention of those who apply themselves to the study of architecture; and have generally been considered as the models and standard of regular and ornamental building. Many representations of them drawn and engraved by skillful artists have been published, by which means the study of the art has been everywhere greatly facilitated, and the general practice of it improved and promoted. Insomuch that what is now esteemed the most elegant manner of decorating buildings was originally formed, and has since been established, on examples which the antiquities of Rome have furnished.

But although the world is enriched with collections of this sort already published, we thought it would be a work not unacceptable to the lovers of architecture if we added to those collections some examples drawn from the antiquities of Greece; and we were confirmed in our opinion by this consideration principally, that as Greece was the great mistress of the arts, and Rome, in this respect, no more than her disciple, it may be presumed all the most admired buildings which adorned that imperial city were but imitations of Grecian originals.

Hence it seemed probable that if accurate representations of these originals were published, the world would be enabled to form, not only more extensive, but juster ideas than have hitherto been obtained concerning architecture, and the state in which it existed during the best ages of antiquity. It even seemed that a performance of this kind might contribute to the improvement of the art itself, which at present appears to be founded on too partial and too scanty a system of ancient examples.

For during those ages of violence and barbarism which began the declension, and continued long after the destruction of the Roman empire, the beautiful edifices which had been erected in Italy with such great labor and expense, were neglected or destroyed; so that, to use a very common expression, it may truly be said that architecture lay for ages buried in its own ruins; and although from these ruins it has phoenixlike received a second birth, we may nevertheless conclude that many of the beauties and elegancies which enhanced its ancient splendor are still wanting, and that it has not yet by any means recovered all its former perfection.

This conclusion becomes sufficiently obvious when we consider that the great artists by whose industry this noble art has been revived, were obliged to shape its present form after those ideas only which the casual remains of Italy suggested to them; and these remains are so far from furnishing all the materials necessary for a complete restoration of architecture in all its parts, that the best collections of them, those published by Palladio and Desgodetz, cannot be said to afford a sufficient variety of examples for restoring even the three orders of columns, for they are deficient in what relates to the Doric and Ionic, the two most ancient of these orders.

From what has been said it should appear that architecture is reduced and restrained within narrower limits than could be wished for want of a greater number of ancient examples than have hitherto been published; it must, then, be granted that every such example of beautiful form or proportion, wherever it may be found, is a valuable addition to the former stock; and does, when published, become a material acquisition to the art.

But of all the countries which were embellished by the ancients with magnificent buildings, Greece appears principally to merit our attention; since, if we believe the ancients themselves, the most beautiful orders and dispositions of columns were invented in that country, and the most celebrated works of architecture were erected there: to which may be added that the most excellent

treatises on the art appear to have been written by Grecian architects.

The city of Greece most renowned for stately edifices, for the
genius of its inhabitants, and for the culture of every art, was
Athens. We therefore resolved to examine that spot rather than
any other; flattering ourselves that the remains we might find there
would excel in true taste and elegance everything hitherto published.

[PREFACE]

A S E L E C T I O N

Richard Hurd

1720–1808

LETTERS ON CHIVALRY AND ROMANCE
1762

[These letters, written under the "magic of the old romances," are another manifestation of the interest in the "Gothick" that flowered in
the Norse poems of Gray and the Rowley poems of Chatterton.]

LETTER I

THE ages we call barbarous present us with many a subject of curious speculation. What, for instance, is more remarkable than the
Gothic chivalry? or than the spirit of *romance*, which took its rise
from that singular institution?

Nothing in human nature, my dear friend, is without its reasons.
The modes and fashions of different times may appear, at first sight,
fantastic and unaccountable. But they who look nearly into them
discover some latent cause of their production.

Nature once known, no prodigies remain,[1]

as sings our philosophical bard; but to come at this knowledge
is the difficulty. Sometimes a close attention to the workings of
the human mind is sufficient to lead us to it: sometimes more than
that, the diligent observation of what passes without us, is necessary.

1 Pope *Moral Essays* I. 208.

This last I take to be the case here. The prodigies we are now contemplating had their origin in the barbarous ages. Why, then, says the fastidious modern, look any farther for the reason? Why not resolve them at once into the usual caprice and absurdity of barbarians?

This, you see, is a short and commodious philosophy. Yet barbarians have their *own*, such as it is, if they are not enlightened by our reason. Shall we then condemn them unheard, or will it not be fair to let them have the telling of their own story?

Would we know from what causes the institution of chivalry was derived? The time of its birth, the situation of the barbarians amongst whom it arose, must be considered; their wants, designs, and policies must be explored; we must inquire when and where and how it came to pass that the western world became familiarized to this prodigy, which we now start at.

Another thing is full as remarkable, and concerns us more nearly. The spirit of chivalry was a fire which soon spent itself; but that of *romance*, which was kindled at it, burnt long, and continued its light and heat even to the politer ages.

The greatest geniuses of our own and foreign countries, such as Ariosto and Tasso in Italy, and Spenser and Milton in England, were seduced by these barbarities of their forefathers, were even charmed by the Gothic romances.[2] Was this caprice and absurdity in them? Or may there not be something in the Gothic romance peculiarly suited to the views of a genius, and to the ends of poetry? And may not the philosophic moderns have gone too far in their perpetual ridicule and contempt of it?

To form a judgment in the case, the rise, progress, and genius of Gothic chivalry must be explained.

The circumstances in the Gothic fictions and manners which are proper to the ends of poetry (if any such there be) must be pointed out.

Reasons for the decline and rejection of the Gothic taste in later times must be given.

You have in these particulars both the subject and the plan of the following *Letters*.

LETTER VI

.   .   .   .

After all, the conclusion is not to be drawn so much from particular passages, as from the general impression left on our minds

---

2 Medieval legend; not the "Gothic romance" of eighteenth-century prose fiction.

in reading the ancient and modern poets. And this is so much in favor of the latter that Mr. Addison [3] scruples not to say, "The ancients have not much of this poetry among them; for, indeed," continues he, "almost the whole substance of it owes its original to the darkness and superstition of later ages.—Our forefathers looked upon nature with more reverence and horror, before the world was enlightened by learning and philosophy, and loved to astonish themselves with the apprehensions of witchcraft, prodigies, charms, and enchantments. There was not a village in England that had not a ghost in it; the churchyards were all haunted; every large common had a circle of fairies belonging to it; and there was scarce a shepherd to be met with who had not seen a spirit."

We are upon enchanted ground, my friend; and you are to think yourself well used that I detain you no longer in this fearful circle. The glimpse you have had of it will help your imagination to conceive the rest. And without more words you will readily apprehend that the fancies of our modern bards are not only more gallant, but, on a change of the scene, more sublime, more terrible, more alarming than those of the classic fablers. In a word, you will find that the manners they paint, and the superstitions they adopt, are the more poetical for being Gothic.

Letter VII

But nothing shows the difference of the two systems under consideration more plainly than the effect they really had on the two greatest of our poets; at least the two which an English reader is most fond to compare with Homer, I mean *Spenser* and *Milton*.

It is not to be doubted but that each of these bards had kindled his poetic fire from classic fables. So that, of course, their prejudices would lie that way. Yet they both appear, when most inflamed, to have been more particularly rapt with the Gothic fables of chivalry.

Spenser, though he had been long nourished with the spirit and substance of Homer and Virgil, chose the times of chivalry for his theme, and fairyland for the scene of his fictions. He could have planned, no doubt, an heroic design on the exact classic model; or he might have trimmed between the Gothic and classic, as his contemporary Tasso did. But the charms of fairy prevailed. And if any think he was seduced by Ariosto into this choice, they should consider that it could be only for the sake of his subject; for the genius and character of these poets was widely different.

3 *Spectator* No. 419.

Under this idea, then, of a Gothic, not classical poem, the *Faerie Queene* is to be read and criticized. And on these principles, it would not be difficult to unfold its merit in another way than has been hitherto attempted.

Milton, it is true, preferred the classic model to the Gothic. But it was after long hesitation; and his favorite subject was Arthur and his knights of the round table. On this he had fixed for the greater part of his life. What led him to change his mind was, partly, as I suppose, his growing fanaticism; partly, his ambition to take a different route from Spenser; but chiefly perhaps, the discredit into which the stories of chivalry had now fallen by the immortal satire of Cervantes. Yet we see through all his poetry, where his enthusiasm flames out most, a certain predilection for the legends of chivalry before the fables of Greece.

This circumstance, you know, has given offense to the austerer and more mechanical critics. They are ready to censure his judgment as juvenile and unformed when they see him so delighted, on all occasions, with the Gothic romances. But do these censors imagine that Milton did not perceive the defects of these works, as well as they? No: it was not the composition of books of chivalry, but the manners described in them, that took his fancy; as appears from his *Allegro:*

> Towered cities please us then
> And the busy hum of men,
> Where throngs of knights and barons bold
> In weeds of peace high triumphs hold,
> With store of ladies, whose bright eyes
> Rain influence, and judge the prize
> Of wit, or arms, while both contend
> To win her grace, whom all commend.

And when in the *Penseroso* he draws, by a fine contrivance, the same kind of image to soothe melancholy which he had before given to excite mirth, he indeed extols an author of one of these romances, as he had before, in general, extolled the subject of them; but it is an author worthy of his praise; not the writer of *Amadis* or *Sir Launcelot of the Lake*, but Chaucer himself, who has left an unfinished story on the Gothic or feudal model:

> Or call up him that left half-told
> The story of Cambuscan bold,
> Of Camball and of Algarsife,
> And who had Canace to wife

That own'd the virtuous ring and glass,
And of the wondrous horse of brass,
On which the Tartar king did ride;
And if aught else great bards beside
In sage and solemn tunes have sung
Of tourneys and of trophies hung,
Of forests and enchantments drear,
Where more is meant than meets the ear.

The conduct, then, of these two poets may incline us to think
with more respect than is commonly done of the Gothic manners,
I mean as adapted to the uses of the greater poetry.

I say nothing of Shakespeare because the sublimity (the divinity, let it be, if nothing else will serve) of his genius kept no certain
route, but rambled at hazard into all the regions of human life and
manners. So that we can hardly say what he preferred or what he
rejected on full deliberation. Yet one thing is clear, that even he
is greater when he uses Gothic manners and machinery than when
he employs classical: which brings us again to the same point,
that the former have, by their nature and genius, the advantage
of the latter in producing the *sublime*.

LETTER X

. . . So little account does this wicked poetry make of philosophical or historical truth: all she allows us to look for is *poetical
truth;* a very slender thing indeed, and which the poet's eye, when
rolling in its finest frenzy, can but just lay hold of. To speak in
the philosophic language of Mr. Hobbes, it is something much
*beyond the actual bounds, and only within the conceived possibil-
ity, of nature.*

But the source of bad criticism, as universally of bad philosophy,
is the abuse of terms. A poet, they say, must follow Nature; and
by Nature we are to suppose can only be meant the known and
experienced course of affairs in this world. Whereas the poet has
a world of his own, where experience has less to do than consistent imagination.

He has, besides, a supernatural world to range in. He has gods
and faeries and witches at his command: and

——O! who can tell
The hidden pow'r of herbes, and might of magic spell?
(Spenser, Book I, canto 2)

Thus in the poet's world, all is marvelous and extraordinary; yet
not *unnatural* in one sense, as it agrees to the conceptions that are

readily entertained of these magical and wonder-working natures. . . .

LETTER XII

The wonders of chivalry were still in the memory of men, were
still existing, in some measure, in real life, when Chaucer undertook
to expose the barbarous relaters of them.

This ridicule, we may suppose, hastened the fall both of chivalry
and romance. At least from that time the spirit of both declined
very fast, and at length fell into such discredit that when now
Spenser arose, and with a genius singularly fitted to immortalize
the land of faery, he met with every difficulty and disadvantage to
obstruct his design. . . .

In short, to keep off the eyes of the profane from prying too
nearly into his subject, he threw about it the mist of allegory: he
moralized his song: and the virtues and vices lay hid under his warriors and enchanters. . . .

. . . The only favorable circumstance that attended him (and
this no doubt encouraged, if it did not produce, his untimely project) was that he was somewhat befriended in these fictions, even
when interpreted according to the letter, by the romantic spirit of
his age, much countenanced, and for a time brought into fresh
credit, by the romantic Elizabeth. Her inclination for the fancies
of chivalry is well known, and obsequious wits and courtiers would
not be wanting to feed and flatter it. In short, tilts and tournaments
were in vogue: the *Arcadia* and the *Faerie Queene* were written.

With these helps the new spirit of chivalry made a shift to support itself for a time, when reason was but dawning, as we may
say, and just about to gain the ascendant over the portentous spec-
ters of the imagination. Its growing splendor, in the end, put them
all to flight, and allowed them no quarter even amongst the poets.
So that Milton, as fond as we have seen he was of the Gothic fictions, durst only admit them on the bye, and in the way of simile
and illustration only. . . .

Thus at length the magic of the old romances was perfectly dissolved. They began with reflecting an image, indeed, of the feudal
manors, but an image magnified and distorted by unskillful designers. Common sense being offended with these perversions of
truth and nature (still accounted the more monstrous as the ancient manners they pretended to copy after were now disused and
of most men forgotten) the next step was to have recourse to allegories. Under this disguise they walked the world awhile; the
excellence of the moral and the ingenuity of the contrivance mak-

ing some amends and being accepted as a sort of apology for the absurdity of the literal story.

Under this form the tales of faery kept their ground and even made their fortune at court, where they became, for two or three reigns, the ordinary entertainment of our princes. But reason, in the end (assisted, however, by party and religious prejudices) drove them off the scene and would endure these *lying wonders* neither in their own proper shape nor as masked in figures.

Henceforth, the taste of wit and poetry took a new turn: and *fancy*, that had wantoned it so long in the world of fiction, was now constrained, against her will, to ally herself with strict truth if she would gain admittance into reasonable company.

What we have gotten by this revolution, you will say, is a great deal of good sense. What we have lost is a world of fine fabling; the illusion of which is so grateful to the *charmed spirit* that in spite of philosophy and fashion, *Faerie* Spenser still ranks highest among the poets; I mean with all those who are either come of that house, or have any kindness for it.

Earth-born critics, my friend, may blaspheme,

> But all the gods are ravish'd with delight,
> Of his celestial song, and music's wondrous might.

A SELECTION

James Macpherson

1736–1796

POEMS OF OSSIAN

1761–1763

[The learned Hugh Blair remarked of these purportedly ancient Celtic poems that "uncouth and abrupt Ossian may sometimes appear by reason of his conciseness, but he is sublime, he is pathetic, in an eminent degree." Exactly how Macpherson composed the "epics" of *Fingal* and *Temora* is not certain. Although Johnson mocked, the fastidious Gray, for all his scholarship, desperately wished to believe that here was authentic bardic verse.]

THE SONGS OF SELMA

1762

ARGUMENT

Address to the evening star. An apostrophe to Fingal and his times. Minona sings before the king the song of the unfortunate Colma; and the bards exhibit other specimens of their poetical talents; according to an annual custom established by the monarchs of the ancient Caledonians.

STAR of descending night! fair is thy light in the west! thou liftest thy unshorn head from thy cloud: thy steps are stately on thy hill. What dost thou behold in the plain? The stormy winds are laid. The murmur of the torrent comes from afar. Roaring waves climb the distant rock. The flies of evening are on their feeble wings; the hum of their course is on the field. What dost thou behold, fair light? But thou dost smile and depart. The waves come with joy around thee: they bathe thy lovely hair. Farewel, thou silent beam! Let the light of Ossian's soul arise!

AND it does arise in its strength! I behold my departed friends. Their gathering is on Lora, as in the days of other years. Fingal comes like a watery column of mist; his heroes are around: And see the bards of song, grey-haired Ullin! stately Ryno! Alpin, with the tuneful voice! the soft complaint of Minona! How are ye changed, my friends, since the days of Selma's feast? when we contended, like gales of spring, as they fly along the hill, and bend by turns the feebly-whistling grass.

MINONA came forth in her beauty; with down-cast look and tearful eye. Her hair flew slowly on the blast, that rushed unfrequent from the hill. The souls of the heroes were sad when she raised the tuneful voice. Often had they seen the grave of Salgar, the dark dwelling of white-bosomed Colma. Colma left alone on the hill, with all her voice of song! Salgar promised to come: but the night descended around. Hear the voice of Colma, when she sat alone on the hill!

COLMA

IT IS night; I am alone, forlorn on the hill of storms. The wind is heard in the mountain. The torrent pours down the rock. No hut receives me from the rain; forlorn on the hill of winds!

RISE, moon! from behind thy clouds. Stars of the night arise! Lead me, some light, to the place, where my love rests from the chase alone! his bow near him, unstrung: his dogs panting around him. But here I must sit alone, by the rock of the mossy stream. The stream and the wind roar aloud. I hear not the voice of my love! Why delays my Salgar, why the chief of the hill, his promise? Here is the rock, and here the tree! here is the roaring stream! Thou didst promise with night to be here. Ah! whither is my Salgar gone? With thee I would fly, from my father; with thee, from my brother of pride. Our race have long been foes; we are not foes, O Salgar!

Cease a little while, O wind! stream, be thou silent awhile! let my voice be heard around. Let my wanderer hear me! Salgar! it is Colma who calls. Here is the tree, and the rock. Salgar, my love! I am here. Why delayest thou thy coming? Lo! the calm moon comes forth. The flood is bright in the vale. The rocks are gray on the steep. I see him not on the brow. His dogs come not before him, with tidings of his near approach. Here I must sit alone!

Who lie on the heath beside me? Are they my love and my brother? Speak to me, O my friends! To Colma they give no reply. Speak to me: I am alone! My soul is tormented with fears! Ah! they are dead! Their swords are red from the fight. O my brother! my brother! why hast thou slain my Salgar? why, O Salgar! hast thou slain my brother? Dear were ye both to me! what shall I say in your praise? Thou wert fair on the hill among thousands! he was terrible in fight. Speak to me; hear my voice; hear me, sons of my love! They are silent; silent forever! Cold, cold are their breasts of clay! Oh! from the rock on the hill; from the top of the windy steep, speak, ye ghosts of the dead! speak, I will not be afraid! Whither are ye gone to rest? In what cave of the hill shall I find the departed? No feeble voice is on the gale; no answer half-drowned in the storm!

I sit in my grief! I wait for morning in my tears! Rear the tomb, ye friends of the dead. Close it not till Colma come. My life flies away like a dream! why should I stay behind? Here shall I rest with my friends, by the stream of the sounding rock. When night comes on the hill; when the loud winds arise; my ghost shall stand in the blast, and mourn the death of my friends. The hunter shall hear from his booth. He shall fear but love my voice! For sweet shall my voice be for my friends: pleasant were her friends to Colma!

Such was thy song, Minona, softly-blushing daughter of Torman. Our tears descended for Colma, and our souls were sad! Ullin came with his harp; he gave the song of Alpin. The voice of Alpin was pleasant: the soul of Ryno was a beam of fire! But they had rested in the narrow house: their voice had ceased in Selma. Ullin had returned, one day, from the chase, before the heroes fell. He heard their strife on the hill; their song was soft but sad. They mourned the fall of Morar, first of mortal men! His soul was like the soul of Fingal; his sword like the sword of Oscar. But he fell, and his father mourned: his sister's eyes were full of tears. Minona's eyes were full of tears, the sister of car-borne Morar. She retired from the song of Ullin, like the moon in the west, when she foresees the shower, and hides her fair head in a cloud. I touched the harp, with Ullin; the song of mourning rose!

RYNO

THE wind and the rain are past: calm is the noon of day. The clouds are divided in heaven. Over the green hills flies the inconstant sun. Red through the stony vale comes down the stream of the hill. Sweet are thy murmurs, O stream! but more sweet is the voice I hear. It is the voice of Alpin, the son of song, mourning for the dead! Bent is his head of age; red his tearful eye. Alpin, thou son of song, why alone on the silent hill? why complainest thou, as a blast in the wood; as a wave on the lonely shore?

ALPIN

MY tears, O Ryno! are for the dead; my voice for those that have passed away. Tall thou art on the hill; fair among the sons of the vale. But thou shall fall like Morar; the mourner shall sit on thy tomb. The hills shall know thee no more; thy bow shall lie in the hall, unstrung!

THOU wert swift, O Morar! as a roe on the desert; terrible as a meteor of fire. Thy wrath was as the storm. Thy sword in battle, as lightning in the field. Thy voice was a stream after rain; like thunder on distant hills. Many fell by thy arm; they were consumed in the flames of thy wrath. But when thou didst return from war, how peaceful was thy brow! Thy face was like the sun after rain; like the moon in the silence of night; calm as the breast of the lake when the loud wind is laid.

NARROW is thy dwelling now! dark the place of thine abode! With three steps I compass thy grave, O thou who wast so great before! Four stones, with their heads of moss, are the only memorial of thee. A tree with scarce a leaf, long grass, which whistles in the wind, mark to the hunter's eye the grave of the mighty Morar. Morar! thou art low indeed. Thou hast no mother to mourn thee; no maid with her tears of love. Dead is she that brought thee forth. Fallen is the daughter of Morglan.

WHO on his staff is this? who is this, whose head is white with age? whose eyes are red with tears? who quakes at every step? It is thy father, O Morar! the father of no son but thee. He heard of thy fame in war; he heard of foes dispersed. He heard of Morar's renown; why did he not hear of his wound? Weep, thou father of Morar! weep; but thy son heareth thee not. Deep is the sleep of the dead; low their pillow of dust. No more shall he hear thy voice; no more awake at thy call. When shall it be morn in the grave, to bid the slumberer awake? Farewell, thou bravest of men! thou conqueror in the field! but the field shall see thee no more; nor the dark wood be lightened with the splendor of thy steel. Thou hast left no son. The song shall preserve thy name. Future times shall hear of thee; they shall hear of the fallen Morar!

THE grief of all arose, but most the bursting sigh of Armin. He remembers the death of his son, who fell in the days of his youth. Carmor was near the hero, the chief of the echoing Galmal. Why bursts the sigh of Armin, he said? Is there a cause to mourn? The song comes, with its music, to melt and please the soul. It is like soft mist, that, rising from a lake, pours on the silent vale; the green flowers are filled with dew, but the sun returns in his strength, and the mist is gone. Why art thou sad, O Armin! chief of sea-surrounded Gorma?

SAD! I am! nor small is my cause of woe! Carmor, thou hast lost no son; thou hast lost no daughter of beauty. Colgar the valiant lives; and Annira fairest maid. The boughs of thy house ascend, O Carmor! but Armin is the last of his race. Dark is thy bed, O Daura! deep thy sleep in the tomb! When shalt thou awake with thy songs? with all thy voice of music?

ARISE, winds of autumn, arise; blow along the heath! streams of the mountains roar! roar, tempests, in the groves of my oaks! walk through broken clouds, O moon! show thy pale face, at intervals! bring to my mind the night, when all my children fell; when Arindal the mighty fell; when Daura the lovely failed! Daura, my daughter! thou wert fair; fair as the moon on Fura; white as the driven snow; sweet as the breathing gale. Arindal, thy bow was strong. Thy spear was swift in the field. Thy look was like mist on the wave: thy shield, a red cloud in a storm. Armar, renowned in war, came, and sought Daura's love. He was not long refused: fair was the hope of their friends!

ERATH, son of Odgal, repined: his brother had been slain by Armar. He came disguised like a son of the sea: fair was his skiff on the wave; white his locks of age; calm his serious brow. Fairest of women, he said, lovely daughter of Armin! a rock not distant in the sea bears a tree on its side; red shines the fruit afar. There Armar waits for Daura. I come to carry his love! She went; she called on Armar. Naught answered, but the son of the rock, Armar, my love! my love! why tormentest thou me with fear? hear, son of Arnart, hear: it is Daura who calleth thee! Erath the traitor fled laughing to the land. She lifted up her voice; she called for her brother and her father. Arindal! Armin! none to relieve your Daura!

HER voice came over the sea. Arindal my son descended from the hill; rough in the spoils of the chase. His arrows rattled by his side; his bow was in his hand: five dark-gray dogs attend his steps. He saw fierce Erath on the shore: he seized and bound him to an oak. Thick wind the thongs of the hide around his limbs; he loads the wind with his groans. Arindal ascends the deep in his boat, to bring Daura to land. Armar came in his wrath, and let fly the gray-feathered shaft. It sung; it sunk in thy heart, O Arindal my son! for Erath the traitor thou diedst. The oar is stopped at once; he panted on the rock and expired. What is thy grief, O Daura, when round thy feet is poured thy brother's blood! the boat is broken in twain. Armar plunges into the sea, to rescue his Daura, or die. Sudden a blast from the hill came over the waves. He sunk, and he rose no more.

ALONE, on the sea-beat rock, my daughter was heard to complain. Frequent and loud were her cries. What could her father do? All night I stood on the shore. I saw her by the faint beam of the moon. All night I heard her cries. Loud was the wind; the rain beat hard on the hill. Before morning appeared, her voice was weak. It died away, like the evening breeze among the grass of the rocks. Spent with grief she expired; and left thee Armin alone. Gone is my strength in war! fallen my pride among women! When the storms aloft arise: when the north lifts the wave on high; I sit by the sounding shore, and look on the fatal rock. Often by the setting moon, I see the ghosts of my children. Half-viewless, they walk in mournful conference together. Will none of you speak in pity? They do not regard their father. I am sad, O Carmor, nor small is my cause of woe!

SUCH were the words of the bards in the days of song; when the king heard the music of harps, the tale of other times! The chiefs gathered from all their hills, and heard the lovely sound. They praised the voice of Cona! the first among a thousand bards! But age is now on my tongue; my soul has failed! I hear, at times, the ghosts of bards, and learn their pleasant song. But memory fails on my mind. I hear the call of years! They say, as they pass along,

why does Ossian sing? Soon shall he lie in the narrow house, and
no bard shall raise his fame! Roll on, ye dark-brown years; ye
bring no joy on your course! Let the tomb open to Ossian, for
his strength has failed. The sons of song are gone to rest. My voice
remains, like a blast, that roars, lonely, on a sea-surrounded rock,
after the winds are laid. The dark moss whistles there; the distant
mariner sees the waving trees!

A SELECTION

Thomas Percy

1729–1811

RELIQUES OF ANCIENT ENGLISH POETRY
1765

[Thomas Percy, later Bishop of Dromore, had a consuming interest in
the Chinese, the Norse, the Hebrew, and the Peruvian, as well as in
"ancient English" poetry. In publishing the *Reliques* from the manuscripts of Humphrey Pitt of Shifnal, Percy cut and altered to suit what
he supposed to be the taste of the day. In spite of this cavalier editing,
the *Reliques* are of greater moment than even *Ossian* in the revival of
the ballad and "romance."]

In a polished age like the present, I am sensible that many of these
reliques of antiquity will require great allowances to be made for
them. Yet have they, for the most part, a pleasing simplicity, and
many artless graces, which in the opinion of no mean critics have
been thought to compensate for the want of higher beauties, and
if they do not dazzle the imagination, are frequently found to interest the heart.

[PREFACE]

I cannot conclude the account of the ancient English minstrels
without remarking that they are most of them represented to
have been of the North of England. There is scarce an old historical song or ballad wherein a minstrel or harper appears, but he
is characterized, by way of eminence, to have been "of the North
Countrie": and indeed the prevalence of the northern dialect in

such compositions shows that this representation is real. On the other hand, the scene of the finest Scottish ballads is laid in the south of Scotland, which should seem to have been peculiarly the nursery of Scottish minstrels. In the old song of "Maggy Lawder," a piper is asked, by way of distinction, "Come ze frae the Border?" The martial spirit constantly kept up and exercised near the frontier of the two kingdoms, as it furnished continual subjects for their songs, so it inspired the inhabitants of the adjacent counties on both sides with the powers of poetry. Besides, as our southern metropolis must have been ever the scene of novelty and refinement, the northern countries, as being most distant, would preserve their ancient manners longest, and of course the old poetry, in which those manners are so peculiarly described.

The reader will observe in the more ancient ballads of this collection a caste of style and measure very different from that of contemporary poets of a higher class; many phrases and idioms which the minstrels seem to have appropriated to themselves, and a very remarkable license of varying the accent of words at pleasure, in order to humor the flow of the verse, particularly in the rhymes; as

| Coun trie′ | harp er′ | bat tel′ | morn ing′ |
| La die′ | sing er′ | dam sel′ | lov ing′ |

instead of *coun'try, la'dy, har'per, sin'ger,* &c.—This liberty is but sparingly assumed by the classical poets of the same age, or even by the latter composers of heroical ballads; I mean by such as professedly wrote for the press. For it is to be observed that so long as the minstrels subsisted, they seem never to have designed their rhymes for publication, and probably never committed them to writing themselves: what copies are preserved of them were doubtless taken down from their mouths. But as the old minstrels gradually wore out, a new race of ballad-writers succeeded, an inferior sort of minor poets who wrote narrative songs merely for the press. Instances of both may be found in the reign of Elizabeth. . . .

The old minstrel ballads are in the northern dialect, abound with antique words and phrases, are extremely incorrect, and run into the utmost license of meter; they have also a romantic wildness, and are in the true spirit of chivalry.—The other sort are written in exacter measure, have a low or subordinate correctness, sometimes bordering on the insipid, yet often well adapted to the pathetic; these are generally in the southern dialect, exhibit a more modern phraseology, and are commonly descriptive of more modern manners.

[An Essay on the Ancient Minstrels in England]

For the Victory at Agincourt

Deo gratias Anglia redde pro victoria! [1]

Owre kynge went forth to Normandy,
With grace and myzt of chivalry;
The God for him wrouzt marvelously,
Wherefore Englonde may calle, and cry
   Deo gratias:
  Deo gratias Anglia redde pro victoria.

He sette a sege, the sothe for to say,
To Harflue toune with ryal array;
That toune he wan and made a fray,
That Fraunce shall rywe tyl domes day.
   Deo gratias, &c.

Then went owre kynge with alle his oste
Thorowe Fraunce for all the Frenshe boste;
He spared for drede of leste ne most,
Tyl he come to Agincourt coste.
   Deo gratias, &c.

Than for sothe that knyzt comely
In Agincourt feld he fauzt manly,
Thorow grace of God most myzty
He had both the felde and the victory:
   Deo gratias, &c.

Ther dukys and erlys, lorde and barone,
Were take and slayne and that wel sone,
And some were ledde in to Lundone
With joye and merthe and grete renone.
   Deo gratias, &c.

Now gracious God he save owre kynge,
His peple and all his wel wyllynge,
Gef him gode lyfe and gode endynge,
That we with merth mowe savely synge
   Deo gratias:
  Deo gratias Anglia redde pro victoria.

1 "Let England give thanks to God for victory."

Thomas Gray

1716–1771

It is revealing that Gray should be named by Dr. Johnson as one of the most learned men in Europe and that at the same time he should be the most fastidious among the thin voices of "taste." Regius Professor of History in Cambridge, commentator upon heraldry and architecture, antiquarian, student of music, botanist and entomologist, sketcher, scholar of Greek, Latin, French, German, Old English, and Old Norse, poet, letter-writer, traveler in search of the picturesque—Gray dreaded pedantry and always thought of himself as an amateur in whatever he did. He remained one of the very influential persons who are little known to the public but who influence persons who are known to the public. His liking for the Highlands and the Lake Country, for example, or for the medieval, is symptomatic of a change of taste. In a famous judgment, Matthew Arnold remarked that Gray never spoke out, that his age was against him. It is unlikely that Gray would have spoken out in any age. There is an air of the precious about almost all that he did. His knowledge was cast into allusions rather than into a system. It is true that he suffered from a "white" melancholy, a lassitude of spirit that belongs to his day. His verve, he writes Mason, is "of so delicate a constitution, and has such weak nerves, as not to stir out of its chamber above three days in a year." But essentially Gray, like Walpole or the Wartons, remains a dilettante. His range in poetry is surprising, from the polished and meditative ode and elegy (in which he values "extreme conciseness of expression, yet pure, perspicuous, and musical") to *vers de société* and the learned "enthusiasm" of the Norse poems. He always writes in key. After all, what saves the *Elegy* from mere sentimentality, or from commonplace? Simply that Gray is unwilling to identify himself too closely with it. His own epitaph, at the close, is kept in a nice removal by having it put into the mouth of a rustic, who is himself a convention. Gray is too well-bred to speak out about even such a personal matter as his own death. And the ardor of the Norse and Welsh odes is a little studied. In supplying the notes for these poems, Gray is unwilling to be clear beyond a certain point: "It is extremely well—nobody understands me, and I am perfectly satisfied," he writes Mason. If he dreads pedantry, he dreads popularity also. In this spirit he refuses the laureateship. His self-consciousness thwarts his impulse even in his letters; having momentarily abandoned himself to a sentence brilliantly describing a scene in Kent, he draws up with the remark, "This last sentence is so fine, I am quite ashamed." When he goes to study at the newly opened British Museum, he explains that with him are three men writing there for someone else "& I, who only read to know if there were anything worth writing, & that not without some difficulty."

BIOGRAPHICAL NOTES

Born in London, the son of a scrivener of violent disposition; his mother and her sister, Mary Antrobus, kept a millinery shop. Gray the only one of twelve children to survive. Reared by his mother. Attended Eton (1727) with Horace Walpole, Richard West, and Thomas Ashton. Studied at Peterhouse, Cambridge (1734–38), as pensioner, but took no degree. Made the grand tour with Walpole (1739–41) and quarreled with him; later made it up. Settled for a short time at Stoke Poges with his mother (1742). Richard West died (1742). Gray returned to Peterhouse as fellow commoner to live as scholarly recluse for most of remaining years. *Elegy in a Country Churchyard* printed anonymously (1751). Death of Gray's mother (1753). *Six Poems* (1753), to accompany designs by Bentley. Moved from Peterhouse to Pembroke College (1756). *Odes by Mr. Gray* printed at Walpole's Strawberry Hill Press (1757). Refused laureateship at death of Colley Cibber (1757). Took lodgings in London to read at the newly opened British Museum (1759). Tour of the north (1761); tours of Scotland (1764–65). Collected edition of the poems (1768). Appointed Regius Professor of History (1768). Tour of the Lake Country (1769). Sudden illness while dining at Pembroke; death within the week (1771) and burial at Stoke Poges.

BIBLIOGRAPHY: *Poetical Works*, ed. A. L. Poole, 1917. *Correspondence*, ed. Paget Toynbee and Leonard Whibley, 3 vols., 1935. Cecil, Lord David, *The Poetry of Thomas Gray*, 1946; *Two Quiet Lives*, 1948. Jones, W. Powell, *Thomas Gray, Scholar: The True Tragedy of an Eighteenth-Century Gentleman*, 1937. Ketton-Cremer, R. W., *Thomas Gray*, 1955. Roberts, Sidney Castle, *Thomas Gray of Pembroke*, 1952.

ODE ON A DISTANT PROSPECT OF ETON COLLEGE

1747

Ye distant spires, ye antique towers,
That crown the watry glade,
Where grateful Science still adores
Her Henry's holy shade; [1]
And ye, that from the stately brow

[handwritten margin note: emphasis falls on the price exacted by knowledge or insight]

1 King Henry the Sixth, founder of the College. [Gray]

Of Windsor's heights th' expanse below
  Of grove, of lawn, of mead survey,
Whose turf, whose shade, whose flowers among
Wanders the hoary Thames along
  His silver-winding way.   10

Ah happy hills, ah pleasing shade,
  Ah fields belov'd in vain,
Where once my careless childhood stray'd,
  A stranger yet to pain!
I feel the gales, that from ye blow,
A momentary bliss bestow,
  As waving fresh their gladsome wing,
My weary soul they seem to sooth,
And, redolent of joy and youth,
  To breathe a second spring.   20

Say, Father Thames, for thou hast seen
  Full many a sprightly race
Disporting on thy margent green
  The paths of pleasure trace,
Who foremost now delight to cleave
With pliant arm thy glassy wave?
  The captive linnet which enthrall?
What idle progeny succeed
To chase the rolling circle's speed,
  Or urge the flying ball?   30

While some on earnest business bent
  Their murm'ring labours ply,
'Gainst graver hours, that bring constraint
  To sweeten liberty:
Some bold adventurers disdain
The limits of their little reign,
  And unknown regions dare descry:
Still as they run they look behind,
They hear a voice in every wind,
  And snatch a fearful joy.   40

Gay hope is theirs by fancy fed,
  Less pleasing when possest;
The tear forgot as soon as shed,
  The sunshine of the breast:

Theirs buxom health of rosy hue,
Wild wit, invention ever-new,
  And lively chear of vigour born;
The thoughtless day, the easy night,
The spirits pure, the slumbers light,
  That fly th' approach of morn.   50

Alas, regardless of their doom,
  The little victims play!
No sense have they of ills to come,
  Nor care beyond to-day:
Yet see how all around 'em wait
The ministers of human fate,
  And black Misfortune's baleful train!
Ah, shew them where in ambush stand
To seize their prey the murth'rous band!
  Ah, tell them they are men!   60

These shall the fury Passions tear,
  The vultures of the mind,
Disdainful Anger, pallid Fear,
  And Shame that sculks behind;
Or pineing Love shall waste their youth,
Or Jealousy with rankling tooth,
  That inly gnaws the secret heart,
And Envy wan, and faded Care,
Grim-visag'd comfortless Despair,
  And Sorrow's piercing dart.   70

Ambition this shall tempt to rise,
  Then whirl the wretch from high,
To bitter Scorn a sacrifice,
  And grinning Infamy.
The stings of Falsehood those shall try,
And hard Unkindness' alter'd eye,
  That mocks the tear it forc'd to flow;
And keen Remorse with blood defil'd,
And moody Madness laughing wild
  Amid severest woe.   80

Lo, in the vale of years beneath
  A griesly troop are seen,
The painful family of Death,

More hideous than their Queen:
This racks the joints, this fires the veins,
That every laboring sinew strains,
   Those in the deeper vitals rage:
Lo, Poverty, to fill the band,
That numbs the soul with icy hand,
   And slow-consuming Age.   90

To each his suff'rings: all are men,
   Condemn'd alike to groan,
The tender for another's pain;
   Th' unfeeling for his own.
Yet ah, why should they know their fate?
Since sorrow never comes too late,
   And happiness too swiftly flies.
Thought would destroy their paradise.
No more; where ignorance is bliss,
   'Tis folly to be wise.   100

SONNET ON THE DEATH OF RICHARD WEST

1775

narrator's grief cuts him off from nature + other men

In vain to me the smiling mornings shine,
   And redd'ning Phœbus lifts his golden fire:
The birds in vain their amorous descant join;
   Or chearful fields resume their green attire:
These ears, alas! for other notes repine,
   A different object do these eyes require.
My lonely anguish melts no heart, but mine;
   And in my breast the imperfect joys expire.
Yet Morning smiles the busy race to chear,
   And new-born pleasure brings to happier men: 10
The fields to all their wonted tribute bear:
   To warm their little loves the birds complain:
I fruitless mourn to him, that cannot hear,
   And weep the more, because I weep in vain.

ODE ON THE SPRING

1748

Lo! where the rosy-bosom'd Hours,
Fair Venus' train appear,
Disclose the long-expecting flowers,
And wake the purple year!
The Attic warbler [1] pours her throat,
Responsive to the cuckow's note,
The untaught harmony of spring:
While whisp'ring pleasure as they fly,
Cool Zephyrs thro' the clear blue sky
Their gather'd fragrance fling.   10

Where'er the oak's thick branches stretch
A broader browner shade;
Where'er the rude and moss-grown beech
O'ercanopies the glade,
Beside some water's rushy brink
With me the Muse shall sit, and think
(At ease reclin'd in rustic state)
How vain the ardour of the crowd,
How low, how little are the proud,
How indigent the great!   20

Still is the toiling hand of Care:
The panting herds repose:
Yet hark, how thro' the peopled air
The busy murmur glows!
The insect youth are on the wing,
Eager to taste the honied spring,
And float amid the liquid noon:
Some lightly o'er the current skim,
Some shew their gaily-gilded trim
Quick-glancing to the sun.   30

To Contemplation's sober eye
Such is the race of man:
And they that creep, and they that fly,

1 The nightingale.

Shall end where they began.
Alike the busy and the gay
But flutter thro' life's little day,
In fortune's varying colours drest:
Brush'd by the hand of rough Mischance,
Or chill'd by age, their airy dance
They leave, in dust to rest.   40

Methinks I hear in accents low
The sportive kind reply:
"Poor moralist! and what art thou?
A solitary fly!
Thy joys no glittering female meets,
No hive hast thou of hoarded sweets,
No painted plumage to display:
On hasty wings thy youth is flown;
    Thy sun is set, thy spring is gone—
We frolick, while 'tis May."   50

ODE ON THE DEATH OF A FAVOURITE CAT

DROWNED IN A TUB OF GOLDFISHES

1748

'Twas on a lofty vase's side,
Where China's gayest art had dy'd
    The azure flow'rs, that blow;
Demurest of the tabby kind,
The pensive Selima, reclin'd,
    Gazed on the lake below.

Her conscious tail her joy declar'd;
The fair round face, the snowy beard,
    The velvet of her paws,
Her coat, that with the tortoise vies,
Her ears of jet, and emerald eyes,
    She saw; and purr'd applause.   10

Still had she gaz'd; but 'midst the tide
Two angel forms were seen to glide,
    The genii of the stream:

Their scaly armour's Tyrian hue
Thro' richest purple to the view
  Betray'd a golden gleam.

The hapless nymph with wonder saw:
A whisker first and then a claw,   20
  With many an ardent wish,
She stretch'd in vain to reach the prize.
What female heart can gold despise?
  What cat's averse to fish?

Presumptuous maid! with looks intent
Again she stretch'd, again she bent,
  Nor knew the gulf between.
(Malignant Fate sat by, and smil'd)
The slipp'ry verge her feet beguil'd,
  She tumbled headlong in.   30

Eight times emerging from the flood,
She mew'd to ev'ry wat'ry god,
  Some speedy aid to send.
No Dolphin came, no Nereid stirr'd:
Nor cruel Tom, nor Susan heard.
  A fav'rite has no friend!

From hence, ye beauties, undeceiv'd,
Know, one false step is ne'er retriev'd,
  And be with caution bold.
Not all that tempts your wand'ring eyes   40
And heedless hearts, is lawful prize;
  Nor all that glisters, gold.

ELEGY WRITTEN IN A COUNTRY CHURCHYARD

1751

The curfew tolls the knell of parting day,
  The lowing herd wind slowly o'er the lea,
The ploughman homeward plods his weary way,
  And leaves the world to darkness and to me.

narrator looks at perspective, present scene surrounding him, evokes the past life of the forefathers, considers the unrealized possibilities for good + evil in the rustics

Now fades the glimmering landscape on the sight,
  And all the air a solemn stillness holds,
Save where the beetle wheels his droning flight,
  And drowsy tinklings lull the distant folds;

adj, noun, verb, adj, noun — golden line from Latin

Save that from yonder ivy-mantled tow'r
  The mopeing owl does to the moon complain
Of such, as wand'ring near her secret bow'r,
  Molest her ancient solitary reign.   10

Beneath those rugged elms, that yew-tree's shade,
  Where heaves the turf in many a mold'ring heap,
Each in his narrow cell for ever laid,
  The rude forefathers of the hamlet sleep.

Milton Book IX — Para Lost

The breezy call of incense-breathing Morn,
  The swallow twitt'ring from the straw-built shed,
The cock's shrill clarion, or the echoing horn,
  No more shall rouse them from their lowly bed.   20

For them no more the blazing hearth shall burn,
  Or busy housewife ply her evening care:
No children run to lisp their sire's return,
  Or climb his knees the envied kiss to share.

Oft did the harvest to their sickle yield,
  Their furrow oft the stubborn glebe has broke;
How jocund did they drive their team afield!
  How bow'd the woods beneath their sturdy stroke!

Stanza 8

Let not Ambition mock their useful toil,
  Their homely joys, and destiny obscure;
Nor Grandeur hear with a disdainful smile,   30
  The short and simple annals of the poor.

The boast of heraldry, the pomp of pow'r,
  And all that beauty, all that wealth e'er gave,
Awaits alike th' inevitable hour.
  The paths of glory lead but to the grave.

Nor you, ye proud, impute to these the fault,
  If Mem'ry o'er their tomb no trophies raise,
Where thro' the long-drawn isle and fretted vault
  The pealing anthem swells the note of praise   40

technical perspective — serves to suggest the complementary nature of form and content

Gray implies — what we are involves the question of perspective, of how we look to others, how we look

Rich

Can <u>storied urn</u> or animated bust
  Back to its mansion call the fleeting breath?
Can Honour's voice provoke the silent dust,
  Or Flatt'ry soothe the dull cold ear of Death?

Perhaps in this neglected spot is laid   *Stanza 12*
  Some heart once pregnant with celestial fire;
Hands, that the rod of empire might have sway'd,
  Or wak'd to extasy the living lyre.

But <u>Knowledge</u> to their eyes her ample page   *Knowledge + penury*
  Rich with the spoils of time did ne'er unroll;   *are parallel —*
Chill <u>Penury</u> repress'd their noble rage,   50
  And froze the genial current of the soul.   *lack of knowledge is deplored*

often consolation to unnumbered
Full many a gem of purest ray serene,   *thousands, who have*
  The dark unfathom'd caves of ocean bear:
Full many a flower is born to blush unseen,   *felt the anguish of*
  And waste its sweetness on the desert air.   *never being discovered*

Some village-Hampden,[1] that with dauntless breast
  The little tyrant of his fields withstood;
Some mute inglorious Milton here may rest,
  Some Cromwell guiltless of his country's blood.   60

Th' applause of list'ning senates to command,
  The threats of pain and ruin to despise,
To scatter plenty o'er a smiling land,
  And read their hist'ry in a nation's eyes,

Can't blame anyone
<u>Their lot forbad</u>: nor circumscrib'd alone   *Stanza 17*
  Their growing virtues, but their crimes confin'd;   *consolatory*
Forbad to wade through slaughter to a throne,
  And shut the gates of mercy on mankind,

The struggling pangs of conscious truth to hide,
  To quench the blushes of ingenuous shame,   70
Or heap the shrine of Luxury and Pride
  With incense kindled at the Muse's flame.

[1] John Hampden, leader of the resistance to Charles I's attempt to collect "ship-money," an ancient tax.

to ourselves

Far from the madding crowd's ignoble strife,
~~Their sober wishes never learn'd to stray;~~
Along the cool sequester'd vale of life
    They kept the noiseless tenour of their way.

Yet ev'n these bones from insult to protect,
    Some frail memorial still erected nigh,
With uncouth rhymes and shapeless sculpture deck'd,
    Implores the passing tribute of a sigh.   80

Their names, their years, spelt by th' unletter'd Muse,
    The place of fame and elegy supply:
And many a holy text around she strews,
    That teach the rustic moralist to die.

For who to dumb forgetfulness a prey,
    This pleasing anxious being e'er resign'd,
Left the warm precincts of the chearful day,
    Nor cast one longing ling'ring look behind?

On some fond breast the parting soul relies,
    Some pious drops the closing eye requires;
Ev'n from the tomb the voice of Nature cries,
    Ev'n in our ashes live their wonted fires.   92

For thee, who mindful of th' unhonour'd dead
    Dost in these lines their artless tale relate;
If chance, by lonely contemplation led,
    Some kindred spirit shall inquire thy fate,

Haply some hoary-headed swain may say,   97
    "Oft have we seen him at the peep of dawn
Brushing with hasty steps the dews away,
    To meet the sun upon the upland lawn.   100

"There, at the foot of yonder nodding beech
    That wreathes its old fantastic roots so high,
His listless length at noontide would he stretch,
    And pore upon the brook that babbles by.

"Hard by yon wood, now smiling as in scorn,
    Mutt'ring his wayward fancies he would rove,
Now drooping, woeful wan, like one forlorn,
    Or craz'd with care, or cross'd in hopeless love.

"One morn I miss'd him on the custom'd hill,
  Along the heath and near his fav'rite tree; 110
Another came; nor yet beside the rill,
  Nor up the lawn, nor at the wood was he;

"The next with dirges due in sad array
  Slow through the church-way path we saw him born.
Approach and read (for thou canst read) the lay,
  Grav'd on the stone beneath yon aged thorn." *116*

The Epitaph

Here rests his head upon the lap of Earth
  A youth to Fortune and to Fame unknown:
Fair Science frown'd not on his humble birth,
  And Melancholy mark'd him for her own.

Large was his bounty, and his soul sincere,
  Heav'n did a recompence as largely send:
He gave to Mis'ry all he had, a tear,
  He gain'd from Heav'n ('twas all he wish'd) a friend. 120

No farther seek his merits to disclose,
  Or draw his frailties from their dread abode,
(There they alike in trembling hope repose)
  The bosom of his Father and his God.

[Handwritten annotations: "Reflective"; "was person of learning — to analyze own life"; "positive feature" (underlining "Large was his bounty"); "melancholic person of Il Penseroso"]

HYMN TO ADVERSITY

1753

Daughter of Jove, relentless Power,
Thou Tamer of the human breast,
Whose iron scourge and tort'ring hour,
The bad affright, afflict the best!
Bound in thy adamantine chain,
The proud are taught to taste of pain,
And purple tyrants vainly groan
With pangs unfelt before, unpitied and alone.

When first thy sire to send on earth
Virtue, his darling child, design'd, 10
To thee he gave the heav'nly birth,

And bad to form her infant mind.
Stern rugged nurse! thy rigid lore
With patience many a year she bore:
What sorrow was, thou bad'st her know,
And from her own she learn'd to melt at others' woe.

Scared at thy frown terrific, fly
Self-pleasing Folly's idle brood,
Wild Laughter, Noise, and thoughtless Joy,
And leave us leisure to be good.   20
Light they disperse, and with them go
The summer friend, the flatt'ring foe;
By vain Prosperity receiv'd,
To her they vow their truth, and are again believ'd.

Wisdom, in sable garb array'd,
Immers'd in rapt'rous thought profound,
And Melancholy, silent maid
With leaden eye, that loves the ground,
Still on thy solemn steps attend:
Warm Charity, the gen'ral friend,   30
With Justice, to herself severe,
And Pity, dropping soft the sadly-pleasing tear.

Oh gently on thy suppliant's head,
Dread Goddess, lay thy chast'ning hand!
Not in thy Gorgon terrors clad,
Nor circled with the vengeful band
(As by the impious thou art seen)
With thund'ring voice, and threat'ning mien,
With screaming Horror's funeral cry,
Despair, and fell Disease, and ghastly Poverty.   40

Thy form benign, O Goddess, wear,
Thy milder influence impart,
Thy philosophic train be there
To soften, not to wound, my heart,
The gen'rous spark extinct revive,
Teach me to love and to forgive,
Exact my own defects to scan,
What others are, to feel, and know myself a man.

ODE ON THE PLEASURE ARISING FROM VICISSITUDE

1775

Now the golden Morn aloft
  Waves her dew-bespangled wing,
With vermeil cheek, and whisper soft
  She wooes the tardy Spring,
Till April starts and calls around
The sleeping fragrance from the ground;
And lightly o'er the living scene
Scatters his freshest, tenderest green.

New-born flocks, in rustic dance,
  Frisking ply their feeble feet;   10
Forgetful of their wintry trance
  The birds his presence greet:
But chief, the skylark warbles high
His trembling thrilling extacy,
And, lessening from the dazzled sight,
Melts into air and liquid light.

Rise, my soul, on wings of fire,
  Rise the rapt'rous choir among;
Hark! 'tis Nature strikes the lyre
  And leads the general song: 20

*   *   *   *   *   *   *

Yesterday the sullen year
  Saw the snowy whirlwind fly;
Mute was the music of the air,
  The herd stood drooping by:
Their raptures now, that wildly flow,
No yesterday, nor morrow know;
'Tis man alone that joy descries
With forward, and reverted eyes.

Smiles on past Misfortune's brow
   Soft Reflection's hand can trace;   30
And o'er the cheek of Sorrow throw
   A melancholy grace;
While Hope prolongs our happier hour,
Or deepest shades, that dimly lower
And blacken round our weary way,
Gilds with a gleam of distant day.

Still, where rosy Pleasure leads,
   See a kindred Grief pursue;
Behind the steps that Misery treads,
   Approaching Comfort view.   40
The hues of Bliss more brightly glow
Chastis'd by sabler tints of woe;
And, blended form, with artful strife
The strength and harmony of life.

See the wretch that long has tost
   On the thorny bed of pain,
At length repair his vigour lost
   And breathe, and walk again:
The meanest floweret of the vale,
The simplest note that swells the gale,   50
The common sun, the air, the skies,
To him are opening Paradise.

Humble Quiet builds her cell
   Near the source where pleasure flows;
She eyes the clear crystalline well
   And tastes it as it goes.

     *   *   *   *   *   *   *

THE PROGRESS OF POESY

1757

I. 1

Awake, Æolian lyre,[1] awake,
And give to rapture all thy trembling strings.
From Helicon's harmonious springs [2]
A thousand rills their mazy progress take:
    The laughing flowers, that round them blow,
    Drink life and fragrance as they flow.
Now the rich stream of music winds along
    Deep, majestic, smooth, and strong,
Thro' verdant vales, and Ceres' golden reign:
    Now rolling down the steep amain,   10
    Headlong, impetuous, see it pour:
The rocks, and nodding groves rebellow to the roar.

I. 2

    O! sovereign of the willing soul,
Parent of sweet and solemn-breathing airs,
    Enchanting shell! the sullen Cares,
And frantic Passions hear thy soft controul.
    On Thracia's hills the Lord of War
    Has curb'd the fury of his car,
And drop'd his thirsty lance at thy command.
    Perching on the sceptred hand   20
Of Jove, thy magic lulls the feather'd king [3]
    With ruffled plumes, and flagging wing:
    Quench'd in dark clouds of slumber lie
The terror of his beak, and light'nings of his eye.

I. 3

    Thee the voice, the dance, obey,
    Temper'd to thy warbled lay.
    O'er Idalia's [4] velvet-green
    The rosy-crowned Loves are seen
        On Cytherea's day

1 That is, the lyre of Pindar.
2 Hippocrene and Aganippe, founts of the Muses, were on Mt. Helicon in Boeotia.
3 The eagle, bearer of the lightning of Zeus.
4 Idalia, a town on Cyprus, had a temple sacred to Cytherea, or Venus.

With antic Sports, and blue-eyed Pleasures,
Frisking light in frolic measures;
Now pursuing, now retreating,
   Now in circling troops they meet:
To brisk notes in cadence beating
   Glance their many-twinkling feet.
Slow melting strains their Queen's approach declare:
   Where'er she turns the Graces homage pay.
With arms sublime, that float upon the air,
   In gliding state she wins her easy way:
O'er her warm cheek, and rising bosom, move   40
The bloom of young Desire, and purple light of Love.

II. 1

   Man's feeble race what ills await,
Labour, and Penury, the racks of Pain,
   Disease, and Sorrow's weeping train,
And Death, sad refuge from the storms of Fate!
   The fond complaint, my song, disprove,
   And justify the laws of Jove.
Say, has he giv'n in vain the heav'nly Muse?
   Night, and all her sickly dews,
   Her spectres wan, and birds of boding cry,   50
   He gives to range the dreary sky:
Till down the eastern cliffs afar
Hyperion's march they spy, and glitt'ring shafts of war.

II. 2

   In climes beyond the solar road,
Where shaggy forms o'er ice-built mountains roam,
   The Muse has broke the twilight-gloom
To chear the shiv'ring native's dull abode.
   And oft, beneath the od'rous shade
   Of Chili's boundless forests laid,
She deigns to hear the savage youth repeat   60
   In loose numbers wildly sweet
Their feather-cinctur'd chiefs, and dusky loves.
   Her track, where'er the goddess roves,
   Glory pursue, and generous Shame,
Th' unconquerable Mind, and Freedom's holy flame.

II. 3

Woods, that wave o'er Delphi's steep,
Isles, that crown th' Ægean deep,
Fields, that cool Ilissus [5] laves,
Or when Mæander's [6] amber waves
  In lingering lab'rinths creep,   70
How do your tuneful echoes languish,
Mute, but to the voice of Anguish?
Where each old poetic mountain
  Inspiration breath'd around:
Ev'ry shade and hallow'd fountain
  Murmur'd deep a solemn sound:
Till the sad Nine in Greece's evil hour
Left their Parnassus for the Latian plains.
Alike they scorn the pomp of tyrant-Power,
And coward Vice, that revels in her chains.   80
When Latium had her lofty spirit lost,
They sought, O Albion! next thy sea-encircled coast.

III. 1

Far from the sun and summer-gale,
In thy green lap was Nature's darling [7] laid,
  What time, where lucid Avon stray'd,
To him the mighty Mother did unveil
  Her aweful face: the dauntless child
  Stretch'd forth his little arms, and smiled.
"This pencil take," she said, "whose colours clear
  Richly paint the vernal year: 90
Thine too these golden keys, immortal boy!
  This can unlock the gates of Joy;
  Of Horror that, and thrilling Fears,
Or ope the sacred source of sympathetic tears."

III. 2

Nor second he,[8] that rode sublime
Upon the seraph-wings of Extasy,
  The secrets of th' Abyss to spy.
He pass'd the flaming bounds of Place and Time:
  The living throne, the saphire-blaze,

---

5 A river that flows by Athens.   7 Shakespeare
6 A river in Asia Minor.   8 Milton.

Where angels tremble, while they gaze,   100
He saw; but blasted with excess of light,
   Clos'd his eyes in endless night.
Behold, where Dryden's less presumptuous car,
   Wide o'er the fields of Glory bear
   Two coursers of ethereal race,
With necks in thunder cloath'd, and long-resounding pace.

III. 3

Hark, his hands the lyre explore!
Bright-eyed Fancy, hovering o'er,
Scatters from her pictur'd urn
Thoughts that breathe, and words that burn.   110
   But ah! 'tis heard no more—
O lyre divine, what daring spirit
Wakes thee now? Though he inherit
Nor the pride, nor ample pinion,
   That the Theban Eagle [9] bear
Sailing, with supreme dominion
   Thro' the azure deep of air:
Yet oft before his infant eyes would run
   Such forms, as glitter in the Muse's ray
With orient hues, unborrow'd of the sun: 120
   Yet shall he mount, and keep his distant way
Beyond the limits of a vulgar fate,
Beneath the good how far—but far above the great.

THE BARD

A PINDARIC ODE [1]

1757

I. 1

"Ruin seize thee, ruthless king!
Confusion on thy banners wait,
   Though fann'd by Conquest's crimson wing,
They mock the air with idle state.

---

9 Pindar, born in the territory of Thebes.
1 The following ode is founded on a tradition current in Wales, that Edward the
First, when he completed the conquest of
that country, ordered all the bards, that fell
into his hands, to be put to death. [Gray]

Helm, nor hauberk's twisted mail,
Nor ev'n thy virtues, tyrant, shall avail
To save thy secret soul from nightly fears,
    From Cambria's [2] curse, from Cambria's tears!"
Such were the sounds, that o'er the crested pride
    Of the first Edward scatter'd wild dismay,   10
As down the steep of Snowdon's shaggy side
He wound with toilsome march his long array.
Stout Glo'ster stood aghast in speechless trance;
"To arms!" cried Mortimer, and couch'd his quiv'ring lance.

I.   2

    On a rock, whose haughty brow
    Frowns o'er old Conway's foaming flood,
    Robed in the sable garb of woe,
With haggard eyes the Poet stood;
    (Loose his beard, and hoary hair
Stream'd, like a meteor, to the troubled air)   20
And with a master's hand, and prophet's fire,
    Struck the deep sorrows of his lyre.
"Hark, how each giant-oak, and desert cave,
    Sighs to the torrent's aweful voice beneath!
O'er thee, O King! their hundred arms they wave,
    Revenge on thee in hoarser murmurs breath;
Vocal no more, since Cambria's fatal day,
To high-born Hoel's harp, or soft Llewellyn's lay.

I.   3

    "Cold is Cadwallo's tongue,
    That hush'd the stormy main: 30
Brave Urien sleeps upon his craggy bed:
    Mountains, ye mourn in vain
    Modred, whose magic song
Made huge Plinlimmon bow his cloud-top'd head.
    On dreary Arvon's shore they lie,
    Smear'd with gore, and ghastly pale:
Far, far aloof th' affrighted ravens sail;
    The famish'd eagle screams, and passes by.
Dear lost companions of my tuneful art,
    Dear, as the light that visits these sad eyes,   40
Dear, as the ruddy drops that warm my heart,
    Ye died amidst your dying country's cries—

2 Wales

No more I weep. They do not sleep.
On yonder cliffs, a griesly band,
    I see them sit, they linger yet,
    Avengers of their native land:
With me in dreadful harmony they join,
And weave with bloody hands the tissue of thy line."

II. 1

"Weave the warp, and weave the woof,
The winding-sheet of Edward's race.   50
    Give ample room, and verge enough
    The characters of hell to trace.
Mark the year, and mark the night,
When Severn shall re-eccho, with affright
The shrieks of death, thro' Berkley's roofs that ring,
    Shrieks of an agonizing King! [3]
She-wolf of France, [4] with unrelenting fangs,
    That tear'st the bowels of thy mangled mate,
From thee be born, who o'er thy country hangs
    The scourge of Heav'n. [5] What Terrors round him wait!   60
Amazement in his van, with Flight combined,
And Sorrow's faded form, and Solitude behind.

II. 2

"Mighty victor, mighty lord,
Low on his funeral couch he lies! [6]
    No pitying heart, no eye, afford
    A tear to grace his obsequies.
Is the Sable Warrior fled? [7]
Thy son is gone. He rests among the dead.
The swarm, that in thy noon-tide beam were born?
    Gone to salute the rising Morn.   70
Fair laughs the Morn, and soft the Zephyr blows, [8]
    While proudly riding o'er the azure realm
In gallant trim the gilded vessel goes;
    Youth on the prow, and Pleasure at the helm;

---

[3] Edward the Second, cruelly butchered in Berkley Castle. [Gray]

[4] Isabel of France, Edward the Second's adulterous queen. [Gray]

[5] Triumphs of Edward the Third in France. [Gray]

[6] Death of that King, abandoned by his children, and even robbed in his last mo-

ments by his courtiers and his mistress. [Gray]

[7] Edward the Black Prince, dead some time before his father. [Gray]

[8] Magnificence of Richard the Second's reign. See Froissard, and other contemporary writers. [Gray]

Regardless of the sweeping Whirlwind's sway,
That, hush'd in grim repose, expects his evening prey.

II. 3

"Fill high the sparkling bowl,
The rich repast prepare,
Reft of a crown, he yet may share the feast:
Close by the regal chair   80
Fell Thirst and Famine scowl
A baleful smile upon their baffled guest.[9]
Heard ye the din of battle bray,
Lance to lance, and horse to horse?[10]
Long years of havock urge their destin'd course,
And thro' the kindred squadrons mow their way.
Ye towers of Julius, London's lasting shame,
With many a foul and midnight murther fed,[11]
Revere his consort's[12] faith, his father's[13] fame,
And spare the meek usurper's holy head.[14]   90
Above, below, the rose of snow,
Twin'd with her blushing foe, we spread:[15]
The bristled Boar[16] in infant-gore
Wallows beneath the thorny shade.
Now, brothers, bending o'er th' accursed loom,
Stamp we our vengeance deep, and ratify his doom.

III. 1

"Edward, lo! to sudden fate
(Weave we the woof. The thread is spun)
Half of thy heart we consecrate.[17]
(The web is wove. The work is done.)"   100
"Stay, oh, stay! nor thus forlorn

9 Richard the Second, as we are told by Archbishop Scroop and the confederate Lords in their manifesto, by Thomas of Walsingham, and all the older writers, was starved to death. The story of his assassination by Sir Piers of Exon is of much later date. [Gray]

10 Ruinous civil wars of York and Lancaster. [Gray]

11 Henry the Sixth, George Duke of Clarence, Edward the Fifth, Richard Duke of York, etc., believed to be murthered secretly in the Tower of London. The oldest part of that structure is vulgarly attributed to Julius Cæsar. [Gray]

12 Margaret of Anjou, a woman of heroic spirit, who struggled hard to save her husband and her crown. [Gray]

13 Henry the Fifth. [Gray]

14 Henry the Sixth, very near being canonized. The line of Lancaster had no right of inheritance to the crown. [Gray]

15 The white and red roses, devices of York and Lancaster. [Gray]

16 The silver boar was the badge of Richard the Third; whence he was usually known in his own time by the name of the Boar. [Gray]

17 Eleanor of Castile died a few years after the conquest of Wales. The heroic proof she gave of her affection for her lord is well known. The monuments of his regret and sorrow for the loss of her, are still to be seen at Northampton, Gaddington, Waltham, and other places. [Gray]

Leave me unbless'd, unpitied, here to mourn:
In yon bright track, that fires the western skies,
   They melt, they vanish from my eyes.
But oh! what solemn scenes on Snowdon's height
   Descending slow their glitt'ring skirts unroll!
Visions of glory, spare my aching sight,
   Ye unborn ages, crowd not on my soul!
No more our long-lost Arthur we bewail.[18]
All-hail, ye genuine kings, Britannia's issue, hail! [19]   110

III.   2

   "Girt with many a baron bold
Sublime their starry fronts they rear;
   And gorgeous dames, and statesmen old
   In bearded majesty, appear.
   In the midst a form divine! [20]
Her eye proclaims her of the Briton-line;
Her lion-port, her awe-commanding face,
   Attemper'd sweet to virgin-grace.
What strings symphonious tremble in the air,
What strains of vocal transport round her play!   120
Hear from the grave, great Taliessin,[21] hear;
   They breathe a soul to animate thy clay.
Bright Rapture calls, and soaring, as she sings,
Waves in the eye of Heav'n her many-colour'd wings.

III.   3

   "The verse adorn again
   Fierce War, and faithful Love,[22]
And Truth severe, by fairy Fiction drest.
   In buskin'd measures move [23]
   Pale Grief, and Pleasing Pain,
With Horror, tyrant of the throbbing breast.   130
   A voice, as of the cherub-choir,
   Gales from blooming Eden bear;
   And distant warblings lessen on my ear,

18 It was the common belief of the Welsh nation that King Arthur was still alive in Fairyland, and should return again to reign over Britain. [Gray]

19 Both Merlin and Taliessin had prophesied that the Welsh should regain their sovreignty over this island; which seemed to be accomplished in the House of Tudor. [Gray]

20 Queen Elizabeth.

21 Taliessin, chief of the bards, flourished in the sixth century. His works are still preserved, and his memory held in high veneration among his countrymen. [Gray]

22 "Fierce wars and faithful loves shall moralize my song." Spenser. Proëme to the Faerie Queene. [Gray]

23 Shakespere. [Gray]

That lost in long futurity expire.[24]
Fond impious man, think'st thou, yon sanguine cloud,
  Rais'd by thy breath, has quench'd the orb of day?
To-morrow he repairs the golden flood,
  And warms the nations with redoubled ray.
    Enough for me: with joy I see
    The different doom our fates assign.   140
    Be thine Despair, and scept'red Care,
    To triumph, and to die, are mine."
He spoke, and headlong from the mountain's height
Deep in the roaring tide he plung'd to endless night.

THE FATAL SISTERS

AN ODE. FROM THE NORSE TONGUE

1768

PREFACE

In the eleventh century, Sigurd, Earl of the Orkney Islands, went with a fleet of ships and a considerable body of troops into Ireland, to the assistance of Sictryg with the silken beard, who was making war on his father-in-law Brian, King of Dublin: the Earl and all his forces were cut to pieces, and Sictryg was in danger of a total defeat; but the enemy had a greater loss by the death of Brian, their king, who fell in the action. On Christmas day (the day of the battle), a native of Caithness in Scotland, of the name of Darrud, saw at a distance a number of persons on horseback riding full speed towards a hill, and seeming to enter into it. Curiosity led him to follow them, till looking through an opening in the rocks he saw twelve gigantic figures resembling women: they were all employed about a loom; and as they wove, they sung the following dreadful song; which when they had finished, they tore the web into twelve pieces, and (each taking her portion) galloped six to the north and as many to the south.[1]

---

24 The succession of poets after Milton's time. [Gray]

1 The *Valkyriur* were female divinities, servants of Odin (or Woden) in the Gothic mythology. Their name signifies *Choosers of the slain.* They were mounted on swift horses, with drawn swords in their hands; and in the throng of battle selected such as were destined to slaughter, and conducted them to *Valhalla,* the hall of Odin, or paradise of the brave; where they attended the banquet, and served the departed heroes with horns of mead and ale. [Gray]

Now the storm begins to lower,
(Haste, the loom of hell prepare,)
Iron-sleet of arrowy shower
Hurtles in the darken'd air.

Glitt'ring lances are the loom,
Where the dusky warp we strain,
Weaving many a soldier's doom,
Orkney's woe and Randver's bane.

See the griesly texture grow,
('Tis of human entrails made,)   10
And the weights, that play below
Each a gasping warrior's head.

Shafts for shuttles, dipp'd in gore,
Shoot the trembling cords along.
Sword, that once a monarch bore,
Keep the tissue close and strong.

Mista black, terrific maid,
Sangrida, and Hilda see,
Join the wayward work to aid:
'Tis the woof of victory.   20

Ere the ruddy sun be set,
Pikes must shiver, javelins sing,
Blade with clattering buckler meet,
Hauberk crash, and helmet ring.

(Weave the crimson web of war)
Let us go, and let us fly,
Where our friends the conflict share,
Where they triumph, where they die.

As the paths of fate we tread,
Wading through th' ensanguin'd field: 30
Gondula, and Geira, spread
O'er the youthful king [2] your shield.

2 Sictryg.

We the reins to slaughter give,
Ours to kill, and ours to spare:
Spite of danger he shall live.
(Weave the crimson web of war.)

They, whom once the desert-beach
Pent within its bleak domain,
Soon their ample sway shall stretch
O'er the plenty of the plain.   40

Low the dauntless earl is laid,
Gor'd with many a gaping wound:
Fate demands a nobler head;
Soon a king [3] shall bite the ground.

Long his loss shall Eirin weep,
Ne'er again his likeness see;
Long her strains in sorrow steep,
Strains of immortality!

Horror covers all the heath,
Clouds of carnage blot the sun.   50
Sisters, weave the web of death;
Sisters, cease, the work is done.

Hail the task, and hail the hands!
Songs of joy and triumph sing!
Joy to the victorious bands;
Triumph to the younger king.

Mortal, thou that hear'st the tale,
Learn the tenour of our song.
Scotland, thro' each winding vale
Far and wide the notes prolong.   60

Sisters, hence with spurs of speed:
Each her thundering faulchion wield;
Each bestride her sable steed.
Hurry, hurry to the field!

---

[3] Brian.

LETTERS *

To Horace Walpole

[April 16, 1734]

I believe by your not making me happy in a longer letter than that I have just received, you had a design to prevent my tiring you with a tedious one; but in revenge for your neglect I'm resolved to send you one five times as long: S^r, do you think, that I'll be fob'd off with eleven lines and a half? after waiting this week in continual expectation, & proposing to myself all the pleasure, that you, if you would, might give me; Gadsbud! I am provoked into a fermentation! when I see you next, I'll firk you, I'll rattle you with a Certiorari: let me tell you; I am at present as full of wrath & choler, as—as—you are of wit & good-nature; though I begin to doubt your title to the last of them, since you have balked me in this manner: what an excuse do you make with your Passion-week & fiddle-faddle, as if you could ever be at a loss what to say; why, I, that am in the country could give you a full & true account of half a dozen Intrigues, nay I have an amour carried on almost under my window between a boar & a sow, people of very good fashion, that come to an assignation, and squeak like ten masquerades; I have a great mind to make you hear the whole progress of the affair, together with the humours of Miss Pigsnies, the lady's Confidente; but you will think perhaps I invent it, & so I shall let it alone: but I wonder you are not ashamed of yourself; in town, and not able to furnish out an epistle as long as a Cows tail! (excuse the rusticity of my simile) in short, I have tryed and condemned you in my mind, all that you can alledge to save yourself won't do; for I find by your excuses you are brought to your derniere Chemise; and as you stand guilty, I adjudge you to be drawn to the place of execution, your chamber; where taking pen in hand, you shall write a letter as long as this, to him, who is nothing, when not

your sincere friend
& most devoted humble Servt

T: Gray

* Reprinted from *The Correspondence of Thomas Gray,* edited by Paget Toynbee and Leonard Whibley by permission of the Clarendon Press, Oxford. Throughout the selection from Gray's letters and journals the eccentricities of Gray's autograph have, when possible, been represented.

To West [1]

You must know that I do not take degrees, and, after this term, shall have nothing more of college impertinencies to undergo, which I trust will be some pleasure to you, as it is a great one to me. I have endured lectures daily and hourly since I came last, supported by the hopes of being shortly at full liberty to give myself up to my friends and classical companions, who, poor souls! though I see them fallen into great contempt with most people here, yet I cannot help sticking to them, and out of a spirit of obstinacy (I think) love them the better for it; and indeed, what can I do else? Must I plunge into metaphysics? Alas, I cannot see in the dark; nature has not furnished me with the optics of a cat. Must I pore upon mathematics? Alas, I cannot see in too much light; I am no eagle. It is very possible that two and two make four, but I would not give four farthings to demonstrate this ever so clearly; and if these be the profits of life, give me the amusements of it. The people I behold all around me, it seems, know all this and more, and yet I do not know one of them who inspires me with any ambition of being like him. Surely it was of this place, now Cambridge, but formerly known by the name of Babylon, that the prophet spoke when he said, 'the wild beasts of the desert shall dwell there, and their houses shall be full of doleful creatures, and owls shall build there, and satyrs shall dance there; their forts and towers shall be a den for ever, a joy of wild asses; there shall the great owl make her nest, and lay and hatch and gather under her shadow; it shall be a court of dragons; the screech owl also shall rest there, and find for herself a place of rest.' You see here is a pretty collection of desolate animals, which is verified in this town to a tittle, and perhaps it may also allude to your habitation, for you know all types may be taken by abundance of handles; however, I defy your owls to match mine.

If the default of your spirits and nerves be nothing but the effect of the hyp, I have no more to say. We all must submit to that wayward Queen; I too in no small degree own her sway,

I feel her influence while I speak her power.

1 Gray, Richard West, Horace Walpole, and Thomas Ashton formed a "quadruple alliance" in close friendship during their days at Eton. The sudden death of West in 1742 was a great shock to Gray. Except for a brief quarrel, Gray was a lifelong friend of Walpole.

But if it be a real distemper, pray take more care of your health, if not for your own at least for our sakes, and do not be so soon weary of this little world: I do not know what refined friendships you may have contracted in the other, but pray do not be in a hurry to see your acquaintance above; among your terrestrial familiars, however, though I say it that should not say it, there positively is not one that has a greater esteem for you than

Yours most sincerely, &c.

Peterhouse, December, 1736.

To West

After a month's expectation of you, and a fortnight's despair, at Cambridge, I am come to town, and to better hopes of seeing you. If what you sent me last [2] be the product of your melancholy, what may I not expect from your more cheerful hours? For by this time the ill health that you complain of is (I hope) quite departed; though, if I were self-interested, I ought to wish for the continuance of any thing that could be the occasion of so much pleasure to me. Low spirits are my true and faithful companions; they get up with me, go to bed with me, make journeys and returns as I do; nay, and pay visits, and will even affect to be jocose, and force a feeble laugh with me; but most commonly we sit alone together, and are the prettiest insipid company in the world. However, when you come, I believe they must undergo the fate of all humble companions, and be discarded. Would I could turn them to the same use that you have done, and make an Apollo of them. If they could write such verses with me, not hartshorn, nor spirit of amber, nor all that furnishes the closet of an apothecary's widow, should persuade me to part with them: But, while I write to you, I hear the bad news of Lady Walpole's death on Saturday night last. Forgive me if the thought of what my poor Horace must feel on that account, obliges me to have done in reminding you that I am

Yours, &c.

London, Aug. 22, 1737.

2 West's letter of July 4, with a poem *Ad Amicos.*

To West

Paris, May 22, 1739.[3]

After the little particulars aforesaid I should have proceeded to a journal of our transactions for this week past, should have carried you post from hence to Versailles, hurried you through the gardens to Trianon, back again to Paris, so away to Chantilly. But the fatigue is perhaps more than you can bear, and moreover I think I have reason to stomach your last piece of gravity. Supposing you were in your soberest mood, I am sorry you should think me capable of ever being so dissipé, so evaporé, as not to be in a condition of relishing any thing you could say to me. And now, if you have a mind to make your peace with me, arouse ye from your megrims and your melancholies, and (for exercise is good for you) throw away your night-cap, call for your jack-boots, and set out with me, last Saturday evening, for Versailles—and so at eight o'clock, passing through a road speckled with vines, and villas, and hares, and partridges, we arrive at the great avenue, flanked on either hand with a double row of trees about half a mile long, and with the palace itself to terminate the view; facing which, on each side of you is placed a semi-circle of very handsome buildings, which form the stables. These we will not enter into, because you know we are no jockies. Well! and is this the great front of Versailles? What a huge heap of littleness! it is composed, as it were, of three courts, all open to the eye at once, and gradually diminishing till you come to the royal apartments, which on this side present but half a dozen windows and a balcony. This last is all that can be called a front, for the rest is only great wings. The hue of all this mass is black, dirty red, and yellow; the first proceeding from stone changed by age; the second, from a mixture of brick; and the last, from a profusion of tarnished gilding. You cannot see a more disagreeable tout-ensemble; and, to finish the matter, it is all stuck over in many places with small busts of a tawny hue between every window. We pass through this to go into the garden, and here the case is indeed altered; nothing can be vaster and more magnificent than the back front; before it a very spacious terrace spreads itself, adorned with two large basons; these are bordered and lined (as most of the others) with white marble, with handsome statues of bronze reclined on

3 Gray was making the grand tour with Horace Walpole.

their edges. From hence you descend a huge flight of steps into a semi-circle formed by woods, that are cut all round into niches, which are filled with beautiful copies of all the famous antique statues in white marble. Just in the midst is the bason of Latona; she and her children are standing on the top of a rock in the middle, on the sides of which are the peasants, some half, some totally changed into frogs, all which throw out water at her in great plenty. From this place runs on the great alley, which brings you into a complete round, where is the bason of Apollo, the biggest in the gardens. He is rising in his car out of the water, surrounded by nymphs and tritons, all in bronze, and finely executed, and these, as they play, raise a perfect storm about him; beyond this is the great canal, a prodigious long piece of water, that terminates the whole: All this you have at one coup d'oeil in entering the garden, which is truly great. I cannot say as much of the general taste of the place; every thing you behold savours too much of art; all is forced, all is constrained about you; statues and vases sowed every where without distinction; sugar-loaves and minced-pies of yew; scrawl-work of box, and little squirting jets-d'eau, besides a great sameness in the walks, cannot help striking one at first sight, not to mention the silliest of labyrinths, and all Æsop's fables in water; since these were designed in usum Delphini [4] only. Here then we walk by moonlight, and hear the ladies and the nightingales sing. Next morning, being Whitsunday, make ready to go to the Installation of nine Knights du Saint Esprit, Cambis is one: high mass celebrated with music, great croud, much incense, King, Queen, Dauphin, Mesdames, Cardinals, and Court: Knights arrayed by his majesty; reverences before the altar, not bows, but curtsies; stiff hams; much tittering among the ladies; trumpets, kettle-drums and fifes. My dear West, I am vastly delighted with Trianon, all of us with Chantilly; if you would know why, you must have patience, for I can hold my pen no longer, except to tell you that I saw Britannicus [5] last Night; all the characters, particularly Agrippina and Nero, done to perfection; to-morrow Phædra and Hippolitus.[6] We are making you a little bundle of petites pieces; there is nothing in them, but they are acting at present; there are too Crebillon's Letters, and Amusemens sur le langage des Bêtes, said

---

4 "For the use of the Dauphin." [The Latin *delphinus*, "dolphin," derived from the proper name of the family of the Counts of Vienne.]

5 By Racine (1669).
6 Undoubtedly *Phèdre* by Racine (1677).

to be of one Bougeant, a Jesuit; they are both esteemed, and lately come out. This day se'nnight we go to Rheims.

To His Mother

Rheims, June 21, N.S. 1739.

We have now been settled almost three weeks in this city, which is more considerable upon account of its size and antiquity, than from the number of its inhabitants, or any advantages of commerce. There is little in it worth a stranger's curiosity, besides the cathedral church, which is a vast Gothic building of a surprising beauty and lightness, all covered over with a profusion of little statues, and other ornaments. It is here the Kings of France are crowned by the Archbishop of Rheims, who is the first Peer, and the Primate of the kingdom: The holy vessel made use of on that occasion, which contains the oil, is kept in the church of St. Nicasius hard by, and is believed to have been brought by an angel from heaven at the coronation of Clovis, the first christian king. The streets in general have but a melancholy aspect, the houses all old; the public walks run along the side of a great moat under the ramparts, where one hears a continual croaking of frogs; the country round about is one great plain covered with vines, which at this time of the year afford no very pleasing prospect, as being not above a foot high. What pleasures the place denies to the sight, it makes up to the palate; since you have nothing to drink but the best champaigne in the world, and all sort of provisions equally good. As to other pleasures, there is not that freedom of conversation among the people of fashion here, that one sees in other parts of France; for though they are not very numerous in this place, and consequently must live a good deal together, yet they never come to any great familiarity with one another. As my Lord Conway had spent a good part of his time among them, his brother, and we with him, were soon introduced into all their assemblies: As soon as you enter, the lady of the house presents each of you a card, and offers you a party at quadrille; you sit down, and play forty deals without intermission, excepting one quarter of an hour, when every body rises to eat of what they call the gouter, which supplies the place of our tea, and is a service of wine, fruits, cream, sweetmeats, crawfish and cheese. People take what they like, and sit down again to play; after that, they make little parties to go to the walks together, and then all the company retire to their separate habitations. Very seldom any suppers or dinners are given; and this is the manner they live among one another; not so much out of any aversion they have to pleasure, as out of a sort of formality they have contracted by not being much frequented by people who have lived at Paris. It is sure they do not hate gaiety any more than the rest of their country-people, and can enter into diversions, that are once proposed, with a good grace enough: for instance, the other evening we happened to be got together in a company of eighteen people, men and women of the best fashion here, at a garden in the town to walk; when one of the ladies bethought herself of asking, Why should not we sup here? Immediately the cloth was laid by the side of a fountain under the trees, and a very elegant supper served up; after which another said, Come, let us sing; and directly began herself: From singing we insensibly fell to dancing, and singing in a round; when somebody mentioned the violins, and immediately a company of them was ordered: Minuets were begun in the open air, and then came country-dances, which held till four o'clock next morning; at which hour the gayest lady there proposed, that such as were weary should get into their coaches, and the rest of them should dance before them with the music in the van; and in this manner we paraded through all the principal streets of the city, and waked every body in it. Mr. Walpole had a mind to make a custom of the thing, and would have given a ball in the same manner next week; but the women did not come into it; so I believe it will drop, and they will return to their dull cards, and usual formalities. We are not to stay above a month longer here, and shall then go to Dijon, the chief city of Burgundy, a very splendid and very gay town; at least such is the present design.

To His Mother

Turin, Nov. 7, N.S. 1739.

I am this night arrived here, and have just set down to rest me after eight days tiresome journey: For the three first we had the same road we before past through to go to Geneva; the fourth we turned out of it, and for that day and the next travelled rather among than upon the Alps; the way commonly running through a deep valley by the side of the river Arc, which works itself a passage, with great difficulty and a mighty noise, among vast quantities of rocks, that have rolled down from the mountain tops. The winter was so far advanced, as in great measure to spoil the beauty of the prospect, however, there was still somewhat fine remaining amidst the savageness and horror of the place: The sixth we began to go up several of these mountains; and as we were passing one, met with an odd accident enough: Mr. Walpole had a little fat black spaniel, that he was very fond of, which he sometimes used to set down, and let it run by the chaise side. We were at that time in a very rough road, not two yards broad at most; on one side was a great wood of pines, and on the other a vast precipice; it was noon-day, and the sun shone bright, when all of a sudden, from the wood-side, (which was as steep upwards, as the other part was downwards) out rushed a great wolf, came close to the head of the horses, seized the dog by the throat, and rushed up the hill again with him in his mouth. This was done in less than a quarter of a minute; we all saw it, and yet the servants had not time to draw their pistols, or do any thing to save the dog. If he had not been there, and the creature had thought fit to lay hold of one of the horses; chaise, and we, and all must inevitably have tumbled above fifty fathoms perpendicular down the precipice. The seventh we came to Lanebourg, the last town in Savoy; it lies at the foot of the famous mount Cenis, which is so situated as to allow no room for any way but over the very top of it. Here the chaise was forced to be pulled to pieces, and the baggage and that to be carried by mules: We ourselves were wrapped up in our furs, and seated upon a sort of matted chair without legs, which is carried upon poles in the manner of a bier, and so begun to ascend by the help of eight men. It was six miles to the top, where a plain opens itself about as many more in breadth, covered perpetually with very deep snow, and in the midst of that a great lake of unfathomable depth, from whence a river takes its rise, and tumbles over monstrous rocks quite down the other side of the mountain. The descent is six miles more, but infinitely more steep than the going up; and here the men perfectly fly down with you, stepping from stone to stone with incredible swiftness in places where none but they could go three paces without falling. The immensity of the precipices, the roaring of the river and torrents that run into it, the huge craggs covered with ice and snow, and the clouds below you and about you, are objects it is impossible to conceive without seeing them; and though we had heard many strange descriptions of the scene, none of them at all came up to it. We were but five hours in performing the whole, from which you may judge of the rapidity of the men's motion. We are now got into Piedmont, and stopped a little while at La Ferriere, a small village about three quarters of the way down, but still among the clouds, where we began to hear a new language spoken round about us; at last we got quite down, went through the Pas de Suse, a narrow road among the Alps, defended by two fortresses, and lay at Bossolens: Next evening through a fine avenue of nine miles in length, as straight as a line, we arrived at this city, which, as you know, is the capital of the Principality, and the residence of the King of Sardinia. . . . We shall stay here, I believe, a fortnight, and proceed for Genoa, which is three or four days journey to go post. I am, etc.

To West

Turin, Nov. 16, N.S. 1739.

. . . I own I have not, as yet, any where met with those grand and simple works of Art, that are to amaze one, and whose sight one is to be the better for: But those of Nature have astonished me beyond expression. In our little journey up to the Grande Chartreuse, I do not remember to have gone ten paces without an exclamation, that there was no restraining: Not a precipice, not a torrent, not a cliff, but is pregnant with religion and poetry. There are certain scenes that would awe an atheist into belief, without the help of other argument. One need not have a very fantastic imagination to see spirits there at noon-day: You have Death perpetually before your eyes, only so far removed, as to compose the mind without frighting it. I am well persuaded St. Bruno was a man of no common genius, to choose such a situation for his retirement; and perhaps should have been a disciple of his, had I been born in his time. You may believe Abelard and Heloïse were not forgot upon this occasion: If I do not mistake, I saw you too every now and then at a distance among the trees; il me semble, que j'ai vu ce chien de visage là quelque part.[7] You seemed to call to me from the other side of the precipice, but the noise of the river below was so great, that I really could not distinguish what you

---

7 "It seems to me I've seen that dogface somewhere before."

said; it seemed to have a cadence like verse. In your next you will be so good to let me know what it was. The week we have since passed among the Alps, has not equalled the single day upon that mountain, because the winter was rather too far advanced, and the weather a little foggy. However, it did not want its beauties; the savage rudeness of the view is inconceivable without seeing it: I reckoned in one day, thirteen cascades, the least of which was, I dare say, one hundred feet in height. . . .

To West

Tivoli, May 20, 1740.

This day being in the palace of his Highness the Duke of Modena, he laid his most serene commands upon me to write to Mr. West, and said he thought it for his glory, that I should draw up an inventory of all his most serene possessions for the said West's perusal.—Imprimis, a house, being in circumference a quarter of a mile, two feet and an inch; the said house containing the following particulars, to wit, a great room. Item, another great room; item, a bigger room; item, another room; item, a vast room; item, a sixth of the same; a seventh ditto; an eighth as before; a ninth as abovesaid; a tenth (see No. 1.); item, ten more such, besides twenty besides, which, not to be too particular, we shall pass over. The said rooms contain nine chairs, two tables, five stools, and a cricket. From whence we shall proceed to the garden, containing two millions of superfine laurel hedges, a clump of cypress trees, and half the river Teverone, that pisses into two thousand several chamberpots. Finis.—Dame Nature desired me to put in a list of her little goods and chattels, and, as they were small, to be very minute about them. She has built here three or four little mountains, and laid them out in an irregular semi-circle; from certain others behind, at a greater distance, she has drawn a canal, into which she has put a little river of hers, called Anio; she has cut a huge cleft between the two innermost of her four hills, and there she has left it to its own disposal; which she has no sooner done, but, like a heedless chit, it tumbles headlong down a declivity fifty feet perpendicular, breaks itself all to shatters, and is converted into a shower of rain, where the sun forms many a bow, red, green, blue and yellow. To get out of our metaphors without any further trouble, it is the most noble sight in the world. The

weight of that quantity of waters, and the force they fall with, have
worn the rocks they throw themselves among into a thousand irregular craggs, and to a vast depth. In this channel it goes boiling
along with a mighty noise till it comes to another steep, where you
see it a second time come roaring down (but first you must walk
two miles farther) a greater height than before, but not with that
quantity of waters; for by this time it has divided itself, being
crossed and opposed by the rocks, into four several streams, each
of which, in emulation of the great one, will tumble down too;
and it does tumble down, but not from an equally elevated place;
so that you have at one view all these cascades intermixed with
groves of olive and little woods, the mountains rising behind them,
and on the top of one (that which forms the extremity of one of
the half-circle's horns) is seated the town itself. At the very extremity of that extremity, on the brink of the precipice, stands the
Sybils' temple, the remains of a little rotunda, surrounded with
its portico, above half of whose beautiful Corinthian pillars are
still standing and entire; all this on one hand. On the other, the
open Campagna of Rome, here and there a little castle on a hillock,
and the city itself on the very brink of the horizon, indistinctly
seen (being 18 miles off) except the dome of St. Peter's; which,
if you look out of your window, wherever you are, I suppose, you
can see. I did not tell you that a little below the first fall, on the
side of the rock, and hanging over that torrent, are little ruins
which they shew you for Horace's house, a curious situation to
observe the

> Præceps Anio, & Tiburni lucus, & uda
> Mobilibus pomaria rivis.[8]

Mæcenas did not care for such a noise, it seems, and built him a
house (which they also carry one to see) so situated that it sees
nothing at all of the matter, and for any thing he knew there might
be no such river in the world. Horace had another house on the
other side of the Teverone, opposite to Mæcenas's; and they told
us there was a bridge of communication, by which 'andava il detto
Signor per trastullarsi coll' istesso Orazio.'[9] In coming hither we
crossed the Aquæ Albulæ, a vile little brook that stinks like a fury,
and they say it has stunk so these thousand years. I forgot the

8 "The headlong Anio, Tiburnus' grove,
and orchards watered by the coursing rills"
(Horace *Odes* I. vii. 13–14).

9 "The aforesaid gentleman went to amuse
himself with the aforesaid Horace."

Piscina of Quintilius Varus, where he used to keep certain little fishes. This is very entire, and there is a piece of the aqueduct that supplied it too; in the garden below is old Rome, built in little, just as it was, they say. There are seven temples in it, and no houses at all: They say there were none.

To West

London, Thursday, April [8], [1742]

You are very good in giving yourself the trouble to read and find fault with my long harangues. Your freedom (as you call it) has so little need of apologies, that I should scarce excuse your treating me any otherwise; which, whatever compliment it might be to my vanity, would be making a very ill one to my understanding. As to matter of stile, I have this to say: The language of the age is never the language of poetry; except among the French, whose verse, where the thought or image does not support it, differs in nothing from prose. Our poetry, on the contrary, has a language peculiar to itself; to which almost every one, that has written, has added something by enriching it with foreign idioms and derivatives: Nay sometimes words of their own composition or invention. Shakespear and Milton have been great creators this way; and no one more licentious than Pope or Dryden, who perpetually borrow expressions from the former. Let me give you some instances from Dryden, whom every body reckons a great master of our poetical tongue.——Full of *museful mopeings*—unlike the *trim* of love—a pleasant *beverage*—a *roundelay* of love—stood silent in his *mood*—with knots and *knares* deformed—his *ireful mood*—in proud *array*—his *boon* was granted—and *disarray* and shameful rout—*wayward* but wise—*furbished* for the field—the *foiled dodderd* oaks—*disherited*—*smouldring* flames—*retchless* of laws—*crones* old and ugly—the *beldam* at his side—the *grandamhag*—*villanize* his Father's fame.——But they are infinite: And our language not being a settled thing (like the French) has an undoubted right to words of an hundred years old, provided antiquity have not rendered them unintelligible. In truth, Shakespear's language is one of his principal beauties; and he has no less advantage over your Addisons and Rowes in this, than in those other great excellencies you mention. Every word in him is a picture. . . .

To West

London, May 27, 1742.

Mine, you are to know, is a white Melancholy, or rather Leucocholy, for the most part; which though it seldom laughs or dances, nor ever amounts to what one calls Joy or Pleasure, yet is a good easy sort of a state, and ça ne laisse que de s'amuser.[10] The only fault of it is insipidity; which is apt now and then to give a sort of Ennui, which makes one form certain little wishes that signify nothing. But there is another sort, black indeed, which I have now and then felt, that has somewhat in it like Tertullian's rule of faith, Credo quia impossibile est;[11] for it believes, nay, is sure of every thing that is unlikely, so it be but frightful; and, on the other hand, excludes and shuts its eyes to the most possible hopes, and every thing that is pleasurable; from this the Lord deliver us! for none but he and sunshiny weather can do it. In hopes of enjoying this kind of weather, I am going into the country for a few weeks. . . .

To Walpole

Camb:ge Feb: 13. 1753.

Sure You are not out of your Wits! this I know, if you suffer my Head to be printed, you infallibly will put me out of mine.[12] I conjure you immediately to put a stop to any such design. who is at the Expence of engraving it, I know not; but if it be Dodsley, I will make up the Loss to him. the thing, as it was, I know will make me ridiculous enough; but to appear in proper Person at the head of my works, consisting of half a dozen Ballads in 30 Pages, would be worse than the Pillory. I do assure you, if I had received such a Book with such a frontispice without any warning, I believe, it would have given me a Palsy. therefore I rejoice to have received this Notice; & shall not be easy, till you tell me all thoughts of it are laid aside. I am extremely in earnest, & can't bear even the Idea!

I had wrote to Dodsley to tell him, how little I liked the Title he had prefix'd, but your letter has put all that out of my Head. if you think it necessary to print these explanations for the use of

10 "That can't help being amusing."
11 "I believe *because* it is impossible."

12 Dodsley proposed to print Gray's portrait (by Eckhardt) as a frontispiece to the poems.

People that have no eyes, I could be glad, they were a little alter'd. I am to my shame in your debt for a long letter, but I can not think of anything else, till you have set me at ease. Adieu, I am

Yours ever,

T: G:

To WHARTON [13]

Dear Doct[r],—I cannot say anything to you about Mason, whose motions I am entirely a stranger to, & have not once heard from him since he left London; till (the 3[d] of this month) a letter came, in w[ch] he tells me, that Gaskarth is at Aston with him, & that the latter end of the month, or the beginning of the next, he shall be in town as he goes into waiting the last fortnight in October. L[d] H. has sent him no less than four Expresses (literally so) with publick News good & bad, w[ch] has made him of infinite importance in the eyes of that neighbourhood. I can not pretend therefore to guess, whether he will be able to come to you. I am sorry to tell you that I try in vain to execute your commission about tapestry. what is so bad, as wry-mouthed histories? and yet for this they ask me at least double the price you talk of. I have seen nothing neither, that would please me at any price: yet I allow tapestry (if at all tolerable) to be a very proper furniture for your sort of house; but doubt, if any bargain of that kind is to be met with, except at some old mansion-sale in the country, where People will disdain tapestry, because they hear, that Paper is all the fashion. Stonhewer has been in Northamptonshire till now: as you told me the subject of your letter, I did not send it thither to him, besides that he was every day expected in Town. at last he is come, and has it; but I have not yet seen him: he is gone to-day (I believe) to Portsmouth to receive a Morocco Embassador, but returns very shortly. there is one advantage in getting into your Abbey at Christmastime: that it will be at its worst, & if you can bear it then, you need not fear for the rest of the year. M[r] W: [14] has lately made a new Bed-chamber, w[ch] as it is in the best tast of anything he has yet done, & in your own Gothic way, I must describe a little. you enter by a peaked door at one corner

---

13 Dr. Thomas Wharton, an old schoolfellow. This letter also mentions William Mason, "a good and well-meaning creature" who wrote some poor verse and had a consuming interest in gardening: he was editor of Gray's letters. Richard Stonehewer was a schoolboy friend of Gray and a life-long admirer.

14 Horace Walpole, who was making Strawberry Hill into a "Gothic" villa.

of the room (out of a narrow winding passage, you may be sure)
into an Alcove, in wch the bed is to stand, formed by a screen of
pierced work opening by one large arch in the middle to the rest
of the chamber, wch is lighted at the other end by a bow-window
of three bays, whose tops are of rich painted glass in mosaic. the
cieling is coved & fretted in star & quatrefoil compartments, with
roses at the intersections, all in papier-maché. the chimney on
your left is the high-altar in the cathedral of Rouen (from whence
the Screen also is taken) consisting of a low surbased Arch between two octagon Towers, whose pinnacles almost reach the
Cieling, all of Nich-work. the chairs & dressing-table are real carved
ebony, pick'd up at auctions. the hangings uniform purple paper,
hung all over with the court of Henry, ye 8th, copied after the Hol-
bein's in the Queen's Closet at Kensington, in black & gold frames.
the bed is to be either from Burleigh (for Ld Exeter is new furnishing it, & means to sell some of his original houshold-stuff) of the
rich old tarnish'd embroidery; or if that is not to be had, & it must
be new, it is to be a cut velvet with a dark purple pattern on a
stone-colour sattin ground, & deep mixt fringes & tassels. there's
for you, but I want you to see it. in the meantime I live in the
Musæum, [15] & write volumes of antiquity. I have got (out of the
original Ledger-book of the Signet) K: Richard 3^d's oath to
Elizabeth, late *calling herself Queen of* England; to prevail upon
her to come out of Sanctuary with her 5 daughters. his Grant to
Lady Hastings & her Son, dated 6 weeks after he had cut off her
Husband's head. a letter to his Mother; another to his Chancellor,
to persuade his Sollicitor General not to marry Jane Shore then in
Ludgate by his command. Sr Tho: Wyat's Defence at his Tryal,
when accused by B^p Bonner of high-treason; Lady Purbeck and
her Son's remarkable Case, and several more odd things unknown
to our Historians. when I come home, I have a great heap of the
Conway Papers [16] wch is a secret) to read, & make out. in short, I
am up to the ears.

The Fish you mention is so accurately described that I know it
at sight. it is the *Ink-fish*, or Loligo of the Romans. in Greek Τευθὸς,
in Italian, Calamaio. in French, Calmar. you will find it ranged by
Linnæus in the class of *Vermes*, the order of *Mollusca*, the genus

---

15 The British Museum, recently opened.
16 The papers of Edward Conway (d.
1631) and his grandson, Edward Conway
(d. 1683); both served as Secretaries of
State.

of *Sepia*, Nᵒ 4, pag: 659. The smaller ones are eaten as a delicacy fried, with their own ink for sauce, by the Italians and others. you may see it in Aldrovandus.[17]

I do not see much myself of the face of nature here, but I enquire. Wheat was cutting in Kent the 23ᵈ of July. the 25ᵗʰ at Enfield. the 27ᵗʰ Wheat, Barley, & Oats cutting all at once about Windsor: the forward Pease all got in, ground plough'd and turnips sow'd. 9ᵗʰ of August Harvest still continued in Buck:ʳᵉ. The 27ᵗʰ about Kennington it was just over, being delay'd for want of hands. in some places 50 mile from London it is but just over now for the same reason. the 3ᵈ of Aug: Catherine-pears, Muscle-Plums, and small black Cherries were sold in wheel barrows. Filberds in plenty the 8ᵗʰ. Mulberries, & fine green-gage plums the 19ᵗʰ. fine Nectarines & Peaches, the 27ᵗʰ. the 4ᵗʰ of Sept:ʳ Melons and Perdrigon-plums. the 8ᵗʰ, Walnuts 20 a penny. this is all I know about fruit. my Weather is not very compleat.

July

20, 1759. London. Therm: 5 in the afternoon,			at 79
21	. . . .		
22	. . . . same hour		76
23 Wind N.N.E.	d:° .	80	⎧ Grass
24	d:° .	—	⎨ burnt
25	d:° .	78	⎩ up
26 wᵈ N:N:W. brisk at noon			71
27 Wind laid at night			—
28 wᵈ N: fair, white flying clouds, ...	9 in mornᵍ		68
29 " S.S.W. still & cloudy sunshine	d:°		69
30. gloomy & hot. wᵈ W:S:W: shower at night . .	d:°		70
31. 8 hours rain. wᵈ S:W: moonshiny night . . .	d:°		70

Aug:

1. cloudy. W:S:W: brisk and chill, bright evenᵍ .	d:°	66
2. cloudy Sun. W:S:W: chill. a little rain. night clear	d:°	65
3. Fine, wᵈ N:W: cool	d:°	64
4. gloomy. S:W: high. seven hours heavy rain .	d:°	64
5. cloudy. N:W: hard rain at night . . .	d:°	66
6. Clouds & sunshine. wᵈ N:W: brisk . . .	Therm: at 9	64
7. wᵈ S:W: fair	d:°	66
8. W: clear and hot	"	74
9. S:S:W: very hot	"	76

[17] Ulysse Aldrovandus, author of a thirteen-volume natural history (1599–1603).

10.	d°.	hot and foggy	.	.	.	.	.	.	"	74
11.		clear and extreme hot	.	.	.	.		"	.	76
12.	N:N:W:	small rain. evening fine	.	.	.	.		"	.	66
13.	N:N:E:	brisk. fine day	.	.	.	.	.	"	.	66
14.		cloudy	.	.	.	.	.	.	"	64
15.	N:N:W:	clouds & sun	.	.	.	.	.	"	.	68
16.		very fine	.	.	.	.	.	.	"	64
17.	S:W:	overcast. some rain	.	.	.	.		"	.	68
18.		very fine	.	.	.	.	.	.	"	64
19.	W:N:W:	cloudy, but fair. at night hard rain	.		"	.	64
20.	W:S:W:	overcast. at night much rain	.	.	"	.	66

I go no farther than you do: but it is down in my book.

what do you say to all our victories? The night we rejoiced for Boscawen,[18] in the midst of squibs and bonfires arrived Lord G. Sackville. He sees company: & to-day has put out a short address to the Publick, saying, he expects a Court-Martial (for no one abroad had authority to try him) and desires people to suspend their judgement. I fear, it is a rueful case.

I believe, I shall go on Monday to Stoke for a time, where Lady Cobh^m has been dying. My best respects to Mrs Wharton. Believe me ever faithfully

Yours

TG:

Southampton-Row, Sept: 18. 1759.

To Wharton

[ca. June 20, 1760]

Dear Doctor,

. . . .

If you have seen Stonhewer he has probably told you of my old Scotch (or rather Irish) poetry. I am gone mad about them. they are said to be translations (literal & in prose) from the *Erse*-tongue, done by one Macpherson, a young Clergyman in the High-lands. he means to publish a Collection he has of these specimens of antiquity, if it be antiquity: but what plagues me is, I cannot come at any certainty on that head. I was so struck, so *extasié* with their

---

18 Edward Boscawen defeated the French fleet off Lagos Bay, Portugal, on August 18, 1759. George Sackville (First Viscount Sackville) was dismissed from the army after the Battle of Minden (1759), in which he failed to follow orders to attack the French.

infinite beauty, that I writ into Scotland to make a thousand enquiries. The letters I have in return are ill-wrote, ill-reason'd, unsatisfactory, calculated (one would imagine) to deceive one, &
yet not cunning enough to do it cleverly. in short, the whole external evidence would make one believe these fragments (for so
he calls them, tho' nothing can be more entire) counterfeit: but
the internal is so strong on the other side, that I am resolved to believe them genuine, spite of the Devil & the Kirk. It is impossible
to convince me, that they were invented by the same Man, that
writes me these letters. on the other hand it is almost as hard to
suppose, if they are original, that he should be able to translate
them so admirably. what can one do? since St:^{r} went, I have received another of a very different & inferior kind (being merely descriptive) much more modern than the former (he says) yet very
old too; this too in its way is extremely fine. In short this Man is
the very Demon of Poetry, or he has lighted on a treasure hid for
ages. the Welch Poets are also coming to light: I have seen a Discourse in MS. about them (by one Mr Evans,[19] a Clergyman) with
specimens of their writings. this is in Latin, & tho' it don't approach
the other, there are fine scraps among it.

You will think I am grown mighty poetical of a sudden; you
would think so still more, if you knew, there was a Satyr printed
against me & Mason jointly. it is call'd *Two Odes*: the one is inscribed to Obscurity (that is me) the other to Oblivion. it tells me
what I never heard before, for (speaking of himself) the Author
says, tho' he has,

> Nor the Pride, nor Self-Opinion,
> That possess the happy pair,
> Each of Taste the fav'rite Minion,
> Prancing thro' the desert air:
> Yet shall he mount, with classick housings graced,
> By help mechanick of equestrian block;
> And all unheedful of the Critick's mock
> Spur his light Courser o'er the bounds of Taste.

The writer is a Mr Coleman, who publish'd the *Connoisseur*,
nephew to the late Lady Bath, & a Friend of Garrick's. I believe
his Odes sell no more than mine did, for I saw a heap of them lie

---

19 Evan Evans, who published *Some Specimens of the Poetry of the Antient Welsh Bards* in 1764.

in a Bookseller's window, who recommended them to me as a very pretty thing.

If I did not mention Tristram [20] to you, it was because I thought I had done so before. there is much good fun in it, & humour sometimes hit & sometimes mist. I agree with your opinion of it, & shall see the two future volumes with pleasure. have you read his Sermons (with his own comic figure at the head of them)? they are in the style I think most proper for the pulpit, and shew a very strong imagination and a sensible heart: but you see him often tottering on the verge of laughter, & ready to throw his periwig in the face of his audience. now for my season.

April 10. I observed the Elm putting out.
 12. That, & the Pear looked green. Therm: at 62.
 13. very fine; White-Poplar & Willow put out.
 15. Standard-Pear (shelter'd) in full bloom.
 18. Lime & Horn-beam green.
 19. Swallows flying.
 20. Th: at 60. w^d S:W: Sky-Lark, Chaffinch, Thrush, Wren, & Robin singing. Horse-Chesnut, Wild-Bryar, Bramble, and Sallow had spread their leaves. Haw-thorn & Lilac had form'd their blossoms. Black-thorn, double-flower'd Peach, & Pears in full bloom; Double Jonquils, Hyacinths, Anemones, single Wall-flowers, & Auriculas in flower. In the fields, Dog-Violets, Daisies, Dandelion, Buttercups, Red-Archangel, & Shepherd's Purse.
 21. Almond out of bloom, & spreading its leaves.
 26. Lilacs flow'ring.
May 1. Gentianella in flower.
 2. Pear goes off. Apple blooms. Th: at 63. W^d N:E: still fair and dry.
 3. Evening & all night hard rain.
 4. Th: at 40. W^d N:E:, rain.
 11. Very fine. W^d N:E: Horse-Chesnut in full bloom. Wallnut & Vine spread. Lilacs, Persian Jasmine, Tulips, Wall-flowers, Pheasant-eye, Lilly in the Valley in flower. in the fields, Furze, Cowslips, Harebells, and Cow-Parsnep.
 13. Jasmine and Acacia spread. fine weather.
 18. Show'ry. W^d high.
 19. Same. Therm: at 56.
 20. Thunder, Rain. . . 54.

20 The first and second volumes of Sterne's *Tristram Shandy* were printed at York in 1760.

21. Rain. W^d N:E: 52.

31. Green Peas 15d a Quart.

June 1. .... at 78.

2. Scarlet Strawberries, Duke-Cherries; hay-making here.

3. W^d S:S:E: Therm: at 84 (the highest I ever saw it) it was at Noon. since wch till last week we had hot dry weather. now it rains like mad. Cherries and Strawberries in bushels.

I believe, there is no fear of War with Spain.

To Mason

[London, Nov. 8, 1765]

Dear Mason

. . . .

I am return'd from Scotland charm'd with my expedition: it is of the Highlands I speak: the Lowlands are worth seeing once, but the Mountains are extatic, & ought to be visited in pilgrimage once a year. none but those monstrous creatures of God know how to join so much beauty with so much horror. a fig for your Poets, Painters, Gardeners, & Clergymen, that have not been among them: their imagination can be made up of nothing but bowling-greens, flowering shrubs, horse-ponds, Fleet ditches, shell-grottoes, & Chinese rails. then I had so beautiful an autumn: Italy could hardly produce a nobler scene of finer season, and this so sweetly contrasted with that perfection of nastiness, & total want of accommodation, that Scotland only can supply. oh! you would have bless'd yourself. I shall certainly go again. what a pity 'tis I can't draw, nor describe, nor ride on horseback!

To Walpole

Pembroke-college, Feb. 25, 1768.

To your friendly accusation, I am glad I can plead not guilty with a safe conscience. Dodsley told me in the spring that the plates from Mr. Bentley's designs [21] were worn out, and he wanted to have them copied and reduced to a smaller scale for a new edition. I dissuaded him from so silly an expense, and desired he would put in no ornaments at all. The *Long Story* was to be totally omitted, as its only use (that of explaining the prints) was gone: but to supply the place of it in bulk, lest *my works* should be mistaken

21 Gray's *Poems* had appeared with the designs in 1753, 1765, and 1766. The volume was first entitled *Designs by Mr. R. Bentley for Six Poems by Mr. T. Gray.*

for the works of a flea, or a pismire, I promised to send him an equal weight of poetry or prose: so, since my return hither, I put up about two ounces of stuff; viz. The Fatal Sisters, The Descent of Odin (of both which you have copies), a bit of something from the Welch, and certain little notes, partly from justice (to acknowledge the debt, where I had borrowed any thing), partly from ill temper, just to tell the gentle reader, that Edward I. was not Oliver Cromwell, nor queen Elizabeth the witch of Endor. This is literally all; and with all this I shall be but a shrimp of an author. I gave leave also to print the same thing at Glasgow; but I doubt my packet has miscarried, for I hear nothing of its arrival as yet. To what you say to me so civilly, that I ought to write more, I reply in your own words (like the pamphleteer, who is going to confute you out of your own mouth), What has one to do, when *turned of fifty*, but really to think of finishing? However, I will be candid (for you seem to be so with me), and avow to you, that till fourscore-and-ten, whenever the humour takes me, I will write, because I like it; and because I like myself better when I do so. If I do not write much, it is because I cannot. As you have not this last plea, I see no reason why you should not continue as long as it is agreeable to yourself, and to all such as have any curiosity or judgment in the subjects you choose to treat. By the way let me tell you (while it is fresh) that lord Sandwich, who was lately dining at Cambridge, speaking (as I am told) handsomely of your book,[22] said, it was pity you did not know that his cousin Manchester had a genealogy of the kings, which came down no lower than to Richard III. and at the end of it were two portraits of Richard and his son, in which that king appeared to be a handsome man. I tell you it as I heard it; perhaps you may think it worth enquiring into.

I have looked into Speed and Leslie.[23] It appears very odd, that Speed in the speech he makes for P. Warbeck, addressed to James IV. of Scotland, should three times cite the *manuscript proclamation* of Perkin, then in the hands of Sir Robert Cotton; and yet when he gives us the proclamation afterwards (on occasion of the insurrection in Cornwall) he does not cite any such manuscript. In Casley's Catalogue of the Cotton Library you may see whether

---

22 Walpole's *Historic Doubts on Richard III* (1768).
23 John Speed, *The Theater of the Empire of Great Britain* (1611) and *The History of Great Britain* (1611); and John Leslie, author of a Latin history of Scotland (1578).

this manuscript proclamation still exists or not: if it does, it may be found at the Musæum. Leslie will give you no satisfaction at all: though no subject of England, he could not write freely on this matter, as the title of Mary his mistress to the crown of England was derived from that of Henry VII. Accordingly, he every where treats Perkin as an impostor; yet drops several little expressions inconsistent with that supposition. He has preserved no proclamation: he only puts a short speech into Perkin's mouth, the substance of which is taken by Speed, and translated in the end of his, which is a good deal longer: the whole matter is treated by Leslie very concisely and superficially. I can easily transcribe it, if you please; but I do not see that it could answer any purpose.

Mr. Boswell's book [24] I was going to recommend to you, when I received your letter: it has pleased and moved me strangely, all (I mean) that relates to Paoli. He is a man born two thousand years after his time! The pamphlet proves what I have always maintained, that any fool may write a most valuable book by chance, if he will only tell us what he heard and saw with veracity. Of Mr. Boswell's truth I have not the least suspicion, because I am sure he could invent nothing of this kind. The true title of this part of his work is, A Dialogue between a Green-goose and a Hero.

. . . .

JOURNAL. 30 SEPT: 1769.[1]

W[d] at NW.; clouds & sunshine. a mile & ½ from Brough on a hill lay a great army encamp'd. to the left open'd a fine valley with green meadows & hedge rows, a Gentleman's house peeping forth from a grove of old trees. on a nearer approach, appear'd myriads of horses & cattle in the road itself & in all the fields round me, a brisk stream hurrying cross the way, thousands of clean healthy People in their best party-color'd apparel, Farmers & their families, Esquires & their daughters, hastening up from the dales & down the fells on every side, glittering in the sun & pressing forward to join the throng: [2] while the dark hills, on many of whose tops the mists were yet hanging, served as a contrast to this gay & moving scene, w[ch] continued for near two miles more along the road, and

---

24 *An Account of Corsica* (1768).
1 The journal of a tour in the Lake Country and Yorkshire. written to be sent to

Wharton, who could not go with Gray.
2 There was a fair at Brough.

the crowd (coming towards it) reach'd on as far as Appleby. On the ascent of the hill above Appleby the thick hanging wood & the long reaches of the Eden (rapid, clear, & full as ever) winding below with views of the Castle & Town gave much employment to the mirror: [3] but the sun was wanting & the sky overcast. oats & barley cut every where, but not carried in. passed Kirby-thore, S^r W: Dalston's house at Acornbank, Whinfield-park, Harthorn-oaks, Countess-pillar, Brougham-Castle, Mr Brown (one of ye six Clerks) his large new house, cross'd the Eden & the Eimot (pronounce *Eeman*) with its green vale, & at 3 o'clock dined with Mrs Buchanan, at *Penrith*, on trout & partridge. in the afternoon walk'd up the *Beacon-hill* a mile to the top, saw Whinfield and Lowther-parks, & thro' an opening in the bosom of that cluster of mountains, wch the Doctor well remembers, the lake of Ulz-water, with the craggy tops of a hundred nameless hills. these to W: & S:, to the N: a great extent of black & dreary plains, to E: *Cross-fell* just visible thro' mists & vapours hovering round it.

Oct: 1. W^d at S:W: a gray autumnal day, air perfectly calm & gentle. Went to see *Ulz-water* 5 miles distant. soon left the Keswick-road & turn'd to the left thro' shady lanes along the Vale of *Eeman*, which runs rapidly on near the way, ripling over the stones. to the right is *Delmaine*, a large fabrick of pale red stone, with 9 windows in front & 7 on the side built by Mr Hassel, behind it a fine lawn surrounded by woods & a long rocky eminence rising over them. a clear & brisk rivulet runs by the house to join the Eeman, whose course is in sight & at a small distance.

Farther on appears *Hatton St John*, a castle-like old mansion of Mr Huddleston. approach'd *Dunmallert*, a fine pointed hill, cover'd with wood planted by old Mr Hassle beforemention'd, who lives always at home & delights in planting. walk'd over a spungy meadow or two & began to mount this hill thro' a broad & strait green alley among the trees, & with some toil gain'd the summit. from hence saw the Lake opening directly at my feet majestic in its calmness, clear & smooth as a blew mirror with winding shores & low points of land cover'd with green inclosures, white farmhouses looking out among the trees, & cattle feeding. the water is almost every where border'd with cultivated lands gently sloping upwards till they reach the feet of the mountains, wch rise very

3 Claude glass, the mirrorlike (or telescopelike) device that "composed" and tinted a scene

rude & aweful with their broken tops on either hand. directly in front, at better than 3 mile's distance, *Place-Fell*, one of the bravest among them, pushes its bold broad breast into the midst of the Lake & forces it to alter its course, forming first a large bay to the left & then bending to the right.

I descended *Dunmallert* again by a side avenue, that was only not perpendicular, & came to *Barton*-bridge over the *Eeman*, then walking thro' a path in the wood round the bottom of the hill came forth, where the *Eeman* issues out of the lake, & continued my way along it's western shore close to the water, & generally on a level with it. Saw a cormorant flying over it & fishing. . . . (to be continued)

1 Oct: 1769.

The figure of *Ulz-water* nothing resembles that laid down in our maps: it is 9 miles long, & (at widest) under a mile in breadth. after extending itself 3 m: & ½ in a line to S: W: it turns at the foot of *Place-Fell*, almost due West, and is here not twice the breadth of the Thames at London. it is soon again interrupted by the roots of *Helvellyn*, a lofty & very rugged mountain, & spreading again turns off to S: E:, and is lost among the deep recesses of the hills. to this second turning I pursued my way about four miles along its borders beyond a village scatter'd among trees & call'd *Water-malloch*, in a pleasant grave day, perfectly calm & warm, but without a gleam of sunshine: then the sky seeming to thicken, the valley to grow more desolate, & evening drawing on, I return'd by the way I came to *Penrith*.

Oct: 2. W^d at S: E:, sky clearing, *Cross-fell* misty, but the outline of the other hills very distinct. set out at 10 for *Keswick*, by the road we went in 1767. saw *Greystock*-town & castle to the right, wch lie only 3 miles (over the Fells) from *Ulz-water*. pass'd through *Penradock & Threlcot* at the feet of *Saddleback*, whose furrow'd sides were gilt by the noon-day Sun, while its brow appear'd of a sad purple from the shadow of the clouds, as they sail'd slowly by it. the broad & green valley of *Gardies* and *Lowside*, with a swift stream glittering among the cottages & meadows lay to the left; and the much finer (but narrower) valley of *St John's* opening into it. *Hill-top* the large, tho' low, mansion of the Gaskarths, now a Farm-house, seated on an eminence among woods under a steep fell, was what appear'd the most conspicuous, & beside it a great rock like some antient tower nodding to its fall. pass'd by the side of *Skiddaw* & its cub called *Latterrig*, & saw from an eminence, at two miles distance, the Vale of Elysium in all its verdure, the sun then playing on the bosom of the lake, & lighting up all the mountains with its lustre.

Dined by two o'clock at the Queen's Head, and then straggled out alone to the *Parsonage*, fell down on my back across a dirty lane, with my glass [4] open in one hand, but broke only my knuckles: stay'd nevertheless, & saw the sun set in all its glory.

Oct: 3. W^d at S: E:; a heavenly day. rose at seven, and walk'd out under the conduct of my Landlord to *Borrodale*. the grass was cover'd with a hoar-frost, wch soon melted, & exhaled in a thin blewish smoke cross'd the meadows obliquely, catching a diversity of views among the hills over the lake & islands, & changing prospect at every ten paces, left *Cockshut* & *Castle-hill* (wch we formerly mounted) behind me, & drew near the foot of *Walla-crag*, whose bare & rocky brow, cut perpendicularly down above 400 feet, as I guess, awefully overlooks the way: our path here tends to the left, & the ground gently rising, & cover'd with a glade of scattering trees & bushes on the very margin of the water, opens both ways the most delicious view, that my eyes ever beheld. behind you are the magnificent heights of *Walla*-crag; opposite lie the thick hanging woods of Ld Egremont, & *Newland*-valley, with green & smiling fields embosom'd in the dark cliffs; to the left the jaws of *Borodale*, with that turbulent Chaos of mountain behind mountain roll'd in confusion; beneath you, & stretching far away to the right, the shining purity of the *Lake*, just ruffled by the breeze enough to shew it is alive, reflecting rocks, woods, fields, & inverted tops of mountains, with the white buildings of *Keswick*, *Crosthwait*-church, & *Skiddaw* for a back ground at distance. oh Doctor! I never wish'd more for you; & pray think, how the glass played its part in such a spot, wch is called *Carf-close-reeds*: I chuse to set down these barbarous names, that any body may enquire on the place, & easily find the particular station, that I mean. this scene continues to *Barrow-gate*, & a little farther, passing a brook called *Barrow-beck*, we enter'd *Borrodale*. the crags, named *Lodoor-banks* now begin to impend terribly over your way;

---

[4] Claude glass.

& more terribly, when you hear, that three years since an immense mass of rock tumbled at once from the brow, & bar'd all access to the dale (for this is the only road) till they could work their way thro' it. luckily no one was passing at the time of this fall; but down the side of the mountain, & far into the lake lie dispersed the huge fragments of this ruin in all shapes & in all directions. something farther we turn'd aside into a coppice, ascending a little in front of *Lodoor* water-fall. the height appears to be about 200 feet, the quantity of water not great, tho' (these three days excepted) it had rain'd daily in the hills for near two months before: but then the stream was nobly broken, leaping from rock to rock, & foaming with fury. on one side a towering crag, that spired up to equal, if not overtop, the neighbouring cliffs (this lay all in shade & darkness) on the other hand a rounder broader projecting hill shag'd with wood & illumined by the sun, wch glanced sideways on the upper part of the cataract. the force of the water wearing a deep channel in the ground hurries away to join the lake. we descended again, & passed the stream over a rude bridge. soon after we came under *Gowder-crag*, a hill more formidable to the eye & to the apprehension than that of *Lodoor;* the rocks atop, deep-cloven perpendicularly by the rains, hanging loose & nodding forwards, seem just starting from their base in shivers: the whole way down & the road on both sides is strew'd with piles of the fragments strangely thrown across each other & of a dreadful bulk. the place reminds one of those passes in the Alps, where the Guides tell you to move on with speed, & say nothing, lest the agitation of the air should loosen the snows above, and bring down a mass, that would overwhelm a caravan. I took their counsel here and hasten'd on in silence.

A SELECTION

Sir William Chambers
1726–1796

DESIGNS OF CHINESE BUILDINGS, FURNITURE, DRESSES, MACHINES, AND UTENSILS
1757

[A taste for chinoiserie led Sir William to believe that the English garden laid "too much stress on nature and simplicity." He preferred the surprising variety of the Oriental garden, which did not exclude the wild, dreary, or horrible. Even in the districts of limekilns and mines, Sir William thought, some astonishing effects could be gained: "a few uncouth straggling trees, some ruins, caverns, rocks, torrents, abandoned villages, in part consumed by fire, solitary hermitages, and other similar objects, artfully introduced and blended with gloomy plantations would complete the aspect of desolation, and serve to fill the mind." In his *Dissertation on Oriental Gardening* (1772) Sir William enlarges the matters mentioned in this earlier volume.]

Of the Art of Laying out Gardens among the Chinese

THEIR artists distinguish three different species of scenes, to which they give the appellations of pleasing, horrid, and enchanted. Their enchanted scenes answer, in a great measure, to what we call romantic, and in these they make use of several artifices to excite surprise. Sometimes they make a rapid stream or torrent pass underground, the turbulent noise of which strikes the ear of the newcomer, who is at a loss to know from whence it proceeds: at other times they dispose the rocks, buildings, and other objects that form the composition in such a manner as that the wind passing through the different interstices and cavities, made in them for that purpose, causes strange and uncommon sounds. They introduce into these scenes all kinds of extraordinary trees, plants, and flowers, form artificial and complicated echoes, and let loose different sorts of monstrous birds and animals.

In their scenes of horror they introduce impending rocks, dark caverns, and impetuous cataracts rushing down the mountains from all sides; the trees are ill formed, and seemingly torn to pieces

by the violence of tempests; some are thrown down and intercept
the course of the torrents, appearing as if they had been brought
down by the fury of the waters; others look as if shattered and
blasted by the force of lightning; the buildings are some in ruins,
others half-consumed by fire, and some miserable huts dispersed in
the mountains serve at once to indicate the existence and wretchedness of the inhabitants. These scenes are generally succeeded by
pleasing ones. The Chinese artists, knowing how powerfully contrast operates on the mind, constantly practice sudden transitions
and a striking opposition of forms, colors, and shades. Thus they
conduct you from limited prospects to extensive views; from objects of horror to scenes of delight; from lakes and rivers to plains,
hills, and woods; to dark and gloomy colors they oppose such as are
brilliant, and to complicated forms, simple ones; distributing by a
judicious arrangement the different masses of light and shade in
such a manner as to render the composition at once distinct in its
parts and striking in the whole.

A SELECTION

Edmund Burke

1729-1797

A PHILOSOPHICAL INQUIRY INTO THE ORIGIN OF OUR IDEAS OF THE SUBLIME AND BEAUTIFUL

1756, 1757

[This is a remarkable treatise for several reasons: it shows the tendency
to explain esthetic qualities as the result of emotions roused within the
observer rather than as qualities in the object observed; it crystallizes
many of the "romantic" ideas concerning the sublime that Addison
and others had suggested; it signalizes, therefore, the passing of
Augustan ideals of taste; it anticipates Lessing's famous *Laocoön* in
suggesting that poetry is not an imitative art in the same sense that the
plastic and visual arts are "imitative"; it anticipates semantic theories
that language is a communication of "attitudes" rather than of precise
and rational "ideas"; on this account, it tacitly justifies the poetry of
"nature" rather than of "art." It is, of course, doubtful whether Burke
was aware of the full implications of his comments.]

Of the Sublime

WHATEVER is fitted in any sort to excite the ideas of pain and danger, that is to say, whatever is in any sort terrible or is conversant about terrible objects, or operates in a manner analogous to terror, is a source of the *sublime;* that is, it is productive of the strongest emotion which the mind is capable of feeling. I say the strongest emotion, because I am satisfied the ideas of pain are much more powerful than those which enter on the part of pleasure. Without all doubt, the torments which we may be made to suffer are much greater in their effect on the body and mind than any pleasures which the most learned voluptuary could suggest, or than the liveliest imagination and the most sound and exquisitely sensible body could enjoy. Nay, I am in great doubt whether any man could be found who would earn a life of the most perfect satisfaction at the price of ending it in the torments which justice inflicted in a few hours on the late unfortunate regicide in France.[1] But as pain is stronger in its operation than pleasure, so death is in general a much more affecting idea than pain; because there are very few pains, however exquisite, which are not preferred to death: nay, what generally makes pain itself, if I may say so, more painful is that it is considered as an emissary of this king of terrors. When danger or pain press too nearly, they are incapable of giving any delight, and are simply terrible; but at certain distances, and with certain modifications, they may be, and they are, delightful, as we every day experience. The cause of this I shall endeavor to investigate hereafter.

[PART I, sec. 7]

Sympathy

It is by [sympathy] that we enter into the concerns of others; that we are moved as they are moved, and are never suffered to be indifferent spectators of almost anything which men can do or suffer. For sympathy must be considered as a sort of substitution, by which we are put into the place of another man, and affected in many respects as he is affected: so that this passion may either partake of the nature of those which regard self-preservation, and turning upon pain may be the source of the sublime; or it may turn upon ideas of pleasure; and then whatever has been said of the social affections, whether they regard society in general, or only some particular modes of it, may be applicable here. It is by this

---

1 Robert Francis Damien, drawn by horses in 1757 for attempting the life of Louis XV.

principle chiefly that poetry, painting, and other affecting arts transfuse their passions from one breast to another, and are often capable of grafting a delight on wretchedness, misery, and death itself. It is a common observation that objects which in the reality would shock are in tragical and suchlike representations the source of a very high species of pleasure. This, taken as a fact, has been the cause of much reasoning. The satisfaction has been commonly attributed, first, to the comfort we receive in considering that so melancholy a story is no more than a fiction; and, next, to the contemplation of our own freedom from the evils which we see represented. I am afraid it is a practice much too common in inquiries of this nature to attribute the cause of feelings which merely arise from the mechanical structure of our bodies, or from the natural frame and constitution of our minds, to certain conclusions of the reasoning faculty on the objects presented to us; for I should imagine that the influence of reason in producing our passions is nothing near so extensive as it is commonly supposed.

[PART I, sec. 13]

The Recapitulation

To draw the whole of what has been said into a few distinct points:—The passions which belong to self-preservation turn on pain and danger; they are simply painful when their causes immediately affect us; they are delightful when we have an idea of pain and danger without being actually in such circumstances; this delight I have not called pleasure, because it turns on pain, and because it is different enough from any idea of positive pleasure. Whatever excites this delight I call *sublime*. The passions belonging to self-preservation are the strongest of all the passions.

The second head to which the passions are referred with relation to their final cause is society. There are two sorts of societies. The first is the society of sex. The passion belonging to this is called love, and it contains a mixture of lust; its object is the beauty of women. The other is the great society with man and all other animals. The passion subservient to this is called likewise love, but it has no mixture of lust, and its object is beauty; which is a name I shall apply to all such qualities in things as induce in us a sense of affection and tenderness, or some other passion the most nearly resembling these. The passion of love has its rise in positive pleasure; it is, like all things which grow out of pleasure, capable of being mixed with a mode of uneasiness, that is, when an idea of its object is excited in the mind with an idea at the same time of having irretrievably lost it. This mixed sense of pleasure I have not called *pain* because it turns upon actual pleasure, and because it is, both in its cause and in most of its effects, of a nature altogether different.

Next to the general passion we have for society, to a choice in which we are directed by the pleasure we have in the object, the particular passion under this head called sympathy has the greatest extent. The nature of this passion is to put us in the place of another in whatever circumstance he is in, and to affect us in a like manner; so that this passion may, as the occasion requires, turn either on pain or pleasure; but with the modifications mentioned in some cases in section 11. As to imitation and preference, nothing more need be said.

[Part I, sec. 18]

Of the Passion Caused by the Sublime

The passion caused by the great and sublime in *nature*, when those causes operate most powerfully, is astonishment: and astonishment is that state of the soul in which all its motions are suspended, with some degree of horror. In this case the mind is so entirely filled with its object that it cannot entertain any other, nor by consequence reason on that object which employs it. Hence arises the great power of the sublime, that, far from being produced by them, it anticipates our reasonings, and hurries us on by an irresistible force. Astonishment, as I have said, is the effect of the sublime in its highest degree; the inferior effects are admiration, reverence, and respect.

[Part II, sec. 1]

Recapitulation

On the whole, the qualities of beauty, as they are merely sensible qualities, are the following: First, to be comparatively small. Secondly, to be smooth. Thirdly, to have a variety in the direction of the parts; but, fourthly, to have those parts not angular, but melted, as it were, into each other. Fifthly, to be of a delicate frame, without any remarkable appearance of strength. Sixthly, to have its colors clear and bright, but not very strong and glaring. Seventhly, or if it should have any glaring color, to have it diversified with others. These are, I believe, the properties on which beauty depends; properties that operate by nature, and are less liable to be altered by caprice or confounded by a diversity of tastes than any other.

[Part III, sec. 18]

Grace

Gracefulness is an idea not very different from beauty; it consists in much the same things. Gracefulness is an idea belonging to *posture* and *motion*. In both these things to be graceful it is requisite that there be no appearance of difficulty; there is required a small inflection of the body; and a composure of the parts in such a manner as not to incumber each other, not to appear divided by sharp and sudden angles. In this case, this roundness, this delicacy of attitude and motion, it is that all the magic of grace consists, and what is called its *je ne sçai quoi;* as will be obvious to any observer who considers attentively the Venus de Medicis, the Antinous; or any statue generally allowed to be graceful in a high degree.

[PART III, sec. 22]

The Sublime and Beautiful Compared

On closing this general view of beauty, it naturally occurs that we should compare it with the sublime; and in this comparison there appears a remarkable contrast. For sublime objects are vast in their dimensions, beautiful ones comparatively small; beauty should be smooth and polished; the great, rugged and negligent: beauty should shun the right line, yet deviate from it insensibly; the great in many cases loves the right line; and when it deviates, it often makes a strong deviation: beauty should not be obscure; the great ought to be dark and gloomy: beauty should be light and delicate; the great ought to be solid, and even massive. They are indeed ideas of a very different nature, one being founded on pain, the other on pleasure; and however they may vary afterwards from the direct nature of their causes, yet these causes keep up an eternal distinction between them, a distinction never to be forgotten by any whose business it is to affect the passions. In the infinite variety of natural combinations, we must expect to find the qualities of things the most remote imaginable from each other united in the same object. We must expect also to find combinations of the same kind in the works of art. But when we consider the power of an object upon our passions, we must know that when anything is intended to affect the mind by the force of some predominant property, the affection produced is like to be the more uniform and perfect if all the other properties or qualities of the object be of the same nature and tending to the same design as the principal.

> If black and white blend, soften, and unite
> A thousand ways, are there no black and white? [2]

If the qualities of the sublime and beautiful are sometimes found
united, does this prove that they are the same; does it prove that
they are anyway allied; does it prove even that they are not opposite and contradictory? Black and white may soften, may
blend; but they are not therefore the same. Nor, when they are
so softened and blended with each other, or with different colors,
is the power of black as black, or of white as white, so strong as
when each stands uniform and undistinguished.

[PART III, sec. 27]

Examples that Words May Affect without Raising Images

. . . I know very well that the mind possesses a faculty of raising such images at pleasure; but then an act of will is necessary to
this; and in ordinary conversation or reading it is very rarely that
any image at all is excited in the mind. If I say, "I shall go to Italy
next summer," I am well understood. Yet I believe nobody has by
this painted in his imagination the exact figure of the speaker
passing by land and by water, or both; sometimes on horseback,
sometimes in a carriage: with all the particulars of the journey.
Still less has he any idea of Italy, the country to which I proposed
to go; or of the greenness of the fields, the ripening of the fruits,
and the warmth of the air, with the change to this from a different season, which are the ideas for which the word *summer* is
substituted; but least of all has he any image for the word *next*;
for this word stands for the idea of many summers, with the exclusion of all but one: and surely the man who says *next summer*
has no images of such a succession and such an exclusion. In
short, it is not only of those ideas which are commonly called
abstract, and of which no image at all can be formed, but even of
particular, real beings, that we converse without having any idea
of them excited in the imagination; as will certainly appear on a
diligent examination of our own minds. Indeed, so little does
poetry depend for its effect on the power of raising sensible
images, that I am convinced it would lose a very considerable part
of its energy if this were the necessary result of description. Because that union of affecting words, which is the most powerful
of all poetical instruments, would frequently lose its force along
with its propriety and consistency if the sensible images were always excited. . . . In reality, poetry and rhetoric do not succeed

2 Pope *Essay on Man* II. 213–14.

in exact description so well as painting does; their business is to affect rather by sympathy than imitation; to display rather the effect of things on the mind of the speaker, or of others, than to present a clear idea of the things themselves. This is their most extensive province, and that in which they succeed the best.

[PART V, sec. 5]

Poetry Not Strictly an Imitative Art

Hence we may observe that poetry, taken in its most general sense, cannot with strict propriety be called an art of imitation. It is indeed an imitation so far as it describes the manners and passions of men which their words can express; where *animi motus effert interprete lingua.*[3] There it is strictly imitation; and all merely dramatic poetry is of this sort. But *descriptive* poetry operates chiefly by *substitution;* by the means of sounds, which by custom have the effect of realities. Nothing is an imitation further than as it resembles some other thing; and words undoubtedly have no sort of resemblance to the ideas for which they stand.

[PART V, sec. 6]

How Words Influence the Passions

. . . The truth is, all verbal description, merely as naked description, though never so exact, conveys so poor and insufficient an idea of the thing described that it could scarcely have the smallest effect if the speaker did not call in to his aid those modes of speech that mark a strong and lively feeling in himself. Then, by the contagion of our passions, we catch a fire already kindled in another, which probably might never have been struck out by the object described. Words, by strongly conveying the passions by those means which we have already mentioned, fully compensate for their weakness in other respects. It may be observed that very polished languages, and such as are praised for their superior clearness and perspicuity, are generally deficient in strength. The French language has that perfection and that defect. Whereas the Oriental tongues, and in general the languages of the most unpolished people, have a great force and energy of expression, and this is but natural. Uncultivated people are but ordinary observers of things, and not critical in distinguishing them; but for that reason they admire more, and are more affected with what they see, and therefore express themselves in a warmer and more

[3] "The tongue acts as interpreter of the mind" (Horace *Ars Poetica.* III).

passionate manner. If the affection be well conveyed, it will work
its effect without any clear idea at all of the thing which has
originally given rise to it. . . .

[PART V, sec. 7]

A SELECTION

William Gilpin
1724–1804

OBSERVATIONS . . . ON SEVERAL PARTS OF ENGLAND: . . . CUMBERLAND AND WESTMORLAND
1786

[This benevolent clergyman (the original of William Combe's "Dr.
Syntax in Search of the Picturesque" satirizing the traveler of the day)
remarked that "Regularity and Exactness excite no manner of Pleasure
in the Imagination." Gilpin, the dean of writers on the picturesque,
thought of this quality as being the beauties "appealing to the Painter."]

. . . IT is not every man who can build a house that can execute
a ruin. To give the stone its moldering appearance; to make the
widening chink run naturally through all the joints; to mutilate
the ornaments; to peel the facing from the internal structure; to
show how correspondent parts have once united, though now the
chasm runs wide between them; and to scatter heaps of ruin
around with negligence and ease are great efforts of art—much
too delicate for the hand of a common workman, and what we
rarely see performed. . . .

THREE ESSAYS
1792

MR. BURKE, enumerating the properties of beauty, considers
smoothness as one of the most essential. . . .

Thus, then, we suppose the matter stands with regard to beautiful objects in general. But in picturesque representation, it seems
somewhat odd, yet perhaps we shall find it equally true, that the
reverse of this is the case, and that the ideas of *neat* and *smooth*.

instead of being picturesque, in reality strip the object in which they reside of all pretensions to *picturesque beauty*.—Nay, farther, we do not scruple to assert that *roughness* forms the most essential point of difference between the *beautiful* and the *picturesque;* as it seems to be that particular quality which makes objects chiefly pleasing in painting.—I use the term *roughness;* but properly speaking roughness relates only to the surfaces of bodies: when we speak of their delineation, we use the word ruggedness. Both ideas, however, equally enter into the picturesque, and both are observable in the smaller as in the larger parts of nature—in the outline and bark of a tree, as in the rude summit and craggy sides of a mountain.

A piece of Palladian architecture may be elegant to the last degree. The proportion of its parts, the propriety of its ornaments, and the symmetry of the whole may be highly pleasing. But if we introduce it in a picture, it immediately becomes a formal object and ceases to please. Should we wish to give it picturesque beauty, we must use the mallet instead of the chisel: we must beat down one half of it, deface the other, and throw the mutilated members around in heaps. In short, from a *smooth* building we must turn it into a *rough* ruin. No painter who had the choice of the two objects would hesitate which to choose.

Again, why does an elegant piece of garden ground make no figure on canvas? The shape is pleasing, the combination of the objects harmonious, and the winding of the walk in the very line of beauty. All this is true; but the *smoothness* of the whole, though right, and as it should be in nature, offends in a picture. Turn the lawn into a piece of broken ground; plant rugged oaks instead of flowering shrubs; break the edges of the walk; give it the rudeness of a road; mark it with wheel tracks; and scatter around a few stones and brushwood—in a word, instead of making the whole *smooth*, make it *rough*, and you make it also *picturesque*. . . .

[Essay I]

But among all the objects of art, the picturesque eye is perhaps most inquisitive after the elegant relics of ancient architecture; the ruined tower, the Gothic arch, the remains of castles and abbeys. These are the richest legacies of art. They are consecrated by time; and almost deserve the veneration we pay to the works of nature itself. . . .

[Essay II]

A SELECTION

Uvedale Price

1747–1829

ESSAYS ON THE PICTURESQUE

1794–1798

[Uvedale Price, Richard Payne Knight, and Humphrey Repton became involved, in the last years of the century, in a wearisome controversy about the real nature of the picturesque. The selections that follow show how Price valued the Gothic architecture for its picturesque value, much as Ruskin was to do some years later.]

I AM therefore persuaded that the . . . qualities of roughness and of sudden variation joined to that of irregularity are the most efficient causes of the picturesque.

This, I think, will appear very clearly if we take a view of those objects, both natural and artificial, that are allowed to be picturesque, and compare them with those which are as generally allowed to be beautiful.

A temple or palace of Grecian architecture in its perfect, entire state, and with its surface and color smooth and even, either in painting or reality is beautiful; in ruin it is picturesque. Observe the process by which time, the great author of such changes, converts a beautiful object into a picturesque one. First, by means of weather stains, partial incrustations, mosses, etc. it at the same time takes off from the uniformity of the surface and of the color; that is, gives a degree of roughness and variety of tint. Next, the various accidents of weather loosen the stones themselves; they tumble in irregular masses upon what was perhaps smooth turf or pavement, or nicely trimmed walks and shrubberies, now mixed and overgrown with wild plants and creepers, that crawl over and shoot among the fallen ruins. Sedums, wallflowers, and other vegetables that bear drought find nourishment in the decayed cement from which the stones have been detached; birds convey their food into the chinks, and yew, elder, and other berried plants project from the sides, while the ivy mantles over other parts and crowns the top. The even, regular lines of the doors and windows are broken, and through their ivy-fringed openings is displayed in a more broken and picturesque manner that striking image in Virgil:

Apparet domus intus, et atria longa patescunt,
Apparent Priami et veterum penetralia regum.[1]

Gothic architecture is generally considered as more pictur-esque, though less beautiful, than Grecian; and upon the same principle that a ruin is more so than a new edifice. The first thing that strikes the eye in approaching any building is the general out-line and the effect of the openings: in Grecian buildings the gen-eral lines of the roof are straight, and even when varied and adorned by a dome or a pediment, the whole has a character of symmetry and regularity. But symmetry, which in works of art, particularly, accords with the beautiful, is in the same degree ad-verse to the picturesque; and among the various causes of the su-perior picturesqueness of ruins compared with entire buildings, the destruction of symmetry is by no means the least powerful.

In Gothic buildings, the outline of the summit presents such a variety of forms, of turrets and pinnacles, some open, some fretted and variously enriched, that even where there is an exact corre-spondence of parts, it is often disguised by an appearance of splendid confusion and irregularity. In the doors and windows of Gothic churches, the pointed arch has as much variety as any reg-ular figure can well have; the eye, too, is less strongly conducted than by the parallel lines in the Grecian style, from the top of one aperture to that of another; and every person must be struck with the extreme richness and intricacy of some of the principal win-dows of our cathedrals and ruined abbeys. In these last is dis-played the triumph of the picturesque; and their charms to a painter's eye are often so great as to rival those which arise from the chaste ornaments and the noble and elegant simplicity of the Grecian architecture. . . .

[CHAP. III]

If we examine our feelings on a warm, genial day in a spot full of the softest beauties of nature, the fragrance of spring breathing around us, pleasure then seems to be our natural state; to be re-ceived, not sought after; it is the happiness of existing to sensations of delight only; we are unwilling to move, almost to think, and desire only to feel, to enjoy. In pursuing the same train of ideas,

---

[1] *Aeneid* II. 483–84. "The home within appears, and the long corridors are laid open; the chambers of Priam and ancient kings are shown."

I may add that the effect of the picturesque is curiosity; an effect which, though less splendid and powerful, has a more general influence. Those who have felt the excitement produced by the intricacies of wild, romantic, mountainous scenes can tell how curiosity, while it prompts us to scale every rocky promontory, to explore every new recess, by its active agency keeps the fibers to their full tone; and thus picturesqueness, when mixed with either of the other characters, corrects the languor of beauty or the tension of sublimity. But as the nature of every corrective must be to take off from the peculiar effect of what it is to correct, so does the picturesque when united to either of the others. It is the coquetry of nature; it makes beauty more amusing, more varied, more playful, but also

Less winning soft, less amiably mild.

Again, by its variety, its intricacy, its partial concealments, it excites that active curiosity which gives play to the mind, loosening those iron bonds with which astonishment chains up its faculties.

[CHAP. IV]

David Hume

1711–1776

HUME described himself as "a man of mild dispositions, of command of temper, of an open, social, and cheerful humor, capable of attachment, but little susceptible of enmity, and of great moderation in all my passions." The enlightenment had a way of distilling its most venomous principles in these mild and genial vessels like Hume or the novelist Robert Bage or William Godwin. Hume is continually advancing the most devastating conclusions with an air of inquiry and even of embarrassment, all the while protesting that he means no harm. There is hardly an enlightened topic that he does not discuss with shrewdness and a disarming suspension of judgment. He has a rigorous Scottish mind, very honest and always seeking the inconvenient exception. Like Bacon, he is fond of casting his speculation into aphoristic hints. He is most "philosophical" in his distrust of "enthusiasm"—"raptures, transports, surprising flights of fancy." He cannot, he says, detect any provable correspondence between what is outside the mind and what is within; he is certain only of a sequence of impressions that apparently group themselves by "association." He urges theorizers upon the social contract to look abroad into the world, where they will "meet with nothing that, in the least, corresponds to their ideas or can warrant so refined and philosophical a system." He suggests that justice is to be determined by utility alone. When he considers the existence of a "standard of taste," he leaves unanswered far more questions than he raises; therein lies the value of the essay. Notorious in his day for his skepticism, he provoked a whole Scottish philosophy of common sense, and ultimately evoked a definitive answer from no less a person than Immanuel Kant. Hume's is one of the most various and active minds of the century.

BIOGRAPHICAL NOTES

Born in Edinburgh "of a good family." After the death of his father, his mother, "a woman of singular merit," devoted herself to rearing her children upon straitened means. Hume "seized with a passion for literature," his "ruling passion." Entered University of Edinburgh (1723); gave up law for "pursuits of philosophy and general learning." Entered business in Bristol (1734), but abandoned it and went to France (1734-37) to study with Jesuits at La Flèche and compose *Treatise of Human Nature*. Returned to London to publish *Treatise* (1739-40), which was "dead born." Published *Essays* (1741-42). Became tutor to Marquis of Annandale (1745-46), then secretary to General St. Clair (1746-49). Recast *Treatise into Inquiry concerning Human Understanding* (1748). Further essays (1749), the *Inquiry concerning Principles of Morals* (1751), and *Political Discourses* (1752). His writings bitterly assailed by churchmen. Appointed Librarian to Faculty of Advocates in Edinburgh (1752). Began publishing *History of Great Britain* (1754). Printed *Natural History of Religion* (1757), attacked by Bishop Hurd. Appointed secretary to Embassy at Paris (1763), where he was "loaded" with "excessive civilities." Returned to Edinburgh "to bury myself in a philosophical retreat" (1766). Befriended Rousseau, whom he brought to England; Rousseau quarreled with him. Hume appointed Under-Secretary of State (1767); and again returned to Edinburgh (1769). Stricken with disease (1775) and died "detached from life."

BIBLIOGRAPHY: *Philosophical Works*, 4 vols., 1854. *Philosophical Works*, ed. T. H. Green and T. H. Grose, 2 vols., 1898. *Letters*, ed. J. Y. T. Greig, 2 vols., 1932. Basson, Anthony Henry, *David Hume*, 1958. Black, John Bennett, *The Art of History; A Study of Four Great Historians of the Eighteenth Century*, 1926. Brunius, Teddy, *David Hume on Criticism*, 1952. Greig, J. Y. T., *David Hume*, 1931. Laing, B. M., *David Hume*, 1932. Lucas, Frank Laurence, *The Art of Living*, 1959. Mossner, Ernest C., *The Forgotten Hume: Le bon David*, 1943; *The Life of David Hume*, 1954. Smith, Norman Kemp, *The Philosophy of David Hume*, 1949.

OF THE STANDARD OF TASTE

1757

The great variety of taste, as well as of opinion, which prevails
in the world, is too obvious not to have fallen under everyone's
observation. Men of the most confined knowledge are able to remark a difference of taste in the narrow circle of their acquaintance,
even where the persons have been educated under the same government and have early imbibed the same prejudices. But those who
can enlarge their view to contemplate distant nations and remote
ages are still more surprised at the great inconsistence and con-
trariety. We are apt to call *barbarous* whatever departs widely
from our own taste and apprehension, but soon find the epithet of
reproach retorted on us. And the highest arrogance and self-conceit
is at last startled on observing an equal assurance on all sides, and
scruples, amidst such a contest of sentiment, to pronounce positively in its own favor.

As this variety of taste is obvious to the most careless inquirer,
so will it be found, on examination, to be still greater in reality
than in appearance. The sentiments of men often differ with regard to beauty and deformity of all kinds, even while their general
discourse is the same. There are certain terms in every language
which import blame, and others praise; and all men who use the
same tongue must agree in their application of them. Every voice
is united in applauding elegance, propriety, simplicity, spirit in
writing, and in blaming fustian, affectation, coldness, and a false
brilliancy. But when critics come to particulars, this seeming unanimity vanishes; and it is found that they had affixed a very
different meaning to their expressions. In all matters of opinion
and science, the case is opposite; the difference among men is there
oftener found to lie in generals than in particulars, and to be less
in reality than in appearance. An explanation of the terms commonly ends the controversy, and the disputants are surprised to
find that they had been quarreling while at bottom they agreed in
their judgment.

Those who found morality on sentiment, more than on reason,
are inclined to comprehend ethics under the former observation,

and to maintain, that, in all questions which regard conduct and manners, the difference among men is really greater than at first sight it appears. It is indeed obvious that writers of all nations and all ages concur in applauding justice, humanity, magnanimity, prudence, veracity, and in blaming the opposite qualities. Even poets and other authors, whose compositions are chiefly calculated to please the imagination, are yet found, from Homer down to Fénelon,[1] to inculcate the same moral precepts, and to bestow their applause and blame on the same virtues and vices. This great unanimity is usually ascribed to the influence of plain reason, which, in all these cases, maintains similar sentiments in all men, and prevents those controversies to which the abstract sciences are so much exposed. So far as the unanimity is real, this account may be admitted as satisfactory. But we must also allow that some part of the seeming harmony in morals may be accounted for from the very nature of language. The word *virtue*, with its equivalent in every tongue, implies praise, as that of *vice* does blame: and no one, without the most obvious and grossest impropriety, could affix reproach to a term which in general acceptation is understood in a good sense, or bestow applause where the idiom requires disapprobation. Homer's general precepts, where he delivers any such, will never be controverted; but it is obvious that when he draws particular pictures of manners, and represents heroism in Achilles and prudence in Ulysses, he intermixes a much greater degree of ferocity in the former and of cunning and fraud in the latter than Fénelon would admit of. The sage Ulysses, in the Greek poet, seems to delight in lies and fictions, and often employs them without any necessity, or even advantage. But his more scrupulous son, in the French epic writer, exposes himself to the most imminent perils, rather than depart from the most exact line of truth and veracity.

The admirers and followers of the Alcoran insist on the excellent moral precepts interspersed throughout that wild and absurd performance. But it is to be supposed that the Arabic words which correspond to the English *equity, justice, temperance, meekness, charity* were such as, from the constant use of that tongue, must always be taken in a good sense; and it would have argued the greatest ignorance, not of morals, but of language, to have men-

---

1 Author of *Télémaque* (1699), an educational story for his pupil, the Duke of Bourgogne.

tioned them with any epithets, besides those of applause and approbation. But would we know whether the pretended prophet had really attained a just sentiment of morals? Let us attend to his narration, and we shall soon find that he bestows praise on such instances of treachery, inhumanity, cruelty, revenge, bigotry, as are utterly incompatible with civilized society. No steady rule of right seems there to be attended to; and every action is blamed or praised, so far only as it is beneficial or hurtful to the true believers. The merit of delivering true general precepts in ethics is indeed very small. Whoever recommends any moral virtues, really does no more than is implied in the terms themselves. That people who invented the word *charity*, and used it in a good sense, inculcated more clearly, and much more efficaciously, the precept, "Be charitable," than any pretended legislator or prophet who should insert such a maxim in his writings. Of all expressions, those which, together with their other meaning, imply a degree either of blame or approbation, are the least liable to be perverted or mistaken.

It is natural for us to seek a *standard of taste*, a rule by which the various sentiments of men may be reconciled, at least a decision afforded, confirming one sentiment and condemning another.

There is a species of philosophy which cuts off all hopes of success in such an attempt, and represents the impossibility of ever attaining any standard of taste. The difference, it is said, is very wide between judgment and sentiment. All sentiment is right; because sentiment has a reference to nothing beyond itself, and is always real, wherever a man is conscious of it. But all determinations of the understanding are not right, because they have a reference to something beyond themselves, to wit, real matter of fact, and are not always conformable to that standard. Among a thousand different opinions which different men may entertain of the same subject, there is one, and but one, that is just and true; and the only difficulty is to fix and ascertain it. On the contrary, a thousand different sentiments excited by the same object are all right, because no sentiment represents what is really in the object. It only marks a certain conformity or relation between the object and the organs or faculties of the mind; and if that conformity did not really exist, the sentiment could never possibly have being. Beauty is no quality in things themselves: it exists merely in the mind which contemplates them; and each mind perceives a different beauty. One person may even perceive deformity, where another is sensible of beauty; and every individual ought to acquiesce in his own sentiment without pretending to regulate those of others. To seek the real beauty, or real deformity, is as fruitless an inquiry as to pretend to ascertain the real sweet or real bitter. According to the disposition of the organs, the same object may be both sweet and bitter, and the proverb has justly determined it to be fruitless to dispute concerning tastes. It is very natural, and even quite necessary, to extend this axiom to mental as well as bodily taste; and thus common sense, which is so often at variance with philosophy, especially with the skeptical kind, is found in one instance, at least, to agree in pronouncing the same decision.

But though this axiom, by passing into a proverb, seems to have attained the sanction of common sense, there is certainly a species of common sense which opposes it, at least serves to modify and restrain it. Whoever would assert an equality of genius and elegance between Ogilby [2] and Milton, or Bunyan and Addison, would be thought to defend no less an extravagance than if he had maintained a molehill to be as high as Teneriffe, or a pond as extensive as the ocean. Though there may be found persons who give the preference to the former authors, no one pays attention to such a taste; and we pronounce without scruple the sentiment of these pretended critics to be absurd and ridiculous. The principle of the natural equality of tastes is then totally forgot, and while we admit it on some occasions, where the objects seem near an equality, it appears an extravagant paradox, or rather a palpable absurdity, where objects so disproportioned are compared together.

It is evident that none of the rules of composition are fixed by reasonings a priori, or can be esteemed abstract conclusions of the understanding, from comparing those habitudes and relations of ideas which are eternal and immutable. Their foundation is the same with that of all the practical sciences, experience; nor are they anything but general observations concerning what has been universally found to please in all countries and in all ages. Many of the beauties of poetry and even of eloquence are founded on falsehood and fiction, on hyperboles, metaphors, and an abuse or perversion of terms from their natural meaning. To check the sallies of the imagination, and to reduce every expression to geometrical

2 John Ogilby (1600–1676), translator of Vergil and Homer, and compiler of travel books.

truth and exactness would be the most contrary to the laws of criticism, because it would produce a work which, by universal experience, has been found the most insipid and disagreeable. But though poetry can never submit to exact truth, it must be confined by rules of art, discovered to the author either by genius or observation. If some negligent or irregular writers have pleased, they have not pleased by their transgressions of rule or order, but in spite of these transgressions; they have possessed other beauties which were conformable to just criticism, and the force of these beauties has been able to overpower censure, and give the mind a satisfaction superior to the disgust arising from the blemishes. Ariosto pleases, but not by his monstrous and improbable fictions, by his bizarre mixture of the serious and comic style, by the want of coherence in his stories, or by the continual interruptions of his narration. He charms by the force and clearness of his expression, by the readiness and variety of his inventions, and by his natural pictures of the passions, especially those of the gay and amorous kind: and however his faults may diminish our satisfaction, they are not able entirely to destroy it. Did our pleasure really arise from those parts of his poem which we denominate faults, this would be no objection to criticism in general; it would only be an objection to those particular rules of criticism which would establish such circumstances to be faults, and would represent them as universally blamable. If they are found to please, they cannot be faults, let the pleasure which they produce be ever so unexpected and unaccountable.

But though all the general rules of art are founded only on experience and on the observation of the common sentiments of human nature, we must not imagine that, on every occasion, the feelings of men will be conformable to these rules. Those finer emotions of the mind are of a very tender and delicate nature, and require the concurrence of many favorable circumstances to make them play with facility and exactness, according to their general and established principles. The least exterior hindrance to such small springs, or the least internal disorder, disturbs their motion, and confounds the operation of the whole machine. When we would make an experiment of this nature, and would try the force of any beauty or deformity, we must choose with care a proper time and place, and bring the fancy to a suitable situation and disposition. A perfect serenity of mind, a recollection of thought, a due attention to the object—if any of these circumstances be wanting, our experiment will be fallacious, and we shall be unable to judge of the catholic and universal beauty. The relation which nature has placed between the form and the sentiment will at least be more obscure, and it will require greater accuracy to trace and discern it. We shall be able to ascertain its influence not so much from the operation of each particular beauty, as from the durable admiration which attends those works that have survived all the caprices of mode and fashion, all the mistakes of ignorance and envy.

The same Homer who pleased at Athens and Rome two thousand years ago is still admired at Paris and at London. All the changes of climate, government, religion, and language have not been able to obscure his glory. Authority or prejudice may give a temporary vogue to a bad poet or orator, but his reputation will never be durable or general. When his compositions are examined by posterity or by foreigners, the enchantment is dissipated, and his faults appear in their true colors. On the contrary, a real genius, the longer his works endure, and the more wide they are spread, the more sincere is the admiration which he meets with. Envy and jealousy have too much place in a narrow circle, and even familiar acquaintance with his person may diminish the applause due to his performances: but when these obstructions are removed, the beauties which are naturally fitted to excite agreeable sentiments immediately display their energy; and while the world endures, they maintain their authority over the minds of men.

It appears, then, that, amidst all the variety and caprice of taste, there are certain general principles of approbation or blame, whose influence a careful eye may trace in all operations of the mind. Some particular forms or qualities, from the original structure of the internal fabric, are calculated to please, and others to displease; and if they fail of their effect in any particular instance, it is from some apparent defect or imperfection in the organ. A man in a fever would not insist on his palate as able to decide concerning flavors, nor would one affected with the jaundice pretend to give a verdict with regard to colors. In each creature there is a sound and a defective state, and the former alone can be supposed to afford us a true standard of taste and sentiment. If, in the sound state of the organ, there be an entire or a considerable uniformity of sentiment among men, we may thence derive an idea of the perfect beauty; in like manner as the appearance of objects in day-light, to the eye of a man in health, is denominated their true and real color, even while color is allowed to be merely a phantasm of the senses.

Many and frequent are the defects in the internal organs which prevent or weaken the influence of those general principles on which depends our sentiment of beauty or deformity. Though some objects, by the structure of the mind, be naturally calculated to give pleasure, it is not to be expected that in every individual the pleasure will be equally felt. Particular incidents and situations occur which either throw a false light on the objects or hinder the true from conveying to the imagination the proper sentiment and perception.

One obvious cause why many feel not the proper sentiment of beauty is the want of that delicacy of imagination which is requisite to convey a sensibility of those finer emotions. This delicacy everyone pretends to; everyone talks of it, and would reduce every kind of taste or sentiment to its standard. But as our intention in this essay is to mingle some light of the understanding with the feelings of sentiment, it will be proper to give a more accurate definition of delicacy than has hitherto been attempted. And not to draw our philosophy from too profound a source, we shall have recourse to a noted story in *Don Quixote*.

"It is with good reason," says Sancho to the squire with the great nose, "that I pretend to have a judgment in wine; this is a quality hereditary in our family. Two of my kinsmen were once called to give their opinion of a hogshead which was supposed to be excellent, being old and of a good vintage. One of them tastes it, considers it, and, after mature reflection, pronounces the wine to be good, were it not for a small taste of leather which he perceived in it. The other, after using the same precautions, gives also his verdict in favor of the wine, but with the reserve of a taste of iron which he could easily distinguish. You cannot imagine how much they were both ridiculed for their judgment. But who laughed in the end? On emptying the hogshead, there was found at the bottom an old key with a leathern thong tied to it."

The great resemblance between mental and bodily taste will easily teach us to apply this story. Though it be certain that beauty and deformity, more than sweet and bitter, are not qualities in objects, but belong entirely to the sentiment, internal or external, it must be allowed that there are certain qualities in objects which are fitted by nature to produce those particular feelings. Now as these qualities may be found in a small degree, or may be mixed and confounded with each other, it often happens that the taste is not affected with such minute qualities, or is not able to distinguish all the particular flavors amidst the disorder in which they are presented. Where the organs are so fine as to allow nothing to escape them, and at the same time so exact as to perceive every ingredient in the composition, this we call delicacy of taste, whether we employ these terms in the literal or metaphorical sense. Here then, the general rules of beauty are of use, being drawn from established models, and from the observation of what pleases or displeases, when presented singly and in a high degree; and if the same qualities, in a continued composition and in a smaller degree, affect not the organs with a sensible delight or uneasiness, we exclude the person from all pretensions to this delicacy. To produce these general rules or avowed patterns of composition is like finding the key with the leathern thong, which justified the verdict of Sancho's kinsmen, and confounded those pretended judges who had condemned them. Though the hogshead had never been emptied, the taste of the one was still equally delicate, and that of the other equally dull and languid; but it would have been more difficult to have proved the superiority of the former to the conviction of every bystander. In like manner, though the beauties of writing had never been methodized or reduced to general principles, though no excellent models had ever been acknowledged, the different degrees of taste would still have subsisted, and the judgment of one man been preferable to that of another; but it would not have been so easy to silence the bad critic, who might always insist upon his particular sentiment, and refuse to submit to his antagonist. But when we show him an avowed principle of art; when we illustrate this principle by examples whose operation, from his own particular taste, he acknowledges to be conformable to the principle; when we prove that the same principle may be applied to the present case, where he did not perceive or feel its influence —he must conclude, upon the whole, that the fault lies in himself, and that he wants the delicacy which is requisite to make him sensible of every beauty and every blemish in any composition or discourse.

It is acknowledged to be the perfection of every sense or faculty to perceive with exactness its most minute objects, and allow nothing to escape its notice and observation. The smaller the objects are which become sensible to the eye, the finer is that organ, and the more elaborate its make and composition. A good palate is not tried by strong flavors, but by a mixture of small ingredients, where we are still sensible of each part, notwithstanding its minuteness and its confusion with the rest. In like manner, a quick and acute perception of beauty and deformity must be the perfection of our mental taste; nor can a man be satisfied with himself while he suspects that any excellence or blemish in a discourse has passed him unobserved. In this case the perfection of the man, and the perfection of the sense of feeling, are found to be united. A very delicate palate, on many occasions, may be a great inconvenience both to a man himself and to his friends. But a delicate taste of wit or beauty must always be a desirable quality, because it is the source of all the finest and most innocent enjoyments of which human nature is susceptible. In this decision the sentiments of all mankind are agreed. Wherever you can ascertain a delicacy of taste, it is sure to meet with approbation; and the best way of ascertaining it is to appeal to those models and principles which have been established by the uniform consent and experience of nations and ages.

But though there be naturally a wide difference, in point of delicacy, between one person and another, nothing tends further to increase and improve this talent than practice in a particular art, and the frequent survey or contemplation of a particular species of beauty. When objects of any kind are first presented to the eye or imagination, the sentiment which attends them is obscure and confused; and the mind is, in a great measure, incapable of pronouncing concerning their merits or defects. The taste cannot perceive the several excellences of the performance, much less distinguish the particular character of each excellency, and ascertain its quality and degree. If it pronounce the whole in general to be beautiful or deformed, it is the utmost that can be expected; and even this judgment a person so unpracticed will be apt to deliver with great hesitation and reserve. But allow him to acquire experience in those objects, his feeling becomes more exact and nice; he not only perceives the beauties and defects of each part, but marks the distinguishing species of each quality, and assigns it suitable praise or blame. A clear and distinct sentiment attends him through the whole survey of the objects; and he discerns that very degree and kind of approbation or displeasure which each part is naturally fitted to produce. The mist dissipates which seemed formerly to hang over the object; the organ acquires greater perfection in its operations, and can pronounce, without danger of mistake, concerning the merits of every performance. In a word, the same address and dexterity which practice gives to the execution of any work, is also acquired by the same means in the judging of it.

So advantageous is practice to the discernment of beauty that, before we can give judgment on any work of importance, it will even be requisite that that very individual performance be more than once perused by us, and be surveyed in different lights with attention and deliberation. There is a flutter or hurry of thought which attends the first perusal of any piece, and which confounds the genuine sentiment of beauty. The relation of the parts is not discerned; the true characters of style are little distinguished. The several perfections and defects seem wrapped up in a species of confusion, and present themselves indistinctly to the imagination. Not to mention that there is a species of beauty, which, as it is florid and superficial, pleases at first; but being found incompatible with a just expression either of reason or passion, soon palls upon the taste, and is then rejected with disdain, at least rated at a much lower value.

It is impossible to continue in the practice of contemplating any order of beauty without being frequently obliged to form comparisons between the several species and degrees of excellence, and estimating their proportion to each other. A man who has had no opportunity of comparing the different kinds of beauty is indeed totally unqualified to pronounce an opinion with regard to any object presented to him. By comparison alone we fix the epithets of praise or blame, and learn how to assign the due degree of each. The coarsest daubing contains a certain luster of colors and exactness of imitation, which are so far beauties, and would affect the mind of a peasant or Indian with the highest admiration. The most vulgar ballads are not entirely destitute of harmony or nature; and none but a person familiarized to superior beauties would pronounce their numbers harsh, or narration uninteresting. A great inferiority of beauty gives pain to a person conversant in the highest excellence of the kind, and is for that reason pronounced a deformity; as the most finished object with which we are acquainted is naturally supposed to have reached the pinnacle of perfection, and to be entitled to the highest applause. One accustomed to see, and examine, and weigh the several performances, admired in different ages and nations, can alone rate the merits of a work exhibited to his view, and assign its proper rank among the productions of genius.

But to enable a critic the more fully to execute this undertaking, he must preserve his mind free from all prejudice, and allow nothing to enter into his consideration but the very object which is submitted to his examination. We may observe that every work of art, in order to produce its due effect on the mind, must be surveyed in a certain point of view, and cannot be fully relished by persons whose situation, real or imaginary, is not conformable to that which is required by the performance. An orator addresses himself to a particular audience, and must have a regard to their particular genius, interests, opinions, passions, and prejudices; otherwise he hopes in vain to govern their resolutions, and inflame their affections. Should they even have entertained some prepossessions against him, however unreasonable, he must not overlook this disadvantage; but, before he enters upon the subject, must endeavor to conciliate their affection, and acquire their good graces. A critic of a different age or nation who should peruse this discourse must have all these circumstances in his eye, and must place himself in the same situation as the audience, in order to form a true judgment of the oration. In like manner, when any work is addressed to the public, though I should have a friendship or enmity with the author, I must depart from this situation, and, considering myself as a man in general, forget, if possible, my individual being and my peculiar circumstances. A person influenced by prejudice complies not with this condition, but obstinately maintains his natural position without placing himself in that point of view which the performance supposes. If the work be addressed to persons of a different age or nation, he makes no allowance for their peculiar views and prejudices; but, full of the manners of his own age and country, rashly condemns what seemed admirable in the eyes of those for whom alone the discourse was calculated. If the work be executed for the public, he never sufficiently enlarges his comprehension, or forgets his interest as a friend or enemy, as a rival or commentator. By this means his sentiments are perverted; nor have the same beauties and blemishes the same influence upon him as if he had imposed a proper violence on his imagination, and had forgotten himself for a moment. So far his taste evidently departs from the true standard, and of consequence loses all credit and authority.

It is well known that in all questions submitted to the understanding, prejudice is destructive of sound judgment, and perverts all operations of the intellectual faculties: it is no less contrary to good taste; nor has it less influence to corrupt our sentiment of beauty. It belongs to *good sense* to check its influence in both cases; and in this respect, as well as in many others, reason, if not an essential part of taste, is at least requisite to the operations of this latter faculty. In all the nobler productions of genius there is a mutual relation and correspondence of parts; nor can either the beauties or blemishes be perceived by him whose thought is not capacious enough to comprehend all those parts, and compare them with each other, in order to perceive the consistence and uniformity of the whole. Every work of art has also a certain end or purpose for which it is calculated; and is to be deemed more or less perfect as it is more or less fitted to attain this end. The object of eloquence is to persuade, of history to instruct, of poetry to please, by means of the passions and the imagination. These ends we must carry constantly in our view when we peruse any performance; and we must be able to judge how far the means employed are adapted to their respective purposes. Besides, every kind of composition, even the most poetical, is nothing but a chain of propositions and reasonings; not always, indeed, the justest and most exact, but still plausible and specious, however disguised by the coloring of the imagination. The persons introduced in tragedy and epic poetry must be represented as reasoning and thinking and concluding and acting suitably to their character and circumstances, and without judgment, as well as taste and invention, a poet can never hope to succeed in so delicate an undertaking. Not to mention that the same excellence of faculties which contributes to the improvement of reason, the same clearness of conception, the same exactness of distinction, the same vivacity of apprehension, are essential to the operations of true taste, and are its infallible concomitants. It seldom or never happens that a man of sense, who has experience in any art, cannot judge of its beauty; and it is no less rare to meet with a man who has a just taste without a sound understanding.

Thus, though the principles of taste be universal, and nearly, if not entirely, the same in all men, yet few are qualified to give judgment on any work of art, or establish their own sentiment as the standard of beauty. The organs of internal sensation are seldom so perfect as to allow the general principles their full play, and produce a feeling correspondent to those principles. They either labor under some defect, or are vitiated by some disorder; and by that means excite a sentiment which may be pronounced erroneous. When the critic has no delicacy, he judges without any distinction, and is only affected by the grosser and more palpable qualities of the object: the finer touches pass unnoticed and disregarded. Where he is not aided by practice, his verdict is attended with confusion and hesitation. Where no comparison has been employed, the most frivolous beauties, such as rather merit the name of defects, are the object of his admiration. Where he lies under the influence of prejudice, all his natural sentiments are perverted. Where good sense is wanting, he is not qualified to discern the beauties of design and reasoning which are the highest and most excellent. Under some or other of these imperfections the generality of men labor, and hence a true judge in the finer arts is observed, even during the most polished ages, to be so rare a character. Strong sense, united to delicate sentiment, improved by practice, perfected by comparison, and cleared of all prejudice, can alone entitle critics to this valuable character; and the joint verdict of such, wherever they are to be found, is the true standard of taste and beauty.

But where are such critics to be found? By what marks are they to be known? How distinguish them from pretenders? These questions are embarrassing; and seem to throw us back into the same uncertainty from which, during the course of this essay, we have endeavored to extricate ourselves.

But if we consider the matter aright, these are questions of fact, not of sentiment. Whether any particular person be endowed with good sense and a delicate imagination, free from prejudice, may often be the subject of dispute, and be liable to great discussion and inquiry; but that such a character is valuable and estimable will be agreed in by all mankind. Where these doubts occur, men can do no more than in other disputable questions which are submitted to the understanding: they must produce the best arguments that their invention suggests to them; they must acknowledge a true and decisive standard to exist somewhere, to wit, real existence and matter of fact; and they must have indulgence to such as differ from them in their appeals to this standard. It is sufficient for our present purpose if we have proved that the taste of all individuals is not upon an equal footing, and that some men in general, however difficult to be particularly pitched upon, will be acknowledged by universal sentiment to have a preference above others.

But, in reality, the difficulty of finding, even in particulars, the standard of taste, is not so great as it is represented. Though in speculation we may readily avow a certain criterion in science, and deny it in sentiment, the matter is found in practice to be much more hard to ascertain in the former case than in the latter. Theories of abstract philosophy, systems of profound theology, have prevailed during one age; in a successive period these have been universally exploded; their absurdity has been detected; other theories and systems have supplied their place, which again gave place to their successors: and nothing has been experienced more liable to the revolutions of chance and fashion than these pretended decisions of science. The case is not the same with the beauties of eloquence and poetry. Just expressions of passion and nature are sure, after a little time, to gain public applause, which they maintain forever. Aristotle and Plato and Epicurus and Descartes, may successively yield to each other; but Terence and Vergil maintain an universal, undisputed empire over the minds of men. The abstract philosophy of Cicero has lost its credit; the vehemence of his oratory is still the object of our admiration.

Though men of delicate taste be rare, they are easily to be distinguished in society by the soundness of their understanding, and the superiority of their faculties above the rest of mankind. The ascendant which they acquire gives a prevalence to that lively approbation with which they receive any productions of genius, and renders it generally predominant. Many men, when left to themselves, have but a faint and dubious perception of beauty, who yet are capable of relishing any fine stroke which is pointed out to them. Every convert to the admiration of the real poet or orator is the cause of some new conversion. And though prejudices may prevail for a time, they never unite in celebrating any rival to the true genius, but yield at last to the force of nature and just sentiment. Thus, though a civilized nation may easily be mistaken in the choice of their admired philosopher, they never have been found long to err in their affection for a favorite epic or tragic author.

But notwithstanding all our endeavors to fix a standard of taste, and reconcile the discordant apprehensions of men, there still remain two sources of variation, which are not sufficient indeed to confound all the boundaries of beauty and deformity, but will often serve to produce a difference in the degrees of our approbation or blame. The one is the different humors of particular men; the other, the particular manners and opinions of our age and country. The general principles of taste are uniform in human nature: where men vary in their judgments, some defect or perversion in the faculties may commonly be remarked, proceeding either from prejudice, from want of practice, or want of delicacy; and there is just reason for approving one taste and condemning another. But where there is such a diversity in the internal frame or external situation as is entirely blameless on both sides, and leaves no room to give one the preference above the other, in that case a certain degree of diversity in judgment is unavoidable, and we seek in vain for a standard by which we can reconcile the contrary sentiments.

A young man whose passions are warm will be more sensibly touched with amorous and tender images than a man more advanced in years, who takes pleasure in wise, philosophical reflections concerning the conduct of life and moderation of the passions. At twenty, Ovid may be the favorite author, Horace at forty, and perhaps Tacitus at fifty. Vainly would we, in such cases, endeavor to enter into the sentiments of others, and divest ourselves of those propensities which are natural to us. We choose our favorite author as we do our friend, from a conformity of humor and disposition. Mirth or passion, sentiment or reflection— whichever of these most predominates in our temper, it gives us a peculiar sympathy with the writer who resembles us.

One person is more pleased with the sublime, another with the tender, a third with raillery. One has a strong sensibility to blemishes, and is extremely studious of correctness; another has a more lively feeling of beauties, and pardons twenty absurdities and defects for one elevated or pathetic stroke. The ear of this man is entirely turned towards conciseness and energy; that man is delighted with a copious, rich, and harmonious expression. Simplicity is affected by one; ornament by another. Comedy, tragedy,

satire, odes have each its partisans, who prefer that particular species of writing to all others. It is plainly an error in a critic to
confine his approbation to one species or style of writing, and
condemn all the rest. But it is almost impossible not to feel a
predilection for that which suits our particular turn and disposition. Such preferences are innocent and unavoidable, and can
never reasonably be the object of dispute, because there is no
standard by which they can be decided.

For a like reason we are more pleased, in the course of our reading, with pictures and characters that resemble objects which are
found in our own age or country than with those which describe
a different set of customs. It is not without some effort that we
reconcile ourselves to the simplicity of ancient manners, and
behold princesses carrying water from the spring, and kings and
heroes dressing their own victuals. We may allow in general that
the representation of such manners is no fault in the author, nor
deformity in the piece; but we are not so sensibly touched with
them. For this reason, comedy is not easily transferred from one
age or nation to another. A Frenchman or Englishman is not
pleased with the *Andria* of Terence, or *Clitia* of Machiavel; where
the fine lady, upon whom all the play turns, never once appears
to the spectators, but is always kept behind the scenes, suitably
to the reserved humor of the ancient Greeks and modern Italians.
A man of learning and reflection can make allowance for these
peculiarities of manners; but a common audience can never divest
themselves so far of their usual ideas and sentiments as to relish
pictures which nowise resemble them.

But here there occurs a reflection, which may, perhaps, be useful in examining the celebrated controversy concerning ancient
and modern learning; where we often find the one side excusing
any seeming absurdity in the ancients from the manners of the
age, and the other refusing to admit this excuse, or at least admitting it only as an apology for the author, not for the performance. In my opinion, the proper boundaries in this subject have
seldom been fixed between the contending parties. Where any innocent peculiarities of manners are represented, such as those above
mentioned, they ought certainly to be admitted; and a man who is
shocked with them gives an evident proof of false delicacy and
refinement. The poet's "monument more durable than brass," must
fall to the ground like common brick or clay, were men to make

no allowance for the continual revolutions of manners and customs, and would admit of nothing but what was suitable to the prevailing fashion. Must we throw aside the pictures of our ancestors, because of their ruffs and farthingales? But where the ideas of morality and decency alter from one age to another, and where vicious manners are described, without being marked with the proper characters of blame and disapprobation, this must be allowed to disfigure the poem, and to be a real deformity. I cannot, nor is it proper I should, enter into such sentiments; and however I may excuse the poet on account of the manners of his age, I can never relish the composition. The want of humanity and of decency so conspicuous in the characters drawn by several of the ancient poets, even sometimes by Homer and the Greek tragedians, diminishes considerably the merit of their noble performances, and gives modern authors an advantage over them. We are not interested in the fortunes and sentiments of such rough heroes; we are displeased to find the limits of vice and virtue so much confounded; and whatever indulgence we may give to the writer on account of his prejudices, we cannot prevail on ourselves to enter into his sentiments, or bear an affection to characters which we plainly discover to be blamable.

The case is not the same with moral principles as with speculative opinions of any kind. These are in continual flux and revolution. The son embraces a different system from the father. Nay, there scarcely is any man who can boast of great constancy and uniformity in this particular. Whatever speculative errors may be found in the polite writings of any age or country, they detract but little from the value of those compositions. There needs but a certain turn of thought or imagination to make us enter into all the opinions which then prevailed, and relish the sentiments or conclusions derived from them. But a very violent effort is requisite to change our judgment of manners, and excite sentiments of approbation or blame, love or hatred, different from those to which the mind, from long custom, has been familiarized. And where a man is confident of the rectitude of that moral standard by which he judges, he is justly jealous of it, and will not pervert the sentiments of his heart for a moment, in complaisance to any writer whatsoever.

Of all speculative errors, those which regard religion are the most excusable in compositions of genius; nor is it ever permitted to judge of the civility or wisdom of any people, or even of single persons, by the grossness or refinement of their theological principles. The same good sense that directs men in the ordinary occurrences of life, is not hearkened to in religious matters, which are supposed to be placed altogether above the cognizance of human reason. On this account all the absurdities of the pagan system of theology must be overlooked by every critic who would pretend to form a just notion of ancient poetry; and our posterity, in their turn, must have the same indulgence to their forefathers. No religious principles can ever be imputed as a fault to any poet while they remain merely principles, and take not such strong possession of his heart as to lay him under the imputation of *bigotry* or *superstition*. Where that happens, they confound the sentiments of morality, and alter the natural boundaries of vice and virtue. They are therefore eternal blemishes, according to the principle above mentioned; nor are the prejudices and false opinions of the age sufficient to justify them.

It is essential to the Roman Catholic religion to inspire a violent hatred of every other worship, and to represent all pagans, Mahometans, and heretics as the objects of divine wrath and vengeance. Such sentiments, though they are in reality very blamable, are considered as virtues by the zealots of that communion, and are represented in their tragedies and epic poems as a kind of divine heroism. This bigotry has disfigured two very fine tragedies of the French theater *Polyeucte* and *Athalie;*[3] where an intemperate zeal for particular modes of worship is set off with all the pomp imaginable, and forms the predominant character of the heroes. "What is this?" says the sublime Joad to Josabet, finding her in discourse with Mathan the priest of Baal. "Does the daughter of David speak to this traitor? Are you not afraid lest the earth should open, and pour forth flames to devour you both! Or lest these holy walls should fall and crush you together? What is his purpose? Why comes that enemy of God hither to poison the air which we breathe with his horrid presence?" Such sentiments are received with great applause on the theater of Paris; but at London the spectators would be full as much pleased to hear Achilles tell Agamemnon that he was a dog in his forehead, and a deer in his heart, or Jupiter threaten Juno with a sound drubbing, if she will not be quiet.

---

[3] Corneille's *Polyeucte* and Racine's *Athalie*

Religious principles are also a blemish in any polite composition when they rise up to superstition, and intrude themselves into every sentiment, however remote from any connection with religion. It is no excuse for the poet that the customs of his country had burdened life with so many religious ceremonies and observances that no part of it was exempt from that yoke. It must forever be ridiculous in Petrarch to compare his mistress, Laura, to Jesus Christ. Nor is it less ridiculous in that agreeable libertine, Boccace, very seriously to give thanks to God Almighty, and the ladies, for their assistance in defending him against his enemies.

A SELECTION

David Hume

1711–1776

[By a sceptical materialism, Hume cast doubt not only upon the possibility of knowing what is outside ourselves, but even reduced our minds to a succession of fleeting impressions. If there is any order in these impressions, Hume remarks, it is due to the almost mechanical principle of association, which operates in the mind somewhat as the law of gravitation operates in the physical world. Hume prepared the way for the transcendentalism of Kant as well as for the impressionism of Walter Pater.]

A TREATISE OF HUMAN NATURE

1739–1740

. . . FOR my part, when I enter most intimately into what I call *myself*, I always stumble on some particular perception or other, of heat or cold, light or shade, love or hatred, pain or pleasure. I never can catch *myself* at any time without a perception, and can never observe anything but the perception. When my perceptions are removed for any time, as by sound sleep, so long am I insensible of myself, and may be truly said not to exist. And were all my perceptions removed by death, and could I neither think nor feel nor see nor love nor hate after the dissolution of my body, I should be entirely annihilated, nor do I conceive what is farther requisite to make me a perfect nonentity. If anyone upon serious and unprejudiced reflection thinks he has a different notion of *himself*, I must confess I can reason no longer with him. All I can allow him is that he may be in the right as well as I, and that we are essentially different in this particular. He may, perhaps, perceive something simple and continued, which he calls *himself*, though I am certain there is no such principle in me.

But setting aside some metaphysicians of this kind, I may venture to affirm of the rest of mankind that they are nothing but a bundle or collection of different perceptions, which succeed each other with an inconceivable rapidity, and are in a perpetual flux and movement. Our eyes cannot turn in their sockets without varying our perceptions. Our thought is still more variable than our sight; and all our other senses and faculties contribute to this change; nor is there any single power of the soul which remains unalterably the same, perhaps for one moment. The mind is a kind of theater, where several perceptions successively make their appearance, pass, repass, glide away, and mingle in an infinite variety of postures and situations. There is properly no simplicity in it at one time, nor identity in different; whatever natural prepension we may have to imagine that simplicity and identity. The comparison of the theater must not mislead us. They are the successive perceptions only that constitute the mind; nor have we the most distant notion of the place where these scenes are represented, or of the materials of which it is composed.

[BOOK I, part iv, sec. 6]

AN INQUIRY CONCERNING HUMAN UNDERSTANDING
1748

. . . AND it is certain we here advance a very intelligible proposition at least, if not a true one, when we assert that after the constant conjunction of two objects—heat and flame, for instance, weight and solidity—we are determined by custom alone to expect the one from the appearance of the other. This hypothesis seems even the only one which explains the difficulty why we draw, from a thousand instances, an inference which we are not able to draw from one instance, that is, in no respect, different from them. Reason is incapable of any such variation. The conclusions which it draws from considering one circle are the same which it would form upon surveying all the circles in the universe. But no man, having seen only one body move after being impelled by another, could infer that every other body will move after a like impulse. All inferences from experience, therefore, are effects of custom, not of reasoning.

Custom, then, is the great guide of human life. It is that principle alone which renders our experience useful to us, and makes us expect for the future a similar train of events with those which have appeared in the past. Without the influence of custom we should be entirely ignorant of every matter of fact beyond what is immediately present to the memory and senses. We should never know how to adjust means to ends, or to employ our natural powers in the production of any effect. There would be an end at once of all action, as well as of the chief part of speculation.

[SECTION V, part i]

A SELECTION

Philip Dormer Stanhope, Fourth Earl of Chesterfield

1694–1773

LETTERS TO HIS SON

[Filled with the shrewd observations of a man of the world, these letters are an almost classic statement of a "genteel tradition" that would "sacrifice to the Graces" and make social life an art. Chesterfield recommends that this natural son of his cultivate "every genteel attitude that the human body can be put into," that he always be "easy and graceful"—even that he learn "to loll genteelly."]

Bath, March 9, O.S.[1] 1748

DEAR BOY:

I must, from time to time, remind you of what I have often recommended to you, and of what you cannot attend to too much; *sacrifice to the Graces*. The different effects of the same things, said or done, when accompanied or abandoned by them, is almost inconceivable. They prepare the way to the heart; and the heart

---

1 "Old Style."—Until 1751, England used the Julian calendar instead of the Gregorian or "new-style" calendar devised by Pope Gregory XIII to bring the solar and the calendar year into agreement. By the Julian calendar there was a difference of about eleven days.

has such an influence over the understanding that it is worth while to engage it in our interest. It is the whole of women, who are guided by nothing else; and it has so much to say, even with men, and the ablest men too, that it commonly triumphs in every struggle with the understanding. Monsieur de Rochefoucault, in his *Maxims*, says, that *l'esprit est souvent la dupe du cœur.*[2] If he had said, instead of *souvent, presque toujours,*[3] I fear he would have been nearer the truth. This being the case, aim at the heart. Intrinsic merit alone will not do: it will gain you the general esteem of all; but not the particular affection, that is, the heart of any. To engage the affection of any particular person, you must, over and above your general merit, have some particular merit to that person, by services done or offered, by expressions of regard and esteem, by complaisance, attentions, etc., for him; and the graceful manner of doing all these things opens the way to the heart, and facilitates, or rather insures, their effects. From your own observation, reflect what a disagreeable impression an awkward address, a slovenly figure, an ungraceful manner of speaking, whether stuttering, muttering, monotony, or drawling, an unattentive behavior, etc., make upon you, at first sight, in a stranger, and how they prejudice you against him, though, for aught you know, he may have great intrinsic sense and merit. And reflect, on the other hand, how much the opposites of all these things prepossess you, at first sight, in favor of those who enjoy them. You wish to find all good qualities in them, and are in some degree disappointed if you do not. A thousand little things, not separately to be defined, conspire to form these graces, this *je ne sais quoi,* that always pleases. A pretty person, genteel motions, a proper degree of dress, an harmonious voice, something open and cheerful in the countenance, but without laughing; a distinct and properly varied manner of speaking: all these things, and many others, are necessary ingredients in the composition of the pleasing *je ne sais quoi,* which everybody feels, though nobody can describe. Observe carefully, then, what displeases or pleases you in others, and be persuaded that, in general, the same thing will please or displease them in you. Having mentioned laughing, I must particularly warn you against it: and I could heartily wish that you may often be seen to smile, but never heard to laugh while you live. Frequent and loud laughter is the characteristic of folly and ill manners: it is the manner in which the mob express their silly joy at silly things; and they call it being merry. In my mind, there is nothing so

2 "The mind is often the dupe of the heart."   3 "Almost always."

illiberal, and so ill bred, as audible laughter. True wit, or sense, never yet made anybody laugh; they are above it: they please the mind, and give a cheerfulness to the countenance. But it is low buffoonery, or silly accidents, that always excite laughter; and that is what people of sense and breeding should show themselves above. A man's going to sit down, in the supposition that he had a chair behind him, and falling down upon his breech for want of one, sets a whole company a-laughing, when all the wit in the world would not do it; a plain proof, in my mind, how low and unbecoming a thing laughter is—not to mention the disagreeable noise that it makes, and the shocking distortion of the face that it occasions. Laughter is easily restrained by a very little reflection; but, as it is generally connected with the idea of gaiety, people do not enough attend to its absurdity. I am neither of a melancholy, nor a cynical disposition; and am as willing and as apt to be pleased as anybody; but I am sure that since I have had the full use of my reason, nobody has ever heard me laugh. Many people, at first from awkwardness and *mauvaise honte*, have got a very disagreeable and silly trick of laughing whenever they speak: and I know a man of very good parts, Mr. Waller, who cannot say the commonest thing without laughing; which makes those who do not know him take him at first for a natural fool. This, and many other very disagreeable habits, are owing to *mauvaise honte* at their first setting out in the world. They are ashamed in company, and so disconcerted that they do not know what they do, and try a thousand tricks to keep themselves in countenance; which tricks afterwards grow habitual to them. Some put their fingers in their nose, others scratch their head, others twirl their hats; in short, every awkward, ill-bred body has his trick. But the frequency does not justify the thing; and all these vulgar habits and awkwardness, though not criminal indeed, are most carefully to be guarded against, as they are great bars in the way of the art of pleasing. Remember that to please is almost to prevail, or at least a necessary previous step to it. You, who have your fortune to make, should more particularly study this art. You had not, I must tell you, when you left England, *les manières prévenantes*; [4] and I must confess they are not very common in England: but I hope that your good sense will make you acquire them abroad. If you desire to make yourself considerable in the world (as, if you have any spirit, you do) it must be entirely your own doing; for I may very possibly be out of the world at the time you come into it. Your own rank and fortune will not assist you; your merit and your manners can

4 "Engaging manners."

alone raise you to figure and fortune. I have laid the foundations of them, by the education which I have given you; but you must build the superstructure yourself. . . .

Dear Boy,

. . . Having mentioned commonplace observations, I will particularly caution you against either using, believing, or approving them. They are the common topics of witlings and coxcombs; those who really have wit have the utmost contempt for them and scorn even to laugh at the pert things that those would-be wits say upon such subjects.

Religion is one of their favorite topics; it is all priestcraft, and an invention contrived and carried on by priests of all religions for their own power and profit; from this absurd and false principle flow the commonplace insipid jokes and insults upon the clergy. With these people, every priest, of every religion, is either a public or concealed unbeliever, drunkard, and whoremaster; whereas I conceive that priests are extremely like other men, and neither the better nor the worse for wearing a gown or a surplice; but if they are different from other people, probably it is rather on the side of religion and morality or, at least, decency, from their education and manner of life.

Another common topic for false wit and cold raillery is matrimony. Every man and his wife hate each other cordially, whatever they may pretend, in public, to the contrary. The husband certainly wishes his wife at the devil, and the wife certainly cuckolds her husband. Whereas I presume that men and their wives neither love nor hate each other the more upon account of the form of matrimony which has been said over them. The cohabitation, indeed, which is the consequence of matrimony makes them either love or hate more, accordingly as they respectively deserve it; but that would be exactly the same between any man and woman who lived together without being married.

These and many other commonplace reflections upon nations or professions in general (which are at least as often false as true) are the poor refuge of people who have neither wit nor invention of their own, but endeavor to shine in company by second-hand finery. I always put these pert jackanapes out of countenance by looking extremely grave when they expect that I should laugh at their pleasantries; and by saying *Well, and so,* as if they had not done, and that the sting were still to come. This disconcerts them, as they have no resources in themselves and have but one set of jokes to live upon. Men of parts are not reduced to these shifts, and have the utmost contempt for them: they find proper subjects enough for either useful or lively conversations; they can be witty without satire or commonplace, and serious without being dull. The frequentation of courts checks this petulancy of manners; the good breeding and circumspection which are necessary, and only to be learned there, correct those pertnesses. I do not doubt but that you are improved in your manners by the short visit which you have made at Dresden; and the other courts, which I intend that you shall be better acquainted with, will gradually smooth you up to the highest polish. In courts a versatility of genius and a softness of manners are absolutely necessary, which some people mistake for abject flattery, and having no opinion of one's own; whereas it is only the decent and genteel manner of maintaining your own opinion and possibly of bringing other people to it. The manner of doing things is often more important than the things themselves, and the very same thing may become either pleasing or offensive by the manner of saying or doing it. *Materiam supera-bat opus,*[5] is often said of works of sculpture; where, though the materials were valuable, as silver, gold, etc., the workmanship was still more so. This holds true, applied to manners, which adorn whatever knowledge or parts people may have, and even make a greater impression upon nine in ten of mankind than the intrinsic value of the materials. On the other hand, remember that what Horace says of good writing is justly applicable to those who would make a good figure in courts and distinguish themselves in the shining parts of life: *Sapere est principium et fons.*[6] A man who, without a good fund of knowledge and parts, adopts a court life makes the most ridiculous figure imaginable. He is a machine, little superior to the court clock; and as this points out the hours, he points out the frivolous employment of them. He is, at most, a comment upon the clock, and according to the hours that it strikes, tells you now it is levee, now dinner, now suppertime, etc. The end which I propose by your education, and which (*if you please*) I shall certainly attain, is to unite in you all the knowledge of a scholar with the manners of a courtier; and to join, what is seldom joined in any of my countrymen, books and the world. They are commonly twenty years old before they have spoken to anybody above their schoolmaster and the fellows of their college. If they happen to have learning, it is only Greek and Latin, but not one word of modern history or modern languages. Thus prepared, they

5 "The art surpassed the substance."   6 "To know is the foundation and the source."

go abroad, as they call it; but, in truth, they stay at home all that while, for, being very awkward, confoundedly ashamed, and not speaking the languages, they go into no foreign company, at least none good; but dine and sup with one another only at the tavern. Such examples, I am sure, you will not imitate, but even carefully avoid. You will always take care to keep the best company in the place where you are, which is the only use of traveling: and (by the way) the pleasures of a gentleman are only to be found in the best company; for that riot which low company most falsely and impudently call pleasure is only the sensuality of a swine.

I ask hard and uninterrupted study from you but one year more; after that, you shall have every day more and more time for your amusements. A few hours each day will then be sufficient for application, and the others cannot be better employed than in the pleasures of good company. Adieu.

London, September 5, O.S., 1748

DEAR BOY:

. . . I will recommend to your attentive perusal, now that you are going into the world, two books, which will let you as much into the characters of men, as books can do. I mean, *Les Réflexions Morales de Monsieur de la Rochefoucauld,* and *Les Caractères de la Bruyère;* but remember, at the same time, that I only recommend them to you as the best general maps to assist you in your journey, and not as marking out every particular turning and winding that you will meet with. There your own sagacity and observation must come to their aid. La Rochefoucauld, is, I know, blamed, but I think without reason, for deriving all our actions from the source of self-love. For my own part, I see a great deal of truth, and no harm at all, in that opinion. It is certain that we seek our own happiness in everything we do; and it is as certain that we can only find it in doing well, and in conforming all our actions to the rule of right reason, which is the great law of nature. It is only a mistaken self-love that is a blamable motive, when we take the immediate and indiscriminate gratification of a passion, or appetite, for real happiness. But am I blamable if I do a good action upon account of the happiness which that honest consciousness will give me? Surely not. On the contrary, that pleasing consciousness is a proof of my virtue. The reflection which is the most censured in Monsieur de la Rochefoucauld's book as a very ill-natured one, is this, *On trouve dans le malheur de son meilleur ami, quelque chose qui ne déplaît pas.*[7] And why not? Why may I not feel a

7 "One finds in the misfortune of his best friend something not entirely distressing."

very tender and real concern for the misfortune of my friend, and yet at the same time feel a pleasing consciousness at having discharged my duty to him, by comforting and assisting him to the utmost of my power in that misfortune? Give me but virtuous actions, and I will not quibble and chicane about the motives. And I will give anybody their choice of these two truths, which amount to the same thing: He who loves himself best is the honestest man; or, The honestest man loves himself best.

The characters of La Bruyère are pictures from the life; most of them finely drawn, and highly colored. Furnish your mind with them first, and when you meet with their likeness, as you will every day, they will strike you the more. You will compare every feature with the original; and both will reciprocally help you to discover the beauties and the blemishes.

As women are a considerable, or at least a pretty numerous part of company, and as their suffrages go a great way towards establishing a man's character in the fashionable part of the world (which is of great importance to the fortune and figure he proposes to make in it), it is necessary to please them. I will therefore, upon this subject, let you into certain *arcana*, that will be very useful for you to know, but which you must with the utmost care conceal, and never seem to know. Women, then, are only children of a larger growth; they have an entertaining tattle and sometimes wit; but for solid, reasoning good sense, I never knew in my life one that had it, or who reasoned or acted consequentially for four-and-twenty hours together. Some little passion or humor always breaks in upon their best resolutions. Their beauty neglected or controverted, their age increased, or their supposed understandings depreciated, instantly kindles their little passions, and overturns any system of consequential conduct that in their most reasonable moments they might have been capable of forming. A man of sense only trifles with them, plays with them, humors and flatters them, as he does with a sprightly, forward child; but he neither consults them about, nor trusts them with, serious matters; though he often makes them believe that he does both, which is the thing in the world that they are proud of; for they love mightily to be dabbling in business (which, by the way, they always spoil), and, being justly distrustful that men in general look upon them in a trifling light, they almost adore that man who talks more seriously to them, and who seems to consult and trust them: I say who seems; for weak men really do, but wise ones only seem to do it. No flattery is either too high or too low for them. They will greedily swallow the highest, and gratefully accept of the lowest; and you may safely flatter any woman, from her understanding down to the exquisite taste of her fan. Women who are either indisputably beautiful or indisputably ugly are best flattered upon the score of their understandings; but those who are in a state of mediocrity are best flattered upon their beauty, or at least their graces; for every woman who is not absolutely ugly thinks herself handsome, but not hearing often that she is so, is the more grateful and the more obliged to the few who tell her so; whereas a decided and conscious beauty looks upon every tribute paid to her beauty only as her due, but wants to shine and to be considered on the side of her understanding; and a woman who is ugly enough to know that she is so, knows that she has nothing left for it but her understanding, which is consequently (and probably in more senses than one) her weak side. But these are secrets which you must keep inviolably, if you would not, like Orpheus, be torn to pieces by the whole sex: on the contrary, a man who thinks of living in the great world must be gallant, polite, and attentive to please the women. They have, from the weakness of men, more or less influence in all courts: they absolutely stamp every man's character in the *beau monde*, and make it either current, or cry it down and stop it in payments. It is, therefore, absolutely necessary to manage, please, and flatter them, and never to discover the least mark of contempt, which is what they never forgive; but in this they are not singular, for it is the same with men, who will much sooner forgive an injustice than an insult. Every man is not ambitious, or covetous, or passionate; but every man has pride enough in his composition to feel and resent the least slight and contempt. Remember, therefore, most carefully to conceal your contempt, however just, wherever you would not make an implacable enemy. Men are much more unwilling to have their weaknesses and their imperfections known than their crimes; and if you hint to a man that you think him silly, ignorant, or even ill bred or awkward, he will hate you more and longer than if you tell him plainly that you think him a rogue. Never yield to that temptation, which to most young men is very strong, of exposing other people's weakness and infirmities, for the sake either of diverting the company, or showing your own superiority. You may get the laugh on your side by it for the present; but you will make enemies by it forever; and even those who laugh with you then, will, upon reflection fear, and consequently hate you; besides that it is ill natured, and a good heart desires rather to conceal than expose other people's weaknesses or misfortunes. If you have wit, use it to please, and not to hurt: you may shine, like the sun in the temperate zones, without scorching. Here it is wished for; under the line it is dreaded.

These are some of the hints which my long experience in the great world enables me to give you, and which, if you attend to them, may prove useful to you in your journey through it. I wish it may be a prosperous one; at least, I am sure that it must be your own fault if it is not. . . .

A SELECTION

Anna Laetitia Barbauld

1743–1825

CORSICA

(WRITTEN IN THE YEAR 1769)

1773

[In 1765, while the Corsicans were struggling against France and Genoa (as well as among themselves) Boswell arrived in the island bearing an introduction from Rousseau himself to the Corsican general Pascal Paoli. Boswell returned to London with a number of Corsican garments that he enjoyed wearing, and set about composing his *Account of Corsica* (1768) and his *Essays in Favor of the Brave Corsicans* (1769)—much to the disgust of Dr. Johnson, who urged his friend "to empty your head of Corsica, which I think has filled it rather too long." When France subdued the Corsicans in 1769, Paoli took refuge in England; even Dr. Johnson was forced to admit that Paoli, this wild friend of Boswell, had "the loftiest port of any man he had ever seen." Mrs. Barbauld's poem is highly representative of eighteenth-century occasional verse.]

Hail, generous Corsica! unconquered isle!
The fort of freedom; that amidst the waves
Stands like a rock of adamant, and dares
The wildest fury of the beating storm.

And are there yet, in this late sickly age,
Unkindly to the towering growths of virtue,

Such bold exalted spirits? Men whose deeds,
To the bright annals of old Greece opposed,
Would throw in shades her yet unrivaled name,
And dim the lustre of her fairest page!   10
And glows the flame of Liberty so strong
In this lone speck of earth! this spot obscure,
Shaggy with woods, and crusted o'er with rock,
By slaves surrounded, and by slaves oppressed!
What then should Britons feel?—should they not catch
The warm contagion of heroic ardour,
And kindle at a fire so like their own?

Such were the working thoughts which swelled the breast
Of generous Boswel; when with nobler aim
And views beyond the narrow beaten track   20
By trivial fancy trod, he turned his course
From polished Gallia's soft delicious vales,
From the grey reliques of imperial Rome,
From her long galleries of laureled stone,
Her chiseled heroes and her marble gods,
Whose dumb majestic pomp yet awes the world,
To animated forms of patriot zeal:
Warm in the living majesty of virtue;
Elate with fearless spirit; firm; resolved;
By fortune nor subdued, nor awed by power.   30

How raptured fancy burns, while warm in thought
I trace the pictured landscape; while I kiss
With pilgrim lips devout the sacred soil
Stained with the blood of heroes. Cyrnus,[1] hail!
Hail to thy rocky, deep indented shores,
And pointed cliffs, which hear the chafing deep
Incessant foaming round their shaggy sides.
Hail to thy winding bays, thy sheltering ports
And ample harbours, which inviting stretch
Their hospitable arms to every sail: 40
Thy numerous streams, that bursting from the cliffs
Down the steep channeled rock impetuous pour
With grateful murmur: on the fearful edge
Of the rude precipice, thy hamlets brown
And straw-roofed cots, which from the level vale
Scarce seen, amongst the craggy hanging cliffs

1 The Greek name for Corsica.

Seem like an eagle's nest aerial built.
Thy swelling mountains, brown with solemn shade
Of various trees, that wave their giant arms
O'er the rough sons of freedom; lofty pines,   50
And hardy fir, and ilex ever green,
And spreading chesnut, with each humbler plant,
And shrub of fragrant leaf, that clothes their sides
With living verdure; whence the clustering bee
Extracts her golden dews: the shining box,
And sweet-leaved myrtle, aromatic thyme,
The prickly juniper, and the green leaf
Which feeds the spinning worm; while glowing bright
Beneath the various foliage, wildly spreads
The arbutus, and rears his scarlet fruit   60
Luxuriant, mantling o'er the craggy steeps;
And thy own native laurel crowns the scene.
Hail to thy savage forests, awful, deep;
Thy tangled thickets, and thy crowded woods,
The haunt of herds untamed; which sullen bound
From rock to rock with fierce unsocial air,
And wilder gaze, as conscious of the power
That loves to reign amid the lonely scenes
Of unquelled nature: precipices huge,
And tumbling torrents; trackless deserts, plains   70
Fenced in with guardian rocks, whose quarries teem
With shining steel, that to the cultured fields
And sunny hills which wave with bearded grain
Defends their homely produce. Liberty,
The mountain Goddess, loves to range at large
Amid such scenes, and on the iron soil
Prints her majestic step. For these she scorns
The green enameled vales, the velvet lap
Of smooth savannahs, where the pillowed head
Of Luxury reposes; balmy gales,   80
And bowers that breathe of bliss. For these, when first
This isle emerging like a beauteous gem
From the dark bosom of the Tyrrhene main
Reared its fair front, she marked it for her own,
And with her spirit warmed. Her genuine sons,
A broken remnant, from the generous stock
Of ancient Greece, from Sparta's sad remains,
True to their high descent, preserved unquenched

The sacred fire through many a barbarous age:
Whom, nor the iron rod of cruel Carthage,   90
Nor the dread sceptre of imperial Rome,
Nor bloody Goth, nor grisly Saracen,
Nor the long galling yoke of proud Liguria,
Could crush into subjection. Still unquelled
They rose superior, bursting from their chains,
And claimed man's dearest birthright, liberty:
And long, through many a hard unequal strife
Maintained the glorious conflict; long withstood,
With single arm, the whole collected force
Of haughty Genoa, and ambitious Gaul.   100
And shall withstand it—Trust the faithful Muse!

It is not in the force of mortal arm,
Scarcely in fate, to bind the struggling soul
That galled by wanton power, indignant swells
Against oppression; breathing great revenge,
Careless of life, determined to be free.
And favouring Heaven approves: for see the Man,
Born to exalt his own, and give mankind
A glimpse of higher natures; just, as great;
The soul of council, and the nerve of war;   110
Of high unshaken spirit, tempered sweet
With soft urbanity, and polished grace,
And attic wit, and gay unstudied smiles:
Whom Heaven in some propitious hour endowed
With every purer virtue: gave him all
That lifts the hero, or adorns the man.
Gave him the eye sublime; the searching glance,
Keen, scanning deep, that smites the guilty soul
As with a beam from heaven; on his brow
Serene, and spacious front, set the broad seal   120
Of dignity and rule; then smiled benign
On this fair pattern of a God below,
High wrought, and breathed into his swelling breast
The large ambitious wish to save his country.
O beauteous title to immortal fame!
The man devoted to the public, stands
In the bright records of superior worth
A step below the skies: if he succeed,

The first fair lot which earth affords, is his;
And if he falls, he falls above a throne.   130
When such their leader, can the brave despair?
Freedom the cause, and Paoli the chief!

.   .   .   .

A SELECTION

James Burnett, Lord Monboddo

1714–1799

ANCIENT METAPHYSICS
(The History of Man)
1779–1799

[Although it has been denied that Monboddo is himself a primitivist,
he was much concerned with the evidences of man's progression from
savagery to civilization. Dr. Johnson was *afraid* ("chuckling and
laughing") that Monboddo did not know he was talking nonsense.]

THE subject of this chapter will be to mark some of the first steps
of this wonderful progression of man. Of these I have seen with
mine own eyes three, which is what very few now living can say.
The first I saw was in the pure natural state when he was catched
in the woods of Hanover, walking on all four. It was Peter the
Wild Boy, as he was called, whom I have mentioned above. I saw
him twice, and I had a very particular account of him from an Oxford gentleman who at my desire went to see him; which account
I have published.[1] He had learned to articulate but few words,
though he was put to school, and no doubt a great deal of pains
bestowed to teach him to speak. But this we should not wonder at
when we consider what trouble it requires to teach deaf men to
speak, though born and brought up among us. Of his being a man,
there never was the least doubt entertained; and that he was not
an idiot or defective in natural capacity I think is evident, from
the several accounts of him which I have published in the passages
above quoted. And indeed, from what I saw of him myself, I think
I can attest that he had as much understanding as could be expected in a man who had learned none of our arts, not even the

---

1 In the third volume of the *Ancient Metaphysics.*

use of his own body so well as to walk erect till he was fifteen years of age; for till then he was a quadruped.

The next step of this progression is the orangutan, or Man of the Woods, as the name imports, by which he is called by the people of Africa, where he is to be seen, and who do not appear to have the least doubt that he is a man; which, as they live in the country with him, they should know better than we can do. Two of them I saw in London some years ago, and one of them I could have purchased for £50; which money, poor as I am, I would have given for him, and been at the expense of his education, if I had not been convinced not only that *he* was a man, but that it was of absolute necessity that, in the progress of the human species, man should at some time or other be such an animal. For if he was originally a quadruped, as I think I have proved by facts incontestable, with only a natural aptitude more than any other animal to walk on two, as Aristotle has said, the first step in his progression was to become a biped, to which, by nature, he was so much adapted. I will not here repeat what I have elsewhere said at so great length [2] in proof of the humanity of the orangutan, where I think I have demonstrated that he is a man, both in mind and body, and particularly as to his mind, by which, as I have observed, Aristotle has chiefly distinguished animals. For I have shown that he has the sense of what is decent and becoming, which is peculiar to man and distinguishes him from the brute as much as anything else. And he has a sense of honor which is really surprising, and such as is not to be found in many men among us; for he cannot bear to be exposed as a show, nor to be laughed at; and travelers mention examples of some of them having died of vexation for being so treated. He has also the feeling of humanity in a strong degree, and a sense of justice, as is evident from a remarkable example given.[3] Further, he has made some progress in the arts of life, for he builds huts, and he has got the use of a stick for attacking or defending, which as Horace observes,[4] was the first artificial weapon man used after he had ceased to use his native weapons, his nails and fists. He has learned also the use of fire, which is more than the inhabitants of the Ladrone Islands had learned when they were discovered by the Portuguese; and lastly, he buries his dead. . . .

The last step of this progression I likewise saw, and it was a great one. It was the wild girl, or *fille sauvage*, as the French called her, who came from a country where the people had learned to articu-

---

2 *The Origin of Language*, Book II, chap. 4. second edition.

3 *Origin of Language*, I.
4 *Sermonum*, I, *sat.* 3.

late very imperfectly indeed, but sufficiently to communicate their wants and desires. I saw her in Paris about twenty-six years ago, and conversed with her much, as she had been then in Paris for several years, and spoke French well enough. She was taken up by a French ship somewhere upon the coast of Labrador, and was carried to one of the West India islands, from whence she sailed in a ship which was wrecked upon the coast of Flanders, and only she and a negro girl were saved. Her first appearance in France was at a village called Songè, near to Chalon in Champagne, whither I went to inquire about her. She was first seen there swimming a river, and coming out of it with a fish in her hand, which she had caught: for she told me that in her country they lived like beavers, always near the water, and caught the fish with their hands, by diving, as the people of the Ladrone Islands do. They were hunters, too; she and the negro girl, in their journey from Flanders, subsisted on game, which they caught by speed of foot. She said that in her country, besides language, they had a certain music, which they had formed in imitation of birds. But they had no use of fire, and in that, too, they resembled the people of the Ladrone Islands; and she told me that when she first came to France, a fire in a room was her terror and abhorrence; and the eating of flesh dressed by fire threw her into a very bad disease, of which she recovered with much difficulty. She was wonderfully swift of foot, and could overtake in that way almost any animal, and then knock it on the head with a bludgeon she wore, which she called a *boutou*, a name given by the inhabitants of the Caribbee Islands to a bludgeon; from which it appears she had been in one of those islands, in her way from America to France. She could climb a tree, too, like a squirrel, and leap from one tree to another; but all these bodily faculties, she told me, with much regret, she had lost at the time I saw her. . . .

[Book I, chap. 2]

(HISTORY OF MAN IN THE CIVILIZED STATE)

In the preceding book I think I have shown very clearly that man, in his natural state, is much happier than he is in his civilized life as it is conducted at present in the nations of Europe. And the reason is plain: that man, as well as other animals in the natural state, is governed by instinct, that is divine intelligence prompting him to do everything that is necessary for the preservation of the individual and the continuation of the kind; whereas the civilized man is guided by his own intelligence, which, however weak or imperfect it may be, is the governing principle in his little world, directing all his operations, particularly those of his animal life. Now this government must be very difficult in the civil societies I speak of, particularly in such of them where money is so predominant and of such general use as it is in Britain. In the natural state, the wants and appetites are very few, none but such as are necessary for the support of the individual and the propagation of the kind, and which all, at the same time, give pleasure to the animal; whereas in the civilized state, the wants and desires are innumerable, especially when money furnishes the means of gratifying them. Then there arise passions the most unnatural. . . .

[BOOK III, chap. 1]

. . . Now I lay it down as a principle that God is wise and good, and consequently that he has allotted to every animal an economy and manner of life best suited to his nature, and which will preserve him longer in health and strength than any other manner of life. That this is the case of other animals has never, I believe, been disputed. Now we cannot suppose that man is an exception from this general law of nature: and that he has invented another manner of life for himself, better than that which God has allotted him, that is more conducive to his health, strength, and longevity, is, I think, impious to maintain. That the civilized life of man, when he is clothed, housed, uses fire, eats flesh, and flesh cooked and prepared by fire, drinks wine, too, and other strong liquors, and even spirits, which are fuel for fire, is not his natural life, I have clearly, I think, proved. . . .

The necessary consequence of men living in so unnatural a way with respect both to houses, clothes, and diet, and continuing to live so for many generations, each generation adding to the vices, diseases, and weaknesses produced by the unnatural life of the preceding, is that they must gradually decline in strength, health, and longevity, till at last the race dies out. To deny this would be to deny that the life allotted by God and nature to man is the best life for the preservation of his health and strength; for, if it be so, I think it is demonstration that the constant deviation from it, going on for very many generations, must end in the extinction of the race. To say otherwise, I think, would be to maintain that man, in defiance of the ordinance of God, could continue his race forever. Besides, I think it would be inconsistent with the wisdom and goodness of God to suppose that he had formed a species of animals that were to continue forever the most miserable and, at the same time, more imperfect of their kind, than any other animal on this earth.   [Book IV, chap. 1]

Samuel Johnson

1709–1784

BECAUSE of his eccentricities and willfulness, it is tempting to present Johnson simply as a grotesque. In fact, Johnson always struggled against his own irregular impulses that carried him on the fullest tide of London life and even led him to believe that he was mad. These turbulent impulses were kept in some order by a rigorous mind that seldom allowed him to be taken in by cant or sham or oversubtlety. He is supposed to have dealt in platitudes; but, as Walter Raleigh says, there are two kinds of platitudes: those that mean nothing to the hearer or speaker, and those bearing such weighty implication for the speaker that they fall heavily upon our own sensibilities. The great conclusions from human experience can thus be, and need to be, stated and re-stated. Johnson, who was never one to reverence "the accidental prescriptions of authority," has a realistic mind in this sense—that he powerfully comprehends and powerfully expresses certain over-whelming conclusions. He is not deluded by either rationalism or senti-mentality; *The Vanity of Human Wishes* and *Rasselas* spring from a conviction that "sorrow is inherent in humanity" and that the world is not so pleasant as the deists supposed. Sometimes, of course, his convic-tions are merely provincial: "For anything I can see," he exclaims, "for-eigners are fools." Yet on the whole the force of Johnson's criticism of literature and life is in the generalities inexorably set forth. His "clas-sicism" is a synthetic ability. "Great thoughts," he remarks, "are always general." Sir Joshua Reynolds, regarding painting as Johnson regards writing, believes that it is desirable to elevate the mind "to the idea of general beauty, and the contemplation of general truth." Johnson does not arrive at his generalities easily; because of his own precarious tem-perament he is aware of the difficulty of living sanely. Here is the deep paradox of Johnson the great moralist, a man of eccentric im-pulses who is continually trying to combat eccentricity; he struggles on between sloth and strenuousness, assertiveness (almost arrogance) and humility, whimsey and stolidity, melancholy (almost despair) and resignation, dread of "imagination" and visions of the Great Wall of China, the sensual and the abstemious. The only reconciliation possible comes through good sense—the sense of congruity mentioned by Reynolds—a "reasonableness" that is not a rational so much as an ethical faculty. Johnson lives by the theological virtue of "prudence," the ability to deal with the immediate situation without abandoning principle. Thus he can profess a Tory creed of "subordination" and at the same time declare that "if a sovereign oppresses his people to a great degree, they will rise and cut off his head. There is a remedy in human nature against tyranny." Quite without the immortality conferred by Boswell, Johnson is a memorable figure. He had his own unruly romantic temperament, and was possessed by what he once called a "hunger of imagination that preys incessantly upon life."

BIOGRAPHICAL NOTES

Son of a Lichfield bookseller. Enduring great poverty and "horrible hypochondria," attended Pembroke College, Oxford (1728-29) but took no degree. Employed as teacher at Market Bosworth; then went to Birmingham to write for *Birmingham Journal* (1732-35). Translated Lobo's *Voyage to Abyssinia* (1735); married Mrs. Elizabeth Porter, a widow, twenty years his elder; opened a school at Edial. Went to London with his pupil David Garrick (1737). Contributed hack work to Edward Cave's *Gentleman's Magazine* (1738-44). Published *London* (1738), and the *Life of Richard Savage* (1744), his friend. Wrote *Plan* of the proposed English dictionary (1747) and began drudging on it. *The Vanity of Human Wishes* published, and *Irene* presented by Garrick at the Drury Lane, without success (1749). *The Rambler* (1750-52). His wife "Tetty" died (1752). Contributed to *The Adventurer* (1753-54). Published *Dictionary of the English Language* (1755). Contributed *Idler* essays to the *Universal Chronicle* (1758-60). The death of his mother; *Rasselas* written in haste (1759). Granted a government pension (1762) and met Boswell in Davies' bookshop (1763). With Reynolds, founded the Club (1764), including Burke, Goldsmith, Garrick, Boswell, Gibbon, Dr. Burney, Topham Beauclerk, Dr. Nugent, Sir John Hawkins, Bennet Langton, Anthony Chamier, and others. Became intimate with the Thrales (1764-65). Edited Shakespeare (1765). Toured the Highlands with Boswell (1773). *Journey to the Western Islands* (1775). Granted LL.D. by Oxford. Death of Thrale (1781). *Lives of the Poets* (1779-81). Last years saddened by ill health, melancholy, and marriage of Mrs. Thrale to Piozzi.

BIBLIOGRAPHY: *Works,* 11 vols., 1825. Yale edition, 1958- . *Poems,* edd. D. N. Smith and E. L. McAdam, Jr., 1941. *Letters,* ed. R. W. Chapman, 1952. *London, The Vanity of Human Wishes,* ed. T. S. Eliot, 1930. Bate, W. J., *The Achievement of Samuel Johnson,* 1955. Bloom, E. A., *Samuel Johnson in Grub Street,* 1957. Boswell, J., *Journal of a Tour to the Hebrides with Samuel Johnson,* edd. F. A. Pottle and C. H. Bennett, 1936; *Life of Samuel Johnson,* edd. G. B. Hill and L. F. Powell, 6 vols., 1934. Bronson, B. J., *Johnson Agonistes,* 1946. Chapman, R. W., *Johnsonian and Other Essays and Reviews,* 1953. Clifford, J. L., *Young Sam Johnson,* 1955. Davis, B. H., *Johnson Before Boswell,* 1960. Greene, D. J., *The Politics of Samuel Johnson,* 1960. Hagstrum, J. H., *Samuel Johnson's Literary Criticism,* 1952. Hill, G. B., ed., *Johnsonian Miscellanies,* 2 vols., 1897. Houston, P. H., *Dr. Johnson, a Study in Eighteenth Century Humanism,* 1923. Lucas, F. L., *The Search for Good Sense,* 1958. [Lunn] Hugh Kingsmill, *Johnson Without Boswell,* 1941. Krutch, J. W., *Samuel Johnson,* 1944. Pearson, H., *Johnson and Boswell,* 1958. Piozzi, H. L., *Anecdotes of the Late Samuel Johnson,* ed. S. C. Roberts, 1925. Raleigh, W. A., *Six Essays on Johnson,* 1927. Reade, A. L., *Johnsonian Gleanings,* 11 vols., 1909-52. Sherbo, A., *Samuel Johnson, Editor of Shakespeare,* 1956. Smith-Dampier, J. L., *Who's Who in Boswell,* 1935. Watkins, W. B. C., *Perilous Balance,* 1939. Wimsatt, W. K., *The Prose of Samuel Johnson,* 1941.

THE VANITY OF HUMAN WISHES

IN IMITATION OF THE TENTH SATIRE OF JUVENAL

1749

Let Observation, with extensive view,
Survey mankind, from China to Peru;
Remark each anxious toil, each eager strife,
And watch the busy scenes of crowded life;
Then say how hope and fear, desire and hate
O'erspread with snares the clouded maze of fate,
Where wav'ring man, betray'd by vent'rous pride
To tread the dreary paths without a guide,
As treach'rous phantoms in the mist delude,
Shuns fancied ills, or chases airy good;   10
How rarely Reason guides the stubborn choice,
Rules the bold hand, or prompts the suppliant voice;
How nations sink, by darling schemes oppress'd,
When Vengeance listens to the fool's request.
Fate wings with ev'ry wish th' afflictive dart,
Each gift of nature, and each grace of art;
With fatal heat impetuous courage glows,
With fatal sweetness elocution flows,
Impeachment stops the speaker's powerful breath,
And restless fire precipitates on death.   20
    But scarce observ'd, the knowing and the bold
Fall in the gen'ral massacre of gold;
Wide-wasting pest! that rages unconfin'd,
And crowds with crimes the records of mankind;
For gold his sword the hireling ruffian draws,
For gold the hireling judge distorts the laws;
Wealth heap'd on wealth, nor truth nor safety buys,
The dangers gather as the treasures rise.
    Let Hist'ry tell where rival kings command,
And dubious title shakes the madded land,   30
When statutes glean the refuse of the sword,
How much more safe the vassal than the lord,
Low skulks the hind beneath the rage of power,
And leaves the wealthy traitor in the Tower,
Untouch'd his cottage, and his slumbers sound,

Tho' confiscation's vultures hover round.
The needy traveller, serene and gay,
Walks the wild heath, and sings his toil away.
Does envy seize thee? crush th' upbraiding joy,
Increase his riches and his peace destroy; 40
New fears in dire vicissitude invade,
The rustling brake alarms, and quiv'ring shade,
Nor light nor darkness bring his pain relief,
One shews the plunder, and one hides the thief.

Yet still one gen'ral cry the skies assails,
And gain and grandeur load the tainted gales;
Few know the toiling statesman's fear or care,
Th' insidious rival and the gaping heir.[1]

Once more, Democritus,[2] arise on earth,
With cheerful wisdom and instructive mirth, 50
See motley life in modern trappings dress'd,
And feed with varied fools th' eternal jest:
Thou who couldst laugh where want enchain'd caprice,
Toil crush'd conceit, and man was of a piece;
Where wealth unlov'd without a mourner dy'd;
And scarce a sycophant was fed by pride;
Where ne'er was known the form of mock debate,
Or seen a new-made mayor's unwieldy state;
Where change of fav'rites made no change of laws,
And senates heard before they judg'd a cause; 60
How wouldst thou shake at Britain's modish tribe,
Dart the quick taunt, and edge the piercing gibe?
Attentive truth and nature to descry,
And pierce each scene with philosophic eye,
To thee were solemn toys or empty show
The robes of pleasures and the veils of woe:
All aid the farce, and all thy mirth maintain,
Whose joys are causeless, or whose griefs are vain.

Such was the scorn that fill'd the sage's mind,
Renew'd at ev'ry glance on human kind; 70
How just that scorn ere yet thy voice declare,
Search ev'ry state, and canvass ev'ry pray'r.

Unnumber'd suppliants crowd Preferment's gate,
Athirst for wealth, and burning to be great;
Delusive Fortune hears th' incessant call,

---

[1] Frederick, Prince of Wales, had quarreled with his father, George II.

[2] Called the "laughing philosopher" because of his geniality; he lived in the fifth century B.C.

They mount, they shine, evaporate, and fall.
On ev'ry stage the foes of peace attend,
Hate dogs their flight, and insult mocks their end.
Love ends with hope, the sinking statesman's door
Pours in the morning worshiper no more;   80
For growing names the weekly scribbler lies,
To growing wealth the dedicator flies;
From ev'ry room descends the painted face,
That hung the bright palladium of the place;
And smok'd in kitchens, or in auctions sold,
To better features yields the frame of gold;
For now no more we trace in ev'ry line
Heroic worth, benevolence divine:
The form distorted justifies the fall,
And detestation rids th' indignant wall.   90
    But will not Britain hear the last appeal,
Sign her foe's doom, or guard her fav'rites' zeal?
Thro' Freedom's sons no more remonstrance rings,
Degrading nobles and controlling kings;
Our supple tribes repress their patriot throats,
And ask no questions but the price of votes;
With weekly libels and septennial ale.[3]
Their wish is full to riot and to rail.
    In full-blown dignity, see Wolsey [4] stand,
Law in his voice, and fortune in his hand: 100
To him the church, the realm, their powers consign,
Through him the rays of regal bounty shine;
Turn'd by his nod the stream of honour flows,
His smile alone security bestows:
Still to new heights his restless wishes tower,
Claim leads to claim, and pow'r advances power;
Till conquest unresisted ceas'd to please,
And rights submitted, left him none to seize.
At length his sov'reign frowns—the train of state
Mark the keen glance, and watch the sign to hate.   110
Where'er he turns, he meets a stranger's eye,
His suppliants scorn him, and his followers fly;
At once is lost the pride of awful state,
The golden canopy, the glitt'ring plate,
The regal palace, the luxurious board,

---

3 The limit of any Parliament was seven
years; "septennial" ale won good will for
the candidates.

4 Thomas, Cardinal Wolsey, Lord Chancellor, who was dismissed from office by
Henry VIII, then arrested for high treason
in 1530

The liv'ried army, and the menial lord.
With age, with cares, with maladies oppress'd,
He seeks the refuge of monastic rest.
Grief aids disease, remember'd folly stings,
And his last sighs reproach the faith of kings.   120
   Speak thou, whose thoughts at humble peace repine,
Shall Wolsey's wealth, with Wolsey's end be thine?
Or liv'st thou now, with safer pride content,
The wisest justice on the banks of Trent?
For why did Wolsey, near the steeps of fate,
On weak foundations raise th' enormous weight?
Why but to sink beneath misfortune's blow,
With louder ruin to the gulfs below?
   What gave great Villiers [5] to th' assassin's knife,
And fix'd disease on Harley's [6] closing life?   130
What murder'd Wentworth,[7] and what exil'd Hyde,[8]
By kings protected and to kings allied?
What but their wish indulg'd in courts to shine,
And pow'r too great to keep or to resign?
   When first the college rolls receive his name,
The young enthusiast quits his ease for fame;
Resistless burns the fever of renown
Caught from the strong contagion of the gown:
O'er Bodley's dome [9] his future labours spread,
And Bacon's mansion trembles o'er his head.[10]   140
Are these thy views? proceed, illustrious youth,
And Virtue guard thee to the throne of Truth!
Yet should thy soul indulge the gen'rous heat,
Till captive Science yields her last retreat;
Should Reason guide thee with her brightest ray,
And pour on misty Doubt resistless day;
Should no false kindness lure to loose delight,
Nor praise relax, nor difficulty fright;
Should tempting Novelty thy cell refrain,
And Sloth effuse her opiate fumes in vain;   150
Should Beauty blunt on fops her fatal dart,

---

5 George Villiers, Duke of Buckingham and favorite of James I, was assassinated by John Felton in 1628.

6 Robert Harley, Earl of Oxford and Tory minister under Anne, impeached for high treason in 1715.

7 Thomas Wentworth, Earl of Strafford, condemned to death in 1641 as a friend of Charles I.

8 Edward Hyde, Earl of Clarendon, and Lord Chancellor under Charles II; in 1667 he was impeached and went into exile.

9 The Bodleian Library at Oxford.

10 The tradition was that Friar Bacon's study over the Folly Bridge at Oxford would fall if one greater than Bacon passed under it.

Nor claim the triumph of a letter'd heart;
Should no disease thy torpid veins invade,
Nor Melancholy's phantoms haunt thy shade;
Yet hope not life from grief or danger free,
Nor think the doom of man revers'd for thee:
Deign on the passing world to turn thine eyes,
And pause a while from letters, to be wise;
There mark what ills the scholar's life assail,
Toil, envy, want, the patron, and the gaol.   160
See nations slowly wise, and meanly just,
To buried merit raise the tardy bust.
If dreams yet flatter, once again attend,
Hear Lydiat's life,[11] and Galileo's, end.
   Nor deem, when Learning her last prize bestows,
The glitt'ring eminence exempt from foes;
See when the vulgar 'scapes, despis'd or aw'd,
Rebellion's vengeful talons seize on Laud.[12]
From meaner minds though smaller fines content,
The plunder'd palace, or sequester'd rent;   170
Mark'd out by dang'rous parts he meets the shock,
And fatal Learning leads him to the block:
Around his tomb let Art and Genius weep,
But hear his death, ye blockheads, hear and sleep.
   The festal blazes, the triumphal show,
The ravish'd standard, and the captive foe,
The senate's thanks, the gazette's pompous tale,
With force resistless o'er the brave prevail.
Such bribes the rapid Greek [13] o'er Asia whirl'd,
For such the steady Romans shook the world;   180
For such in distant lands the Britons shine,
And stain with blood the Danube or the Rhine;
This pow'r has praise, that virtue scarce can warm,
Till fame supplies the universal charm.
Yet Reason frowns on War's unequal game,
Where wasted nations raise a single name,
And mortgag'd states their grandsires' wreaths regret
From age to age in everlasting debt;
Wreaths which at last the dear-bought right convey
To rust on medals, or on stones decay.   190

11 Thomas Lydiat (1572–1646), a scholar who was ruined by his Royalist sympathies; Galileo (1564–1642) was persecuted by the Inquisition for advocating the Copernican theory.

12 William Laud, Archbishop of Canterbury, condemned to death by the Long Parliament in 1645.

13 Alexander the Great.

On what foundation stands the warrior's pride,
How just his hopes, let Swedish Charles [14] decide;
A frame of adamant, a soul of fire,
No dangers fright him, and no labours tire;
O'er love, o'er fear, extends his wide domain,
Unconquer'd lord of pleasure and of pain;
No joys to him pacific sceptres yield,
War sounds the trump, he rushes to the field;
Behold surrounding kings their powers combine,
And one capitulate,[15] and one resign;   200
Peace courts his hand, but spreads her charms in vain;
"Think nothing gain'd," he cries, "till naught remain,
On Moscow's walls till Gothic standards fly,
And all be mine beneath the polar sky."
The march begins in military state,
And nations on his eye suspended wait;
Stern Famine guards the solitary coast,
And Winter barricades the realms of Frost;
He comes, nor want nor cold his course delay;—
Hide, blushing Glory, hide Pultowa's day: [16]   210
The vanquish'd hero leaves his broken bands,
And shows his miseries in distant lands;
Condemn'd a needy supplicant to wait,
While ladies interpose, and slaves debate.
But did not Chance at length her error mend?
Did no subverted empire mark his end?
Did rival monarchs give the fatal wound?
Or hostile millions press him to the ground?
His fall was destin'd to a barren strand,
A petty fortress, and a dubious hand;   220
He left the name at which the world grew pale,
To point a moral, or adorn a tale.
    All times their scenes of pompous woes afford,
From Persia's tyrant to Bavaria's lord.[17]
In gay hostility, and barb'rous pride,
With half mankind embattled at his side,
Great Xerxes comes to seize the certain prey,

14 Charles XII of Sweden, whose power was broken by the Russians at the battle of Pultowa in 1709.
15 Frederick IV of Denmark, allied with Augustus II of Poland against Charles XII, capitulated to Charles in 1700; Augustus resigned his crown to Charles in 1704.
16 See note 14.

17 Xerxes, King of Persia, whose invasion of Greece ended at the disastrous battle of Salamis (480 B.C.); he was so proud that he supposed himself master of the sea and winds. Charles Albert, Elector of Bavaria, claimed the crown of the Holy Roman Empire and precipitated the War of the Austrian Succession.

And starves exhausted regions in his way;
Attendant Flatt'ry counts his myriads o'er,
Till counted myriads sooth his pride no more;   230
Fresh praise is tried till madness fires his mind,
The waves he lashes, and enchains the wind;
New pow'rs are claim'd, new pow'rs are still bestow'd,
Till rude resistance lops the spreading god;
The daring Greeks deride the martial show,
And heap their valleys with the gaudy foe;
Th' insulted sea with humbler thought he gains,
A single skiff to speed his flight remains;
Th' incumber'd oar scarce leaves the dreaded coast
Through purple billows and a floating host.   240
    The bold Bavarian, in a luckless hour,
Tries the dread summits of Cæsarean pow'r,
With unexpected legions bursts away,
And sees defenseless realms receive his sway;
Short sway! fair Austria spreads her mournful charms,
The queen, the beauty, sets the world in arms;
From hill to hill the beacon's rousing blaze
Spreads wide the hope of plunder and of praise;
The fierce Croatian, and the wild Hussar,
With all the sons of ravage crowd the war;   250
The baffled prince, in honour's flatt'ring bloom
Of hasty greatness finds the fatal doom;
His foes' derision, and his subjects' blame,
And steals to death from anguish and from shame.
    Enlarge my life with multitude of days!
In health, in sickness, thus the suppliant prays;
Hides from himself his state, and shuns to know,
That life protracted is protracted woe.
Time hovers o'er, impatient to destroy,
And shuts up all the passages of joy;   260
In vain their gifts the bounteous seasons pour,
The fruit autumnal, and the vernal flower;
With listless eyes the dotard views the store,
He views, and wonders that they please no more;
Now pall the tasteless meats, and joyless wines,
And Luxury with sighs her slave resigns.
Approach, ye minstrels, try the soothing strain,
Diffuse the tuneful lenitives of pain:
No sounds, alas! would touch th' impervious ear,

Though dancing mountains witness'd Orpheus near; 270
Nor lute nor lyre his feeble powers attend,
Nor sweeter music of a virtuous friend,
But everlasting dictates crowd his tongue,
Perversely grave, or positively wrong.
The still returning tale, and ling'ring jest,
Perplex the fawning niece and pamper'd guest,
While growing hopes scarce awe the gath'ring sneer,
And scarce a legacy can bribe to hear;
The watchful guests still hint the last offence;
The daughter's petulance, the son's expense, 280
Improve his heady rage with treach'rous skill,
And mould his passions till they make his will.
   Unnumber'd maladies his joints invade,
Lay siege to life and press the dire blockade;
But unextinguish'd Av'rice still remains,
And dreaded losses aggravate his pains;
He turns, with anxious heart and crippled hands,
His bonds of debt, and mortgages of lands;
Or views his coffers with suspicious eyes,
Unlocks his gold, and counts it till he dies. 290
   But grant, the virtues of a temp'rate prime
Bless with an age exempt from scorn or crime;
An age that melts with unperceiv'd decay,
And glides in modest innocence away;
Whose peaceful day Benevolence endears,
Whose night congratulating Conscience cheers;
The gen'ral fav'rite as the gen'ral friend:
Such age there is, and who shall wish its end?
   Yet ev'n on this her load Misfortune flings,
To press the weary minutes' flagging wings; 300
New sorrow rises as the day returns,
A sister sickens, or a daughter mourns.
Now kindred Merit fills the sable bier,
Now lacerated Friendship claims a tear;
Year chases year, decay pursues decay,
Still drops some joy from with'ring life away;
New forms arise, and diff'rent views engage,
Superfluous lags the vet'ran on the stage,
Till pitying Nature signs the last release,
And bids afflicted worth retire to peace. 310
   But few there are whom hours like these await,

Who set unclouded in the gulfs of Fate.
From Lydia's monarch [18] should the search descend,
By Solon caution'd to regard his end,
In life's last scene what prodigies surprise,
Fears of the brave, and follies of the wise!
From Marlb'rough's eyes the streams of dotage flow,
And Swift expires a driv'ler and a show.

The teeming mother, anxious for her race,
Begs for each birth the fortune of a face: 320
Yet Vane [19] could tell what ills from beauty spring;
And Sedley [20] curs'd the form that pleas'd a king.
Ye nymphs of rosy lips and radiant eyes,
Whom Pleasure keeps too busy to be wise,
Whom joys with soft varieties invite,
By day the frolic, and the dance by night;
Who frown with vanity, who smile with art,
And ask the latest fashion of the heart;
What care, what rules your heedless charms shall save,
Each nymph your rival, and each youth your slave?   330
Against your fame with fondness hate combines,
The rival batters, and the lover mines.
With distant voice neglected Virtue calls,
Less heard and less, the faint remonstrance falls;
Tir'd with contempt, she quits the slipp'ry reign,
And Pride and Prudence take her seat in vain.
In crowd at once, where none the pass defend,
The harmless freedom, and the private friend.
The guardians yield, by force superior plied:
To Int'rest, Prudence; and to Flatt'ry, Pride.   340
Now Beauty falls betray'd, despis'd, distress'd,
And hissing Infamy proclaims the rest.

Where then shall Hope and Fear their objects find?
Must dull suspense corrupt the stagnant mind?
Must helpless man, in ignorance sedate,
Roll darkling down the torrent of his fate?
Must no dislike alarm, no wishes rise,
No cries invoke the mercies of the skies?
Inquirer, cease; petitions yet remain,
Which Heaven may hear, nor deem Religion vain.   350

18 Croesus, King of Lydia, warned by
Solon, the wise man of Greece, that no man
can be considered happy until he has finished life happily.
19 Anne Vane, mistress of Frederick,
Prince of Wales, who cast her off.

20 Catherine Sedley, daughter of the poet
Sir Charles Sedley, mistress of the Duke of
York (later James II), who deserted her
after making her Countess of Dorchester.

Still raise for good the supplicating voice,
But leave to Heaven the measure and the choice.
Safe in His power, whose eyes discern afar
The secret ambush of a specious prayer.
Implore His aid, in His decisions rest,
Secure, whate'er He gives, He gives the best.
Yet when the sense of sacred presence fires,
And strong devotion to the skies aspires,
Pour forth thy fervours for a healthful mind,
Obedient passions, and a will resign'd;   360
For love, which scarce collective man can fill;
For patience sov'reign o'er transmuted ill;
For faith, that panting for a happier seat,
Counts death kind Nature's signal of retreat:
These goods for man the laws of Heaven ordain,
These goods He grants, who grants the power to gain;
With these celestial Wisdom calms the mind,
And makes the happiness she does not find.

THE RAMBLER *(849-74)* Dec 4

No. 4.   Saturday, March 31, 1750

Simul et jucunda et idonea dicere vitae.
                                    —HOR. *Art of Poetry*, 334
And join both profit and delight in one.

                                    —CREECH

The works of fiction with which the present generation seems
more particularly delighted are such as exhibit life in its true state,
diversified only by accidents that daily happen in the world, and
influenced by passions and qualities which are really to be found
in conversing with mankind.

This kind of writing may be termed, not improperly, the comedy of romance, and is to be conducted nearly by the rules of
comic poetry. Its province is to bring about natural events by easy
means, and to keep up curiosity without the help of wonder: it is
therefore precluded from the machines and expedients of the
heroic romance, and can neither employ giants to snatch away a
lady from the nuptial rites, nor knights to bring her back from

captivity; it can neither bewilder its personages in deserts, nor lodge them in imaginary castles.

I remember a remark made by Scaliger upon Pontanus, that all his writings are filled with the same images; and that if you take from him his lilies and his roses, his satyrs and his dryads, he will have nothing left that can be called poetry. In like manner, almost all the fictions of the last age will vanish if you deprive them of a hermit and a wood, a battle and a shipwreck.

Why this wild strain of imagination found reception so long in polite and learned ages, it is not easy to conceive; but we cannot wonder that while readers could be procured, the authors were willing to continue it; for when a man had by practice gained some fluency of language, he had no further care than to retire to his closet, let loose his invention, and heat his mind with incredibilities; a book was thus produced without fear of criticism, without the toil of study, without knowledge of nature, or acquaintance with life.

The task of our present writers is very different; it requires, together with that learning which is to be gained from books, that experience which can never be attained by solitary diligence, but must arise from general converse and accurate observation of the living world. Their performances have, as Horace expresses it, *plus oneris quanto venio minus*, little indulgence, and therefore more difficulty. They are engaged in portraits of which everyone knows the original, and can detect any deviation from exactness of resemblance. Other writings are safe, except from the malice of learning, but these are in danger from every common reader; as the slipper ill executed was censured by a shoemaker who happened to stop in his way at the Venus of Apelles.

But the fear of not being approved as just copiers of human manners is not the most important concern that an author of this sort ought to have before him. These books are written chiefly to the young, the ignorant, and the idle, to whom they serve as lectures of conduct, and introductions into life. They are the entertainment of minds unfurnished with ideas, and therefore easily susceptible of impressions; not fixed by principles, and therefore easily following the current of fancy; not informed by experience, and consequently open to every false suggestion and partial account.

That the highest degree of reverence should be paid to youth, and that nothing indecent should be suffered to approach their eyes or ears, are precepts extorted by sense and virtue from an ancient writer by no means eminent for chastity of thought. The same kind, though not the same degree, of caution, is required in everything which is laid before them, to secure them from unjust prejudices, perverse opinions, and incongruous combinations of images.

In the romances formerly written, every transaction and sentiment was so remote from all that passes among men, that the reader was in very little danger of making any applications to himself; the virtues and crimes were equally beyond his sphere of activity; and he amused himself with heroes and with traitors, deliverers and persecutors, as with beings of another species, whose actions were regulated upon motives of their own, and who had neither faults nor excellencies in common with himself.

But when an adventurer is leveled with the rest of the world, and acts in such scenes of the universal drama as may be the lot of any other man, young spectators fix their eyes upon him with closer attention, and hope, by observing his behavior and success, to regulate their own practices when they shall be engaged in the like part.

For this reason these familiar histories may perhaps be made of greater use than the solemnities of professed morality, and convey the knowledge of vice and virtue with more efficacy than axioms and definitions. But if the power of example is so great as to take possession of the memory by a kind of violence, and produce effects almost without the intervention of the will, care ought to be taken that when the choice is unrestrained, the best examples only should be exhibited; and that which is likely to operate so strongly should not be mischievous or uncertain in its effects.

The chief advantage which these fictions have over real life is that their authors are at liberty, though not to invent, yet to select objects, and to cull from the mass of mankind those individuals upon which the attention ought most to be employed; as a diamond, though it cannot be made, may be polished by art, and placed in such situation as to display that luster which before was buried among common stones.

It is justly considered as the greatest excellency of art to imitate nature; but it is necessary to distinguish those parts of nature which are most proper for imitation: greater care is still required in representing life, which is so often discolored by passion or deformed by wickedness. If the world be promiscuously described, I cannot see of what use it can be to read the account; or why it may not be as safe to turn the eye immediately upon mankind as upon a mirror which shows all that presents itself without discrimination.

It is therefore not a sufficient vindication of a character that it is drawn as it appears; for many characters ought never to be drawn: nor of a narrative that the train of events is agreeable to observation and experience; for that observation which is called knowledge of the world will be found much more frequently to make men cunning than good. The purpose of these writings is surely not only to show mankind, but to provide that they may be seen hereafter with less hazard; to teach the means of avoiding the snares which are laid by Treachery for Innocence, without infusing any wish for that superiority with which the betrayer flatters his vanity; to give the power of counteracting fraud without the temptation to practice it; to initiate youth by mock encounters in the art of necessary defense, and to increase prudence without impairing virtue.

Many writers, for the sake of following nature, so mingle good and bad qualities in their principal personages that they are both equally conspicuous; and as we accompany them through their adventures with delight, and are led by degrees to interest ourselves in their favor, we lose the abhorrence of their faults because they do not hinder our pleasure, or perhaps regard them with some kindness for being united with so much merit.

There have been men, indeed, splendidly wicked, whose endowments threw a brightness on their crimes, and whom scarce any villainy made perfectly detestable because they never could be wholly divested of their excellencies; but such have been in all ages the great corrupters of the world, and their resemblance ought no more to be preserved than the art of murdering without pain.

Some have advanced, without due attention to the consequence of this notion, that certain virtues have their correspondent faults, and therefore that to exhibit either apart is to deviate from probability. Thus men are observed by Swift to be "grateful in the same degree as they are resentful." This principle, with others of the same kind, supposes man to act from a brute impulse, and pursue a certain degree of inclination without any choice of the object; for, otherwise, though it should be allowed that gratitude and resentment arise from the same constitution of the passions, it follows not that they will be equally indulged when reason is consulted; yet, unless that consequence be admitted, this sagacious maxim becomes an empty sound, without any relation to practice or to life.

Nor is it evident that even the first motions to these effects are always in the same proportion. For pride, which produces quickness of resentment, will obstruct gratitude by unwillingness to admit that inferiority which obligation implies; and it is very unlikely that he who cannot think he receives a favor will acknowledge or repay it.

It is of the utmost importance to mankind that positions of this tendency should be laid open and confuted; for while men consider good and evil as springing from the same root, they will spare the one for the sake of the other, and in judging, if not of others at least of themselves, will be apt to estimate their virtues by their vices. To this fatal error all those will contribute who confound the colors of right and wrong, and, instead of helping to settle their boundaries, mix them with so much art that no common mind is able to disunite them.

In narratives where historical veracity has no place, I cannot discover why there should not be exhibited the most perfect idea of virtue; of virtue not angelical, nor above probability (for what we cannot credit, we shall never imitate) but the highest and purest that humanity can reach, which, exercised in such trials as the various revolutions of things shall bring upon it, may, by conquering some calamities and enduring others, teach us what we may hope, and what we can perform. Vice (for vice is necessary to be shown) should always disgust; nor should the graces of gaiety, nor the dignity of courage, be so united with it as to reconcile it to the mind. Wherever it appears, it should raise hatred by the malignity of its practices, and contempt by the meanness of its stratagems: for while it is supported by either parts or spirit, it will be seldom heartily abhorred. The Roman tyrant was content to be hated if he was but feared; and there are thousands of the readers of romances willing to be thought wicked if they may be allowed to be wits. It is therefore to be steadily inculcated that virtue is the highest proof of understanding, and the only solid basis of greatness; and that vice is the natural consequence of narrow thoughts; that it begins in mistake, and ends in ignominy.

RASSELAS

1759

CHAPTER X

IMLAC'S HISTORY CONTINUED. A DISSERTA-
TION UPON POETRY [1]

"Wherever I went I found that poetry was considered as the highest learning, and regarded with a veneration somewhat approaching to that which man would pay to the angelic nature. And yet it fills me with wonder that in almost all countries, the most ancient poets are considered as the best; whether it be that every other kind of knowledge is an acquisition gradually attained, and poetry is a gift conferred at once; or that the first poetry of every nation surprised them as a novelty, and retained the credit by consent which it received by accident at first; or whether, as the province of poetry is to describe nature and passion, which are always the same, the first writers took possession of the most striking objects for description and the most probable occurrences for fiction, and left nothing to those that followed them but transcription of the same events and new combinations of the same images. Whatever be the reason, it is commonly observed that the early writers are in possession of nature, and their followers of art; that the first excel in strength and invention, and the latter in elegance and refinement.

"I was desirous to add my name to this illustrious fraternity. I read all the poets of Persia and Arabia, and was able to repeat by memory the volumes that are suspended in the mosque of Mecca. But I soon found that no man was ever great by imitation. My desire of excellence impelled me to transfer my attention to nature and to life. Nature was to be my subject, and men to be my auditors: I could never describe what I had not seen; I could not hope

---

1 Imlac the old philosopher is none other than Johnson. He acts as adviser to the young Prince Rasselas and his sister Nekayah, who have left their sheltered royal life in the Happy Valley to study the life of men in the world. Rasselas seeks to find whether true happiness for man is not possible. Yet he finds only that philosophers cannot face misfortune with equanimity, that hermits are not necessarily holy, that prosperity does not mean content, and that power brings no peace of mind. They return to Abyssinia resigned to the limitations of living. The discourse on poetry is part of Imlac's "history" of himself.

to move those with delight or terror whose interests and opinions I did not understand.

"Being now resolved to be a poet, I saw everything with a new purpose; my sphere of attention was suddenly magnified: no kind of knowledge was to be overlooked. I ranged mountains and deserts for images and resemblances, and pictured upon my mind every tree of the forest and flower of the valley. I observed with equal care the crags of the rock and the pinnacles of the palace. Sometimes I wandered along the mazes of the rivulet, and sometimes watched the changes of the summer clouds. To a poet nothing can be useless. Whatever is beautiful and whatever is dreadful must be familiar to his imagination; he must be conversant with all that is awfully vast or elegantly little. The plants of the garden, the animals of the wood, the minerals of the earth, and meteors of the sky, must all concur to store his mind with inexhaustible variety; for every idea is useful for the enforcement or decoration of moral or religious truth; and he who knows most will have most power of diversifying his scenes, and of gratifying his reader with remote allusions and unexpected instruction.

"All the appearances of nature I was therefore careful to study, and every country which I have surveyed has contributed something to my poetical powers."

"In so wide a survey," said the prince, "you must surely have left much unobserved. I have lived till now within the circuit of these mountains, and yet cannot walk abroad without the sight of something which I had never beheld before, or never heeded."

"The business of a poet," said Imlac, "is to examine, not the individual, but the species; to remark general properties and large appearances; he does not number the streaks of the tulip, or describe the different shades in the verdure of the forest. He is to exhibit in his portraits of nature such prominent and striking features as recall the original to every mind, and must neglect the minuter discriminations, which one may have remarked and another have neglected, for those characteristics which are alike obvious to vigilance and carelessness.

"But the knowledge of nature is only half the task of a poet; he must be acquainted likewise with all the modes of life. His character requires that he estimate the happiness and misery of every condition, observe the power of all the passions in all their combinations, and trace the changes of the human mind as they are modified by various institutions and accidental influences of climate or custom, from the sprightliness of infancy to the despondence of decrepitude. He must divest himself of the prejudices of his age or country; he must consider right and wrong in their abstracted and invariable state; he must disregard present laws and opinions, and rise to general and transcendental truths, which will always be the same; he must therefore content himself with the slow progress of his name, contemn the applause of his own time, and commit his claims to the justice of posterity. He must write as the interpreter of nature and the legislator of mankind, and consider himself as presiding over the thoughts and manners of future generations, as a being superior to time and place.

"His labor is not yet at an end; he must know many languages and many sciences; and, that his style may be worthy of his thoughts, must by incessant practice familiarize to himself every delicacy of speech and grace of harmony."

THE IDLER

No. 85. Saturday, December 1, 1759

One of the peculiarities which distinguish the present age is the multiplication of books. Every day brings new advertisements of literary undertakings, and we are flattered with repeated promises of growing wise on easier terms than our progenitors.

How much either happiness or knowledge is advanced by this multitude of authors, it is not very easy to decide.

He that teaches us anything which we knew not before is undoubtedly to be reverenced as a master.

He that conveys knowledge by more pleasing ways may very properly be loved as a benefactor; and he that supplies life with innocent amusement will certainly be caressed as a pleasing companion.

But few of those who fill the world with books have any pretensions to the hope either of pleasing or instructing. They have often no other task than to lay two books before them out of which they compile a third, without any new materials of their own, and with very little application of judgment to those which former authors have supplied.

That all compilations are useless I do not assert. Particles of science are often very widely scattered. Writers of extensive comprehension have incidental remarks upon topics very remote from the principal subject, which are often more valuable than formal treatises, and which yet are not known because they are not promised in the title. He that collects those under proper heads is very laudably employed, for though he exerts no great abilities in the work, he facilitates the progress of others, and, by making that easy of attainment which is already written, may give some mind more vigorous or more adventurous than his own leisure for new thoughts and original designs.

But the collections poured lately from the press have been seldom made at any great expense of time or inquiry, and therefore only serve to distract choice without supplying any real want.

It is observed that a corrupt society has many laws; I know not whether it is not equally true that *an ignorant age has many books*. When the treasures of ancient knowledge lie unexamined, and original authors are neglected and forgotten, compilers and plagiaries are encouraged, who give us again what we had before, and grow great by setting before us what our own sloth had hidden from our view.

Yet are not even these writers to be indiscriminately censured and rejected. Truth, like beauty, varies its fashions, and is best recommended by different dresses to different minds; and he that recalls the attention of mankind to any part of learning which time has left behind it may be truly said to advance the literature of his own age. As the manners of nations vary, new topics of persuasion become necessary, and new combinations of imagery are produced; and he that can accommodate himself to the reigning taste may always have readers who perhaps would not have looked upon better performances.

To exact of every man who writes that he should say something new would be to reduce authors to a small number; to oblige the most fertile genius to say only what is new would be to contract his volumes to a few pages. Yet surely there ought to be some bounds to repetition; libraries ought no more to be heaped forever with the same thoughts differently expressed than with the same books differently decorated.

The good or evil which these secondary writers produce is seldom of any long duration. As they owe their existence to change of fashion, they commonly disappear when a new fashion becomes prevalent. The authors that in any nation last from age to age are very few, because there are very few that have any other claim to notice than that they catch hold on present curiosity, and gratify some accidental desire, or produce some temporary conveniency.

But however the writers of the day may despair of future fame, they ought at least to forbear any present mischief. Though they cannot arrive at eminent heights of excellence, they might keep themselves harmless. They might take care to inform themselves before they attempt to inform others, and exert the little influence which they have for honest purposes.

But such is the present state of our literature that the ancient sage [1] who thought *a great book a great evil* would now think the multitude of books a multitude of evils. He would consider a bulky writer who engrossed a year and a swarm of pamphleteers who stole each an hour as equal wasters of human life, and would make no other difference between them than between a beast of prey and a flight of locusts.

PREFACE TO SHAKESPEARE
1765

That praises are without reason lavished on the dead, and that the honors due only to excellence are paid to antiquity, is a complaint likely to be always continued by those who, being able to add nothing to truth, hope for eminence from the heresies of paradox; or those who, being forced by disappointment upon consolatory expedients, are willing to hope from posterity what the present age refuses, and flatter themselves that the regard which is yet denied by envy will be at last bestowed by time.

Antiquity, like every other quality that attracts the notice of mankind, has undoubtedly votaries that reverence it not from reason but from prejudice. Some seem to admire indiscriminately whatever has been long preserved, without considering that time has sometimes cooperated with chance; all perhaps are more willing to honor past than present excellence; and the mind contem-

---

1 The poet Callimachus, third century B.C.

plates genius through the shades of age, as the eye surveys the sun through artificial opacity. The great contention of criticism is to find the faults of the moderns and the beauties of the ancients. While an author is yet living, we estimate his powers by his worst performance; and when he is dead, we rate them by his best.

To works, however, of which the excellence is not absolute and definite, but gradual and comparative, to works not raised upon principles demonstrative and scientific, but appealing wholly to observation and experience, no other test can be applied than length of duration and continuance of esteem. What mankind have long possessed they have often examined and compared; and if they persist to value the possession, it is because frequent comparisons have confirmed opinion in its favor. As among the works of nature no man can properly call a river deep or a mountain high without the knowledge of many mountains and many rivers, so, in the production of genius, nothing can be styled excellent till it has been compared with other works of the same kind. Demonstration immediately displays its power, and has nothing to hope or fear from the flux of years; but works tentative and experimental must be estimated by their proportion to the general and collective ability of man as it is discovered in a long succession of endeavors. Of the first building that was raised, it might be with certainty determined that it was round or square; but whether it was spacious or lofty must have been referred to time. The Pythagorean scale of numbers was at once discovered to be perfect; but the poems of Homer we yet know not to transcend the common limits of human intelligence but by remarking that nation after nation, and century after century, has been able to do little more than transpose his incidents, new-name his characters, and paraphrase his sentiments.

The reverence due to writings that have long subsisted arises therefore not from any credulous confidence in the superior wisdom of past ages, or gloomy persuasion of the degeneracy of mankind, but is the consequence of acknowledged and indubitable positions that what has been longest known has been most considered, and what is most considered is best understood.

The poet of whose works I have undertaken the revision may now begin to assume the dignity of an ancient and claim the privilege of established fame and prescriptive veneration. He has long outlived his century, the term commonly fixed as the test of literary merit. Whatever advantages he might once derive from personal allusions, local customs, or temporary opinions, have for many years been lost; and every topic of merriment or motive of sorrow which the modes of artificial life afforded him now only obscure the scenes which they once illuminated. The effects of favor and competition are at an end; the tradition of his friendships and his enmities has perished; his works support no opinion with arguments nor supply any faction with invectives; they can neither indulge vanity nor gratify malignity; but are read without any other reason than the desire of pleasure, and are therefore praised only as pleasure is obtained; yet, thus unassisted by interest or passion, they have passed through variations of taste and changes of manners, and, as they devolved from one generation to another, have received new honors at every transmission.

But because human judgment, though it be gradually gaining upon certainty, never becomes infallible, and approbation, though long continued, may yet be only the approbation of prejudice or fashion, it is proper to inquire by what peculiarities of excellence Shakespeare has gained and kept the favor of his countrymen.

Nothing can please many, and please long, but just representations of general nature. Particular manners can be known to few, and therefore few only can judge how nearly they are copied. The irregular combinations of fanciful invention may delight awhile by that novelty of which the common satiety of life sends us all in quest; but the pleasures of sudden wonder are soon exhausted, and the mind can only repose on the stability of truth.

Shakespeare is, above all writers, at least above all modern writers, the poet of nature, the poet that holds up to his readers a faithful mirror of manners and of life. His characters are not modified by the customs of particular places, unpracticed by the rest of the world; by the peculiarities of studies or professions, which can operate but upon small numbers; or by the accidents of transient fashions or temporary opinions: they are the genuine progeny of common humanity, such as the world will always supply and observation will always find. His persons act and speak by the influence of those general passions and principles by which all minds are agitated and the whole system of life is continued in motion. In the writings of other poets a character is too often an individual: in those of Shakespeare it is commonly a species.

It is from this wide extension of design that so much instruction is derived. It is this which fills the plays of Shakespeare with practical axioms and domestic wisdom. It was said of Euripides that every verse was a precept; and it may be said of Shakespeare that from his works may be collected a system of civil and economical prudence. Yet his real power is not shown in the splendor of particular passages, but by the progress of his fable and the tenor of his dialogue; and he that tries to recommend him by select quotations will succeed like the pedant in Hierocles [1] who, when he offered his house to sale, carried a brick in his pocket as a specimen.

It will not easily be imagined how much Shakespeare excels in accommodating his sentiments to real life but by comparing him with other authors. It was observed of the ancient schools of declamation that the more diligently they were frequented, the more was the student disqualified for the world, because he found nothing there which he should ever meet in any other place. The same remark may be applied to every stage but that of Shakespeare. The theater, when it is under any other direction, is peopled by such characters as were never seen, conversing in a language which was never heard, upon topics which will never arise in the commerce of mankind. But the dialogue of this author is often so evidently determined by the incident which produces it, and is pursued with so much ease and simplicity, that it seems scarcely to claim the merit of fiction, but to have been gleaned by diligent selection out of common conversation and common occurrences.

Upon every other stage the universal agent is love, by whose power all good and evil is distributed and every action quickened or retarded. To bring a lover, a lady, and a rival into the fable; to entangle them in contradictory obligations, perplex them with oppositions of interest, and harass them with violence of desires inconsistent with each other; to make them meet in rapture, and part in agony; to fill their mouths with hyperbolical joy and outrageous sorrow; to distress them as nothing human ever was distressed; to deliver them as nothing human ever was delivered, is the business of a modern dramatist. For this, probability is violated, life is misrepresented, and language is depraved. But love is only one of many passions; and as it has no great influence upon the sum of

---

[1] An Alexandrine philosopher of the fifth century A.D. *Asteia* (attributed to Hierocles) No. 9 (*Hieroclis Commentarius in Aurea Carmina* [ed. Needham, 1709], p. 462) [C. H. Conley, *The Reader's Johnson*].

life, it has little operation in the dramas of a poet who caught his ideas from the living world and exhibited only what he saw before him. He knew that any other passion, as it was regular or exorbitant, was a cause of happiness or calamity.

Characters thus ample and general were not easily discriminated and preserved; yet perhaps no poet ever kept his personages more distinct from each other. I will not say with Pope that every speech may be assigned to the proper speaker, because many speeches there are which have nothing characteristical; but perhaps though some may be equally adapted to every person, it will be difficult to find that any can be properly transferred from the present possessor to another claimant. The choice is right when there is reason for choice.

Other dramatists can only gain attention by hyperbolical or aggravated characters, by fabulous and unexampled excellence or depravity, as the writers of barbarous romances invigorated the reader by a giant and a dwarf; and he that should form his expectations of human affairs from the play or from the tale would be equally deceived. Shakespeare has no heroes; his scenes are occupied only by men, who act and speak as the reader thinks that he should himself have spoken or acted on the same occasion; even where the agency is supernatural, the dialogue is level with life. Other writers disguise the most natural passions and most frequent incidents so that he who contemplates them in the book will not know them in the world: Shakespeare approximates the remote, and familiarizes the wonderful; the event which he represents will not happen, but, if it were possible, its effects would probably be such as he has assigned; and it may be said that he has not only shown human nature as it acts in real exigencies, but as it would be found in trials to which it cannot be exposed.

This therefore is the praise of Shakespeare, that his drama is the mirror of life; that he who has mazed his imagination in following the phantoms which other writers raise up before him, may here be cured of his delirious ecstasies by reading human sentiments in human language, by scenes from which a hermit may estimate the transactions of the world, and a confessor predict the progress of the passions.

His adherence to general nature has exposed him to the censure of critics, who form their judgments upon narrower principles. Dennis and Rymer think his Romans not sufficiently Roman; and

Voltaire censures his kings as not completely royal.[2] Dennis is offended that Menenius, a senator of Rome, should play the buffoon; and Voltaire perhaps thinks decency violated when the Danish usurper is represented as a drunkard. But Shakespeare always makes nature predominate over accident; and, if he preserves the essential character, is not very careful of distinctions superinduced and adventitious. His story requires Romans or kings, but he thinks only on men. He knew that Rome, like every other city, had men of all dispositions; and wanting a buffoon, he went into the senate-house for that which the senate-house would certainly have afforded him. He was inclined to show an usurper and a murderer not only odious, but despicable; he therefore added drunkenness to his other qualities, knowing that kings love wine like other men, and that wine exerts its natural power upon kings. These are the petty cavils of petty minds; a poet overlooks the casual distinction of country and condition, as a painter, satisfied with the figure, neglects the drapery.

The censure which he has incurred by mixing comic and tragic scenes, as it extends to all his works, deserves more consideration. Let the fact be first stated, and then examined. *class Dec/H₂*

Shakespeare's plays are not in the rigorous and critical sense either tragedies or comedies, but compositions of a distinct kind; exhibiting the real state of sublunary nature, which partakes of *nature that we know* good and evil, joy and sorrow, mingled with endless variety of proportion and innumerable modes of combination; and expressing the course of the world, in which the loss of one is the gain of another; in which, at the same time, the reveler is hasting to his wine, and the mourner burying his friend; in which the malignity of one is sometimes defeated by the frolic of another; and many mischiefs and many benefits are done and hindered without design.

Out of this chaos of mingled purposes and casualties the ancient poets, according to the laws which custom had prescribed, selected some the crimes of men, and some their absurdities; some the momentous vicissitudes of life, and some the lighter occurrences; some the terrors of distress, and some the gaieties of prosperity. Thus rose the two modes of imitation, known by the names of *tragedy*

2 Johnson refers to John Dennis's *Essay on the Genius and Writings of Shakespeare* (1712), Thomas Rymer's *Short View of Tragedy* (1693) and *The Tragedies of the Last Age Considered* (1678), and Voltaire's various depreciating comments in works like *Discours sur la tragédie* (1730), *Lettres philosophiques* (Letter 18) (1733–34), and *L'Appel à toutes les nations de l'Europe* (1761).

and *comedy*, compositions intended to promote different ends by contrary means, and considered as so little allied that I do not recollect among the Greeks or Romans a single writer who attempted both.

Shakespeare has united the powers of exciting laughter and sorrow not only in one mind, but in one composition. Almost all his plays are divided between serious and ludicrous characters, and, in the successive evolutions of the design, sometimes produce seriousness and sorrow, and sometimes levity and laughter.

That this is a practice contrary to the rules of criticism will be readily allowed; but there is always an appeal open from criticism to nature. The end of writing is to instruct; the end of poetry is to instruct by pleasing. That the mingled drama may convey all the instruction of tragedy or comedy cannot be denied, because it includes both in its alternations of exhibition, and approaches nearer than either to the appearance of life, by showing how great machinations and slender designs may promote or obviate one another, and the high and the low co-operate in the general system by unavoidable concatenation.

It is objected that by this change of scenes the passions are interrupted in their progression, and that the principal event, being not advanced by a due gradation of preparatory incidents, wants at last the power to move, which constitutes the perfection of dramatic poetry. This reasoning is so specious that it is received as true even by those who in daily experience feel it to be false. The interchanges of mingled scenes seldom fail to produce the intended vicissitudes of passion. Fiction cannot move so much but that the attention may be easily transferred; and though it must be allowed that pleasing melancholy be sometimes interrupted by unwelcome levity, yet let it be considered likewise that melancholy is often not pleasing, and that the disturbance of one man may be the relief of another; that different auditors have different habitudes; and that, upon the whole, all pleasure consists in variety.

The players who in their edition divided our author's works into comedies, histories, and tragedies seem not to have distinguished the three kinds by any very exact or definite ideas.

An action which ended happily to the principal persons, however serious or distressful through its intermediate incidents, in their opinion constituted a comedy. This idea of a comedy continued long amongst us; and plays were written, which, by changing the catastrophe, were tragedies today, and comedies tomorrow.

Tragedy was not in those times a poem of more general dignity or elevation than comedy; it required only a calamitous conclusion, with which the common criticism of that age was satisfied, whatever lighter pleasure it afforded in its progress.

History was a series of actions, with no other than chronological succession, independent on each other, and without any tendency to introduce or regulate the conclusion. It is not always very nicely distinguished from tragedy. There is not much nearer approach to unity of action in the tragedy of *Antony and Cleopatra* than in the history of *Richard the Second*. But a history might be continued through many plays; as it had no plan, it had no limits.

Through all these denominations of the drama, Shakespeare's mode of composition is the same; an interchange of seriousness and merriment, by which the mind is softened at one time and exhilarated at another. But whatever be his purpose, whether to gladden or depress, or to conduct the story without vehemence or emotion through tracts of easy and familiar dialogue, he never fails to attain his purpose; as he commands us, we laugh or mourn, or sit silent with quiet expectation, in tranquillity without indifference.

When Shakespeare's plan is understood, most of the criticisms of Rymer and Voltaire vanish away. The play of *Hamlet* is opened, without impropriety, by two sentinels; Iago bellows at Brabantio's window without injury to the scheme of the play, though in terms which a modern audience would not easily endure; the character of Polonius is seasonable and useful; and the grave-diggers themselves may be heard with applause.

Shakespeare engaged in dramatic poetry with the world open before him; the rules of the ancients were yet known to few; the public judgment was unformed; he had no example of such fame as might force him upon imitation, nor critics of such authority as might restrain his extravagance: he therefore indulged his natural disposition; and his disposition, as Rymer has remarked, led him to comedy. In tragedy he often writes, with great appearance of toil and study, what is written at last with little felicity; but in his comic scenes he seems to produce, without labor, what no labor can improve. In tragedy he is always struggling after some occasion to be comic; but in comedy he seems to repose, or to luxuriate, as in a mode of thinking congenial to his nature. In his tragic scenes there is always something wanting, but his comedy often surpasses expectation or desire. His comedy pleases by the thoughts and the language, and his tragedy for the greater part by incident and action. His tragedy seems to be skill, his comedy to be instinct.

The force of his comic scenes has suffered little diminution from the changes made by a century and a half, in manners or in words. As his personages act upon principles arising from genuine passion, very little modified by particular forms, their pleasures and vexations are communicable to all times and to all places; they are natural, and therefore durable: the adventitious peculiarities of personal habits are only superficial dyes, bright and pleasing for a little while, yet soon fading to a dim tinct, without any remains of former luster; but the discriminations of true passion are the colors of nature: they pervade the whole mass, and can only perish with the body that exhibits them. The accidental compositions of heterogeneous modes are dissolved by the chance which combined them; but the uniform simplicity of primitive qualities neither admits increase nor suffers decay. The sand heaped by one flood is scattered by another, but the rock always continues in its place. The stream of time, which is continually washing the dissoluble fabrics of other poets, passes without injury by the adamant of Shakespeare.

If there be, what I believe there is, in every nation a style which never becomes obsolete, a certain mode of phraseology so consonant and congenial to the analogy and principles of its respective language as to remain settled and unaltered, this style is probably to be sought in the common intercourse of life, among those who speak only to be understood, without ambition of elegance. The polite are always catching modish innovations, and the learned depart from established forms of speech, in hope of finding or making better; those who wish for distinction forsake the vulgar when the vulgar is right, but there is a conversation above grossness, and below refinement, where propriety resides, and where this poet seems to have gathered his comic dialogue. He is therefore more agreeable to the ears of the present age than any other author equally remote, and among his other excellencies deserves to be studied as one of the original masters of our language.

These observations are to be considered not as unexceptionably constant, but as containing general and predominant truth. Shakespeare's familiar dialogue is affirmed to be smooth and clear, yet not wholly without ruggedness or difficulty; as a country may be eminently fruitful, though it has spots unfit for cultivation: his characters are praised as natural, though their sentiments are sometimes forced, and their actions improbable; as the earth upon the whole is spherical, though its surface is varied with protuberances and cavities.

Shakespeare with his excellencies has likewise faults, and faults sufficient to obscure and overwhelm any other merit. I shall show them in the proportion in which they appear to me, without envious malignity or superstitious veneration. No question can be more innocently discussed than a dead poet's pretensions to renown; and little regard is due to that bigotry which sets candor higher than truth.

His first defect is that to which may be imputed most of the evil in books or in men. He sacrifices virtue to convenience, and is so much more careful to please than to instruct that he seems to write without any moral purpose. From his writings indeed a system of social duty may be selected, for he that thinks reasonably must think morally, but his precepts and axioms drop casually from him; he makes no just distribution of good or evil, nor is always careful to show in the virtuous a disapprobation of the wicked; he carries his persons indifferently through right and wrong, and at the close dismisses them without further care, and leaves their examples to operate by chance. This fault the barbarity of his age cannot extenuate; for it is always a writer's duty to make the world better, and justice is a virtue independent on time or place.

The plots are often so loosely formed that a very slight consideration may improve them, and so carelessly pursued that he seems not always fully to comprehend his own design. He omits opportunities of instructing or delighting which the train of his story seems to force upon him, and apparently rejects those exhibitions which would be more affecting for the sake of those which are more easy.

It may be observed that in many of his plays the latter part is evidently neglected. When he found himself near the end of his work, and in view of his reward, he shortened the labor to snatch the profit. He therefore remits his efforts where he should most vigorously exert them, and his catastrophe is improbably produced or imperfectly represented.

He had no regard to distinction of time or place, but gives to one age or nation, without scruple, the customs, institutions, and opinions of another, at the expense not only of likelihood, but of possibility. These faults Pope has endeavored, with more zeal than judgment, to transfer to his imagined interpolators.[3] We need not wonder to find Hector quoting Aristotle, when we see the loves of Theseus and Hippolyta combined with the Gothic mythology of fairies. Shakespeare, indeed, was not the only violator of chronology, for in the same age Sidney, who wanted not the advantages of learning, has, in his *Arcadia,* confounded the pastoral with the feudal times, the days of innocence, quiet, and security with those of turbulence, violence, and adventure.

In his comic scenes he is seldom very successful when he engages his characters in reciprocations of smartness and contests of sarcasm; their jests are commonly gross, and their pleasantry licentious; neither his gentlemen nor his ladies have much delicacy, nor are sufficiently distinguished from his clowns by any appearance of refined manners. Whether he represented the real conversation of his time is not easy to determine: the reign of Elizabeth is commonly supposed to have been a time of stateliness, formality, and reserve; yet perhaps the relaxations of that severity were not very elegant. There must, however, have been always some modes of gaiety preferable to others, and a writer ought to choose the best.

In tragedy his performance seems constantly to be worse as his labor is more. The effusions of passion, which exigence forces out, are for the most part striking and energetic; but whenever he solicits his invention, or strains his faculties, the offspring of his throes is tumor, meanness, tediousness, and obscurity.

In narration he affects a disproportionate pomp of diction and a wearisome train of circumlocution, and tells the incident imperfectly in many words which might have been more plainly delivered in few. Narration in dramatic poetry is naturally tedious, as it is unanimated and inactive, and obstructs the progress of the action; it should therefore always be rapid and enlivened by frequent interruption. Shakespeare found it an encumbrance, and instead of lightening it by brevity, endeavored to recommend it by dignity and splendor.

His declamations or set speeches are commonly cold and weak, for his power was the power of nature; when he endeavored, like other tragic writers, to catch opportunities of amplification and, instead of inquiring what the occasion demanded, to show how

---

3 Preface to Pope's edition of Shakespeare (1725).

much his stores of knowledge could supply, he seldom escapes without the pity or resentment of his reader.

It is incident to him to be now and then entangled with an unwieldy sentiment which he cannot well express, and will not reject; he struggles with it awhile, and, if it continues stubborn, comprises it in words such as occur, and leaves it to be disentangled and evolved by those who have more leisure to bestow upon it.

Not that always where the language is intricate the thought is subtle, or the image always great where the line is bulky; the equality of words to things is very often neglected, and trivial sentiments and vulgar ideas disappoint the attention, to which they are recommended by sonorous epithets and swelling figures.

But the admirers of this great poet have most reason to complain when he approaches nearest to his highest excellence, and seems fully resolved to sink them in dejection and mollify them with tender emotions by the fall of greatness, the danger of innocence, or the crosses of love. What he does best, he soon ceases to do. He is not long soft and pathetic without some idle conceit or contemptible equivocation. He no sooner begins to move than he counteracts himself; and terror and pity, as they are rising in the mind, are checked and blasted by sudden frigidity.

A quibble is to Shakespeare what luminous vapors are to the traveler: he follows it at all adventures; it is sure to lead him out of his way, and sure to engulf him in the mire. It has some malignant power over his mind, and its fascinations are irresistible. Whatever be the dignity or profundity of his disquisitions, whether he be enlarging knowledge or exalting affection, whether he be amusing attention with incidents, or enchaining it in suspense, let but a quibble spring up before him, and he leaves his work unfinished. A quibble is the golden apple for which he will always turn aside from his career or stoop from his elevation. A quibble, poor and barren as it is, gave him such delight that he was content to purchase it by the sacrifice of reason, propriety, and truth. A quibble was to him the fatal Cleopatra for which he lost the world, and was content to lose it.

It will be thought strange that in enumerating the defects of this writer, I have not yet mentioned his neglect of the unities; his violation of those laws which have been instituted and established by the joint authority of poets and critics.

For his other deviations from the art of writing, I resign him to critical justice without making any other demand in his favor than that which must be indulged to all human excellence: that his virtues be rated with his failings. But from the censure which this irregularity may bring upon him I shall, with due reverence to that learning which I must oppose, adventure to try how I can defend him.

His histories, being neither tragedies nor comedies, are not subject to any of their laws; nothing more is necessary to all the praise which they expect than that the changes of action be so prepared as to be understood; that the incidents be various and affecting, and the characters consistent, natural, and distinct. No other unity is intended, and therefore none is to be sought.

In his other works he has well enough preserved the unity of action. He has not, indeed, an intrigue regularly perplexed and regularly unraveled: he does not endeavor to hide his design only to discover it, for this is seldom the order of real events, and Shakespeare is the poet of nature: but his plan has commonly what Aristotle requires, a beginning, a middle, and an end; one event is concatenated with another, and the conclusion follows by easy consequence. There are, perhaps, some incidents that might be spared, as in other poets there is much talk that only fills up time upon the stage; but the general system makes gradual advances, and the end of the play is the end of expectation.

To the unities of time and place he has shown no regard; and perhaps a nearer view of the principles on which they stand will diminish their value and withdraw from them the veneration which, from the time of Corneille,[4] they have very generally received, by discovering that they have given more trouble to the poet than pleasure to the auditor.

The necessity of observing the unities of time and place arises from the supposed necessity of making the drama credible. The critics hold it impossible that an action of months or years can be possibly believed to pass in three hours; or that the spectator can suppose himself to sit in the theater while ambassadors go and return between distant kings, while armies are levied and towns besieged, while an exile wanders and returns, or till he whom they saw courting his mistress shall lament the untimely fall of his son. The mind revolts from evident falsehood, and fiction loses its force when it departs from the resemblance of reality.

4 Corneille in 1660 printed the *Discours des trois unités.*

From the narrow limitation of time necessarily arises the contraction of place. The spectator who knows that he saw the first
act at Alexandria cannot suppose that he sees the next at Rome, at
a distance to which not the dragons of Medea could, in so short a
time, have transported him; he knows with certainty that he has
not changed his place; and he knows that place cannot change
itself, that what was a house cannot become a plain, that what was
Thebes can never be Persepolis.

Such is the triumphant language with which a critic exults over
the misery of an irregular poet, and exults commonly without resistance or reply. It is time, therefore, to tell him by the authority
of Shakespeare that he assumes, as an unquestionable principle, a
position which, while his breath is forming it into words, his understanding pronounces to be false. It is false that any representation
is mistaken for reality; that any dramatic fable in its materiality
was ever credible or, for a single moment, was ever credited.

The objection arising from the impossibility of passing the first
hour at Alexandria and the next at Rome supposes that when the
play opens the spectator really imagines himself at Alexandria, and
believes that his walk to the theater has been a voyage to Egypt,
and that he lives in the days of Antony and Cleopatra. Surely he
that imagines this may imagine more. He that can take the stage
at one time for the palace of the Ptolemies may take it in half an
hour for the promontory of Actium. Delusion, if delusion be admitted, has no certain limitation; if the spectator can be once persuaded that his old acquaintances are Alexander and Caesar, that
a room illuminated with candles is the plain of Pharsalia or the
bank of Granicus, he is in a state of elevation above the reach of
reason or of truth, and from the heights of empyrean poetry may
despise the circumscriptions of terrestrial nature. There is no reason why a mind thus wandering in ecstasy should count the clock,
or why an hour should not be a century in that calenture of the
brain that can make the stage a field.

The truth is that the spectators are always in their senses, and
know, from the first act to the last, that the stage is only a stage, and
that the players are only players. They came to hear a certain number of lines recited with just gesture and elegant modulation. The
lines relate to some action, and an action must be in some place;
but the different actions that complete a story may be in places
very remote from each other; and where is the absurdity of allow-

ing that space to represent first Athens, and then Sicily, which was always known to be neither Sicily nor Athens but a modern theater?

By supposition, as place is introduced, time may be extended; the time required by the fable elapses, for the most part, between the acts; for, of so much of the action as is represented, the real and poetical duration is the same. If, in the first act, preparations for war against Mithridates are represented to be made in Rome, the event of the war may, without absurdity, be represented, in the catastrophe, as happening in Pontus; we know that there is neither war nor preparation for war; we know that we are neither in Rome nor Pontus, that neither Mithridates nor Lucullus are before us. The drama exhibits successive imitations of successive actions; and why may not the second imitation represent an action that happened years after the first, if it be so connected with it that nothing but time can be supposed to intervene? Time is, of all modes of existence, most obsequious to the imagination; a lapse of years is as easily conceived as a passage of hours. In contemplation we easily contract the time of real actions, and therefore willingly permit it to be contracted when we only see their imitation.

It will be asked how the drama moves if it is not credited. It is credited with all the credit due to a drama. It is credited, whenever it moves, as a just picture of a real original; as representing to the auditor what he would himself feel if he were to do or suffer what is there feigned to be suffered or to be done. The reflection that strikes the heart is not that the evils before us are real evils, but that they are evils to which we ourselves may be exposed. If there be any fallacy, it is not that we fancy the players, but that we fancy ourselves, unhappy for a moment; but we rather lament the possibility than suppose the presence of misery, as a mother weeps over her babe when she remembers that death may take it from her. The delight of tragedy proceeds from our consciousness of fiction; if we thought murders and treasons real, they would please no more.

Imitations produce pain or pleasure not because they are mistaken for realities, but because they bring realities to mind. When the imagination is recreated by a painted landscape, the trees are not supposed capable to give us shade or the fountains coolness; but we consider how we should be pleased with such fountains playing beside us and such woods waving over us. We are agitated in reading the history of *Henry the Fifth;* yet no man takes his book for the field of Agincourt. A dramatic exhibition is a book recited with concomitants that increase or diminish its effect. Familiar comedy is often more powerful on the theater than in the page; imperial tragedy is always less. The humor of Petruchio may be heightened by grimace; but what voice or what gesture can hope to add dignity or force to the soliloquy of Cato?

A play read affects the mind like a play acted. It is therefore evident that the action is not supposed to be real; and it follows that between the acts a longer or shorter time may be allowed to pass, and that no more account of space or duration is to be taken by the auditor of a drama than by the reader of a narrative, before whom may pass in an hour the life of a hero or the revolutions of an empire.

Whether Shakespeare knew the unities and rejected them by design or deviated from them by happy ignorance, it is, I think, impossible to decide, and useless to inquire. We may reasonably suppose that, when he rose to notice, he did not want the counsels and admonitions of scholars and critics, and that he at last deliberately persisted in a practice which he might have begun by chance. As nothing is essential to the fable but unity of action, and as the unities of time and place arise evidently from false assumptions, and, by circumscribing the extent of the drama, lessen its variety, I cannot think it much to be lamented that they were not known by him, or not observed: nor, if such another poet could arise, should I very vehemently reproach him that his first act passed at Venice and his next in Cyprus. Such violations of rules merely positive become the comprehensive genius of Shakespeare, and such censures are suitable to the minute and slender criticism of Voltaire.

> Non usque adeo permiscuit imis
> Longus summa dies, ut non, si voce Metelli
> Serventur leges, malint a Caesare tolli.[5]

Yet when I speak thus slightly of dramatic rules, I cannot but recollect how much wit and learning may be produced against me; before such authorities I am afraid to stand: not that I think the present question one of those that are to be decided by mere authority, but because it is to be suspected that these precepts

---

5 Lucan *Pharsalia* III. 138–140: "The long day has not so confounded the highest with the lowest that the laws might not better be set aside by Caesar than preserved by Metellus."

have not been so easily received but for better reasons than I have yet been able to find. The result of my inquiries, in which it would be ludicrous to boast of impartiality, is that the unities of time and place are not essential to a just drama, that though they may sometimes conduce to pleasure, they are always to be sacrificed to the nobler beauties of variety and instruction; and that a play written with nice observation of critical rules is to be contemplated as an elaborate curiosity, as the product of superfluous and ostentatious art, by which is shown rather what is possible than what is necessary.

He that, without diminution of any other excellence, shall preserve all the unities unbroken deserves the like applause with the architect who shall display all the orders of architecture in a citadel without any deduction from its strength; but the principal beauty of a citadel is to exclude the enemy, and the greatest graces of a play are to copy nature and instruct life.

Perhaps what I have here not dogmatically but deliberately written may recall the principles of the drama to a new examination. I am almost frighted at my own temerity; and when I estimate the fame and the strength of those that maintain the contrary opinion, am ready to sink down in reverential silence; as Æneas withdrew from the defence of Troy when he saw Neptune shaking the wall and Juno heading the besiegers. . . .

A JOURNEY TO THE WESTERN ISLANDS OF SCOTLAND

1775

I had desired to visit the Hebrides, or Western Islands of Scotland, so long that I scarcely remember how the wish was originally excited; and was in the autumn of the year 1773 induced to undertake the journey by finding in Mr. Boswell a companion whose acuteness would help my inquiry, and whose gaiety of conversation and civility of manners are sufficient to counteract the inconveniences of travel in countries less hospitable than we have passed. . . .

At Inverness . . . we procured three horses for ourselves and a servant, and one more for our baggage, which was no very heavy load. We found in the course of our journey the convenience of having disencumbered ourselves by laying aside whatever we could spare; for it is not to be imagined without experience how in climbing crags and treading bogs and winding through narrow and obstructed passages a little bulk will hinder and a little weight will burden; or how often a man that has pleased himself at home with his own resolution will, in the hour of darkness and fatigue, be content to leave behind him everything but himself. . . .

Lough Ness is about twenty-four miles long, and from one to two miles broad. It is remarkable that Boethius [1] in his description of Scotland gives it twelve miles of breadth. When historians or geographers exhibit false accounts of places far distant, they may be forgiven, because they can tell but what they are told; and that their accounts exceed the truth may be justly supposed, because most men exaggerate to others, if not to themselves: but Boethius lived at no great distance; if he never saw the lake, he must have been very incurious, and if he had seen it, his veracity yielded to very slight temptations.

Lough Ness, though not twelve miles broad, is a very remarkable diffusion of water without islands. . . .

Near the way by the waterside we espied a cottage. This was the first Highland hut that I had seen; and as our business was with life and manners, we were willing to visit it. To enter a habitation without leave seems to be not considered here as rudeness or intrusion. The old laws of hospitality still give this license to a stranger.

A hut is constructed with loose stones ranged for the most part with some tendency to circularity. It must be placed where the wind cannot act upon it with violence, because it has no cement; and where the water will run easily away, because it has no floor but the naked ground. The wall, which is commonly about six feet high, declines from the perpendicular a little inward. Such rafters as can be procured are then raised for a roof and covered with heath, which makes a strong and warm thatch, kept from flying off by ropes of twisted heath, of which the ends, reaching from the center of the thatch to the top of the wall, are held firm by the weight of a large stone. No light is admitted but at the entrance and through a hole in the thatch, which gives vent to the

1 Hector Boece (1465?–1536) wrote a history of Scotland.

smoke. This hole is not directly over the fire, lest the rain should extinguish it; and the smoke, therefore, naturally fills the place before it escapes. Such is the general structure of the houses in which one of the nations of this opulent and powerful island has been hitherto content to live. Huts, however, are not more uniform than palaces; and this which we were inspecting was very far from one of the meanest, for it was divided into several apartments; and its inhabitants possessed such property as a pastoral poet might exalt into riches.

When we entered, we found an old woman boiling goat's flesh in a kettle. She spoke little English, but we had interpreters at hand, and she was willing enough to display her whole system of economy. She has five children, of which none are yet gone from her. The eldest, a boy of thirteen, and her husband, who is eighty years old, were at work in the wood. Her two next sons were gone to Inverness to buy meal, by which oatmeal is always meant. Meal she considered as expensive food, and told us that in spring, when the goats gave milk, the children could live without it. She is mistress of sixty goats, and I saw many kids in an enclosure at the end of her house. She had also some poultry. By the lake we saw a potato garden and a small spot of ground on which stood four shocks, containing each twelve sheaves of barley. She has all this from the labor of their own hands, and, for what is necessary to be bought, her kids and her chickens are sent to market.

With the true pastoral hospitality she asked us to sit down and drink whisky. She is religious, and though the kirk is four miles off (probably eight English miles) she goes thither every Sunday. We gave her a shilling, and she begged snuff, for snuff is the luxury of a Highland cottage. . . .

Towards evening we crossed, by a bridge, the river which makes the celebrated Fall of Fiers. The country at the bridge strikes the imagination with all the gloom and grandeur of Siberian solitude. The way makes a flexure, and the mountains, covered with trees, rise at once on the left hand and in front. We desired our guides to show us the Fall, and dismounting, clambered over very rugged crags, till I began to wish that our curiosity might have been gratified with less trouble and danger. We came at last to a place where we could overlook the river, and saw a channel torn, as it seems, through black piles of stone, by which the stream is obstructed and broken till it comes to a very steep descent, of such dreadful depth that we were naturally inclined to turn aside our eyes.

But we visited the place at an unseasonable time, and found it divested of its dignity and terror. Nature never gives everything at once. A long continuance of dry weather, which made the rest of the way easy and delightful, deprived us of the pleasure expected from the Fall of Fiers. The river having now no water but what the springs supply, showed us only a swift current, clear and shallow, fretting over the asperities of the rocky bottom; and we were left to exercise our thoughts by endeavoring to conceive the effect of a thousand streams poured from the mountains into one channel, struggling for expansion in a narrow passage, exasperated by rocks rising in their way, and at last discharging all their violence of waters by a sudden fall through the horrid chasm. . . .

Early in the afternoon we came to Anoch, a village in Glenmollison of three huts, one of which is distinguished by a chimney. Here we were to dine and lodge. . . .

Our host, having amused us for a time, resigned us to our guides. The journey of this day was long, not that the distance was great but that the way was difficult. We were now in the bosom of the Highlands with full leisure to contemplate the appearance and properties of mountainous regions such as have been in many countries the last shelters of national distress, and are everywhere the scenes of adventures, stratagems, surprises, and escapes.

Mountainous countries are not passed but with difficulty, not merely from the labor of climbing; for to climb is not always necessary: but because that which is not mountain is commonly bog, through which the way must be picked with caution. Where there are hills, there is much rain, and the torrents pouring down into the intermediate spaces seldom find so ready an outlet as not to stagnate till they have broken the texture of the ground.

Of the hills which our journey offered to the view on either side, we did not take the height, nor did we see any that astonished us with their loftiness. Towards the summit of one there was a white spot which I should have called a naked rock, but the guides, who had better eyes and were acquainted with the phenomena of the country, declared it to be snow. It had already lasted to the end of August and was likely to maintain its contest with the sun till it should be reinforced by winter.

The height of mountains, philosophically considered, is properly computed from the surface of the next sea; but as it affects the eye or imagination of the passenger, as it makes either a spectacle or an obstruction, it must be reckoned from the place where the rise begins to make a considerable angle with the plain. In extensive continents the land may by gradual elevation attain great height without any other appearance than that of a plain gently inclined, and if a hill placed upon such raised ground be described as having its altitude equal to the whole space above the sea, the representation will be fallacious.

These mountains may be properly enough measured from the inland base; for it is not much above the sea. As we advanced at evening towards the western coast, I did not observe the declivity to be greater than is necessary for the discharge of the inland waters.

We passed many rivers and rivulets, which commonly ran with a clear shallow stream over a hard pebbly bottom. These channels, which seem so much wider than the water that they convey would naturally require, are formed by the violence of the wintry floods, produced by the accumulation of innumerable streams that fall in rainy weather from the hills and, bursting away with resistless impetuosity, make themselves a passage proportionate to their mass.

Such capricious and temporary waters cannot be expected to produce many fish. The rapidity of the wintry deluge sweeps them away, and the scantiness of the summer stream would hardly sustain them above the ground. This is the reason why in fording the northern rivers no fishes are seen, as in England, wandering in the water.

Of the hills many may be called, with Homer's Ida, abundant in springs; but few can deserve the epithet which he bestows upon Pelion by waving their leaves. They exhibit very little variety, being almost wholly covered with dark heath, and even that seems to be checked in its growth. What is not heath is nakedness, a little diversified by now and then a stream rushing down the steep. An eye accustomed to flowery pastures and waving harvests is astonished and repelled by this wide extent of hopeless sterility. The appearance is that of matter incapable of form or usefulness, dismissed by Nature from her care and, disinherited of her favors, left in its original elemental state, or quickened only with one sullen power of useless vegetation.

It will very readily occur that this uniformity of barrenness can afford very little amusement to the traveler; that it is easy to sit at home and conceive rocks and heath and waterfalls; and that these journeys are useless labors which neither impregnate the imagination nor enlarge the understanding. It is true that of far the greater part of things we must content ourselves with such knowledge as description may exhibit or analogy supply; but it is true likewise that these ideas are always incomplete and that at least till we have compared them with realities, we do not know them to be just. As we see more, we become possessed of more certainties and consequently gain more principles of reasoning and found a wider basis of analogy.

Regions mountainous and wild, thinly inhabited, and little cultivated make a great part of the earth, and he that has never seen them must live unacquainted with much of the face of nature and with one of the great scenes of human existence.

As the day advanced towards noon, we entered a narrow valley, not very flowery, but sufficiently verdant. Our guides told us that horses could not travel all day without rest or meat, and entreated us to stop here, because no grass would be found in any other place. The request was reasonable and the argument cogent. We therefore willingly dismounted and diverted ourselves as the place gave us opportunity.

I sat down on a bank such as a writer of romance might have delighted to feign. I had, indeed, no trees to whisper over my head, but a clear rivulet streamed at my feet. The day was calm, the air was soft, and all was rudeness, silence, and solitude. Before me and on either side were high hills which, by hindering the eye from ranging, forced the mind to find entertainment for itself. Whether I spent the hour well I know not; for here I first conceived the thought of this narration. . . .

At Dunvegan I had tasted lotus, and was in danger of forgetting that I was ever to depart, till Mr. Boswell sagely reproached me with my sluggishness and softness. I had no very forcible defense to make; and we agreed to pursue our journey. Macleod [2] accompanied us to Ulinish, where we were entertained by the sheriff of the island. . . .

We were then told of a cavern by the seaside, remarkable for the powerful reverberation of sounds. After dinner we took a boat

2 Laird of Dunvegan.

to explore this curious cavity. The boatmen, who seemed to be of a rank above that of common drudges, inquired who the strangers were; and being told we came one from Scotland and the other from England, asked if the Englishman could recount a long genealogy. What answer was given them, the conversation being in Erse, I was not much inclined to examine.

They expected no good event of the voyage; for one of them declared that he heard the cry of an English ghost. This omen I was not told till after our return, and therefore cannot claim the dignity of despising it.

The sea was smooth. We never left the shore, and came without any disaster to the cavern, which we found rugged and misshapen, about one hundred and eighty feet long, thirty wide in the broadest part, and in the loftiest, as we guessed, about thirty high. It was now dry, but at high water the sea rises in it near six feet. Here I saw what I had never seen before, limpets and mussels in their natural state. But as a new testimony of the veracity of common fame, here was no echo to be heard. . . .

In our way to Armidel was Coriatachan, where we had already been, and to which, therefore, we were very willing to return. We stayed, however, so long at Talisker that a great part of our journey was performed in the gloom of the evening. In traveling even thus almost without light through naked solitude, when there is a guide whose conduct may be trusted, a mind not naturally too much disposed to fear may preserve some degree of cheerfulness; but what must be the solicitude of him who should be wandering among the crags and hollows, benighted, ignorant, and alone?

The fictions of the Gothic romances were not so remote from credibility as they are now thought. In the full prevalence of the feudal institution, when violence desolated the world, and every baron lived in a fortress, forests and castles were regularly succeeded by each other, and the adventurer might very suddenly pass from the gloom of woods, or the ruggedness of moors, to seats of plenty, gaiety, and magnificence. Whatever is imagined in the wildest tale, if giants, dragons, and enchantment be excepted, would be felt by him who, wandering in the mountains without a guide, or upon the sea without a pilot, should be carried, amidst his terror and uncertainty, to the hospitality and elegance of Raasay or Dunvegan. . . .

Of the Erse language, as I understand nothing, I cannot say more than I have been told. It is the rude speech of a barbarous people, who had few thoughts to express, and were content, as they conceived grossly, to be grossly understood. . . .

In an unwritten speech, nothing that is not very short is transmitted from one generation to another. Few have opportunities of hearing a long composition often enough to learn it, or have inclination to repeat it so often as is necessary to retain it: and what is once forgotten is lost forever. I believe there cannot be recovered in the whole Erse language five hundred lines of which there is any evidence to prove them a hundred years old. Yet I hear that the father of Ossian [3] boasts of two chests more of ancient poetry, which he suppresses because they are too good for the English.

He that goes into the Highlands with a mind naturally acquiescent and a credulity eager for wonders may come back with an opinion very different from mine: for the inhabitants, knowing the ignorance of all strangers in their language and antiquities, perhaps are not very scrupulous adherents to truth; yet I do not say that they deliberately speak studied falsehood or have a settled purpose to deceive. They have inquired and considered little, and do not always feel their own ignorance. They are not much accustomed to be interrogated by others, and seem never to have thought upon interrogating themselves: so that if they do not know what they tell to be true, they likewise do not distinctly perceive it to be false.

Mr. Boswell was very diligent in his inquiries; and the result of his investigations was that the answer to the second question was commonly such as nullified the answer to the first.

We were awhile told that they had an old translation of the Scriptures, and told it till it would appear obstinacy to inquire again. Yet by continued accumulation of questions we found that the translation meant, if any meaning there were, was nothing else than the Irish Bible.

We heard of manuscripts that were, or that had been, in the hands of somebody's father or grandfather; but at last we had no reason to believe they were other than Irish. Martin [4] mentions Irish, but never any Erse manuscripts, to be found in the islands of his time.

I suppose my opinion of the poems of Ossian is already discovered. I believe they never existed in any other form than that

---

[3] James Macpherson. [4] Thomas Martin, antiquary (1697–1771).

which we have seen. The editor, or author, never could show the original; nor can it be shown by any other. To revenge reasonable incredulity by refusing evidence is a degree of insolence with which the world is not yet acquainted: and stubborn audacity is the last refuge of guilt. It would be easy to show it if he had it; but whence could it be had? It is too long to be remembered, and the language formerly had nothing written. He has doubtless inserted names that circulate in popular stories, and may have translated some wandering ballads, if any can be found; and the names, and some of the images, being recollected, make an inaccurate auditor imagine, by the help of Caledonian bigotry, that he has formerly heard the whole. . . .

Having waited some days at Armidel, we were flattered at last with a wind that promised to convey us to Mull. We went on board a boat that was taking in kelp, and left the isle of Skye behind us. We were doomed to experience, like others, the danger of trusting to the wind, which blew against us in a short time with such violence that we, being no seasoned sailors, were willing to call it a tempest. I was seasick, and lay down. Mr. Boswell kept the deck. The master knew not well whither to go, and our difficulties might perhaps have filled a very pathetic page had not Mr. Maclean of Col, who, with every other qualification which insular life requires, is a very active and skillful mariner, piloted us safe into his own harbor.

In the morning we found ourselves under the isle of Col, where we landed, and passed the first day and night with Captain Maclean, a gentleman who has lived some time in the East Indies, but having dethroned no nabob, is not too rich to settle in his own country. . . .

Here I first mounted a little Highland steed; and if there had been many spectators, should have been somewhat ashamed of my figure in the march. The horses of the islands, as of other barren countries, are very low; they are indeed musculous and strong beyond what their size gives reason for expecting; but a bulky man upon one of their backs makes a very disproportionate appearance. . . .

In the morning we went again into the boat, and were landed on Inch Kenneth, an island about a mile long and perhaps half a mile broad, remarkable for pleasantness and fertility. It is verdant and grassy, and fit both for pasture and tillage; but it has no trees.

Its only inhabitants were Sir Allan Maclean and two young ladies, his daughters, with their servants.

Romance does not often exhibit a scene that strikes the imagination more than this little desert in these depths of western obscurity, occupied not by a gross herdsman, or amphibious fisherman, but by a gentleman and two ladies, of high birth, polished manners, and elegant conversation, who, in a habitation raised not very far above the ground, but furnished with unexpected neatness and convenience, practiced all the kindness of hospitality and refinement of courtesy. . . .

Inch Kenneth was once a seminary of ecclesiastics, subordinate, I suppose, to Icolmkill.[5] Sir Allan had a mind to trace the foundations of the college, but neither I nor Mr. Boswell, who bends a keener eye on vacancy, were able to perceive them.

Our attention, however, was sufficiently engaged by a venerable chapel, which stands yet entire, except that the roof is gone. It is about sixty feet in length and thirty in breadth. On one side of the altar is a bas-relief of the blessed virgin, and by it lies a little bell, which, though cracked, and without a clapper, has remained there for ages, guarded only by the venerableness of the place. The ground round the chapel is covered with gravestones of chiefs and ladies, and still continues to be a place of sepulture.

Inch Kenneth is a proper prelude to Icolmkill. It was not without some mournful emotion that we contemplated the ruins of religious structures and the monuments of the dead. . . .

At last we came to Icolmkill, but found no convenience for landing. Our boat could not be forced very near the dry ground, and our Highlanders carried us over the water.

We were now treading that illustrious island which was once the luminary of the Caledonian regions, whence savage clans and roving barbarians derived the benefits of knowledge and the blessings of religion. To abstract the mind from all local emotion would be impossible if it were endeavored, and would be foolish if it were possible. Whatever withdraws us from the power of our senses; whatever makes the past, the distant, or the future predominate over the present advances us in the dignity of thinking beings. Far from me and from my friends be such frigid philosophy as may conduct us indifferent and unmoved over any ground which has been dignified by wisdom, bravery, or virtue. That man is little

5 Iona, where in 565 St. Columba founded a monastery.

to be envied whose patriotism would not gain force upon the plain of Marathon or whose piety would not grow warmer among the ruins of Iona. . . .

That these edifices are of different ages seems evident. The arch of the first church is Roman, being part of a circle; that of the additional building is pointed and therefore Gothic or Saracenical; the tower is firm and wants only to be floored and covered.

Of the chambers or cells belonging to the monks there are some walls remaining, but nothing approaching to a complete apartment.

The bottom of the church is so encumbered with mud and rubbish that we could make no discoveries of curious inscriptions, and what there are have been already published. The place is said to be known where the black stones lie concealed on which the old Highland chiefs, when they made contracts and alliances, used to take the oath, which was considered as more sacred than any other obligation, and which could not be violated without the blackest infamy. In those days of violence and rapine, it was of great importance to impress upon savage minds the sanctity of an oath by some particular and extraordinary circumstances. They would not have recourse to the black stones upon small or common occasions, and when they had established their faith by this tremendous sanction, inconstancy and treachery were no longer feared.

The chapel of the nunnery is now used by the inhabitants as a kind of general cowhouse, and the bottom is consequently too miry for examination. Some of the stones which covered the later abbesses have inscriptions which might yet be read if the chapel were cleansed. The roof of this, as of all the other buildings, is totally destroyed, not only because timber quickly decays when it is neglected, but because in an island utterly destitute of wood, it was wanted for use, and was consequently the first plunder of needy rapacity.

The chancel of the nuns' chapel is covered with an arch of stone, to which time has done no injury; and a small apartment communicating with the choir, on the north side, like the chapterhouse in cathedrals, roofed with stone in the same manner, is likewise entire.

In one of the churches was a marble altar which the superstition of the inhabitants has destroyed. Their opinion was that a fragment of this stone was a defense against shipwrecks, fire, and miscarriages. In one corner of the church the basin for holy water is yet unbroken.

The cemetery of the nunnery was, till very lately, regarded with such reverence that only women were buried in it. These reliques of veneration always produce some mournful pleasure. I could have forgiven a great injury more easily than the violation of this imaginary sanctity.

South of the chapel stand the walls of a large room which was probably the hall or refectory of the nunnery. This apartment is capable of repair. Of the rest of the convent there are only fragments.

Besides the two principal churches, there are, I think, five chapels yet standing, and three more remembered. There are also crosses, of which two bear the names of St. John and St. Matthew.

A large space of ground about these consecrated edifices is covered with gravestones, few of which have any inscription. He that surveys it attended by an insular antiquary may be told where the kings of many nations are buried, and if he loves to soothe his imagination with the thoughts that naturally rise in places where the great and the powerful lie mingled with the dust, let him listen in submissive silence; for if he asks any questions, his delight is at an end.

Iona has long enjoyed, without any very credible attestation, the honor of being reputed the cemetery of the Scottish kings. It is not unlikely that when the opinion of local sanctity was prevalent, the chieftains of the isles, and perhaps some of the Norwegian or Irish princes, were reposited in this venerable enclosure. But by whom the subterraneous vaults are peopled is now utterly unknown. The graves are very numerous, and some of them undoubtedly contain the remains of men who did not expect to be so soon forgotten.

Not far from this awful ground may be traced the garden of the monastery; the fishponds are yet discernible, and the aqueduct which supplied them is still in use.

There remains a broken building which is called the Bishop's House, I know not by what authority. It was once the residence of some man above the common rank, for it has two stories and a chimney. We were shown a chimney at the other end, which was only a niche without perforation; but so much does antiquarian credulity or patriotic vanity prevail that it was not much more safe to trust the eye of our instructor than the memory.

There is in the island one house more, and only one, that has a chimney; we entered it and found it neither wanting repair nor inhabitants; but to the farmers who now possess it the chimney is of no great value, for their fire was made on the floor in the middle of the room, and notwithstanding the dignity of their mansion, they rejoiced like their neighbors in the comforts of smoke.

It is observed that ecclesiastical colleges are always in the most pleasant and fruitful places. While the world allowed the monks their choice, it is surely no dishonor that they chose well. This island is remarkably fruitful. The village near the churches is said to contain seventy families, which, at five in a family, is more than a hundred inhabitants to a mile. There are perhaps other villages; yet both corn and cattle are annually exported.

But the fruitfulness of Iona is now its whole prosperity. The inhabitants are remarkably gross and remarkably neglected: I know not if they are visited by any minister. The island which was once the metropolis of learning and piety has now no school for education nor temple for worship, only two inhabitants that can speak English, and not one that can write or read.

The people are of the clan of Maclean; and though Sir Allan had not been in the place for many years, he was received with all the reverence due to their chieftain. One of them, being sharply reprehended by him for not sending him some rum, declared after his departure, in Mr. Boswell's presence, that he had no design of disappointing him. "For," said he, "I would cut my bones for him; and if he had sent his dog for it, he should have had it."

When we were to depart, our boat was left by the ebb at a great distance from the water, but no sooner did we wish it afloat than the islanders gathered round it and by the union of many hands pushed it down the beach; every man who could contribute his help seemed to think himself happy in the opportunity of being for a moment useful to his chief.

We now left those illustrious ruins by which Mr. Boswell was much affected, nor would I willingly be thought to have looked upon them without some emotion. Perhaps in the revolutions of the world Iona may be sometime again the instructress of the western regions. . . .

On the next day we began our journey southwards. The weather was tempestuous. For half the day the ground was rough, and our horses were still small. Had they required much restraint, we might have been reduced to difficulties; for, I think, we had among us but one bridle. We fed the poor animals liberally, and they performed their journey well. In the latter part of the day we came to a firm and smooth road made by the soldiers, on which we traveled with great security, busied with contemplating the scene about us. The night came on while we had yet a great part of the way to go, though not so dark but that we could discern the cataracts which poured down the hills on one side and fell into one general channel that ran with great violence on the other. The wind was loud, the rain was heavy, and the whistling of the blast, the fall of the shower, the rush of the cataracts, and the roar of the torrent, made a nobler chorus of the rough music of nature than it had ever been my chance to hear before. The streams which ran across the way from the hills to the main current were so frequent that after a while I began to count them, and in ten miles reckoned fifty-five, probably missing some, and having let some pass before they forced themselves on my notice. At last we came to Inverary, where we found an inn not only commodious but magnificent. . . .

Such are the things which this journey has given me an opportunity of seeing, and such are the reflections which that sight has raised. Having passed my time almost wholly in cities, I may have been surprised by modes of life and appearances of nature that are familiar to men of wider survey and more varied conversation. Novelty and ignorance must always be reciprocal, and I cannot but be conscious that my thoughts on national manners are the thoughts of one who has seen but little.

PRAYERS AND MEDITATIONS

1785

April 25, 1752 [1]

O Lord, our heavenly Father, almighty and most merciful God, in whose hands are life and death, who givest and takest away, castest down and raisest up, look with mercy on the affliction of thy unworthy servant, turn away thine anger from me, and speak peace to my troubled soul. Grant me the assistance and comfort of thy Holy Spirit that I may remember with thankfulness the blessings so long enjoyed by me in the society of my departed wife; make me so to think on her precepts and example that I may imitate whatever was in her life acceptable in thy sight and avoid all by which she offended Thee. Forgive me, O merciful Lord, all my sins, and enable me to begin and perfect that reformation which I promised her, and to persevere in that resolution which she implored Thee to continue, in the purposes which I recorded in thy sight when she lay dead before me, in obedience to thy laws and faith in thy word. And now, O Lord, release me from my sorrow, fill me with just hopes, true faith, and holy consolations, and enable me to do my duty in that state of life to which Thou hast been pleased to call me, without disturbance from fruitless grief or tumultuous imaginations; that in all my thoughts, words, and actions, I may glorify thy Holy Name, and finally obtain what I hope Thou hast granted to thy departed servant, everlasting joy and felicity, through our Lord Jesus Christ. Amen.

April 22, 1753

O Lord, who givest the grace of repentance, and hearest the prayers of the penitent, grant that by true contrition, I may obtain forgiveness of all the sins committed and of all duties neglected in my union with the wife whom Thou hast taken from me; for the neglect of joint devotion, patient exhortation, and mild instruction. And, O Lord, who canst change evil to good, grant that the loss of my wife may so mortify all inordinate affections in me that I may henceforth please Thee by holiness of life.

1 Mrs. Johnson ("Tetty") had died on March 28.

And, O Lord, so far as it may be lawful for me, I commend to thy fatherly goodness the soul of my departed wife; beseeching Thee to grant her whatever is best in her present state, and finally to receive her to eternal happiness. All this I beg for Jesus Christ's sake, whose death I am now about to commemorate. To whom, &c. Amen.

This I repeated sometimes at church.

Sept. 18, 1760

Resolved, *Deo juvante:*

To combat notions of obligation.

To apply to study.

To reclaim imaginations.

To consult the resolves on Tetty's coffin.

To rise early.

To study religion.

To go to church.

To drink less strong liquors.

To keep a journal.

To oppose laziness, by doing what is to be done tomorrow.

Rise as early as I can.

Send for books for Hist. of War.

Put books in order.

Scheme of life.

Easter Eve, 1761

Since the communion of last Easter, I have led a life so dissipated and useless, and my terrors and perplexities have so much increased, that I am under great depression and discouragement; yet I propose to present myself before God tomorrow with humble hope that He will not break the bruised reed.

Come unto me all ye that travail.

I have resolved, I hope not presumptuously, till I am afraid to resolve again. Yet, hoping in God, I steadfastly purpose to lead a new life. O God, enable me, for Jesus Christ's sake.

My purpose is:

To avoid idleness.

To regulate my sleep as to length and choice of hours.

To set down every day what shall be done the day following.

To keep a journal.
To worship God more diligently.
To go to church every Sunday.
To study the Scriptures.
To read a certain portion every week.

April 21st, 1764, 3 in the morning

My indolence, since my last reception of the Sacrament, has sunk into grosser sluggishness, and my dissipation spread into wilder negligence. My thoughts have been clouded with sensuality; and except that from the beginning of this year I have in some measure forborne excess of strong drink, my appetites have predominated over my reason. A kind of strange oblivion has overspread me, so that I know not what has become of the last year; and perceive that incidents and intelligence pass over me without leaving any impression.

This is not the life to which heaven is promised. I purpose to approach the altar again tomorrow. Grant, O Lord, that I may receive the Sacrament with such resolutions of a better life as may by thy grace be effectual, for the sake of Jesus Christ. Amen.

April 22, 1764

Having, before I went to bed, composed the foregoing meditation and the following prayer, I tried to compose myself, but slept unquietly. I rose, took tea, and prayed for resolution and perseverance. Thought on Tetty, dear poor Tetty, with my eyes full.

I went to church; came in at the first of the Psalms, and endeavored to attend the service, which I went through without perturbation. After sermon, I recommended Tetty in a prayer by herself; and my father, mother, brother, and Bathurst,[2] in another. I did it only once, so far as it might be lawful for me.

I then prayed for resolution and perseverance to amend my life. I received soon; the communicants were many. At the altar, it occurred to me that I ought to form some resolutions. I resolved, in the presence of God, but without a vow, to repel sinful thoughts, to study eight hours daily, and, I think, to go to church every Sunday, and read the Scriptures. I gave a shilling; and, seeing a poor girl at the Sacrament in a bedgown, gave her privately a

2 Either Dr. Richard Bathurst or his father, Colonel Bathurst.

crown, though I saw Hart's *Hymns* in her hand.[3] I prayed earnestly for amendment, and repeated my prayer at home. Dined with Miss W[illiams], went to prayers at church; went to —— ——, spent the evening not pleasantly. Avoided wine, and tempered a very few glasses with sherbet. Came home and prayed.

August 17th, 1767

From that time by abstinence I have had more ease. I have read five books of Homer, and hope to end the 6th tonight. I have given Mrs. —— a guinea.

By abstinence from wine and suppers, I obtained sudden and great relief, and had freedom of mind restored to me; which I have wanted for all this year, without being able to find any means of obtaining it.

I am now about to receive, with my old friend Kitty Chambers,[4] the Sacrament, preparatory to her death. Grant, O God, that it may fit me. I purpose temperance for my resolution. O God, enable me to keep my purpose to thy glory.

5:32 P.M.

I have communicated with Kitty, and kissed her. I was for some time distracted, but at last more composed. I commended my friends and Kitty. Lucy [5] and I were much affected. Kitty is, I think, going to heaven.

Townmalling, in Kent
Sept. 18th, 1768, at night

I have now begun the sixtieth year of my life. How the last year has passed, I am unwilling to terrify myself with thinking. This day has been passed in great perturbation; I was distracted at church in an uncommon degree, and my distress has had very little intermission. I have found myself somewhat relieved by reading, which I therefore intend to practice when I am able.

This day it came into my mind to write the history of my melancholy. On this I purpose to deliberate; I know not whether it may not too much disturb me.

---

3 Joseph Hart was a dissenting minister. His *Hymns* (1759) were widely used by Nonconformists.

4 A servant for Johnson for over forty years. Johnson says that she "came to live with my mother about 1724, and has been but little parted from us since. She buried my father, my brother, and my mother. She is now [1767] fifty-eight years old."

5 His stepdaughter.

I this day read a great part of Pascal's life.

O Lord, who hast safely brought me, &c.

Sept. 18, 1771, 9 at night

I am now come to my sixty-third year. For the last year I have been slowly recovering both from the violence of my last illness and, I think, from the general disease of my life. My breath is less obstructed, and I am more capable of motion and exercise. My mind is less encumbered, and I am less interrupted in mental employment. Some advances, I hope, have been made towards regularity. I have missed church since Easter only two Sundays, both which, I hope, I have endeavored to supply by attendance on divine worship in the following week. Since Easter my evening devotions have been lengthened. But indolence and indifference has been neither conquered or opposed. No plan of study has been pursued or formed, except that I have commonly read every week, if not on Sunday, a stated portion of the New Testament in Greek. But what is most to be considered, I have neither attempted nor formed any scheme of life by which I may do good and please God.

One great hindrance is want of rest; my nocturnal complaints grow less troublesome towards morning; and I am tempted to repair the deficiencies of the night. I think, however, to try to rise every day by eight and to combat indolence as I shall obtain strength. Perhaps Providence has yet some use for the remnant of my life.

April 7th [1776]

The time is again at which, since the death of my poor dear Tetty, on whom God have mercy, I have annually commemorated the mystery of Redemption, and annually purposed to amend my life. My reigning sin, to which perhaps many others are appendant, is waste of time, and general sluggishness, to which I was always inclined, and, in part of my life, have been almost compelled by morbid melancholy and disturbance of mind. Melancholy has had in me its paroxysms and remissions, but I have not improved the intervals, nor sufficiently resisted my natural inclination, or sickly habits. I will resolve, henceforth, to rise at eight in the morning, so far as resolution is proper, and will pray that God will strengthen me. I have begun this morning.

Though for the past week I have had an anxious design of communicating today, I performed no particular act of devotion till on Friday I went to church. My design was to pass part of the day in exercises of piety, but Mr. Boswell interrupted me; of him, however, I could have rid myself, but poor Thrale, *orbus et exspes*,[6] came for comfort, and sat till seven, when we all went to church.

In the morning I had at church some radiations of comfort.

I fasted, though less rigorously than at other times. I, by negligence, poured milk into the tea, and, in the afternoon, drank one dish of coffee with Thrale; yet at night, after a fit of drowsiness, I felt myself very much disordered by emptiness, and called for tea, with peevish and impatient eagerness. My distress was very great.

Yesterday, I do not recollect that to go to church came into my thoughts; but I sat in my chamber, preparing for preparation; interrupted I know not how. I was near two hours at dinner.

I go now with hope,

To rise in the morning at eight.

To use my remaining time with diligence.

To study more accurately the Christian religion.

Monday, April 20th, 1778

After a good night, as I am forced to reckon, I rose seasonably, and prayed, using the Collect for yesterday.

In reviewing my time from Easter 1777, I found a very melancholy and shameful blank. So little has been done that days and months are without any trace. My health has, indeed, been very much interrupted. My nights have been commonly not only restless but painful and fatiguing. My respiration was once so difficult that an asthma was suspected. I could not walk, but with great difficulty, from Stowhill to Greenhill. Some relaxation of my breast has been procured, I think, by opium, which, though it never gives me sleep, frees my breast of spasms.

I have written a little of the *Lives of the Poets*, I think with all my usual vigor. I have made sermons, perhaps as readily as formerly. My memory is less faithful in retaining names, and, I am afraid, in retaining occurrences. Of this vacillation and vagrancy of mind, I impute a great part to a fortuitous and unsettled life, and therefore purpose to spend my time with more method.

This year the 28th of March passed away without memorial.

---

6 "Destitute and hopeless." Harry, Thrale's only son, had died suddenly on March 23.

Poor Tetty, whatever were our faults and failings, we loved each other! I did not forget thee yesterday. Couldst thou have lived!— I am now, with the help of God, to begin a new life.

GOOD FRIDAY

April 2 [1779]

After a night restless and oppressive, I rose this morning somewhat earlier than is usual; and having taken tea, which was very necessary to compose the disorder in my breast, having eaten nothing, I went to church with Boswell. We came late; I was able to attend the Litany with little perturbation. When we came home, I began the First to the Thessalonians, having prayed by the Collect for the right use of the Scriptures. I gave Boswell *Les Pensées de Pascal* that he might not interrupt me. I did not, I believe, read very diligently; and before I had read far, we went to church again; I was again attentive. At home I read again, then drank tea, with a bun and an half, thinking myself less able to fast than at former times; and then concluded the Epistle. Being much oppressed with drowsiness, I slept about an hour by the fire.

11 P.M.

I am now to review the last year and find little but dismal vacuity, neither business nor pleasure; much intended and little done. My health is much broken; my nights afford me little rest. I have tried opium, but its help is counterbalanced with great disturbance; it prevents the spasms but it hinders sleep. O God, have mercy on me.

Last week I published [the first part of] the *Lives of the Poets*, written I hope in such a manner as may tend to the promotion of piety.

In this last year I have made little acquisition; I have scarcely read anything. I maintain Mrs. [Desmoulins] [7] and her daughter. Other good of myself I know not where to find, except a little charity.

But I am now in my seventieth year; what can be done ought not to be delayed.

[7] Daughter of Dr. Swinfen of Lichfield, Johnson's godfather; Mrs Desmoulins, like Anna Williams, lived with Johnson, whose charity was always ministering to the unfortunate.

[March 28, 1782]

This is the day on which, in 1752, dear Tetty died. I have now uttered a prayer of repentance and contrition; perhaps Tetty knows that I prayed for her. Perhaps Tetty is now praying for me. God help me. Thou, God, art merciful, hear my prayers and enable me to trust in Thee.

We were married almost seventeen years and have now been parted thirty.

AGAINST INQUISITIVE AND PERPLEXING THOUGHTS

August 12, 1784

O Lord, my Maker and Protector, who has graciously sent me into this world to work out my salvation, enable me to drive from me all such unquiet and perplexing thoughts as may mislead or hinder me in the practice of those duties which Thou hast required. When I behold the works of thy hands and consider the course of thy providence, give me grace always to remember that thy thoughts are not my thoughts, nor thy ways my ways. And while it shall please Thee to continue me in this world, where much is to be done and little to be known, teach me by thy Holy Spirit to withdraw my mind from unprofitable and dangerous inquiries, from difficulties vainly curious, and doubts impossible to be solved. Let me rejoice in the light which Thou hast imparted, let me serve Thee with active zeal and humble confidence, and wait with patient expectation for the time in which the soul which Thou receivest shall be satisfied with knowledge. Grant this, O Lord, for Jesus Christ's sake. Amen.

James Boswell

1740–1795

THE nineteenth century was prone to regard Boswell as the most efficient stenographer and the most celebrated toady in the annals of English literature: Boswell was simply another Johnsonian satellite. Then were found Boswell's "private papers" at Malahide Castle—jottings, first drafts, records putting beyond question the position of James Boswell as among the consummate literary craftsmen of the ages. And Boswell the man proves no stenographer or toady, but of a temperament vivid enough to rival that of Johnson. After all, the friendship with Johnson was only an episode (though one of the most satisfying episodes) in the rich life of Boswell the Laird, the advocate, the rake, the social lion, the traveler, the clubbable man. The conflicts within Boswell were as violent as those within Johnson: devoted as he was to his wife and children, he would plunge at any moment into the grossest drunkenness and lechery (which sometimes threatened to destroy his health); egoistic and ambitious as he was, he was always willing to humble himself for the sake of observing great men like Rousseau, Hume, Voltaire, or Johnson; apprehensive as he was in pious moments regarding the hereafter, he never controlled the wayward, robust appetites that drove him to vice; impersonal and literal as his remarks appear, each passage in his biography is artfully arranged, phrased, and modulated; although he seems most himself when lost in scenes of wild sociability, he confessed that he had "at bottom a melancholy cast; which dissipation relieves by making me thoughtless, and therefore, an easier, tho' a more contemptible animal." No one of the age had so keen a relish for human experience; driven by his discordant moods, watching himself yielding to them, selflessly reporting his responses, Boswell becomes almost a symbol of average human nature itself: "I am, I flatter myself, completely a citizen of the world," he says. Probably nobody has been more curious about the possibilities and ranges of human behavior than Boswell, or more concerned to record his discoveries. He has defended this gusto for observing the human being: "Let me value my forwardness. It has procured me much happiness. I do not think it is impudence. It is eagerness to share the best society, and a diligence to attain what I desire." His knowledge was never complete until it was recorded, and it was never finally recorded until the finer sort of memory played over it. Boswell explains: "Scenes through which a man has gone improve by lying in the memory. They grow mellow. And I don't know how it is, but even pleasing scenes improve by time, and seem more exquisite in recollection." Then Boswell reveals the secret of his art—the shaping imagination with which he worked: "Perhaps there is so much evil in every human enjoyment when present, so much dross mixed with it, that it requires to be refined by time; and yet I do not see why time should not melt away the good and the evil in equal proportions, why the shade should decay, and the light remain in preservation." In short, the experience preserved in all its immediacy has, by the imaginative memory, become art. In this art it is safe to say that James Boswell has no competitor. He said he had "all Dr. Johnson's principles, with some degree of relaxation."

BIOGRAPHICAL NOTES

Son of Alexander Boswell, Laird of Auchinleck. Study at the University of Edinburgh. Succeeds in meeting and questioning David Hume (1758). On May 16, 1763, meets Dr. Johnson in the London bookshop of Tom Davies. Travel and study abroad (1763-66)—the Grand Tour; meets Voltaire and Rousseau; affair with Isabella de Zuylen (Zélide); visits Corsica and meets General Paoli. Admitted to the Scottish bar (1766). Prints *An Account of Corsica* (1768). Marries Margaret Montgomerie (1769). Law practice in Edinburgh, with periods of dissipation and trips to London to see Johnson. Admitted to The Club (1773), and journey to the Hebrides with Johnson. Succeeds to family estate (1782). Death of Johnson (1784). Prints *Journal of a Tour to the Hebrides* (1785). Called to the English bar and settles in London (1789). Spells of dissipation. Relies on Lord Lonsdale for patronage. Under encouragement of Edmond Malone undertakes to compose the *Life of Johnson*. Mrs. Boswell dies (1789). The *Life* appears (1791).

BIBLIOGRAPHY: *The Journal of a Tour to the Hebrides,* edd. Frederick A. Pottle and Charles H. Bennett, 1936. *Life of Johnson,* edd. Birkbeck Hill and L. F. Powell, 1934. *Private Papers of James Boswell from Malahide Castle,* edd. Geoffrey Scott and Frederick A. Pottle, 1928-1934. *Private Papers of James Boswell,* Yale Edition, 1950– . Pottle, Frederick A., "The Life of Boswell," *Yale Review,* XXXV, no. 3, Spring, 1946, pp. 445-460. Quennell, Peter, *The Profane Virtues,* 1945. Tinker, C. B., *Young Boswell,* 1922.

JOURNAL OF A TOUR TO THE HEBRIDES
WITH SAMUEL JOHNSON, LL.D.*

1785

Dr. Johnson had for many years given me hopes that we should go together and visit the Hebrides. Martin's Account of those islands had impressed us with a notion that we might there contemplate a system of life almost totally different from what we had been accustomed to see; and to find simplicity and wildness, and all the circumstances of remote time or place, so near to our native great island, was an object within the reach of reasonable curiosity. Dr. Johnson has said in his *Journey* that he scarcely remembered how the wish to visit the Hebrides was excited; but he told me, in summer 1763, that his father put Martin's Account into his hands when he was very young, and that he was much pleased with it. We reckoned there would be some inconveniences and hardships, and perhaps a little danger; but these we were persuaded were magnified in the imagination of everybody. When I was at Ferney in 1764, I mentioned our design to Voltaire. He looked at me as if I had talked of going to the North Pole, and said, "You do not insist on my accompanying you?" "No, sir." "Then I am very willing you should go." I was not afraid that our curious expedition would be prevented by such apprehensions, but I doubted that it would not be possible to prevail on Dr. Johnson to relinquish for some time the felicity of a London life, which, to a man who can enjoy it with full intellectual relish, is apt to make existence in any narrower sphere seem insipid or irksome. I doubted that he would not be willing to come down from his elevated state of philosophical dignity; from a superiority of wisdom among the wise and of learning among the learned; and from flashing his wit upon minds bright enough to reflect it.

He had disappointed my expectations so long that I began to despair; but in spring 1773, he talked of coming to Scotland that

* The passages enclosed in brackets are from Boswell's early and more personal draft, lately found in the private papers at Malahide Castle. These are reprinted from *Journal of a Tour to the Hebrides with* *Samuel Johnson, LL.D.* by James Boswell. Copyright 1936 by Ralph H. Isham. By permission of the Viking Press, Inc., New York.

year with so much firmness that I hoped he was at last in earnest. I knew that if he were once launched from the metropolis, he would go forward very well; and I got our common friends there to assist in setting him afloat. To Mrs. Thrale in particular, whose enchantment over him seldom failed, I was much obliged. It was, "I'll give thee a wind." "Thou art kind." [1] To *attract* him we had invitations from the chiefs Macdonald and MacLeod, and for additional aid I wrote to Lord Elibank, Dr. William Robertson, and Dr. Beattie . . .

Dr. Samuel Johnson's character—religious, moral, political, and literary—nay, his figure and manner, are, I believe, more generally known than those of almost any man; yet it may not be superfluous here to attempt a sketch of him. Let my readers then remember that he was a sincere and zealous Christian, of high-Church-of-England and monarchical principles, which he would not tamely suffer to be questioned; steady and inflexible in maintaining the obligations of piety and virtue, both from a regard to the order of society and from a veneration for the Great Source of all order; correct, nay stern, in his taste; hard to please and easily offended, impetuous and irritable in his temper, but of a most humane and benevolent heart; having a mind stored with a vast and various collection of learning and knowledge, which he communicated with peculiar perspicuity and force, in rich and choice expression. He united a most logical head with a most fertile imagination, which gave him an extraordinary advantage in arguing, for he could reason close or wide as he saw best for the moment. He could when he chose it be the greatest sophist that ever wielded a weapon in the schools of declamation, but he indulged this only in conversation, for he owned that he sometimes talked for victory; he was too conscientious to make error permanent and pernicious by deliberately writing it. He was conscious of his superiority. He loved praise when it was brought to him, but was too proud to seek for it. He was somewhat susceptible of flattery. His mind was so full of imagery that he might have been perpetually a poet. It has been often remarked that in his poetical pieces, which it is to be regretted are so few, because so excellent, his style is easier than in his prose. There is deception in this: it is not easier but better suited to the dignity of verse; as one may dance with grace whose motions in ordinary walking—in the common step—are

---

1 *Macbeth* I. iii. 11–12.

awkward. He had a constitutional melancholy, the clouds of which darkened the brightness of his fancy and gave a gloomy cast to his whole course of thinking; yet, though grave and awful in his deportment when he thought it necessary or proper, he frequently indulged himself in pleasantry and sportive sallies. He was prone to superstition but not to credulity. Though his imagination might incline him to a belief of the marvelous and the mysterious, his vigorous reason examined the evidence with jealousy. He had a loud voice and a slow, deliberate utterance which no doubt gave some additional weight to the sterling metal of his conversation. Lord Pembroke said once to me at Wilton, with a happy pleasantry and some truth, that "Dr. Johnson's sayings would not appear so extraordinary were it not for his *bow-wow way*": but I admit the truth of this only on some occasions. The *Messiah* played upon the Canterbury organ is more sublime than when played upon an inferior instrument, but very slight music will seem grand when conveyed to the ear through that majestic medium. *While therefore Doctor Johnson's sayings are read, let his manner be taken along with them.* Let it, however, be observed that the sayings themselves are generally great; that, though he might be an ordinary composer at times, he was for the most part a Handel.—His person was large, robust, I may say approaching to the gigantic, and grown unwieldy from corpulency. His countenance was naturally of the cast of an ancient statue, but somewhat disfigured by the scars of that *evil* which it was formerly imagined the *royal touch* could cure. He was now in his sixty-fourth year, and was become a little dull of hearing. His sight had always been somewhat weak; yet so much does mind govern and even supply the deficiency of organs that his perceptions were uncommonly quick and accurate. His head and sometimes also his body shook with a kind of motion like the effect of a palsy; he appeared to be frequently disturbed by cramps or convulsive contractions, of the nature of that distemper called St. Vitus's dance.[2] He wore a full suit of plain brown clothes with twisted-hair buttons of the same color, a large bushy greyish wig, a plain shirt, black worsted stock-

2 Such they appeared to me; but since the first edition, Sir Joshua Reynolds has observed to me that Dr. Johnson's extraordinary gestures were only habits in which he indulged himself at certain times. When in company where he was not free, or when engaged earnestly in conversation, he never gave way to such habits, which proves that they were not involuntary. I still, however, think that these gestures were involuntary; for surely had not that been the case, he would have restrained them in the public streets. [Boswell]

ings, and silver buckles. Upon this tour, when journeying, he wore boots and a very wide brown cloth greatcoat with pockets which might have almost held the two volumes of his folio dictionary, and he carried in his hand a large English oak stick. Let me not be censured for mentioning such minute particulars. Everything relative to so great a man is worth observing. I remember Dr. Adam Smith, in his rhetorical lectures at Glasgow, told us he was glad to know that Milton wore latchets in his shoes instead of buckles. When I mention the oak stick, it is but letting *Hercules* have his club; and by and by my readers will find this stick will bud and produce a good joke.

This imperfect sketch of "the *combination* and the *form*" of that Wonderful Man whom I venerated and loved while in this world, and after whom I gaze with humble hope now that it has pleased Almighty God to call him to a better world, will serve to introduce to the fancy of my readers the capital object of the following journal, in the course of which I trust they will attain to a considerable degree of acquaintance with him.

His prejudice against Scotland was announced almost as soon as he began to appear in the world of letters. In his *London, a Poem,* are the following nervous lines:

> For who would leave, unbrib'd, Hibernia's land?
> Or change the rocks of Scotland for the Strand?
> There none are swept by sudden fate away;
> But all, whom hunger spares, with age decay.

The truth is, like the ancient Greeks and Romans, he allowed himself to look upon all nations but his own as barbarians: not only Hibernia and Scotland, but Spain, Italy, and France are attacked in the same poem. If he was particularly prejudiced against the Scots, it was because they were more in his way; because he thought their success in England rather exceeded the due proportion of their real merit; and because he could not but see in them that nationality which I believe no liberal-minded Scotsman will deny. He was indeed, if I may be allowed the phrase, at bottom much of a *John Bull,* much of a blunt *true-born Englishman.* There was a stratum of common clay under the rock of marble. He was voraciously fond of good eating, and he had a great deal of that quality called *humor,* which gives an oiliness and a gloss to every other quality.

I am, I flatter myself, completely a citizen of the world.—In my travels through Holland, Germany, Switzerland, Italy, Corsica, France, I never felt myself from home; and I sincerely love "every kindred and tongue and people and nation." I subscribe to what my late truly learned and philosophical friend Mr. Crosbie said: that the English are better animals than the Scots; they are nearer the sun, their blood is richer and more mellow: but when I humor any of them in an outrageous contempt of Scotland, I fairly own I treat them as children. And thus I have, at some moments, found myself obliged to treat even Dr. Johnson.

To Scotland, however, he ventured; and he returned from it in great good humor, with his prejudices much lessened, and with very grateful feelings of the hospitality with which he was treated, as is evident from that admirable work, his *Journey to the Western Islands of Scotland*, which, to my utter astonishment, has been misapprehended, even to rancor, by many of my countrymen.

To have the company of Chambers and Scott,[3] he delayed his journey so long that the Court of Session, which rises on the eleventh of August, was broke up before he got to Edinburgh.

On Saturday, the fourteenth of August, 1773, late in the evening, I received a note from him that he was arrived at Boyd's Inn, at the head of the Canongate. I went to him directly. He embraced me cordially, and I exulted in the thought that I now had him actually in Caledonia. Mr. Scott's amiable manners and attachment to our Socrates at once united me to him. He told me that before I came in the Doctor had unluckily had a bad specimen of Scottish cleanliness. He then drank no fermented liquor. He asked to have his lemonade made sweeter; upon which the waiter with his greasy fingers lifted a lump of sugar and put it into it. The Doctor in indignation threw it out of the window. Scott said he was afraid he would have knocked the waiter down. Mr. Johnson told me that such another trick was played him at the house of a lady in Paris. He was to do me the honor to lodge under my roof. I regretted sincerely that I had not also a room for Mr. Scott. Mr. Johnson and I walked arm-in-arm up the High Street to my house in James's Court; it was a dusky night; I could not prevent his being assailed by the evening effluvia of Edinburgh. I heard a late

---

3 Robert Chambers and William Scott were Johnson's "propitious convoys" on his way to Scotland.

baronet of some distinction in the political world in the beginning of the present reign observe that "walking the streets of Edinburgh at night was pretty perilous and a good deal odoriferous." The peril is much abated by the care which the magistrates have taken to enforce the city laws against throwing foul water from the windows; but from the structure of the houses in the old town, which consist of many storeys, in each of which a different family lives, and there being no covered sewers, the odor still continues. A zealous Scotsman would have wished Mr. Johnson to be without one of his five senses upon this occasion. As we marched slowly along, he grumbled in my ear, "I smell you in the dark!" But he acknowledged that the breadth of the street and the loftiness of the buildings on each side made a noble appearance.

My wife had tea ready for him, which it is well known he delighted to drink at all hours, particularly when sitting up late, and of which his able defense against Mr. Jonas Hanway should have obtained him a magnificent reward from the East India Company. He showed much complacency upon finding that the mistress of the house was so attentive to his singular habit; and as no man could be more polite when he chose to be so, his address to her was most courteous and engaging, and his conversation soon charmed her into a forgetfulness of his external appearance . . .

Wednesday, 18th August. On this day we set out from Edinburgh. We should gladly have had Mr. Scott to go with us, but he was obliged to return to England.—I have given a sketch of Dr. Johnson; my readers may wish to know a little of his fellow-traveler. Think, then, of a gentleman of ancient blood, the pride of which was his predominant passion. He was then in his thirty-third year, and had been about four years happily married. His inclination was to be a soldier, but his father, a respectable judge, had pressed him into the profession of the law. He had traveled a good deal and seen many varieties of human life. He had thought more than anybody supposed, and had a pretty good stock of general learning and knowledge. He had all Dr. Johnson's principles, with some degree of relaxation. He had rather too little than too much prudence, and his imagination being lively, he often said things of which the effect was very different from the intention. He resembled sometimes

The best good man, with the worst natured muse.

He cannot deny himself the vanity of finishing with the encomium of Dr. Johnson, whose friendly partiality to the companion of his tour represents him as one "whose acuteness would help my inquiry, and whose gaiety of conversation and civility of manners are sufficient to counteract the inconveniences of travel in countries less hospitable than we have passed."

Dr. Johnson thought it unnecessary to put himself to the additional expense of bringing with him Francis Barber, his faithful black servant, so we were attended only by my man, Joseph Ritter, a Bohemian, a fine stately fellow above six feet high, who had been over a great part of Europe, and spoke many languages. He was the best servant I ever saw. Let not my readers disdain his introduction. For Dr. Johnson gave him this character: "Sir, he is a civil man, and a wise man."

From an erroneous apprehension of violence, Dr. Johnson had provided a pair of pistols, some gunpowder, and a quantity of bullets: but upon being assured we should run no risk of meeting any robbers, he left his arms and ammunition in an open drawer, of which he gave my wife the charge. He also left in that drawer one volume of a pretty full and curious diary of his life, of which I have a few fragments, but the book has been destroyed. I wish female curiosity had been strong enough to have had it all transcribed, which might easily have been done; and I should think the theft, being *pro bono publico*, might have been forgiven. But I may be wrong. My wife told me she never once looked into it.— She did not seem quite easy when we left her, but away we went!

Mr. Nairne, advocate, was to go with us as far as St. Andrews. It gives me pleasure that by mentioning his *name* I connect his title to the just and handsome compliment paid him by Dr. Johnson in his book: "A gentleman who could stay with us only long enough to make us know how much we lost by his leaving us." When we came to Leith, I talked with perhaps too boasting an air how pretty the Frith of Forth looked; as indeed, after the prospect from Constantinople, of which I have been told, and that from Naples, which I have seen, I believe the view of that Frith and its environs from the Castle Hill of Edinburgh is the finest prospect in Europe. "Ay," said Dr. Johnson, "that is the state of the world. Water is the same everywhere:

Una est injusti caerula forma maris." [4]

I told him the port here was the mouth of the river or water of Leith. "Not *Lethe*," said Mr. Nairne.—"Why, sir," said Dr. Johnson, "when a Scotchman sets out from this port for England, he forgets his native country." NAIRNE. "I hope, sir, you will forget England here." JOHNSON. "Then 'twill be still more Lethe." He observed of the pier or quay, "You have no occasion for so large a one: your trade does not require it; but you are like a shopkeeper who takes a shop, not only for what he has to put into it, but that it may be believed he has a great deal to put into it." It is very true that there is now comparatively little trade upon the eastern coast of Scotland. The riches of Glasgow show how much there is in the west; and perhaps we shall find trade travel westward on a great scale as well as a small.

We talked of a man's drowning himself.—JOHNSON. "I should never think it time to make away with myself." I put the case of Eustace Budgell, who was accused of forging a will and sunk himself in the Thames before the trial of its authenticity came on. "Suppose, sir," said I, "that a man is absolutely sure that if he lives a few days longer, he shall be detected in a fraud, the consequence of which will be utter disgrace and expulsion from society." JOHNSON. "Then, sir, let him go abroad to a distant country; let him go to some place where he is *not* known. Don't let him go to the devil where he *is* known!"

He then said, "I see a number of people barefooted here; I suppose you all went so before the Union. Boswell, your ancestors went so when they had as much land as your family has now. Yet 'Auchinleck' is the 'Field of Stones'; there would be bad going barefooted there. The Lairds, however, did it." I bought some speldings, fish (generally whitings) salted and dried in a particular manner, being dipped in the sea and dried in the sun, and eaten by the Scots by way of a relish. He had never seen them, though they are sold in London. I insisted on *scottifying* his palate, but he was very reluctant. With difficulty I prevailed with him to let a bit of one of them lie in his mouth. He did not like it . . .

Saturday, 21st August. . . . About a mile from Monboddo,

---

4 Non illic urbes, non tu mirabere silvas: Nor groves nor towns the ruthless ocean
  Una est injusti caerula forma maris.   shows;
       —*Ovid, Amor.* L. II. El. xi.   Unvaried still its azure surface flows.
                                                          [Boswell]

where you turn off the road, Joseph was waiting to tell us my lord expected us to dinner. We drove over a wild moor. It rained and the scene was somewhat dreary. Dr. Johnson repeated with solemn emphasis Macbeth's speech on meeting the witches. As we traveled on, he told me, "Sir, you got into our Club by doing what a man can do.[5] Several of the members wished to keep you out. Burke told me he doubted if you were fit for it: but now you are in, none of them are sorry. Burke says that you have so much good humor naturally, it is scarce a virtue." BOSWELL. "They were afraid of you, sir, as it was you who proposed me." JOHNSON. "Sir, they knew that if they refused you, they'd probably never have got in another. I'd have kept them all out. Beauclerk was very earnest for you." BOSWELL. "Beauclerk has a keenness of mind which is very uncommon." JOHNSON. "Yes, sir; and everything comes from him so easily. It appears to me that I labor when I say a good thing." BOSWELL. "You are loud, sir, but it is not an effort of mind." . . .

I started the subject of emigration. JOHNSON. "To a man of mere animal life, you can urge no argument against going to America but that it will be some time before he will get the earth to produce. But a man of any intellectual enjoyment will not easily go and immerse himself and his posterity for ages in barbarism."

. . . My lord [6] and Dr. Johnson disputed a little whether the savage or the London shopkeeper had the best existence, his lordship, as usual, preferring the savage. My lord was extremely hospitable, and I saw both Dr. Johnson and him liking each other better every hour.

Dr. Johnson having retired for a short time, his lordship spoke of his conversation as I could have wished. Dr. Johnson had said, "I have done greater feats with my knife than this," though he had eaten a very hearty dinner. My lord, who affects or believes he follows an abstemious system, seemed struck with Dr. Johnson's manner of living. I had a particular satisfaction in being under the roof of Monboddo, my lord being my father's old friend, and having been always very good to me. We were cordial together. He asked Dr. Johnson and me to stay all night. When I said we *must* be at Aberdeen, he replied, "Well, I am like the Romans: I shall say

---

5 This, I find, is considered as obscure. I suppose Dr. Johnson meant that I assiduously and earnestly recommended myself to some of the members, as in a canvass for an election into Parliament. [Boswell]

6 James Burnett, Lord Monboddo.

to you 'happy to come, happy to depart.'" He thanked Dr. Johnson for his visit. JOHNSON. "I little thought, when I had the honor to meet your lordship in London, that I should see you at Monboddo." After dinner, as the ladies were going away, Dr. Johnson would stand up. He insisted that politeness was of great consequence in society. "It is," said he, "fictitious benevolence. It supplies the place of it among those who see each other only in public, or but little. Depend upon it, the want of it never fails to produce something disagreeable to one or other. I have always applied to good breeding what Addison in his *Cato* says of Honor:

> Honor's a sacred tie; the law of Kings;
> The noble mind's distinguishing perfection,
> That aids and strengthens Virtue where it meets her,
> And imitates her actions where she is not."

When he took up his large oak stick, he said, "My lord, that's *Homeric*." . . .

Wednesday, 1st September. I awaked very early. I began to imagine that the landlord, being about to emigrate, might murder us to get our money and lay it upon the soldiers in the barn. Such groundless fears will arise in the mind before it has resumed its vigor after sleep! Dr. Johnson had had the same kind of ideas; for he told me afterwards that he considered so many soldiers, having seen us, would be witnesses should any harm be done; and that circumstance, I suppose, he considered as a security. When I got up, I found him sound asleep in his miserable sty, as I may call it, with a colored handkerchief tied round his head. With difficulty could I awaken him. It reminded me of Henry IV's fine soliloquy on sleep; for there was here as "uneasy a pallet" as the poet's imagination could possibly conceive.

A redcoat of the 15th regiment, whether officer or only sergeant I could not be sure, came to the house in his way to the mountains to shoot deer, which it seems the Laird of Glenmorison does not hinder anybody to do. Few, indeed, can do them harm. We had him to breakfast with us. We got away about eight. Macqueen walked some miles to give us a convoy. He had in 1745 joined the Highland army at Fort Augustus, and continued in it till after the battle of Culloden. As he narrated the particulars of that ill-advised but brave attempt, I could not refrain from tears. There is a certain association of ideas in my mind upon that subject, by which

I am strongly affected. The very Highland names, or the sound of a bagpipe, will stir my blood and fill me with a mixture of melancholy and respect for courage; with pity for an unfortunate and superstitious regard for antiquity, and thoughtless inclination for war; in short, with a crowd of sensations with which sober rationality has nothing to do.

We passed through Glen Shiel, with prodigious mountains on each side. We saw where the battle was fought in the year 1719. Dr. Johnson owned he was now in a scene of as wild nature as he could see; but he corrected me sometimes in my inaccurate observations. "There," said I, "is a mountain like a cone." JOHNSON. "No, sir. It would be called so in a book; and when a man comes to look at it, he sees it is not so. It is indeed pointed at the top; but one side of it is larger than the other." Another mountain I called immense. JOHNSON. "No; it is no more than a considerable protuberance."

Tuesday, 7th September. . . . It was a very wet, stormy day. So we were obliged to remain here, as it was impossible to cross the sea to Raasay.

[Mr. Johnson called me to his bedside this morning, and to my astonishment he *took off* Lady Macdonald leaning forward with a hand on each cheek and her mouth open—quite insipidity on a monument grinning at sense and spirit. To see a beauty represented by Mr. Johnson was excessively high. I told him it was a masterpiece and that he must have studied it much. "Ay," said he.]

I employed a part of the forenoon in writing this Journal. The rest of it was somewhat dreary from the gloominess of the weather and the uncertain state which we were in, as we could not tell but it might clear up every hour. Nothing is more painful to the mind than a state of suspense, especially when it depends upon the weather, concerning which there can be so little calculation. As Dr. Johnson said of our weariness on the Monday at Aberdeen, "Sensation is sensation." Corrichatachin, which was last night a hospitable house, was in my mind changed today into a prison. [A Mr. Macdonald of Breakish came at dinner. We had a good plentiful one: roast mutton, a chicken-pie, and I forget how many good dishes. After it we had several Erse songs, and a bowl of stout punch. I was plagued somewhat with the toothache. I had a slight return of that spleen or hypochondria or whatever it should be called, which formerly made me so miserable, and which operates not only as to the present, but throws a gloom upon everything, whether past or future. The blackness of the imagination blackens every object that it takes in. How much reason have I to thank God that I have now hardly any remains of so direful a malady! The cheerfulness and constant good sense of my valuable spouse have had the happiest influence upon my mind.] . . .

Sunday, 12th September. . . . We spoke of death. Dr. Johnson on this subject observed that the boastings of some men as to dying easily were idle talk, proceeding from partial views. I mentioned Hawthornden's *Cypress Grove*, where it is said that the world is a mere show; and that it is unreasonable for a man to wish to continue in the show-room after he has seen it. Let him go cheerfully out and give place to other spectators. JOHNSON. "Yes, sir, if he is sure he is to be well after he goes out of it. But if he is to grow blind after he goes out of the show-room, and never to see anything again; or if he does not know whither he is to go next, a man will not go cheerfully out of a show-room. No wise man will be contented to die if he thinks he is to go into a state of punishment. Nay, no wise man will be contented to die if he thinks he is to fall into annihilation: for however unhappy any man's existence may be, he yet would rather have it than not exist at all. No, there is no rational principle by which a man can die contented, but a trust in the mercy of God, through the merits of Jesus Christ." This short sermon delivered with manly eloquence in a boat on the sea, which was perfectly calm, on a day appropriated to religious worship, while everyone listened with an air of satisfaction, had a most pleasing effect upon my mind . . .

I was highly pleased to see Dr. Johnson safely arrived at Kingsburgh and received by the hospitable Mr. Macdonald, who with a most respectful attention supported him into the house. Kingsburgh was completely the figure of a gallant Highlander, exhibiting "the graceful mien and manly looks" which our popular Scotch song has justly attributed to that character. He had his tartan plaid thrown about him, a large blue bonnet with a knot of black ribbon like a cockade, a brown short coat of a kind of duffle, a tartan waistcoat with gold buttons and gold buttonholes, a bluish filibeg, and tartan hose. He had jet-black hair tied behind, and was a large stately man, with a steady sensible countenance.

[There was a comfortable parlour with a good fire, and a dram of admirable Holland's gin went round. By and by supper came, when there appeared his spouse, the celebrated Miss Flora. She was a little woman, of a mild and genteel appearance, mighty soft and well-bred. To see Mr. Samuel Johnson salute Miss Flora Macdonald was a wonderful romantic scene to me. There was a Mrs. Macdonald, wife to James, a brother of Kingsburgh's, and one of his sons. We had as genteel a supper as one would wish to see, in particular an excellent roasted turkey, porter to drink at table, and after supper claret and punch. But what I admired was the perfect ease with which everything went on. My *facility of manners*, as Adam Smith said of me, had fine play.]

Miss Flora Macdonald (for so I shall call her) told me she heard upon the mainland, as she was returning home about a fortnight before, that Mr. Boswell was coming to Sky, and one Mr. Johnson, a young English buck, with him. He was highly entertained with this fancy. Giving an account of the afternoon which we passed at Anoch, he said, "I, being a *buck*, had Miss in to make tea."—He was rather quiescent tonight and went early to bed. I was in a cordial humor and promoted a cheerful glass. The punch was excellent. Honest Mr. MacQueen observed that I was in high glee, "my *governor* being gone to bed." Yet in reality my heart was grieved when I recollected that Kingsburgh was embarrassed in his affairs and intended to go to America. However, nothing but what was good was present, and I pleased myself in thinking that so spirited a fellow would be well everywhere. I slept in the same room with Dr. Johnson. Each had a neat bed with tartan curtains in an upper chamber.

Monday, 13th September. [Last night's jovial bout disturbed me somewhat, but not long.] The room where we lay was a celebrated one. Dr. Johnson's bed was the very bed in which the grandson of the unfortunate King James II lay on one of the nights after the failure of his rash attempt in 1745–6 while he was eluding the pursuit of the emissaries of government, which had offered thirty thousand pounds as a reward for apprehending him. To see Dr. Samuel Johnson lying in that bed, in the Isle of Sky, in the house of Miss Flora Macdonald, struck me with such a group of ideas as it is not easy for words to describe as they passed through the mind. He smiled, and said, "I have had no ambitious thoughts in it." The room was decorated with a great variety of maps and prints. Among others was Hogarth's print of Wilkes grinning with the cap of liberty on a pole by him. That, too, was a curious circumstance in the scene this morning, such a contrast was Wilkes to the above group! It reminded me of Sir William Chambers's account of oriental gardening in which we are told all odd, strange, ugly, and even terrible objects, are introduced for the sake of variety: a wild extravagance of taste which is so well ridiculed in the celebrated *Epistle* to him. The following lines of that poem immediately occurred to me:

> Here too, O King of vengeance! in thy fane,
> Tremendous Wilkes shall rattle his gold chain.

Upon the table in our room I found in the morning a slip of paper on which Dr. Johnson had written with his pencil these words: "Quantum cedat virtutibus aurum." [7] What he meant by writing it I could not tell. He had caught cold a day or two ago, and the rain yesterday having made it worse, he was become very deaf. At breakfast he said he would have given a good deal rather than not have lain in that bed. I owned he was the lucky man; and observed that without doubt it had been contrived between Mrs. Macdonald and him. She seemed to acquiesce, adding "You know young *bucks* are always favorites of the ladies." He spoke of Prince Charles being here, and asked Mrs. Macdonald, "*Who* was with him? We were told, Madam, in England, there was one Miss Flora Macdonald with him." She said, "They were very right." [She then very obligingly told him out of her own mouth, how she had agreed to carry the Prince with her out of Lewis when it was known he was there; the country was full of troops and the coast surrounded with ships. He passed as her maid, an Irish girl, Betty Bourke. They set off in a small boat. The people on shore fired after them to bring them to. But they went forward. They landed in Sky. She got a horse and her maid walked beside her, which it seems is common in this part of the world, but Betty looked somewhat awkward in women's clothes. They came to Monkstadt. She dined at table with Lady Margaret Macdonald, where was an officer who commanded a party watching for the Prince, at whom she often laughed in good humour afterwards as having deceived him; and her maid was—I do not remember where.

Mr. Johnson said all this should be written down. She said Bishop

---

7 "With virtue weigh'd, what worthless trash is gold!"—[Boswell]

Forbes at Leith had it. Mr. Johnson and I were both visibly of the *old interest* (to use the Oxford expression), kindly affectioned at least, and perhaps too openly so.

Sandie MacLeod had assured us that the Prince was in London in 1759 when there was a plan in agitation for him. We could hardly believe it, and Mr. Johnson said there could be no probable plan then. Dr. MacLeod said with warmth that there was. The present Royal Family were all to have been seized and put aboard a ship; he was to have been in London; a number of persons of great consequence, among which was the Lord Mayor of London, were in the plot, and James III of Britain would have been proclaimed at Charing Cross; the Prince Regent would have issued writs and called a Parliament, and all would have gone well. "But," said the Doctor, "it failed from the pusillanimity of some of those who were to have acted." Mr. Johnson said it could not have done, unless the King of Prussia had stopped the Army in Germany; for that the Army would have fought without orders, and the fleet would have fought without orders, for the king under whom they served.

I must here explain a little Mr. Johnson's political notions as well as my own. We are both *Tories;* both convinced of the utility of monarchial power, and both lovers of that reverence and affection for a sovereign which constitute loyalty, a principle which I take to be absolutely extinguished in Britain, which is one of the worst consequences of the Revolution. Mr. Johnson is not properly a *Jacobite.* He does not hold the *jus divinum* of kings. He founds their right on long possession, which ought not to be disturbed upon slight grounds. He said to me once that he did not know but it was become necessary to remove the King at the time of the Revolution; and after the present family have had so long a possession, it appears to him that their right becomes the same that the Stuarts had. His difficulty is as to the right still in some measure belonging to that unfortunate family. In short, he is dubious; and he would not involve a nation in a civil war to restore the Stuarts. Nay, I have heard him say he was so dubious that if holding up his right hand would have gained the victory to the Highland army in 1745, he does not know if he would have done it. Beauclerk told me he heard him say so before he had his pension. I, again, have all that Mr. Johnson has, and something more, for my high notions of male succession make me mount up to distant times; and when I find how the Stuart family's right has been formed, it appears to me as but very casual and artificial. I find not the firm feudal hold for which I wish and which my imagination figures. I might fix my eye at the point of James IV, from whom my ancestor Thomas Boswell got the estate of Auchinleck, and look no further, had I a line of males from that Prince. But Queen Mary comes in the way; and I see the sons of Lennox on the throne. Besides, I consider that even supposing Prince Charles to have the right, it may be very generous for one to support another's right at every risk, but it is not wise, and I would not do it. Mr. Johnson's argument of right being formed by possession and acknowledgment of the people, settles my mind, and I have now no uneasiness. With all this, he and I have a kind of *liking* for Jacobitism, something that it is not easy to define. I should guard against it; for from what I have now put down, it is certain that my calm reasoning stops short at action, so that doing anything violent in support of the cause would only be following a sort of passion or warm whim. And talking much in favour of it may even in this secure and liberal reign hurt a man in his rising in life.]

Kingsburgh conducted us in his boat across one of the lochs, as they call them, or arms of the sea, which flow in upon all the coasts of Sky, to a mile beyond a place called Grishinish. Our horses had been sent round by land to meet us. By this sail we saved eight miles of bad riding. Dr. Johnson said, "When we take into the computation what we have saved and what we have gained by this agreeable sail, it is a great deal." He observed, "It is very disagreeable riding in Sky. The way is so narrow, one only at a time can travel, so it is quite unsocial; and you cannot indulge in meditation by yourself, because you must be always attending to the steps which your horse takes." This was a just and clear description of its inconveniences . . .

During our sail, Dr. Johnson asked about the use of the dirk with which he imagined the Highlanders cut their meat. He was told they had a knife and fork besides to eat with. He asked, how did the women do? and was answered, some of them had a knife and fork too, but in general the men when they had cut their meat, handed the knives and forks to the women, and they themselves eat with their fingers. The old Tutor of Macdonald always eat fish with his fingers, alleging that a knife and fork gave it a bad taste. I took the liberty to observe to Dr. Johnson that he did so. "Yes," said he; "but it is because I am short-sighted and afraid of bones, for which reason I am not fond of eating many kinds of fish, because I must use my fingers." [Perhaps I put down too many things in this Journal. I have no fanners in my head, at least no good ones, to separate wheat from chaff. Yet for as much as I put down, what is written falls greatly short of the quantity of thought. A page of my Journal is like a cake of portable soup. A little may be diffused into a considerable portion.] . . .

Tuesday, 14th September. Dr. Johnson said in the morning, "Is not this a fine lady?" [8] There was not a word now of his "impatience to be in civilized life"—though indeed I should beg pardon: he found it here. We had slept well and lain long. After breakfast we surveyed the castle and the garden. Mr. Bethune, the parish minister, Magnus McLeod of Claggan, brother to Talisker, and McLeod of Bay, two substantial gentlemen of the clan, dined with us. We had admirable venison, generous wine; in a word, all that a good table has. This was really the hall of a chief. Lady MacLeod had been much obliged to my father, who had settled by arbitration a variety of perplexed claims between her and her relation, the Laird of Brodie, which she now repaid by particular attention to me.—MacLeod started the subject of making women do penance in the church for fornication. JOHNSON. "It is right, sir. Infamy is attached to the crime by universal opinion as soon as it is known. I would not be the man who would discover it, if I alone knew it, for a woman may reform; nor would I commend a parson who divulges a woman's first offense; but being once divulged, it ought to be infamous. Consider of what importance to society the chastity of women is. Upon that all the property in the world depends. We hang a thief for stealing a sheep; but the unchastity of a woman transfers sheep and farm and all from the right owner. I have much more reverence for a common prostitute than for a woman who conceals her guilt. The prostitute is known. She cannot deceive; she cannot bring a strumpet into the arms of an honest man without his knowledge." BOSWELL. "There is, however, a great difference between the licentiousness of a single woman and that of a married woman." JOHNSON. "Yes, sir; there is a great difference between stealing a shilling and stealing a thousand pounds; between simply taking a man's purse, and murdering him first and then taking it. But when one begins to be vicious, it is

8 Lady MacLeod.

easy to go on. Where single women are licentious, you rarely find faithful married women." BOSWELL. "And yet we are told that in some nations in India, the distinction is strictly observed." JOHNSON. "Nay, don't give us India. That puts me in mind of Montesquieu, who is really a fellow of genius, too, in many respects; whenever he wants to support a strange opinion, he quotes you the practice of Japan or of some other distant country, of which he knows nothing. To support polygamy, he tells you of the island of Formosa, where there are ten women for one man. He had but to suppose another island, where there are ten men born for one woman, and so make marriage between them." . . .

Lady MacLeod asked if no man was naturally good. JOHNSON. "No, madam, no more than a wolf." BOSWELL. "Nor no woman, sir?" JOHNSON. "No, sir." Lady MacLeod started at this, saying in a low voice, "This is worse than Swift." . . .

Thursday, 16th September. Last night much care was taken of Dr. Johnson, who was still distressed by his cold. He had hitherto most strangely slept without a night-cap. Miss MacLeod made him a large flannel one, and he was prevailed with to drink a little brandy when he was going to bed. He has great virtue in not drinking wine or any fermented liquor, because, as he acknowledged to us, he could not do it in moderation.—Lady MacLeod would hardly believe him, and said, "I'm sure, sir, you would not carry it too far." JOHNSON. "Nay, madam, it carried me. I took the opportunity of a long illness to leave it off. It was then prescribed to me not to drink wine; and having broken off the habit, I have never returned to it."

In the argument on Tuesday night about natural goodness, Dr. Johnson denied that any child was better than another, but by difference of instruction; though in consequence of greater attention being paid to instruction by one child than another, and of a variety of imperceptible causes, such as instruction being counteracted by servants, a notion was conceived that of two children equally well educated, one was naturally much worse than another. He owned this morning that one might have a greater aptitude to learn than another, and that we inherit dispositions from our parents. "I inherited," said he, "a vile melancholy from my father, which has made me mad all my life, at least not sober." Lady MacLeod wondered he should tell this. "Madam," said I, "he knows that with that madness he is superior to other men."

I have often been astonished with what exactness and perspicuity he will explain the whole process of any art. He this morning explained to us all the operation of coining, and at night he gave us all the operation of brewing so very clearly that Mr. MacQueen said, when he heard the first, he thought he had been bred in the Mint; when he heard the second, that he had been bred a brewer.

I was elated by the thought of having been able to entice such a man to this remote part of the world. A ludicrous, yet just, image presented itself to my mind, which I expressed to the company. I compared myself to a dog who has got hold of a large piece of meat, and runs away with it to a corner, where he may devour it in peace, without any fear of others taking it from him. "In London, Reynolds, Beauclerk, and all of them are contending who shall enjoy Dr. Johnson's conversation. We are feasting upon it, undisturbed, at Dunvegan."

It was still a storm of wind and rain. Dr. Johnson, however, walked out with MacLeod, and saw Rorie More's cascade in full perfection. Colonel MacLeod, instead of being all life and gaiety, as I have seen him, was at present grave and somewhat depressed by his anxious concern about MacLeod's affairs, and by finding some gentlemen of the clan by no means disposed to act a generous or affectionate part to their chief in his distress, but bargaining with him as with a stranger. However, he was agreeable and polite, and Dr. Johnson said he was a very pleasing man. [Mr. Johnson said he would go to Sweden with me. I said we should like to be with the King. Said Mr. Johnson, "I doubt if he would speak to us." Said the Colonel, "I'm sure Mr. Boswell would speak to him." This was a good remark as to my forwardness. He added with a genteel civility, "and with great propriety." Let me value my forwardness. It has procured me much happiness. I do not think it is impudence. It is an eagerness to share the best society, and a diligence to attain what I desire. If a man is praised for seeking knowledge though mountains and seas are in his way, is it not laudable in me to seek it at the risk of mortification from repulses? I have never yet exerted ambition in rising in the state. But sure I am, no man has made his way better to the best of company. Were my *places* to be ranged after my name, as "Member of the Club at the Turk's Head," etc., I should make as great a figure as most peers. There is a meaning in this if it were well expressed.]

After the ladies were gone from table, we talked of the Highlanders' not having sheets; and this led us to consider the advantage of wearing linen. JOHNSON. "All animal substances are less cleanly than vegetables. Wool, of which flannel is made, is an animal substance; flannel therefore is not so cleanly as linen. I remember I used to think tar dirty; but when I knew it to be only a preparation of the juice of the pine, I thought so no longer. It is not disagreeable to have the gum that oozes from a plum-tree upon your fingers, because it is vegetable; but if you have any candlegrease, any tallow upon your fingers, you are uneasy till you rub it off.—I have often thought that if I kept a seraglio, the ladies should all wear linen gowns—or cotton; I mean stuffs made of vegetable substances. I would have no silk; you cannot tell when it is clean. It will be very nasty before it is perceived to be so. Linen detects its own dirtiness."

[To hear Mr. Johnson, while sitting solemn in arm-chair, talk of his keeping a seraglio and saying too, "I have *often* thought," was truly curious. Mr. Macqueen asked him if he would admit me. "Yes," said he, "if he were properly prepared; and he'd make a very good eunuch. He'd be a fine gay animal. He'd do his part well." "I take it," said I, "better than you would do your part." Though he treats his friends with uncommon freedom, he does not like a return. He seemed to me to be a little angry. He got off from my joke by saying, "I have not told you what was to be my part"—and then at once he returned to my office as eunuch and expatiated upon it with such fluency that it really hurt me. He made me quite contemptible for the moment. Luckily the company did not take it so clearly as I did. Perhaps, too, I imagined him to be more serious in this extraordinary raillery than he really was. But I am of a firmer metal than Langton and can stand a rub better.] . . . .

We talked tonight of Luther's allowing the Landgrave of Hesse two wives, and that it was with the consent of the wife to whom he was first married. JOHNSON. "There was no harm in this so far as she was only concerned, because *volenti non fit injuria*.[9] But it was an offense against the general order of society, and against the law of the Gospel, by which one man and one woman are to be united. No man can have two wives but by preventing somebody else from having one."

Monday, 20th September. . . . MacLeod was too late in com-

9 "No harm is done when a person consents."

ing to breakfast. Dr. Johnson said laziness was worse than the toothache. BOSWELL. "I cannot agree with you, sir; a basin of cold water or a horsewhip will cure laziness." JOHNSON. "No, sir, it will only put off the fit; it will not cure the disease. I have been trying to cure laziness all my life, and could not do it." BOS-WELL. "But if a man does in a shorter time what might be the labor of a life, there is nothing to be said against him." JOHN-SON (perceiving at once that I alluded to him and his dictionary). "Suppose that flattery to be true, the consequence would be that the world would have no right to censure a man; but that will not justify him to himself." . . .

Thursday, 23d September. . . . There is a beautiful little island in the Loch of Dunvegan, called Isa. MacLeod said he would give it to Dr. Johnson, on condition of his residing on it three months in the year; nay, one month. Dr. Johnson was highly amused with the fancy. I have seen him please himself with little things, even with mere ideas like the present. He talked a great deal of this island—how he would build a house there,—how he would fortify it,—how he would have cannon,—how he would plant,—how he would sally out and *take* the Isle of Muck; and then he laughed with uncommon glee, and could hardly leave off. I have seen him do so at a small matter that struck him, and was a sport to no one else . . .

Saturday, 25th September. . . . Dr. Johnson went to bed soon. When one bowl of punch was finished, I rose, and was near the door, in my way upstairs to bed; but Corrichatachin said it was the first time Col had been in his house, and he should have his bowl;—and would not I join in drinking it? The heartiness of my honest landlord, and the desire of doing social honor to our very obliging conductor, induced me to sit down again. Col's bowl was finished; and by that time we were well warmed. A third bowl was soon made, and that too was finished. We were cordial, and merry to a high degree; but of what passed I have no recollection, with any accuracy. I remember calling Corrichatachin by the familiar appellation of "Corri," which his friends do. A fourth bowl was made, by which time Col and young Mackinnon, Corrichatachin's son, slipped away to bed. I continued a little with Corri and Knockoe; but at last I left them. It was near five in the morning when I got to bed.

Sunday, 26th September. I awaked at noon with a severe headache. I was much vexed that I should have been guilty of such a riot, and afraid of a reproof from Dr. Johnson. I thought it very inconsistent with that conduct which I ought to maintain while the companion of the Rambler. About one he came into my room, and accosted me, "What, drunk yet?"—His tone of voice was not that of severe upbraiding; so I was relieved a little.—"Sir," said I, "they kept me up."—He answered, "No, you kept them up, you drunken dog."—This he said with good-humored *English* pleasantry. Soon afterwards, Corrichatachin, Col, and other friends assembled round my bed. Corri had a brandy bottle and glass with him, and insisted I should take a dram.—"Ay," said Dr. Johnson, "fill him drunk again. Do it in the morning, that we may laugh at him all day. It is a poor thing for a fellow to get drunk at night, and skulk to bed, and let his friends have no sport."—Finding him thus jocular, I became quite easy; and when I offered to get up, he very good-naturedly said, "You need be in no such hurry now." [10] —I took my host's advice and drank some brandy, which I found an effectual cure for my headache. When I rose, I went into Dr. Johnson's room, and taking up Mrs. Mackinnon's prayer-book, I opened it at the twentieth Sunday after Trinity, in the epistle for which I read, "And be not drunk with wine, wherein there is excess." Some would have taken this as a divine interposition . . .

This was another day of wind and rain, but good cheer and good society helped to beguile the time. I felt myself comfortable enough in the afternoon. I then thought that my last night's riot was no more than such a social excess as may happen without much moral blame; and recollected that some physicians maintained that a fever produced by it was, upon the whole, good for health: so different are our reflections on the same subject at different periods, and such the excuses with which we palliate what we know to be wrong . . .

Monday, 27th September. . . . [I had a good cup of coffee this

[10] My ingeniously relating this occasional instance of intemperance has I find been made the subject both of severe criticism and ludicrous banter. With the banterers I shall not trouble myself, but I wonder that those who pretend to the appellation of serious critics should not have had sagacity enough to perceive that here, as in every other part of the present work, my principal object was to delineate Dr. Johnson's manners and character. In justice to him I would not omit an anecdote, which, though in some degree to my own disadvantage, exhibits in so strong a light the indulgence and good humor with which he could treat those excesses in his friends, of which he highly disapproved.

In some other instances, the critics have been equally wrong as to the true motive of my recording particulars, the objections to which I saw as clearly as they. But it would be an endless task for an author to point out upon every occasion the precise object he has in view. Contenting himself with the approbation of readers of discernment and taste, he ought not to complain that some are found who cannot or will not understand him. [Boswell]

afternoon. Dr. Macdonald's wife, "Mrs. Dr. Roy" (i.e., red Doctor), as Malcolm MacLeod toasted her, was a neat, pretty little girl. She sat down upon Mr. Johnson's knee, and upon being bid by some of the company, put her hands round his neck and kissed him. "Do it again," said he, "and let us see who will tire first." He kept her on his knee some time, while he and she drank tea. He was now like a *buck* indeed. All the company laughed in great glee, and they were all pleased to see him have so much good humour. To me it was a very high scene. To see the grave philosopher—the Rambler —toying with a little Highland wench! There was a coincidence of opposed ideas. But what could he do? He must have been surly, and weak too, had he not behaved as he did. He would have been laughed at, and not more respected, though less loved.

He read tonight, as he sat in the company, a great deal of this volume of my Journal, and said to me, "The more I read of this, I think the more highly of you." "Are you in earnest?" said I. Said he, "It is true, whether I am in earnest or no." I went to bed at two in the morning, but the rest of the company sat still. They drank on and sung Erse songs till near five. I lay in great uneasiness. I was quite somber in the dark, and could get no rest. I tried to think how long I had been free now, but all the gloomy chances that imagination can figure disturbed me. I had the utmost impatience to get home. I was tormented for some time, till at last those who lay in the same room with me came up. Unluckily Col found a bottle of punch standing; upon which in tumbled all the company, and they drank it, and another which Corrichatachin brought. They made many apologies for disturbing me. I said I once thought of rising and going down to them. Honest Corri said that to have had me do that, he would have given a cow. I thought I suffered so much tonight that the scene would make a figure in my Journal, but it makes but a wretched one.]

Tuesday, 28th September. The weather was worse than yesterday. I felt as if imprisoned. Dr. Johnson said it was irksome to be detained thus; yet he seemed to have less uneasiness, or more patience, than I had. What made our situation worse here was that we had no rooms that we could command, for the good people had no notion that a man could have any occasion but for a mere sleeping place; so, during the day, the bedrooms were common to all the house. Servants eat in Dr. Johnson's, and mine was a kind of general rendezvous for all under the roof, children and dogs not excepted. As the gentlemen occupied the parlor, the ladies had no place to sit in, during the day, but Dr. Johnson's room. I had always some quiet time for writing in it, before he was up; and by degrees I accustomed the ladies to let me sit in it after breakfast at my Journal, without minding me.

Dr. Johnson was this morning for going to see as many islands as we could, not recollecting the uncertainty of the season, which might detain us in one place for many weeks. He said to me, "I have more the spirit of adventure than you."—For my part I was anxious to get to Mull, from whence we might almost any day reach the mainland . . .

Sunday, 3d October. Joseph reported that the wind was still against us. Dr. Johnson said, "A wind or not a wind? that is the question"; for he can amuse himself at times with a little play of words, or rather of sentences. I remember when he turned his cup at Aberbrothock, where we drank tea, he muttered, "*Claudite jam rivos, pueri.*" [11] I must again and again apologize to fastidious readers for recording such minute particulars. They prove the scrupulous fidelity of my Journal. Dr. Johnson said it was a very exact picture of a portion of his life.

While we were chatting in the indolent style of men who were to stay here all this day at least, we were suddenly roused with being told that the wind was fair, that a little fleet of herring-busses was passing by for Mull, and that Mr. Simpson's vessel was about to sail. Hugh Macdonald, the skipper, came to us, and was impatient that we should get ready, which we soon did. Dr. Johnson with composure and solemnity repeated the observation of Epictetus, that, "as man has the voyage of death before him, whatever may be his employment, he should always be ready at the master's call; and an old man should never be far from the shore, lest he should not be able to get himself ready." He rode, and I and the other gentlemen walked about an English mile to the shore, where the vessel lay. Dr. Johnson said he should never forget Sky, and returned thanks for all civilities. We were carried to the vessel in a small boat which she had, and we set sail very briskly about one o'clock. I was much pleased with the motion for many hours. Dr. Johnson grew sick, and retired under cover, as it rained a good deal. I kept above, that I might have fresh air. [I eat bread and

11 "Dam up the ditches, boys; the meadows have drunk enough." Vergil *Eclogues* III. iii.

cheese, and drank whiskey and rum and brandy. The worthy Bailie had sent with us half a sheep and biscuits and apples and beer and brandy. There was a little room or den at the forecastle, with two beds, and a fire in it. Dinner was dressed, and I was persuaded to go down. I eat boiled mutton and boiled salt herring, and drank beer and punch. I exulted in being a stout seaman, while Mr. Johnson was quite in a state of annihilation. But I soon had a change; for after imagining that I could go with ease to America or the East Indies, I turned woefully sick, and was obliged to get aboveboard, though it rained hard.] . . .

Mr. Simpson was sanguine in his hopes for a while, the wind being fair for us. He said he would land us at Icolmkill that night. But when the wind failed, it was resolved we should make for the Sound of Mull, and land in the harbor of Tobermory. We kept near the five herring vessels for some time; but afterwards four of them got before us, and one little wherry fell behind us. When we got in full view of the point of Ardnamurchan, the wind changed, and was directly against our getting into the Sound. We were then obliged to tack, and get forward in that tedious manner. As we advanced, the storm grew greater, and the sea very rough. Col then began to talk of making for Eigg or Canna or his own island. Our skipper said he would get us into the Sound. Having struggled for this a good while in vain, he said he would push forward till we were near the land of Mull, where we might cast anchor and lie till the morning; for although before this there had been a good moon, and I had pretty distinctly seen not only the land of Mull, but up the Sound, and the country of Movern as at one end of it, the night was now grown very dark. Our crew consisted of one Macdonald our skipper, and two sailors, one of whom had but one eye; Mr. Simpson himself, Col, and Hugh Macdonald his servant, all helped. Simpson said he would willingly go for Col if young Col or his servant would undertake to pilot us to a harbor; but as the island is low land, it was dangerous to run upon it in the dark. Col and his servant appeared a little dubious. The scheme of running for Canna seemed then to be embraced; but Canna was ten leagues off, all out of our way; and they were afraid to attempt the harbor of Eigg. All these different plans were successively in agitation. The old skipper still tried to make for the land of Mull; but then it was considered that there was no place there where we could anchor in safety. Much time was lost in striving against the storm. At last it became so rough, and threatened to be so much worse, that Col and his servant took more courage and said they would undertake to hit one of the harbors in Col.—"Then let us run for it, in God's name," said the skipper; and instantly we turned towards it. The little wherry which had fallen behind us had hard work. The master begged that if we made for Col, we should put out a light to him. Accordingly one of the sailors waved a glowing peat for some time. The various difficulties that were started gave me a good deal of apprehension, from which I was relieved when I found we were to run for a harbor before the wind. But my relief was but of short duration; for I soon heard that our sails were very bad, and were in danger of being torn in pieces, in which case we would be driven upon the rocky shore of Col. It was very dark, and there was a heavy and incessant rain. The sparks of the burning peat flew so much about that I dreaded the vessel might take fire. Then, as Col was a sportsman, and had powder on board, I figured that we might be blown up. Simpson and he appeared a little frightened, which made me more so; and the perpetual talking, or rather shouting, which was carried on in Erse, alarmed me still more. A man is always suspicious of what is saying in an unknown tongue; and if fear be his passion at the time, he grows more afraid. Our vessel often lay so much on one side that I trembled lest she should be overset; and indeed they told me afterwards that they had run her sometimes to within an inch of the water, so anxious were they to make what haste they could before the night should be worse. I now saw what I never saw before, a prodigious sea with immense billows coming upon a vessel, so that it seemed hardly possible to escape. There was something grandly horrible in the sight. I am glad I have seen it once. Amidst all these terrifying circumstances, I endeavored to compose my mind. It was not easy to do it; for all the stories that I had heard of the dangerous sailing among the Hebrides, which is proverbial, came full upon my recollection. [It distressed me to think how much my dearest wife would suffer should I now be lost, and in what a destitute, or at least wretchedly dependent, state she would be left. I upbraided myself as not having a sufficient cause for putting myself in such danger. Piety afforded me a good deal of comfort. I prayed fervently to God, but I was confused, for I remember I used a strange expression: that if it should please him to preserve me, *I would be-*

have myself ten times better. Be the expression what it may, I shall never forget—at least I hope so—the good resolutions which I then formed. While I prayed, I was disturbed by the objections against a particular providence and against hoping that the petitions of an individual would have any influence with the Divinity; objections which have been often made, and which Dr. Hawkesworth has lately revived in his preface to the *Voyages to the South Seas;* but Dr. Ogden's excellent doctrine on the efficacy of intercession prevailed. I was really in very great fear this night.]

It was half an hour after eleven before we set ourselves in the course for Col. As I saw them all busy doing something, I asked Col with much earnestness what I could do. He with a happy readiness put into my hand a rope which was fixed to the top of one of the masts, and told me to hold it till he bade me pull. If I had considered the matter, I might have seen that this could not be of the least service; but his object was to keep me out of the way of those who were busy working the vessel; and at the same time to divert my fear by employing me and making me think that I was of use. Thus did I stand firm to my post while the wind and rain beat upon me, always expecting a call to pull my rope.

The man with one eye steered; old Macdonald and Col and his servant lay upon the forecastle looking sharp out for the harbor. It was necessary to carry much *cloth,* as they termed it, that is to say, much sail, in order to keep the vessel off the shore of Col. This made violent plunging in a rough sea. At last they spied the harbor of Lochiern, and Col cried, "Thank God, we are safe!" We ran up till we were opposite to it, and soon afterwards we got into it and cast anchor.

Dr. Johnson had all this time been quiet and unconcerned. He had lain down on one of the beds, and having got free from sickness, was satisfied. The truth is, he knew nothing of the danger we were in; but fearless and unconcerned, might have said in the words which he has chosen for the motto to his Rambler *Quo me cunque rapit tempestas, deferor hospes.*[12] Once during the doubtful consultations he asked whither we were going; and upon being told that it was not certain whether to Mull or Col, he cried, "Col for my money!"—I now went down, with Col and Mr. Simpson, to visit him. He was lying in philosophic tranquillity, with a greyhound of Col's at his back, keeping him warm . . .

12 "For as the tempest drives, I shape my way." [Francis]

Sunday, 17th October. . . . [It was the 19th Sunday after Trinity. I shall ever remember it. Mr. Johnson said it was the most agreeable Sunday evening that he had ever passed in his life. We were all in a good frame. I was truly pious.

I walked out in the dark to the cross, knelt before it, and holding it with both my hands, I prayed with strong devotion, while I had before me the image of that on which my Saviour died for the sins of the world. The sanctity of venerable Columbus [13] filled my imagination. I considered that to ask the intercession of a departed saint was at least innocent, and might be of service. I indulged my inclination to what is called superstitious prayer. I said, "*Sancte Columbe, ora pro me.* O Columbus, thou venerable Saint, as we have all the reason that can be to believe that thou art in heaven, I beseech thee to pray God that I may attain to everlasting felicity." I cannot be sure of the exact words (I am now writing at Glasgow, October 28). But what I said was to the above purpose. I felt a kind of pleasing awful confusion. I was for going into the chapel; but a tremor seized me for ghosts, and I hastened back to the house. It was exceedingly dark, and in my timorous hurry I stepped suddenly into a hollow place, and strained a sinew on my right foot. It was painful a while; but rubbing it with rum and vinegar cured it by next day at breakfast.] . . .

Tuesday, 19th October. . . . [We went ashore [14] upon a little rising ground, which is an island at high water. We sat down upon a seat of rock, and took a repast of cold mutton, bread and cheese and apples, and punch. Lauchlan Dow in the mean time ran to Lauchlan Maclean's house. When he returned with Lauchlan Maclean, we had the disappointment of finding that no spirits of any kind were to be found. A burial some days before had exhausted them. Mr. Campbell of ——, a tacksman of the Duke of Argyll's, lived not far off. Sir Allan sent the two Lauchlans thither, begging the loan of two bottles of rum. We got them, with a message that Mr. Campbell had expected us to dinner, having heard that we were to pass; that he was sorry he had not then seen us, and hoped we would be with him next day. We refreshed our crew. The weather grew coldish. I proposed an expedient to keep our feet warm, which was to strew the boat plentifully with heath, the chief production of the island where we dined. Accordingly I fell to work and pulled, as did some of our men, and Mr. Johnson

13 St. Columba. They are at Inchkenneth.   14 Mull.

pulled very assiduously. Sir Allen,[15] who had been used to command men, and had no doubt superintended soldiers making roads or throwing up ramparts or doing some other kind of work, never stopped, but stood by *grieving* us (the Scottish expressive term for overseeing as a taskmaster, an overseer being called a *grieve;* as my lord Loudoun tells, a countryman said to him, Mr. Dun our minister was *grieving* my father, who was busy gathering stones to mend a road). We made ourselves very comfortable with the heath. The wind was now against us, but we had very little of it.

We coasted along Mull, which was on our left. On our right was the Atlantic, with Staffa and other islands in it for some part of the way. Then we came to a large black rock in the sea; then to Nun's Island, which it is said belonged to the nuns of Icolmkill, and that from it the stone for the buildings of Icolmkill was taken; as the rocks still there are of the same kind of stone, and there is none such in Icolmkill. It became very dusky, or rather dark, about seven; for our voyage, by going along the turnings of the coast, would be, Sir Allan said, forty miles from Inchkenneth to Iona; so that we were benighted. Mr. Johnson said, as we were going up the narrow sound between Mull and Nun's Island, with solemn-like rocks on each side of us, and the waves rising and falling, and our boat proceeding with a dancing motion, "This is roving among the Hebrides, or nothing is." A man has a pleasure in applying things to words, and comparing the reality with the picture of fancy. We had long talked of "roving among the Hebrides." It was curious to repeat the words previously used, and which had impressed our imaginations by frequent use; and then to feel how the immediate impression from actually roving differed from the one in fancy, or agreed with it. It will be curious too, to perceive how the impression made by reading this my Journal some years after our roving will affect the mind, when compared with the recollection of what was felt at the time. Mr. Johnson said I should read my Journal about every three years. Joseph made a very good observation. "Your journey," said he, "will always be more agreeable to you."

I often do not observe chronology, for fear of losing a thing by waiting till I can put it in its exact place. Joseph said this one night as I was going to bed, and was resuming to him with much complacency some of our past scenes on this expedition. He meant

15 Sir Allan Maclean.

what I have often experienced: that scenes through which a man has gone improve by lying in the memory. They grow mellow. It is said, "*Acti labores sunt jucundi.*" [16] This may be owing to comparing them with present ease. But I also think that even harsh scenes acquire a softness by length of time; and many scenes are like very loud sounds, which do not please till you are at a distance from them, or at least do not please so much; or like strong coarse pictures, which must be viewed at a distance. And I don't know how it is, but even pleasing scenes improve by time, and seem more exquisite in recollection than when they were present, if they have not faded to dimness in the memory. Perhaps there is so much evil in every human enjoyment when present, so much dross mixed with it, that it requires to be refined by time; and yet I do not see why time should not melt away the good and the evil in equal proportions, why the shade should decay and the light remain in preservation. I must hear Mr. Johnson upon this subject.

The boat had so much motion tonight that I had a renewal of the uneasiness of fear at sea; and I wondered how I could so soon totally forget what I had endured when driven to Col. People accustomed to sail give every little direction with so loud a tone that a fresh-water man is alarmed. Sir William Temple's observation on the boisterous manners of seamen from their being used to contend with a boisterous element, will apply in some degree to all "who go down into the sea"—at least while they are upon it. Col talks loud at sea, and Sir Allan talks loud at sea. I asked if we should not be quieter when we were in the Sound between Mull and Icolmkill. Sir Allan said no. We should have a rougher sea, as we should then have a stronger current against us, and have the Atlantic quite open from each end of the Sound. I yielded so much to fear as to ask if it would not be better that we should go ashore for that night on Mull, and cross the Sound in the morning with daylight. Sir Allan was for going on. Mr. Johnson said, "I suppose Sir Allan, who knows, thinks there is no danger." "No, sir," said Sir Allan. Mr. Johnson was satisfied. I therefore had nothing to say, but kept myself calm. I am so much a disciple of Dr. Ogden's [17] that I venture to pray even upon small occasions if I feel myself much concerned. Perhaps when a man is much concerned, the occasions ought not to be called small. I put up a petition to God

[16] "Past labors are sweet." [Cicero's *De Finibus*]

[17] Samuel Ogden, author of *Sermons on Prayer*.

to make the waves more still. I know not if I ought to draw a conclusion from what happened; but so it was, that after we had turned the point of Nun's Island and got into the Sound of Icolmkill, the tide was for us, and we went along with perfect smoothness, which made me feel a most pleasing tranquillity.] . . .

Saturday, 23d October. . . . It rained very hard as we journeyed on after dinner. The roar of torrents from the mountains, as we passed along in the dusk, and the other circumstances attending our ride this evening have been mentioned with so much animation by Dr. Johnson that I shall not attempt to say anything on the subject.

We got at night to Inveraray, where we found an excellent inn. Even here Dr. Johnson would not change his wet clothes.

The prospect of good accommodation cheered us much. We supped well; and after supper, Dr. Johnson, whom I had not seen taste any fermented liquor during all our travels, called for a gill of whisky. "Come," said he, "let me know what it is that makes a Scotchman happy!" He drank it all but a drop, which I begged leave to pour into my glass, that I might say we had drunk whisky together. I proposed Mrs. Thrale should be our toast. He would not have *her* drunk in whisky, but rather some insular lady; so we drank one of the ladies whom we had lately left.—He owned tonight that he got as good a room and bed as at an English inn.

[I had here the comfort of a letter from my dear wife, of whom I had not heard for many weeks; and I had the regale of a letter from Mr. Garrick, in answer to mine to him from Inverness. My feelings this night were as agreeable as can be imagined.] . . .

Tuesday, 2d November. We were now in a country not only "of saddles and bridles," but of post-chaises; and having ordered one from Kilmarnock, we got to Auchinleck before dinner.

My father was not quite a year and a half older than Dr. Johnson, but his conscientious discharge of his laborious duty as a judge in Scotland (where the law proceedings are almost all in writing), a severe complaint which ended in his death, and the loss of my mother, a woman of almost unexampled piety and goodness, had before this time in some degree affected his spirits, and rendered him less disposed to exert his faculties; for he had originally a very strong mind and cheerful temper. He assured me he never had felt one moment of what is called low spirits, or uneasiness without a real cause. He had a great many good stories, which he told uncommonly well, and he was remarkable for "humor, *incolumni gravitate*," as Lord Monboddo used to characterize it. His age, his office, and his character had long given him an acknowledged claim to great attention, in whatever company he was; and he could ill brook any diminution of it. He was as sanguine a Whig and Presbyterian as Dr. Johnson was a Tory and Church of England man; and as he had not much leisure to be informed of Dr. Johnson's great merits by reading his works, he had a partial and unfavorable notion of him, founded on his supposed political tenets, which were so discordant to his own that, instead of speaking of him with that respect to which he was entitled, he used to call him "a *Jacobite fellow*." Knowing all this, I should not have ventured to bring them together, had not my father, out of kindness to me, desired me to invite Dr. Johnson to his house.

I was very anxious that all should be well, and begged of my friend to avoid three topics, as to which they differed very widely: Whiggism, Presbyterianism, and—Sir John Pringle.[18] He said courteously, "I shall certainly not talk on subjects which I am told are disagreeable to a gentleman under whose roof I am; especially, I shall not do so to *your father*."

Our first day went off very smoothly. It rained, and we could not get out; but my father showed Dr. Johnson his library, which, in curious editions of the Greek and Roman classics, is, I suppose, not excelled by any private collection in Great Britain. My father had studied at Leyden and been very intimate with the Gronovii and other learned men there. He was a sound scholar, and, in particular, had collated manuscripts and different editions of Anacreon, and others of the Greek lyric poets, with great care; so that my friend and he had much matter for conversation, without touching on the fatal topics of difference . . .

Saturday, 6th November. I cannot be certain whether it was on this day or a former that Dr. Johnson and my father came in collision. If I recollect right, the contest began while my father was showing him his collection of medals; and Oliver Cromwell's coin unfortunately introduced Charles the First, and Toryism. They became exceedingly warm and violent, and I was very much distressed by being present at such an altercation between two men, both of whom I reverenced; yet I durst not interfere. It would certainly be very unbecoming in me to exhibit my honored father

18 Of liberal religious views; friend of Benjamin Franklin.

and my respected friend as intellectual gladiators, for the entertainment of the public; and therefore I suppress what would, I dare say, make an interesting scene in this dramatic sketch—this account of the transit of Johnson over the Caledonian Hemisphere.

Yet I think I may, without impropriety, mention one circumstance, as an instance of my father's address. Dr. Johnson challenged him, as he did us all at Talisker, to point out any theological works of merit written by Presbyterian ministers in Scotland. My father, whose studies did not lie much in that way, owned to me afterwards that he was somewhat at a loss how to answer, but that luckily he recollected having read in catalogues the title of *Durham on the Galatians;* upon which he boldly said, "Pray, sir, have you read Mr. Durham's excellent commentary on the Galatians?" "No, sir," said Dr. Johnson. By this lucky thought my father kept him at bay, and for some time enjoyed his triumph; but his antagonist soon made a retort, which I forbear to mention.

In the course of their altercation, Whiggism and Presbyterianism, Toryism and Episcopacy, were terribly buffeted. My worthy hereditary friend Sir John Pringle, never having been mentioned, happily escaped without a bruise.

My father's opinion of Dr. Johnson may be conjectured from the name he afterwards gave him, which was "Ursa Major."

THE LIFE OF SAMUEL JOHNSON, LL.D.

1791

To write the Life of him who excelled all mankind in writing the lives of others, and who, whether we consider his extraordinary endowments, or his various works, has been equaled by few in any age, is an arduous, and may be reckoned in me a presumptuous, task.

Had Dr. Johnson written his own Life, in conformity with the opinion which he has given,[1] that every man's life may be best written by himself; had he employed in the preservation of his own history, that clearness of narration and elegance of language in which he has embalmed so many eminent persons, the world would probably have had the most perfect example of biography that

1 *Idler,* No. 84.

was ever exhibited. But although he at different times, in a desultory manner, committed to writing many particulars of the progress of his mind and fortunes, he never had persevering diligence enough to form them into a regular composition. Of these memorials a few have been preserved; but the greater part was consigned by him to the flames, a few days before his death.

As I had the honor and happiness of enjoying his friendship for upwards of twenty years; as I had the scheme of writing his life constantly in view; as he was well apprised of this circumstance, and from time to time obligingly satisfied my enquiries, by communicating to me the incidents of his early years; as I acquired a facility in recollecting, and was very assiduous in recording, his conversation, of which the extraordinary vigor and vivacity constituted one of the first features of his character; and as I have spared no pains in obtaining materials concerning him, from every quarter where I could discover that they were to be found, and have been favored with the most liberal communications by his friends; I flatter myself that few biographers have entered upon such a work as this, with more advantages; independent of literary abilities, in which I am not vain enough to compare myself with some great names who have gone before me in this kind of writing.

Since my work was announced, several Lives and Memoirs of Dr. Johnson have been published, the most voluminous of which is one compiled for the booksellers of London, by Sir John Hawkins, Knight, a man, whom, during my long intimacy with Dr. Johnson, I never saw in his company, I think, but once, and I am sure not above twice. Johnson might have esteemed him for his decent, religious demeanor, and his knowledge of books and literary history; but from the rigid formality of his manners, it is evident that they never could have lived together with companionable ease and familiarity; nor had Sir John Hawkins that nice perception which was necessary to mark the finer and less obvious parts of Johnson's character. His being appointed one of his executors, gave him an opportunity of taking possession of such fragments of a diary and other papers as were left; of which, before delivering them up to the residuary legatee, whose property they were, he endeavored to extract the substance. In this he has not been very successful, as I have found upon a perusal of those papers, which have been since transferred to me. Sir John Hawkins's ponderous labors, I must acknowledge, exhibit a *farrago*, of

[handwritten margin note: Hawkins slighted Boswell]

[handwritten note at bottom: class dec 13]

which a considerable portion is not devoid of entertainment to the lovers of literary gossiping; but besides its being swelled out with long unnecessary extracts from various works, (even one of several leaves from Osborne's Harleian Catalogue, and those not compiled by Johnson, but by Oldys) a very small part of it relates to the person who is the subject of the book; and, in that, there is such an inaccuracy in the statement of facts, as in so solemn an author is hardly excusable, and certainly makes his narrative very unsatisfactory. But what is still worse, there is throughout the whole of it a dark uncharitable cast, by which the most unfavorable construction is put upon almost every circumstance in the character and conduct of my illustrious friend; who, I trust, will, by a true and fair delineation, be vindicated both from the injurious misrepresentations of this author, and from the slighter aspersions of a lady who once lived in great intimacy with him. . . .

Instead of melting down my materials into one mass, and constantly speaking in my own person, by which I might have appeared to have more merit in the execution of the work, I have resolved to adopt and enlarge upon the excellent plan of Mr. Mason, in his Memoirs of Gray. Wherever narrative is necessary to explain, connect, and supply, I furnish it to the best of my abilities; but in the chronological series of Johnson's life, which I trace as distinctly as I can, year by year, I produce, wherever it is in my power, his own minutes, letters, or conversation, being convinced that this mode is more lively, and will make my readers better acquainted with him, than even most of those were who actually knew him, but could know him only partially; whereas there is here an accumulation of intelligence from various points, by which his character is more fully understood and illustrated.

Indeed I cannot conceive a more perfect mode of writing any man's life, than not only relating all the most important events of it in their order, but interweaving what he privately wrote, and said, and thought; by which mankind are enabled as it were to see him live, and to "live o'er each scene" with him, as he actually advanced through the several stages of his life. Had his other friends been as diligent and ardent as I was, he might have been almost entirely preserved. As it is, I will venture to say that he will be seen in this work more completely than any man who has ever yet lived.

And he will be seen as he really was; for I profess to write, not his panegyric, which must be all praise, but his life; which, great and good as he was, must not be supposed to be entirely perfect. To be as he was, is indeed subject of panegyric enough to any man in this state of being; but in every picture there should be shade as well as light, and when I delineate him without reserve, I do what he himself recommended, both by his precept and his example.

"If the biographer writes from personal knowledge, and makes haste to gratify the public curiosity, there is danger lest his interest, his fear, his gratitude, or his tenderness, overpower his fidelity, and tempt him to conceal, if not to invent. There are many who think it an act of piety to hide the faults or failings of their friends, even when they can no longer suffer by their detection; we therefore see whole ranks of characters adorned with uniform panegyric, and not to be known from one another but by extrinsic and casual circumstances. 'Let me remember (says Hale) when I find myself inclined to pity a criminal, that there is likewise a pity due to the country.' If we owe regard to the memory of the dead, there is yet more respect to be paid to knowledge, to virtue, and to truth." [2]

What I consider as the peculiar value of the following work, is the quantity it contains of Johnson's conversation; which is universally acknowledged to have been eminently instructive and entertaining; and of which the specimens that I have given upon a former occasion, have been received with so much approbation, that I have good grounds for supposing that the world will not be indifferent to more ample communications of a similar nature.

That the conversation of a celebrated man, if his talents have been exerted in conversation, will best display his character, is, I trust, too well established in the judgment of mankind, to be at all shaken by a sneering observation of Mr. Mason, in his Memoirs of Mr. William Whitehead, in which there is literally no *Life*, but a mere dry narrative of facts. I do not think it was quite necessary to attempt a depreciation of what is universally esteemed, because it was not to be found in the immediate object of the ingenious writer's pen; for in truth, from a man so still and so tame, as to be contented to pass many years as the domestic companion of a superannuated lord and lady, conversation could no more be expected, than from a Chinese mandarin on a chimney-piece, or the fantastic figures on a gilt leather screen.

2 *Rambler*, No. 60.

If authority be required let us appeal to Plutarch, the prince of
ancient biographers. "Nor is it always in the most distinguished
achievements that men's virtues or vices may be best discerned; but
very often an action of small note, a short saying, or a jest, shall
distinguish a person's real character more than the greatest sieges,
or the most important battles." [3]

To this may be added the sentiments of the very man whose
life I am about to exhibit. "The business of the biographer is often
to pass slightly over those performances and incidents which produce vulgar greatness, to lead the thoughts into domestic privacies,
and display the minute details of daily life, whose exterior append-
ages are cast aside, and men excel each other only by prudence
and by virtue. The account of Thuanus is with great propriety
said by its author to have been written, that it might lay open to
posterity the private and familiar character of that man, *cujus ingenium et candorem ex ipsius scriptis sunt olim semper miraturi,*
whose candor and genius will to the end of time be by his writings
preserved in admiration.

"There are many invisible circumstances, which whether we
read as enquirers after natural or moral knowledge, whether we
intend to inlarge our science or increase our virtue, are more important than public occurrences. Thus Sallust, the great master of
nature, has not forgot in his account of Catiline to remark that his
walk was now quick, and again slow, as an indication of a mind
revolving with violent commotion. Thus the story of Melanchthon
affords a striking lecture on the value of time, by informing us
that when he had made an appointment, he expected not only the
hour but the minute to be fixed, that the day might not run out
in the idleness of suspense; and all the plans and enterprises of
De Witt are now of less importance to the world than that part
of his personal character, which represents him as careful of his
health, and negligent of his life.

"But biography has often been allotted to writers, who seem
very little acquainted with the nature of their task, or very negligent about the performance. They rarely afford any other account than might be collected from public papers, but imagine
themselves writing a life, when they exhibit a chronological series
of actions or preferments; and have so little regard to the manners
or behavior of their heroes, that more knowledge may be gained

---

[3] Plutarch's Life of Alexander.—Langhorne's Translation.

of a man's real character, by a short conversation with one of his
servants, than from a formal and studied narrative, begun with his
pedigree, and ended with his funeral.

"There are indeed, some natural reasons why these narratives
are often written by such as were not likely to give much instruction or delight, and why most accounts of particular persons are
barren and useless. If a life be delayed till interest and envy are at
an end, we may hope for impartiality, but must expect little intelligence; for the incidents which give excellence to biography are
of a volatile and evanescent kind, such as soon escape the memory,
and are rarely transmitted by tradition. We know how few can
portray a living acquaintance, except by his most prominent and
observable particularities, and the grosser features of his mind;
and it may be easily imagined how much of this little knowledge
may be lost in imparting it, and how soon a succession of copies
will lose all resemblance of the original." [4]

I am fully aware of the objections which may be made to the
minuteness on some occasions of my detail of Johnson's conversation, and how happily it is adapted for the petty exercise of ridicule, by men of superficial understanding, and ludicrous fancy; but
I remain firm and confident in my opinion that minute particulars
are frequently characteristic, and always amusing, when they relate to a distinguished man. I am therefore exceedingly unwilling
that anything, however slight, which my illustrious friend thought
it worth his while to express, with any degree of point, should
perish. For this almost superstitious reverence, I have found very
old and venerable authority, quoted by our great modern prelate,
Secker, in whose tenth sermon there is the following passage:

"*Rabbi David Kimchi*, a noted Jewish commentator, who lived
about five hundred years ago, explains that passage in the first
Psalm, *His leaf also shall not wither*, from Rabbins yet older than
himself, thus: That *even the idle talk*, so he expresses it, *of a good
man ought to be regarded*; the most superfluous things he saith are
always of some value. And other ancient authors have the same
phrase, nearly in the same sense."

Of one thing I am certain, that considering how highly the
small portion which we have of the table-talk and other anecdotes
of our celebrated writers is valued, and how earnestly it is regretted
that we have not more, I am justified in preserving rather too many

4 *Rambler*, No. 60.

of Johnson's sayings, than too few; especially as from the diversity of dispositions it cannot be known with certainty beforehand, whether what may seem trifling to some, and perhaps to the collector himself, may not be most agreeable to many; and the greater number that an author can please in any degree, the more pleasure does there arise to a benevolent mind.

To those who are weak enough to think this a degrading task, and the time and labor which have been devoted to it misemployed, I shall content myself with opposing the authority of the greatest man of any age, JULIUS CÆSAR, of whom Bacon observes, that "in his book of Apothegms which he collected, we see that he esteemed it more honor to make himself but a pair of tables, to take the wise and pithy words of others, than to have every word of his own to be made an apothegm or an oracle." [5]

Having said thus much by way of introduction, I commit the following pages to the candor of the public.

Samuel Johnson was born in Lichfield, in Staffordshire, on the 18th of September, N.S. 1709; and his initiation into the Christian church was not delayed; for his baptism is recorded in the register of St. Mary's parish in that city, to have been performed on the day of his birth: His father is there styled *Gentleman*, a circumstance of which an ignorant panegyrist has praised him for not being proud; when the truth is that the appellation of Gentleman, though now lost in the indiscriminate assumption of *Esquire*, was commonly taken by those who could not boast of gentility. His father was Michael Johnson, a native of Derbyshire, of obscure extraction, who settled in Lichfield as a bookseller and stationer. His mother was Sarah Ford, descended of an ancient race of substantial yeomanry in Warwickshire. They were well advanced in years when they married, and never had more than two children, both sons, Samuel, their first-born, who lived to be the illustrious character whose various excellence I am to endeavor to record, and Nathanael, who died in his twenty-fifth year.

Mr. Michael Johnson was a man of a large and robust body, and of a strong and active mind; yet, as in the most solid rocks, veins of unsound substance are often discovered, there was in him a mixture of that disease, the nature of which eludes the most minute

5 Bacon's *Advancement of Learning*, Book I.

enquiry, though the effects are well known to be a weariness of life, an unconcern about those things which agitate the greater part of mankind, and a general sensation of gloomy wretchedness. From him then his son inherited, with some other qualities, "a vile melancholy," which in his too strong expression of any disturbance of mind, "made him mad all his life, at least not sober." Michael was, however, forced by the narrowness of his circumstances to be very diligent in business, not only in his shop, but by occasionally resorting to several towns in the neighborhood, some of which were at a considerable distance from Lichfield. At that time booksellers' shops in the provincial towns of England were very rare, so that there was not one even in Birmingham, in which town old Mr. Johnson used to open a shop every market-day. He was a pretty good Latin scholar, and a citizen so creditable as to be made one of the magistrates of Lichfield; and, being a man of good sense, and skill in his trade, he acquired a reasonable share of wealth, of which however he afterwards lost the greatest part by engaging unsuccessfully in a manufacture of parchment. He was a zealous high-church man and royalist, and retained his attachment to the unfortunate house of Stuart, though he reconciled himself, by casuistical arguments of expediency and necessity, to take the oaths imposed by the prevailing power.

There is a circumstance in his life somewhat romantic, but so well authenticated, that I shall not omit it. A young woman of Leek, in Staffordshire, while he served his apprenticeship there, conceived a violent passion for him; and though it met with no favorable return, followed him to Lichfield, where she took lodgings opposite to the house in which he lived, and indulged her hopeless flame. When he was informed that it so preyed upon her mind that her life was in danger, he with a generous humanity went to her and offered to marry her, but it was then too late: Her vital power was exhausted; and she actually exhibited one of the very rare instances of dying for love. She was buried in the cathedral of Lichfield; and he, with a tender regard, placed a stone over her grave with this inscription:

Here lies the body of
MRS. ELIZABETH BLANEY, a stranger:
She departed this life
20 of September, 1694.

Johnson's mother was a woman of distinguished understanding. I asked his old school-fellow, Mr. Hector, surgeon, of Birmingham, if she was not vain of her son. He said, "she had too much good sense to be vain, but she knew her son's value." Her piety was not inferior to her understanding; and to her must be ascribed those early impressions of religion upon the mind of her son, from which the world afterwards derived so much benefit. He told me, that he remembered distinctly having had the first notice of Heaven, "a place to which good people went," and hell, "a place to which bad people went," communicated to him by her, when a little child in bed with her; and that it might be the better fixed in his memory, she sent him to repeat it to Thomas Jackson, their man-servant; he not being in the way, this was not done; but there was no occasion for any artificial aid for its preservation. . . .

Young Johnson had the misfortune to be much afflicted with the scrophula, or king's-evil, which disfigured a countenance naturally well formed, and hurt his visual nerves so much, that he did not see at all with one of his eyes, though its appearance was little different from that of the other. There is amongst his prayers, one inscribed *"When my* EYE *was restored to its use,"* which ascertains a defect that many of his friends knew he had, though I never perceived it. I supposed him to be only near-sighted; and indeed I must observe that in no other respect could I discern any defect in his vision; on the contrary, the force of his attention and perceptive quickness made him see and distinguish all manner of objects, whether of nature or of art, with a nicety that is rarely to be found. When he and I were traveling in the Highlands of Scotland, and I pointed out to him a mountain which I observed resembled a cone, he corrected my inaccuracy, by showing me, that it was indeed pointed at the top, but that one side of it was larger than the other. And the ladies with whom he was acquainted agree that no man was more nicely and minutely critical in the elegance of female dress. When I found that he saw the romantic beauties of Islam, in Derbyshire, much better than I did, I told him that he resembled an able performer upon a bad instrument. How false and contemptible then are all the remarks which have been made to the prejudice either of his candor or of his philosophy, founded upon a supposition that he was almost blind. It has been said that he contracted this grievous malady from his nurse. His mother, yielding to the superstitious notion, which, it is wonderful to think, prevailed so long in this country, as to the virtue of the regal touch—a notion, which our kings encouraged, and to which a man of such enquiry and such judgment as Carte could give credit—carried him to London, where he was actually touched by Queen Anne. Mrs. Johnson indeed, as Mr. Hector informed me, acted by the advice of the celebrated Sir John Floyer, then a physician in Lichfield. Johnson used to talk of this very frankly; and Mrs. Piozzi has preserved his very picturesque description of the scene, as it remained upon his fancy. Being asked if he could remember Queen Anne,— "He had (he said) a confused, but somehow a sort of solemn recollection of a lady in diamonds, and a long black hood." This touch, however, was without any effect. I ventured to say to him, in allusion to the political principles in which he was educated, and of which he ever retained some odor, that "his mother had not carried him far enough; she should have taken him to ROME." . . .

1729: Aetat. 20

The "morbid melancholy," which was lurking in his constitution, and to which we may ascribe those particularities, and that aversion to regular life, which, at a very early period, marked his character, gathered such strength in his twentieth year, as to afflict him in a dreadful manner. While he was at Lichfield, in the college vacation of the year 1729, he felt himself overwhelmed with an horrible hypochondria, with perpetual irritation, fretfulness, and impatience; and with a dejection, gloom, and despair, which made existence misery. From this dismal malady he never afterwards was perfectly relieved; and all his labors, and all his enjoyments, were but temporary interruptions of its baleful influence. How wonderful, how unsearchable are the ways of God! Johnson, who was blest with all the powers of genius and understanding in a degree far above the ordinary state of human nature, was at the same time visited with a disorder so afflictive, that they who know it by dire experience, will not envy his exalted endowments. That it was, in some degree, occasioned by a defect in his nervous system, that inexplicable part of our frame, appears highly probable. He told Mr. Paradise that he was sometimes so languid and inefficient that he could not distinguish the hour upon the town-clock.

Johnson, upon the first violent attack of this disorder, strove to overcome it by forcible exertions. He frequently walked to Birmingham and back again, and tried many other expedients, but all in vain. His expression concerning it to me was "I did not then know how to manage it." His distress became so intolerable, that he applied to Dr. Swinfen, physician in Lichfield, his god-father, and put into his hands a state of his case, written in Latin. Dr. Swinfen was so much struck with the extraordinary acuteness, research, and eloquence of this paper, that in his zeal for his god-son he showed it to several people. His daughter, Mrs. Desmoulins, who was many years humanely supported in Dr. Johnson's house in London, told me that upon his discovering that Dr. Swinfen had communicated his case, he was so much offended that he was never afterwards fully reconciled to him. He indeed had good reason to be offended; for though Dr. Swinfen's motive was good, he in-considerately betrayed a matter deeply interesting and of great delicacy, which had been entrusted to him in confidence: and ex-posed a complaint of his young friend and patient, which, in the superficial opinion of the generality of mankind, is attended with contempt and disgrace.

But let not little men triumph upon knowing that Johnson was an HYPOCHONDRIAC, was subject to what the learned, philosophical, and pious Dr. Cheyne has so well treated under the title of "The English Malady." Though he suffered severely from it, he was not therefore degraded. The powers of his great mind might be troubled, and their full exercise suspended at times; but the mind itself was ever entire. As a proof of this, it is only necessary to consider, that, when he was at the very worst, he composed that state of his own case, which showed an uncommon vigor, not only of fancy and taste, but of judgment. I am aware that he himself was too ready to call such a complaint by the name of *madness;* in conformity with which notion, he has traced its gradations, with exquisite nicety, in one of the chapters of his RASSELAS. But there is surely a clear distinction between a disorder which affects only the imagination and spirits, while the judgment is sound, and a disorder by which the judgment itself is impaired. The distinction was made to me by the late Professor Gaubius of Leyden, physi-cian to the Prince of Orange, in a conversation which I had with him several years ago, and he explained it thus: "If (said he) a man tells me that he is grievously disturbed, for that he *imagines* he sees a ruffian coming against him with a drawn sword, though at the same time he is *conscious* it is a delusion, I pronounce him to have a disordered imagination; but if a man tells me that he *sees* this, and in consternation calls to me to look at it, I pronounce him to be *mad*."

It is a common effect of low spirits or melancholy, to make those who are afflicted with it imagine that they are actually suffering those evils which happen to be most strongly presented to their minds. Some have fancied themselves to be deprived of the use of their limbs, some to labor under acute diseases, others to be in extreme poverty; when, in truth, there was not the least reality in any of the suppositions; so that when the vapors were dispelled, they were convinced of the delusion. To Johnson, whose supreme enjoyment was the exercise of his reason, the disturbance or obscuration of that faculty was the evil most to be dreaded. Insanity, therefore, was the object of his most dismal apprehension; and he fancied himself seized by it, or approaching to it, at the very time when he was giving proofs of a more than ordinary soundness and vigor of judgment. That his own diseased imagination should have so far deceived him, is strange; but it is stranger still that some of his friends should have given credit to his groundless opinion, when they had such undoubted proofs that it was totally fallacious; though it is by no means surprising that those who wish to depreciate him, should, since his death, have laid hold of this circumstance, and insisted upon it with very unfair aggravation.

Amidst the oppression and distraction of a disease which very few have felt in its full extent, but many have experienced in a slighter degree, Johnson, in his writings, and in his conversation, never failed to display all the varieties of intellectual excellence. In his march through this world to a better, his mind still appeared grand and brilliant, and impressed all around him with the truth of Virgil's noble sentiment—

"Igneus est ollis vigor et cœlestis origo." [6]

The history of his mind as to religion is an important article. I have mentioned the early impressions made upon his tender imagination by his mother, who continued her pious cares with assiduity, but, in his opinion, not with judgment. "Sunday (said he) was a heavy day to me when I was a boy. My mother confined me on that day, and made me read 'The Whole Duty of Man,' from a great part of which I could derive no instruction. When, for instance, I had read the chapter on theft, which from my infancy

6 "Theirs is a fiery energy and heavenly origin."

I had been taught was wrong, I was no more convinced that theft was wrong than before; so there was no accession of knowledge. A boy should be introduced to such books by having his attention directed to the arrangement, to the style, and other excellencies of composition; that the mind being thus engaged by an amusing variety of objects may not grow weary."

He communicated to me the following particulars upon the subject of his religious progress. "I fell into an inattention to religion, or an indifference about it, in my ninth year. The church at Lichfield, in which we had a seat, wanted reparation, so I was to go and find a seat in other churches; and having bad eyes, and being awkward about this, I used to go and read in the fields on Sunday. This habit continued till my fourteenth year; and still I find a great reluctance to go to church. I then became a sort of lax *talker* against religion, for I did not much *think* against it; and this lasted till I went to Oxford, where it would not be *suffered*. When at Oxford I took up Law's 'Serious Call to a Holy Life,' expecting to find it a dull book, (as such books generally are) and perhaps to laugh at it. But I found Law quite an overmatch for me; and this was the first occasion of my thinking in earnest of religion, after I became capable of rational enquiry." From this time forward religion was the predominant object of his thoughts; though, with the just sentiments of a conscientious Christian, he lamented that his practice of its duties fell far short of what it ought to be.

This instance of a mind such as that of Johnson being first disposed, by an unexpected incident, to think with anxiety of the momentous concerns of eternity, and of "what he should do to be saved," may for ever be produced in opposition to the superficial and sometimes profane contempt that has been thrown upon those occasional impressions which it is certain many Christians have experienced; though it must be acknowledged that weak minds, from an erroneous supposition that no man is in a state of grace who has not felt a particular conversion, have, in some cases, brought a degree of ridicule upon them; a ridicule, of which it is inconsiderate or unfair to make a general application.

How seriously Johnson was impressed with a sense of religion, even in the vigor of his youth, appears from the following passage in his minutes kept by way of diary: Sept. 7, 1736. I have this day entered upon my 28th year. "Mayest thou, O God, enable me, for

Jesus Christ's sake, to spend this in such a manner, that I may receive comfort from it at the hour of death, and in the day of judgment! Amen."

The particular course of his reading while at Oxford, and during the time of vacation which he passed at home, cannot be traced. Enough has been said of his irregular mode of study. He told me, that from his earliest years he loved to read poetry, but hardly ever read any poem to an end; that he read Shakspeare at a period so early that the speech of the Ghost in Hamlet terrified him when he was alone; that Horace's Odes were the compositions in which he took most delight, and it was long before he liked his Epistles and Satires. He told me what he read *solidly* at Oxford was Greek; not the Grecian historians, but Homer and Euripides, and now and then a little epigram; that the study of which he was the most fond was metaphysics, but he had not read much, even in that way. I always thought that he did himself injustice in his account of what he had read, and that he must have been speaking with reference to the vast portion of study which is possible, and to which a few scholars in the whole history of literature have attained; for when I once asked him whether a person whose name I have now forgotten, studied hard, he answered "No, Sir. I do not believe he studied hard. I never knew a man who studied hard. I conclude, indeed, from the effects, that some men have studied hard, as Bentley and Clarke." Trying him by that criterion upon which he formed his judgment of others, we may be absolutely certain, both from his writings and his conversation, that his reading was very extensive. Dr. Adam Smith, than whom few were better judges on this subject, once observed to me, that "Johnson knew more books than any man alive." He had a peculiar facility in seizing at once what was valuable in any book, without submitting to the labor of perusing it from beginning to end. He had, from the irritability of his constitution, at all times, an impatience and hurry when he either read or wrote. A certain apprehension arising from novelty, made him write his first exercise at College twice over; but he never took that trouble with any other composition: and we shall see that his most excellent works were struck off at a heat, with rapid exertion.

Yet he appears, from his early notes or memorandums in my possession, to have at various times attempted, or at least planned, a methodical course of study, according to computation, of which he was all his life fond, as it fixed his attention steadily upon something without, and prevented his mind from preying upon itself. Thus I find in his handwriting the number of lines in each of two of Euripides's tragedies, of the Georgics of Virgil, of the first six books of the Æneid, of Horace's Art of Poetry, of three of the books of Ovid's Metamorphoses, of some parts of Theocritus, and of the tenth satire of Juvenal; and a table, showing at the rate of various numbers a day (I suppose verses to be read) what would be, in each case, the total amount in a week, month, and year.

No man had a more ardent love of literature, or a higher respect for it, than Johnson. His apartment in Pembroke College was that upon the second floor over the gateway. The enthusiast of learning will ever contemplate it with veneration. One day, while he was sitting in it quite alone, Dr. Panting, then master of the College, whom he called "a fine Jacobite fellow," overheard him uttering this soliloquy in his strong emphatic voice: "Well, I have a mind to see what is done in other places of learning. I'll go and visit the universities abroad. I'll go to France and Italy. I'll go to Padua.— And I'll mind my business. For an *Athenian* blockhead is the worst of all blockheads."

Dr. Adams told me that Johnson, while he was at Pembroke College, "was caressed and loved by all about him, was a gay and frolicsome fellow, and passed there the happiest part of his life." But this is a striking proof of the fallacy of appearances, and how little any of us know of the real internal state even of those whom we see most frequently; for the truth is that he was then depressed by poverty, and irritated by disease. When I mentioned to him this account as given me by Dr. Adams, he said, "Ah, Sir, I was mad and violent. It was bitterness which they mistook for frolic. I was miserably poor, and I thought to fight my way by my literature and my wit; so I disregarded all power and all authority."

The Bishop of Dromore observes in a letter to me, "The pleasure he took in vexing the tutors and fellows has been often mentioned. But I have heard him say, what ought to be recorded to the honor of the present venerable master of that College, the Reverend William Adams, D.D., who was then very young, and one of the junior fellows; that the mild but judicious expostulations of this worthy man, whose virtue awed him, and whose learning he revered, made him really ashamed of himself, 'though I fear (said he) I was too proud to own it.'

"I have heard from some of his contemporaries that he was generally seen lounging at the College gate, with a circle of young students round him, whom he was entertaining with wit, and keeping from their studies, if not spiriting them up to rebellion against the College discipline, which in his maturer years he so much extolled." . . .

1736: Aetat. 27

In a man whom religious education has secured from licentious indulgences, the passion of love, when once it has seized him, is exceedingly strong; being unimpaired by dissipation, and totally concentrated in one object. This was experienced by Johnson when he became the fervent admirer of Mrs. Porter, after her first husband's death. Miss Porter told me that when he was first introduced to her mother, his appearance was very forbidding: he was then lean and lank, so that his immense structure of bones was hideously striking to the eye, and the scars of the scrophula were deeply visible. He also wore his hair, which was straight and stiff, and separated behind: and he often had, seemingly, convulsive starts and odd gesticulations, which tended to excite at once surprise and ridicule. Mrs. Porter was so much engaged by his conversation that she overlooked all these external disadvantages, and said to her daughter, "this is the most sensible man that I ever saw in my life."

Though Mrs. Porter was double the age of Johnson, and her person and manner, as described to me by the late Mr. Garrick, were by no means pleasing to others, she must have had a superiority of understanding and talents as she certainly inspired him with a more than ordinary passion; and she having signified her willingness to accept of his hand, he went to Lichfield to ask his mother's consent to the marriage; which he could not but be conscious was a very imprudent scheme, both on account of their disparity of years, and her want of fortune. But Mrs. Johnson knew too well the ardor of her son's temper, and was too tender a parent to oppose his inclinations.

I know not for what reason the marriage ceremony was not performed at Birmingham; but a resolution was taken that it should be at Derby, for which place the bride and bridegroom set out on horseback, I suppose in very good humor. But though Mr. Topham Beauclerk used archly to mention Johnson's having told him with much gravity, "Sir, it was a love marriage on both sides," I have had from my illustrious friend the following curious account of their journey to church upon the nuptial morn:—"Sir, she had read the old romances, and had got into her head the fantastical notion that a woman of spirit should use her lover like a dog. So, Sir, at first she told me that I rode too fast, and she could not keep up with me: and, when I rode a little slower, she passed me, and complained that I lagged behind. I was not to be made the slave of caprice; and I resolved to begin as I meant to end. I therefore pushed on briskly, till I was fairly out of her sight. The road lay between two hedges, so I was sure she could not miss it; and I contrived that she should soon come up with me. When she did, I observed her to be in tears."

This, it must be allowed, was a singular beginning of connubial felicity; but there is no doubt that Johnson, though he thus showed a manly firmness, proved a most affectionate and indulgent husband to the last moment of Mrs. Johnson's life: and in his "Prayers and Meditations," we find very remarkable evidence that his regard and fondness for her never ceased, even after her death.

He now set up a private academy, for which purpose he hired a large house, well situated near his native city. In the Gentleman's Magazine for 1736, there is the following advertisement: "At Edial, near Lichfield, in Staffordshire, young gentlemen are boarded and taught the Latin and Greek Languages, by SAMUEL JOHNSON." But the only pupils that were put under his care were the celebrated David Garrick and his brother George, and a Mr. Offely, a young gentleman of good fortune who died early. . . .

Johnson was not more satisfied with his situation as the master of an academy, than with that of the usher of a school; we need not wonder, therefore, that he did not keep his academy above a year and a half. From Mr. Garrick's account he did not appear to have been profoundly reverenced by his pupils. His oddities of manner, and uncouth gesticulations, could not but be the subject of merriment to them; and in particular, the young rogues used to listen at the door of his bed-chamber, and peep through the key-hole, that they might turn into ridicule his tumultuous and awkward fondness for Mrs. Johnson, whom he used to name by the familiar appellation of *Tetty* or *Tetsey*, which, like *Betty* or *Betsey*, is provincially used as a contraction for *Elizabeth*, her Christian name, but which to us seems ludicrous, when applied to a woman of her age and appearance. Mr. Garrick described her to me as very fat, with a bosom of more than ordinary protuberance, with swelled cheeks, of a florid red, produced by thick painting, and increased by the liberal use of cordials; flaring and fantastic in her dress, and affected both in her speech and her general behavior. I have seen Garrick exhibit her, by his exquisite talent of mimicry, so as to excite the heartiest burst of laughter; but he, probably, as is the case in all such representations, considerably aggravated the picture. . . .

1749: Aetat. 40

Garrick being now vested with theatrical power by being manager of Drury-lane theater, he kindly and generously made use of it to bring out Johnson's tragedy, which had been long kept back for want of encouragement. But in this benevolent purpose he met with no small difficulty from the temper of Johnson, which could not brook that a drama which he had formed with much study, and had been obliged to keep more than the nine years of Horace, should be revised and altered at the pleasure of an actor. Yet Garrick knew well, that without some alterations it would not be fit for the stage. A violent dispute having ensued between them, Garrick applied to the Reverend Dr. Taylor to interpose. Johnson was at first very obstinate. "Sir, (said he) the fellow wants me to make Mahomet run mad, that he may have an opportunity of tossing his hands and kicking his heels." He was, however, at last, with difficulty, prevailed on to comply with Garrick's wishes, so as to allow of some changes; but still there were not enough.

Dr. Adams was present the first night of the representation of IRENE, and gave me the following account: "Before the curtain drew up, there were catcalls whistling, which alarmed Johnson's friends. The Prologue, which was written by himself in a manly strain, soothed the audience, and the play went off tolerably, till it came to the conclusion, when Mrs. Pritchard, the heroine of the piece, was to be strangled upon the stage, and was to speak two lines with the bow-string round her neck. The audience cried out 'Murder! Murder!' She several times attempted to speak; but in vain. At last she was obliged to go off the stage alive." This passage was afterwards struck out, and she was carried off to be put to death behind the scenes, as the play now has it. The Epilogue, as Johnson informed me, was written by Sir William Yonge. I know not how his play came to be thus graced by the pen of a person then so eminent in the political world.

Notwithstanding all the support of such performers as Garrick, Barry, Mrs. Cibber, Mrs. Pritchard, and every advantage of dress and decorations, the tragedy of Irene did not please the public. Mr. Garrick's zeal carried it through for nine nights, so that the author had his three nights' profits; and from a receipt signed by him, now in the hands of Mr. James Dodsley, it appears that his friend, Mr. Robert Dodsley, gave him one hundred pounds for the copy, with his usual reservation of the right of one edition.

IRENE, considered as a poem, is entitled to the praise of superior excellence. Analyzed into parts, it will furnish a rich store of noble sentiments, fine imagery, and beautiful language; but it is deficient in pathos, in that delicate power of touching the human feelings, which is the principal end of the drama. Indeed Garrick has complained to me, that Johnson not only had not the faculty of producing the impressions of tragedy, but that he had not the sensibility to perceive them. His great friend Mr. Walmsley's prediction, that he would "turn out a fine tragedy writer," was, therefore, ill-founded. Johnson was wise enough to be convinced that he had not the talents necessary to write successfully for the stage, and never made another attempt in that species of composition.

When asked how he felt upon the ill success of his tragedy, he replied, "Like the Monument!" meaning that he continued firm and unmoved as that column. And let it be remembered, as an admonition to the *genus irritabile* of dramatic writers, that this great man, instead of peevishly complaining of the bad taste of the town, submitted to its decision without a murmur. He had indeed, upon all occasions a great deference for the general opinion: "A man (said he) who writes a book, thinks himself wiser or wittier than the rest of mankind; he supposes that he can instruct or amuse them, and the public to whom he appeals, must, after all, be the judges of his pretensions."

On occasion of this play being brought upon the stage, Johnson had a fancy that as a dramatic author his dress should be more gay than what he ordinarily wore; he therefore appeared behind the scenes, and even in one of the side boxes, in a scarlet waistcoat, with rich gold lace, and a gold-laced hat. He humorously observed to Mr. Langton, "that when in that dress he could not treat people with the same ease as when in his usual plain clothes." Dress indeed, we must allow, has more effect even upon strong minds than one should suppose, without having had the experience of it. His necessary attendance while his play was in rehearsal, and during its performance, brought him acquainted with many of the performers of both sexes, which produced a more favorable opinion of their profession than he had harshly expressed in his Life of Savage. With some of them he kept up an acquaintance as long as he and they lived, and was ever ready to show them acts of kindness. He for a considerable time used to frequent the *Green-Room*, and seemed to take delight in dissipating his gloom by mixing in the sprightly chit-chat of the motley circle then to be found there. Mr. David Hume related to me from Mr. Garrick, that Johnson at last denied himself this amusement, from considerations of rigid virtue; saying, "I'll come no more behind your scenes, David; for the silk stockings and white bosoms of your actresses excite my amorous propensities." . . . .

1763: Aetat. 54

Mr. Thomas Davies the actor, who then kept a bookseller's shop in Russel-street, Covent-garden, told me that Johnson was very much his friend, and came frequently to his house, where he more than once invited me to meet him: but by some unlucky accident or other he was prevented from coming to us.

Mr. Thomas Davies was a man of good understanding and talents, with the advantage of a liberal education. Though somewhat pompous, he was an entertaining companion; and his literary performances have no inconsiderable share of merit. He was a friendly and very hospitable man. Both he and his wife (who has been celebrated for her beauty) though upon the stage for many years, maintained an uniform decency of character; and Johnson esteemed them, and lived in as easy an intimacy with them as with any family which he used to visit. Mr. Davies recollected several of Johnson's remarkable sayings, and was one of the best of the many imitators of his voice and manner, while relating them. He increased my impatience more and more to see the extraordinary man whose works I highly valued, and whose conversation was reported to be so peculiarly excellent.

At last, on Monday the 16th of May, when I was sitting in Mr. Davies's back-parlor, after having drunk tea with him and Mrs. Davies, Johnson unexpectedly came into the shop; and Mr. Davies having perceived him through the glass-door in the room in which we were sitting, advancing towards us,—he announced his awful approach to me, somewhat in the manner of an actor in the part of Horatio, when he addresses Hamlet on the appearance of his father's ghost, "Look, my Lord, it comes." I found that I had a very perfect idea of Johnson's figure, from the portrait of him painted by Sir Joshua Reynolds soon after he had published his Dictionary, in the attitude of sitting in his easy chair in deep meditation; which was the first picture his friend did for him, which Sir Joshua very kindly presented to me, and from which an engraving has been made for this work. Mr. Davies mentioned my name, and respectfully introduced me to him. I was much agitated; and recollecting his prejudice against the Scotch, of which I had heard much, I said to Davies, "Don't tell where I come from."—"From Scotland," cried Davies, roguishly. "Mr. Johnson, (said I) I do indeed come from Scotland, but I cannot help it." I am willing to flatter myself that I meant this as light pleasantry to soothe and conciliate him, and not as an humiliating abasement at the expense of my country. But however that might be, this speech was somewhat unlucky; for with that quickness of wit for which he was so remarkable, he seized the expression "come from Scotland," which I used in the sense of being of that country; and, as if I had said that I had come away from it, or left it, retorted, "That, Sir, I find, is what a very great many of your countrymen cannot help." This stroke stunned me a good deal; and when we had sat down, I felt myself not a little embarrassed, and apprehensive of what might come next. He then addressed himself to Davies: "What do you think of Garrick? He has refused me an order for the play for Miss Williams, because he knows the house will be full, and that an order would be worth three shillings." Eager to take any opening to get into conversation with him, I ventured to say, "O, Sir, I cannot think Mr. Garrick would grudge such a trifle to you." "Sir, (said he, with a stern look) I have known David Garrick longer than you have done: and I know no right you have to talk to me on the subject." Perhaps I deserved this check; for it was rather presumptuous in me, an entire stranger, to express any doubt of the justice of his animadversion upon his old acquaintance and pupil. I now felt myself much mortified, and began to think that the hope which I had long indulged of obtaining his acquaintance was blasted. And, in truth, had not my ardor been uncommonly strong, and my resolution uncommonly persevering, so rough a reception might have deterred me for ever from making any further attempts. Fortunately, however, I remained upon the field not wholly discomfited; and was soon rewarded by hearing some of his conversation, of which I preserved the following short minute, without marking the questions and observations by which it was produced.

"People (he remarked) may be taken in once, who imagine that an author is greater in private life than other men. Uncommon parts require uncommon opportunities for their exertion.

"In barbarous society, superiority of parts is of real consequence. Great strength or great wisdom is of much value to an individual. But in more polished times there are people to do every thing for money; and then there are a number of other superiorities, such as those of birth and fortune, and rank, that dissipate men's attention, and leave no extraordinary share of respect for personal and intellectual superiority. This is wisely ordered by Providence, to preserve some equality among mankind."

"Sir, this book ('The Elements of Criticism,' which he had taken up) is a pretty essay, and deserves to be held in some estimation, though much of it is chimerical."

Speaking of one who with more than ordinary boldness attacked public measures and the royal family, he said, "I think he is safe from the law, but he is an abusive scoundrel; and instead of applying to my Lord Chief Justice to punish him, I would send half a dozen footmen and have him well ducked."

"The notion of liberty amuses the people of England, and helps to keep off the *tedium vitæ*. When a butcher tells you that *his heart bleeds for his country*, he has, in fact, no uneasy feeling."

"Sheridan will not succeed at Bath with his oratory. Ridicule has gone down before him, and I doubt, Derrick is his enemy.[7]

"Derrick may do very well, as long as he can outrun his character; but the moment his character gets up with him, it is all over."

It is, however, but just to record, that some years afterwards, when I reminded him of this sarcasm, he said, "Well, but Derrick has now got a character that he need not run away from."

I was highly pleased with the extraordinary vigor of his conversation, and regretted that I was drawn away from it by an en-

7 Mr. Sheridan was then reading lectures upon Oratory at Bath, where Derrick was Master of the Ceremonies; or, as the phrase is, KING.

gagement at another place. I had, for a part of the evening, been left alone with him, and had ventured to make an observation now and then, which he received very civilly; so that I was satisfied that though there was a roughness in his manner, there was no ill-nature in his disposition. Davies followed me to the door, and when I complained to him a little of the hard blows which the great man had given me, he kindly took upon him to console me by saying, "Don't be uneasy. I can see he likes you very well."

A few days afterwards I called on Davies, and asked him if he thought I might take the liberty of waiting on Mr. Johnson at his chambers in the Temple. He said I certainly might, and that Mr. Johnson would take it as a compliment. So on Tuesday the 24th of May, after having been enlivened by the witty sallies of Messieurs Thornton, Wilkes, Churchill, and Lloyd, with whom I had passed the morning, I boldly repaired to Johnson. His chambers were on the first floor of No. 1, Inner-Temple-lane, and I entered them with an impression given me by the Reverend Dr. Blair, of Edinburgh, who had been introduced to him not long before, and described his having "found the Giant in his den"; an expression which, when I came to be pretty well acquainted with Johnson, I repeated to him, and he was diverted at this picturesque account of himself. Dr. Blair had been presented to him by Dr. James Fordyce. At this time the controversy concerning the pieces published by Mr. James Macpherson, as translations of Ossian, was at its height. Johnson had all along denied their authenticity; and, what was still more provoking to their admirers, maintained that they had no merit. The subject having been introduced by Dr. Fordyce, Dr. Blair, relying on the internal evidence of their antiquity, asked Dr. Johnson whether he thought any man of a modern age could have written such poems? Johnson replied, "Yes, Sir, many men, many women, and many children." Johnson at this time, did not know that Dr. Blair had just published a Dissertation, not only defending their authenticity, but seriously ranking them with the poems of Homer and Virgil; and when he was afterwards informed of this circumstance, he expressed some displeasure at Dr. Fordyce's having suggested the topic, and said, "I am not sorry that they got thus much for their pains. Sir, it was like leading one to talk of a book, when the author is concealed behind the door."

He received me very courteously: but, it must be confessed, that his apartment, and furniture, and morning dress, were sufficiently uncouth. His brown suit of clothes looked very rusty: he had on a little old shriveled unpowdered wig, which was too small for his head; his shirt-neck and knees of his breeches were loose; his black worsted stockings ill drawn up; and he had a pair of unbuckled shoes by way of slippers. But all these slovenly particularities were forgotten the moment that he began to talk. Some gentlemen, whom I do not recollect, were sitting with him; and when they went away, I also rose; but he said to me, "Nay, don't go."—"Sir, (said I) I am afraid that I intrude upon you. It is benevolent to allow me to sit and hear you." He seemed pleased with this compliment, which I sincerely paid him, and answered, "Sir, I am obliged to any man who visits me."—I have preserved the following short minute of what passed this day.

"Madness frequently discovers itself merely by unnecessary deviation from the usual modes of the world. My poor friend Smart showed the disturbance of his mind, by falling upon his knees, and saying his prayers in the street, or in any other unusual place. Now although, rationally speaking, it is greater madness not to pray at all, than to pray as Smart did, I am afraid there are so many who do not pray, that their understanding is not called in question."

Concerning this unfortunate poet, Christopher Smart, who was confined in a mad-house, he had, at another time, the following conversation with Dr. Burney.—BURNEY. "How does poor Smart do, Sir; is he likely to recover?" JOHNSON. "It seems as if his mind had ceased to struggle with the disease; for he grows fat upon it." BURNEY. "Perhaps, Sir, that may be from want of exercise." JOHNSON. "No, Sir; he has partly as much exercise as he used to have, for he digs in the garden. Indeed, before his confinement, he used for exercise to walk to the alehouse; but he was *carried* back again. I did not think he ought to be shut up. His infirmities were not noxious to society. He insisted on people praying with him; and I'd as lief pray with Kit Smart as any one else. Another charge was, that he did not love clean linen; and I have no passion for it."

Johnson continued. "Mankind have a great aversion to intellectual labor; but even supposing knowledge to be easily attainable, more people would be content to be ignorant than would take even a little trouble to acquire it.

"The morality of an action depends on the motive from which we act. If I fling half a crown to a beggar with intention to break his head, and he picks it up and buys victuals with it, the physical effect is good; but, with respect to me, the action is very wrong. So, religious exercises, if not performed with an intention to please GOD, avail us nothing. As our Saviour says of those who perform them from other motives, 'Verily they have their reward.' "

"The Christian religion has very strong evidences. It, indeed, appears in some degree strange to reason; but in history we have undoubted facts, against which, in reasoning à priori, we have more arguments than we have for them; but then, testimony has great weight, and casts the balance. I would recommend to every man whose faith is yet unsettled, Grotius,—Dr. Pearson,—and Dr. Clarke."

Talking of Garrick, he said, "He is the first man in the world for sprightly conversation."

When I rose a second time, he again pressed me to stay, which I did.

He told me, that he generally went abroad at four in the afternoon, and seldom came home till two in the morning. I took the liberty to ask if he did not think it wrong to live thus, and not make more use of his great talents. He owned it was a bad habit. On reviewing, at the distance of many years, my journal of this period, I wonder how, at my first visit, I ventured to talk to him so freely, and that he bore it with so much indulgence.

Before we parted, he was so good as to promise to favor me with his company one evening at my lodgings: and, as I took my leave, shook me cordially by the hand. It is almost needless to add, that I felt no little elation at having now so happily established an acquaintance of which I had been so long ambitious.

My readers will, I trust, excuse me for being thus minutely circumstantial, when it is considered that the acquaintance of Dr. Johnson was to me a most valuable acquisition, and laid the foundation of whatever instruction and entertainment they may receive from my collections concerning the great subject of the work which they are now perusing.

I did not visit him again till Monday, June 13, at which time I recollect no part of his conversation, except that when I told him I had been to see Johnson ride upon three horses, he said, "Such a man, Sir, should be encouraged; for his performances show the extent of the human power in one instance, and thus tend to raise our opinion of the faculties of man. He shows what may be attained by persevering application; so that every man may hope, that by giving as much application, although perhaps he may never ride three horses at a time, or dance upon a wire, yet he may be equally expert in whatever profession he has chosen to pursue."

He again shook me by the hand at parting, and asked me why I did not come oftener to him. Trusting that I was now in his good graces, I answered, that he had not given me much encouragement, and reminded him of the check I had received from him at our first interview. "Poh, poh! (said he, with a complacent smile) never mind these things. Come to me as often as you can. I shall be glad to see you."

I had learnt that his place of frequent resort was the Mitre tavern in Fleet-street, where he loved to sit up late, and I begged I might be allowed to pass an evening with him there soon, which he promised I should. A few days afterwards I met him near Temple-bar, about one o'clock in the morning, and asked him if he would then go to the Mitre. "Sir, (said he) it is too late; they won't let us in. But I'll go with you another night with all my heart."

A revolution of some importance in my plan of life had just taken place; for instead of procuring a commission in the foot-guards, which was my own inclination, I had, in compliance with my father's wishes, agreed to study the law, and was soon to set out for Utrecht, to hear the lectures of an excellent Civilian in that University, and then to proceed on my travels. Though very desirous of obtaining Dr. Johnson's advice and instructions on the mode of pursuing my studies, I was at this time so occupied, shall I call it? or so dissipated, by the amusements of London, that our next meeting was not till Saturday, June 25, when happening to dine at Clifton's eating-house, in Butcher-row, I was surprised to perceive Johnson come in and take his seat at another table. The mode of dining, or rather being fed, at such houses in London, is well known to many to be particularly unsocial, as there is no ordinary, or united company, but each person has his own mess, and is under no obligation to hold any intercourse with any one. A liberal and full-minded man, however, who loves to talk, will break through this churlish and unsocial restraint. Johnson and an Irish gentleman got into a dispute concerning the cause of some part of mankind being black. "Why, Sir, (said Johnson) it has been accounted for in three ways: either by supposing that they are the posterity of Ham, who was cursed; or that God at first created two kinds of men, one black and another white; or that by the heat of the sun the skin is scorched, and so acquires a sooty hue. This matter has been much canvassed among naturalists, but has never been brought to any certain issue." What the Irishman said is totally obliterated from my mind; but I remember that he became very warm and intemperate in his expressions: upon which Johnson rose, and quietly walked away. When he had retired, his antagonist took his revenge, as he thought, by saying, "He has a most ungainly figure, and an affectation of pomposity, unworthy of a man of genius."

Johnson had not observed that I was in the room. I followed him, however, and he agreed to meet me in the evening at the Mitre. I called on him, and we went thither at nine. We had a good supper, and port wine, of which he then sometimes drank a bottle. The orthodox high-church sound of the MITRE,—the figure and manner of the celebrated SAMUEL JOHNSON,—the extraordinary power and precision of his conversation, and the pride arising from finding myself admitted as his companion, produced a variety of sensations, and a pleasing elevation of mind beyond what I had ever before experienced. I find in my journal the following minute of our conversation, which, though it will give but a very faint notion of what passed, is, in some degree, a valuable record; and it will be curious in this view, as showing how habitual to his mind were some opinions which appear in his works.

"Colley Cibber, Sir, was by no means a blockhead; but by arrogating to himself too much, he was in danger of losing that degree of estimation to which he was entitled. His friends gave out that he *intended* his birth-day odes should be bad: but that was not the case, Sir; for he kept them many months by him, and a few years before he died he showed me one of them, with great solicitude to render it as perfect as might be, and I made some corrections, to which he was not very willing to submit. I remember the following couplet in allusion to the King and himself:

> 'Perch'd on the eagle's soaring wing,
> The lowly linnet loves to sing.'

Sir, he had heard something of the fabulous tale of the wren sitting upon the eagle's wing, and he had applied it to a linnet. Cibber's familiar style, however, was better than that which Whitehead has assumed. *Grand* nonsense is insupportable. Whitehead is but a little man to inscribe verses to players."

I did not presume to controvert this censure, which was tinctured with his prejudice against players, but I could not help thinking that a dramatic poet might with propriety pay a compliment to an eminent performer, as Whitehead has very happily done in his verses to Mr. Garrick.

"Sir, I do not think Gray a first-rate poet. He has not a bold imagination, nor much command of words. The obscurity in which he has involved himself will not persuade us that he is sublime. His Elegy in a church-yard has a happy selection of images, but I don't like what are called his great things. His ode which begins

> 'Ruin seize thee, ruthless King,
> Confusion on thy banners wait!'

has been celebrated for its abruptness, and plunging into the subject all at once. But such arts as these have no merit, unless when they are original. We admire them only once; and this abruptness has nothing new in it. We have had it often before. Nay, we have it in the old song of Johnny Armstrong:

> 'Is there ever a man in all Scotland,
> From the highest estate to the lowest degree, &c.'

And then, Sir,

> 'Yes, there is a man in Westmoreland
> And Johnny Armstrong they do him call.'

There, now, you plunge at once into the subject. You have no previous narration to lead you to it.—The two next lines in that ode are, I think, very good:

> 'Though fann'd by conquest's crimson wing,
> They mock the air with idle state.' "

Here let it be observed, that although his opinion of Gray's poetry was widely different from mine, and I believe from that of most men of taste, by whom it is with justice highly admired, there is certainly much absurdity in the clamor which has been raised, as if he had been culpably injurious to the merit of that bard, and had been actuated by envy. Alas! ye little short-sighted critics, could Johnson be envious of the talents of any of his contemporaries? That his opinion on this subject was what in private and in public he uniformly expressed, regardless of what others might think, we may wonder, and perhaps regret; but it is shallow and unjust to charge him with expressing what he did not think.

Finding him in a placid humor, and wishing to avail myself of the opportunity which I fortunately had of consulting a sage, to hear whose wisdom, I conceived, in the ardor of youthful imagination, that men filled with a noble enthusiasm for intellectual improvement would gladly have resorted from distant lands;—I opened my mind to him ingenuously, and gave him a little sketch of my life, to which he was pleased to listen with great attention.

I acknowledged, that though educated very strictly in the principles of religion, I had for some time been misled into a certain degree of infidelity; but that I was come now to a better way of thinking, and was fully satisfied of the truth of the Christian revelation, though I was not clear as to every point considered to be orthodox. Being at all times a curious examiner of the human mind, and pleased with an undisguised display of what had passed in it, he called to me with warmth, "Give me your hand; I have taken a liking to you." He then began to descant upon the force of testimony, and the little we could know of final causes; so that the objections of, why was it so? or why was it not so? ought not to disturb us; adding, that he himself had at one period been guilty of a temporary neglect of religion, but that it was not the result of argument, but mere absence of thought.

After having given credit to reports of his bigotry, I was agreeably surprised when he expressed the following very liberal sentiment, which has the additional value of obviating an objection to our holy religion, founded upon the discordant tenets of Christians themselves: "For my part, Sir, I think all Christians, whether Papists or Protestants, agree in the essential articles, and that their differences are trivial, and rather political than religious."

We talked of belief in ghosts. He said, "Sir, I make a distinction between what a man may experience by the mere strength of his imagination, and what imagination cannot possibly produce. Thus, suppose I should think that I saw a form, and heard a voice cry, 'Johnson, you are a very wicked fellow, and unless you repent you will certainly be punished'; my own unworthiness is so deeply impressed upon my mind, that I might *imagine* I thus saw and heard, and therefore I should not believe that an external communication had been made to me. But if a form should appear, and a voice should tell me that a particular man had died at a particular place, and a particular hour, a fact which I had no apprehension of, nor any means of knowing, and this fact, with all its circumstances, should afterwards be unquestionably proved, I should, in that case, be persuaded that I had supernatural intelligence imparted to me."

Here it is proper, once for all, to give a true and fair statement of Johnson's way of thinking upon the question, whether departed spirits are ever permitted to appear in this world, or in any way to operate upon human life. He has been ignorantly misrepresented as weakly credulous upon that subject; and, therefore, though I feel an inclination to disdain and treat with silent contempt so foolish a notion concerning my illustrious friend, yet as I find it has gained ground, it is necessary to refute it. The real fact then is, that Johnson had a very philosophical mind, and such a rational respect for testimony, as to make him submit his understanding to what was authentically proved, though he could not comprehend why it was so. Being thus disposed, he was willing to enquire into the truth of any relation of supernatural agency, a general belief of which has prevailed in all nations and ages. But so far was he from being the dupe of implicit faith, that he examined the matter with a jealous attention, and no man was more ready to refute its falsehood when he had discovered it. Churchill in his poem entitled "The Ghost," availed himself of the absurd credulity imputed to Johnson, and drew a caricature of him under the name of "Pomposo," representing him as one of the believers of the story of a Ghost in Cock-lane, which, in the year 1762, had gained very general credit in London. Many of my readers, I am convinced, are to this hour under an impression that Johnson was thus foolishly deceived. It will therefore surprise them a good deal when they are informed upon undoubted authority, that Johnson was one of those by whom the imposture was detected. The story had become so popular, that he thought it should be investigated; and in this research he was assisted by the Reverend Dr. Douglas, now Bishop of Salisbury, the great detector of impostures; who informs me, that after the gentlemen who went and examined into the evidence were satisfied of its falsity, Johnson wrote in their presence an account of it, which was published in the news-papers and Gentleman's Magazine, and undeceived the world.

Our conversation proceeded. "Sir, (said he) I am a friend to subordination, as most conducive to the happiness of society. There is a reciprocal pleasure in governing and being governed."

"Dr. Goldsmith is one of the first men we now have as an author, and he is a very worthy man too. He has been loose in his principles, but he is coming right."

I mentioned Mallet's tragedy of ELVIRA, which had been acted the preceding winter at Drury-lane, and that the Honorable Andrew Erskine, Mr. Dempster, and myself, had joined in writing a pamphlet, entitled "Critical Strictures" against it. That the mildness of Dempster's disposition had, however, relented; and he had candidly said, "We have hardly a right to abuse this tragedy; for bad as it is, how vain should either of us be to write one not near so good." JOHNSON. "Why no, Sir; this is not just reasoning. You *may* abuse a tragedy, though you cannot write one. You may scold a carpenter who has made you a bad table, though you cannot make a table. It is not your trade to make tables."

When I talked to him of the paternal estate to which I was heir, he said, "Sir, let me tell you, that to be a Scotch landlord, where you have a number of families dependent upon you, and attached to you, is, perhaps as high a situation as humanity can arrive at. A merchant upon the 'Change of London, with a hundred thousand pounds, is nothing; an English Duke, with an immense fortune, is nothing: he has no tenants who consider themselves as under his patriarchal care, and who will follow him to the field upon an emergency."

His notion of the dignity of a Scotch landlord had been formed upon what he had heard of the Highland Chiefs; for it is long since a lowland landlord has been so curtailed in his feudal authority, that he has little more influence over his tenants than an English landlord; and of late years most of the Highland Chiefs have destroyed, by means too well known, the princely power which they once enjoyed.

He proceeded: "Your going abroad, Sir, and breaking off idle habits, may be of great importance to you. I would go where there are courts and learned men. There is a good deal of Spain that has not been perambulated. I would have you go thither. A man of inferior talents to yours may furnish us with useful observations upon that country." His supposing me, at that period of life, capable of writing an account of my travels that would deserve to be read, elated me not a little.

I appeal to every impartial reader whether this faithful detail of his frankness, complacency, and kindness to a young man, a stranger and a Scotchman, does not refute the unjust opinion of the harshness of his general demeanor. His occasional reproofs of folly, impudence, or impiety, and even the sudden sallies of his constitutional irritability of temper, which have been preserved for the poignancy of their wit, have produced that opinion among those who have not considered that such instances, though collected by Mrs. Piozzi into a small volume, and read over in a few hours, were, in fact, scattered through a long series of years: years, in which his time was chiefly spent in instructing and delighting mankind by his writings and conversation, in acts of piety to GOD, and good-will to men.

I complained to him that I had not yet acquired much knowledge, and asked his advice as to my studies. He said, "Don't talk of study now. I will give you a plan; but it will require some time to consider of it." "It is very good in you (I replied) to allow me to be with you thus. Had it been foretold to me some years ago that I should pass an evening with the author of the RAMBLER, how should I have exulted!" What I then expressed was sincerely from the heart. He was satisfied that it was, and cordially answered, "Sir, I am glad we have met. I hope we shall pass many evenings and mornings too, together." We finished a couple of bottles of port, and sat till between one and two in the morning.

He wrote this year in the Critical Review the account of "Telemachus, a Mask," by the Reverend George Graham, of Eton College. The subject of this beautiful poem was particularly interesting to Johnson, who had much experience of "the conflict of opposite principles," which he describes as "The contention between pleasure and virtue, a struggle which will always be continued while the present system of nature shall subsist: nor can history or poetry exhibit more than pleasure triumphing over virtue, and virtue subjugating pleasure."

As Dr. Oliver Goldsmith will frequently appear in this narrative, I shall endeavor to make my readers in some degree acquainted with his singular character. He was a native of Ireland, and a contemporary with Mr. Burke, at Trinity College, Dublin, but did not then give much promise of future celebrity. He, however, observed to Mr. Malone that "though he made no great figure in mathematics, which was a study in much repute there, he could turn an ode of Horace into English better than any of them." He afterwards studied physic at Edinburgh, and upon the Continent: and I have been informed, was enabled to pursue his travels on foot, partly by demanding at universities to enter the lists as a disputant, by which, according to the custom of many of them, he was entitled to the premium of a crown, when luckily for him his challenge was not accepted; so that, as I once observed to Dr. Johnson, he *disputed* his passage through Europe. He then came to England, and was employed successively in the capacities of an usher to an academy, a corrector of the press, a reviewer, and a writer for a news-paper. He had sagacity enough to cultivate assiduously the acquaintance of Johnson, and his faculties were gradually enlarged by the contemplation of such a model. To me and many others it appeared that he studiously copied the manner of Johnson, though, indeed, upon a smaller scale.

At this time I think he had published nothing with his name, though it was pretty generally known that *one Dr. Goldsmith* was the author of "An Enquiry into the Present State of Polite Learning in Europe," and of "The Citizen of the World," a series of letters supposed to be written from London by a Chinese. No man had the art of displaying with more advantage as a writer, whatever literary acquisitions he made. "*Nihil quod tetigit non ornavit.*" [8] His mind resembled a fertile, but thin soil. There was a quick, but not a strong vegetation, of whatever chanced to be thrown upon it. No deep root could be struck. The oak of the forest did not grow there: but the elegant shrubbery and the fragrant parterre appeared in gay succession. It has been generally circulated and believed that he was a mere fool in conversation; but, in truth, this has been greatly exaggerated. He had, no doubt, a more than common share of that hurry of ideas which we often find in his countrymen, and which sometimes produces a laughable confusion in expressing them. He was very much what the French call *un étourdi*, and from vanity and an eager desire of being conspicuous wherever he was, he frequently talked carelessly without knowledge of the subject, or even without thought. His person was short, his countenance coarse and vulgar, his deportment that of a scholar awkwardly affecting the easy gentleman. Those who were in any way distinguished, excited envy in him to so ridiculous an excess, that the instances of it are hardly credible. When accompanying

8 He improved all that he touched.

two beautiful young ladies with their mother on a tour in France, he was seriously angry that more attention was paid to them than to him; and once at the exhibition of the *Fantoccini* in London, when those who sat next him observed with what dexterity a puppet was made to toss a pike, he could not bear that it should have such praise, and exclaimed with some warmth, "Pshaw! I can do it better myself."

He, I am afraid, had no settled system of any sort, so that his conduct must not be strictly scrutinized; but his affections were social and generous, and when he had money he gave it away very liberally. His desire of imaginary consequence predominated over his attention to truth. When he began to rise into notice, he said he had a brother who was Dean of Durham, a fiction so easily detected, that it is wonderful how he should have been so inconsiderate as to hazard it. He boasted to me at this time of the power of his pen in commanding money, which I believe was true in a certain degree, though in the instance he gave he was by no means correct. He told me that he had sold a novel for four hundred pounds. This was his "Vicar of Wakefield." But Johnson informed me, that he had made the bargain for Goldsmith, and the price was sixty pounds. "And, Sir, (said he) a sufficient price too, when it was sold; for then the fame of Goldsmith had not been elevated, as it afterwards was, by his 'Traveller'; and the bookseller had such faint hopes of profit by his bargain, that he kept the manuscript by him a long time, and did not publish it till after the 'Traveller' had appeared. Then, to be sure, it was accidentally worth more money."

Mrs. Piozzi and Sir John Hawkins have strangely misstated the history of Goldsmith's situation and Johnson's friendly interference, when this novel was sold. I shall give it authentically from Johnson's own exact narration:

"I received one morning a message from poor Goldsmith that he was in great distress, and as it was not in his power to come to me, begging that I would come to him as soon as possible. I sent him a guinea, and promised to come to him directly. I accordingly went as soon as I was dressed, and found that his landlady had arrested him for his rent, at which he was in a violent passion. I perceived that he had already changed my guinea, and had got a bottle of Madeira and a glass before him. I put the cork into the bottle, desired he would be calm, and began to talk to him of the means by which he might be extricated. He then told me that he had a novel ready for the press, which he produced to me. I looked into it, and saw its merit; told the landlady I should soon return, and having gone to a bookseller sold it for sixty pounds. I brought Goldsmith the money, and he discharged his rent, not without rating his landlady in a high tone for having used him so ill."

My next meeting with Johnson was on Friday the 1st of July, when he and I and Dr. Goldsmith supped at the Mitre. I was before this time pretty well acquainted with Goldsmith, who was one of the brightest ornaments of the Johnsonian school. Goldsmith's respectful attachment to Johnson was then at its height; for his own literary reputation had not yet distinguished him so much as to excite a vain desire of competition with his great Master. He had increased my admiration of the goodness of Johnson's heart, by incidental remarks in the course of conversation, such as, when I mentioned Mr. Levet, whom he entertained under his roof, "He is poor and honest, which is recommendation enough to Johnson"; and when I wondered that he was very kind to a man of whom I had heard a very bad character, "He is now become miserable, and that insures the protection of Johnson."

Goldsmith attempted this evening to maintain, I suppose from an affectation of paradox, "that knowledge was not desirable on its own account, for it often was a source of unhappiness." JOHNSON. "Why, Sir, that knowledge may in some cases produce unhappiness, I allow. But, upon the whole, knowledge, *per se*, is certainly an object which every man would wish to attain, although, perhaps, he may not take the trouble necessary for attaining it."

Dr. John Campbell, the celebrated political and biographical writer, being mentioned, Johnson said, "Campbell is a man of much knowledge, and has a good share of imagination. His 'Hermippus Redivivus' is very entertaining, as an account of the Hermetic philosophy, and as furnishing a curious history of the extravagances of the human mind. If it were merely imaginary, it would be nothing at all. Campbell is not always rigidly careful of truth in his conversation; but I do not believe there is any thing of this carelessness in his books. Campbell is a good man, a pious man. I am afraid he has not been in the inside of a church for many years; but he never passes a church without pulling off his hat. This shows that he has good principles. I used to go pretty often to Campbell's on a Sunday evening till I began to consider that the shoals of

Scotchmen who flocked about him might probably say, when any thing of mine was well done, 'Ay, ay, he has learned this of CAW-MELL!'"

He talked very contemptuously of Churchill's poetry, observing that "it had a temporary currency, only from its audacity of abuse, and being filled with living names, that it would sink into oblivion." I ventured to hint that he was not quite a fair judge, as Churchill had attacked him violently. JOHNSON. "Nay, Sir, I am a very fair judge. He did not attack me violently till he found I did not like his poetry; and his attack on me shall not prevent me from continuing to say what I think of him, from an apprehension that it may be ascribed to resentment. No, Sir, I called the fellow a blockhead at first, and I will call him a blockhead still. However, I will acknowledge that I have a better opinion of him now, than I once had; for he has shown more fertility than I expected. To be sure, he is a tree that cannot produce good fruit; he only bears crabs. But, Sir, a tree that produces a great many crabs is better than a tree which produces only a few."

In this depreciation of Churchill's poetry I could not agree with him. It is very true that the greatest part of it is upon the topics of the day, on which account, as it brought him great fame and profit at the time, it must proportionately slide out of the public attention as other occasional objects succeed. But Churchill had extraordinary vigor both of thought and expression. His portraits of the players will ever be valuable to the true lovers of the drama; and his strong caricatures of several eminent men of his age, will not be forgotten by the curious. Let me add that there are in his works many passages which are of a general nature; and his "Prophecy of Famine" is a poem of no ordinary merit. It is, indeed, falsely injurious to Scotland; but therefore may be allowed a greater share of invention.

Bonnell Thornton had just published a burlesque "Ode on St. Cecilia's day, adapted to the ancient British music, viz. the salt-box, the jews-harp, the marrow-bones and cleaver, the humstrum or hurdy-gurdy, &c." Johnson praised its humor, and seemed much diverted with it. He repeated the following passage:

"In strains more exalted the salt-box shall join,
   And clattering and battering and clapping combine;
   With a rap and a tap while the hollow side sounds,
   Up and down leaps the flap, and with rattling rebounds."

I mentioned the periodical paper called THE CONNOISSEUR. He said it wanted matter.—No doubt it had not the deep thinking of Johnson's writings. But surely it has just views of the surface of life, and a very sprightly manner. His opinion of THE WORLD was not much higher than of THE CONNOISSEUR.

Let me here apologize for the imperfect manner in which I am obliged to exhibit Johnson's conversation at this period. In the early part of my acquaintance with him, I was so wrapt in admiration of his extraordinary colloquial talents, and so little accustomed to his peculiar mode of expression, that I found it extremely difficult to recollect and record his conversation with its genuine vigor and vivacity. In progress of time, when my mind was, as it were, *strongly impregnated with the Johnsonian œther*, I could with much more facility and exactness, carry in my memory and commit to paper the exuberant variety of his wisdom and wit.

At this time, *Miss* Williams, as she was then called, though she did not reside with him in the Temple under his roof, but had lodgings in Bolt-court, Fleet-street, had so much of his attention, that he every night drank tea with her before he went home, however late it might be, and she always sat up for him. This, it may be fairly conjectured, was not alone a proof of his regard for *her*, but of his own unwillingness to go into solitude, before that unseasonable hour at which he had habituated himself to expect the oblivion of repose. Dr. Goldsmith, being a privileged man, went with him this night, strutting away, and calling to me with an air of superiority, like that of an esoteric over an exoteric disciple of a sage of antiquity, "I go to see Miss Williams." I confess, I then envied him this mighty privilege, of which he seemed so proud; but it was not long before I obtained the same mark of distinction.

On Tuesday the 5th of July, I again visited Johnson. He told me he had looked into the poems of a pretty voluminous writer, Mr. (now Dr.) John Ogilvie, one of the Presbyterian ministers of Scotland, which had lately come out, but could find no thinking in them. BOSWELL. "Is there not imagination in them, Sir?" JOHNSON. "Why, Sir, there is in them what *was* imagination, but it is no more imagination in *him*, than sound is sound in the echo. And his diction too is not his own. We have long ago seen *white-robed innocence*, and *flower-bespangled meads*."

Talking of London, he observed, "Sir, if you wish to have a just notion of the magnitude of this city, you must not be satisfied with seeing its great streets and squares, but must survey the innumerable little lanes and courts. It is not in the showy evolutions of buildings, but in the multiplicity of human habitations which are crowded together, that the wonderful immensity of London consists."—I have often amused myself with thinking how different a place London is to different people. They, whose narrow minds are contracted to the consideration of some one particular pursuit, view it only through that medium. A politician thinks of it merely as the seat of government in its different departments; a grazier, as a vast market for cattle; a mercantile man, as a place where a prodigious deal of business is done upon 'Change; a dramatic enthusiast, as the grand scene of theatrical entertainments; a man of pleasure, as an assemblage of taverns, and the great emporium for ladies of easy virtue. But the intellectual man is struck with it, as comprehending the whole of human life in all its variety, the contemplation of which is inexhaustible.

On Wednesday, July 6, he was engaged to sup with me at my lodgings in Downing-street, Westminster. But on the preceding night my landlord having behaved very rudely to me and some company who were with me, I had resolved not to remain another night in his house. I was exceedingly uneasy at the awkward appearance I supposed I should make to Johnson and the other gentleman whom I had invited, not being able to receive them at home, and being obliged to order supper at the Mitre. I went to Johnson in the morning, and talked of it as of a serious distress. He laughed, and said, "Consider, Sir, how insignificant this will appear a twelve-month hence."—Were this consideration to be applied to most of the little vexatious incidents of life, by which our quiet is too often disturbed, it would prevent many painful sensations. I have tried it frequently with good effect. "There is nothing (continued he) in this mighty misfortune; nay, we shall be better at the Mitre." I told him that I had been at Sir John Fielding's office, complaining of my landlord, and had been informed, that though I had taken my lodgings for a year, I might, upon proof of his bad behavior, quit them when I pleased, without being under an obligation to pay rent for any longer time than while I possessed them. The fertility of Johnson's mind could show itself even upon so small a matter as this. "Why, Sir, (said he) I suppose this must be the law, since you have been told so in Bow-street. But if your landlord could hold you to your bargain, and the lodgings should be yours for a year, you may certainly use them as you think fit. So, Sir, you may quarter two life-guardmen upon him; or you may send the greatest scoundrel you can find into your apartments; or you may say that you want to make some experiments in natural philosophy, and may burn a large quantity of assafœtida in his house."

I had as my guests this evening at the Mitre tavern, Dr. Johnson, Dr. Goldsmith, Mr. Thomas Davies, Mr. Eccles, an Irish gentleman, for whose agreeable company I was obliged to Mr. Davies, and the Reverend Mr. John Ogilvie, who was desirous of being in company with my illustrious friend, while I in my turn, was proud to have the honor of showing one of my countrymen upon what easy terms Johnson permitted me to live with him.

Goldsmith, as usual, endeavored, with too much eagerness, to *shine*, and disputed very warmly with Johnson against the well known maxim of the British constitution, "the King can do no wrong"; affirming, that, "what was morally false could not be politically true; and as the King might, in the exercise of his regal power, command and cause the doing of what was wrong, it certainly might be said, in sense and in reason, that he could do wrong." JOHNSON. "Sir, you are to consider, that in our constitution, according to its true principles, the King is the head, he is supreme: he is above every thing, and there is no power by which he can be tried. Therefore, it is, Sir, that we hold the King can do no wrong; that whatever may happen to be wrong in government may not be above our reach, by being ascribed to Majesty. Redress is always to be had against oppression, by punishing the immediate agents. The King, though he should command, cannot force a judge to condemn a man unjustly; therefore it is the judge whom we prosecute and punish. Political institutions are formed upon the consideration of what will most frequently tend to the good of the whole, although now and then exceptions may occur. Thus it is better in general that a nation should have a supreme legislative power, although it may at times be abused. And then, Sir, there is this consideration, that *if the abuse be enormous, Nature will rise up, and claiming her original rights, overturn a corrupt political system.*" I mark this animated sentence with peculiar pleasure, as a noble instance of that truly dignified spirit of freedom which ever glowed in his heart, though he was charged with slavish tenets by superficial observers; because he was at all times indignant against that false patriotism, that pretended love of freedom, that unruly restlessness which is inconsistent with the stable authority of any good government.

This generous sentiment, which he uttered with great fervor, struck me exceedingly, and stirred my blood to that pitch of fancied resistance, the possibility of which I am glad to keep in mind, but to which I trust I never shall be forced.

"Great abilities (said he) are not requisite for an historian; for in historical composition, all the greatest powers of the human mind are quiescent. He has facts ready to his hand, so there is no exercise of invention. Imagination is not required in any high degree; only about as much as is used in the lower kinds of poetry. Some penetration, accuracy, and coloring, will fit a man for the task, if he can give the application which is necessary."

"Bayle's Dictionary is a very useful work for those to consult who love the biographical part of literature, which is what I love most."

Talking of the eminent writers in Queen Anne's reign, he observed, "I think Dr. Arbuthnot the first man among them. He was the most universal genius, being an excellent physician, a man of deep learning, and a man of much humor. Mr. Addison was, to be sure, a great man; his learning was not profound; but his morality, his humor, and his elegance of writing, set him very high."

Mr. Ogilvie was unlucky enough to choose for the topic of his conversation the praises of his native country. He began with saying, that there was very rich land around Edinburgh. Goldsmith, who had studied physic there, contradicted this, very untruly, with a sneering laugh. Disconcerted a little by this, Mr. Ogilvie then took a new ground, where, I suppose, he thought himself perfectly safe; for he observed, that Scotland had a great many noble wild prospects. JOHNSON. "I believe, Sir, you have a great many. Norway, too, has noble wild prospects; and Lapland is remarkable for prodigious noble wild prospects. But, Sir, let me tell you, the noblest prospect which a Scotchman ever sees, is the high road that leads him to England!" This unexpected and pointed sally produced a roar of applause. After all, however, those who admire the rude grandeur of Nature, cannot deny it to Caledonia.

On Saturday, July 9, I found Johnson surrounded with a numerous levee, but have not preserved any part of his conversation. On the 14th we had another evening by ourselves at the Mitre. It happening to be a very rainy night, I made some commonplace observations on the relaxation of nerves and depression of spirits which such weather occasioned; [9] adding, however, that it was good for the vegetable creation. Johnson, who, as we have already seen, denied that the temperature of the air had any influence on the human frame, answered, with a smile of ridicule, "Why, yes, Sir, it is good for vegetables, and for the animals who eat those vegetables, and for the animals who eat those animals." This observation of his aptly enough introduced a good supper; and I soon forgot, in Johnson's company, the influence of a moist atmosphere.

Feeling myself now quite at ease as his companion, though I had all possible reverence for him, I expressed a regret that I could not be so easy with my father, though he was not much older than Johnson, and certainly however respectable had not more learning and greater abilities to depress me. I asked him the reason of this. JOHNSON. "Why, Sir, I am a man of the world. I live in the world, and I take in some degree, the color of the world as it moves along. Your father is a judge in a remote part of the island, and all his notions are taken from the old world. Besides, Sir, there must always be a struggle between a father and son, while one aims at power and the other at independence." I said, I was afraid my father would force me to be a lawyer. JOHNSON. "Sir, you need not be afraid of his forcing you to be a laborious practicing lawyer; that is not in his power. For as the proverb says, 'One man may lead a horse to the water, but twenty cannot make him drink.' He may be displeased that you are not what he wishes you to be; but that displeasure will not go far. If he insists only on your having as much law as is necessary for a man of property, and then endeavors to get you into Parliament, he is quite in the right."

He enlarged very convincingly upon the excellence of rhyme over blank verse in English poetry. I mentioned to him that Dr. Adam Smith, in his lectures upon composition, when I studied under him in the College of Glasgow, had maintained the same opinion strenuously, and I repeated some of his arguments. JOHNSON. "Sir, I was once in company with Smith, and we did not take to each other; but had I known that he loved rhyme as much as you tell me he does, I should have HUGGED him."

Talking of those who denied the truth of Christianity, he said. "It is always easy to be on the negative side. If a man were now to deny that there is salt upon the table, you could not reduce him to an absurdity. Come, let us try this a little further. I deny that Canada is taken, and I can support my denial by pretty good arguments. The French are a much more numerous people than we; and it is not likely that they would allow us to take it. 'But the ministry have assured us, in all the formality of the Gazette, that it is taken.' —Very true. But the ministry have put us to an enormous expense by the war in America, and it is their interest to persuade us that we have got something for our money.—'But the fact is confirmed by thousands of men who were at the taking of it.'—Ay, but these men have still more interest in deceiving us. They don't want that you should think the French have beat them, but that they have beat the French. Now suppose you should go over and find that it really is taken, that would only satisfy yourself; for when you come home, we will not believe you. We will say, you have been bribed.—Yet, Sir, notwithstanding all these plausible objections, we have no doubt that Canada is really ours. Such is the weight of common testimony. How much stronger are the evidences of the Christian religion?"

"Idleness is a disease which must be combatted; but I would not advise a rigid adherence to a particular plan of study. I myself have never persisted in any plan for two days together. A man ought to read just as inclination leads him: for what he reads as a task will do him little good. A young man should read five hours in a day, and so may acquire a great deal of knowledge."

To a man of vigorous intellect and ardent curiosity like his own, reading without a regular plan may be beneficial; though even such a man must submit to it, if he would attain a full understanding of any of the sciences.

To such a degree of unrestrained frankness had he now accustomed me, that in the course of this evening I talked of the numerous reflections which had been thrown out against him on account of his having accepted a pension from his present Majesty. "Why, Sir, (said he, with a hearty laugh) it is a mighty foolish noise that they make. I have accepted of a pension as a reward which has been thought due to my literary merit; and now that I have this pension, I am the same man in every respect that I have ever been; I retain the same principles. It is true, that I cannot now curse (smiling) the House of Hanover; nor would it be decent for me to drink King James's health in the wine that King George gives me money to pay

for. But, Sir, I think that the pleasure of cursing the House of Hanover, and drinking King James's health, are amply overbalanced by
three hundred pounds a year."

There was here, most certainly, an affectation of more Jacobitism than he really had; and indeed an intention of admitting, for
the moment, in a much greater extent than it really existed, the
charge of disaffection imputed to him by the world, merely for the
purpose of showing how dexterously he could repel an attack, even
though he were placed in the most disadvantageous position; for I
have heard him declare, that if holding up his right hand would
have secured victory at Culloden to Prince Charles's army, he was
not sure he would have held it up; so little confidence had he in
the right claimed by the house of Stuart, and so fearful was he of
the consequences of another revolution on the throne of Great-
Britain; and Mr. Topham Beauclerk assured me he had heard him
say this before he had his pension. At another time he said to Mr.
Langton, "Nothing has ever offered that has made it worth my
while to consider the question fully." He, however, also said to the
same gentleman, talking of King James the Second, "It was become
impossible for him to reign any longer in this country." He no
doubt had an early attachment to the House of Stuart; but his zeal
had cooled as his reason strengthened. Indeed, I heard him once say
"that after the death of a violent Whig, with whom he used to contend with great eagerness, he felt his Toryism much abated." I suppose he meant Mr. Walmsley.

Yet there is no doubt that at earlier periods he was wont often
to exercise both his pleasantry and ingenuity in talking Jacobitism.
My much respected friend, Dr. Douglas, now Bishop of Salisbury,
has favored me with the following admirable instance from his
Lordship's own recollection. One day when dining at old Mr.
Langton's, where Miss Roberts, his niece, was one of the company,
Johnson, with his usual complacent attention to the fair sex, took
her by the hand and said, "My dear, I hope you are a Jacobite."
Old Mr. Langton, who, though a high and steady Tory, was at-
tached to the present Royal Family, seemed offended, and asked
Johnson, with great warmth, what he could mean by putting such
a question to his niece! "Why, Sir, (said Johnson) I meant no offense to your niece, I meant her a great compliment. A Jacobite,
Sir, believes in the divine right of Kings. He that believes in the
divine right of Kings believes in a Divinity. A Jacobite believes

in the divine right of Bishops. He that believes in the divine right of Bishops believes in the divine authority of the Christian religion. Therefore, Sir, a Jacobite is neither an Atheist nor a Deist. That cannot be said of a Whig; for *Whiggism is a negation of all principle.*"

He advised me when abroad to be as much as I could with the Professors in the Universities, and with the Clergy; for from their conversation I might expect the best accounts of everything in whatever country I should be, with the additional advantage of keeping my learning alive.

It will be observed that when giving me advice as to my travels, Dr. Johnson did not dwell upon cities, and palaces, and pictures, and shows, and Arcadian scenes. He was of Lord Essex's opinion, who advises his kinsman Roger Earl of Rutland, "rather to go a hundred miles to speak with one wise man, than five miles to see a fair town."

I described to him an impudent fellow from Scotland, who affected to be a savage, and railed at all established systems. JOHNSON. "There is nothing surprizing in this, Sir. He wants to make himself conspicuous. He would tumble in a hogsty, as long as you looked at him and called to him to come out. But let him alone, never mind him, and he'll soon give it over."

I added that the same person maintained that there was no distinction between virtue and vice. JOHNSON. "Why, Sir, if the fellow does not think as he speaks, he is lying; and I see not what honor he can propose to himself from having the character of a liar. But if he does really think that there is no distinction between virtue and vice, why, Sir, when he leaves our houses let us count our spoons."

Sir David Dalrymple, now one of the Judges of Scotland by the title of Lord Hailes, had contributed much to increase my high opinion of Johnson, on account of his writings, long before I attained to a personal acquaintance with him; I, in return, had informed Johnson of Sir David's eminent character for learning and religion; and Johnson was so much pleased, that at one of our evening meetings he gave him for his toast. I at this time kept up a very frequent correspondence with Sir David; and I read to Dr. Johnson to-night the following passage from the letter which I had last received from him:

"It gives me pleasure to think that you have obtained the friendship of Mr. Samuel Johnson. He is one of the best moral writers which England has produced. At the same time, I envy you the free and undisguised converse with such a man. May I beg you to present my best respects to him, and to assure him of the veneration which I entertain for the author of the Rambler and of Rasselas? Let me recommend this last work to you; with the Rambler you certainly are acquainted. In Rasselas you will see a tender-hearted operator, who probes the wound only to heal it. Swift, on the contrary, mangles human nature. He cuts and slashes, as if he took pleasure in the operation, like the tyrant who said *Ita feri ut se sentia emori.*" Johnson seemed to be much gratified by this just and well-turned compliment.

He recommended to me to keep a journal of my life, full and unreserved. He said it would be a very good exercise, and would yield me great satisfaction when the particulars were faded from my remembrance. I was uncommonly fortunate in having had a previous coincidence of opinion with him upon this subject, for I had kept such a journal for some time; and it was no small pleasure to me to have this to tell him, and to receive his approbation. He counseled me to keep it private, and said I might surely have a friend who would burn it in case of my death. From this habit I have been enabled to give the world so many anecdotes, which would otherwise have been lost to posterity. I mentioned that I was afraid I put into my journal too many little incidents. JOHNSON. "There is nothing, Sir, too little for so little a creature as man. It is by studying little things that we attain the great art of having as little misery and as much happiness as possible."

Next morning Mr. Dempster happened to call on me, and was so much struck even with the imperfect account which I gave him of Dr. Johnson's conversation, that to his honor be it recorded, when I complained that drinking port and sitting up late with him, affected my nerves for some time after, he said, "One had better be palsied at eighteen than not keep company with such a man." . . .

Rousseau's treatise on the inequality of mankind was at this time a fashionable topic. It gave rise to an observation by Mr. Dempster, that the advantages of fortune and rank were nothing to a wise man, who ought to value only merit. JOHNSON. "If man were savage, living in the woods by himself, this might be true; but in civilized society we all depend upon each other, and our happiness is very much owing to the good opinion of mankind. Now,

Sir, in civilized society, external advantages make us more respected. A man with a good coat upon his back meets with a better reception than he who has a bad one. Sir, you may analyze this, and say what is there in it? But that will avail you nothing, for it is a part of a general system. Pound St. Paul's church into atoms, and consider any single atom; it is, to be sure, good for nothing; but, put all these atoms together, and you have St. Paul's church. So it is with human felicity, which is made up of many ingredients, each of which may be shown to be very insignificant. In civilized society, personal merit will not serve you so much as money will. Sir, you may make the experiment. Go into the street, and give one man a lecture on morality, and another a shilling, and see which will respect you most. If you wish only to support nature, Sir William Petty fixes your allowance at three pounds a year; but as times are much altered, let us call it six pounds. This sum will fill your belly, shelter you from the weather, and even get you a strong lasting coat, supposing it to be made of good bull's hide. Now, Sir, all beyond this is artificial, and is desired in order to obtain a greater degree of respect from our fellow-creatures. And, Sir, if six hundred pounds a year procure a man more consequence, and, of course, more happiness than six pounds a year, the same proportion will hold as to six thousand, and so on, as far as opulence can be carried. Perhaps he who has a large fortune may not be so happy as he who has a small one; but that must proceed from other causes than from his having the large fortune: for, *cœteris paribus*, he who is rich in a civilized society, must be happier than he who is poor; as riches, if properly used, (and it is a man's own fault if they are not) must be productive of the highest advantages. Money, to be sure, of itself is of no use; for its only use is to part with it. Rousseau, and all those who deal in paradoxes, are led away by a childish desire of novelty. When I was a boy, I used always to choose the wrong side of a debate, because most ingenious things, that is to say, most new things, could be said upon it. Sir, there is nothing for which you may not muster up more plausible arguments, than those which are urged against wealth and other external advantages. Why, now, there is stealing; why should it be thought a crime? When we consider by what unjust methods property has been often acquired, and that what was unjustly got it must be unjust to keep, where is the harm in one man's taking the property of another from him? Besides, Sir, when we consider the bad use that many people make of their property, and how much better use the thief may make of it, it may be defended as a very allowable practice. Yet, Sir, the experience of mankind has discovered stealing to be so very bad a thing, that they make no scruple to hang a man for it. When I was running about this town a very poor fellow, I was a great arguer for the advantages of poverty; but I was, at the same time, very sorry to be poor. Sir, all the arguments which are brought to represent poverty as no evil, show it to be evidently a great evil. You never find people laboring to convince you that you may live very happily upon a plentiful fortune.—So you hear people talking how miserable a King must be; and yet they all wish to be in his place."

It was suggested that kings must be unhappy, because they are deprived of the greatest of all satisfactions, easy and unreserved society. JOHNSON. "That is an ill-founded notion. Being a king does not exclude a man from such society. Great kings have always been social. The King of Prussia, the only great king at present, is very social. Charles the Second, the last King of England who was a man of parts, was social; and our Henrys and Edwards were all social."

Mr. Dempster having endeavored to maintain that intrinsic merit *ought* to make the only distinction amongst mankind. JOHNSON. "Why, Sir, mankind have found that this cannot be. How shall we determine the proportion of intrinsic merit? Were that to be the only distinction amongst mankind, we should soon quarrel about the degrees of it. Were all distinctions abolished, the strongest would not long acquiesce, but would endeavor to obtain a superiority by their bodily strength. But, Sir, as subordination is very necessary for society, and contentions for superiority very dangerous, mankind, that is to say, all civilized nations, have settled it upon a plain invariable principle. A man is born to hereditary rank; or his being appointed to certain offices, gives him a certain rank. Subordination tends greatly to human happiness. Were we all upon an equality, we should have no other enjoyment than mere animal pleasure."

I said, I considered distinction of rank to be of so much importance in civilized society, that if I were asked on the same day to dine with the first Duke in England, and with the first man in Britain for genius, I should hesitate which to prefer. JOHNSON. "To be sure, Sir, if you were to dine only once, and it were never to be known where you dined, you would choose rather to dine with the first man for genius; but to gain most respect, you should dine with the first Duke in England. For nine people in ten that you meet with, would have a higher opinion of you for having dined with a Duke; and the great genius himself would receive you better, because you had been with the great Duke."

He took care to guard himself against any possible suspicion that his settled principles of reverence for rank and respect for wealth were at all owing to mean or interested motives; for he asserted his own independence as a literary man. "No man (said he) who ever lived by literature, has lived more independently than I have done." He said he had taken longer time than he needed to have done in composing his Dictionary. He received our compliments upon that great work with complacency, and told us that the Academy *della Crusca* could scarcely believe that it was done by one man.

Next morning I found him alone, and have preserved the following fragments of his conversation. Of a gentleman who was mentioned, he said, "I have not met with any man for a long time who has given me such general displeasure. He is totally unfixed in his principles, and wants to puzzle other people." I said his principles had been poisoned by a noted infidel writer, but that he was, nevertheless, a benevolent good man. JOHNSON. "We can have no dependance upon that instinctive, that constitutional goodness which is not founded upon principle. I grant you that such a man may be a very amiable member of society. I can conceive him placed in such a situation that he is not much tempted to deviate from what is right; and as every man prefers virtue, when there is not some strong incitement to transgress its precepts, I can conceive him doing nothing wrong. But if such a man stood in need of money, I should not like to trust him; and I should certainly not trust him with young ladies, for *there* there is always temptation. Hume, and other sceptical innovators, are vain men, and will gratify themselves at any expense. Truth will not afford sufficient food to their vanity; so they have betaken themselves to error. Truth, Sir, is a cow which will yield such people no more milk, and so they are gone to milk the bull. If I could have allowed myself to gratify my vanity at the expense of truth, what fame might I have acquired. Everything which Hume has advanced against Christianity had passed through my mind long before he wrote. Always remember this, that after a system is well settled upon positive evidence, a few partial objections ought not to shake it. The human mind is so limited, that it cannot take in all the parts of a subject, so that there may be objections raised against any thing. There are objections against a *plenum*, and objections against a *vacuum;* yet one of them must certainly be true."

I mentioned Hume's argument against the belief of miracles, that it is more probable that the witnesses to the truth of them are mistaken, or speak falsely, than that the miracles should be true. JOHNSON. "Why, Sir, the great difficulty of proving miracles should make us very cautious in believing them. But let us consider; although GOD has made Nature to operate by certain fixed laws, yet it is not unreasonable to think that he may suspend those laws, in order to establish a system highly advantageous to mankind. Now the Christian religion is a most beneficial system, as it gives us light and certainty where we were before in darkness and doubt. The miracles which prove it are attested by men who had no interest in deceiving us; but who, on the contrary, were told that they should suffer persecution, and did actually lay down their lives in confirmation of the truth of the facts which they asserted. Indeed, for some centuries the heathens did not pretend to deny the miracles; but said they were performed by the aid of evil spirits. This is a circumstance of great weight. Then, Sir, when we take the proofs derived from prophecies which have been so exactly fulfilled, we have most satisfactory evidence. Supposing a miracle possible, as to which, in my opinion, there can be no doubt, we have as strong evidence for the miracles in support of Christianity, as the nature of the thing admits."

At night, Mr. Johnson and I supped in a private room at the Turk's Head coffee-house, in the Strand. "I encourage this house (said he) for the mistress of it is a good civil woman, and has not much business."

"Sir, I love the acquaintance of young people; because, in the first place, I don't like to think myself growing old. In the next place, young acquaintances must last longest, if they do last; and then, Sir, young men have more virtue than old men; they have more generous sentiments in every respect. I love the young dogs of this age, they have more wit and humor and knowledge of life than we had; but then the dogs are not so good scholars. Sir, in my early years I read very hard. It is a sad reflection but a true one, that I knew almost as much at eighteen as I do now. My judgment, to be sure, was not so good; but, I had all the facts. I remember very well, when I was at Oxford, an old gentleman said to me, 'Young man, ply your book diligently now, and acquire a stock of knowledge; for when years come upon you, you will find that poring upon books will be but an irksome task.' "

This account of his reading, given by himself in plain words, sufficiently confirms what I have already advanced upon the disputed question as to his application. It reconciles any seeming inconsistency in his way of talking upon it at different times; and shows that idleness and reading hard were with him relative terms, the import of which, as used by him, must be gathered from a comparison with what scholars of different degrees of ardor and assiduity have been known to do. And let it be remembered, that he was now talking spontaneously, and expressing his genuine sentiments; whereas at other times he might be induced, from his spirit of contradiction, or more properly from his love of argumentative contest, to speak lightly of his own application to study. It is pleasing to consider that the old gentleman's gloomy prophecy as to the irksomeness of books to men of an advanced age, which is too often fulfilled, was so far from being verified in Johnson, that his ardor for literature never failed, and his last writings had more ease and vivacity than any of his earlier productions.

He mentioned to me now, for the first time, that he had been distressed by melancholy, and for that reason had been obliged to fly from study and meditation, to the dissipating variety of life. Against melancholy he recommended constant occupation of mind, a great deal of exercise, moderation in eating and drinking, and especially to shun drinking at night. He said melancholy people were apt to fly to intemperance for relief, but that it sunk them much deeper in misery. He observed, that laboring men who work hard, and live sparingly, are seldom or never troubled with low spirits.

He again insisted on the duty of maintaining subordination of rank. "Sir, I would no more deprive a nobleman of his respect, than of his money. I consider myself as acting a part in the great system of society, and I do to others as I would have them to do to me. I would behave to a nobleman as I should expect he would behave to me, were I a nobleman and he Sam. Johnson. Sir, there is one Mrs. Macaulay in this town, a great republican. One day when I was at her house, I put on a very grave countenance, and said to her, 'Madam, I am now become a convert to your way of thinking. I am convinced that all mankind are upon an equal footing; and to give you an unquestionable proof, Madam, that I am in earnest, here is a very sensible, civil, well-behaved fellow-citizen, your footman; I desire that he may be allowed to sit down and dine with us.' I thus, Sir, showed her the absurdity of the leveling doctrine. She has never liked me since. Sir, your levelers wish to level *down* as far as themselves; but they cannot bear leveling *up* to themselves. They would all have some people under them; why not then have some people above them?" I mentioned a certain author who disgusted me by his forwardness, and by showing no deference to noblemen into whose company he was admitted. JOHNSON. "Suppose a shoemaker should claim an equality with him, as he does with a Lord: how he would stare. 'Why, Sir, do you stare? (says the shoemaker) I do great service to society. 'Tis true, I am paid for doing it; but so are you, Sir: and I am sorry to say it, better paid than I am, for doing something not so necessary. For mankind could do better without your books, than without my shoes.' Thus, Sir, there would be a perpetual struggle for precedence, were there no fixed invariable rules for the distinction of rank, which creates no jealousy, as it is allowed to be accidental."

He said, Dr. Joseph Warton was a very agreeable man, and his "Essay on the Genius and Writings of Pope," a very pleasing book. I wondered that he delayed so long to give us the continuation of it. JOHNSON. "Why, Sir, I suppose he finds himself a little disappointed, in not having been able to persuade the world to be of his opinion as to Pope."

We have now been favored with the concluding volume, in which, to use a parliamentary expression, he has *explained*, so as not to appear quite so adverse to the opinion of the world, concerning Pope, as was at first thought; and we must all agree, that his work is a most valuable accession to English literature.

A writer of deserved eminence being mentioned, Johnson said, "Why, Sir, he is a man of good parts, but being originally poor, he has got a love of mean company and low jocularity; a very bad thing, Sir. To laugh is good, and to talk is good. But you ought no more to think it enough if you laugh, than you are to think it enough if you talk. You may laugh in as many ways as you talk;

and surely *every* way of talking that is practiced cannot be esteemed."

I spoke of Sir James Macdonald as a young man of most distinguished merit, who united the highest reputation at Eton and Oxford, with the patriarchal spirit of a great Highland Chieftain. I mentioned that Sir James had said to me, that he had never seen Mr. Johnson, but he had a great respect for him, though at the same time it was mixed with some degree of terror. JOHNSON. "Sir, if he were to be acquainted with me, it might lessen both."

The mention of this gentleman led us to talk of the Western Islands of Scotland, to visit which he expressed a wish that then appeared to be a very romantic fancy, which I little thought would be afterwards realized. He told me, that his father had put Martin's account of those islands into his hands when he was very young, and that he was highly pleased with it; that he was particularly struck with the St. Kilda man's notion that the high church of Glasgow had been hollowed out of a rock; a circumstance to which old Mr. Johnson had directed his attention. He said, he would go to the Hebrides with me, when I returned from my travels, unless some very good companion should offer when I was absent, which he did not think probable; adding, "There are few people whom I take so much to, as you." And when I talked of my leaving England, he said with a very affectionate air, "My dear Boswell, I should be very unhappy at parting, did I think we were not to meet again."—I cannot too often remind my readers, that although such instances of his kindness are doubtless very flattering to me, yet I hope my recording them will be ascribed to a better motive than to vanity; for they afford unquestionable evidence of his tenderness and complacency, which some, while they were forced to acknowledge his great powers, have been so strenuous to deny.

He maintained that a boy at school was the happiest of human beings. I supported a different opinion, from which I have never yet varied, that a man is happier: and I enlarged upon the anxiety and sufferings which are endured at school. JOHNSON. "Ah! Sir, a boy's being flogged is not so severe as a man's having the hiss of the world against him. Men have a solicitude about fame; and the greater share they have of it, the more afraid they are of losing it." I silently asked myself, "Is it possible that the great SAMUEL JOHNSON really entertains any such apprehension, and is not confident that his exalted fame is established upon a foundation never to be shaken?"

He this evening drank a bumper to Sir David Dalrymple, "as a man of worth, a scholar, and a wit." "I have (said he) never heard of him, except from you; but let him know my opinion of him: for as he does not show himself much in the world, he should have the praise of the few who hear of him."

On Tuesday, July 26, I found Mr. Johnson alone. It was a very wet day, and I again complained of the disagreeable effects of such weather. JOHNSON. "Sir, this is all imagination, which physicians encourage; for man lives in air, as a fish lives in water, so that if the atmosphere press heavy from above, there is an equal resistance from below. To be sure, bad weather is hard upon people who are obliged to be abroad; and men cannot labor so well in the open air in bad weather, as in good: but, Sir, a smith or a tailor, whose work is within doors, will surely do as much in rainy weather, as in fair. Some very delicate frames, indeed, may be affected by wet weather; but not common constitutions."

We talked of the education of children; and I asked him what he thought was best to teach them first. JOHNSON. "Sir, it is no matter what you teach them first, any more than what leg you shall put into your breeches first. Sir, you may stand disputing which is best to put in first, but in the mean time your breech is bare. Sir, while you are considering which of two things you should teach your child first, another boy has learnt them both."

On Thursday, July 28, we again supped in private at the Turk's Head coffee-house. JOHNSON. "Swift has a higher reputation than he deserves. His excellence is strong sense; for his humor, though very well, is not remarkably good. I doubt whether the 'Tale of a Tub' be his; for he never owned it, and it is much above his usual manner."

"Thomson, I think, had as much of the poet about him as most writers. Everything appeared to him through the medium of his favorite pursuit. He could not have viewed those two candles burning but with a poetical eye."

"Has not —— a great deal of wit, Sir?" JOHNSON. "I do not think so, Sir. He is, indeed, continually attempting wit, but he fails. And I have no more pleasure in hearing a man attempting wit and failing, than in seeing a man trying to leap over a ditch and tumbling into it."

He laughed heartily when I mentioned to him a saying of his concerning Mr. Thomas Sheridan, which Foote took a wicked pleasure to circulate. "Why, Sir, Sherry is dull, naturally dull; but it must have taken him a great deal of pains to become what we now see him. Such an excess of stupidity, Sir, is not in Nature."— "So (said he) I allowed him all his own merit."

He now added, "Sheridan cannot bear me. I bring his declamation to a point. I ask him a plain question, 'What do you mean to teach?' Besides, Sir, what influence can Mr. Sheridan have upon the language of this great country, by his narrow exertions? Sir, it is burning a farthing candle at Dover, to show light at Calais."

Talking of a young man who was uneasy from thinking that he was very deficient in learning and knowledge, he said, "A man has no reason to complain who holds a middle place, and has many below him; and perhaps he has not six of his years above him;— perhaps not one. Though he may not know any thing perfectly, the general mass of knowledge that he has acquired is considerable. Time will do for him all that is wanting."

The conversation then took a philosophical turn. JOHNSON. "Human experience, which is constantly contradicting theory, is the great test of truth. A system, built upon the discoveries of a great many minds, is always of more strength, than what is produced by the mere workings of any one mind, which, of itself, can do little. There is not so poor a book in the world that would not be a prodigious effort were it wrought out entirely by a single mind, without the aid of prior investigators. The French writers are superficial, because they are not scholars, and so proceed upon the mere power of their own minds, and we see how very little power they have."

"As to the Christian religion, Sir, besides the strong evidence which we have for it, there is a balance in its favor from the number of great men who have been convinced of its truth, after a serious consideration of the question. Grotius was an acute man, a lawyer, a man accustomed to examine evidence, and he was convinced. Grotius was not a recluse, but a man of the world, who certainly had no bias to the side of religion. Sir Isaac Newton set out an infidel, and came to be a very firm believer."

He this evening again recommended to me to perambulate Spain. I said it would amuse him to get a letter from me dated at Sala·manca. JOHNSON. "I love the University of Salamanca; for when the Spaniards were in doubt as to the lawfulness of their conquering America, the University of Salamanca gave it as their opinion that it was not lawful." He spoke this with great emotion, and with that generous warmth which dictated the lines in his "London," against Spanish encroachment.

I expressed my opinion of my friend Derrick as but a poor writer. JOHNSON. "To be sure, Sir, he is; but you are to consider that his being a literary man has got for him all that he has. It has made him King of Bath. Sir, he has nothing to say for himself but that he is a writer. Had he not been a writer, he must have been sweeping the crossings in the streets, and asking halfpence from everybody that past."

In justice, however, to the memory of Mr. Derrick, who was my first tutor in the ways of London, and showed me the town in all its variety of departments, both literary and sportive, the particulars of which Dr. Johnson advised me to put in writing, it is proper to mention what Johnson, at a subsequent period, said of him both as a writer and an editor: "Sir, I have often said, that if Derrick's letters had been written by one of a more established name, they would have been thought very pretty letters." And, "I sent Derrick to Dryden's relations to gather materials for his life; and I believe he got all that I myself should have got."

Poor Derrick! I remember him with kindness. Yet I cannot withhold from my readers a pleasant humorous sally which could not have hurt him had he been alive, and now is perfectly harmless. In his collection of poems, there is one upon entering the harbor of Dublin, his native city, after a long absence. It begins thus:

"Eblana! much lov'd city, hail!
Where first I saw the light of day."

And after a solemn reflection on his being "numbered with forgotten dead," there is the following stanza:

"Unless my lines protract my fame,
And those, who chance to read them, cry,
I knew him! Derrick was his name,
In yonder tomb his ashes lie."

which was thus happily parodied by Mr. John Home, to whom we owe the beautiful and pathetic tragedy of "Douglas":

> "Unless my *deeds* protract my fame,
>   And he who passes sadly sings,
>   I knew him! Derrick was his name,
>   *On yonder tree his carcase swings!*"

I doubt much whether the amiable and ingenious author of these burlesque lines will recollect them; for they were produced extempore one evening while he and I were walking together in the dining-room at Eglingtoune Castle, in 1760, and I have never mentioned them to him since.

Johnson said once to me, "Sir, I honor Derrick for his presence of mind. One night, when Floyd, another poor author, was wandering about the streets in the night, he found Derrick fast asleep upon a bulk; upon being suddenly waked, Derrick started up, 'My dear Floyd, I am sorry to see you in this destitute state: will you go home with me to *my lodgings?*' "

I again begged his advice as to my method of study at Utrecht. "Come, (said he) let us make a day of it. Let us go down to Greenwich and dine, and talk of it there." The following Saturday was fixed for this excursion.

As we walked along the Strand to-night, arm in arm, a woman of the town accosted us, in the usual enticing manner. "No, no, my girl, (said Johnson) it won't do." He, however, did not treat her with harshness; and we talked of the wretched life of such women, and agreed, that much more misery than happiness, upon the whole, is produced by illicit commerce between the sexes.

On Saturday, July 30, Dr. Johnson and I took a sculler at the Temple-stairs, and set out for Greenwich. I asked him if he really thought a knowledge of the Greek and Latin languages an essential requisite to a good education. JOHNSON. "Most certainly, Sir; for those who know them have a very great advantage over those who do not. Nay, Sir, it is wonderful what a difference learning makes upon people even in the common intercourse of life, which does not appear to be much connected with it." "And yet, (said I) people go through the world very well, and carry on the business of life to good advantage, without learning." JOHNSON. "Why, Sir, that may be true in cases where learning cannot possibly be of any use; for instance, this boy rows us as well without learning, as if he could sing the song of Orpheus to the Argonauts, who were the first sailors." He then called to the boy, "What would you give, my lad, to know about the Argonauts?" "Sir, (said the boy) I would give what I have." Johnson was much pleased with his answer, and we gave him a double fare. Dr. Johnson then turning to me, "Sir, (said he) a desire of knowledge is the natural feeling of mankind; and every human being, whose mind is not debauched, will be willing to give all that he has, to get knowledge."

We landed at the Old Swan, and walked to Billingsgate, where we took oars and moved smoothly along the silver Thames. It was a very fine day. We were entertained with the immense number and variety of ships that were lying at anchor, and with the beautiful country on each side of the river.

I talked of preaching, and of the great success which those called Methodists have. JOHNSON. "Sir, it is owing to their expressing themselves in a plain and familiar manner, which is the only way to do good to the common people, and which clergymen of genius and learning ought to do from a principle of duty, when it is suited to their congregations; a practice, for which they will be praised by men of sense. To insist against drunkenness as a crime, because it debases reason, the noblest faculty of man, would be of no service to the common people; but to tell them that they may die in a fit of drunkenness, and show them how dreadful that would be, cannot fail to make a deep impression. Sir, when your Scotch clergy give up their homely manner, religion will soon decay in that country." Let this observation, as Johnson meant it, be ever remembered.

I was much pleased to find myself with Johnson at Greenwich, which he celebrates in his "London" as a favorite scene. I had the poem in my pocket, and read the lines aloud with enthusiasm:

> "On Thames's banks in silent thought we stood,
> Where Greenwich smiles upon the silver flood:
> Pleas'd with the seat which gave ELIZA birth,
> We kneel, and kiss the consecrated earth."

He remarked that the structure of Greenwich hospital was too magnificent for a place of charity, and that its parts were too much detached, to make one great whole.

Buchanan, he said, was a very fine poet; and observed, that he was the first who complimented a lady, by ascribing to her the different perfections of the heathen goddesses; but that Johnson improved upon this, by making his lady, at the same time, free from their defects.

He dwelt upon Buchanan's elegant verses to Mary, Queen of Scots, *Nympha Caledoniæ*, &c. and spoke with enthusiasm of the beauty of Latin verse. "All the modern languages (said he) cannot furnish so melodious a line as

"Formosam resonare doces Amarillida silvas."

Afterwards he entered upon the business of the day, which was to give me his advice as to a course of study. And here I am to mention with much regret, that my record of what he said is miserably scanty. I recollect with admiration an animating blaze of eloquence, which roused every intellectual power in me to the highest pitch, but must have dazzled me so much, that my memory could not preserve the substance of his discourse; for the note which I find of it is no more than this:—"He ran over the grand scale of human knowledge; advised me to select some particular branch to excel in, but to acquire a little of every kind." The defect of my minutes will be fully supplied by a long letter upon the subject, which he favored me with, after I had been some time at Utrecht, and which my readers will have the pleasure to peruse in its proper place.

We walked in the evening in Greenwich Park. He asked me, I suppose, by way of trying my disposition, "Is not this very fine?" Having no exquisite relish of the beauties of Nature, and being more delighted with "the busy hum of men," I answered, "Yes, Sir; but not equal to Fleet-street." JOHNSON. "You are right, Sir."

I am aware that many of my readers may censure my want of taste. Let me, however, shelter myself under the authority of a very fashionable Baronet in the brilliant world, who, on his attention being called to the fragrance of a May evening in the country, observed, "This may be very well; but for my part, I prefer the smell of a flambeau at the play-house."

We stayed so long at Greenwich, that our sail up the river, in our return to London, was by no means so pleasant as in the morning; for the night air was so cold that it made me shiver. I was the more sensible of it from having sat up all the night before recollecting and writing in my journal what I thought worthy of preservation; an exertion, which, during the first part of my acquaintance with Johnson, I frequently made. I remember having sat up four nights in one week, without being much incommoded in the day time.

Johnson, whose robust frame was not in the least affected by the cold, scolded me, as if my shivering had been a paltry effeminacy, saying, "Why do you shiver?" Sir William Scott, of the Commons, told me, that when he complained of a headache in the post-chaise, as they were traveling together to Scotland, Johnson treated him in the same manner: "At your age, Sir, I had no headache." It is not easy to make allowance for sensations in others, which we ourselves have not at the time. We must all have experienced how very differently we are affected by the complaints of our neighbors, when we are well and when we are ill. In full health, we can scarcely believe that they suffer much; so faint is the image of pain upon our imagination; when softened by sickness, we readily sympathize with the sufferings of others.

We concluded the day at the Turk's Head coffee-house very socially. He was pleased to listen to a particular account which I gave him of my family, and of its hereditary estate, as to the extent and population of which he asked questions, and made calculations; recommending, at the same time, a liberal kindness to the tenantry, as people over whom the proprietor was placed by Providence. He took delight in hearing my description of the romantic seat of my ancestors. "I must be there, Sir, (said he) and we will live in the old castle; and if there is not a room in it remaining, we will build one." I was highly flattered, but could scarcely indulge a hope that Auchinleck would indeed be honored by his presence, and celebrated by a description, as it afterwards was, in his "Journey to the Western Islands."

After we had again talked of my setting out for Holland, he said, "I must see thee out of England; I will accompany you to Harwich." I could not find words to express what I felt upon this unexpected and very great mark of his affectionate regard.

Next day, Sunday, July 31, I told him I had been that morning at a meeting of the people called Quakers, where I had heard a woman preach. JOHNSON. "Sir, a woman's preaching is like a dog's walking on his hind legs. It is not done well; but you are surprised to find it done at all."

On Tuesday, August 2, (the day of my departure from London having been fixed for the 5th) Dr. Johnson did me the honor to pass a part of the morning with me at my chambers. He said, that "he always felt an inclination to do nothing." I observed, that it was strange to think that the most indolent man in Britain had written the most laborious work, THE ENGLISH DICTIONARY.

I mentioned an imprudent publication, by a certain friend of his, at an early period of life, and asked him if he thought it would hurt him. JOHNSON. "No, Sir; not much. It may, perhaps, be mentioned at an election."

I had now made good my title to be a privileged man, and was carried by him in the evening to drink tea with Miss Williams, whom, though under the misfortune of having lost her sight, I found to be agreeable in conversation; for she had a variety of literature, and expressed herself well; but her peculiar value was the intimacy in which she had long lived with Johnson, by which she was well acquainted with his habits, and knew how to lead him on to talk.

After tea he carried me to what he called his walk, which was a long narrow paved court in the neighborhood, overshadowed by some trees. There we sauntered a considerable time; and I complained to him that my love of London and of his company was such, that I shrunk almost from the thought of going away even to travel, which is generally so much desired by young men. He roused me by manly and spirited conversation. He advised me, when settled in any place abroad, to study with an eagerness after knowledge, and to apply to Greek an hour every day; and when I was moving about, to read diligently the great book of mankind.

On Wednesday, August 3, we had our last social evening at the Turk's Head coffee-house, before my setting out for foreign parts. I had the misfortune, before we parted, to irritate him unintentionally. I mentioned to him how common it was in the world to tell absurd stories of him, and to ascribe to him very strange sayings. JOHNSON. "What do they make me say, Sir?" BOSWELL. "Why, Sir, as an instance very strange indeed, (laughing heartily as I spoke) David Hume told me, you said that you would stand before a battery of cannon to restore the Convocation to its full powers."— Little did I apprehend that he had actually said this: but I was soon convinced of my error; for, with a determined look, he thundered out, "And would I not, Sir? Shall the Presbyterian *Kirk* of Scotland have its General Assembly, and the Church of England be denied its Convocation?" He was walking up and down the room, while I told him the anecdote; but when he uttered this explosion of high-church zeal, he had come close to my chair, and his eye flashed with indignation. I bowed to the storm, and diverted the force of it, by leading him to expatiate on the influence which religion derived from maintaining the church with great external respectability.

I must not omit to mention that he this year wrote "The Life of Ascham," and the Dedication to the Earl of Shaftesbury, prefixed to the edition of that writer's English works, published by Mr. Bennet.

On Friday, August 5, we set out early in the morning in the Harwich stage-coach. A fat elderly gentlewoman, and a young Dutchman, seemed the most inclined among us to conversation. At the inn where we dined, the gentlewoman said that she had done her best to educate her children; and, particularly, that she had never suffered them to be a moment idle. JOHNSON. "I wish, Madam, you would educate me too; for I have been an idle fellow all my life." "I am sure, Sir, (said she) you have not been idle." JOHNSON. "Nay, Madam, it is very true; and that gentleman there, (pointing to me) has been idle. He was idle at Edinburgh. His father sent him to Glasgow, where he continued to be idle. He then came to London, where he has been very idle; and now he is going to Utrecht, where he will be as idle as ever." I asked him privately how he could expose me so. JOHNSON. "Poh, poh! (said he) they knew nothing about you, and will think of it no more." In the afternoon the gentlewoman talked violently against the Roman Catholics, and of the horrors of the Inquisition. To the utter astonishment of all the passengers but myself, who knew that he could talk upon any side of a question, he defended the Inquisition, and maintained, that "false doctrine should be checked on its first appearance; that the civil power should unite with the church in punishing those who dare to attack the established religion, and that such only were punished by the Inquisition." He had in his pocket *Pomponius Mela de Situ Orbis*, in which he read occasionally, and seemed very intent upon ancient geography. Though by no means niggardly, his attention to what was generally right was so minute, that having observed at one of the stages that I ostentatiously gave a shilling to the coachman, when the custom was for each passenger to give only six-pence, he took me aside and scolded me, saying that what I had done would make the coachman dissatisfied with all the rest of the passengers who gave him no more than his due. This was a just reprimand; for in whatever way a man may indulge his generosity or his vanity in spending his money, for the sake of others he ought not to raise the price of any article for which there is a constant demand.

He talked of Mr. Blacklock's poetry, so far as it was descriptive of visible objects; and observed, that "as its author had the misfortune to be blind, we may be absolutely sure that such passages are combinations of what he has remembered of the works of other writers who could see. That foolish fellow, Spence, has labored to explain philosophically how Blacklock may have done, by means of his own faculties, what it is impossible he should do. The solution, as I have given it, is plain. Suppose, I know a man to be so lame that he is absolutely incapable to move himself, and I find him in a different room from that in which I left him; shall I puzzle myself with idle conjectures, that, perhaps, his nerves have by some unknown change all at once become effective? No, Sir, it is clear how he got into a different room: he was *carried*."

Having stopped a night at Colchester, Johnson talked of that town with veneration, for having stood a siege for Charles the First. The Dutchman alone now remained with us. He spoke English tolerably well; and thinking to recommend himself to us by expatiating on the superiority of the criminal jurisprudence of this country over that of Holland, he inveighed against the barbarity of putting an accused person to the torture, in order to force a confession. But Johnson was as ready for this, as for the Inquisition. "Why, Sir, you do not, I find, understand the law of your own country. To torture in Holland is considered as a favor to an accused person; for no man is put to the torture there, unless there is as much evidence against him as would amount to conviction in England. An accused person among you, therefore, has one chance more to escape punishment, than those who are tried among us."

At supper this night he talked of good eating with uncommon satisfaction. "Some people (said he) have a foolish way of not minding, or pretending not to mind, what they eat. For my part, I mind my belly very studiously, and very carefully; for I look upon it, that he who does not mind his belly, will hardly mind any thing else." He now appeared to me *Jean Bull philosophe*, and he was for the moment, not only serious, but vehement. Yet I have heard him, upon other occasions, talk with great contempt of people who were anxious to gratify their palates; and the 206th number of his Rambler is a masterly essay against gulosity. His practice, indeed, I must acknowledge, may be considered as casting the balance of his different opinions upon this subject; for I never knew any man who relished good eating more than he did. When at table, he was totally absorbed in the business of the moment; his looks seemed riveted to his plate; nor would he, unless when in very high company, say one word, or even pay the least attention to what was said by others, till he had satisfied his appetite: which was so fierce, and indulged with such intenseness, that while in the act of eating, the veins of his forehead swelled, and generally a strong perspiration was visible. To those whose sensations were delicate, this could not but be disgusting; and it was doubtless not very suitable to the character of a philosopher, who should be distinguished by self-command. But it must be owned, that Johnson, though he could be rigidly *abstemious*, was not a *temperate* man either in eating or drinking. He could refrain, but he could not use moderately. He told me, that he had fasted two days without inconvenience, and that he had never been hungry but once. They who beheld with wonder how much he eat upon all occasions, when his dinner was to his taste, could not easily conceive what he must have meant by hunger; and not only was he remarkable for the extraordinary quantity which he eat but he was, or affected to be, a man of very nice discernment in the science of cookery. He used to descant critically on the dishes which had been at table where he had dined or supped, and to recollect very minutely what he had liked. I remember when he was in Scotland, his praising "*Gordon's palates*" (a dish of palates at the Honorable Alexander Gordon's) with a warmth of expression which might have done honor to more important subjects. "As for Maclaurin's imitation of a *made dish*, it was a wretched attempt." He about the same time was so much displeased with the performances of a nobleman's French cook, that he exclaimed with vehemence, "I'd throw such a rascal into the river"; and he then proceeded to alarm a lady at whose house he was to sup, by the following manifesto of his skill: "I, Madam, who live at a variety of good tables, am a much better judge of cookery than any person who has a very tolerable cook, but lives much at home; for his palate is gradually adapted to the taste of his cook: whereas, Madam, in trying by a wider range, I can more exquisitely judge." When invited to dine, even with an intimate friend, he was not pleased if something better than a plain dinner was not prepared for him. I have heard him say on such an occasion, "This was a good dinner enough, to be sure: but it was not a dinner to *ask* a man to." On the other hand, he was wont to express, with great glee, his satisfaction when he had been entertained quite to his mind. One day when he had dined with his neighbor and landlord, in Bolt-court, Mr. Allen, the printer, whose old housekeeper had studied his taste in every thing, he pronounced this eulogy: "Sir, we could not have had a better dinner, had there been a *Synod of Cooks*."

While we were left by ourselves, after the Dutchman had gone to bed, Dr. Johnson talked of that studied behavior which many have recommended and practiced. He disapproved of it; and said, "I never considered whether I should be a grave man, or a merry man, but just let inclination, for the time, have its course."

He flattered me with some hopes that he would, in the course of the following summer, come over to Holland, and accompany me in a tour through the Netherlands.

I teased him with fanciful apprehensions of unhappiness. A moth having fluttered round the candle, and burned itself, he laid hold of this little incident to admonish me; saying, with a sly look, and in a solemn but a quiet tone, "That creature was its own tormentor, and I believe its name was BOSWELL."

Next day we got to Harwich, to dinner; and my passage in the packet-boat to Helvoetsluys being secured, and my baggage put on board, we dined at our inn by ourselves. I happened to say, it would be terrible if he should not find a speedy opportunity of returning to London, and be confined in so dull a place. JOHNSON. "Don't, Sir, accustom yourself to use big words for little matters. It would *not* be *terrible*, though I *were* to be detained some time here." The practice of using words of disproportionate magnitude, is, no doubt, too frequent every where; but, I think, most remarkable among the French, of which, all who have traveled in France must have been struck with innumerable instances.

We went and looked at the church, and having gone into it, and walked up to the altar, Johnson, whose piety was constant and fervent, sent me to my knees, saying, "Now that you are going to leave your native country, recommend yourself to the protection of your CREATOR and REDEEMER."

After we came out of the church, we stood talking for some

time together of Bishop Berkeley's ingenious sophistry to prove the non-existence of matter, and that every thing in the universe is merely ideal. I observed, that though we are satisfied his doctrine is not true, it is impossible to refute it. I never shall forget the alacrity with which Johnson answered, striking his foot with mighty force against a large stone, till he rebounded from it,—"I refute it *thus*." This was a stout exemplification of the *first truths of Pere Bouffier*, or the *original principles* of Reid and of Beattie; without admitting which, we can no more argue in metaphysics, than we can argue in mathematics without axioms. To me it is not conceivable how Berkeley can be answered by pure reasoning; but I know that the nice and difficult task was to have been undertaken by one of the most luminous minds of the present age, had not politics "turned him from calm philosophy aside." What an admirable display of subtlety, united with brilliance, might his contending with Berkeley have afforded us! How must we, when we reflect on the loss of such an intellectual feast, regret that he should be characterized as the man,

Class   dec 13th "Who born for the universe narrow'd his mind,
         And to party gave up what was meant for mankind?"

My revered friend walked down with me to the beach, where we embraced and parted with tenderness, and engaged to correspond by letters. I said, "I hope, Sir, you will not forget me in my absence." JOHNSON. "Nay, Sir, it is more likely you should forget me, than that I should forget you." As the vessel put out to sea, I kept my eyes upon him for a considerable time, while he remained rolling his majestic frame in his usual manner; and at last I perceived him walk back into the town, and he disappeared. . . .

majestic constantly used

1765: Aetat. 56

This year was distinguished by his being introduced into the family of Mr. Thrale, one of the most eminent brewers in England, and member of Parliament for the borough of Southwark. Foreigners are not a little amazed, when they hear of brewers, distillers, and men in similar departments of trade, held forth as persons of considerable consequence. In this great commercial country it is natural that a situation which produces much wealth should be considered as very respectable; and, no doubt, honest industry is entitled to esteem. But, perhaps, the too rapid advances of men of low extraction tends to lessen the value of that distinction by birth and gentility, which has ever been found beneficial to the grand scheme of subordination. Johnson used to give this account of the rise of Mr. Thrale's father: "He worked at six shillings a week for twenty years in the great brewery, which afterwards was his own. The proprietor of it had an only daughter, who was married to a nobleman. It was not fit that a peer should continue the business. On the old man's death, therefore, the brewery was to be sold. To find a purchaser for so large a property was a difficult matter; and, after some time, it was suggested, that it would be advisable to treat with Thrale, a sensible, active, honest man, who had been employed in the house, and to transfer the whole to him for thirty thousand pounds, security being taken upon the property. This was accordingly settled. In eleven years Thrale paid the purchase-money. He acquired a large fortune, and lived to be a member of Parliament for Southwark. But what was most remarkable was the liberality with which he used his riches. He gave his son and daughters the best education. The esteem which his good conduct procured him from the nobleman who had married his master's daughter, made him to be treated with much attention; and his son, both at school and at the University of Oxford, associated with young men of the first rank. His allowance from his father, after he left college, was splendid; not less than a thousand a year. This, in a man who had risen as old Thrale did, was a very extraordinary instance of generosity. He used to say, 'If this young dog does not find so much after I am gone as he expects, let him remember that he has had a great deal in my own time.' "

The son, though in affluent circumstances, had good sense enough to carry on his father's trade, which was of such extent that I remember he once told me, he would not quit it for an annuity of ten thousand a year; "Not (said he) that I get ten thousand a year by it, but it is an estate to a family." Having left daughters only, the property was sold for the immense sum of one hundred and thirty-five thousand pounds; a magnificent proof of what may be done by fair trade in a long period of time.

There may be some who think that a new system of gentility might be established, upon principles totally different from what have hitherto prevailed. Our present heraldry, it may be said, is suited to the barbarous times in which it had its origin. It is chiefly founded upon ferocious merit, upon military excellence. Why, in civilized times, we may be asked, should there not be rank and honors upon principles, which, independent of long custom, are certainly not less worthy, and which, when once allowed to be connected with elevation and precedency, would obtain the same dignity in our imagination? Why should not the knowledge, the skill, the expertness, the assiduity, and the spirited hazards of trade and commerce, when crowned with success, be entitled to give those flattering distinctions by which mankind are so universally captivated?

Such are the specious, but false, arguments for a proposition which always will find numerous advocates, in a nation where men are every day starting up from obscurity to wealth. To refute them is needless. The general sense of mankind cries out, with irresistible force, "Un gentilhomme est toujours gentilhomme."

Mr. Thrale had married Miss Hester Lynch Salusbury, of good Welch extraction, a lady of lively talents, improved by education. That Johnson's introduction into Mr. Thrale's family, which contributed so much to the happiness of his life, was owing to her desire for his conversation, is a very probable and the general supposition: but it is not the truth. Mr. Murphy, who was intimate with Mr. Thrale, having spoken very highly of Dr. Johnson, he was requested to make them acquainted. This being mentioned to Johnson, he accepted of an invitation to dinner at Thrale's, and was so much pleased with his reception, both by Mr. and Mrs. Thrale, and they so much pleased with him, that his invitations to their house were more and more frequent, till at last he became one of the family, and an apartment was appropriated to him, both in their house at Southwark and in their villa at Streatham.

Johnson had a very sincere esteem for Mr. Thrale, as a man of excellent principles, a good scholar, well skilled in trade, of a sound understanding, and of manners such as presented the character of a plain independent English squire. As this family will frequently be mentioned in the course of the following pages, and as a false notion has prevailed that Mr. Thrale was inferior, and in some degree insignificant, compared with Mrs. Thrale, it may be proper to give a true state of the case from the authority of Johnson himself in his own words.

"I know no man, (said he) who is more master of his wife and family than Thrale. If he but holds up a finger, he is obeyed. It is a great mistake to suppose that she is above him in literary attainments. She is more flippant; but he has ten times her learning: he is a regular scholar; but her learning is that of a school-boy in one of the lower forms." My readers may naturally wish for some representation of the figures of this couple. Mr. Thrale was tall, well proportioned, and stately. As for *Madam*, or *my Mistress*, by which epithets Johnson used to mention Mrs. Thrale, she was short, plump, and brisk. She has herself given us a lively view of the idea which Johnson had of her person, on her appearing before him in a dark-colored gown: "You little creatures should never wear those sort of clothes, however; they are unsuitable in every way. What! have not all insects gay colors!" Mr. Thrale gave his wife a liberal indulgence, both in the choice of their company, and in the mode of entertaining them. He understood and valued Johnson, without remission, from their first acquaintance to the day of his death. Mrs. Thrale was enchanted with Johnson's conversation for its own sake, and had also a very allowable vanity in appearing to be honored with the attention of so celebrated a man.

Nothing could be more fortunate for Johnson than this connection. He had at Mr. Thrale's all the comforts and even luxuries of life: his melancholy was diverted, and his irregular habits lessened by association with an agreeable and well ordered family. He was treated with the utmost respect, and even affection. The vivacity of Mrs. Thrale's literary talk roused him to cheerfulness and exertion, even when they were alone. But this was not often the case; for he found here a constant succession of what gave him the highest enjoyment: the society of the learned, the witty, and the eminent in every way, who were assembled in numerous companies, called forth his wonderful powers, and gratified him with admiration, to which no man could be insensible. . . .

1776: Aetat. 67

I am now to record a very curious incident in Dr. Johnson's life, which fell under my own observation; of which *pars magna fui*, and which I am persuaded will, with the liberal-minded, be much to his credit.

My desire of being acquainted with celebrated men of every description, had made me, much about the same time, obtain an introduction to Dr. Samuel Johnson and to John Wilkes, Esq. Two men more different could perhaps not be selected out of all mankind. They had even attacked one another with some asperity in their writings; yet I lived in habits of friendship with both. I could fully relish the excellence of each; for I have ever delighted in that intellectual chemistry, which can separate good qualities from evil in the same person.

Sir John Pringle, "mine own friend and my Father's friend," between whom and Dr. Johnson I in vain wished to establish an acquaintance, as I respected and lived in intimacy with both of them, observed to me once, very ingeniously, "It is not in friendship as in mathematics, where two things, each equal to a third, are equal between themselves. You agree with Johnson as a middle quality, and you agree with me as a middle quality; but Johnson and I should not agree." Sir John was not sufficiently flexible; so I desisted; knowing, indeed, that the repulsion was equally strong on the part of Johnson; who, I know not from what cause, unless his being a Scotchman, had formed a very erroneous opinion of Sir John. But I conceived an irresistible wish, if possible, to bring Dr. Johnson and Mr. Wilkes together. How to manage it, was a nice and difficult matter.

My worthy booksellers and friends, Messieurs Dilly in the Poultry, at whose hospitable and well-covered table I have seen a greater number of literary men, than at any other, except that of Sir Joshua Reynolds, had invited me to meet Mr. Wilkes and some more gentlemen, on Wednesday, May 15. "Pray (said I) let us have Dr. Johnson."—"What with Mr. Wilkes? not for the world, (said Mr. Edward Dilly) Dr. Johnson would never forgive me." —"Come, (said I) if you'll let me negotiate for you, I will be answerable that all shall go well." DILLY. "Nay, if you will take it upon you, I am sure I shall be very happy to see them both here."

Notwithstanding the high veneration which I entertained for Dr. Johnson, I was sensible that he was sometimes a little actuated by the spirit of contradiction, and by means of that I hoped I should gain my point. I was persuaded that if I had come upon him with a direct proposal, "Sir, will you dine in company with Jack Wilkes?" he would have flown into a passion, and would probably have answered, "Dine with Jack Wilkes, Sir! I'd as soon dine with Jack Ketch." I therefore, while we were sitting quietly by ourselves at his house in an evening, took occasion to open my plan thus:—"Mr. Dilly, Sir, sends his respectful compliments to you, and would be happy if you would do him the honor to dine with him on Wednesday next along with me, as I must soon go to Scotland." JOHNSON. "Sir, I am obliged to Mr. Dilly. I will wait upon him—" BOSWELL. "Provided, Sir, I suppose, that the company which he is to have, is agreeable to you." JOHNSON. "What do you mean, Sir? What do you take me for? Do you think I am so ignorant of the world, as to imagine that I am to prescribe to a gentleman what company he is to have at his table?" BOSWELL. "I beg your pardon, Sir, for wishing to prevent you from meeting people whom you might not like. Perhaps he may have some of what he calls his patriotic friends with him." JOHNSON. "Well, Sir, and what then? What care I for his *patriotic friends?* Poh!" BOSWELL. "I should not be surprised to find Jack Wilkes there." JOHNSON. "And if Jack Wilkes *should* be there, what is that to *me,* Sir? My dear friend, let us have no more of this. I am sorry to be angry with you; but really it is treating me strangely to talk to me as if I could not meet any company whatever, occasionally." BOSWELL. "Pray, forgive me, Sir: I meant well. But you shall meet whoever comes, for me." Thus I secured him, and told Dilly that he would find him very well pleased to be one of his guests on the day appointed.

Upon the much-expected Wednesday, I called on him about half an hour before dinner, as I often did when we were to dine out together, to see that he was ready in time, and to accompany him. I found him buffeting his books, as upon a former occasion, covered with dust, and making no preparation for going abroad. "How is this, Sir? (said I). Don't you recollect that you are to dine at Mr. Dilly's?" JOHNSON. "Sir, I did not think of going to Dilly's: it went out of my head. I have ordered dinner at home with Mrs. Williams." BOSWELL. "But, my dear Sir, you know you were engaged to Mr. Dilly, and I told him so. He will expect you, and will be much disappointed if you don't come." JOHNSON. "You must talk to Mrs. Williams about this."

Here was a sad dilemma. I feared that what I was so confident I had secured, would yet be frustrated. He had accustomed himself to show Mrs. Williams such a degree of humane attention, as frequently imposed some restraint upon him; and I knew that if she should be obstinate, he would not stir. I hastened down stairs to the blind lady's room, and told her I was in great uneasiness, for Dr. Johnson had engaged to me to dine this day at Mr. Dilly's, but that he had told me he had forgotten his engagement, and had ordered dinner at home. "Yes, Sir, (said she, pretty peevishly) Dr.

Johnson is to dine at home."—"Madam, (said I) his respect for you is such, that I know he will not leave you, unless you absolutely desire it. But as you have so much of his company, I hope you will be good enough to forego it for a day: as Mr. Dilly is a very worthy man, has frequently had agreeable parties at his house for Dr. Johnson, and will be vexed if the Doctor neglects him to-day. And then, Madam, be pleased to consider my situation; I carried the message, and I assured Mr. Dilly that Dr. Johnson was to come; and no doubt he has made a dinner, and invited a company, and boasted of the honor he expected to have. I shall be quite disgraced if the Doctor is not there." She gradually softened to my solicitations, which were certainly as earnest as most entreaties to ladies upon any occasion, and was graciously pleased to empower me to tell Dr. Johnson, "That all things considered, she thought he should certainly go." I flew back to him, still in dust, and careless of what should be the event, "indifferent in his choice to go or stay"; but as soon as I had announced to him Mrs. Williams's consent, he roared, "Frank, a clean shirt," and was very soon dressed. When I had him fairly seated in a hackney-coach with me, I exulted as much as a fortune-hunter who has got an heiress into a post-chaise with him to set out for Gretna-Green.

When we entered Mr. Dilly's drawing-room, he found himself in the midst of a company he did not know. I kept myself snug and silent, watching how he would conduct himself. I observed him whispering to Mr. Dilly, "Who is that gentleman, Sir?"—"Mr. Arthur Lee."—JOHNSON. "Too, too, too," (under his breath) which was one of his habitual mutterings. Mr. Arthur Lee could not but be very obnoxious to Johnson, for he was not only a *patriot*, but an *American*. He was afterwards minister from the United States at the court of Madrid. "And who is the gentleman in lace?"—"Mr. Wilkes, Sir." This information confounded him still more; he had some difficulty to restrain himself, and taking up a book, sat down upon a window-seat and read, or at least kept his eye upon it intently for some time, till he composed himself. His feelings, I dare say, were awkward enough. But he no doubt recollected his having rated me for supposing that he could be at all disconcerted by any company, and he, therefore, resolutely set himself to behave quite as an easy man of the world, who could adapt himself at once to the disposition and manners of those whom he might chance to meet.

The cheering sound of "Dinner is upon the table," dissolved his reverie, and we *all* sat down without any symptom of ill humor. There were present, beside Mr. Wilkes, and Mr. Arthur Lee, who was an old companion of mine when he studied physic at Edinburgh, Mr. (now Sir John) Miller, Dr. Lettsom, and Mr. Slater, the druggist. Mr. Wilkes placed himself next to Dr. Johnson, and behaved to him with so much attention and politeness, that he gained upon him insensibly. No man eat more heartily than Johnson, or loved better what was nice and delicate. Mr. Wilkes was very assiduous in helping him to some fine veal. "Pray give me leave, Sir;—It is better here—A little of the brown—Some fat, Sir—A little of the stuffing—Some gravy—Let me have the pleasure of giving you some butter—Allow me to recommend a squeeze of this orange;—or the lemon, perhaps, may have more zest."— "Sir, Sir, I am obliged to you, Sir," cried Johnson, bowing, and turning his head to him with a look for some time of "surly virtue," [10] but, in a short while, of complacency.

Foote being mentioned, Johnson said, "He is not a good mimic." One of the company added, "A merry Andrew, a buffoon." JOHNSON. "But he has wit too, and is not deficient in ideas, or in fertility and variety of imagery, and not empty of reading; he has knowledge enough to fill up his part. One species of wit he has in an eminent degree, that of escape. You drive him into a corner with both hands; but he's gone, Sir, when you think you have got him —like an animal that jumps over your head. Then he has a great range for wit; he never lets truth stand between him and a jest, and he is sometimes mighty coarse. Garrick is under many restraints from which Foote is free." WILKES. "Garrick's wit is more like Lord Chesterfield's." JOHNSON. "The first time I was in company with Foote was at Fitzherbert's. Having no good opinion of the fellow, I was resolved not to be pleased; and it is very difficult to please a man against his will. I went on eating my dinner pretty sullenly, affecting not to mind him. But the dog was so very comical, that I was obliged to lay down my knife and fork, throw myself back upon my chair, and fairly laugh it out. No, Sir, he was irresistible. He upon one occasion experienced, in an extraordinary degree, the efficacy of his powers of entertaining. Amongst the many and various modes which he tried of getting money, he became a partner with a small-beer brewer, and he was to have a

10 Johnson's "London, a Poem," v. 145.

share of the profits for procuring customers amongst his numerous acquaintance. Fitzherbert was one who took his small-beer; but it was so bad that the servants resolved not to drink it. They were at some loss how to notify their resolution, being afraid of offending their master, who they knew liked Foote much as a companion. At last they fixed upon a little black boy, who was rather a favorite, to be their deputy, and deliver their remonstrance; and having invested him with the whole authority of the kitchen, he was to inform Mr. Fitzherbert, in all their names, upon a certain day, that they would drink Foote's small-beer no longer. On that day Foote happened to dine at Fitzherbert's, and this boy served at table; he was so delighted with Foote's stories, and merriment, and grimace, that when he went down stairs, he told them, 'This is the finest man I have ever seen. I will not deliver your message. I will drink his small-beer.' "

Somebody observed that Garrick could not have done this. WILKES. "Garrick would have made the small-beer still smaller. He is now leaving the stage; but he will play *Scrub* all his life." I knew that Johnson would let nobody attack Garrick but himself, as Garrick said to me, and I had heard him praise his liberality; so to bring out his commendation of his celebrated pupil, I said, loudly, "I have heard Garrick is liberal." JOHNSON. "Yes, Sir, I know that Garrick has given away more money than any man in England that I am acquainted with, and that not from ostentatious views. Garrick was very poor when he began life; so when he came to have money, he probably was very unskillful in giving away, and saved when he should not. But Garrick began to be liberal as soon as he could; and I am of opinion, the reputation of avarice which he has had, has been very lucky for him, and prevented his having many enemies. You despise a man for avarice, but do not hate him. Garrick might have been much better attacked for living with more splendor than is suitable to a player: if they had had the wit to have assaulted him in that quarter, they might have galled him more. But they have kept clamoring about his avarice, which has rescued him from much obloquy and envy."

Talking of the great difficulty of obtaining authentic information for biography, Johnson told us, "When I was a young fellow I wanted to write the 'Life of Dryden,' and in order to get materials, I applied to the only two persons then alive who had seen him; these were old Swinney, and old Cibber. Swinney's information was no more than this, 'That at Will's coffee-house Dryden had a particular chair for himself, which was set by the fire in winter, and was then called his winter-chair; and that it was carried out for him to the balcony in summer, and was then called his summer-chair.' Cibber could tell no more but 'That he remembered him a decent old man, arbiter of critical disputes at Will's.' You are to consider that Cibber was then at a great distance from Dryden, had perhaps one leg only in the room, and durst not draw in the other." BOSWELL. "Yet Cibber was a man of observation?" JOHNSON. "I think not." BOSWELL. "You will allow his 'Apology' to be well done." JOHNSON. "Very well done, to be sure, Sir. That book is a striking proof of the justice of Pope's remark:

'Each might his several province well command,
Would all but stoop to what they understand.'"

BOSWELL. "And his plays are good." JOHNSON. "Yes; but that was his trade; l'esprit du corps; he had been all his life among players and play-writers. I wondered that he had so little to say in conversation, for he had kept the best company, and learned all that can be got by the ear. He abused Pindar to me, and then showed me an ode of his own, with an absurd couplet, making a linnet soar on an eagle's wing. I told him that when the ancients made a simile, they always made it like something real."

Mr. Wilkes remarked, that "among all the bold flights of Shakespeare's imagination, the boldest was making Birnam Wood march to Dunsinane; creating a wood where there never was a shrub; a wood in Scotland! ha! ha! ha!" And he also observed, that "the clannish slavery of the Highlands of Scotland was the single exception to Milton's remark of 'The Mountain Nymph, sweet Liberty,' being worshiped in all hilly countries."—"When I was at Inverary (said he) on a visit to my old friend Archibald, Duke of Argyle, his dependents congratulated me on being such a favorite of his Grace. I said, 'It is then, gentlemen, truly lucky for me; for if I had displeased the Duke, and he had wished it, there is not a Campbell among you but would have been ready to bring John Wilkes's head to him in a charger. It would have been only

"Off with his head! so much for Aylesbury."'

I was then member for Aylesbury."

Dr. Johnson and Mr. Wilkes talked of the contested passage in

Horace's Art of Poetry, "*Difficile est propriè communia dicere.*"
Mr. Wilkes, according to my note, gave the interpretation thus:
"It is difficult to speak with propriety of common things; as, if a
poet had to speak of Queen Caroline drinking tea, he must endeavor to avoid the vulgarity of cups and saucers." But upon reading my note, he tells me that he meant to say, that "the word *communia*, being a Roman law-term, signifies here things *communis
juris*, that is to say, what have never yet been treated by any body;
and this appears clearly from what followed,

> '———Tuque
> Rectiùs Iliacum carmen deducis in actus
> Quàm si proferres ignota indictaque primus.'

You will easier make a tragedy out of the Iliad than on any subject not handled before." JOHNSON. "He means that it is difficult
to appropriate to particular persons qualities which are common
to all mankind, as Homer has done."

WILKES. "We have no City-Poet now: that is an office which has
gone into disuse. The last was Elkanah Settle. There is something
in *names* which one cannot help feeling. Now *Elkanah Settle*
sounds so *queer*, who can expect much from that name? We should
have no hesitation to give it for John Dryden, in preference to
Elkanah Settle, from the names only, without knowing their different merits." JOHNSON. "I suppose, Sir, Settle did as well for
Aldermen in his time, as John Home could do now. Where did
Beckford, and Trecothick learn English?"

Mr. Arthur Lee mentioned some Scotch who had taken possession of a barren part of America, and wondered why they
should choose it. JOHNSON. "Why, Sir, all barrenness is comparative. The *Scotch* would not know it to be barren." BOSWELL.
"Come, come, he is flattering the English. You have now been in
Scotland, Sir, and say if you did not see meat and drink enough
there." JOHNSON. "Why yes, Sir; meat and drink enough to give
the inhabitants sufficient strength to run away from home." All
these quick and lively sallies were said sportively, quite in jest, and
with a smile, which showed that he meant only wit. Upon this
topic he and Mr. Wilkes could perfectly assimilate; here was a
bond of union between them, and I was conscious that as both of
them had visited Caledonia, both were fully satisfied of the strange

Dr. Samuel Johnson
An engraving from the painting
by Sir Joshua Reynolds

Samuel Johnson and James Boswell
Contemporary cartoon

Vauxhall Garden, Famous Rotunda with Madam Weichesel Singing. Supper box, left, Boswell, Johnson, Mrs. Thrale

narrow ignorance of those who imagine that it is a land of famine. But they amused themselves with persevering in the old jokes. When I claimed a superiority for Scotland over England in one respect, that no man can be arrested there for a debt merely because another swears it against him; but there must first be the judgment of a court of law ascertaining its justice; and that a seizure of the person, before judgment is obtained, can take place only, if his creditor should swear that he is about to fly from the country, or, as it is technically expressed, is *in meditatione fugæ:* WILKES. "That, I should think, may be safely sworn of all the Scotch nation." JOHNSON. (To Mr. Wilkes) "You must know, Sir. I lately took my friend Boswell, and showed him genuine civilized life in an English provincial town. I turned him loose at Lichfield, my native city, that he might see for once real civility: for you know he lives among savages in Scotland, and among rakes in London." WILKES. "Except when he is with grave, sober, decent people, like you and me." JOHNSON. (smiling) "And we ashamed of him."

They were quite frank and easy. Johnson told the story of his asking Mrs. Macaulay to allow her footman to sit down with them, to prove the ridiculousness of the arguments for the equality of mankind; and he said to me afterwards, with a nod of satisfaction, "You saw Mr. Wilkes acquiesced." Wilkes talked with all imaginable freedom of the ludicrous title given to the Attorney-General, *Diabolus Regis;* adding, "I have reason to know something about that officer; for I was prosecuted for a libel." Johnson, who many people would have supposed must have been furiously angry at hearing this talked of so lightly, said not a word. He was now, *indeed,* "a good-humored fellow."

After dinner we had an accession of Mrs. Knowles, the Quaker lady, well known for her various talents, and of Mr. Alderman Lee. Amidst some patriotic groans, somebody (I think the Alderman) said, "Poor old England is lost." JOHNSON. "Sir, it is not so much to be lamented that old England is lost, as that the Scotch have found it." WILKES. "Had Lord Bute governed Scotland only, I should not have taken the trouble to write his eulogy, and dedicate 'MORTIMER' to him."

Mr. Wilkes held a candle to show a fine print of a beautiful female figure which hung in the room, and pointed out the elegant contour of the bosom with the finger of an arch connoisseur. He afterwards in a conversation with me waggishly insisted, that all the time Johnson showed visible signs of a fervent admiration of the corresponding charms of the fair Quaker.

This record, though by no means so perfect as I could wish, will serve to give a notion of a very curious interview, which was not only pleasing at the time, but had the agreeable and benignant effect of reconciling any animosity, and sweetening any acidity, which, in the various bustle of political contest, had been produced in the minds of two men, who though widely different, had so many things in common—classical learning, modern literature, wit and humor, and ready repartee—that it would have been much to be regretted if they had been for ever at a distance from each other.

Mr. Burke gave me much credit for this successful *negotiation;* and pleasantly said, "that there was nothing equal to it in the whole history of the *Corps Diplomatique.*"

I attended Dr. Johnson home, and had the satisfaction to hear him tell Mrs. Williams how much he had been pleased with Mr. Wilkes's company, and what an agreeable day he had passed. . . .

1781: Aetat. 72

On Friday, April 20, I spent with him one of the happiest days that I remember to have enjoyed in the whole course of my life. Mrs. Garrick, whose grief for the loss of her husband was, I believe, as sincere as wounded affection and admiration could produce, had this day, for the first time since his death, a select party of his friends to dine with her. The company was, Miss Hannah More, who lived with her, and whom she called her Chaplain; Mrs. Boscawen, Mrs. Elizabeth Carter, Sir Joshua Reynolds, Dr. Burney, Dr. Johnson, and myself. We found ourselves very elegantly entertained at her house in the Adelphi, where I have passed many a pleasing hour with him "who gladdened life." She looked well, talked of her husband with complacency, and while she cast her eyes on his portrait, which hung over the chimney-piece, said, that "death was now the most agreeable object to her." The very semblance of David Garrick was cheering. Mr. Beauclerk, with happy propriety, inscribed under that fine portrait of him, which by Lady Diana's kindness is now the property of my friend Mr. Langton, the following passage from his beloved Shakespeare:

> "————A merrier man,
> Within the limit of becoming mirth,
> I never spent an hour's talk withal.
> His eye begets occasion for his wit;
> For every object that the one doth catch
> The other turns to a mirth-moving jest;
> Which his fair tongue (Conceit's expositor)
> Delivers in such apt and gracious words,
> That aged ears play truant at his tales,
> And younger hearings are quite ravished;
> So sweet and voluble is his discourse."

We were all in fine spirits; and I whispered to Mrs. Boscawen, "I believe this is as much as can be made of life." In addition to a splendid entertainment, we were regaled with Lichfield ale, which had a peculiar appropriate value. Sir Joshua, and Dr. Burney, and I, drank cordially of it to Dr. Johnson's health; and though he would not join us, he as cordially answered, "Gentlemen, I wish you all as well as you do me."

The general effect of this day dwells upon my mind in fond remembrance, but I do not find much conversation recorded. What I have preserved shall be faithfully given.

One of the company mentioned Mr. Thomas Hollis, the strenuous Whig, who used to send over Europe presents of democratical books, with their boards stamped with daggers and caps of liberty. Mrs. Carter said, "He was a bad man: he used to talk uncharitably." JOHNSON. "Poh! poh! Madam; who is the worse for being talked of uncharitably? Besides, he was a dull poor creature as ever lived: and I believe he would not have done harm to a man whom he knew to be of very opposite principles to his own. I remember once at the Society of Arts, when an advertisement was to be drawn up, he pointed me out as the man who could do it best. This, you will observe, was kindness to me. I however slipped away and escaped it."

Mrs. Carter having said of the same person, "I doubt he was an Atheist." JOHNSON. "I don't know that. He might perhaps have become one, if he had had time to ripen (smiling). He might have *exuberated* into an Atheist."

Sir Joshua Reynolds praised "Mudge's Sermons." JOHNSON. "Mudge's Sermons are good, but not practical. He grasps more sense than he can hold; he takes more corn than he can make into meal; he opens a wide prospect, but it is so distant, it is indistinct.

I love 'Blair's Sermons.' Though the dog is a Scotchman, and a Presbyterian, and every thing he should not be, I was the first to praise them. Such was my candor" (smiling). MRS. BOSCAWEN. "Such his great merit, to get the better of your prejudices." JOHNSON. "Why, Madam, let us compound the matter; let us ascribe it to my candor, and his merit."

In the evening we had a large company in the drawing-room; several ladies, the Bishop of Killaloe, Dr. Percy, Mr. Chamberlayne of the Treasury, &c. &c. Somebody said, the life of a mere literary man could not be very entertaining. JOHNSON. "But it certainly may. This is a remark which has been made, and repeated, without justice; why should the life of a literary man be less entertaining than the life of any other man? Are there not as interesting varieties in such a life? As a *literary life* it may be very entertaining." BOS-WELL. "But it must be better surely, when it is diversified with a little active variety—such as his having gone to Jamaica:—or—his having gone to the Hebrides." Johnson was not displeased at this.

Talking of a very respectable author, he told us a curious circumstance in his life, which was, that he had married a printer's devil. REYNOLDS. "A printer's devil, Sir! Why, I thought a printer's devil was a creature with a black face and in rags." JOHNSON. "Yes, Sir. But I suppose he had her face washed, and put clean clothes on her. (Then looking very serious, and very earnest.) And she did not disgrace him;—the woman had a bottom of good sense." The word *bottom* thus introduced, was so ludicrous when contrasted with his gravity, that most of us could not forbear tittering and laughing; though I recollect that the Bishop of Killaloe kept his countenance with perfect steadiness, while Miss Hannah More slyly hid her face behind a lady's back who sat on the same settee with her. His pride could not bear that any expression of his should excite ridicule, when he did not intend it; he therefore resolved to assume and exercise despotic power, glanced sternly around, and called out in a strong tone, "Where's the merriment?" Then collecting himself, and looking awful, to make us feel how he could impose restraint, and as it were searching his mind for a still more ludicrous word, he slowly pronounced, "I say the *woman* was *fundamentally* sensible"; as if he had said, hear this now, and laugh if you dare. We all sat composed as at a funeral.

He and I walked away together; we stopped a little while by the rails of the Adelphi, looking on the Thames, and I said to him with some emotion, that I was now thinking of two friends we had lost, who once lived in the buildings behind us, Beauclerk and Garrick. "Ay, Sir, (said he, tenderly) and two such friends as cannot be supplied."

For some time after this day I did not see him very often, and of the conversation which I did enjoy, I am sorry to find I have preserved but little. I was at this time engaged in a variety of other matters, which required exertion and assiduity, and necessarily occupied almost all my time. . . .

About this time it was much the fashion for several ladies to have evening assemblies, where the fair sex might participate in conversation with literary and ingenious men, animated by a desire to please. These societies were denominated *Blue-stocking Clubs*, the origin of which title being little known, it may be worth while to relate it. One of the most eminent members of those societies, when they first commenced, was Mr. Stillingfleet, whose dress was remarkably grave, and in particular it was observed, that he wore blue stockings. Such was the excellence of his conversation that his absence was felt as so great a loss, that it used to be said, "We can do nothing without the *blue-stockings*"; and thus by degrees the title was established. Miss Hannah More has admirably described a *Blue-stocking Club*, in her "*Bas Bleu*," a poem in which many of the persons who were most conspicuous there are mentioned.

Johnson was prevailed with to come sometimes into these circles, and did not think himself too grave even for the lively Miss Monckton (now Countess of Corke) who used to have the finest *bit of blue* at the house of her mother, Lady Galway. Her vivacity enchanted the Sage, and they used to talk together with all imaginable ease. A singular instance happened one evening, when she insisted that some of Sterne's writings were very pathetic. Johnson bluntly denied it. "I am sure (said she) they have affected *me*."—"Why (said Johnson, smiling, and rolling himself about) that is, because, dearest, you're a dunce." When she sometimes afterwards mentioned this to him, he said with equal truth and politeness: "Madam, if I had thought so, I certainly should not have said it."

Another evening Johnson's kind indulgence towards me had a pretty difficult trial. I had dined at the Duke of Montrose's with a very agreeable party, and his grace, according to his usual custom, had circulated the bottle very freely. Lord Graham and I went together to Miss Monckton's, where I certainly was in extraordinary spirits, and above all fear or awe. In the midst of a great number of persons of the first rank, amongst whom I recollect with confusion, a noble lady of the most stately decorum, I placed myself next to Johnson, and thinking myself now fully his match, talked to him in a loud and boisterous manner, desirous to let the company know how I could contend with *Ajax*. I particularly remember pressing him upon the value of the pleasures of the imagination and as an illustration of my argument, asking him, "What, Sir, supposing I were to fancy that the —— (naming the most charming Duchess in his Majesty's dominions) were in love with me should I not be very happy?" My friend with much address evaded my interrogatories, and kept me as quiet as possible; but it may easily be conceived how he must have felt. However, when a few days afterwards I waited upon him and made an apology, he behaved with the most friendly gentleness.

While I remained in London this year, Johnson and I dined together at several places. I recollect a placid day at Dr. Butler's, who had now removed from Derby to Lower Grosvenor-street, London; but of his conversation on that and other occasions during this period, I neglected to keep any regular record, and shall therefore insert here some miscellaneous articles which I find in my Johnsonian notes.

His disorderly habits, when "making provision for the day that was passing over him," appear from the following anecdote, communicated to me by Mr. John Nichols:—"In the year 1763, a young bookseller, who was an apprentice to Mr. Whiston, waited on him with a subscription to his 'Shakespeare': and observing that the Doctor made no entry in any book of the subscriber's name, ventured diffidently to ask, whether he would please to have the gentleman's address, that it might be properly inserted in the printed list of subscribers.—'I shall print no List of Subscribers,' said Johnson, with great abruptness: but almost immediately recollecting himself, added, very complacently, 'Sir, I have two very cogent reasons for not printing any list of subscribers;—one, that I have lost all the names,—the other, that I have spent all the money.'"

Johnson could not brook appearing to be worsted in argument, even when he had taken the wrong side, to show the force and dexterity of his talents. When, therefore, he perceived that his opponent gained ground, he had recourse to some sudden mode of robust sophistry. Once when I was pressing upon him with visible advantage, he stopped me thus:—"My dear Boswell, let's have no more of this; you'll make nothing of it. I'd rather have you whistle a Scotch tune."

Care, however, must be taken to distinguish between Johnson when he "talked for victory," and Johnson when he had no desire but to inform and illustrate.—"One of Johnson's principal talents (says an eminent friend of his) was shown in maintaining the wrong side of an argument, and in a splendid perversion of the truth.—If you could contrive to have his fair opinion on a subject, and without any bias from personal prejudice, or from a wish to be victorious in argument, it was wisdom itself, not only convincing, but overpowering."

He had, however, all his life habituated himself to consider conversation as a trial of intellectual vigor and skill; and to this I think, we may venture to ascribe that unexampled richness and brilliancy which appeared in his own. As a proof at once of his eagerness for colloquial distinction, and his high notion of this eminent friend, he once addressed him thus: "——, we now have been several hours together; and you have said but one thing for which I envied you." . . .

1784: Aetat. 75

My readers are now, at last, to behold SAMUEL JOHNSON preparing himself for that doom, from which the most exalted powers afford no exemption to man. Death had always been to him an object of terror; so that though by no means happy, he still clung to life with an eagerness at which many have wondered. At any time when he was ill, he was very pleased to be told that he looked better. An ingenious member of the *Eumelian Club* informs me, that upon one occasion, when he said to him that he saw health returning to his cheek, Johnson seized him by the hand and exclaimed. "Sir, you are one of the kindest friends I ever had."

His own state of his views of futurity will appear truly rational; and may, perhaps, impress the unthinking with seriousness.

"You know, (says he) I never thought confidence with respect to futurity, any part of the character of a brave, a wise, or a good man. Bravery has no place where it can avail nothing; wisdom impresses strongly the consciousness of those faults, of which it is, perhaps, itself an aggravation; and goodness, always wishing to be better, and imputing every deficience to criminal negligence, and every fault to voluntary corruption, never dares to suppose the condition of forgiveness fulfilled, nor what is wanting in the crime supplied by penitence.

"This is the state of the best; but what must be the condition of him whose heart will not suffer him to rank himself among the best, or among the good? Such must be his dread of the approaching trial as will leave him little attention to the opinion of those whom he is leaving forever; and the serenity that is not felt, it can be no virtue to feign."

His great fear of death, and the strange dark manner in which Sir John Hawkins imparts the uneasiness which he expressed on account of offenses with which he charged himself, may give occasion to injurious suspicions, as if there had been something of more than ordinary criminality weighing upon his conscience. On that account, therefore, as well as from the regard to truth which he inculcated, I am to mention, (with all possible respect and delicacy, however) that his conduct after he came to London, and had associated with Savage and others, was not so strictly virtuous, in one respect, as when he was a younger man. It was well known, that his amorous inclinations were uncommonly strong and impetuous. He owned to many of his friends, that he used to take women of the town to taverns, and hear them relate their history. —In short, it must not be concealed that like many other good and pious men, among whom we may place the apostle Paul upon his own authority, Johnson was not free from propensities which were ever "warring against the law of his mind"—and that in his combats with them, he was sometimes overcome.

Here let the profane and licentious pause; let them not thoughtlessly say that Johnson was an *hypocrite*, or that his *principles* were not firm, because his *practice* was not uniformly conformable to what he professed.

Let the question be considered independent of moral and religious associations; and no man will deny that thousands, in many instances, act against conviction. Is a prodigal, for example, an *hypocrite*, when he owns he is satisfied that his extravagance will bring him to ruin and misery? We are *sure* he *believes* it; but immediate inclination, strengthened by indulgence, prevails over that belief in influencing his conduct. Why then shall credit be refused to the *sincerity* of those who acknowledge their persuasion of moral and religious duty, yet sometimes fail of living as it requires? I heard Dr. Johnson once observe, "There is something noble in publishing truth, though it condemns one's self." And one who said in his presence, "he had no notion of people being in earnest in their good professions, whose practice was not suitable to them," was thus reprimanded by him:—"Sir, are you so grossly ignorant of human nature as not to know that a man may be very sincere in good principles, without having good practice?"

But let no man encourage or soothe himself in "presumptuous sin," from knowing that Johnson was sometimes hurried into indulgences which he thought criminal. I have exhibited this circumstance as a shade in so great a character, both from my sacred love of truth, and to show that he was not so weakly scrupulous as he has been represented by those who imagine that the sins, of which a deep sense was upon his mind, were merely such little venial trifles as pouring milk into his tea on Good-Friday. His understanding will be defended by my statement, if his consistency of conduct be in some degree impaired. But what wise man would, for momentary gratifications, deliberately subject himself to suffer such uneasiness as we find was experienced by Johnson in reviewing his conduct as compared with his notion of the ethics of the gospel? Let the following passages [11] be kept in remembrance: "O, GOD, giver and preserver of all life, by whose power I was created, and by whose providence I am sustained, look down upon me with tenderness and mercy; grant that I may not have been created to be finally destroyed; that I may not be preserved to add wickedness to wickedness."—"O, LORD, let me not sink into total depravity; look down upon me, and rescue me at last from the captivity of sin."—"Almighty and most merciful Father, who hast continued my life from year to year, grant that by longer life I may become less desirous of sinful pleasures, and more careful of eternal happiness."—"Let not my years be multiplied to increase my guilt; but, as my age advances, let me become more pure in my thoughts, more regular in my desires, and more obedient to thy laws."— "Forgive, O merciful LORD, whatever I have done contrary to thy laws. Give me such a sense of my wickedness as may produce true contrition and effectual repentance; so that when I shall be called into another state, I may be received among the sinners to whom

11 From Johnson's *Prayers and Meditations.*

sorrow and reformation have obtained pardon, for Jesus Christ's sake. Amen."

Such was the distress of mind, such the penitence of Johnson, in his hours of privacy, and in his devout approaches to his Maker. His *sincerity*, therefore, must appear to every candid mind unquestionable.

It is of essential consequence to keep in view, that there was in this excellent man's conduct no false principle of *commutation*, no *deliberate* indulgence in sin, in consideration of a counterbalance of duty. His offending, and his repenting, were distinct and separate: and when we consider his almost unexampled attention to truth, his inflexible integrity, his constant piety, who will dare to "cast a stone at him"? Besides, let it never be forgotten, that he cannot be charged with any offense indicating badness of *heart*, any thing dishonest, base, or malignant; but, that, on the contrary, he was charitable in an extraordinary degree: so that even in one of his own rigid judgments of himself, (Easter eve, 1781) while he says, "I have corrected no external habits"; he is obliged to own, "I hope that since my last communion I have advanced, by pious reflections, in my submission to God, and my benevolence to man."

I am conscious that this is the most difficult and dangerous part of my biographical work, and I cannot but be very anxious concerning it. I trust that I have got through it, preserving at once my regard to truth,—to my friend,—and to the interests of virtue and religion. Nor can I apprehend that more harm can ensue from the knowledge of the irregularities of Johnson, guarded as I have stated it, than from knowing that Addison and Parnell were intemperate in the use of wine; which he himself, in his Lives of those celebrated writers and pious men, has not forborne to record.

It is not my intention to give a very minute detail of the particulars of Johnson's remaining days, of whom it was now evident, that the crisis was fast approaching, when he must *"die like men, and fall like one of the Princes."* Yet it will be instructive, as well as gratifying to the curiosity of my readers, to record a few circumstances, on the authenticity of which they may perfectly rely, as I have been at the utmost pains to obtain an accurate account of his last illness, from the best authority.

Dr. Heberden, Dr. Brocklesby, Dr. Warren, and Dr. Butter, physicians, generously attended him, without accepting any fees, as did Mr. Cruickshank, surgeon; and all that could be done from professional skill and ability, was tried, to prolong a life so truly valuable. He himself, indeed, having, on account of his very bad constitution, been perpetually applying himself to medical inquiries, united his own efforts with those of the gentlemen who attended him; and imagining that the dropsical collection of water which oppressed him might be drawn off by making incisions in his body, he, with his usual resolute defiance of pain, cut deep, when he thought that his surgeon had done it too tenderly.

About eight or ten days before his death, when Dr. Brocklesby paid him his morning visit, he seemed very low and desponding, and said, "I have been as a dying man all night." He then emphatically broke out in the words of Shakespeare,

> "Can'st thou not minister to a mind diseas'd;
> Pluck from the memory a rooted sorrow;
> Raze out the written troubles of the brain;
> And, with some sweet oblivious antidote,
> Cleanse the stuff'd bosom of that perilous stuff,
> Which weighs upon the heart?" [12]

To which Dr. Brocklesby readily answer'd, from the same great poet:

> "————————therein the patient
> Must minister to himself."

Johnson expressed himself much satisfied with the application.

On another day after this, when talking on the subject of prayer, Dr. Brocklesby repeated from Juvenal,

> "*Orandum est, ut sit mens sana in corpore sano,*" [13]

and so on to the end of the tenth satire; but in running it quickly over, he happened, in the line,

> "*Qui spatium vitæ extremum inter munera ponat,*"

to pronounce *supremum* for *extremum;* at which Johnson's critical ear instantly took offense, and discoursing vehemently on the unmetrical effect of such a lapse, he showed himself as full as ever of the spirit of the grammarian.

Having no other relations, it had been for some time Johnson's intention to make a liberal provision for his faithful servant, Mr.

---

12 See *Macbeth* V. iii. 40–46.
13 "You need to pray to have a sound mind in a sound body," followed by the line in Juvenal's Satire X, "that considers the last scene of life among one's blessings." See Johnson's own imitation of Juvenal's satire in "The Vanity of Human Wishes."

Francis Barber, whom he looked upon as particularly under his protection, and whom he had all along treated truly as an humble friend. Having asked Dr. Brocklesby what would be a proper annuity to a favorite servant, and being answered that it must depend on the circumstances of the master; and, that in the case of a nobleman, fifty pounds a year was considered as an adequate reward for many years' faithful service;—"Then, (said Johnson) shall I be *nobilissimus*, for I mean to leave Frank seventy pounds a year, and I desire you to tell him so." It is strange, however, to think, that Johnson was not free from that general weakness of being averse to execute a will, so that he delayed it from time to time; and had it not been for Sir John Hawkins's repeatedly urging it, I think it is probable that his kind resolution would not have been fulfilled. After making one, which, as Sir John Hawkins informs us, extended no further than the promised annuity, Johnson's final disposition of his property was established by a will and codicil, of which copies are subjoined.

The consideration of numerous papers of which he was possessed, seems to have struck Johnson's mind with a sudden anxiety, and as they were in great confusion, it is much to be lamented that he had not entrusted some faithful and discreet person with the care and selection of them; instead of which, he, in a precipitate manner, burned large masses of them, with little regard, as I apprehend, to discrimination. Not that I suppose we have thus been deprived of any compositions which he had ever intended for the public eye; but from what escaped the flames, I judge that many curious circumstances relating both to himself and other literary characters, have perished.

Two very valuable articles, I am sure we have lost, which were two quarto volumes, containing a full, fair, and most particular account of his own life, from his earliest recollection. I owned to him, that having accidentally seen them, I had read a great deal in them; and apologizing for the liberty I had taken, asked him if I could help it. He placidly answered, "Why, Sir, I do not think you could have helped it." I said that I had, for once in my life, felt half an inclination to commit theft. It had come into my mind to carry off those two volumes, and never see him more. Upon my enquiring how this would have affected him, "Sir, (said he) I believe I should have gone mad." . . .

Johnson, with that native fortitude, which, amidst all his bodily distress and mental sufferings, never forsook him, asked Dr. Brocklesby, as a man in whom he had confidence, to tell him plainly whether he could recover. "Give me (said he) a direct answer." The Doctor having first asked him if he could bear the whole truth, which way soever it might lead, and being answered that he could, declared that, in his opinion, he could not recover without a miracle. "Then, (said Johnson) I will take no more physic, not even my opiates: for I have prayed that I may render up my soul to GOD unclouded." In this resolution he persevered, and, at the same time, used only the weakest kinds of sustenance. Being pressed by Mr. Windham to take somewhat more generous nourishment, lest too low a diet should have the very effect which he dreaded, by debilitating his mind, he said, "I will take anything but inebriating sustenance."

The Reverend Mr. Strahan, who was the son of his friend, and had been always one of his great favorites, had, during his last illness, the satisfaction of contributing to soothe and comfort him. That gentleman's house at Islington, of which he is Vicar, afforded Johnson, occasionally and easily, an agreeable change of place and fresh air; and he attended also upon him in town in the discharge of the sacred offices of his profession.

Mr. Strahan has given me the agreeable assurance, that, after being in much agitation, Johnson became quite composed, and continued so till his death.

Dr. Brocklesby, who will not be suspected of fanaticism, obliged me with the following accounts:

"For some time before his death, all his fears were calmed and absorbed by the prevalence of his faith, and his trust in the merits and *propitiation* of JESUS CHRIST.

"He talked often to me about the necessity of faith in the *sacrifice* of Jesus, as necessary beyond all good works whatever, for the salvation of mankind.

"He pressed me to study Dr. Clarke and to read his sermons. I asked him why he pressed Dr. Clarke, an Arian. 'Because, (said he) he is fullest on the *propitiatory sacrifice.*'"

Johnson having thus in his mind the true Christian scheme, at once rational and consolatory, uniting justice and mercy in the

DIVINITY, with the improvement of human nature, previous to his receiving the Holy Sacrament, in his apartment, composed and fervently uttered his prayer:

"Almighty and most merciful Father, I am now as to human eyes it seems, about to commemorate, for the last time, the death of thy Son JESUS CHRIST, our Saviour and Redeemer. Grant, O LORD, that my whole hope and confidence may be in his merits, and thy mercy; enforce and accept my imperfect repentance; make this commemoration available to the confirmation of my faith, the establishment of my hope, and the enlargement of my charity; and make the death of thy Son JESUS CHRIST effectual to my redemption. Have mercy upon me, and pardon the multitude of my offenses. Bless my friends; have mercy upon all men. Support me, by thy Holy Spirit, in the days of weakness, and at the hour of death; and receive me, at my death, to everlasting happiness, for the sake of JESUS CHRIST. Amen."

Having, as has been already mentioned, made his will on the 8th and 9th of December, and settled all his worldly affairs, he languished till Monday, the 13th of that month, when he expired, about seven o'clock in the evening, with so little apparent pain that his attendants hardly perceived when his dissolution took place.

Of his last moments, my brother, Thomas David, has furnished me with the following particulars:

"The Doctor, from the time that he was certain his death was near, appeared to be perfectly resigned, was seldom or never fretful or out of temper, and often said to his faithful servant, who gave me this account, 'Attend, Francis, to the salvation of your soul, which is the object of greatest importance': he also explained to him passages in the scripture, and seemed to have pleasure in talking upon religious subjects.

"On Monday, the 13th of December, the day on which he died, a Miss Morris, daughter to a particular friend of his, called, and said to Francis, that she begged to be permitted to see the Doctor, that she might earnestly request him to give her his blessing. Francis went into his room, followed by the young lady, and delivered the message. The Doctor turned himself in the bed, and said, 'GOD bless you, my dear!' These were the last words he spoke.—His difficulty of breathing increased till about seven o'clock in the evening, when Mr. Barber and Mrs. Desmoulins, who were sitting in the room, observing that the noise he made in breathing had ceased, went to the bed, and found he was dead."

About two days after his death, the following very agreeable account was communicated to Mr. Malone, in a letter by the Honorable John Byng, to whom I am much obliged for granting me permission to introduce it in my work.

"DEAR SIR,

"SINCE I saw you, I have had a long conversation with Cawston, who sat up with Dr. Johnson, from nine o'clock on Sunday evening, till ten o'clock on Monday morning. And, from what I can gather from him, it should seem, that Dr. Johnson was perfectly composed, steady in hope, and resigned to death. At the interval of each hour, they assisted him to sit up in his bed, and moved his legs, which were in much pain; when he regularly addressed himself to fervent prayer; and though, sometimes, his voice failed him, his sense never did, during that time. The only sustenance he received, was cyder and water. He said his mind was prepared, and the time to his dissolution seemed long. At six in the morning, he enquired the hour, and, on being informed, said that all went on regularly, and he felt he had but a few hours to live.

"At ten o'clock in the morning, he parted from Cawston, saying, 'You should not detain Mr. Windham's servant:—I thank you; bear my remembrance to your master.' Cawston says, that no man could appear more collected, more devout, or less terrified at the thoughts of the approaching minute.

"This account, which is so much more agreeable than, and somewhat different from, yours, has given us the satisfaction of thinking that that great man died as he lived, full of resignation, strengthened in faith, and joyful in hope."

A few days before his death, he had asked Sir John Hawkins, as one of his executors, where he should be buried; and on being answered, "Doubtless, in Westminster-Abbey," seemed to feel a satisfaction, very natural to a poet; and indeed in my opinion very natural to every man of any imagination, who has no family sepulcher in which he can be laid with his fathers. Accordingly, upon Monday, December 20, his remains were deposited in that noble and renowned edifice; and over his grave was placed a large blue flag-stone, with this inscription:

"SAMUEL JOHNSON, LL.D.
Obit XIII *die Decembris,*
Anno Domini
M.DCC.LXXXIV.
Ætatis suæ LXXV."

His funeral was attended by a respectable number of his friends, particularly such of the members of THE LITERARY CLUB as were then in town; and was also honored with the presence of several of the Reverend Chapters of Westminster. Mr. Burke, Sir Joseph Banks, Mr. Windham, Mr. Langton, Sir Charles Bunbury, and Mr. Coleman, bore his pall. His school-fellow, Dr. Taylor, performed the mournful office of reading the burial service.

I trust, I shall not be accused of affectation, when I declare, that I find myself unable to express all that I felt upon the loss of such a "Guide, Philosopher, and Friend." I shall, therefore, not say one word of my own, but adopt those of an eminent friend, which he uttered with an abrupt felicity, superior to all studied compositions:—"He has made a chasm, which not only nothing can fill up, but which nothing has a tendency to fill up.—Johnson is dead.— Let us go to the next best:—there is nobody; no man can be said to put you in mind of Johnson."

Sir Joshua Reynolds

1723–1792

DR. JOHNSON said that Reynolds was the most invulnerable man he knew, "whom if he should quarrel with him, he should find the most difficulty how to abuse." The *Discourses,* given over the years from 1769 to 1790, while Reynolds was President of the Royal Academy, are also invulnerable; in spite of their patent shallowness and inconsistencies, they are hard to abuse. What are we to think of a painter (a President of the Royal Academy at that) who can gravely remark that the chief attention of a painter of portraits is "employed in planting the features in their proper places, which so much contributes to giving the effect and true impression of the whole"! Absurd as this sounds, Reynolds was making the admissible point that great portraiture demands a simplification of details. Thus it is with all the *Discourses,* which have been called the most adequate summation of a "classic" point of view which Dr. Johnson shared. A more unpleasant word for this point of view is "academic." This point of view denied that genius is possible without knowledge or without a tradition; it also denied that taste and genius are the result of rules alone; it believed that the grandeur of art results from getting above "all singular forms, local customs, particularities, and details of every kind"; it recognized what the nineteenth century often forgot—that "art has boundaries though imagination has none"; it contradicted the still prevalent belief that art is deception, that a painter is only a camera eye; it held that each art has a singular purpose, not to be confused with the purpose of other arts. Every one of these principles was violated not only in the nineteenth century, but in the very years when the discourses were being delivered. Admittedly a great deal of esthetic discussion is quibbling about terms; yet the admiration of many modern painters and critics for the carefully constructed and "artificial" pastoral landscapes by Nicholas Poussin, for example, indicates the pertinence of Sir Joshua's opinions. If Wordsworth misled us into believing that all poetry must be simple and spontaneous, the Victorian critics like John Ruskin misled us into believing that all painting must reproduce the greatest possible number of "facts."

BIOGRAPHICAL NOTES

Born at Plympton, Devonshire, son of the master of the grammar school; educated by his father. Apprenticed to Thomas Hudson, portrait-painter (1740–43); set up as portrait-painter in Plymouth and London (1744–49). Met Admiral Keppel in Plymouth and journeyed on his ship to Italy for study (1749–52). Portrait of Keppel (1753) established reputation; painted the royal family. Met Garrick and Johnson and contributed three papers to the *Idler* (1759). Elected governor and guardian of Foundling Hospital. Moved to Leicester Square (1760). Founded the Club with Johnson, Burke, Goldsmith, and others (1764). Became a close friend of Goldsmith. Elected to the Society of Dilettanti (1766). President of the new Royal Academy (1768). Knighted (1769). Granted D.C.L. from Oxford (1773). Painted "Three Ladies Adorning a Term of Hymen" (1774) and "Mrs. Sheridan as Saint Cecilia" (1775). Published the first seven *Discourses* (1778). Met Fanny Burney. Traveled in France and the Netherlands (1782). Edited DuFresnoy's *Art of Painting* (1783). Painted "Mrs. Siddons as the Tragic Muse" (1784). Became chief painter to George III (1784). Deeply shocked by the death of Johnson (1784). Visited Flanders (1785). Failing eyesight; stopped painting (1789). Quarreled with the Royal Academy (1790). Increasing ill health; died, and was buried in St. Paul's (1792).

BIBLIOGRAPHY: *Discourses*, ed. Roger Fry, 1905; ed. R. R. Wark, 1959; also in Everyman's Library, 1907. *Letters*, ed. F. W. Hilles, 1929. Armstrong, Sir Walter, *Sir Joshua Reynolds*, 1900. Hilles, F. W., *The Literary Career of Sir Joshua Reynolds*, 1936. Hudson, Derek, *Sir Joshua Reynolds*, 1958. Waterhouse, E. K., *Reynolds* (English Master Painters), 1939.

DISCOURSE XIII

1786

*Art not merely Imitation, but under the Direction of the
Imagination. In what Manner Poetry, Painting,
Acting, Gardening, and Architecture de-
part from Nature.*

GENTLEMEN,

To discover beauties, or to point out faults, in the works of celebrated masters, and to compare the conduct of one artist with another, is certainly no mean or inconsiderable part of criticism; but
this is still no more than to know the art through the artist. This
test of investigation must have two capital defects; it must be narrow, and it must be uncertain. To enlarge the boundaries of the
art of painting, as well as to fix its principles, it will be necessary
that *that* art and *those* principles should be considered in their
correspondence with the principles of the other arts which, like
this, address themselves primarily and principally to the imagination. When those connected and kindred principles are brought
together to be compared, another comparison will grow out of
this; that is, the comparison of them all with those of human nature, from whence arts derive the materials upon which they are
to produce their effects.

When this comparison of art with art, and of all arts with the
nature of man, is once made with success, our guiding lines are as
well ascertained and established as they can be in matters of this
description.

This, as it is the highest style of criticism, is at the same time the
soundest; for it refers to the eternal and immutable nature of things.

You are not to imagine that I mean to open to you at large, or
to recommend to your research, the whole of this vast field of
science. It is certainly much above my faculties to reach it; and
though it may not be above yours to comprehend it fully, if it were
fully and properly brought before you, yet perhaps the most perfect criticism requires habits of speculation and abstraction not
very consistent with the employment which ought to occupy and
the habits of mind which ought to prevail in a practical artist. I

only point out to you these things, that when you do criticize (as all who work on a plan will criticize more or less), your criticism may be built on the foundation of true principles; and that though you may not always travel a great way, the way that you do travel may be the right road.

I observe, as a fundamental ground, common to all the arts with which we have any concern in this discourse, that they address themselves only to two faculties of the mind, its imagination and its sensibility.

All theories which attempt to direct or to control the art, upon any principles falsely called rational, which we form to ourselves upon a supposition of what ought in reason to be the end or means of art, independent of the known first effect produced by objects on the imagination, must be false and delusive. For though it may appear bold to say it, the imagination is here the residence of truth. If the imagination be affected, the conclusion is fairly drawn; if it be not affected, the reasoning is erroneous, because the end is not obtained; the effect itself being the test, and the only test, of the truth and efficacy of the means.

There is in the commerce of life, as in art, a sagacity which is far from being contradictory to right reason, and is superior to any occasional exercise of that faculty; which supersedes it; and does not wait for the slow progress of deduction, but goes at once, by what appears a kind of intuition, to the conclusion. A man endowed with this faculty feels and acknowledges the truth, though it is not always in his power, perhaps, to give a reason for it; because he cannot recollect and bring before him all the materials that gave birth to his opinion; for very many and very intricate considerations may unite to form the principle, even of small and minute parts, involved in, or dependent on, a great system of things: though these in process of time are forgotten, the right impression still remains fixed in his mind.

This impression is the result of the accumulated experience of our whole life, and has been collected, we do not always know how, or when. But this mass of collective observation, however acquired, ought to prevail over that reason, which, however powerfully exerted on any particular occasion, will probably comprehend but a partial view of the subject; and our conduct in life as well as in the arts is, or ought to be, generally governed by this habitual reason: it is our happiness that we are enabled to draw on such funds. If we were obliged to enter into a theoretical deliberation on every occasion before we act, life would be at a stand, and art would be impracticable.

It appears to me, therefore, that our first thoughts, that is, the effect which anything produces on our minds, on its first appearance, is never to be forgotten; and it demands for that reason, because it is the first, to be laid up with care. If this be not done, the artist may happen to impose on himself by partial reasoning; by a cold consideration of those animated thoughts which proceed, not perhaps from caprice or rashness (as he may afterwards conceit), but from the fullness of his mind, enriched with the copious stores of all the various inventions which he had ever seen, or had ever passed in his mind. These ideas are infused into his design without any conscious effort; but if he be not on his guard, he may reconsider and correct them, till the whole matter is reduced to a commonplace invention.

This is sometimes the effect of what I mean to caution you against; that is to say, an unfounded distrust of the imagination and feeling, in favor of narrow, partial, confined, argumentative theories, and of principles that seem to apply to the design in hand, without considering those general impressions on the fancy in which real principles of *sound reason*, and of much more weight and importance, are involved, and, as it were, lie hid, under the appearance of a sort of vulgar sentiment.

Reason, without doubt, must ultimately determine everything; at this minute it is required to inform us when that very reason is to give way to feeling.

Though I have often spoken of that mean conception of our art which confines it to mere imitation, I must add that it may be narrowed to such a mere matter of experiment as to exclude from it the application of science, which alone gives dignity and compass to any art. But to find proper foundations for science is neither to narrow nor to vulgarize it; and this is sufficiently exemplified in the success of experimental philosophy. It is the false system of reasoning, grounded on a partial view of things, against which I would most earnestly guard you. And I do it the rather because those narrow theories, so coincident with the poorest and most miserable practice, and which are adopted to give it countenance, have not had their origin in the poorest minds, but in the mistakes, or possibly in the mistaken interpretations, of great and commanding authorities. We are not therefore in this case misled by feeling, but by false speculation.

When such a man as Plato speaks of painting as only an imitative art, and that our pleasure proceeds from observing and acknowledging the truth of the imitation, I think he misleads us by a partial theory. It is in this poor, partial, and so far false view of the art, that Cardinal Bembo [1] has chosen to distinguish even Raffaelle himself, whom our enthusiasm honors with the name of Divine. The same sentiment is adopted by Pope in his epitaph on Sir Godfrey Kneller; and he turns the panegyric solely on imitation, as it is a sort of deception.

I shall not think my time misemployed, if by any means I may contribute to confirm your opinion of what ought to be the object of your pursuit; because, though the best critics must always have exploded this strange idea, yet I know that there is a disposition towards a perpetual recurrence to it, on account of its simplicity and superficial plausibility. For this reason I shall beg leave to lay before you a few thoughts on this subject; to throw out some hints that may lead your minds to an opinion (which I take to be the truth) that painting is not only to be considered as an imitation, operating by deception, but that it is, and ought to be, in many points of view, and strictly speaking, no imitation at all of external nature. Perhaps it ought to be as far removed from the vulgar idea of imitation as the refined civilized state in which we live is removed from a gross state of nature; and those who have not cultivated their imaginations, which the majority of mankind certainly have not, may be said, in regard to arts, to continue in this state of nature. Such men will always prefer imitation to that excellence which is addressed to another faculty that they do not possess; but these are not the persons to whom a painter is to look, any more than a judge of morals and manners ought to refer controverted points upon those subjects to the opinions of people taken from the banks of the Ohio or from New Holland.

It is the lowest style only of arts, whether of painting, poetry, or music, that may be said, in the vulgar sense, to be naturally pleasing. The higher efforts of those arts, we know by experience, do not affect minds wholly uncultivated. This refined taste is the consequence of education and habit; we are born only with a capacity

1 See the passage toward the end of the first book of Baldassare Castiglione's *Book of the Courtier* (1528); not Bembo but Count Lewis advances the theory mentioned by Reynolds.

of entertaining this refinement, as we are born with a disposition to receive and obey all the rules and regulations of society; and so far it may be said to be natural to us, and no further.

What has been said may show the artist how necessary it is, when he looks about him for the advice and criticism of his friends, to make some distinction of the character, taste, experience, and observation in this art of those from whom it is received. An ignorant, uneducated man may, like Apelles's critic, be a competent judge of the truth of the representation of a sandal; or to go somewhat higher, like Molière's old woman,[2] may decide upon what is nature, in regard to comic humor; but a critic in the higher style of art ought to possess the same refined taste which directed the artist in his work.

To illustrate this principle by a comparison with other arts, I shall now produce some instances to show that they, as well as our own art, renounce the narrow idea of nature, and the narrow theories derived from that mistaken principle, and apply to that reason only which informs us not what imitation is—a natural representation of a given object—but what it is natural for the imagination to be delighted with. And perhaps there is no better way of acquiring this knowledge than by this kind of analogy: each art will corroborate and mutually reflect the truth on the other. Such a kind of juxtaposition may likewise have this use, that whilst the artist is amusing himself in the contemplation of other arts, he may habitually transfer the principles of those arts to that which he professes; which ought to be always present to his mind, and to which everything is to be referred.

So far is art from being derived from, or having any immediate intercourse with, particular nature as its model, that there are many arts that set out with a professed deviation from it.

This is certainly not so exactly true in regard to painting and sculpture. Our elements are laid in gross common nature—an exact imitation of what is before us: but when we advance to the higher state, we consider this power of imitation, though first in the order of acquisition, as by no means the highest in the scale of perfection.

Poetry addresses itself to the same faculties and the same dispositions as painting, though by different means. The object of both is to accommodate itself to all the natural propensities and inclina-

<hr>

2 Before they were performed Molière read his comedies to his old housekeeper to test their humor. See *Spectator* 70.

tions of the mind. The very existence of poetry depends on the license it assumes of deviating from actual nature, in order to gratify natural propensities by other means, which are found by experience full as capable of affording such gratification. It sets out with a language in the highest degree artificial, a construction of measured words, such as never is, nor ever was, used by man. Let this measure be what it may, whether hexameter or any other meter used in Latin or Greek—or rhyme, or blank verse varied with pauses and accents, in modern languages—they are all equally removed from nature, and equally a violation of common speech. When this artificial mode has been established as the vehicle of sentiment, there is another principle in the human mind, to which the work must be referred, which still renders it more artificial, carries it still further from common nature, and deviates only to render it more perfect. That principle is the sense of congruity, coherence, and consistency, which is a real existing principle in man; and it must be gratified. Therefore having once adopted a style and a measure not found in common discourse, it is required that the sentiments also should be in the same proportion elevated above common nature, from the necessity of there being an agreement of the parts among themselves, that one uniform whole may be produced.

To correspond therefore with this general system of deviation from nature, the manner in which poetry is offered to the ear, the tone in which it is recited, should be as far removed from the tone of conversation as the words of which that poetry is composed. This naturally suggests the idea of modulating the voice by art, which I suppose may be considered as accomplished to the highest degree of excellence in the recitative of the Italian opera; as we may conjecture it was in the chorus that attended the ancient drama. And though the most violent passions, the highest distress, even death itself, are expressed in singing or recitative, I would not admit as sound criticism the condemnation of such exhibitions on account of their being unnatural.

If it is natural for our senses and our imaginations to be delighted with singing, with instrumental music, with poetry, and with graceful action, taken separately (none of them being in the vulgar sense natural, even in that separate state), it is conformable to experience, and therefore agreeable to reason as connected with and referred to experience, that we should also be delighted with this

union of music, poetry, and graceful action, joined to every circumstance of pomp and magnificence calculated to strike the senses
of the spectator. Shall reason stand in the way and tell us that we
ought not to like what we know we do like, and prevent us from
feeling the full effect of this complicated exertion of art? This is
what I would understand by poets and painters being allowed to
dare everything; for what can be more daring than accomplishing
the purpose and end of art by a complication of means, none of
which have their archetypes in actual nature?

So far therefore is servile imitation from being necessary, that
whatever is familiar, or in any way reminds us of what we see and
hear every day, perhaps does not belong to the higher provinces of
art, either in poetry or painting. The mind is to be transported, as
Shakespeare expresses it, *beyond the ignorant present* to ages past.
Another and a higher order of beings is supposed; and to those
beings everything which is introduced into the work must correspond. Of this conduct, under these circumstances, the Roman and
Florentine schools afford sufficient examples. Their style by this
means is raised and elevated above all others; and by the same means
the compass of art itself is enlarged.

We often see grave and great subjects attempted by artists of
another school; who, though excellent in the lower class of art,
proceeding on the principles which regulate that class, and not
recollecting, or not knowing, that they were to address themselves
to another faculty of the mind, have become perfectly ridiculous.
The picture which I have at present in my thoughts is a sacrifice
of Iphigenia, painted by Jan Steen, a painter of whom I have formerly had occasion to speak with the highest approbation; and
even in this picture, the subject of which is by no means adapted
to his genius, there is nature and expression; but it is such expression, and the countenances are so familiar, and consequently so
vulgar, and the whole accompanied with such finery of silks and
velvets, that one would be almost tempted to doubt whether the
artist did not purposely intend to burlesque his subject.

Instances of the same kind we frequently see in poetry. Parts
of Hobbes's translation of Homer are remembered and repeated
merely for the familiarity and meanness of their phraseology, so ill
corresponding with the ideas which ought to have been expressed,
and, as I conceive, with the style of the original.

We may proceed in the same manner through the comparatively

inferior branches of art. There are in works of that class the same distinction of a higher and a lower style; and they take their rank and degree in proportion as the artist departs more, or less, from common nature, and makes it an object of his attention to strike the imagination of the spectator by ways belonging specially to art—unobserved and untaught out of the school of its practice.

If our judgments are to be directed by narrow, vulgar, untaught, or rather ill-taught reason, we must prefer a portrait by Denner or any other high finisher, to those of Titian or Vandyck; and a landscape of Vanderheyden to those of Titian or Rubens; for they are certainly more exact representations of nature.

If we suppose a view of nature represented with all the truth of the *camera obscura*, and the same scene represented by a great artist, how little and mean will the one appear in comparison of the other, where no superiority is supposed from the choice of the subject. The scene shall be the same, the difference only will be in the manner in which it is presented to the eye. With what additional superiority, then, will the same artist appear when he has the power of selecting his materials, as well as elevating his style? Like Nicolas Poussin, he transports us to the environs of ancient Rome, with all the objects which a literary education makes so precious and interesting to man; or, like Sebastian Bourdon, he leads us to the dark antiquity of the Pyramids of Egypt; or, like Claude Lorrain, he conducts us to the tranquillity of arcadian scenes and fairyland.

Like the history-painter, a painter of landscapes in this style and with this conduct sends the imagination back into antiquity; and, like the poet, he makes the elements sympathize with his subject; whether the clouds roll in volumes, like those of Titian or Salvator Rosa, or, like those of Claude, are gilded with the setting sun; whether the mountains have sudden and bold projections, or are gently sloped; whether the branches of his trees shoot out abruptly in right angles from their trunks, or follow each other with only a gentle inclination. All these circumstances contribute to the general character of the work, whether it be of the elegant, or of the more sublime kind. If we add to this the powerful materials of lightness and darkness, over which the artist has complete dominion, to vary and dispose them as he pleases, to diminish or increase them as will best suit his purpose and correspond to the general idea of his work, a landscape thus conducted, under the influence of a poetical mind, will have the same superiority over the more ordinary and common views as Milton's *Allegro* and *Penseroso* have over a cold prosaic narration or description; and such a picture would make a more forcible impression on the mind than the real scenes, were they presented before us.

If we look abroad to other arts, we may observe the same distinction, the same division into two classes; each of them acting under the influence of two different principles, in which the one follows nature, the other varies it and sometimes departs from it.

The theater, which is said *to hold the mirror up to nature*, comprehends both those ideas. The lower kind of comedy or farce, like the inferior style of painting, the more naturally it is represented, the better; but the higher appears to me to aim no more at imitation, so far as it belongs to anything like deception, or to expect that the spectators should think that the events there represented are really passing before them, than Raffaelle in his cartoons, or Poussin in his sacraments, expected it to be believed, even for a moment, that what they exhibited were real figures.

For want of this distinction, the world is filled with false criticism. Raffaelle is praised for naturalness and deception, which he certainly has not accomplished, and as certainly never intended; and our late great actor Garrick has been as ignorantly praised by his friend Fielding; who doubtless imagined he had hit upon an ingenious device by introducing in one of his novels [3] (otherwise a work of the highest merit) an ignorant man mistaking Garrick's representation of a scene in Hamlet for reality. A very little reflection will convince us that there is not one circumstance in the whole scene that is of the nature of deception. The merit and excellence of Shakespeare, and of Garrick, when they were engaged in such scenes, is of a different and much higher kind. But what adds to the falsity of this intended compliment is that the best stage representation appears even more unnatural to a person of such a character, who is supposed never to have seen a play before, than it does to those who have had a habit of allowing for those necessary deviations from nature which the art requires.

In theatric representation, great allowances must always be made for the place in which the exhibition is represented; for the surrounding company, the lighted candles, the scenes visibly shifted in your sight, and the language of blank verse, so different from common English, which merely as English must appear surprising

---

3 *Tom Jones* (Bk. XVI, chap. 5), in which Partridge sees *Hamlet*.

in the mouths of Hamlet, and all the court and natives of Denmark. These allowances are made; but their being made puts an end to all manner of deception: and further, we know that the more low, illiterate, and vulgar any person is, the less he will be disposed to make these allowances, and of course to be deceived by any imitation; the things in which the trespass against nature and common probability is made in favor of the theater being quite within the sphere of such uninformed men.

Though I have no intention of entering into all the circumstances of unnaturalness in theatrical representations, I must observe that even the expression of violent passion is not always the most excellent in proportion as it is the most natural; so great terror and such disagreeable sensations may be communicated to the audience that the balance may be destroyed by which pleasure is preserved and holds its predominance in the mind: violent distortion of action, harsh screamings of the voice, however great the occasion, or however natural on such occasion, are therefore not admissible in the theatric art. Many of these allowed deviations from nature arise from the necessity which there is that everything should be raised and enlarged beyond its natural state, that the full effect may come home to the spectator, which otherwise would be lost in the comparatively extensive space of the theater. Hence the deliberate and stately step, the studied grace of action, which seems to enlarge the dimensions of the actor and alone to fill the stage. All this unnaturalness, though right and proper in its place, would appear affected and ridiculous in a private room; *quid enim deformius, quam scenam in vitam transferre?* [4]

And here I must observe, and I believe it may be considered as a general rule, that no art can be engrafted with success on another art. For though they all profess the same origin, and to proceed from the same stock, yet each has its own peculiar modes both of imitating nature, and of deviating from it, each for the accomplishment of its own particular purpose. These deviations, more especially, will not bear transplantation to another soil.

If a painter should endeavor to copy the theatrical pomp and parade of dress and attitude, instead of that simplicity which is not a greater beauty in life than it is in painting, we should condemn such pictures as painted in the meanest style.

4 "For what could be more unfitting than to carry a scene from the drama into actual life?"

So also gardening, as far as gardening is an art, or entitled to that appellation, is a deviation from nature; for if the true taste consists, as many hold, in banishing every appearance of art or any traces of the footsteps of man, it would then be no longer a garden. Even though we define it "Nature to advantage dress'd," [5] and in some sense is such, and much more beautiful and commodious for the recreation of man, it is, however, when so dressed, no longer a subject for the pencil of a landscape-painter, as all landscape-painters know, who love to have recourse to nature herself and to dress her according to the principles of their own art; which are far different from those of gardening, even when conducted according to the most approved principles, and such as a landscape-painter himself would adopt in the disposition of his own grounds for his own private satisfaction.

I have brought together as many instances as appear necessary to make out the several points which I wished to suggest to your consideration in this discourse, that your own thoughts may lead you further in the use that may be made of the analogy of the arts, and of the restraint which a full understanding of the diversity of many of their principles ought to impose on the employment of that analogy.

The great end of all those arts is to make an impression on the imagination and the feeling. The imitation of nature frequently does this. Sometimes it fails, and something else succeeds. I think therefore the true test of all the arts is not solely whether the production is a true copy of nature, but whether it answers the end of art, which is to produce a pleasing effect upon the mind.

It remains only to speak a few words of architecture, which does not come under the denomination of an imitative art. It applies itself, like music (and I believe we may add poetry), directly to the imagination, without the intervention of any kind of imitation.

There is in architecture, as in painting, an inferior branch of art in which the imagination appears to have no concern. It does not, however, acquire the name of a polite and liberal art from its usefulness, or administering to our wants or necessities, but from some higher principle: we are sure that in the hands of a man of genius it is capable of inspiring sentiment, and of filling the mind with great and sublime ideas.

It may be worth the attention of artists to consider what ma-

5 Pope *Essay on Criticism* II. 97

terials are in their hands that may contribute to this end; and whether this art has it not in its power to address itself to the imagination with effect by more ways than are generally employed by architects.

To pass over the effect produced by that general symmetry and proportion by which the eye is delighted, as the ear is with music, architecture certainly possesses many principles in common with poetry and painting. Among those which may be reckoned as the first is that of affecting the imagination by means of association of ideas. Thus, for instance, as we have naturally a veneration for antiquity, whatever building brings to our remembrance ancient customs and manners, such as the castles of the barons of ancient chivalry, is sure to give this delight. Hence it is that *towers and battlements* [6] are so often selected by the painter and the poet to make a part of the composition of their ideal landscape; and it is from hence, in a great degree, that in the buildings of Vanbrugh, who was a poet as well as an architect, there is a greater display of imagination than we shall find perhaps in any other, and this is the ground of the effect we feel in many of his works, notwithstanding the faults with which many of them are justly charged. For this purpose, Vanbrugh appears to have had recourse to some of the principles of the Gothic architecture; which, though not so ancient as the Grecian, is more so to our imagination, with which the artist is more concerned than with absolute truth.

The barbaric splendor of those Asiatic buildings, which are now publishing by a member of this Academy,[7] may possibly, in the same manner, furnish an architect not with models to copy, but with hints of composition and general effect, which would not otherwise have occurred.

It is, I know, a delicate and hazardous thing (and as such I have already pointed it out), to carry the principles of one art to another, or even to reconcile in one object the various modes of the same art, when they proceed on different principles. The sound rules of the Grecian architecture are not to be lightly sacrificed. A deviation from them, or even an addition to them, is like a deviation or addition to, or from, the rules of other arts—fit only for a great master, who is thoroughly conversant in the nature of man, as well as all combinations in his own art.

6 Towers and battlements it sees
  Bosom'd high in tufted trees.
    Milton, *L'Allegro* [Reynolds].

7 William Hodges, who had published a portfolio on India.

It may not be amiss for the architect to take advantage *sometimes* of that to which I am sure the painter ought always to have his eyes open, I mean the use of accidents; to follow when they lead, and to improve them, rather than always to trust to a regular plan. It often happens that additions have been made to houses, at various times, for use or pleasure. As such buildings depart from regularity, they now and then acquire something of scenery by this accident, which I should think might not unsuccessfully be adopted by an architect, in an original plan, if it does not too much interfere with convenience. Variety and intricacy is a beauty and excellence in every other of the arts which address the imagination; and why not in architecture?

The forms and turnings of the streets of London and other old towns are produced by accident, without any original plan or design; but they are not always the less pleasant to the walker or spectator on that account. On the contrary, if the city had been built on the regular plan of Sir Christopher Wren, the effect might have been, as we know it is in some new parts of the town, rather unpleasing; the uniformity might have produced weariness and a slight degree of disgust.

I can pretend to no skill in the detail of architecture. I judge now of the art merely as a painter. When I speak of Vanbrugh, I mean to speak of him in the language of our art. To speak then of Vanbrugh in the language of a painter, he had originality of invention, he understood light and shadow, and had great skill in composition. To support his principal object he produced his second and third groups or masses; he perfectly understood in his art what is the most difficult in ours, the conduct of the background, by which the design and invention is set off to the greatest advantage. What the background is in painting, in architecture is the real ground on which the building is erected; and no architect took greater care than he that his work should not appear crude and hard: that is, it did not abruptly start out of the ground without expectation or preparation.

This is a tribute which a painter owes to an architect who composed like a painter; and was defrauded of the due reward of his merit by the wits of his time, who did not understand the principles of composition in poetry better than he; and who knew little or nothing of what he understood perfectly, the general ruling principles of architecture and painting. His fate was that of the great

Perrault;[8] both were the objects of the petulant sarcasms of factious men of letters; and both have left some of the fairest ornaments which to this day decorate their several countries—the façade of the Louvre, Blenheim, and Castle Howard.

Upon the whole, it seems to me, that the object and intention of all the arts is to supply the natural imperfection of things, and often to gratify the mind by realizing and embodying what never existed but in the imagination.

It is allowed on all hands that facts and events, however they may bind the historian, have no dominion over the poet or the painter. With us, history is made to bend and conform to this great idea of art. And why? Because these arts, in their highest province, are not addressed to the gross senses, but to the desires of the mind, to that spark of divinity which we have within, impatient of being circumscribed and pent up by the world which is about us. Just so much as our art has of this, just so much of dignity, I had almost said of divinity, it exhibits; and those of our artists who possessed this mark of distinction in the highest degree acquired from thence the glorious appellation of Divine.

A SELECTION

Oliver Goldsmith

1728–1774

THE LIFE OF RICHARD NASH, ESQ., LATE MASTER OF CEREMONIES AT BATH

1762

[This account of the famous "Beau Nash," known as "King of Bath," is perhaps the best introduction to the life at the most celebrated English resort, that inspired scene after scene in the prose fiction of the century.]

PROBABLY . . . by the arrival of Queen Anne there, for her health, about the year 1703, the city of Bath became in some measure frequented by people of distinction. . . .

8 Claude Perrault, one of the architects who designed the Louvre (1667–74).

Still, however, the amusements of this place were neither elegant nor conducted with delicacy. General society among people of rank or fortune was by no means established. The nobility still preserved a tincture of Gothic haughtiness, and refused to keep company with the gentry at any of the public entertainments of the place. Smoking in the rooms was permitted; gentlemen and ladies appeared in a disrespectful manner at public entertainments in aprons and boots. With an eagerness common to those whose pleasures come but seldom, they generally continued them too long; and thus they were rendered disgusting by too free an enjoyment. If the company liked each other, they danced till morning; if any person lost at cards, he insisted on continuing the game till luck should turn. The lodgings for visitants were paltry, though expensive; the dining rooms and other chambers were floored with boards, colored brown with soot and small beer, to hide the dirt; the walls were covered with unpainted wainscot; the furniture corresponded with the meanness of the architecture; a few oak chairs, a small looking glass, with a fender and tongs, composed the magnificence of these temporary habitations. The city was in itself mean and contemptible; no elegant buildings, no open streets, nor uniform squares! The pumphouse was without any director; the chairmen permitted no gentlemen or ladies to walk home by night without insulting them; and to add to all this, one of the greatest physicians of his age conceived a design of ruining the city by writing against the efficacy of the waters. It was from a resentment of some affronts he had received there that he took this resolution; and accordingly published a pamphlet by which he said "he would cast a toad into the spring."

In this situation of things it was, that Nash first came into that city, and hearing the threat of this physician, he humorously assured the people that if they would give him leave, he would charm away the poison of the doctor's toad, as they usually charmed the venom of the tarantula, by music. He therefore was immediately empowered to set up the force of a band of music against the poison of the doctor's reptile. The company very sensibly increased; Nash triumphed, and the sovereignty of the city was decreed to him by every rank of people. . . .

His first care when made Master of Ceremonies, or King of Bath, as it is called, was to promote a music subscription, of one guinea each, for a band, which was to consist of six performers, who were to receive a guinea a week each for their trouble. He allowed also two guineas a week for lighting and sweeping the rooms; for which he accounted to the subscribers by receipt.

Contemplation. A portrait of Mrs. Stanhope by Sir Joshua Reynolds

Frances, Marchioness Camden by Sir Joshua Reynolds

The pumphouse was immediately put under the care of an officer, by the name of the pumper; for which he paid the corporation an annual rent. A row of new houses was begun on the south side of the gravel walks, before which a handsome pavement was then made for the company to walk on. Not less than seventeen or eighteen hundred pounds was raised this year and in the beginning of 1706, by subscription, and laid out in repairing the roads near the city. The streets began to be better paved, cleaned, and lighted; the licenses of the chairmen were repressed, and by an act of Parliament procured on this occasion, the invalids who came to drink or bathe were exempted from all manner of toll as often as they should go out of the city for recreation.

The houses and streets now began to improve, and ornaments were lavished upon them even to profusion. But in the midst of this splendor the company were still obliged to assemble in a booth to drink tea and chocolate, or to game. Mr. Nash undertook to remedy this inconvenience, and by his direction one Thomas Harrison erected a handsome assemblyhouse for these purposes. A better band of music was also procured, and the former subscription of one guinea was raised to two. Harrison had three guineas a week for the room and candles, and the music two guineas a man. The money Mr. Nash received and accounted for with the utmost exactness and punctuality. To this house were also added gardens for people of rank and fashion to walk in; and the beauty of the suburbs continued to increase, notwithstanding the opposition that was made by the corporation, who at that time looked upon every useful improvement, particularly without the walls, as dangerous to the inhabitants within.

His dominion was now extensive and secure, and he determined to support it with the strictest attention. But in order to proceed in everything like a king, he was resolved to give his subjects a law, and the following rules were accordingly put up in the pump-room:—

RULES TO BE OBSERVED AT BATH

1. That a visit of ceremony at first coming and another at going away, are all that are expected or desired, by ladies of quality and fashion,—except impertinents.

2. That ladies coming to the ball appoint a time for their footmen coming to wait on them home, to prevent disturbance and inconveniences to themselves and others.

3. That gentlemen of fashion never appearing in a morning before the ladies in gowns and caps, show breeding and respect.

4. That no person take it ill that anyone goes to another's play, or breakfast, and not theirs;—except captious by nature.

5. That no gentleman give his ticket for the balls to any but gentlewomen.—N.B. Unless he has none of his acquaintance.

6. That gentlemen crowding before the ladies at a ball show ill manners; and that none do so for the future—except such as respect nobody but themselves.

7. That no gentleman or lady takes it ill that another dances before them;—except such as have no pretense to dance at all.

8. That the elder ladies and children be content with a second bench at the ball, as being past or not come to perfection.

9. That the younger ladies take notice how many eyes observe them. —N.B. This does not extend to the *Have-at-alls.*

10. That all whisperers of lies and scandal be taken for their authors.

11. That all repeaters of such lies and scandal be shunned by all company,—except such as have been guilty of the same crime.—N.B. *Several men of no character, old women and young ones of questioned reputation are great authors of lies in these places, being of the sect of levellers.*

. . . . It is certain they were in general religiously observed by his subjects, and executed by him with impartiality; neither rank nor fortune shielded the refractory from his resentment.

The balls, by his directions, were to begin at six and to end at eleven. Nor would he suffer them to continue a moment longer, lest invalids might commit irregularities to counteract the benefit of the waters. Everything was to be performed in proper order. Each ball was to open with a minuet, danced by two persons of the highest distinction present. When the minuet concluded, the lady was to return to her seat, and Nash was to bring the gentleman a new partner. This ceremony was to be observed by every succeeding couple; every gentleman being obliged to dance with two ladies till the minuets were over, which generally continued two hours. At eight the country dances were to begin; ladies of quality, according to their rank, standing up first. About nine o'clock a short interval was allowed for rest, and for the gentlemen to help their partners to tea. That over, the company were to pursue their amusements till the clock struck eleven. Then the master of ceremonies, entering the ballroom, ordered the music to desist by lifting up his finger. The dances discontinued, and some time allowed for becoming cool, the ladies were handed to their chairs.

Even the royal family themselves had not influence enough to make him deviate from any of these rules. The Princess Amelia once applying to him for one dance more after he had given the signal to withdraw, he assured her royal highness that the established rules of Bath resembled the laws of Lycurgus, which would admit of no alteration without an utter subversion of all his authority. . . .

The city of Bath, by such assiduity, soon became the theater of summer amusements for all people of fashion; and the manner of spending the day there must amuse any but such as disease or spleen had made uneasy to themselves. The following is a faint picture of the pleasures that scene affords. Upon a stranger's arrival at Bath he is welcomed by a peal of the Abbey bells, and in the next place by the voice and music of the city waits. For these civilities, the ringers have generally a present made them of half a guinea, and the waits of half a crown, or more, in proportion to the person's fortune, generosity, or ostentation. These customs, though disagreeable, are, however, liked, or they would not continue. The greatest incommodity attending them is the disturbance the bells must give the sick. But the pleasure of knowing the name of every family that comes to town recompenses the inconvenience. Invalids are fond of news, and upon the first sound of the bells, everybody sends out to inquire for whom they ring.

After the family is thus welcomed to Bath, it is the custom for the master of it to go to the public places and subscribe two guineas at the assemblyhouses towards the balls and music in the pumphouse, for which he is entitled to three tickets every ball night. His next subscription is a crown, half a guinea, or a guinea, according to his rank and quality, for the liberty of walking in the private walks belonging to Simpson's assemblyhouse; a crown or half a guinea is also given to the booksellers, for which the gentleman is to have what books he pleases to read at his lodgings, and at the coffeehouse another subscription is taken for pen, ink, and paper, for such letters as the subscriber shall write at it during his stay. The ladies, too, may subscribe to the booksellers, and to an house by the pumproom, for the advantage of reading the news, and for enjoying each other's conversation.

Things being thus adjusted, the amusements of the day are generally begun by bathing, which is no unpleasing method of passing away an hour or so. . . .

The hours for bathing are commonly between six and nine in the morning, and the baths are every morning supplied with fresh water. . . .

In the morning the lady is brought in a close chair, dressed in her bathing clothes, to the bath; and, being in the water, the woman who attends presents her with a little floating dish like a basin; into which the lady puts a handkerchief, a snuffbox, and a nosegay. She then traverses the bath; if a novice, with a guide, if otherwise, by herself; and having amused herself thus while she thinks proper, calls for her chair, and returns to her lodgings.

The amusement of bathing is immediately succeeded by a general assembly of people at the pumphouse; some for pleasure, and some to drink the hot waters. Three glasses at three different times is the usual portion for every drinker; and the intervals between every glass are enlivened by the harmony of a small band of music, as well as by the conversation of the gay, the witty, or the forward.

From the pumphouse the ladies, from time to time, withdraw to a female coffeehouse, and from thence return to their lodgings to breakfast. The gentlemen withdraw to their coffeehouses to read the papers, or converse on the news of the day, with a freedom and ease not to be found in the metropolis.

People of fashion make public breakfasts at the assemblyhouses, to which they invite their acquaintances, and they sometimes order private concerts; or, when so disposed, attend lectures on the arts and sciences, which are frequently taught there in a pretty superficial manner, so as not to tease the understanding, while they afford the imagination some amusement. The private concerts are performed in the ballrooms; the tickets a crown each.

Concert breakfasts at the assemblyhouse sometimes make also a part of the morning's amusement here, the expenses of which are defrayed by a subscription among the men. Persons of rank and fortune who can perform are admitted into the orchestra, and find a pleasure in joining with the performers.

Thus we have the tedious morning fairly over. When noon approaches, and church (if any please to go there) is done, some of the company appear upon the parade, and other public walks, where they continue to chat and amuse each other, till they have formed parties for the play, cards, or dancing for the evening. Another part of the company divert themselves with reading in the booksellers' shops, or are generally seen taking the air and exercise, some on horseback, some in coaches. Some walk in the meadows round the town, winding along the side of the river Avon and the neighboring canal; while others are seen scaling some of those romantic precipices that overhang the city.

When the hour of dinner draws nigh, and the company are returned from their different recreations, the provisions are generally served with the utmost elegance and plenty. Their mutton, butter, fish, and fowl, are all allowed to be excellent, and their cookery still exceeds their meat.

After dinner is over, and evening prayers ended, the company meet a second time at the pumphouse. From this they retire to the walks, and from thence go to drink tea at the assemblyhouses, and the rest of the evenings are concluded either with balls, plays, or visits. A theater was erected in the year 1705, by subscription, by people of the highest rank, who permitted their arms to be engraven on the inside of the house, as a public testimony of their liberality towards it. Every Tuesday and Friday evening is concluded with a public ball, the contributions to which are so numerous that the price of each ticket is trifling. Thus Bath yields a continued rotation of diversions, and people of all ways of thinking, even from the libertine to the Methodist, have it in their power to complete the day with employments suited to their inclinations.

A SELECTION

Christopher Anstey

1724–1805

THE NEW BATH GUIDE

1766

[Among the most-read poems of the century, *The New Bath Guide* belongs with Smollett's *Humphry Clinker* as a high-spirited commentary upon life at the resorts. Anstey's poem is distinguished by its lively anapests and its clever adaptation of the verse letter.]

Mr. Simkin B-n-r-d to Lady B-n-r-d, at —— Castle, North

LETTER VII

A Panegyric on Bath, *and a* Moravian Hymn

Of all the gay places the world can afford,
By gentle and simple for pastime ador'd,
Fine balls, and fine concerts, fine buildings, and springs,
Fine walks, and fine views, and a thousand fine things,
(Not to mention the sweet situation and air)
What place, my dear mother, with *Bath* can compare?
Let *Bristol* for commerce and dirt be renown'd,
At *Sals'bury* pen-knives and scissars be ground;

The towns of *Devizes*, of *Bradford* and *Frome*,
May boast that they better can manage the loom;   10
I believe that they may;—but the world to refine
In manners, in dress, in politeness to shine,
O *Bath!* let the art, let the glory be thine.
I'm sure that I've travell'd our country all o'er,
And ne'er was so civilly treated before;
Would you think, my dear mother, (without the least hint
That we all should be glad of appearing in print)
The news-writers here were so kind as to give all
The world an account of our happy arrival?—
You scarce can imagine what numbers I've met,   20
(Tho' to me they are perfectly strangers as yet)
Who all with address and civility came,
And seem'd vastly proud of SUBSCRIBING our name.
Young TIMOTHY CANVASS is charm'd with the place,
Who, I hear, is come hither, his fibres to brace;
Poor man! at th'election he threw, t'other day,
All his victuals, and liquor, and money away;
And some people think with such haste he began,
That soon he the constable greatly outran,
And is qualify'd now for a parliament-man: 30
Goes every day to the coffee-house, where
The wits and the great politicians repair;
Harangues on the funds and the state of the nation,
And plans a good speech for an administration,
In hopes of a place which he thinks he deserves,
As the love of his country has ruin'd his nerves.—
Our neighbour, Sir EASTERLIN WIDGEON, has swore
He ne'er will return to his bogs any more;
The *Thicksculls* are settled; we've had invitations
With a great many more on the score of relations: 40
The *Loungers* are come too.—Old STUCCO has just sent
His plan for a house to be built in the *Crescent;*
'Twill soon be complete, and they say all their work
Is as strong as *St. Paul's*, or the minster at *York.*
Don't you think 'twould be better to lease our estate,
And buy a good house here before 'tis too late?
You never can go, my dear mother, where you
So much have to see, and so little to do.
    I write this in haste, for the Captain is come,
And so kind as to go with us all to the Room;   50
But be sure by the very next post you shall hear

Of all I've the pleasure of meeting with there:
For I scribble my verse with a great deal of ease,
And can send you a letter whenever I please;
And while at this place I've the honour to stay,
I think I can never want something to say.
But now, my dear mother, &c. &c.

S—— B–n–r–d

Bath, 1766

POSTSCRIPT

I'm sorry to find at the city of *Bath*,   60
Many folks are uneasy concerning their faith:
NICODEMUS, the preacher, strives all he can do
To quiet the conscience of good sister PRUE;
But TABBY from scruples of mind is releas'd
Since she met with a learned MORAVIAN priest,
Who says, *There is neither transgression nor sin;*
A doctrine that brings many customers in.
She thinks this the prettiest ode upon earth,
Which he made on his infant that dy'd in the birth.

ODE

Chicken blessed   70
And caressed,
Little bee on JESU'S breast!
From the hurry
And the flurry
Of the earth thou'rt now at rest.

Mr. Simkin B-n-r-d to Lady B-n-r-d, at —— Hall, North

LETTER XI

A Description of the Ball, *with an Episode on* Beau Nash

What joy at the ball, what delight I have found,
Of all the bright circle encompass'd around!
Each moment with transport my bosom felt warm,
For what, my dear mother, like beauty can charm?
The remembrance alone, while their praise I rehearse,
Gives life to my numbers, and strength to my verse:
Then allow for the rapture the muses inspire,
Such themes call aloud for poetical fire.

I've read how the Goddesses meet all above,
And throng the immortal assemblies of JOVE,   10
When join'd with the Graces fair VENUS appears,
Ambrosial sweet odours perfume all the spheres;
But the Goddess of Love, and the Graces and all,
Must yield to the beauties I've seen at the ball;
For JOVE never felt such a joy at his heart,
Such a heat as these charming sweet creatures impart.
In short—there is something in very fine women,
When they meet all together—that's quite overcoming.
     Then say, O ye nymphs that inhabit the shades
Of *Pindus'* sweet banks, *Heliconian* maids,   20
Celestial Muses, ye powers divine,
O say, for your memory's better than mine,
What troops of fair virgins assembled around,
What squadrons of heroes for dancing renown'd,
Were rous'd by the fiddles' harmonious sound.
What goddess shall first be the theme of my song,
Whose name the clear AVON may murmur along,
And Echo repeat all the vallies among!
Lady TETTATON'S sister, Miss FUBBY FATARMIN,
Was the first that presented her person so charming,   30
Than whom more engaging, more beautiful none,
A goddess herself among goddesses shone,
Excepting the lovely Miss TOWZER alone.
'Tis she that has long been the toast of the town,
Tho' all the world knows her complexion is brown:
If some people think that her mouth be too wide,
Miss TOWZER has numberless beauties beside;
A countenance noble, with sweet pouting lips,
And a delicate shape from her waist to her hips;
Besides a prodigious rough black head of hair   40
All frizzled and curl'd o'er her neck that is bare;
I've seen the sweet creature but once, I confess,
But her air, and her manner, and pleasing address,
All made me feel something I ne'er can express.
     But lo! on a sudden what multitudes pour
From *Cambrian* mountains, from *Indian* shore;
Bright maidens, bright widows, and fortunate swains,
Who cultivate LIFFY'S sweet borders and plains,
And they who their flocks in fair ALBION feed,
Rich flocks and rich herds (so the gods have decreed)   50
Since they quitted the pleasanter banks of the *Tweed*.

Yet here no confusion, no tumult is known,
Fair order and beauty establish their throne;
For order, and beauty, and just regulation,
Support all the works of this ample creation.
For this, in compassion to mortals below,
The gods, their peculiar favour to shew,
Sent HERMES to *Bath* in the shape of a BEAU:
That grandson of ATLAS came down from above
To bless all the regions of pleasure and love;   60
To lead the fair nymph thro' the various maze,
Bright beauty to marshal, his glory and praise;
To govern, improve, and adorn the gay scene,
By the Graces instructed, and *Cyprian* queen:
As when in a garden delightful and gay,
Where FLORA is wont all her charms to display,
The sweet hyacinthus with pleasure we view
Contend with narcissus in delicate hue;
The gard'ner industrious trims out his border,
Puts each odoriferous plant in its order;   70
The myrtle he ranges, the rose and the lilly,
With iris, and crocus, and daffa-down-dilly;
Sweet peas and sweet oranges all he disposes
At once to regale both your eyes and your noses:
Long reign'd the great NASH, this omnipotent Lord,
Respected by youth, and by parents ador'd;
For him not enough at a ball to preside,
The unwary and beautiful nymph would he guide;
Oft tell her a tale, how the credulous maid
By man, by perfidious man, is betray'd;   80
Taught Charity's hand to relieve the distrest,
While tears have his tender compassion exprest:
But alas! he is gone, and the city can tell
How in years and in glory lamented he fell;
Him mourn'd all the Dryads on CLAVERTON'S mount;
Him AVON deplor'd, him the nymph of the Fount,
The crystalline streams.
Then perish his picture, his statue decay,
A tribute more lasting the Muses shall pay.
If true what philosophers all will assure us,   90
Who dissent from the doctrine of great EPICURUS,
That the spirit's immortal: as poets allow,
If life's occupations are follow'd below:
In reward of his labours, his virtues and pains,

He is footing it now in th'Elysian plains,
Indulg'd, as a token of PROSPERINE'S favour,
To preside at her balls in a cream-colour'd beaver:
Then peace to his ashes—our grief be supprest,
Since we find such a phoenix has sprung from his nest:
Kind Heaven has sent us another professor,[1]   100
Who follows the steps of his great predecessor.
   But hark! now they strike the melodious string,
The vaulted roof echoes, the mansions all ring;
At the sound of the hautboy, the bass and the fiddle,
Sir BOREAS BLUBBER steps forth in the middle,
Like a holy-hock, noble, majestic, and tall,
Sir BOREAS BLUBBER first opens the ball:
Sir BOREAS, great in the minuet known,
Since the day that for dancing his talents were shewn,
Where the science is practised by gentlemen grown.   110
For in every science, in ev'ry profession,
We make the best progress at years of discretion.
How he puts on his hat, with a smile on his face,
And delivers his hand with an exquisite grace!
How genteely he offers Miss CARROT before us,
Miss CARROT FITZ-OOZER, a niece of Lord PORUS!
How nimbly he paces, how active and light!
One never can judge of a man at first sight;
But as near as I guess, from the size of his calf,
He may weigh about twenty-three stone and a half.   120
Now why should I mention a hundred or more,
Who went the same circle as others before,
To a tune that they play'd us a hundred times o'er?
See little BOB JEROM, old CHRYSOSTOM'S son,
With a chitterlin shirt, and a buckle of stone:
What a cropt head of hair the young parson has on!
Emerg'd from his grizzle, th' unfortunate sprig
Seems as if he was hunting all night for his wig;
Not perfectly pleas'd with the coat on his back,
Tho' the coat's a good coat, but alas! it is black!   130
With envious eyes he is doom'd to behold
The Captain's red suit that's embroider'd with gold!
How seldom mankind are content with their lot!
BOB JEROM two very good livings has got:

1 After the death of Nash in 1761, vari- / Irishman, held the office from *ca.* 1763 to
ous persons acted as King of Bath, or Mas- / 1769.
ter of Ceremonies. Samuel Derrick, an

Yet still he accuses his parents deceas'd,
For making a man of such spirit a priest.
  Not so master MARMOZET, sweet little boy,
Mrs. DANGLECUB'S hopes, her delight and her joy:
Her pigeon-wing'd head was not drest quite so soon,
For it took up a barber the whole afternoon: 140
His jacket's well lac'd, and the ladies protest
Master MARMOZET dances as well as the best:
Yet some think the boy would be better at school;
But I hear Mrs. DANGLECUB'S not such a fool
To send a poor thing with a spirit so meek,
To be flogg'd by a tyrant for Latin and Greek;
She wonders that parents to *Eton* should send
Five hundred great boobies their manners to mend,
She says that her son will his fortune advance,
By learning so early to fiddle and dance;   150
So she brings him to *Bath*, which I think is quite right,
For they do nothing else here from morning till night;
And this is a lesson all parents should know,
To train up a child in the way he should go:
For, as SOLOMON says, you may safely uphold,
He ne'er will depart from the same when he's old.
No doubt she's a woman of fine understanding,
Her air and her presence there's something so grand in;
So wise and discreet; and, to give her her due,
Dear mother, she's just such a woman as you.   160
  But who is that bombazine lady so gay,
So profuse of her beauties in sable array?
How she rests on her heel, how she turns out her toe,
How she pulls down her stays, with her head up, to shew
Her lily-white bosom that rivals the snow!
'Tis the widow QUICKLACKIT, whose husband last week,
Poor STEPHEN, went suddenly forth in a pique,
And push'd off his boat for the *Stygian* creek:
Poor STEPHEN! he never return'd from the bourn,
But left the disconsolate widow to mourn: 170
Three times did she faint when she heard of the news;
Six days did she weep, and all comfort refuse;
But STEPHEN, no sorrow, no tears can recall!—
So she hallows the seventh, and comes to the ball.
  For music, sweet music, has charms to controul,
And tune up each passion that ruffles the soul!
What things I have read, and what stories been told

Of feats that were done by musicians of old!
I saw, t'other day, in a *thing call'd an ode*,
As it lay in a snug little house on the road,   180
How SAUL was restor'd, tho' his sorrow was sharp,
When DAVID, the *Bethlemite*, play'd on the harp:
'Twas music that brought a man's wife from *Old Nick*,
And at *Bath* has the pow'r to recover the sick:
Thus a lady was cur'd t'other day.—But 'tis time
To seal up my letter, and finish my rhyme.

                                        S—— B–n–r–d
Bath, 1766

Oliver Goldsmith

1728–1774

In a way, Goldsmith is one of the last Augustans who without method can talk us into sense. In him the "polite" note is once more heard as he moves through and about a matter with an engaging ease. His characteristic manner is an informal, almost negligent, one, a kind of genial and slovenly rococo that is ceasing to be rococo. His fondness for whimsey is more pronounced than Addison's and foreshadows the gusto of Charles Lamb; both are "humorists" in the exact sense of the word. The mood of Goldsmith, as well as of Lamb, is a "good nature" that were it not for a mellowness of character would deteriorate into sentimentality. In fact, Goldsmith's Augustan politeness, like that of Dick Steele, is always about to be dissolved into sentiment. Yet the sentimentality of Goldsmith is not the usual eighteenth-century sentimentality because it is not cultivated for its own sake. His grace is usually a little burdened with some useful precept or morality not very gravely held. *The Traveller* is filled with this sort of commonplace. *The Citizen of the World* essays are pleasing and often witty instances of the "foreign visitor" convention for mild satire. *The Deserted Village*, like *The Vicar of Wakefield*, is an idyl; it would be easy enough to argue that neither has much bearing upon life as it is or was. But sweet Auburn composes into an attractive little genre piece; one can see the same sort of picturesque composition in Gainsborough's *Market Cart* or in Constable's *Hay Wain*.

BIOGRAPHICAL NOTES

Born at Pallasmore, County Longford, Ireland, son of a rural clergyman of the Anglican church at Kilkenny West, at Lissoy, Ireland. Attended local schools (*ca.* 1736-44); then Trinity College, Dublin (1744-49), and barely secured a degree. Rejected for orders (1751); intended to study law, but lost the means at play (1752). Studied medicine, after a fashion, at Edinburgh (1752) and Leyden (1754) and wandered about the Continent (1755-56). Back in London (1756), became apothecary's assistant, physician "in a humble way," schoolteacher, corrector of press for Samuel Richardson, and finally a lifelong dweller in Grub Street. *Inquiry into the Present State of Polite Learning* and essays for *The Bee* (1759). Hack writing for *The British Magazine*, *The Monthly Review*, *The Critical Review*, and other periodicals. Met Johnson. *Citizen of the World* (1762). Became a charter member of the Club founded by Johnson, Reynolds, Burke, and others (1764). Moved into lodgings in the Temple. *The Traveller* completed with the advice of Johnson (1764). *Essays* (1765). Resumed medical practice (1765). *The Vicar of Wakefield* (1766). *The Good-natured Man* (1768). Several compilations and translations undertaken. Appointed Professor of History to the Royal Academy (1769). *The Deserted Village* (1770). *She Stoops to Conquer* (1773). Died in debt, and a victim of his own medical prescriptions. Buried in the grounds of the Temple Church.

BIBLIOGRAPHY: *Works*, ed. J. W. M. Gibbs, 5 vols., 1884-1908. *Selected Works*, ed. Richard Garnett, 1950. *New Essays*, ed. Ronald S. Crane, 1927. *Collected Letters*, ed. K. C. Balderston, 1928. Dobson, Austin, *Life of Oliver Goldsmith*, 1888. Forster, John, *Life and Times of Oliver Goldsmith*, 1871. Freeman, William, *Oliver Goldsmith*, 1951. Gwynn, Stephen, *Oliver Goldsmith*, 1935. Lucas, Frank Laurence, *In Search of Good Sense*, 1958. Wardle, Ralph M., *Oliver Goldsmith*, 1957.

THE TRAVELLER; OR, A PROSPECT OF SOCIETY

TO THE REV. HENRY GOLDSMITH

1764

Remote, unfriended, melancholy, slow,
Or by the lazy Scheld, or wandering Po;
Or onward, where the rude Carinthian boor
Against the houseless stranger shuts the door;
Or where Campania's plain forsaken lies,
A weary waste expanding to the skies;
Where'er I roam, whatever realms to see,
My heart untravell'd fondly turns to thee:
Still to my brother turns, with ceaseless pain,

And drags at each remove a lengthening chain.[1]
   Eternal blessings crown my earliest friend,
And round his dwelling guardian saints attend;
Blest be that spot, where chearful guests retire
To pause from toil, and trim their evening fire;
Blest that abode, where want and pain repair,
And every stranger finds a ready chair:
Blest be those feasts with simple plenty crown'd,
Where all the ruddy family around,
Laugh at the jests or pranks that never fail,
Or sigh with pity at some mournful tale;   20
Or press the bashful stranger to his food,
And learn the luxury of doing good.
   But me, not destin'd such delights to share,
My prime of life in wandering spent and care,
Impell'd, with steps unceasing, to pursue
Some fleeting good, that mocks me with the view;
That, like the circle bounding earth and skies,
Allures from far, yet, as I follow, flies;
My fortune leads to traverse realms alone,
And find no spot of all the world my own.   30
   Ev'n now, where Alpine solitudes ascend,
I sit me down a pensive hour to spend;
And, plac'd on high above the storm's career,
Look downward where an hundred realms appear;
Lakes, forests, cities, plains extending wide,
The pomp of kings, the shepherd's humbler pride.
   When thus Creation's charms around combine,
Amidst the store, should thankless pride repine?
Say, should the philosophic mind disdain
That good which makes each humbler bosom vain?   40
Let school-taught pride dissemble all it can,
These little things are great to little man;
And wiser he, whose sympathetic mind
Exults in all the good of all mankind.
Ye glittering towns, with wealth and splendor crown'd,
Ye fields, where summer spreads profusion round,
Ye lakes, whose vessels catch the busy gale,
Ye bending swains, that dress the flowery vale,
For me your tributary stores combine:
Creation's heir, the world, the world is mine.   50

1 See the first paragraph of Letter III of *The Citizen of the World*, where Goldsmith uses the same phrase to express nostalgia.

As some lone miser visiting his store,
Bends at his treasure, counts, recounts it o'er;
Hoards after hoards his rising raptures fill,
Yet still he sighs, for hoards are wanting still:
Thus to my breast alternate passions rise,
Pleas'd with each good that heaven to man supplies:
Yet oft a sigh prevails, and sorrows fall,
To see the hoard of human bliss so small;
And oft I wish, amidst the scene, to find
Some spot to real happiness consign'd,   60
Where my worn soul, each wandering hope at rest,
May gather bliss to see my fellows blest.
    But where to find that happiest spot below,
Who can direct, when all pretend to know?
The shudd'ring tenant of the frigid zone
Boldly proclaims that happiest spot his own;
Extols the treasures of his stormy seas,
And his long nights of revelry and ease;
The naked negro, panting at the line,
Boasts of his golden sands and palmy wine,   70
Basks in the glare, or stems the tepid wave,
And thanks his gods for all the good they gave.
Such is the patriot's boast, where'er we roam,
His first, best country ever is, at home.
And yet, perhaps, if countries we compare,
And estimate the blessings which they share;
Though patriots flatter, still shall wisdom find
An equal portion dealt to all mankind,
As different good, by art or nature given,
To different nations makes their blessings even.   80
    Nature, a mother kind alike to all,
Still grants her bliss at labour's earnest call;
With food as well the peasant is supply'd
On Idra's cliffs as Arno's shelvy side;
And though the rocky crested summits frown,
These rocks, by custom, turn to beds of down.
From art more various are the blessings sent;
Wealth, commerce, honour, liberty, content.
Yet these each other's power so strong contest.
That either seems destructive of the rest.   90
Where wealth and freedom reign contentment fails,
And honour sinks where commerce long prevails.
Hence every state to one lov'd blessing prone,

Conforms and models life to that alone.
Each to the fav'rite happiness attends,
And spurns the plan that aims at other ends;
'Till carried to excess in each domain,
This fav'rite good begets peculiar pain.

But let us try these truths with closer eyes,
And trace them through the prospect as it lies:　　　　100
Here for a while my proper cares resign'd,
Here let me sit in sorrow for mankind;
Like yon neglected shrub at random cast,
That shades the steep, and sighs at every blast.

Far to the right where Appennine ascends,
Bright as the summer, Italy extends;
Its uplands sloping deck the mountain's side,
Woods over woods in gay theatric pride;
While oft some temple's mould'ring tops between,
With venerable grandeur mark the scene.　　　　110

Could Nature's bounty satisfy the breast,
The sons of Italy were surely blest.
Whatever fruits in different climes were found,
That proudly rise, or humbly court the ground;
Whatever blooms in torrid tracts appear,
Whose bright succession decks the varied year;
Whatever sweets salute the northern sky
With vernal lives, that blossom but to die;
These here disporting own the kindred soil,
Nor ask luxuriance from the planter's toil;　　　　120
While sea-born gales their gelid wings expand
To winnow fragrance round the smiling land.

But small the bliss that sense alone bestows,
And sensual bliss is all the nation knows.
In florid beauty groves and fields appear,
Man seems the only growth that dwindles here.
Contrasted faults through all his manners reign:
Though poor, luxurious; though submissive, vain;
Though grave, yet trifling; zealous, yet untrue,
And even in penance planning sins anew.　　　　130
All evils here contaminate the mind,
That opulence departed leaves behind;
For wealth was theirs, nor far remov'd the date,
When commerce proudly flourish'd through the state;
At her command the palace learnt to rise,
Again the long-fall'n column sought the skies;

The canvas glow'd beyond e'en Nature warm,
The pregnant quarry teem'd with human form.
Till, more unsteady than the southern gale,
Commerce on other shores display'd her sail;   140
While nought remain'd of all that riches gave,
But towns unmann'd, and lords without a slave:
And late the nation found with fruitless skill
Its former strength was but plethoric ill.

Yet, still the loss of wealth is here supplied
By arts, the splendid wrecks of former pride;
From these the feeble heart and long-fallen mind
An easy compensation seem to find.
Here may be seen, in bloodless pomp array'd,
The paste-board triumph and the cavalcade;   150
Processions form'd for piety and love,
A mistress or a saint in every grove.
By sports like these are all their cares beguil'd,
The sports of children satisfy the child;
Each nobler aim represt by long controul,
Now sinks at last, or feebly mans the soul;
While low delights, succeeding fast behind,
In happier meanness occupy the mind:
As in those domes, where Cæsars once bore sway,
Defac'd by time and tott'ring in decay,   160
There in the ruin, heedless of the dead,
The shelter-seeking peasant builds his shed;
And, wondering man could want the larger pile,
Exults, and owns his cottage with a smile.

My soul turn from them, turn we to survey
Where rougher climes a nobler race display,
Where the bleak Swiss their stormy mansion tread,
And force a churlish soil for scanty bread;
No product here the barren hills afford,
But man and steel, the soldier and his sword.   170
No vernal blooms their torpid rocks array,
But winter lingering chills the lap of May;
No zephyr fondly sues the mountain's breast,
But meteors glare, and stormy glooms invest.

Yet still, even here, content can spread a charm,
Redress the clime, and all its rage disarm.
Though poor the peasant's hut, his feasts though small,
He sees his little lot the lot of all;
Sees no contiguous palace rear its head

To shame the meanness of his humble shed;   180
No costly lord the sump.uous banquet deal
To make him loath his vegetable meal;
But calm, and bred in ignorance and toil,
Each wish contracting, fits him to the soil.
Chearful at morn he wakes from short repose,
Breathes the keen air, and carols as he goes;
With patient angle trolls the finny deep,
Or drives his vent'rous plow-share to the steep;
Or seeks the den where snow-tracks mark the way,
And drags the struggling savage [2] into day.   190
At night returning, every labour sped,
He sits him down the monarch of a shed;
Smiles by his chearful fire, and round surveys
His children's looks, that brighten at the blaze;
While his lov'd partner, boastful of her hoard,
Displays her cleanly platter on the board:
And haply too some pilgrim, thither led,
With many a tale repays the nightly bed.
    Thus every good his native wilds impart,
Imprints the patriot passion on his heart;   200
And even those ills, that round his mansion rise,
Enhance the bliss his scanty fund supplies.
Dear is that shed to which his soul conforms,
And dear that hill which lifts him to the storms;
And as a child, when scaring sounds molest,
Clings close and closer to the mother's breast,
So the loud torrent, and the whirlwind's roar,
But bind him to his native mountains more.
    Such are the charms to barren states assign'd;
Their wants but few, their wishes all confin'd.   210
Yet let them only share the praises due,
If few their wants. their pleasures are but few;
For every want that stimulates the breast,
Becomes a source of pleasure when redrest.
Whence from such lands each pleasing science flies,
That first excites desire, and then supplies;
Unknown to them, when sensual pleasures cloy,
To fill the languid pause with finer joy;
Unknown those powers that raise the soul to flame,
Catch every nerve, and vibrate through the frame.   220
Their level life is but a smouldering fire.

[2] Wild beast.

Unquench'd by want, unfann'd by strong desire;
Unfit for raptures, or, if raptures chear
On some high festival of once a year,
In wild excess the vulgar breast takes fire,
Till, buried in debauch, the bliss expire.
But not their joys alone thus coarsely flow:
Their morals, like their pleasures, are but low,
For, as refinement stops, from sire to son
Unalter'd, unimprov'd the manners run,   230
And love's and friendship's finely pointed dart
Fall blunted from each indurated heart.
Some sterner virtues o'er the mountain's breast
May sit, like falcons cow'ring on the nest;
But all the gentler morals, such as play
Through life's more cultur'd walks, and charm the way,
These far dispers'd, on timorous pinions fly,
To sport and flutter in a kinder sky.
To kinder skies, where gentler manners reign,
I turn; and France displays her bright domain.   240
Gay sprightly land of mirth and social ease,
Pleas'd with thyself, whom all the world can please,
How often have I led thy sportive choir,
With tuneless pipe, beside the murmuring Loire?
Where shading elms along the margin grew,
And freshen'd from the wave the zephyr flew;
And haply, though my harsh touch falt'ring still,
But mock'd all tune, and marr'd the dancer's skill;
Yet would the village praise my wonderous power,
And dance, forgetful of the noon-tide hour.   250
Alike all ages. Dames of ancient days
Have led their children through the mirthful maze,
And the gay grandsire, skill'd in gestic lore,
Has frisk'd beneath the burthen of threescore.
So blest a life these thoughtless realms display,
Thus idly busy rolls their world away:
Theirs are those arts that mind to mind endear,
For honour forms the social temper here.
Honour, that praise which real merit gains,
Or even imaginary worth obtains,   260
Here passes current; paid from hand to hand,
It shifts in splendid traffick round the land:
From courts, to camps, to cottages it strays,
And all are taught an avarice of praise;

They please, are pleas'd, they give to get esteem,
Till, seeming blest, they grow to what they seem.
But while this softer art their bliss supplies,
It gives their follies also room to rise;
For praise too dearly lov'd, or warmly sought,
Enfeebles all internal strength of thought.   270
And the weak soul, within itself unblest,
Leans for all pleasure on another's breast.
Hence ostentation here, with tawdry art,
Pants for the vulgar praise which fools impart;
Here vanity assumes her pert grimace,
And trims her robes of frize with copper lace,
Here beggar pride defrauds her daily cheer,
To boast one splendid banquet once a year;
The mind still turns where shifting fashion draws,
Nor weighs the solid worth of self applause.   280
To men of other minds my fancy flies,
Embosom'd in the deep where Holland lies,
Methinks her patient sons before me stand,
Where the broad ocean leans against the land,
And, sedulous to stop the coming tide,
Lift the tall rampire's artificial pride.
Onward methinks, and diligently slow,
The firm connected bulwark seems to grow.
Spreads its long arms amidst the watery roar,
Scoops out an empire, and usurps the shore.   290
While the pent ocean rising o'er the pile,
Sees an amphibious world beneath him smile;
The slow canal, the yellow blossom'd vale,
The willow tufted bank, the gliding sail,
The crouded mart, the cultivated plain,
A new creation rescu'd from his reign.
Thus, while around the wave-subjected soil
Impels the native to repeated toil,
Industrious habits in each bosom reign,
And industry begets a love of gain.   300
Hence all the good from opulence that springs,
With all those ills superfluous treasure brings,
Are here displayed. Their much-lov'd wealth imparts
Convenience, plenty, elegance, and arts;
But view them closer, craft and fraud appear,
Even liberty itself is barter'd here.
At gold's superior charms all freedom flies,

The needy sell it, and the rich man buys;
A land of tyrants, and a den of slaves,
Here wretches seek dishonourable graves,   310
And calmly bent, to servitude conform,
Dull as their lakes that slumber in the storm.
  Heavens! how unlike their Belgic sires of old!
Rough, poor, content, ungovernably bold;
War in each breast, and freedom on each brow;
How much unlike the sons of Britain now!
  Fir'd at the sound my genius spreads her wing,
And flies where Britain courts the western spring;
Where lawns extend that scorn Arcadian pride,
And brighter streams than fam'd Hydaspis glide.   320
There all around the gentlest breezes stray,
There gentle music melts on every spray;
Creation's mildest charms are there combin'd.
Extremes are only in the master's mind!
Stern o'er each bosom Reason holds her state.
With daring aims irregularly great;
Pride in their port, defiance in their eye,
I see the lords of human kind pass by;
Intent on high designs, a thoughtful band,
By forms unfashion'd, fresh from Nature's hand;   330
Fierce in their native hardiness of soul,
True to imagin'd right, above controul,
While even the peasant boasts these rights to scan,
And learns to venerate himself as man.
  Thine, Freedom, thine the blessings pictur'd here,
Thine are those charms that dazzle and endear;
Too blest indeed, were such without alloy,
But foster'd even by Freedom ills annoy:
That independence Britons prize too high,
Keeps man from man, and breaks the social tie;   340
The self-dependent lordlings stand alone,
All claims that bind and sweeten life unknown;
Here by the bonds of nature feebly held,
Minds combat minds, repelling and repell'd.
Ferments arise, imprison'd factions roar,
Represt ambition struggles round her shore,
Till over-wrought, the general system feels
Its motions stopt, or phrenzy fire the wheels.
  Nor this the worst. As nature's ties decay,
As duty, love, and honour fail to sway,   350

Fictitious bonds, the bonds of wealth and law,
Still gather strength, and force unwilling awe.
Hence all obedience bows to these alone,
And talent sinks, and merit weeps unknown;
Till time may come, when stript of all her charms,
The land of scholars, and the nurse of arms,
Where noble stems transmit the patriot flame,
Where kings have toil'd, and poets wrote for fame,
One sink of level avarice shall lie,
And scholars, soldiers, kings, unhonour'd die.   360

    Yet think not, thus when Freedom's ills I state,
I mean to flatter kings, or court the great;
Ye powers of truth that bid my soul aspire,
Far from my bosom drive the low desire;
And thou fair Freedom, taught alike to feel
The rabble's rage, and tyrant's angry steel;
Thou transitory flower, alike undone
By proud contempt, or favour's fostering sun,
Still may thy blooms the changeful clime endure,
I only would repress them to secure: 370
For just experience tells; in every soil,
That those who think must govern those that toil;
And all that freedom's highest aims can reach,
Is but to lay proportion'd loads on each.
Hence, should one order disproportion'd grow,
Its double weight must ruin all below.

    O then how blind to all that truth requires,
Who think it freedom when a part aspires!
Calm is my soul, nor apt to rise in arms,
Except when fast approaching danger warms: 380
But when contending chiefs blockade the throne,
Contracting regal power to stretch their own,
When I behold a factious band agree
To call it freedom when themselves are free;
Each wanton judge new penal statutes draw,
Laws grind the poor, and rich men rule the law;
The wealth of climes, where savage nations roam,
Pillag'd from slaves to purchase slaves at home;
Fear, pity, justice, indignation start,
Tear off reserve, and bare my swelling heart;   390
'Till half a patriot, half a coward grown,
I fly from petty tyrants to the throne.

Yes, brother, curse with me that baleful hour,
When first ambition struck at regal power;
And thus polluting honour in its source,
Gave wealth to sway the mind with double force.
Have we not seen, round Britain's peopled shore,
Her useful sons exchang'd for useless ore?
Seen all her triumphs but destruction haste,
Like flaring tapers bright'ning as they waste;   400
Seen opulence, her grandeur to maintain,
Lead stern depopulation in her train,
And over fields where scatter'd hamlets rose,
In barren solitary pomp repose?
Have we not seen at pleasure's lordly call,
The smiling long-frequented village fall?
Beheld the duteous son, the sire decay'd,
The modest matron, and the blushing maid,
Forc'd from their homes, a melancholy train,
To traverse climes beyond the western main;   410
Where wild Oswego spreads her swamps around,
And Niagara stuns with thund'ring sound?
    Even now, perhaps, as there some pilgrim strays
Through tangled forests, and through dangerous ways;
Where beasts with man divided empire claim,
And the brown Indian marks with murd'rous aim;
There, while above the giddy tempest flies,
And all around distressful yells arise,
The pensive exile, bending with his woe,
To stop too fearful, and too faint to go,   420
Casts a long look where England's glories shine,
And bids his bosom sympathize with mine.
    Vain, very vain, my weary search to find
That bliss which only centers in the mind:
Why have I stray'd, from pleasure and repose,
To seek a good each government bestows?
In every government, though terrors reign,
Though tyrant kings, or tyrant laws restrain,
How small of all that human hearts endure,
That part which laws or kings can cause or cure.   430
Still to ourselves in every place consign'd,
Our own felicity we make or find:
With secret course, which no loud storms annoy,
Glides the smooth current of domestic joy.

The lifted ax, the agonizing wheel,
Luke's iron crown,[3] and Damiens' bed of steel,
To men remote from power but rarely known,
Leave reason, faith, and conscience, all our own.

THE DESERTED VILLAGE, A POEM

1770

Sweet Auburn! loveliest village of the plain,
Where health and plenty cheer'd the labouring swain,
Where smiling spring its earliest visit paid,
And parting summer's ling'ring blooms delay'd,
Dear lovely bowers of innocence and ease,
Seats of my youth, when every sport could please,
How often have I loiter'd o'er thy green,
Where humble happiness endear'd each scene!
How often have I paus'd on every charm,
The shelter'd cot, the cultivated farm,   10
The never-failing brook, the busy mill,
The decent church that topt the neighb'ring hill,
The hawthorn bush, with seats beneath the shade,
For talking age and whisp'ring lovers made;
How often have I blest the coming day,
When toil remitting lent its turn to play,
And all the village train, from labour free,
Led up their sports beneath the spreading tree,
While many a pastime circled in the shade,
The young contending as the old survey'd;   20
And many a gambol frolick'd o'er the ground,
And sleights of art and feats of strength went round;
And still as each repeated pleasure tir'd,
Succeeding sports the mirthful band inspir'd;
The dancing pair that simply sought renown,
By holding out to tire each other down;
The swain mistrustless of his smutted face,
While secret laughter titter'd round the place;
The bashful virgin's side-long looks of love,

---

[3] George (not Luke) Dosza, a Hungarian patriot, was punished in 1514 for rebellion by having placed on his head a red-hot crown. Robert François Damiens in 1757 was tortured, then drawn by horses, for attempting to kill Louis XV of France

The matron's glance that would those looks reprove. 30
These were thy charms, sweet village! sports like these,
With sweet succession, taught ev'n toil to please;
These round thy bowers their chearful influence shed,
These were thy charms—But all these charms are fled.
   Sweet smiling village, loveliest of the lawn,
Thy sports are fled, and all thy charms withdrawn;
Amidst thy bowers the tyrant's hand is seen,
And desolation saddens all thy green:
One only master grasps the whole domain,
And half a tillage stints thy smiling plain; 40
No more thy glassy brook reflects the day,
But choak'd with sedges, works its weedy way;
Along thy glades, a solitary guest,
The hollow sounding bittern guards its nest;
Amidst thy desert walks the lapwing flies,
And tires their echoes with unvary'd cries.
Sunk are thy bowers, in shapeless ruin all,
And the long grass o'ertops the mould'ring wall,
And, trembling, shrinking from the spoiler's hand,
Far, far away thy children leave the land. 50
   Ill fares the land, to hast'ning ills a prey,
Where wealth accumulates, and men decay;
Princes and lords may flourish, or may fade;
A breath can make them, as a breath has made;
But a bold peasantry, their country's pride,
When once destroy'd, can never be supply'd.
   A time there was, ere England's griefs began,
When every rood of ground maintain'd its man;
For him light labour spread her wholesome store,
Just gave what life requir'd, but gave no more: 60
His best companions, innocence and health;
And his best riches, ignorance of wealth.
   But times are altered; trade's unfeeling train
Usurp the land and dispossess the swain;
Along the lawn, where scatter'd hamlets rose,
Unwieldy wealth, and cumb'rous pomp repose;
And every want to oppulence ally'd,
And every pang that folly pays to pride.
These gentle hours that plenty bade to bloom,
Those calm desires that ask'd but little room, 70
Those healthful sports that grac'd the peaceful scene,
Liv'd in each look, and brighten'd all the green;

These far departing seek a kinder shore,
And rural mirth and manners are no more.
   Sweet Auburn! parent of the blissful hour,
Thy glades forlorn confess the tyrant's power.
Here, as I take my solitary rounds,
Amidst thy tangling walks, and ruin'd grounds,
And, many a year elaps'd, return to view
Where once the cottage stood, the hawthorn grew,   80
Remembrance wakes with all her busy train,
Swells at my breast, and turns the past to pain.
   In all my wand'rings round this world of care,
In all my griefs—and God has giv'n my share—
I still had hopes my latest hours to crown,
Amidst these humble bowers to lay me down;
To husband out life's taper at the close,
And keep the flame from wasting by repose.
I still had hopes, for pride attends us still,
Amidst the swains to shew my book-learn'd skill,   90
Around my fire an evening group to draw,
And tell of all I felt, and all I saw;
And, as an hare whom hounds and horns pursue,
Pants to the place from whence at first she flew,
I still had hopes, my long vexations past,
Here to return—and die at home at last.
   O blest retirement, friend to life's decline,
Retreats from care that never must be mine,
How happy he who crowns in shades like these,
A youth of labour with an age of ease;   100
Who quits a world where strong temptations try,
And, since 'tis hard to combat, learns to fly.
For him no wretches, born to work and weep,
Explore the mine, or tempt the dang'rous deep;
No surly porter stands in guilty state
To spurn imploring famine from the gate;
But on he moves to meet his latter end,
Angels around befriending virtue's friend;
Sinks to the grave with unperceiv'd decay,
While resignation gently slopes the way;   110
And, all his prospects bright'ning to the last,
His Heaven commences ere the world be past!
   Sweet was the sound when oft at ev'ning's close,
Up yonder hill the village murmur rose;
There, as I past with careless steps and slow,

The mingling notes came soften'd from below;
The swain responsive as the milk-maid sung,
The sober herd that low'd to meet their young,
The noisy geese that gabbled o'er the pool,
The playful children just let loose from school; 120
The watch-dog's voice that bay'd the whisp'ring wind,
And the loud laugh that spoke the vacant mind;
These all in sweet confusion sought the shade,
And fill'd each pause the nightingale had made.
But now the sounds of population fail,
No cheerful murmurs fluctuate in the gale,
No busy steps the grass-grown foot-way tread,
For all the bloomy flush of life is fled.
All but yon widow'd, solitary thing
That feebly bends beside the plashy spring; 13
She, wretched matron, forc'd, in age, for bread,
To strip the brook with mantling cresses spread,
To pick her wintry faggot from the thorn,
To seek her nightly shed, and weep till morn;
She only left of all the harmless train,
The sad historian of the pensive plain.
   Near yonder copse, where once the garden smil'd,
And still where many a garden flower grows wild;
There, where a few torn shrubs the place disclose,
The village preacher's modest mansion rose. 1 μ
A man he was, to all the country dear,
And passing rich with forty pounds a year;
Remote from towns he ran his godly race,
Nor e'er had changed, nor wish'd to change his place;
Unpractised he to fawn, or seek for power,
By doctrines fashion'd to the varying hour;
Far other aims his heart had learn'd to prize,
More skilled to raise the wretched than to rise.
His house was known to all the vagrant train,
He chid their wand'rings, but reliev'd their pain; 150
The long remember'd beggar was his guest,
Whose beard descending swept his aged breast;
The ruin'd spendthrift, now no longer proud,
Claim'd kindred there, and had his claims allow'd;
The broken soldier, kindly bade to stay,
Sate by his fire, and talk'd the night away;
Wept o'er his wounds, or tales of sorrow done,
Shoulder'd his crutch, and shew'd how fields were won.

Pleas'd with his guests, the good man learn'd to glow, 160
And quite forgot their vices in their woe;
Careless their merits, or their faults to scan,
His pity gave ere charity began.
Thus to relieve the wretched was his pride,
And even his failings lean'd to Virtue's side;
But in his duty prompt at every call,
He watch'd and wept, he pray'd and felt, for all.
And, as a bird each fond endearment tries,
To tempt its new fledg'd offspring to the skies;
He tried each art, reprov'd each dull delay,
Allur'd to brighter worlds, and led the way. 170
Beside the bed where parting life was laid,
And sorrow, guilt, and pain, by turns dismay'd,
The rev'rend champion stood. At his controul,
Despair and anguish fled the struggling soul;
Comfort came down the trembling wretch to raise,
And his last fault'ring accents whisper'd praise.
At church, with meek and unaffected grace,
His looks adorn'd the venerable place;
Truth from his lips prevail'd with double sway,
And fools, who came to scoff, remain'd to pray. 180
The service past, around the pious man,
With steady zeal each honest rustic ran;
Even children follow'd with endearing wile,
And pluck'd his gown, to share the good man's smile.
His ready smile a parent's warmth exprest,
Their welfare pleas'd him, and their cares distrest;
To them his heart, his love, his griefs were given,
But all his serious thoughts had rest in heaven.
As some tall cliff that lifts its awful form,
Swells from the vale, and midway leaves the storm, 190
Though round its breast the rolling clouds are spread,
Eternal sunshine settles on its head.
Beside yon straggling fence that skirts the way,
With blossom'd furze unprofitably gay,
There, in his noisy mansion, skill'd to rule,
The village master taught his little school;
A man severe he was, and stern to view,
I knew him well, and every truant knew;
Well had the boding tremblers learn'd to trace
The day's disasters in his morning face; 200
Full well they laugh'd with counterfeited glee,

At all his jokes, for many a joke had he;
Full well the busy whisper circling round,
Convey'd the dismal tidings when he frown'd;
Yet he was kind, or if severe in aught,
The love he bore to learning was in fault;
The village all declar'd how much he knew;
'Twas certain he could write, and cypher too;
Lands he could measure, terms and tides presage,
And even the story ran that he could gauge.   210
In arguing too, the parson own'd his skill,
For even though vanquish'd, he could argue still;
While words of learned length, and thundering sound,
Amaz'd the gazing rustics rang'd around;
And still they gaz'd, and still the wonder grew,
That one small head could carry all he knew.
   But past is all his fame. The very spot
Where many a time he triumph'd, is forgot.
Near yonder thorn, that lifts its head on high,
Where once the sign-post caught the passing eye,   220
Low lies that house where nut-brown draughts inspir'd,
Where grey-beard mirth and smiling toil retir'd,
Where village statesmen talk'd with looks profound,
And news much older than their ale went round.
Imagination fondly stoops to trace
The parlour splendours of that festive place;
The white-wash'd wall, the nicely sanded floor,
The varnish'd clock that click'd behind the door;
The chest contriv'd a double debt to pay,
A bed by night, a chest of drawers by day;   230
The pictures plac'd for ornament and use,
The twelve good rules, the royal game of goose;
The hearth, except when winter chill'd the day,
With aspen boughs, and flowers, and fennel gay,
While broken tea-cups, wisely kept for shew,
Rang'd o'er the chimney, glisten'd in a row.
   Vain transitory splendor! Could not all
Reprieve the tott'ring mansion from its fall!
Obscure it sinks, nor shall it more impart
An hour's importance to the poor man's heart;   240
Thither no more the peasant shall repair
To sweet oblivion of his daily care;
No more the farmer's news, the barber's tale,
No more the wood-man's ballad shall prevail;

No more the smith his dusky brow shall clear,
Relax his pond'rous strength, and lean to hear;
The host himself no longer shall be found
Careful to see the mantling bliss go round;
Nor the coy maid, half willing to be prest,
Shall kiss the cup to pass it to the rest.   250
    Yes! let the rich deride, the proud disdain,
These simple blessings of the lowly train,
To me more dear, congenial to my heart,
One native charm, than all the gloss of art;
Spontaneous joys, where Nature has its play,
The soul adopts, and owns their first-born sway;
Lightly they frolic o'er the vacant mind,
Unenvi'd, unmolested, unconfin'd.
But the long pomp, the midnight masquerade,
With all the freaks of wanton wealth array'd,   260
In these, ere triflers half their wish obtain,
The toiling pleasure sickens into pain;
And, even while fashion's brightest arts decoy,
The heart distrusting asks, if this be joy.
    Ye friends to truth, ye statesmen, who survey
The rich man's joys encrease, the poor's decay,
'Tis yours to judge, how wide the limits stand
Between a splendid and an happy land.
Proud swells the tide with loads of freighted ore,
And shouting Folly hails them from her shore;   270
Hoards, even beyond the miser's wish abound,
And rich men flock from all the world around.
Yet count our gains. This wealth is but a name
That leaves our useful products still the same.
Not so the loss. The man of wealth and pride,
Takes up a space that many poor supply'd;
Space for his lake, his park's extended bounds,
Space for his horses, equipage, and hounds;
The robe that wraps his limbs in silken sloth,
Has robb'd the neighbouring fields of half their growth;   280
His seat, where solitary sports are seen,
Indignant spurns the cottage from the green;
Around the world each needful product flies,
For all the luxuries the world supplies.
While thus the land adorn'd for pleasure, all
In barren splendor feebly waits the fall.
    As some fair female unadorn'd and plain,

Secure to please while youth confirms her reign,
Slights every borrowed charm that dress supplies,
Nor shares with art the triumph of her eyes: 290
But when those charms are past, for charms are frail,
When time advances, and when lovers fail,
She then shines forth, sollicitous to bless,
In all the glaring impotence of dress.
Thus fares the land, by luxury betray'd;
In nature's simplest charms at first array'd;
But verging to decline, its splendors rise,
Its vistas strike, its palaces surprise;
While scourg'd by famine from the smiling land,
The mournful peasant leads his humble band;   300
And while he sinks without one arm to save,
The country blooms—a garden, and a grave.
    Where then, ah! where shall poverty reside,
To scape the pressure of contiguous pride?
If to some common's fenceless limits stray'd,
He drives his flock to pick the scanty blade,
Those fenceless fields the sons of wealth divide,
And even the bare-worn common is deny'd.
    If to the city sped—What waits him there?
To see profusion that he must not share;   310
To see ten thousand baneful arts combin'd
To pamper luxury, and thin mankind;
To see those joys the sons of pleasure know,
Extorted from his fellow-creature's woe.
Here, while the courtier glitters in brocade,
There the pale artist [1] plies the sickly trade;
Here, while the proud their long-drawn pomps display,
There the black gibbet glooms beside the way.
The dome where Pleasure holds her midnight reign,
Here, richly deckt, admits the gorgeous train;   320
Tumultuous grandeur crouds the blazing square,
The rattling chariots clash, the torches glare.
Sure scenes like these no troubles e'er annoy!
Sure these denote one universal joy!
Are these thy serious thoughts?—Ah, turn thine eyes
Where the poor houseless shiv'ring female lies.
She once, perhaps, in village plenty blest,
Has wept at tales of innocence distrest;
Her modest looks the cottage might adorn,

1 Artisan.

Sweet as the primrose peeps beneath the thorn;   330
Now lost to all; her friends, her virtue fled,
Near her betrayer's door she lays her head,
And pinch'd with cold, and shrinking from the shower,
With heavy heart deplores that luckless hour,
When idly first, ambitious of the town,
She left her wheel and robes of country brown.

Do thine, sweet AUBURN, thine, the loveliest train,
Do thy fair tribes participate her pain?
Even now, perhaps, by cold and hunger led,
At proud men's doors they ask a little bread!   340
Ah, no. To distant climes, a dreary scene,
Where half the convex world intrudes between,
Through torrid tracts with fainting steps they go,
Where wild Altama [2] murmurs to their woe.
Far different there from all that charm'd before,
The various terrors of that horrid shore;
Those blazing suns that dart a downward ray,
And fiercely shed intolerable day;
Those matted woods where birds forget to sing,
But silent bats in drowsy clusters cling,   350
Those pois'nous fields with rank luxuriance crown'd,
Where the dark scorpion gathers death around;
Where at each step the stranger fears to wake
The rattling terrors of the vengeful snake;
Where crouching tigers wait their hapless prey,
And savage men, more murd'rous still than they;
While oft in whirls the mad tornado flies,
Mingling the ravag'd landschape with the skies.
Far different these from every former scene,
The cooling brook, the grassy vested green,   360
The breezy covert of the warbling grove,
That only shelter'd thefts of harmless love.

Good Heaven! what sorrows gloom'd that parting day,
That called them from their native walks away;
When the poor exiles, every pleasure past,
Hung round their bowers, and fondly look'd their last,
And took a long farewel, and wish'd in vain
For seats like these beyond the western main;
And shudd'ring still to face the distant deep,
Return'd and wept, and still return'd to weep.   37c
The good old sire, the first prepar'd to go

2 A river in Georgia.

To new-found worlds, and wept for other's woe.
But for himself, in conscious virtue brave,
He only wish'd for worlds beyond the grave.
His lovely daughter, lovelier in her tears,
The fond companion of his helpless years,
Silent went next, neglectful of her charms,
And left a lover's for a father's arms.
With louder plaints the mother spoke her woes,
And blest the cot where every pleasure rose;   380
And kist her thoughtless babes with many a tear,
And claspt them close in sorrow doubly dear;
Whilst her fond husband strove to lend relief
In all the silent manliness of grief.

   O luxury! Thou curst by heaven's decree,
How ill exchang'd are things like these for thee!
How do thy potions, with insidious joy,
Diffuse their pleasures only to destroy!
Kingdoms, by thee, to sickly greatness grown,
Boast of a florid vigour not their own.   390
At every draught more large and large they grow,
A bloated mass of rank unwieldy woe;
Till sapp'd their strength, and every part unsound,
Down, down they sink, and spread a ruin round.

   Even now the devastation is begun,
And half the business of destruction done;
Even now, methinks, as pond'ring here I stand,
I see the rural virtues leave the land.
Down where yon anchoring vessel spreads the sail,
That idly waiting flaps with every gale,   400
Downward they move, a melancholy band,
Pass from the shore, and darken all the strand.
Contented toil, and hospitable care,
And kind connubial tenderness, are there;
And piety, with wishes plac'd above,
And steady loyalty, and faithful love:
And thou, sweet Poetry, thou loveliest maid,
Still first to fly where sensual joys invade;
Unfit in these degen'rate times of shame,
To catch the heart, or strike for honest fame;   410
Dear charming nymph, neglected and decry'd,
My shame in crouds, my solitary pride;
Thou source of all my bliss, and all my woe,
That found'st me poor at first, and keep'st me so;

Thou guide by which the nobler arts excel,
Thou nurse of every virtue, fare thee well.
Farewel, and O! where'er thy voice be try'd,
On Torno's cliffs, or Pambamarca's side,
Whether where equinoctial fervours glow,
Or winter wraps the polar world in snow,   420
Still let thy voice prevailing over time,
Redress the rigours of th' inclement clime;
Aid slighted truth, with thy persuasive strain
Teach erring man to spurn the rage of gain;
Teach him, that states of native strength possest,
Though very poor, may still be very blest;
That trade's proud empire hastes to swift decay,
As ocean sweeps the labour'd mole away;
While self-dependent power can time defy,
As rocks resist the billows and the sky.   430

AN INQUIRY INTO THE PRESENT STATE OF POLITE LEARNING IN EUROPE

1759, 1774

CHAPTER XI

Of the Marks of Literary Decay in France and England

The faults already mentioned are such as learning is often found to flourish under; but there is one of a much more dangerous nature, which has begun to fix itself among us. I mean criticism, which may properly be called the natural destroyer of polite learning. We have seen that critics, or those whose only business is to write books upon other books, are always more numerous as learning is more diffused; and experience has shown that, instead of promoting its interest, which they profess to do, they generally injure it. This decay which criticism produces may be deplored, but can scarcely be remedied, as the man who writes against the critics is obliged to add himself to the number. Other depravations in the republic of letters, such as affectation in some popular writer, leading others into vicious imitation; political struggles in the state; a depravity of morals among the people; ill-directed encouragement, or no encouragement, from the great,—these have been often found to co-operate in the decline of literature; and it has sometimes declined, as in modern Italy, without them; but an increase of criticism has always portended a decay. Of all misfortunes, therefore, in the commonwealth of letters, this of judging from rule, and not from feeling, is the most severe. At such a tribunal no work of original merit can please. Sublimity, if carried to an exalted height, approaches burlesque, and humor sinks into vulgarity. The person who cannot feel may ridicule both as such, and bring rules to corroborate his assertion. There is, in short, no excellence in writing that such judges may not place among the neighboring defects. Rules render the reader more difficult to be pleased, and abridge the author's power of pleasing.

If we turn to either country, we shall perceive evident symptoms of this natural decay beginning to appear. Upon a moderate calculation, there seem to be as many volumes of criticism published in those countries as of all other kinds of polite erudition united. Paris sends forth not less than four literary journals every month: the *Année Littéraire* and the *Feuille*, by Fréron; the *Journal Etrangère* by the Chevalier d'Arc; and *Le Mercure*, by Marmontel. We have two literary reviews in London,[1] with critical newspapers and magazines without number. The compilers of these resemble the commoners of Rome; they are all for leveling property not by increasing their own, but by diminishing that of others. The man who has any good nature in his disposition must, however, be somewhat displeased to see distinguished reputations often the sport of ignorance,—to see, by one false pleasantry, the future peace of a worthy man's life disturbed, and this only because he has unsuccessfully attempted to instruct or amuse us. Though ill nature is far from being wit, yet it is generally laughed at as such. The critic enjoys the triumph and ascribes to his parts what is only due to his effrontery. I fire with indignation when I see persons wholly destitute of education and genius indent to the press, and thus turn bookmakers, adding to the sin of criticism the sin of ignorance also; whose trade is a bad one, and who are bad workmen in the trade.

When I consider those industrious men as indebted to the works of others for a precarious subsistence; when I see them coming

---

[1] The *Monthly Review* and the *Critical Review;* Goldsmith had contributed to the *Monthly,* and Smollett had edited the *Critical* from 1756 to 1759.

down at stated intervals to rummage the bookseller's counter for materials to work upon, it raises a smile, though mixed with pity. It reminds me of an animal called by naturalists the soldier. "This little creature," says the historian, "is passionately fond of a shell, but not being supplied with one by nature, has recourse to the deserted shell of some other. I have seen these harmless reptiles," continues he, "come down once a year from the mountains, rank and file, cover the whole shore, and ply busily about, each in quest of a shell to please it. Nothing can be more amusing than their industry upon this occasion. One shell is too big, another too little: they enter and keep possession sometimes for a good while, until one is, at last, found entirely to please. When all are thus properly equipped, they march up again to the mountains, and live in their new acquisition till under a necessity of changing."

There is, indeed, scarcely an error of which our present writers are guilty that does not arise from their opposing systems; there is scarcely an error that criticism cannot be brought to excuse. From this proceeds the affected security of our odes, the tuneless flow of our blank verse, the pompous epithet, labored diction, and every other deviation from common sense which procures the poet the applause of the month: he is praised by all, read by a few, and soon forgotten.

There never was an unbeaten path trodden by the poet that the critic did not endeavor to reclaim him by calling his attempt innovation. This might be instanced in Dante, who first followed nature, and was persecuted by the critics as long as he lived. Thus novelty, one of the greatest beauties in poetry, must be avoided, or the connoisseur be displeased. It is one of the chief privileges, however, of genius to fly from the herd of imitators by some happy singularity; for, should he stand still, his heavy pursuers will at length certainly come up and fairly dispute the victory.

The ingenious Mr. Hogarth used to assert that everyone except the connoisseur was a judge of painting. The same may be asserted of writing. The public, in general, set the whole piece in the proper point of view; the critic lays his eye close to all its minuteness, and condemns or approves in detail. And this may be the reason why so many writers at present are apt to appeal from the tribunal of criticism to that of the people.

From a desire in the critic of grafting the spirit of ancient languages upon the English have proceeded of late several disagreeable instances of pedantry. Among the number I think we may reckon blank verse. Nothing but the greatest sublimity of subject can render such a measure pleasing; however, we now see it used upon the most trivial occasions. It has particularly found its way into our didactic poetry, and is likely to bring that species of composition into disrepute for which the English are deservedly famous.

Those who are acquainted with writing know that our language runs almost naturally into blank verse. The writers of our novels, romances, and all of this class who have no notion of style, naturally hobble into this unharmonious measure. If rhymes, therefore, be more difficult, for that very reason I would have our poets write in rhyme. Such a restriction upon the thought of a good poet often lifts and increases the vehemence of every sentiment; for fancy, like a fountain, plays highest by diminishing the aperture. But rhymes, it will be said, are a remnant of monkish stupidity, an innovation upon the poetry of the ancients. They are but indifferently acquainted with antiquity who make the assertion. Rhymes are probably of older date than either the Greek or Latin dactyl and spondee. The Celtic, which is allowed to be the first language spoken in Europe, has ever preserved them, as we may find in the Edda of Iceland and the Irish carols, still sung among the original inhabitants of that island. Olaus Wormius gives us some of the Teutonic poetry in this way; and Pantoppidan, Bishop of Bergen, some of the Norwegian. In short, this jingle of sounds is almost natural to mankind; at least it is so to our language, if we may judge from many unsuccessful attempts to throw it off.

I should not have employed so much time in opposing this erroneous innovation if it were not apt to introduce another in its train—I mean, a disgusting solemnity of manner into our poetry; and, as the prose-writer has been ever found to follow the poet, it must consequently banish in both all that agreeable trifling which, if I may so express it, often deceives us into instruction. The finest sentiment and the most weighty truth may put on a pleasant face, and it is even virtuous to jest when serious advice must be disgusting. But, instead of this, the most trifling performance among us now assumes all the didactic stiffness of wisdom. The most diminutive son of fame or of famine has his *we* and his *us*, his *firstlies* and his *secondlies*, as methodical as if bound in cowhide and closed with clasps of brass. Were these monthly reviews and magazines frothy, pert, or absurd, they might find some pardon; but to be dull and dronish is an encroachment on the prerogative of a folio. These things should be considered as pills to purge melancholy; they should be made up in our splenetic climate to be taken as physic, and not so as to be used when we take it.

However, by the power of one single monosyllable our critics have almost got the victory over humor amongst us. Does the poet paint the absurdities of the vulgar, then he is *low;* does he exaggerate the features of folly to render it more thoroughly ridiculous, he is then *very low.* In short, they have proscribed the comic or satirical muse from every walk but high life, which, though abounding in fools as well as the humblest station, is by no means so fruitful in absurdity. Among well-bred fools we may despise much, but have little to laugh at; nature seems to present us with an universal blank of silk, ribbons, smiles, and whispers. Absurdity is the poet's game, and good breeding is the nice concealment of absurdities. The truth is, the critic generally mistakes humor for wit, which is a very different excellence. Wit raises human nature above its level; humor acts a contrary part, and equally depresses it. To expect exalted humor is a contradiction in terms; and the critic, by demanding an impossibility from the comic poet, has, in effect, banished new comedy from the stage. But, to put the same thought in a different light, when an unexpected similitude in two objects strikes the imagination—in other words, when a thing is *wittily* expressed—all our pleasure turns into admiration of the artist who had fancy enough to draw the picture. When a thing is *humorously* described, our burst of laughter proceeds from a very different cause; we compare the absurdity of the character represented with our own, and triumph in our conscious superiority. No natural defect can be a cause of laughter because it is a misfortune to which ourselves are liable. A defect of this kind changes the passion into pity or horror. We only laugh at those instances of moral absurdity to which we are conscious we ourselves are not liable. For instance, should I describe a man as wanting his nose, there is no humor in this, as it is an accident to which human nature is subject, and may be any man's case; but should I represent this man without his nose as extremely curious in the choice of his snuff-box, we here see him guilty of an absurdity of which we imagine it impossible for ourselves to be guilty, and therefore applaud our own good sense on the comparison. Thus, then, the pleasure we receive from wit turns on the admiration of another; that which we feel from humor centers in the admiration of ourselves. The poet, therefore, must place the object he would have the subject of humor in a state of inferiority; in other words, the subject of humor must be *low*.

The solemnity worn by many of our modern writers is, I fear, often the mask of dullness; for certain it is, it seems to fit every author who pleases to put it on. By the complexion of many of our late publications one might be apt to cry out with Cicero, *Civem, mehercule, non puto esse qui his temporibus ridere possit*,[2]—"On my conscience, I believe we have all forgot to laugh in these days." Such writers probably make no distinction between what is praised and what is pleasing; between those commendations which the reader pays his own discernment, and those which are the genuine result of his sensations.

It were to be wished, therefore, that we no longer found pleasure with the inflated style that has for some years been looked upon as fine writing, and which every young writer is now obliged to adopt if he chooses to be read. We should now dispense with loaded epithet and dressing up trifles with dignity. For, to use an obvious instance, it is not those who make the greatest noise with their wares in the streets that have most to sell. Let us, instead of writing finely, try to write naturally; not hunt after lofty expressions to deliver mean ideas, nor be for ever gaping when we only mean to deliver a whisper.

THE CITIZEN OF THE WORLD

1762

LETTER III

From Lien Chi Altangi to the care of Fipsihi, resident in Moscow, to be forwarded by the Russian caravan to Fum Hoam, First President of the Ceremonial Academy at Pekin, in China.

Think not, O thou guide of my youth! that absence can impair my respect, or interposing trackless deserts blot your reverend

2 *Letters to his Friends* II. 4.

figure from my memory. The farther I travel, I feel the pain of separation with stronger force; those ties that bind me to my native country and you are still unbroken. By every remove I only drag a greater length of chain.

Could I find ought worth transmitting from so remote a region as this to which I have wandered, I should gladly send it; but, instead of this, you must be contented with a renewal of my former professions, and an imperfect account of a people with whom I am as yet but superficially acquainted. The remarks of a man who has been but three days in the country can only be those obvious circumstances which force themselves upon the imagination. I consider myself here as a newly created being introduced into a new world. Every object strikes with wonder and surprise. The imagination, still unsated, seems the only active principle of the mind. The most trifling occurrences give pleasure till the gloss of novelty is worn away. When I have ceased to wonder, I may possibly grow wise; I may then call the reasoning principle to my aid, and compare those objects with each other which were before examined without reflection.

Behold me, then, in London, gazing at the strangers, and they at me. It seems they find somewhat absurd in my figure; and had I been never from home, it is possible I might find an infinite fund of ridicule in theirs; but by long traveling I am taught to laugh at folly alone, and to find nothing truly ridiculous but villainy and vice.

When I had just quitted my native country, and crossed the Chinese wall, I fancied every deviation from the customs and manners of China was a departing from nature. I smiled at the blue lips and red foreheads of the Tonguese; and could hardly contain when I saw the Daures dress their heads with horns. The Ostiacs powdered with red earth, and the Calmuck beauties tricked out in all the finery of sheepskin appeared highly ridiculous. But I soon perceived that the ridicule lay not in them, but in me; that I falsely condemned others of absurdity because they happened to differ from a standard originally founded in prejudice or partiality.

I find no pleasure, therefore, in taxing the English with departing from nature in their external appearance, which is all I yet know of their character: it is possible they only endeavor to improve her simple plan, since every extravagance in dress proceeds from a desire of becoming more beautiful than nature made us;

and this is so harmless a vanity that I not only pardon, but approve it. A desire to be more excellent than others is what actually makes us so; and as thousands find a livelihood in society by such appetites, none but the ignorant inveigh against them.

You are not insensible, most reverend Fum Hoam, what numberless trades, even among the Chinese, subsist by the harmless pride of each other. Your nose-borers, feet-swathers, tooth-stainers, eyebrow-pluckers would all want bread, should their neighbors want vanity. These vanities, however, employ much fewer hands in China than in England; and a fine gentleman or a fine lady here, dressed up to the fashion, seems scarcely to have a single limb that does not suffer some distortions from art.

To make a fine gentleman, several trades are required, but chiefly a barber. You have undoubtedly heard of the Jewish champion whose strength lay in his hair. One would think that the English were for placing all wisdom there. To appear wise, nothing more is requisite here than for a man to borrow hair from the heads of all his neighbors, and clap it like a bush on his own. The distributors of law and physic stick on such quantities that it is almost impossible, even in idea, to distinguish between the head and the hair.

Those whom I have now been describing affect the gravity of the lion; those I am going to describe more resemble the pert vivacity of smaller animals. The barber, who is still master of the ceremonies, cuts their hair close to the crown; and then, with a composition of meal and hog's lard, plasters the whole in such a manner as to make it impossible to distinguish whether the patient wears a cap or a plaster: but, to make the picture more perfectly striking, conceive the tail of some beast, a greyhound's tail, or a pig's tail, for instance, appended to the back of the head, and reaching down to that place where tails in other animals are generally seen to begin: thus betailed and bepowdered, the man of taste fancies he improves in beauty, dresses up his hard-featured face in smiles, and attempts to look hideously tender. Thus equipped, he is qualified to make love, and hopes for success more from the powder on the outside of his head than the sentiments within.

Yet when I consider what sort of a creature the fine lady is to whom he is supposed to pay his addresses, it is not strange to find him thus equipped in order to please. She is herself every whit as fond of powder, and tails, and hog's lard as he. To speak my secret sentiments, most reverend Fum, the ladies here are horridly ugly;

I can hardly endure the sight of them; they no way resemble the beauties of China: the Europeans have a quite different idea of beauty from us. When I reflect on the small-footed perfections of an Eastern beauty, how is it possible I should have eyes for a woman whose feet are ten inches long? I shall never forget the beauties of my native city of Nangfew. How very broad their faces! How very short their noses! How very little their eyes! How very thin their lips! How very black their teeth! The snow on the tops of Bao is not fairer than their cheeks; and their eyebrows as small as the line by the pencil of Quamsi. Here a lady with such perfections would be frightful. Dutch and Chinese beauties, indeed, have some resemblance, but English women are entirely different; red cheeks, big eyes, and teeth of a most odious whiteness are not only seen here, but wished for; and then they have such masculine feet as actually serve *some* for walking!

Yet, uncivil as Nature has been, they seem resolved to outdo her in unkindness; they use white powder, blue powder, and black powder for their hair, and a red powder for the face on some particular occasions.

They like to have the face of various colors, as among the Tartars of Koreki, frequently sticking on, with spittle, little black patches on every part of it, except on the tip of the nose, which I have never seen with a patch. You'll have a better idea of their manner of placing these spots when I have finished a map of an English face patched up to the fashion, which shall shortly be sent to increase your curious collection of paintings, medals, and monsters.

But what surprises more than all the rest is what I have just now been credibly informed by one of this country. "Most ladies here," says he, "have two faces; one face to sleep in, and another to show in company. The first is generally reserved for the husband and family at home; the other put on to please strangers abroad: the family face is often indifferent enough, but the outdoor one looks something better; this is always made at the toilet, where the looking glass and toad-eater sit in council, and settle the complexion of the day."

I can't ascertain the truth of this remark: however, it is actually certain that they wear more clothes within doors than without; and I have seen a lady who seemed to shudder at a breeze in her own apartment appear half naked in the streets. Farewell.

LETTER XXI

To the Same

The English are as fond of seeing plays acted as the Chinese; but there is a vast difference in the manner of conducting them. We play our pieces in the open air, the English theirs under cover; we act by daylight, they by the blaze of torches. One of our plays continues eight or ten days successively; an English piece seldom takes up above four hours in the representation.

My companion in black, with whom I am now beginning to contract an intimacy, introduced me a few nights ago to the playhouse, where we placed ourselves conveniently at the foot of the stage. As the curtain was not drawn before my arrival, I had an opportunity of observing the behavior of the spectators, and indulging those reflections which novelty generally inspires.

The richest in general were placed in the lowest seats, and the poor rose above them in degrees proportioned to their poverty. The order of precedence seemed here inverted; those who were undermost all the day now enjoyed a temporary eminence, and became masters of the ceremonies. It was they who called for the music, indulging every noisy freedom and testifying all the insolence of beggary in exaltation.

They who held the middle region seemed not so riotous as those above them, nor yet so tame as those below: to judge by their looks, many of them seemed strangers there as well as myself. They were chiefly employed, during this period of expectation, in eating oranges, reading the story of the play, or making assignations.

Those who sat in the lowest rows, which are called the pit, seemed to consider themselves as judges of the merit of the poet and the performers; they were assembled partly to be amused and partly to show their taste; appearing to labor under that restraint which an affectation of superior discernment generally produces. My companion, however, informed me that not one in a hundred of them knew even the first principles of criticism; that they assumed the right of being censors because there was none to contradict their pretensions; and that every man who now called himself a connoisseur became such to all intents and purposes.

Those who sat in the boxes appeared in the most unhappy situation of all. The rest of the audience came merely for their own amusement; these, rather to furnish out a part of the entertainment themselves. I could not avoid considering them as acting parts in dumb show—not a curtsey or nod that was not the result of art; not a look nor a smile that was not designed for murder. Gentlemen and ladies ogled each other through spectacles; for my companion observed that blindness was of late become fashionable; all affected indifference and ease while their hearts at the same time burned for conquest. Upon the whole, the lights, the music, the ladies in their gayest dresses, the men with cheerfulness and expectation in their looks, all conspired to make a most agreeable picture, and to fill a heart that sympathizes at human happiness with inexpressible serenity.

The expected time for the play to begin at last arrived; the curtain was drawn, and the actors came on. A woman who personated a queen came in curtseying to the audience, who clapped their hands upon her appearance. Clapping of hands is, it seems, the manner of applauding in England; the manner is absurd, but every country, you know, has its peculiar absurdities. I was equally surprised, however, at the submission of the actress, who should have considered herself as a queen, as at the little discernment of the audience who gave her such marks of applause before she attempted to deserve them. Preliminaries between her and the audience being thus adjusted, the dialogue was supported between her and a most hopeful youth, who acted the part of her confidant. They both appeared in extreme distress, for it seems the queen had lost a child some fifteen years before, and still kept its dear resemblance next her heart, while her kind companion bore a part in her sorrows.

Her lamentations grew loud; comfort is offered, but she detests the very sound: she bids them preach comfort to the winds. Upon this her husband comes in, who, seeing the queen so much afflicted, can himself hardly refrain from tears, or avoid partaking in the soft distress. After thus grieving through three scenes, the curtain dropped for the first act.

"Truly," said I to my companion, "these kings and queens are very much disturbed at no very great misfortune: certain I am, were people of humbler stations to act in this manner, they would be thought divested of common sense." I had scarcely finished this observation, when the curtain rose and the king came on in a vio-

lent passion. His wife had, it seems, refused his proffered tenderness, had spurned his royal embrace, and he seemed resolved not
to survive her fierce disdain. After he had thus fretted, and the
queen had fretted through the second act, the curtain was let down
once more.

"Now," says my companion, "you perceive the king to be a man
of spirit; he feels at every pore: one of your phlegmatic sons of
clay would have given the queen her own way, and let her come
to herself by degrees; but the king is for immediate tenderness or
instant death: death and tenderness are leading passions of every
modern buskined hero; this moment they embrace, and the next
stab, mixing daggers and kisses in every period."

I was going to second his remarks when my attention was engrossed by a new object; a man came in balancing a straw upon his
nose, and the audience were clapping their hands in all the raptures
of applause. "To what purpose," cried I, "does this unmeaning
figure make his appearance? Is he a part of the plot?" "Unmeaning
do you call him?" replied my friend in black. "This is one of the
most important characters of the whole play; nothing pleases the
people more than seeing a straw balanced: there is a great deal of
meaning in the straw; there is something suited to every apprehension in the sight; and a fellow possessed of talents like these is
sure of making his fortune."

The third act now began with an actor who came to inform us
that he was the villain of the play, and intended to show strange
things before all was over. He was joined by another who seemed
as much disposed for mischief as he; their intrigues continued
through this whole division. "If that be a villain," said I, "he must
be a very stupid one to tell his secrets without being asked; such
soliloquies of late are never admitted in China."

The noise of clapping interrupted me once more; a child of six
years old was learning to dance on the stage, which gave the ladies
and mandarins infinite satisfaction. "I am sorry," said I, "to see the
pretty creature so early learning so very bad a trade; dancing being, I presume, as contemptible here as it is in China." "Quite the
reverse," interrupted my companion; "dancing is a very reputable
and genteel employment here; men have a greater chance for encouragement from the merit of their heels than their heads. One
who jumps up and flourishes his toes three times before he comes to
the ground may have three hundred a year; he who flourishes them

four times gets four hundred; but he who arrives at five is inestimable, and may demand what salary he thinks proper. The female dancers, too, are valued for this sort of jumping and crossing;
and it is a cant word amongst them that she deserves most who
shows highest. But the fourth act is begun; let us be attentive."

In the fourth act the queen finds her long-lost child, now grown
up into a youth of smart parts and great qualifications; wherefore
she wisely considers that the crown will fit his head better than
that of her husband, whom she knows to be a driveler. The king
discovers her design, and here comes on the deep distress: he loves
the queen, and he loves the kingdom; he resolves therefore, in order
to possess both, that her son must die. The queen exclaims at his
barbarity, is frantic with rage, and at length, overcome with sorrow, falls into a fit; upon which the curtain drops, and the act is
concluded.

"Observe the art of the poet," cries my companion. "When the
queen can say no more, she falls into a fit. While thus her eyes are
shut, while she is supported in the arms of Abigail, what horrors
do we not fancy! We feel it in every nerve; take my word for it,
that fits are the true aposiopesis of modern tragedy."

The fifth act began, and a busy piece it was. Scenes shifting,
trumpets sounding, mobs hallooing, carpets spreading, guards bustling from one door to another; gods, demons, daggers, racks, and
ratsbane. But whether the king was killed, or the queen was
drowned, or the son was poisoned, I have absolutely forgotten.

When the play was over, I could not avoid observing that the
persons of the drama appeared in as much distress in the first act as
the last. "How is it possible," said I, "to sympathize with them
through five long acts? Pity is but a short-lived passion. I hate to
hear an actor mouthing trifles: neither startings, strainings, nor attitudes affect me, unless there be cause: after I have been once or
twice deceived by those unmeaning alarms, my heart sleeps in
peace, probably unaffected by the principal distress. There should
be one great passion aimed at by the actor as well as the poet; all
the rest should be subordinate, and only contribute to make that
the greater; if the actor, therefore, exclaims upon every occasion
in tones of despair, he attempts to move us too soon; he anticipates
the blow, he ceases to affect, though he gains our applause."

I scarce perceived that the audience were almost all departed;
wherefore, mixing with the crowd. my companion and I got into

the street, where, essaying an hundred obstacles from coach wheels and palanquin poles, like birds in their flight through the branches of a forest, after various turnings, we both at length got home in safety. Adieu.

The people of London are as fond of walking as our friends at Pekin of riding; one of the principal entertainments of the citizens here in summer is to repair about nightfall to a garden not far from town, where they walk about, show their best clothes and best faces, and listen to a concert provided for the occasion.

I accepted an invitation a few evenings ago from my old friend, the man in black, to be one of a party that was to sup there; and at the appointed hour waited upon him at his lodgings. There I found the company assembled and expecting my arrival. Our party consisted of my friend, in superlative finery, his stockings rolled, a black velvet waistcoat which was formerly new, and a gray wig combed down in imitation of hair; a pawnbroker's widow, of whom, by the by, my friend was a professed admirer, dressed out in green damask, with three gold rings on every finger; Mr. Tibbs, the second-rate beau I have formerly described, together with his lady, in flimsy silk, dirty gauze instead of linen, and a hat as big as an umbrella.

Our first difficulty was in settling how we should set out. Mrs. Tibbs had a natural aversion to the water, and the widow, being a little in flesh, as warmly protested against walking; a coach was therefore agreed upon, which being too small to carry five, Mr. Tibbs consented to sit in his wife's lap.

In this manner, therefore, we set forward, being entertained by the way with the bodings of Mr. Tibbs, who assured us he did not expect to see a single creature for the evening above the degree of a cheesemonger; that this was the last night of the gardens, and that consequently we should be pestered with the nobility and gentry from Thames Street and Crooked Lane, with several other prophetic ejaculations, probably inspired by the uneasiness of his situation.

The illuminations began before we arrived, and I must confess that upon entering the gardens, I found every sense overpaid with more than expected pleasure: the lights everywhere glimmering through the scarcely moving trees, the full-bodied concert bursting on the stillness of the night, the natural concert of the birds in the more retired part of the grove vying with that which was formed by art, the company gaily dressed looking satisfaction, and the tables spread with various delicacies, all conspired to fill my imagination with the visionary happiness of the Arabian lawgiver, and lifted me into an ecstasy of admiration. "Head of Confucius," cried I to my friend, "this is fine! This unites rural beauty with courtly magnificence! If we except the virgins of immortality that hang on every tree, and may be plucked at every desire, I do not see how this falls short of Mahomet's Paradise!"—"As for virgins," cries my friend, "it is true, they are a fruit that do not much abound in our gardens here; but if ladies as plenty as apples in autumn and as complying as any *houri* of them all, can content you, I fancy we have no need to go to Heaven for Paradise."

I was going to second his remarks, when we were called to a consultation by Mr. Tibbs and the rest of the company to know in what manner we were to lay out the evening to the greatest advantage. Mrs. Tibbs was for keeping the genteel walk of the garden, where she observed there was always the very best company; the widow, on the contrary, who came but once a season, was for securing a good standing place to see the waterworks, which she assured us would begin in less than an hour at farthest; a dispute therefore began, and as it was managed between two of very opposite characters, it threatened to grow more bitter at every reply. Mrs. Tibbs wondered how people could pretend to know the polite world who had received all their rudiments of breeding behind a counter; to which the other replied that though some people sat behind counters, yet they could sit at the head of their own tables too, and carve three good dishes of hot meat whenever they thought proper, which was more than some people could say for themselves that hardly knew a rabbit and onions from a green goose and gooseberries.

It is hard to say where this might have ended had not the husband, who probably knew the impetuosity of his wife's disposition, proposed to end the dispute by adjourning to a box and try if there was anything to be had for supper that was supportable. To this we all consented; but here a new distress arose: Mr. and Mrs. Tibbs would sit in none but a genteel box, a box where they might see and be seen; one, as they expressed it, in the very focus of public view; but such a box was not easy to be obtained, for though we were perfectly convinced of our own gentility and the gentility of our appearance, yet we found it a difficult matter to persuade the keepers of the boxes to be of our opinion; they chose to reserve genteel boxes for what they judged more genteel company.

At last, however, we were fixed, though somewhat obscurely, and supplied with the usual entertainment of the place. The widow found the supper excellent, but Mrs. Tibbs thought everything detestable. "Come, come, my dear," cries the husband, by way of consolation, "to be sure we can't find such dressing here as we have at Lord Crump's or Lady Crimp's; but for Vauxhall dressing it is pretty good; it is not their victuals, indeed, I find fault with, but their wine; their wine," cries he, drinking off a glass, "indeed is most abominable."

By this last contradiction the widow was fairly conquered in point of politeness. She perceived now that she had no pretensions in the world to taste, her very senses were vulgar, since she had praised detestable custard and smacked at wretched wine; she was therefore content to yield the victory, and for the rest of the night to listen and improve. It is true she would now and then forget herself and confess she was pleased, but they soon brought her back again to miserable refinement. She once praised the painting of the box in which we were sitting, but was soon convinced that such paltry pieces ought rather to excite horror than satisfaction; she ventured again to commend one of the singers, but Mrs. Tibbs soon let her know, in the style of a connoisseur, that the singer in question had neither ear, voice, nor judgment.

Mr. Tibbs, now willing to prove that his wife's pretensions to music were just, entreated her to favor the company with a song; but to this she gave a positive denial, "For you know very well, my dear," says she, "that I am not in voice today, and when one's voice is not equal to one's judgment, what signifies singing? besides, as there is no accompaniment, it would be but spoiling music." All these excuses, however, were overruled by the rest of the company, who, though one would think they already had music enough, joined in the entreaty. But particularly the widow, now willing to convince the company of her breeding, pressed so warmly, that she seemed determined to take no refusal. At last, then, the lady complied, and after humming for some minutes, began with such a voice, and such affectation, as I could perceive gave but little satisfaction to any except her husband. He sat with rapture in his eye, and beat time with his hand on the table.

You must observe, my friend, that it is the custom of this country when a lady or gentleman happens to sing for the company to sit as mute and motionless as statues. Every feature, every limb, must seem to correspond in fixed attention, and while the song continues, they are to remain in a state of universal petrifaction. In this mortifying situation we had continued for some time, listening to the song and looking with tranquillity, when the master of the box came to inform us that the waterworks were going to begin. At this information I could instantly perceive the widow bounce from her seat; but correcting herself, she sat down again, repressed by motives of good breeding. Mrs. Tibbs, who had seen the waterworks a hundred times, resolving not to be interrupted, continued her song without any share of mercy, nor had the smallest pity on our impatience. The widow's face, I own, gave me high entertainment; in it I could plainly read the struggle she felt between good breeding and curiosity; she talked of the waterworks the whole evening before, and seemed to have come merely in order to see them; but then she could not bounce out in the very middle of a song, for that would be forfeiting all pretensions to high life, or high-lived company, ever after. Mrs. Tibbs therefore kept on singing, and we continued to listen, till at last, when the song was just concluded, the waiter came to inform us that the waterworks were over.

"The waterworks over!" cried the widow. "The waterworks over already! That's impossible! They can't be over so soon!" "It is not my business," replied the fellow, "to contradict your ladyship; I'll run again and see." He went, and soon returned with a confirmation of the dismal tidings. No ceremony could now bind my friend's disappointed mistress; she testified her displeasure in the openest manner; in short, she now began to find fault in turn, and at last insisted upon going home just at the time that Mr. and Mrs. Tibbs assured the company that the polite hours were going to begin and that the ladies would instantaneously be entertained with the horns. Adieu!

ESSAY ON THE THEATER;
OR, A COMPARISON BETWEEN SENTIMENTAL AND LAUGHING COMEDY

1773

The theater, like all other amusements, has its fashions and its prejudices; and when satiated with its excellence, mankind begin to mistake change for improvement. For some years tragedy was the reigning entertainment; but of late it has entirely given way to comedy, and our best efforts are now exerted in these lighter kinds of composition. The pompous train, the swelling phrase, and the unnatural rant are displaced for that natural portrait of human folly and frailty of which all are judges because all have sat for the picture.

But as in describing nature, it is presented with a double face, either of mirth or sadness, our modern writers find themselves at a loss which chiefly to copy from; and it is now debated whether the exhibition of human distress is likely to afford the mind more entertainment than that of human absurdity.

Comedy is defined by Aristotle to be a picture of the frailties of the lower part of mankind, to distinguish it from tragedy, which is an exhibition of the misfortunes of the great. When comedy, therefore, ascends to produce the characters of princes or generals upon the stage, it is out of its walk, since low life and middle life are entirely its object. The principal question, therefore, is, whether in describing low or middle life, an exhibition of its follies be not preferable to a detail of its calamities? Or, in other words, which deserves the preference, the weeping sentimental comedy, so much in fashion at present, or the laughing and even low comedy, which seems to have been last exhibited by Vanbrugh and Cibber?

If we apply to authorities, all the great masters in the dramatic art have but one opinion. Their rule is that as tragedy displays the calamities of the great, so comedy should excite our laughter by ridiculously exhibiting the follies of the lower part of mankind. Boileau, one of the best modern critics, asserts that comedy will not admit of tragic distress:

Le Comique, ennemi des soupirs et des pleurs,
N'admet point dans ses vers de tragiques douleurs.[1]

Nor is this rule without the strongest foundation in nature, as the distresses of the mean by no means affect us so strongly as the calamities of the great. When tragedy exhibits to us some great man fallen from his height and struggling with want and adversity, we feel his situation in the same manner as we suppose he himself must feel, and our pity is increased in proportion to the height from which he fell. On the contrary, we do not so strongly sympathize with one born in humbler circumstances, and encountering accidental distress: so that whilst we melt for Belisarius, we scarcely give halfpence to the beggar who accosts us in the street. The one has our pity, the other our contempt. Distress, therefore, is the proper object of tragedy, since the great excite our pity by their fall; but not equally so of comedy, since the actors employed in it are originally so mean that they sink but little by their fall.

Since the first origin of the stage, tragedy and comedy have run in distinct channels, and never till of late encroached upon the provinces of each other. Terence, who seems to have made the nearest approaches, always judiciously stops short before he comes to the downright pathetic; and yet he is even reproached by Caesar for wanting the *vis comica*.[2] All the other comic writers of antiquity aim only at rendering folly or vice ridiculous, but never exalt their characters into buskined pomp or make what Voltaire humorously calls a *tradesman's tragedy*.

Yet notwithstanding this weight of authority and the universal practice of former ages, a new species of dramatic composition has been introduced under the name of *sentimental* comedy, in which the virtues of private life are exhibited rather than the vices exposed; and the distresses rather than the faults of mankind make our interest in the piece. These comedies have had of late great success, perhaps from their novelty, and also from their flattering every man in his favorite foible. In these plays almost all the characters are good and exceedingly generous; they are lavish enough of their *tin* money on the stage; and though they want humor, have abundance of sentiment and feeling. If they happen to have faults or foibles, the spectator is taught not only to pardon but to applaud them, in consideration of the goodness of their hearts; so that folly,

---

1 L'Art poétique III. 401–2.   2 The comic spirit.

instead of being ridiculed, is commended, and the comedy aims at touching our passions without the power of being truly pathetic. In this manner we are likely to lose one great source of entertainment on the stage; for while the comic poet is invading the province of the tragic muse, he leaves her lovely sister quite neglected. Of this, however, he is no way solicitous, as he measures his fame by his profits.

But it will be said that the theater is formed to amuse mankind, and that it matters little, if this end be answered, by what means it is obtained. If mankind find delight in weeping at comedy, it would be cruel to abridge them in that or any other innocent pleasure. If those pieces are denied the name of comedies, yet call them by any other name, and if they are delightful, they are good. Their success, it will be said, is a mark of their merit, and it is only abridging our happiness to deny us an inlet to amusement.

These objections, however, are rather specious than solid. It is true that amusement is a great object of the theater; and it will be allowed that these sentimental pieces do often amuse us; but the question is whether the true comedy would not amuse us more. The question is whether a character supported throughout a piece with its ridicule still attending would not give us more delight than this species of bastard tragedy, which only is applauded because it is new.

A friend of mine who was sitting unmoved at one of these sentimental pieces was asked how he could be so indifferent. "Why, truly," says he, "as the hero is but a tradesman, it is indifferent to me whether he be turned out of his countinghouse on Fish Street Hill, since he will still have enough left to open shop in St. Giles's."

The other objection is as ill grounded; for though we should give these pieces another name, it will not mend their efficacy. It will continue a kind of *mulish* production, with all the defects of its opposite parents, and marked with sterility. If we are permitted to make comedy weep, we have an equal right to make tragedy laugh, and to set down in blank verse the jests and repartees of all the attendants in a funeral procession.

But there is one argument in favor of sentimental comedy which will keep it on the stage in spite of all that can be said against it. It is of all others the most easily written. Those abilities that can hammer out a novel are fully sufficient for the production of a sentimental comedy. It is only sufficient to raise the characters a little; to deck out the hero with a riband, or give the heroine a title; then to put an insipid dialogue, without character or humor, into their mouths, give them mighty good hearts, very fine clothes, furnish a new set of scenes, make a pathetic scene or two, with a sprinkling of tender melancholy conversation through the whole; and there is no doubt but all the ladies will cry and all the gentlemen applaud.

Humor at present seems to be departing from the stage, and it will soon happen that our comic players will have nothing left for it but a fine coat and a song. It depends upon the audience whether they will actually drive those poor merry creatures from the stage, or sit at a play as gloomy as at the tabernacle. It is not easy to recover an art when once lost; and it will be but a just punishment that when, by our being too fastidious, we have banished humor from the stage, we should ourselves be deprived of the art of laughing.

A SELECTION

Horace Walpole

1717–1797

A DESCRIPTION OF THE VILLA OF HORACE WALPOLE AT STRAWBERRY HILL

1774

[As soon as Walpole bought Strawberry Hill in 1747, he began to transform it into "a little Gothic castle" with all the "fragments of old painted glass, arms, or anything" that was, or looked, medieval. Presently Walpole was admitting tourists by ticket only, to gape at his Gallery, his Round Tower, his Chapel, and his Great Cloister, all designed with the aid of his friends Bentley and John Chute, of the Vine in Hampshire. Strawberry Hill was elaborated into a precious "fantastic fabric" of rococo-Gothic filigree work that finds its counterpart in the *Reliques* of Percy and the preposterous archaisms of the Rowley poems.]

.   .   .   .

ENTERING by the great north gate, the first object that presents itself is a small oratory enclosed with iron rails; in front, an altar, on which stands a saint in bronze; open niches, and stone basins for holy water; designed by John Chute, Esq., of the Vine in Hampshire. On the right hand is a small garden called the abbot's garden, parted off by an open screen, taken from the tomb of Roger Niger, Bishop of London, in old St. Paul's. Passing on the left, by a small cloister, is the entrance to the house, the narrow front of which was designed by Richard Bentley, only son of Dr. Bentley, the learned master of Trinity College, Cambridge. Over the door are three shields of Walpole, Shorter, and Robsart. . . .

The Library: The books are ranged within Gothic arches of pierced work, taken from a side-door case to the choir in Dugdale's St. Paul's. The doors themselves were designed by Mr. Chute. The chimney piece is imitated from the tomb of John of Eltham, Earl of Cornwall, in Westminster Abbey; the stonework from that of Thomas, Duke of Clarence, at Canterbury. The ceiling was painted by Clermont, from Mr. Walpole's design drawn out by Mr. Bentley. In the middle is the shield of Walpole surrounded with the quarters borne by the family. At each end in a round is a knight on horseback, in the manner of ancient seals; that next to the window bears the arms of Fitz Osbert, the other of Robsart. . . .

The large window and the two rose windows have a great deal of fine painted glass, particularly Faith, Hope, and Charity, whole figures in colors; a large shield with the arms of England, and heads of Charles Ist and Charles IInd. . . .

The Gallery: Fifty-six feet long, seventeen feet high, and thirteen wide without the five recesses. The ceiling is taken from one of the side aisles of Henry VII's chapel. In the windows, painted by Peckett, are all the quarterings of the family. The great door is copied from the north door of Saint Albans, and the two smaller are parts of the same design. The side with recesses, which are finished with a gold network over looking glass, is taken from the tomb of Archbishop Bourchier at Canterbury. . . .

Thomas Chatterton

1752–1770

WITH Chatterton we enter upon those "enchanted grounds" that "are the more poetical for being Gothic." This uneasy, embittered youth, when he was not chafing under the rather depressing circumstances of his life, withdrew into visions of old romance with which his brain, like that of Keats, was stuffed. Thus his verses strangely mingle fancy with disillusion. Upon occasion he could write with all the virulence of the enlightenment that

> Religion's but opinion's bastard son,
> A perfect mystery, more than three in one.

Then, resorting to a chicanery that gained him only scorn, he attempted to convince Horace Walpole and others that the grotesquely spelled lyrics and ballads that he composed with the aid of dictionaries of Old English were authentic medieval poems by one Thomas Rowley. It is curious that Walpole, addicted as he was to the "antiquarian Gothic" of Strawberry Hill, no less artificial than the Rowley poems, should have been the one to rebuff Chatterton. Many of these pseudomedieval poems, inspired by hours of poring over manuscripts from the muniment room of St. Mary Redcliffe, the famous Bristol church, would be only of historical interest were it not for the lyric passages that distinguish them above the ordinary eighteenth-century archaizing verse. The three "African Eclogues" have a fantastic charm not unlike that of Coleridge's "Kubla Khan."

BIOGRAPHICAL NOTES

Son of a Bristol schoolmaster, who died before Chatterton was born. Educated at Colston's School, Bristol, as a charity pupil (1760). Wrote verses and was attracted by the documents in the muniment room of St. Mary Redcliffe, where his ancestors had been sextons. Apprenticed to John Lambert, an attorney (1767). Began composing the Rowley Poems, purportedly by a fifteenth-century poet-priest, friend of William Canynge of Bristol. Wrote in vain to Dodsley and Horace Walpole to interest them in these poems (1768–69). Chafed at Lambert's; contributed to *Town and Country Magazine*. Went to London to live by his pen (1770), but earned barely a pittance. Drank poison in a London lodging house (August 24, 1770).

BIBLIOGRAPHY: *Complete Poetical Works*, ed. H. D. Roberts, 2 vols., 1906. *Poetical Works*, ed. W. W. Skeat, 2 vols., 1875. Dixon, W. M., *Chatterton*, 1930. Meyerstein, E. H. W., *A Life of Thomas Chatterton*, 1930–31. Nevill, John Cranstoun, *Thomas Chatterton*, 1948.

NARVA AND MORED

AN AFRICAN ECLOGUE

1770

Recite the loves of Narva and Mored,
The priest of Chalma's triple idol said.
High from the ground the youthful warriors sprung,
Loud on the concave shell the lances rung:
In all the mystic mazes of the dance,
The youths of Banny's burning sands advance,
Whilst the soft virgin panting looks behind,
And rides upon the pinions of the wind;
Ascends the mountain's brow, and measures round
The steepy cliffs of Chalma's sacred ground,   10
Chalma, the god whose noisy thunders fly
Thro' the dark covering of the midnight sky,
Whose arm directs the close embattled host,
And sinks the labouring vessels on the coast;
Chalma, whose excellence is known from far,
From Lupa's rocky hill to Calabar:
The guardian god of Afric and the isles,
Where nature in her strongest vigour smiles;
Where the blue blossom of the forky thorn,
Bends with the nectar of the opening morn: 20
Where ginger's aromatic, matted root,
Creep through the mead, and up the mountains shoot.
    Three times the virgin, swimming on the breeze,
Danc'd in the shadow of the mystic trees:
When, like a dark cloud spreading to the view,
The first-born sons of war and blood pursue;
Swift as the elk they pour along the plain;
Swift as the flying clouds distilling rain;
Swift as the boundings of the youthful roe,
They course around, and lengthen as they go.   30
Like the long chain of rocks, whose summits rise
Far in the sacred regions of the skies;
Upon whose top the black'ning tempest lours,
Whilst down its side the gushing torrent pours,
Like the long cliffy mountains which extend

From Lorbar's cave, to where the nations end,
Which sink in darkness, thick'ning and obscure,
Impenetrable, mystic, and impure;
The flying terrors of the war advance,
And round the sacred oak, repeat the dance.   40
Furious they twist around the gloomy trees,
Like leaves in autumn twirling with the breeze.
So when the splendour of the dying day
Darts the red lustre of the watery way,
Sudden beneath Toddida's whistling brink,
The circling billows in wild eddies sink,
Whirl furious round, and the loud bursting wave
Sinks down to Chalma's sacerdotal cave,
Explores the palaces on Zira's coast,
Where howls the war-song of the chieftain's ghost;   50
Where the artificer in realms below,
Gilds the rich lance or beautifies the bow,
From the young palm-tree spins the useful twine,
Or makes the teeth of elephants divine;
Where the pale children of the feeble sun,
In search of gold, thro' every climate run:
From burning heat to freezing torments go,
And live in all vicissitudes of woe.
Like the loud eddies of Toddida's sea,
The warriors circle the mysterious tree: 60
'Till spent with exercise they spread around
Upon the op'ning blossoms of the ground.
The priestess rising, sings the sacred tale,
And the loud chorus echoes thro' the dale.

Priestess

Far from the burning sands of Calabar;
Far from the lustre of the morning-star;
Far from the pleasure of the holy morn;
Far from the blessedness of Chalma's horn:
Now rest the souls of Narva and Mored,
Laid in the dust, and number'd with the dead.   70
Dear are their memories to us, and long,
Long shall their attributes be known in song.
Their lives were transient as the meadow flow'r,
Ripen'd in ages, wither'd in an hour.
Chalma, reward them in his gloomy cave,
And open all the prisons of the grave!

Bred to the service of the godhead's throne,
And living but to serve his god alone,
Narva was beauteous as the opening day
When on the spangling waves the sunbeams play,   80
When the mackaw, ascending to the sky,
Views the bright splendour with a steady eye.
Tall, as the house of Chalma's dark retreat;
Compact and firm, as Rhadal Ynca's fleet,
Completely beauteous as a summer's sun,
Was Narva, by his excellence undone.
Where the soft Togla creeps along the meads,
Thro' scented calamus and fragrant reeds:
Where the sweet zinsa spreads its matted bed,
Liv'd the still sweeter flower, the young Mored.   90
Black was her face as Togla's hidden cell;
Soft as the moss where hissing adders dwell.
As to the sacred court she brought a fawn,
The sportive tenant of the spicy lawn,
She saw and loved! and Narva too forgot
His sacred vestment and his mystic lot.
Long had the mutual sigh, the mutual tear,
Burst from the breast and scorn'd confinement there;
Existence was a torment! O my breast!
Can I find accents to unfold the rest?   100
Lock'd in each other's arms, from Hyga's cave
They plung'd relentless to a wat'ry grave;
And falling murmured to the powers above,
"Gods! take our lives, unless we live to love."

BRISTOWE TRAGEDIE: OR THE DETHE OF SYR CHARLES BAWDIN [1]

1772

The featherd songster chaunticleer
    Han wounde hys bugle horne,
And tolde the earlie villager
    The commynge of the morne:

---

[1] Sir Charles is evidently a Lancastrian executed by Edward IV, who deposed Henry VI. Chatterton may have had in mind Sir Baldwin Fulford. This is a "Rowley" poem. These "Rowley" poems were presented by Chatterton as having been written by one Thomas Rowley, who was patronized by William Canynge, a fifteenth-century mayor of Bristol.

Kynge EDWARDE sawe the ruddie streakes
   Of lyghte eclypse the greie;
And herde the raven's crokynge throte
   Proclayme the fated daie.

"Thou'rt ryght," quod hee, "for, by the Godde
   That syttes enthron'd on hyghe!   10
CHARLES BAWDIN, and hys fellowes twaine,
   To-daie shall surelie die."

Thenne wythe a jugge of nappy ale
   Hys Knyghtes dydd onne hymm waite;
"Goe tell the traytour, thatt to-daie
   Hee leaves thys mortall state."

Syr CANTERLONE thenne bendedd lowe,
   Wythe harte brymm-fulle of woe;
Hee journey'd to the castle-gate,
   And to Syr CHARLES dydd goe.   20

Butt whenne hee came, hys children twaine,
   And eke hys lovynge wyfe,
Wythe brinie tears dydd wett the floore,
   For goode Syr CHARLESES lyfe.

"O goode Syr CHARLES!" sayd CANTERLONE,
   "Badde tydyngs I doe brynge."
"Speke boldlie, manne," sayd brave Syr CHARLES,
   "Whatte says thie traytor kynge?"

"I greeve to telle, before yonne sonne
   Does fromme the welkinn flye,   30
Hee hath uponne hys honour sworne,
   Thatt thou shalt surelie die."

"Wee all must die," quod brave Syr CHARLES;
   "Of thatte I'm not affearde;
Whatte bootes to lyve a little space?
   Thanke JESU, I'm prepar'd:

"Butt telle thye kynge, for myne hee's not,
   I'de sooner die to-daie
Thanne lyve hys slave, as manie are,
   Tho' I shoulde lyve for aie."   40

Thenne CANTERLONE hee dydd goe out,
　To telle the maior straite
To gett all thynges ynne reddyness
　For goode Syr CHARLESES fate.

Thenne Maisterr CANYNGE saughte the kynge,
　And felle down onne hys knee;
"I'm come," quod hee, "unto your grace
　To move your clemencye."

Thenne quod the kynge, "Youre tale speke out,
　You have been much oure friende;　　　　50
Whatever youre request may bee,
　Wee wylle to ytte attende."

"My nobile leige! alle my request
　Ys for a nobile knyghte,
Who, tho' may hap hee has donne wronge,
　He thoghte ytte stylle was ryghte:

"Hee has a spouse and children twaine,
　Alle rewyn'd are for aie;
Yff thatt you are resolv'd to lett
　CHARLES BAWDIN die to-daie."　　　　60

"Speke nott of such a traytour vile,"
　The kynge ynne furie sayde;
"Before the evening starre doth sheene,
　BAWDIN shall loose hys hedde:

"Justice does loudlie for hym calle,
　And hee shalle have hys meede:
Speke, Maister CANYNGE! Whatte thynge else
　Att present doe you neede?"

"My nobile leige!" goode CANYNGE sayde,
　"Leave justice to our Godde,　　　　70
And laye the yronne rule asyde;
　Be thyne the olyve rodde.

"Was Godde to serche our hertes and reines,
　The best were synners grete;
CHRIST'S vycarr only knowes ne synne,
　Ynne alle thys mortall state.

"Lett mercie rule thyne infante reigne,
  'Twylle faste thye crowne fulle sure;
From race to race thy familie
  Alle sov'reigns shall endure: 80

"But yff wythe bloode and slaughter thou
  Beginne thy infante reigne,
Thy crowne uponne thy childrennes brows
  Wylle never long remayne."

"CANYNGE, awaie! thys traytour vile
  Has scorn'd my power and mee;
Howe canst thou thenne for such a man..e
  Intreate my clemencye?"

"My nobile leige! the trulie brave
  Wylle val'rous actions prize,   90
Respect a brave and nobile mynde,
  Altho' ynne enemies."

"CANYNGE, awaie! By Godde ynne Heav'n
  Thatt dydd mee beinge gyve,
I wylle nott taste a bitt of breade
  Whilst thys Syr CHARLES dothe lyve.

"By MARIE, and alle Seinctes ynne Heav'n,
  Thys sunne shall be hys laste."
Thenne CANYNGE dropt a brinie teare,
  And from the presence paste.   100

Wyth herte brymm-fulle of gnawynge grief,
  Hee to Syr CHARLES dydd goe,
And satt hymm downe uponne a stoole,
  And teares beganne to flowe.

"Wee all must die," quod brave Syr CHARLES;
  "Whatte bootes ytte howe or whenne;
Dethe ys the sure, the certaine fate
  Of all wee mortall menne.

"Saye why, my friend, thie honest soul
  Runns overr att thyne eye;   110
Is ytte for my most welcome doome
  Thatt thou dost child-lyke crye?"

Quod godlie CANYNGE, "I doe weepe,
  Thatt thou so soone must dye,
And leave thy sonnes and helpless wyfe;
  'Tys thys thatt wettes myne eye."

"Thenne drie the tears thatt out thyne eye
  From godlie fountaines sprynge;
Dethe I despise, and alle the power
  Of EDWARDE, traytor kynge.   12

"Whan throgh the tyrant's welcom means
  I shall resigne my lyfe,
The Godde I serve wylle soone provyde
  For bothe mye sonnes and wyfe.

"Before I sawe the lyghtsome sunne,
  Thys was appointed mee;
Shall mortal manne repyne or grudge
  Whatt Godde ordeynes to bee?

"Howe oft ynne battaile have I stoode,
  Whan thousands dy'd arounde;   130
Whan smokynge streemes of crimson bloode
  Imbrew'd the fatten'd grounde:

"Howe dydd I knowe thatt ev'ry darte,
  Thatt cutte the airie waie,
Myghte nott fynde passage toe my harte,
  And close myne eyes for aie?

"And shall I nowe, forr feere of dethe,
  Looke wanne and bee dysmayde?
Ne! fromm my herte flie childyshe feere,
  Bee alle the manne display'd.   140

"Ah, goddelyke HENRIE! Godde forefende,
  And guarde thee and thye sonne,
Yff 'tis hys wylle; but yff 'tis nott,
  Why thenne hys wylle bee donne.

"My honest friende, my faulte has beene
  To serve Godde and mye prynce;
And thatt I no tyme-server am,
  My dethe wylle soone convynce.

"Ynne Londonne citye was I borne,
    Of parents of grete note;   150
My fadre dydd a nobile armes
    Emblazon onne hys cote:

"I make ne doubte butt hee ys gone
    Where soone I hope to goe;
Where wee for ever shall bee blest,
    From oute the reech of woe:

"Hee taughte mee justice and the laws
    Wyth pitie to unite;
And eke hee taughte mee howe to knowe
    The wronge cause fromm the ryghte: 160

"Hee taughte mee wythe a prudent hande
    To feede the hungrie poore,
Ne lett mye sarvants dryve awaie
    The hungrie fromme my doore:

"And none can saye, butt alle mye lyfe
    I have hys wordyes kept;
And summ'd the actyonns of the daie
    Eche nyghte before I slept.

"I have a spouse, goe aske of her,
    Yff I defyl'd her bedde?   170
I have a kynge, and none can laie
    Blacke treason onne my hedde.

"Ynne Lent, and onne the holie eve,
    Fromm fleshe I dydd refrayne;
Whie should I thenne appeare dismay'd
    To leave thys worlde of payne?

"Ne! hapless HENRIE! I rejoyce,
    I shalle ne see thye dethe;
Moste willynglie ynne thye just cause
    Doe I resign my brethe.   180

"Oh, fickle people! rewyn'd londe!
    Thou wylt kenne peace ne moe;
Whyle RICHARD's sonnes exalt themselves,
    Thye brookes wythe bloude wylle flowe.

"Saie, were ye tyr'd of godlie peace,
    And godlie HENRIE's reigne,
Thatt you dydd choppe youre easie daies
    For those of bloude and peyne?

"Whatte tho' I onne a sledde bee drawne,
    And mangled by a hynde,   190
I doe defye the traytor's pow'r,
    Hee can ne harm my mynde;

"Whatte tho', uphoisted onne a pole,
    Mye lymbes shall rotte ynne ayre,
And ne ryche monument of brasse
    CHARLES BAWDIN's name shall bear;

"Yett ynne the holie booke above,
    Whyche tyme can't eate awaie,
There wythe the sarvants of the Lorde
    Mye name shall lyve for aie.   200

"Thenne welcome dethe! for lyfe eterne
    I leave thys mortall lyfe:
Farewell, vayne worlde, and alle that's deare,
    Mye sonnes and lovynge wyfe!

"Nowe dethe as welcome to mee comes,
    As e'er the moneth of Maie;
Nor woulde I even wyshe to lyve,
    Wyth my dere wyfe to staie."

Quod CANYNGE, " 'Tys a goodlie thynge
    To bee prepar'd to die;   210
And from thys world of peyne and grefe
    To Godde ynne Heav'n to flie."

And nowe the bell beganne to tolle,
    And claryonnes to sounde;
Syr CHARLES hee herde the horses feete
    A prauncyng onne the grounde:

And just before the officers,
    His lovynge wyfe came ynne,
Weepynge unfeigned teeres of woe,
    Wythe loude and dysmalle dynne.   220

"Sweet FLORENCE! nowe I praie forbere,
   Ynne quiet lett mee die;
Praie Godde, thatt ev'ry Christian soule
   Maye looke onne dethe as I.

"Sweet FLORENCE! why these brinie teeres?
   Theye washe my soule awaie,
And almost make mee wyshe for lyfe,
   Wyth thee, sweete dame, to staie.

" 'Tys butt a journie I shalle goe
   Untoe the lande of blysse;
Nowe, as a proofe of husbande's love,
   Receive thys holie kysse."   230

Thenne FLORENCE, fault'ring ynne her saie,
   Tremblynge these wordyes spoke,
"Ah, cruele EDWARDE! bloudie kynge!
   My herte ys welle nyghe broke:

"Ah, sweete Syr CHARLES! why wylt thou goe,
   Wythoute thye lovynge wyfe?
The cruelle axe thatt cuttes thye necke,
   Ytte eke shall ende mye lyfe."   240

And nowe the officers came ynne
   To brynge Syr CHARLES awaie,
Whoe turnedd toe his lovynge wyfe,
   And thus toe her dydd saie:

"I goe to lyfe, and nott to dethe;
   Truste thou ynne Godde above,
And teache thye sonnes to feare the Lorde,
   And ynne theyre hertes hym love:

"Teache them to runne the nobile race
   Thatt I theyre fader runne:
FLORENCE! shou'd dethe thee take—adieu!   250
   Yee officers, leade onne."

Thenne FLORENCE rav'd as anie madde,
   And dydd her tresses tere;
"Oh! staie, mye husbande! lorde! and lyfe!"—
   Syr CHARLES thenne dropt a teare.

'Tyll tyredd oute wythe ravynge loud,
    Shee fellen onne the flore;
Syr CHARLES exerted alle hys myghte,
    And march'd fromm oute the dore.   260

Uponne a sledde hee mounted thenne,
    Wythe lookes fulle brave and swete;
Lookes, thatt enshone ne moe concern
    Thanne anie ynne the strete.

Before hym went the council-menne,
    Ynne scarlett robes and golde,
And tassils spanglynge ynne the sunne,
    Muche glorious to beholde:

The Freers of Seincte AUGUSTYNE next
    Appeared to the syghte,   270
All cladd ynne homelie russett weedes,
    Of godlie monkysh plyghte: [2]

Ynne diffraunt partes a godlie psaume
    Moste sweetlie theye dydd chaunt;
Behynde theyre backes syx mynstrelles came,
    Who tun'd the strunge bataunt. [3]

Thenne fyve-and-twentye archers came;
    Echone the bowe dydd bende,
From rescue of kynge HENRIES friends
    Syr CHARLES forr to defend.   280

Bolde as a lyon came Syr CHARLES,
    Drawne onne a clothe-layde sledde,
Bye two blacke stedes ynne trappynges white,
    Wyth plumes uponne theyre hedde:

Behynde hym fyve-and-twentye moe
    Of archers stronge and stoute,
Wyth bended bowe echone ynne hande,
    Marched ynne goodlie route:

2 Condition.
3 The adjective "eager," which Chatter-   ton uses as a name for some sort of musical
    instrument!

Seincte JAMESES Freers marched next,
    Echone hys parte dydd chaunt;   290
Behynde theyre backs syx mynstrelles came,
    Who tun'd the strunge bataunt:

Thenne came the maior and eldermenne,
    Ynne clothe of scarlett deck't;
And theyre attendyng menne echone,
    Lyke Easterne princes trickt:

And after them, a multitude
    Of citizenns dydd thronge;
The wyndowes were alle fulle of heddes,
    As hee dydd passe alonge.   300

And whenne hee came to the hyghe crosse,
    Syr CHARLES dydd turne and saie,
"O Thou, thatt savest manne fromme synne,
    Washe mye soule clean thys daie!"

Att the grete mynsterr wyndowe sat
    The kynge ynne myckle state,
To see CHARLES BAWDIN goe alonge
    To hys most welcom fate.

Soone as the sledde drewe nyghe enowe,
    Thatt EDWARDE hee myghte heare,   310
The brave Syr CHARLES hee dydd stande uppe,
    And thus hys wordes declare:

"Thou seest mee, EDWARDE! traytour vile!
    Expos'd to infamie;
Butt bee assur'd, disloyall manne!
    I'm greaterr nowe thanne thee.

"Bye foule proceedyngs, murdre, bloude,
    Thou wearest nowe a crowne;
And hast appoynted mee to dye,
    By power nott thyne owne.   320

"Thou thynkest I shall dye to-daie;
    I have beene dede 'till nowe,
And soone shall lyve to weare a crowne
    For aie uponne my browe:

'Whylst thou, perhapps, for som few yeares,
  Shalt rule thys fickle lande,
To lett them knowe howe wyde the rule
  'Twixt kynge and tyrant hande:

"Thye pow'r unjust, thou traytour slave!
  Shall falle onne thye owne hedde"—   330
Fromm out of hearyng of the kynge
  Departed thenne the sledde.

Kynge EDWARDE's soule rush'd to hys face,
  Hee turn'd hys hedde awaie,
And to hys broder GLOUCESTER
  Hee thus dydd speke and saie:

"To hym that soe-much-dreaded dethe
  Ne ghastlie terrors brynge,
Beholde the manne! hee spake the truthe,
  Hee's greater thanne a kynge!"   340

"Soe lett hym die!" Duke RICHARD sayde;
  "And maye echone oure foes
Bende downe theyre neckes to bloudie axe,
  And feede the carryon crowes."

And nowe the horses gentlie drewe
  Syr CHARLES uppe the hyghe hylle;
The axe dydd glysterr ynne the sunne,
  Hys pretious bloude to spylle.

Syrr CHARLES dydd uppe the scaffold goe,
  As uppe a gilded carre   350
Of victorye, bye val'rous chiefs
  Gayn'd ynne the bloudie warre:

And to the people hee dydd saie,
  "Beholde you see mee dye,
For servynge loyally mye kynge,
  Mye kynge most rightfullie.

"As longe as EDWARDE rules thys lande,
  Ne quiet you wylle knowe;
Youre sonnes and husbandes shalle bee slayne,
  And brookes wythe bloude shalle flowe.   360

"You leave youre goode and lawfulle kynge,
 Whenne ynne adversitye;
Lyke mee, untoe the true cause stycke,
 And for the true cause dye."

Thenne hee, wyth preestes, uponne hys knees,
 A pray'r to Godde dydd make,
Besecchynge hym unto hymselfe
 Hys partynge soule to take.

Thenne, kneelynge downe, hee layd his hedde
 Most seemlie onne the blocke;   370
Whyche fromme hys bodie fayre at once
 The able heddes-manne stroke:

And oute the bloude beganne to flowe,
 And rounde the scaffolde twyne;
And teares, enow to washe't awaie,
 Dydd flowe fromme each mann's eyne.

The bloudie axe hys bodie fayre
 Ynnto foure parties cutte;
And ev'rye parte, and eke hys hedde,
 Uponne a pole was putte.   380

One parte dydd rotte onne Kynwulph-hylle,
 One onne the mynster-tower,
And one from off the castle-gate
 The crowen dydd devoure:

The other onne Seyncte Powle's goode gate,
 A dreery spectacle;
Hys hedde was plac'd onne the hyghe crosse,
 Ynne hyghe-streete most nobile.

Thus was the ende of BAWDIN's fate:
 Godde prosper longe oure kynge,   390
And grante hee maye, wyth BAWDIN's soule,
 Ynne heav'n Godd's mercie synge!

MYNSTRELLES SONGE [1]

1777

O! synge untoe mie roundelaie,
O! droppe the brynie teare wythe mee,
Daunce ne moe atte hallie daie,
Lycke a reynynge [2] ryver bee;
    Mie love ys dedde,
    Gon to hys death-bedde,
    Al under the wyllowe tree.

Blacke hys cryne [3] as the wyntere nyghte,
Whyte hys rode [4] as the sommer snowe,
Rodde hys face as the mornynge lyghte,   10
Cale [5] he lyes ynne the grave belowe;
    Mie love ys dedde,
    Gon to hys deathe-bedde,
    Al under the wyllowe tree.

Swote hys tyngue as the throstles note,
Quycke ynn daunce as thoughte canne bee,
Defte hys taboure, codgelle stote,
O! hee lyes bie the wyllowe tree:
    Mie love ys dedde,
    Gonne to hys deathe-bedde,   20
    All underre the wyllowe tree.

Harke! the ravenne flappes hys wynge,
In the briered delle belowe;
Harke! the dethe-owle loude dothe synge,
To the nyghte-mares as heie [6] goe;
    Mie love ys dedde,
    Gon to hys deathe-bedde,
    Al under the wyllowe tree.

See! the whyte moone sheenes onne hie;
Whyterre ys mie true loves shroude;   30
Whyterre yanne [7] the mornynge skie,
Whyterre yanne the evenynge cloude;

1 In Ælla, a Tragycal Enterlude, 1777.   5 Cold.
2 Running.   6 They.
3 Hair.   7 Than.
4 Complexion.

Mie love ys dedde,
Gon to hys deathe-bedde,
Al under the wyllowe tree.

Heere, uponne mie true loves grave,
Schalle the baren fleurs be layde,
Nee one hallie Seyncte to save
Al the celness [8] of a mayde.
    Mie love ys dedde,   40
    Gonne to hys death-bedde,
    Alle under the wyllowe tree.

Wythe mie hondes I'lle dente the brieres
Rounde his hallie corse to gre,[9]
Ouphante [10] fairie, lyghte youre fyres,
Heere mie boddie stylle schalle bee.
    Mie love ys dedde,
    Gon to hys deathe-bedde,
    Al under the wyllowe tree.

Comme, wythe acorne-coppe & thorne,   50
Drayne mie hartys blodde awaie;
Lyfe & all yttes goode I scorne,
Daunce bie nete, or feaste by daie.
    Mie love ys dedde,
    Gon to hys death-bedde,
    Al under the wyllowe tree.

Waterre wytches, crownede wythe reytes,[11]
Bere mee to yer leathalle tyde.
I die; I comme; mie true love waytes.
Thos the damselle spake, and dyed.   60

Edward Gibbon

1737–1794

LIKE Boswell, Gibbon could pride himself upon being completely a
man of the world. His life, his temperament, his historical method

---

8 Coldness.   10 Elfin.
9 Grow.   11 Water flags.

would not be possible except in the cosmopolitan atmosphere of the eighteenth century. As he says of himself after his life in Lausanne, he had ceased to be entirely an Englishman and had assumed a "world view" that made provincialism impossible. His egoism, his equanimity, are of a curious sort: he writes to his father, "Whatever else I may be ignorant of, I think I know myself, and shall always endeavour to mention my good qualities without vanity, and my defects without repugnance." Here is the "justness" of view toward one's self that we find in Boswell, the honesty and poise of the century that is too cool and self-possessed to seem like exhibitionism. This poise makes Gibbon's autobiography disarming; he can tell with composure how his passion for Susanne Curchod ended with a prudent decision not to marry her— "I sighed as a lover; I obeyed as a son." Later, when Gibbon was even more self-possessed, he could write to his mother, "The intelligence you received of fair eyes, bleeding hearts, and an approaching daughter-in-law, is all very agreeable Romance. A pair of very tolerable eyes, I must confess, made their appearance at Sheffield, and what is more extraordinary were accompanied by good sense and good humour, without one grain of affectation. Yet, still I am *indifferent*, and she is *poor*." This self-possession is the note of the famous *History of the Decline and Fall of the Roman Empire*, easily the greatest of the "enlightened" histories, in which Gibbon takes the cool secular world view of the religious, political, and social earthquakes by which the ancient world crumbled away. That is why the *History* was composed with such certainty and firmness of development; that is why it was so hated by those who considered themselves Christians (Gibbon regarded them as provincial, not "enlightened"). Gibbon was, in a sense, finding a predetermined pattern in the course of history and offering, as encyclopedist and "philosophe," his observation on this pattern. Although the Autobiography, composed of carefully written and rewritten fragments, is not so dramatic a record as those by Boswell, or so rich in texture, it is a major document of the cosmopolitan attitudes of the enlightenment.

BIOGRAPHICAL NOTES

Born of a good family at Putney-on-Thames and reared chiefly by a maiden-aunt, Catherine Porten. Entered Westminster School (1749). Entered Magdalen College, Oxford, as gentleman-commoner (1752), but felt contempt for Oxford and was soon converted to Romanism. Sent by father to Lausanne (1753) to be re-converted by M. Pavillard. Love for Susanne Curchod. Returned to England (1758) and was commissioned captain in the militia; published an *Essai sur l'Étude de la Littérature*. In 1763–64 revisited the Continent: Lausanne and Rome, where he determined to write the *History*. After death of his father (1770), Gibbon settled in London, read for the *History*, entered Parliament, and became a member of the Club. First volume of the *History* printed (1776). Left England to settle at Lausanne to complete the *History* (1783). Last volumes of *History* appeared, and Gibbon began writing his memoirs (1787–88). Visit to England and death in London (1793).

BIBLIOGRAPHY: *Gibbon's Journal,* ed. D. M. Low, N.Y., n.d. *Private Letters of Edward Gibbon,* ed. Rowland E. Prothero, London, 1896. *Memoirs of the Life of Edward Gibbon,* ed. George Birkbeck Hill, London, 1900. Black, John Bennett, *The Art of History: A Study of Four Great Historians of the Eighteenth Century,* London and N.Y., 1926. Bond, Harold Lewis, *The Literary Art of Edward Gibbon,* 1960. Dawson, Christopher, *Edward Gibbon,* 1935. Low, David Morrice, *Edward Gibbon,* 1937. Mowat, Robert Balmain, *Gibbon,* 1936. Quennell, Peter, *The Profane Virtues,* 1945. Young, George Malcolm, *Gibbon,* 1948.

MEMOIRS OF MY LIFE AND WRITINGS

1795

In my ninth year (January, 1746), in a lucid interval of comparative health, my father adopted the convenient and customary mode of English education; and I was sent to Kingston-upon-Thames, to a school of about seventy boys, which was kept by Dr. Woodeson and his assistants. Every time I have since passed over Putney Common, I have always noticed the spot where my mother, as we drove along in the coach, admonished me that I was now going into the world, and must learn to think and act for myself. The expression may appear ludicrous, yet there is not in the course of life a more remarkable change than the removal of a child from the luxury and freedom of a wealthy house to the frugal diet and strict subordination of a school; from the tenderness of parents and obsequiousness of servants to the rude familiarity of his equals, the insolent tyranny of his seniors, and the rod, perhaps, of a cruel and capricious pedagogue. Such hardships may steel the mind and body against the injuries of fortune; but my timid reserve was astonished by the crowd and tumult of the school; the want of strength and activity disqualified me for the sports of the playfield; nor have I forgot how often in the year 'forty-six I was reviled and buffeted for the sins of my Tory ancestors. By the common methods of discipline, at the expense of many tears and some blood, I purchased the knowledge of the Latin syntax: and not long since I was possessed of the dirty volumes of Phaedrus and

Cornelius Nepos, which I painfully construed and darkly understood. . . .

At the conclusion of this first period of my life, I am tempted to enter a protest against the trite and lavish praise of the happiness of our boyish years, which is echoed with so much affectation in the world. That happiness I have never known, that time I have never regretted; and were my poor aunt still alive, she would bear testimony to the early and constant uniformity of my sentiments. It will indeed be replied that *I* am not a competent judge; that pleasure is incompatible with pain; that joy is excluded from sickness; and that the felicity of a schoolboy consists in the perpetual motion of thoughtless and playful agility, in which I was never qualified to excel. My name, it is most true, could never be enrolled among the sprightly race, the idle progeny of Eton or Westminster,

> Who foremost might delight to cleave,
> With pliant arm, the glassy wave,
> Or urge the flying ball.[1]

The poet may gaily describe the short hours of recreation; but he forgets the daily tedious labors of the school, which is approached each morning with anxious and reluctant steps.

. . . My own introduction to the university of Oxford forms a new era in my life; and at the distance of forty years I still remember my first emotions of surprise and satisfaction. In my fifteenth year I felt myself suddenly raised from a boy to a man; the persons whom I respected as my superiors in age and academical rank entertained me with every mark of attention and civility; and my vanity was flattered by the velvet cap and silk gown which distinguish a gentleman-commoner [2] from a plebeian student. A decent allowance, more money than a schoolboy had ever seen, was at my own disposal; and I might command among the tradesmen of Oxford an indefinite and dangerous latitude of credit. A key was delivered into my hands, which gave me the free use of a numerous and learned library: my apartment consisted of three elegant and well-furnished rooms in the new building—a stately pile—of Magdalen College; and the adjacent walks, had they been frequented by Plato's disciples, might have been compared to the Attic shade on the banks of the Ilissus. Such was the fair prospect

1 Gray's "Ode on a Distant Prospect of Eton College."

2 A special rank of Oxford student between graduate and undergraduate.

of my entrance (April 3, 1752) into the university of Oxford. A venerable prelate, whose taste and erudition must reflect honor on the society in which they were formed, has drawn a very interesting picture of his academical life. "I was educated," says Bishop Lowth,[3] "in the university of Oxford. I enjoyed all the advantages, both public and private, which that famous seat of learning so largely affords. I spent many years in that illustrious society, in a well-regulated course of useful discipline and studies, and in the agreeable and improving commerce of gentlemen and of scholars; in a society where emulation without envy, ambition without jealousy, contention without animosity, incited industry, and awakened genius; where a liberal pursuit of knowledge, and a genuine freedom of thought, was raised, encouraged, and pushed forward by example, by commendation, and by authority. I breathed the same atmosphere that the Hookers, the Chillingworths, and the Lockes had breathed before; whose benevolence and humanity were as extensive as their vast genius and comprehensive knowledge; who always treated their adversaries with civility and respect; who made candor, moderation, and liberal judgment as much the rule and law as the subject of their discourse. And do you reproach me with my education in this place, and with my relation to this most respectable body, which I shall always esteem my greatest advantage and my highest honor?" I transcribe with pleasure this eloquent passage, without examining what benefits or what rewards were derived by Hooker, or Chillingworth, or Locke, from their academical institution; without inquiring whether in this angry controversy the spirit of Lowth himself is purified from the intolerant zeal which Warburton had ascribed to the genius of the place. It may indeed be observed that the atmosphere of Oxford did not agree with Mr. Locke's constitution, and that the philosopher justly despised the academical bigots who expelled his person and condemned his principles. The expression of gratitude is a virtue and a pleasure: a liberal mind will delight to cherish and celebrate the memory of its parents; and the teachers of science are the parents of the mind. I applaud the filial piety which it is impossible for me to imitate; since I must not confess an imaginary debt, to assume the merit of a just or generous retribution. To the university of Oxford I

---

3 Robert Lowth, bishop of London, who was replying to an attack by William Warburton, bishop of Gloucester, in a controversy regarding Biblical interpretation.

acknowledge no obligation; and she will as cheerfully renounce me for a son as I am willing to disclaim her for a mother. I spent fourteen months at Magdalen College; they proved the fourteen months the most idle and unprofitable of my whole life. The reader will pronounce between the school and the scholar; but I cannot affect to believe that nature had disqualified me for all literary pursuits. The specious and ready excuse of my tender age, imperfect preparation, and hasty departure, may doubtless be alleged; nor do I wish to defraud such excuses of their proper weight. Yet in my sixteenth year I was not devoid of capacity or application; even my childish reading had displayed an early though blind propensity for books; and the shallow flood might have been taught to flow in a deep channel and a clear stream. In the discipline of a well-constituted academy, under the guidance of skillful and vigilant professors, I should gradually have risen from translations to originals, from the Latin to the Greek classics, from dead languages to living science: my hours would have been occupied by useful and agreeable studies, the wanderings of fancy would have been restrained, and I should have escaped the temptations of idleness, which finally precipitated my departure from Oxford.

Perhaps in a separate annotation I may coolly examine the fabulous and real antiquities of our sister universities, a question which has kindled such fierce and foolish disputes among their fanatic sons. In the meanwhile it will be acknowledged that these venerable bodies are sufficiently old to partake of all the prejudices and infirmities of age. The schools of Oxford and Cambridge were founded in a dark age of false and barbarous science; and they are still tainted with the vices of their origin. Their primitive discipline was adapted to the education of priests and monks; and the government still remains in the hands of the clergy, an order of men whose manners are remote from the present world, and whose eyes are dazzled by the light of philosophy. The legal incorporation of these societies by the charters of popes and kings had given them a monopoly of the public instruction; and the spirit of monopolists is narrow, lazy, and oppressive: their work is more costly and less productive than that of independent artists; and the new improvements so eagerly grasped by the competition of freedom are admitted with slow and sullen reluctance in those proud corporations, above the fear of a rival and below the confession of an error. We may scarcely hope that any reformation will be a voluntary act; and so deeply are they rooted in law and prejudice that even the omnipotence of Parliament would shrink from an inquiry into the state and abuses of the two universities.

The use of academical degrees, as old as the thirteenth century, is visibly borrowed from the mechanic corporations, in which an apprentice, after serving his time, obtains a testimonial of his skill, and a license to practice his trade and mystery. It is not my design to depreciate those honors, which could never gratify or disappoint my ambition; and I should applaud the institution, if the degrees of bachelor or licentiate were bestowed as the reward of manly and successful study; if the name and rank of doctor or master were strictly reserved for the professors of science who have approved their title to the public esteem.

In all the universities of Europe, excepting our own, the languages and sciences are distributed among a numerous list of effective professors: the students, according to their taste, their calling, and their diligence, apply themselves to the proper masters; and in the annual repetition of public and private lectures these masters are assiduously employed. Our curiosity may inquire what number of professors has been instituted at Oxford? (for I shall now confine myself to my own university); by whom are they appointed, and what may be the probable chances of merit or incapacity? how many are stationed to the three faculties,[4] and how many are left for the liberal arts? what is the form, and what the substance, of their lessons? But all these questions are silenced by one short and singular answer, "That in the university of Oxford the greater part of the public professors have for these many years given up altogether even the pretense of teaching." Incredible as the fact may appear, I must rest my belief on the positive and impartial evidence of a master of moral and political wisdom, who had himself resided at Oxford. Dr. Adam Smith assigns as the cause of their indolence, that instead of being paid by voluntary contributions, which would urge them to increase the number and to deserve the gratitude of their pupils, the Oxford professors are secure in the enjoyment of a fixed stipend, without the necessity of labor, or the apprehension of control. It has indeed been observed, nor is the observation absurd, that excepting in experimental sciences,

---

4 Since medieval days, the chief "faculties" were those in theology, law, and medicine and the arts.

which demand a costly apparatus and a dexterous hand, the many valuable treatises that have been published on every subject of learning may now supersede the ancient mode of oral instruction. Were this principle true in its utmost latitude, I should only infer that the offices and salaries which are become useless ought without delay to be abolished. But there still remains a material difference between a book and a professor; the hour of the lecture enforces attendance; attention is fixed by the presence, the voice, and the occasional questions, of the teacher; the most idle will carry something away; and the more diligent will compare the instructions which they have heard in the school, with the volumes which they peruse in their chamber. The advice of a skillful professor will adapt a course of reading to every mind and every situation; his authority will discover, admonish, and at last chastise, the negligence of his disciples; and his vigilant inquiries will ascertain the steps of their literary progress. Whatever science he professes he may illustrate in a series of discourses, composed in the leisure of his closet, pronounced on public occasions, and finally delivered to the press. I observe with pleasure, that in the university of Oxford Dr. Lowth, with equal eloquence and erudition, has executed this task in his incomparable *Praelectiones* on the poetry of the Hebrews.

The college of St. Mary Magdalen was founded in the fifteenth century by Wainfleet, bishop of Winchester; and now consists of a president, forty fellows, and a number of inferior students. It is esteemed one of the largest and most wealthy of our academical corporations, which may be compared to the Benedictine abbeys of Catholic countries; and I have loosely heard that the estates belonging to Magdalen College, which are leased by those indulgent landlords at small quitrents and occasional fines, might be raised, in the hands of private avarice, to an annual revenue of nearly thirty thousand pounds. Our colleges are supposed to be schools of science, as well as of education; nor is it unreasonable to expect that a body of literary men, devoted to a life of celibacy, exempt from the care of their own subsistence, and amply provided with books, should devote their leisure to the prosecution of study, and that some effects of their studies should be manifested to the world. The shelves of their library groan under the weight of the Benedictine folios, of the editions of the Fathers, and the collections of the Middle Ages, which have issued from the single abbey of St.

Germain de Préz at Paris. A composition of genius must be the offspring of one mind; but such works of industry as may be divided among many hands, and must be continued during many years, are the peculiar province of a laborious community. If I inquire into the manufactures of the monks of Magdalen, if I extend the inquiry to the other colleges of Oxford and Cambridge, a silent blush, or a scornful frown, will be the only reply. The fellows or monks of my time were decent easy men, who supinely enjoyed the gifts of the founder: their days were filled by a series of uniform employments—the chapel and the hall, the coffee-house and the common room, till they retired, weary and well satisfied, to a long slumber. From the toil of reading, or thinking, or writing, they had absolved their conscience; and the first shoots of learning and ingenuity withered on the ground, without yielding any fruits to the owners or the public. As a gentleman-commoner, I was admitted to the society of the fellows, and fondly expected that some questions of literature would be the amusing and instructive topics of their discourse. Their conversation stagnated in a round of college business, Tory politics, personal anecdotes, and private scandal: their dull and deep potations excused the brisk intemperance of youth: and their constitutional toasts were not expressive of the most lively loyalty for the house of Hanover. A general election was now approaching: the great Oxfordshire contest already blazed with all the malevolence of party zeal. Magdalen College was devotedly attached to the old interest; and the names of Wenman and Dashwood were more frequently pronounced than those of Cicero and Chrysostom. The example of the senior fellows could not inspire the undergraduates with a liberal spirit or studious emulation; and I cannot describe, as I never knew, the discipline of college. Some duties may possibly have been imposed on the poor scholars, whose ambition aspired to the peaceful honors of a fellowship (*ascribi quietis ordinibus . . . Deorum*);[5] but no independent members were admitted below the rank of a gentleman-commoner, and our velvet cap was the cap of liberty. A tradition prevailed that some of our predecessors had spoken Latin declamations in the hall; but of this ancient custom no vestige remained: the obvious methods of public exercises and examinations were totally unknown; and I have never

5 Horace *Odes* III. iii. 35: "To be enrolled in the serene ranks of the gods."

heard that either the president or the society interfered in the private economy of the tutors and their pupils.

The silence of the Oxford professors, which deprives the youth of public instruction, is imperfectly supplied by the tutors, as they are styled, of the several colleges. Instead of confining themselves to a single science, which had satisfied the ambition of Burmann or Bernoulli,[6] they teach, or promise to teach, either history or mathematics, or ancient literature, or moral philosophy; and as it is possible that they may be defective in all, it is highly probable that of some they will be ignorant. They are paid indeed by private contributions, but their appointment depends on the head of the house; their diligence is voluntary, and will consequently be languid, while the pupils themselves, or their parents, are not indulged in the liberty of choice or change. The first tutor into whose hands I was resigned appears to have been one of the best of the tribe: Dr. Waldegrave was a learned and pious man, of a mild disposition, strict morals, and abstemious life, who seldom mingled in the politics or the jollity of the college. But his knowledge of the world was confined to the university; his learning was of the last rather than of the present age; his temper was indolent; his faculties, which were not of the first rate, had been relaxed by the climate; and he was satisfied, like his fellows, with the slight and superficial discharge of an important trust. As soon as my tutor had sounded the insufficiency of his disciple in school learning, he proposed that we should read, every morning from ten to eleven, the comedies of Terence. The sum of my improvement in the university of Oxford is confined to three or four Latin plays; and even the study of an elegant classic, which might have been illustrated by a comparison of ancient and modern theaters, was reduced to a dry and literal interpretation of the author's text. During the first weeks I constantly attended these lessons in my tutor's room; but as they appeared equally devoid of profit and pleasure, I was once tempted to try the experiment of a formal apology. The apology was accepted with a smile. I repeated the offense with less ceremony; the excuse was admitted with the same indulgence: the slightest motive of laziness or indisposition, the most trifling avocation at home or abroad, was allowed as a worthy impediment;

6 Pieter Burmann (1668–1741), a Dutch classical scholar. Jacques, Jean, and Nicolas Bernoulli were all famous in early eighteenth-century mathematics.

nor did my tutor appear conscious of my absence or neglect. . . .

After the departure of Dr. Waldegrave, I was transferred, with his other pupils, to his academical heir, whose literary character did not command the respect of the college. Dr. Winchester well remembered that he had a salary to receive, and only forgot that he had a duty to perform. Instead of guiding the studies, and watching over the behavior of his disciple, I was never summoned to attend even the ceremony of a lecture; and, excepting one voluntary visit to his rooms, during the eight months of his titular office, the tutor and pupil lived in the same college as strangers to each other. The want of experience, of advice, and of occupation, soon betrayed me into some improprieties of conduct, ill-chosen company, late hours, and inconsiderate expense. My growing debts might be secret; but my frequent absence was visible and scandalous, and a tour to Bath, a visit into Buckinghamshire, and four excursions to London, in the same winter, were costly and dangerous frolics. They were, indeed, without a meaning, as without an excuse. The irksomeness of a cloistered life repeatedly tempted me to wander; but my chief pleasure was that of traveling; and I was too young and bashful to enjoy, like a manly Oxonian in town, the pleasures of London. In all these excursions I eloped from Oxford; I returned to college: in a few days I eloped again, as if I had been an independent stranger in a hired lodging, without once hearing the voice of admonition, without once feeling the hand of control. Yet my time was lost, my expenses were multiplied, my behavior abroad was unknown; folly as well as vice should have awakened the attention of my superiors, and my tender years would have justified a more than ordinary degree of restraint and discipline.

It might at least be expected that an ecclesiastical school should inculcate the orthodox principles of religion. But our venerable mother had contrived to unite the opposite extremes of bigotry and indifference: an heretic, or unbeliever, was a monster in her eyes; but she was always, or often, or sometimes, remiss in the spiritual education of her own children. According to the statutes of the university, every student, before he is matriculated, must subscribe his assent to the thirty-nine articles of the Church of England, which are signed by more than read, and read by more than believe them. My insufficient age excused me, however, from the immediate performance of this legal ceremony; and the vice-chancellor directed me to return as soon as I should have accomplished my fifteenth year; recommending me, in the meanwhile, to the instruction of my college. My college forgot to instruct: I forgot to return, and was myself forgotten by the first magistrate of the university. Without a single lecture, either public or private, either Christian or Protestant, without any academical subscription, without any episcopal confirmation, I was left by the dim light of my catechism to grope my way to the chapel and communion table, where I was admitted without a question how far, or by what means, I might be qualified to receive the sacrament. Such almost incredible neglect was productive of the worst mischiefs. From my childhood I had been fond of religious disputation: my poor aunt has been often puzzled by the mysteries which she strove to believe; nor had the elastic spring been totally broken by the weight of the atmosphere of Oxford. The blind activity of idleness urged me to advance without armor into the dangerous mazes of controversy; and at the age of sixteen I bewildered myself into the errors of the Church of Rome.

The progress of my conversion may tend to illustrate, at least, the history of my own mind. It was not long since Dr. Middleton's *Free Inquiry* had sounded an alarm in the theological world: much ink and much gall had been spilt in the defense of the primitive miracles; and the two dullest of their champions were crowned with academical honors by the university of Oxford.[7] The name of Middleton was unpopular; and his proscription very naturally led me to peruse his writings, and those of his antagonists. His bold criticism, which approaches the precipice of infidelity, produced on my mind a singular effect; and had I persevered in the communion of Rome, I should now apply to my own fortune the prediction of the Sybil,

> ——Via prima salutis,
> Quod minime reris, Graia, pandetur ab urbe.[8]

The elegance of style and freedom of argument were repelled by a shield of prejudice. I still revered the character, or rather the names, of the saints and fathers whom Dr. Middleton exposes; nor could he destroy my implicit belief, that the gift of miraculous powers was continued in the church during the first four or five

7 William Dodwell and Thomas Church.
8 *Aeneid* VI. 96–97:   to crown,
"Hope, where unlooked for, comes thy toils   Thy road to safety from a Grecian town."

centuries of Christianity. But I was unable to resist the weight of historical evidence, that within the same period most of the leading doctrines of popery were already introduced in theory and practice: nor was my conclusion absurd—that miracles are the test of truth, and that the church must be orthodox and pure which was so often approved by the visible interposition of the Deity. The marvelous tales which are so boldly attested by the Basils and Chrysostoms, the Augustins and Jeromes, compelled me to embrace the superior merits of celibacy, the institution of the monastic life, the use of the sign of the cross, of holy oil, and even of images, the invocation of saints, the worship of relics, the rudiments of purgatory in prayers for the dead, and the tremendous mystery of the sacrifice of the body and blood of Christ, which insensibly swelled into the prodigy of transubstantiation. In these dispositions, and already more than half a convert, I formed an unlucky intimacy with a young gentleman of our college. With a character less resolute, Mr. Molesworth had imbibed the same religious opinions; and some popish books, I know not through what channel, were conveyed into his possession. I read, I applauded, I believed; the English translation of two famous works of Bossuet, bishop of Meaux, the *Exposition of the Catholic Doctrine* and the *History of the Protestant Variations*, achieved my conversion; and I surely fell by a noble hand. I have since examined the originals with a more discerning eye, and shall not hesitate to pronounce that Bossuet is indeed a master of all the weapons of controversy. In the *Exposition*, a specious apology, the orator assumes, with consummate art, the tone of candor and simplicity; and the ten-horned monster is transformed, at his magic touch, into the milk-white hind who must be loved as soon as she is seen. In the *History*, a bold and well-aimed attack, he displays, with a happy mixture of narrative and argument, the faults and follies, the changes and contradictions, of our first reformers; whose variations (as he dexterously contends) are the mark of historical error, while the perpetual unity of the Catholic church is the sign and test of infallible truth. To my present feelings it seems incredible that I should ever believe that I believed in transubstantiation. But my conqueror oppressed me with the sacramental words, "Hoc est corpus meum," and dashed against each other the figurative half-meanings of the Protestant sects: every objection was resolved into omnipotence;

and after repeating at St. Mary's the Athanasian Creed, I humbly
acquiesced in the mystery of the real presence.

> To take up half on trust, and half to try,
> Name it not faith, but bungling bigotry.
> Both knave and fool the merchant we may call,
> To pay great sums, and to compound the small:
> For who would break with Heaven, and would not break for all? [9]

No sooner had I settled my new religion than I resolved to profess
myself a Catholic. Youth is sincere and impetuous; and a momentary glow of enthusiasm had raised me above all temporal considerations.

By the keen Protestants, who would gladly retaliate the example
of persecution, a clamor is raised of the increase of popery: and
they are always loud to declaim against the toleration of priests
and Jesuits, who pervert so many of His Majesty's subjects from
their religion and allegiance. On the present occasion the fall of
one or more of her sons directed this clamor against the university;
and it was confidently affirmed that popish missionaries were suffered, under various disguises, to introduce themselves into the
colleges of Oxford. But justice obliges me to declare that, as far
as relates to myself, this assertion is false; and that I never conversed with a priest, or even with a papist, till my resolution from
books was absolutely fixed. In my last excursion to London I addressed myself to Mr. Lewis, a Roman Catholic bookseller in Rus-
sell Street, Covent Garden, who recommended me to a priest, of
whose name and order I am at present ignorant. In our first interview he soon discovered that persuasion was needless. After sounding the motives and merits of my conversion, he consented to admit me into the pale of the church; and at his feet, on the eighth
of June, 1753, I solemnly, though privately, abjured the errors
of heresy. The seduction of an English youth of family and fortune
was an act of as much danger as glory; but he bravely overlooked
the danger, of which I was not then sufficiently informed.
"Where a person is reconciled to the see of Rome, or procures
others to be reconciled, the offense (says Blackstone) amounts
to high treason." And if the humanity of the age would prevent
the execution of this sanguinary statute, there were other laws of

9 Dryden, *The Hind and the Panther*, I.

a less odious cast, which condemned the priest to perpetual imprisonment, and transferred the proselyte's estate to his nearest relation. An elaborate controversial epistle, approved by my director, and addressed to my father, announced and justified the step which I had taken. My father was neither a bigot nor a philosopher; but his affection deplored the loss of an only son, and his good sense was astonished at my strange departure from the religion of my country. In the first sally of passion he divulged a secret which prudence might have suppressed, and the gates of Magdalen College were forever shut against my return. Many years afterwards, when the name of Gibbon was become as notorious as that of Middleton, it was industriously whispered at Oxford, that the historian had formerly "turned papist"; my character stood exposed to the reproach of inconstancy; and this invidious topic would have been handled without mercy by my opponents, could they have separated my cause from that of the university. For my own part, I am proud of an honest sacrifice of interest to conscience. I can never blush, if my tender mind was entangled in the sophistry that seduced the acute and manly understandings of Chillingworth and Bayle, who afterwards emerged from superstition to scepticism. . . .

After carrying me to Putney, to the house of his friend Mr. Mallet, by whose philosophy I was rather scandalized than reclaimed, it was necessary for my father to form a new plan of education, and to devise some method which, if possible, might effect the cure of my spiritual malady. After much debate it was determined, from the advice and personal experience of Mr. Eliot (now Lord Eliot) to fix me, during some years, at Lausanne in Switzerland. Mr. Frey, a Swiss gentleman of Basel, undertook the conduct of the journey: we left London the 19th of June, crossed the sea from Dover to Calais, traveled post through several provinces of France, by the direct road of St. Quentin, Rheims, Langres, and Besançon, and arrived the 30th of June at Lausanne, where I was immediately settled under the roof and tuition of Mr. Pavilliard, a Calvinist minister. . . .

My obligations to the lessons of Mr. Pavilliard gratitude will not suffer me to forget; he was endowed with a clear head and a warm heart; his innate benevolence had assuaged the spirit of the church; he was rational, because he was moderate; in the course of his studies he had acquired a just though superficial knowledge of most branches of literature; by long practice he was skilled in the arts of teaching; and he labored with assiduous patience to know the character, gain the affection, and open the mind, of his English pupil. As soon as we began to understand each other, he gently led me, from a blind and undistinguished love of reading, into the path of instruction. I consented with pleasure that a portion of the morning hours should be consecrated to a plan of modern history and geography, and to the critical perusal of the French and Latin classics; and at each step I felt myself invigorated by the habits of application and method. His prudence repressed and dissembled some youthful sallies; and as soon as I was confirmed in the habits of industry and temperance, he gave the reins into my own hands. His favorable report of my behavior and progress gradually obtained some latitude of action and expense; and he wished to alleviate the hardships of my lodging and entertainment. The principles of philosophy were associated with the examples of taste; and by a singular chance, the book, as well as the man, which contributed the most effectually to my education, has a stronger claim on my gratitude than on my admiration. M. de Crousaz, the adversary of Bayle and Pope, is not distinguished by lively fancy or profound reflection; and even in his own country, at the end of a few years, his name and writings are almost obliterated. But his philosophy had been formed in the school of Locke, his divinity in that of Limborch and Le Clerc; in a long and laborious life, several generations of pupils were taught to think, and even to write; his lessons rescued the academy of Lausanne from Calvinistic prejudice; and he had the rare merit of diffusing a more liberal spirit among the clergy and people of the Pays de Vaud. His system of logic, which in the last editions has swelled to six tedious and prolix volumes, may be praised as a clear and methodical abridgment of the art of reasoning, from our simple ideas to the most complex operations of the human understanding. This system I studied, and meditated, and abstracted, till I obtained the free command of an universal instrument, which I soon presumed to exercise on my Catholic opinions. Pavilliard was not unmindful that his first task, his most important duty, was to reclaim me from the errors of popery. The intermixture of sects has rendered the Swiss clergy acute and learned on the topics of controversy; and I have some of his letters in which he celebrates the dexterity of his attack, and my gradual concessions after a firm and well-managed defense. I was willing, and I am now willing, to allow him a handsome share of the honor of my conversion; yet I must observe, that it was principally effected by my private reflections; and I still remember my solitary transport at the discovery of a philosophical argument against the doctrine of transubstantiation—that the text of Scripture which seems to inculcate the real presence is attested only by a single sense—our sight; while the real presence itself is disproved by three of our senses—the sight, the touch, and the taste. The various articles of the Romish creed disappeared like a dream; and after a full conviction, on Christmas day, 1754, I received the sacrament in the church of Lausanne. It was here that I suspended my religious inquiries, acquiescing with implicit belief in the tenets and mysteries which are adopted by the general consent of Catholics and Protestants. . . .

I hesitate, from the apprehension of ridicule, when I approach the delicate subject of my early love. By this word I do not mean the polite attention, the gallantry, without hope or design, which has originated in the spirit of chivalry and is interwoven with the texture of French manners. I understand by this passion the union of desire, friendship, and tenderness, which is inflamed by a single female, which prefers her to the rest of her sex, and which seeks her possession as the supreme or the sole happiness of our being. I need not blush at recollecting the object of my choice; and though my love was disappointed of success, I am rather proud that I was once capable of feeling such a pure and exalted sentiment. The personal attractions of Mademoiselle Susan Curchod were embellished by the virtues and talents of the mind. Her fortune was humble, but her family was respectable. Her mother, a native of France, had preferred her religion to her country. The profession of her father did not extinguish the moderation and philosophy of his temper, and he lived content, with a small salary and laborious duty, in the obscure lot of minister of Crassy, in the mountains that separate the Pays de Vaud from the county of Burgundy. In the solitude of a sequestered village he bestowed a liberal and even learned education on his only daughter. She surpassed his hopes by her proficiency in the sciences and languages; and in her short visits to some relations at Lausanne, the wit, the beauty, and erudition of Mademoiselle Curchod were the theme of universal applause. The report of such a prodigy awakened my curiosity; I saw and loved. I found her learned without pedantry, lively in conversation, pure in sentiment, and elegant in manners; and the first sudden emotion was fortified by the habits and knowledge of a more familiar acquaintance. She permitted me to make her two or three visits at her father's house. I passed some happy days there in the mountains of Burgundy, and her parents honorably encouraged the connection. In a calm retirement the gay vanity of youth no longer fluttered in her bosom; she listened to the voice of truth and passion; and I might presume to hope that I had made some impression on a virtuous heart. At Crassy and Lausanne I indulged my dream of felicity; but on my return to England, I soon discovered that my father would not hear of this strange alliance, and that without his consent I was myself destitute and helpless. After a painful struggle I yielded to my fate: I sighed as a lover, I obeyed as a son; my wound was insensibly healed by time, absence, and the habits of a new life. My cure was accelerated by a faithful report of the tranquillity and cheerfulness of the lady herself; and my love subsided in friendship and esteem. The minister of Crassy soon afterwards died; his stipend died with him; his daughter retired to Geneva, where, by teaching young ladies, she earned a hard subsistence for herself and her mother; but in her lowest distress she maintained a spotless reputation, and a dignified behavior. A rich banker of Paris, a citizen of Geneva, had the good fortune and good sense to discover and possess this inestimable treasure; and in the capital of taste and luxury she resisted the temptations of wealth, as she had sustained the hardships of indigence. The genius of her husband has exalted him to the most conspicuous station in Europe. In every change of prosperity and disgrace he has reclined on the bosom of a faithful friend; and Mademoiselle Curchod is now the wife of M. Necker, the minister, and perhaps the legislator, of the French monarchy.

Whatsoever have been the fruits of my education, they must be ascribed to the fortunate banishment which placed me at Lausanne. I have sometimes applied to my own fate the verses of Pindar, which remind an Olympic champion that his victory was the consequence of his exile; and that at home, like a domestic fowl, his days might have rolled away inactive or inglorious. If my childish revolt against the religion of my country had not stripped me in time of my academic gown, the five important years so liberally improved in the studies and conversation of Lausanne would have been steeped in port and prejudice among the monks of Oxford.

Had the fatigue of idleness compelled me to read, the path of learning would not have been enlightened by a ray of philosophic freedom. I should have grown to manhood ignorant of the life and language of Europe, and my knowledge of the world would have been confined to an English cloister. But my religious error fixed me at Lausanne in a state of banishment and disgrace. The rigid course of discipline and abstinence to which I was condemned invigorated the constitution of my mind and body; poverty and pride estranged me from my countrymen. One mischief however, and in their eyes a serious and irreparable mischief, was derived from the success of my Swiss education—I had ceased to be an Englishman. At the flexible period of my youth, from the age of sixteen to twenty-one, my opinions, habits, and sentiments were cast in a foreign mold; the faint and distant remembrance of England was almost obliterated; my native language was grown less familiar; and I should have cheerfully accepted the offer of a moderate independence on the terms of perpetual exile. By the good sense and temper of Pavilliard my yoke was insensibly lightened: he left me master of my time and actions; but he could neither change my situation, nor increase my allowance; and with the progress of my years and reason I impatiently sighed for the moment of my deliverance. At length, in the spring of the year 1758, my father signified his permission and his pleasure that I should immediately return home. We were then in the midst of a war; the resentment of the French at our taking their ships without a declaration had rendered that polite nation somewhat peevish and difficult. They denied a passage to English travelers, and the road through Germany was circuitous, toilsome, and perhaps in the neighborhood of the armies exposed to some danger. In this perplexity, two Swiss officers of my acquaintance in the Dutch service, who were returning to their garrisons, offered to conduct me through France as one of their companions; nor did we sufficiently reflect that my borrowed name and regimentals might have been considered, in case of a discovery, in a very serious light. I took my leave of Lausanne on the 11th April, 1758, with a mixture of joy and regret, in the firm resolution of revisiting, as a man, the persons and places which had been so dear to my youth. . . .

As I am now entering on a more ample field of society and study, I can only hope to avoid a vain and prolix garrulity, by overlooking the vulgar crowd of my acquaintance, and confining myself to such intimate friends among books and men as are best entitled to my notice by their own merit and reputation, or by the deep impression which they have left on my mind. Yet I will embrace this occasion of recommending to the young student a practice which about this time I myself adopted. After glancing my eye over the design and order of a new book, I suspended the perusal till I had finished the task of self-examination, till I had revolved, in a solitary walk, all that I knew or believed, or had thought, on the subject of the whole work, or of some particular chapter: I was then qualified to discern how much the author added to my original stock; and if I was sometimes satisfied by the agreement, I was sometimes alarmed by the opposition, of our ideas. The favorite companions of my leisure were our English writers since the Revolution: they breathe the spirit of reason and liberty; and they most seasonably contributed to restore the purity of my own language, which had been corrupted by the long use of a foreign idiom. By the judicious advice of Mr. Mallet I was directed to the writings of Swift and Addison; wit and simplicity are their common attributes: but the style of Swift is supported by manly original vigor; that of Addison is adorned by the female graces of elegance and mildness. The old reproach that no British altars had been raised to the muse of history was recently disproved by the first performances of Robertson and Hume, the histories of Scotland and of the Stuarts. I will assume the presumption of saying that I was not unworthy to read them: nor will I disguise my different feelings in the repeated perusals. The perfect composition, the nervous language, the well-turned periods of Dr. Robertson inflamed me to the ambitious hope that I might one day tread in his footsteps; the calm philosophy, the careless inimitable beauties of his friend and rival often forced me to close the volume with a mixed sensation of delight and despair. . . .

My temper is not very susceptible of enthusiasm, and the enthusiasm which I do not feel, I have ever scorned to affect. But at the distance of twenty-five years I can neither forget nor express the strong emotions which agitated my mind as I first approached and entered the *eternal city*. After a sleepless night I trod, with a lofty step, the ruins of the Forum; each memorable spot where Romulus *stood*, or Tully spoke, or Caesar fell, was at once present to my eye; and several days of intoxication were lost or enjoyed before I could descend to a cool and minute investigation. My guide was Mr. Byers, a Scotch antiquary of experience and taste; but in the daily labor of eighteen weeks the powers of attention were sometimes fatigued, till I was myself qualified, in a last review, to select and study the capital works of ancient and modern art. Six weeks were borrowed for my tour of Naples, the most populous of cities relative to its size, whose luxurious inhabitants seem to dwell on the confines of paradise and hell fire. I was presented to the boy-king by our new envoy, Sir William Hamilton, who, wisely diverting his correspondence from the secretary of state to the Royal Society and British Museum, has elucidated a country of such inestimable value to the naturalist and antiquarian. On my return I fondly embraced, for the last time, the miracles of Rome; but I departed without kissing the foot of Rezzonico (Clement XIII), who neither possessed the wit of his predecessor Lambertini, nor the virtues of his successor Ganganelli.

In my pilgrimage from Rome to Loretto, I again crossed the Apennine; from the coast of the Adriatic I traversed a fruitful and populous country, which could alone disprove the paradox of Montesquieu, that modern Italy is a desert. Without adopting the exclusive prejudice of the natives, I sincerely admire the paintings of the Bologna school. I hastened to escape from the sad solitude of Ferrara, which in the age of Caesar was still more desolate. The spectacle of Venice afforded some hours of astonishment; the university of Padua is a dying taper; but Verona still boasts her amphitheater; and his native Vicenza is adorned by the classic architecture of Palladio: the road of Lombardy and Piedmont— (did Montesquieu find them without inhabitants?)—led me back to Milan, Turin, and the passage of Mount Cenis, where I again crossed the Alps in my way to Lyons.

The use of foreign travel has been often debated as a general question; but the conclusion must be finally applied to the character and circumstances of each individual. With the education of boys, *where* or *how* they may pass over some juvenile years with the least mischief to themselves or others, I have no concern. But after supposing the previous and indispensable requisites of age, judgment, a competent knowledge of men and books, and a freedom from domestic prejudices, I will briefly describe the qualifications which I deem most essential to a traveler. He should be endowed with an active, indefatigable vigor of mind and body, which can seize every mode of conveyance, and support, with a careless smile, every hardship of the road, the weather, or the inn. The benefits of foreign travel will correspond with the degrees of these qualifications; but in this sketch those to whom I am known will not accuse me of framing my own panegyric. It was at Rome, on the 15th of October, 1764, as I sat musing amidst the ruins of the Capitol, while the barefooted friars were singing vespers in the temple of Jupiter, that the idea of writing the decline and fall of the city first started to my mind. But my original plan was circumscribed to the decay of the city rather than of the Empire: and, though my reading and reflections began to point towards that object, some years elapsed, and several avocations intervened, before I was seriously engaged in the execution of that laborious work. . . .

I had now attained the first of earthly blessings, independence: I was the absolute master of my hours and actions: nor was I deceived in the hope that the establishment of my library in town would allow me to divide the day between study and society. Each year the circle of my acquaintance, the number of my dead and living companions, was enlarged. To a lover of books the shops and sales of London present irresistible temptations; and the manufacture of my history required a various and growing stock of materials. The militia, my travels, the House of Commons, the fame of an author, contributed to multiply my connections: I was chosen a member of the fashionable clubs; and, before I left England in 1783, there were few persons of any eminence in the literary or political world to whom I was a stranger. It would most assuredly be in my power to amuse the reader with a gallery of portraits and a collection of anecdotes. But I have always condemned the practice of transforming a private memorial into a vehicle of satire or praise. By my own choice I passed in town the greatest part of the year: but whenever I was desirous of breathing the air of the country, I possessed an hospitable retreat at Sheffield Place in Sussex, in the family of my valuable friend, Mr. Holroyd, whose character, under the name of Lord Sheffield, has since been more conspicuous to the public.

No sooner was I settled in my house and library, than I undertook the composition of the first volume of my history. At the outset all was dark and doubtful—even the title of the work, the true era of the decline and fall of the Empire, the limits of the introduction, the division of the chapters, and the order of the narrative; and I was often tempted to cast away the labor of seven years. The style of an author should be the image of his mind, but the choice and command of language is the fruit of exercise. Many experiments were made before I could hit the middle tone between a dull chronicle and a rhetorical declamation: three times did I compose the first chapter, and twice the second and third, before I was tolerably satisfied with their effect. In the remainder of the way I advanced with a more equal and easy pace; but the fifteenth and sixteenth chapters have been reduced, by three successive revisals, from a large volume to their present size; and they might still be compressed without any loss of facts or sentiments. An opposite fault may be imputed to the concise and superficial narrative of the first reigns, from Commodus to Alexander; a fault of which I have never heard, except from Mr. Hume in his last journey to London. Such an oracle might have been consulted and obeyed with rational devotion; but I was soon disgusted with the modest practice of reading the manuscript to my friends. Of such friends, some will praise from politeness, and some will criticize from vanity. The author himself is the best judge of his own performance; no one has so deeply meditated on the subject; no one is so sincerely interested in the event. . . .

I am at a loss how to describe the success of the work, without betraying the vanity of the writer. The first impression was exhausted in a few days; a second and third edition were scarcely adequate to the demand; and the bookseller's property was twice invaded by the pirates of Dublin. My book was on every table, and almost on every toilette; the historian was crowned by the taste or fashion of the day; nor was the general voice disturbed by the barking of any *profane* critic. The favor of mankind is most freely bestowed on a new acquaintance of any original merit; and the mutual surprise of the public and their favorite is productive of those warm sensibilities which at a second meeting can no longer be rekindled. If I listened to the music of praise, I was more seriously satisfied with the approbation of my judges. The candor of Dr. Robertson embraced his disciple. A letter from Mr. Hume overpaid the labor of ten years; but I have never presumed to accept a place in the triumvirate of British historians. . . .

Nearly two years had elapsed between the publication of my first and the commencement of my second volume; and the causes must be assigned of this long delay. 1. After a short holiday, I indulged my curiosity in some studies of a very different nature; a course of anatomy, which was demonstrated by Dr. Hunter, and some lessons of chemistry, which were delivered by Mr. Higgins. The principles of these sciences, and a taste for books of natural history, contributed to multiply my ideas and images; and the anatomist and chemist may sometimes track me in their own snow. 2. I dived, perhaps too deeply, into the mud of the Arian controversy; and many days of reading, thinking, and writing, were consumed in the pursuit of a phantom.   3. It is difficult to arrange, with order and perspicuity, the various transactions of the age of Constantine; and so much was I displeased with the first essay, that I committed to the flames above fifty sheets.   4. The six months of Paris and pleasure must be deducted from the account. But when I resumed my task I felt my improvement; I was now master of my style and subject, and while the measure of my daily performance was enlarged, I discovered less reason to cancel or correct. It has always been my practice to cast a long paragraph in a single mold, to try it by my ear, to deposit it in my memory, but to suspend the action of the pen till I had given the last polish to my work. Shall I add that I never found my mind more vigorous, nor my composition more happy, than in the winter hurry of society and parliament?

Had I believed that the majority of English readers were so fondly attached even to the name and shadow of Christianity; had I foreseen that the pious, the timid, and the prudent, would feel, or affect to feel, with such exquisite sensibility, I might perhaps have softened the two invidious chapters [10] which would create many enemies, and conciliate few friends. But the shaft was shot, the alarm was sounded, and I could only rejoice that if the voice of our priests was clamorous and bitter, their hands were disarmed from the powers of persecution. I adhered to the wise resolution of trusting myself and my writings to the candor of the public, till Mr. Davies of Oxford presumed to attack, not the faith, but the fidelity, of the historian. *My Vindication*, expressive of less anger than contempt, amused for a moment the busy and idle metropolis; and the most rational part of the laity, and even of the clergy, appear to have been satisfied of my innocence and accuracy. . . .

My transmigration from London to Lausanne could not be effected without interrupting the course of my historical labors.

10 The fifteenth and sixteenth, on the spread of Christianity.

The hurry of my departure, the joy of my arrival, the delay of my tools, suspended their progress; and a full twelvemonth was lost before I could resume the thread of regular and daily industry. A number of books most requisite and least common had been previously selected; the academical library of Lausanne, which I could use as my own, contained at least the fathers and councils; and I have derived some occasional succor from the public collections of Berne and Geneva. The fourth volume was soon terminated by an abstract of the controversies of the Incarnation, which the learned Dr. Prideaux [11] was apprehensive of exposing to profane eyes. It had been the original design of the learned Dean Prideaux to write the history of the ruin of the Eastern church. In this work it would have been necessary, not only to unravel all those controversies which the Christians made about the hypostatical union, but also to unfold all the niceties and subtle notions which each sect entertained concerning it. The pious historian was apprehensive of exposing that incomprehensible mystery to the cavils and objections of unbelievers; and he durst not, "seeing the nature of this book, venture it abroad in so wanton and lewd an age."

In the fifth and sixth volumes the revolutions of the Empire and the world are most rapid, various, and instructive; and the Greek or Roman historians are checked by the hostile narratives of the barbarians of the East and the West.

It was not till after many designs, and many trials, that I preferred, as I still prefer, the method of grouping my picture by nations; and the seeming neglect of chronological order is surely compensated by the superior merits of interest and perspicuity. The style of the first volume is, in my opinion, somewhat crude and elaborate; in the second and third it is ripened into ease, correctness, and numbers; but in the three last I may have been seduced by the facility of my pen, and the constant habit of speaking one language and writing another may have infused some mixture of Gallic idioms. Happily for my eyes I have always closed my studies with the day, and commonly with the morning; and a long but temperate labor has been accomplished without fatiguing either the mind or body; but when I computed the remainder of my time and my task, it was apparent that, according to the season of publication, the delay of a month would be productive of that of a year. I was now straining for the goal, and in the last winter

11 Humphrey Prideaux, dean of Norwich.

many evenings were borrowed from the social pleasures of Lausanne. I could now wish that a pause, an interval, had been allowed for a serious revisal.

I have presumed to mark the moment of conception: I shall now commemorate the hour of my final deliverance. It was on the day, or rather night, of the 27th of June, 1787, between the hours of eleven and twelve, that I wrote the last lines of the last page, in a summerhouse in my garden. After laying down my pen, I took several turns in a *berceau*, or covered walk of acacias, which commands a prospect of the country, the lake, and the mountains. The air was temperate, the sky was serene, the silver orb of the moon was reflected from the waters, and all nature was silent. I will not dissemble the first emotions of joy on recovery of my freedom, and perhaps the establishment of my fame. But my pride was soon humbled, and a sober melancholy was spread over my mind, by the idea that I had taken an everlasting leave of an old and agreeable companion, and that whatsoever might be the future date of my history, the life of the historian must be short and precarious. I will add two facts which have seldom occurred in the composition of six, or at least of five, quartos.   1. My first rough manuscript, without any intermediate copy, has been sent to the press. 2. Not a sheet has been seen by any human eyes excepting those of the author and the printer: the faults and the merits are exclusively my own. . . .

The conclusion of my work was generally read and variously judged. The style has been exposed to much academical criticism; a religious clamor was revived; and the reproach of indecency has been loudly echoed by the rigid censors of morals. I never could understand the clamor that has been raised against the indecency of my three last volumes.   1. An equal degree of freedom in the former part, especially in the first volume, had passed without reproach.   2. I am justified in painting the manners of the times; the vices of Theodora form an essential feature in the reign and character of Justinian; and the most naked tale in my history is told by the Rev. Mr. Joseph Warton, an instructor of youth. (*Essay on the Genius and Writings of Pope*, pp. 322–24).   3. My English text is chaste, and all licentious passages are left in the obscurity of a learned language. "Le Latin dans ses mots brave l'honnêteté," says the correct Boileau, in a country and idiom more scrupulous than our own. Yet, upon the whole, the *History of the*

Decline and Fall seems to have struck root both at home and abroad, and may perhaps a hundred years hence still continue to be abused. . . .

Within the last two or three years our tranquillity has been clouded by the disorders of France; many families at Lausanne were alarmed and affected by the terrors of an impending bankruptcy; but the revolution, or rather the dissolution of the kingdom, has been heard and felt in the adjacent lands.

I beg leave to subscribe my assent to Mr. Burke's creed on the revolution of France. I admire his eloquence, I approve his politics, I adore his chivalry, and I can almost excuse his reverence for church establishments. I have sometimes thought of writing a dialogue of the dead, in which Lucian, Erasmus, and Voltaire should mutually acknowledge the danger of exposing an old superstition to the contempt of the blind and fanatic multitude.

A swarm of emigrants of both sexes, who escaped from the public ruin, has been attracted by the vicinity, the manners, and the language of Lausanne; and our narrow habitations in town and country are now occupied by the first names and titles of the departed monarchy. These noble fugitives are entitled to our pity; they may claim our esteem; but they cannot, in their present state of mind and fortune, much contribute to our amusement. Instead of looking down as calm and idle spectators on the theater of Europe, our domestic harmony is somewhat embittered by the infusion of party spirit: our ladies and gentlemen assume the character of self-taught politicians; and the sober dictates of wisdom and experience are silenced by the clamor of the triumphant *democrates*. The fanatic missionaries of sedition have scattered the seeds of discontent in our cities and villages, which have flourished above two hundred and fifty years without fearing the approach of war or feeling the weight of government. Many individuals, and some communities, appear to be infected with the Gallic frenzy, the wild theories of equal and boundless freedom; but I trust that the body of the people will be faithful to their sovereign and to themselves; and I am satisfied that the failure or success of a revolt would equally terminate in the ruin of the country. While the aristocracy of Berne protects the happiness, it is superfluous to inquire whether it be founded in the rights, of man: the economy of the state is liberally supplied without the aid of taxes; and the magistrates *must* reign with prudence and equity, since they are unarmed in the midst of an armed nation. The revenue of Berne, excepting some small duties, is derived from church lands, tithes, feudal rights, and interest of money. The republic has nearly 500,000*l.* sterling in the English funds, and the amount of their treasure is unknown to the citizens themselves. For myself (may the omen be averted!) I can only declare, that the first stroke of a rebel drum would be the signal of my immediate departure.

When I contemplate the common lot of mortality, I must acknowledge that I have drawn a high prize in the lottery of life. The far greater part of the globe is overspread with barbarism or slavery: in the civilized world the most numerous class is condemned to ignorance and poverty; and the double fortune of my birth in a free and enlightened country, in an honorable and wealthy family, is the lucky chance of an unit against millions. The general probability is about three to one, that a newborn infant will not live to complete his fiftieth year. I have now passed that age, and may fairly estimate the present value of my existence in the threefold division of mind, body, and estate.

1. The first and indispensable requisite of happiness is a clear conscience, unsullied by the reproach or remembrance of an unworthy action:—

            ————Hic murus aheneus esto,
        Nil conscire sibi, nulla pallescere culpa.¹²

I am endowed with a cheerful temper, a moderate sensibility, and a natural disposition to repose rather than to activity: some mischievous appetites and habits have perhaps been corrected by philosophy or time. The love of study, a passion which derives fresh vigor from enjoyment, supplies each day, each hour, with a perpetual source of independent and rational pleasure; and I am not sensible of any decay of the mental faculties. The original soil has been highly improved by cultivation; but it may be questioned whether some flowers of fancy, some grateful errors, have not been eradicated with the weeds of prejudice. 2. Since I have escaped from the long perils of my childhood, the serious advice

---

¹² Horace *Epistles* I. i. 59–60: "Let this be a brazen wall of defense, to know your- self guilty of no evil to cause you to go pale."

of a physician has seldom been requisite. "The madness of superfluous health" I have never known, but my tender constitution
has been fortified by time, and the inestimable gift of the sound
and peaceful slumbers of infancy may be imputed both to the
mind and body.   3. I have already described the merits of my society and situation; but these enjoyments would be tasteless or
bitter, if their possession were not assured by an annual and adequate supply. According to the scale of Switzerland, I am a rich
man; and I am indeed rich, since my income is superior to my
expense, and my expense is equal to my wishes. My friend Lord
Sheffield has kindly relieved me from the cares to which my taste
and temper are most adverse. Shall I add, that since the failure of
my first wishes, I have never entertained any serious thoughts of
a matrimonial connection?

I am disgusted with the affectation of men of letters who complain that they have renounced a substance for a shadow, and that
their fame (which sometimes is no insupportable weight) affords
a poor compensation for envy, censure, and persecution. My own
experience, at least, has taught me a very different lesson; twenty
happy years have been animated by the labor of my *History*, and
its success has given me a name, a rank, a character, in the world,
to which I should not otherwise have been entitled. The freedom
of my writings has indeed provoked an implacable tribe; but as I
was safe from the stings, I was soon accustomed to the buzzing of
the hornets: my nerves are not tremblingly alive, and my literary
temper is so happily framed that I am less sensible of pain than of
pleasure. The rational pride of an author may be offended, rather
than flattered, by vague indiscriminate praise; but he cannot, he
should not, be indifferent to the fair testimonies of private and
public esteem. Even his moral sympathy may be gratified by the
idea that now, in the present hour, he is imparting some degree of
amusement or knowledge to his friends in a distant land; that one
day his mind will be familiar to the grandchildren of those who are
yet unborn. I cannot boast of the friendship or favor of princes;
the patronage of English literature has long since been devolved on
our booksellers, and the measure of their liberality is the least am-
biguous test of our common success. Perhaps the golden mediocrity of my fortune has contributed to fortify my application.

The present is a fleeting moment; the past is no more; and our
prospect of futurity is dark and doubtful. This day may *possibly*

be my last; but the laws of probability, so true in general, so fallacious in particular, still allow about fifteen years. I shall soon enter
into the period which, as the most agreeable of his long life, was
selected by the judgment and experience of the sage Fontenelle.
His choice is approved by the eloquent historian of nature,[13] who
fixes our moral happiness to the mature season in which our passions are supposed to be calmed, our duties fulfilled, our ambition
satisfied, our fame and fortune established on a solid basis. In private conversation that great and amiable man added the weight of
his own experience; and this autumnal felicity might be exemplified in the lives of Voltaire, Hume, and many other men of letters.
I am far more inclined to embrace than to dispute this comfortable
doctrine. I will not suppose any premature decay of the mind or
body; but I must reluctantly observe that two causes, the abbrevi-
ation of time, and the failure of hope, will always tinge with a
browner shade the evening of life.

THE DECLINE AND FALL OF
THE ROMAN EMPIRE
1776–1788

CHAPTER XV

The Progress of the Christian Religion, and the Sentiments,
Manners, Numbers, and Condition of the Primitive Christians.

A candid but rational inquiry into the progress and establishment of Christianity may be considered as a very essential part of
the history of the Roman Empire. While that great body was invaded by open violence, or undermined by slow decay, a pure
and humble religion gently insinuated itself into the minds of men,
grew up in silence and obscurity, derived new vigor from opposition, and finally erected the triumphant banner of the cross on the
ruins of the Capitol. Nor was the influence of Christianity confined
to the period or to the limits of the Roman Empire. After a revolution of thirteen or fourteen centuries, that religion is still professed by the nations of Europe, the most distinguished portion of
humankind in arts and learning as well as in arms. By the industry

13 Buffon.

and zeal of the Europeans it has been widely diffused to the most distant shores of Asia and Africa; and by the means of their colonies has been firmly established from Canada to Chile, in a world unknown to the ancients.

But this inquiry, however useful or entertaining, is attended with two peculiar difficulties. The scanty and suspicious materials of ecclesiastical history seldom enable us to dispel the dark cloud that hangs over the first age of the church. The great law of impartiality too often obliges us to reveal the imperfections of the uninspired teachers and believers of the gospel; and, to a careless observer, *their* faults may seem to cast a shade on the faith which they professed. But the scandal of the pious Christian, and the fallacious triumph of the infidel, should cease as soon as they recollect not only *by whom*, but likewise *to whom*, the Divine Revelation was given. The theologian may indulge the pleasing task of describing Religion as she descended from Heaven, arrayed in her native purity. A more melancholy duty is imposed on the historian. He must discover the inevitable mixture of error and corruption which she contracted in a long residence upon earth, among a weak and degenerate race of beings.

Our curiosity is naturally prompted to inquire by what means the Christian faith obtained so remarkable a victory over the established religions of the earth. To this inquiry an obvious but satisfactory answer may be returned; that it was owing to the convincing evidence of the doctrine itself, and to the ruling providence of its great Author. But as truth and reason seldom find so favorable a reception in the world, and as the wisdom of Providence frequently condescends to use the passions of the human heart, and the general circumstances of mankind, as instruments to execute its purpose, we may still be permitted, though with becoming submission, to ask not, indeed, what were the first, but what were the secondary causes of the rapid growth of the Christian church. It will, perhaps, appear that it was most effectually favored and assisted by the five following causes: I. The inflexible, and, if we may use the expression, the intolerant zeal of the Christians, derived, it is true, from the Jewish religion, but purified from the narrow and unsocial spirit which, instead of inviting, had deterred the Gentiles from embracing the law of Moses. II. The doctrine of a future life, improved by every additional circumstance which could give weight and efficacy to that important truth. III. The miraculous powers ascribed to the primitive church. IV. The pure and austere morals of the Christians. V. The union and discipline of the Christian republic, which gradually formed an independent and increasing state in the heart of the Roman Empire.

We have already described the religious harmony of the ancient world, and the facility with which the most different and even hostile nations embraced, or at least respected, each other's superstitions. A single people refused to join in the common intercourse of mankind. The Jews, who, under the Assyrian and Persian monarchies, had languished for many ages the most despised portion of their slaves, emerged from obscurity under the successors of Alexander; and as they multiplied to a surprising degree in the East, and afterwards in the West, they soon excited the curiosity and wonder of other nations. The sullen obstinacy with which they maintained their peculiar rites and unsocial manners seemed to mark them out a distinct species of men, who boldly professed, or who faintly disguised, their implacable hatred to the rest of humankind. Neither the violence of Antiochus, nor the arts of Herod, nor the example of the circumjacent nations, could ever persuade the Jews to associate with the institutions of Moses the elegant mythology of the Greeks. According to the maxims of universal toleration, the Romans protected a superstition which they despised. The polite Augustus condescended to give orders that sacrifices should be offered for his prosperity in the temple of Jerusalem; while the meanest of the posterity of Abraham, who should have paid the same homage to the Jupiter of the Capitol, would have been an object of abhorrence to himself and to his brethren. But the moderation of the conquerors was insufficient to appease the jealous prejudices of their subjects, who were alarmed and scandalized at the ensigns of paganism, which necessarily introduced themselves into a Roman province. . . .

The writings of Cicero represent in the most lively colors the ignorance, the errors, and the uncertainty of the ancient philosophers with regard to the immortality of the soul. When they are desirous of arming their disciples against the fear of death, they inculcate, as an obvious though melancholy position, that the fatal stroke of our dissolution releases us from the calamities of life, and that those can no longer suffer who no longer exist. Yet there were a few sages of Greece and Rome who had conceived a more exalted, and, in some respects, a juster idea of human nature; though it must be confessed that, in the sublime inquiry, their reason had been often guided by their imagination, and that their imagination had been prompted by their vanity. When they viewed with complacency the extent of their own mental powers, when they exercised the various faculties of memory, of fancy, and of judgment, in the most profound speculations or the most important labors, and when they reflected on the desire of fame, which transported them into future ages, far beyond the bounds of death and of the grave, they were unwilling to confound themselves with the beasts of the field, or to suppose that a being, for whose dignity they entertained the most sincere admiration, could be limited to a spot of earth and to a few years of duration. With this favorable prepossession they summoned to their aid the science, or rather the language, of metaphysics. They soon discovered that as none of the properties of matter will apply to the operations of the mind, the human soul must consequently be a substance distinct from the body, pure, simple, and spiritual, incapable of dissolution, and susceptible of a much higher degree of virtue and happiness after the release from its corporeal prison. From these specious and noble principles the philosophers who trod in the footsteps of Plato deduced a very unjustifiable conclusion, since they asserted not only the future immortality, but the past eternity of the human soul, which they were too apt to consider as a portion of the infinite and self-existing spirit which pervades and sustains the universe. A doctrine thus removed beyond the senses and the experience of mankind might serve to amuse the leisure of a philosophic mind; or, in the silence of solitude, it might sometimes impart a ray of comfort to desponding virtue; but the faint impression which had been received in the schools was soon obliterated by the commerce and business of active life. We are sufficiently acquainted with the eminent persons who flourished in the age of Cicero and of the first Caesars, with their actions, their characters, and their motives, to be assured that their conduct in this life was never regulated by any serious conviction of the rewards or punishments of a future state. At the bar and in the senate of Rome the ablest orators were not apprehensive of giving offense to their hearers by exposing that doctrine as an idle and extravagant opinion, which was rejected with contempt by every man of a liberal education and understanding.

Since, therefore, the most sublime efforts of philosophy can extend no farther than feebly to point out the desire, the hope, or, at most, the probability of a future state, there is nothing, except a divine revelation, that can ascertain the existence and describe the condition of the invisible country which is destined to receive the souls of men after their separation from the body. But we may perceive several defects inherent to the popular religions of Greece and Rome which rendered them very unequal to so arduous a task. 1. The general system of their mythology was unsupported by any solid proofs; and the wisest among the pagans had already disclaimed its usurped authority. 2. The description of the infernal regions had been abandoned to the fancy of painters and of poets, who peopled them with so many phantoms and monsters who dispensed their rewards and punishments with so little equity that a solemn truth, the most congenial to the human heart, was oppressed and disgraced by the absurd mixture of the wildest fictions. 3. The doctrine of a future state was scarcely considered among the devout polytheists of Greece and Rome as a fundamental article of faith. The providence of the gods, as it related to public communities rather than to private individuals, was principally displayed on the visible theater of the present world. The petitions which were offered on the altars of Jupiter or Apollo expressed the anxiety of their worshipers for temporal happiness, and their ignorance or indifference concerning a future life. The important truth of the immortality of the soul was inculcated with more diligence as well as success in India, in Assyria, in Egypt, and in Gaul; and, since we cannot attribute such a difference to the superior knowledge of the barbarians, we must ascribe it to the influence of an established priesthood, which employed the motives of virtue as the instrument of ambition.

We might naturally expect that a principle so essential to religion would have been revealed in the clearest terms to the chosen people of Palestine, and that it might safely have been intrusted to the hereditary priesthood of Aaron. It is incumbent on us to adore the mysterious dispensations of Providence when we discover that the doctrine of the immortality of the soul is omitted in the law of Moses; it is darkly insinuated by the prophets; and during the long period which elapsed between the Egyptian and the Babylonian servitudes, the hopes as well as fears of the Jews appear to have been confined within the narrow compass of the present life. After Cyrus had permitted the exiled nation to return into the promised land, and after Ezra had restored the ancient records of their religion, two celebrated sects, the Sadducees and the Pharisees, insensibly arose at Jerusalem. The former, selected from the more opulent and distinguished ranks of society, were strictly attached to the literal sense of the Mosaic law, and they piously rejected the immortality of the soul as an opinion that received no countenance from the divine book which they revered as the only rule of their faith. To the authority of scripture the Pharisees added that of tradition, and they accepted, under the name of traditions, several speculative tenets from the philosophy or religion of the eastern nations. The doctrines of fate or predestination, of angels and spirits, and of a future state of rewards and punishments were in the number of these new articles of belief; and as the Pharisees, by the austerity of their manners, had drawn into their party the body of the Jewish people, the immortality of the soul became the prevailing sentiment of the synagogue under the reign of the Asmonaean princes and pontiffs. The temper of the Jews was incapable of contenting itself with such a cold and languid assent as might satisfy the mind of a polytheist; and, as soon as they admitted the idea of a future state, they embraced it with the zeal which has always formed the characteristic of the nation. Their zeal, however, added nothing to its evidence, or even probability: and it was still necessary that the doctrine of life and immortality, which had been dictated by nature, approved by reason, and received by superstition, should obtain the sanction of divine truth from the authority and example of Christ.

When the promise of eternal happiness was proposed to mankind, on condition of adopting the faith and of observing the precepts of the gospel, it is no wonder that so advantageous an offer should have been accepted by great numbers of every religion, of every rank, and of every province in the Roman Empire. The ancient Christians were animated by a contempt for their present existence, and by a just confidence of immortality, of which the doubtful and imperfect faith of modern ages cannot give us any adequate notion. In the primitive church the influence of truth was very powerfully strengthened by an opinion which, however it may deserve respect for its usefulness and antiquity, has not been found agreeable to experience. It was universally believed that the end of the world and the kingdom of Heaven were at hand. The near approach of this wonderful event had been predicted by the apostles; the tradition of it was preserved by their earliest disciples, and those who understood in their literal sense the discourses of Christ himself were obliged to expect the second and glorious coming of the Son of Man in the clouds, before that generation was totally extinguished which had beheld his humble condition upon earth, and which might still be witness of the calamities of the Jews under Vespasian or Hadrian. The revolution of seventeen centuries has instructed us not to press too closely the mysterious language of prophecy and revelation; but, as long as, for wise purposes, this error was permitted to subsist in the church, it was productive of the most salutary effects on the faith and practice of Christians, who lived in the awful expectation of that moment when the globe itself, and all the various race of mankind, should tremble at the appearance of their divine judge. . . .

The condemnation of the wisest and most virtuous of the pagans on account of their ignorance or disbelief of the divine truth seems to offend the reason and the humanity of the present age. But the primitive church, whose faith was of a much firmer consistence, delivered over, without hesitation, to eternal torture the far greater part of the human species. A charitable hope might perhaps be indulged in favor of Socrates, or some other sages of antiquity, who had consulted the light of reason before that of the Gospel had arisen. But it was unanimously affirmed that those who since the birth or the death of Christ had obstinately persisted in the worship of the demons, neither deserved, nor could expect, a pardon from the irritated justice of the Deity. These rigid sentiments, which had been unknown to the ancient world, appear to have infused a spirit of bitterness into a system of love and harmony. The ties of blood and friendship were frequently torn asunder by the difference of religious faith; and the Christians, who in this world found themselves oppressed by the power of the pagans, were sometimes seduced by resentment and spiritual pride to delight in the prospect of their future triumph. "You are fond of spectacles," exclaims the stern Tertullian; "expect the greatest of all spectacles, the last and eternal judgment of the universe. How shall I admire, how laugh, how rejoice, how exult, when I behold so many proud monarchs, and fancied gods, groaning in the lowest abyss of darkness; so many magistrates who persecuted the name of the Lord, liquefying in fiercer fires than they ever kindled against the Christians; so many sage philosophers blushing in red-hot flames with their deluded scholars; so many celebrated poets trembling before the tribunal, not of Minos, but of Christ; so many tragedians, more tuneful in the expression of their own sufferings; so many dancers—" But the humanity of the reader will permit me to draw a veil over the rest of this infernal description, which the zealous African pursues in a long variety of affected and unfeeling witticisms. . . .

The supernatural gifts which even in this life were ascribed to the Christians above the rest of mankind, must have conduced to their own comfort, and very frequently to the conviction of infidels. Besides the occasional prodigies, which might sometimes be effected by the immediate interposition of the Deity when he suspended the laws of Nature for the service of religion, the Christian church, from the time of the apostles and their first disciples, has claimed an uninterrupted succession of miraculous powers, the gift of tongues, of vision, and of prophecy, the power of expelling demons, of healing the sick, and of raising the dead. The knowledge of foreign languages was frequently communicated to the contemporaries of Irenaeus, though Irenaeus himself was left to struggle with the difficulties of a barbarous dialect whilst he preached the Gospel to the natives of Gaul. The divine inspiration, whether it was conveyed in the form of a waking or of a sleeping vision, is described as a favor very liberally bestowed on all ranks of the faithful, on women as on elders, on boys as well as upon bishops. When their devout minds were sufficiently prepared by a course of prayer, of fasting, and of vigils, to receive the extraordinary impulse, they were transported out of their senses, and delivered in ecstasy what was inspired, being mere organs of the Holy Spirit, just as a pipe or flute is of him who blows into it. We may add that the design of these visions was, for the most part, either to disclose the future history, or to guide the present administration, of the church. The expulsion of the demons from the bodies of those unhappy persons whom they had been permitted to torment was considered as a signal, though ordinary, triumph of religion, and is repeatedly alleged by the ancient apologists as the most convincing evidence of the truth of Christianity. The awful ceremony was usually performed in a public manner, and in the presence of a great number of spectators; the patient was relieved by the power or skill of the exorcist, and the vanquished demon was heard to confess that he was one of the fabled gods of antiquity, who had impiously usurped the adoration of mankind. But the miraculous cure of diseases of the most inveterate or even preternatural kind can no longer occasion any surprise when we recollect that in the days of Irenaeus, about the end of the second century, the resurrection of the dead was very far from being esteemed an uncommon event; that the miracle was frequently performed on necessary occasions by great fasting and the joint supplication of the church of the place, and that the persons thus restored to their prayers had lived afterwards among them many years. At such a period, when faith could boast of so many wonderful victories over death, it seems difficult to account for the skepticism of those philosophers who still rejected and derided the doctrine of the resurrection. A noble Grecian had rested on this important ground the whole controversy, and promised Theophilus, bishop of Antioch, that, if he could be gratified with the sight of a single person who had been actually raised from the dead, he would immediately embrace the Christian religion. It is somewhat remarkable that the prelate of the first eastern church, however anxious for the conversion of his friend, thought proper to decline this fair and reasonable challenge. . . .

It is a very honorable circumstance for the morals of the primitive Christians that even their faults, or rather errors, were derived from an excess of virtue. The bishops and doctors of the church, whose evidence attests, and whose authority might influence, the professions, the principles, and even the practice of their contemporaries, had studied the Scriptures with less skill than devotion, and they often received in the most literal sense those rigid precepts of Christ and the apostles to which the prudence of succeeding commentators has applied a looser and more figurative mode of interpretation. Ambitious to exalt the perfection of the Gospel above the wisdom of philosophy, the zealous fathers have carried the duties of self-mortification, of purity, and of patience, to a height which it is scarcely possible to attain, and much less to preserve, in our present state of weakness and corruption. A doctrine so extraordinary and so sublime must inevitably command the veneration of the people; but it was ill calculated to obtain the suffrage of those worldly philosophers who, in the conduct of this transitory life, consult only the feelings of nature and the interest of society.

There are two very natural propensities which we may distinguish in the most virtuous and liberal dispositions, the love of pleasure and the love of action. If the former is refined by art and learning, improved by the charms of social intercourse, and corrected by a just regard to economy, to health, and to reputation, it is productive of the greatest part of the happiness of private life. The love of action is a principle of a much stronger and more doubtful nature. It often leads to anger, to ambition, and to revenge; but when it is guided by the sense of propriety and benevolence, it becomes the parent of every virtue; and, if those virtues are accompanied with equal abilities, a family, a state, or an empire may be indebted for their safety and prosperity to the undaunted courage of a single man. To the love of pleasure we may therefore ascribe most of the agreeable, to the love of action we may attribute most of the useful and respectable, qualifications. The character in which both the one and the other should be united and harmonized would seem to constitute the most perfect idea of human nature. The insensible and inactive disposition, which should be supposed alike destitute of both, would be rejected, by the common consent of mankind, as utterly incapable of procuring any happiness to the individual, or any public benefit to the world. But it was not in *this* world that the primitive Christians were desirous of making themselves either agreeable or useful.

The acquisition of knowledge, the exercise of our reason or

fancy, and the cheerful flow of unguarded conversation may employ the leisure of a liberal mind. Such amusements, however, were rejected with abhorrence, or admitted with the utmost caution, by the severity of the fathers, who despised all knowledge that was not useful to salvation, and who considered all levity of discourse as a criminal abuse of the gift of speech. In our present state of existence the body is so inseparably connected with the soul that it seems to be our interest to taste, with innocence and moderation, the enjoyments of which that faithful companion is susceptible. Very different was the reasoning of our devout predecessors; vainly aspiring to imitate the perfection of angels, they disdained, or they affected to disdain, every earthly and corporeal delight. Some of our senses indeed are necessary for our preservation, others for our subsistence, and others again for our information; and thus far it was impossible to reject the use of them. The first sensation of pleasure was marked as the first moment of their abuse. The unfeeling candidate for Heaven was instructed not only to resist the grosser allurements of the taste or smell, but even to shut his ears against the profane harmony of sounds, and to view with indifference the most finished productions of human art. Gay apparel, magnificent houses, and elegant furniture were supposed to unite the double guilt of pride and of sensuality: a simple and mortified appearance was more suitable to the Christian who was certain of his sins and doubtful of his salvation. In their censures of luxury the fathers are extremely minute and circumstantial; and among the various articles which excite their pious indignation we may enumerate false hair, garments of any color except white, instruments of music, vases of gold or silver, downy pillows (as Jacob reposed his head on a stone), white bread, foreign wines, public salutations, the use of warm baths, and the practice of shaving the beard, which, according to the expression of Tertullian, is a lie against our own faces, and an impious attempt to improve the works of the Creator. When Christianity was introduced among the rich and the polite, the observation of these singular laws was left, as it would be at present, to the few who were ambitious of superior sanctity. But it is always easy, as well as agreeable, for the inferior ranks of mankind to claim a merit from the contempt of that pomp and pleasure which fortune has placed beyond their reach. The virtue of the primitive Christians, like that of the first Romans, was very frequently guarded by poverty and ignorance.

The chaste severity of the fathers in whatever related to the commerce of the two sexes flowed from the same principle; their abhorrence of every enjoyment which might gratify the sensual, and degrade the spiritual, nature of man. It was their favorite opinion that if Adam had preserved his obedience to the Creator, he would have lived forever in a state of virgin purity, and that some harmless mode of vegetation might have peopled paradise with a race of innocent and immortal beings. The use of marriage was permitted only to his fallen posterity, as a necessary expedient to continue the human species, and as a restraint, however imperfect, on the natural licentiousness of desire. The hesitation of the orthodox casuists on this interesting subject betrays the perplexity of men unwilling to approve an institution which they were compelled to tolerate. The enumeration of the very whimsical laws which they most circumstantially imposed on the marriage bed would force a smile from the young, and a blush from the fair. It was their unanimous sentiment that a first marriage was adequate to all the purposes of nature and of society. The sensual connection was refined into a resemblance of the mystic union of Christ with his church, and was pronounced to be indissoluble either by divorce or by death. The practice of second nuptials was branded with the name of a legal adultery; and the persons who were guilty of so scandalous an offense against Christian purity were soon excluded from the honors, and even from the alms, of the church. Since desire was imputed as a crime, and marriage was tolerated as a defect, it was consistent with the same principles to consider a state of celibacy as the nearest approach to the divine perfection. It was with the utmost difficulty that ancient Rome could support the institution of six vestals; but the primitive church was filled with a great number of persons of either sex who had devoted themselves to the profession of perpetual chastity. A few of these, among whom we may reckon the learned Origen, judged it the most prudent to disarm the tempter. Some were insensible and some were invincible against the assaults of the flesh. Disdaining an ignominious flight, the virgins of the warm climate of Africa encountered the enemy in the closest engagement; they permitted priests and deacons to share their bed, and gloried amidst the flames in their unsullied purity. But insulted Nature sometimes vindicated her rights, and this new species of martyrdom served only to introduce a new scandal into the church. Among the Christian ascetics, however (a name which they soon acquired from their painful exercise), many, as they were less presumptuous, were probably more successful. The loss of sensual pleasure was supplied and compensated by spiritual pride. Even the multitude of pagans were inclined to estimate the merit of the sacrifice by its apparent difficulty; and it was in the praise of these chaste spouses of Christ that

the fathers have poured forth the troubled stream of their eloquence. Such are the early traces of monastic principles and institutions, which, in a subsequent age, have counterbalanced all the
temporal advantages of Christianity. . . .

But how shall we excuse the supine inattention of the pagan and
philosophic world to those evidences which were presented by
the hand of Omnipotence, not to their reason, but to their senses?
During the age of Christ, of his apostles, and of their first disciples,
the doctrine which they preached was confirmed by innumerable
prodigies. The lame walked, the blind saw, the sick were healed,
the dead were raised, demons were expelled, and the laws of Nature
were frequently suspended for the benefit of the church. But the
sages of Greece and Rome turned aside from the awful spectacle,
and, pursuing the ordinary occupations of life and study, appeared
unconscious of any alterations in the moral or physical government of the world. Under the reign of Tiberius, the whole earth,
or at least a celebrated province of the Roman Empire, was involved in a preternatural darkness of three hours. Even this miraculous event, which ought to have excited the wonder, the curiosity,
and the devotion of mankind, passed without notice in an age of
science and history. It happened during the lifetime of Seneca and
the elder Pliny, who must have experienced the immediate effects,
or received the earliest intelligence, of the prodigy. Each of these
philosophers, in a laborious work, has recorded all the great phenomena of Nature, earthquakes, meteors, comets, and eclipses,
which his indefatigable curiosity could collect. Both the one and
the other have omitted to mention the greatest phenomenon to
which the mortal eye has been witness since the creation of the
globe. A distinct chapter of Pliny is designed for eclipses of an extraordinary nature and unusual duration; but he contents himself
with describing the singular defect of light which followed the
murder of Caesar, when, during the greatest part of a year, the
orb of the sun appeared pale and without splendor. This season of
obscurity, which cannot surely be compared with the preternatural darkness of the Passion, had been already celebrated by most
of the poets and historians of that memorable age.

A SELECTION

John Wesley

1703-1791

JOURNAL

["Methodism," the great religious revival of eighteenth-century England under the leadership of John and Charles Wesley and George Whitefield, has left its literary record in this *Journal* and in the great number of hymns by the two brothers. Although the Wesleys began, in 1729, at Oxford, to be "methodists" in the piety with which they followed the observances of the Church of England, it was inevitable that their followers should become an independent church. The program of "good works" effected by the Methodists, and their concern for the humbler Englishmen, had incalculable social effects.]

WED., May 24, 1738 . . . In the evening I went very unwillingly to a society in Aldersgate Street, where one was reading Luther's preface to the *Epistle to the Romans*. About a quarter before nine, while he was describing the change which God works in the heart through faith in Christ, I felt my heart strangely warmed. I felt I did trust in Christ, Christ alone for salvation; and an assurance was given me that He had taken away *my* sins, even *mine*, and saved *me* from the law of sin and death.

I began to pray with all my might for those who had in a more especial manner despitefully used me and persecuted me. I then testified openly to all there what I now first felt in my heart. But it was not long before the enemy suggested, "This cannot be faith; for where is thy joy?" Then was I taught that peace and victory over sin are essential to faith in the Captain of our salvation; but that, as to the transports of joy that usually attend the beginning of it, especially in those who have mourned deeply, God sometimes giveth, sometimes withholdeth them, according to the counsels of His own will.

After my return home, I was much buffeted with temptations; but cried out, and they fled away. They returned again and again. I as often lifted up my eyes, and He "sent me help from His holy place." And herein I found the difference between this and my former state chiefly consisted. I was striving, yea, fighting with all my might under the law, as well as under grace. But then I was sometimes, if not often, conquered; now, I was always conqueror.

Sat., [March] 31st [1739]—In the evening I reached Bristol, and met Mr. Whitefield there. I could scarce reconcile myself at first to this strange way of preaching in the fields, of which he set me an example on Sunday; having been all my life (till very lately) so tenacious of every point relating to decency and order, that I should have thought the saving of souls almost a sin if it had not been done in a church.

Monday, [April] 2, [1739]—At four in the afternoon, I submitted to be more vile, and proclaimed in the highways the glad tidings of salvation, speaking from a little eminence in a ground adjoining to the city to about three thousand people. The scripture on which I spoke was this (is it possible anyone should be ignorant that it is fulfilled in every true minister of Christ?): "The Spirit of the Lord is upon me, because He hath anointed me to preach the Gospel to the poor. He hath sent me to heal the broken-hearted; to preach deliverance to the captives, and recovery of sight to the blind; to set at liberty them that are bruised, to proclaim the acceptable year of the Lord."

Sat., [April] 14, [1739]—I preached at the poorhouse: three or four hundred were within, and more than twice that number were without: to whom I explained those comfortable words, "When they had nothing to pay, he frankly forgave them both."

Fri., [April] 26, [1739]—All Newgate rang with the cries of those whom the word of God cut to the heart. Two of them were in a moment filled with joy, to the astonishment of those that beheld them.

Sun., [May] 13, [1739]— . . . My ordinary employment (in public) was now as follows: every morning I read prayers and preached at Newgate. Every evening I expounded a portion of Scripture at one or more of the Societies. On Monday, in the afternoon, I preached abroad, near Bristol; on Tuesday, at Bath and Two Mile Hill alternately; on Wednesday, at Baptist Mills; every other Thursday, near Pensford; every other Friday, in another part of Kingswood; on Saturday in the afternoon, and Sunday morning, in the Bowling Green (which lies near the middle of the city); on Sunday, at eleven, near Hannam Mount; at two, at Clifton; and at five, on Rose Green. And hitherto, as my day is, so my strength hath been.

Tues., [June] 5, [1739]—There was a great expectation at Bath of what a noted man was to do to me there; and I was much entreated not to preach, because no one knew what might happen.

By this report I also gained a much larger audience, among whom were many of the rich and great. I told them plainly the Scripture had concluded them all under sin, high and low, rich and poor, one with another. Many of them seemed to be a little surprised, and were sinking apace into seriousness, when their champion appeared, and coming close to me, asked by what authority I did these things? I replied, "By the authority of Jesus Christ, conveyed to me by the (now) Archbishop of Canterbury, when he laid his hands upon me and said, 'Take thou authority to preach the Gospel.' " He said, "This is contrary to Act of Parliament. This is a conventicle." I answered, "Sir, the conventicles mentioned in that Act (as the preamble shows) are seditious meetings; but this is not such; here is no shadow of sedition; therefore it is not contrary to that Act." He replied, "I say it is: and beside, your preaching frightens people out of their wits." "Sir, did you ever hear me preach?" "No." "How then can you judge of what you never heard?" "Sir, by common report." "Common report is not enough. Give me leave, Sir, to ask, is not your name Nash?" "My name is Nash." "Sir, I dare not judge of you by common report. I think it not enough to judge by." Here he paused awhile, and having recovered himself, said, "I desire to know what this people comes here for?" On which one replied, "Sir, leave him to me. Let an old woman answer him. You, Mr. Nash, take care of your body. We take care of our souls; and for the food of our souls we come here." He replied not a word, but walked away.

Tues., [October] 23, [1739]— . . . Returning [from Bradford] in the evening I was exceedingly pressed to go back to a young woman in Kingswood. The fact I nakedly relate, and leave every man to his own judgment of it. I went. She was nineteen or twenty years old, but, it seems, could not write or read. I found her on the bed, two or three persons holding her. It was a terrible sight. Anguish, horror, and despair, above all description, appeared in her pale face. The thousand distortions of her whole body showed how the dogs of hell were gnawing her heart. The shrieks intermixed were scarce to be endured. But her stony eyes could not weep. She screamed out, as soon as words could find their way, "I am damned, damned; lost forever. Six days ago you might have helped me; but it is past. I am the Devil's now; I have given myself to him. His I am. Him I must serve. With him I must go to hell. I will be his; I will serve him; I will go with him to hell. I cannot be saved. I will not be saved. I must, I will, I will be damned." She then began praying to the Devil. We began,

"Arm of the Lord, awake, awake!"

She immediately sunk down as asleep; but, as soon as we left off, broke out again with inexpressible vehemence: "Stony hearts, break! I am a warning to you. Break, break, poor stony hearts! Will you not break? What can be done more for stony hearts? I am damned that ye may be saved. Now break, now break, poor stony hearts! You need not be damned, though I must." She then fixed her eyes on the corner of the ceiling, and said, "There he is, aye, there he is; come, good Devil, come. Take me away. You said you would dash my brains out; come, do it quickly. I am yours. I will be yours. Come just now. Take me away." We interrupted her by calling again upon God; on which she sunk down as before; and another young woman began to roar out as loud as she had done. My brother now came in, it being nine o'clock. We continued in prayer till past eleven, when God in a moment spoke into the soul, first of the first tormented, and then of the other. And they both joined in singing praise to Him, who had stilled the enemy and the avenger.

Mon., [August] 11, [1740]—Forty or fifty of those who were seeking salvation desired leave to spend the night together at the Society Room, in prayer and giving thanks. Before ten I left them, and lay down. But I could have no quiet rest, being quite uneasy in my sleep, as I found others were too, that were asleep in other parts of the house. Between two and three in the morning I was waked and desired to come downstairs. I immediately heard such a confused noise, as if a number of men were all putting to the sword. It increased when I came into the room, and began to pray. One whom I particularly observed to be roaring aloud for pain, was J—— W——, who had been always, till then, very sure that "none cried out but hypocrites:" so had Mrs. S——ms also; but she too now cried to God with a loud and bitter cry. It was not long before God heard from his holy place: He spake, and all our souls were comforted. He bruised Satan under our feet; and sorrow and sighing fled away.

Sat., [March] 28, [1741]—Having heard much of Mr. Whitefield's unkind behavior, since his return from Georgia, I went to him to hear him speak for himself, that I might know how to judge. I much approved of his plainness of speech. He told me he and I preached two different Gospels, and, therefore, he not only would not join with or give me the right hand of fellowship, but was resolved publicly to preach against me and my brother, wheresoever he preached at all. Mr. Hall (who went with me) put him in mind of the promise he had made but a few days before, that whatever his private opinion was, he would never publicly preach against us. He said that promise was only an effect of human weakness, and he was now of another mind.

Thurs., [May] 7, [1741]—I reminded the United Society that many of our brethren and sisters had not needful food; many were destitute of convenient clothing; many were out of business, and that without their own fault; and many were sick and ready to perish: that I had done what in me lay to feed the hungry, to clothe the naked, to employ the poor, and to visit the sick; but was not alone sufficient for these things; and therefore desired all whose hearts were as my heart:

1. To bring what clothes each could spare, to be distributed among those that wanted most.

2. To give weekly a penny, or what they could afford, for the relief of the poor and sick.

My design, I told them, is to employ for the present all the women who are out of business, and desire it, in knitting. To these we will first give the common price for what work they do, and then add, according as they need. Twelve persons are appointed to inspect these, and to visit and provide things needful for the sick. Each of these is to visit all the sick within their district, every other day; and to meet on Tuesday evening, to give an account of what they had done, and consult what can be done farther.

Sat., [March] 12, [1743]— . . . I observed the number of those who had left the Society, since December 30, was seventy-six:—

Fourteen of these (chiefly Dissenters) said, they left it because otherwise their Ministers would not give them the Sacrament.
Nine more, because their husbands or wives were not willing they should stay in it.
Twelve, because their parents were not willing.
Five, because their master and mistress would not let them come.
Seven, because their acquaintance persuaded them to leave it.
Five, because people said such bad things of the Society.
Nine, because they would not be laughed at.
Three, because they would not lose the poor's allowance.
Three more, because they could not spare time to come.
Two, because it was too far off.
One, because she was afraid of falling into fits.
One, because people were so rude in the street.
Two, because Thomas Naisbit was in the Society.
One, because he would not turn his back on his baptism.
One, because we were mere Church of England men. And,
One, because it was time enough to serve God yet.

The number of those who were expelled the Society was sixty-four:—

Two for cursing and swearing.
Two for habitual Sabbath-breaking.
Seventeen for drunkenness.
Two for retailing spirituous liquors.
Three for quarreling and brawling.
One for beating his wife.
Three for habitual, willful lying.
Four for railing and evil-speaking.
One for idleness and laziness. And
Nine-and-twenty for lightness and carelessness.

Wed., Nov. 2, [1743], [Newcastle]—The following advertisement was published: "For the benefit of Mr. Este. By the Edinburgh Company of Comedians, on Friday, November 4, will be
acted a comedy, called, *The Conscious Lovers*: to which will be
added, a Farce, called *Trick upon Trick; or Methodism Displayed*." On Friday a vast multitude of spectators were assembled
in the Moot Hall to see this. It was believed, there could not be
less than fifteen hundred people, some hundreds of whom sat on
rows of seats built upon the stage. Soon after the comedians had
begun the first act of the play, on a sudden all those seats fell down
at once, the supporters of them breaking like a rotten stick; the
people were thrown one upon another, about five foot forward,
but not one of them hurt. After a short time, the rest of the spectators were quiet, and the actors went on. In the middle of the second
act, all the shilling seats gave a crack, and sunk several inches down.
A great noise and shrieking followed, and as many as could readily
get at the door, went out and returned no more. Notwithstanding
this, when the noise was over, the actors went on with the play.
In the beginning of the third act, the entire stage suddenly sunk
about six inches; the players retired with great precipitation; yet
in a while they began again. At the latter end of the third act, all
the sixpenny seats, without any kind of notice, fell to the ground.
There was now a cry on every side, it being supposed that many
were crushed to pieces; but upon inquiry, not a single person (such
was the mercy of God!) was either killed or dangerously hurt;
two or three hundred remaining still in the hall. Mr. Este (who
was to act the Methodist) came upon the stage, and told them for
all this, he was resolved the farce should be acted. While he was
speaking, the stage sunk six inches more, on which he ran back in
the utmost confusion, and the people as fast as they could out of
the door, none staying to look behind him.

Sat., [Nov.] 24, [1759]—We rode to Everton, Mr. Berridge

being gone to preach before the University at Cambridge. Many people came to his house in the evening, and it was a season of great refreshment.

Sun. 25.—I was a little afraid my strength would not suffice for reading prayers and preaching, and administering the Lord's Supper alone, to a large number of communicants; but all was well. Mr. Hicks began his own service early, and came before I had ended my sermon. So we finished the whole before two, and I had time to breathe before the evening service. In the afternoon God was eminently present with us, though rather to comfort than to convince. But I observed a remarkable difference since I was here before as to the manner of the work. None now were in trances, none cried out, none fell down or were convulsed; only some trembled exceedingly, a low murmur was heard, and many were refreshed with the multitude of peace.

The danger *was* to regard extraordinary circumstances too much, such as outcries, convulsions, visions, trances; as if these were essential to the inward work, so that it could not go on without them. Perhaps the danger *is* to regard them too little, to condemn them altogether; to imagine they had nothing of God in them, and were a hindrance to His work. Whereas the truth is: (1) God suddenly and strongly convinced many that they were lost sinners, the natural consequence whereof were sudden outcries and strong bodily convulsions; (2) to strengthen and encourage them that believed, and to make His work more apparent, He favored several of them with divine dreams, others with trances and visions; (3) in some of these instances, after a time, nature mixed with grace; (4) Satan likewise mimicked this work of God, in order to discredit the whole work. And yet it is not wise to give up this part, any more than to give up the whole. At first it was, doubtless, wholly from God. It is partly so at this day; and He will enable us to discern how far, in every case, the work is pure, and where it mixes or degenerates.

Let us even suppose that, in some few cases, there was a mixture of dissimulation—that persons pretended to see or feel what they did not, and imitated the cries or convulsive motions of those who were really overpowered by the Spirit of God; yet even this should not make us either deny or undervalue the real work of the Spirit. The shadow is no disparagement of the substance, nor the counterfeit of the real diamond. We may further suppose that Satan will make these visions an occasion of pride. But what can be inferred from hence? Nothing, but that we should guard against it; that we should diligently exhort all to be little in their own eyes, knowing that nothing avails with God but humble love. But still, to slight or censure visions in general would be both irrational and unchristian.

Fri., [June] 28, [1776]—I am seventy-three years old, and far abler to preach than I was at three-and-twenty. What natural means has God used to produce so wonderful an effect? (1) Continual exercise and change of air, by traveling above four thousand miles in a year; (2) constant rising at four; (3) the ability, if ever I want, to sleep immediately; (4) the never losing a night's sleep in my life; (5) two violent fevers, and two deep consumptions. These, it is true, were rough medicines; but they were of admirable service; causing my flesh to come again as the flesh of a little child. May I add, lastly, evenness of temper? I *feel* and *grieve;* but, by the grace of God, I *fret* at nothing. But still "the help that is done upon earth, He doeth it Himself." And this He doeth in answer to many prayers.

Thurs., [September] 12, [1776]—I spent about two hours in Mr. Hoare's gardens at Stourton. I have seen the most celebrated gardens in England, but these far exceed them all: 1. In the situation, being laid out on the sloping sides of a semicircular mountain; 2. in the vast basin of water enclosed between them, covering, I suppose, sixty acres of ground; 3. in the delightful interchange of shady groves and sunny glades, curiously mixed together. Above all, in the lovely grottos, two of which excel everything of the kind which I ever saw; the fountain grotto, made entirely of rock-work, admirably well imitating nature, and the castle grotto, into which you enter unawares beneath a heap of ruins. This is within totally built of roots of trees, wonderfully interwoven. On one side of it is a little hermitage, with a lamp, a chair, a table, and bones upon it.

Others were delighted with the temples, but I was not: (1) because several of the statues about them were mean; (2) because I cannot admire the images of devils, and we know the gods of the heathens are but devils; (3) because I defy all mankind to reconcile statues with nudities, either to common sense or common decency.

Thurs., [March] 24, [1785]— . . . . I was now considering how strangely the grain of mustardseed, planted about fifty years ago, has grown up. It has spread through all Great Britain and Ireland; the Isle of Wight, and the Isle of Man; then to America, from the Leeward Islands, through the whole Continent, into Canada, and

Newfoundland. And the Societies in all these parts walk by one rule, knowing religion is holy tempers, and striving to worship God, not in form only, but likewise "in spirit and in truth."

On Tuesday [March 4, 1788] I gave notice of my design to preach on Thursday evening upon (what is now the general topic) Slavery. In consequence of this, on Thursday, the house, from end to end, was filled with high and low, rich and poor. I preached on that ancient prophecy, "God shall enlarge Japhet. And he shall dwell in the tents of Shem; and Canaan shall be his servant." About the middle of the discourse, while there was on every side attention still as night, a vehement noise arose, none could tell why, and shot like lightning through the whole congregation. The terror and confusion were inexpressible. You might have imagined it was a city taken by storm. The people rushed upon each other with the utmost violence, the benches were broken in pieces; and nine-tenths of the congregation appeared to be struck with the same panic. In about six minutes the storm ceased, almost as suddenly as it rose, and all being calm, I went on without the least interruption.

It was the strangest incident of the kind I ever remember; and I believe none can account for it without supposing some preter-natural influence. Satan fought lest his kingdom should be deliver-ed up. We set *Friday* apart as a day of fasting and prayer, that God would remember those poor outcasts of men, and (what seems impossible with men, considering the wealth and power of their oppressors) make a way for them to escape, and break their chains in sunder.

Sun., [April] 12, [1789]—Being Easter Day, we had a solemn as-sembly indeed; many hundred communicants in the morning; and in the afternoon far more hearers than our room would contain, though it is now considerably enlarged. Afterwards I met the So-ciety, and explained to them at large the original design of the Methodists, viz., Not to be a distinct party, but to stir up all par-ties, Christians or heathens, to worship God in spirit and in truth; but the Church of England in particular, to which they belonged from the beginning. With this view I have uniformly gone on for fifty years, never varying from the doctrine of the Church at all, nor from her discipline of choice, but of necessity. So, in a course of years, necessity was laid upon me (as I have proved elsewhere) (1) to preach in the open air; (2) to pray extempore; (3) to form societies; (4) to accept of the assistance of lay preachers; and in a few other instances to use such means as occurred to prevent or remove evils that we either felt or feared.

THOUGHTS UPON METHODISM
1768

. . . .

It nearly concerns us to understand how the case stands with us at present. I fear, wherever riches have increased (exceeding few are the exceptions), the essence of religion, the mind that was in Christ, has decreased in the same proportion. Therefore do I not see how it is possible, in the nature of things, for any revival of true religion to continue long. For religion must necessarily produce both industry and frugality; and these cannot but produce riches. But as riches increase, so will pride, anger, and love of the world in all its branches.

How, then, is it possible that Methodism, that is, a religion of the heart, though it flourishes now as a green bay tree, should continue in this state? For the Methodists in every place grow diligent and frugal; consequently, they increase in goods. Hence they proportionably increase in pride, in anger, in the desire of the flesh, the desire of the eyes, and the pride of life. So, although the form of religion remains, the spirit is swiftly vanishing away.

Is there no way to prevent this? This continual decay of pure religion? We ought not to forbid people to be diligent and frugal; we must exhort all Christians to gain all they can, and to save all they can; that is, in effect, to grow rich! What way, then (I ask again), can we take, that our money may not sink us to the nethermost hell?—There is one way, and there is no other under heaven. If those who gain all they can, and save all they can, will likewise give all they can, then the more they gain, the more they will grow in grace, and the more treasure they will lay up in heaven.

William Cowper

1731–1800

In Cowper the eighteenth-century depression of spirit darkened occasionally into insanity. Spells of abysmal melancholy brought with them a sense of defilement before God and a conviction that "everybody hated me" or that "all my food was poisoned." For a time he submitted himself to the inquisition of John Newton, an evangelical clergyman who had a reputation for preaching people mad. Cowper's spirits would break even at "the pressure of too much joy." The only terms upon which he could maintain the momentary composure of his mind was by a retirement with Mrs. Unwin so close and so evenly regulated as to be hermitlike. Shut up in the bleak house overlooking the dismal square at Olney, he explained, "I should miss the minutest object, and be disagreeably affected by its removal." The later seclusion at Weston was no different. When he visited Eartham in 1792, he felt "terrors" at journeying over the Sussex Downs, and complained that Weston suited him better—"it has an air of snug concealment in which a disposition like mine feels itself peculiarly gratified; whereas here I see from every window woods like forests and hills like mountains—a wilderness, in short, that rather increases my natural melancholy." Cowper was soothed and secured by the cozy Bedfordshire scene and mild domestic amenities—a walk by the Ouse on a winter morning when the icicles tinkled on the withered leaves, or a newspaper unhurriedly read in the evening light. This is the level of Cowper's best verse. The earth and every common sight are as unpretentiously recorded as in Wordsworth, but without Wordsworth's contemplative breadth. Unfortunately Cowper often wrote mere metrical prose when he thought of himself as a satirist or reformer. Usually he scribbled off his letters in that chatty, whimsical mood in which he wrote "The Diverting History of John Gilpin." There is something pathetic about even the humor of Cowper, who trifled when he was "reduced to it by necessity." "And strange as it may seem," he writes, "the most ludicrous lines I ever wrote have been written in the saddest mood."

BIOGRAPHICAL NOTES

Son of the rector of Great Berkhamstead, Hertfordshire; his mother, a descendant of John Donne, died in 1737—a great shock to Cowper, who suffered from melancholy. Attended private school, where he was bullied. Entered Westminster School (1741); then was articled to a solicitor (1749). Fell in love with a cousin, Theodora Cowper, but her father forbade the match. Studied at the Middle Temple; admitted to the bar (1754). Suffered great "dejection of spirits"; read George Herbert. Began writing light verse; befriended by Theodora's sister, later Lady Hesketh. Unable to face examination for Clerkship of Journals of House of Lords (1763); attempted suicide; confined in an asylum at St. Albans. Met Unwin family at home of his brother John, in Huntingdon (1765). After death of Mr. Unwin, moved to Olney with Mrs. Unwin, and accepted the guidance of evangelical John Newton (1767). Complete "retirement." Recurrence of insanity (1773–74); was convinced of his damnation. Composed the *Olney Hymns* with Newton (1771–79). Found relative contentment caring for his garden, hares, and other pets. Met Lady Austen (1781) and published *Poems* with *Table Talk* and *Retirement* (1782). At hint from Lady Austen composed *The Task* (1785). Estrangement from Lady Austen. Received financial aid from Lady Hesketh. Moved to Weston Underwood, to house owned by the Throckmortons (1786). Began translating Homer. Recurrence of insanity (1787). Mrs. Unwin ailing. Translation of Homer published (1791). Mrs. Unwin died (1796). Infirm nerves and health; accepted spiritual guidance of an ignorant schoolteacher, Samuel Teedon. After 1795, lived with a relative, John Johnson, at East Dereham; increasing depression until death.

BIBLIOGRAPHY: *Poetical Works,* ed. H. S. Milford, 1913. *Poems,* Everyman ed., 1950. *Correspondence,* ed. T. Wright, 4 vols., 1904. Cecil, Lord David, *The Stricken Deer,* 1938. Fausset. H. I'A., *William Cowper,* 1928. Hartley, L. C., *William Cowper, Humanitarian,* 1938. Huang, R., *William Cowper, Nature Poet,* 1957. Nicholson, N., *William Cowper,* 1951. Quinlan, M., *William Cowper,* 1953. Ryscamp, C., *William Cowper of the Inner Temple,* 1959. Thomas, G., *William Cowper and the Eighteenth Century,* 1948. Wright, T., *William Cowper,* 1921.

THE SHRUBBERY

WRITTEN IN A TIME OF AFFLICTION

1782

O happy shades—to me unblest!
    Friendly to peace, but not to me!
How ill the scene that offers rest,
    And heart that cannot rest, agree!

This glassy stream, that spreading pine,
    Those alders quiv'ring to the breeze,
Might soothe a soul less hurt than mine,
    And please, if anything could please.

But fix'd, unalterable care
    Foregoes not what she feels within,   10
Shows the same sadness ev'rywhere,
    And slights the season and the scene.

For all that pleas'd in wood or lawn,
    While peace possess'd these silent bow'rs,
Her animating smile withdrawn,
    Has lost its beauties and its pow'rs.

The saint or moralist should tread
    This moss-grown alley, musing, slow;
They seek, like me, the secret shade,
    But not, like me, to nourish woe!   20

Me fruitful scenes and prospects waste
    Alike admonish not to roam;
These tell me of enjoyments past,
    And those of sorrows yet to come.

EPITAPH ON A HARE

1784

Here lies, whom hound did ne'er pursue,
    Nor swifter greyhound follow,
Whose foot ne'er tainted morning dew,
    Nor ear heard huntsman's hallo;

Old Tiney, surliest of his kind,
    Who, nurs'd with tender care,
And to domestic bounds confin'd,
    Was still a wild Jack-hare.

Though duly from my hand he took
    His pittance ev'ry night,   10
He did it with a jealous look,
    And, when he could, would bite.

His diet was of wheaten bread,
    And milk, and oats, and straw;
Thistles, or lettuces instead,
    With sand to scour his maw.

On twigs of hawthorn he regal'd,
    On pippins' russet peel,
And, when his juicy salads fail'd,
    Slic'd carrot pleased him well.   20

A Turkey carpet was his lawn,
    Whereon he lov'd to bound,
To skip and gambol like a fawn,
    And swing his rump around.

His frisking was at evening hours,
    For then he lost his fear;
But most before approaching show'rs,
    Or when a storm drew near.

Eight years and five round-rolling moons
He thus saw steal away,   30
Dozing out all his idle noons,
And ev'ry night at play.

I kept him for his humour' sake,
For he would oft beguile
My heart of thoughts that made it ache,
And force me to a smile.

And now beneath this walnut-shade
He finds his long, last home,
And waits, in snug concealment laid,
Till gentler Puss shall come.   40

He, still more aged, feels the shocks
From which no care can save,
And, partner once of Tiney's box,
Must soon partake his grave.

THE TASK

1785

BOOK I

The Sofa

I sing the Sofa. I, who lately sang
Truth, Hope, and Charity, and touch'd with awe
The solemn chords, and with a trembling hand,
Escap'd with pain from that advent'rous flight,
Now seek repose upon an humbler theme:
The theme though humble, yet august and proud
Th' occasion—for the Fair commands the song.
    Time was, when clothing sumptuous or for use,
Save their own painted skins, our sires had none.
As yet black breeches were not; satin smooth,   10
Or velvet soft, or plush with shaggy pile:
The hardy chief upon the rugged rock
Wash'd by the sea, or on the grav'ly bank
Thrown up by wintry torrents roaring loud,

Fearless of wrong, repos'd his weary strength.
Those barb'rous ages past, succeeded next
The birth-day of invention; weak at first,
Dull in design, and clumsy to perform.
Joint-stools were then created; on three legs
Upborn they stood. Three legs upholding firm   20
A massy slab, in fashion square or round.
On such a stool immortal Alfred sat,
And sway'd the sceptre of his infant realms:
And such in ancient halls and mansions drear
May still be seen; but perforated sore,
And drill'd in holes, the solid oak is found,
By worms voracious eating through and through.

    At length a generation more refin'd
Improv'd the simple plan; made three legs four,
Gave them a twisted form vermicular,   30
And o'er the seat, with plenteous wadding stuff'd,
Induc'd a splendid cover, green and blue,
Yellow and red, of tap'stry richly wrought,
And woven close, or needle-work sublime.
There might ye see the piony spread wide,
The full-blown rose, the shepherd and his lass,
Lap-dog and lambkin with black staring eyes,
And parrots with twin cherries in their beak.

    Now came the cane from India, smooth and bright
With Nature's varnish; sever'd into stripes   40
That interlac'd each other, these supplied
Of texture firm a lattice-work, that brac'd
The new machine, and it became a chair.
But restless was the chair; the back erect
Distress'd the weary loins, that felt no ease;
The slipp'ry seat betray'd the sliding part
That press'd it, and the feet hung dangling down,
Anxious in vain to find the distant floor.
These for the rich: the rest, whom fate had plac'd
In modest mediocrity, content   50
With base materials, sat on well-tann'd hides,
Obdurate and unyielding, glassy smooth,
With here and there a tuft of crimson yarn,
Or scarlet crewel, in the cushion fixt;
If cushion might be call'd, what harder seem'd
Than the firm oak of which the frame was form'd.
No want of timber then was felt or fear'd

In Albion's happy isle. The lumber stood
Pond'rous and fixt by its own massy weight.
But elbows still were wanting; these, some say,   60
An alderman of Cripplegate contriv'd:
And some ascribe th' invention to a priest
Burly and big, and studious of his ease.
But, rude at first, and not with easy slope
Receding wide, they press'd against the ribs,
And bruis'd the side; and, elevated high,
Taught the rais'd shoulders to invade the ears.
Long time elaps'd or e'er our rugged sires
Complain'd, though incommodiously pent in,
And ill at ease behind. The ladies first   70
'Gan murmur, as became the softer sex.
Ingenious fancy, never better pleas'd
Than when employ'd t'accommodate the fair,
Heard the sweet moan with pity, and devis'd
The soft settee; one elbow at each end,
And in the midst an elbow it receiv'd,
United yet divided, twain at once.
So sit two kings of Brentford [1] on one throne;
And so two citizens who take the air,
Close pack'd, and smiling, in a chaise and one.   80
But relaxation of the languid frame,
By soft recumbency of outstretch'd limbs,
Was bliss reserv'd for happier days. So slow
The growth of what is excellent; so hard
T' attain perfection in this nether world.
Thus first necessity invented stools,
Convenience next suggested elbow-chairs,
And luxury th'accomplish'd SOFA last.
    The nurse sleeps sweetly, hir'd to watch the sick,
Whom snoring she disturbs. As sweetly he,   90
Who quits the coach-box at the midnight hour
To sleep within the carriage more secure,
His legs depending at the open door.
Sweet sleep enjoys the curate in his desk,
The tedious rector drawling o'er his head;
And sweet the clerk below. But neither sleep
Of lazy nurse, who snores the sick man dead,
Nor his who quits the box at midnight hour

---

1 In *The Rehearsal* (1672), a satirical play written by George Villiers, Duke of Buckingham, and his friends appear two ridiculous Kings of Brentford.

To slumber in the carriage more secure,
Nor sleep enjoy'd by curate in his desk, 100
Nor yet the dozings of the clerk, are sweet,
Compar'd with the repose the sofa yields.
　　Oh may I live exempted (while I live
Guiltless of pamper'd appetite obscene)
From pangs arthritic, that infest the toe
Of libertine excess. The sofa suits
The gouty limb, 'tis true; but gouty limb,
Though on a sofa, may I never feel:
For I have lov'd the rural walk through lanes
Of grassy swarth, close cropt by nibbling sheep, 110
And skirted thick with intertexture firm
Of thorny boughs; have lov'd the rural walk
O'er hills, through valleys, and by rivers' brink,
E'er since a truant boy I pass'd my bounds
T' enjoy a ramble on the banks of Thames;
And still remember, nor without regret
Of hours that sorrow since has much endear'd,
How oft, my slice of pocket store consum'd,
Still hung'ring, pennyless and far from home,
I fed on scarlet hips and stony haws, 120
Or blushing crabs, or berries, that imboss
The bramble, black as jet, or sloes austere.
Hard fare! but such as boyish appetite
Disdains not; nor the palate, undeprav'd
By culinary arts, unsav'ry deems.
No sofa then awaited my return;
Nor sofa then I needed. Youth repairs
His wasted spirits quickly, by long toil
Incurring short fatigue; and, though our years
As life declines speed rapidly away, 130
And not a year but pilfers as he goes
Some youthful grace that age would gladly keep;
A tooth or auburn lock, and by degrees
Their length and colour from the locks they spare;
Th' elastic spring of an unwearied foot
That mounts the style with ease, or leaps the fence,
That play of lungs, inhaling and again
Respiring freely the fresh air, that makes
Swift pace or steep ascent no toil to me,
Mine have not pilfer'd yet; nor yet impair'd 140
My relish of fair prospect; scenes that sooth'd

Or charm'd me young, no longer young, I find
Still soothing and of pow'r to charm me still.
And witness, dear companion of my walks,[2]
Whose arm this twentieth winter I preceive
Fast lock'd in mine, with pleasure such as love,
Confirm'd by long experience of thy worth
And well-tried virtues, could alone inspire—
Witness a joy that thou hast doubled long.
Thou know'st my praise of nature most sincere,   150
And that my raptures are not conjur'd up
To serve occasions of poetic pomp,
But genuine, and art partner of them all.
How oft upon yon eminence our pace
Has slacken'd to a pause, and we have born
The ruffling wind, scarce conscious that it blew,
While admiration, feeding at the eye,
And still unsated, dwelt upon the scene.
Thence with what pleasure have we just discern'd
The distant plough slow moving, and beside   160
His lab'ring team, that swerv'd not from the track,
The sturdy swain diminish'd to a boy!
Here Ouse, slow winding through a level plain
Of spacious meads with cattle sprinkled o'er,
Conducts the eye along its sinuous course
Delighted. There, fast rooted in their bank,
Stand, never overlook'd, our fav'rite elms,
That screen the herdsman's solitary hut;
While far beyond, and overthwart the stream
That, as with molten glass, inlays the vale,   170
The sloping land recedes into the clouds;
Displaying on its varied side the grace
Of hedge-row beauties numberless, square tow'r,
Tall spire, from which the sound of cheerful bells
Just undulates upon the list'ning ear,
Groves, heaths, and smoking villages, remote.
Scenes must be beautiful, which, daily view'd,
Please daily, and whose novelty survives
Long knowledge and the scrutiny of years.
Praise justly due to those that I describe.   180
    Nor rural sights alone, but rural sounds,
Exhilarate the spirit, and restore
The tone of languid Nature. Mighty winds,

2 Mrs. Unwin.

That sweep the skirt of some far-spreading wood
Of ancient growth, make music not unlike
The dash of ocean on his winding shore,
And lull the spirit while they fill the mind;
Unnumber'd branches waving in the blast,
And all their leaves fast flutt'ring, all at once.
Nor less composure waits upon the roar   190
Of distant floods, or on the softer voice
Of neighb'ring fountain, or of rills that slip
Through the cleft rock, and, chiming as they fall
Upon loose pebbles, lose themselves at length
In matted grass, that with a livelier green
Betrays the secret of their silent course.
Nature inanimate employs sweet sounds,
But animated nature sweeter still,
To sooth and satisfy the human ear.
Ten thousand warblers cheer the day, and one   200
The live-long night: nor these alone, whose notes
Nice finger'd art must emulate in vain,
But cawing rooks, and kites that swim sublime
In still repeated circles, screaming loud,
The jay, the pie, and ev'n the boding owl
That hails the rising moon, have charms for me.
Sounds inharmonious in themselves and harsh,
Yet heard in scenes where peace for ever reigns,
And only there, please highly for their sake.
    Peace to the artist, whose ingenious thought   210
Devis'd the weather-house,[3] that useful toy!
Fearless of humid air and gathering rains,
Forth steps the man—an emblem of myself!
More delicate, his tim'rous mate retires.
When Winter soaks the fields, and female feet,
Too weak to struggle with tenacious clay,
Or ford the rivulets, are best at home,
The task of new discov'ries falls on me.
At such a season, and with such a charge,
Once went I forth; and found, till then unknown,   220
A cottage, whither oft we since repair:
'Tis perch'd upon the green-hill top, but close
Environ'd with a ring of branching elms
That overhang the thatch, itself unseen
Peeps at the vale below; so thick beset

3 A box that predicts weather by the advance or retreat of small figures.

With foliage of such dark redundant growth,
I call'd the low-roof'd lodge the *peasant's nest*.
And, hidden as it is, and far remote
From such unpleasing sounds as haunt the ear
In village or in town, the bay of curs   230
Incessant, clinking hammers, grinding wheels,
And infants clam'rous whether pleas'd or pain'd,
Oft have I wish'd the peaceful covert mine.
Here, I have said, at least I should possess
The poet's treasure, silence, and indulge
The dreams of fancy, tranquil and secure.
Vain thought! the dweller in that still retreat
Dearly obtains the refuge it affords.
Its elevated site forbids the wretch
To drink sweet waters of the crystal well;   240
He dips his bowl into the weedy ditch,
And, heavy-laden, brings his bev'rage home,
Far-fetch'd and little worth; nor seldom waits,
Dependant on the baker's punctual call,
To hear his creaking panniers at the door,
Angry and sad, and his last crust consum'd.
So farewell envy of the *peasant's nest!*
If solitude make scant the means of life,
Society for me!—thou seeming sweet,
Be still a pleasing object in my view;   250
My visit still, but never mine abode.

    Not distant far, a length of colonnade
Invites us. Monument of ancient taste,
Now scorn'd, but worthy of a better fate.
Our fathers knew the value of a screen
From sultry suns; and, in their shaded walks
And long protracted bow'rs, enjoy'd at noon
The gloom and coolness of declining day.
We bear our shades about us; self-depriv'd
Of other screen, the thin umbrella spread,   260
And range an Indian waste without a tree.
Thanks to Benevolus [4]—he spares me yet
These chesnuts rang'd in corresponding lines;
And, though himself so polish'd, still reprieves
The obsolete prolixity of shade.

    Descending now (but cautious, lest too fast)
A sudden steep, upon a rustic bridge

4 John Courtenay Throckmorton, of Weston Underwood.

We pass a gulph, in which the willows dip
Their pendent boughs, stooping as if to drink.
Hence, ancle-deep in moss and flow'ry thyme,   270
We mount again, and feel at ev'ry step
Our foot half sunk in hillocks green and soft,
Raised by the mole, the miner of the soil.
He, not unlike the great ones of mankind,
Disfigures earth; and, plotting in the dark,
Toils much to earn a monumental pile,
That may record the mischiefs he has done.
    The summit gain'd, behold the proud alcove
That crowns it! yet not all its pride secures
The grant retreat from injuries impress'd   280
By rural carvers, who with knives deface
The pannels, leaving an obscure, rude name,
In characters uncouth, and spelt amiss.
So strong the zeal t' immortalize himself
Beats in the breast of man, that ev'n a few
Few transient years, won from th' abyss abhorr'd
Of blank oblivion, seem a glorious prize,
And even to a clown. Now roves the eye;
And, posted on this speculative height,
Exults in its command. The sheep-fold here   290
Pours out its fleecy tenants o'er the glebe.
At first, progressive as a stream, they seek
The middle field; but, scatter'd by degrees,
Each to his choice, soon whiten all the land.
There from the sun-burnt hay-field, homeward creeps
The loaded wain; while, lighten'd of its charge,
The wain that meets it passes swiftly by;
The boorish driver leaning o'er his team
Vocif'rous, and impatient of delay.
Nor less attractive is the woodland scene,   300
Diversified with trees of ev'ry growth,
Alike, yet various. Here the gray smooth trunks
Of ash, or lime, or beech, distinctly shine,
Within the twilight of their distant shades;
There, lost behind a rising ground, the wood
Seems sunk, and shorten'd to its topmost boughs.
No tree in all the grove but has its charms,
Though each its hue peculiar; paler some,
And of a wannish gray; the willow such,
And poplar, that with silver lines his leaf,   310

And ash far-stretching his umbrageous arm;
Of deeper green the elm; and deeper still,
Lord of the woods, the long-surviving oak.
Some glossy-leav'd, and shining in the sun,
The maple, and the beech of oily nuts
Prolific, and the lime at dewy eve
Diffusing odours: nor unnoted pass
The sycamore, capricious in attire,
Now green, now tawny, and, ere autumn yet
Have chang'd the woods, in scarlet honours bright.   320
O'er these, but far beyond (a spacious map
Of hill and valley interpos'd between),
The Ouse, dividing the well-water'd land,
Now glitters in the sun, and now retires,
As bashful, yet impatient to be seen.
     Hence the declivity is sharp and short,
And such the re-ascent; between them weeps
A little naiad her impov'rish'd urn
All summer long, which winter fills again.
The folded gates would bar my progress now,   330
But that the lord of this enclos'd demesne,[5]
Communicative of the good he owns,
Admits me to a share; the guiltless eye
Commits no wrong, nor wastes what it enjoys.
Refreshing change! where now the blazing sun?
By short transition we have lost his glare,
And stepp'd at once into a cooler clime.
Ye fallen avenues! once more I mourn
Your fate unmerited, once more rejoice
That yet a remnant of your race survives.   340
How airy and how light the graceful arch,
Yet awful as the consecrated roof
Re-echoing pious anthems! while beneath
The chequer'd earth seems restless as a flood
Brush'd by the wind. So sportive is the light
Shot through the boughs, it dances as they dance,
Shadow and sunshine intermingling quick,
And dark'ning and enlight'ning, as the leaves
Play wanton, ev'ry moment, ev'ry spot.
     And now, with nerves new-brac'd and spirits cheer'd,   350
We tread the wilderness, whose well-roll'd walks,
With curvature of slow and easy sweep—

5 See note 4.

Deception innocent—give ample space
To narrow bounds. The grove receives us next;
Between the upright shafts of whose tall elms
We may discern the thresher at his task.
Thump after thump resounds the constant flail,
That seems to swing uncertain, and yet falls
Full on the destin'd ear. Wide flies the chaff.
The rustling straw sends up a frequent mist　　　360
Of atoms, sparkling in the noon-day beam.
Come hither, ye that press your beds of down,
And sleep not: see him sweating o'er his bread
Before he eats it.—'Tis the primal curse,
But soften'd into mercy; made the pledge
Of cheerful days, and nights without a groan.
　By ceaseless action all that is subsists.
Constant rotation of th' unwearied wheel
That nature rides upon maintains her health,
Her beauty, her fertility. She dreads　　　370
An instant's pause, and lives but while she moves.
Its own revolvency upholds the world.
Winds from all quarters agitate the air,
And fit the limpid element for use,
Else noxious: oceans, rivers, lakes, and streams,
All feel the fresh'ning impulse, and are cleans'd
By restless undulation: ev'n the oak
Thrives by the rude concussion of the storm:
He seems indeed indignant, and to feel
Th' impression of the blast with proud disdain,　　　380
Frowning as if in his unconscious arm
He held the thunder: but the monarch owes
His firm stability to what he scorns—
More fixt below, the more disturb'd above.
The law, by which all creatures else are bound,
Binds man the lord of all. Himself derives
No mean advantage from a kindred cause,
From strenuous toil his hours of sweetest ease.
The sedentary stretch their lazy length
When custom bids, but no refreshment find,　　　390
For none they need: the languid eye, the cheek
Deserted of its bloom, the flaccid, shrunk,
And wither'd muscle, and the vapid soul,
Reproach their owner with that love of rest
To which he forfeits ev'n the rest he loves.

Not such th' alert and active. Measure life
By its true worth, the comforts it affords,
And theirs alone seems worthy of the name.
Good health, and, its associate in most,
Good temper; spirits prompt to undertake,   400
And not soon spent, though in an arduous task;
The pow'rs of fancy and strong thought are theirs;
Ev'n age itself seems privileg'd in them,
With clear exemption from its own defects.
A sparkling eye beneath a wrinkled front
The vet'ran shows, and, gracing a gray beard
With youthful smiles, descends toward the grave
Sprightly, and old almost without decay.

Like a coy maiden, ease, when courted most,
Farthest retires—an idol, at whose shrine   410
Who oft'nest sacrifice are favour'd least.
The love of Nature, and the scenes she draws,
Is Nature's dictate. Strange! there should be found,
Who, self-imprison'd in their proud saloons,
Renounce the odours of the open field
For the unscented fictions of the loom;
Who, satisfied with only pencil'd scenes,
Prefer to the performance of a God
Th' inferior wonders of an artist's hand!
Lovely indeed the mimic works of art;   420
But Nature's works far lovelier. I admire—
None more admires—the painter's magic skill,
Who shows me that which I shall never see,
Conveys a distant country into mine,
And throws Italian light on English walls:
But imitative strokes can do no more
Than please the eye—sweet Nature ev'ry sense.
The air salubrious of her lofty hills,
The cheering fragrance of her dewy vales,
And music of her woods—no works of man   430
May rival these; these all bespeak a pow'r
Peculiar, and exclusively her own.
Beneath the open sky she spreads the feast;
'Tis free to all—'tis ev'ry day renew'd;
Who scorns it starves deservedly at home.
He does not scorn it, who, imprison'd long
In some unwholesome dungeon, and a prey
To sallow sickness, which the vapours, dank

And clammy, of his dark abode have bred,
Escapes at last to liberty and light: 440
His cheek recovers soon its healthful hue;
His eye relumines its extinguish'd fires;
He walks, he leaps, he runs—is wing'd with joy,
And riots in the sweets of ev'ry breeze.
He does not scorn it, who has long endur'd
A fever's agonies, and fed on drugs.
Nor yet the mariner, his blood inflam'd
With acrid salts; his very heart athirst
To gaze at Nature in her green array,
Upon the ship's tall side he stands, possess'd   450
With visions prompted by intense desire:
Fair fields appear below, such as he left,
Far distant, such as he would die to find—
He seeks them headlong, and is seen no more.
    The spleen is seldom felt where Flora reigns;
The low'ring eye, the petulance, the frown,
And sullen sadness, that o'ershade, distort,
And mar the face of beauty, when no cause
For such immeasurable woe appears,
These Flora banishes, and gives the fair   460
Sweet smiles, and bloom less transient than her own.
It is the constant revolution, stale
And tasteless, of the same repeated joys,
That palls and satiates, and makes languid life
A pedlar's pack, that bows the bearer down.
Health suffers, and the spirits ebb; the heart
Recoils from its own choice—at the full feast
Is famish'd—finds no music in the song,
No smartness in the jest; and wonders why.
Yet thousands still desire to journey on,   470
Though halt, and weary of the path they tread.
The paralytic, who can hold her cards,
But cannot play them, borrows a friend's hand
To deal and shuffle, to divide and sort,
Her mingled suits and sequences; and sits,
Spectatress both and spectacle, a sad
And silent cypher, while her proxy plays.
Others are dragg'd into the crowded room
Between supporters; and, once seated, sit,
Through downright inability to rise,   480
Till the stout bearers lift the corpse again.

These speak a loud memento. Yet ev'n these
Themselves love life, and cling to it, as he
That overhangs a torrent to a twig.
They love it, and yet loath it; fear to die,
Yet scorn the purposes for which they live.
Then wherefore not renounce them? No—the dread,
The slavish dread of solitude, that breeds
Reflection and remorse, the fear of shame,
And their invet'rate habits, all forbid.   490
    Whom call we gay? That honour has been long
The boast of mere pretenders to the name.
The innocent are gay—the lark is gay,
That dries his feathers, saturate with dew,
Beneath the rosy cloud, while yet the beams
Of day-spring overshoot his humble nest.
The peasant too, a witness of his song,
Himself a songster, is as gay as he.
But save me from the gaiety of those
Whose head-aches nail them to a noon-day bed;   500
And save me too from theirs whose haggard eyes
Flash desperation, and betray their pangs
For property stripp'd off by cruel chance;
From gaiety that fills the bones with pain,
The mouth with blasphemy, the heart with woe.
    The earth was made so various, that the mind
Of desultory man, studious of change,
And pleas'd with novelty, might be indulg'd.
Prospects, however lovely, may be seen
Till half their beauties fade; the weary sight,   510
Too well acquainted with their smiles, slides off,
Fastidious, seeking less familiar scenes.
Then snug enclosures in the shelter'd vale,
Where frequent hedges intercept the eye,
Delight us; happy to renounce awhile,
Not senseless of its charms, what still we love,
That such short absence may endear it more.
Then forests, or the savage rock, may please,
That hides the sea-mew in his hollow clefts
Above the reach of man. His hoary head,   520
Conspicuous many a league, the mariner
Bound homeward, and in hope already there,
Greets with three cheers exulting. At his waist
A girdle of half-wither'd shrubs he shows,

And at his feet the baffled billows die.
The common, overgrown with fern, and rough
With prickly gorse, that, shapeless and deform'd,
And dang'rous to the touch, has yet its bloom,
And decks itself with ornaments of gold,
Yields no unpleasing ramble; there the turf   530
Smells fresh, and, rich in odorif'rous herbs
And fungous fruits of earth, regales the sense
With luxury of unexpected sweets.
   There often wanders one, whom better days
Saw better clad, in cloak of satin trimm'd
With lace, and hat with splendid ribband bound.
A serving maid was she, and fell in love
With one who left her, went to sea, and died.
Her fancy follow'd him through foaming waves
To distant shores; and she would sit and weep   540
At what a sailor suffers; fancy, too,
Delusive most where warmest wishes are,
Would oft anticipate his glad return,
And dream of transports she was not to know.
She heard the doleful tidings of his death—
And never smil'd again! And now she roams
The dreary waste; there spends the livelong day,
And there, unless when charity forbids,
The livelong night. A tatter'd apron hides,
Worn as a cloak, and hardly hides, a gown   550
More tatter'd still; and both but ill conceal
A bosom heav'd with never-ceasing sighs.
She begs an idle pin of all she meets,
And hoards them in her sleeve; but needful food,
Though press'd with hunger oft, or comelier clothes,
Though pinch'd with cold, asks never.—Kate is craz'd!
   I see a column of slow rising smoke
O'ertop the lofty wood that skirts the wild.
A vagabond and useless tribe there eat
Their miserable meal. A kettle, slung   560
Between two poles upon a stick transverse,
Receives the morsel—flesh obscene of dog,
Or vermin, or, at best, of cock purloin'd
From his accustom'd perch. Hard faring race!
They pick their fuel out of ev'ry hedge,
Which, kindled with dry leaves, just saves unquench'd
The spark of life. The sportive wind blows wide

Their flutt'ring rags, and shows a tawny skin,
The vellum of the pedigree they claim.
Great skill have they in palmistry, and more   570
To conjure clean away the gold they touch,
Conveying worthless dross into its place;
Loud when they beg, dumb only when they steal.
Strange! that a creature rational, and cast
In human mould, should brutalize by choice
His nature; and, though capable of arts
By which the world might profit, and himself,
Self-banish'd from society, prefer
Such squalid sloth to honourable toil!
Yet even these, though, feigning sickness oft,   580
They swathe the forehead, drag the limping limb,
And vex their flesh with artificial sores,
Can change their whine into a mirthful note
When safe occasion offers; and, with dance,
And music of the bladder and the bag,
Beguile their woes, and make the woods resound.
Such health and gaiety of heart enjoy
The houseless rovers of the sylvan world;
And, breathing wholesome air, and wand'ring much,
Need other physic none to heal th' effects   590
Of loathsome diet, penury, and cold.
    Blest he, though undistinguish'd from the crowd
By wealth or dignity, who dwells secure,
Where man, by nature fierce, has laid aside
His fierceness, having learnt, though slow to learn,
The manners and the arts of civil life.
His wants, indeed, are many; but supply
Is obvious, plac'd within the easy reach
Of temp'rate wishes and industrious hands.
Here virtue thrives as in her proper soil;   600
Not rude and surly, and beset with thorns,
And terrible to sight, as when she springs
(If e'er she spring spontaneous) in remote
And barb'rous climes, where violence prevails,
And strength is lord of all; but gentle, kind,
By culture tam'd, by liberty refresh'd,
And all her fruits by radiant truth matur'd.
War and the chase engross the savage whole;
War follow'd for revenge, or to supplant
The envied tenants of some happier spot,   610

The chase for sustenance, precarious trust!
His hard condition with severe constraint
Binds all his faculties, forbids all growth
Of wisdom, proves a school in which he learns
Sly circumvention, unrelenting hate,
Mean self-attachment, and scarce aught beside.
Thus fare the shiv'ring natives of the north,
And thus the rangers of the western world,
Where it advances far into the deep,
Towards th' antarctic. Ev'n the favour'd isles,   620
So lately found, although the constant sun
Cheer all their seasons with a grateful smile,
Can boast but little virtue; and, inert
Through plenty, lose in morals what they gain
In manners—victims of luxurious ease.
These therefore I can pity, plac'd remote
From all that science traces, art invents,
Or inspiration teaches; and enclosed
In boundless oceans, never to be pass'd
By navigators uninform'd as they,   630
Or plough'd perhaps by British bark again:
But, far beyond the rest, and with most cause,
Thee, gentle savage! [6] whom no love of thee
Or thine, but curiosity perhaps,
Or else vain glory, prompted us to draw
Forth from thy native bow'rs, to show thee here
With what superior skill we can abuse
The gifts of Providence, and squander life.
The dream is past; and thou hast found again
Thy cocoas and bananas, palms and yams,   640
And homestall thatch'd with leaves. But hast thou found
Their former charms? And, having seen our state,
Our palaces, our ladies, and our pomp
Of equipage, our gardens, and our sports,
And heard our music; are thy simple friends,
Thy simple fare, and all thy plain delights,
As dear to thee as once? And have thy joys
Lost nothing by comparison with ours?
Rude as thou art, (for we return'd thee rude
And ignorant, except of outward show)   650

[6] Omai, a native of Otaheite, brought to England when Captain Cook returned from his second voyage; before he returned to Otaheite with Cook in 1776, he had met the brightest London society, including Frances Burney, Sir Joshua Reynolds, and Dr. Johnson.

I cannot think thee yet so dull of heart
And spiritless, as never to regret
Sweets tasted here, and left as soon as known.
Methinks I see thee straying on the beach,
And asking of the surge that bathes thy foot
If ever it has wash'd our distant shore.
I see thee weep, and thine are honest tears,
A patriot's for his country: thou art sad
At thought of her forlorn and abject state,
From which no pow'r of thine can raise her up.   660
Thus fancy paints thee, and, though apt to err,
Perhaps errs little when she paints thee thus.
She tells me, too, that duly ev'ry morn
Thou climb'st the mountain top, with eager eye
Exploring far and wide the wat'ry waste
For sight of ship from England. Ev'ry speck
Seen in the dim horizon turns thee pale
With conflict of contending hopes and fears.
But comes at last the dull and dusky eve,
And sends thee to thy cabin, well prepar'd   670
To dream all night of what the day denied.
Alas! expect it not. We found no bait
To tempt us in thy country. Doing good,
Disinterested good, is not our trade.
We travel far, 'tis true, but not for nought;
And must be brib'd, to compass earth again,
By other hopes and richer fruits than yours.
    But, though true worth and virtue in the mild
And genial soil of cultivated life
Thrive most, and may perhaps thrive only there,   680
Yet not in cities oft: in proud and gay
And gain-devoted cities. Thither flow,
As to a common and most noisome sew'r,
The dregs and feculence of ev'ry land.
In cities foul example on most minds
Begets its likeness. Rank abundance breeds
In gross and pamper'd cities sloth and lust,
And wantonness and gluttonous excess.
In cities vice is hidden with most ease,
Or seen with least reproach; and virtue, taught   690
By frequent lapse, can hope no triumph there
Beyond th' achievement of successful flight.

I do confess them nurs'ries of the arts,
In which they flourish most; where, in the beams
Of warm encouragement, and in the eye
Of public note, they reach their perfect size.
Such London is, by taste and wealth proclaim'd
The fairest capital of all the world,
By riot and incontinence the worst.
There, touch'd by Reynolds, a dull blank becomes   700
A lucid mirror, in which Nature sees
All her reflected features. Bacon [7] there
Gives more than female beauty to a stone,
And Chatham's eloquence to marble lips.
Nor does the chissel occupy alone
The pow'rs of sculpture, but the style as much;
Each province of her art her equal care.
With nice incision of her guided steel
She ploughs a brazen field, and clothes a soil
So sterile with what charms soe'er she will,   710
The richest scen'ry and the loveliest forms.
Where finds philosophy her eagle eye,
With which she gazes at yon burning disk
Undazzled, and detects and counts his spots?
In London: where her implements exact,
With which she calculates, computes, and scans,
All distance, motion, magnitude, and now
Measures an atom, and now girds a world?
In London. Where has commerce such a mart,
So rich, so throng'd, so drain'd, and so supplied,   720
As London—opulent, enlarg'd, and still
Increasing, London? Babylon of old
Not more the glory of the earth than she,
A more accomplish'd world's chief glory now.
   She has her praise. Now mark a spot or two,
That so much beauty would do well to purge;
And show this queen of cities, that so fair
May yet be foul; so witty, yet not wise.
It is not seemly, nor of good report,
That she is slack in discipline; more prompt   730
T' avenge than to prevent the breach of law:
That she is rigid in denouncing death
On petty robbers, and indulges life

7 John Bacon, R.A., sculptor.

And liberty, and oft-times honour too,
To peculators of the public gold:
That thieves at home must hang; but he, that puts
Into his overgorg'd and bloated purse
The wealth of Indian provinces, escapes.
Nor is it well, nor can it come to good,
That, through profane and infidel contempt   740
Of holy writ, she has presum'd t' annul
And abrogate, as roundly as she may,
The total ordinance and will of God;
Advancing fashion to the post of truth,
And cent'ring all authority in modes
And customs of her own, till sabbath rites
Have dwindled into unrespected forms,
And knees and hassocks are well-nigh divorc'd.
    God made the country, and man made the town.
What wonder then that health and virtue, gifts   750
That can alone make sweet the bitter draught
That life holds out to all, should most abound
And least be threaten'd in the fields and groves?
Possess ye, therefore, ye, who, borne about
In chariots and sedans, know no fatigue
But that of idleness, and taste no scenes
But such as art contrives, possess ye still
Your element; there only can ye shine;
There only minds like yours can do no harm.
Our groves were planted to console at noon   760
The pensive wand'rer in their shades. At eve
The moon-beam, sliding softly in between
The sleeping leaves, is all the light they wish,
Birds warbling all the music. We can spare
The splendour of your lamps; they but eclipse
Our softer satellite. Your songs confound
Our more harmonious notes: the thrush departs
Scar'd, and th' offended nightingale is mute.
There is a public mischief in your mirth;
It plagues your country. Folly such as yours,   770
Grac'd with a sword, and worthier of a fan,
Has made, what enemies could ne'er have done,
Our arch of empire, stedfast but for you,
A mutilated structure, soon to fall.

ON THE RECEIPT OF MY MOTHER'S PICTURE OUT OF NORFOLK

The Gift of My Cousin Ann Bodham

1798

Oh that those lips had language! Life has pass'd
With me but roughly since I heard thee last.
Those lips are thine—thy own sweet smiles I see,
The same that oft in childhood solaced me;
Voice only fails, else, how distinct they say,
"Grieve not, my child, chase all thy fears away!"
The meek intelligence of those dear eyes
(Blest be the art that can immortalize,
The art that baffles time's tyrannic claim
To quench it) here shines on me still the same.　10
　Faithful remembrancer of one so dear,
Oh welcome guest, though unexpected, here!
Who bidd'st me honour with an artless song,
Affectionate, a mother lost so long,
I will obey, not willingly alone,
But gladly, as the precept were her own;
And, while that face renews my filial grief,
Fancy shall weave a charm for my relief—
Shall steep me in Elysian reverie,
A momentary dream, that thou art she.　20
　My mother! when I learn'd that thou wast dead,
Say, wast thou conscious of the tears I shed?
Hover'd thy spirit o'er thy sorrowing son,
Wretch even then, life's journey just begun?
Perhaps thou gav'st me, though unseen, a kiss;
Perhaps a tear, if souls can weep in bliss—
Ah that maternal smile! it answers—Yes.
I heard the bell toll'd on thy burial day,
I saw the hearse that bore thee slow away,
And, turning from my nurs'ry window, drew　30
A long, long sigh, and wept a last adieu!
But was it such?—It was.—Where thou art gone
Adieus and farewells are a sound unknown.
May I but meet thee on that peaceful shore,

The parting sound shall pass my lips no more!
Thy maidens griev'd themselves at my concern,
Oft gave me promise of a quick return.
What ardently I wish'd, I long believ'd,
And, disappointed still, was still deceiv'd;
By disappointment every day beguil'd,   40
Dupe of *to-morrow* even from a child.
Thus many a sad to-morrow came and went,
Till, all my stock of infant sorrow spent,
I learn'd at last submission to my lot;
But, though I less deplor'd thee, ne'er forgot.
   Where once we dwelt our name is heard no more,
Children not thine have trod my nurs'ry floor;
And where the gard'ner Robin, day by day,
Drew me to school along the public way,
Delighted with my bauble coach, and wrapt   50
In scarlet mantle warm, and velvet capt,
'Tis now become a history little known,
That once we call'd the past'ral house our own.
Short-liv'd possession! but the record fair
That mem'ry keeps of all thy kindness there,
Still outlives many a storm that has effac'd
A thousand other themes less deeply trac'd.
Thy nightly visits to my chamber made,
That thou might'st know me safe and warmly laid;
Thy morning bounties ere I left my home,   60
The biscuit, or confectionary plum;
The fragrant waters on my cheeks bestow'd
By thy own hand, till fresh they shone and glow'd;
All this, and more endearing still than all,
Thy constant flow of love, that knew no fall,
Ne'er roughen'd by those cataracts and breaks
That humour interpos'd too often makes;
All this still legible in mem'ry's page,
And still to be so, to my latest age,
Adds joy to duty, makes me glad to pay   70
Such honours to thee as my numbers may;
Perhaps a frail memorial, but sincere,
Not scorn'd in heav'n, though little notic'd here.
   Could time, his flight revers'd, restore the hours,
When, playing with thy vesture's tissued flow'rs,
The violet, the pink, and jessamine,
I prick'd them into paper with a pin,

(And thou wast happier than myself the while,
Would'st softly speak, and stroke my head and smile)
Could those few pleasant hours again appear,   80
Might one wish bring them, would I wish them here?
I would not trust my heart—the dear delight
Seems so to be desir'd, perhaps I might.—
But no—what here we call our life is such,
So little to be lov'd, and thou so much,
That I should ill requite thee to constrain
Thy unbound spirit into bonds again.
   Thou, as a gallant bark from Albion's coast
(The storms all weather'd and the ocean cross'd)
Shoots into port at some well-haven'd isle,   90
Where spices breathe and brighter seasons smile,
There sits quiescent on the floods that show
Her beauteous form reflected clear below,
While airs impregnated with incense play
Around her, fanning light her streamers gay;
So thou, with sails how swift! hast reach'd the shore
"Where tempests never beat nor billows roar," [1]
And thy lov'd consort on the dang'rous tide.
Of life, long since, has anchor'd at thy side.
But me, scarce hoping to attain that rest,   100
Always from port withheld, always distress'd—
Me howling winds drive devious, tempest toss'd,
Sails ript, seams op'ning wide, and compass lost,
And day by day some current's thwarting force
Sets me more distant from a prosp'rous course.
But oh the thought, that thou art safe, and he!
That thought is joy, arrive what may to me.
My boast is not that I deduce my birth
From loins enthron'd, and rulers of the earth;
But higher far my proud pretensions rise—   110
The son of parents pass'd into the skies.
And now, farewell—time, unrevok'd, has run
His wonted course, yet what I wish'd is done.
By contemplation's help, not sought in vain,
I seem t' have liv'd my childhood o'er again;
To have renew'd the joys that once were mine,
Without the sin of violating thine:
And, while the wings of fancy still are free,
And I can view this mimic shew of thee,

1 Samuel Garth *Dispensary* III. 226.

Time has but half succeeded in his theft—   120
Thyself remov'd, thy power to soothe me left.

TO MARY

1803

The twentieth year is well-nigh past
Since first our sky was overcast;
Ah, would that this might be the last,
           My Mary!

Thy spirits have a fainter flow,
I see thee daily weaker grow—
'Twas my distress that brought thee low,
           My Mary!

Thy needles, once a shining store,
For my sake restless heretofore,
Now rust disus'd, and shine no more,
           My Mary.   10

For though thou gladly wouldst fulfil
The same kind office for me still,
Thy sight now seconds not thy will,
           My Mary.

But well thou play'd'st the housewife's part,
And all thy threads with magic art
Have wound themselves about this heart,
           My Mary.   20

Thy indistinct expressions seem
Like language utter'd in a dream,
Yet me they charm, whate'er the theme,
           My Mary.

Thy silver locks, once auburn bright,
Are still more lovely in my sight
Than golden beams of orient light,
           My Mary.

For, could I view nor them nor thee,
What sight worth seeing could I see?   30
The sun would rise in vain for me,
       My Mary!

Partakers of thy sad decline,
Thy hands their little force resign,
Yet, gently prest, press gently mine,
       My Mary.

And then I feel that still I hold
A richer store ten thousandfold
Than misers fancy in their gold,
       My Mary.   40

Such feebleness of limbs thou prov'st
That now at every step thou mov'st
Upheld by two; yet still thou lov'st,
       My Mary!

And still to love, though prest with ill,
In wintry age to feel no chill,
With me is to be lovely still,
       My Mary.

But ah, by constant heed I know
How oft the sadness that I show
Transforms thy smiles to looks of woe,   50
       My Mary.

And should my future lot be cast
With much resemblance of the past,
Thy worn-out heart will break at last,
       My Mary.

Robert Burns (1185-1218)
1759-1796
Dec 13

MORE than a decade before Wordsworth announced that his own
poetry would deal with "incidents and situations from common life,"
Robert Burns had found themes of simple, sure effect in what Mat-

thew Arnold called Scotch drink, Scotch religion, and Scotch manners. This plowman is the only justification of the eighteenth-century hope of finding a poetry of nature. There had been poetical shoemakers, poetical milkwomen, and even poetical washerwomen; but they were all disappointing. Burns, the "heaven-taught" poetical farmer, was not entirely, as the anonymous poem prefacing the first edition of his verses announced, "unbroke by rules of Art." He simply had a gift of song, as did Blake. His range is limited, as his attempts in English verse show, but within this range of hearty friendship and hearty scorn, momentary love, and unsophisticated delight in living, he is unexcelled. This is the range of his experience as a Scottish peasant. His humor is quick and often bitter, and he has a knack of telling a story. All this is not to deny his occasional vulgarity and sentimentalism. Pre-eminently, however, his art is the lyric that suddenly filled the cadences he felt so subtly. It is paradoxical that the eighteenth century should have prepared the way for a poet of nature, and that when this poet of nature came, he was one of the extremely few who do not belong to any century.

BIOGRAPHICAL NOTES

Born at Alloway, Ayrshire, in a two-room cottage, the son of a peasant-farmer, who worked himself to death, bankrupt (1784). Struggle to support the Burns family at Mossgiel Farm, Mauchline Parish, where Burns wrote some early verses mocking Scottish religion. Affair with Elizabeth Paton, who bore Burns a daughter (1785). Affair with Jean Armour, who bore Burns the twins Robert and Jean (1786); her father spurned Burns's offer to marry her. Burns continued to write satires. In need of money, considered emigrating to Jamaica. Printed his poems in Kilmarnock (1786) with success. Death of Mary Campbell, to whom Burns had been attracted. Burns postponed emigration and went to Edinburgh to be feted as "Caledonia's Bard" and to publish a new edition of the poems, by subscription (1787). Toured the Border (1787). Found that patronage fails, but collected and wrote songs for James Johnson's *Scots Musical Museum*. Jean Armour bore him twin daughters (1788). Burns rented a farm in Ellisland, Dumfriesshire (1788) and acknowledged Jean as wife. Friendship with Agnes M'Lehose ("Clarinda") and Maria Riddell. Jenny Clow bore him a child (1788). Appointed exciseman (1789) and moved to Dumfries (1791). Anne Park bore Burns a daughter (1791). Burns began to collect songs for Thomson's *Select Collection of Scottish Airs* (1792). Third edition of poems (1793). Serious ill health (1795) and death from rheumatic fever.

BIBLIOGRAPHY: *Poetry*, ed. W. E. Henley and T. F. Henderson, 4 vols., 1896–97. *Poems and Songs*, ed. J. Barke, 1955. *Letters*, ed. J. de Lancey Ferguson, 2 vols., 1931. Carswell, Catherine, *Life of Robert Burns*, 1930. Crawford, Thomas, *A Study of the Poems and Songs*, 1960. Ferguson, J. de L., *Pride and Passion: Robert Burns*, 1939. Daiches, David, *Robert Burns*, 1950. Lindsay, Maurice, *Burns Encyclopaedia*, 1959; *Robert Burns*, 1954. Snyder, Franklin Bliss, *Life of Robert Burns*, 1932.

THE COTTER'S SATURDAY NIGHT

INSCRIBED TO ROBERT AIKEN, ESQ.[1]

Let not Ambition mock their useful toil,
Their homely joys, and destiny obscure;
Nor Grandeur hear, with a disdainful smile,
The short and simple annals of the poor.
—GRAY.

1786

My lov'd, my honour'd, much respected friend!
No mercenary bard his homage pays;
With honest pride, I scorn each selfish end,
My dearest meed, a friend's esteem and praise.
To you I sing, in simple Scottish lays,
The lowly train in life's sequester'd scene;
The native feelings strong, the guileless ways;
What Aiken in a cottage would have been;
Ah! tho' his worth unknown, far happier there I ween!

November chill blaws loud wi' angry sugh;   10
The short'ning winter day is near a close;
The miry beasts retreating frae the pleugh;
The black'ning trains o' craws to their repose:
The toil-worn cotter frae his labor goes,—
This night his weekly moil is at an end,—
Collects his spades, his mattocks, and his hoes,
Hoping the morn in ease and rest to spend,
And weary, o'er the moor, his course does hameward bend.

At length his lonely cot appears in view,
Beneath the shelter of an aged tree;   20
Th' expectant wee-things, toddlin, stacher through
To meet their dad, wi' flichterin' noise and glee.
His wee bit ingle, blinkin bonilie,
His clean hearth-stane, his thrifty wifie's smile,
The lisping infant, prattling on his knee,

flichterin': fluttering   stacher: stagger

---

1 Robert Aiken, a solicitor, was an old friend of Burns, who called him his "chief patron"; Aiken, he said, "read him into fame" before Burns had published his verse.

Does a' his weary kiaugh and care beguile,
An' makes him quite forget his labor and his toil.

Belyve, the elder bairns come drapping in,
At service out, amang the farmers roun';
Some ca the pleugh, some herd, some tentie rin   30
A cannie errand to a neebor town:
Their eldest hope, their Jenny, woman grown,
In youthfu' bloom, love sparkling in her e'e,
Comes hame; perhaps, to shew a braw new gown,
Or deposite her sair-won penny-fee,
To help her parents dear, if they in hardship be.

With joy unfeign'd, brothers and sisters meet,
And each for other's weelfare kindly spiers:
The social hours, swift-wing'd, unnotic'd fleet;
Each tell the uncos that he sees or hears.   40
The parents partial eye their hopeful years;
Anticipation forward points the view;
The mother, wi' her needle and her sheers,
Gars auld claes look amaist as weel's the new;
The father mixes a' wi' admonition due.

Their master's and their mistress's command
The younkers a' are warned to obey;
And mind their labors wi' an eydent hand,
And ne'er, tho' out o' sight, to jauk or play:
"And O! be sure to fear the Lord alway,   50
And mind your duty, duly, morn and night;
Lest in temptation's path ye gang astray,
Implore his counsel and assisting might:
They never sought in vain that sought the Lord aright."

But hark! a rap comes gently to the door;
Jenny, wha kens the meaning o' the same,
Tells how a neebor lad came o'er the moor,
To do some errands, and convoy her hame.
The wily mother sees the conscious flame
Sparkle in Jenny's e'e, and flush her cheek;   60
With heart-struck anxious care, inquires his name,

belyve: by-and-by	kiaugh: anxiety
ca: drive	spiers: inquires
eydent: diligent	tentie: attentive
gars: makes	uncos: news

While Jenny hafflins is afraid to speak;
Weel-pleas'd the mother hears, it's nae wild, worthless rake.

With kindly welcome, Jenny brings him ben;
A strappin' youth, he takes the mother's eye;
Blythe Jenny sees the visit's no ill taen;
The father cracks of horses, pleughs, and kye.
The youngster's artless heart o'erflows wi' joy,
But blate and laithfu', scarce can weel behave;
The mother, wi' a woman's wiles, can spy
What makes the youth sae bashfu' and sae grave;   70
Weel-pleas'd to think her bairn's respected like the lave.

O happy love! where love like this is found:
O heart-felt raptures! bliss beyond compare!
I've pacèd much this weary, mortal round,
And sage experience bids me this declare:—
"If Heaven a draught of heavenly pleasure spare,
One cordial in this melancholy vale,
'Tis when a youthful, loving, modest pair,
In other's arms, breathe out the tender tale   80
Beneath the milk-white thorn that scents the ev'ning gale."

Is there, in human form, that bears a heart,
A wretch! a villain! lost to love and truth!
That can, with studied, sly, ensnaring art,
Betray sweet Jenny's unsuspecting youth?
Curse on his perjur'd arts! dissembling, smooth!
Are honor, virtue, conscience, all exil'd?
Is there no pity, no relenting ruth,
Points to the parents fondling o'er their child?
Then paints the ruin'd maid, and their distraction wild?   90

But now the supper crowns their simple board,
The healsome porritch, chief o' Scotia's food;
The soupe their only hawkie does afford,
That 'yont the hallan snugly chows her cood;
The dame brings forth, in complimental mood,
To grace the lad, her well-hain'd kebbuck, fell;
And aft he's prest, and aft he ca's it guid;

blate and laithfu': shy and bashful	hallan: partition
cracks: talks	hawkie: cow
fell: strong	kebbuck: cheese
hafflins: half	lave: rest

The frugal wifie, garrulous, will tell,
How 'twas a towmond auld, sin' lint was i' the bell.

The cheerfu' supper done, wi' serious face,   100
They, round the ingle, form a circle wide;
The sire turns o'er, with patriarchal grace,
The big ha'-Bible, ance his father's pride.
His bonnet rev'rently is laid aside,
His lyart haffets wearing thin and bare;
Those strains that once did sweet in Zion glide,
He wales a portion with judicious care,
And, "Let us worship God!" he says, with solemn air.

They chant their artless notes in simple guise,
They tune their hearts, by far the noblest aim;   110
Perhaps *Dundee's* wild-warbling measures rise,
Or plaintive *Martyrs*, worthy of the name;
Or noble *Elgin* beets the heaven-ward flame,
The sweetest far of Scotia's holy lays.
Compar'd with these, Italian trills are tame;
The tickl'd ears no heart-felt raptures raise;
Nae unison hae they, with our Creator's praise.

The priest-like father reads the sacred page,
How Abram was the friend of God on high;
Or Moses bade eternal warfare wage   120
With Amalek's ungracious progeny;
Or, how the royal bard [2] did groaning lie
Beneath the stroke of Heaven's avenging ire;
Or Job's pathetic plaint, and wailing cry;
Or rapt Isaiah's wild, seraphic fire;
Or other holy seers that tune the sacred lyre.

Perhaps the Christian volume is the theme:
How guiltless blood for guilty man was shed;
How he, who bore in Heaven the second name,
Had not on earth whereon to lay his head;   130
How his first followers and servants sped;
The precepts sage they wrote to many a land;
How he, who lone in Patmos banished,[3]

lint was i' the bell: flax was in blossom   wales: chooses
lyart haffets: gray hair   beets: fans

2 David.   3 St. John.

Saw in the sun a mighty angel stand,
And heard great Bab'lon's doom pronounc'd by Heav'n's com-
    mand.

Then kneeling down to Heaven's Eternal King,
The saint, the father, and the husband prays:
Hope "springs exulting on triumphant wing," [4]
That thus they all shall meet in future days,
There, ever bask in uncreated rays,   140
No more to sigh or shed the bitter tear,
Together hymning their Creator's praise,
In such society, yet still more dear;
While circling Time moves round in an eternal sphere.

Compar'd with this, how poor Religion's pride,
In all the pomp of method, and of art;
When men display to congregations wide
Devotion's ev'ry grace, except the heart.
The Power, incens'd, the pageant will desert,
The pompous strain, the sacerdotal stole;   150
But haply, in some cottage far apart,
May hear, well-pleas'd, the language of the soul,
And in his Book of Life the inmates poor enroll.

Then homeward all take off their sev'ral way;
The youngling cottagers retire to rest;
The parent-pair their secret homage pay,
And proffer up to Heaven the warm request,
That He who stills the raven's clam'rous nest,
And decks the lily fair in flow'ry pride,
Would, in the way His wisdom sees the best,   160
For them and for their little ones provide;
But, chiefly, in their hearts with grace divine preside.

From scenes like these, old Scotia's grandeur springs,
That makes her lov'd at home, rever'd abroad:
Princes and lords are but the breath of kings,
"An honest man's the noblest work of God." [5]
And certes, in fair Virtue's heavenly road,
The cottage leaves the palace far behind;
What is a lordling's pomp? a cumbrous load,

4 Pope *Windsor Forest* 112.   5 Pope *Essay on Man* IV. 248.

Disguising oft the wretch of humankind, 170
Studied in arts of hell, in wickedness refin'd!

O Scotia! my dear, my native soil!
For whom my warmest wish to Heaven is sent!
Long may thy hardy sons of rustic toil
Be blest with health, and peace, and sweet content!
And oh! may Heaven their simple lives prevent
From Luxury's contagion, weak and vile!
Then, howe'er crowns and coronets be rent,
A virtuous populace may rise the while,
And stand a wall of fire around their much-lov'd isle. 180

O Thou, who pour'd the patriotic tide,
That stream'd thro' Wallace's undaunted heart,
Who dar'd to, nobly, stem tyrannic pride,
Or nobly die, the second glorious part:
(The patriot's God, peculiarly Thou art,
His friend, inspirer, guardian, and reward!)
Oh never, never Scotia's realm desert;
But still the patriot, and the patriot-bard
In bright succession raise, her ornament and guard!

TO A MOUSE

ON TURNING HER UP IN HER NEST WITH THE PLOUGH, NOVEMBER, 1785
1786

Wee, sleeket, cowrin, tim'rous beastie,
Oh, what a panic's in thy breastie!
Thou need na start awa sae hasty,
   Wi' bickering brattle!
I wad be laith to rin an' chase thee,
   Wi' murdering pattle!

I'm truly sorry man's dominion
Has broken Nature's social union,
An' justifies that ill opinion
   Which makes thee startle 10
At me, thy poor, earth-born companion,
   An' fellow mortal!

bickering brattle: hasty scamper   pattle: plow-staff

I doubt na, whyles, but thou may thieve;
What then? Poor beastie, thou maun live!
A daimen icker in a thrave
    'S a sma' request:
I'll get a blessin wi' the lave,
    An' never miss't!

Thy wee-bit housie, too, in ruin!
Its silly wa's the win's are strewin!   20
An' naething, now, to big a new ane,
    O' foggage green!
An' bleak December's win's ensuin,
    Baith snell an' keen!

Thou saw the fields laid bare an' wast,
An' weary winter comin fast,
An' cozie here, beneath the blast,
    Thou thought to dwell,
Till crash! the cruel coulter past
    Out thro' thy cell.   30

That wee-bit heap o' leaves an' stibble,
Has cost thee monie a weary nibble!
Now thou's turn'd out, for a' thy trouble,
    But house or hald,
To thole the winter's sleety dribble,
    An' cranreuch cauld!

But, Mousie, thou art no thy lane,
In proving foresight may be vain:
The best-laid schemes o' mice an' men
    Gang aft agley,   40
An' lea'e us nought but grief an' pain,
    For promis'd joy!

Still thou are blest, compar'd wi' me!
The present only toucheth thee:
But och! I backward cast my e'e,
    On prospects drear!
An' forward, tho' I canna see,
    I guess an' fear!

agley: awry	foggage: grass
cranreuch: frost	snell: sharp
daimen icker in a thrave: occasional ear in a	thole: suffer
shock	

EPITAPH ON A HENPECKED SQUIRE

1786

As father Adam first was fool'd,
A case that's still too common,
Here lies a man a woman rul'd:
The Devil ruled the woman.

TO A MOUNTAIN DAISY

ON TURNING ONE DOWN WITH THE PLOUGH IN APRIL, 1786

1786

Wee, modest, crimson-tipped flow'r,
Thou's met me in an evil hour;
For I maun crush amang the stoure
  Thy slender stem:
To spare thee now is past my pow'r,
  Thou bonie gem.

Alas! it's no thy neebor sweet,
The bonie lark, companion meet,
Bending thee 'mang the dewy weet,
  Wi' spreckl'd breast!   10
When upward-springing, blythe, to greet
  The purpling east.

Cauld blew the bitter-biting north
Upon thy early, humble birth;
Yet cheerfully thou glinted forth
  Amid the storm,
Scarce rear'd above the parent-earth
  Thy tender form.

The flaunting flow'rs our gardens yield,
High shelt'ring woods and wa's maun shield; 20
But thou, beneath the random bield

bield: shelter   stoure: dust

O' clod or stane,
Adorns the histie stibble-field,
                    Unseen, alane.

There, in thy scanty mantle clad,
Thy snawie bosom sun-ward spread,
Thou lifts thy unassuming head
                    In humble guise;
But now the share uptears thy bed,
                    And low thou lies!   30

Such is the fate of artless maid,
Sweet flow'ret of the rural shade!
By love's simplicity betray'd,
                    And guileless trust;
Till she, like thee, all soil'd, is laid
                    Low i' the dust.

Such is the fate of simple bard,
On life's rough ocean, luckless starr'd!
Unskillful he to note the card
                    Of prudent lore,
Till billows rage, and gales blow hard,   40
                    And whelm him o'er!

Such fate to suffering Worth is giv'n,
Who long with wants and woes has striv'n,
By human pride or cunning driv'n
                    To mis'ry's brink;
Till, wrench'd of ev'ry stay but Heav'n,
                    He, ruin'd, sink!

Ev'n thou who mourn'st the daisy's fate,
That fate is thine—no distant date;
Stern Ruin's ploughshare drives elate,   50
                    Full on thy bloom,
Till crush'd beneath the furrow's weight
                    Shall be thy doom!

histie: bare

TO A LOUSE

ON SEEING ONE ON A LADY'S BONNET AT CHURCH

1786

Ha! whare ye gaun, ye crowlin ferlie?
Your impudence protects you sairly:
I canna say but ye strunt rarely
　　　Owre gauze and lace;
Tho', faith! I fear ye dine but sparely
　　　On sic a place.

Ye ugly, creepin, blastet wonner,
Detested, shunn'd by saunt an' sinner,
How daur ye set your fit upon her—
　　　Sae fine a lady!
Gae somewhere else, and seek your dinner
　　　On some poor body.

Swith! in some beggar's hauffet squattle;
There ye may creep, and sprawl, and sprattle,
Wi' ither kindred, jumping cattle,
　　　In shoals and nations;
Whare horn nor bane ne'er daur unsettle
　　　Your thick plantations.

Now haud you there! ye're out o' sight,
Below the fatt'rels, snug an' tight;
Na, faith ye yet! ye'll no be right
　　　Till ye've got on it—
The vera tapmost, tow'rin height
　　　O' Miss's bonnet.

My sooth! right bauld ye set your nose out,
As plump an' gray as onie grozet:
O for some rank, mercurial rozet,
　　　Or fell, red smeddum,

10

20

blastet wonner: blasted wonder	rozet: rosin
crowlin ferlie: crawling marvel	smeddum: powder
fatt'rels: trimmings	sairly: well
fit: foot	sprattle: struggle
grozet: gooseberry	strunt: strut
hauffet: temple	swith: quick

I'd gie you sic a hearty dose o't,
    Wad dress your droddum.   30

I wad na been surpris'd to spy
You on an auld wife's flainen toy;
Or aiblins some bit duddie boy,
    On's wyliecoat;
But Miss's fine Lunardi! fye!
    How daur ye do't?

O Jenny, dinna toss your head,
An' set your beauties a' abroad!
Ye little ken what cursed speed
    The blastie's makin!   40
Thae winks an' finger-ends, I dread,
    Are notice takin!

O wad some Power the giftie gie us
To see oursels as ithers see us!
It wad frae monie a blunder free us,
    An' foolish notion:
What airs in dress an' gait wad lea'e us,
    An' ev'n devotion!

EPISTLE TO J. LAPRAIK

AN OLD SCOTTISH BARD

April 1, 1785

1786

While briers an' woodbines budding green,
And paitricks scraichin loud at e'en,
An' morning poussie whiddin seen,
    Inspire my Muse,
This freedom, in an unknown frien'
    I pray excuse.

aiblins: perhaps	flainen: flannel
blastie: wretch	Lunardi: balloon bonnet
droddum: breech	paitricks scraichin: partridges screeching
duddie: ragged	poussie whiddin: hare scampering

On Fasten-e'en we had a rockin,
To ca' the crack and weave our stockin;
And there was muckle fun and jokin,
  Ye need na doubt;
At length we had a hearty yokin,
  At *sang about*.

There was ae sang, amang the rest,
Aboon them a' it pleas'd me best,
That some kind husband had addrest
  To some sweet wife;
It thirl'd the heart-strings thro' the breast,
  A' to the life.

I've scarce heard ought describ'd sae weel,
What gen'rous, manly bosoms feel;
Thought I, "Can this be Pope, or Steele,
  Or Beattie's wark?"
They tauld me 'twas an odd kind chiel
  About Muirkirk.

It pat me fidgin-fain to hear't,
An' sae about him there I spier't;
Then a' that kent him round declar'd
  He had ingine;
That nane excell'd it, few cam near't,
  It was sae fine.

That, set him to a pint of ale,
An' either douce or merry tale,
Or rhymes an' sangs he'd made himsel,
  Or witty catches—
'Tween Inverness an' Teviotdale,
  He had few matches.

Then up I gat, an' swoor an aith,
Tho' I should pawn my pleugh an' graith,

ca' the crack: gossip	ingine: genius
chiel: fellow	rockin: gathering
douce: sad	spier't: asked
Fasten-e'en: evening before Lent	thirl'd: thrilled
fidgin-fain: fidgeting	yokin: bout
graith: gear	

Or die a cadger pownie's death,
          At some dyke-back,   40
A pint an' gill I'd gie them baith,
          To hear your crack.

But, first an' foremost, I should tell,
Amaist as soon as I could spell,
I to the crambo-jingle fell;
          Tho' rude an' rough—
Yet crooning to a body's sel
          Does weel eneugh.

I am nae poet, in a sense,
But just a rhymer like by chance,   50
An' hae to learning nae pretense;
          Yet, what the matter?
Whene'er my Muse does on me glance,
          I jingle at her.

Your critic-folk may cock their nose,
And say, "How can you e'er propose,
You wha ken hardly verse frae prose,
          To mak a sang?"
But, by your leaves, my learned foes,
          Ye're maybe wrang.   60

What's a' your jargon o' your schools,
Your Latin names for horns an' stools?
If honest Nature made you fools,
          What sairs your grammars?
Ye'd better ta'en up spades and shools,
          Or knappin-hammers.

A set o' dull, conceited hashes
Confuse their brains in college classes,
They gang in stirks, and come out asses,
          Plain truth to speak;   70
An syne they think to climb Parnassus
          By dint o' Greek!

cadger pownie's: hawker pony's	knappin-hammers: tonebreakers' hammers
crambo-jingle: rhyme	sairs: serves
dyke-back: wall	stirks: bullocks
hashes: dunces	

Gie me ae spark o' Nature's fire!
That's a' the learning I desire;
Then, tho' I drudge thro' dub an' mire
    At pleugh or cart,
My Muse, tho' hamely in attire,
    May touch the heart.

O for a spunk o' Allan's [1] glee,
Or Fergusson's, the bauld an' slee,
Or bright Lapraik's, my friend to be,
    If I can hit it!
That would be lear eneugh for me,
    If I could get it.

Now, Sir, if ye hae friends enow,
Tho' real friends, I b'lieve, are few;
Yet, if your catalogue be fow,
    I'se no insist:
But, gif ye want ae friend that's true,
    I'm on your list.

I winna blaw about mysel,
As ill I like my fauts to tell;
But friends, an' folk that wish me well,
    They sometimes roose me;
Tho' I maun own, as monie still
    As far abuse me.

There's ae wee faut they whyles lay to me,
I like the lasses—Gude forgie me!
For monie a plack they wheedle frae me
    At dance or fair;
Maybe some ither thing they gie me,
    They weel can spare.

80

90

100

dub: puddle   roose: flatter
fow: full   slee: sly
plack: coin

1 Allan Ramsay (1686–1758), Edinburgh wig-maker, bookseller, and poet, who had printed *The Tea-Table Miscellany* and *The Evergreen*, collections of traditional Scottish and English songs; he also wrote *The Gentle Shepherd*, a pastoral drama. He was an important influence in reviving Scottish vernacular poetry. Robert Fergusson (1750–1774), mentioned in the following line, was another writer of Scottish lyrics before Burns.

But Mauchline Race, or Mauchline Fair,
I should be proud to meet you there;
We'se gie ae night's discharge to care,
  If we forgather;
And hae a swap o' rhymin-ware
  Wi' ane anither.

The four-gill chap, we'se gar him clatter,
An' kirsen him wi' reekin water;   110
Syne we'll sit down an' tak our whitter,
  To cheer our heart;
An' faith, we'se be acquainted better
  Before we part.

Awa, ye selfish, warly race,
Wha think that havins, sense, an' grace,
Ev'n love an' friendship, should give place
  To catch-the-plack!
I dinna like to see your face,
  Nor hear your crack.   120

But ye whom social pleasure charms,
Whose hearts the tide of kindness warms,
Who hold your being on the terms,
  "Each aid the others,"
Come to my bowl, come to my arms,
  My friends, my brothers!

But, to conclude my lang epistle,
As my auld pen's worn to the grissle,
Twa lines frae you wad gar me fissle,
  Who am most fervent,   130
While I can either sing or whistle,
  Your friend and servant.

catch-the-plack: money-grubbing	reekin: steaming
fissle: tingle	warly: worldly
kirsen: christen	whitter: drink

ADDRESS TO THE UNCO GUID,
OR THE RIGIDLY RIGHTEOUS

My Son, these maxims make a rule,
An' lump them ay thegither:
The Rigid Righteous is a fool,
The Rigid Wise anither;
The cleanest corn that e'er was dight
May hae some pyles o' caff in;
So ne'er a fellow-creature slight
For random fits o' daffin.
              SOLOMON.—*Eccles.*, vii, 16.

1787

O ye who are sae guid yoursel,
  Sae pious and sae holy,
Ye've nought to do but mark and tell
  Your neebors' fauts and folly;
Whase life is like a weel-gaun mill,
  Supplied wi' store o' water;
The heaped happer's ebbing still,
  An' still the clap plays clatter!

Hear me, ye venerable core,
  As counsel for poor mortals   10
That frequent pass douce Wisdom's door
  For glaiket Folly's portals;
I, for their thoughtless, careless sakes,
  Would here propone defenses—
Their donsie tricks, their black mistakes,
  Their failings and mischances.

Ye see your state wi' theirs compar'd,
  And shudder at the niffer,
But cast a moment's fair regard,
  What makes the mighty differ?   20

clap: clapper
daffin: fun
dight: threshed
donsie: vicious
douce: grave

glaiket: giddy
happer's: hopper's
niffer: exchange
pyles o' caff: grains of chaff

Discount what scant occasion gave,
   That purity ye pride in,
And (what's aft mair than a' the lave)
   Your better art o' hidin.

Think, when your castigated pulse
   Gies now and then a wallop,
What ragings must his veins convulse,
   That still eternal gallop!
Wi' wind and tide fair i' your tail,
   Right on ye scud your sea-way;   30
But in the teeth o' baith to sail,
   It makes an unco lee-way.

See Social-life and Glee sit down,
   All joyous and unthinking,
Till, quite transmugrify'd, they're grown
   Debauchery and Drinking:
Oh would they stay to calculate
   Th' eternal consequences,
Or—your more dreadful hell to state—
   Damnation of expences!   40

Ye high, exalted, virtuous dames,
   Tied up in godly laces,
Before ye gie poor Frailty names,
   Suppose a change o' cases;
A dear-lov'd lad, convenience snug,
   A treach'rous inclination—
But, let me whisper i' your lug,
   Ye're aiblins nae temptation.

Then gently scan your brother man,
   Still gentler sister woman;   50
Tho' they may gang a kennin wrang,
   To step aside is human:
One point must still be greatly dark,
   The moving *why* they do it;
And just as lamely can ye mark
   How far perhaps they rue it.

aiblins: perhaps   lug: ear
kennin: trifle   unco: remarkable

Who made the heart, 'tis He alone
    Decidedly can try us;
He knows each chord, its various tone,
    Each spring, its various bias: 60
Then at the balance let's be mute,
    We never can adjust it;
What's done we partly may compute,
    But know not what's resisted.

GREEN GROW THE RASHES, O

1787

CHORUS

Green grow the rashes, O;
    Green grow the rashes, O;
The sweetest hours that e'er I spend,
    Are spent amang the lasses, O.

There's nought but care on ev'ry han',
    In ev'ry hour that passes, O:
What signifies the life o' man,
    An' 'twere na for the lasses, O?

The war'ly race may riches chase,
    An' riches still may fly them, O;   10
An' tho' at last they catch them fast,
    Their hearts can ne'er enjoy them, O.

But gie me a cannie hour at e'en,
    My arms about my dearie, O:
An' war'ly cares, an' war'ly men,
    May a' gae tapsalteerie, O.

For you sae douce, ye sneer at this,
    Ye're nought but senseless asses, O:
The wisest man the warl' e'er saw,
    He dearly lov'd the lasses, O.   20

cannie: quiet   tapsalteerie: topsy-turvy
douce: grave   war'ly: worldly
rashes: rushes

Auld Nature swears, the lovely dears
Her noblest work she classes, O:
Her prentice han' she tried on man,
An' then she made the lasses, O.

CHORUS

Green grow the rashes, O;
Green grow the rashes, O;
The sweetest hours that e'er I spend,
Are spent amang the lasses, O.

WHISTLE O'ER THE LAVE O'T

1790

First when Maggie was my care,
Heav'n, I thought, was in her air;
Now we're married—spier nae mair—
But—whistle o'er the lave o't!

Meg was meek, and Meg was mild,
Sweet and harmless as a child:
Wiser men than me's beguil'd—
Whistle o'er the lave o't!

How we live, my Meg and me,
How we love, and how we gree,
I care na by how few may see—
Whistle o'er the lave o't!

Wha I wish were maggots' meat,
Dish'd up in her winding-sheet,
I could write (but Meg wad see't)—
Whistle o'er the lave o't!

lave: rest   spier: ask

THOU LINGERING STAR

1790

Thou ling'ring star with less'ning ray,
   That lov'st to greet the early morn,
Again thou usher'st in the day
   My Mary from my soul was torn.
O Mary, dear departed shade!
   Where is thy place of blissful rest?
See'st thou thy lover lowly laid?
   Hear'st thou the groans that rend his breast?

That sacred hour can I forget,
   Can I forget the hallow'd grove,   10
Where, by the winding Ayr, we met
   To live one day of parting love?
Eternity cannot efface
   Those records dear of transports past,
Thy image at our last embrace—
   Ah! little thought we 'twas our last!

Ayr, gurgling, kiss'd his pebbled shore,
   O'erhung with wild woods, thick'ning green;
The fragrant birch and hawthorn hoar
   Twin'd am'rous round the raptur'd scene;   20
The flowers sprang wanton to be prest,
   The birds sang love on every spray,
Till too, too soon, the glowing west
   Proclaim'd the speed of winged day.

Still o'er these scenes my mem'ry wakes
   And fondly broods with miser-care.
Time but th' impression stronger makes,
   As streams their channels deeper wear.
O Mary, dear departed shade!
   Where is thy place of blissful rest?   30
See'st thou thy lover lowly laid?
   Hear'st thou the groans that rend his breast?

TAM O' SHANTER

A TALE

Of Brownyis and of Bogillis full is this Buke.
—GAWIN DOUGLAS.

1791

When chapman billies leave the street,
And drouthy neebors neebors meet;
As market-days are wearin late,
An' folk begin to tak the gate;
While we sit bousing at the nappy,
An' gettin' fou and unco happy,
We think na on the lang Scots miles,
The mosses, waters, slaps, and stiles,
That lie between us and our hame,
Whare sits our sulky, sullen dame,   10
Gathering her brows like gathering storm,
Nursing her wrath to keep it warm.
   This truth fand honest Tam o' Shanter,
As he frae Ayr ae night did canter:
(Auld Ayr, wham ne'er a town surpasses,
For honest men and bonie lasses).
   O Tam, hadst thou but been sae wise,
As taen thy ain wife Kate's advice!
She tauld thee weel thou was a skellum,
A blethering, blustering, drunken blellum;   20
That frae November till October,
Ae market-day thou was nae sober;
That ilka melder wi' the miller,
Thou sat as lang as thou had siller;
That ev'ry naig was ca'd a shoe on,
The smith and thee gat roaring fou on;
That at the Lord's house, ev'n on Sunday,
Thou drank wi' Kirkton Jean till Monday.
She prophesied that, late or soon,

blellum: babbler
ca'd: driven
chapman billies: pedlar fellows
ilka: each
melder: milling

nappy: ale
skellum: rascal
slaps: gaps in fences
unco: extremely

Thou would be found deep drown'd in Doon,   30
Or catch'd wi' warlocks in the mirk
By Alloway's auld, haunted kirk.
   Ah, gentle dames! it gars me greet
To think how monie counsels sweet,
How monie lengthen'd, sage advices,
The husband frae the wife despises!
   But to our tale:—Ae market-night,
Tam had got planted unco right,
Fast by an ingle, bleezing finely,
Wi' reaming swats, that drank divinely;   40
And at his elbow, Souter Johnie,
His ancient, trusty, drouthy cronie;
Tam lo'ed him like a very brither;
They had been fou for weeks thegither.
The night drave on wi' sangs and clatter;
And ay the ale was growing better:
The landlady and Tam grew gracious
Wi' secret favours, sweet and precious:
The Souter tauld his queerest stories;
The landlord's laugh was ready chorus: 50
The storm without might rair and rustle,
Tam did na mind the storm a whistle.
   Care, mad to see a man sae happy,
E'en drown'd himsel amang the nappy.
As bees flee hame wi' lades o' treasure,
The minutes wing'd their way wi' pleasure:
Kings may be blest, but Tam was glorious,
O'er a' the ills o' life victorious!
   But pleasures are like poppies spread;
You seize the flow'r, its bloom is shed;   60
Or like the snow falls in the river,
A moment white—then melts forever;
Or like the borealis race,
That flit ere you can point their place;
Or like the rainbow's lovely form
Evanishing amid the storm.
Nae man can tether time or tide;
The hour approaches Tam maun ride:
That hour, o' night's black arch the key-stane,
That dreary hour Tam mounts his beast in;   70

gars: makes   reaming swats: frothing ale
greet: weep   Souter: cobbler

And sic a night he taks the road in,
As ne'er poor sinner was abroad in.

The wind blew as 'twad blawn its last;
The rattling show'rs rose on the blast;
The speedy gleams the darkness swallow'd;
Loud, deep, and lang the thunder bellow'd:
That night, a child might understand,
The Deil had business on his hand.

Weel mounted on his gray mare, Meg,
A better never lifted leg,   80
Tam skelpet on thro' dub and mire,
Despising wind, and rain, and fire;
Whiles holding fast his guid blue bonnet,
Whiles crooning o'er some auld Scots sonnet,
Whiles glow'ring round wi' prudent cares,
Lest bogles catch him unawares;
Kirk-Alloway was drawing nigh,
Where ghaists and houlets nightly cry.

By this time he was cross the ford,
Whare in the snaw the chapman smoor'd;   90
And past the birks and meikle stane,
Whare drunken Charlie brak's neck-bane;
And thro' the whins, and by the cairn,
Whare hunters fand the murder'd bairn;
And near the thorn, aboon the well,
Whare Mungo's mither hang'd hersel.
Before him Doon pours all his floods;
The doubling storm roars thro' the woods;
The lightnings flash from pole to pole;
Near and more near the thunders roll: 100
When, glimm'ring thro' the groaning trees,
Kirk-Alloway seem'd in a bleeze,
Thro' ilka bore the beams were glancing,
And loud resounded mirth and dancing.

Inspiring bold John Barleycorn,
What dangers thou canst make us scorn!
Wi' tippenny, we fear nae evil;
Wi' usquabae, we'll face the Devil!
The swats sae ream'd in Tammie's noddle,

bogles: hobgoblins   skelpet: clattered
bore: crack   smoor'd: smothered
dub: puddle   usquabae: whiskey
houlets: owls   whins: furze

Fair play, he car'd na deils a boddle.   110
But Maggie stood, right sair astonish'd,
Till, by the heel and hand admonish'd,
She ventur'd forward on the light;
And, vow! Tam saw an unco sight!
    Warlocks and witches in a dance:
Nae cotillion, brent new frae France,
But hornpipes, jigs, strathspeys, and reels,
Put life and mettle in their heels.
At winnock-bunker in the east,
There sat Auld Nick, in shape o' beast;   120
A tousie tyke, black, grim, and large,
To gie them music was his charge;
He screw'd the pipes and gart them skirl,
Till roof and rafters a' did dirl.
Coffins stood round, like open presses,
That shaw'd the dead in their last dresses;
And, by some devilish cantraip sleight,
Each in its cauld hand held a light:
By which heroic Tam was able
To note upon the haly table   130
A murderer's banes in gibbet-airns;
Twa span-lang, wee, unchristen'd bairns;
A thief, new-cutted frae a rape—
Wi' his last gasp his gab did gape;
Five tomahawks, wi' bluid red-rusted;
Five scymitars, wi' murder crusted;
A garter which a babe had strangled;
A knife a father's throat had mangled—
Whom his ain son o' life bereft—
The gray-hairs yet stack to the heft;   140
Wi' mair o' horrible an' awefu',
Which ev'n to name wad be unlawfu'.
    As Tammie glowr'd, amaz'd, and curious,
The mirth and fun grew fast and furious:
The piper loud and louder blew,
The dancers quick and quicker flew,
They reel'd, they set, they cross'd, they cleeket,

boddle: twopence
brent: bright
cantraip sleight: magic trick
cleeket: joined hands
dirl: rattle

gab: mouth
skirl: scream
tousie tyke: shaggy cur
winnock-bunker: window-seat

Till ilka carlin swat and reeket,
And coost her duddies to the wark,
And linket at it in her sark!   150
    Now, Tam, O Tam, had thae been queans,
A' plump and strapping in their teens!
Their sarks, instead o' cresshie flannen,
Been snaw-white seventeen hunder linen! [1]
Thir breeks o' mine, my only pair,
That ance were plush, o' guid blue hair,
I wad hae gi'en them aff my hurdies,
For ae blink o' the bonie burdies!
    But wither'd beldams, auld and droll,
Rigwoodie hags wad spean a foal,   160
Louping and flinging on a crummock,
I wonder did na turn thy stomach!
    But Tam kend what was what fu' brawlie:
There was ae winsome wench and wawlie,
That night enlisted in the core,
Lang after kend on Carrick shore
(For monie a beast to dead she shot,
An' perish'd monie a bonie boat,
And shook baith meikle corn and bear,
And kept the country-side in fear),   170
Her cutty sark, o' Paisley harn,
That while a lassie she had worn,
In longitude tho' sorely scanty,
It was her best, and she was vauntie.
Ah! little kend thy reverend grannie,
That sark she coft for her wee Nannie,
Wi' twa pund Scots ('twas a' her riches),
Wad ever grac'd a dance of witches!
    But here my Muse her wing maun cour;
Sic flights are far beyond her pow'r!   180
To sing how Nannie lap and flang
(A souple jad she was, and strang),

bear: barley	duddies: clothes
brawlie: finely	harn: coarse cloth
breeks: breeches	hurdies: buttocks
carlin: hag	linket: danced
coft: bought	rigwoodie: lean
coost: threw out	sark: shirt
cresshie: greasy	spean: wean
crummock: staff	wawlie: jolly
cutty: short	vauntie: proud

1 Finely woven linen with 1,700 threads to the width.

And how Tam stood like ane bewitch'd,
And thought his very een enrich'd;
Even Satan glowr'd, and fidg'd fu' fain,
And hotch'd and blew wi' might and main:
Till first ae caper, syne anither,
Tam tint his reason a' thegither,
And roars out: "Weel done, Cutty-sark!"
And in an instant all was dark;   190
And scarcely had he Maggie rallied,
When out the hellish legion sallied.

    As bees bizz out wi' angry fyke,
When plundering herds assail their byke;
As open pussie's mortal foes,
When, pop! she starts before their nose;
As eager runs the market-crowd,
When "Catch the thief!" resounds aloud:
So Maggie runs, the witches follow,
Wi' monie an eldritch skriech and hollo.   200

    Ah, Tam! ah, Tam! thou'lt get thy fairin!
In hell they'll roast thee like a herrin!
In vain thy Kate awaits thy comin!
Kate soon will be a woefu' woman!
Now, do thy speedy utmost, Meg,
And win the key-stane of the brig;
There, at them thou thy tail may toss,
A running stream they dare na cross.
But ere the key-stane she could make,
The fient a tail she had to shake;   210
For Nannie, far before the rest,
Hard upon noble Maggie prest,
And flew at Tam wi' furious ettle;
But little wist she Maggie's mettle!
Ae spring brought off her master hale,
But left behind her ain gray tail:
The carlin claught her by the rump,
And left poor Maggie scarce a stump.

    Now, wha this tale o' truth shall read,
Ilk man and mother's son take heed: 220
Whene'er to drink you are inclin'd,
Or cutty sarks run in your mind,

byke: hive	fient a tail: devil a tail
eldritch: ghastly	fyke: bustle
ettle: intent	hotch'd: jerked
fairin: reward	pussie's: hare's
fidg'd: fidgeted	tint: lost

Think! ye may buy the joys o'er dear,
Remember Tam o' Shanter's mare.

AE FOND KISS

1792

Ae fond kiss, and then we sever!
Ae farewell, and then forever!
Deep in heart-wrung tears I'll pledge thee,
Warring sighs and groans I'll wage thee.
Who shall say that Fortune grieves him
While the star of hope she leaves him?
Me, nae cheerfu' twinkle lights me;
Dark despair around benights me.

I'll ne'er blame my partial fancy,
Naething could resist my Nancy: 10
But to see her was to love her;
Love but her, and love forever.
Had we never lov'd sae kindly,
Had we never lov'd sae blindly,
Never met—or never parted—
We had ne'er been broken-hearted.

Fare thee weel, thou first and fairest!
Fare thee weel, thou best and dearest!
Thine be ilka joy and treasure,
Peace, enjoyment, love, and pleasure!   20
Ae fond kiss, and then we sever;
Ae farewell, alas, forever!
Deep in heart-wrung tears I'll pledge thee,
Warring sighs and groans I'll wage thee!

ilka: each

THE BANKS O' DOON

1792

Ye banks and braes o' bonie Doon,
  How can ye bloom sae fresh and fair;
How can ye chant, ye little birds,
  And I sae weary fu' o' care!
Thou'll break my heart, thou warbling bird,
  That wantons thro' the flowering thorn:
Thou minds me o' departed joys,
  Departed never to return.

Aft hae I rov'd by bonie Doon,
  To see the rose and woodbine twine;   10
And ilka bird sang o' its luve,
  And fondly sae did I o' mine.
Wi' lightsome heart I pu'd a rose,
  Fu' sweet upon its thorny tree;
And my fause lover staw my rose,
  But, ah! he left the thorn wi' me.

staw: stole

SCOTS, WHA HAE

1794

Scots, wha hae wi' Wallace bled,
Scots, wham Bruce has aften led,
Welcome to your gory bed,
      Or to victorie!

Now's the day, and now's the hour;
See the front o' battle lour;
See approach proud Edward's [1] pow'r—
      Chains and slaverie!

1 Edward II in 1314 was routed at Bannockburn by the Scottish forces under Bruce.

Wha will be a traitor knave?
Wha can fill a coward's grave?
Wha sae base as be a slave?—
    Let him turn and flee!

Wha for Scotland's king and law
Freedom's sword will strongly draw,
Freeman stand, or freeman fa',
    Let him follow me!

By Oppression's woes and pains,
By your sons in servile chains,
We will drain our dearest veins,
    But they shall be free!   20

Lay the proud usurpers low!
Tyrants fall in every foe!
Liberty's in every blow!
    Let us do or die!

IS THERE FOR HONEST POVERTY

1795

Is there for honest poverty,
    That hings his head, an' a' that?
The coward slave, we pass him by—
    We dare be poor for a' that!
For a' that, an' a' that,
    Our toil's obscure, an' a' that,
The rank is but the guinea's stamp,
    The man's the gowd for a' that.

What though on hamely fare we dine,
    Wear hoddin gray, an' a' that?   10
Gie fools their silks, and knaves their wine—
    A man's a man for a' that!
For a' that, an' a' that,
    Their tinsel show, an' a' that,

gowd: gold   hoddin: coarse cloth

The honest man, tho' e'er sae poor,
    Is king o' men for a' that.

Ye see yon birkie, ca'd a lord,
    Wha struts, an' stares, an' a' that?
Tho' hundreds worship at his word,
    He's but a cuif for a' that: 20
For a' that, an' a' that,
    His ribband, star, an' a' that,
The man o' independent mind,
    He looks an' laughs at a' that.

A prince can mak a belted knight,
    A marquis, duke, an' a' that;
But an honest man's aboon his might—
    Guid faith, he mauna fa' that!
For a' that, an' a' that,
    Their dignities, an' a' that,   30
The pith o' sense, and pride o' worth,
    Are higher rank than a' that.

Then let us pray that come it may,
    (As come it will for a' that)
That sense and worth, o'er a' the earth,
    Shall bear the gree an' a' that!
For a' that, an' a' that,
    It's comin yet for a' that,
That man to man, the world o'er,
    Shall brithers be for a' that!   40

birkie: fellow   gree: prize
cuif: ninny   mauna: must not

A RED, RED ROSE

1796

Oh my luve is like a red, red rose,
    That's newly sprung in June;
Oh my luve is like the melodie,
    That's sweetly play'd in tune.

As fair art thou, my bonie lass,
　So deep in luve am I;
And I will luve thee still, my dear,
　Till a' the seas gang dry.

Till a' the seas gang dry, my dear,
　And the rocks melt wi' the sun;
And I will luve thee still, my dear,
　While the sands o' life shall run.

And fare thee weel, my only luve,
　And fare thee weel a while!
And I will come again, my luve,
　Tho' it were ten thousand mile!

HIGHLAND MARY

1799

Ye banks and braes and streams around
　The castle o' Montgomery,
Green be your woods, and fair your flowers,
　Your waters never drumlie!
There Summer first unfald her robes,
　And there the langest tarry;
For there I took the last fareweel,
　O' my sweet Highland Mary.

How sweetly bloom'd the gay, green birk,
　How rich the hawthorn's blossom,
As underneath their fragrant shade
　I clasp'd her to my bosom!
The golden hours on angel wings,
　Flew o'er me and my dearie;
For dear to me as light and life,
　Was my sweet Highland Mary.

Wi' monie a vow and lock'd embrace
　Our parting was fu' tender;
And, pledging aft to meet again,
　We tore oursels asunder.

birk: birch　　　　　　drumlie: muddy

But oh, fell Death's untimely frost,
    That nipt my flower sae early!
Now green's the sod, and cauld's the clay,
    That wraps my Highland Mary!

Oh pale, pale now, those rosy lips
    I aft hae kiss'd sae fondly;
And clos'd for aye the sparkling glance
    That dwalt on me sae kindly;
And mold'ring now in silent dust,
    That heart that lo'ed me dearly!
But still within my bosom's core   30
    Shall live my Highland Mary.

YE FLOWERY BANKS

1808

Ye flowery banks o' bonie Doon,
    How can ye blume sae fair;
How can ye chant, ye little birds,
    And I sae fu' o' care!

Thou'll break my heart, thou bonie bird,
    That sings upon the bough;
Thou minds me o' the happy days
    When my fause luve was true.

Thou'll break my heart, thou bonie bird,
    That sings beside thy mate;   10
For sae I sat, and sae I sang,
    And wist na o' my fate.

Aft hae I rov'd by bonie Doon,
    To see the woodbine twine,
And ilka bird sang o' its luve,
    And sae did I o' mine.

Wi' lightsome heart I pu'd a rose,
    Frae aff its thorny tree;
And my fause luver staw my rose,
    But left the thorn wi' me.   20

fause: false   staw: stole

A SELECTION

Adam Smith

1723–1790

[Smith never intended that his *Wealth of Nations* should be taken alone; he evidently believed that the tendency to "truck, barter, and exchange" in man is counteracted by "sympathy." The nineteenth century, however, disregarded the *Theory* and proceeded to divorce "business" from the ethics of pity, or "benevolence," with what consequences the twentieth century has observed.]

THE THEORY OF MORAL SENTIMENTS

1759

How selfish soever man may be supposed, there are evidently some principles in his nature which interest him in the fortune of others, and render their happiness necessary to him, though he derives nothing from it except the pleasure of seeing it. Of this kind is pity or compassion, the emotion which we feel for the misery of others when we see it or are made to conceive it in a very lively manner. That we often derive sorrow from the sorrow of others is a matter of fact too obvious to require any instances to prove it; for this sentiment, like all the other original passions of human nature, is by no means confined to the virtuous and humane, though they perhaps may feel it with the most exquisite sensibility. The greatest ruffian, the most hardened violator of the laws of society, is not altogether without it.

[PART I, section i, chap. 1]

AN INQUIRY INTO THE NATURE AND CAUSES OF THE WEALTH OF NATIONS

1776

Of the Principle which Gives Occasion to the Division of Labor

THIS division of labor from which so many advantages are derived is not originally the effect of any human wisdom, which foresees and intends that general opulence to which it gives occasion. It is the necessary, though very slow and gradual, consequence of a certain propensity in human nature which has in view no such extensive utility; the propensity to truck, barter, and exchange one thing for another.

Whether this propensity be one of those original principles in human nature of which no further account can be given, or whether, as seems more probable, it be the necessary consequence of the faculties of reason and speech, it belongs not to our present subject to inquire. It is common to all men, and to be found in no other race of animals, which seem to know neither this nor any other species of contracts. Two greyhounds in running down the same hare have sometimes the appearance of acting in some sort of concert. Each turns her towards his companion, or endeavors to intercept her when his companion turns her towards himself. This, however, is not the effect of any contract, but of the accidental concurrence of their passions in the same object at that particular time. Nobody ever saw a dog make a fair and deliberate exchange of one bone for another with another dog. . . . In almost every other race of animals, each individual, when it is grown up to maturity, is entirely independent, and in its natural state has occasion for the assistance of no other living creature. But man has almost constant occasion for the help of his brethren, and it is in vain for him to expect it from their benevolence only. He will be more likely to prevail if he can interest their self-love in his favor, and show them that it is for their own advantage to do for him what he requires of them. Whoever offers to another a bargain of any kind proposes to do this. Give me that which I want, and you shall have this which you want, is the meaning of every such offer; and it is in this manner that we obtain from one another the far greater part of those good offices which we stand in need of. It is not from the benevolence of the butcher, the brewer, or the baker that we expect our dinner, but from their regard to their own interest. We address ourselves not to their humanity, but to their self-love, and never talk to them of our own necessities, but of their advantages. . . .

As it is by treaty, by barter, and by purchase that we obtain from one another the greater part of those mutual good offices which we stand in need of, so it is this same trucking disposition which originally gives occasion to the division of labor. In a tribe of hunters or shepherds, a particular person makes bows and arrows, for example, with more readiness and dexterity than any other. He frequently exchanges them for cattle or for venison with his companions; and he finds at last that he can, in this manner, get more cattle and venison than if he himself went to the field to catch them. From a regard to his own interest, therefore, the making of bows and arrows grows to be his chief business, and he becomes a sort of armorer. Another excels in making the frames and covers of their little huts or movable houses. He is accustomed to be of use in this way to his neighbors, who reward him in the same manner with cattle and with venison, till at last he finds it his interest to dedicate himself entirely to this employment, and to become a sort of house-carpenter. In the same manner a third becomes a smith or a brazier; a fourth, a tanner or dresser of hides or skins, the principal part of the clothing of savages. And thus the certainty of being able to exchange all that surplus part of the produce of his own labor, which is over and above his own consumption, for such parts of the produce of other men's labor as he may have occasion for encourages every man to apply himself to a particular occupation, and to cultivate and bring to perfection whatever talent of genius he may possess for that particular species of business. . . .

A SELECTION

Thomas Day
1748–1789

THE DESOLATION OF AMERICA
1777

[Day, like many Englishmen, was an ardent supporter of the Americans.]

. . . .

Howl, howl, thou genius of the Western Shore!
Thy hopes extinguish'd, and thy fame no more!
The labours of an age at once laid low,
Beneath the vengeance of a mightier foe!
Wide o'er the ruin'd fields which once were thine,
See! the proud bands of adverse Europe shine!
See! daring prows thy vanquish'd waves divide,
Sport on thy billows, and insult thy tide!
All that rewarded once thy children's toil,
Riches and arts become the victor's spoil.   10
Thy swelling columns, thy majestic spires,

Bow to their base, and moulder in the fires.
The impious steel thy sacred haunt invades,
And guilt and tyranny pollute thy shades.
O'er all the scene insatiate vengeance reigns,
Nor Heaven itself can vindicate its fanes.
   But oh! what rage these guilty deeds inspires?
Who wields the faulchion, and who hurls the fires?
No foreign hate impels this storm of death,
That rolls impetuous down, and crushes all beneath.   20
Each claim rejected now, that once was priz'd,
All piety contemn'd, and faith despis'd,
See! the fell parent by the fiends possest,
Plants her keen dagger in the offspring's breast!
Inexorably fierce, alike unaw'd
By shame, by nature, or by nature's God!
   Vainly our fields have all their gifts supplied,
To sate her luxury, or sooth her pride.
Patient of sufferings, and unbroke by toils,
In vain our race has yielded up their spoils;   30
And seen the sons of idle pomp consume
Their fragrant treasures, and nectareous bloom,
While fetter'd industry stood weeping by,
And mark'd the teeming earth, and favouring sky;
Mark'd, but not dar'd to use—Oh! impious pride!—
The blessings Heaven bestow'd, but man denied.
For her alone our commerce spread the sail,
Through all our harbours, to the western gale:
And every wave some precious offering bore,
To deck her cities, or increase her store.—   40
Too fond of fame, and prodigal of life,
Our warriors bled where'er she wag'd the strife:
On every shore, in every combat tried,
For her they conquer'd, and for her they died.—
Our industry and valour rear'd the mound,
Where now she sits, and darts her rays around;
And imp'd her flight, when touch'd by glory's flame,
She spread her eagle wings, and soar'd to fame.
   But now no thought, nor memory remains,   50
Of all our former merits and our pains.
The future, Heaven; the past, oblivion hides;
And friendship's slighted bonds the sword divides.
Lo! Britain bended to the servile yoke,
Her fire extinguish'd, and her spirit broke,

Beneath the pressure of [a tyrant's] sway,
Herself at once the spoiler and the prey,
Detest[s] the virtues she can boast no more
And envies every right to every shore!
At once to nature and to pity blind, 60
Wages abhorred war with humankind;
And wheresoe'er her ocean rolls his wave,
Provokes an enemy, or meets a slave.—
But free-born minds inspir'd with noble flame,
Attest their origin, and scorn the claim.
Beyond the sweets of pleasure and of rest,
The joys which captivate the vulgar breast;
Beyond the dearer ties of kindred blood;
Or brittle life's too transitory good;
The sacred charge of liberty they prize, 70
That last, and noblest, present of the skies.—
These are the crimes, for which, in ruin hurl'd,
The wrath of Britain bursts upon the world.—
These are the crimes, for which our race must feel
The flames of vengeance, and the ruthless steel;
All ills, all wrongs that e'er the vanquish'd shar'd;
All crimes remorseless conquest ever dar'd;
Whate'er vindictive tyrants can decree,
For souls that train'd to honour dar'd be free;
Whatever horrors stigmatize the time, 80
When guilt prevails, and virtue is a crime.—
For impotent in rage, oppression calls
The banded world to our devoted walls.
Where'er the crimes of lawless power degrade
The harden'd breast and blood becomes a trade;
Thence, lur'd by British gold the spoiler leads
His squadrons, and the brib'd assassin bleeds.
Here, lost to all their former virtue, shine
The venal legions of the servile Rhine:
Hither, as to a certain quarry flies 90
The gloomy hunter from his frozen skies:
But far more fell, more dreadful than the rest,
From his dark forest springs the savage pest
Untaught in open fields the fight to dare;
Or with firm foot await the coming war;
Through woods and wastes the silent mischief glides,
As hope of spoil, or thirst of vengeance guides:
Then like a tyger crouching by the way,

Forth rushes on his unsuspecting prey;
Torture and death alone his thoughts employ: 100
Blood his delight, and havoc all his joy:
The minister of hell, and Britain's hate,
Nature's abhorrence, and the scourge of hate!
Yet, gracious Heaven! tho' clouds may intervene,
And transitory horrors shade the scene;
Though for an instant virtue sink depressed,
While vice exulting rears her bloody crest;
Thy sacred truth shall still inspire my mind,
To cast the terrors of my fate behind!
Thy power which nature's utmost bound pervades, 110
Beams thro' the void, and cheers destruction's shades,
Can blast the laurel on the victor's head,
And smooth the good man's agonizing bed,
To songs of triumph change the captive's groans,
And hurl the powers of darkness from their thrones!

Edmund Burke

1729–1797

IF Paine is an "idealist," Burke, like Johnson, is a "realist" in the sense that he is willing to adjust his principles to meet an existing situation. He compromises. This is not to say that he is without principles. He holds his principles more loosely than Paine; his mind is less rigid, because he recognizes that "the nature of man is intricate; the objects of society are of the greatest possible complexity." For this reason he never ventures to place solid interests upon only speculative grounds. This flexibility enables Burke to "return upon himself," as Arnold said. He is willing to justify Wilkes, the "radical," and he asserts that the poorest being that crawls the earth is a noble object when it defends itself against oppression; he is also ready to abandon any number of constitutional principles to prevent "a fruitless, hopeless, unnatural civil war" with the American colonies. Yet he bitterly opposes the French Revolution because he sees that government cannot be founded upon abstract rights; it is a contrivance to meet human wants. Thus, although Burke seems to be without principles, he is not, for his principles are establishments. Establishments are the repositories of human experience. Nevertheless he perceives that "when the reason of the old establishments is gone, it is absurd to preserve nothing but the burden of them." He wishes to modify, not to innovate; thus he would regard establishments as a guide and a tradition. This attitude represents a sort of "classicism" that Dr. Johnson and Sir Joshua Reynolds express in literature and the fine arts. Innovation proceeds more entirely upon principle alone than Burke wishes; and principles are apt to be rationalistic abstractions. He has a more historical and organic view of the state and society than Paine, who is a systematizer. Burke is experiential and empirical: no idea is a thoroughly sound idea unless it has some chance of being effected; the past enables us to decide what this chance is. Unlike Paine, Burke would use his principles instead of being used by them. This knack for looking at the existing situation is characteristically British. The British constitution is a matter of usage rather than abstract principle; the principles underlying it are largely a heritage of past experience. Thus it maintains contact with the past while it is brought to bear upon the situation at hand. We cannot understand either the British government or the British mind unless we understand Burke. Of course, Paine's accusation that when Burke attacked the French Revolution he pitied the plumage and forgot the dying bird is just; at moments Burke failed to adapt himself to the existing situation. Yet it should be clear that Burke's defense of property and prerogative is not defense of a principle so much as a comment made in the light of historical experience. It is not very helpful to deal with Burke and Paine by names like "conservative" and "radical." The issue between them is that Paine is addicted to an "ideology," whereas Burke is not. Burke more successfully than Paine escapes from the tyranny of a concept.

BIOGRAPHICAL NOTES

Born in Dublin, the son of a Protestant father and a Roman Catholic mother. Attended a Quaker school at Ballitore (1741), then entered Trinity College, Dublin (1743), and went to London to study law at the Middle Temple (1750) but gave up law for literature. *A Vindication of Natural Society* (1756), a satire on the deism and political views of Bolingbroke. *Philosophical Inquiry into the Sublime and Beautiful* (1756), a revolutionary, though imperfect, treatise on esthetics. Married Jane Mary Nugent (1756). Began editing the *Annual Register* (1759). Appointed private secretary to William Gerard Hamilton, an official in Ireland (1761); then private secretary to the Marquis of Rockingham (1765). Began Parliamentary career as member for Wendover, a Rockingham or liberal Whig (1765). Purchased estate, Gregories (1769), and began to run up debts. *Thoughts on the Present Discontents* (1770), provoked by the exclusion of Wilkes from Parliament. Visit to France (1773). Elected M.P. for Bristol (1774) and defended

the American Colonies in Parliament: speeches on American taxation
and conciliation with America (1774–75). *Letter to the Sheriffs of Bristol* (1777) defending his American policy. Close friendships with
Johnson, Garrick, Reynolds, Goldsmith, Fanny Burney, and members
of the Club. Aided George Crabbe. Projected reforms in government
finance. Undertook impeachment of Warren Hastings; speech on *The
Nabob of Arcot's Debts* (1785). The trial of Hastings (1788–95). *Reflections on the Revolution in France* (1790). Break with Fox upon the
Revolution. *An Appeal from the New to the Old Whigs* (1791).
Granted a pension by Pitt (1794). Death of his son Richard, a heavy
blow (1794). Criticized by Duke of Bedford for accepting a pension;
replied by the *Letter to a Noble Lord* (1796). Never recuperated from
shock of Richard's death.

BIBLIOGRAPHY: *Works*, 8 vols., 1854–61. *Selected Writings*, ed. L. J. Bate, 1960.
Cobban, A., *Edmund Burke and the Revolt against the Eighteenth Century*, 1960.
Copeland, T. W., *Edmund Burke*, 1950. Morley, J., *Burke*, 1879, etc. Osborn, A. M.,
Rousseau and Burke, 1940. Parkin, C., *The Moral Basis of Burke's Political Thought*,
1956. Stanlis, P. J., *Edmund Burke and the Natural Law*, 1958.

A LETTER TO JOHN FARR AND JOHN HARRIS, ESQRS., SHERIFFS OF THE CITY OF BRISTOL, ON THE AFFAIRS OF AMERICA

1777

. . . .

I am charged with being an American. If warm affection towards
those over whom I claim any share of authority be a crime, I am
guilty of this charge. But I do assure you (and they who know me
publicly and privately will bear witness to me) that if ever one
man lived more zealous than another for the supremacy of Parliament and the rights of this imperial crown, it was myself. Many
others indeed might be more knowing in the extent or the foundation of these rights. I do not pretend to be an antiquary, a lawyer,
or qualified for the chair of professor in metaphysics. I never ventured to put your solid interests upon speculative grounds. My
having constantly declined to do so has been attributed to my incapacity for such disquisitions; and I am inclined to believe it is
partly the cause. I never shall be ashamed to confess that where
I am ignorant I am diffident. I am indeed not very solicitous to
clear myself of this imputed incapacity, because men even less

conversant than I am in this kind of subtleties and placed in stations
to which I ought not to aspire, have, by the mere force of civil
discretion, often conducted the affairs of great nations with distinguished felicity and glory.

When I first came into a public trust, I found your Parliament
in possession of an unlimited legislative power over the colonies.
I could not open the statute book without seeing the actual exercise
of it, more or less, in all cases whatsoever. This possession passed
with me for a title. It does so in all human affairs. No man examines
into the defects of his title to his paternal estate or to his established
government. Indeed, common sense taught me that a legislative
authority not actually limited by the express terms of its foundation or by its own subsequent acts cannot have its powers parceled
out by argumentative distinctions so as to enable us to say that here
they can, and there they cannot, bind. Nobody was so obliging as
to produce to me any record of such distinctions, by compact or
otherwise, either at the successive formation of the several colonies
or during the existence of any of them. If any gentlemen were able
to see how one power could be given up (merely on abstract reasoning) without giving up the rest, I can only say that they saw
farther than I could; nor did I ever presume to condemn anyone
for being clear sighted when I was blind. I praise their penetration
and learning, and hope that their practice has been correspondent
to their theory.

I had indeed very earnest wishes to keep the whole body of this
authority perfect and entire as I found it, and to keep it so, not for
our advantage solely, but principally for the sake of those on whose
account all just authority exists; I mean the people to be governed.
For I thought I saw that many cases might well happen in which
the exercise of every power comprehended in the broadest idea
of legislature might become, in its time and circumstances, not a
little expedient for the peace and union of the colonies amongst
themselves as well as for their perfect harmony with Great Britain.
Thinking so (perhaps erroneously) but being honestly of that opinion, I was at the same time very sure that the authority of which I
was so jealous could not under the actual circumstances of our
plantations be at all preserved in any of its members but by the
greatest reserve in its application, particularly in those delicate
points in which the feelings of mankind are the most irritable.
They who thought otherwise have found a few more difficulties

in their work than (I hope) they were thoroughly aware of when they undertook the present business. I must beg leave to observe that it is not only the invidious branch of taxation that will be resisted, but that no other given part of legislative rights can be exercised without regard to the general opinion of those who are to be governed. That general opinion is the vehicle and organ of legislative omnipotence. Without this, it may be a theory to entertain the mind, but it is nothing in the direction of affairs. The completeness of the legislative authority of Parliament *over this kingdom* is not questioned; and yet many things indubitably included in the abstract idea of that power, and which carry no absolute injustice in themselves, yet being contrary to the opinions and feelings of the people, can as little be exercised as if Parliament in that case had been possessed of no right at all. I see no abstract reason which can be given why the same power which made and repealed the High Commission Court and the Star Chamber [1] might not revive them again; and these courts, warned by their former fate, might possibly exercise their powers with some degree of justice. But the madness would be as unquestionable as the competence of that Parliament which should attempt such things. If anything can be supposed out of the power of human legislature, it is religion; I admit, however, that the established religion of this country has been three or four times altered by act of Parliament and therefore that a statute binds even in that case. But we may very safely affirm that, notwithstanding this apparent omnipotence, it would be now found as impossible for King and Parliament to alter the established religion of this country as it was to King James alone when he attempted to make such an alteration without a Parliament.[2] In effect, to follow, not to force the public inclination; to give a direction, a form, a technical dress, and a specific sanction to the general sense of the community, is the true end of legislature.

It is so with regard to the exercise of all the powers which our constitution knows in any of its parts, and indeed to the substantial existence of any of the parts themselves. The King's negative to bills is one of the most indisputed of the royal prerogatives; and

---

1 The Court of High Commission was established in 1583 to exact conformity among the clergy; the Court of Star Chamber (named from the gilded roof of the chamber in which it sat) developed from the King's council into an instrument for dealing arbitrary justice under James I and Charles I.

2 Burke refers to the Romanist schemes of James II.

it extends to all cases whatsoever. I am far from certain that if several laws which I know had fallen under the stroke of that scepter, that the public would have had a very heavy loss. But it is not the *propriety* of the exercise which is in question. The exercise itself is wisely forborne. Its repose may be the preservation of its existence; and its existence may be the means of saving the constitution itself on an occasion worthy of bringing it forth. As the disputants whose accurate and logical reasonings have brought us into our present condition think it absurd that powers or members of any constitution should exist rarely or never to be exercised, I hope I shall be excused in mentioning another instance that is material. We know that the Convocation of the Clergy had formerly been called and sat with nearly as much regularity to business as Parliament itself. It is now called for form only. It sits for the purpose of making some polite ecclesiastical compliments to the King and, when that grace is said, retires and is heard of no more. It is, however, *a part of the constitution*, and may be called out into act and energy whenever there is occasion, and whenever those who conjure up that spirit will choose to abide the consequences. It is wise to permit its legal existence; it is much wiser to continue it a legal existence only. So truly has prudence (constituted as the god of this lower world) the entire dominion over every exercise of power committed into its hands; and yet I have lived to see prudence and conformity to circumstances wholly set at nought in our late controversies and treated as if they were the most contemptible and irrational of all things. I have heard it a hundred times very gravely alleged that in order to keep power in wind it was necessary, by preference, to exert it in those very points in which it was most likely to be resisted and the least likely to be productive of any advantage.

These were the considerations, gentlemen, which led me early to think that, in the comprehensive dominion which the Divine Providence had put into our hands, instead of troubling our understandings with speculations concerning the unity of empire and the identity or distinction of legislative powers and inflaming our passions with the heat and pride of controversy, it was our duty, in all soberness, to conform our government to the character and circumstances of the several people who composed this mighty and strangely diversified mass. I never was wild enough to conceive that one method would serve for the whole, that the natives of Hindostan and those of Virginia could be ordered in the same manner, or that the Cutchery [3] court and the grand jury of Salem could be regulated on a similar plan. I was persuaded that government was a practical thing, made for the happiness of mankind and not to furnish out a spectacle of uniformity to gratify the schemes of visionary politicians. Our business was to rule, not to wrangle; and it would have been a poor compensation that we had triumphed in a dispute whilst we lost an empire.

If there be one fact in the world perfectly clear, it is this: "That the disposition of the people of America is wholly averse to any other than a free government"; and this is indication enough to any honest statesman how he ought to adapt whatever power he finds in his hands to their case. If any ask me what a free government is, I answer that, for any practical purpose, it is what the people think so, and that they, and not I, are the natural, lawful, and competent judges of this matter. If they practically allow me a greater degree of authority over them than is consistent with any correct ideas of perfect freedom, I ought to thank them for so great a trust and not to endeavor to prove from thence that they have reasoned amiss and that, having gone so far, by analogy they must hereafter have no enjoyment but by my pleasure.

If we had seen this done by any others, we should have concluded them far gone in madness. It is melancholy as well as ridiculous to observe the kind of reasoning with which the public has been amused in order to divert our minds from the common sense of our American policy. There are people who have split and anatomized the doctrine of free government as if it were an abstract question concerning metaphysical liberty and necessity and not a matter of moral prudence and natural feeling. They have disputed whether liberty be a positive or a negative idea; whether it does not consist in being governed by laws, without considering what are the laws or who are the makers; whether man has any rights by nature; and whether all the property he enjoys be not the alms of his government, and his life itself their favor and indulgence. Others, corrupting religion as these have perverted philosophy, contend that Christians are redeemed into captivity, and the blood of the Saviour of mankind has been shed to make them the slaves of a few proud and insolent sinners. These shocking ex-

3 Cutchery was a province in Hindostan.

tremes provoking to extremes of another kind, speculations are let loose as destructive to all authority as the former are to all freedom; and every government is called tyranny and usurpation which is not formed on their fancies. In this manner the stirrers-up of this contention, not satisfied with distracting our dependencies and filling them with blood and slaughter, are corrupting our understandings: they are endeavoring to tear up, along with practical liberty, all the foundations of human society, all equity and justice, religion and order.

Civil freedom, gentlemen, is not, as many have endeavored to persuade you, a thing that lies hid in the depth of abstruse science. It is a blessing and a benefit, not an abstract speculation; and all the just reasoning that can be put upon it is of so coarse a texture as perfectly to suit the ordinary capacities of those who are to enjoy and of those who are to defend it. Far from any resemblance to those propositions in geometry and metaphysics which admit no medium, but must be true or false in all their latitude, social and civil freedom, like all other things in common life, are variously mixed and modified, enjoyed in very different degrees, and shaped into an infinite diversity of forms, according to the temper and circumstances of every community. The *extreme* of liberty (which is its abstract perfection, but its real fault) obtains nowhere, nor ought to obtain anywhere; because extremes, as we all know, in every point which relates either to our duties or satisfactions in life, are destructive both to virtue and enjoyment. Liberty, too, must be limited in order to be possessed. The degree of restraint it is impossible in any case to settle precisely. But it ought to be the constant aim of every wise public council to find out by cautious experiments and rational, cool endeavors with how little, not how much, of this restraint the community can subsist. For liberty is a good to be improved, and not an evil to be lessened. It is not only a private blessing of the first order, but the vital spring and energy of the state itself, which has just so much life and vigor as there is liberty in it. But whether liberty be advantageous or not (for I know it is a fashion to decry the very principle), none will dispute that peace is a blessing; and peace must in the course of human affairs be frequently bought by some indulgence and toleration at least to liberty. For as the Sabbath (though of divine institution) was made for man, not man for the Sabbath, government, which can claim no higher origin or authority, in its exercise at least, ought to conform to the exigencies of the time and the temper and character of the people with whom it is concerned, and not always to attempt violently to bend the people to their theories of subjection. The bulk of mankind, on their part, are not excessively curious concerning any theories whilst they are really happy; and one sure symptom of an ill-conducted state is the propensity of the people to resort to them.

But when subjects, by a long course of such ill conduct, are once thoroughly inflamed and the state itself violently distempered, the people must have some satisfaction to their feelings more solid than a sophistical speculation on law and government. Such was our situation; and such a satisfaction was necessary to prevent recourse to arms: it was necessary towards laying them down; it will be necessary to prevent the taking them up again and again. Of what nature this satisfaction ought to be, I wish it had been the disposition of Parliament seriously to consider. It was certainly a deliberation that called for the exertion of all their wisdom.

I am, and ever have been, deeply sensible of the difficulty of reconciling the strong presiding power that is so useful towards the conservation of a vast, disconnected, infinitely diversified empire with that liberty and safety of the provinces which they must enjoy (in opinion and practice at least) or they will not be provinces at all. I know, and have long felt, the difficulty of reconciling the unwieldy haughtiness of a great ruling nation, habituated to command, pampered by enormous wealth, and confident from a long course of prosperity and victory, to the high spirit of free dependencies, animated with the first glow and activity of juvenile heat, and assuming to themselves, as their birthright, some part of that very pride which oppresses them. They who perceive no difficulty in reconciling these tempers (which, however, to make peace must some way or other be reconciled) are much above my capacity or much below the magnitude of the business. Of one thing I am perfectly clear, that it is not by deciding the suit, but by compromising the difference, that peace can be restored or kept. They who would put an end to such quarrels by declaring roundly in favor of the whole demands of either party have mistaken, in my humble opinion, the office of a mediator. . . .

REFLECTIONS ON THE REVOLUTION IN FRANCE

AND

ON THE PROCEEDINGS IN CERTAIN SOCIETIES IN LONDON RELATIVE TO THAT EVENT

IN A LETTER

INTENDED TO HAVE BEEN SENT TO A GENTLEMAN IN PARIS

1790

. . . .

On the forenoon of the 4th of November last, Doctor Richard Price, a nonconforming minister of eminence, preached at the dissenting meetinghouse of the Old Jewry, to his club or society,[1] a very extraordinary miscellaneous sermon, in which there are some good moral and religious sentiments, and not ill expressed, mixed up in a sort of porridge of various political opinions and reflections: but the Revolution in France is the grand ingredient in the caldron. . . .

. . . His doctrines affect our constitution in its vital parts. He tells the Revolution Society, in this political sermon, that his Majesty "is almost the *only* lawful king in the world, because the *only* one who owes his crown to the *choice of his people*." As to the kings of *the world*, all of whom (except one) this archpontiff of the *rights of men*, with all the plenitude, and with more than the boldness of the papal deposing power in its meridian fervor of the twelfth century, puts into one sweeping clause of ban and anathema, and proclaims usurpers by circles of longitude and latitude, over the whole globe, it behoves them to consider how they admit into their territories these apostolic missionaries, who are to tell their subjects they are not lawful kings That is their concern. It is ours, as a domestic interest of some moment, seriously to consider the solidity of the *only* principle upon which these gentlemen acknowledge a king of Great Britain to be entitled to their allegiance.

---

[1] The Revolution Society, commemorating the Revolution of 1688.

This doctrine, as applied to the prince now on the British throne, either is nonsense, and therefore neither true nor false, or it affirms a most unfounded, dangerous, illegal, and unconstitutional position. According to this spiritual doctor of politics, if his Majesty does not owe his crown to the choice of his people, he is no *lawful king*. Now nothing can be more untrue than that the crown of this kingdom is so held by his Majesty. Therefore if you follow their rule, the king of Great Britain, who most certainly does not owe his high office to any form of popular election, is in no respect better than the rest of the gang of usurpers, who reign, or rather rob, all over the face of this our miserable world, without any sort of right or title to the allegiance of their people. The policy of this general doctrine, so qualified, is evident enough. The propagators of this political gospel are in hopes that their abstract principle (their principle that a popular choice is necessary to the legal existence of the sovereign magistracy) would be overlooked whilst the king of Great Britain was not affected by it. In the mean time the ears of their congregations would be gradually habituated to it, as if it were a first principle admitted without dispute. For the present it would only operate as a theory, pickled in the preserving juices of pulpit eloquence, and laid by for future use. *Condo et compono quae mox depromere possim.*[2] By this policy, whilst our government is soothed with a reservation in its favor to which it has no claim, the security which it has in common with all governments, so far as opinion is security, is taken away. . . .

Whatever may be the success of evasion in explaining away the gross error of *fact* which supposes that his Majesty (though he holds it in concurrence with the wishes) owes his crown to the choice of his people, yet nothing can evade their full explicit declaration concerning the principle of a right in the people to choose, which right is directly maintained and tenaciously adhered to. All the oblique insinuations concerning election bottom in this proposition, and are referable to it. Lest the foundation of the king's exclusive legal title should pass for a mere rant of adulatory freedom, the political divine proceeds dogmatically to assert that by the principles of the Revolution [3] the people of England have acquired three fundamental rights, all which, with him, compose one system,

2 Horace *Epistles* I. i. 12: "I collect and store what presently I may be able to use."   3 The Revolution of 1688.

and lie together in one short sentence; namely, that we have acquired a right,

1. "To choose our own governors."
2. "To cashier them for misconduct."
3. "To frame a government for ourselves."

This new and hitherto unheard-of bill of rights, though made in the name of the whole people, belongs to those gentlemen and their faction only. The body of the people of England have no share in it. They utterly disclaim it. They will resist the practical assertion of it with their lives and fortunes. They are bound to do so by the laws of their country, made at the time of that very Revolution which is appealed to in favor of the fictitious rights claimed by the society which abuses its name. . . .

You will observe that from Magna Charta to the Declaration of Right,[4] it has been the uniform policy of our constitution to claim and assert our liberties as an *entailed inheritance* derived to us from our forefathers, and to be transmitted to our posterity, as an estate specially belonging to the people of this kingdom, without any reference whatever to any other more general or prior right. By this means our constitution preserves a unity in so great a diversity of its parts. We have an inheritable crown, an inheritable peerage, and a House of Commons and a people inheriting privileges, franchises, and liberties, from a long line of ancestors.

This policy appears to me to be the result of profound reflection; or rather the happy effect of following nature, which is wisdom without reflection, and above it. A spirit of innovation is generally the result of a selfish temper and confined views. People will not look forward to posterity who never look backward to their ancestors. Besides, the people of England well know that the idea of inheritance furnishes a sure principle of conservation and a sure principle of transmission, without at all excluding a principle of improvement. It leaves acquisition free; but it secures what it acquires. Whatever advantages are obtained by a state proceeding on these maxims are locked fast as in a sort of family settlement, grasped as in a kind of mortmain forever. By a constitutional policy working after the pattern of nature, we receive, we hold, we

---

[4] The act that settled the rights of subjects and the succession of the crown after the Revolution of 1688.

transmit our government and our privileges in the same manner in which we enjoy and transmit our property and our lives. The institutions of policy, the goods of fortune, the gifts of Providence, are handed down, to us and from us, in the same course and order. Our political system is placed in a just correspondence and symmetry with the order of the world and with the mode of existence decreed to a permanent body composed of transitory parts, wherein, by the disposition of a stupendous wisdom, molding together the great mysterious incorporation of the human race, the whole, at one time, is never old, or middle-aged, or young, but, in a condition of unchangeable constancy, moves on through the varied tenor of perpetual decay, fall, renovation, and progression. Thus, by preserving the method of nature in the conduct of the state, in what we improve, we are never wholly new, in what we retain we are never wholly obsolete. By adhering in this manner and on those principles to our forefathers, we are guided not by the superstition of antiquarians, but by the spirit of philosophic analogy. In this choice of inheritance we have given to our frame of polity the image of a relation in blood, binding up the constitution of our country with our dearest domestic ties, adopting our fundamental laws into the bosom of our family affections, keeping inseparable, and cherishing with the warmth of all their combined and mutually reflected charities, our state, our hearths, our sepulchers, and our altars. . . .

Far am I from denying in theory, full as far is my heart from withholding in practice (if I were of power to give or to withhold), the *real* rights of men. In denying their false claims of right, I do not mean to injure those which are real and are such as their pretended rights would totally destroy. If civil society be made for the advantage of man, all the advantages for which it is made become his right. It is an institution of beneficence; and law itself is only beneficence acting by a rule. Men have a right to live by that rule; they have a right to do justice, as between their fellows, whether their fellows are in public function or in ordinary occupation. They have a right to the fruits of their industry and to the means of making their industry fruitful. They have a right to the acquisitions of their parents, to the nourishment and improvement of their offspring, to instruction in life, and to consolation in death. Whatever each man can separately do without trespassing upon others, he has a right to do for himself; and he has a right to a fair portion of all which society, with all its combinations of skill and force, can do in his favor. In this partnership all men have equal rights; but not to equal things. He that has but five shillings in the partnership has as good a right to it as he that has five hundred pounds has to his larger proportion. But he has not a right to an equal dividend in the product of the joint stock; and as to the share of power, authority, and direction which each individual ought to have in the management of the state, that I must deny to be amongst the direct original rights of man in civil society; for I have in my contemplation the civil social man, and no other. It is a thing to be settled by convention.

If civil society be the offspring of convention, that convention must be its law. That convention must limit and modify all the descriptions of constitution which are formed under it. Every sort of legislative, judicial, or executory power are its creatures. They can have no being in any other state of things; and how can any man claim, under the conventions of civil society, rights which do not so much as suppose its existence? Rights which are absolutely repugnant to it? One of the first motives to civil society, and which becomes one of its fundamental rules, is *that no man should be judge in his own cause.* By this each person has at once divested himself of the first fundamental right of uncovenanted man, that is, to judge for himself and to assert his own cause. He abdicates all right to be his own governor. He inclusively, in a great measure, abandons the right of self-defense, the first law of nature. Men cannot enjoy the rights of an uncivil and of a civil state together. That he may obtain justice, he gives up his right of determining what it is in points the most essential to him. That he may secure some liberty, he makes a surrender in trust of the whole of it.

Government is not made in virtue of natural rights, which may and do exist in total independence of it, and exist in much greater clearness and in a much greater degree of abstract perfection; but their abstract perfection is their practical defect. By having a right to everything, they want everything. Government is a contrivance of human wisdom to provide for human *wants.* Men have a right that these wants should be provided for by this wisdom. Among these wants is to be reckoned the want, out of civil society, of a sufficient restraint upon their passions. Society requires not only that the passions of individuals should be subjected, but that even in the mass and body, as well as in the individuals, the inclinations of men should frequently be thwarted, their will controlled, and their passions brought into subjection. This can only be done *by a power out of themselves*, and not, in the exercise of its function, subject to that will and to those passions which it is its office to bridle and subdue. In this sense the restraints on men, as well as their liberties, are to be reckoned among their rights. But as the liberties and the restrictions vary with times and circumstances and admit of infinite modifications, they cannot be settled upon any abstract rule; and nothing is so foolish as to discuss them upon that principle.

The moment you abate anything from the full rights of men, each to govern himself, and suffer any artificial, positive limitation upon those rights, from that moment the whole organization of government becomes a consideration of convenience. This it is which makes the constitution of a state and the due distribution of its powers a matter of the most delicate and complicated skill. It requires a deep knowledge of human nature and human necessities and of the things which facilitate or obstruct the various ends which are to be pursued by the mechanism of civil institutions. The state is to have recruits to its strength and remedies to its distempers. What is the use of discussing a man's abstract right to food or medicine? The question is upon the method of procuring and administering them. In that deliberation I shall always advise to call in the aid of the farmer and the physician rather than the professor of metaphysics.

The science of constructing a commonwealth or renovating it or reforming it is, like every other experimental science, not to be taught a priori. Nor is it a short experience that can instruct us in that practical science, because the real effects of moral causes are not always immediate; but that which in the first instance is prejudicial may be excellent in its remoter operation, and its excellence may arise even from the ill effects it produces in the beginning. The reverse also happens; and very plausible schemes, with very pleasing commencements, have often shameful and lamentable conclusions. In states there are often some obscure and almost latent causes, things which appear at first view of little moment, on which a very great part of its prosperity or adversity may most essentially depend. The science of government being, therefore, so practical in itself and intended for such practical purposes, a matter which requires experience and even more experience than any person can gain in his whole life, however sagacious and observing he may be, it is with infinite caution that any man ought to venture upon pulling down an edifice which has answered in any tolerable degree for ages the common purposes of society, or on building it up again, without having models and patterns of approved utility before his eyes.

These metaphysic rights entering into common life, like rays of light which pierce into a dense medium, are, by the laws of nature, refracted from their straight line. Indeed, in the gross and complicated mass of human passions and concerns, the primitive rights of men undergo such a variety of refractions and reflections that it becomes absurd to talk of them as if they continued in the simplicity of their original direction. The nature of man is intricate; the objects of society are of the greatest possible complexity; and therefore no simple disposition or direction of power can be suitable either to man's nature or to the quality of his affairs. When I hear the simplicity of contrivance aimed at and boasted of in any new political constitutions, I am at no loss to decide that the artificers are grossly ignorant of their trade or totally negligent of their duty. The simple governments are fundamentally defective, to say no worse of them. If you were to contemplate society in but one point of view, all these simple modes of polity are infinitely captivating. In effect each would answer its single end much more perfectly than the more complex is able to attain all its complex purposes. But it is better that the whole should be imperfectly and anomalously answered than that, while some parts are provided for with great exactness, others might be totally neglected, or perhaps materially injured, by the overcare of a favorite member.

The pretended rights of these theorists are all extremes; and in proportion as they are metaphysically true, they are morally and politically false. The rights of men are in a sort of *middle*, incapable of definition, but not impossible to be discerned. The rights of men in governments are their advantages; and these are often in balances between differences of good, in compromises sometimes between good and evil, and sometimes between evil and evil. Political reason is a computing principle; adding, subtracting, multiplying, and dividing, morally and not metaphysically or mathematically, true moral denominations.

By these theorists the right of the people is almost always sophistically confounded with their power. The body of the community, whenever it can come to act, can meet with no effectual resistance; but till power and right are the same, the whole body of them has no right inconsistent with virtue and the first of all virtues, prudence. Men have no right to what is not reasonable and to what is not for their benefit; for though a pleasant writer said, *Liceat perire poetis*, when one of them, in cold blood, is said to have leaped into the flames of a volcanic revolution, *Ardentem frigidus Aetnam insiluit*,[5] I consider such a frolic rather as an unjustifiable poetic license than as one of the franchises of Parnassus; and whether he were poet or divine or politician that chose to exercise this kind of right, I think that more wise, because more charitable, thoughts would urge me rather to save the man than to preserve his brazen slippers as the monuments of his folly. . . .

. . . . History will record that on the morning of the 6th of October, 1789, the King and Queen of France, after a day of confusion, alarm, dismay, and slaughter, lay down, under the pledged security of public faith, to indulge nature in a few hours of respite and troubled, melancholy repose. From this sleep the queen was first startled by the voice of the sentinel at her door, who cried out to her to save herself by flight—that this was the last proof of fidelity he could give—that they were upon him and he was dead. Instantly he was cut down. A band of cruel ruffians and assassins, reeking with his blood, rushed into the chamber of the queen and pierced with a hundred strokes of bayonets and poniards the bed from whence this persecuted woman had but just time to fly almost naked, and through ways unknown to the murderers had escaped to seek refuge at the feet of a king and husband, not secure of his own life for a moment.

This king, to say no more of him, and this queen, and their infant children (who once would have been the pride and hope of a great and generous people) were then forced to abandon the sanctuary of the most splendid palace in the world, which they left swimming in blood, polluted by massacre, and strewed with scattered limbs and mutilated carcasses. Thence they were conducted into the capital of their kingdom. Two had been selected from the unprovoked, unresisted, promiscuous slaughter which was made

---

5 Horace *Ars Poetica* 465-66:
"Leaped into fiery Aetna in cold blood.—

These bards are licensed (be it understood)
To perish as they list."

[Howes]

of the gentlemen of birth and family who composed the king's bodyguard. These two gentlemen, with all the parade of an execution of justice, were cruelly and publicly dragged to the block and beheaded in the great court of the palace. Their heads were stuck upon spears and led the procession, whilst the royal captives who followed in the train were slowly moved along, amidst the horrid yells and shrilling screams and frantic dances and infamous contumelies and all the unutterable abominations of the furies of hell, in the abused shape of the vilest of women. After they had been made to taste, drop by drop, more than the bitterness of death in the slow torture of a journey of twelve miles, protracted to six hours, they were, under a guard composed of those very soldiers who had thus conducted them through this famous triumph, lodged in one of the old palaces of Paris, now converted into a bastille for kings.

Is this a triumph to be consecrated at altars? to be commemorated with grateful thanksgiving? to be offered to the divine humanity with fervent prayer and enthusiastic ejaculation?—These Theban and Thracian orgies, acted in France and applauded only in the Old Jewry, I assure you, kindle prophetic enthusiasm in the minds but of very few people in this kingdom; although a saint and apostle, who may have revelations of his own, and who has so completely vanquished all the mean superstitions of the heart, may incline to think it pious and decorous to compare it with the entrance into the world of the Prince of Peace, proclaimed in a holy temple by a venerable sage, and not long before not worse announced by the voice of angels to quiet the innocence of shepherds.

At first I was at a loss to account for this fit of unguarded transport. I knew, indeed, that the sufferings of monarchs make a delicious repast to some sort of palates. There were reflections which might serve to keep this appetite within some bounds of temperance. But when I took one circumstance into my consideration, I was obliged to confess that much allowance ought to be made for the society, and that the temptation was too strong for common discretion; I mean, the circumstance of the Io Paean of the triumph, the animating cry which called "for *all* the BISHOPS to be hanged on the lamp-posts," might well have brought forth a burst of enthusiasm on the foreseen consequences of this happy day. I allow to so much enthusiasm some little deviation from prudence. I allow this prophet to break forth into hymns of joy and thanksgiving on an event which appears like the precursor of the millennium and the projected Fifth Monarchy, in the destruction of all church establishments. There was, however (as in all human affairs there is), in the midst of this joy something to exercise the patience of these worthy gentlemen and to try the long-suffering of their faith. The actual murder of the king and queen and their child was wanting to the other auspicious circumstances of this "*beautiful day.*" The actual murder of the bishops, though called for by so many holy ejaculations, was also wanting. A group of regicide and sacrilegious slaughter was indeed boldly sketched, but it was only sketched. It unhappily was left unfinished, in this great history-piece of the massacre of innocents. What hardy pencil of a great master from the school of the rights of men will finish it is to be seen hereafter. The age has not yet the complete benefit of that diffusion of knowledge that has undermined superstition and error; and the King of France wants another object or two to consign to oblivion, in consideration of all the good which is to arise from his own sufferings and the patriotic crimes of an enlightened age.

Although this work of our new light and knowledge did not go to the length that in all probability it was intended it should be carried, yet I must think that such treatment of any human creatures must be shocking to any but those who are made for accomplishing revolutions. But I cannot stop here. Influenced by the inborn feelings of my nature and not being illuminated by a single ray of this new-sprung modern light, I confess to you, sir, that the exalted rank of the persons suffering, and particularly the sex, the beauty, and the amiable qualities of the descendant of so many kings and emperors, with the tender age of royal infants, insensible only through infancy and innocence of the cruel outrages to which their parents were exposed, instead of being a subject of exultation adds not a little to my sensibility on that most melancholy occasion.

I hear that the august person who was the principal object of our preacher's triumph, though he supported himself, felt much on that shameful occasion. As a man, it became him to feel for his wife and his children and the faithful guards of his person that were massacred in cold blood about him. As a prince, it became him to feel for the strange and frightful transformation of his civilized subjects, and to be more grieved for them than solicitous for himself. It derogates little from his fortitude, while it adds infinitely to the honor of his humanity. I am very sorry to say it, very sorry indeed, that such personages are in a situation in which it is not becoming in us to praise the virtues of the great.

I hear, and I rejoice to hear, that the great lady, the other object of the triumph, has borne that day (one is interested that beings made for suffering should suffer well) and that she bears all the succeeding days, that she bears the imprisonment of her husband and her own captivity and the exile of her friends and the insulting adulation of addresses and the whole weight of her accumulated wrongs, with a serene patience, in a manner suited to her rank and race and becoming the offspring of a sovereign distinguished for her piety and her courage; that, like her, she has lofty sentiments; that she feels with the dignity of a Roman matron; that in the last extremity she will save herself from the last disgrace; and that if she must fall, she will fall by no ignoble hand.

It is now sixteen or seventeen years since I saw the Queen of France, then the dauphiness, at Versailles; and surely never lighted on this orb, which she hardly seemed to touch, a more delightful vision. I saw her just above the horizon, decorating and cheering the elevated sphere she just began to move in,—glittering like the morning star, full of life and splendor and joy. Oh! what a revolution! and what a heart must I have, to contemplate without emotion that elevation and that fall! Little did I dream, when she added titles of veneration to those of enthusiastic, distant, respectful love, that she should ever be obliged to carry the sharp antidote against disgrace concealed in that bosom; little did I dream that I should have lived to see such disasters fallen upon her in a nation of gallant men, in a nation of men of honor, and of cavaliers. I thought ten thousand swords must have leaped from their scabbards to avenge even a look that threatened her with insult.—But the age of chivalry is gone. That of sophisters, economists, and calculators has succeeded; and the glory of Europe is extinguished forever. Never, never more shall we behold that generous loyalty to rank and sex, that proud submission, that dignified obedience, that subordination of the heart, which kept alive, even in servitude itself, the spirit of an exalted freedom. The unbought grace of life, the cheap defense of nations, the nurse of manly sentiment and heroic enterprise is gone! It is gone, that sensibility of principle, that chastity of honor which felt a stain like a wound, which inspired courage whilst it mitigated ferocity, which ennobled whatever it touched, and under which vice itself lost half its evil by losing all its grossness.

This mixed system of opinion and sentiment had its origin in the ancient chivalry; and the principle, though varied in its appearance by the varying state of human affairs, subsisted and influenced through a long succession of generations, even to the time we live in. If it should ever be totally extinguished, the loss I fear will be great. It is this which has given its character to modern Europe. It is this which has distinguished it under all its forms of government, and distinguished it to its advantage, from the states of Asia and possibly from those states which flourished in the most brilliant periods of the antique world. It was this which, without confounding ranks, had produced a noble equality and handed it down through all the gradations of social life. It was this opinion which mitigated kings into companions and raised private men to be fellows with kings. Without force or opposition, it subdued the fierceness of pride and power; it obliged sovereigns to submit to the soft collar of social esteem, compelled stern authority to submit to elegance, and gave a dominating vanquisher of laws to be subdued by manners.

But now all is to be changed. All the pleasing illusions which made power gentle and obedience liberal, which harmonized the different shades of life, and which, by a bland assimilation, incorporated into politics the sentiments which beautify and soften private society are to be dissolved by this new conquering empire of light and reason. All the decent drapery of life is to be rudely torn off. All the superadded ideas, furnished from the wardrobe of a moral imagination, which the heart owns and the understanding ratifies as necessary to cover the defects of our naked, shivering nature and to raise it to dignity in our own estimation, are to be exploded as a ridiculous, absurd, and antiquated fashion.

On this scheme of things, a king is but a man; a queen is but a woman; a woman is but an animal, and an animal not of the highest order. All homage paid to the sex in general as such, and without distinct views, is to be regarded as romance and folly. Regicide and parricide and sacrilege are but fictions of superstition, corrupting jurisprudence by destroying its simplicity. The murder of a king or a queen or a bishop or a father are only common homicide, and if the people are by any chance or in any way gainers by it, a sort of homicide much the most pardonable, and into which we ought not to make too severe a scrutiny.

On the scheme of this barbarous philosophy, which is the off-spring of cold hearts and muddy understandings, and which is as void of solid wisdom as it is destitute of all taste and elegance, laws are to be supported only by their own terrors and by the concern which each individual may find in them from his own private speculations or can spare to them from his own private interests. In the groves of *their* academy, at the end of every vista, you see nothing but the gallows. Nothing is left which engages the affec-tions on the part of the commonwealth. On the principles of this mechanic philosophy, our institutions can never be embodied, if I may use the expression, in persons, so as to create in us love, venera-tion, admiration, or attachment. But that sort of reason which banishes the affections is incapable of filling their place. These public affections, combined with manners, are required some-times as supplements, sometimes as correctives, always as aids to law. The precept given by a wise man, as well as a great critic, for the construction of poems is equally true as to states: *Non satis est pulchra esse poemata, dulcia sunto.*[6] There ought to be a system of manners in every nation which a well-formed mind would be disposed to relish. To make us love our country, our country ought to be lovely.

But power, of some kind or other, will survive the shock in which manners and opinions perish; and it will find other and worse means for its support. The usurpation which, in order to subvert ancient institutions, has destroyed ancient principles, will hold power by arts similar to those by which it has acquired it. When the old feudal and chivalrous spirit of *fealty*, which, by freeing kings from fear, freed both kings and subjects from the precautions of tyranny, shall be extinct in the minds of men, plots and assassinations will be anticipated by preventive murder and preventive confiscation and that long roll of grim and bloody max-ims which form the political code of all power not standing on its own honor and the honor of those who are to obey it. Kings will be tyrants from policy when subjects are rebels from principle.

When ancient opinions and rules of life are taken away, the loss cannot possibly be estimated. From that moment we have no com-

---

[6] Horace *Ars Poetica* 99. "It is not enough that poems should be beautiful; let them be endearing."

pass to govern us, nor can we know distinctly to what port we steer. Europe undoubtedly, taken in a mass, was in a flourishing condition the day on which your Revolution was completed. How much of that prosperous state was owing to the spirit of our old manners and opinions is not easy to say; but as such causes cannot be indifferent in their operation, we must presume that, on the whole, their operation was beneficial.

We are but too apt to consider things in the state in which we find them without sufficiently adverting to the causes by which they have been produced and possibly may be upheld. Nothing is more certain than that our manners, our civilization, and all the good things which are connected with manners and with civilization have, in this European world of ours, depended for ages upon two principles, and were indeed the result of both combined; I mean the spirit of a gentleman and the spirit of religion. The nobility and the clergy, the one by profession, the other by patronage, kept learning in existence, even in the midst of arms and confusions, and whilst governments were rather in their causes than formed. Learning paid back what it received to nobility and to priesthood, and paid it with usury, by enlarging their ideas and by furnishing their minds. Happy if they had all continued to know their indissoluble union and their proper place! Happy if learning, not debauched by ambition, had been satisfied to continue the instructor and not aspired to be the master! Along with its natural protectors and guardians, learning will be cast into the mire and trodden down under the hoofs of a swinish multitude.

If, as I suspect, modern letters owe more than they are always willing to own to ancient manners, so do other interests which we value full as much as they are worth. Even commerce and trade and manufacture, the gods of our economical politicians, are themselves perhaps but creatures, are themselves but effects which, as first causes, we choose to worship. They certainly grew under the same shade in which learning flourished. They too may decay with their natural protecting principles. With you, for the present at least, they all threaten to disappear together. Where trade and manufactures are wanting to a people and the spirit of nobility and religion remains, sentiment supplies, and not always ill supplies, their place; but if commerce and the arts should be lost in an experiment to try how well a state may stand without these old fundamental principles, what sort of a thing must be a nation of gross, stupid, ferocious, and, at the same time, poor and sordid barbarians, destitute of religion, honor, or manly pride, possessing nothing at present and hoping for nothing hereafter?

I wish you may not be going fast, and by the shortest cut, to that horrible and disgustful situation. Already there appears a poverty of conception, a coarseness and vulgarity in all the proceedings of the assembly and of all their instructors. Their liberty is not liberal. Their science is presumptuous ignorance. Their humanity is savage and brutal. . . .

I almost venture to affirm that not one in a hundred amongst us participates in the "triumph" of the Revolution Society. If the King and Queen of France and their children were to fall into our hands by the chance of war, in the most acrimonious of all hostilities (I deprecate such an event, I deprecate such hostility), they would be treated with another sort of triumphal entry into London. We formerly have had a king of France in that situation;[7] you have read how he was treated by the victor in the field and in what manner he was afterwards received in England. Four hundred years have gone over us; but I believe we are not materially changed since that period. Thanks to our sullen resistance to innovation, thanks to the cold sluggishness of our national character, we still bear the stamp of our forefathers. We have not (as I conceive) lost the generosity and dignity of thinking of the fourteenth century; nor as yet have we subtilized ourselves into savages. We are not the converts of Rousseau; we are not the disciples of Voltaire; Helvetius has made no progress amongst us. Atheists are not our preachers; madmen are not our lawgivers. We know that *we* have made no discoveries, and we think that no discoveries are to be made in morality, nor many in the great principles of government, nor in the ideas of liberty, which were understood long before we were born altogether as well as they will be after the grave has heaped its mold upon our presumption and the silent tomb shall have imposed its law on our pert loquacity. In England we have not yet been completely emboweled of our natural entrails; we still feel within us, and we cherish and cultivate, those inbred sentiments which are the faithful guardians, the active monitors of our duty, the true supporters of all liberal and manly morals. We have not been drawn and trussed in order that we may be filled, like stuffed birds in a museum, with chaff and rags and

7 King John of France was captured by the English at Poitiers in 1356.

paltry blurred shreds of paper about the rights of man. We preserve the whole of our feelings still native and entire, unsophisticated by pedantry and infidelity. We have real hearts of flesh and blood beating in our bosoms. We fear God; we look up with awe to kings, with affection to parliaments, with duty to magistrates, with reverence to priests, and with respect to nobility. Why? Because when such ideas are brought before our minds, it is *natural* to be so affected; because all other feelings are false and spurious and tend to corrupt our minds, to vitiate our primary morals, to render us unfit for rational liberty, and, by teaching us a servile, licentious, and abandoned insolence, to be our low sport for a few holidays, to make us perfectly fit for and justly deserving of slavery through the whole course of our lives.

You see, sir, that in this enlightened age I am bold enough to confess that we are generally men of untaught feelings, that instead of casting away all our old prejudices, we cherish them to a very considerable degree, and, to take more shame to ourselves, we cherish them because they are prejudices; and the longer they have lasted and the more generally they have prevailed, the more we cherish them. We are afraid to put men to live and trade each on his own private stock of reason, because we suspect that this stock in each man is small and that the individuals would do better to avail themselves of the general bank and capital of nations and of ages. Many of our men of speculation, instead of exploding general prejudices, employ their sagacity to discover the latent wisdom which prevails in them. If they find what they seek (and they seldom fail) they think it more wise to continue the prejudice, with the reason involved, than to cast away the coat of prejudice and to leave nothing but the naked reason; because prejudice, with its reason, has a motive to give action to that reason and an affection which will give it permanence. Prejudice is of ready application in the emergency; it previously engages the mind in a steady course of wisdom and virtue and does not leave the man hesitating in the moment of decision, skeptical, puzzled, and unresolved. Prejudice renders a man's virtue his habit, and not a series of unconnected acts. Through just prejudice, his duty becomes a part of his nature.

Your literary men and your politicians (and so do the whole clan of the enlightened among us) essentially differ in these points. They have no respect for the wisdom of others, but they pay it

off by a very full measure of confidence in their own. With them
it is a sufficient motive to destroy an old scheme of things because
it is an old one. As to the new, they are in no sort of fear with regard to the duration of a building run up in haste, because duration
is no object to those who think little or nothing has been done
before their time and who place all their hopes in discovery. They
conceive, very systematically, that all things which give perpetuity are mischievous, and therefore they are at inexpiable war with
all establishments. They think that government may vary like
modes of dress and with as little ill effect; that there needs no principle of attachment, except a sense of present conveniency, to any
constitution of the state. They always speak as if they were of opinion that there is a singular species of compact between them and
their magistrates, which binds the magistrate, but which has nothing reciprocal in it, but that the majesty of the people has a right
to dissolve it without any reason but its will. Their attachment to
their country itself is only so far as it agrees with some of their
fleeting projects; it begins and ends with that scheme of polity
which falls in with their momentary opinion.

  These doctrines, or rather sentiments, seem prevalent with your
new statesmen. But they are wholly different from those on which
we have always acted in this country.

  I hear it is sometimes given out in France that what is doing
among you is after the example of England. I beg leave to affirm
that scarcely anything done with you has originated from the practice or the prevalent opinions of this people, either in the act or
in the spirit of the proceeding. Let me add that we are as unwilling
to learn these lessons from France as we are sure that we never
taught them to that nation. The cabals here who take a sort of
share in your transactions as yet consist of but a handful of people.
If unfortunately by their intrigues, their sermons, their publications, and by a confidence derived from an expected union with
the counsels and forces of the French nation, they should draw
considerable numbers into their faction and in consequence should
seriously attempt anything here in imitation of what has been done
with you, the event, I dare venture to prophesy, will be that, with
some trouble to their country, they will soon accomplish their own
destruction. This people refused to change their law in remote
ages from respect to the infallibility of popes, and they will not
now alter it from a pious implicit faith in the dogmatism of philos-

ophers, though the former was armed with the anathema and crusade and though the latter should act with the libel and the lamp iron.

Formerly your affairs were your own concern only. We felt for them as men; but we kept aloof from them because we were not citizens of France. But when we see the model held up to ourselves, we must feel as Englishmen, and feeling, we must provide as Englishmen. Your affairs, in spite of us, are made a part of our interest, so far at least as to keep at a distance your panacea or your plague. If it be a panacea, we do not want it. We know the consequences of unnecessary physic. If it be a plague, it is such a plague that the precautions of the most severe quarantine ought to be established against it.

I hear on all hands that a cabal calling itself philosophic receives the glory of many of the late proceedings, and that their opinions and systems are the true actuating spirit of the whole of them. I have heard of no party in England, literary or political, at any time known by such a description. It is not with you composed of those men, is it, whom the vulgar, in their blunt, homely style, commonly call atheists and infidels? If it be, I admit that we too have had writers of that description who made some noise in their day. At present they repose in lasting oblivion. Who born within the last forty years has read one word of Collins and Toland and Tindal and Chubb and Morgan and that whole race who called themselves freethinkers? Who now reads Bolingbroke? [8] Who ever read him through? Ask the booksellers of London what is become of all these lights of the world. In as few years their few successors will go to the family vault of "all the Capulets." But whatever they were or are with us, they were and are wholly unconnected individuals. With us they kept the common nature of their kind and were not gregarious. They never acted in corps or were known as a faction in the state nor presumed to influence in that name or character or for the purposes of such a faction any of our public concerns. Whether they ought so to exist and so be permitted to act is another question. As such cabals have not existed in England, so neither has the spirit of them had any influence in establishing

---

8 Henry St. John, Viscount Bolingbroke, author of *The Idea of a Patriot King* (1749) and a number of philosophical essays with a deistic leaning. The influence of Bolingbroke appears in Pope's *Essay on Man*.

the original frame of our constitution or in any one of the several reparations and improvements it has undergone. The whole has been done under the auspices and is confirmed by the sanctions of religion and piety. The whole has emanated from the simplicity of our national character and from a sort of native plainness and directness of understanding which for a long time characterized those men who have successively obtained authority amongst us. This disposition still remains, at least in the great body of the people.

We know and, what is better, we feel inwardly that religion is the basis of civil society and the source of all good and of all comfort. In England we are so convinced of this that there is no rust of superstition with which the accumulated absurdity of the human mind might have crusted it over in the course of ages, that ninety-nine in a hundred of the people of England would not prefer to impiety. We shall never be such fools as to call in an enemy to the substance of any system to remove its corruptions, to supply its defects, or to perfect its construction. If our religious tenets should ever want a further elucidation, we shall not call on atheism to explain them. We shall not light up our temple from that unhallowed fire. It will be illuminated with other lights. It will be perfumed with other incense than the infectious stuff which is imported by the smugglers of adulterated metaphysics. If our ecclesiastical establishment should want a revision, it is not avarice or rapacity, public or private, that we shall employ for the audit or receipt or application of its consecrated revenue. Violently condemning neither the Greek nor the Armenian, nor, since heats are subsided, the Roman system of religion, we prefer the Protestant; not because we think it has less of the Christian religion in it, but because, in our judgment, it has more. We are Protestants not from indifference but from zeal.

We know, and it is our pride to know, that man is by his constitution a religious animal; that atheism is against, not only our reason, but our instincts; and that it cannot prevail long. But if, in the moment of riot, and in a drunken delirium from the hot spirit drawn out of the alembic of hell, which in France is now so furiously boiling, we should uncover our nakedness by throwing off that Christian religion which has hitherto been our boast and comfort and one great source of civilization amongst us, and amongst many other nations, we are apprehensive (being well aware that the mind will not endure a void) that some uncouth, pernicious, and degrading superstition might take place of it.

For that reason, before we take from our establishment the natural human means of estimation, and give it up to contempt, as you have done, and in doing it have incurred the penalties you well deserve to suffer, we desire that some other may be presented to us in the place of it. We shall then form our judgment.

On these ideas, instead of quarreling with establishments, as some do who have made a philosophy and a religion of their hostility to such institutions, we cleave closely to them. We are resolved to keep an established church, an established monarchy, an established aristocracy, and an established democracy, each in the degree it exists, and in no greater. I shall show you presently how much of each of these we possess.

It has been the misfortune (not, as these gentlemen think it, the glory) of this age, that everything is to be discussed, as if the constitution of our country were to be always a subject rather of altercation than enjoyment. For this reason, as well as for the satisfaction of those among you (if any such you have among you) who may wish to profit of examples, I venture to trouble you with a few thoughts upon each of these establishments. I do not think they were unwise in ancient Rome, who, when they wished to new-model their laws, sent commissioners to examine the best constituted republics within their reach.

First, I beg leave to speak of our church establishment, which is the first of our prejudices; not a prejudice destitute of reason, but involving in it profound and extensive wisdom. I speak of it first. It is first, and last, and midst in our minds. For, taking ground on that religious system of which we are now in possession, we continue to act on the early received and uniformly continued sense of mankind. That sense not only, like a wise architect, hath built up the august fabric of states, but like a provident proprietor, to preserve the structure from profanation and ruin, as a sacred temple purged from all the impurities of fraud and violence and injustice and tyranny, hath solemnly and forever consecrated the commonwealth and all that officiate in it. This consecration is made, that all who administer in the government of men, in which they stand in the person of God himself, should have high and worthy notions of their function and destination; that their hope should be full of immortality; that they should not look to the paltry pelf of the moment, nor to the temporary and transient praise of the vulgar, but to a solid, permanent existence, in the permanent part of their nature, and to a permanent fame and glory, in the example they leave as a rich inheritance to the world.

Such sublime principles ought to be infused into persons of exalted situations, and religious establishments provided that may continually revive and enforce them. Every sort of moral, every sort of civil, every sort of politic institution, aiding the rational and natural ties that connect the human understanding and affections to the divine, are not more than necessary, in order to build up that wonderful structure, Man, whose prerogative it is to be in a great degree a creature of his own making, and who, when made as he ought to be made, is destined to hold no trivial place in the creation. But whenever man is put over men, as the better nature ought ever to preside, in that case more particularly, he should as nearly as possible be approximated to his perfection.

The consecration of the state, by a state religious establishment, is necessary also to operate with a wholesome awe upon free citizens; because, in order to secure their freedom, they must enjoy some determinate portion of power. To them, therefore, a religion connected with the state, and with their duty towards it, becomes even more necessary than in such societies where the people, by the terms of their subjection, are confined to private sentiments and the management of their own family concerns. All persons possessing any portion of power ought to be strongly and awefully impressed with an idea that they act in trust; and that they are to account for their conduct in that trust to the one great Master, Author, and Founder of society.

This principle ought even to be more strongly impressed upon the minds of those who compose the collective sovereignty than upon those of single princes. Without instruments, these princes can do nothing. Whoever uses instruments, in finding helps, finds also impediments. Their power is, therefore, by no means complete; nor are they safe in extreme abuse. Such persons, however elevated by flattery, arrogance, and self-opinion, must be sensible that, whether covered or not by positive law, in some way or other they are accountable even here for the abuse of their trust. If they are not cut off by a rebellion of their people, they may be strangled by the very janissaries kept for their security against all other rebellion. Thus we have seen the King of France sold by his soldiers for an increase of pay. But where popular authority is absolute and unrestrained, the people have an infinitely greater, because a far better founded, confidence in their own power. They are themselves, in a great measure, their own instruments. They are nearer to their objects. Besides, they are less under responsibility to one of the greatest controlling powers on earth, the sense of fame and estimation. The share of infamy that is likely to fall to the lot of each individual in public acts is small indeed; the operation of opinion being in the inverse ratio to the number of those who abuse power. Their own approbation of their own acts has to them the appearance of a public judgment in their favor. A perfect democracy is, therefore, the most shameless thing in the world. As it is the most shameless, it is also the most fearless. No man apprehends in his person that he can be made subject to punishment. Certainly the people at large never ought: for as all punishments are for example towards the conservation of the people at large, the people at large can never become the subject of punishment by any human hand. It is therefore of infinite importance that they should not be suffered to imagine that their will, any more than that of kings, is the standard of right and wrong. They ought to be persuaded that they are full as little entitled, and far less qualified, with safety to themselves, to use any arbitrary power whatsoever; that therefore they are not, under a false show of liberty, but in truth, to exercise an unnatural, inverted domination, tyrannically to exact, from those who officiate in the state, not an entire devotion to their interest, which is their right, but an abject submission to their occasional will; extinguishing thereby, in all those who serve them, all moral principle, all sense of dignity, all use of judgment, and all consistency of character; whilst by the very same process they give themselves up a proper, a suitable, but a most contemptible prey to the servile ambition of popular sycophants or courtly flatterers.

When the people have emptied themselves of all the lust of selfish will, which without religion it is utterly impossible they ever should, when they are conscious that they exercise, and exercise perhaps in a higher link of the order of delegation, the power which to be legitimate must be according to that eternal, immutable law in which will and reason are the same, they will be more careful how they place power in base and incapable hands. In their nomination to office, they will not appoint to the exercise of authority, as to a pitiful job, but as to a holy function; not according to their sordid, selfish interest, nor to their wanton caprice, nor to their arbitrary will; but they will confer that power (which any man may well tremble to give or to receive) on those only in whom they may discern that predominant proportion of active virtue and wisdom, taken together and fitted to the charge, such, as in the great and inevitable mixed mass of human imperfections and infirmities, is to be found.

When they are habitually convinced that no evil can be acceptable, either in the act or the permission, to him whose essence is good, they will be better able to extirpate out of the minds of all magistrates, civil, ecclesiastical, or military, anything that bears the least resemblance to a proud and lawless domination.

But one of the first and most leading principles on which the commonwealth and the laws are consecrated is lest the temporary possessors and life-renters in it, unmindful of what they have received from their ancestors, or of what is due to their posterity, should act as if they were the entire masters; that they should not think it among their rights to cut off the entail, or commit waste on the inheritance, by destroying at their pleasure the whole original fabric of their society; hazarding to leave to those who come after them a ruin instead of an habitation, and teaching these successors as little to respect their contrivances as they had themselves respected the institutions of their forefathers. By this unprincipled facility of changing the state as often and as much and in as many ways as there are floating fancies or fashions, the whole chain and continuity of the commonwealth would be broken. No one generation could link with the other. Men would become little better than the flies of a summer.

And first of all, the science of jurisprudence, the pride of the human intellect, which, with all its defects, redundancies, and errors, is the collected reason of ages, combining the principles of original justice with the infinite variety of human concerns, as a heap of old exploded errors, would be no longer studied. Personal self-sufficiency and arrogance (the certain attendants upon all those who have never experienced a wisdom greater than their own) would usurp the tribunal. Of course no certain laws, establishing invariable grounds of hope and fear, would keep the actions of men in a certain course, or direct them to a certain end.

Nothing stable in the modes of holding property, or exercising function, could form a solid ground on which any parent could speculate in the education of his offspring, or in a choice for their future establishment in the world. No principles would be early worked into the habits. As soon as the most able instructor had completed his laborious course of institution, instead of sending forth his pupil accomplished in a virtuous discipline, fitted to procure him attention and respect in his place in society, he would find everything altered; and that he had turned out a poor creature to the contempt and derision of the world, ignorant of the true grounds of estimation. Who would insure a tender and delicate sense of honor to beat almost with the first pulses of the heart, when no man could know what would be the test of honor in a nation continually varying the standard of its coin? No part of life would retain its acquisitions. Barbarism with regard to science and literature, unskillfulness with regard to arts and manufactures, would infallibly succeed to the want of a steady education and settled principle; and thus the commonwealth itself would, in a few generations, crumble away, be disconnected into the dust and powder of individuality, and at length dispersed to all the winds of heaven.

To avoid therefore the evils of inconstancy and versatility, ten thousand times worse than those of obstinacy and the blindest prejudice, we have consecrated the state, that no man should approach to look into its defects or corruptions but with due caution; that he should never dream of beginning its reformation by its subversion; that he should approach to the faults of the state as to the wounds of a father, with pious awe and trembling solicitude. By this wise prejudice we are taught to look with horror on those children of their country who are prompt rashly to hack that aged parent in pieces and put him into the kettle of magicians in hopes that by their poisonous weeds and wild incantations they may regenerate the paternal constitution and renovate their father's life.

Society is indeed a contract. Subordinate contracts for objects of mere occasional interest may be dissolved at pleasure; but the state ought not to be considered as nothing better than a partnership agreement in a trade of pepper and coffee, calico or tobacco, or some other such low concern, to be taken up for a little temporary interest and to be dissolved by the fancy of the parties. It is to be looked on with other reverence; because it is not a partnership in things subservient only to the gross animal existence of a temporary and perishable nature. It is a partnership in all science, a partnership in all art, a partnership in every virtue, and in all perfection. As the ends of such a partnership cannot be obtained in many generations, it becomes a partnership not only between those who are living but between those who are living, those who are dead, and those who are to be born. Each contract of each particular state is but a clause in the great primeval contract of eternal society, linking the lower with the higher natures, connecting the visible and invisible world, according to a fixed compact sanctioned by the inviolable oath which holds all physical and all moral natures, each in their appointed place. This law is not subject to the will of those who by an obligation above them, and infinitely superior, are bound to submit their will to that law. The municipal corporations of that universal kingdom are not morally at liberty at their pleasure, and on their speculations of a contingent improvement, wholly to separate and tear asunder the bands of their subordinate community, and to dissolve it into an unsocial, uncivil, unconnected chaos of elementary principles. It is the first and supreme necessity only, a necessity that is not chosen, but chooses, a necessity paramount to deliberation, that admits no discussion, and demands no evidence, which alone can justify a resort to anarchy. This necessity is no exception to the rule; because this necessity itself is a part too of that moral and physical disposition of things to which man must be obedient by consent or force. But if that which is only submission to necessity should be made the object of choice, the law is broken, nature is disobeyed, and the rebellious are outlawed, cast forth, and exiled from this world of reason and order and peace and virtue and fruitful penitence, into the antagonist world of madness, discord, vice, confusion, and unavailing sorrow.

Thomas Paine

1737–1809

THE virtues and failings of the revolutionist are both apparent in Tom Paine, the universal "friend of man" and ardent hater of "tyranny." He heroically exposes social abuses and religious superstition, and he can inflame the American colonists against a wrongheaded English policy. He is above all the successful pamphleteer who can instigate a program of "direct action." He became in America and France, as well as in England, a symbol of "enlightened" defiance against every sort of oppression. Yet he is the victim of an ideology. Like the French *philosophe* or encyclopedist, he is addicted to the stark rational abstractions that run through eighteenth-century democratic thought—the equality of man, the state of nature, the social compact, natural rights, and so on. His value is often a critical, destructive one. He is honest and unselfish and courageous, but he cannot deal with the complexities of an actual situation. Unlike Burke, Paine can draw an issue simply and clearly: Here is the principle; follow it. Thus he fails in tact and perception—"The composition of poetry," he explains, "differs from that of prose in the manner of mixing long and short syllables together." (One recalls Bentham's distinction that "Prose *is when* all the lines except the last go on to the margin; poetry is when some of them fall short of it!") The same want of perception makes Paine's attack upon Christianity not blasphemous (because it is honestly and indignantly meant) but simply incompetent: "The Christian theory is little else than the idolatry of the ancient mythologists accommodated to the purposes of power and revenue." To Paine, God is a scientist governing the universe, and at the same time a great philanthropist "of the most benevolent kind." As in Diderot and the other radical "friends of humanity," the rational abstractions of Paine are heated by strong social affections. But for all his limitations, the democratic tradition would be much poorer without its Tom Paine. He is a necessary corrective to the traditionalism of Burke and vigorously states the case against prerogative and inequality.

BIOGRAPHICAL NOTES

Son of a Quaker stay-maker of Thetford. At school "repressed" his "tendency to poetry." Employed as stay-maker, sailor, tobacconist, and schoolteacher. Married Mary Lambert (1759); she died the next year. Twice discharged as excise officer (1765, 1774). Developed strong interest in mechanical devices. Married Elizabeth Ollive (1771). Sold property to satisfy creditors. Separated from wife and, bearing a letter of introduction from Benjamin Franklin, went to Philadelphia for "subsistence" (1774). Edited *Pennsylvania Magazine*. Devoted self to the cause of American independence; printed *Common Sense* (1776), urging separation from England. *The Crisis* (1776–83) designed to bolster American morale during the war. Accompanied John Laurens to France (1781) to negotiate a loan to the colonies. In return for these services, was granted an estate at New Rochelle. Visited Paris to discuss plans for a suspension bridge (1787). In London, met Godwin, Blake, Thomas Holcroft, and Horne Tooke. *The Rights of Man* (1791–92), asserting, in reply to Burke's *Reflections,* the principles of the French Revolution. Fled from England to Paris under indictment for high treason. Elected a member of the National Assembly (1792), but imprisoned after pleading against the execution of Louis XVI and sundry intrigues against him. *The Age of Reason* finished during this imprisonment (1793). Escaped guillotine through the aid of James Monroe. Took refuge in New Rochelle (1804). Regarded as an atheist and completely neglected; died in poverty and obscurity in New York.

BIBLIOGRAPHY: *Writings,* ed. M. D. Conway, 4 vols., 1894–96. Aldridge, Alfred Owen, *Man of Reason,* 1959. Best, Mary Agnes, *Thomas Paine, Prophet and Martyr of Democracy,* 1927. Gould, Frederick John, *Thomas Paine,* 1925. Pearson, Hesketh, *Tom Paine, Friend of Mankind,* 1937.

THE RIGHTS OF MAN

1791–1792

PART I

Among the incivilities by which nations or individuals provoke and irritate each other, Mr. Burke's pamphlet on the French Revolution [1] is an extraordinary instance. Neither the people of France nor the National Assembly were troubling themselves about the affairs of England or the English Parliament; and that Mr. Burke should commence an unprovoked attack upon them, both in Parliament and in public, is a conduct that cannot be pardoned on the score of manners, nor justified on that of policy.

There is scarcely an epithet of abuse to be found in the English language with which Mr. Burke has not loaded the French nation and the National Assembly. Everything which rancor, prejudice, ignorance, or knowledge could suggest is poured forth in the copious fury of near four hundred pages. In the strain and on the plan

1 Burke's *Reflections on the Revolution in France* (1790)—hardly a pamphlet!

Mr. Burke was writing, he might have written on to as many thousands. When the tongue or the pen is let loose in a frenzy of passion, it is the man, and not the subject, that becomes exhausted.

Hitherto Mr. Burke has been mistaken and disappointed in the opinions he had formed of the affairs of France; but such is the ingenuity of his hope, or the malignancy of his despair, that it furnishes him with new pretenses to go on. There was a time when it was impossible to make Mr. Burke believe there would be any revolution in France. His opinion then was that the French had neither spirit to undertake it nor fortitude to support it; and now that there is one, he seeks an escape by condemning it.

Not sufficiently content with abusing the National Assembly, a great part of his work is taken up with abusing Dr. Price (one of the best-hearted men that lives) and the two societies in England known by the name of the Revolution and the Constitutional Societies.

Dr. Price had preached a sermon on the 4th of November, 1789, being the anniversary of what is called in England the Revolution, which took place in 1688. Mr. Burke, speaking of this sermon, says, "The political divine proceeds dogmatically to assert that by the principles of the Revolution the people of England have acquired three fundamental rights:

1. To choose our own governors.
2. To cashier them for misconduct.
3. To frame a government for ourselves."

Dr. Price does not say that the right to do these things exists in this or in that person, or in this or in that description of persons, but that it exists in the *whole*—that it is a right resident in the nation. Mr. Burke, on the contrary, denies that such a right exists in the nation, either in whole or in part, or that it exists anywhere; and, what is still more strange and marvelous, he says "that the people of England utterly disclaim such a right, and that they will resist the practical assertion of it with their lives and fortunes." That men should take up arms and spend their lives and fortunes, *not* to maintain their rights, but to maintain they have *not* rights, is an entirely new species of discovery, and suited to the paradoxical genius of Mr. Burke.

The method which Mr. Burke takes to prove that the people of England have no such rights, and that such rights do not now exist

Skirts of the Wood by Thomas Gainsborough

Scene in Bedlam from "The Rake's Progress" by William Hogarth

Prison Scene from "The Rake's Progress" by William Hogarth

in the nation, either in whole or in part, or anywhere at all, is of the same marvelous and monstrous kind with what he has already said; for his arguments are that the persons, or the generation of persons, in whom they did exist, are dead, and with them the right is dead also. To prove this, he quotes a declaration made by Parliament about a hundred years ago, to William and Mary, in these words: "The Lords Spiritual and Temporal, and Commons, do, in the name of the people aforesaid [meaning the people of England then living], most humbly and faithfully *submit* themselves, their *heirs* and *posterity*, for EVER." He also quotes a clause of another act of Parliament made in the same reign, the terms of which, he says, "bind us [meaning the people of that day], our *heirs* and our *posterity*, to *them*, their *heirs* and *posterity*, to the end of time."

Mr. Burke conceives his point sufficiently established by producing those clauses, which he enforces by saying that they exclude the right of the nation for *ever;* and not yet content with making such declarations, repeated over and over again, he further says "that if the people of England possessed such a right before the Revolution [which he acknowledges to have been the case, not only in England, but throughout Europe, at an early period], yet that the *English nation* did, at the time of the Revolution, most solemnly renounce and abdicate it, for themselves, and *for all their posterity, for ever.*"

As Mr. Burke occasionally applies the poison drawn from his horrid principles (if it is not profanation to call them by the name of principles), not only to the English nation, but to the French Revolution and the National Assembly, and charges that august, illuminated, and illuminating body of men with the epithet of *usurpers*, I shall, *sans cérémonie*, place another system of principles in opposition to his.

The English Parliament of 1688 did a certain thing which, for themselves and their constituents, they had a right to do, and which it appeared right should be done; but, in addition to this right, which they possessed by delegation, *they set up another right by assumption*, that of binding and controlling posterity to the end of time. The case, therefore, divides itself into two parts: the right which they possessed by delegation and the right which they set up by assumption. The first is admitted; but with respect to the second, I reply—

There never did, there never will, and there never can, exist a parliament, or any description of men, or any generation of men, in any country, possessed of the right or the power of binding and controlling posterity to the *"end of time,"* or of commanding forever how the world shall be governed, or who shall govern it; and therefore all such clauses, acts, or declarations by which the makers of them attempt to do what they have neither the right nor the power to do, nor the power to execute, are in themselves null and void. Every age and generation must be as free to act for itself *in all cases* as the ages and generations which preceded it. The vanity and presumption of governing beyond the grave is the most ridiculous and insolent of all tyrannies. Man has no property in man; neither has any generation a property in the generations which are to follow. The Parliament or the people of 1688, or of any other period, had no more right to dispose of the people of the present day, or to bind or to control them *in any shape whatever*, than the Parliament or the people of the present day have to dispose of, bind or control those who are to live a hundred or a thousand years hence. Every generation is, and must be, competent to all the purposes which its occasions require. It is the living, and not the dead, that are to be accommodated. When man ceases to be, his power and his wants cease with him; and having no longer any participation in the concerns of this world, he has no longer any authority in directing who shall be its governors, or how its government shall be organized, or how administered.

I am not contending for nor against any form of government, nor for nor against any party, here or elsewhere. That which a whole nation chooses to do, it has a right to do. Mr. Burke says, No. Where, then, does the right exist? I am contending for the rights of the *living*, and against their being willed away, and controlled and contracted for, by the manuscript-assumed authority of the dead; and Mr. Burke is contending for the authority of the dead over the rights and freedom of the living. There was a time when kings disposed of their crowns by will upon their deathbeds, and consigned the people, like beasts of the field, to whatever successor they appointed. This is now so exploded as scarcely to be remembered, and so monstrous as hardly to be believed; but the parliamentary clauses upon which Mr. Burke builds his political church are of the same nature.

The laws of every country must be analogous to some common principle. In England no parent or master, nor all the authority of

Parliament, omnipotent as it has called itself, can bind or control the personal freedom even of an individual beyond the age of twenty-one years. On what ground of right, then, could the Parliament of 1688, or any other Parliament, bind all posterity forever? . . .

I have now to follow Mr. Burke through a pathless wilderness of rhapsodies, and a sort of descant upon governments, in which he asserts whatever he pleases, on the presumption of its being believed, without offering either evidence or reasons for so doing.

Before anything can be reasoned upon to a conclusion, certain facts, principles, or data to reason from, must be established, admitted, or denied. Mr. Burke, with his usual outrage, abuses the "Declaration of the Rights of Man," published by the National Assembly of France, as the basis on which the constitution of France is built. This he calls "paltry and blurred sheets of paper about the rights of man." Does Mr. Burke mean to deny that *man* has any rights? If he does, then he must mean that there are no such things as rights anywhere, and that he has none himself; for who is there in the world but man? But if Mr. Burke means to admit that man has rights, the question then will be: What are those rights, and how man came by them originally?

The error of those who reason by precedents drawn from antiquity, respecting the rights of man, is that they do not go far enough into antiquity. They do not go the whole way. They stop in some of the intermediate stages of an hundred or a thousand years, and produce what was then done as a rule for the present day. This is no authority at all. If we travel still farther into antiquity, we shall find a direct contrary opinion and practice prevailing; and, if antiquity is to be authority, a thousand such authorities may be produced, successively contradicting each other; but if we proceed on, we shall at last come out right; we shall come to the time when man came from the hand of his Maker. What was he then? Man. Man was his high and only title, and a higher cannot be given him.—But of titles I shall speak hereafter.

We are now got at the origin of man, and at the origin of his rights. As to the manner in which the world has been governed from that day to this, it is no farther any concern of ours than to make a proper use of the errors or the improvements which the history of it presents. Those who lived a hundred or a thousand years ago were then moderns, as we are now. They had *their* ancients, and those ancients had others, and we also shall be ancients in our turn. If the mere name of antiquity is to govern in the affairs of life, the people who are to live an hundred or a thousand years hence may as well take us for a precedent, as we make a precedent of those who lived an hundred or a thousand years ago. The fact is that portions of antiquity, by proving everything, establish nothing. It is authority against authority all the way, till we come to the divine origin of the rights of man, at the creation. Here our inquiries find a resting place, and our reason finds a home. If a dispute about the rights of man had arisen at the distance of an hundred years from the creation, it is to this source of authority they must have referred, and it is to this same source of authority that we must now refer.

Though I mean not to touch upon any sectarian principle of religion, yet it may be worth observing that the genealogy of Christ is traced to Adam. Why, then, not trace the rights of man to the creation of man? I will answer the question. Because there have been upstart governments, thrusting themselves between, and presumptuously working to *unmake* man.

If any generation of men ever possessed the right of dictating the mode by which the world should be governed forever, it was the first generation that existed; and if that generation did not do it, no succeeding generation can show any authority for doing it, nor set any up. The illuminating and divine principle of the equal rights of man (for it has its origin from the Maker of man) relates not only to the living individuals, but to generations of men succeeding each other. Every generation is equal in rights to the generations which preceded it, by the same rule that every individual is born equal in rights with his contemporary.

Every history of the creation, and every traditionary account, whether from the lettered or unlettered world, however they may vary in their opinion or belief of certain particulars, all agree in establishing one point, *the unity of man;* by which I mean that men are all of *one degree,* and consequently that all men are born equal, and with equal natural rights, in the same manner as if posterity had been continued by creation instead of generation, the latter being the only mode by which the former is carried forward; and consequently, every child born into the world must be considered as deriving its existence from God. The world is as new to him as it was to the first man that existed, and his natural right in it is of the same kind.

The Mosaic account of the creation, whether taken as divine authority or merely historical, is fully up to this point, *the unity or equality of man.* The expression admits of no controversy. "And God said, let us make man in our own image. In the image of God created he him; male and female created he them." The distinction of sexes is pointed out, but no other distinction is even implied. If this be not divine authority, it is at least historical authority, and shows that the equality of man, so far from being a modern doctrine, is the oldest upon record.

It is also to be observed that all the religions known in the world are founded, so far as they relate to man, on the *unity of man,* as being all of one degree. Whether in heaven or in hell, or in whatever state man may be supposed to exist hereafter, the good and the bad are the only distinctions. Nay, even the laws of governments are obliged to slide into this principle, by making degrees to consist in crimes, and not in persons.

It is one of the greatest of all truths, and of the highest advantage to cultivate. By considering man in this light, and by instructing him to consider himself in this light, it places him in a close connection with all his duties, whether to his Creator, or to the creation of which he is a part; and it is only when he forgets his origin, or, to use a more fashionable phrase, his birth and family, that he becomes dissolute. It is not among the least of the evils of the present existing governments in all parts of Europe that man, considered as man, is thrown back to a vast distance from his Maker, and the artificial chasm filled up by a succession of barriers, or a sort of turnpike gates, through which he has to pass. I will quote Mr. Burke's catalogue of barriers that he has set up between man and his Maker. Putting himself in the character of a herald, he says: "We fear God—we look with awe to kings—with affection to Parliaments—with duty to magistrates—with reverence to priests—and with respect to nobility." Mr. Burke has forgotten to put in "chivalry." He has also forgot to put in Peter.

The duty of man is not a wilderness of turnpike gates, through which he is to pass by tickets from one to the other. It is plain and simple, and consists but of two points: his duty to God, which every man must feel, and, with respect to his neighbor, to do as he would be done by. If those to whom power is delegated do well, they will be respected: if not, they will be despised; and with regard to those to whom no power is delegated, but who assume it, the rational world can know nothing of them.

Hitherto we have spoken only (and that but in part) of the natural rights of man. We have now to consider the civil rights of man, and to show how the one originates from the other. Man did not enter into society to become *worse* than he was before, nor to have less rights than he had before, but to have those rights better secured. His natural rights are the foundation of all his civil rights. But in order to pursue this distinction with more precision, it will be necessary to mark the different qualities of natural and civil rights.

A few words will explain this. Natural rights are those which appertain to man in right of his existence. Of this kind are all the intellectual rights, or rights of the mind, and also all those rights of acting as an individual for his own comfort and happiness, which are not injurious to the natural rights of others. Civil rights are those which appertain to man in right of his being a member of society. Every civil right has for its foundation some natural right preexisting in the individual, but to which his individual power is not, in all cases, sufficiently competent. Of this kind are all those which relate to security and protection.

From this short review it will be easy to distinguish between that class of natural rights which man retains after entering into society and those which he throws into the common stock as a member of society.

The natural rights which he retains are all those in which the *power* to execute is as perfect in the individual as the right itself. Among this class, as is before mentioned, are all the intellectual rights, or rights of the mind; consequently religion is one of those rights. The natural rights which are not retained are all those in which, though the right is perfect in the individual, the power to execute them is defective. They answer not his purpose. A man by natural right has a right to judge in his own cause; and so far as the right of the mind is concerned, he never surrenders it. But what availeth it him to judge, if he has not power to redress? He therefore deposits this right in the common stock of society, and takes the arm of society, of which he is a part, in preference and in addition to his own. Society *grants* him nothing. Every man is a proprietor in society, and draws on the capital as a matter of right.

From these premises two or three certain conclusions will follow:

First, That every civil right grows out of a natural right; or, in other words, is a natural right exchanged.

Secondly, That civil power properly considered as such is made up of the aggregate of that class of the natural rights of man which becomes defective in the individual in point of power, and answers not his purpose, but when collected to a focus becomes competent to the purpose of everyone.

Thirdly, That the power produced from the aggregate of natural rights, imperfect in power in the individual, cannot be applied to invade the natural rights which are retained in the individual, and in which the power to execute is as perfect as the right itself.

We have now, in a few words, traced man from a natural individual to a member of society, and shown, or endeavored to show, the quality of the natural rights retained, and of those which are exchanged for civil rights. Let us now apply these principles to governments.

In casting our eyes over the world, it is extremely easy to distinguish the governments which have arisen out of society, or out of the social compact, from those which have not; but to place this in a clearer light than what a single glance may afford, it will be proper to take a review of the several sources from which governments have arisen and on which they have been founded.

They may be all comprehended under three heads. First, superstition. Secondly, power. Thirdly, the common interest of society and the common rights of man.

The first was a government of priestcraft, the second of conquerors, and the third of reason.

When a set of artful men pretended, through the medium of oracles, to hold intercourse with the Deity as familiarly as they now march up the back stairs in European courts, the world was completely under the government of superstition. The oracles were consulted, and whatever they were made to say became the law; and this sort of government lasted as long as this sort of superstition lasted.

After these a race of conquerors arose, whose government, like that of William the Conqueror, was founded in power, and the sword assumed the name of a scepter. Governments thus established last as long as the power to support them lasts; but that they might avail themselves of every engine in their favor, they united fraud to force, and set up an idol which they called divine right, and which, in imitation of the Pope, who affects to be spiritual and temporal, and in contradiction to the founder of the Christian religion, twisted itself afterwards into an idol of another shape, called Church and State. The key of St. Peter and the key of the treasury became quartered on one another, and the wondering cheated multitude worshiped the invention.

When I contemplate the natural dignity of man, when I feel (for nature has not been kind enough to me to blunt my feelings) for the honor and happiness of its character, I become irritated at the attempt to govern mankind by force and fraud, as if they were all knaves and fools, and can scarcely avoid disgust at those who are thus imposed upon.

We have now to review the governments which arise out of society, in contradistinction to those which arose out of superstition and conquest.

It has been thought a considerable advance towards establishing the principles of freedom to say that government is a compact between those who govern and those who are governed; but this cannot be true, because it is putting the effect before the cause; for as man must have existed before governments existed, there necessarily was a time when governments did not exist, and consequently there could originally exist no governors to form such a compact with.

The fact therefore must be that the *individuals themselves*, each in his own personal and sovereign right, *entered into a compact with each other* to produce a government; and this is the only mode in which governments have a right to arise, and the only principle on which they have a right to exist.

To possess ourselves of a clear idea of what government is, or ought to be, we must trace it to its origin. In doing this we shall easily discover that governments must have arisen either *out* of the people or *over* the people. Mr. Burke has made no distinction. He investigates nothing to its source, and therefore he confounds everything; but he has signified his intention of undertaking, at some future opportunity, a comparison between the constitution of England and France. As he thus renders it a subject of controversy by throwing the gauntlet, I take him upon his own ground. It is in high challenges that high truths have the right of appearing; and I accept it with the more readiness because it affords me, at the same time, an opportunity of pursuing the subject with respect to governments arising out of society.

But it will be first necessary to define what is meant by a constitution. It is not sufficient that we adopt the word; we must fix also a standard signification to it.

A constitution is not a thing in name only, but in fact. It has not an ideal, but a real existence; and wherever it cannot be produced in a visible form, there is none. A constitution is a thing *antecedent* to a government, and a government is only the creature of a constitution. The constitution of a country is not the act of its government, but of the people constituting its government. It is the body of elements to which you can refer, and quote article by article; and which contains the principles on which the government shall be established, the manner in which it shall be organized, the powers it shall have, the mode of elections, the duration of parliaments, or by what other name such bodies may be called; the powers which the executive part of the government shall have; and in fine, everything that relates to the complete organization of a civil government, and the principles on which it shall act, and by which it shall be bound. A constitution, therefore, is to a government what the laws made afterwards by that government are to a court of judicature. The court of judicature does not make laws, neither can it alter them; it only acts in conformity to the laws made: and the government is in like manner governed by the constitution.

Can, then, Mr. Burke produce the English constitution? If he cannot, we may fairly conclude that though it has been so much talked about, no such thing as a constitution exists, or ever did exist, and consequently that the people have yet a constitution to form.

Mr. Burke will not, I presume, deny the position I have already advanced—namely, that governments arise either *out* of the people or *over* the people. The English government is one of those which arose out of a conquest, and not out of society, and consequently it arose over the people; and though it has been much modified from the opportunity of circumstances since the time of William the Conqueror, the country has never yet regenerated itself, and is therefore without a constitution. . . .

THE AGE OF REASON

1795

PART FIRST

I

It has been my intention, for several years past, to publish my thoughts upon religion. I am well aware of the difficulties that attend the subject, and, from that consideration, had reserved it to a more advanced period of life. I intended it to be the last offering I should make to my fellow citizens of all nations; and that at a time when the purity of the motive that induced me to it could not admit of a question, even by those who might disapprove the work.

The circumstance that has now taken place in France, of the total abolition of the whole national order of priesthood and of everything appertaining to compulsive systems of religion and compulsive articles of faith, has not only precipitated my intention, but rendered a work of this kind exceedingly necessary; lest, in the general wreck of superstition, of false systems of government, and false theology, we lose sight of morality, of humanity, and of the theology that is true.

As several of my colleagues, and others of my fellow citizens of France, have given me the example of making their voluntary and individual profession of faith, I also will make mine; and I do this with all that sincerity and frankness with which the mind of man communicates with itself.

I believe in one God, and no more; and I hope for happiness beyond this life.

I believe in the equality of man, and I believe that religious duties consist in doing justice, loving mercy, and endeavoring to make our fellow creatures happy.

But, lest it should be supposed that I believe many other things in addition to these, I shall, in the progress of this work, declare the things I do not believe, and my reasons for not believing them.

I do not believe in the creed professed by the Jewish church, by the Roman church, by the Greek church, by the Turkish church, by the Protestant church, nor by any church that I know of. My own mind is my own church.

All national institutions of churches, whether Jewish, Christian, or Turkish, appear to me no other than human inventions set up to terrify and enslave mankind and monopolize power and profit.

I do not mean by this declaration to condemn those who believe otherwise. They have the same right to their belief as I have to mine. But it is necessary to the happiness of man that he be mentally faithful to himself. Infidelity does not consist in believing, or in disbelieving; it consists in professing to believe what he does not believe.

It is impossible to calculate the moral mischief, if I may so express it, that mental lying has produced in society. When a man has so far corrupted and prostituted the chastity of his mind as to subscribe his professional belief to things he does not believe, he has prepared himself for the commission of every other crime. He takes up the trade of a priest for the sake of gain, and, in order to *qualify* himself for that trade, he begins with a perjury. Can we conceive anything more destructive to morality than this?

Soon after I had published the pamphlet *Common Sense* in America, I saw the exceeding probability that a revolution in the system of government would be followed by a revolution in the system of religion. The adulterous connection of church and state, wherever it had taken place, whether Jewish, Christian, or Turkish, had so effectually prohibited, by pains and penalties, every discussion upon established creeds, and upon first principles of religion that, until the system of government should be changed, those subjects could not be brought fairly and openly before the world; but that whenever this should be done, a revolution in the system of religion would follow. Human inventions and priestcraft would be detected, and man would return to the pure, unmixed, and unadulterated belief of one God, and no more.

Every national church or religion has established itself by pretending some special mission from God, communicated to certain individuals. The Jews have their Moses; the Christians their Jesus Christ, their apostles and saints; and the Turks their Mahomet—as if the way to God was not open to every man alike.

Each of those churches show certain books which they call *revelation*, or the word of God. The Jews say that their word of God was given by God to Moses face to face; the Christians say that their word of God came by divine inspiration; and the Turks say that their word of God (the Koran) was brought by an angel from heaven. Each of those churches accuse the other of unbelief; and, for my own part, I disbelieve them all.

As it is necessary to affix right ideas to words, I will, before I proceed further into the subject, offer some observations on the word *revelation.* Revelation, when applied to religion, means something communicated *immediately* from God to man.

No one will deny or dispute the power of the Almighty to make such a communication, if he pleases. But admitting, for the sake of a case, that something has been revealed to a certain person, and not revealed to any other person, it is revelation to that person only. When he tells it to a second person, a second to a third, a third to a fourth, and so on, it ceases to be a revelation to all those persons. It is a revelation to the first person only, and *hearsay* to every other; and, consequently, they are not obliged to believe it.

It is a contradiction in terms and ideas to call anything a revelation that comes to us at second hand, either verbally or in writing. Revelation is necessarily limited to the first communication. After this, it is only an account of something which that person says was a revelation made to him; and though he may find himself obliged to believe it, it cannot be incumbent upon me to believe it in the same manner, for it was not a revelation to *me,* and I have only his word for it that it was made to *him.*

When Moses told the children of Israel that he received the two tables of the commandments from the hand of God, they were not obliged to believe him, because they had no other authority for it than his telling them so; and I have no other authority for it than some historian telling me so. The commandments carry no internal evidence of divinity with them. They contain some good moral precepts, such as any man qualified to be a lawgiver or a legislator could produce himself, without having recourse to supernatural intervention.[1]

When I am told that the Koran was written in Heaven and brought to Mahomet by an angel, the account comes to near the same kind of hearsay evidence and second-hand authority as the former. I did not see the angel myself, and therefore I have a right not to believe it.

When also I am told that a woman called the Virgin Mary said,

[1] It is, however, necessary to except the declaration which says that God *visits the sins of the fathers upon the children.* This is contrary to every principle of moral justice. [Paine.]

or gave out, that she was with child without any cohabitation with a man, and that her betrothed husband, Joseph, said that an angel told him so, I have a right to believe them or not: such a circumstance required a much stronger evidence than their bare word for it; but we have not even this; for neither Joseph nor Mary wrote any such matter themselves. It is only reported by others that *they said so*. It is hearsay upon hearsay, and I do not choose to rest my belief upon such evidence.

It is, however, not difficult to account for the credit that was given to the story of Jesus Christ being the Son of God. He was born at a time when the heathen mythology had still some fashion and repute in the world, and that mythology had prepared the people for the belief of such a story. Almost all the extraordinary men that lived under the heathen mythology were reputed to be the sons of some of their gods. It was not a new thing, at that time, to believe a man to have been celestially begotten; the intercourse of gods with women was then a matter of familiar opinion. Their Jupiter, according to their accounts, had cohabited with hundreds; the story therefore had nothing in it either new, wonderful, or obscene; it was conformable to the opinions that then prevailed among the people called Gentiles, or mythologists, and it was those people only that believed it. The Jews, who had kept strictly to the belief of one God and no more, and who had always rejected the heathen mythology, never credited the story.

It is curious to observe how the theory of what is called the Christian church sprung out of the tail of the heathen mythology. A direct incorporation took place in the first instance, by making the reputed founder to be celestially begotten. The trinity of gods that then followed was no other than a reduction of the former plurality, which was about twenty or thirty thousand. The statue of Mary succeeded the statue of Diana of Ephesus. The deification of heroes changed into the canonization of saints. The mythologists had gods for everything; the Christian mythologists had saints for everything. The church became as crowded with the one as the pantheon had been with the other; and Rome was the place of both. The Christian theory is little else than the idolatry of the ancient mythologists, accommodated to the purposes of power and revenue; and it yet remains to reason and philosophy to abolish the amphibious fraud.

Nothing that is here said can apply, even with the most distant disrespect, to the *real* character of Jesus Christ. He was a virtuous and an amiable man. The morality that he preached and practiced was of the most benevolent kind; and though similar systems of morality had been preached by Confucius, and by some of the Greek philosophers, many years before, by the Quakers since, and by many good men in all ages, it has not been exceeded by any.

Jesus Christ wrote no account of himself, of his birth, parentage, or anything else. Not a line of what is called the New Testament is of his writing. The history of him is altogether the work of other people; and as to the account given of his resurrection and ascension, it was the necessary counterpart to the story of his birth. His historians, having brought him into the world in supernatural manner, were obliged to take him out again in the same manner, or the first part of the story must have fallen to the ground.

The wretched contrivance with which this latter part is told exceeds everything that went before it. The first part, that of the miraculous conception, was not a thing that admitted of publicity; and therefore the tellers of this part of the story had this advantage, that though they might not be credited they could not be detected. They could not be expected to prove it, because it was not one of those things that admitted of proof, and it was impossible that the person of whom it was told could prove it himself.

But the resurrection of a dead person from the grave, and his ascension through the air, is a thing very different, as to the evidence it admits of, to the invisible conception of a child in the womb. The resurrection and ascension, supposing them to have taken place, admitted of public and ocular demonstration, like that of the ascension of a balloon, or the sun at noonday, to all Jerusalem at least. A thing which everybody is required to believe requires that the proof and evidence of it should be equal to all, and universal; and as the public visibility of this last related act was the only evidence that could give sanction to the former part, the whole of it falls to the ground, because that evidence never was given. Instead of this, a small number of persons, not more than eight or nine, are introduced as proxies for the whole world, to say they *saw it*, and all the rest of the world are called upon to believe it. But it appears that Thomas did not believe the resurrection; and, as they say, would not believe without having ocular and manual demonstration himself. *So neither will I;* and the reason is equally as good for me, and for every other person, as for Thomas. It is in vain to attempt to palliate or disguise this matter. The story, so far as relates to the supernatural part, has every mark of fraud and imposition stamped upon the face of it. Who were the authors of it is as impossible for us now to know as it is for us to be assured that the books in which the account is related were written by the persons whose names they bear. The best surviving evidence we now have respecting this affair is the Jews. They are regularly descended from the people who lived in the times this resurrection and ascension is said to have happened, and they say *it is not true*. It has long appeared to me a strange inconsistency to cite the Jews as a proof of the truth of the story. It is the same as if a man were to say, "I will prove the truth of what I have told you by producing the people who say it is false."

That such a person as Jesus Christ existed, and that he was crucified, which was the mode of execution at that day, are historical relations strictly within the limits of probability. He preached most excellent morality and the equality of man; but he preached also against the corruptions and avarice of the Jewish priests; and this brought upon him the hatred and vengeance of the whole order of priesthood. The accusation which those priests brought against him was that of sedition and conspiracy against the Roman government, to which the Jews were then subject and tributary; and it is not improbable that the Roman government might have some secret apprehension of the effects of his doctrine as well as the Jewish priests; neither is it improbable that Jesus Christ had in contemplation the delivery of the Jewish nation from the bondage of the Romans. Between the two, however, this virtuous reformer and revolutionist lost his life.

It is upon this plain narrative of facts, together with another case I am going to mention, that the Christian mythologists, calling themselves the Christian church, have erected their fable, which for absurdity and extravagance is not exceeded by anything that is to be found in the mythology of the ancients.

The ancient mythologists tell that the race of giants made war against Jupiter, and that one of them threw an hundred rocks against him at one throw; that Jupiter defeated him with thunder, and confined him afterwards under Mount Aetna; and that every time the giant turns himself, Mount Aetna belches fire. It is here easy to see that the circumstance of the mountain, that of its being a volcano, suggested the idea of the fable; and that the fable is made to fit and wind itself up with that circumstance.

The Christian mythologists tell that their Satan made war against the Almighty, who defeated him, and confined him afterwards, not under a mountain, but in a pit. It is here easy to see that the first fable suggested the idea of the second; for the fable of Jupiter and the giants was told many hundred years before that of Satan.

Thus far the ancient and the Christian mythologists differ very little from each other. But the latter have contrived to carry the matter much farther. They have contrived to connect the fabulous part of the story of Jesus Christ with the fable originating from Mount Aetna; and, in order to make all the parts of the story tie together, they have taken to their aid the tradition of the Jews; for the Christian mythology is made up partly from the ancient mythology and partly from the Jewish traditions.

The Christian mythologists, after having confined Satan in a pit, were obliged to let him out again, to bring on the sequel of the fable. He is then introduced into the garden of Eden in the shape of a snake, or a serpent, and in that shape he enters into familiar conversation with Eve, who is noways surprised to hear a snake talk, and the issue of this *tête-à-tête* is that he persuades her to eat an apple, and the eating of that apple damns all mankind.

After giving Satan this triumph over the whole creation, one would have supposed that the church mythologists would have been kind enough to send him back again to the pit; or, if they had not done this, that they would have put a mountain upon him (for they say that their faith can remove a mountain) or have him put *under* a mountain, as the former mythologists had done, to prevent his getting again among the women and doing more mischief. But instead of this, they leave him at large without even obliging him to give his parole. The secret of which is that they could not do without him; and after being at the trouble of making him, they bribed him to stay. They promised him ALL the Jews, ALL the Turks by anticipation, nine-tenths of the world beside, and Mahomet into the bargain. After this, who can doubt the bountifulness of the Christian mythology?

Having thus made an insurrection and a battle in Heaven, in which none of the combatants could be either killed or wounded—put Satan into the pit—let him out again—given him a triumph over the whole creation—damned all mankind by the eating of an apple, these Christian mythologists bring the two ends of their fable together. They represent this virtuous and amiable man, Jesus Christ, to be at once both God and man, and also the Son of God, celestially begotten on purpose to be sacrificed, because, they say, that Eve in her longing had eaten an apple.

Putting aside everything that might excite laughter by its absurdity, or detestation by its profaneness, and confining ourselves merely to an examination of the parts, it is impossible to conceive a story more derogatory to the Almighty, more inconsistent with his wisdom, more contradictory to his power, than this story is.

In order to make for it a foundation to rise upon, the inventors were under the necessity of giving to the being whom they call Satan a power equally as great, if not greater, than they attribute to the Almighty. They have not only given him the power of liberating himself from the pit, after what they call his fall, but they have made that power increase afterwards to infinity. Before this fall, they represent him only as an angel of limited existence, as they represent the rest. After his fall, he becomes, by their account, omnipresent. He exists everywhere, and at the same time. He occupies the whole immensity of space.

Not content with this deification of Satan, they represent him as defeating, by stratagem, in the shape of an animal of the creation, all the power and wisdom of the Almighty. They represent him as having compelled the Almighty to the *direct necessity* either of surrendering the whole of the creation to the government and sovereignty of this Satan or of capitulating for its redemption by coming down upon earth and exhibiting himself upon a cross in the shape of a man.

Had the inventors of this story told it the contrary way—that is, had they represented the Almighty as compelling Satan to exhibit *himself* on a cross in the shape of a snake, as a punishment for his new transgression—the story would have been less absurd, less contradictory. But, instead of this, they make the transgressor triumph and the Almighty fall.

That many good men have believed this strange fable, and lived very good lives under that belief (for credulity is not a crime), is what I have no doubt of. In the first place, they were educated to believe it, and they would have believed anything else in the same manner. There are also many who have been so enthusiastically enraptured by what they conceived to be the infinite love of God to man in making a sacrifice of himself that the vehemence of the idea has forbidden and deterred them from examining into the absurdity and profaneness of the story. The more unnatural anything is, the more is it capable of becoming the object of dismal admiration.

But if objects for gratitude and admiration are our desire, do they not present themselves every hour to our eyes? Do we not see a fair creation prepared to receive us the instant we were born—a world furnished to our hands that cost us nothing? Is it we that light up the sun, that pour down the rain, and fill the earth with abundance? Whether we sleep or wake, the vast machinery of the universe still goes on. Are these things, and the blessings they indicate in future, nothing to us? Can our gross feelings be excited by no other subjects than tragedy and suicide? Or is the gloomy pride of man become so intolerable that nothing can flatter it but a sacrifice of the Creator?

I know that this bold investigation will alarm many, but it would be paying too great a compliment to their credulity to forbear it upon that account. The times and the subject demand it to be done. The suspicion that the theory of what is called the Christian church is fabulous is becoming very extensive in all countries; and it will be a consolation to men staggering under that suspicion, and doubting what to believe and what to disbelieve, to see the subject freely investigated. I therefore pass on to an examination of the books called the Old and the New Testament.

These books, beginning with Genesis and ending with Revelations (which by the bye is a book of riddles that requires a revelation to explain it), are, we are told, the word of God. It is, therefore, proper for us to know who told us so, that we may know what credit to give to the report. The answer to this question is that nobody can tell, except that we tell one another so. The case, however, historically appears to be as follows:

When the church mythologists established their system, they collected all the writings they could find, and managed them as they pleased. It is a matter altogether of uncertainty to us whether such of the writings as now appear under the name of the Old and the New Testament are in the same state in which those collectors say they found them; or whether they added, altered, abridged, or dressed them up.

Be this as it may, they decided by *vote* which of the books out of the collection they had made should be the WORD OF GOD, and which should not. They rejected several; they voted others to be doubtful, such as the books called the Apocrypha; and those books which had a majority of votes were voted to be the word of God. Had they voted otherwise, all the people since calling themselves Christians had believed otherwise; for the belief of the one comes from the vote of the other. Who the people were that did all this, we know nothing of; they called themselves by the general name of the church; and this is all we know of the matter.

As we have no other external evidence or authority for believing those books to be the word of God than what I have mentioned, which is no evidence or authority at all, I come, in the next place, to examine the internal evidence contained in the books themselves.

In the former part of this essay I have spoken of revelation. I now proceed further with that subject, for the purpose of applying it to the books in question.

Revelation is a communication of something which the person to whom that thing is revealed did not know before. For if I have done a thing or seen it done, it needs no revelation to tell me I have done it or seen it, nor to enable me to tell it or to write it.

Revelation, therefore, cannot be applied to anything done upon earth of which man is himself the actor or the witness; and consequently, all the historical and anecdotal part of the Bible, which is almost the whole of it, is not within the meaning and compass of the word *revelation*, and therefore is not the word of God.

When Samson ran off with the gateposts of Gaza, if he ever did so (and whether he did or not is nothing to us), or when he visited his Delilah, or caught his foxes, or did anything else, what has revelation to do with these things? If they were facts, he could tell them himself; or his secretary, if he kept one, could write them, if they were worth either telling or writing; and if they were fictions, revelation could not make them true; and whether true or not, we are neither the better nor the wiser for knowing them.—When we contemplate the immensity of that Being who directs and governs the incomprehensible WHOLE, of which the utmost ken of human sight can discover but a part, we ought to feel ashamed at calling such paltry stories the word of God.

As to the account of the creation, with which the book of Genesis opens, it has all the appearance of being a tradition which the

Israelites had among them before they came into Egypt; and after their departure from that country they put it at the head of their history, without telling, as it is most probable they did not know, how they came by it. The manner in which the account opens shows it to be traditionary. It begins abruptly. It is nobody that speaks. It is nobody that hears. It is addressed to nobody. It has neither first, second, nor third person. It has every criterion of being a tradition. It has no voucher. Moses does not take it upon himself by introducing it with the formality that he uses on other occasions, such as that of saying, *"The Lord spake unto Moses, saying."*

Why it has been called the Mosaic account of the creation I am at a loss to conceive. Moses, I believe, was too good a judge of such subjects to put his name to that account. He had been educated among the Egyptians, who were a people as well skilled in science, and particularly in astronomy, as any people of their day; and the silence and caution that Moses observes, in not authenticating the account, is a good negative evidence that he neither told it nor believed it.—The case is that every nation of people has been world-makers, and the Israelites had as much right to set up the trade of world-making as any of the rest; and as Moses was not an Israelite, he might not choose to contradict the tradition. The account, however, is harmless, and this is more than can be said for many other parts of the Bible.

When we read the obscene stories, the voluptuous debaucheries, the cruel and torturous executions, the unrelenting vindictiveness with which more than half the Bible is filled, it would be more consistent that we called it the word of a demon than the word of God. It is a history of wickedness, that has served to corrupt and brutalize mankind; and, for my own part, I sincerely detest it, as I detest everything that is cruel. . . .

But some perhaps will say: "Are we to have no word of God—no revelation?" I answer: "Yes. There is a word of God; there is a revelation."

THE WORD OF GOD IS THE CREATION WE BEHOLD: and it is in *this word*, which no human invention can counterfeit or alter, that God speaketh universally to man.

Human language is local and changeable, and is therefore incapable of being used as the means of unchangeable and universal information. The idea that God sent Jesus Christ to publish, as they say, the glad tidings to all nations, from one end of the earth unto the other, is consistent only with the ignorance of those who knew nothing of the extent of the world, and who believed, as those world-saviors believed and continued to believe for several centuries (and that in contradiction to the discoveries of philosophers and the experience of navigators), that the earth was flat like a trencher; and that a man might walk to the end of it.

But how was Jesus Christ to make anything known to all nations? He could speak but one language, which was Hebrew; and there are in the world several hundred languages. Scarcely any two nations speak the same language, or understand each other; and as to translations, every man who knows anything of languages knows that it is impossible to translate from one language into another not only without losing a great part of the original, but frequently of mistaking the sense; and, besides all this, the art of printing was wholly unknown at the time Christ lived.

It is always necessary that the means that are to accomplish any end be equal to the accomplishment of that end, or the end cannot be accomplished. It is in this that the difference between finite and infinite power and wisdom discovers itself. Man frequently fails in accomplishing his end from a natural inability of the power to the purpose, and frequently from the want of wisdom to apply power properly. But it is impossible for infinite power and wisdom to fail as man faileth. The means it useth are always equal to the end; but human language, more especially as there is not a universal language, is incapable of being used as a universal means of unchangeable and uniform information; and therefore it is not the means that God useth in manifesting himself universally to man.

It is only in the CREATION that all our ideas and conceptions of a *word of God* can unite. The creation speaketh a universal language, independently of human speech or human language, multiplied and various as they be. It is an ever existing original which every man can read. It cannot be forged; it cannot be counterfeited; it cannot be lost; it cannot be altered; it cannot be suppressed. It does not depend upon the will of man whether it shall be published or not; it publishes itself from one end of the earth to the other. It preaches to all nations and to all worlds; and this *word of God* reveals to man all that is necessary for man to know of God.

Do we want to contemplate his power? We see it in the immensity of the creation. Do we want to contemplate his wisdom? We see it in the unchangeable order by which the incomprehensible Whole is governed. Do we want to contemplate his munificence? We see it in the abundance with which he fills the earth. Do we want to contemplate his mercy? We see it in his not withholding that abundance even from the unthankful. In fine, do we want to know what God is? Search not the book called the Scripture, which any human hand might make, but the scripture called the Creation.

. . . .

A SELECTION

William Godwin

1756–1836

INQUIRY CONCERNING POLITICAL JUSTICE

1793, 1796, 1798

[Godwin was among the most utopian of the "perfectibilitarians." Trusting entirely in the power of "reason," he repudiated violence as a means of reforming and equalizing mankind. So assured was he of the supremacy of "truth" and "reason" that he looked forward eagerly to the day when government will disappear and man will order his life by the dictates of his own mind. In this day, all such "tyranny" as marriage will be dissolved, and man will be exempt from the necessity of co-operating with his fellows even in playing music or acting a drama. Thus will dawn the era of "liberty"—a philosophic anarchy. Godwin attributes many of the ills of society to the inequality of property. As father-in-law of Shelley and the inspiration of many of the ideas of that poet, Godwin perpetuated his notions well beyond the eighteenth century.]

THE VOLUNTARY ACTIONS OF MEN ORIGINATE IN THEIR OPINIONS

. . . .

THE corollaries respecting political truth, deducible from the simple proposition which seems clearly established by the reasonings of the present chapter, that the voluntary actions of men are in all instances conformable to the deductions of their understanding, are of the highest importance. Hence, we may infer what are the hopes and prospects of human improvement. The doctrine which may be founded upon these principles may, perhaps, best be expressed in the five following propositions: sound reasoning and truth, when adequately communicated, must always be victorious over error; sound reasoning and truth are capable of being so communicated; truth is omnipotent; the vices and moral weakness of man are not invincible; man is perfectible, or, in other words, susceptible of perpetual improvement. . . .

The first of these propositions is so evident that it needs only be stated in order to the being universally admitted. Is there anyone who can imagine that when sound argument and sophistry are fairly brought into comparison, the victory can be doubtful? Sophistry may assume a plausible appearance, and contrive to a certain extent to bewilder the understanding. But it is one of the prerogatives of truth to follow it in its mazes and strip it of disguise. Nor does any difficulty from this consideration interfere with the establishment of the present proposition. We suppose truth not merely to be exhibited, but adequately communicated; that is, in other words, distinctly apprehended by the person to whom it is addressed. In this case the victory is too sure to admit of being controverted by the most inveterate skepticism.

The second proposition is that sound reasoning and truth are capable of being adequately communicated by one man to another. This proposition may be understood of such communication either as it affects the individual or the species. First of the individual.

In order to its due application in this point of view, opportunity for the communication must necessarily be supposed. The incapacity of human intellect at present requires that this opportunity should be of long duration or repeated recurrence. We do not always know how to communicate all the evidence we are capable of communicating, in a single conversation, and much less in a single instant. But if the communicator be sufficiently master of his subject, and if the truth be altogether on his side, he must ultimately succeed in his undertaking. We suppose him to have sufficient urbanity to conciliate the good will, and sufficient energy to engage the attention of the party concerned. In that case there is no prejudice, no blind reverence for established systems, no false fear of the inferences to be drawn, that can resist him. He will encounter these one after the other, and he will encounter them with success. Our prejudices, our undue reverence and imaginary fears flow out of some views the mind has been induced to entertain; they are founded in the belief of some propositions. But every one of these propositions is capable of being refuted. The champion we describe proceeds from point to point; if in any his success have been doubtful, that he will retrace and put out of the reach of mistake; and it is evidently impossible that with such qualifications and such perseverance he should not ultimately accomplish his purpose.

Such is the appearance which this proposition assumes when examined in a loose and practical view. In strict consideration, it will not admit of debate. Man is a rational being. If there be any man who is incapable of making inferences for himself, or understanding, when stated in the most explicit terms, the inferences of another, him we consider as an abortive production, and not in strictness belonging to the human species. It is absurd, therefore, to say that sound reasoning and truth cannot be communicated by one man to another. Whenever in any case he fails, it is that he is not sufficiently laborious, patient, and clear. We suppose, of course, the person who undertakes to communicate the truth really to possess it, and be master of his subject; for it is scarcely worth an observation to say that that which he has not himself he cannot communicate to another.

If truth, therefore, can be brought home to the conviction of the individual, let us see how it stands with the public or the world. Now in the first place, it is extremely clear that if no individual can resist the force of truth, it can only be necessary to apply this proposition from individual to individual and we shall at length comprehend the whole. Thus the affirmation in its literal sense is completely established. . . .

The third of the propositions enumerated is that truth is omnipotent. This proposition, which is convenient for its brevity, must be understood with limitations. It would be absurd to affirm that truth unaccompanied by the evidence which proves it to be such, or when that evidence is partially and imperfectly stated, has any such property. But it has sufficiently appeared from the arguments already adduced, that truth, when adequately communicated, is, so far as relates to the conviction of the understanding, irresistible. There may, indeed, be propositions which, though true in themselves, may be beyond the sphere of human knowledge, or respecting which human beings have not yet discovered sufficient arguments for their support. In that case, though true in themselves, they are not truths to us. The reasoning by which they are attempted to be established, is not sound reasoning. It may, perhaps, be found that the human mind is not capable of arriving at absolute certainty upon any subject of inquiry; and it must be admitted that human science is attended with all degrees of certainty, from the highest moral evidence to the slightest balance of probability. But human beings are capable of apprehending and weighing all these degrees; and to know the exact quantity of probability which I ought to ascribe to any proposition may be said to be in one sense the possessing certain knowledge. It would farther be absurd, if we regard truth in relation to its empire over our conduct, to suppose that it is not limited in its operations by the faculties of our frame. It may be compared to a connoisseur, who, however consummate be his talents, can extract from a given instrument only such tones as that instrument will afford. But within these limits the deduction which forms the principal substance of this chapter, proves to us that whatever is brought home to the conviction of the understanding, so long as it is present to the mind, possesses an undisputed empire over the conduct. Nor will he who is sufficiently conversant with the science of intellect be hasty in assigning the bounds of our capacity. There are some things which the structure of our bodies will render us forever unable to effect; but in many cases the lines which appear to prescribe a term to our efforts will, like the mists that arise from a lake, retire farther and farther, the more closely we endeavor to approach them.

Fourthly, the vices and moral weakness of man are not invincible. This is the preceding proposition with a very slight variation in the statement. Vice and weakness are founded upon ignorance and error; but truth is more powerful than any champion that can be brought into the field against it; consequently, truth has the faculty of expelling weakness and vice, and placing nobler and more beneficent principles in their stead.

Lastly, man is perfectible. This proposition needs some explanation.

By perfectible it is not meant that he is capable of being brought to perfection. But the word seems sufficiently adapted to express the faculty of being continually made better and receiving perpetual improvement; and in this sense it is here to be understood. The term perfectible, thus explained, not only does not imply the capacity of being brought to perfection, but stands in express opposition to it. If we could arrive at perfection, there would be an end of our improvement. There is, however, one thing of great importance that it does imply; every perfection or excellence that human beings are competent to conceive, human beings, unless in cases that are palpably and unequivocally excluded by the structure of their frame, are competent to attain.

This is an inference which immediately follows from the omnipotence of truth. Every truth that is capable of being communicated is capable of being brought home to the conviction of the mind. Every principle which can be brought home to the conviction of the mind will infallibly produce a correspondent effect upon the conduct. If there were not something in the nature of man incompatible with absolute perfection, the doctrine of the omnipotence of truth would afford no small probability that he would one day reach it. Why is the perfection of man impossible?

The idea of absolute perfection is scarcely within the grasp of human understanding. If science were more familiarized to speculations of this sort, we should perhaps discover that the notion itself was pregnant with absurdity and contradiction.

It is not necessary in this argument to dwell upon the limited nature of human faculties. We can neither be present to all places nor to all times. We cannot penetrate into the essences of things; or rather, we have no sound and satisfactory knowledge of things external to ourselves, but merely of our own sensations. We cannot discover the causes of things, or ascertain that in the antecedent which connects it with the consequent, and discern nothing but their contiguity. With what pretense can a being thus shut in on all sides lay claim to absolute perfection?

But not to insist upon these considerations, there is one principle in the human mind which must forever exclude us from arriving at a close of our acquisitions, and confine us to perpetual progress. The human mind, so far as we are acquainted with it, is nothing else but a faculty of perception. All our knowledge, all our ideas, everything we possess as intelligent beings, comes from impression. All the minds that exist set out from absolute ignorance. They received first one impression, and then a second. As the impressions became more numerous, and were stored by the help of memory, and combined by the faculty of association, so the experience increased, and with the experience, the knowledge, the wisdom, everything that distinguishes man from what we understand by a "clod of the valley." [1] This seems to be a simple and incontrovertible history of intellectual beings; and if it be true, then as our accumulations have been incessant in the time that is gone; so, as long as we continue to perceive, to remember or reflect, they must perpetually increase.

[Book I, chap. 5]

1 Job 21:33.

A SELECTION

THE ANTI-JACOBIN

[George Canning, J. H. Frere, William Gifford, George Ellis]

[The enthusiasm of English "levelers" for French liberty, equality, and fraternity provoked in *The Anti-Jacobin* what has been called the best satire between Pope and Byron. Paine, Thelwall, Southey, Coleridge, Charles Lloyd, Joseph Priestley, Gilbert Wakefield, Richard Price, and a whole group of dissenters and followers of Fox were the victims of a somewhat indiscriminate onslaught that revived satire as a "sacred weapon" in the defence of conservatism. Many contributions to the journal were the result of simply leaving a manuscript open, upon a desk, in the editorial room and permitting those in the office to add to it at will.]

THE NEW MORALITY
July 9, 1798

From mental mists to purge a nation's eyes;
To animate the weak, unite the wise;
To trace the deep infection, that pervades
The crowded town, and taints the rural shades;
To mark how wide extends the mighty waste
O'er the fair realms of Science, Learning, Taste;
To drive and scatter all the brood of lies,
And chase the varying falsehood as it flies;
The long arrears of ridicule to pay,
To drag reluctant Dullness back to day;   10
Much yet remains.—To you these themes belong,
Ye favour'd sons of virtue and of song!
   Say, is the field too narrow? are the times
Barren of folly, and devoid of crimes?

. . . .

   Awake! for shame! or e'er thy nobler sense
Sink in the oblivious pool of indolence!
Must wit be found alone on falsehood's side,
Unknown to truth, to virtue unallied?

Arise! nor scorn thy country's just alarms;
Wield in her cause thy long-neglected arms: 20
Of lofty satire pour th' indignant strain,
Leagued with her friends, and ardent to maintain
'Gainst Learning's, Virtue's, Truth's, Religion's foes,
A kingdom's safety, and the world's repose.
   If Vice appal thee,—if thou view with awe
Insults that brave, and crimes that 'scape the law;—
Yet may the specious bastard brood, which claim
A spurious homage under Virtue's name,
Sprung from that parent of ten thousand crimes,
The *New Philosophy* of modern times,—   30
Yet, these may rouse thee!—With unsparing hand,
Oh, lash the vile impostures from the land!
   First, stern Philanthropy:—not she, who dries
The orphan's tears, and wipes the widow's eyes;
Not she, who, sainted Charity her guide,
Of British bounty pours the annual tide:—
But *French* Philanthropy;—whose boundless mind
Glows with the general love of all mankind;—
Philanthropy,—beneath whose baneful sway
Each patriot passion sinks, and dies away.   40
   Taught in her school to imbibe thy mawkish strain,
Condorcet, filter'd through the dregs of Paine,
Each pert adept disowns a Briton's part,
And plucks the name of England from his heart.
   What, shall a name, a word, a sound control
The aspiring thought, and cramp the expansive soul?
Shall one half-peopled Island's rocky round
A love, that glows for all Creation, bound?
And social charities contract the plan
Framed for thy freedom, UNIVERSAL MAN?   50
—No—through the extended globe his feelings run
As broad and general as the unbounded sun!
No narrow bigot *he*;—*his* reason'd view
Thy interests, England, ranks with thine, Peru!
France at our doors, *he* sees no danger nigh,
But heaves for Turkey's woes the impartial sigh;
A steady Patriot of the World alone,
The Friend of every Country—but his own.
   Next comes a gentler Virtue.—Ah! beware
Lest the harsh verse her shrinking softness scare.   60
Visit her not too roughly;—the warm sigh

Breathes on her lips;—the tear-drop gems her eye.
Sweet Sensibility, who dwells enshrin'd
In the fine foldings of the feeling mind;—
With delicate Mimosa's sense endued,
Who shrinks instinctive from a hand too rude;
Or, like the *anagallis*, prescient flower,
Shuts her soft petals at the approaching shower.

    Sweet child of sickly Fancy!—her of yore
From her lov'd France Rousseau to exile bore;   70
And, while midst lakes and mountains wild he ran,
Full of himself, and shunn'd the haunts of man,
Taught her o'er each lone vale and Alpine steep
To lisp the story of his wrongs, and weep;
Taught her to cherish still in either eye,   ⎤
Of tender tears a plentiful supply,   ⎬
And pour them in the brooks that babbled by;— ⎦
—Taught by nice scale to mete her feelings strong,
False by degrees, and exquisitely wrong;—
—For the crush'd beetle *first*,—the widow'd dove,   80
And all the warbled sorrows of the grove;—
Next for poor suff'ring *guilt*;—and *last* of all,
For parents, friends, a king and country's fall.

    Mark her fair votaries, prodigal of grief,
With cureless pangs, and woes that mock relief,
Droop in soft sorrow o'er a faded flower;
O'er a dead jack-ass [1] pour the pearly shower;—
But hear, unmov'd, of *Loire's* ensanguin'd flood,
Chok'd up with slain;—of *Lyons* drench'd in blood;
Of crimes that blot the age, the world with shame,   90
Foul crimes, but sicklied o'er with Freedom's name;
Altars and thrones subverted, social life
Trampled to earth,—the husband from the wife,
Parent from child, with ruthless fury torn,—
Of talents, honour, virtue, wit, forlorn,
In friendless exile,—of the wise and good
Staining the daily scaffold with their blood,—
Of savage cruelties, that scare the mind,
The rage of madness with hell's lusts combined—
Of hearts torn reeking from the mangled breast,—   100
They hear—and hope, that ALL IS FOR THE BEST.

---

1 A reference to the Nampont episode in Sterne's *Sentimental Journey.*

Ere long, perhaps, to this astonish'd Isle,
Fresh from the shores of subjugated Nile,
Shall Buonaparte's victor fleet protect
The genuine Theo-Philanthropic sect,—
The sect of Marat, Mirabeau, Voltaire,—
Led by their Pontiff, good La Reveillère.[2]
—Rejoiced our CLUBS shall greet him, and install
The holy Hunch-back in thy dome, St. Paul!
While countless votaries thronging in his train   110
Wave their red caps, and hymn this jocund strain:
"*Couriers* and *Stars*, Sedition's Evening Host,
Thou *Morning Chronicle*, and *Morning Post*,
Whether ye make the Rights of Man your theme,
Your country libel, and your God blaspheme,
Or dirt on private worth and virtue throw,
Still blasphemous or blackguard, praise Lepaux.
"And ye five other wandering bards, that move
In sweet accord of harmony and love,
Coleridge and Southey, Lloyd, and Lambe and Co.   120
Tune all your mystic harps to praise Lepaux!
Priestley and Wakefield, humble, holy men,
Give praises to his name with tongue and pen!
Thelwall, and ye that lecture as ye go,
And for your pains get pelted, praise Lepaux!
Praise him each Jacobin, or fool, or knave,
And your cropp'd heads in sign of worship wave!
All creeping creatures, venomous and low,
Paine, Williams, Godwin, Holcroft, praise Lepaux!
——— and ——— with ——— join'd,   130
And every other beast after his kind.
And thou *Leviathan!* on ocean's brim
Hugest of living things that sleep and swim;
Thou in whose nose by Burke's gigantic hand
The hook was fix'd to drag thee to the land,[3]
With ———, ———, and ——— in thy train,
And ——— wallowing in the yeasty main—
Still as ye snort, and puff, and spout, and blow,
In puffing, and in spouting, praise Lepaux!"
Britain, beware; nor let the insidious foe,   140
Of force despairing, aim a deadlier blow.

Thy peace, thy strength, with devilish wiles assail,
And when her arms are vain, by arts prevail.
True, thou art rich, art powerful!—thro' thine Isle
Industrious skill, contented labour, smile;
Far seas are studded with thy countless sails;
What wind but wafts them, and what shore but hails!
True, thou art brave!—o'er all the busy land
In patriot ranks embattled myriads stand;
Thy foes behold with impotent amaze,   150
And drop the lifted weapon as they gaze!
   But what avails to guard each outward part,
If subtlest poison, circling at thy heart,
Spite of thy courage, of thy pow'r, and wealth,
Mine the sound fabric of thy vital health?

. . . .

   Guard we but our own hearts: with constant view
To ancient morals, ancient manners true,
True to the manlier virtues, such as nerv'd
Our fathers' breasts, and this proud Isle preserv'd   160
For many a rugged age:—and scorn the while,—
Each philosophic atheist's specious guile.—
The soft seductions, the refinements nice,
Of gay morality, and easy vice:—
So shall we brave the storm;—our 'stablish'd pow'r
Thy refuge, Europe, in some happier hour.—
—But, French *in heart*—tho' victory crown our brow,
Low at our feet though prostrate nations bow,
Wealth gild our cities, commerce crowd our shore,—
London may shine, but England is no more.   170

William Blake

1757–1827

OF the many astonishing stories told about Blake the least apocryphal
are those about his visions: how he saw the prophet Ezekiel sitting in
the fields, how he attended a fairy's funeral, how when his brother died
he saw his soul flying off and heard its wings flapping. Whatever one
wishes to think of these anecdotes, the poetry of Blake, like his draw-

ing, is "imagination heightened to the point of vision." He accepts the imagination as "the divine body in every man"; it breaks through the order of time, space, and matter, into transcendental flight. Blake hated science ("God is not a mathematical diagram"); he was repelled by Wordsworth ("I fear Wordsworth loves nature, and nature is the work of the devil"). Both "reason" and "nature" signify to him man's limitations, his loss of vision and denial of desire; for all restriction is evil. Blake's "mysticism," far from being a mere ecstasy of feeling, expresses itself in symbols. His imagination is visionary in that it concentrates itself into imagery, both in poetry and engraving. These symbols evidently arranged themselves for him in a relation so complicated and obscure that many of his longer prophetic poems are unintelligible. But the isolated symbols in the lyrics have an almost hypnotic effectiveness, partly because Blake's verse is literally incantation. The rhythms of the nursery rhyme accentuate the intensely realized images. In the obscure "prophetic" books emanating from his reading on Swedenborg, Gnosticism, and the Druids, Blake swings into the longer cadences of Ossianic prose-poetry. In the lyric, his art is one of intensity with little complexity. It is the same in his illustrations for Milton, Young, Blair, and Dante, where his supple line bears the entire rhythm. For Blake is no colorist; a sharp and wiry line is the token of perfection, he says, although he tinted with water color the engravings with which he illuminated his own poetry. Many of these designs are "sublime" in the Michelangelesque and Gothic manner. The visionary Blake naturally could not tolerate the academism of Sir Joshua Reynolds, whose *Discourses* irritated him to the marginal comment "Damned fool!" Although Blake habitually dwelt within the splendor of his visions, he welcomed the French Revolution as ecstatically as any Jacobin, and even took to wearing a liberty cap. In his hatred of inhumanity in any form he was as bitter as Tom Paine. Perhaps it was inevitable that the enlightened eighteenth century should rouse a Blake

> To cast off Rational Demonstration . . .
> To cast off the rotten rags of Memory by Inspiration,
> To cast off Bacon, Locke, & Newton . .
> To cast aside from Poetry all that is not Inspiration.

BIOGRAPHICAL NOTES

Son of a London hosier. Experienced strange childhood visions and daily "messengers from Heaven." Early familiarity with Swedenborg's writings. Apprenticed to the engraver Basire (1771), who roused his admiration for "Gothic" instead of "classical" by sending him to sketch monuments in Westminster Abbey. Engraved plates for books. Met Fuseli and Flaxman (1780). Married Catherine Boucher, who could not write (1782). Lived in Leicester Fields and opened a print shop.

The Temptation by William Blake

Flight into Egypt by William Blake

Poetical Sketches (1783). *Songs of Innocence* and the *Book of Thel* (1789) printed by his own "illuminated" method. Accepted the French Revolution enthusiastically; knew Paine, Godwin, Mary Wollstonecraft, Priestley, and other "Jacobins." The "minor prophecies" written and engraved: *The French Revolution* (1791), *The Marriage of Heaven and Hell* (ca. 1793), *Visions of the Daughters of Albion* (1793), etc. Moved to Lambeth; met Thomas Butts, a patron. *America* (1793), *A Song of Liberty* (1793), *Songs of Experience* (1794) written and engraved. Designs for Young's *Night Thoughts* (1796), *The Four Zoas* (ca. 1795–1804). Visited at William Hayley's cottage at Felpham, Sussex (1800–1803), his only extended absence from London. Quarrel with Hayley and return to London. Further "enlightenment" and "turn to the eternal" (ca. 1804). Engraving of the designs for Blair's *Grave*, Milton, *Job*, Dante, etc. Began engraving the "major prophecies": Parts of *Vala*, *Milton*, *Jerusalem* (1804–20). An exhibition of Blake's work (1809) received by Southey and others as lunacy. *The Canterbury Pilgrims* engraved (1810). Obscure life in London. Died after lingering illness.

BIBLIOGRAPHY: *Complete Writings*, ed. G. Keynes, 1957. *Poetry and Prose*, ed. G. Keynes, 1939. *Letters*, ed. G. Keynes, 1956. Binyon, L., *Drawings and Engravings of William Blake*, 1922; *Engraved Designs of William Blake*, 1926. Adams, H., *Blake and Yeats*, 1955. Blackstone, B., *English Blake*, 1949. Blunt, A., *The Art of William Blake*, 1959. Bronowski, J., *William Blake*, 1943. Damon, S. F., *William Blake, His Philosophy and Symbols*, 1947. Digby, G. W., *Symbol and Image in William Blake*, 1957. Erdman, D. V., *Blake, Prophet Against Empire*, 1954. Frye, N., *Fearful Symmetry*, 1953. Gaunt, W., *Arrows of Desire*, 1956. Gardner, S., *Infinity on the Anvil*, 1954. Gleckner, R. F., *The Piper and the Bard*, 1959. Keynes, G., *Blake Studies*, 1949. Margoliouth, H. M., *William Blake*, 1951. Murry, J. M., *William Blake*, 1933. Pinto, V. de S., *The Divine Vision*, 1957. Plowman, M., *Introduction to the Study of Blake*, 1952. Rudd, M., *Divided Image*, 1953. Schorer, M., *William Blake*, 1946. White, H. C., *The Mysticism of William Blake*, 1927. Wilson, M., *Life of William Blake*, 1927.

POETICAL SKETCHES

1783

TO THE EVENING STAR

Thou fair-hair'd angel of the evening,
Now, whilst the sun rests on the mountains, light
Thy bright torch of love; thy radiant crown
Put on, and smile upon our evening bed!
Smile on our loves, and, while thou drawest the
Blue curtains of the sky, scatter thy silver dew
On every flower that shuts its sweet eyes
In timely sleep. Let thy west wind sleep on
The lake; speak silence with thy glimmering eyes,
And wash the dusk with silver. Soon, full soon,   10
Dost thou withdraw; then the wolf rages wide,

And the lion glares thro' the dun forest:
The fleeces of our flocks are cover'd with
Thy sacred dew: protect them with thine influence.

SONG

How sweet I roam'd from field to field,
    And tasted all the summer's pride,
Till I the prince of love beheld,
    Who in the sunny beams did glide!

He shew'd me lilies for my hair,
    And blushing roses for my brow;
He led me through his gardens fair,
    Where all his golden pleasures grow.

With sweet May dews my wings were wet,
    And Phœbus fir'd my vocal rage;   10
He caught me in his silken net,
    And shut me in his golden cage.

He loves to sit and hear me sing,
    Then, laughing, sports and plays with me;
Then stretches out my golden wing,
    And mocks my loss of liberty.

SONG

My silks and fine array,
    My smiles and languish'd air,
By love are driv'n away;
    And mournful lean Despair
Brings me yew to deck my grave:
Such end true lovers have.

His face is fair as heav'n,
    When springing buds unfold;
Oh why to him was't giv'n
    Whose heart is wintry cold?   10
His breast is love's all-worship'd tomb,
Where all love's pilgrims come.

Bring me an axe and spade,
    Bring me a winding-sheet;

When I my grave have made,
  Let winds and tempests beat:
Then down I'll lie, as cold as clay.
True love doth pass away!

THERE IS NO NATURAL RELIGION

ca. 1788

I

The Argument. Man has no notion of moral fitness but from education. Naturally he is only a natural organ subject to Sense.
I. Man cannot naturally perceive but through his natural or bodily organs.
II. Man by his reasoning power can only compare & judge of what he has already perceiv'd.
III. From a perception of only 3 senses or 3 elements none could deduce a fourth or fifth.
IV. None could have other than natural or organic thoughts if he had none but organic perceptions.
V. Man's desires are limited by his perceptions, none can desire what he has not perceiv'd.
VI. The desires & perceptions of man, untaught by any thing but organs of sense, must be limited to objects of sense.
Conclusion. If it were not for the poetic or prophetic character the philosophic & experimental would soon be at the ratio of all things, & stand still, unable to do other than repeat the same dull round over again.

II

I. Man's perceptions are not bounded by organs of perception; he perceives more than sense (tho' ever so acute) can discover.
II. Reason, or the ratio of all we have already known, is not the same that it shall be when we know more.
III. [Lacking]
IV. The bounded is loathed by its possessor. The same dull round, even of a universe, would soon become a mill with complicated

wheels.

V. If the many become the same as the few when possess'd, More! More! is the cry of a mistaken soul; less than All cannot satisfy man.

VI. If any could desire what he is incapable of possessing, despair must be his eternal lot.

VII. The desire of Man being infinite, the possession is infinite & himself infinite.

Application. He who sees the Infinite in all things, sees God. He who sees the Ratio only, sees himself only.

Therefore God becomes as we are, that we may be as he is.

SONGS OF INNOCENCE

1789

INTRODUCTION

Piping down the valleys wild,
Piping songs of pleasant glee,
On a cloud I saw a child,
And he laughing said to me:

"Pipe a song about a Lamb!"
So I piped with merry chear.
"Piper, pipe that song again";
So I piped: he wept to hear.

"Drop thy pipe, thy happy pipe;
Sing thy songs of happy chear":
So I sang the same again,
While he wept with joy to hear.

"Piper, sit thee down, and write
In a book, that all may read."
So he vanish'd from my sight,
And I pluck'd a hollow reed,

And I made a rural pen,
And I stain'd the water clear,

And I wrote my happy songs
Every child may joy to hear.   20

THE LAMB

Little lamb, who made thee?
Dost thou know who made thee?
Gave thee life, and bid thee feed,
By the stream and o'er the mead;
Gave thee clothing of delight,
Softest clothing, woolly, bright;
Gave thee such a tender voice,
Making all the vales rejoice?
Little lamb, who made thee?
Dost thou know who made thee?   10

Little lamb, I'll tell thee,
Little lamb, I'll tell thee:
He is called by thy name,
For he calls himself a Lamb.
He is meek, and he is mild;
He became a little child.
I a child, and thou a lamb,
We are called by his name.
Little lamb, God bless thee!
Little lamb, God bless thee!   20

THE DIVINE IMAGE

To Mercy, Pity, Peace, and Love
All pray in their distress;
And to these virtues of delight
Return their thankfulness.

For Mercy, Pity, Peace, and Love
Is God, our father dear,
And Mercy, Pity, Peace, and Love
Is Man, his child and care.

For Mercy has a human heart,
Pity, a human face,   10
And Love, the human form divine,
And Peace, the human dress.

Then every man, of every clime,
  That prays in his distress,
Prays to the human form divine,
  Love, Mercy, Pity, Peace.

And all must love the human form,
  In heathen, Turk, or Jew;
Where Mercy, Love, and Pity dwell,
  There God is dwelling too.   20

NIGHT

The sun descending in the west,
The evening star does shine;
The birds are silent in their nest,
And I must seek for mine.
  The moon like a flower
  In heaven's high bower,
  With silent delight
  Sits and smiles on the night.

Farewell, green fields and happy groves,
Where flocks have took delight.   10
Where lambs have nibbled, silent moves
The feet of angels bright;
  Unseen they pour blessing
  And joy without ceasing,
  On each bud and blossom,
  And each sleeping bosom.

They look in every thoughtless nest,
Where birds are cover'd warm;
They visit caves of every beast,
To keep them all from harm.   20
  If they see any weeping
  That should have been sleeping,
  They pour sleep on their head,
  And sit down by their bed.

When wolves and tygers howl for prey,
They pitying stand and weep;
Seeking to drive their thirst away,

And keep them from the sheep;
But if they rush dreadful,
The angels, most heedful,   30
Receive each mild spirit,
New worlds to inherit.

And there the lion's ruddy eyes
Shall flow with tears of gold,
And pitying the tender cries,
And walking round the fold,
Saying, "Wrath, by his meekness,
And by his health, sickness
Is driven away
From our immortal day.   40

"And now beside thee, bleating lamb,
I can lie down and sleep;
Or think on him who bore thy name,
Graze after thee and weep.
For, wash'd in life's river,
My bright mane for ever
Shall shine like the gold
As I guard o'er the fold."

THE BOOK OF THEL

1789

Thel's Motto

Does the Eagle know what is in the pit?
Or wilt thou go ask the Mole?
Can Wisdom be put in a silver rod,
Or Love in a golden bowl?

I

The daughters of the Seraphim led round their sunny flocks,—
All but the youngest: she in paleness sought the secret air,

To fade away like morning beauty from her mortal day.
Down by the river of Adona her soft voice is heard,
And thus her gentle lamentation falls like morning dew:

"O life of this our spring! why fades the lotus of the water,
Why fade these children of the spring, born but to smile and fall?
Ah! Thel is like a wat'ry bow, and like a parting cloud;
Like a reflection in a glass; like shadows in the water;
Like dreams of infants, like a smile upon an infant's face;   10
Like the dove's voice; like transient day; like music in the air.
Ah! gentle may I lay me down, and gentle rest my head,
And gentle sleep the sleep of death, and gentle hear the voice
Of him that walketh in the garden in the evening time."
The lilly of the valley, breathing in the humble grass,
Answer'd the lovely maid and said: "I am a wat'ry weed,
And I am very small and love to dwell in lowly vales;
So weak, the gilded butterfly scarce perches on my head.
Yet I am visited from heaven; and he that smiles on all
Walks in the valley and each morn over me spreads his hand,   20
Saying, 'Rejoice, thou humble grass, thou new-born lilly flower,
Thou gentle maid of silent valleys and of modest brooks;
For thou shalt be clothed in light, and fed with morning manna,
Till summer's heat melts thee beside the fountains and the springs
To flourish in eternal vales.' Then why should Thel complain?
Why should the mistress of the vales of Har utter a sigh?"

She ceas'd, and smil'd in tears, then sat down in her silver shrine.

Thel answer'd: "O thou little virgin of the peaceful valley,
Giving to those that cannot crave, the voiceless, the o'ertired;
Thy breath doth nourish the innocent lamb, he smells thy milky
          garments.   30
He crops thy flowers while thou sittest smiling in his face,
Wiping his mild and meekin mouth from all contagious taints.
Thy wine doth purify the golden honey; thy perfume,
Which thou dost scatter on every little blade of grass that springs,
Revives the milked cow, and tames the fire-breathing steed.
But Thel is like a faint cloud kindled at the rising sun:
I vanish from my pearly throne, and who shall find my place?"

"Queen of the vales," the lilly answer'd, "ask the tender cloud,
And it shall tell thee why it glitters in the morning sky,
And why it scatters its bright beauty thro' the humid air.   40

Descend, O little cloud, and hover before the eyes of Thel."

The cloud descended; and the lilly bow'd her modest head,
And went to mind her numerous charge among the verdant grass.

II

"O little cloud," the virgin said, "I charge thee tell to me
Why thou complainest not when in one hour thou fade away:
Then we shall seek thee, but not find. Ah! Thel is like to thee:
I pass away: yet I complain, and no one hears my voice."
The cloud then shew'd his golden head and his bright form
    emerg'd,
Hovering and glittering on the air, before the face of Thel.

"O virgin, know'st thou not our steeds drink of the golden
    springs   50
Where Luvah doth renew his horses? Look'st thou on my youth,
And fearest thou, because I vanish and am seen no more,
Nothing remains? O maid, I tell thee, when I pass away,
It is to tenfold life, to love, to peace, and raptures holy:
Unseen descending, weigh my light wings upon balmy flowers,
And court the fair-eyed dew to take me to her shining tent:
The weeping virgin, trembling kneels before the risen sun,
Till we arise link'd in a golden band and never part,
But walk united, bearing food to all our tender flowers."

"Dost thou, O little cloud? I fear that I am not like thee, 60
For I walk thro' the vales of Har, and smell the sweetest flowers,
But I feed not the little flowers; I hear the warbling birds,
But I feed not the warbling birds; they fly and seek their food:
But Thel delights in these no more, because I fade away;
And all shall say, 'Without a use this shining woman liv'd,
Or did she only live to be at death the food of worms?'"

The cloud reclin'd upon his airy throne, and answer'd thus:

"Then if thou art the food of worms, O virgin of the skies,
How great thy use, how great thy blessing! Every thing that lives
Lives not alone nor for itself. Fear not, and I will call 70
The weak worm from its lowly bed, and thou shalt hear its voice.
Come forth, worm of the silent valley, to thy pensive queen."

The helpless worm arose, and sat upon the lilly's leaf,
And the bright cloud sail'd on to find his partner in the vale.

III

Then Thel astonish'd view'd the worm upon its dewy bed.

"Art thou a worm? Image of weakness, art thou but a worm?
I see thee like an infant, wrapped in the lilly's leaf.
Ah! weep not, little voice, thou canst not speak, but thou canst
    weep.
Is this a worm? I see thee lay helpless and naked, weeping,
And none to answer, none to cherish thee with mother's
    smiles." 80

The clod of clay heard the worm's voice and rais'd her pitying
    head:
She bow'd over the weeping infant, and her life exhal'd
In milky fondness: then on Thel she fix'd her humble eyes.

"O beauty of the vales of Har! we live not for ourselves.
Thou seest me the meanest thing, and so I am indeed.
My bosom of itself is cold, and of itself is dark;
But He, that loves the lowly, pours his oil upon my head,
And kisses me, and binds his nuptial bands around my breast,
And says, 'Thou mother of my children, I have loved thee,
And I have given thee a crown that none can take away.' 90
But how this is, sweet maid, I know not, and I cannot know;
I ponder, and I cannot ponder; yet I live and love."

The daughter of beauty wip'd her pitying tears with her white
    veil,
And said: "Alas! I knew not this, and therefore did I weep.
That God would love a worm I knew, and punish the evil foot
That wilful bruis'd its helpless form; but that he cherish'd it
With milk and oil, I never knew, and therefore did I weep;
And I complain'd in the mild air, because I fade away,
And lay me down in thy cold bed, and leave my shining lot."

"Queen of the vales," the matron clay answer'd, "I heard thy
    sighs, 100
And all thy moans flew o'er my roof, but I have call'd them down.

Wilt thou, O Queen, enter my house? 'Tis given thee to enter
And to return: fear nothing, enter with thy virgin feet."

IV

The eternal gates' terrific porter lifted the northern bar;
Thel enter'd in and saw the secrets of the land unknown.
She saw the couches of the dead, and where the fibrous roots
Of every heart on earth infixes deep its restless twists;
A land of sorrows and of tears where never smile was seen.

She wander'd in the land of clouds thro' valleys dark, list'ning
Dolours and lamentations; waiting oft beside a dewy grave,   110
She stood in silence, list'ning to the voices of the ground,
Till to her own grave plot she came, and there she sat down,
And heard this voice of sorrow breathed from the hollow pit.

"Why cannot the ear be closed to its own destruction?
Or the glist'ning eye to the poison of a smile?
Why are eyelids stor'd with arrows ready drawn,
Where a thousand fighting men in ambush lie?
Or an eye of gifts and graces show'ring fruits and coined gold?
Why a tongue impress'd with honey from every wind?
Why an ear, a whirlpool fierce to draw creations in?   120
Why a nostril wide inhaling terror, trembling, and affright?
Why a tender curb upon the youthful burning boy?
Why a little curtain of flesh on the bed of our desire?"

The virgin started from her seat, and with a shriek
Fled back unhinder'd till she came into the vales of Har.

THE MARRIAGE OF HEAVEN AND HELL

ca. 1793

The Argument

RINTRAH roars & shakes his fires in the burden'd air;
Hungry clouds swag on the deep.

Once meek, and in a perilous path,

The just man kept his course along
The vale of death.
Roses are planted where thorns grow,
And on the barren heath
Sing the honey bees.

Then the perilous path was planted;
And a river, and a spring   10
On every cliff and tomb;
And on the bleached bones
Red clay brought forth;

Till the villain left the paths of ease,
To walk in perilous paths, and drive
The just man into barren climes.
Now the sneaking serpent walks
In mild humility,
And the just man rages in the wilds
Where lions roam.   20

Rintrah roars & shakes his fires in the burden'd air;
Hungry clouds swag on the deep.

¶

As a new heaven is begun, and it is now thirty-three years since
its advent: the Eternal Hell revives. And lo! Swedenborg is the
Angel sitting at the tomb; his writings are the linen clothes folded
up. Now is the dominion of Edom, & the return of Adam into Paradise; see Isaiah xxxiv & xxxv Chap.

Without Contraries is no progression. Attraction and Repulsion, Reason and Energy, Love and Hate, are necessary to Human
existence.

From these contraries spring what the religious call Good &
Evil. Good is the passive that obeys Reason. Evil is the active
springing from Energy.

Good is Heaven. Evil is Hell.

The Voice of the Devil

ALL Bibles or sacred codes have been the causes of the following
Errors:

1. That Man has two real existing principles, Viz: a Body & a Soul.

2. That Energy, call'd Evil, is alone from the Body, & that Reason, call'd Good, is alone from the Soul.

3. That God will torment Man in Eternity for following his Energies.

But the following Contraries to these are True:

1. Man has no Body distinct from his Soul; for that call'd Body is a portion of Soul discern'd by the five Senses, the chief inlets of Soul in this age.

2. Energy is the only life, and is from the Body, and Reason is the bound or outward circumference of Energy.

3. Energy is Eternal Delight.

¶

THOSE who restrain desire, do so because theirs is weak enough to be restrained; and the restrainer or reason usurps its place & governs the unwilling.

And being restrain'd, it by degrees becomes passive, till it is only the shadow of desire.

The history of this is written in Paradise Lost, & the Governor or Reason is call'd Messiah.

And the original Archangel, or possessor of the command of the heavenly host, is call'd the Devil or Satan and his children are call'd Sin & Death.

But in the Book of Job, Milton's Messiah is call'd Satan.

For this history has been adopted by both parties.

It indeed appear'd to Reason as if Desire was cast out, but the Devil's account is, that the Messiah fell, & formed a heaven of what he stole from the Abyss.

This is shewn in the Gospel, where he prays to the Father to send the comforter or Desire, that Reason may have Ideas to build on, the Jehovah of the Bible being no other than he who dwells in flaming fire.

Know that after Christ's death, he became Jehovah.

But in Milton, the Father is Destiny, the Son a Ratio of the five senses, & the Holy-ghost, Vacuum!

Note. The reason Milton wrote in fetters when he wrote of

Angels & God, and at liberty when of Devils & Hell, is because he was a true Poet and of the Devil's party without knowing it.

A Memorable Fancy

As I was walking among the fires of hell, delighted with the enjoyments of Genius, which to Angels look like torment and insanity, I collected some of their Proverbs; thinking that as the sayings used in a nation mark its character, so the Proverbs of Hell shew the nature of Infernal wisdom better than any description of buildings or garments.

When I came home: on the abyss of the five senses, where a flat sided steep frowns over the present world, I saw a mighty Devil folded in black clouds, hovering on the sides of the rock; with corroding fires he wrote the following sentence now perceived by the minds of men, & read by them on earth:

How do you know but ev'ry Bird that cuts the airy way,
Is an immense world of delight, clos'd by your senses five?

Proverbs of Hell

In seed time learn, in harvest teach, in winter enjoy.
Drive your cart and your plow over the bones of the dead.
The road of excess leads to the palace of wisdom.
Prudence is a rich ugly old maid courted by Incapacity.
He who desires but acts not, breeds pestilence.
The cut worm forgives the plow.
Dip him in the river who loves water.
A fool sees not the same tree that a wise man sees.
He whose face gives no light, shall never become a star.
Eternity is in love with the productions of time.
The busy bee has no time for sorrow.
The hours of folly are measur'd by the clock, but of wisdom, no clock can measure.
All wholsom food is caught without a net or a trap.
Bring out number, weight & measure in a year of dearth.
No bird soars too high, if he soars with his own wings.
A dead body revenges not injuries.
The most sublime act is to set another before you.

If the fool would persist in his folly he would become wise.

Folly is the cloke of knavery.

Shame is Pride's cloke.

Prisons are built with stones of Law, Brothels with bricks of Religion.

The pride of the peacock is the glory of God.

The lust of the goat is the bounty of God.

The wrath of the lion is the wisdom of God.

The nakedness of woman is the work of God.

Excess of sorrow laughs. Excess of joy weeps.

The roaring of lions, the howling of wolves, the raging of the stormy sea, and the destructive sword, are portions of eternity, too great for the eye of man.

The fox condemns the trap, not himself.

Joys impregnate. Sorrows bring forth.

Let man wear the fell of the lion, woman the fleece of the sheep.

The bird a nest, the spider a web, man friendship.

The selfish, smiling fool, & the sullen, frowning fool, shall be both thought wise, that they may be a rod.

What is now proved was once only imagin'd.

The rat, the mouse, the fox, the rabbet watch the roots, the lion, the tyger, the horse, the elephant watch the fruits.

The cistern contains: the fountain overflows.

One thought fills immensity.

Always be ready to speak your mind, and a base man will avoid you.

Every thing possible to be believ'd is an image of truth.

The eagle never lost so much time as when he submitted to learn of the crow.

The fox provides for himself, but God provides for the lion.

Think in the morning. Act in the noon. Eat in the evening. Sleep in the night.

He who has suffer'd you to impose on him knows you.

As the plow follows words, so God rewards prayers.

The tygers of wrath are wiser than the horses of instruction.

Expect poison from the standing water.

You never know what is enough unless you know what is more than enough.

Listen to the fool's reproach! it is a kingly title!

The eyes of fire, the nostrils of air, the mouth of water, the beard of earth.

The weak in courage is strong in cunning.

The apple tree never asks the beech how he shall grow, nor the lion, the horse, how he shall take his prey.

The thankful reciever bears a plentiful harvest.

If others had not been foolish, we should be so.

The soul of sweet delight can never be defil'd.

When thou seest an Eagle, thou seest a portion of Genius: lift up thy head!

As the catterpiller chooses the fairest leaves to lay her eggs on, so the priest lays his curse on the fairest joys.

To create a little flower is the labour of ages.

Damn braces: Bless relaxes.

The best wine is the oldest, the best water the newest.

Prayers plow not! Praises reap not!

Joys laugh not! Sorrows weep not!

The head Sublime, the heart Pathos, the genitals Beauty, the hands & feet Proportion.

As the air to a bird or the sea to a fish, so is contempt to the contemptible.

The crow wish'd every thing was black, the owl that every thing was white.

Exuberance is Beauty.

If the lion was advised by the fox, he would be cunning.

Improvement makes strait roads; but the crooked roads without Improvement are roads of Genius.

Sooner murder an infant in its cradle than nurse unacted desires.

Where man is not, nature is barren.

Truth can never be told so as to be understood, and not be believ'd.

Enough! or Too much.

¶

THE ancient Poets animated all sensible objects with Gods or Geniuses, calling them by the names and adorning them with the properties of woods, rivers, mountains, lakes, cities, nations, and whatever their enlarged & numerous senses could percieve.

And particularly they studied the genius of each city & country, placing it under its mental deity;

Till a system was formed, which some took advantage of & enslav'd the vulgar by attempting to realize or abstract the mental deities from their objects: thus began Priesthood;

Choosing forms of worship from poetic tales.

And at length they pronounc'd that the Gods had order'd such things.

Thus men forgot that All deities reside in the human breast. . . .

¶

THE ancient tradition that the world will be consumed in fire at the end of six thousand years is true, as I have heard from Hell.

For the cherub with his flaming sword is hereby commanded to leave his guard at tree of life; and when he does, the whole creation will be consumed and appear infinite and holy, whereas it now appears finite & corrupt.

This will come to pass by an improvement of sensual enjoyment.

But first the notion that man has a body distinct from his soul is to be expunged; this I shall do by printing in the infernal method, by corrosives, which in Hell are salutary and medicinal, melting apparent surfaces away, and displaying the infinite which was hid.

If the doors of perception were cleansed every thing would appear to man as it is, infinite.

For man has closed himself up, till he sees all things thro' narrow chinks of his cavern. . . .

A Memorable Fancy

ONCE I saw a Devil in a flame of fire, who arose before an Angel that sat on a cloud, and the Devil utter'd these words:

"The worship of God is: Honouring his gifts in other men, each according to his genius, and loving the greatest men best: those who envy or calumniate great men hate God; for there is no other God."

The Angel hearing this became almost blue; but mastering himself he grew yellow, & at last white, pink, & smiling, and then replied:

"Thou Idolater! is not God One? & is not he visible in Jesus Christ? and has not Jesus Christ given his sanction to the law of ten commandments? and are not all other men fools, sinners, & nothings?"

The Devil answer'd: "Bray a fool in a morter with wheat, yet shall not his folly be beaten out of him; if Jesus Christ is the greatest man, you ought to love him in the greatest degree; now hear how he has given his sanction to the law of ten commandments: did he not mock at the sabbath, and so mock the sabbath's God? murder those who were murder'd because of him? turn away the law from the woman taken in adultery? steal the labor of others to support him? bear false witness when he omitted making a defence before Pilate? covet when he pray'd for his disciples, and when he bid them shake off the dust of their feet against such as refused to lodge them? I tell you, no virtue can exist without breaking these ten commandments. Jesus was all virtue, and acted from impulse, not from rules."

When he had so spoken, I beheld the Angel, who stretched out his arms, embracing the flame of fire, & he was consumed and arose as Elijah.

Note: This Angel, who is now become a Devil, is my particular friend; we often read the Bible together in its infernal or diabolical sense, which the world shall have if they behave well.

I have also The Bible of Hell, which the world shall have whether they will or no.

ONE Law for the Lion & Ox is Oppression.

A Song of Liberty

I.

THE Eternal Female groan'd! it was heard over all the Earth.

2. Albion's coast is sick, silent; the American meadows faint!

3. Shadows of Prophecy shiver along by the lakes and the rivers, and mutter across the ocean. France, rend down thy dungeon;

4. Golden Spain, burst the barriers of old Rome;

5. Cast thy keys, O Rome, into the deep down falling, even to eternity down falling,

6. And weep.

7. In her trembling hands she took the new born terror, howling.

8. On those infinite mountains of light now barr'd out by the atlantic sea, the new born fire stood before the starry king!

9. Flag'd with grey brow'd snows and thunderous visages, the jealous wings wav'd over the deep.

10. The speary hand burned aloft, unbuckled was the shield, forth went the hand of jealousy among the flaming hair, and hurl'd the new born wonder thro' the starry night.

11. The fire, the fire is falling!

12. Look up! look up! O citizen of London, enlarge thy countenance! O Jew, leave counting gold! return to thy oil and wine. O African! black African! (go, winged thought, widen his forehead.)

13. The fiery limbs, the flaming hair, shot like the sinking sun into the western sea.

14. Wak'd from his eternal sleep, the hoary element roaring fled away;

15. Down rush'd, beating his wings in vain, the jealous king; his grey brow'd councellors, thunderous warriors, curl'd veterans, among helms, and shields, and chariots, horses, elephants, banners, castles, slings, and rocks.

16. Falling, rushing, ruining! buried in the ruins, on Urthona's dens;

17. All night beneath the ruins, then their sullen flames faded emerge round the gloomy king.

18. With thunder and fire, leading his starry hosts thro' the waste wilderness, he promulgates his ten commands, glancing his beamy eyelids over the deep in dark dismay,

19. Where the son of fire in his eastern cloud, while the morning plumes her golden breast,

20. Spurning the clouds written with curses, stamps the stony law to dust, loosing the eternal horses from the dens of night, crying EMPIRE IS NO MORE! AND NOW THE LION & WOLF SHALL CEASE.

CHORUS

Let the Priests of the Raven of dawn no longer in deadly black,
with hoarse note curse the sons of joy. Nor his accepted brethren
whom, tyrant, he calls free, lay the bound or build the roof. Nor
pale religious letchery call that virginity that wishes but acts not!

For every thing that lives is Holy.

NEVER SEEK TO TELL THY LOVE

ca. 1793

Never seek to tell thy love
Love that never told can be;
For the gentle wind does move
Silently, invisibly.

I told my love, I told my love,
I told her all my heart,
Trembling, cold, in ghastly fears—
Ah, she doth depart.

Soon as she was gone from me
A traveller came by
Silently, invisibly—   10
O, was no deny.

I SAW A CHAPEL ALL OF GOLD

ca. 1793

I saw a chapel all of gold
That none did dare to enter in,
And many weeping stood without,
Weeping, mourning, worshipping.

I saw a serpent rise between
The white pillars of the door,

And he forc'd and forc'd and forc'd,
Down the golden hinges tore.

And along the pavement sweet,
Set with pearls and rubies bright,   10
All his slimy length he drew,
Till upon the altar white

Vomiting his poison out
On the bread and on the wine.
So I turn'd into a sty
And laid me down among the swine.

SONGS OF EXPERIENCE

1794

The Clod and the Pebble

"Love seeketh not itself to please,
  Nor for itself hath any care,
But for another gives its ease,
  And builds a heaven in hell's despair."

So sung a little clod of clay,
  Trodden with the cattle's feet,
But a pebble of the brook
  Warbled out these metres meet:

"Love seeketh only self to please,
  To bind another to its delight,   10
Joys in another's loss of ease,
  And builds a hell in heaven's despite."

Holy Thursday

Is this a holy thing to see
  In a rich and fruitful land,
Babes reduc'd to misery,
  Fed with cold and usurous hand?

Is that trembling cry a song?
   Can it be a song of joy?
And so many children poor?
   It is a land of poverty!

And their sun does never shine,
   And their fields are bleak and bare,
And their ways are fill'd with thorns:
   It is eternal winter there.

For where'er the sun does shine,
   And where'er the rain does fall,
Babe can never hunger there,
   Nor poverty the mind appall.

The Chimney-Sweeper

A little black thing among the snow,
Crying, "'Weep! 'weep!" in notes of woe!
"Where are thy father and mother? say?"—
"They are both gone up to the church to pray.

"Because I was happy upon the heath,
And smil'd among the winter's snow,
They clothed me in the clothes of death,
And taught me to sing the notes of woe.

"And because I am happy and dance and sing,
They think they have done me no injury,
And are gone to praise God and his priest and king,
Who make up a heaven of our misery."

The Tyger

Tyger! tyger! burning bright
In the forests of the night,
What immortal hand or eye
Could frame thy fearful symmetry?

In what distant deeps or skies
Burnt the fire of thine eyes?
On what wings dare he aspire?
What the hand dare seize the fire?

And what shoulder, and what art,
Could twist the sinews of thy heart? 10
And when thy heart began to beat,
What dread hand? and what dread feet?

What the hammer? what the chain?
In what furnace was thy brain?
What the anvil? what dread grasp
Dare its deadly terrors clasp?

When the stars threw down their spears,
And water'd heaven with their tears,
Did he smile his work to see?
Did he who made the Lamb make thee? 20

Tyger! tyger! burning bright
In the forests of the night,
What immortal hand or eye,
Dare frame thy fearful symmetry?

Ah, Sun-Flower

Ah, Sun-flower! weary of time,
    Who countest the steps of the sun,
Seeking after that sweet golden clime,
    Where the traveller's journey is done:

Where the youth pined away with desire,
    And the pale virgin shrouded in snow,
Arise from their graves, and aspire
    Where my Sun-flower wishes to go.

The Garden of Love

I went to the Garden of Love,
    And saw what I never had seen:
A chapel was built in the midst,
    Where I used to play on the green.

And the gates of this chapel were shut,
    And "Thou shalt not" writ over the door;
So I turn'd to the Garden of Love
    That so many sweet flowers bore;

And I saw it was filled with graves,
And tombstones where flowers should be;
And priests in black gowns were walking their rounds,
And binding with briars my joys and desires.

LONDON

I wander thro' each charter'd street,
Near where the charter'd Thames does flow,
And mark in every face I meet
Marks of weakness, marks of woe.

In every cry of every man,
In every infant's cry of fear,
In every voice, in every ban,
The mind-forg'd manacles I hear.

How the chimney-sweeper's cry
Every black'ning church appalls; 10
And the hapless soldier's sigh
Runs in blood down palace walls.

But most thro' midnight streets I hear
How the youthful harlot's curse
Blasts the new-born infant's tear,
And blights with plagues the marriage hearse.

THE HUMAN ABSTRACT

Pity would be no more
If we did not make somebody poor;
And mercy no more could be
If all were as happy as we.

And mutual fear brings peace,
Till the selfish loves increase:
Then cruelty knits a snare,
And spreads his baits with care.

He sits down with holy fears,
And waters the ground with tears; 10
Then humility takes its root
Underneath his foot.

Soon spreads the dismal shade
Of mystery over his head;
And the catterpiller and fly
Feed on the mystery.

And it bears the fruit of deceit,
Ruddy and sweet to eat;
And the raven his nest has made
In its thickest shade.   20

The Gods of the earth and sea
Sought thro' nature to find this tree;
But their search was all in vain:
There grows one in the human brain.

A POISON TREE

I was angry with my friend:
I told my wrath, my wrath did end.
I was angry with my foe:
I told it not, my wrath did grow.

And I watr'd it in fears,
Night and morning with my tears;
And I sunned it with smiles,
And with soft deceitful wiles.

And it grew both day and night,
Till it bore an apple bright;   10
And my foe beheld it shine,
And he knew that it was mine,

And into my garden stole
When the night had veil'd the pole:
In the morning glad I see
My foe outstretch'd beneath the tree.

MOCK ON, MOCK ON, VOLTAIRE, ROUSSEAU

(Written ca. 1800–1803)

Mock on, mock on, Voltaire, Rousseau:
Mock on, mock on; 'tis all in vain!
You throw the sand against the wind,
And the wind blows it back again.

And every sand becomes a gem
Reflected in the beams divine;
Blown back they blind the mocking eye,
But still in Israel's paths they shine.

The atoms of Democritus
And Newton's particles of light   10
Are sands upon the Red Sea shore,
Where Israel's tents do shine so bright.

AUGURIES OF INNOCENCE

(Written ca. 1803)

To see a World in a grain of sand
And a Heaven in a wild flower,
Hold Infinity in the palm of your hand
And Eternity in an hour.

A robin redbreast in a cage
Puts all Heaven in a rage.
A dove-house fill'd with doves and pigeons
Shudders Hell thro' all its regions.
A dog starved at his master's gate
Predicts the ruin of the State.   10
A horse misus'd upon the road

Calls to Heaven for human blood.
Each outcry of the hunted hare
A fiber from the brain does tear.
A skylark wounded in the wing,
A cherubim does cease to sing.
The game-cock clip'd and arm'd for fight
Does the rising sun affright.
Every wolf's and lion's howl
Raises from Hell a Human soul.   20
The wild deer, wand'ring here and there,
Keeps the Human soul from care.
The lamb misus'd breeds public strife
And yet forgives the butcher's knife.
The bat that flits at close of eve
Has left the brain that won't believe.
The owl that calls upon the night
Speaks the unbeliever's fright.
He who shall hurt the little wren
Shall never be belov'd by men.   30
He who the ox to wrath has mov'd
Shall never be by woman lov'd.
The wanton boy that kills the fly
Shall feel the spider's enmity.
He who torments the chafer's sprite
Weaves a bower in endless night.
The catterpiller on the leaf
Repeats to thee thy mother's grief.
Kill not the moth nor butterfly,
For the Last Judgment draweth nigh.   40
Who shall train the horse to war
Shall never pass the polar bar.
The beggar's dog and widow's cat,
Feed them and thou wilt grow fat.
The gnat that sings his summer's song
Poison gets from Slander's tongue.
The poison of the snake and newt
Is the sweat of Envy's foot.
The poison of the honey-bee
Is the artist's jealousy.   50
The prince's robes and beggar's rags
Are toadstools on the miser's bags.
A truth that's told with bad intent

Beats all the lies you can invent.
It is right it should be so;
Man was made for joy and woe;
And when this we rightly know
Thro' the world we safely go.
Joy and woe are woven fine,
A clothing for the soul divine;   60
Under every grief and pine
Runs a joy with silken twine.
The babe is more than swadling-bands;
Throughout all these human lands
Tools were made, and born were hands,
Every farmer understands.
Every tear from every eye
Becomes a babe in Eternity;
This is caught by females bright
And return'd to its own delight.   70
The bleat, the bark, bellow, and roar
Are waves that beat on Heaven's shore.
The babe that weeps the rod beneath
Writes revenge in realms of death.
The beggar's rags, fluttering in air,
Does to rags the heavens tear.
The soldier, arm'd with sword and gun,
Palsied strikes the summer's sun.
The poor man's farthing is worth more
Than all the gold on Afric's shore.   80
One mite wrung from the lab'rer's hands
Shall buy and sell the miser's lands:
Or, if protected from on high,
Does that whole nation sell and buy.
He who mocks the infant's faith
Shall be mock'd in age and death.
He who shall teach the child to doubt
The rotting grave shall ne'er get out.
He who respects the infant's faith
Triumphs over Hell and Death.   90
The child's toys and the old man's reasons
Are the fruits of the two seasons.
The questioner, who sits so sly,
Shall never know how to reply.
He who replies to words of Doubt

Doth put the light of Knowledge out.
The strongest poison ever known
Came from Caesar's laurel crown.
Naught can deform the human race
Like to the armour's iron brace. 100
When gold and gems adorn the plow
To peaceful arts shall Envy bow.
A riddle, or the cricket's cry,
Is to Doubt a fit reply.
The emmet's inch and eagle's mile
Make lame Philosophy to smile.
He who doubts from what he sees
Will ne'er believe, do what you please.
If the Sun and Moon should doubt,
They'd immediately go out. 110
To be in a passion you good may do,
But no good if a passion is in you.
The whore and gambler, by the state
Licenc'd, build that nation's fate.
The harlot's cry from street to street
Shall weave Old England's winding sheet.
The winner's shout, the loser's curse,
Dance before dead England's hearse.
Every night and every morn
Some to misery are born. 120
Every morn and every night
Some are born to sweet delight.
Some are born to sweet delight,
Some are born to endless night.
We are led to believe a lie
When we see not thro' the eye,
Which was born in a night, to perish in a night,
When the Soul slept in beams of Light.
God appears and God is light
To those poor souls who dwell in night, 130
But does a human form display
To those who dwell in realms of day.

PREFACE TO MILTON

1804

And did those feet in ancient time
Walk upon England's mountains green?
And was the holy Lamb of God
On England's pleasant pastures seen?

And did the countenance divine
Shine forth upon our clouded hills?
And was Jerusalem builded here
Among these dark Satanic mills?

Bring me my bow of burning gold:
Bring me my arrows of desire: 10
Bring me my spear: O clouds, unfold!
Bring me my chariot of fire.

I will not cease from mental fight,
Nor shall my sword sleep in my hand,
Till we have built Jerusalem
In England's green and pleasant land.

MILTON

From BOOK THE SECOND

(*ca.* 1804–1808)

. . . But turning toward Ololon in terrible majesty Milton
Replied: "Obey thou the words of the Inspired Man.
All that can be annihilated must be annihilated
That the Children of Jerusalem may be saved from slavery.
There is a Negation, & there is a Contrary:
The Negation must be destroy'd to redeem the Contraries.
The Negation is the Spectre, the Reasoning Power in Man:

This is a false body, in incrustation over my immortal
Spirit, a Selfhood which must be put off & annihilated alway.
To cleanse the face of my spirit by self-examination,
To bathe in the waters of Life, to wash off the Not Human,
I come in Self-annihilation & the grandeur of Inspiration,
To cast off Rational Demonstration by faith in the Saviour,
To cast off the rotten rags of Memory by Inspiration,
To cast off Bacon, Locke & Newton from Albion's covering,
To take off his filthy garments & clothe him with Imagination,
To cast aside from Poetry all that is not Inspiration,
That it no longer shall dare to mock with the aspersion of Madness
Cast on the Inspired by the tame high finisher of paltry blots
Indefinite, or paltry rhymes, or paltry harmonies,
Who creeps into state government like a caterpiller to destroy;
To cast off the idiot Questioner who is always questioning
But never capable of answering, who sits with a sly grin
Silent plotting when to question, like a thief in a cave,
Who publishes doubt & calls it knowledge, whose Science is
   Despair,
Whose pretence to knowledge is Envy, whose whole Science is
To destroy the wisdom of ages to gratify ravenous Envy
That rages round him like a wolf day & night without rest:
He smiles with condescension, he talks of benevolence & virtue,
And those who act with benevolence & virtue they murder time
   on time.
These are the destroyers of Jerusalem, these are the murderers
Of Jesus, who deny the Faith & mock at Eternal Life,
Who pretend to Poetry that they may destroy Imagination
By imitation of Nature's images drawn from remembrance.
These are the sexual garments, the abomination of desolation,
Hiding the human lineaments as with an ark & curtains
Which Jesus rent & now shall wholly purge away with fire
Till Generation is swallow'd up in Regeneration."

EPIGRAM

(*Written ca.* 1808–1811)

The only man that e'er I knew
Who did not make me almost spew
Was Fuseli: [1] he was both Turk and Jew—
And so, dear Christian friends, how do you do?

A SELECTION

William Paley

1743–1805

[The leading Anglican theologian of his day, Paley, like the deists, turned to nature for his proof that God exists. The sum of his argument is that "the world abounds in contrivances" that *must* have been made especially by an intelligent God for our happiness. The universe is as nicely designed as a watch—and the existence of a watch proves that there was a maker. Paley accumulates instances of what today would be called "adaptation" of organs to special uses. In short, he is a Darwin without Darwin's evolutionary view. To Darwin, the adaptation of organs to their uses proves evolution; to Paley, it proves special "contrivance" on the part of God.]

THE PRINCIPLES OF MORAL AND POLITICAL PHILOSOPHY

1785

CONTRIVANCE proves design; and the predominant tendency of the contrivance indicates the disposition of the designer. The world abounds with contrivances: and all the contrivances which we are acquainted with are directed to beneficial purposes. Evil, no doubt, exists; but is never, that we can perceive, the object of contrivance. Teeth are contrived to eat, not to ache; their aching now and then is incidental to the contrivance, perhaps inseparable from it:

---

1 Henry Fuseli (1741–1825), a Swiss painter and author who came to England in 1763. His most famous picture was the "Gothic" *Nightmare*, done in 1781.

or even, if you will, let it be called a defect in the contrivance; but it is not the *object* of it. . . . We never discover a train of contrivance to bring about an evil purpose. No anatomist ever discovered a system of organization calculated to produce pain and disease; or, in explaining the parts of the human body, ever said "This is to irritate; this to inflame; this duct is to convey the gravel to the kidneys; this gland to secrete the humor which forms the gout": if by chance he come at a part of which he knows not the use, the most he can say is that it is useless: no one ever suspects that it is put there to incommode, to annoy, or to torment. Since then God hath called forth his consummate wisdom to contrive and provide for our happiness, and the world appears to have been constituted with this design at first; so long as this constitution is upholden by him, we must in reason suppose the same design to continue.

[BOOK II, chap. v]

NATURAL THEOLOGY
1802

IN comparing different animals, I know no part of their structure which exhibits greater variety, or, in that variety, a nicer accommodation to their respective conveniency, than that which is seen in the different formations of their *mouths*. Whether the purpose be the reception of aliment merely, or the catching of prey, the picking up of seeds, the cropping of herbage, the extraction of juices, the suction of liquids, the breaking and grinding of food, the taste of that food, together with the respiration of air, and, in conjunction with it, the utterance of sound; these various offices are assigned to this one part, and, in different species, provided for, as they are wanted, by its different constitution. In the human species, forasmuch as there are hands to convey the food to the mouth, the mouth is flat, and by reason of its flatness, fitted only for *reception;* whereas the projecting jaws, the wide rictus, the pointed teeth of the dog and his affinities, enable them to apply their mouths to *snatch and seize* the objects of their pursuit. The full lips, the rough tongue, the corrugated cartilaginous palate, the broad cutting teeth of the ox, the deer, the horse, and the sheep, qualify this tribe for *browsing* upon their pasture; either gathering large mouthfuls at once, where the grass is long, which is the case with the ox in particular; or biting close, where it is short, which the horse and the sheep are able to do, in a degree that one could hardly expect. The retired underjaw of the swine *works in the ground*, after the protruding snout, like a prong or plowshare, has made its way to the roots upon which it feeds. A conformation so happy, was not the gift of chance.

[CHAPTER XII]

Upon the whole, after all the schemes and struggles of a reluctant philosophy, the necessary resort is to a Deity. The marks of *design* are too strong to be gotten over. Design must have had a designer. That designer must have been a person. That person is GOD.

[CHAPTER XXIII]

A SELECTION

Jeremy Bentham

1748–1832

AN INTRODUCTION TO THE PRINCIPLES OF MORALS AND LEGISLATION

1780–1789

[In Bentham, the benevolism of the eighteenth century culminates in a full utilitarianism, which was transmitted to the nineteenth century by thinkers like James Mill and his son, John Stuart Mill. The thoroughgoing materialism of Bentham was repudiated by the latter. It is curious how the benevolence of the esthetic Shaftesbury runs through a line of thinkers including Hutcheson, Hume, and Adam Smith, to terminate in the crass utility of Bentham (who is said to have loved everything with four, as well as two, legs). Among the most important of Bentham's influences today is that upon semantics, the scrutiny of words, contexts, and meanings.]

NATURE has placed mankind under the governance of two sovereign masters, *pain* and *pleasure*. It is for them alone to point out what we ought to do, as well as to determine what we shall do. On the one hand the standard of right and wrong, on the other the chain of causes and effects, are fastened to their throne. They govern us in all we do, in all we say, in all we think: every effort we can make to throw off our subjection will serve but to demonstrate and confirm it. In words a man may pretend to abjure their empire, but in reality he will remain subject to it all the while. The *principle of utility* recognizes this subjection, and assumes it for the foundation of that system the object of which is to rear the fabric of felicity by the hands of reason and of law. Systems which attempt to question it deal in sounds instead of sense, in caprice instead of reason, in darkness instead of light. . . .

. . . By the principle of utility is meant that principle which approves or disapproves of every action whatsoever according to the tendency which it appears to have to augment or diminish the happiness of the party whose interest is in question: or, what is the same thing in other words, to promote or to oppose that happiness. I say of every action whatsoever, and therefore not only of every action of a private individual, but of every measure of government.

By utility is meant that property in any object whereby it tends to produce benefit, advantage, pleasure, good, or happiness (all this in the present case comes to the same thing) or (what comes again to the same thing) to prevent the happening of mischief, pain, evil, or unhappiness to the party whose interest is considered. . . .

An action then may be said to be conformable to the principle of utility, or, for shortness' sake, to utility (meaning with respect to the community at large) when the tendency it has to augment the happiness of the community is greater than any it has to diminish it. . . .

Of an action that is conformable to the principle of utility, one may always say either that it is one that ought to be done, or at least that it is not one that ought not to be done. One may also say that it is right it should be done; at least that it is not wrong it should be done; that it is a right action; at least that it is not a wrong action. When thus interpreted, the words *ought*, and *right* and *wrong*, and others of that stamp, have a meaning: when otherwise, they have none.

[CHAPTER I]

To a person considered *by himself*, the value of a pleasure or pain considered *by itself* will be greater or less according to the four following circumstances:

(1) Its *intensity*.
(2) Its *duration*.

(3) Its *certainty* or *uncertainty*.
(4) Its *propinquity* or *remoteness*. ...

To a *number* of persons, with reference to each of whom the value of a pleasure or a pain is considered, it will be greater or less, according to seven circumstances: to wit . . .

(1) Its *intensity*.
(2) Its *duration*.
(3) Its *certainty* or *uncertainty*.
(4) Its *propinquity* or *remoteness*.
(5) Its *fecundity*.
(6) Its *purity*.[1]

And one other; to wit:
(7) Its *extent;* that is, the number of persons to whom it *extends*.

Sum up all the values of all the *pleasures* on the one side, and those of all the pains on the other. The balance, if it be on the side of pleasure, will give the *good* tendency of the act upon the whole, with respect to the interests of that *individual* person; if on the side of pain, the *bad* tendency of it upon the whole.

Take an account of the *number* of persons whose interests appear to be concerned, and repeat the above process with respect to each. . . . Take the *balance*, which, if on the side of *pleasure*, will give the general *good tendency* of the act, with respect to the total number or community of individuals concerned; if on the side of pain, the general *evil tendency*, with respect to the same community.

[CHAPTER IV]

The general tendency of an act is more or less pernicious according to the sum total of its consequences: that is, according to the difference between the sum of such as are good and the sum of such as are evil.

It is to be observed that here, as well as henceforward, whenever consequences are spoken of, such only are meant as are *material*. Of the consequences of any act, the multitude and variety must needs be infinite, but such of them only as are material are worth regarding.

[CHAPTER VII]

With respect to goodness and badness, as it is with everything else that is not itself either pain or pleasure, so is it with motives.

1 That is, its unmixed quality.

If they are good or bad, it is only on account of their effects: good, on account of their tendency to produce pleasure or avert pain; bad, on account of their tendency to produce pain or avert pleasure. Now the case is that from one and the same motive, and from every kind of motive, may proceed actions that are good, others that are bad, and others that are indifferent. . . .

It appears then that there is no such thing as any sort of motive which is a bad one in itself; nor, consequently, any such thing as a sort of motive which in itself is exclusively a good one. . . .

What, then (it will be said) are not lust, cruelty, avarice, bad motives? . . . The fact is that these are names which, if properly applied, are never applied but in the cases where the motives they signify happen to be bad. The names of these motives, considered apart from their effects, are sexual desire, displeasure, and pecuniary interest. To sexual desire, when the effects of it are looked upon as bad, is given the name of lust. Now lust is always a bad motive. Why? Because if the case be such that the effects of the motive are not bad, it does not go, or at least ought not to go, by the name of lust. The case is, then, that when I say "Lust is a bad motive," it is a proposition that merely concerns the import of the word *lust;* and which would be false if transferred to the other word used for the same motive, *sexual desire.* Hence we see the emptiness of all those rhapsodies of commonplace morality, which consist in the taking of such names as lust, cruelty, and avarice, and branding them with marks of reprobation: applied to the *thing,* they are false; applied to the *name,* they are true indeed, but nugatory. Would you do a real service to mankind, show them the cases in which sexual desire *merits* the name of lust; displeasure, that of cruelty; and pecuniary interest, that of avarice.

[CHAPTER X]

A SELECTION

Thomas Robert Malthus

1766–1834

AN ESSAY ON THE PRINCIPLE OF POPULATION

1798

[The second edition of the *Essay* (1803) was enlarged and more scientifically argued and documented. Malthus claims that all of his opinions are to be found in Hume, Robert Wallace, Adam Smith, and Richard Price. His attack on Godwin is particularly devastating.]

I THINK I may fairly make two postulata:

First, that food is necessary to the existence of man.

Secondly, that the passion between the sexes is necessary, and will remain nearly in its present state.

These two laws ever since we have had any knowledge of mankind appear to have been fixed laws of our nature; and as we have not hitherto seen any alteration in them, we have no right to conclude that they will ever cease to be what they are now, without an immediate act of power in that Being who first arranged the system of the universe, and for the advantage of his creatures still executes, according to fixed laws, all its various operations.

I do not know that any writer has supposed that on this earth man will ultimately be able to live without food. But Mr. Godwin has conjectured that the passion between the sexes may in time be extinguished. As, however, he calls this part of his work a deviation into the land of conjecture, I will not dwell longer upon it at present than to say that the best arguments for the perfectibility of man are drawn from a contemplation of the great progress that he has already made from the savage state, and the difficulty of saying where he is to stop. But towards the extinction of the passion between the sexes no progress has hitherto been made. It appears to exist in as much force at present as it did two thousand or four thousand years ago. . . .

Assuming, then, my postulata as granted, I say that the power of population is indefinitely greater than the power in the earth to produce subsistence for man.

Population when unchecked increases in a geometrical ratio. Subsistence increases only in an arithmetical ratio. A slight acquaintance with numbers will show the immensity of the first power in comparison of the second.

By that law of our nature which makes food necessary to the life of man, the effects of these two unequal powers must be kept equal.

This implies a strong and constantly operating check on population from the difficulty of subsistence. This difficulty must fall somewhere, and must necessarily be severely felt by a large portion of mankind.

Through the animal and vegetable kingdoms, nature has scattered the seeds of life abroad with the most profuse and liberal hand. She has been comparatively sparing in the room, and the nourishment, necessary to rear them. The germs of existence contained in this spot of earth, with ample food and ample room to expand in, would fill millions of worlds in the course of a few thousand years. Necessity, that imperious and all-pervading law of nature, restrains them within the prescribed bounds. The race of plants and the race of animals shrink under this great restrictive law. And the race of man cannot, by any efforts of reason, escape from it. Among plants and animals its effects are waste of seed, sickness, and premature death. Among mankind, misery and vice. . . .

This natural inequality of the two powers of population and of production in the earth, and that great law of our nature which must constantly keep their effects equal, form the great difficulty that to me appears insurmountable in the way to the perfectibility of society. All other arguments are of slight and subordinate consideration in comparison of this. I see no way by which man can escape from the weight of this law which pervades all animated nature. . . .

Consequently, if the premises are just, the argument is conclusive against the perfectibility of the mass of mankind.

[CHAPTER I]

George Crabbe

1754–1832

CRABBE should appeal to the twentieth century because of his unflinching and at times repellent observation that had better be called literal than realistic. In a great number of tales he presents the social conditions in the village he knew best, Aldborough, on the impoverished Suffolk coast. This strongly "social" attitude should be another reason for present-day interest in his work. Crabbe offsets the idyllic *Deserted Village* of Goldsmith as well as the more monumental and contemplative pastoral of Wordsworth. Possibly it is unfortunate that Crabbe chose to write in verse at all, for the heroic couplet is not very well suited to his plain narrative, although there are certain memorable snatches—"the muddy ecstasies of beer," for example. If he had turned to the novel, or, better, the short story, he might have secured his effects more easily. In several of his prefatory notes he has presented a very adequate theory of prose fiction. Howbeit, there is undeniable power in his stories of the beggared, the illegitimate, the drunkard, the insane, the unwedded mother. In his earlier and best work he prefers to deal with these "underprivileged" and, more remarkably, to deal with them against their environment—the poorhouse, the church, the hospital, the slums, and domestic industry. With cumulative force he places before us a whole social "level." Crabbe also knows how to tell a story, although his range is obviously not that of Chaucer. In brief, there are values in Crabbe that can hardly be found elsewhere in the poetry of his day. As he says of his own *Tales,* "while much is lost for want of unity of subject and grandeur of design, something is gained by greater variety of incident and more minute display of character, by accuracy of description and diversity of scene."

BIOGRAPHICAL NOTES

Born at Aldborough, Suffolk, a "mean and scrambling" seaport; son of a schoolmaster and collector of salt duties. Attended school at Stow-market. Apprenticed to a surgeon near Bury St. Edmunds; also worked on a farm nearby (1768). Next worked at Woodbridge, where he met Sarah Elmy, "Mira" of the poems. *Inebriety* printed at Ipswich (1775). Returned to Aldborough to serve as apothecary, write verses, and study botany and theology. Went to London (1780), determined to give up medicine for literature. In distress, appealed to Edmund Burke, who took him into his household, aided him in publishing *The Library* (1781), and introduced him to Sir Joshua Reynolds and Dr. Johnson. Took orders and served as chaplain to Duke of Rutland (1782). Published *The Village* (1783), revised with Johnson's aid. Married Sarah Elmy and held several small livings secured by patronage. *The Newspaper* published (1785); then twenty years of writing and burning manuscripts (among them novels) without publishing. *The Parish Register* (1807). *The Borough* (1810), called "disgusting." *Tales in Verse* (1812). Death of Sarah, who had become insane (1813). *Tales of the Hall* (1819). Last years spent at Trowbridge.

BIBLIOGRAPHY: *Poems,* ed. A. W. Ward, 3 vols., 1905–07. *Poetical Works,* ed. A. J. and R. M. Carlyle, 1914. Crabbe, George [the poet's son], *The Life of George Crabbe,* 1834, 1932. Haddokin, Lillian, *The Poetry of Crabbe,* 1955.

THE VILLAGE

1783

BOOK I

The Village Life, and every care that reigns
O'er youthful peasants and declining swains;

What labour yields, and what, that labour past,
Age, in its hour of languor, finds at last;
What form the real picture of the poor,
Demand a song—the Muse can give no more.

Fled are those times when, in harmonious strains,
The rustic poet praised his native plains.
No shepherds now, in smooth alternate verse,
Their country's beauty or their nymphs' rehearse; 10
Yet still for these we frame the tender strain,
Still in our lays fond Corydons complain,
And shepherds' boys their amorous pains reveal,
The only pains, alas! they never feel.

On Mincio's banks, in Cæsar's bounteous reign,
If Tityrus found the Golden Age again,
Must sleepy bards the flattering dream prolong,
Mechanic echoes of the Mantuan song?
From Truth and Nature shall we widely stray,
Where Virgil, not where Fancy, leads the way? 20

Yes, thus the Muses sing of happy swains,
Because the Muses never knew their pains.
They boast their peasants' pipes; but peasants now
Resign their pipes and plod behind the plough;
And few, amid the rural-tribe, have time
To number syllables, and play with rhyme;
Save honest Duck,[1] what son of verse could share
The poet's rapture, and the peasant's care?
Or the great labours of the field degrade,
With the new peril of a poorer trade? 30

From this chief cause these idle praises spring,
That themes so easy few forbear to sing;
For no deep thought the trifling subjects ask:
To sing of shepherds is an easy task.
The happy youth assumes the common strain,
A nymph his mistress, and himself a swain;
With no sad scenes he clouds his tuneful prayer,
But all, to look like her, is painted fair.

I grant indeed that fields and flocks have charms
For him that grazes or for him that farms; 40
But when amid such pleasing scenes I trace
The poor laborious natives of the place,

1 Stephen Duck, the thresher-poet; one of the "uneducated poets of nature." Duck was patronized by Pope, Joseph Spence, and Queen Caroline, who appointed him chaplain at Kew and librarian at the "Gothic" hut, called Merlin's Cave, in Richmond Gardens.

And see the mid-day sun, with fervid ray,
On their bare heads and dewy temples play;
While some, with feebler heads and fainter hearts,
Deplore their fortune, yet sustain their parts:
Then shall I dare these real ills to hide
In tinsel trappings of poetic pride?
　　No; cast by Fortune on a frowning coast,
Which neither groves nor happy valleys boast;　　50
Where other cares than those the Muse relates,
And other shepherds dwell with other mates;
By such examples taught, I paint the cot,
As Truth will paint it, and as bards will not:
Nor you, ye poor, of letter'd scorn complain,
To you the smoothest song is smooth in vain;
O'ercome by labour, and bow'd down by time,
Feel you the barren flattery of a rhyme?
Can poets soothe you, when you pine for bread,
By winding myrtles round your ruin'd shed?　　60
Can their light tales your weighty griefs o'erpow'r,
Or glad with airy mirth the toilsome hour?
　　Lo! where the heath, with withering brake grown o'er,
Lends the light turf that warms the neighbouring poor;
From thence a length of burning sand appears,
Where the thin harvest waves its wither'd ears;
Rank weeds, that every art and care defy,
Reign o'er the land, and rob the blighted rye:
There thistles stretch their prickly arms afar,
And to the ragged infant threaten war;　　70
There poppies, nodding, mock the hope of toil;
There the blue bugloss paints the sterile soil;
Hardy and high, above the slender sheaf,
The slimy mallow waves her silky leaf;
O'er the young shoot the charlock throws a shade,
And clasping tares cling round the sickly blade;
With mingled tints the rocky coasts abound,
And a sad splendour vainly shines around.
So looks the nymph whom wretched arts adorn,
Betray'd by man, then left for man to scorn;　　80
Whose cheek in vain assumes the mimic rose,
While her sad eyes the troubled breast disclose;
Whose outward splendour is but folly's dress,
Exposing most, when most it gilds distress.
　　Here joyless roam a wild amphibious race,

With sullen woe display'd in every face;
Who far from civil arts and social fly,
And scowl at strangers with suspicious eye.
    Here too the lawless merchant of the main
Draws from his plough th' intoxicated swain;   90
Want only claim'd the labour of the day,
But vice now steals his nightly rest away.
    Where are the swains, who, daily labour done,
With rural games play'd down the setting sun;
Who struck with matchless force the bounding ball,
Or made the pond'rous quoit obliquely fall;
While some huge Ajax, terrible and strong,
Engaged some artful stripling of the throng,
And fell beneath him, foil'd, while far around
Hoarse triumph rose, and rocks return'd the sound?   100
Where now are these?—Beneath yon cliff they stand,
To show the freighted pinnace where to land; [2]
To load the ready steed with guilty haste;
To fly in terror o'er the pathless waste;
Or, when detected in their straggling course,
To foil their foes by cunning or by force;
Or, yielding part (which equal knaves demand),
To gain a lawless passport through the land.
    Here, wand'ring long amid these frowning fields,
I sought the simple life that Nature yields;   110
Rapine and Wrong and Fear usurp'd her place,
And a bold, artful, surly, savage race;
Who, only skill'd to take the finny tribe,
The yearly dinner, or septennial [3] bribe,
Wait on the shore, and, as the waves run high,
On the tost vessel bend their eager eye,
Which to their coast directs its vent'rous way;
Theirs, or the ocean's, miserable prey.
    As on their neighbouring beach yon swallows stand,
And wait for favouring winds to leave the land,   120
While still for flight the ready wing is spread:
So waited I the favouring hour, and fled—
Fled from these shores where guilt and famine reign,
And cried, "Ah! hapless they who still remain;
Who still remain to hear the ocean roar,
Whose greedy waves devour the lessening shore;

---

2 Crabbe refers to the common crime of   3 Cf. Johnson's *Vanity of Human Wishes*,
smuggling.   lines 96–97.

Till some fierce tide, with more imperious sway,
Sweeps the low hut and all it holds away;
When the sad tenant weeps from door to door,
And begs a poor protection from the poor!"   130

But these are scenes where Nature's niggard hand
Gave a spare portion to the famish'd land;
Hers is the fault, if here mankind complain
Of fruitless toil and labour spent in vain.
But yet in other scenes, more fair in view,
Where Plenty smiles—alas! she smiles for few—
And those who taste not, yet behold her store,
Are as the slaves that dig the golden ore,
The wealth around them makes them doubly poor.

Or will you deem them amply paid in health,   140
Labour's fair child, that languishes with wealth?
Go, then! and see them rising with the sun,
Through a long course of daily toil to run;
See them beneath the dog-star's raging heat,
When the knees tremble and the temples beat;
Behold them, leaning on their scythes, look o'er
The labour past, and toils to come explore;
See them alternate suns and showers engage,
And hoard up aches and anguish for their age;
Through fens and marshy moors their steps pursue,   150
When their warm pores imbibe the evening dew;
Then own that labour may as fatal be
To these thy slaves, as thine excess to thee.

Amid this tribe too oft a manly pride
Strives in strong toil the fainting heart to hide;
There may you see the youth of slender frame
Contend, with weakness, weariness, and shame;
Yet, urged along, and proudly loth to yield,
He strives to join his fellows of the field;
Till long-contending nature droops at last,   160
Declining health rejects his poor repast,
His cheerless spouse the coming danger sees,
And mutual murmurs urge the slow disease.

Yet grant them health, 'tis not for us to tell,
Though the head droops not, that the heart is well;
Or will you praise that homely, healthy fare,
Plenteous and plain, that happy peasants share?
Oh! trifle not with wants you cannot feel,
Nor mock the misery of a stinted meal—

Homely, not wholesome; plain, not plenteous; such   170
As you who praise would never deign to touch.

Ye gentle souls, who dream of rural ease,
Whom the smooth stream and smoother sonnet please;
Go! if the peaceful cot your praises share,
Go, look within, and ask if peace be there:
If peace be his—that drooping weary sire,
Or theirs, that offspring round their feeble fire;
Or hers, that matron pale, whose trembling hand
Turns on the wretched hearth th' expiring brand!

Nor yet can Time itself obtain for these   180
Life's latest comforts, due respect and ease:
For yonder see that hoary swain, whose age
Can with no cares except his own engage;
Who, propp'd on that rude staff, looks up to see
The bare arms broken from the withering tree,
On which, a boy, he climb'd the loftiest bough,
Then his first joy, but his sad emblem now.

He once was chief in all the rustic trade;
His steady hand the straightest furrow made;
Full many a prize he won, and still is proud   190
To find the triumphs of his youth allow'd.
A transient pleasure sparkles in his eyes;
He hears and smiles, then thinks again and sighs;
For now he journeys to his grave in pain;
The rich disdain him, nay, the poor disdain;
Alternate masters now their slave command,
Urge the weak efforts of his feeble hand;
And, when his age attempts its task in vain,
With ruthless taunts, of lazy poor complain.

Oft may you see him, when he tends the sheep,   200
His winter-charge, beneath the hillock weep;
Oft hear him murmur to the winds that blow
O'er his white locks and bury them in snow,
When, roused by rage and muttering in the morn
He mends the broken hedge with icy thorn:—
"Why do I live, when I desire to be
At once from life and life's long labour free?
Like leaves in spring, the young are blown away,
Without the sorrows of a slow decay;
I, like yon wither'd leaf, remain behind,   210
Nipp'd by the frost, and shivering in the wind;
There it abides till younger buds come on,

As I, now all my fellow-swains are gone;
Then, from the rising generation thrust,
It falls, like me, unnoticed to the dust.
 "These fruitful fields, these numerous flocks I see,
Are others' gain, but killing cares to me:
To me the children of my youth are lords,
Cool in their looks, but hasty in their words:
Wants of their own demand their care; and who   220
Feels his own want and succours others too?
A lonely, wretched man, in pain I go,
None need my help, and none relieve my wo;
Then let my bones beneath the turf be laid,
And men forget the wretch they would not aid!"
 Thus groan the old, till, by disease oppress'd,
They taste a final wo, and then they rest.
 Theirs is yon house that holds the parish poor,
Whose walls of mud scarce bear the broken door;
There, where the putrid vapours, flagging, play,   230
And the dull wheel hums doleful through the day—
There children dwell, who know no parents' care;
Parents, who know no children's love, dwell there!
Heart-broken matrons on their joyless bed,
Forsaken wives, and mothers never wed;
Dejected widows with unheeded tears,
And crippled age with more than childhood fears;
The lame, the blind, and, far the happiest they!
The moping idiot and the madman gay.
Here too the sick their final doom receive,   240
Here brought, amid the scenes of grief, to grieve,
Where the loud groans from some sad chamber flow,
Mix'd with the clamours of the crowd below;
Here, sorrowing, they each kindred sorrow scan,
And the cold charities of man to man:
Whose laws indeed for ruin'd age provide,
And strong compulsion plucks the scrap from pride;
But still that scrap is bought with many a sigh,
And pride embitters what it can't deny.
 Say ye, oppress'd by some fantastic woes,   250
Some jarring nerve that baffles your repose;
Who press the downy couch, while slaves advance
With timid eye to read the distant glance;
Who with sad prayers the weary doctor tease,
To name the nameless ever-new disease;

Who with mock patience dire complaints endure,
Which real pain, and that alone, can cure—
How would ye bear in real pain to lie,
Despised, neglected, left alone to die?
How would ye bear to draw your latest breath,   260
Where all that's wretched paves the way for death?
  Such is that room which one rude beam divides,
And naked rafters form the sloping sides;
Where the vile bands that bind the thatch are seen,
And lath and mud are all that lie between,
Save one dull pane, that, coarsely patch'd, gives way
To the rude tempest, yet excludes the day.
Here, on a matted flock, with dust o'erspread,
The drooping wretch reclines his languid head;
For him no hand the cordial cup applies,   270
Or wipes the tear that stagnates in his eyes;
No friends with soft discourse his pain beguile,
Or promise hope till sickness wears a smile.
  But soon a loud and hasty summons calls,
Shakes the thin roof, and echoes round the walls.
Anon, a figure enters, quaintly neat,
All pride and business, bustle and conceit;
With looks unalter'd by these scenes of wo,
With speed that, entering, speaks his haste to go,
He bids the gazing throng around him fly,   280
And carries fate and physic in his eye:
A potent quack, long versed in human ills,
Who first insults the victim whom he kills;
Whose murd'rous hand a drowsy Bench protect,
And whose most tender mercy is neglect.
  Paid by the parish for attendance here,
He wears contempt upon his sapient sneer;
In haste he seeks the bed where Misery lies,
Impatience mark'd in his averted eyes;
And, some habitual queries hurried o'er,   290
Without reply, he rushes on the door.
His drooping patient, long inured to pain,
And long unheeded, knows remonstrance vain;
He ceases now the feeble help to crave
Of man; and silent sinks into the grave.
  But ere his death some pious doubts arise,
Some simple fears, which "bold bad" men despise:
Fain would he ask the parish-priest to prove

His title certain to the joys above;
For this he sends the murmuring nurse, who calls 300
The holy stranger to these dismal walls;
And doth not he, the pious man, appear,
He, "passing rich with forty pounds a year"? [4]
Ah! no; a shepherd of a different stock,
And far unlike him, feeds this little flock:
A jovial youth, who thinks his Sunday's task
As much as God or man can fairly ask;
The rest he gives to loves and labours light,
To fields the morning, and to feasts the night;
None better skill'd the noisy pack to guide, 310
To urge their chase, to cheer them or to chide;
A sportsman keen, he shoots through half the day,
And, skill'd at whist, devotes the night to play.
Then, while such honours bloom around his head,
Shall he sit sadly by the sick man's bed,
To raise the hope he feels not, or with zeal
To combat fears that e'en the pious feel?
  Now once again the gloomy scene explore,
Less gloomy now; the bitter hour is o'er,
The man of many sorrows sighs no more.— 320
Up yonder hill, behold how sadly slow
The bier moves winding from the vale below;
There lie the happy dead, from trouble free,
And the glad parish pays the frugal fee.
No more, O Death! thy victim starts to hear
Churchwarden stern, or kingly overseer;
No more the farmer claims his humble bow,
Thou art his lord, the best of tyrants thou!
  Now to the church behold the mourners come,
Sedately torpid and devoutly dumb; 330
The village children now their games suspend,
To see the bier that bears their ancient friend:
For he was one in all their idle sport,
And like a monarch ruled their little court;
The pliant bow he form'd, the flying ball,
The bat, the wicket, were his labours all;
Him now they follow to his grave, and stand
Silent and sad, and gazing, hand in hand;
While bending low, their eager eyes explore
The mingled relics of the parish poor. 340

4 *The Deserted Village* 142.

The bell tolls late, the moping owl flies round,
Fear marks the flight and magnifies the sound;
The busy priest, detain'd by weightier care,
Defers his duty till the day of prayer;
And, waiting long, the crowd retire distress'd,
To think a poor man's bones should lie unbless'd.

THE PARISH REGISTER

1807

PART III. BURIALS

There was, 'tis said, and I believe, a time,
When humble Christians died with views sublime:
When all were ready for their faith to bleed,
But few to write or wrangle for their creed;
When lively Faith upheld the sinking heart,
And friends, assured to meet, prepared to part;
When Love felt hope, when Sorrow grew serene,
And all was comfort in the death-bed scene.

Alas! when now the gloomy king they wait,
'Tis weakness yielding to resistless fate;   10
Like wretched men upon the ocean cast,
They labour hard and struggle to the last;
"Hope against hope," and wildly gaze around,
In search of help that never shall be found:
Nor, till the last strong billow stops the breath,
Will they believe them in the jaws of Death!

When these my records I reflecting read,
And find what ills these numerous births succeed;
What powerful griefs these nuptial ties attend,
With what regret these painful journeys end;   20
When from the cradle to the grave I look,
Mine I conceive a melancholy book.

Where now is perfect resignation seen?
Alas! it is not on the village-green:—
I've seldom known, though I have often read
Of happy peasants on their dying-bed;
Whose looks proclaim'd that sunshine of the breast,
That more than hope, that Heaven itself express'd.

What I behold are feverish fits of strife,
'Twixt fears of dying and desire of life:
Those earthly hopes, that to the last endure;
Those fears, that hopes superior fail to cure;
At best a sad submission to the doom,
Which, turning from the danger, lets it come.
    Sick lies the man, bewilder'd, lost, afraid,
His spirits vanquish'd and his strength decay'd;
No hope the friend, the nurse, the doctor lend—
"Call then a priest, and fit him for his end."
A priest is call'd; 'tis now, alas! too late,
Death enters with him at the cottage-gate;
Or time allow'd—he goes, assured to find
The self-commending, all-confiding mind;
And sighs to hear, what we may justly call
Death's commonplace, the train of thought in all.
    "True, I'm a sinner," feebly he begins,
"But trust in Mercy to forgive my sins:"
(Such cool confession no past crimes excite!
Such claim on Mercy seems the sinner's right!)
"I know mankind are frail, that God is just,
And pardons those who in his mercy trust;
We're sorely tempted in a world like this,
All men have done, and I like all, amiss;
But now, if spared, it is my full intent
On all the past to ponder and repent:
Wrongs against me I pardon great and small,
And if I die, I die in peace with all."
    His merits thus and not his sins confess'd,
He speaks his hopes, and leaves to Heaven the rest.
Alas! are these the prospects, dull and cold,
That dying Christians to their priests unfold?
Or mends the prospect when th' enthusiast cries,
"I die assured!" and in a rapture dies?
    Ah, where that humble, self-abasing mind,
With that confiding spirit, shall we find—
The mind that, feeling what repentance brings,
Dejection's terrors and Contrition's stings,
Feels then the hope, that mounts all care above,
And the pure joy that flows from pardoning love?
    Such have I seen in death, and much deplore,
So many dying, that I see no more:
Lo! now my records, where I grieve to trace,

How Death has triumph'd in so short a space;
Who are the dead, how died they, I relate,
And snatch some portion of their acts from fate.
  With Andrew Collett we the year begin,
The blind, fat landlord of the Old Crown Inn—
Big as his butt, and, for the self-same use,
To take in stores of strong fermenting juice.
On his huge chair beside the fire he sate,
In revel chief, and umpire in debate;
Each night his string of vulgar tales he told;
When ale was cheap and bachelors were bold:
His heroes all were famous in their days,
Cheats were his boast and drunkards had his praise;
"One, in three draughts, three mugs of ale took down,
As mugs were then—the champion of the Crown;
For thrice three days another lived on ale,
And knew no change but that of mild and stale;
Two thirsty soakers watch'd a vessel's side,
When he the tap with dexterous hand applied;
Nor from their seats departed till they found
That butt was out and heard the mournful sound."
  He praised a poacher, precious child of fun!
Who shot the keeper with his own spring-gun;
Nor less the smuggler who the exciseman tied,
And left him hanging at the birch-wood side,
There to expire; but one who saw him hang
Cut the good cord—a traitor of the gang.
  His own exploits with boastful glee he told,
What ponds he emptied and what pikes he sold;
And how, when bless'd with sight alert and gay,
The night's amusements kept him through the day.
  He sang the praises of those times, when all
"For cards and dice, as for their drink, might call;
When justice wink'd on every jovial crew,
And ten-pins tumbled in the parson's view."
  He told, when angry wives, provoked to rail,
Or drive a third-day drunkard from his ale,
What were his triumphs, and how great the skill
That won the vex'd virago to his will;
Who raving came;—then talk'd in milder strain,—
Then wept, then drank, and pledged her spouse again.
  Such were his themes: how knaves o'er laws prevail,
Or, when made captives, how they fly from jail;

80

90

100

110

The young how brave, how subtle were the old:
And oaths attested all that Folly told.

On death like his what name shall we bestow,
So very sudden! yet so very slow?
'Twas slow:—Disease, augmenting year by year,
Show'd the grim king by gradual steps brought near: 120
'Twas not less sudden; in the night he died,
He drank, he swore, he jested, and he lied;
Thus aiding folly with departing breath—
"Beware, Lorenzo, the slow-sudden death." [1]

Next died the Widow Goe, an active dame,
Famed ten miles round, and worthy all her fame;
She lost her husband when their loves were young,
But kept her farm, her credit, and her tongue:
Full thirty years she ruled with matchless skill,
With guiding judgment and resistless will;   130
Advice she scorn'd, rebellions she suppress'd,
And sons and servants bow'd at her behest.
Like that great man's, who to his Saviour came,
Were the strong words of this commanding dame:—
"Come," if she said, they came; if "go," were gone;
And if "do this,"—that instant it was done.
Her maidens told she was all eye and ear,
In darkness saw and could at distance hear;—
No parish-business in the place could stir,
Without direction or assent from her;   140
In turn she took each office as it fell,
Knew all their duties, and discharged them well;
The lazy vagrants in her presence shook,
And pregnant damsels fear'd her stern rebuke;
She look'd on want with judgment clear and cool,
And felt with reason and bestow'd by rule;
She match'd both sons and daughters to her mind,
And lent them eyes—for Love, she heard, was blind;
Yet ceaseless still she throve, alert, alive,
The working bee, in full or empty hive;   150
Busy and careful, like that working bee,
No time for love nor tender cares had she;
But when our farmers made their amorous vows,
She talk'd of market-streets and patent ploughs.
Not unemploy'd her evenings passed away,
Amusement closed, as business waked the day;

1 Young *Night Thoughts* I. 387.

When to her toilet's brief concern she ran,
And conversation with her friends began,
Who all were welcome, what they saw, to share;
And joyous neighbours praised her Christmas fare, 160
That none around might, in their scorn, complain
Of Gossip Goe as greedy in her gain.

   Thus long she reign'd, admired, if not approved;
Praised, if not honor'd; fear'd, if not beloved;—
When, as the busy days of spring drew near,
That call'd for all the forecast of the year;
When lively hope the rising crops survey'd,
And April promised what September paid;
When stray'd her lambs where gorse and greenweed grow;
When rose her grass in richer vales below; 170
When pleased she look'd on all the smiling land,
And view'd the hinds who wrought at her command;
(Poultry in groups still follow'd where she went;)
Then dread o'ercame her—that her days were spent.
"Bless me! I die, and not a warning giv'n,—
With *much* to do on earth, and *all* for Heav'n!—
No reparation for my soul's affairs,
No leave petition'd for the barn's repairs;
Accounts perplex'd, my interest yet unpaid,
My mind unsettled, and my will unmade;— 180
A lawyer, haste, and in your way, a priest;
And let me die in one good work at least."
She spake, and, trembling, dropp'd upon her knees,
Heaven in her eye and in her hand her keys;
And still the more she found her life decay,
With greater force she grasp'd those signs of sway:
Then fell and died!—In haste her sons drew near,
And dropp'd, in haste, the tributary tear;
Then from th' adhering clasp the keys unbound,
And consolation for their sorrow found. 190

  • • • • • • • • • •

A LIST OF USEFUL READINGS

THE POLITICAL AND SOCIAL BACKGROUND

Allen, Robert Joseph, *The Clubs of Augustan London*, 1933
Allen, Robert Joseph, *Life in Eighteenth Century England* (Museum Extension Publications, Boston Museum of Fine Arts), 1941
Ashton, John, *Social Life in the Reign of Queen Anne*, 1897
Bayne-Powell, Rosamond, *Housekeeping in the Eighteenth Century*, 1956
Botsford, Jay Barrett, *English Society in the Eighteenth Century as Influenced from Oversea*, 1924
Brown, Philip Anthony, *The French Revolution in English History*, 1923
Chancellor, Edwin Beresford, *The XVIIIth Century in London*, 1920
George, Mary Dorothy, *England in Transition; Life and Work in the Eighteenth Century*, 1931
George, Mary Dorothy, *London Life in the XVIIIth Century*, 1930
Gilboy, Elizabeth Waterman, *Wages in Eighteenth Century England*, 1934
Gray, Benjamin Kirkman, *A History of English Philanthropy*, 1905
Hammond, J. L. and Barbara, *The Town Laborer*, 1925, etc.; *The Village Laborer*, 1927, etc.
Irving, William Henry, *John Gay's London, Illustrated from the Poetry of the Time*, 1928
Jones, Louis Clark, *The Clubs of the Georgian Rakes*, 1942
Lecky, William E. Hartpole, *A History of England in the Eighteenth Century*, 8 vols., 1888
Lewis, Wilmarth Sheldon, *Three Tours Through London, in the Years 1748, 1776, 1797*, 1941
Malcolm, James Peller, *Anecdotes of the Manners and Customs of London During the Eighteenth Century*, 1808, 1810
Marshall, Dorothy, *The English Poor in the Eighteenth Century*, 1926
Mowat, Robert Balmain, *England in the Eighteenth Century*, 1932
Namier, Lewis Bernstein, *England in the Age of the American Revolution*, 1930
Quinlan, Maurice James, *Victorian Prelude; a History of English Manners, 1700–1830*, 1941

Richardson, Albert Edward, *Georgian England; a Survey of Social Life, Trades, Industries, and Art from 1700 to 1820*, 1931

Southworth, James Granville, *Vauxhall Gardens; a Chapter in the Social History of England*, 1941

Stebbins, Lucy Poate, *London Ladies: True Tales of the Eighteenth Century*, 1952

Sykes, Norman, *Church and State in England in the XVIIIth Century*, 1934

Sypher, Wylie, *Guinea's Captive Kings: British Anti-Slavery Literature of the XVIIIth Century*, 1942

Timbs, John, *Clubs and Club Life in London, with Anecdotes of Its Famous Coffee-Houses, Hostelries, and Taverns*, 1872

Timbs, John, *English Eccentrics and Eccentricities*, 1898

Trevelyan, George Macaulay, *England Under Queen Anne*, 3 vols., 1930–1934

Turberville, Arthur Stanley, *English Men and Manners in the Eighteenth Century; an Illustrated Narrative*, 1932

Turberville, Arthur Stanley, ed., *Johnson's England; an Account of the Life and Manners of His Age*, 2 vols., 1933

Williams, Basil, *The Whig Supremacy, 1714–1760*, 1939

Wroth, Warwick, *The London Pleasure Gardens of the Eighteenth Century*, 1896

THE INTELLECTUAL BACKGROUND

Babbitt, Irving, *The New Laocoon; an Essay on the Confusion of the Arts*, 1910

Becker, Carl Lotus, *The Heavenly City of the Eighteenth Century Philosophers*, 1935

Benn, Alfred William, *A History of English Rationalism in the Nineteenth Century*, Vol. I, 1906

Bonar, James, *Moral Sense*, 1930

Brinton, Crane, *The Political Ideas of the English Romanticists*, 1926

Burtt, Edwin Arthur, *The Metaphysical Foundations of Modern Science*, 1927

Bury, John Bagnell, *The Idea of Progress; an Inquiry into Its Origin and Growth*, 1932

Cassirer, Ernst, *Philosophy of the Enlightenment*, 1951

Clark, Henry William, *A History of English Nonconformity*, Vol. II; *From the Restoration to the Close of the Nineteenth Century*, 1913

Cobban, Alfred, *In Search of Humanity: The Role of the Enlightenment in Modern History*, 1960

Havens, George, *The Age of Ideas*, 1955

Hazard, Paul, *European Thought in the Eighteenth Century*, 1954

Hearnshaw, Fossey John Cobb, ed., *The Social and Political Ideas of Some English Thinkers of the Augustan Age, A.D. 1650–1750*, 1928

Hearnshaw, Fossey John Cobb, ed., *The Social and Political Ideas of Some Great French Thinkers of the Age of Reason*, 1930

Hearnshaw, Fossey John Cobb, ed., *The Social and Political Ideas of Some Representative Thinkers of the Revolutionary Era*, 1931

Laski, Harold Joseph, *Political Thought in England from Locke to Bentham*, 1932

Lincoln, Anthony, *Some Political and Social Ideas of English Dissent, 1763–1800*, 1938

Lovejoy, Arthur O., *The Great Chain of Being; a Study in the History of an Idea*, 1936

Lovejoy, Arthur O., "Nature as an Aesthetic Norm," *Modern Language Notes*, XLII, 1927

Martin, Kingsley, *French Liberal Thought in the Eighteenth Century*, 1954

Mornet, Daniel, *French Thought in the Eighteenth Century* (Translated by L. M. Levin), 1929

Nicolson, Marjorie Hope, *The Microscope and English Imagination*, 1935; *Mountain Gloom and Mountain Glory*, 1959; *Newton Demands the Muse*, 1946; *Science and Imagination*, 1956

Robertson, John George, *Studies in the Genesis of Romantic Theory in the Eighteenth Century*, 1923

Stephen, Sir Leslie, *History of English Thought in the Eighteenth Century*, Third Ed., 2 vols., 1927

Tawney, Richard Henry, *Religion and the Rise of Capitalism; a Historical Study*, 1926

Tinker, Chauncey Brewster, *Nature's Simple Plan; a Phase of Radical Thought in the Mid-Eighteenth Century*, 1922

Warner, Wellman Joel, *The Wesleyan Movement in the Industrial Revolution*, 1930

Weber, Max, *The Protestant Ethic and the Spirit of Capitalism* (Translated by Talcott Parsons), 1930

Whitney, Lois, *Primitivism and the Idea of Progress in English Popular Literature of the Eighteenth Century*, 1934

THE LITERARY BACKGROUND

Babbitt, Irving, *Rousseau and Romanticism*, 1930

Baker, Ernest Albert, *The History of the English Novel*, Vols. III–VI, 1929–1935

Barbeau, A., *Life and Letters at Bath in the XVIIIth Century*, 1904

Bate, Walter Jackson, *From Classic to Romantic*, 1946

Bernbaum, Ernest, *The Drama of Sensibility*, 1915

Bernbaum, Ernest, *Guide Through the Romantic Movement*, 1930

Bond, Richmond P., *English Burlesque Poetry, 1700–1750*, 1932

Butt, John, *The Augustan Age*, 1950

Chapin, Chester F., Jr., *Personification in Eighteenth-Century English Poetry*, 1955

Churchill, R. C., *English Literature of the Eighteenth Century*, 1953

Collins, Arthur Simons, *Authorship in the Days of Johnson, 1726–1780*, 1927

Deane, Cecil Victor, *Aspects of Eighteenth Century Nature Poetry*, 1935

Dobson, Austin, *Eighteenth Century Vignettes*, 1892–1896

Doughty, Oswald, "The English Malady of the Eighteenth Century," *Review of English Studies*, II, 1926

Durling, Dwight L., *Georgic Tradition in English Poetry*, 1935

Elton, Oliver, "Reason and Enthusiasm in the Eighteenth Century," *Essays and Studies by Members of the English Association*, X, 1924

Elton, Oliver, *A Survey of English Literature, 1730–1780*, 2 vols., 1928

Elton, Oliver, *A Survey of English Literature, 1780–1830*, 2 vols., 1920

Fairchild, Hoxie Neale, *The Noble Savage; a Study in Romantic Naturalism*, 1928

Fairchild, Hoxie Neale, *Religious Trends in English Poetry*, 2 vols., 1939–1942

Gallaway, Francis, *Reason, Rule, and Revolt in English Classicism*, 1940

Graham, Walter, *English Literary Periodicals*, 1930

Green, Frederick Charles, *Minuet: a Critical Survey of French and English Literary Ideas in the Eighteenth Century*, 1935

Grierson, Sir Herbert John Clifford, *Classical and Romantic*, 1923 (Reprinted in *The Background of English Literature*, 1934)

Havens, Raymond Dexter, *The Influence of Milton on English Poetry*, 1922

Hesselgrave, Ruth Avaline, *Lady Miller and the Batheaston Literary Circle*, 1927

Humphreys, A. R., *The Augustan World*, 1954

Jack, Ian, *Augustan Satire*, 1952

Kitchin, George, *A Survey of Burlesque and Parody in English*, 1931

Lesher, Clara R., *The South Sea Islanders in English Literature, 1519–1798*, Chicago, 1938

Lovejoy, Arthur O., "The Parallel of Deism and Classicism," *Modern Philology*, XXIX, 1932

McKenzie, Gordon, *Critical Responsiveness*, 1949

Marks, Emerson R., *Relativist and Absolutist: The Early Neo-Classical Debate in England*, 1955

Marr, George Simpson, *The Periodical Essayists of the Eighteenth Century, with Illustrative Extracts from the Rarer Periodicals*, 1924

Monk, Samuel Holt, *The Sublime; a Study of Critical Theories in XVIII Century England*, 1935

More, Paul Elmer, *With the Wits (Shelburne Essays, Tenth Series)*, 1919

Nichols, John, *Illustrations of the Literary History of the Eighteenth Century*, 8 vols., 1817–1858

Nichols, John, *Literary Anecdotes of the Eighteenth Century*, 9 vols., 1812–1816

Nicoll, Allardyce, *A History of Early Eighteenth Century Drama, 1700–1750*, 1925

Nicoll, Allardyce, *A History of Late Eighteenth Century Drama, 1750–1800*, 1927

Odell, George C. D., *Shakespeare from Betterton to Irving*, 2 vols., 1920

Quayle, Thomas, *Poetic Diction; a Study of Eighteenth Century Verse*, 1924

Reed, Amy Louise, *The Background of Gray's Elegy; a Study in the Taste for Melancholy Poetry, 1700–1751*, 1924

Sherburn, George, *The Restoration and Eighteenth Century*, 1950

Smith, Andrew Cannon, *Theories of the Nature and Standard of Taste in England, 1700–1790*, 1937

Smith, David Nichol, *Some Observations on Eighteenth-Century Poetry*, 1937

Smith, Logan Pearsall, *Four Words: Romantic, Originality, Creative, Genius*, 1924 (Reprinted in *Words and Idioms*, 1925)

Snyder, Edward D., *The Celtic Revival in English Literature*, 1923

Spence, Joseph, *Observations, Anecdotes, and Characters of Books and Men*, 1820

Stauffer, Donald Alfred, *The Art of Biography in Eighteenth Century England*, 1941

Stephen, Sir Leslie, *English Literature and Society in the Eighteenth Century*, 1907

Stern, Bernard Herbert, *The Rise of Romantic Hellenism in English Literature, 1732–1786*, 1940

Stuart, Dorothy M., "Landscape in Augustan Verse," *Essays and Studies by Members of the English Association*, XXVI, 1940

Sutherland, James, *Preface to Eighteenth Century Poetry*, 1948

Tillotson, Geoffrey, *Essays in Criticism and Research*, 1942

Tinker, Chauncey Brewster, *The Salon and English Letters; Chapters on the Interrelations of Literature and Society in the Age of Johnson*, 1915

Tompkins, J. M. S., *The Popular Novel in England, 1770–1800*, 1932

Vines, Sherard, *The Course of English Classicism from the Tudor to the Victorian Age*, 1930

Willey, Basil, *The Eighteenth Century Background; Studies on the Idea of Nature in the Thought of the Period*, 1940

Williamson, George, "The Rhetorical Pattern of Neo-Classical Wit," *Modern Philology*, XXXIII, 1935

Wright, Thomas, *A History of Caricature and Grotesque in Literature and Art*, 1875

THE FINE ARTS

Allen, Beverley Sprague, *Tides in English Taste; A Background for the Study of Literature*, 2 vols., 1937

Baker, Charles Henry Collins, *British Painting*, 1933

Blomfield, Reginald, *History of Renaissance Architecture in England, 1500–1800*, 1897

Borenius, Tancred, *English Painting in the XVIIIth Century*, 1938

Burney, Charles, *A General History of Music* (Edited by Frank Mercer), 2 vols., 1935

Chase, Isabel W. V., *Horace Walpole, Gardenist*, 1943

Clark, Kenneth, *The Gothic Revival; an Essay in the History of Taste*, 1929

Erdberg, Eleanor von, *Chinese Influence on European Garden Structures*, 1936

Fry, Roger Eliot, *Reflections on British Painting*, 1934

Fuller-Maitland, John Alexander, *The Age of Bach and Handel* (*The Oxford History of Music*, Vol. IV), 1931

Georgian Art (1760–1820), (*Burlington Magazine Monograph*, III), 1929

Gloag, John, *Georgian Grace*, 1956

Gothein, Marie Luise, *A History of Garden Art* (Translated by Mrs. Archer-Hind), 2 vols., 1928

Hadow, William Henry, *The Viennese Period* (*The Oxford History of Music*, Vol. V), 1931

Hagstrum, Jean H., *The Sister Arts: The Tradition of Literary Pictorialism and English Poetry from Dryden to Gray*, 1958

Hayden, Arthur, and Stowe, Charles Messer, edd., *Furniture Designs of Chippendale, Hepplewhite, and Sheraton*, 1940

Hipple, Walter J., Jr., *The Beautiful, The Sublime, and the Pictur-*

esque, 1957

Hogarth, William, *The Analysis of Beauty*, ed. Joseph Burke, 1955

Hussey, Christopher, *The Picturesque: Studies in a Point of View*, 1927

Jourdain, Eleanor, *The Work of William Kent*, 1948

Kimball, Fiske, *The Creation of the Rococo*, 1943

Klingender, Francis D., *Art and the Industrial Revolution*, 1947

Lang, Paul Henry, *Music in Western Civilization*, 1941

Larrabee, Stephen A., *English Bards and Grecian Marbles*, 1943

Manwaring, Elizabeth Wheeler, *Italian Landscape in Eighteenth-Century England; a Study Chiefly of the Influence of Claude Lorrain and Salvator Rosa on English Taste, 1700–1800*, 1925

Molloy, Fitzgerald, *Sir Joshua and His Circle*, 2 vols., n.d.

Moore, Robert E., *Hogarth's Literary Relationships*, 1948

Sitwell, Sacheverell, *British Architects and Craftsmen*, 1946

Steegman, John, *The Rule of Taste from George I to George IV*, 1936

Stroud, Dorothy, *Capability Brown*, 1950

Swarbrick, John, *Robert Adam and His Brothers*, [1915]

Sypher, Wylie, *Rococo to Cubism in Art and Literature*, 1960

Tinker, Chauncey Brewster, *Painter and Poet; Studies in the Literary Relations of English Painting*, 1938

Tipping, H. Avray, *English Houses*, (Periods IV–VI), 1920–28

Whistler, Lawrence, *Sir John Vanbrugh, Architect and Dramatist*, 1938

Whitley, William Thomas, *Artists and Their Friends in England, 1700–1799*, 2 vols., 1928

Wilenski, Reginald Howard, *English Painting*, 1937

BIBLIOGRAPHY

The Cambridge Bibliography of English Literature (Ed. F. W. Bateson), 4 vols., 1941

Tobin, James E., *Eighteenth Century English Literature and Its Cultural Background*, 1939

INDEX

1353